USING COMPUTERS AND APPLICATION SOFTWARE

SECOND EDITION

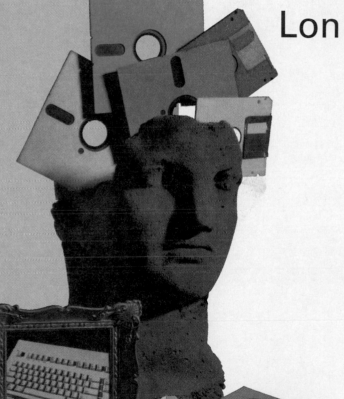

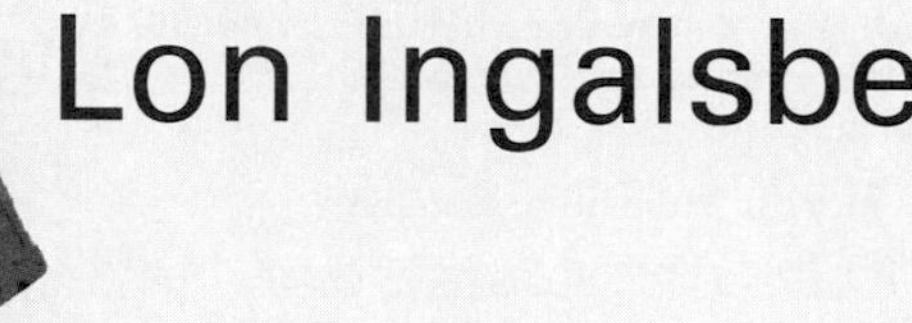

Lon Ingalsbe

Macmillan Publishing Company
NEW YORK

Maxwell Macmillan Canada
TORONTO

Maxwell Macmillan International
NEW YORK OXFORD SINGAPORE SYDNEY

Cover Art: Chas Krider/Photography
Editor: Vernon R. Anthony
Production Editor: JoEllen Gohr
Cover Designer: Russ Maselli
Production Buyer: Pamela D. Bennett

This book was set in Century Schoolbook by York Graphic Services, Inc., and Publication Services and was printed and bound by Von Hoffmann Press, Inc. The cover was printed by Von Hoffmann Press, Inc.

Printed in the United States of America

Macmillan Publishing Company
866 Third Avenue
New York, New York 10022

Macmillan Publishing Company is part of the
Maxwell Communication Group of Companies.

Maxwell Macmillan Canada, Inc.
1200 Eglinton Avenue East, Suite 200
Don Mills, Ontario M3C 3N1

Library of Congress Cataloging-in-Publication Data

Ingalsbe, Lon.
Using computers and application software / Lon Ingalsbe. — 2nd ed.
p. cm.
Includes index.
ISBN 0-02-359640-6
1. Electronic digital computers. 2. Application software.
3. WordPerfect (Computer program) 4. Lotus 1-2-3 (Computer program)
5. dBase III Plus (Computer program) I. Title.
QA76.5.I443 1992
005.36—dc20 91-35998
CIP

Printing: 1 2 3 4 5 6 7 8 9 Year: 2 3 4 5

Photographs without specific credits below their captions are by Macmillan Publishing/Cobalt Productions. Credits for photographs on Part Opening pages: Part 1, left page, Hewlett-Packard Company; right page, top, IBM; right page, bottom, Photofest; Part 2, left page, IBM; right page, Innervisions. Photos in Figures 2.3, 2.4, 2.11, 2.12, 2.13, 2.17, and 2.19 by Innervisions.

To my wife, Marita
and our children, Marguerite, Claire, and Brent

PREFACE

The widespread use of personal computers has brought about revolutionary changes in the way people interact with information in their academic, business, and everyday social environments. This textbook presents the fundamental concepts of computer technologies and introduces the problem-solving potential of popular application software packages to the new user of computers. No previous experience with computers is required for users of this text.

Coverage and Organization

This textbook is organized into two distinct parts—concepts and application software.

Part One offers students a compact yet comprehensive introduction to computer and information processing concepts that is visually striking, enjoyable to read, and highly accessible. The purpose of this section is to provide students with the basic knowledge to make them effective users of computers. In this "Concepts" section, the terminology and concepts essential to computer literacy (from the new user's point of view) are described. This section defines what a computer is, discusses microcomputers and their applications, and describes the information processing cycle, communications, computer networks, information systems, and programming.

The "Concepts" section covers the full range of computer and information processing concepts in a pedagogically sound manner, including a wealth of review questions and vocabulary terms at the end of each chapter. Designed in a visually striking manner, with over 150 full-color photographs and line drawings, this section includes high-interest chapter opening vignettes on pioneers in the computer field.

Part Two provides thorough coverage of WordPerfect Version 5.1, Lotus 1-2-3 Version 2.2, dBASE III Plus, and DOS. (If coverage of additional, or alternate, software packages is required, your Macmillan sales representative will be delighted to describe a full line of other software package text-tutorials.) In addition, and following the software tutorials, this text covers data transfer between applications, a topic ignored by most other books of this kind. From this section students gain conceptual understanding of data structures and the ability to use each application software to its maximum potential.

The "Application Software" section is organized into self-contained modules. The software tutorial modules take the user, command by command, through the specific software packages, their capabilities, and their advantages or disadvantages for given problem-solving applications. The modular format of this textbook allows instructors to choose which software packages to teach and in what order.

The "Application Software" section consists of application software modules with the following features:

- Each software module begins with an "Introduction" that provides the user with a fundamental understanding of the software's principal application and the key terminology associated with it.
- "Tutorial" lessons take students step by step through the basics of the software, introducing its essential commands, concepts, and structures in order to develop in the user a basic competency with the software.
- "Exercises" following the tutorial provide a problem-solving environment which reinforces that which was taught in the tutorial and eases the student into the Command Summary reference section, which emulates "real world" software usage.
- "Cases" provide the most challenge to students' problem-solving skills. This case-study approach presents business scenarios and provides students with the opportunity to analyze, design, test, and implement business solutions using their new software skills.
- "Hints and Hazards" provide tips for students to improve their efficiency with using software and guides students away from frustrating pitfalls.
- "Study Questions" test the student's understanding of the conceptual issues involved in using the software.
- "Additional Topics" explore important advanced topics that are more appropriately taught by example-based discussions than by tutorial or command summary presentations.
- The "Operation and Command Summary" at the end of each software module provides a unique reference which students will find useful throughout the course and long after it is completed. These extensive summaries include brief explanations and examples of the use of the software's commands, functions, and control keys.

Design Features

For this edition, the concepts section has been enhanced by a full-color design. In the application software section, color is used extensively as a pedagogical device. Color is used to signal to students hands-on work at the computer keyboard and is also used to separate the computer's output response from the user's input. In this fashion, students are systematically guided through the tutorials and are able to see easily the results of their input.

It is important for students to be able to check their work against what is happening on the computer screen. As such, accurate representations of the screens are included throughout all instructional steps. Illustrating these steps is the single most effective manner of ensuring that students in a hands-on environment are able to complete their work with the lowest possible level of anxiety and frustration.

Acknowledgments

In 1982, the Earle A. Chiles Foundation provided a grant to the School of Business Administration at Portland State University for the purchase of a microcomputing laboratory, enabling me to create the original versions of the tutorials which are the heart of this textbook. Without this farsighted gift, and the Foundation's continued support, this textbook would not still exist ten years and eighteen iterations later.

During the past ten years hundreds of individuals have contributed to my work: through written reviews, participation in focus groups, responding to surveys, and during countless office visits by Macmillan editors, marketing managers, and sales representatives. To all of you, my personal thanks for all that you have contributed.

I would also like to thank the student, whose thirst for knowledge and self-improvement and whose use of this material in previous iterations have made this textbook the successful teaching tool that it is today.

Special acknowledgment is given to Pat Fenton of West Valley College, for his guidance, constructive criticism, and revisions to the concepts material. Brent Simonson's research, writing, technical expertise, and standards of excellence are evidenced in the revision of the software tutorials.

Finally, the staff of Macmillan Publishing Company deserves special recognition for their efforts in the development and production of this textbook. Their attention to detail, concern for pedagogy, and commitment of resources have resulted in producing the best possible textbook.

CONTENTS

Lotus 1-2-3 Version 2.2

USING COMPUTERS AND APPLICATION SOFTWARE

PART 1

CONCEPTS

OUTLINE

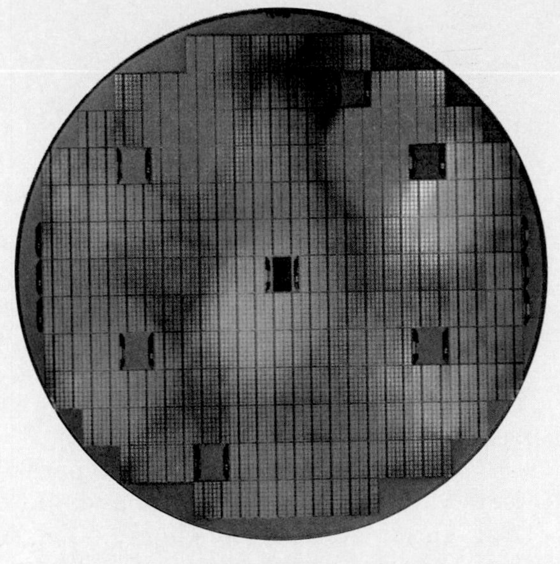

RAYMOND KURZWEIL

Kurzweil developed equipment and programs that link computers to musical instruments, thus allowing musicians to create a wide variety of new sounds.

(Courtesy Martin L. Schneider/ Associates)

PROFILE

Raymond Kurzweil is an impatient man—and a hopeful one. So when he gets an idea for a computer application, his first thought seems to be, "How quickly can we get it on the market?"

It is no wonder, then, that the native New Yorker didn't bother with a lot of formal schooling before plunging into the infant computer world of the late 1950s and early 1960s. In fact, he was only twelve years old when he developed a software package so useful and well constructed that IBM agreed to distribute it.

In 1964, when he was sixteen, Kurzweil won seven national awards, including first prize at the International Science Fair in Electronics and Communications for his pioneering work in artificial intelligence. By the mature age of eighteen, he had sold a software package for $100,000 to a New York publishing company. Clearly, the bright young man had a promising future before him.

The child of a music professor who was a refugee from Nazi Germany, Kurzweil spent his early years in a middle-class neighborhood in New York City. His two passions as a youngster were the piano and computer technology, and he found ways to exploit both enthusiasms.

Stevie Wonder, the famous singer and composer who is blind, first encountered Kurzweil after the young computer whiz began marketing a machine that could scan books and then read them aloud by translating the signals it picked up visually into a synthesized voice. Wonder bought one of the first reading machines.

In talking to Kurzweil about the exotic work being performed by computers, Wonder complained that the music synthesizers available, while useful in their own right, could not simulate the richly varied sounds of traditional acoustic instruments. Out of this conversation grew the idea for the Kurzweil Model 250 keyboard. Although some professional musicians say the Model 250 lacks the depth and range of a grand piano, others are enthusiastic, praising both its "natural" sound and its portability. Prince, Paul Schaefer, Herbie Hancock, Lynn Stanford of the American Ballet Theater, and other top musicians also have used the Kurzweil Model 250. These days, Kurzweil's name and inventions are as well known to performers as they are to the U.S. Patent Office.

Another Kurzweil enthusiasm is the Voice Report, a system that "hears" the spoken word and instantly prints it onto paper.

A great deal of the inventor's success is attributable to his zeal for combining advanced technology with practical business. He is remarkably agile in both the laboratory and the boardroom. Kurzweil founded and presently directs several companies; and he personally raised the money to get them started.

In 1982, at the age of thirty-four, Kurzweil was inducted into the Computer Industry Hall of Fame.

CHAPTER 1

A WORLD WITH COMPUTERS

IN THIS CHAPTER YOU WILL LEARN ABOUT

- **The computing system**
- **An information system**
- **Differences between types of computers**
- **Essential computer functions**

Courtesy International Business Machines Corp.

NEED FOR COMPUTER LITERACY

Unless you intend to be a hermit, computers will affect you. What is computer literacy, and why would you want or need it? **Computer literacy** means having a general knowledge about computers—knowing who uses them and what kinds of functions they perform. Computer literacy is understanding how people use computers and where they use them. Literacy involves learning how computers affect society and how they can benefit your own life or work. Some experts think that, eventually, the person who does not know how to use a computer will be just as handicapped in performing his or her job as the person today who cannot read.

Personal computers have brought computing power to the desk of almost anyone who wants to use them. In many cases, jobs that formerly required no computer skills now have that requirement. Even in jobs that do not require computer use, personal computers can help increase the quality and quantity of work accomplished. Of course, to get the most benefit from a personal computer, you should be comfortable with its fundamental operations.

Part One of this text is designed to give you a solid foundation in computer fundamentals. Part Two is designed to give you hands-on experience with a personal computer.

In subsequent chapters of Part One, you will learn about the operation of the computer and its specific parts, find out what devices are used in conjunction with the computer, and discover how those devices are related. You will learn how computers communicate with each other and the rules that govern that communication. You'll see how managers at various levels of an organization use computers in different ways. You will also learn how computers receive instructions to solve problems.

In this chapter, you will be introduced to the basic concepts of a computing system and to the definitions of key terms used in computing. The emphasis is on *you,* the person who will use, and control, the personal computer as a powerful productivity tool.

PERSONAL WORLD OF COMPUTING

Most likely you have already had a great deal of exposure to computers. Some children receive lessons on computers in kindergarten. Students might learn, in the fourth grade, to create computer instructions using a simplified computer language. Sixth graders are encouraged to use computers to write book reports or personal stories. Junior high students incorporate computer-based instruction as a supplement to mathematics or physical science classes.

High schools increasingly offer word processing courses, beginning programming classes, and introductory computer science courses. Colleges, vocational schools, and other training programs offer a wide variety of computer-related courses for both general and specialized uses of the computer. Colleges also offer computer training in computer sciences, information systems, engineering, and other advanced fields that use computers.

In the workplace, regardless of the type of enterprise—business, industry, government, the armed forces, or education—the computer has become a basic instrument (Figure 1.1). Some classic jobs, such as secretarial or clerical positions, have undergone major change due to the use of the computer.

So, most likely you have been introduced to computing in some way, either directly through your own use or indirectly through your daily activities. You may not, however, fully understand what computers are, how they work, or how you can make the best use of a computer. That is the goal of this first section of the book.

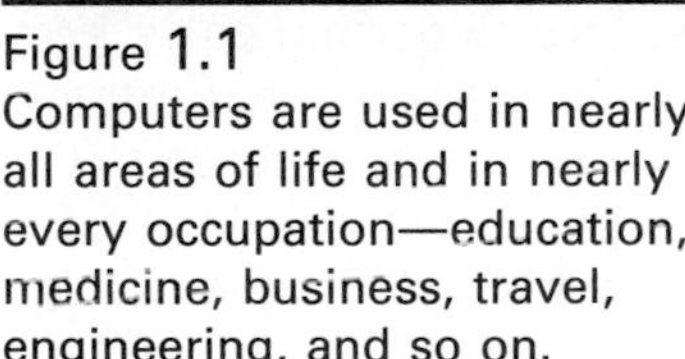

Figure 1.1
Computers are used in nearly all areas of life and in nearly every occupation—education, medicine, business, travel, engineering, and so on.

(Photos top left, middle, and right: Courtesy International Business Machines Corp.)

THE COMPUTING SYSTEM

If you were asked to show someone a computer, you would probably point to a specific box or two of electronic parts. We are comfortable in pointing to a "thing" because it is easiest conceptually for us to understand. A **computer** is a machine composed of separate parts, each working with the others to provide problem-solving functions. But a **computing system** includes more; it consists of hardware, software, data, procedures, and people.

Hardware

When you look more carefully at a computer, you will see various individual parts, or what are usually called components: the display, disk drives, keyboard, mouse, and printer, for example. You are still looking only at **hardware,** the physical, tangible parts of the computing system.

Certainly hardware plays an important role (Figure 1.2). The keyboard and mouse serve as **input devices;** that is, they allow you to send data into the computer in a form the computer can understand. (Data, we'll soon see, consist of the "raw facts" the computer transforms into information.) **Output devices,** such as the display and printer, permit the computer to communicate with you by presenting computer-prepared information in a form you can understand. **Storage devices,** such as the computer's fixed disk or your diskette, provide a place to permanently keep data and programs so that you can use them when needed. The **central processing unit,** or CPU as it is called, is the part of the computer where the actual computing activity occurs. The CPU contains the computer's main memory, also called primary storage, which holds the program and data currently being used. Permanent storage of programs and data is provided by such **secondary storage devices** as the computer's fixed disk or your diskette.

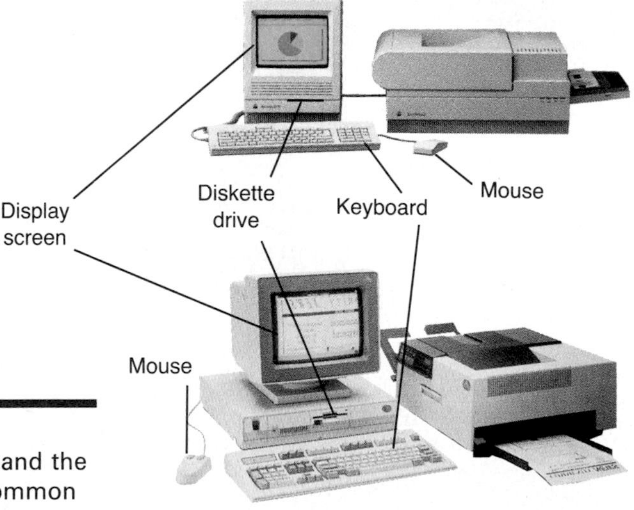

Figure 1.2
The Apple Macintosh and the IBM PS/2 share the common characteristics of computer hardware: input devices such as a keyboard and a mouse; display screens for output; storage on both a diskette drive and an internal fixed disk; and a central processing unit installed inside the system's base.

(Courtesy Apple Computer, Inc. (top) and International Business Machines Corp. (bottom))

The CPU together with the other hardware components—input, output, and storage devices—forms one important part of a computing system. The data you input from a keyboard are transformed by the CPU into information which is then output to you via the printer or display in a timely, accurate, and usable way.

Software

Software, or **programs,** are the instructions needed to direct the computer to complete specific tasks (Figure 1.3). The CPU follows the step-by-step instructions in a program to complete the tasks you need. For example, a **word processing** program contains instructions that permit you to use the computer to enter and save text, to format it or change its appearance on the page, to include figures and charts along with the words, and to output it on a printer. A **spreadsheet** program allows you to use the same computer to enter and manipulate rows and columns of numbers and words, to perform mathematical

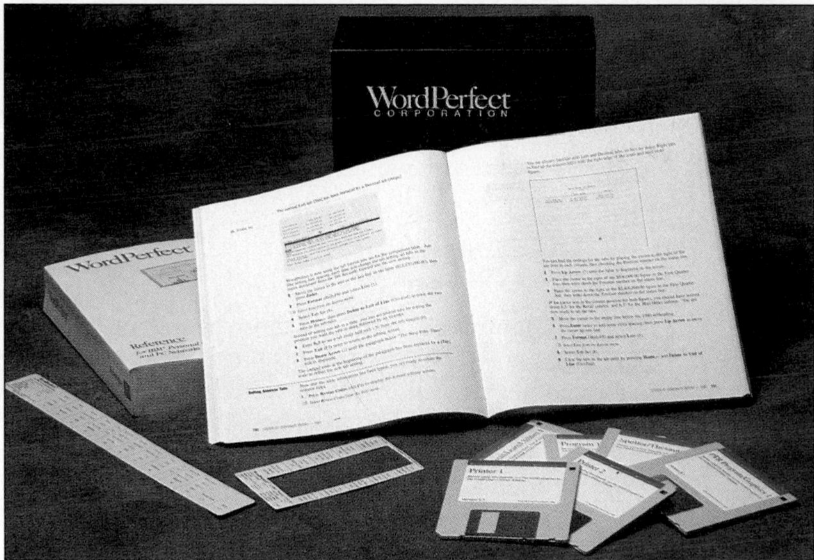

Figure 1.3
The program, contained on the diskettes, is ready to be loaded into the computer.

(Courtesy Innervisions)

processes, and to create graphs to more easily understand information. So, it is software, the list of instructions controlling the computer's operations, that permits you to apply the computer as a general-purpose tool to help you in a variety of tasks.

Data

Data, too, are required as the raw material from which the computer produces information. **Data** are simply the numbers, letters, symbols, or words input to the computer in order to be transformed into information. Data are also called **raw facts** because data alone may have no meaning. **Data processing** is the activity that converts data into an organized, useful form called information (Figure 1.4). Some sources refer to data processing as information processing; however, it is data—not information—that are processed.

Figure 1.4
This clerk is entering data from tax forms. The data will later be processed by the computer.

John Smith, Mary Jones, 38.5, and 45.8 may all be data, but they have no particular meaning here. However, when a computer with an appropriate program reads this data as input, combines it with a pay rate, and produces a payroll check, the data has become information. **Information** is data that has been processed according to a program's instructions and output in a form that is useful, relevant, accurate, and timely when communicated to the person who needs to use it.

Procedures

Procedures, such as those found in operating manuals and other forms of documentation, are another critical part of the computing system. Without proper procedures, you would be at a loss about how to use the computer correctly. Processing data into information requires careful planning and appropriate instructions. If accurate data are not input, the information delivered as output is useless. This phenomenon is called **garbage-in, garbage-out;** it means that the output is only as accurate as the input and the program that processes the data. If you enter a meaningless series of numbers and letters, the computer will not automatically process those data into a list of names and addresses. By the same token, the accuracy of a program's operations has to be verified so that subsequent processes can be performed correctly.

Though the computer follows a program's instructions, you as the computer user must know which program to use and how to use it. The documentation provided in a manual can tell you how to start the program, which data need to be input, and how to verify that the results are accurate. Most software is supplied with a manual explaining the program's operation. A company's procedure manual may have instructions for certain programs to be used at specific times, such as accounting programs that are used to prepare financial statements at the end of the month.

People

By far, the most important component of the computing system is *you,* the person using the computer. You are the controlling force behind the computing system. By knowing the power and the limitations of computing, you are able to select the proper applications to solve problems, produce information, and become more efficient in your work.

Figure 1.5
A computing system brings together computer hardware, software, data, procedures, and people—all working together to produce accurate, useful, and timely information.

(Jo Hall/Macmillan)

A **computing system,** then, is the combination of hardware, software, data, procedures, and you—all working together to get the most out of using the computer (Figure 1.5).

AN INFORMATION SYSTEM

No organization can function without its people, and people have difficulty functioning unless they have timely and accurate information for making decisions, solving problems, or managing their tasks. An **information system** is any combination of people, data, and procedures formed to create and distribute information throughout an organization.

You may have noticed that this definition of an information system does not include the computer. Information systems have existed for as long as civilization has required the need for understanding and using facts. Today's information systems would most likely include a computing system as the primary tool used to acquire, store, retrieve, manipulate, and present facts as information. But information systems go beyond the boundaries of the computing system. They incorporate three important activities: (1) gathering accurate, reliable facts to use as data for the computing system; (2) processing and distributing timely information to those who need it; and (3) responding to the needs of the people within the organization.

During the latter part of the twentieth century, emphasis in the job market has changed dramatically from a muscle orientation to a knowledge orientation. Education in today's information society is geared more toward preparing people to provide services and information rather than toward teaching them physical or industrial skills. Many experts say that most jobs in the future will involve either creating or handling information.

Access to the right information and the latest computer technology no doubt gives a company a competitive edge and a potential for growth. However, too much or unnecessary information can become overwhelming and counterproductive. So, there must be a balance—get the right information to the right person at the right time.

TYPES OF COMPUTERS

Getting timely information to the person who needs it is not always easy. An information system needs to use the right tools. In addition to varying in size and cost, computers differ in their purposes.

Although there are many types of computers, it is not as easy to define them now as it was a decade or two ago. Then the differences between types of computers were fairly obvious: If a computer filled up a room with equipment, it was probably called a mainframe computer; anything else was a minicomputer. Now, the room full of equipment has been replaced by a cabinet that fits on, next to or underneath a desk, and the smaller systems can rest in the palms of your hands.

A more appropriate distinction than size or cost, then, is one that arises from how computers are used and the services they are capable of providing (Figure 1.6). Computers can be grouped into five categories: supercomputers, mainframe computers, minicomputers, personal computers, and embedded processors.

Supercomputers

Supercomputers are the most expensive and most powerful computers. They are used where vast quantities of data must be manipulated, primarily by government agencies, scientists, and large corporations. A supercomputer is especially designed to process complicated mathematical applications, such as weather forecasting and wind-tunnel testing of aircraft. Such applications require the processing of several millions of numeric data values. The analyses

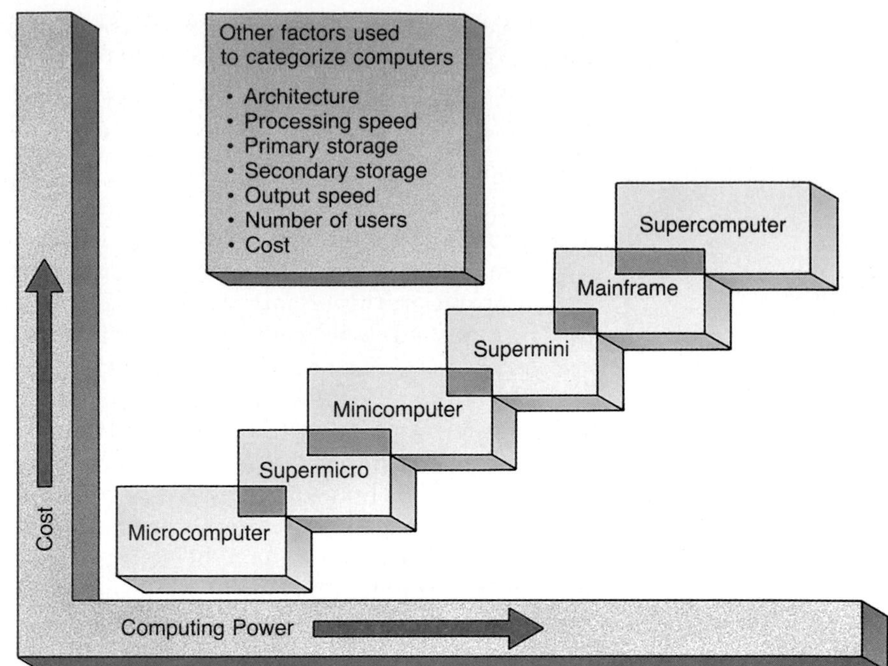

Figure 1.6
Technological advances have increased computing power while reducing computing costs. Categories once used to distinguish computer types have become increasingly blurred.

provided by the programs run on supercomputers might take hours to complete, but they would take much longer—perhaps weeks—on other types of computing hardware.

It is not size or cost that classifies a computer as a supercomputer; it is processing speed and the special ability to process numerically intensive mathematical operations quickly. At the National Energy Research Supercomputer Center, supercomputers provide computing resources for projects ranging from magnetic fusion energy to basic energy sciences and health and environmental research. The center's four Cray supercomputers are linked together to provide a computing capacity of 8.2 *billion* arithmetic operations per second (Figure 1.7). In the time it took you to read this paragraph, the computers would have completed more than 180 billion arithmetic operations. Truly, that is super computing.

Mainframe Computers

The origin of the term *mainframe* lies in computing history. In the 1940s, computers were indeed large "frames" in which electrical and electronic gear

Figure 1.7
The CRAY-2 computer, introduced in June of 1985, has an internal memory capacity of 2 billion bytes and a top speed of 1.2 billion flops (floating point, or arithmetical, operations per second). It is six to twelve times faster than its predecessor, the CRAY-1, and 40,000 to 50,000 times faster than a personal computer. Two hundred and forty thousand computer chips are packed into the CRAY-2's C-shaped cabinet, which measures 53 inches across and 45 inches high.

(Courtesy U.S. Dept. of Energy, Visual Library)

Figure 1.8
ENIAC, a computer developed in the 1940s, filled a room with equipment, wires, and cooling fans. The large metal cabinets holding the equipment gave rise to the term *mainframe* computer.

(Courtesy of International Business Machines Corp.)

was mounted. The "main" frame housed the CPU (Figure 1.8). Today, **mainframe** is a type of computer architecture that has the ability to quickly process a high volume of data; control and use a wide range of data storage, input, and output devices; and support a very large number of users at one time (Figure 1.9). Applications for a mainframe computer include banking, engineering, business information systems, and any large-scale, general-purpose computing needs.

Figure 1.9
ENIAC and other early computers were based on vacuum-tube technology which was responsible for the large size and excessive heat of these systems. Today's computers use integrated circuits which, though much smaller than vacuum tubes, are much faster, less expensive, and more reliable.

(Courtesy of National Semiconductor Corp.)

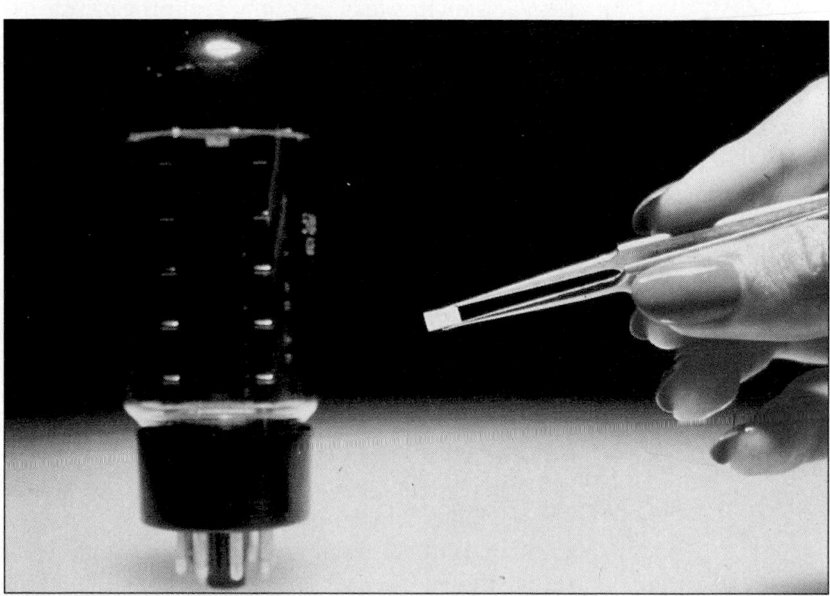

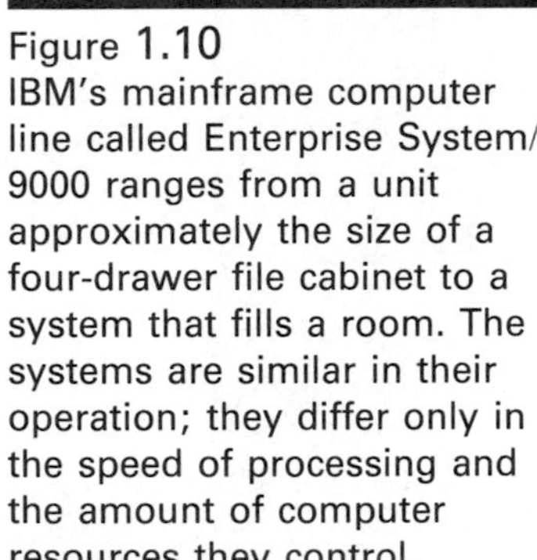

Figure 1.10
IBM's mainframe computer line called Enterprise System/9000 ranges from a unit approximately the size of a four-drawer file cabinet to a system that fills a room. The systems are similar in their operation; they differ only in the speed of processing and the amount of computer resources they control.

(Courtesy of International Business Machines Corp.)

A wide range of systems can be classified as having a mainframe architecture. A system may be the size of a four-drawer filing cabinet, or of a room (Figure 1.10). The difference is in the number and types of computing resources that can be attached to these mainframe systems. The larger scale systems operate at much faster speeds and have the ability to handle a greater number of users than the systems at the lower end of the range. Importantly, in many product lines the same type of software can be run on the line's entire range of computers.

Minicomputers

Minicomputers, the next step down, are smaller and less expensive and contain somewhat less memory and processing capabilities than mainframe computers. Minicomputers can serve several users simultaneously, but not the hundreds supported by mainframes. Minicomputers are often employed by organizations that do not need the processing capability of a mainframe, but do have a need for computing power beyond that of a personal computer.

The term *minicomputer* was created to distinguish this smaller-sized system from the only other system around at that time—mainframes. Over the years, mainframes have become so reduced in scale that they are now smaller than some older minicomputers, and personal computers now have computing power rivaling both minicomputer and mainframe systems. Today, you will probably hear the term **departmental computer** to describe the same type of system once called a minicomputer (Figure 1.11).

Once again, it is not the size, power, or cost of the computer that classifies it as a minicomputer or departmental computer; rather, it is the nature of the computer's use and the resources it can provide. These systems are often used to support business applications such as accounting, inventory control, order entry, payroll and personnel, and manufacturing management. Although minicomputers do not support the extensive resources of large mainframe systems, they can easily support dozens of users.

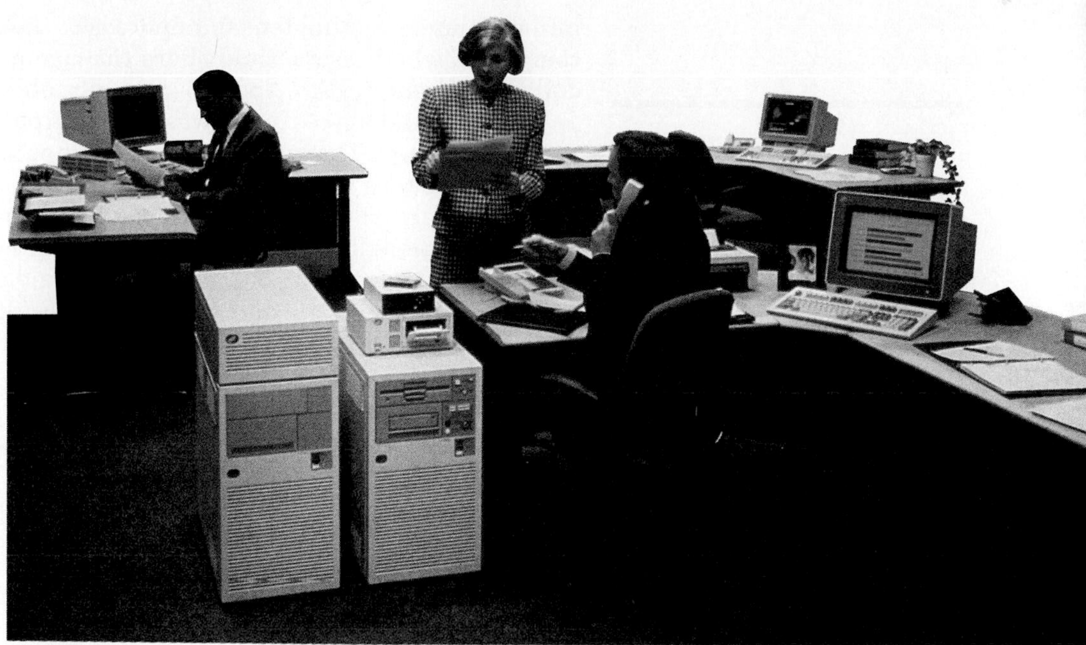

Figure 1.11
The AS/400, IBM's departmental or minicomputer system, is designed to be used in a variety of business applications.

(Courtesy International Business Machines Corp.)

Personal Computers

Personal computers are cheaper, smaller, and contain less memory than mainframe systems and minicomputers. A single personal computer is generally used by only one person at a time. That certainly does not mean, however, that a personal computer is less capable than its larger cousins. Applications for personal computers range through the full array of applications found on minicomputers and mainframe computers, though often scaled down in size for a single user's needs.

Personal computers were made possible by the development of the **microprocessor,** an integrated electronic circuit the size of your thumbnail that contains all of the needed parts of the computer's central processing unit. And don't let the size of a personal computer fool you—the personal computer used to write this text has greater computing speed and power than a mainframe of only ten years ago.

The Apple II computer launched the personal computer revolution (Figure 1.12). For the first time, a practical and somewhat cost-effective computer was available. When the Apple II became available, the only alternatives were

Figure 1.12
The Apple II personal computer launched the personal computer revolution. Left: The original Apple; right: the Apple II.

(Courtesy of Apple Computer, Inc.)

minicomputers costing tens to hundreds of thousands of dollars or mainframe computers where users could share the computer but at a cost of a hundred dollars per minute. An Apple II cost only about $3,000.

Many would agree that it was not the Apple II alone that caused the computer revolution. Though many Apple computers were sold, they did not capture the market's attention until software for use with the Apple II was also sold. Early programs such as Electric Pencil and VisiCalc made possible the use of computers by those who had no idea of how they worked. After reading some of the software's instruction manual, and through a bit of trial-and-error, a novice could start producing valuable results on his or her own personal computer. The world has not been the same since (Figure 1.13).

Figure 1.13
Two of the most popular models of personal computers: (left) the Apple Macintosh and (right) an IBM PS/2.

(Courtesy of Apple Computer, Inc. and International Business Machines Corp.)

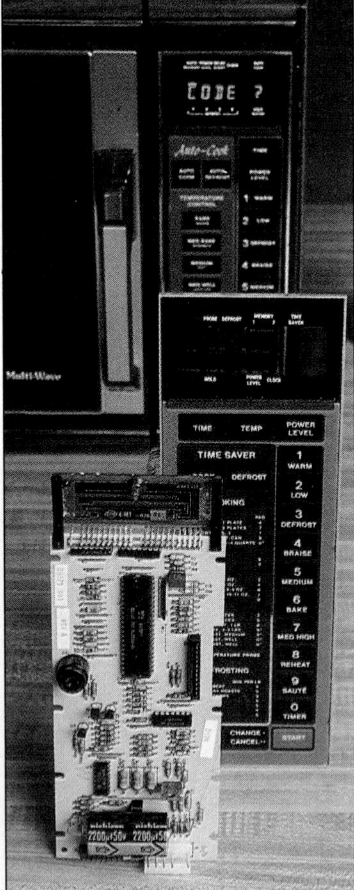

Figure 1.14
This microwave oven has an embedded microprocessor to control its many sophisticated functions.

Embedded Processors

There is an even smaller classification of computer. Using microprocessors, some manufacturers put special-purpose computers inside many of the items they produce as **embedded processors.** Automobile manufacturers place embedded processors in many of their new models to control climate inside the car, adjust power seats and steering wheel settings, and monitor electronic sensors that control gasoline flow, ignition spark, and coolant sensors; signals even warn the driver of road hazards. You can also find these processors in microwave ovens, conventional stoves, televisions, music systems, and an endless variety of similar products (Figure 1.14).

Though embedded processors will not be discussed in this text, they remind us that the power and flexibility of computing is constantly being applied to a wide range of activities in our society. Such flexibility is at the heart of the reason the computer as a tool has value to us.

HOW COMPUTERS FUNCTION

A computer, regardless of its size and computing performance, solves problems by accepting data, performing certain operations on those data, and presenting the results of those operations. Its operations are guided by instructions in the form of a program written by a person who identified an activity that would benefit from the application of a computer to a task.

Before processing can occur, the data must get into the system by means of an input device. Then the computer performs the necessary calculations or manipulations on the data; finally, the organized information is displayed by output devices. Therefore, data flow through the system according to the following steps: input, processing, and output (Figure 1.15).

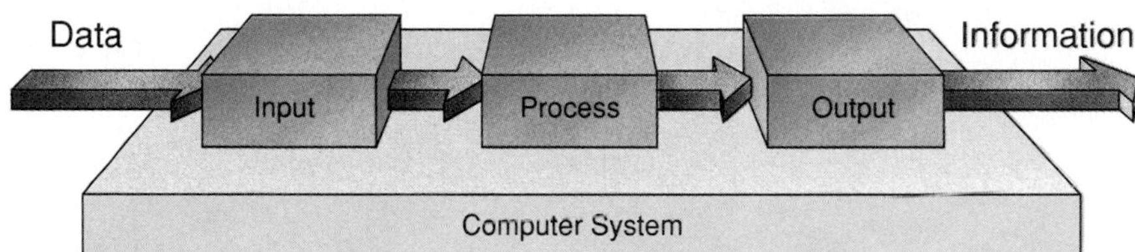

Figure 1.15
The flow of a computing operation begins with data being input to the computer. The computer then processes the data—transforming it into information that is output.

Input involves collecting, verifying, and encoding data into a machine-readable form for the computer. **Processing** means the computer creates useful information from those data by classifying, sorting, calculating, summarizing, and storing the results. **Output** includes converting the information into a human-readable form and displaying it to the user. Output may also include sending the results of computer processing in non-human-readable form in applications such as computer-controlled robotics.

Although computers have many applications, they can perform only three basic tasks:

1. Arithmetic functions on numeric data (adding, subtracting, multiplying, and dividing)
2. Testing of relationships between data items (by comparing values)
3. Storage and retrieval of data

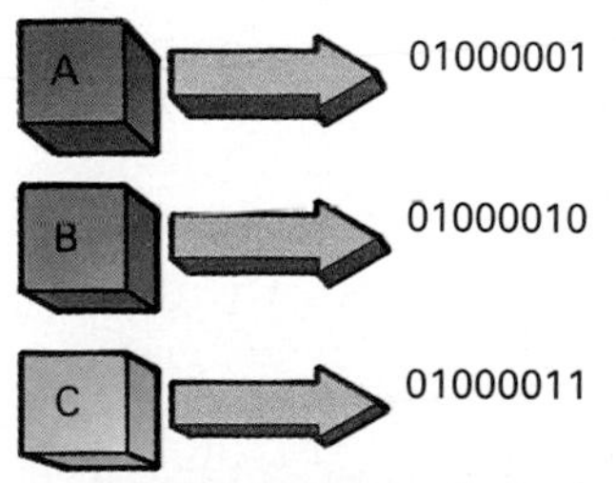

Figure 1.16
The computer can recognize only those characters that are coded as a series of 1s and 0s. In this example, the binary codes for the letters A, B, and C are shown.

These tasks accomplish really no more than people can, but the computer can do the tasks faster, more accurately, and more reliably than the average person. A computer can solve complex mathematical problems in fractions of a second, work with the greatest accuracy imaginable, and store great volumes of data. A disparity of performance between a computer and a person would be readily evident if the task, for example, involved the multiplication of two thirty-two-digit numbers.

To do functions with the speed and accuracy we desire, computers perform all of their work in the most simplistic forms possible. We can recognize and use data in a variety of forms, including alphabetic characters, numeric digits, and special symbols. Computers, in contrast, recognize data by counting discrete signals representing either a high (on) or low (off) voltage state of electricity. For the computer, numbers, alphabetic characters, and special symbols must be reduced to representation by 1s (on) and 0s (off). Figure 1.16 shows how various data can be reduced to representation by a number system of 1s and 0s, called **binary numbers.** So as you press the letter "A" on a keyboard, for example, the computer senses "01000001"—not the letter you see.

Similarly, the computer's own instructions are constructed from this binary numeric code, called **machine language.** All programs we use must eventually be simplified to the numeric language understood by the computer. Because of their reliance on a language comprised of only the binary digits 0 and 1, these systems are called **digital computers.**

TYPES OF SOFTWARE

Computers are capable of performing many varied and valuable tasks, but they are not capable of accomplishing these tasks on their own. We have already seen that computer programs, the software, provide the hardware with a series of instructions to follow in completing an assigned task. These instructions carry out the computer's basic functions—arithmetic, relational, and storage—and determine the sequence in which these activities occur. Program instructions are also responsible for controlling the use of the computer's many individual components; for example, they determine when data are to be read from a disk, displayed on the screen, or printed as output.

There are two general types of computer software: system software and application software. In brief, the computer's **operating system** (which on your system might be called **DOS** for disk operating system) controls and supervises the functions of the computer hardware, provides for the efficient use of the computer by application software, and provides an interface, which is a

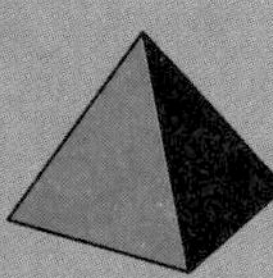

HIGHLIGHT

Is That a Bug on the Menu?

The most enduring importance of an invention is neither the amount of money it makes for its developers nor the number of jobs that result from its manufacture. Rather, it is the impact the invention has on our language. Computers have changed our language a great deal already, and the changes continue.

To begin with, words such as *byte, microchip, bubble memory, bar code, floppy disk, microprocessor,* and *artificial intelligence* were coined as names for devices and processes that didn't exist (or which had limited uses) until the computer came into its own. Then, some commonly used terms began to have specific computer-related meanings: boot, address, BASIC, bit, bug, bus, disk, dump, execute, file, flag, input, interpreter, list, load, loop, menu, monitor, mouse, network, output, plotter, program, PROM, prompt, RAM, swapping, terminal, and track. Although some of these words will no doubt become obsolete, the perseverance of our computer-based society will assure others a long, active life. In 1987, when Merriam-Webster Inc. published a supplement to its 1961 *Third International Dictionary,* the list of new terms contained 12,000 words, many of them originating from their use in the computer field. A supplement to the *Oxford English Dictionary* (the final volume of the dictionary's update) also contains some new American computer terminology (for example, *update* and *user-friendly*).

Perhaps it is poetic justice that the machine that brought so many new words into the language is now the main tool for helping those who prepare dictionaries to keep track of the changing language.

means by which you and the computer can communicate. All computers require an operating system of some sort to function, but the operating system does not provide the services for which we use the computer.

When we use the computer to do word processing, search a database, or to play a game, we are using **application software.** It is application software that solves the problems or provides the information, and therefore it is application software that we recognize most easily. Application software will get the most attention in this text, but remember that application software and the operating system are both required for the computer to function.

Software is available for an extensive range of applications. Word processing software, such as WordPerfect or Microsoft Word, is perhaps the most frequently purchased software. It permits you to do things that are not possible with handwritten or typed documents, such as saving, retrieving, and manipulating the text.

A close second to word processing software is spreadsheet software, such as Lotus 1-2-3 or Microsoft's Excel. Spreadsheet programs manage data stored in row and column format and provide features to perform arithmetic as well as text functions.

Other popular programs provide the ability to manage data. Such programs have the ability to define data storage areas where entries can be saved and manipulated. Anything from a listing of friends for your Christmas cards to a listing of stocks and bonds can be stored. More complicated lists can also be created and accessed via a special language which will be discussed in a subsequent chapter.

You can even write your own applications if you learn a computer language such as BASIC, C, or Pascal. Although writing a program is not simple, it is not terribly difficult to learn, and it gives you the ultimate power to instruct the computer to do things your way.

WHAT COMPUTERS *CANNOT* DO

Computers are very good at what they do, but there are many tasks that they can't do. They can't do anything unless they are first given specific instructions. Computers can't *decide* which program is to be used or provide their own input, *interpret* the information they generate, *implement* any decisions that they suggest, or *think*.

Computers can keep track of scientific data, but they can't conceive or express ideas for continued research. Their memories can contain the contents of encyclopedias, but they cannot decide what to do with that knowledge.

WHAT PEOPLE *CAN* DO

Computers have no ethics built into them; they only follow rules given to them by people. People must determine to use them wisely.

By creating and following precise procedures for gathering, storing, entering, and protecting data, people help computers to produce more valuable information. A person who knows which program is to be used and knows how the program operates is able to use the computer to produce the right information at the right time. If a problem arises for which there are no data or programs already available, people who understand information and computing systems—systems analysts and programmers—can help design application software to solve the problem and procedures that will guide the computer user in both obtaining the data required and using the program to create information.

Remember that a computer is only a tool used by a person who follows the correct procedures to process data into information. In the end, the most important component in the computing system may be the person who understands and controls the system.

Summary

- Computer literacy means having a general knowledge about computers, that is, knowing (1) who uses them; (2) what kinds of functions they perform; (3) how people use them; (4) where they are used; (5) how they affect society; and (6) how to use them to benefit your own life or work.
- A computer is a machine that can solve problems by accepting data, performing certain operations on those data, and presenting the results of those operations.
- Computer programs (software) are the instructions that tell the computer how to complete specific tasks.
- A computing system is the combination of hardware, software, data, procedures and people working together to provide the benefits of using the computer.
- Data are simply the numbers, letters, symbols, words, or phrases that are input to the computer to be transformed into information. Data are also called "raw facts."
- Data processing is the activity that converts data into information.
- Information is valuable if it is on time, relevant, accurate, and communicated to the appropriate person(s). Some information has more value to people than other information.
- The phrase "garbage-in, garbage-out" means that the output is only as accurate as the input and the program that processes the data.
- An information system is any combination of people, data, and procedures used to create and distribute information throughout an organization.
- Large computers are categorized as supercomputers, mainframe computers, and minicomputers. Small computers are called personal computers. Computers built into other products are called embedded processors.
- Input involves collecting, verifying, and encoding data for the computer to read. Processing means the computer creates useful information from data by classifying, sorting, calculating, summarizing, and storing the results. Output includes retrieving data and converting them so that the results can be used.
- Computers can perform only three basic tasks—arithmetic functions, comparisons, and storage and retrieval—but they can do these tasks faster, more accurately, and more reliably than people.
- Data and computer instructions can be reduced to representation by a number system of 1s and 0s, called binary numbers, or machine language. Because of their reliance upon a language comprised of only the binary digits 0 and 1, these systems are called digital computers.
- There are two general types of computer software: operating systems and application software. Operating systems control the computer hardware whereas application software solves problems and provides information.
- Computers cannot decide which program should be used, provide input, interpret data, implement decisions, or think.
- Computers have no ethics built into them; they only follow rules given to them by people. It is up to the people using computers to determine to use them wisely.

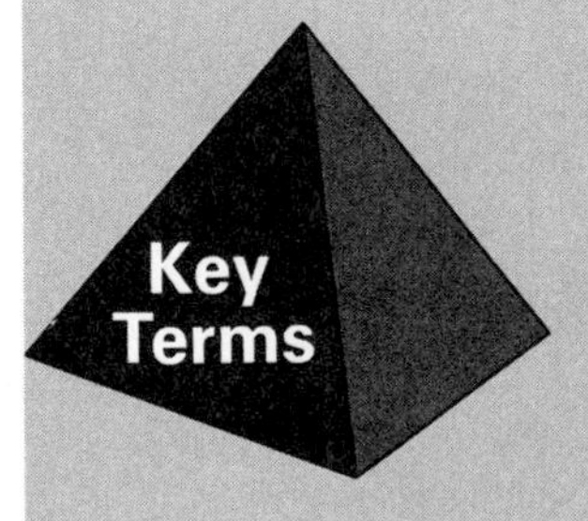

Computer
Hardware
Input device
Output device
Storage device
Central processing unit
Secondary storage device
Data
Information
Input
Processing
Output
Binary number
Machine language
Operating system
Application software

Review Questions

1. Explain why computer literacy is important today.
2. How have personal computers affected us?
3. List the components of a computing system.
4. What are the typical hardware components of a computer?
5. Define software and name several kinds of software packages that make today's computers easy to use.
6. Explain the difference between data and information. How is the value of information determined?
7. List the components of an information system.
8. What are the three categories in which large computer systems are grouped?
9. What are the characteristics of a personal computer?
10. List the steps in the flow of data through a computer and explain what is involved during each step.
11. What are the three functions of a computer?
12. Computers have three advantages over people when it comes to solving problems. What are they?
13. How are data represented in the computer?
14. What is a digital computer?
15. Name and explain the general types of software.
16. List things that computers *cannot* do.
17. What is the most interesting or unusual fact that you learned about computers in this chapter?

PROFILE

DAN BRICKLIN (left) and BOB FRANKSTON (right)

(Courtesy of Slate Corp., Watertown, MA)

Dan Bricklin, like many other students, was not fond of the tedious mathematical calculations that were required when he attended the Harvard Business School in 1978. Many of his assignments involved preparation of financial planning sheets for mock organizations. The work was repetitive and required numerous hand calculations to obtain meaningful results. At times, Bricklin would discover that a calculation he had made in the middle of the worksheet was wrong. To correct the error, that and all dependent calculations had to be redone—a time-consuming and frustrating process. Unlike most of us, however, Dan Bricklin did not just wish for a better way, he eventually did something about it.

At about that same time, microcomputers were starting to enter the marketplace. Initially, they were hardly more than high-tech toys for hobbyists and game-players. But Bricklin saw a more practical and productive use for them. Bricklin thought that an electronic spreadsheet would be a practical idea for small computers. He teamed up with a friend, Bob Frankston, and they developed an electronic spreadsheet. The product was called VisiCalc and was the first spreadsheet of its kind.

The two partners literally worked around the clock to get their programming idea off the drawing board. Recalling those early days (and late nights) for *Datamation* magazine, Bricklin said: "We settled into a routine that would carry us through the end of my term at Harvard. I would go to school during the day, and Bob would sleep. We would meet in the evenings to discuss progress and problems. Then Bob would go to work on the computer for the rest of the night, when the time-sharing rates were cheaper."

In January 1979, Bricklin and Frankston incorporated as Software Arts, Inc., and soon after, in conjunction with

Personal Software (later to become VisiCorp), began marketing VisiCalc. It was truly a revolutionary product that changed the microcomputer into a useful business tool. This was the beginning of the microcomputer application software industry.

VisiCalc went on to become the best-selling software package. In 1983, however, problems between Software Arts and VisiCorp led to lawsuits between the two companies over the rights to VisiCalc. The lawsuits left Software Arts in limbo in regard to further development and upgrades. Bricklin and Software Arts were eventually awarded the rights to VisiCalc; but because they had failed to react quickly to the new 16-bit technology while other companies developed new products for it, they lost their number one position in the marketplace.

Eventually, Bricklin sold the company and the rights to VisiCalc to Lotus, Inc., where Frankston is employed. Bricklin reentered the software business with a new product and a new company, Software Garden, Inc. Without his vision of the electronic spreadsheet and his commitment to make it a reality, the application software industry might not be where it is today.

CHAPTER 2

SOFTWARE AND APPLICATIONS: PERSONAL PRODUCTIVITY TOOLS

IN THIS CHAPTER YOU WILL LEARN ABOUT

- **System software and application software**
- **The operating system and what it does**
- **User interfaces**
- **Types of application software**

Courtesy of Innervisions

SYSTEMS OF SOFTWARE

Your first thought about using a computer might have been, "Great! Now I can really save some time; this computer will do lots of work for me." Perhaps you are interested in using a word processing program to create lengthy reports or to write letters. A business management student may have been told to use the computer because, "It will do budgets for you." You are probably excited about getting your hands on the keyboard and starting to make the computer work for you.

Look again at the last few words in the preceding sentence: "starting to make the computer work for you." That is a key statement because the computer's value is in our ability to put it to work for us in solving problems and producing information as we need it and under our control.

The key to making the computer useful is to combine it with software to perform a particular application. An **application** is the job or task a user wants the computer to do. For example, word processing used for working with text or spreadsheet programs used for statistical calculations are applications. An **application package** is software that, in conjunction with system software, instructs the computer how to do the job (Figure 2.1). Application software helps the user work faster, more efficiently, and thus more productively than if the job were done manually.

Programs that control and direct the operation of the computer hardware are **system software.** System software works behind the scene to allow you to save a letter created with a word processing application program onto a disk or to print the graph produced from a spreadsheet application.

In other words, you work with application software in order to have the computer help you with your tasks. The application program works with the system software to access the computer's hardware resources and thus do the work you request of it. Truly, this is a system of software. Now, let us see how we can make use of this system.

OPERATING SYSTEMS

You are right to be anxious about getting to those programs that most interest you—the applications. Nevertheless, it will be beneficial to learn about software in the order in which you will encounter it when you use the computer. Before any of your work can be accomplished by the computer, indeed before you can even ask the computer to use your favorite application software, the computer must first receive its own essential instructions from the operating system.

What an Operating System Is

When computers were first invented, every detail of how the hardware operated had to be programmed into the computer manually by setting switches or hand-wiring circuits. The process was long and tedious and had to be repeated for each program executed. Anyone wishing to use the computer needed specific and detailed knowledge about how a particular computer system's hardware operated. This process was so inefficient that it reduced the amount of work that could be accomplished on these expensive machines. Users, wishing to increase the system's efficiency, wanted to shift more of the work to the computer's CPU. To accomplish this, a program called an operating system was created.

An **operating system** is a set of programs that controls and supervises a computer system's hardware. Its purpose is to manage the hardware for the most efficient use of computer resources and to provide an interface between a user or an application program and the hardware. The operating system dramatically increased the efficiency of the CPU. By providing a standard set of instructions for commonly used hardware functions, it took the burden of programming every detail of an operation off the programmer.

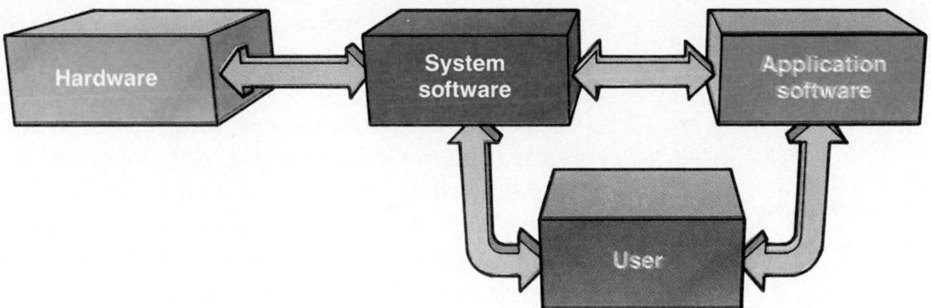

Figure 2.1
A computer interacts with both the system software and application software to accomplish a task.

While the computer is running, the operating system resides in the computer's memory, so the details of an operation are received and executed by the computer at computer speeds. Long delays that occurred when humans had to intervene were thus eliminated. An operating system can also execute another program, such as your application program, immediately without human intervention.

Control and Service Programs

The programs that make up an operating system are generally divided into two categories: control programs and service programs.

Control programs manage the computer hardware and resources. Three of the major functions of control programs are resource allocation, job management, and data management. Computer resources, such as processor time, primary storage, and input and output devices, are allocated for use by control programs. Programs that are being used are scheduled, controlled, and monitored by control programs to ensure the most efficient processing. Access to data for input and output of information to printers, disks, or displays are also managed by the control programs.

The main program in most operating systems is the supervisor program. The **supervisor program** is a control program that is also known in some operating systems as the monitor, executive, or kernel. It is responsible for controlling all the other operating system programs as well as other system and application programs. The activities of all the hardware components of the computer system are controlled by the supervisor program.

Service programs provide a service to the user or programmer of the computer system. Examples include language-translator programs and utility programs. **Language-translator programs** convert instructions written by programmers into machine-language instructions that can be executed by the computer. Language-translator programs are usually called assemblers, compilers, or interpreters; some examples are BASIC, Pascal, COBOL, or C programming languages. **Utility programs** perform common or routine functions, such as loading, saving, or copying a program; keeping track of the files stored on a disk; sorting data; and preparing a disk for use.

Figure 2.2
Every computer has an operating system. Some computers permit you to choose from several alternatives.

(Courtesy of International Business Machines Corporation)

Popular Microcomputer Operating Systems

Probably the operating systems most familiar to you are those found on microcomputers (Figure 2.2). All or part of these operating systems usually reside on a disk and are referred to as a **disk operating system** (DOS). Most likely you will be using MS-DOS (Microsoft Disk Operating System) or PC-DOS, which is a specific version of the MS-DOS software for IBM's Personal Computers. Several other of the most common systems are various versions of the UNIX operating system, CP/M (Control Program for Microcomputers), Apple PRODOS, and the Apple Macintosh operating system. Multitasking operating systems for microcomputers, such as OS/2 designed by IBM and Microsoft, are also available.

Most of the currently available operating systems have more than one version in use. Generally, the developers of operating systems use a numbering scheme to let you know which version you are using. For example, you may be using MS-DOS 4.0. The numbers 4.0 stand for version 4 (the number to the left of the decimal) and release 0 (the number to the right of the decimal). Although each developer has a particular set of rules for assigning the numbers to a program, most agree that a major change to the software will result in a change of the version number, whereas a minor revision such as correcting a program error will result in a new release number.

In most cases, programs designed for an earlier version or release will run on later editions. This characteristic is called **upward compatibility;** for example, a program designed to function with MS-DOS 2.1 will most likely continue to give you good service even though your computer may be running MS-DOS 3.3 or 5.0. The reverse, downward compatibility, is usually not possible. Programs developed for later versions of an operating system will usually not run on earlier versions.

What an Operating System Does

At another point in this book you will learn more specifically how to start your computer and the exact commands to use to put the computer to work. For now, though, let us just take a quick look at the essentials of the operating system.

When you first turn on a computer—and this applies generally to all computers, whether a mainframe system or your own personal computer—the operating system will first check out the computer's hardware functions to make certain that they are working in the way expected. If a component fails to operate correctly, an error message of some sort is usually generated to alert the computer's operator. Perhaps this will be a message on the screen or a series of beeps from the system.

Once the computer has successfully started functioning, the operating system's control programs go to work to "load" the supervisor portion of the operating system into the computer's memory. This is the stage of operations most of us call **booting** the computer. Once the supervisor control program is in memory, the system signals you that it is ready to go to work. That signal is what we call the **prompt,** and it is perhaps the most evident aspect of the operating system's influence over the "personality" of the computing system.

User-Friendly Operating Systems

Many computer users have a fear that they will have to learn a somewhat baffling list of mysterious commands to use their computer. Unfortunately, a computer *can* be made to act that way; the fear can be well founded if the operating system or application programs use commands and keystrokes with hidden meanings, if help is not easily available, or if a program seems to defy a seemingly obvious operation.

User-friendly is a term which implies that the computer somehow assists you; it provides a better means by which you can communicate your needs to it and by which it can guide you when necessary. User-friendly has acquired the popular definition of "easy to learn and easy to use," but that depends on your needs, sophistication, and expectations. Spartan-appearing operating environments may be quite comfortable for those with a high level of computer experience. In contrast, a novice may wish more helpful features and computer-aided assistance.

One way in which the operating system influences the computer's ease of use is in the style of user interface provided. The **user interface** is the means by which you are able to issue commands and instructions to the computer and by which the computer can inform you of actions you must take or errors in operation. Many forms of user interfaces exist, each with its own sort of personality in terms of what it implies for your use of the computer.

Prompts

A prompt is simply a program-generated signal to you that lets you know the system is ready for an action by you. Prompts are created by both application programs and operating systems and are one of the most characteristic forms of the user interface.

You are probably already aware of at least one form of a prompt. The **DOS prompt** seen on most machines using the MS-DOS or PC-DOS operating systems generally looks like this: C:\> (Figure 2.3). This simple form of user interface is said to be **character based,** or **command-line oriented,** because it indicates to you that you are to respond by typing in a series of characters to issue a command to the computer. For example, to start the word processing program, you might enter "WP" and press the enter key on the keyboard. If you enter the command correctly, the operating system responds by starting the word processing program. If you enter a command that is not understood by the operating system, you will receive a brief error message on the display screen (Figure 2.4).

Figure 2.3
The DOS prompt indicates the command line. Entering the command DIR will list the directory of files.

```
C:\>dir

 Volume in drive C has no label
 Directory of C:\

COMMAND  COM    47845   04-09-91   5:00a
CONFIG   SYS      305   08-12-91   6:47p
AUTOEXEC BAT      229   08-13-91   1:57p
PHOTO1   DED    58959   04-17-91   3:20p
PHOTO2   DED    11853   04-25-91   9:54a
PHOTO3   DBD     8585   04-25-91  10:57a
PHOTO4   DED     4708   04-25-91   8:12p
        7 File(s)   2910548 bytes free

C:\>
```

Figure 2.4
When an error is made, the operating system responds with a message. Here, an error was made in entering DIR.

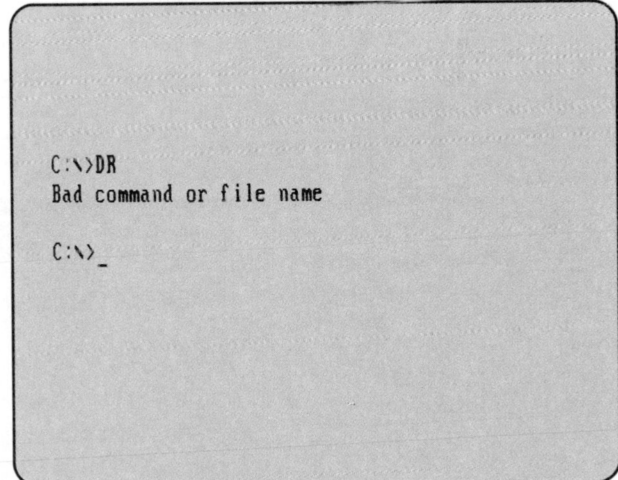
C:\>DR
Bad command or file name
C:\>_

The command-line user interface is not viewed as being very helpful, especially to novice computer users who not surprisingly, have a difficult time trying to sort through and remember many different and strange-appearing commands. Also, this form of interface does not always provide any computer-aided assistance to help guide you in selecting the correct command or overcoming an error message.

Lack of guidance is not always the case with a command-line interface, though, even with the most brief-appearing prompts. dBASE, a popular database program, has a command-line user interface that is simply a period,

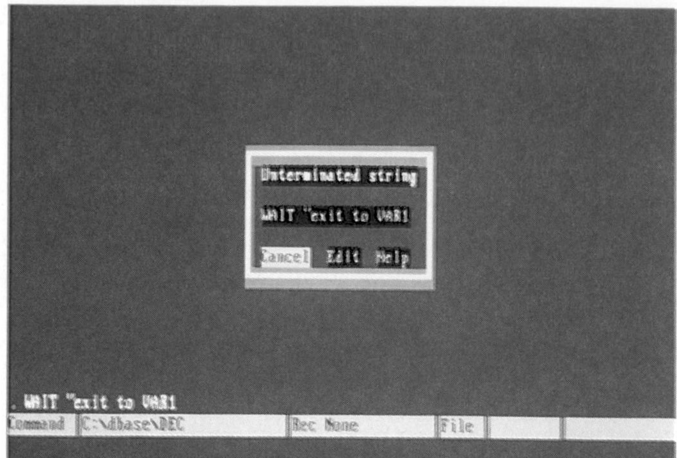

Figure 2.5
dBASE dot prompt. The question mark (?) indicates an error in the dBASE command.

(Courtesy Innervisions)

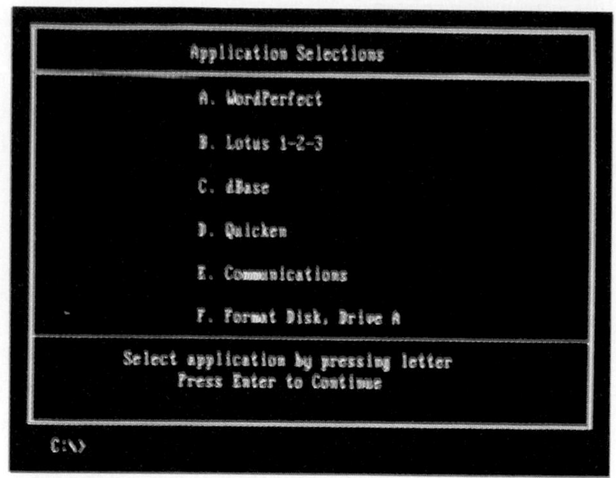

Figure 2.6
A menu of alternative choices simplifies the selection and entry of commands.

(Courtesy Innervisions)

called the dot prompt. Although this is a character-based command line, the error messages attempt to show users where in their command entry the error occurred (Figure 2.5). Also, pressing a function key on the keyboard or typing "HELP" will access a help system.

Menus

When you go to your favorite restaurant, someone usually hands you a menu. **Menus** are simply lists of alternative selections from which you may choose the one you desire. A menu on the computer's screen is an attempt to improve the user's interface by providing a listing of commonly used commands or actions which may be selected to initiate a computing activity (Figure 2.6).

In some cases, menus are simply listings of alternative selections on the screen. You must then indicate your choice to the computer by responding to

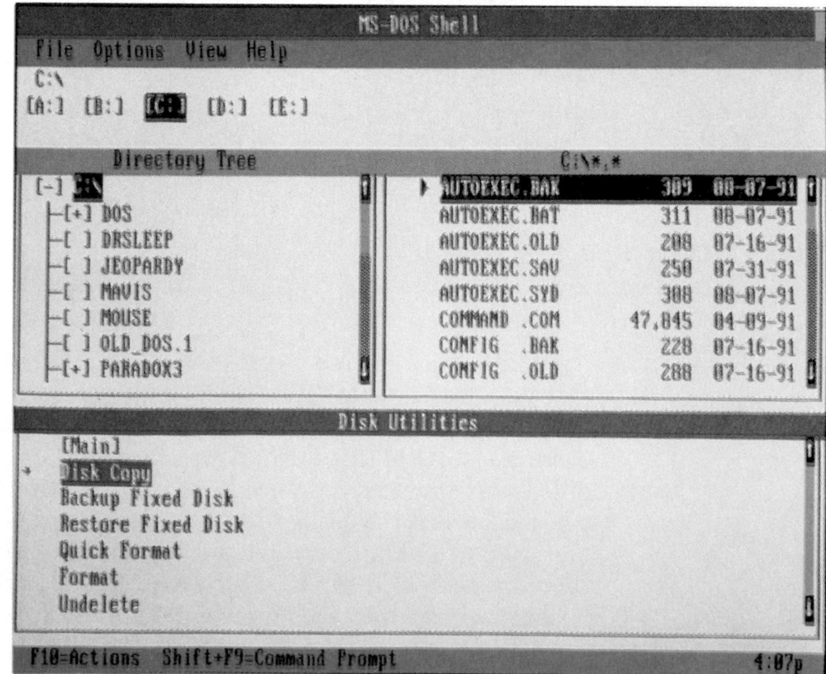

Figure 2.7
A DOS 4.0 menu. Choices are made with either the cursor control and enter keys or by using the mouse. Choices with ". . ." after the entry indicate additional menu listings.

(Courtesy Innervisions)

the same type of command-line prompt already discussed. Although such a menu simplifies the system somewhat in that you might not need to remember frequently used commands, you would still have to recall less obvious commands that were not listed due to the limitations of space on the screen.

An alternative form of menu is one in which a selection of one of the alternatives shown leads to the display of another menu with more specific alternatives relating to the earlier choice. Figure 2.7 on the preceding page is an example: The first screen lists several alternative selections. Choosing "DOS Utilities" leads to another menu listing several DOS functions from which you may choose the one you need.

Frequently, the more advanced menu interfaces do away with the requirement to type in an entry at a command prompt. You may be allowed instead to point to your choice by moving the **cursor** (the flashing line that usually appears on the screen directly in front of where you are typing) to the indicated alternative and to then press the enter key. The cursor, which by the way is simply another form of user interface that lets you know where your next entry will be made as you type on the keyboard, might be moved by using one of the cursor control keys (the arrow keys on the right side of your keyboard), pressing the tab key, or some other method as indicated by the program (for example, pressing the space bar).

By far, the most popular pointing device for personal computers is the **mouse,** a hand-controlled device that may be moved around the desktop in order to move the cursor around the screen (Figure 2.8). When the mouse is being used, the cursor on the screen is usually changed to a small arrow to indicate the selection at which you are pointing.

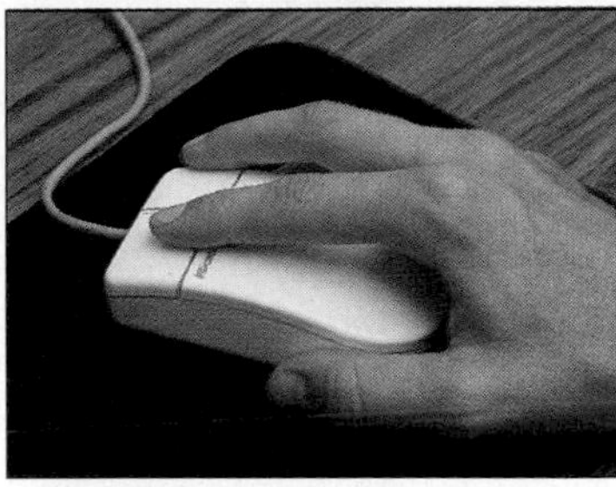

Figure 2.8
The mouse allows you to point to a choice on the screen and to click a button to confirm your selection.

The mouse is only one of several hardware devices that allow pointing of this type. A trackball might be used (Figure 2.9), as well as various other mechanisms, including your finger if the computer has a touch-sensitive screen (Figure 2.10).

Figure 2.9
A trackball is another pointing device.

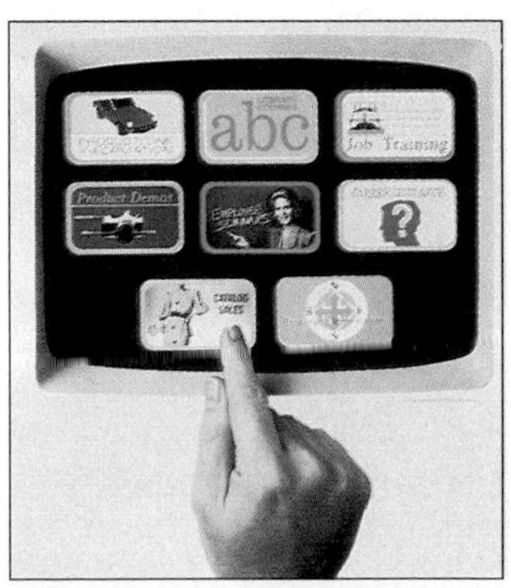

Figure 2.10
A touch-sensitive screen also allows pointing.

Graphic User Interfaces

To use a mouse or other pointing device, the computer must be able to sense any area on the screen where the cursor is moved. These so-called **all-points-addressable screens** are also called **graphics displays** because they are capable of producing images other than only characters—the letters, numbers, and symbols found on the keyboard.

Because they are able to use a variety of graphic images and characters, program designers are able to produce attractive user interfaces by using text for titles, lines for borders, and colors for visual enhancement. A principal difference between earlier versions of MS-DOS and version 4.0, for example, was the appearance of DOS 4.0's graphic user interface which incorporated the use of the mouse, colors, and menu selections in contrast to the older version's interface of a command line only. (Compare Figures 2.3 and 2.7.)

Icons

If a picture is worth a thousand words, an icon must be worth at least a thousand commands to some computer users. An **icon** is a graphic symbol on the screen which represents a command or action (Figure 2.11). Rather than remember to type a command to start your word processing program, for example, "WORD," or having to select the "WORD" alternative from a menu's listing, you simply use the mouse to point to a drawing of a pencil symbolizing your desire to write using the word processing program called WORD.

The use of icons to symbolize actions or options has dramatically altered the way in which we communicate with the computer. Although popularized by Apple Computer's Macintosh line of personal computers, the use of both the mouse and icons was begun by Xerox Corporation in the early 1970s. Certainly

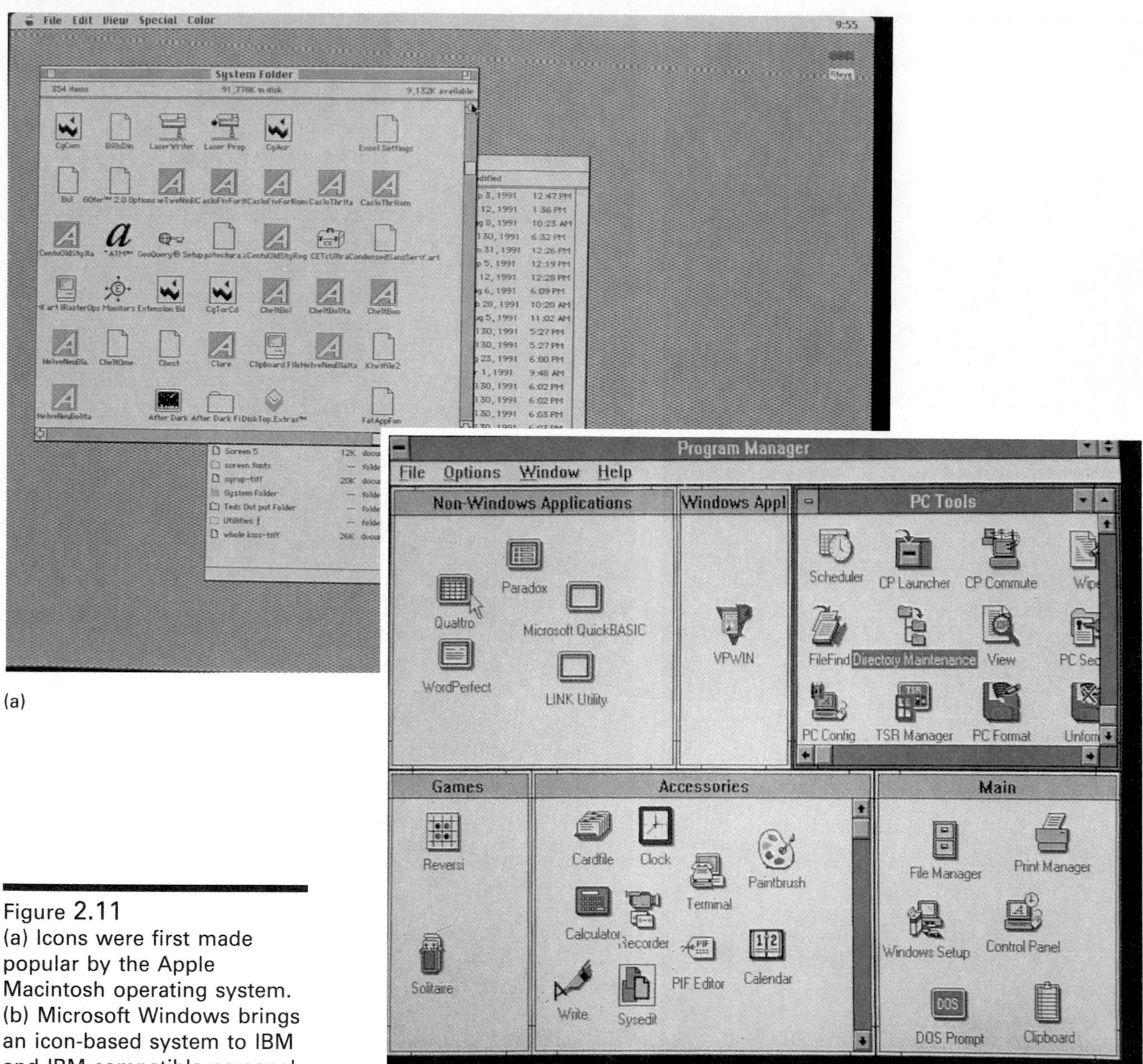

(a)

(b)

Figure 2.11
(a) Icons were first made popular by the Apple Macintosh operating system. (b) Microsoft Windows brings an icon-based system to IBM and IBM-compatible personal computers.

the use of icons has made learning to use the computer more intuitive. New computer users have only to become accustomed to moving the mouse and selecting the proper icon for their tasks in order to become productive. Some actions are almost comic: One of Apple's most famous icons is the trash can; in order to erase a file, for instance, you simply move the file's icon symbol to the trash can, which then plumps up a bit to let you know it is full of trash (Figure 2.12).

Windows and Desktops

Another feature resulting from Xerox's research, and also popularized by the Macintosh computer, is the concept of windowing, or viewing multiple images at one time. A **window** is a specifically defined area of the screen in which may be displayed data, menus, program applications, icons, and other windows. By using multiple windows, for example, a user may view a letter in one

Figure 2.12
The Macintosh trash can is one of the most well-known icons. The icon plumps up when trash has been deposited.

area of the screen while looking up an address from a file in another (Figure 2.13).

The metaphor used to explain the windowing environment is the **desktop.** In this graphical environment, as it is called by Microsoft developers of the Windows program for MS-DOS computers, you are able to arrange your work on the computer screen similar to the way you might arrange your work on top of an actual desk. The most current item, the one you are working on now, would be on top and perhaps would be most prominently in view. Other tasks, represented by additional windows, would appear beneath or to one side or another of the current window. If you discover that you need information from one of the other windows, you can rearrange your electronic desktop to shuffle the desired information to the forefront of the screen—much like you might pull a note out from beneath a stack of other papers. If you decide that you should be able to see the note while you are working on the first application,

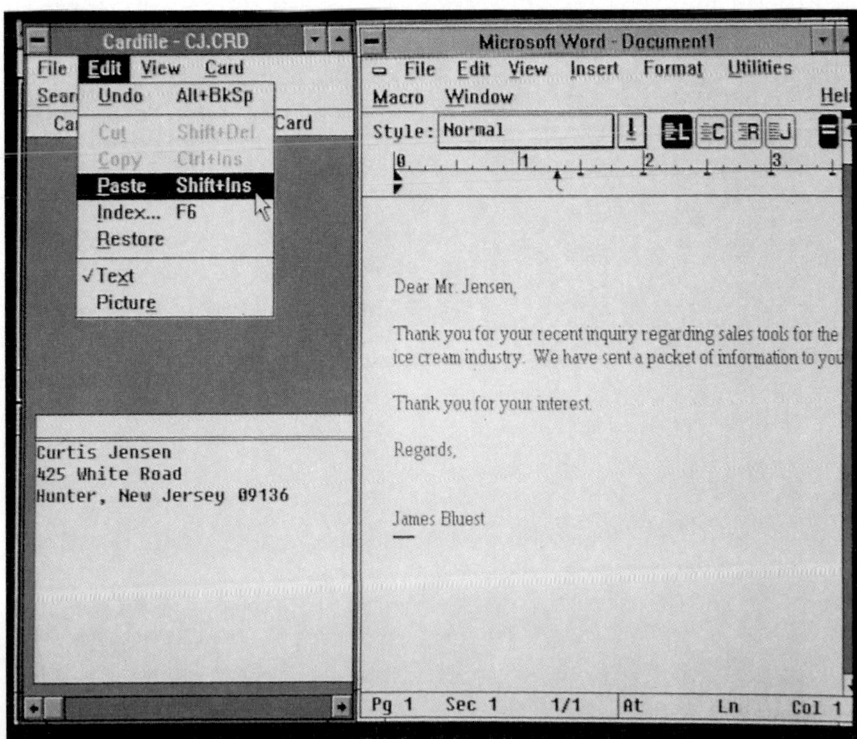

Figure 2.13
Windows give the ability to see multiple images at one time. Here, an address is being accessed in one window in order to be copied to a memo being typed in another window.

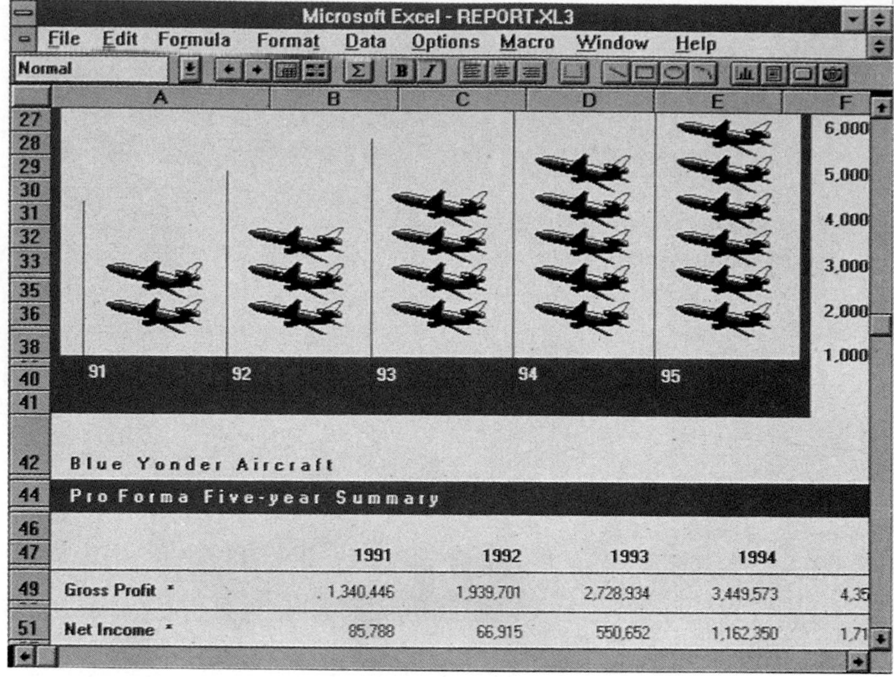

Figure 2.14
While one window shows the annual budget, other windows display charts highlighting key figures from the budget.

(Courtesy of Microsoft Corp.)

you can rearrange the size and location of the two windows so that both are in view on the "desktop" (Figure 2.14).

Operating systems are increasingly incorporating windowing techniques because they can simplify the user interface while they give greater access to applications. The Apple Macintosh operating system is a windowing environment, as is OS/2 for IBM and compatible computers (Figure 2.15). The program called Windows makes this environment available for personal computers that use the MS-DOS system. UNIX, too, has a windowing interface known as X-Windows (Figure 2.16).

One subtle benefit of the intense development of windowing environments is that each of the different systems is becoming more like the others. In the long run, this may mean that once you have mastered one system, you will have basically learned to use them all. It may also mean that applications begun on one computing system could be continued on another without fear that they would be incompatible. That happy circumstance would permit users

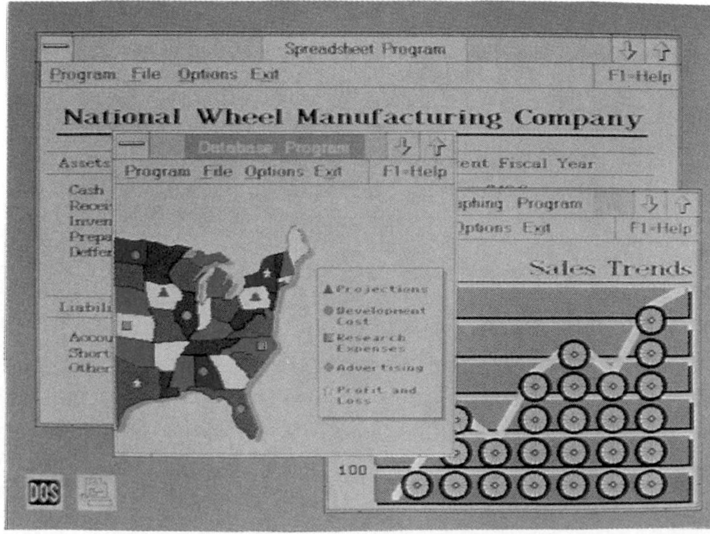

Figure 2.15
The OS/2 operating system for personal computers includes the icon-based Presentation Manager graphic user interface.

(Courtesy of International Business Machines Corporation)

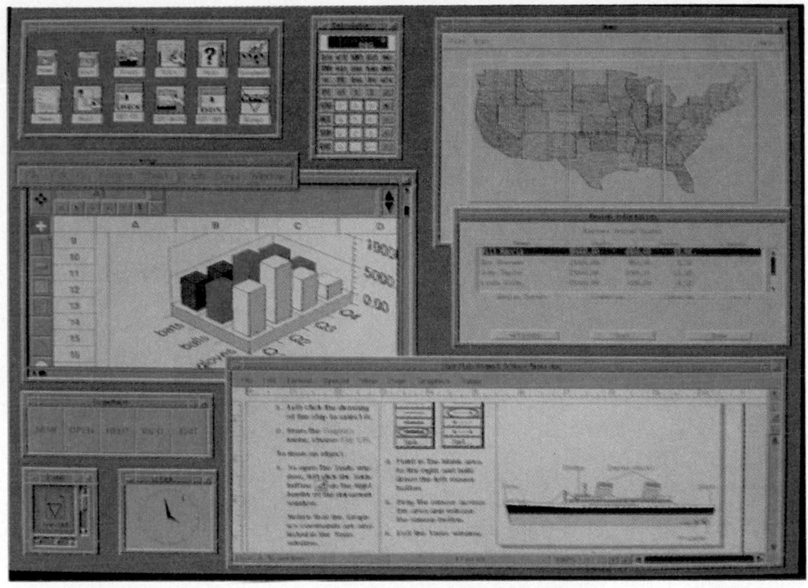

Figure 2.16
X-Windows provides UNIX systems with a graphic environment.

(Courtesy of The Santa Cruz Operation, Inc.)

to focus on the computer as a problem-solving tool in general, rather than on one type of computer hardware versus another.

Is Easier Always Better?

The trend in operating systems is to simplify the user interface—to make it more intuitive and less technical so that users can point to a selection and press a button to initiate a task or perform some action. The apparent benefit is to let the computer do more of the routine work and to let you concentrate on the application you are using to solve your problem. But does this benefit apply to all computer users? Does each improvement enhance operations in the same way for all users?

"Not necessarily" would be the safe answer. As you use the computer more and more, you depend less on the computer to provide you with a menu of choices; instead, you start to remember the choices yourself. You might find that help screens and messages are useful as you begin to use the computer, but that they start to bog you down or to annoy you once you have become more comfortable in your own use of the system.

Those who know the keyboard well and are good touch-typists may find that they are slowed down too much when they have to reach off of the keyboard to find and move the mouse. Perhaps a simple keystroke is better than using the mouse to point to a menu.

On the other hand, even those who may be comfortable using keyboard-oriented commands, and who may have even memorized them, may discover that using the mouse makes certain work faster. And though a user may decide that keyboarding is faster for some tasks, such as word processing, the same user may find the mouse and menus to be more productive for an application such as a spreadsheet.

The point is no one style of computing is best for everyone. No matter how popular or efficient one method may seem to be, that method may not work well for all. Therefore, whether incorporated as a part of the operating system, added on to it (as Windows is to DOS), or part of the application, the best user interface will have a variety of ways to accomplish any task. For example, although DOS 4.0 uses a menu and the mouse, it gives you access to the older command prompt as well. Though Windows is built around a graphic user interface, the operating system permits selection of actions with multiple tools, including the mouse, keyboarded instructions, and function keys (Figure 2.17).

A well-designed user interface permits you to begin your use of the computer with simple tools and as much computer-aided assistance as possible. It also includes, however, the ability to adapt to your increasing sophistication by enabling you to change the way in which you communicate with the computer and its software. Perhaps you will start by using the mouse alone, then gradually learn some keyboard shortcuts, and finally use a combination of methods at one time or another as you desire.

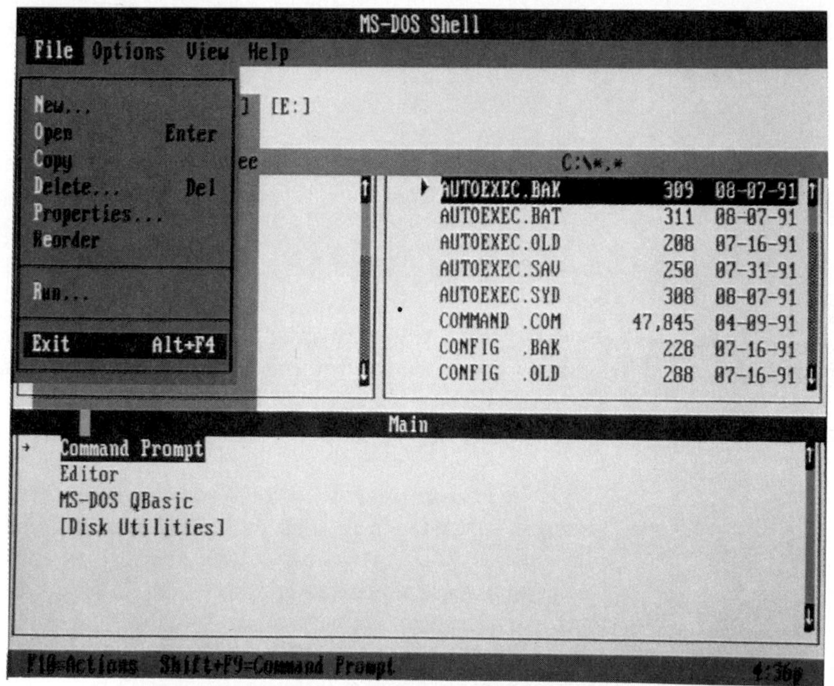

(a)

```
Microsoft(R) MS-DOS(R) Version 5.00
             (C)Copyright Microsoft Corp 1981-1991.

Enter 'EXIT' to return to WordPerfect
D:\WP51>exit_
```

(b)

Figure 2.17
(a) Though DOS 5.0 provides a graphic user interface, it still permits access to the standard DOS prompt through the command prompt option on the menu.
(b) Typing "EXIT" at the command prompt will return the screen to the DOS 5.0 menu.

APPLICATION SOFTWARE

Application software packages come in varying levels of sophistication and complexity (Figure 2.18). The demand for user-friendly application software is no less than that for user-friendly operating systems. So software developers have become more sensitive to the needs of the novice and nontechnical user. At the same time, though, the average level of sophistication continues to increase as more of us use computers more often. This has the effect of raising our expectations of what can be done with application software; so, while paying more attention to novice users, software developers have to continually increase the functions their programs are able to perform.

Two main sources of software exist: (1) so-called packaged software developed commercially by firms or groups who then sell the applications to the computer user, and (2) software developed specifically by or for computer users themselves.

Figure 2.18
A wide variety of application software is available.

(Courtesy Innervisions)

PACKAGED SOFTWARE

Most likely you will be using packaged software. **General application software** is developed for a wide variety of applications and meets most of the needs encountered by computer users. **Specialized application programs** perform very specific tasks, often for very narrowly defined markets. If the task is related to one of the more popular types of application packages, such as word processors, spreadsheets, or data managers, at least one of the hundreds of general application packages available for purchase will probably work for most users. However, the more specialized the task, the more difficult it is to find a package that meets a user's exact needs.

Prewritten, packaged software has several advantages. First, the packages can be set up and running quickly; they are ready for immediate use. If you need application software now, it is probably available. Once purchased and installed on the computer, it is ready to put the computer to use.

A second advantage is that prewritten software packages are usually less expensive than those produced in-house by the user company or an individual. In-house developmental costs for software are high because development is time consuming and requires skilled personnel.

A third advantage is that prewritten software has already been tested. Any new software requires a great deal of testing before it is ready to use. Commercially produced software will not be marketed successfully if the buying audience is not convinced that the software is reliable and efficient. The testing of the software package begins inside the developer's own organization. The program undergoes a quality assurance process to look for errors in the software and to review the accompanying manuals and documentation. Next, the developer often selects several knowledgeable computer users who try out a test copy of the program—so-called beta-test versions that have passed the firm's internal quality assurance process.

When the developers are satisfied that the program is as error-free as it can be, that the documentation is prepared, and that the production of a marketable version is underway, then the program is released for sale in the marketplace. When you need an application, you may simply visit a computer or software retail store to purchase your copy of the program.

You then help to continue the testing, in effect, by using the software. Although the developer tries to remove all possible errors, software produced today is of such complexity and high sophistication that it is virtually impossible to foresee every problem or deficiency. Therefore, as you use the program and perhaps call the developer for assistance with problems or to inquire about features, you are helping to improve the program by providing valuable feedback about its actual use. The more popular programs benefit from having perhaps several hundreds of thousands of users providing feedback. In turn, everyone benefits when a new version incorporates improved features based on user feedback.

Shareware and Public Domain Software

Software can be expensive, but it does not have to be. A computer user with a number of needs could easily spend as much on software as he or she spent to purchase the computer hardware. Some software developers, realizing that not everyone is able to spend hundreds of dollars on each application, have taken an alternative road to the retail market.

Shareware is one avenue for acquiring software. A software developer owns the rights to the software, but elects to distribute it free of charge or for a nominal fee. If you like the software, you are encouraged to send a payment to the developer for an improved version, manuals, or other privileges such as future updates.

Public domain software earns its name from the fact that the developers have given up their rights to the software, or because it was produced from public funds, such as in a university research project underwritten by a government grant. This software is also distributed free of charge.

You might learn of shareware or public domain software through a computer users' group or an electronic bulletin board, from friends or fellow computer users, at computer trade shows, or from advertisements in computer magazines. Be aware, though, that while some software available in this way is very good, most of it has limited support and perhaps is not as completely tested as is commercially available software.

Ethics of Copying Software, and Software Licenses

Unauthorized copying and distribution of software is illegal, period. It is also an unethical use of the software to which you have access.

When an author creates a new book, such as the one you are reading, the author can obtain a copyright, which provides legal protection against unauthorized copying or use of the author's work. Similarly, computer software can be protected legally by a copyright, which establishes a limitation on how a person may legally use the program (Figure 2.19). Other legal protections, such as trademark registration and coverage by patent law, are also granted.

Generally, you do not really buy the software when you acquire an application software package; you actually are buying the right to use the package according to instructions contained within a software license. The software license is often printed on the box or envelope containing the software, with a warning that opening the wrapping containing the software constitutes your acceptance of the developer's conditions of use.

In most cases, you are given the right to use the software on one computer and to make a single **archival copy** of the software as a backup to guard against accidental loss. Sometimes a software company will grant the buyer the right to use the software on more than one computer; a **site license,** for example, grants the right to use the software on all computers installed at a single location or within a company.

Although you may "get away" with making a copy for a friend, you really are breaking the law, unless the software you are using is public domain software or shareware that gives you the right to copy it. Actually, you do not gain

Figure 2.19
Copyright notices accompany application software packages.

IMPORTANT–PLEASE READ CAREFULLY BEFORE OPENING THIS SEALED PACKAGE

NOTIFICATION OF COPYRIGHT

THIS SOFTWARE PROGRAM ("SOFTWARE") IS A PROPRIETARY PRODUCT OF WORDPERFECT CORPORATION ("WPCORP") AND IN CERTAIN INSTANCES CONTAINS MATERIAL PROPRIETARY TO GRAPHIC SOFTWARE SYSTEMS, INC. THESE PROPRIETARY PRODUCTS ARE PROTECTED BY COPYRIGHT LAWS AND INTERNATIONAL TREATY. YOU MUST TREAT THE SOFTWARE LIKE ANY OTHER COPYRIGHTED MATERIAL, EXCEPT THAT YOU MAY MAKE AN ARCHIVAL COPY OF THE SOFTWARE FOR EACH COPY WHICH IS LICENSED TO YOU. YOU MAY NOT COPY THE WRITTEN MATERIALS ACCOMPANYING THE SOFTWARE.

SOFTWARE LICENSE AGREEMENT

LICENSE FOR SINGLE COPY

READ THIS LICENSE AGREEMENT BEFORE OPENING THIS SEALED PACKAGE. THIS AGREEMENT IS A LEGAL CONTRACT BETWEEN YOU, THE END USER, AND WPCORP GOVERNING YOUR USE OF THE SOFTWARE. OPENING THIS SEALED PACKAGE INDICATES YOUR ACCEPTANCE OF THIS AGREEMENT. THIS AGREEMENT SHALL ALSO BE BINDING ON ANY SUBSEQUENT, AUTHORIZED LICENSEE. IF YOU DO NOT WISH TO AGREE TO THE TERMS OF THIS AGREEMENT, PROMPTLY RETURN THE COMPLETE SOFTWARE PROGRAM PACKAGE, WITH THE SEALED MEDIA PACKAGE(S) UNOPENED (IF APPLICABLE), TO THE RESELLER FROM WHOM YOU OBTAINED THIS PRODUCT. YOU WILL RECEIVE A FULL REFUND PROVIDED (i) YOU RETURN THE FULL SOFTWARE PACKAGE, AND (ii) THE SEALED MEDIA PACKAGE(S) IS/ARE UNOPENED. IF YOU HAVE ANY QUESTIONS CONCERNING THIS AGREEMENT, CONTACT WORDPERFECT CORPORATION, ATTN: INFORMATION SERVICES, 1555 N. TECHNOLOGY WAY, OREM, UT 84057-9915, OR CALL (801) 225-5000.

LICENSE

1. If the Software package containing this license is a "Standalone/First Station" version, WPCorp grants you the right to use as many copies of the Software and associated GSS graphics drivers (if applicable) as are indicated above on single-user computers, file servers or on workstations/terminals of a local area network. If, however, the Software package containing this license is a "Network Additional Station" version, you may use the Software only in connection with a workstation/terminal of a local area network. Each copy of the Software on a single-user computer or on a workstation/terminal of a multi-user computer or a local area network, whether only executing from memory in a local area network or multiuser system or stored on a hard disk or other storage device, must be separately licensed. If this is a license for a single copy of the Software and if this sealed package contains multiple forms of media, you are licensed to use only one of the media forms at a time.

2. You may not sublicense, rent or lease the Software, but you may permanently transfer your license to use the Software and accompanying materials by delivering the original media and materials comprising the software package, including the Certificate of License, to a third party who accepts the terms and conditions of this Agreement, and by simultaneously destroying all copies of the Software and accompanying materials in your possession. Such transfer terminates your license to use the Software. The new recipient of the Software and accompanying materials accepts this Agreement and is licensed under the terms of this Agreement upon initially using the Software. If this is a multipack license, you may only transfer this license in its entirety; you may not divide the multipack license and transfer any portion of the licensed materials or separate copies of the Software to any party.

3. If the Software contains GSS graphics drivers, and for any reason your license to use the GSS graphics drivers is terminated, whether by GSS or WPCorp, you must either destroy them or return them to WPCorp.

4. If the licensee is a qualified educational institution, special licensing provisions apply. For information concerning these special educational licensing procedures, contact the WPCorp Education Department at 1555 N. Technology Way, Orem, Utah 84057-9915, or call (801) 222-2300.

5. WPCorp further grants you the right to make an archival copy of the software media as set forth in the Notification of Copyright above. You may not decompile, disassemble, reverse engineer, copy, transfer, or otherwise use the Software except as stated in this Agreement.

6. WPCorp warrants the operation of the Software only with the operating system for which it was designed (e.g., DOS, OS/2, UNIX, etc.). Use of the Software with an operating system other than that for which it was designed may not be supported by WPCorp.

7. Use of the Software in conjunction with any non-WPCorp product which decompiles or recompiles the Software or in any way creates a derivative or modified copy of the Software is not an authorized use. Further, such unauthorized use is not supported by WPCorp and voids the WPCorp product warranty set forth below.

LIMITED WARRANTY/LIMITATION OF REMEDIES

WPCorp will replace, at no charge, defective media and product materials that are returned within 90 days of the original date of purchase. WPCorp warrants that the Software will perform in substantial compliance with the written materials accompanying the Software. If you report, in writing, a significant defect to WPCorp and WPCorp is unable to correct it within 90 days of the date you report the defect, you may return the Software and accompanying materials and WPCorp will refund the purchase price. By opening this sealed package, you agree that the only remedy available to you will be a refund of the purchase price of this software program package.

SUCH WARRANTIES ARE IN LIEU OF OTHER WARRANTIES, EXPRESS OR IMPLIED, INCLUDING, BUT NOT LIMITED TO, THE IMPLIED WARRANTIES OF MERCHANTABILITY AND FITNESS FOR A PARTICULAR PURPOSE WITH RESPECT TO THE SOFTWARE AND THE ACCOMPANYING WRITTEN MATERIALS. IN NO EVENT WILL WPCORP BE LIABLE TO YOU FOR DAMAGES, INCLUDING ANY LOSS OF PROFITS, LOST SAVINGS, OR OTHER INCIDENTAL OR CONSEQUENTIAL DAMAGES ARISING OUT OF YOUR USE OF OR INABILITY TO USE THE SOFTWARE, EVEN IF WPCORP OR AN AUTHORIZED WPCORP REPRESENTATIVE HAS BEEN ADVISED OF THE POSSIBILITY OF SUCH DAMAGES.

This limited warranty gives you specific legal rights. Some states provide other rights, and some states do not allow excluding or limiting implied warranties or limiting liability for incidental or consequential damages. As a result, the above limitations and/or exclusions may not apply to you. Furthermore, some jurisdictions have statutory consumer protection provisions which may supersede this section of the Agreement.

GENERAL

If any provision of this Agreement shall be unlawful, void, or for any reason unenforceable, then that provision shall be deemed severable from this Agreement and shall not affect the validity and enforceability of the remaining provisions of this Agreement. This Agreement is governed by the laws of the State of Utah.

U.S. GOVERNMENT RESTRICTED RIGHTS

The Software and accompanying materials are provided with Restricted Rights. Use, duplication, or disclosure by the Government is subject to restrictions as set forth in subparagraph (c)(1)(ii) of the Rights in Technical Data and Computer Software clause at DFARS 252.227-7013, or subparagraphs (c)(1) and (2) of the Commercial Computer Software–Restricted Rights at 48 CFR 52.227-19, as applicable. Contractor/manufacturer is WordPerfect Corporation, 1555 N. Technology Way, Orem, Utah 84057-9915.

© Copyright WordPerfect Corporation, 1991

LBUGXAMXXXTA—7/91
74 - 42 - 20

by "pirating" a copy of software. If you do not have a legally obtained copy of the software, you will not be able to get assistance from the developer, and you will not be notified of special offers for updated versions. Very importantly, you probably will not have access to the program's operating instructions which are usually contained in the manual shipped with the legal copies.

USER-DEVELOPED SOFTWARE

As an alternative to commercially packaged software, some users write their own. **User-written application packages** are those that are designed and coded by the user or that are written by developers according to the user's specifications. A user can be either an individual, such as yourself, or an organization, such as a business.

An added advantage to writing one's own software is that the creator may, in turn, be able to market and sell it to others. As you saw at the beginning of this chapter, the whole application software industry for microcomputers got its start when Bricklin and Frankston created and sold the first electronic spreadsheet. What was user-written software to them quickly became prewritten software to us.

HIGHLIGHT

Using "User-Friendly"

Of all the terms spun out by the computer revolution, none has become more popular than *user-friendly*. In fact, advertisers and salespeople now apply it indiscriminately to any product that has any interaction with human beings—which is to say, all products. Consequently, a car with power steering becomes user-friendly because it is easier to drive than a car without it. Conceivably, a book with large type and widely spaced lines is more user-friendly than a telephone directory with small type.

Even when the term is applied to computers, software, and accessories, its use is commonly overdone to the point that it can mean anything. Does the computer use a mouse instead of a keyboard for interaction? Does the system support color graphics? Does it use icons instead of text? If the answer is "yes," then there are plenty of computer salespeople and advertisers ready to assure you that you are in the friendliest of territories.

People who are more concerned with precise description than with sales slogans believe that *user-friendly* can still be a valuable phrase when it is applied to the real world and not the sales-driven imaginary one. For a computer or its software to be truly user-friendly, it has to be considered in relation to the work being done as well as to the skills and demands of the operator. The term is relative, not absolute.

One user-friendly quality, for example, is the group of features that actively assists the particular user in the execution of a task by anticipating potential mistakes and keeping them from being catastrophic. The term should mean that a system is designed to encourage rather than discourage use. Capability is a big factor, in addition to friendliness, because ease of use and error compensation mean little if the system can't do the job that is assigned to it.

Until speakers and writers concede to use it precisely, the term *user-friendly* remains too user-friendly.

SPECIALIZED AND GENERALIZED APPLICATION PACKAGES

Application packages can be grouped into two broad categories: specialized and generalized. A **specialized application package** performs a specific task and cannot be changed or programmed to perform a different task. For example, a payroll package is designed to be used exclusively for payroll functions. Another specialized package might be designed to choreograph musical productions. It has not been programmed to do, and cannot be used for, other tasks such as cost analysis.

A **generalized application package** is one that can be applied to a wide variety of tasks. A spreadsheet, for example, has features and capabilities to create one worksheet to calculate a payroll and another worksheet to monitor personal investments.

TYPES OF APPLICATION PACKAGES

New application packages are being developed as microcomputers become faster and more powerful. Applications that were traditionally large-system applications, such as computer-aided design (CAD) systems and expert systems, are now available for microcomputers.

The applications themselves have grown in number, size, speed, power, and capabilities. For example, when Bricklin first conceived the electronic spreadsheet, most microcomputers had 48,000 characters or less of memory to work with. This capacity severely limited the size and capabilities of the software that would run on those microcomputers. Today, however, most microcomputers have at least 640,000 to 1 million characters of memory and most can add more. Obviously, today's spreadsheets can be a lot more powerful than the original one.

Application packages such as accounting and financial packages (including payroll, accounts receivable, accounts payable, general ledger, budgeting, and financial planning) are used in almost every kind of business. **Vertical market packages,** software designed to handle the unique needs of specific markets (businesses) such as medical offices, law firms, car dealerships, and hotel management, are also being sold. It would be impossible to detail all the types of application software in this chapter.

Several application packages have emerged, however, as the most popular and widely used with microcomputers. Word processing programs clearly lead the field as the most widely purchased application; nearly everyone who purchases a personal computer wants to do some word processing. Spreadsheet programs, presentation graphics, desktop publishing, and electronic communication programs are all examples of commonly requested applications.

Word Processing

At some time, you probably have been required to handwrite or type a long term paper or similar document; and you know just how time consuming editing and rewriting the text can be. A **word processor** can make the job simpler, easier, and faster. A word processor is software that lets the user edit, manipulate, and print text (Figure 2.20). It automates many manual tasks

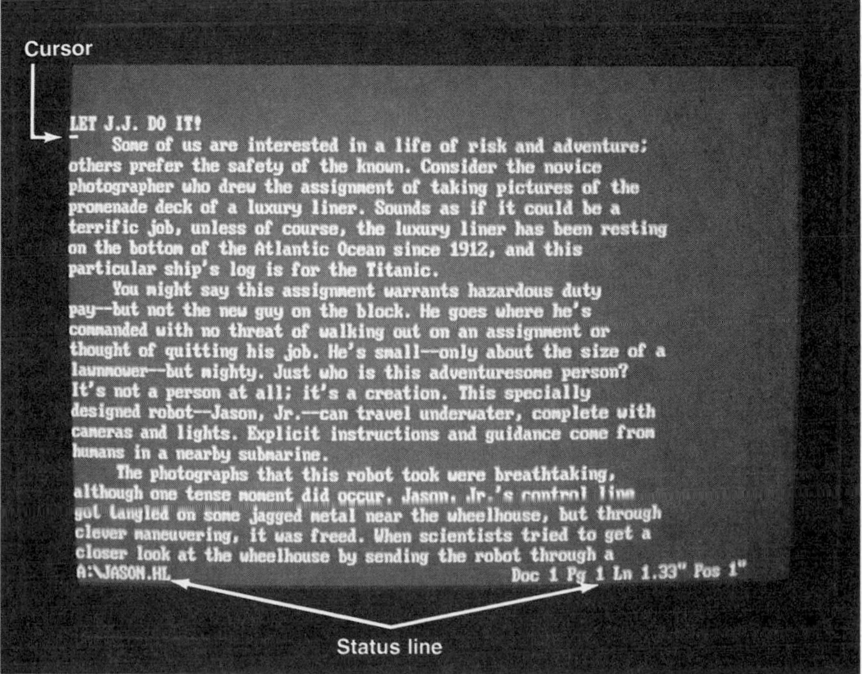

Figure 2.20
A word processing program is used to enter, edit, save, and print text.

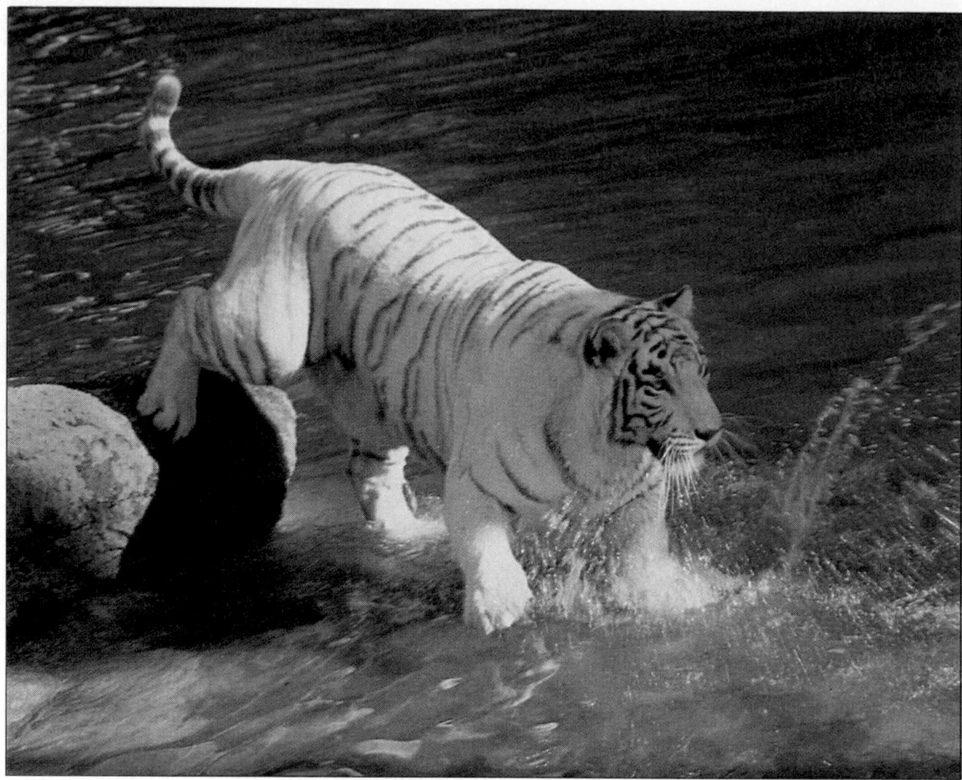

Figure 2.21
Zoos in North America and Europe have created a database containing information on more than 70,000 animals in over 200 zoos from 16 countries. Zoologists use the data to study animal population, breeding, age and sex distribution, and other factors.

(Courtesy Kjell B. Sandved)

associated with writing in longhand or typing, such as cutting and pasting, centering, and setting margins. WordStar, MultiMate Advantage, and WordPerfect are three of the most popular word processors.

Data Managers

The demand that data and information be organized and accessible in different formats has exceeded what can be done manually in a reasonable amount of time. Data managers were developed in answer to this demand.

Data managers store, organize, manipulate, retrieve, display, and print data. The term *data manager* describes file management systems and database management systems. A file management system is a program that stores, manipulates, and prints data stored in separate files. Only one file can be accessed and manipulated at a time. A **database management system** (DBMS) is the program that stores, manipulates, and prints data in a database. In a database, data from more than one file can be accessed at the same time. Data managers are essential to corporations and federal and state governments because they keep track of the vast amounts of data these organizations gather and store (Figure 2.21).

At home you might use a data manager to itemize valuable personal items or to list addresses and phone numbers of friends, relatives, or business contacts. A fund-raising campaign might use a data manager to keep track of the thousands of businesses to be contacted and related information. When a fund-

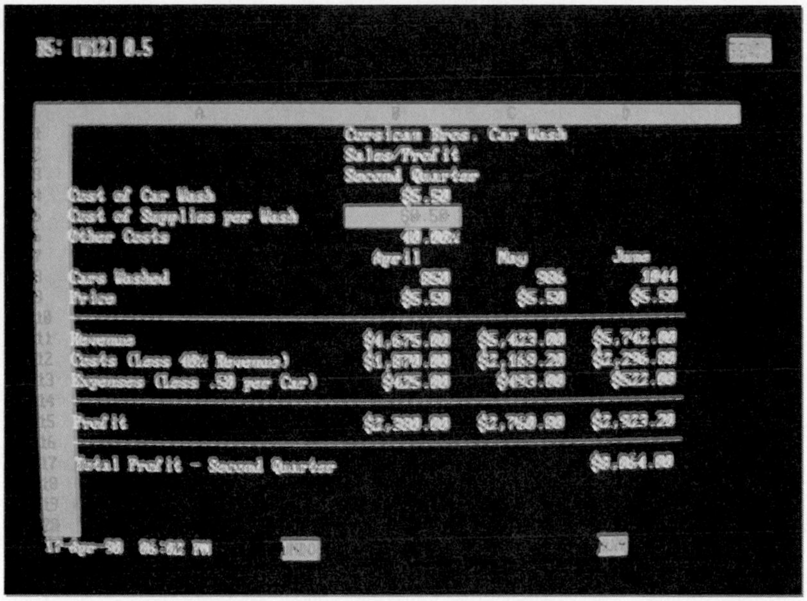

Figure 2.22
A spreadsheet program is used to manipulate rows and columns of data.

(Jo Hall/Macmillan)

raiser makes a contact for a donation or receives a pledge, the pertinent data are available on the computer. dBASE, Paradox, RBASE, and Foxbase are popular data managers.

Electronic Spreadsheets

A **spreadsheet program** is software that displays, manipulates, and prints rows and columns of data (Figure 2.22). It is similar to a paper spreadsheet in that both have columns and rows in which data and labels are entered. The difference lies in the fact that data in an electronic spreadsheet can be easily edited by the user, and all other dependent figures in the spreadsheet are then recalculated automatically and the results stored.

Electronic spreadsheets can perform a variety of tasks from budgeting personal income to financial planning for a corporation. Lotus 1-2-3, Microsoft Excel, Borland's Quattro, and SuperCalc are popular spreadsheets.

Graphics Packages

Graphics packages display data visually in the form of graphic images (Figure 2.23). For example, someone using a spreadsheet or data manager to manipulate and organize data may find it difficult to see relationships or interpret the information. Presenting the information visually (graphically) is one way to make the task easier. One type of graphics package can extract and display data graphically in line, pie, or bar charts. Business managers use graphics packages to present statistics and other data and their relationships to staff or to clients. At home, you could use graphics to create a bar graph that shows if your monthly spending varied from your budget. A popular independent, or stand-alone, graphics package is Harvard Graphics. Graphics software may also be part of a larger package, such as the ones in Lotus 1-2-3, Excel, or Quattro.

Graphics packages are available that enable artists to create pictures (Figure 2.24) and engineers to create designs. Some of these, such as Autodesk Animator, even permit the artist to use the computer to create an animated image or edit input from a video source.

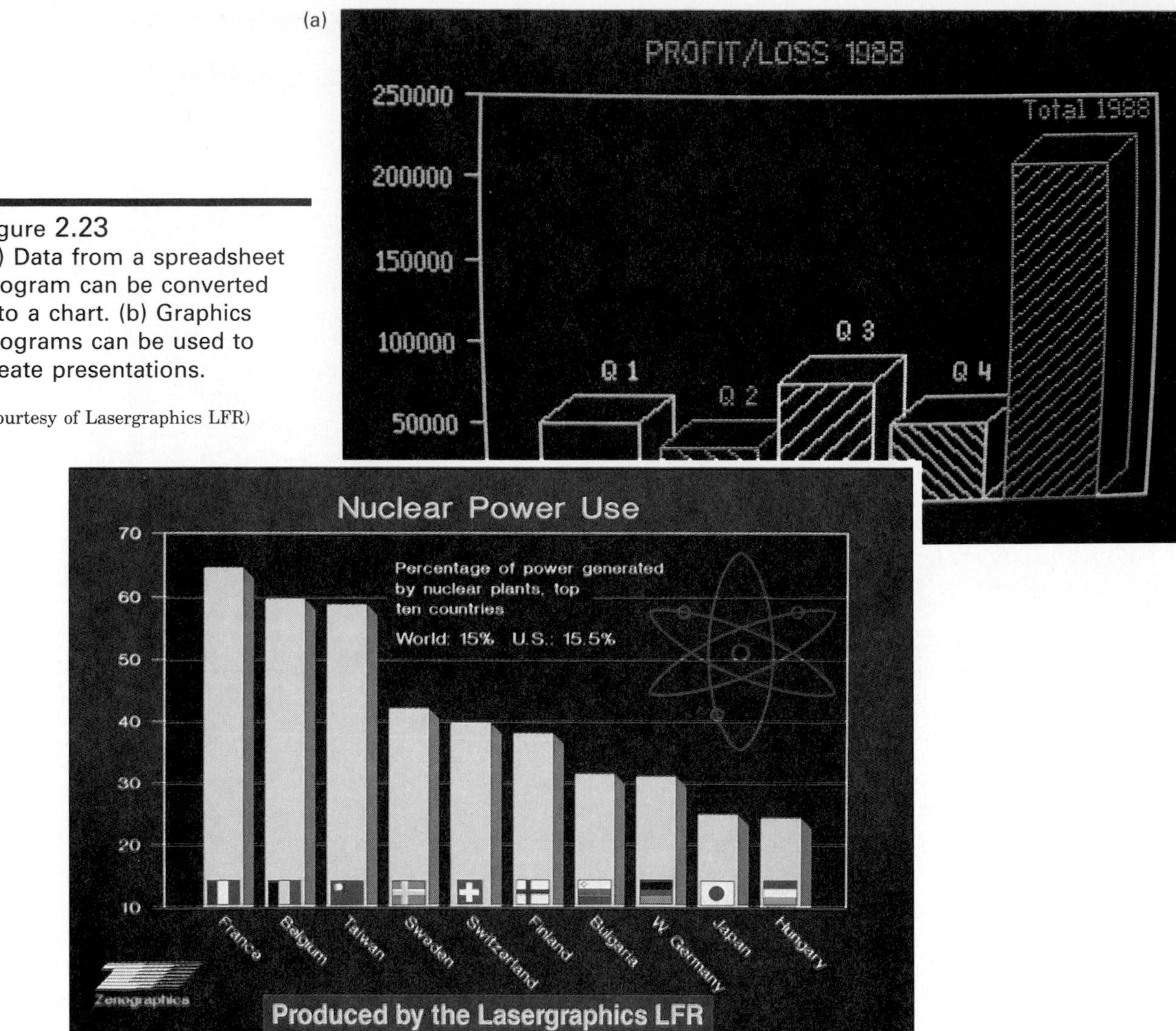

Figure 2.23
(a) Data from a spreadsheet program can be converted into a chart. (b) Graphics programs can be used to create presentations.

(Courtesy of Lasergraphics LFR)

Presentation Graphics

Another form of graphics software is one that assists in preparing materials for presentation purposes—slides and handouts for speakers or instructors. IBM's Storyboard or Microsoft's Power Point can use input from a variety of sources, including video images or computer-created art, which can then be combined with text and other images. Output from these programs can be to photographic slides, printed output, or a video projection device for a computer-aided presentation.

Communication Packages

As more individuals and organizations use computers, the need to transfer data from one computer to another has increased. Law enforcement agencies exchange information on criminals, home users access information services such as CompuServe or Prodigy, and some individuals and businesses send electronic mail (Figure 2.25). To facilitate such communication between computers, **communication packages,** such as the popular Pro-Com, are used.

Figure 2.24
Artists use computer graphics as another medium of expression.

(Courtesy of Time Arts)

Desktop Publishing

Desktop publishing is a concept that combines the use of a microcomputer with word processor, page-composition, and graphics software, and high-quality laser printers to create newsletters, magazines, and other publications (Figure 2.26).

Page-composition software such as PageMaker has been developed for both the MS-DOS system using Microsoft Windows and the Apple Macintosh. The term *desktop publishing* was coined by Paul Brainard of Aldus Corporation when that company's PageMaker software was introduced. With the combination of the Apple Macintosh microcomputer, Apple LaserWriter (a laser printer), and PageMaker, the concept of desktop publishing took off.

Anyone can use such a system to create and publish documents, for example, departments within corporations that want to publish in-house, small businesses, small-magazine publishers, and writers who like the idea of self-

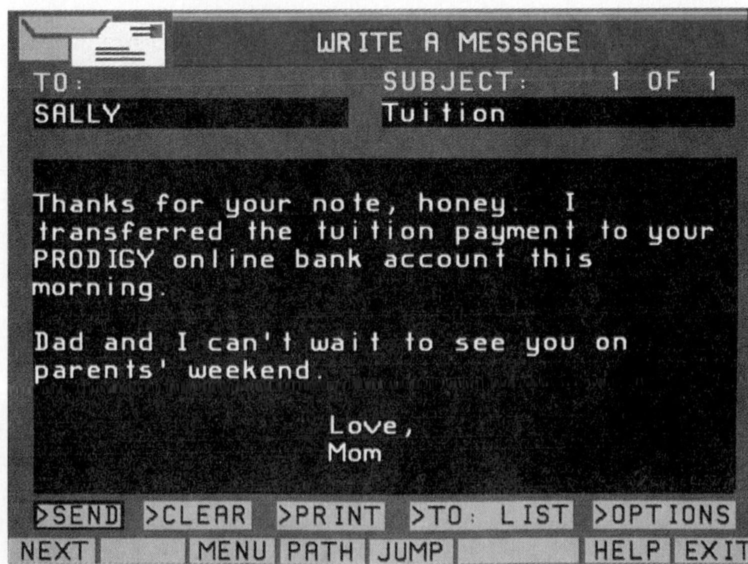

Figure 2.25
Prodigy, an interactive information service, provides members with an electronic mail facility.

(Courtesy of Prodigy Service, Inc.)

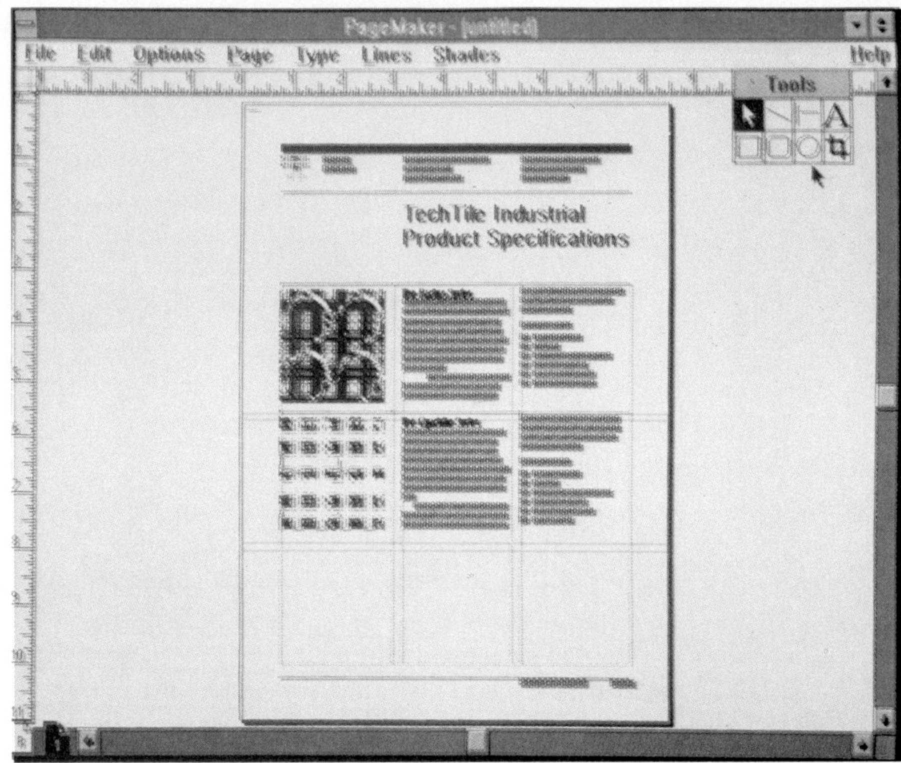

Figure 2.26
A desktop publishing program is used to create finished copy, ready to print.

(Courtesy Innervisions)

publishing. Booklets, brochures, newsletters, and annual reports are produced with desktop-publishing software. Even a fifty-page magazine can be designed, have pages made-up, and be printed.

Integrated Packages—All-in-One Solutions

The data files in many of the early programs designed for microcomputers were not always compatible with each other. The programs were not integrated; that is, data could not be electronically moved from one program to the other. Transferring data from one program to another was either impossible or complex and tedious. Typically, the user's only recourse was to rekey all the data into the receiving program.

For example, if you were asked to analyze and make a presentation of the sales performance of all thirty-six sales regions for company X, you could use a spreadsheet for the necessary calculations and a separate graphics package to produce the graphs. Although it takes five hours to enter data and formulas into the spreadsheet, the results are impressive. Now you are ready to produce bar graphs for the presentation. You spend the next hour pouring over the manuals to find a way to transfer the data from the spreadsheet to the graphics program. No luck! Your only option is to spend another several hours reentering the spreadsheet figures into the graphics program. This duplication of effort could have been avoided if the data in the spreadsheet could have been electronically transferred to the graphics program—if the two programs had been integrated.

Integrated software allows several programs to share the same data. For example, a graphics package can use data directly from the spreadsheet file to draw a graph. Integration also implies the use of similar functions and a common set of commands and keystrokes among programs. In reality, however, this happens in varying degrees. Nevertheless, the result of integration is the user can work faster, more efficiently, and thus more productively, than if nonintegrated programs were used.

The demand for integrated software has led to the development of four distinct approaches to integration: the integrated family of programs; the all-in-one integrated package; the integrated operating environment; and background integration.

Integrated Family of Programs

An **integrated family of programs** is a group of independent application programs that can share data and use common commands and keystrokes. For example, if one program in the set uses the function key F10 to save (store), then all the other programs will also use F10 to save. It is faster and easier to learn each program if they all have the same commands and keystrokes for the same operation.

Each program works independently. Because only one program is loaded into the computer at a time, more memory is available for it. Thus, the integrated family can be more powerful and have more features than its counterpart, the all-in-one integrated package (which we'll discuss next). One disadvantage of the integrated family is that merging data into one application or sharing data between applications can be slower and more awkward than in an all-in-one integrated package.

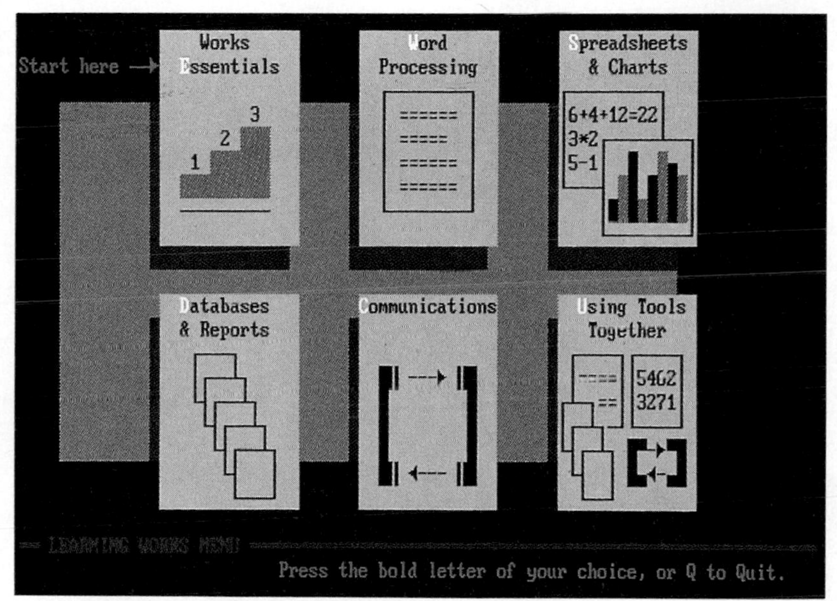

Figure 2.27
Microsoft Works is a popular integrated application package with word processing, spreadsheet, database, and communication capabilities.

(Courtesy of Microsoft Corp.)

All-in-One Integrated Packages

The **all-in-one integrated package** combines several applications into one single program. Most of these packages combine some or all of the word processor, spreadsheet, data manager, graphics, and communication programs (Figure 2.27). The user can conveniently switch between applications and use a common set of commands. With this kind of integrated package, the user can also transfer data from one application to another, or combine data from several applications and transfer that collection of data to another application. It is also possible to store data in one application that automatically updates related data in other applications.

A limitation of an all-in-one package, however, is that it requires large amounts of the computer's memory, or primary storage. Because of this large memory requirement, some of the individual applications in an all-in-one package do not have as many features as their stand-alone equivalents. Some developers have eliminated this problem by including some special functions that conserve memory and allow individual applications to retain their power.

Popular all-in-one integrated packages include Works, Enable, Framework, and Symphony. Two reasons for choosing an all-in-one package are the lower cost of acquiring several functions in one package and the ease of learning one set of commands to use the program.

Integrated Operating Environment

As discussed earlier in this chapter, one way to share data and information among several programs is to run them within a windowing environment such as Microsoft Windows or the Apple Macintosh. The use of this environment

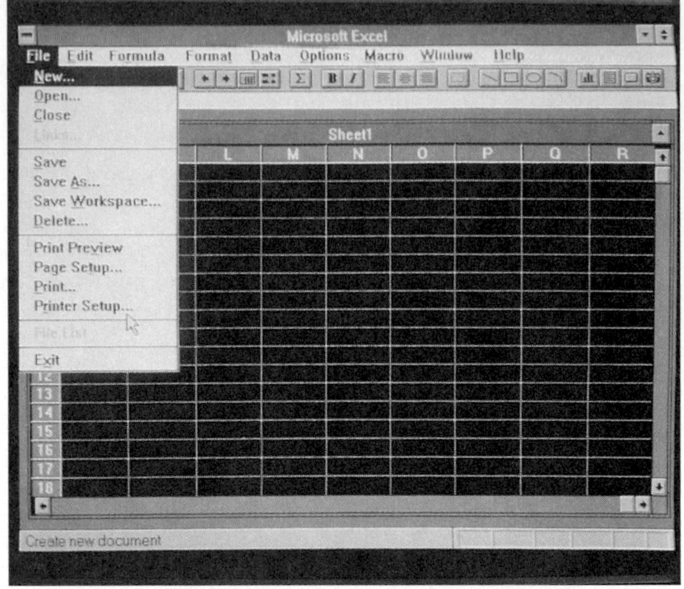

Figure 2.28
The menu bar of windowing programs provides a consistent style of operation.

(Courtesy of Microsoft Corp.)

enforces a common user interface and standard commands (Figure 2.28). The windowing system provides the ability to "cut and paste," that is, to move information from one program application to another.

Background Integration

Utility programs assist the user in various administrative tasks. **Background integration** places these utilities in memory so that they are available instantly at the touch of a key while other software is still running. Programs that run in this way are often called **TSR programs,** for "terminate, stay resident." This terminology simply means that the program is loaded into the computer's memory but does not do anything until the user performs a special keystroke. Then the program "wakes up" to perform its assigned function.

Typical utilities in background integration are a calculator, calendar, appointment book, notepad, and telephone directory and dialer. These utilities

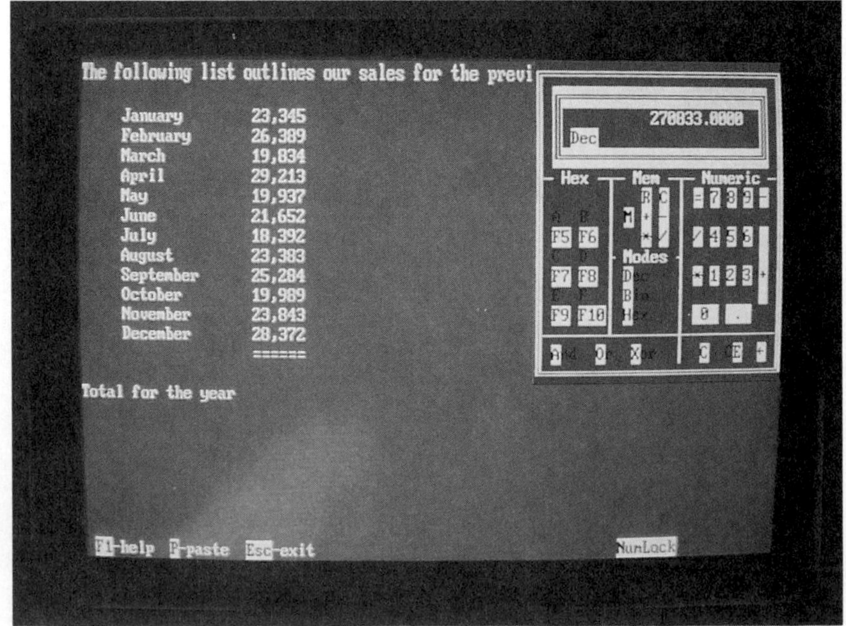

Figure 2.29
SideKick is a TSR program. The SideKick calculator shown on the screen "pops up" when a special key is used.

(Jo Hall/Macmillan)

can be useful additions to any software. For example, the user could access a calculator while using word processing for a document, or use a notepad to take notes while working in a database. SideKick is a popular example of this type of program (Figure 2.29). Within the windowing environment, your ability to choose from several alternative windowed applications might make a background program unnecessary.

Summary

- The computer's value is in our ability to put it to work for us in solving problems and producing information as we need it and under our control.
- Programs that control and direct the operation of the computer hardware are system software. An application package is software that, in conjunction with system software, instructs the computer how to do the job. Application software helps the user work faster, more efficiently, and thus more productively than if the job were done manually.
- An operating system is a set of programs that controls and supervises a computer system's hardware.
- The programs that make up an operating system are generally divided into two categories: control programs and service programs.
- The main program in most operating systems is the supervisor program.
- Service programs provide a service to the user or programmer of the computer system.
- Most of the currently available operating systems have more than one version in use; each version is numbered. Numbers to the left of the decimal represent the version number; numbers to the right of the decimal indicate the release number.
- The operating system's control programs "load" the supervisor portion of the operating system into the computer's memory. This is the stage of operations most of us call booting the computer.
- User-friendly is a term which implies that the computer somehow assists you; it provides a better means by which you can communicate your needs to it and by which it can guide you when necessary.
- A prompt is simply a program-generated signal to you that lets you know the system is ready for an action by you.
- The DOS prompt seen on most machines using the MS-DOS or PC-DOS operating systems generally looks like this: C:\>.
- Menus are simply lists of alternative selections from which you may choose the one you desire.
- An icon is a graphic symbol on the screen which represents a command or action.
- A window is a specifically defined area of the screen in which may be displayed data, menus, program applications, icons, and other windows.
- Two main sources of software exist: (1) so-called packaged software developed commercially by firms or groups who then sell the applications to the computer user, and (2) software developed specifically by or for computer users themselves.
- Shareware is software for which the developer owns the rights but allows it to be distributed free or for a nominal charge. Public domain software includes programs developed with public funds, such as government grants, or software for which the developer elects not to retain any rights and allows free distribution.
- The unauthorized copying and distribution of software is illegal.
- An alternative to commercially packaged software is software written by users.
- Application packages can be grouped into two broad categories: specialized and generalized. A specialized application package performs a specific task and cannot be changed or programmed to perform a different task. A generalized application package is one that can be applied to a wide variety of tasks.
- A vertical market package is software designed to handle the unique needs of a specific market.
- A word processor is software that lets the user edit, manipulate, and print text.
- Data managers store, organize, manipulate, retrieve, display, and print data.
- A spreadsheet program is software that displays, manipulates, and prints rows and columns of data.
- Graphics packages display data visually in the form of graphic images. A form of graphics software is presentation graphics, which assists in the preparation of materials for presentation purposes, such as slides and handouts for speakers or instructors.
- Desktop publishing is a concept that combines the use of a microcomputer with word processor, page-composition, and graphics software, and high-quality laser printers to create newsletters, magazines, and other publications.
- Integrated software allows several programs to share the same data more productively than if nonintegrated programs were used. There are four distinct approaches to integration: the integrated family of programs; the all-in-one integrated package; the integrated operating environment; and background integration.

Key Terms

- **Application**
- **System software**
- **Operating system**
- **Prompt**
- **Mouse**
- **Graphics display**
- **Icon**
- **Window**
- **Word processor**
- **Data manager**
- **Spreadsheet program**
- **Graphics package**
- **Communication package**
- **Desktop publishing**
- **Integrated software**

Review Questions

1. What is the name of a program that helps a user accomplish a task using a computer?
2. Describe a DOS prompt.
3. What does the term *user-friendly software* generally mean?
4. How is a menu used?
5. What is the user interface?
6. Describe the purpose of the mouse.
7. What is an icon and how does it help the user?
8. Application software is developed from two main sources. What are they?
9. With regard to use, what are the two broad categories of application software?
10. Discuss the advantages and disadvantages of using user-written and prewritten software.
11. Compare the costs involved in purchasing ready-to-use, prewritten application software to the costs of writing software in-house.
12. How can an application package be obtained to meet a user's exact specifications?
13. Define a specialized application package and give some examples.
14. What is a generalized application package?
15. Name some of the most popular microcomputer applications and give examples of how you might use each of them.
16. Describe the functions of a word processor.
17. Describe the functions of a data manager.
18. Describe the functions of a spreadsheet.
19. Why is a spreadsheet considered a generalized application package?
20. How can a user display data in graphic form?
21. Which type of application package facilitates sending data from one computer to another?
22. What are the main features of integrated software?
23. Identify the independent application packages that are designed to share data and use common commands and keystrokes.
24. List several features of all-in-one integrated packages.
25. Which kind of integrated package allows independent, nonrelated applications to work concurrently in an integrated environment?
26. How are utilities programs related to application software packages?
27. What is a TSR program?
28. Give some examples of utility programs.
29. Summarize the different approaches to integration.

PROFILE

STEPHEN WOZNIAK and STEVEN P. JOBS

(Courtesy Apple Computer, Inc.)

When Stephen Wozniak and Steven P. Jobs joined forces in the mid-1970s to form Apple Computer, Inc., it was an ideal partnership of science and salesmanship. While both men were well versed in the computer technology of the time, Wozniak was the scientific whiz kid. Jobs had a vision of creating a computer so small, powerful, and easy to use that it would have the sales appeal of a handy home appliance. That his vision was more fact than fantasy was demonstrated within a remarkably short time. The first Apple computer went on sale in 1977; by 1980, when Apple stock became available to the public, the company registered sales of $139 million—not a bad record for an enterprise that was founded on just $1,300.

Neither Wozniak nor Jobs was a college graduate when their company was established. Wozniak had attended the University of California at Berkeley before dropping out in 1972, and Jobs had spent one semester at Reed College in Oregon.

In 1974, Jobs went to work briefly for Nolan Bushnell's video game company, Atari. There he witnessed the intellectually demanding but socially loose work style that would become a trademark at Apple.

A year after joining the Atari staff, Jobs began dropping in on meetings of the Home Brew Computer Club, a group of computer and software enthusiasts that included Wozniak. At the time, Wozniak was on the payroll of the Hewlett-Packard computer company, but Jobs (already with visions of microcomputers dancing in his head) persuaded "Woz" to leave his job and go into business with him. The result was Apple Computer, Inc., a firm devoted from the start to changing the computer from an exotic and scary piece of mysterious hardware into a small, attractive, "user-friendly" workhorse for the office and home.

Success eventually drove the pair of pioneers from the top of the Apple barrel. As early as 1982, Wozniak was experimenting with rock concert promotion—an interest that cost him $30 million in two years. He returned to college at Berkeley and graduated in 1986 with a bachelor's degree in computer science.

Wozniak left Apple in 1985. For a time he joined forces with fellow computer wizard Nolan Bushnell to produce and market a line of toy robots that are directed by audio signals encoded on the soundtracks of television programs or videocassettes. More recently, Wozniak has been returning some of his success to the public by helping to create the Children's Discovery Museum in San Jose, California. In fact, the museum is located on Woz Way as a tribute to his civic interests.

Jobs also left Apple in 1985 and has since formed Next, Inc., a company that builds powerful personal computers for university scholars and educators. Jobs continues to be at the forefront of technology; the NextStep program that controls the Next computer is said to be a new model for software development.

CHAPTER 3

THE INFORMATION PROCESSING CYCLE—CREATING INFORMATION FROM DATA

IN THIS CHAPTER YOU WILL LEARN ABOUT

- **The information processing cycle—IPOS**
- **The way a computer represents data**
- **Input and output equipment**

Courtesy of Hewlett-Packard Company

THE INFORMATION PROCESSING CYCLE—IPOS

The purpose of the computer is to help you turn data into useful information. In this chapter, you will learn about data and the information processing cycle that transforms data into information. You will also see how computer hardware does this work. In addition, we will look at methods and devices for getting the data into the computer, methods and devices to output the results of data processing, storage media, and methods of storing and organizing data.

To help explain the computer's task of creating information from data, we will use a simplified computer model, called the **information processing cycle,** to describe the four basic operations performed by a computer. The first three of these operations—**input, processing,** and **output**—are the tasks performed by the computer when it converts data into information. **Storage,** the fourth operation, refers to the computing system's ability to store and retrieve data and programs for future use. This information processing cycle is often referred to by its initials, IPOS—an easy way to remember the four functions (Figure 3.1).

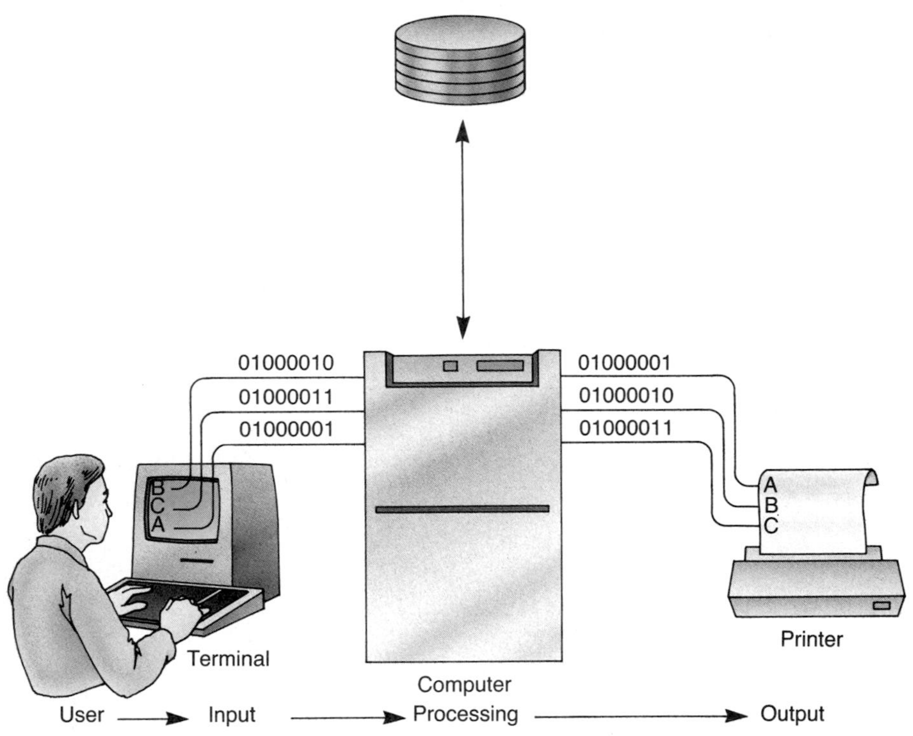

Figure 3.1
The information processing cycle involves four steps: input, processing, output, and storage. Data are entered as input where the computer converts them to machine-readable form. Processing steps convert the data into information which is then output, perhaps to a printer. The computer can also store data for later use.

We will use this model to help relate the various parts of the computer to each other and to describe their basic functions. First, though, you should better understand the nature of data, and how data are related to information.

DATA VERSUS INFORMATION

You will recall from Chapter 1 that data are simply the numbers, letters, symbols, words, or phrases that are input to a computer. Data are only "raw facts" that have no specific meaning to us until they are converted into information. **Information,** then, is data that have been processed into a form that is accessible, useful, and meaningful to its recipient. Thus, before we can obtain information, we need to understand the nature of data from the computing system's perspective.

DATA REPRESENTATION

When you think of data, you may imagine all sorts of facts that a computer might process: names, dates, amounts of money, addresses, and so on. The computer sees data even more simply than this—more simplistically even than the individual characters you might use to enter a name or data.

Data, in a computing system, are represented by specific machine-oriented codes. These codes are then arranged in larger groupings in a **data storage hierarchy** so that your program can access the data conveniently. Let us take a look at data, from its smallest element to its larger collection.

BITS AND BYTES

You are probably comfortable counting and manipulating numbers with the decimal system and can picture in your mind the quantities that each number represents. The computer, however, only identifies signals in the form of digital pulses that represent either a high voltage state (on) or a low voltage state (off). The on and off conditions are commonly labeled with the numbers 1 and 0, respectively. This number system is called the **binary system.**

The ones and zeros can be arranged in various combinations to represent all the numbers, letters, and symbols that can be entered into the computer. While you see numbers and letters assembled to form English words and phrases, the computer sees things differently.

Encoding systems such as **EBCDIC** (Extended Binary Coded Decimal Interchange Code) and **ASCII** (American Standard Code for Information Interchange) were developed to convert alphanumeric characters into codes using ones and zeros (Figure 3.2). For example, in the ASCII encoding system used by your personal computer the small letter "d" is represented by the binary number 10110010, while capital "D" is 11000100.

Data entered into the computer must be interpreted into binary code before they can be used. Fortunately, you do not have to remember all these codes because computer software and hardware convert the data you use into the correct codes.

Figure 3.2
ASCII and EBCDIC systems convert alphanumeric characters into codes computers understand.

Character	8-Bit ASCII	8-Bit EBCDIC	Character	8-Bit ASCII	8-Bit EBCDIC
0	1011 0000	1111 0000	K	1100 1011	1101 0010
1	1011 0001	1111 0001	L	1100 1100	1101 0011
2	1011 0010	1111 0010	M	1100 1101	1101 0100
3	1011 0011	1111 0011	N	1100 1110	1101 0101
4	1011 0100	1111 0100	O	1100 1111	1101 0110
5	1011 0101	1111 0101	P	1101 0000	1101 0111
6	1011 0110	1111 0110	Q	1101 0001	1101 1000
7	1011 0111	1111 0111	R	1101 0010	1101 1001
8	1011 1000	1111 1000	S	1101 0011	1110 0010
9	1011 1001	1111 1001	T	1101 0100	1110 0011
A	1100 0001	1100 0001	U	1101 0101	1110 0100
B	1100 0010	1100 0010	V	1101 0110	1110 0101
C	1100 0011	1100 0011	W	1101 0111	1110 0110
D	1100 0100	1100 0100	X	1101 1000	1110 0111
E	1100 0101	1100 0101	Y	1101 1001	1110 1000
F	1100 0110	1100 0110	Z	1101 1010	1110 1001
G	1100 0111	1100 0111	+	1010 1011	0100 1110
H	1100 1000	1100 1000	$	1010 0100	0101 1011
I	1100 1001	1100 1001	.	1010 1110	0100 1011
J	1100 1010	1101 0001	<	1011 1000	0100 1100

The smallest piece of data that can be recognized and used by the computer is the **bit,** which is a word made up from ***binary digit.*** A bit is a single binary value, either a one or a zero. Because the bit is either "on," a one, or "off," a zero, a single bit can have either one of only two machine codes. To represent all of the letters, numbers, symbols, and computer instructions, a larger number of machine-language codes is needed. A grouping of eight bits, called a **byte,** provides 256 codes. You might be more comfortable in thinking of a byte as equal to a single character, such as a letter or number.

The byte is the basic unit for measuring the size of memory, but it is more common to hear the term **kilobyte** (represented as K or KB) or **megabyte** (MB). You may have heard someone say, for example, that her computer has 640K of memory. In strict scientific notation, "kilo" means 1,000 and "mega" means 1,000,000. However, in the language of computers, the prefix kilo- actually means 1,024 and mega- is 1,048,576. Thus a computer with 640K of memory actually has 655,356 bytes of memory (640 × 1,024). The disparity occurs because the binary number system is based on the powers of 2. When 2 is raised to the 10th power (2^{10}), the result is 1,024. Because of the proximity to 1,000 (10^3), the prefix kilo- was adopted for computer use. The same rationale was used for the prefixes mega- (1 million) and giga- (1 billion). Memory capacities in the terabytes (1 trillion bytes) may soon be common in some of the largest computer systems.

HIGHLIGHT

When Eight Is Not Enough

Surely 256 different 8-bit codes should be enough to satisfy all of the possible characters and symbols you might want to use on a computer, right? Well, actually that number is many codes fewer than the world of computing could use. That reference to the *world* of computing is deliberate, for computing has truly become a universal human activity.

Since 1967, the American Standard Code for Information Interchange, ASCII, has been the recognized standard for coding characters, digits, and symbols. IBM's mainframe computers use a different coding scheme, Extended Binary Coded Decimal Interchange Code (EBCDIC), which necessitates translation when data is exchanged between IBM and non-IBM systems.

Also, ASCII was not designed to represent the special characters used in non-English languages. Other countries have had to design their own 8-bit codes. ASCII is widely used but certainly not universal.

In 1990, a group of twelve computer companies, including IBM, Apple, Microsoft, Xerox and others, met to form a consortium to develop and promote a new code to be known as Unicode. If the new code is successful and becomes a worldwide standard, it would change computing significantly.

With the new code, computers anywhere would be able to understand Chinese ideographs, the Russian Cyrillic alphabet, Hebrew, Arabic, French, Norwegian or any other language—even English. To do this, Unicode would expand the 8-bit byte to a sequence of 16 bits, permitting up to 65,536 possible codes, enough for characters from all current languages.

Characters, Fields, Records, and Files

Bits and bytes are the building blocks of data. To handle the input, output, and storage of data, we need to define larger data structures involving characters, fields, records, files, and databases. These structures are all part of the data storage hierarchy (Figure 3.3).

The smallest unit of data with which you are likely to be concerned is the byte. You just learned some technical aspects about the byte, but it is perhaps easier to think about a byte in terms of characters—one byte can be considered to be one character. To store the name Sharon Smith would require 12 bytes, one for each character in the name plus one more for the space between the first and last name. Yes, the space is a character, not an empty void, to the computer.

Individual data items, or individual facts, are stored as groups of characters (bytes) in a **field.** A name, address, city, state, and zip code would each be contained in five individual data fields. Collected together, these fields would be stored in a **record.** You might have several records of names and addresses for each of your friends. Finally, all of the records containing similar data would be stored in a **file.** In some applications, many files may be combined in what is known as a **database.**

How the computer goes about storing and retrieving data will be covered later in Chapter 5. For now, just remember that data are handled according to the data storage hierarchy: First a file is accessed to obtain the data record; then each data item is found in its own field, which consists of a number of characters, or bytes.

Figure 3.3
The data storage hierarchy: Eight bits make up a byte; several bytes, or characters, create a field. Fields are grouped into records, and records are grouped into files.

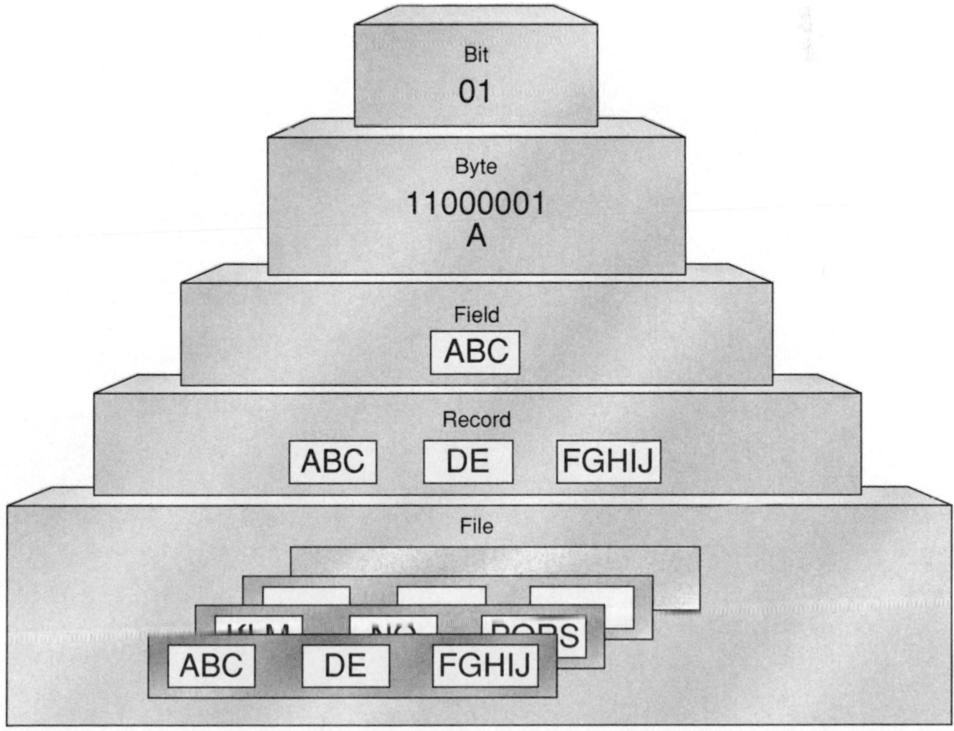

Data Storage Hierarchy

PUTTING THE INFORMATION PROCESSING CYCLE TO WORK

I–P–O–S—the initials tell it all. Data are first *i*nput to the computer, which then *p*rocesses them, transforming the data to information which is then *o*utput for you to use. Along the way, you may *s*tore the data for later access and further processing, or you may use *s*torage to save the information produced. Each of these steps can be identified with some components of your computer system. It may be best to start with those steps most familiar to you, input and output.

INPUT

Before discussing input devices, let's define some terms. **Hardware,** you'll recall, includes all the physical components of a computer system. Any hardware item that is attached to the main unit of a computer, the central processing unit, is referred to as a **peripheral device.** An **input device** is a peripheral device through which data are entered and transformed into machine-readable form. This section will introduce you to a variety of input devices (Figure 3.4).

Input Devices

One of today's most common and familiar input devices is the **keyboard** (Figure 3.5). The traditional QWERTY keys (so called because the first six letters on the top row are Q, W, E, R, T, and Y) form the basic portion of today's computer keyboard (Figure 3.5). A typical computer keyboard also contains a variety of other keys that were added to increase efficiency in programming and in using applications such as a word processor. They may include (1) a **numeric keypad** that looks and functions much like a calculator; (2) **function keys** whose operations can be determined by the user or preprogrammed by the software being used; and (3) **special keys** such as those used to control

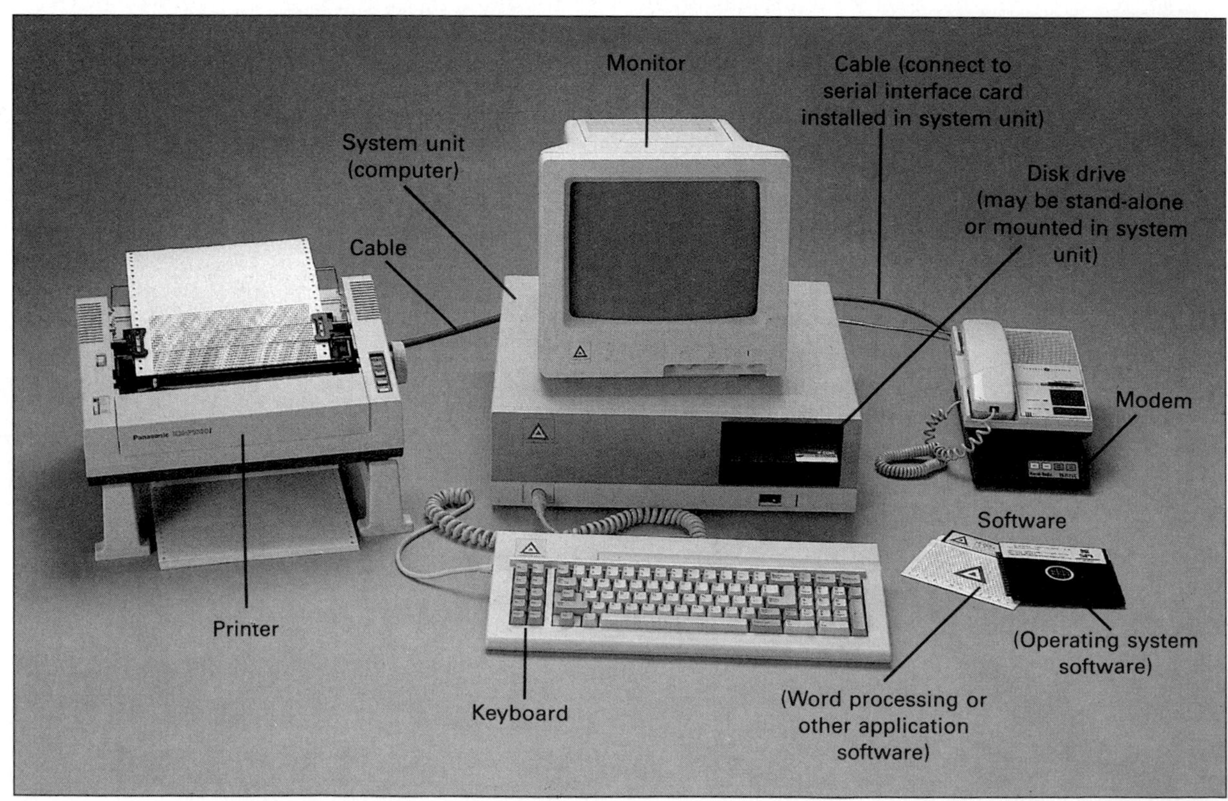

Figure 3.4
A typical microcomputer system has various input and output devices.

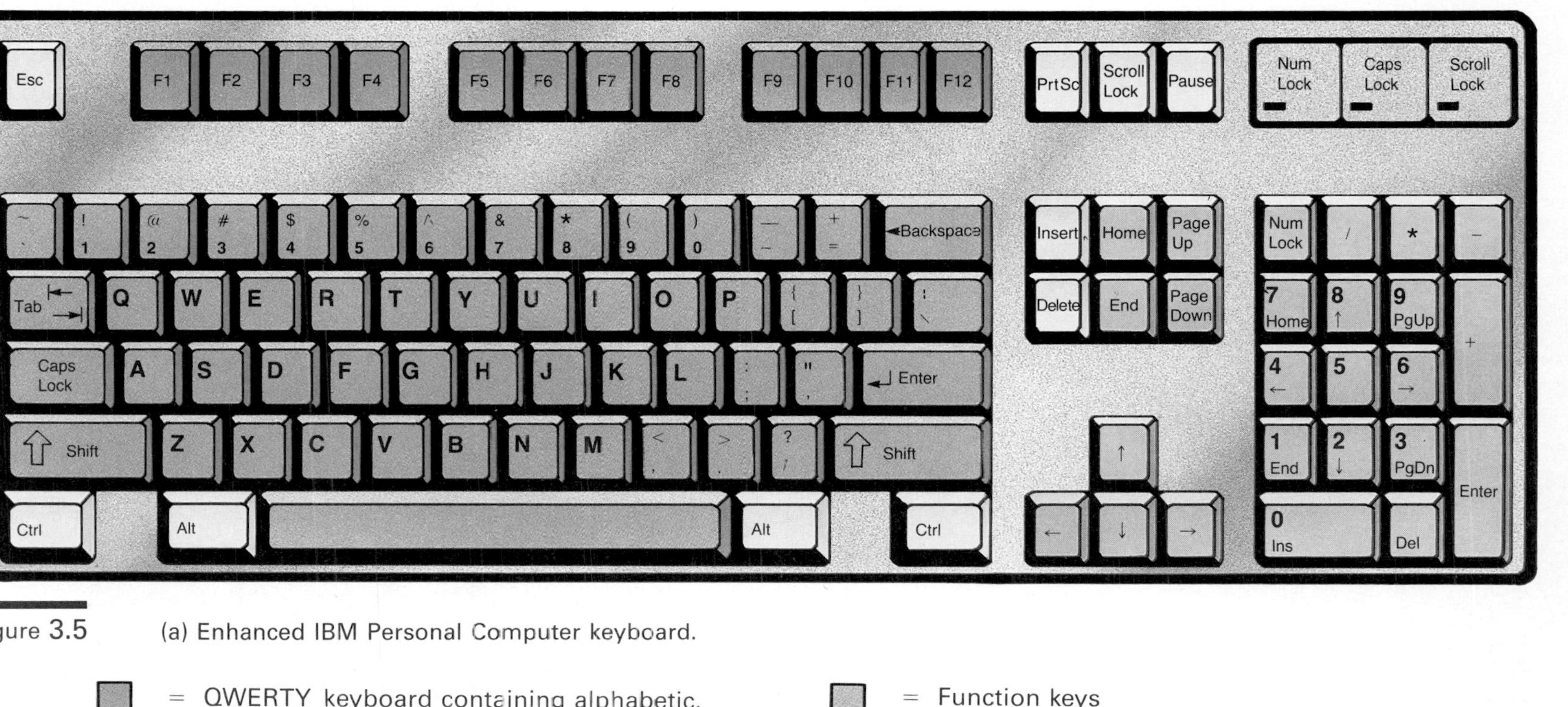

Figure 3.5 (a) Enhanced IBM Personal Computer keyboard.

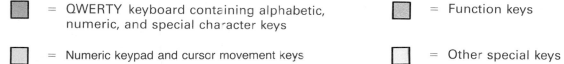

= QWERTY keyboard containing alphabetic, numeric, and special character keys

= Function keys

= Numeric keypad and cursor movement keys

= Other special keys

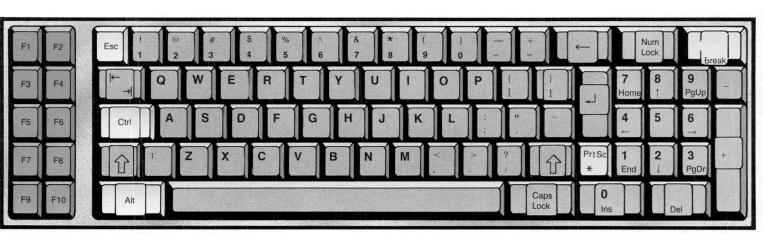

(b) Standard IBM Personal Computer keyboard.

(a)

(b)

(c)

(d)

(e)

(f)

(g)

Figure 3.6
Common input devices.
(a) Mouse (b) Joystick
(c) Trackball (d) Light pen
(e) Digitizing tablet (f) Touch-sensitive screen (g) Scanner

(Courtesy of (a) International Business Machines Corp.; (b) Innervisions; (c) Innervisions; (e) NCR; (f) Travenol Laboratories, Inc.; (g) Hewlett-Packard Company)

the movement of the cursor on the computer screen. The **cursor** is a special character or symbol that indicates the user's position on the screen or focuses attention to a specific area to allow communication and interaction between the user and the program.

When you use the keyboard to enter data into the computer, you are involved in **transcription,** which is defined as a process of transferring from one recording and storage system into another. Often, you might enter data from handwritten originals, called **source documents.**

Naturally, the more often you handle data, the greater the chance of making a mistake. **Transcription errors,** which arise from mishandling data, are common when your data entry takes the form of manual transcription.

Other common input devices include the mouse, joystick, trackball, light pen, digitizing tablet, touch-sensitive screen, and scanner (Figure 3.6).

Source Data Entry

Data may be entered directly into a computer system without transcription in a process referred to as **source data entry.** Examples include the use of **magnetic-ink character recognition** (MICR) on your bank checks (Figure 3.7),

Figure 3.7
Magnetic-ink character recognition (MICR) equipment is used by banks to process checks efficiently.

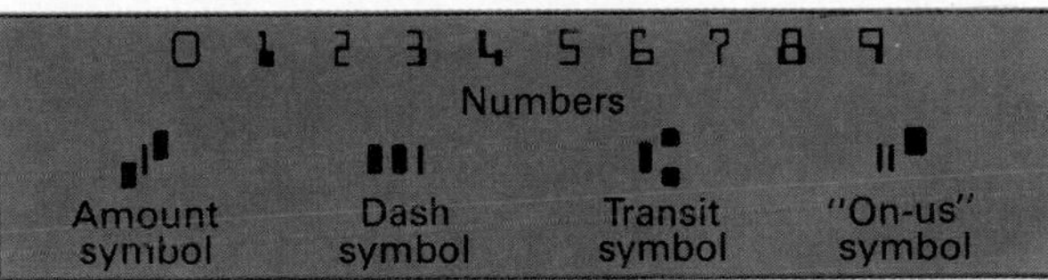

(a) Magnetic-ink character set

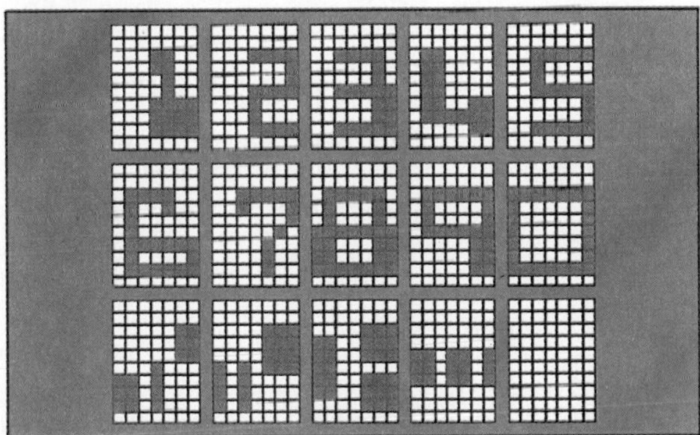

(b) Matrix patterns for magnetic-ink characters

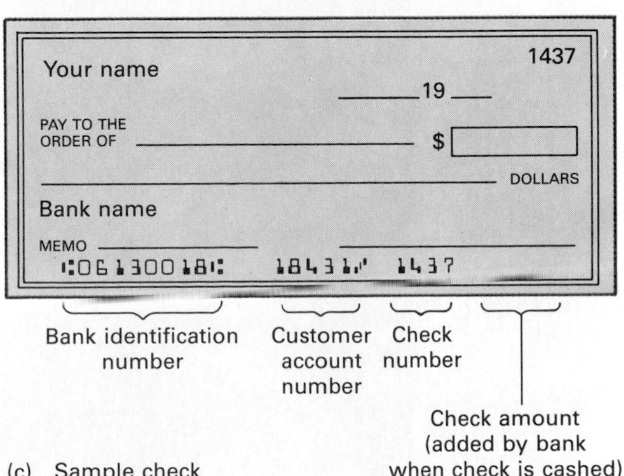

(c) Sample check

Figure 3.8
Automatic teller machine (ATM) cards and most credit cards have a magnetic strip on which the account number and other information are recorded.

(Courtesy of The Huntington National Bank)

magnetic strips on credit cards and automated teller machine (ATM) cards (Figure 3.8), and optical character recognition (OCR), such as the bar codes used in the supermarket (Figure 3.9).

In source data entry, data are prepared at the source in a machine-readable form that can be used by a computer without a separate, intermediate, and manual data transcription step. The source data entry method reduces the number of errors made during input by eliminating the transcription process. Many sources report that approximately 85 percent of all errors detected in data are due to transcription errors and only 15 percent occur in the source data.

By reducing the manual effort and increasing the accuracy of data, source data entry has a beneficial economic impact on the cost of information. By improving the access to data and processing it quickly in a machine-readable form, source data entry has improved the timeliness of information. For these reasons, source data entry has become a popular method for input (Figure 3.10).

Figure 3.9
Bar codes, such as the Universal Product Code (UPC) used in the grocery store, can be read by a laser scanner.

(b, Courtesy of National Semiconductor Co.)

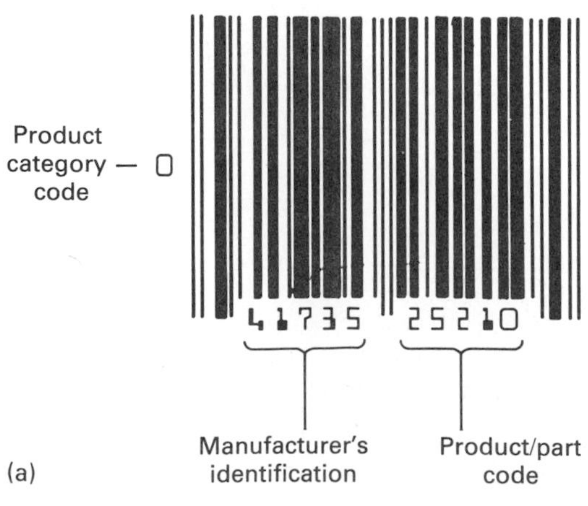

(b)

SIDE 1

GENERAL PURPOSE - NCS - ANSWER SHEET
FOR USE WITH ALL NCS SENTRY OPTICAL MARK READING SYSTEMS
SEE IMPORTANT MARKING INSTRUCTIONS ON SIDE 2

A B C D E	A B C D E	A B C D E	A B C D E	A B C D E
1 ① ② ③ ④ ⑤	11 ① ② ③ ④ ⑤	21 ① ② ③ ④ ⑤	31 ① ② ③ ④ ⑤	41 ① ② ③ ④ ⑤
2 ① ② ③ ④ ⑤	12 ① ② ③ ④ ⑤	22 ① ② ③ ④ ⑤	32 ① ② ③ ④ ⑤	42 ① ② ③ ④ ⑤
3 ① ② ③ ④ ⑤	13 ① ② ③ ④ ⑤	23 ① ② ③ ④ ⑤	33 ① ② ③ ④ ⑤	43 ① ② ③ ④ ⑤
4 ① ② ③ ④ ⑤	14 ① ② ③ ④ ⑤	24 ① ② ③ ④ ⑤	34 ① ② ③ ④ ⑤	44 ① ② ③ ④ ⑤
5 ① ② ③ ④ ⑤	15 ① ② ③ ④ ⑤	25 ① ② ③ ④ ⑤	35 ① ② ③ ④ ⑤	45 ① ② ③ ④ ⑤
6 ① ② ③ ④ ⑤	16 ① ② ③ ④ ⑤	26 ① ② ③ ④ ⑤	36 ① ② ③ ④ ⑤	46 ① ② ③ ④ ⑤
7 ① ② ③ ④ ⑤	17 ① ② ③ ④ ⑤	27 ① ② ③ ④ ⑤	37 ① ② ③ ④ ⑤	47 ① ② ③ ④ ⑤
8 ① ② ③ ④ ⑤	18 ① ② ③ ④ ⑤	28 ① ② ③ ④ ⑤	38 ① ② ③ ④ ⑤	48 ① ② ③ ④ ⑤
9 ① ② ③ ④ ⑤	19 ① ② ③ ④ ⑤	29 ① ② ③ ④ ⑤	39 ① ② ③ ④ ⑤	49 ① ② ③ ④ ⑤
10 ① ② ③ ④ ⑤	20 ① ② ③ ④ ⑤	30 ① ② ③ ④ ⑤	40 ① ② ③ ④ ⑤	50 ① ② ③ ④ ⑤

Figure 3.10
Optical mark recognition (OMR) forms, such as those you may use for tests, provide a means by which pencil marks can be read by the computer.

(NCS General Purpose answer sheet courtesy of National Computer Systems, Inc. © 1977)

OUTPUT

Output involves presenting information that results from processing in a form understandable to humans, or storing data or information in a storage device readable by other machines. An **output device** is a peripheral device that allows a computer to communicate information to humans or another machine by accepting data from the computer and transforming it into a usable form.

Most people and organizations require clear, legible output—a major consideration when purchasing output devices. Output that can be understood by humans can be categorized as hard copy and soft copy. **Hard copy** is output, such as paper, that can be read immediately or stored and read later. It is a relatively stable and permanent form of output. **Soft copy** is usually screen-displayed output. It is a transient form of output and is lost when the computer is turned off. However, if the data needed to create the soft copy has been saved on disk or tape, the soft copy can be reproduced on the screen anytime. Although most soft-copy output is seen on a display device, voice synthesis devices let us *hear* the output as well.

Output Devices

Graphics and text material can be produced with a wide selection of printers and plotters. A printer produces output, usually in the form of text, on paper; however, some printers produce graphics. A plotter produces graphic images on paper. In this section, we will look at only the major categories of printers and plotters. First, let's consider print quality, an important feature of any hard-copy device.

Print Quality

The print quality available from hard-copy output can vary considerably. Figure 3.11 shows examples of each. **Near-typeset-quality print** is similar in quality to the print produced by a typesetting machine; the print you see in a magazine or this text is **typeset-quality print. Letter-quality print** is made by fully formed (solid line) characters as opposed to characters made up of dots or lines. On some printers, **near-letter-quality print** is achieved when the

This is an example of typeset-quality print.

This is an example of near-typeset quality print.

This is an example of letter-quality print.

This is an example of near-letter quality print.

This is an example of standard-quality print.

This is an example of draft-quality (compressed) print.

Figure 3.11
Compare the different qualities of print.

printing mechanism makes multiple passes over the same letters, filling in the spaces between the dots or lines. **Standard-quality print** is produced when characters composed of dots or lines are formed by a single pass of the printing mechanism. **Draft-quality print** forms characters with a minimum number of dots or lines to achieve faster output than standard-quality printing, but at a somewhat reduced quality.

The quality of type that a printer produces is determined by its printing mechanism. Printers have two basic types of printing mechanisms: impact and nonimpact.

Impact Printers

An **impact printer** produces characters by using a hammer or pins to strike an ink ribbon, which in turn presses against a sheet of paper, leaving an impression of the character on the paper. An ordinary typewriter also works in this way.

The impact printer used most often with microcomputers is the **dot-matrix printer.** It is a **character-at-a-time printer,** meaning it prints one character at a time. The **dot-matrix** printer uses a print mechanism, called a print head, containing from nine to twenty-four pins. These pins produce patterns of dots on the paper to form the individual characters (Figure 3.12).

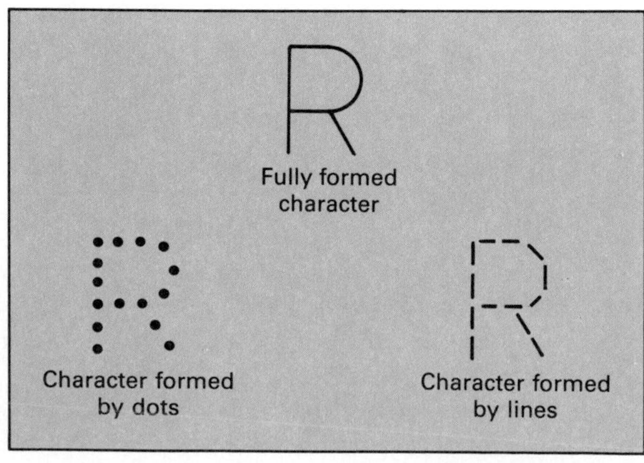

Figure 3.12
Fully formed characters are printed by an impact printer. Dot-matrix printers form a character by printing dots or lines in the pattern of the character.

This is an example of 24-pin dot-matrix print.

This is an example of 9-pin dot-matrix print.

Figure 3.13
Print quality is improved when more dots are printed. Compare these images made by nine-pin and twenty-four-pin printers.

Nine-pin printers are good general-quality printers; twenty-four-pin printers are considered to have superior type and graphics capability (Figure 3.13).

In businesses where enormous amounts of material are printed, character-at-a-time printers are just too slow; these users need line-at-a-time printers. **Line-at-a-time printers,** or **line printers,** use special mechanisms that can print a whole line at once; typically, they can print in the range of 1,200 to 6,000 lines per minute. Drum, chain, and band printers are line-at-a-time printers. Although some line-at-a-time printers are used with microcomputers, more commonly they are used with minicomputer and mainframe systems.

Nonimpact Printers

Nonimpact printers do not use a striking device to produce characters on paper; and because these printers do not hammer against the paper, they are much quieter. Major technologies in this area are the ink-jet, thermal-transfer, and laser printers.

Ink-jet printers form characters on paper by spraying ink from tiny nozzles through an electrical field that arranges the charged ink particles into characters at the rate of approximately 250 characters per second (Figure 3.14).

The **thermal-transfer printer** uses heat to transfer ink to paper. These printers bond the ink onto the paper by heating pins, which press against a special ink ribbon (Figure 3.15).

When speed and quality comparable to typeset material are required, a laser printer is the solution (Figure 3.16). **Laser printers** produce an image on paper by directing a laser beam at a mirror which bounces the image onto a

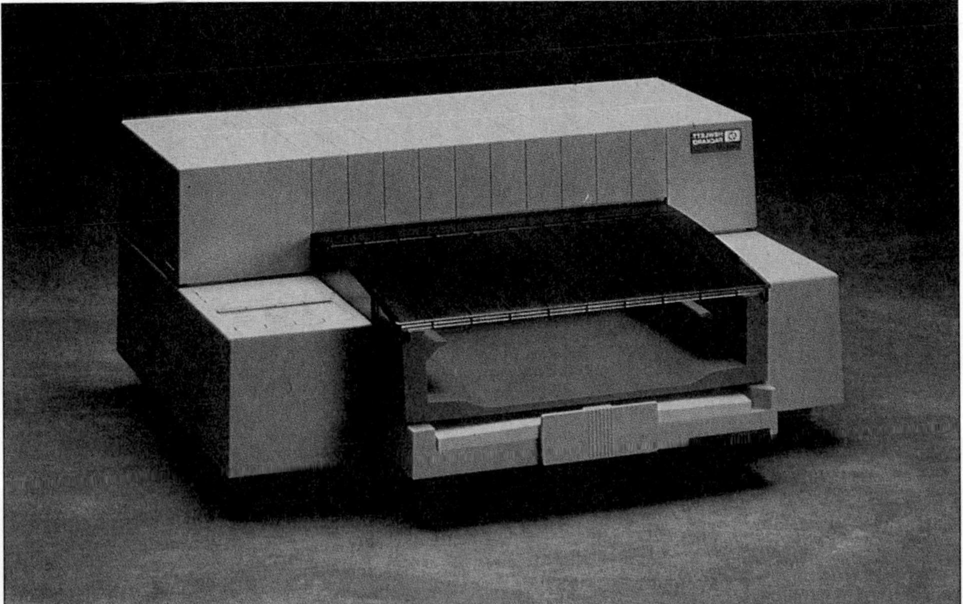

Figure 3.14
An ink-jet printer forms images with droplets of ink.

(Courtesy Hewlett-Packard Company)

Figure 3.15
Thermal-transfer printers form characters by a heat process onto special paper. Here, a color thermal printer is shown. The image is formed by heating dots of red, green, blue, and black ink from a four-color ribbon.

(Courtesy of NEC)

printing drum. The laser-drawn image leaves a negative charge on the drum to which positively charged black toner powder will stick. As the paper rolls by the drum, the toner is transferred to the paper. A hot roller bonds the toner to the paper.

Laser printers are more expensive than other types of printers, but they have the advantages of fast printing speeds, excellent quality, and ability to reproduce high-quality graphics as well as text. Some laser printers have exceptionally high image quality and are used as typesetters or for desktop publishing systems. Often, these printers are also equipped to be compatible with PostScript, a popular page description language developed by Adobe Systems. The printers recognize PostScript's specific coding system for reproducing a wide range of type styles, called fonts, and for achieving better graphic images

Figure 3.16
Laser printers produce high-quality images through a process very much like that of a small copying machine.

(Courtesy of Hewlett-Packard Company)

using curved lines and filled areas. Another plus is PostScript's ability to print color images—a feature of some laser printer models.

Plotters

A **plotter** produces high-quality graphics in multiple colors using pens that are attached to movable arms. The pens are directed across the surface of a stationary piece of paper. Many plotters, however, combine a movable pen arm with paper that can also roll back and forth (Figure 3.17). This two-way movement allows any configuration to be drawn.

Monitors

The most popular and certainly the most viewed form of soft-copy output is found on the monitor, also called simply a screen or display. A **monitor** is a television-like device used to display data or information. Monitors can be combined with keyboards so that input data can be viewed and checked as it is entered. Such a combination is often called a **terminal** or **workstation.**

Monitor quality is often compared in terms of **resolution,** a measure of the number of picture elements, or **pixels,** that a screen contains. A pixel is the smallest increment of a display screen that can be controlled individually—the more pixels, the clearer and sharper the image. A 640-by-460-pixel screen means 640 horizontal pixels and 460 vertical pixels.

Two kinds of viewing screens are used for monitors: cathode-ray tube and flat-panel display. To produce a data image on a **cathode-ray tube** (CRT), an electron beam moves across a phosphor-coated screen. By intensifying the strength of the beam, the phosphor coating glows in certain places, forming the characters. The most common type of CRT has a display screen of twenty-five lines of eighty characters each. Other sizes are available, including those that can display a full $8\frac{1}{2}$-by-11-inch page.

The least expensive of the CRTs is the single-color, or **monochrome, monitor.** Monochrome monitors are used if output is mainly text and numbers; with the appropriate circuitry, however, some can display graphics. Monochrome monitors usually display either green, amber, or white characters on a black screen.

Figure 3.17
Plotters are used to output graphic images, especially for line drawings such as this circuit diagram.

(Courtesy of Houston Instrument)

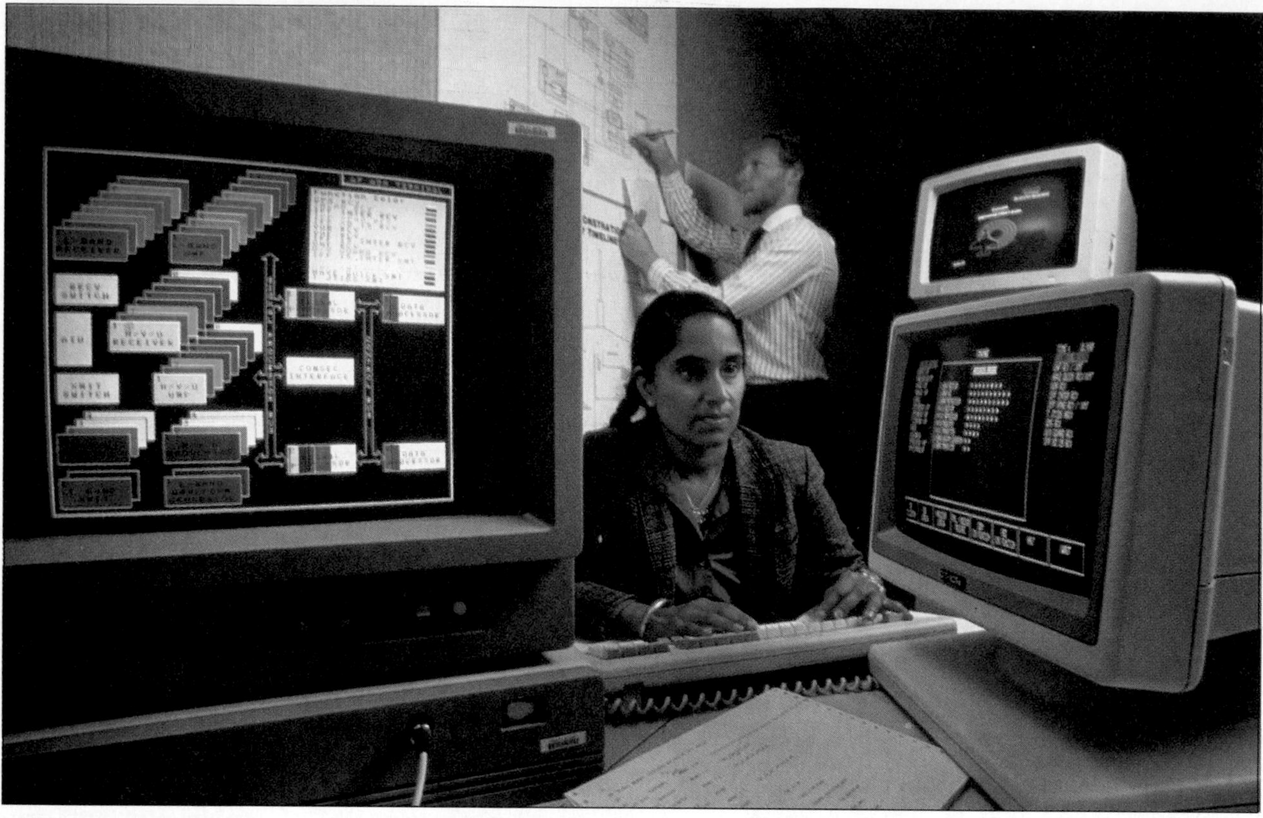

Figure 3.18
The two standard types of monitors are color and monochrome. Compare the image shown on the color monitor on the left to that shown on the monochrome, or single-color, monitor on the right.

(Courtesy of TRW, Inc.)

A color monitor is often preferable for output containing graphics (Figure 3.18). Three colors of phosphor dots form a pixel on color monitors. These colors are blended to make other colors by varying the intensity of the electron beam focused on the phosphor dots (Figure 3.19).

Computers are becoming smaller and more powerful. Flat-panel displays can be manufactured to fit on small, battery-powered portables. Some desktop microcomputers also use flat-panel displays.

The most common flat-panel display is the **liquid-crystal display** (LCD), which produces images by aligning molecular crystals (Figure 3.20). When an electrical charge is applied, the crystals line up in a way that blocks light from passing through them; that absence of light is seen as characters on the screen.

Besides size, another advantage of LCD displays over CRTs is that flat panels do not flicker. The flicker of a CRT is caused by the electron beam

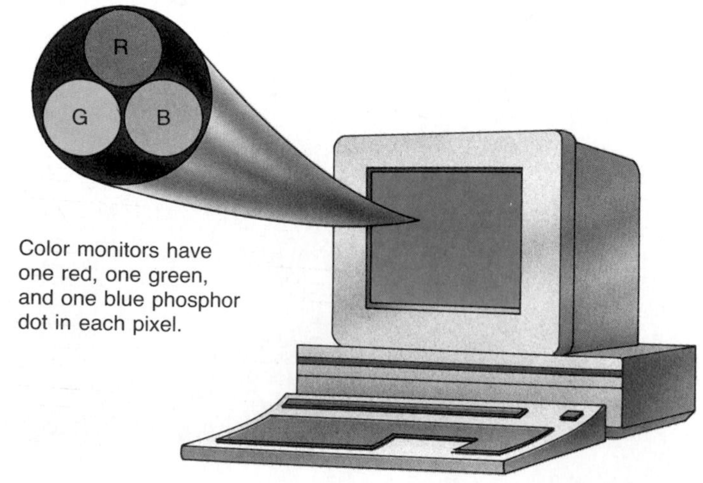

R
G
B
Color monitors have one red, one green, and one blue phosphor dot in each pixel.

Figure 3.19
The smallest dot of light on the computer's screen is called a pixel—for picture element. Varying amounts of red, green, and blue are mixed to achieve a pixel of a specific color.

(a)

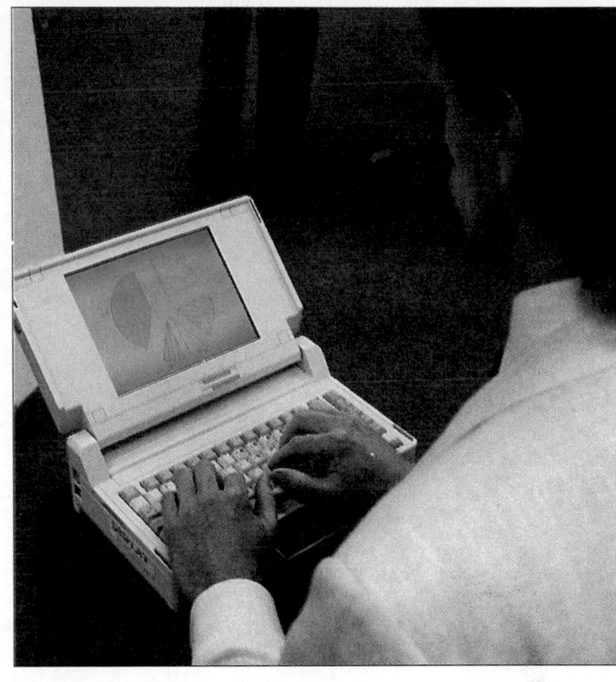

(b)

Figure 3.20
(a) LCD display (b) Gas-plasma display

moving across the screen. It can cause eye strain and fatigue during prolonged sessions at the computer.

New advances are continually being introduced for flat-panel displays. Improved LCD screens have enhanced the visible image. One complaint was that they were difficult to read in either sunlight or dimly lit rooms. Variations in the way the liquid crystals are manufactured and a technique called back-lighting have both contributed to improved LCD panels. Now, color LCD panels are becoming available.

An alternative method for producing a flat panel is gas plasma. **Gas-plasma displays** use electrically charged, ionized gas plasma to create an image of very high quality. Current plasma panels are monochrome, with either a reddish or reddish-orange background and black letters.

Voice Synthesis and Voice Recognition

Another emerging technology involves voice. **Voice synthesis** is the process of electronically reproducing the human voice in recognizable patterns. **Voice recognition** is the ability of the computer to understand spoken words or phrases (Figure 3.21). Both input and output technologies are being developed using voice systems. The obvious advantage is the ease with which you could communicate with the computer if it could recognize your spoken command and respond to you with an audible answer.

TRENDS IN INPUT AND OUTPUT

When computing first became widespread, the most common form of input to the computer was the punched card, and output was nearly always a large stack of paper. These forms of computer communication did the job for their time, but as we began to rely more and more on the computer's ability to provide information, the disadvantages of cards and paper became apparent.

For one thing, punching data into cards meant that someone had to transcribe previously written data into a form understood by the computer. That introduced the possibility of mistakes (transcription errors) caused by misreading or miskeying the data. Also, there was a delay between the time the data were actually captured and when it was input to the computer for process-

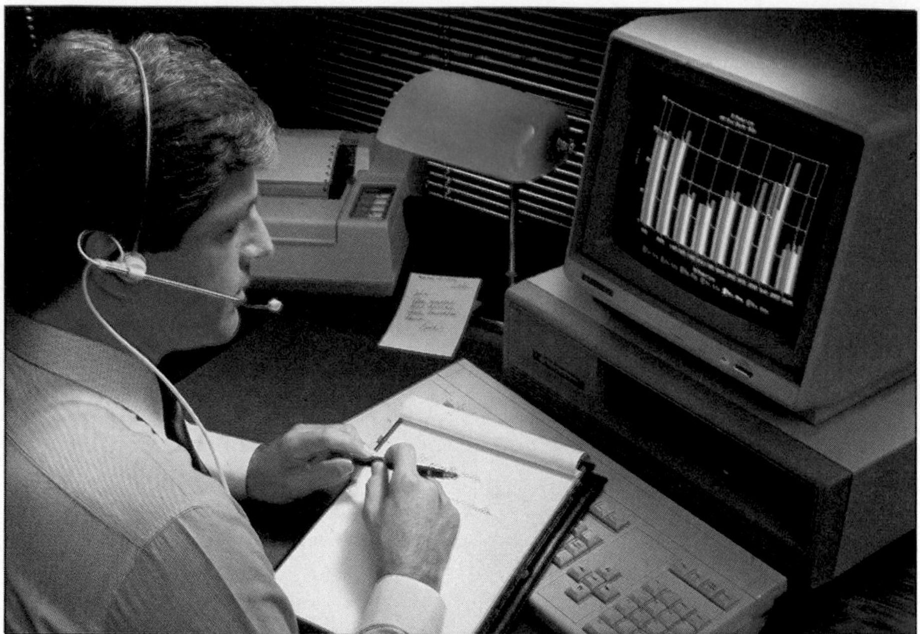

Figure 3.21
Voice-recognition systems free the computer user's hands so work can continue while user and computer communicate.

(Courtesy of Texas Instruments)

ing. Output, too, needed improvement because the stacks of paper did not always provide current information, and sometimes they were a bit too cumbersome to handle.

Since the value of information depends on the timeliness and accuracy of the data used, better methods of input and output were needed. Some of the input and output devices we discussed point to trends in newer equipment and applications.

Source data entry through methods such as bar-code reading, and voice recognition permits us to gather data at the point where they are created. Errors are reduced, and the data are available for immediate processing if needed. On the output side, displays and printers, voice synthesis, and other techniques provide the results of data processing—information—where and when needed.

The trend seems to be to provide technology to gather data at the source where they are best controlled and most accurate. Then the data are either processed immediately or stored until requested. When information is required, the trend is to use the most recently acquired data, or to have immediate access to the data from storage, and to route results directly from processing to the user.

You can observe the effects of these trends everywhere. At the supermarket or gas station, you may use your ATM card to pay for your purchases. You may use computing services to access information about your checking or savings account, to transfer money, or to pay bills. A store might use the computer to check the status of inventory at another location so that you can make the purchase you need today rather than next week. Information that is available when and where it is needed is a powerful resource.

Summary

- The information processing cycle describes the four basic operations performed by a computer. The first three of these operations—input, processing, and output—are the tasks performed by the computer when it converts data into information. Storage, the fourth operation, refers to the computing system's ability to store and retrieve data and programs for future use.
- Data are the numbers, letters, symbols, words, or phrases that are input to a computer; data are only "raw facts."
- Information is data that have been processed into a form that is accessible, useful, and meaningful to its recipient.
- Encoding systems such as EBCDIC (Extended Binary Coded Decimal Interchange Code) and ASCII (American Standard Code for Information Interchange) were developed to convert alphanumeric characters into codes the computer understands, that is, codes consisting of ones and zeros.
- Kilobyte (represented as K or KB) means 1,024 bytes; megabyte (MB) means 1,048,576 bytes.
- The data storage hierarchy is bit, byte, field, record, file, and database.
- Individual data items, or individual facts, are stored as groups of characters (bytes) in a field. Fields are stored in a record. Records containing similar data are stored in a file. In some applications, many files are combined in what is known as a database.
- I–P–O–S stands for the information processing cycle: Data are first *input* to the computer, which then *processes* them into information which is then *output*. Data or information may be *stored* for later access or use.
- Any hardware item that is attached to the main unit of a computer, the central processing unit, is referred to as a peripheral device.
- An input device is a peripheral device through which data are entered and transformed into machine-readable form.
- One of the most common and familiar input devices is the keyboard. Using the keyboard to enter data into the computer is called transcription, which is defined as a process of transferring from one recording and storage system into another. Handwritten originals are called source documents. Transcription errors arise from mishandling data.
- The cursor is a special character or symbol that indicates the user's position on the screen or focuses attention to a specific area to allow communication and interaction between the user and the program.
- Data may be entered directly into a computer system without transcription in a process referred to as source data entry.
- Output involves presenting information that results from processing in a form understandable to humans, or storing data or information in a storage device readable by other machines. An output device is a peripheral device that allows a computer to communicate information to humans or another machine by accepting data from the computer and transforming it into a usable form.
- Hard copy is output, such as paper, that can be read immediately or stored and read later. Soft copy is usually screen-displayed output.
- A printer produces output, usually in the form of text, on paper; however, some printers produce graphics. A plotter produces graphic images on paper.
- Printers have two basic types of printing mechanisms: impact and nonimpact.
- The dot-matrix printer uses print heads containing from nine to twenty-four pins to produce patterns of dots on paper to form individual characters.
- Ink-jet printers form characters on paper by spraying ink from tiny nozzles through an electrical field that arranges the charged ink particles into characters.
- The thermal-transfer printer uses heat to transfer ink to paper.
- Laser printers produce an image on paper by directing a laser beam at a mirror which bounces the image onto a printing drum.
- A plotter produces high-quality graphics in multiple colors using pens that are attached to movable arms.
- A monitor is a television-like device used to display data or information. Monitors can be combined with keyboards so that input data can be viewed and checked as they are entered. This combination is often called a terminal or workstation.
- Monitor quality is often compared in terms of resolution, a measure of the number of picture elements, or pixels, that a screen contains. The least expensive of the CRTs is the single-color, or monochrome, monitor. A color monitor is often preferable for output containing graphics.
- Voice synthesis is the process of electronically reproducing the human voice in recognizable patterns. Voice recognition is the ability of the computer to understand spoken words or phrases.

Key Terms

Information processing cycle
EBCDIC
ASCII
Bit
Byte
Field
Record
File
Database
Function key
Cursor
Hard copy
Soft copy
Monitor

Review Questions

1. How are data different from information?
2. Describe how the binary system is used to store data for use by the computer.
3. What are the two encoding systems commonly used to represent characters for use by the computer?
4. What is the smallest piece of data that can be recognized and used by the computer?
5. A single character, such as a letter or numeric digit, is represented by what computer code?
6. How is the bit used to represent data?
7. Name that data structure that could contain a name, address, or zip code.
8. Describe how a file fits in the data storage hierarchy.
9. What word encompasses all of the physical components of the computer?
10. Give the term used for components attached to the central processing unit.
11. What is the most commonly used input device for the personal computer?
12. Describe the function of the cursor.
13. What is a transcription error and how does it occur?
14. How can source data entry increase the accuracy of data?
15. Describe output.
16. What is the difference between hard copy and soft copy?
17. List the various types of printers and print qualities available.
18. How does a laser printer differ from a dot-matrix printer?
19. Describe the types of monitors used for personal computers.
20. Why would you choose a color monitor rather than a monochrome monitor?

M. E. (TED) HOFF

(Courtesy of Intel Corp.)

PROFILE

It's hard to imagine where we would be today if it weren't for people with vision like Ted Hoff. Even he probably didn't realize what would become of the work he started on that fateful day in 1969.

Ted Hoff joined Intel Corporation in 1969, after working at Stanford University as a research assistant. At Intel, Hoff led a team that helped a Japanese firm, Busicom, design a custom circuit for its calculator.

The Busicom design called for twelve integrated circuit chips, each with 3,000 to 5,000 transistors. The chips that made up the processor were matched to the specific tasks of the calculator. After reviewing the design, however, Hoff decided it was too complex and would be too expensive to produce; consequently, he creatively solved these problems by using a totally different approach. He decided to design the calculator around a general-purpose processor and to rely more on software for specific tasks than on a lot of electronics. Although more memory space was needed to store the software, this approach enabled Hoff to put the entire processor on a single integrated circuit chip—a microprocessor.

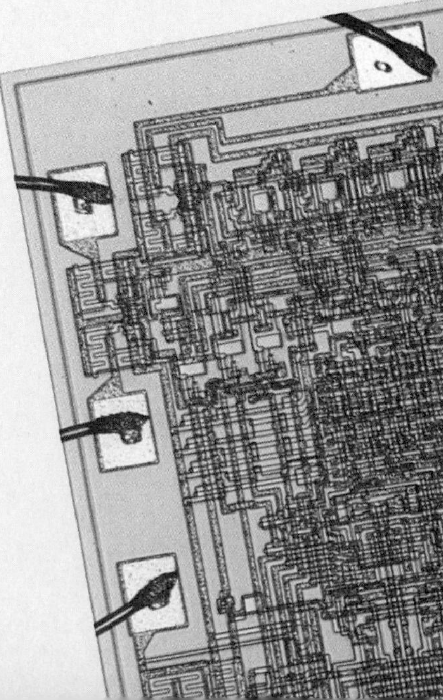

And what a chip it was! The Intel 4004 could handle 4 bits of information at a time, and its computational powers came close to those of the ENIAC, one of the early electronic, digital computers which required an entire room to house. This single microprocessor performed as well as some of the IBM machines of the early 1960s that cost around $30,000 and had processing units the size of a large desk. Hoff's microprocessor was about one-sixth by one-eighth of an inch and cost about $200. The reductions in size and cost made it possible to design small, relatively inexpensive computers. This discovery heralded the beginning of the microcomputer revolution.

Thanks to Ted Hoff's creativeness, microprocessors are everywhere—in our computers, homes, cars, factories, and yes, still in our calculators.

Courtesy of Intel Corp.

CHAPTER 4

CENTRAL PROCESSING UNIT

IN THIS CHAPTER YOU WILL LEARN ABOUT

- **The central processing unit (CPU)**
- **How the CPU processes data**
- **Factors influencing computer performance**
- **Expanding the computer's resources**

A SURPRISING HISTORY

When you stop to consider the computer and the technology that has brought it to your desktop, you probably think of the gleaming windowed walls and controlled workspaces of high-tech manufacturing facilities and of engineers designing the next generation of powerful yet relatively inexpensive systems. Certainly all of that is a part of today's world of computing, but you may be surprised to learn that many of the computer's basic concepts have roots hundreds of years old.

You may also be somewhat surprised that, like Ted Hoff's invention, much of the computer's technology and ability to perform stems from attempts to simplify problem solving rather than to handle complicated tasks. Consider, for instance, the use of the bit, or binary digit, to represent codes inside the computer.

Binary logic, the cornerstone of all operations within the computer, was developed in the 1850s by a self-taught English mathematician, George Boole. **Boolean logic,** the practice of reducing complex problems to a series of simple questions answered only by "yes" or "no" (binary logic) is reflected in the computer's 1 for on, or yes, and 0 for off, or no.

Perhaps even more astonishing, the computer's "brain," the central processing unit, is based on the original work of Charles P. Babbage, who designed an all-purpose problem-solving machine in the early 1800s. Babbage used mechanical components and steam power in his designs for his Difference Engine (Figure 4.1) and Analytical Engine. Though his machines could not be completed during his lifetime, he has been titled "father of the computer" for the concepts they established.

Babbage realized that a problem-solving machine would need some way to obtain its data as input and that it would have to be able to give some answer as output. He also determined that the machine would require (1) a control unit to enable it to follow directions; (2) a device, which he called the "mill," to perform the arithmetic and logical operations; and (3) a place to store data and

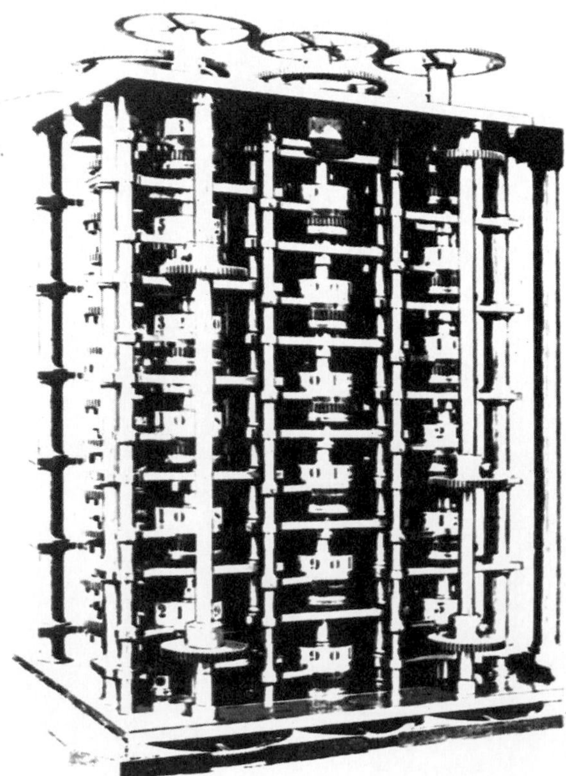

Figure 4.1
Charles Babbage's Difference Engine.

(Courtesy of International Business Machines Corp.)

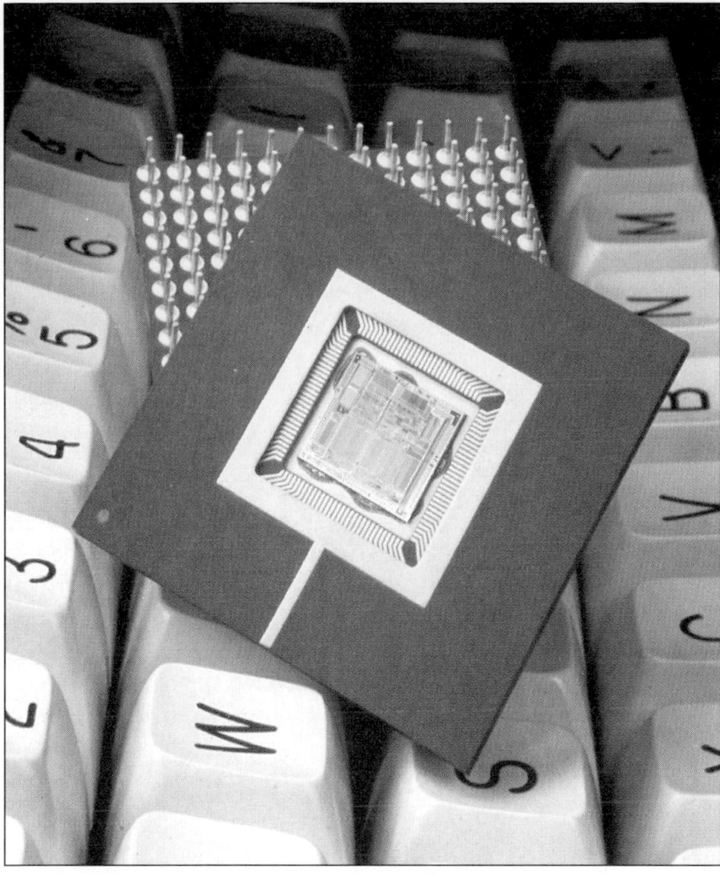

Figure 4.2
A microprocessor mounted in its protective ceramic package.

(Courtesy of Motorola, Inc.)

partial answers while the machine worked through the problem. Babbage actually described the functions of each of the computer's major components: input and output devices, and a central processing unit containing a control unit, arithmetic and logic unit, and memory.

MAIN COMPONENTS OF A CPU

The computer's central processing unit (CPU) consists of a control unit, arithmetic and logic unit (ALU), and memory. Each of these devices has a specific purpose in enabling the computer to carry out its functions. To understand how each works, it is easiest to discuss them as if they were easily distinguishable, separate machines, but that is not really the case.

An **integrated circuit** (IC), also called a microchip or chip, is a small piece of silicon containing one or more complete electronic circuits. Until the developmental work by Ted Hoff, the parts of the CPU were separate units; Hoff combined the ALU and the control unit on a single chip called a **microprocessor** (Figure 4.2). To be called a microprocessor, a chip must contain at least the ALU and control unit, but it may also contain primary storage. The microprocessor led to the rapid development of the microcomputer. In a microcomputer, the components of the CPU are mounted on the main circuit board, often called the "motherboard" or "system board."

If you were to look inside your personal computer, you might be able to locate two of the parts of the CPU. One would be the microprocessor chip, housing the control unit and ALU. Separately, you might be able to find a bank of circuits making up the computer's memory. Some systems are designed so that only a limited amount of memory can be installed on the system board, and additional memory is located on an adapter card plugged into one of the slots provided. Though these units making up the CPU appear to be physically separate circuits, they are treated as one system component.

Control Unit

The **control unit** is the computer's manager; it receives the instructions, interprets them and directs other components to perform their activities (Figure 4.3). The control unit performs four activities: fetching, or receiving instructions stored in the computer's memory; decoding, or translating the instructions into specific sequences of actions to be taken by the computer's other components; executing, or actually carrying out the processing tasks; and storing, or moving the result of processing activities into the computer's memory.

Arithmetic and Logic Unit

The **arithmetic and logic unit (ALU)** is the part of the CPU where all mathematical and logical functions are performed. The basic **mathematical functions** include addition, subtraction, multiplication, and division. Software can combine these four basic math functions to perform logarithmic, trigonometric, and other mathematical functions. In a **logic function** numbers or characters are compared with each other based on their relationships, for example, greater than, less than, equal to, not equal to, greater than or equal to, and less than or equal to. Such comparisons are also called **conditional operations** and are phrased so that they are able to be answered "yes" or "no" according to the rules of Boolean logic.

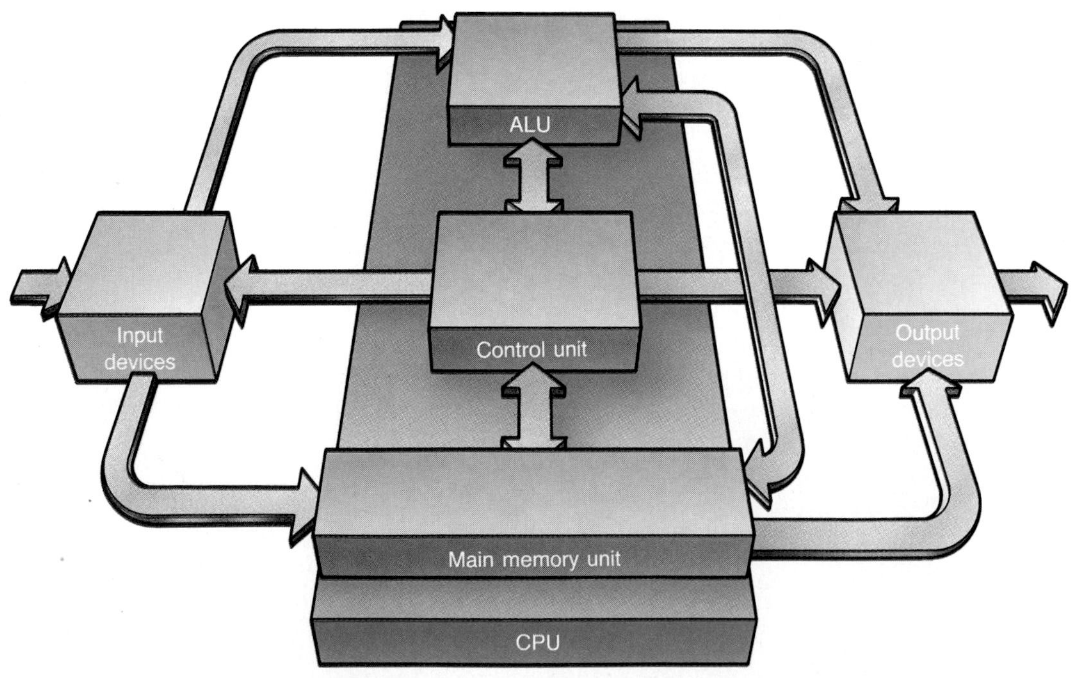

Figure 4.3
The relationship of the CPU and input and output devices is illustrated. The arrows indicate movement of data or instructions among the devices. The CPU's internal structure is represented by the ALU, control unit, and main memory unit.

Memory—The Primary Storage Unit

The **primary storage unit** refers to the internal storage unit of the computer, where programs and their data are stored—what we usually call the computer's memory. **Primary storage,** or **primary memory,** provides temporary storage during program execution. Part of primary storage may also contain permanently stored instructions, such as those that tell the computer what to do when it is turned on. Because primary storage is located inside the computer and is linked directly to the other components of the CPU, access time to data located there is very fast.

The process of entering data into storage is called **writing.** When data are placed in, or written to, storage, they replace what was originally there. The process of retrieving data from storage is called **reading.** Reading does not change the data in any way. The specific location in memory into which data are written or from which they can be read is defined as an **address.**

Most primary storage today is comprised of semiconductor technology. Semiconductor memory is made by "etching" electronic circuits onto a silicon chip (Figure 4.4). The two most common forms are random-access memory and read-only memory.

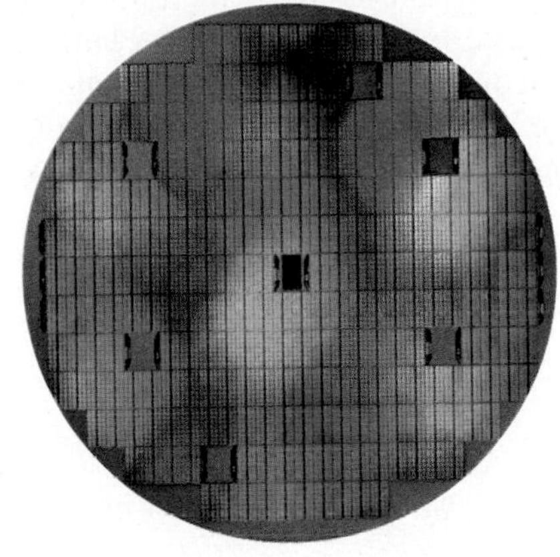

Figure 4.4
This 8-inch silicon wafer holds more than 400 one-million bit (megabit) memory chips. The wafer will be tested and diced, and individual memory chips will be mounted in protective packages before becoming memory chips for personal computers.

(Courtesy of International Business Machines Corp.)

Random-access memory (RAM) is that part of primary storage where data and program instructions are held temporarily while being manipulated or executed. This type of memory allows the user to enter data into memory (write) and then to retrieve them (read).

RAM is **volatile;** it depends on a steady supply of electricity to maintain data storage. When the power to the computer is shut off, everything that was stored in RAM is lost. It is this characteristic of RAM memory that necessitates the use of **secondary storage** (disks, tapes, and so forth) for permanent storage of data and programs.

As the name implies, **read-only memory** (ROM) can only be read; data cannot be written into it. ROM may contain information on how to start the computer and even instructions to the entire operating system. The actual contents of ROM are usually set by the computer manufacturer; they are unchangeable and permanent. Because the contents cannot be altered in any way, and they are not lost when the electric current is turned off, ROM is nonvolatile.

The amount of primary storage is important in determining the capabilities of the computer. You have already heard the description of memory as "640K" or "1MB." The more primary storage available means that more instructions and data can be loaded into the computer. Many applications require a specific amount of memory, or the application package cannot be used. Most computers have provisions for adding individual RAM chips to the main circuit board or adding RAM via expansion cards, a group of integrated circuits already assembled on a printed circuit board.

Additional Memory—Expanded Versus Extended

In early IBM and IBM-compatible microcomputers, the computer's memory was designed so that total accessible memory was physically limited to 1MB. The operating system, DOS, and application programs were allowed to use the first 640K of this memory, which is why 640K is such a popular memory size for so many IBM-compatible computers. The additional space up to 1MB was reserved for system functions (Figure 4.5).

As newer processors with the ability to address more memory were introduced, designers had to develop a way to access this added memory without making older software or systems obsolete. This desire to retain the value of older equipment and software is part of what is meant when you hear the term **compatible.**

Two solutions have emerged: extended and expanded memory. **Extended memory** is all of the memory above 1MB; it is accessed either by software applications specifically written to use extended memory beyond 1MB, or by special additions to the operating system. **Expanded memory** also increases memory access, but it incorporates both hardware and software to address memory and may include locations below 1MB as well as above. Expanded memory, defined in a specification developed jointly by Lotus Development Corporation, Intel Corporation, and Microsoft Corporation, is often called LIM-Specification.

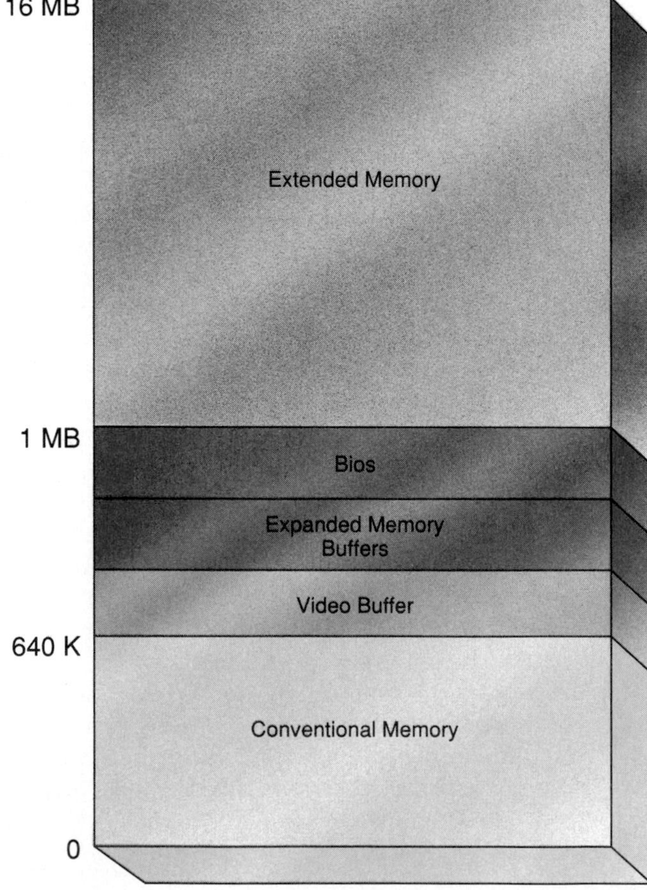

Figure 4.5
The computer's memory is allocated in several ways. Conventional memory reaches 640K. Extended memory is all memory above 1MB. Expanded memory uses temporary storage to reach memory addresses beyond 640K.

HOW THE CPU PROCESSES DATA

How does the computer turn data into information? Just what does the CPU really do? How does it use its three components—memory, ALU, and control unit? How can you judge a system's performance? These questions are all better answered by a more complete description of how the CPU does its work.

Machine Cycle

Earlier, the CPU was described as having four functions: fetching, decoding, executing, and storing. These functions, carried out in that sequence during what is called the **machine cycle,** are at the heart of how the CPU's work is accomplished.

The machine cycle consists of two parts. The first part is the **instruction cycle,** which includes the activity of fetching and decoding an instruction, that is, retrieving it from an address in the computer's main memory and determining what task the instruction requires. The second part of the cycle is called the **execution cycle,** where the required operations are actually carried out and the new data resulting from the operation are stored in memory (Figure 4.6).

Registers and Buffers

To carry out its operations, the computer relies on special data storage areas, called registers and buffers. A **register** is a temporary storage location in memory that very quickly accepts, stores, or transfers data or instructions while in use. The control unit, for instance, fetches an instruction from memory and places it in a decoding register before determining its purpose. **Buffers** are also temporary data-holding areas built into either the CPU or into input or output devices. No matter how fast your disk drive or printer may appear to be, it is much slower than the CPU, so data being sent to or from input/output devices are placed by the CPU into buffers so that the slower devices do not hold back efficient processing (Figure 4.7).

Measuring System Performance

The speed at which the computer is able to complete the machine cycle is considered one measurement of the computer's performance. The number of machine instructions processed per second, called MIPS for **millions of instructions per second,** is often quoted as a performance statistic. Actually, the speed at which the computer is able to complete the machine cycle depends on three characteristics: the system clock, bus width, and word size.

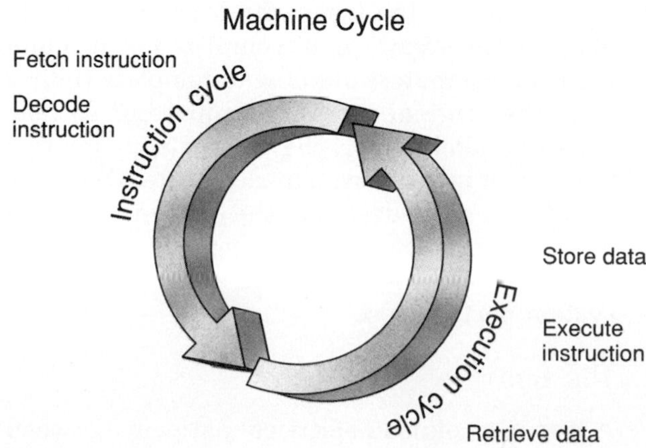

Figure 4.6
The machine cycle.

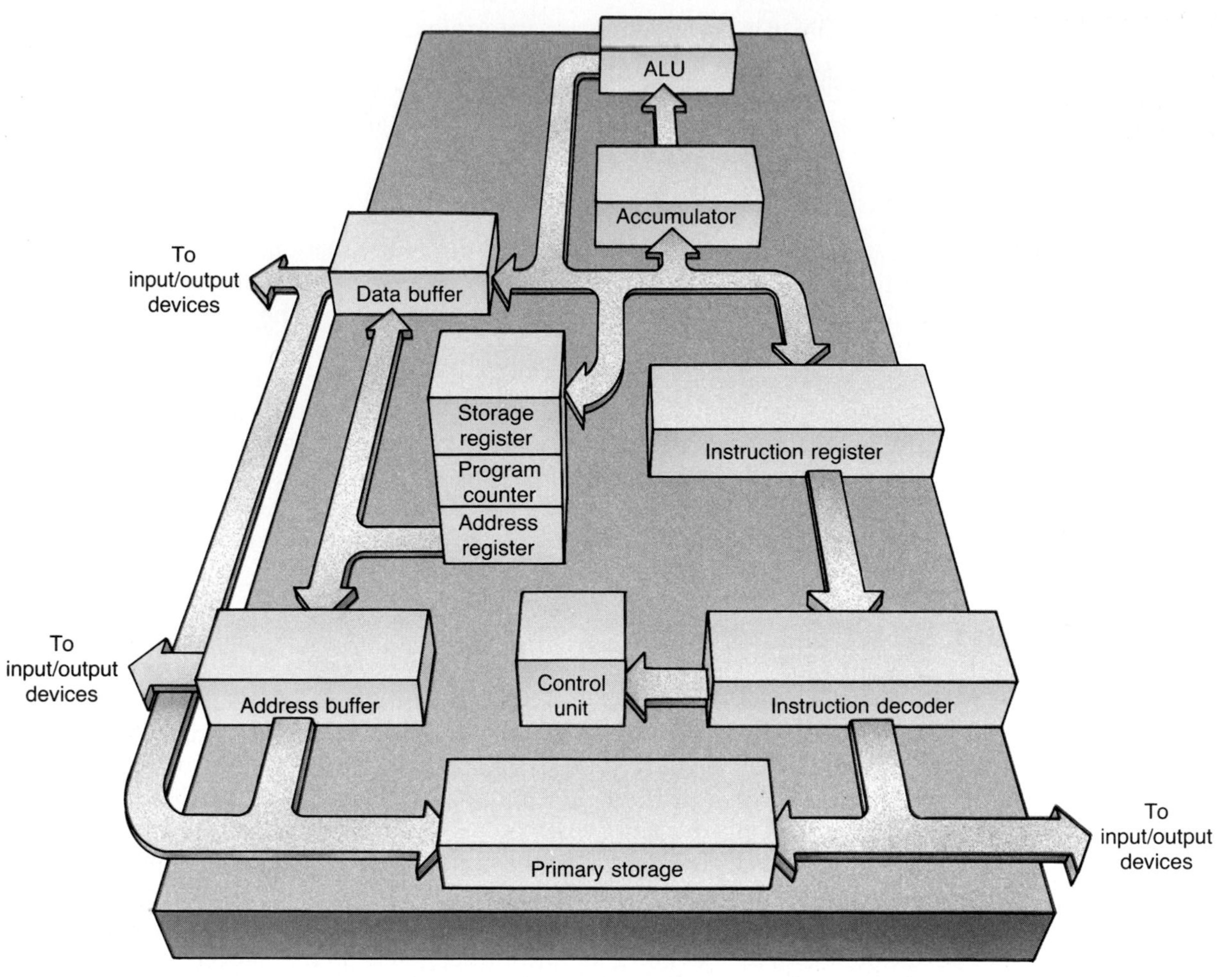

Figure 4.7
Data move along the paths indicated by the arrows in this illustration. Note the use of buffers and registers as temporary holding areas for certain operations.

System Clock

IBM's earliest personal computer models, the PC and PC/XT, performed operations at a rate of 4.77 megahertz. Today's personal computers often work at 16 to 33 megahertz. **Megahertz,** which is translated as millions of cycles per second, is simply the measurement of how fast the computer is able to turn a circuit on and off.

Obviously, the faster the computer can use a circuit, the faster the work done by the circuit can be completed. Is it therefore just as obvious that today's personal computers are able to complete their work more than six times faster than the original personal computers? Although it is true that now the circuitry is much faster, the ability to complete a machine cycle is governed by more than just the system-clock rate. Depending on the nature of the instruction, and on the design of the computer's bus width and word size, more than one cycle may be needed to complete a single machine operation. Therefore, the speed of the system clock alone is not necessarily a good measurement of system performance.

The Bus

A **bus** is a common electrical pathway between the various components of the computer. The bus connects all parts of the CPU and the input and output

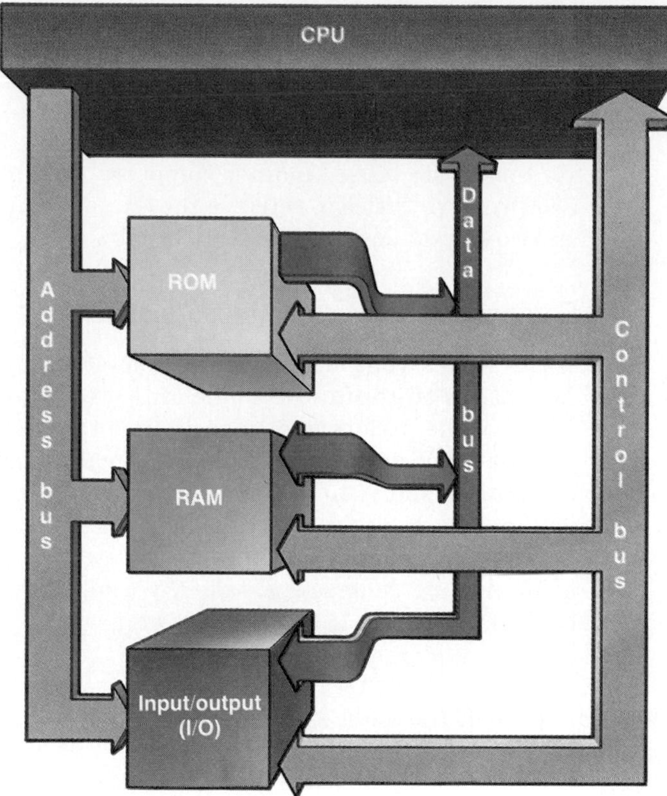

Figure 4.8
Three buses are used to carry data and instructions inside the computing system.

devices as well. Several different types of buses are used, but the one that concerns us now is the data bus, the pathway that carries data throughout the computer (Figure 4.8).

Think of the data bus as a road. A narrow, single-lane road permits limited, one-way traffic, whereas a superhighway has the capacity for many vehicles at one time, going in different directions. The concept applies fairly well to the computer.

Earlier personal computers used an 8-bit data bus design. The design limited data traffic to one direction of travel, and only one byte at a time could be transmitted. As processor capacity developed, newer buses with 16-bit or 32-bit paths were introduced. A 32-bit data bus can transmit four times the data in the same timeframe as an 8-bit bus. Therefore, the width of your computer's data bus will have an impact on performance. Imagine transferring a twenty-page word processing document through an 8-bit bus, one character at a time, versus transferring it through a 32-bit bus at four characters at a time.

The latest developments in bus design include multidirectional data buses. IBM introduced its Micro-Channel Architecture (MCA) design with the PS/2 in 1987. Compaq and other manufacturers followed with EISA (Enhanced Industry Standard Architecture) some time later. These bus designs permit faster data flow because they permit multiple operations to be completed, such as sending output to the printer while taking in keyboard input. Older designs would have made you wait to key in new data until the printer's buffer was full and the data bus released.

Word Size

A computer **word** is the number of adjacent bits that can be stored and manipulated as a unit. Some of the newer microcomputers manipulate a 32-bit word, whereas older models have word lengths of 8 and 16 bits. Word lengths range up to 128 bits for supercomputers. In general, the longer the length of the word that the computer can manipulate, the faster data can be processed.

Word length relates directly to the other two factors of system performance. If a computer uses a 32-bit word, can access that much data in one cycle, and can transmit it in one burst down a 32-bit data bus, it will complete its task faster than another computer that perhaps has only a 16-bit word, requires two cycles to retrieve the data from memory, and must send the data in two bursts down a 16-bit data bus.

Throughput—A Better Measurement

If you really want to determine a computer's relative performance, you should look at **throughput,** the computer's ability to start and end a complete task. Many of the performance measurement statistics used to promote computers, such as MIPS or the system clock's megahertz rating, overlook the fact that the computer's ability to perform efficiently depends on an overall balance of components working together, including software. Therefore, always test a computer's performance on some more relevant factor that you understand; for example, how long does it take the computer to calculate and output a financial analysis from a spreadsheet program?

FAMILIES OF MICROPROCESSORS

Although the CPU of every computer goes about its work in essentially the same way, not every CPU is the same. Engineers have designed several variations of CPUs, each with special characteristics relating to performance, ease of programming, ability to access data, and so on. At the machine instruction level, each variation of a CPU may be different from others. A program written to be run on one type of CPU may not be able to function on a CPU of a different type.

Microprocessors are no exception to these design characteristics and indeed, without realizing it, you are probably influenced by these differences. Personal computing systems have been designed around "families" of microprocessor chips (Figure 4.9).

Ted Hoff's original product began the lineage for one important family of microprocessors: the Intel 80X86, as it is popularly known today. Hoff's design was called the 4004. A later improvement was called the 8008, then revised again as the Intel 8080. A competitor firm, Zilog, manufactured a compatible chip called the Z80. The Z80 was called compatible because a program written to function with the 8080 chip would work in a computer using the Z80 microprocessor.

As more improvements to the circuits were introduced, Intel announced the 8088, 8086, 80286, 80386, and 80486 microprocessors. Each version has more computing capability than earlier designs. Nevertheless, within the family of processors, there is a similarity of machine-language instruction, so that there is a potential of running a program from an earlier version on the latest one. It is not a guarantee, however, because many factors, including the operating system used, are involved.

IBM selected the Intel design for its personal computers beginning with the original IBM PC introduced in 1981. IBM's current PS/2 line of microcomputers still incorporates the 80X86 series of processors, which gives its latest products a strong measure of compatibility with its oldest models.

Another important family of microprocessors is the Motorola 68000, used as the CPU in the Apple Macintosh computers. Latest models of this series of processors provide a similar measure of compatibility within the Macintosh family of computers, but changes to Apple's operating system within various models have made compatibility a bit more tricky.

Figure 4.9
Some popular personal computers and the microprocessors they contain.

Microcomputer	Microprocessor
Apple Macintosh	Motorola 68000
Apple Macintosh II	Motorola 68020
Apple Macintosh SE/30	Motorola 68030
Apple II	MOS Technology 6502
Apple IIc	MOS Technology 65C02
Atari 520ST	Motorola 68000
AT&T UNIX PC	Motorola 68010
AT&T 6300	Intel 8086
Commodore Amiga	Motorola 68000
Compaq Deskpro 286	Intel 80286
Compaq Deskpro 386	Intel 80386
Compaq Portable Computer	Intel 8088
DataWorld's Data 386-16	Intel 80386
Dell System 310	Intel 80386
IBM PC AT	Intel 80286
IBM PC XT	Intel 8088
IBM PS/2 Model 80	Intel 80386
Kaypro II	Zilog Z-80A
Leading Edge Model D	Intel 8088
NeXT	Motorola 68030
Tandy 1000	Intel 8088
Tandy 3000	Intel 80286
TRS-80 Model 4	Zilog Z-80A
TRS-80 Model 16	Intel 8086

OPEN ARCHITECTURE

The term **open architecture** in computing refers to a style or design of construction used to build the system. It refers most specifically to the system unit, and to your ability to change the unit's components. Put somewhat simply, it is a reference to your ability to open up the cabinet and insert or remove parts. If the system unit cannot be opened so that new hardware can be added, it is a **closed architecture** system.

Though two people may buy identical personal computers, they are not likely to use them in an identical way. Perhaps one is an architect who wants to use a computer-aided design program, while the other is a writer interested primarily in word processing. One's work may be entirely within the office, whereas the other may need to use the computer to send and receive material electronically. Over time, many people who own a personal computer consider adding some new hardware feature to it.

Another meaning of open architecture is that manufacturers other than the original computer manufacturer should have access to design information so that they can sell products that work with the basic system unit. The first Apple II computers were, and still are, open architecture systems, as were most early computers. Not only did the originating computer companies offer extra features, but they allowed many specialty products to be designed by so-called third-party vendors. The large and rapidly expanding market for these products stimulated growth in the industry.

HIGHLIGHT

Gilbert Hyatt—Patently the Father of the Micro-processor

As the story goes, Alexander Graham Bell is considered the "father" of the telephone because he got to the patent office first. A similar case of legal genetics surrounds the development of the microprocessor, though it seems that the inventor may have arrived at the patent office last.

For two decades, a common belief has been that the microprocessor was designed at Intel Corporation by Ted Hoff along with other engineers, including Frederico Faggin, who later founded Zilog Corporation and manufactured the Z80 microprocessor.

In 1990, after nearly twenty years of applications, reapplications, and court fights, a patent for the basic design of the microprocessor was awarded to Gilbert Hyatt, a California inventor. If his patent claims are interpreted in his favor, he could demand a royalty payment for nearly every microprocessor sold and for any product that uses a microprocessor in its design.

Substantial amounts of money ride on the potential answers to challenges to Hyatt's patent claims. Opponents argue that Hyatt never constructed a working model of his design, only a hypothetical one, and that he did not provide enough information to demonstrate he could build one. Others argue that he had access to previously documented microprocessor design information and used it in his own work. Certainly, no money will change hands over this issue without major legal challenges.

A more interesting issue arises, though, for you to consider: Is it fair to give Hyatt this patent after the industry has used the design for over twenty years believing, with the federal patent office's backing, that others designed the microprocessor? Could this problem have been avoided if patent designs were published at the time of application? Should patents, which can protect designs for seventeen years, be enforced from the date of filing rather than from the date the patent is granted, which may be years after the date it was submitted?

Patent rights in the United States date back to the Constitution, Article 1, Section 8, Clause 8, which states: "The Congress shall have the power to promote the progress of science and useful arts by securing for limited times to authors and inventors the exclusive right to their respective writings and discoveries." How the government fulfills this responsibility directly affects innovation in this industry.

IBM's personal computers, both the PC and PS/2, are designed as open architecture. Apple initially designed the Macintosh as a closed system, but apparently the popularity of and demand for third-party accessories was so strong that the Macintosh II family of systems is again an open system design.

New accessories and features made available for a personal computer enable you to attach a variety of additional equipment. Thus you can enhance the system's performance and tailor the system to your special needs (Figure 4.10).

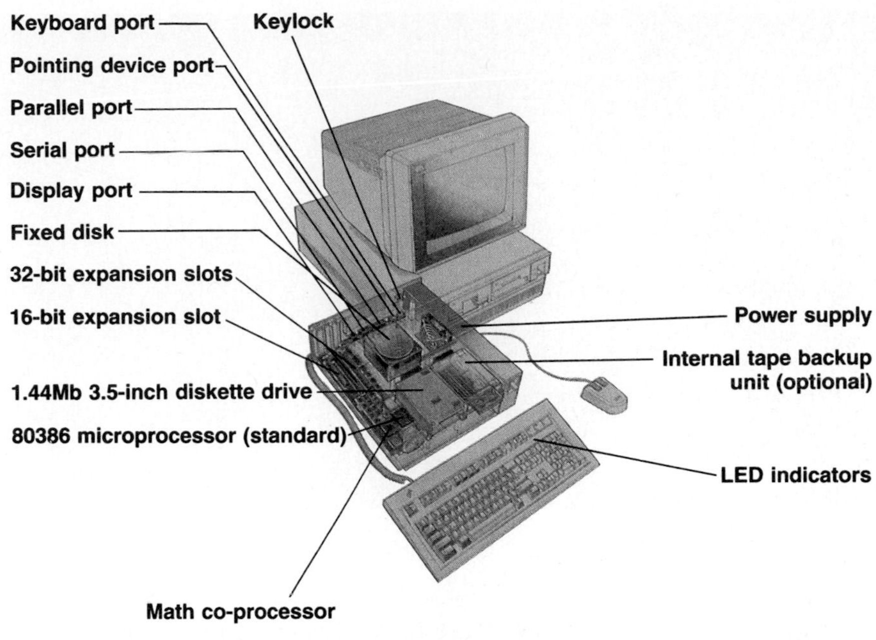

Figure 4.10
A personal computer has several ports and expansion slots that can be used to tailor the system to special needs.

(Courtesy of International Business Machines Corp.)

Coprocessors

A processor, as you know, performs all of the computer's instructions in order to complete a task. A **coprocessor** cooperates with the CPU in completing the computer's work by adding specialized processing capabilities. One of the most common coprocessors, the math coprocessor, is a good example of the cooperative nature involved.

Normally, the computer's ability to perform mathematical calculations is somewhat limited. Certainly, it can do ordinary math at blazing speeds, but the CPU is busy with other functions, too, so a long or complex calculation may be interrupted when the CPU is busy with other duties. Also, even though the CPU is very accurate in its calculations, it may not be accurate enough for some extremely detailed ones.

A math coprocessor, such as the Intel 80287 or 80387 chips, senses when a math or logic operation is about to be performed. Rather than sending the instruction to the CPU's ALU, the math coprocessor receives the work and completes it faster and with greater accuracy than the CPU. It is able to do this because the chip was designed specifically to be very efficient and highly accurate with math or logic instructions.

Coprocessors are not limited to math, however. Specialized graphics and communication accessories often use coprocessors to take over the more complicated, specific tasks related to their purpose. This frees the CPU to handle routine tasks more efficiently.

Expansion Slots and Accessory Cards

The range of available extra features for the computer is almost endless, and no system design could hope to anticipate the many alternative electronic connections that would be needed to accommodate them. To give you the opportunity and flexibility of adding extra features, personal computers such as the

Figure 4.11
Accessory or expansion cards are inserted into the expansion slots to add features to the computer. Shown here is a multifunction card that adds extra RAM memory, parallel and serial ports, and a battery-powered system clock.

IBM PC and PS/2 or Macintosh are equipped with **expansion slots** built into the system boards (Figure 4.11).

By following the computer's design specifications published by the original computer manufacturer, proper electronic connections for attaching printed circuit cards can be made. Expansion or accessory cards, so called because they may expand the machine's capability or add features, can be inserted into these slots to equip the system with new capabilities.

Ports—Making the Connection

Computers require special hardware to connect the central processing system to peripheral devices, such as a printer. The connection is called an **interface,** or more popularly a **port.** It may be available as a plug-in expansion card, but now it is more frequently built into the circuitry on the system board by the manufacturer (Figure 4.12). Data are transferred in one of two ways: serial or parallel.

When a **serial interface** is used, data are transferred either to or from the CPU and a peripheral device one bit at a time (Figure 4.13a). The most common serial interface on microcomputers is called the RS-232C.

In a **parallel interface,** data are transferred either to or from the CPU and a peripheral device one byte at a time, that is, eight bits at a time (Figure 4.13b). Parallel interfaces are faster and more expensive than serial interfaces. Data are sent over conductors running parallel to each other. The

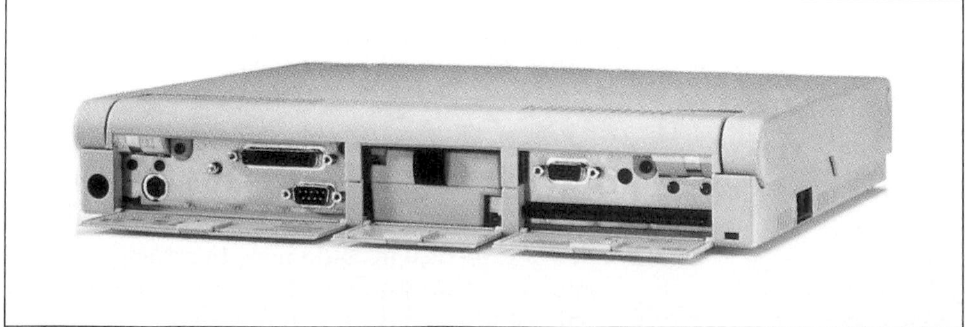

Figure 4.12
Most personal computers contain a variety of built-in connections.

(Courtesy of International Business Machines, Inc.)

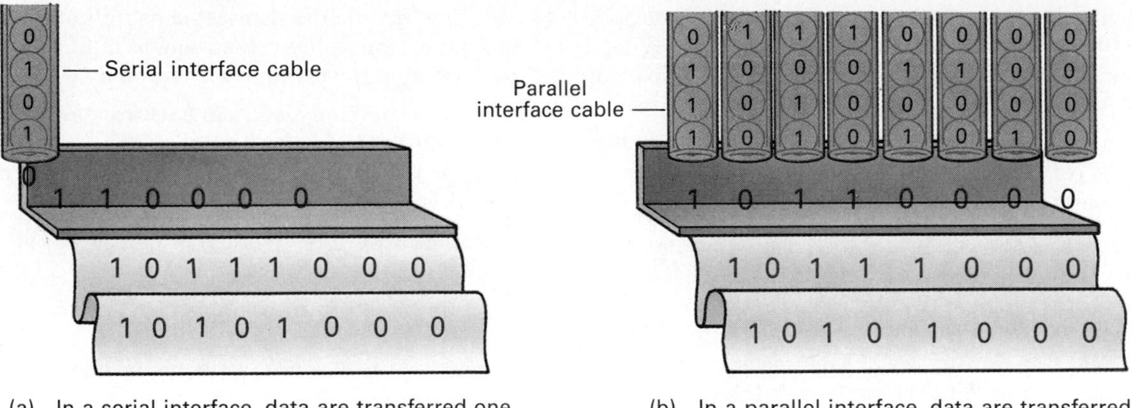
Serial interface cable
Parallel interface cable
(a) In a serial interface, data are transferred one bit at a time.
(b) In a parallel interface, data are transferred one byte at a time.

Figure 4.13
Serial versus parallel data transfer.

Centronics standard and the IEEE-488 standard are parallel interfaces used in many microcomputers.

Although your personal computer may have disk drive storage equipment built into the same cabinet that contains the central processing unit, the disk units are still considered to be peripheral devices. They require some form of an interface, usually called a **controller,** to provide communication to the system. The controller is often installed as an accessory card. Sometimes, there is insufficient space to house all of the components in the personal computer's cabinet so you may have an external disk drive connected by a cable.

One form of interface used for disk drives and other high-speed computer peripherals is the SCSI (pronounced "scuzzy") interface. SCSI stands for **small computer systems interface.** It provides a common interface through which one or more devices can be linked to the computing system. Devices frequently attached to SCSI connections include external disk drives, scanners, and tape backup systems.

To enhance the performance of the system, accessory cards are sometimes equipped with coprocessors that are able to do some part of the computing operations without assistance from the computer's CPU. These so-called **bus-master accessory cards** can be used for several purposes: (1) communication with other computers on a network; (2) control of devices connected to the computer, such as machine tools; or (3) other operations that would reduce the efficiency of the computing system if the system's CPU were the only processor controlling these tasks.

Summary

- Many of the computer's basic concepts have roots hundreds of years old. Binary logic was developed in the 1850s by George Boole. Boolean logic, the practice of reducing complex problems to a series of simple questions answered only by "yes" or "no," is reflected in the computer's 1 for on, or yes, and 0 for off, or no.
- The central processing unit is based on the work of Charles P. Babbage.
- The computer's central processing unit consists of a control unit, arithmetic and logic unit (ALU), and memory. Ted Hoff combined the ALU and the control unit on a single chip called a microprocessor.
- The control unit is the computer's manager; it receives the instructions, interprets them, and directs other components to perform their activities. The control unit performs four activities: fetching, or receiving instructions stored in the computer's memory; decoding, or translating the instructions into specific sequences of actions to be taken by the computer's other components; executing, or actually carrying out the processing tasks; and storing, or moving the result of processing activities into the computer's memory.
- The arithmetic and logic unit is the part of the CPU where all mathematical and logical functions are per-

formed. The basic mathematical functions include addition, subtraction, multiplication, and division. A logic function is one in which numbers or characters are compared with each other based on their relationships.

- The primary storage unit refers to the internal storage unit of the computer, where programs and their data are stored during program execution.
- The process of entering data into storage is called writing. When data are placed in, or written to, storage, they replace what was originally there. The process of retrieving data from storage is called reading. Reading does not change the data in any way. The specific location in memory into which data are written or from which they can be read is defined as an address.
- Random-access memory (RAM) is that part of primary storage where data and program instructions are held temporarily while being manipulated or executed. RAM is volatile. Read-only memory (ROM) can only be read; data cannot be written into it.
- The machine cycle consists of two parts. The first part is the instruction cycle, which includes the activity of fetching and decoding an instruction. The second part of the cycle is called the execution cycle, where the required operations are actually carried out and the new data resulting from the operation are stored in memory.
- A register is a temporary storage location in memory. Buffers are also temporary data-holding areas built into either the CPU or into input or output devices.
- The number of machine instructions processed per second, called MIPS for millions of instructions per second, is often quoted as a performance statistic.
- Megahertz, which is translated as millions of cycles per second, is simply the measurement of how fast the computer is able to turn a circuit on and off.
- A bus is a common electrical pathway between the various components of the computer. The bus connects all parts of the CPU and the input and output devices as well.
- A computer word is the number of adjacent bits that can be stored and manipulated as a unit.
- Open architecture in computing refers to the ability to change a unit's components. If the system unit cannot be opened so that new hardware can be added, it is a closed architecture system.
- A coprocessor cooperates with the CPU in completing the computer's work by adding specialized processing capabilities. One of the most common coprocessors is the math coprocessor.
- Expansion or accessory cards can be inserted into slots to expand the machine's capability or to add features.
- Computers require special hardware to connect the central processing system to peripheral devices; the connection is called an interface, or, more popularly, a port.
- When a serial interface is used, data are transferred either to or from the CPU and a peripheral device one bit at a time. In a parallel interface, data are transferred either to or from the CPU and a peripheral device one byte at a time, that is, eight bits at a time.
- One form of interface used for disk drives and other high-speed computer peripherals is the SCSI ("scuzzy") interface. SCSI stands for small computer systems interface.

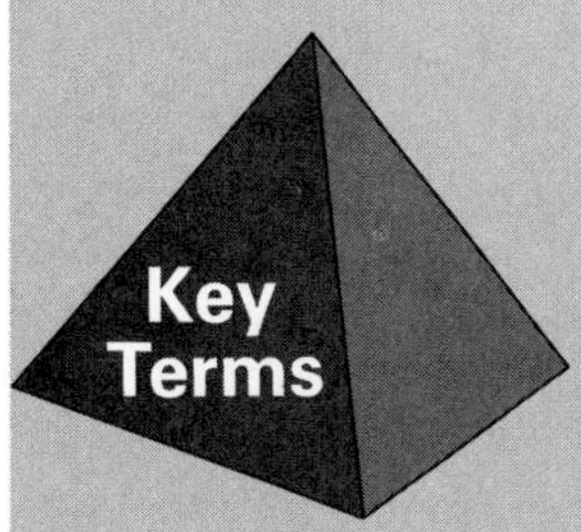

Boolean logic
Integrated circuit
Microprocessor
Control unit
Arithmetic and logic unit
Mathematical function
Logic function
Primary memory
Address
Random-access memory
Read-only memory
Port

Review Questions

1. Discuss George Boole's contribution to the field of computing.
2. List the three main components of the central processing unit and describe their functions.
3. What is a microprocessor?
4. Describe the four activities of the computer's control unit.
5. List the types of mathematical and logic functions performed by the arithmetic and logic unit.
6. What is a conditional operation?
7. Give the phrase used to describe the internal storage unit of the computer.
8. Name the processes for entering data into storage and retrieving data from storage.
9. Define RAM; what does the term *volatile* mean?
10. What is the purpose of read-only memory?
11. Describe what is meant by the term *compatible.*
12. Differentiate between extended and expanded memory.
13. Describe the two parts of the machine cycle.
14. Define and differentiate registers and buffers.
15. What is measured by MIPS?
16. The computer's operating speed is often stated in megahertz; what is this actually measuring?
17. Describe a computer bus; how does it affect computer processing?
18. Describe word size; how does it affect computer processing?
19. What might be considered the best measurement of a computer's processing performance and why?
20. How can a family of microprocessors contribute to computer's compatibility?
21. What is the difference between open and closed computer architectures?
22. Describe the purpose of a coprocessor, giving some examples.
23. How can you add new features to your computer's capabilities?
24. What are ports and how are they used?
25. Differentiate between serial and parallel interfaces.

PROFILE

ALAN SHUGART

(Courtesy Seagate Technology)

The first magnetic-disk filing system, IBM's RAMAC (Random Access Method of Accounting and Control), was introduced in 1955. Work on the RAMAC system began in 1952 in a small IBM facility in San Jose, California, the same year Alan Shugart joined IBM as an engineer.

The careers of certain innovators seem to push technology along into new areas. You will recognize some of the important names in the field of computing—certainly such names as Steve Wozniak and Steve Jobs are familiar as early innovators in the personal computing arena. Alan Shugart, in a much more quiet way, has been equally innovative in the field of disk storage.

IBM's San Jose facility became the center of magnetic storage development for IBM's computers. Many large disk storage systems were developed and manufactured in this plant. Searching for a more inexpensive, convenient form of disk storage, IBM also developed the first floppy disk storage system. Apparently Shugart learned the value of disk storage devices from his experience at IBM.

CHAPTER 5

DATA: STORAGE, ACCESS, AND FILE MANAGEMENT

IN THIS CHAPTER YOU WILL LEARN ABOUT

- **Data stored by the computer**
- **Data storage and retrieval hardware**
- **Methods used to access stored data**
- **Types of data files**

In the early 1970s, Shugart left IBM and founded Shugart Associates. Notably, Shugart Associates pioneered floppy disk storage by introducing the 8-in. floppy as a more efficient storage unit than the magnetic tape cassette recorders being used for personal computers at the time. This was just the product the market needed, and the firm became a leading supplier of diskettes. It was, in fact, so highly regarded that Xerox Corporation acquired Shugart's firm.

Subsequently, Shugart founded Seagate Technology, which became the first firm to supply $3\frac{1}{2}$-in. hard disks for personal computers. Alan Shugart, as the CEO of this pacesetter in the disk storage industry, still leads the way.

(Courtesy International Business Machines, Inc.)

DATA STORAGE HIERARCHY

The fourth stage of the information processing cycle is storage. Data are not always used immediately upon input; they may be stored for later use or to be combined with additional data. Output is not always sent to a display or printer; a program may read data, modify them in some way, and then store them for use with another program. And although it is implied that information is immediately output for use, in fact it may be output in a form that is stored for later access. For example, a graph generated by a spreadsheet program may be stored for access by a presentation graphics program for use at a later meeting.

To understand how the storage operation works, you need to learn about the data storage hierarchy—the way in which the computer organizes data for storage and retrieval. Also, you must understand the relationship of data storage to the specific hardware devices used. Let us start with the way in which data are organized for storage.

Fields: Single Facts

Just as a single bit is too limited to represent all of the characters used for data, a byte is too limited to store all of the data needed. Although a character, or byte, is the smallest element of data you may deal with, most likely you will be handling several characters of data at one time—in the form of words, names, numeric amounts, and so on. Each individual fact, or unique element of data, is stored as a collection of characters of a length as long as is needed to contain the data. These groupings of characters representing a single fact are called **fields** (Figure 5.1).

Fields are classified by the type of data, or characters, they contain. Data can be represented as numeric, alphabetic, and special data types. **Numeric data** consist only of the numeric digits (0–9) and characters used to modify a numeric value, such as signs (+ or −) and a decimal point. **Alphabetic data** contain only alphabetic characters (A–Z and a–z) and the space character.

Data can also be a combination of alphabetic and numeric characters, called **alphanumeric data** (Figure 5.2). This data type is very common; all you have to do is to look at fields that contain some familiar things such as a date expressed as 2/14/95, or a name such as A-1 Radiator Service. Notice, too, that alphanumeric data often contain additional special characters: the hy-

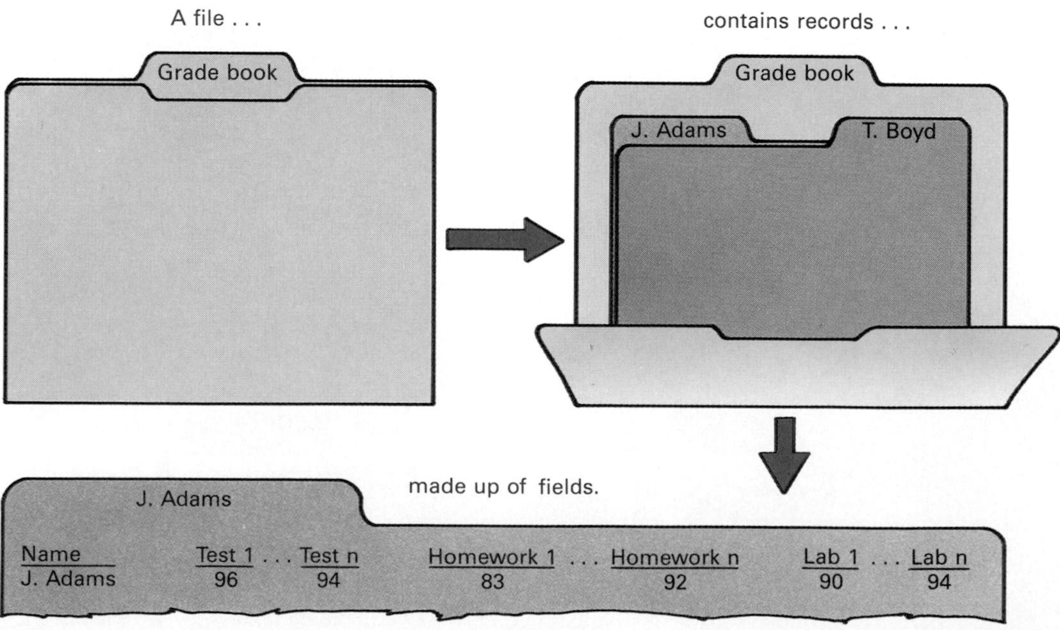

Figure 5.1
Organization of data by field, record, and file.

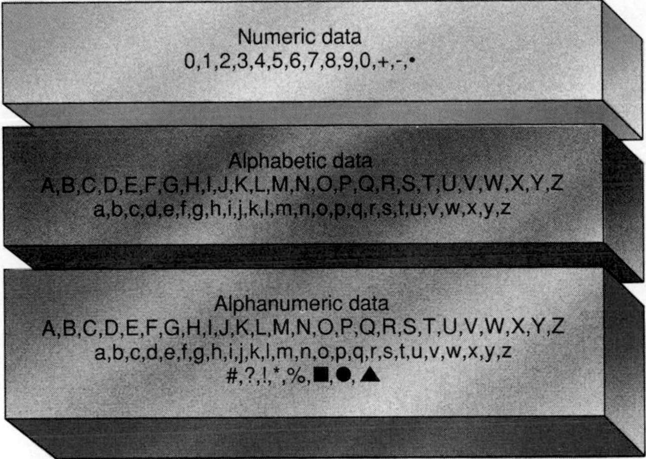

Figure 5.2
Data types.

phen (-) or slash (/) or other commonly used characters such as the top row of characters on your keyboard (! @ # $ % ^ & * ( ) _ – + =). Some programs simplify terminology by referring to fields as either numeric, meaning that the number can be used in a computation, or character, meaning any character or symbol that needs to be stored or displayed.

Records: Collections of Related Facts

A collection of fields, each containing a unique fact but each field related to the other in some way, forms a **record.** Records contain facts that are used together to form a more complete set of facts or a description of something. For example, a personnel department's record usually has fields that can contain several unique facts about an employee (Figure 5.3).

There is another way to view this. Each fact, or field, describes one or another specific attribute about you; but taken together, all of these facts uniquely describe you as a particular person, or entity. The term **attribute** is used to define a specific characteristic about something. We all share many attributes, such as those listed in the personnel record example. So when designing a program to process data, a programmer will define a field to contain data specific to some attribute, such as a field to contain a name or rate of pay. The field then is simply a place to store a specific data value that we can recognize as a name, "John Jones" or "Mary Smith," or pay rate, "12.75" or "14.80." Taken together, all of these unique data values stored in fields within a single record will uniquely identify an **entity,** a special individual who possesses each of these attributes' specific characteristics (Figure 5.4).

Note in Figure 5.4 on page 91 that even though some fields may store the same value for a particular attribute, the collection of data for each individual is unique and pertains only to that single person. Also, some of the fields contain data that would immediately identify the individual, such as the Social Security number; in contrast, it might take several of the other fields together to uniquely identify a single person.

Files: Collections of Related Records

All of the personnel department's records, each containing fields of data for each of the employees in the company, are stored together as a file. Therefore, a **file** is a collection of records related by their content and use.

Figure 5.3
A personnel record.

```
FIELDS

your name:
street address:
city:
state:
zip code:
telephone number:
date of birth:
gender:
social security number:
rate of pay:
job classification:
department:
date of hire:
height:
weight:
color of eyes:
```

At the next level of sophistication, a computer may use a database rather than a single file of records to store and maintain data. A **database** is a specially constructed system of files which is integrated through relationships of data contained within each file. Using the same illustration, a personnel department's database may contain several files of data, one with a record of your personal statistics and another with data related to your specific job within the company. If each record contained an identifier such as an employee number, the database system would be able to associate the two data records by logically relating them via an employee number recorded in the two records.

Files—A Bit More than Data

Perhaps you are somewhat confused by what appears to be an inconsistent use of the word *file*. As just explained, a file is a collection of related records, each containing fields of data. This definition is the most common one, and it is precise when you are discussing a program's need to access data for processing.

But you may have also heard the term *file* used to describe a program itself, as in "the file containing the word processing program." Also, you may have saved a file while using a word processing program, and you may not recognize specific fields or facts in the form of records as being saved in your file.

To clarify this seeming lack of discipline in using the term, you might think of the word *file* as meaning any collection of machine codes stored and

FIELDS	Record 1	Record 2
your name:	John Jones	Mary Smith
street address:	123 Main Street	456 Valley Drive
city:	Centerville	Centerville
state:	California	California
zip code:	95123	95123
telephone number:	555-1256	555-9852
date of birth:	10/24/46	02/19/71
gender:	Male	Female
social security number:	555-12-3456	987-65-4321
rate of pay:	12.75	14.80
job classification:	Assembler	Accounting staff
department:	Production	Accounting
date of hire:	03/17/91	03/17/91
height:	5'11"	5'6"
weight:	175	115
color of eyes:	Brown	Hazel

Figure 5.4
Completed personnel records.

accessed together. In this way, a traditional data file, which does contain individual records, is stored under one file name and is accessed by the computer as a file, although your program may use the file by processing each record one at a time. A word processing document, which you may not recognize as having individual records, is accessed by the word processing program as a single file; the document you saved is data as far as the word processing program is concerned. A program, too, is accessed as a single file when you issue a command to the operating system to use it.

DATA MANAGEMENT

The value of information exists in its being timely, accurate, and useful. If the data on which the information is based is of poor quality in any way, then the value of the information produced by these data is lessened. That is what is at the heart of the phrase "garbage-in, garbage-out (GIGO)." Data management ensures that the data used are of a high quality and that they are adequately maintained and secured. Proper data management changes GIGO to mean, "good-in, good-out."

One term used to describe good data is **data integrity,** which simply means that the data are unimpaired. And one way of achieving data integrity is to promote and follow sound rules for acquiring and handling data. These rules can be very simple, covering such basics as making sure the data are available for input when needed, but the rules must be accurate and must be entered reliably for processing.

Perhaps this seems too simple, but it is easy to make mistakes. For example, you are asked to calculate a home mortgage. You need to find the current mortgage interest rate, but you cannot find your latest interest rate sheet. To get the task done, you borrow your neighbor's file copy without realizing that it is last week's version with a higher percentage. Then, you type in 9.75% for the interest rate, not .0975 as the program expected. If you do not discover the mistakes, you will get very poor information.

Even if your data are entered carefully, mistakes can occur. One way to find mistakes is by verification—corroborating the data entered by checking them against a known source such as the original paper document. Error checking can also be accomplished by the computer. The computer can be programmed to accept only a certain range of data, or to check if the data are in the correct format. Checking for erroneous data items is called **data validation.**

Eliminating Data Errors

Whenever you handle data, you have a risk of error. In entering data, for example, you might mean to key in 18.25, but type instead 18.52. This is a **transposition error,** an error caused when the digits are entered in the wrong order. Such errors are common, especially when data are manually entered into a system. Manual processes for entering data always have the potential for error.

Transcription errors, or simply the errors resulting from inaccurate copying of data from one format to another, can always occur, but they can be reduced. Equipment for source data entry reduces the potential for data transcription errors; machines read data in one form and convert them into computer input. By automating the process, the potential for data entry errors is reduced significantly. Recall, for example, the bar-code scanners discussed in Chapter 3.

STORAGE

As you learned earlier, RAM—the main memory located in the central processing unit—is volatile; it loses its contents as soon as you turn off your computer. Also, when you stop using one program and load the next one, the data and program instructions in memory are changed. Thus, some means of permanent storage is an important consideration, because the computer's memory cannot hold all of the program and data files you might have.

The computer's main processing memory is limited in size. For instance, let us agree that you have a computer with 1MB (1 megabyte or 1 million characters) of main memory. Some application software packages require well above that amount of storage for all of the related program files. In fact, your computer may use diskettes with a capacity of more than 1MB. So, while the computer's memory is adequate for using a particular program, it is not adequate for long-term storage.

By now you realize that the terms *memory* and *storage* are confusingly similar. Try to think of memory as relating to the computer's "brain" with access to data while it is working. Think of storage as the computer's "file cabinet," a repository for keeping things until they are needed to do the work. If someone wants to know how much memory your computer has, as your answer give the amount of main memory, such as 640K or 1MB. The amount of storage you have depends on which specific storage device is being discussed; a hard disk, which we will discuss later in this chapter, may store from 30MB to well over 100MB of files.

Storage, then, refers to the nonvolatile storage external to the computer. This form of storage is called **secondary storage,** or **auxiliary storage.** A secondary-storage medium is usually used for the storage of large amounts of data or for permanent or long-term storage of data or programs. Secondary storage is also used for storing backups, or copies, of data and programs so that they are not permanently lost if power to the computer is interrupted.

Secondary-storage media common to all sizes of computers include magnetic tapes and magnetic disks. Although these media can hold much more data than the computer's primary memory, access to the data is not as fast as it would be if the data were available in the computer's main memory.

Magnetic Tape

Typically, **magnetic tape** is a one-half-inch or one-fourth-inch ribbon of Mylar (a plastic-like material) coated with a thin layer of iron-oxide material (Figure 5.5). In the tape drive (an input/output, or I/O, device), the tape passes by a read/write head, the electromagnetic component in the drive. When the tiny, haphazardly arranged particles of iron oxide are aligned through magnetization, data are stored, or written, as magnetized spots in a pattern that represents 1s and 0s. To read the tape, the drive passes the tape by the read head and the patterns of 1s and 0s are interpreted as pieces of data.

Magnetic tape stores records, or groups of related data, sequentially, that is, one after another. To get to the data required, every record preceding that data must be read. Tapes can store large quantities of data inexpensively and so are often used as backup storage media. Magnetic tapes are erasable, reusable, and durable.

Magnetic tapes can be used with all sizes of computers. They are made in reel-to-reel, cassette, and cartridge forms. Each form stores data magnetically, but each holds different amounts of data and accesses them at different rates. So-called streaming tapes have become an efficient form of storage for use in conveniently backing up the data found on many microcomputers with larger hard disks.

Magnetic Disk

A **magnetic disk** is a Mylar or metallic platter on which electronic data can be stored (Figure 5.6). Data files on the disk can be read sequentially or directly. A magnetic disk's main advantages over magnetic tape include the following:

Figure 5.5
(a) Magnetic reel-to-reel tape with raw iron oxide. (b) Magnetic reel-to-reel tape mounted on tape drives.

((a) Courtesy of BASF Corporation Information Systems; (b) Courtesy of U.S. Department of the Navy)

Figure 5.6
High-speed disk storage units, called disk packs, are constructed of several platters mounted on a common spindle.

(Courtesy of BASF Corporation Information Systems)

1. The ability to access the data stored on it directly
2. The ability to hold more data in a smaller space
3. The ability to attain faster data transfer speeds

Magnetic disks are manufactured in both floppy diskette and hard disk styles.

Floppy Diskette

A **floppy diskette,** also called simply a **diskette** or **disk,** is a small, flexible, Mylar disk coated with iron oxide (similar to magnetic tape) on which data are stored. It is typically available in two sizes for personal computers: $3\frac{1}{2}$ inch and $5\frac{1}{4}$ inch.

The $5\frac{1}{4}$-inch diskettes are covered by a stiff, protective jacket with various holes and cutouts that serve special functions (Figure 5.8). The hub ring is where the disk drive (the I/O device) holds the disk to rotate it. The elongated read/write window allows the read/write head of the drive to write data on, or read data from, the floppy diskette. The small hole next to the hub ring is the index hole through which the computer determines the relative position of the disk for locating data. The cutout on the side of the floppy diskette is the

Figure 5.7
Floppy diskettes are available in $5\frac{1}{4}$-inch and $3\frac{1}{2}$-inch sizes.

(Courtesy Innervisions)

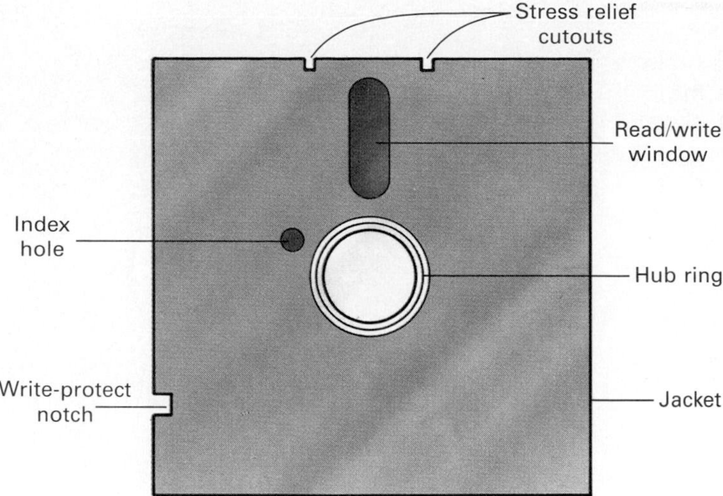

Figure 5.8
A $5\frac{1}{4}$-inch diskette.

write-protect notch. By covering this opening with a piece of tape, data on the disk are protected from being erased or written over.

The $3\frac{1}{2}$-inch diskettes have a hard plastic covering and a protective metal piece that covers the read/write window when the disk is not in use (Figure 5.9). This additional protection makes the disk less prone to damage from handling, dust, or other contaminants. The $3\frac{1}{2}$-inch disk has become favored over the $5\frac{1}{4}$-inch disk in the personal computer market, but both formats are in widespread use.

The amount of data held by a floppy diskette is determined by the disk's recording density. The term **density** refers to how much data are able to be recorded in a given space. Both the $5\frac{1}{4}$-inch and the $3\frac{1}{2}$-inch diskettes are typically sold in two densities: **double density** and **high density.** By compressing the data recorded on the surface of the diskette, a high-density diskette can store much more data than the double-density design.

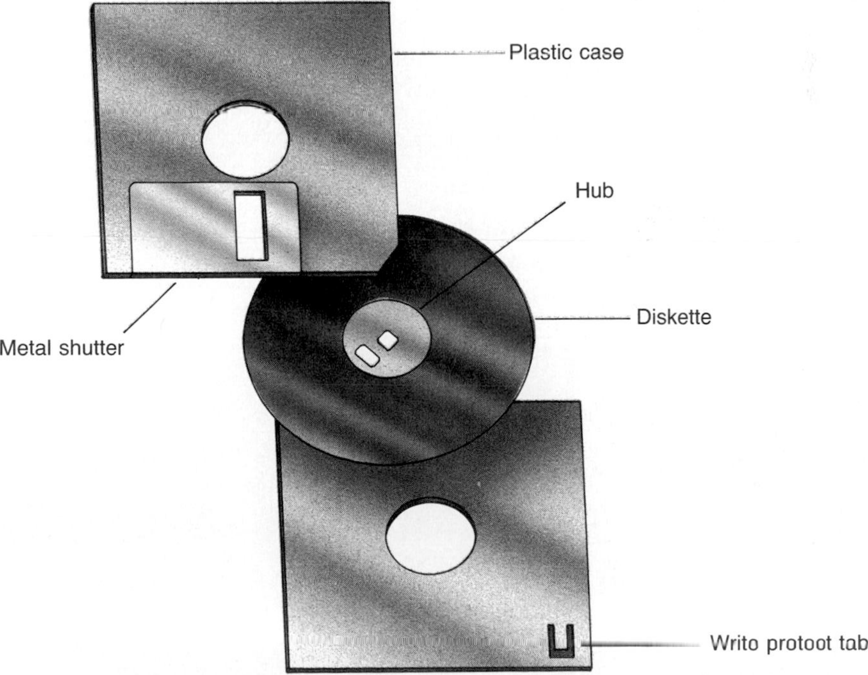

Figure 5.9
A $3\frac{1}{2}$-inch diskette.

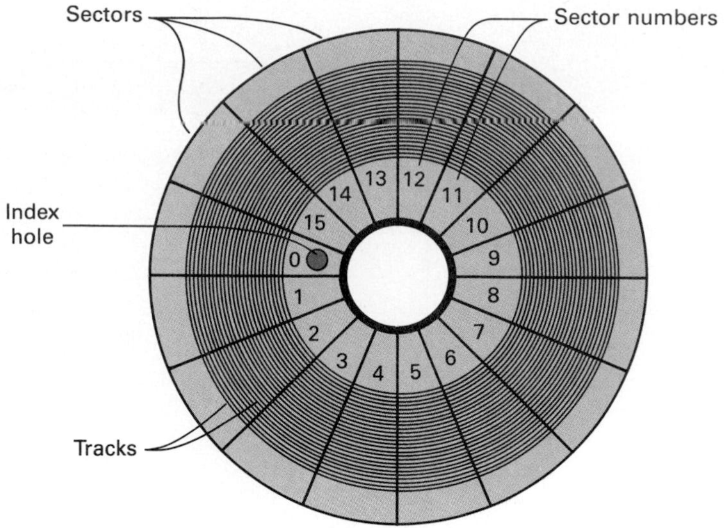

Figure 5.10
Formatting a diskette electronically divides the storage space into tracks and sectors.

Which diskette may be used on your personal computer is determined by two factors. First, the system will have a disk drive of a particular size. A 5¼-inch diskette fits only in a 5¼-inch disk drive, and a 3½-inch diskette requires a 3½-inch drive. Second, the recording capability of the diskette drive determines which density diskette is usable. A high-density drive, generally, can read or record data on either the double- or high-density-type diskette, but a double-density drive cannot read or record data using a high-density diskette unless that diskette is first formatted for the lower-capacity disk drive.

Formatting, or **initializing** a disk, prepares the disk to store data in a way that the operating system can recognize (Figure 5.10). That may not sound right, but it is correct to say that the format of data stored on a diskette is determined largely by the operating system. A 3½-inch double-density diskette may be used on either an IBM PS/2 or an Apple Macintosh computer, but once the diskette is prepared for data storage by either machine, the other system may not be able to read the data. That is, a diskette prepared to store data by a Macintosh may not be used on a PS/2—the IBM system would not be able to recognize the data format used by the Macintosh. One slight modification, however, makes this statement more accurate. Data conversion programs may be used to help one type of computer recognize data prepared by another type.

Hard Disk

To compensate for the limited space on the floppy diskette, the hard disk is widely used. A **hard disk** is hard and inflexible and is made from materials

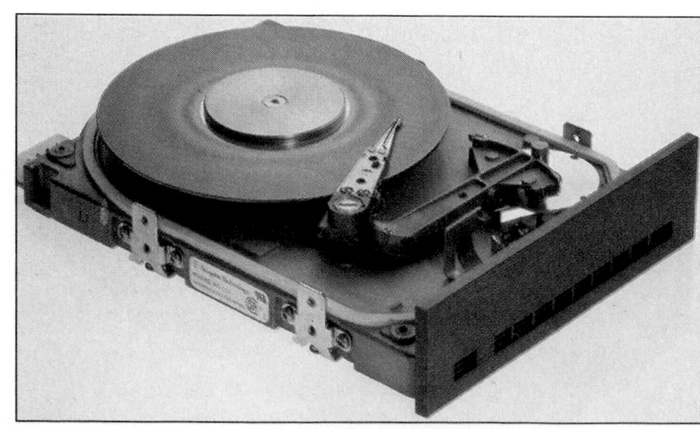

Figure 5.11
This hard disk's case has been removed to show the platters and the read/write head.

(Courtesy of Seagate)

such as aluminum instead of Mylar. The I/O device that transfers data to and from a hard disk is called a hard-disk drive.

The read/write head (Figure 5.11) of a hard-disk drive floats above the surface of the disk at a height of about 50 millionths of an inch (0.00005 inch). In comparison, a human hair is a hundred times larger in diameter. Because of the high rotation speed of the hard disk—approximately 3,600 revolutions per minute (rpm)—if the read/write head runs into any particles of dirt, dust, or even smoke, a head crash results (Figure 5.12). When this occurs, a foreign particle is pushed into the disk, and the head actually bounces and comes into physical contact with the disk. Severe damage can result to the head or the disk, destroying the data stored there.

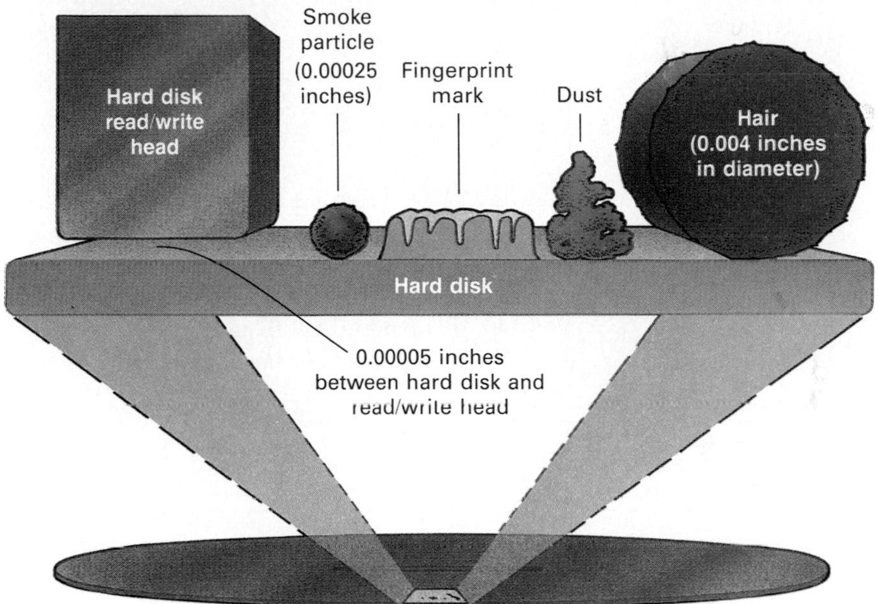

Figure 5.12
The hard disk's read/write head floats on a thin cushion of air. Just how thin is illustrated by comparing the size of disk contaminants to the clearance of the read/write head.

The hard disk has several advantages over a floppy diskette. The rigid construction of a hard disk allows it to be rotated at 3,600 rpm compared with a floppy diskette at 360 rpm. Thus, data can be transferred much faster to or from a hard disk because it takes less time to find the storage location. Also, because of its hard construction, more data can be placed in a smaller area, which gives the hard disk more storage capacity than a floppy diskette of the same size.

Hard-disk drives are available for all sizes of computers. They may be (1) fixed-disk systems that are permanently installed in a drive; (2) removable cartridges; or (3) disk packs, most commonly used with larger computers, that also can be removed from the drive.

Optical Technology

Optical technology involves the use of lasers—highly concentrated beams of light. This technology has created new types of secondary-storage media for the computer, including optical laser disks, optical cards, and optical tape. Most optical media are of the read-only type; however, some of the more recent technology has produced optical disks that can be written on and erased.

Optical laser disks (Figure 5.13) are hard metal disks ranging in size from 4.72 to 14 inches in diameter. They were originally developed as compact disks for video and audio applications. Laser beams encode binary data by burning microscopic "pits," to represent 1s and 0s, onto optical laser disks. The so-called

Figure 5.13
The *Academic American Encyclopedia,* a 9-million-word (20 volumc) encyclopedia, is stored on a compact disk less than 5 inches in diameter, with room to spare. Grolier Electronic Publishers sells it to consumers for about $200. A typical 14-inch disk can store as much as twenty reel-to-reel tapes.

(Courtesy of Grolier Electronic Publishing, Inc.)

CD-ROM (compact-disk, read-only memory) is actually a specially equipped version of the popular CD player you may already use for your favorite music.

The optical card, or laser card, is the size of a credit card and has an optical laser-encoded strip that can store approximately 2 megabytes of data. These cards have many potential uses, most notably credit records or medical histories.

ACCESS TO STORED DATA

You now know that data are stored in files on some sort of storage medium, a disk or tape. These files may take various forms, however, depending on both the type of medium on which the file has been stored, and upon the way in which a program needs to access individual data items. Three common methods to store and retrieve data are sequential access, direct access, and indexed-sequential access.

Sequential Access

The records in a **sequential-access file** are stored and accessed in a row (sequentially), one after another. To access a particular record, all preceding records must be read first (Figure 5.14). Records are processed in the order in which they are stored in the sequential file. When records are recorded in a sequential file in the order in which they have been input to the computer, they are said to be in **entry sequence.**

If you want to process the file in some specific order, say by order of employees' last name or Social Security number, you would have to organize the file in that sequence. You can achieve this by first organizing your input and then entering the data in the desired sequence, or more efficiently, by using a program to sort the data after they have been entered. When this second alternative is used, you select a specific field of the data, sometimes referred to as a **key field,** to use in establishing the order of the data. The resulting organization of data is then written to a new sequential file in either ascending or descending data sequence. **Ascending sequence** would be from lowest to highest value (1 to 10, for example) and **descending sequence** is just the reverse (from Z to A). This process does not change the data stored in the file; it only organizes the retrieval of the data into some predictable, orderly sequence.

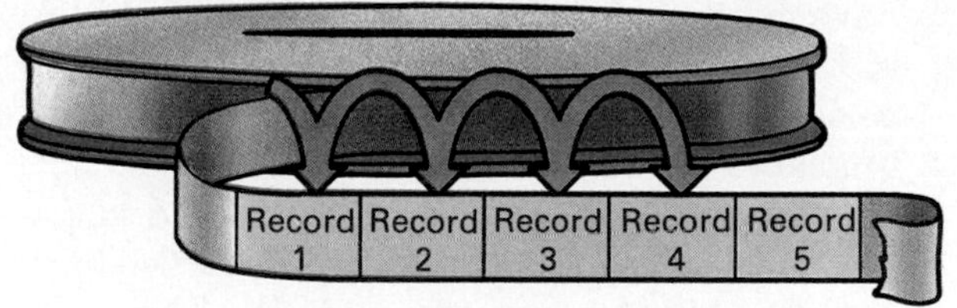

Figure 5.14
In a sequential-access file, records are stored and accessed one after the other (sequentially). To access any one record, record 4 for example, all preceding records (1, 2, and 3) must be accessed first.

Sequential files are used most often when all or most of the data in the file is to be processed. A payroll file, for example, would be an appropriate sequential file because everyone in the file would want his or her record processed. Sequential files are not efficient, however, for files where data are needed on some unpredictable basis, or when the majority of the file is not processed. An example of this might be a file of airline flights; you need only the record for the flight in which you have an interest, and the airline certainly has no idea when you might call.

Maintaining Data in a Sequential File

Maintaining accurate data is important, so some consideration must be given to how data are kept up-to-date in any file. Sequential files can be updated by adding, changing, or deleting records. The process of updating a sequential file requires reading the original file, modifying existing records, and adding new ones or deleting old ones. There is no way to insert new records *in sequence* between existing records or to squeeze together records on each side of a deleted one. Sometimes the old file is kept as a backup in case the updated file is damaged. Although the old file would have to be updated if it were necessary to replace the new file, the amount of work required would be less than if the entire file had to be re-created.

Magnetic tape is a storage medium that is sequential in nature. When you want to read a certain file on a tape, you must process all of the tape preceding the file, then all of the tape for the particular file from beginning to end. Sequential files may also be created on a disk storage system, and in fact, sequential files are perhaps the most common type of file on any storage medium.

Direct Access

A faster type of access that can be used only with disks is direct access. **Direct access** allows a record to be read directly from a disk without reading all preceding records (Figure 5.15). The order in which the records were stored does not matter.

Direct access is the fastest of the three access methods, but it is also the one that is difficult to manage from the programmer's perspective. One reason for the difficulty is that the programmer has to choose a process that can determine the exact record location for each record in the file. Sometimes this is done by picking a key field which uniquely identifies the record. A Social Security number, for example, is better than a name, which might be duplicated—such as John Smith. The program uses the data from the key field to determine a record's address, or specific location within the file; then it accesses the record without processing any other records from the file. This method is also called **random access**, because accessing the record does not depend on any specific order of processing.

Figure 5.15
Records can be accessed directly and individually with the direct-access method. In this example, record 4 can be accessed directly without reading any other record.

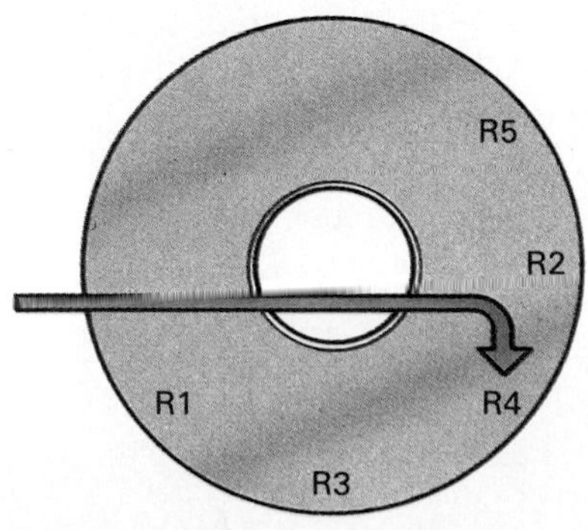

Maintaining Data in a Direct-Access File

With direct access, we can access individual records, or storage locations. Therefore, a direct-access file may be maintained in place; that is, it does not have to be re-created to add, change, or modify records as long as storage space in the file is available. It is wise, however, to make backup copies of the file periodically to guard against accidental loss of data should the file become unusable for any reason.

The reason why this access method is used only with disk has to do with the mechanical aspects of a disk. Disk storage units are also called **direct-access storage devices** (DASD). The system can position the read/write mechanism directly wherever required on the surface of the disk, something impossible to do with tape without first dragging all of the preceding tape along. Think of your music system; if you have a CD or record player, you know that you can play anything directly from any spot on the "disk" as long as you know the location.

Indexed Files

The third technique, indexed access, allows both sequential and direct access to records stored on a disk. This access method also works only on disk and not on tape.

An **index** is simply a list of record addresses. Your program accepts as input the value of the key field from the record you need to locate and, using the index, determines the specific address of the desired record. The record itself is then accessed individually.

An indexed file can be set up in many ways. A common way is to create an **indexed-sequential file** (Figure 5.16). This method of file organization attempts to store records in ascending sequence in order of the key field used to uniquely identify each record. It also creates an index to assist in locating

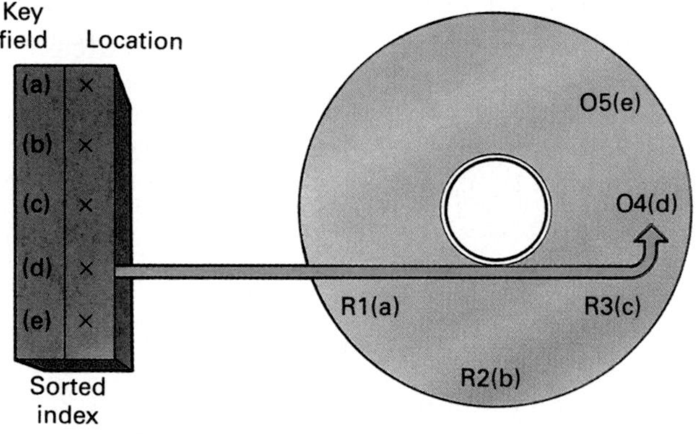

R = Record
O = Record stored in overflow area

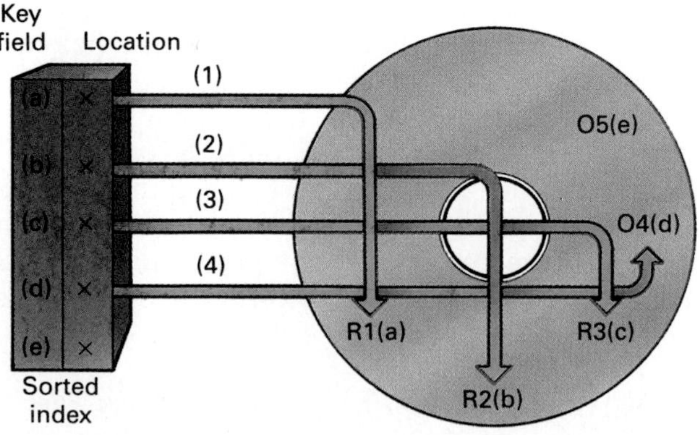

Figure 5.16
The indexed-sequential file maintains an index showing the location of records contained in the file. This file-access method provides for both sequential and direct processing of records.

specific records. An index-sequential file may then be accessed in sequence, in which case the data are processed record by record in a manner similar to a sequential file. Alternatively, a program could access individual records randomly, in a manner somewhat like the direct-file method, using the index to locate the desired record. Also, like direct files, indexed files are able to be maintained in place without creating a new file.

USING A DATABASE TO MANAGE DATA

You may have heard someone remark about his or her computer's database, referring to all of the many files of data stored on the computer's storage equipment. A database may indeed be a number of files, but it is much more than simply a collection of files.

A database is an integrated collection of data items that are stored and retrieved under the control of a database management system. A **database management system** (DBMS) is a program, or system of programs, that creates an organization of data, often in multiple files. The DBMS allows you to create, store, retrieve, and manipulate data without regard to which file it is in, which access method is used, or indeed whether the data you seek are contained in one or more records or files.

A database is built on data **relationships,** which are logical associations of data that enable the DBMS to find each part of data and relate it to another. For example, your personnel record contains data about you such as your name and rate of pay. A payroll record contains the hours you work. Because your employee number appears on both the personnel and payroll records, the DBMS is able to associate these records and process them as if they were in the same record, in the same file.

Recall the terms *attribute* and *entity* from the earlier discussion about fields of data. These terms are used extensively in the development of database systems. The associations of data formed by a database are based on the identification or selection of specific attributes; the group of associated data is an entity.

A DBMS may improve the quality of data. By storing any single fact in only one place, data redundancy is reduced. This means that you will make fewer mistakes when updating, because there is only one place to update data as opposed to several. Data are also independent from programs, which makes the data available as a general resource rather than as a file specific to one program.

DBMS software can be expensive, and the effort to create a database may be significant. On the benefits side, however, data contained within a database can be used more flexibly and thus potentially has greater value. The following section discusses some of the basic concepts of designing databases.

Database Design Concepts

Designing a database in a business environment can be a complex project involving many people. In some organizations, a **database administrator** is in charge of designing, implementing, and maintaining the database and all related activities. The database administrator, along with the users and other specialists, analyzes the requirements of the proposed database. Of course, the main factor to be considered is the user's needs.

After determining the database requirements, a schema and subschemas are developed. The **schema** is the logical, or conceptual, design showing the relationships among data elements in a database. To help maintain database security, various subsets of the schema, or **subschemas,** can be designed to limit access of individual users. Users are then limited to accessing only the data in the subschemas that they are authorized to use. The schema and subschemas compose the database's **logical design,** which is the user's view of how the data appear to be arranged on the secondary storage media.

To complete the design of the database, the **physical design**—how the data are actually stored on secondary storage media and how data are accessed—has to be determined. Users of prepackaged DBMS products need not be concerned with these issues because the physical design is already established and implemented by the program. With a prepackaged DBMS, the user must only make sure that the software's physical design fits the user's needs.

Database Structures

The relationships shown in a schema are often complex. Three basic structures are used to organize the data elements: hierarchical, network, and relational. In practice, the structure used is determined by the application and is sometimes a combination of features from all three database structures.

The **hierarchical database structure** resembles an organizational chart of a corporation. Data can be structured in the same hierarchical way. One might view the structure as an upside-down family tree. At the top, or main, level of data is the **parent,** or root, level. Data under the root level are at the **child,** or subordinate, level. Each parent can have numerous children, but each child can have only one parent (Figure 5.17). Each child level may also be broken down into further levels with the child becoming the parent for the next level.

Because relationships between data items follow defined paths, access to the data is very fast. However, any relationships between data items must be defined when the database is being created. If a manager, for example, wants to retrieve or manipulate data in a manner not defined when the database was originally created, the database will have to be redesigned at great cost.

The **network database structure** is similar to the hierarchical structure; it is more complex in nature but more flexible in accessing data items. Similar to a hierarchical structure, each parent can have more than one child, but in a

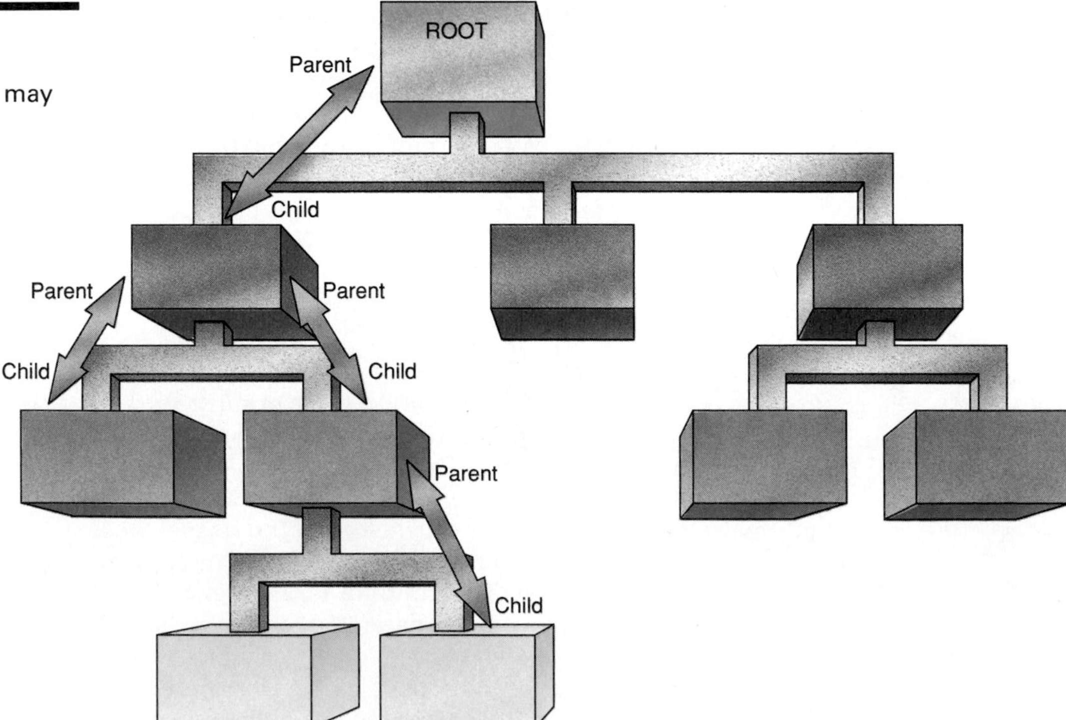

Figure 5.17
In a hierarchical data relationship, each child may have only one parent relationship.

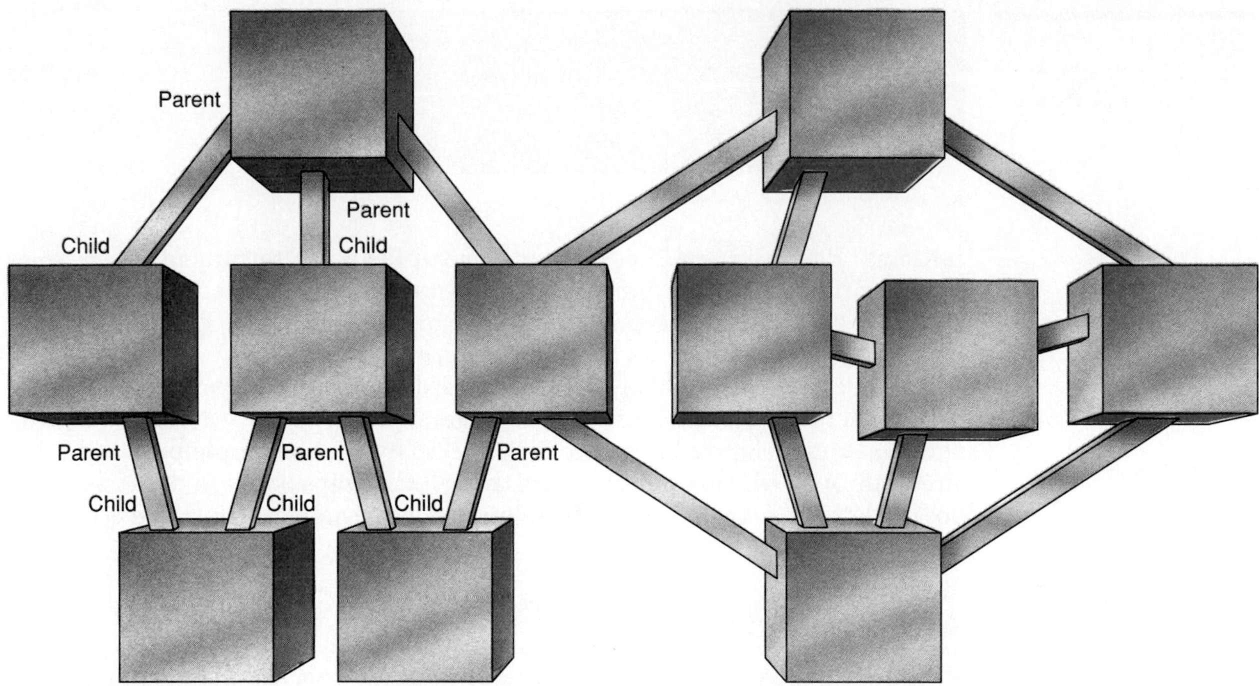

Figure 5.18
A network database structure permits each parent or child to have multiple parent-child relationships.

network structure each child can have more than one parent (Figure 5.18). Therefore, more than one path can lead to the desired data level. The network database structure is a more versatile and flexible data-access structure than the hierarchical type because the route to data is not necessarily downward; it can be from any direction.

In the network structure, again similar to the hierarchical structure, data access is fast because relationships follow predefined paths, and any data relationship must be defined during the database design.

The **relational database structure** does not rely on a parent-child relationship. Instead, the relational structure groups all the data into tables from which the actual data relationships can be built. A **table** consists of rows and

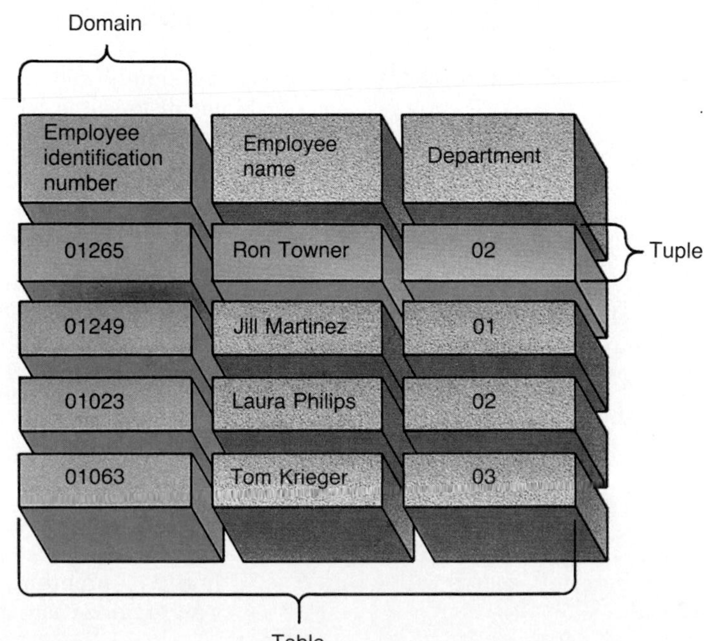

Figure 5.19
A relational database is viewed as a table of data.

Figure 5.20
This example of a database query uses Structured Query Language (SQL).

```
SELECT    EMPNAM, EMPNUM, DEPTNUM, SAL
FROM      EMPF
WHERE     SALARY > 25000
ORDER     BY DEPTNUM
```

columns. Each row specifies a record, or **tuple** in the terminology of a relational database. Each column, called a **domain,** represents individual data items. The entire table represents one or more files. Tables can be linked to pull various data elements together (Figure 5.19).

The relationships between data items do not have to be defined during development of the database. As managers require new ways of analyzing data, they can simply instruct the DBMS to extract and manipulate the desired information. However, because the relationships between data items are not predefined, access time can be relatively slow compared with the other two structures.

Database Query Language

Database query languages help users formulate queries that act as an interface between the users and the DBMS. Such languages help users of relational databases to easily manipulate, analyze, and create reports from data contained in a database. They are composed of simple, easy-to-use commands and statements that allow people other than programmers to use the database. One standard form of query language is **Structured Query Language** (SQL), which has been adapted for many DBMS products (Figure 5.20).

Summary

- Each individual fact, or unique element of data, is stored as a collection of characters of a length as long as is needed to contain the data. These groupings of characters representing a single fact are called fields.
- Fields are classified by the type of data, or characters, they contain.
- A collection of fields, each containing a unique fact but each field related to the other in some way, forms a record.
- A file is a collection of records related by their content and use.
- Data management ensures that the data used are of a high quality and that they are adequately maintained and secured.
- Data integrity means that the data are unimpaired.
- Storage refers to the nonvolatile storage external to the computer. This form of storage is called secondary storage, or auxiliary storage.
- Magnetic tape is a one-half-inch or one-fourth inch ribbon of Mylar (a plastic-like material), coated with a thin layer of iron-oxide material.
- Magnetic tape stores records, or groups of related data, sequentially.
- A magnetic disk is a Mylar or metallic platter on which electronic data can be stored. A floppy diskette, also called simply a diskette or disk, is a small, flexible, Mylar disk coated with iron oxide. A hard disk is hard and inflexible and is made from materials such as aluminum.
- Three common methods to store and retrieve data are sequential access, direct access, and indexed-sequential access.
- The records in a sequential-access file are stored and accessed in a row (sequentially), one after another. Direct access allows a record to be read directly from a disk without reading all preceding records. The third technique, indexed access, allows both sequential and direct access to records stored on a disk.
- A database is an integrated collection of data items that are stored and retrieved under the control of a database management system. A database management system (DBMS) is a program, or system of programs, that creates an organization of data, often in multiple files.

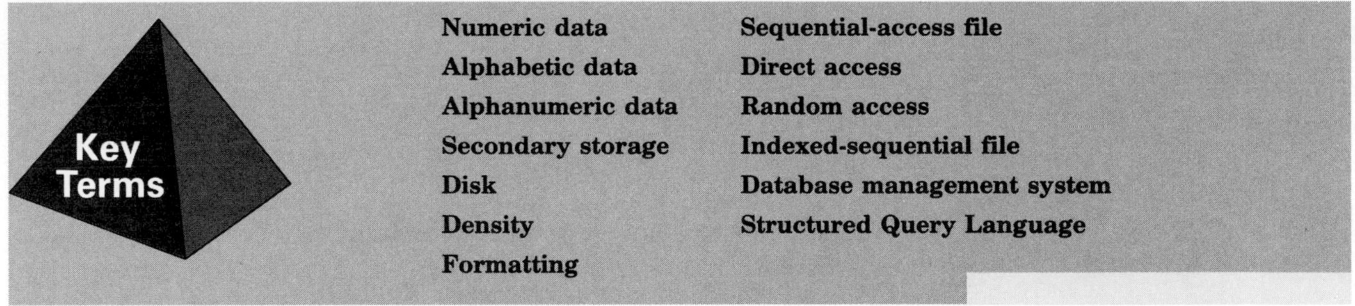

Key
Terms
Numeric data
Alphabetic data
Alphanumeric data
Secondary storage
Disk
Density
Formatting
Sequential-access file
Direct access
Random access
Indexed-sequential file
Database management system
Structured Query Language

Review Questions

1. Explain the term *storage* as part of the information processing cycle.
2. What is the data storage hierarchy?
3. Give the term for a group of characters representing a single fact.
4. Describe how data are classified by the type of characters used.
5. What do we call a collection of individual facts related to each other in some way?
6. Describe the use of the terms *entity* and *attribute.*
7. What is a file of data?
8. Discuss the seemingly conflicting ways in which the term *file* is used.
9. What gives value to information?
10. What is meant by the term *data integrity*?
11. Explain transcription errors and transposition errors.
12. Discuss the difference between the terms *memory* and *storage.*
13. Describe magnetic tape and how it works.
14. Describe the various types of disks and how they work.
15. Discuss the three alternative methods used to store data in and retrieve data from files.
16. What is a DBMS?
17. How does a database differ from a file?
18. What is a relationship in a database?
19. Define the term *schema.*
20. What three database design structures might be used and how do they differ?

PROFILE

CLIFF STOLL

(AP/Wide World Photos)

Astronomers are trained to find minute but significant changes in our endless universe. Perhaps that is why Cliff Stoll, who was trained as an astronomer, was able to find a 75-cent accounting error among the thousands of lines of output produced at the Lawrence Berkeley Lab. That minute monetary error led Stoll to discover the electronic break-in of "Hunter," a mystery user hiding within the labyrinth of international electronic connections used to transmit data and information around the world.

Lawrence Berkeley Labs interconnects its computers to several other computer networks, just as do many other universities, colleges, research institutions, and government agencies. These networks, through interconnections, allow a computer to span the world, literally, to share information, ideas, and sometimes simply personal friendships. They are also, collectively, vast storehouses of sometimes very sensitive data, including military secrets.

When one of the programs that tracks computer usage was unable to assign a specific user account to 75-cents worth of computer time, Stoll uncovered a hacker, someone who writes computer programs or uses other means to break into computer resources. Before long, Stoll knew that Hunter had assigned himself superuser status. The computer term *superuser* means the user can do anything inside the system—look at or copy any file, install or delete any program, and view any computer activity.

By tapping into the Lawrence Berkeley Labs' computers, Hunter was electronically looking over everyone's shoulder to read personal electronic mail messages, track changes to the computer system, and investigate personnel files and user accounts for the information they might contain. The mystery user also searched the computer for connections it might have to other computers on other networks, and it found some very powerful ones. One was the link to the Lawrence Livermore Labs where defense systems such as the Star Wars strategic missile system are created. Other links tie Lawrence Berkeley Labs to Arpanet and Milnet, two important research and military networks with links into secure facilities inside Air Force and Army bases.

Initially, no one took Stoll seriously; after all, most hackers are just bright kids having fun, aren't they? We all know that something like the plot in the movie *War Games* could never really happen, don't we?

After several exhausting months of individual effort, Stoll finally convinced others, including U.S. government counterintelligence agents, that Hunter posed a real and potentially dangerous threat. Nearly a year after he first became aware of the accounting error, Stoll's detective work paid off. A spy ring with ties to the KGB was uncovered operating out of a home in Germany to obtain military and government secrets through electronic computer communications.

Today, Cliff Stoll, an unlikely American Hero, is an astronomer at the Harvard-Smithsonian Center for Astrophysics. He has appeared before the U.S. Senate and has become recognized as a leading authority on computer network security. His best-selling book, *The Cuckoo's Egg,* chronicles his journey through electronic espionage. At the beginning of his book, Stoll even lets you know how to contact him—through electronic mail, of course.

CHAPTER 6

COMMUNICATION AND NETWORKS

IN THIS CHAPTER YOU WILL LEARN ABOUT

- **The ways in which computers communicate**
- **The difference between digital and analog data**
- **Modems and their use in computer communications**
- **Computer networks**
- **Ways to use computer communications**

Courtesy Photofest

CONNECTING TO SOLUTIONS

Your focus, and that of this book, is on microcomputing applications—making good use of the personal computer. Perhaps you are now using an IBM-compatible, MS-DOS computer to do your work. Others may favor an Apple Macintosh or another type of computing resource such as a mainframe or minicomputer.

There is a tendency for those who prefer one particular type of computing to suggest that it is the "best" type of computing for everything. Ask a Macintosh user if he or she might consider using an IBM-compatible system, and you are likely to hear a resolute, "No!" To be fair, you are likely to hear the same answer from anyone who promotes any one particular type of computing system to do his or her work.

The purpose of information systems is to provide information that can contribute to solutions to problems. If the focus shifts to that of justifying the type of computer used, the result is counterproductive and leads to more problems. This tends to be especially true when the discussion turns to the future of mainframe computing. Many suggest that there is no longer any need for large-scale computer giants; they say that all useful work can be done on personal computers, even if it takes several of them. The counterargument is that large-scale mainframes are necessary to perform the huge processing tasks required by engineers and large organizations.

The truth, as always, encompasses both of these philosophies. There is no one "best" computer. Based on this reality, why not simply take advantage of all appropriate technologies? Why not view all computing resources as an **open system** where one can tap into the best resource available to complete a task?

One critical and rapidly evolving technology that has contributed to the open system concept is that of data communication and networking. By connecting computers electronically, information systems can be viewed as an integrated, multi-platform, comprehensive resource. In this new electronic world, it makes no difference whatsoever if the work is completed on a personal computer, mainframe, minicomputer, or supercomputer; all that matters is that there is a specific business need to be settled.

DATA COMMUNICATION

Perhaps you have used your computer to connect to one of the popular computer utilities such as Prodigy, CompuServe, or Dialog. If you have, you have used data communication to expand your computer's capabilities by sharing the use of a much larger computing system resource.

Data communication is the process of sending data from one point to another. The communication link between the two points may be electronic, optical, or perhaps some newly emerging method of transmission. The term **network** refers to the way in which the data are transmitted and to the physical connections used.

Computers that are physically located close to each other, either in the same room or building, can communicate data through a direct-cable link. Computers located far apart may use a particular form of data communication—telecommunication. The process of using communication facilities such as the telephone system and microwave relays to send data between computers is a form of data communication referred to as **telecommunication,** or **teleprocessing.**

To understand data communication and networking, you should first be familiar with the terms and technical side of the subject.

ANALOG AND DIGITAL DATA TRANSMISSION

The two forms of data transmission are analog and digital. **Analog** data transmission is the passage of data in a continuous wave form (Figure 6.1a). The telephone system, sending the sound of our voices, is an example of a system designed for analog data transmission.

Digital data transmission is the passage of data using distinct on and off electrical states (Figure 6.1b). Recall that data in digital form are represented as either on (1) or off (0). Because the computer "understands" and works in digital form, and because digital data communication is faster and more efficient than analog, it would seem that all data communication between computers would be in digital form; but, that is not the case.

Totally digital transmission is possible and is growing; however, the telephone system, designed as an analog system, is used for a great percentage of data communication because it is the largest and most widely used communication system in place. Because of the expense involved in converting to a digital system or running a duplicate digital system, a method was devised that allows the digital signal to be transmitted over telephone lines. The process is called **modulation-demodulation.**

Have you used a modem, or have you even heard that term? Well, if you use the telephone to connect your computer to another system, as you would do if you use CompuServe or Prodigy or an electronic bulletin board, you have used a modem. This communication device has become so popular that some models of personal computers even come with one built in as a standard feature. Let us now look at what a modem is and what it does.

Figure 6.1
Analog and digital transmission.

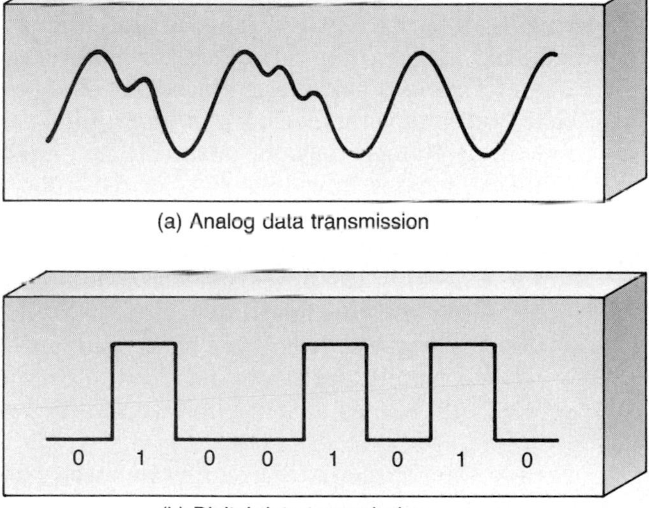

MODEMS

Data in a computer are formatted as digital signals. However, because telephone lines were designed to transmit the human voice, they format data as analog signals. For communication between computers to take place over a telephone line, the digital signal must be converted to an analog signal before it is transmitted. After its journey over the telephone lines, the analog signal must then be reconverted back to a digital signal so that it can be used by the receiving computer. The process of converting a digital signal to an analog signal is called **modulation** (Figure 6.2a). **Demodulation** is the process of reconverting the analog signal back to a digital signal (Figure 6.2b). The device that accomplishes both of these processes is a **modem,** short for modulator-demodulator.

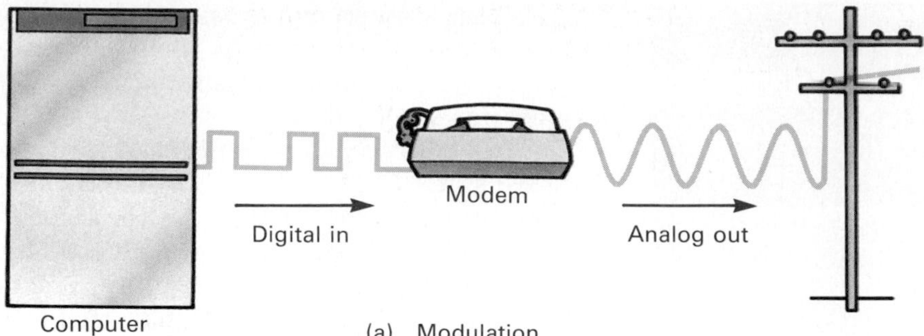

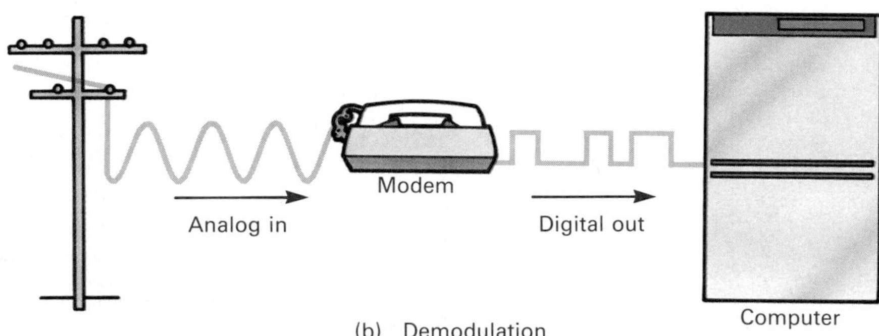

Figure 6.2
Modulation converts a digital signal to an analog signal. Demodulation converts an analog signal to a digital signal.

The two basic types of modems used most often with microcomputers are external direct-connect and internal direct-connect modems. An **external direct-connect modem** is placed outside the computer and connects directly to the telephone line with a modular phone jack (Figure 6.3). A popular external direct-connect modem is the Hayes Smartmodem. Most external direct-connect modems have a variety of features, including the ability to handle these activities:

1. Checking the operating status using status lights and speakers
2. Changing the speed at which data are transmitted
3. Dialing and answering the phone automatically
4. Responding to commands from a communication program
5. Self-testing to verify its own ability to correctly transmit data

Because the specialized circuitry in these modems allows them (rather than the computer) to perform these and other functions, they are often called **smart,** or **intelligent devices.**

The external direct-connect modem requires that a computer be equipped with a communication adapter or other serial port with a connector used as a serial interface. This interface provides a standard method for serial transmission of data. A modem cable connecting the modem to the serial port is also needed.

An **internal direct-connect modem** has all the needed communication circuitry on a plug-in board that fits into one of the expansion slots inside the computer (Figure 6.4). A separate communication board or serial port is not needed. Internal direct-connect modems also are linked directly to the telephone line with a modular phone jack. These modems have many of the same special features as external direct-connect modems. In addition, they take up no desk space and are ideal for use in portable computers.

Figure 6.3
An external direct-connect modem is attached to the computer via a serial cable and to the telephone line via a modular phone jack.

(Larry Hamill/Macmillan)

Figure 6.4
Internal direct-connect modems are inserted into one of the computer system's expansion slots. A modular phone jack connects the modem to the telephone line.

COMMUNICATION CHANNELS

A **communication channel** is the medium, or pathway, through which data are transmitted between devices. Communication channels fall into three basic types: wire cable, microwave, and fiber optics.

Wire cable includes telegraph lines, telephone lines, and coaxial cables; it is the most common type of data communication channel in use today (Figure 6.5). Because it is easier and cheaper to use the extensive wire-cable networks that already exist, wire-cable channels are popular. Another reason for their popularity is that the technology used to transmit data over wire cables is standardized, thus reducing compatibility problems.

A disadvantage of wire cable is that data must be transmitted in analog form. Therefore, digital data must be converted to analog signals before they reach the wire cable. This conversion not only requires special hardware, but it also slows down the transmission of digital data. Another disadvantage is that wire cable is subject to electrical interference, which makes it less reliable than other types of communication channels. Finally, if users are separated by long distances or natural barriers such as mountains or large bodies of water, it is difficult to create the physical links needed to complete transmissions.

Another type of analog communication channel is microwave. **Microwave** signals are transmitted through the atmosphere rather than through wire cables; they are similar to radio and television signals. Microwave signals are transmitted in a straight line; they do not bend around corners or around the curve of the Earth. Transmitter stations redirect and boost the signals. Satellites are also used to direct microwaves over large, geographically dispersed areas.

Compared with wire cable, microwave has a much lower error rate, making it more reliable. Because there are no physical links between the sending and receiving systems, communication links can be made over long distances and rough terrains. A disadvantage, however, is the high cost of ground stations and satellites to support a microwave network.

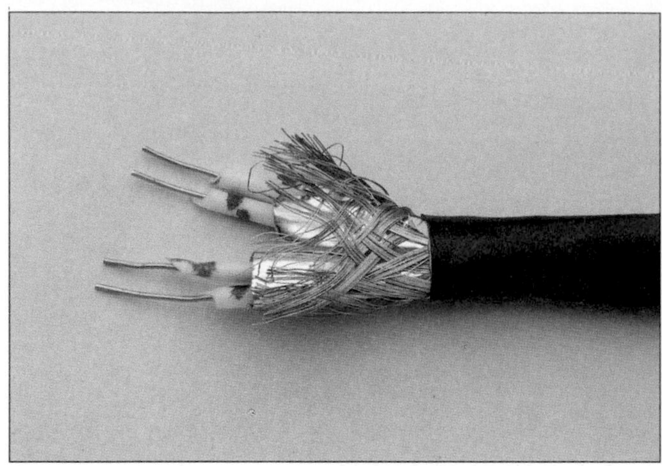
(a)

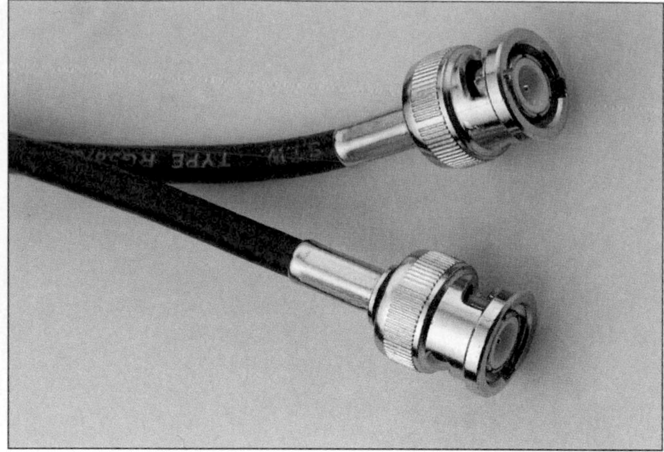
(b)

Figure 6.5
Two types of wire cable: (a) copper-twisted pairs and (b) coaxial copper cable.

(Courtesy Innervisions)

The third type of communication channel is **fiber optics** (Figure 6.6). Unlike wire cable and microwave, a fiber optic channel transmits data in digital form. It uses light impulses that travel through clear flexible tubing. The tubing is thinner than a human hair, and hundreds of tubes can fit in the same amount of space required for one wire cable. Fiber optic channels may become the standard method for connecting data communication systems, but that conversion will be expensive and cannot be done quickly. Too many wire cable installations still exist, and there is no practical way to remove and replace all of those connections.

Figure 6.6
Fiber optic cables, which transmit signals at the speed of light, are replacing the older wire cables used for computer communication.

(Courtesy of United Telecommunications)

HIGHLIGHT

Wireless Networks

What if your portable personal computer could be connected to the office's local area network just by your walking into the building? That possibility is not as remote as you might think, given the rapid development of various methods of wireless data communication.

Packet radio and cellular radio, which you might recognize from the growth in the use of cellular telephones, can be used to replace the modems now used to connect computers. With these methods, your computer could be connected to an office computer wherever you are, in a car or in another building, through a series of transceivers. Just as some cellular telephone services can be used from various cities, your computer could be connected while you travel from place to place. Ardis, a company backed by IBM and Motorola, has 8,000 transceivers in place, and claims that they now cover 80 percent of the nation's population centers.

Within an office or complex of buildings, spread-spectrum radio can replace the more expensive wire or fiber cable installations. Spread-spectrum radio broadcasts over several frequencies to decrease interference and increase the number of communication connections. NCR has begun marketing a product called WaveLan which is installed in a personal computer's expansion slot and enables the computer to communicate at a rate of 2 megabits per second over several hundred feet—without wires.

Infrared light can also be used to transmit data over short distances of 600 feet or less. Photonics has developed a product that bounces infrared light off walls and ceilings to enable computers to communicate without wires within offices.

Wireless technology is still emerging. Many factors have to be considered, for example, allocating airwave frequencies for radio transmissions and preventing interference from similar devices already in place. Imagine pressing the wrong key on your wireless computer and changing channels on your TV or calling your own cellular phone!

Channel Configurations

The two principal communication channel configurations are point-to-point and multipoint (Figure 6.7). In a **point-to-point channel configuration,** a device (for example, a terminal or computer) is connected directly to another device by a dedicated communication channel, that is, a channel that gives those devices sole use of that line. Point-to-point can be an inefficient and costly configuration if a terminal is not active enough to keep the line busy. On the other hand, point-to-point connections are simple to understand and easier to install than other options.

An alternative is the **multipoint channel configuration** in which three or more devices are connected to the same line. The multipoint configuration uses the communication channel more efficiently and reduces the amount of intercabling needed, thus lowering costs. An easy example to understand is one in which a multipoint channel is used to connect several devices that

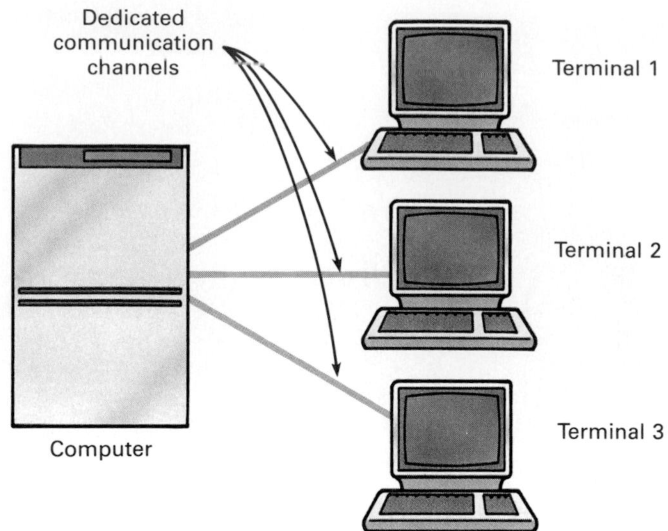

(a) Point-to-point channel configuration

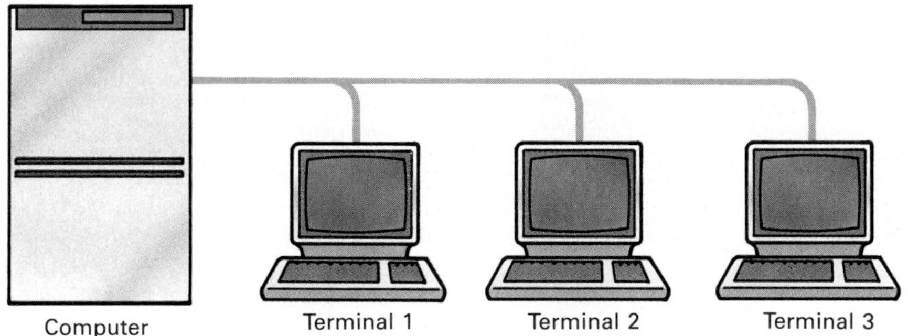

(b) Multipoint channel configuration

Figure 6.7
Point-to-point and multipoint channel configurations.

transmit over a single telephone line rather than several independent lines; the reduction in the number of telephone lines translates directly to a lower cost.

A **multiplexer** is one means of sharing a communication channel among several terminals (Figure 6.8). Multiplexing combines signals from several devices by sending characters from each device in a mixed stream along one communication channel. When the data are received, another multiplexer decodes the mixed signal back into individual data transmissions.

Rate of Data Transmission

If you do have a modem, you will probably recognize terms such as *baud rate* or *2400 bps*. These two terms relate to the measurement of the rate of data transmission. Generally, the speed of transmission is given as bps, or **bits per second.** It means just about what the term implies—the number of bits that can be sent or received in one second. Although **baud rate** is often used interchangeably with bps, they are technically different measurements; however, this technical difference will be ignored for the moment and you may use the terms as if they were similar.

Although higher speeds are possible, typical data transmission speeds are 300, 1,200, 2,400, 4,800, and 9,600 bps. Modems used with microcomputers typically use 300, 1,200, or 2,400 bps. Larger computer systems use high-speed modems for business communication that typically transmit data at speeds of 4,800 bps or higher. Two factors determine the rate at which data can be trans-

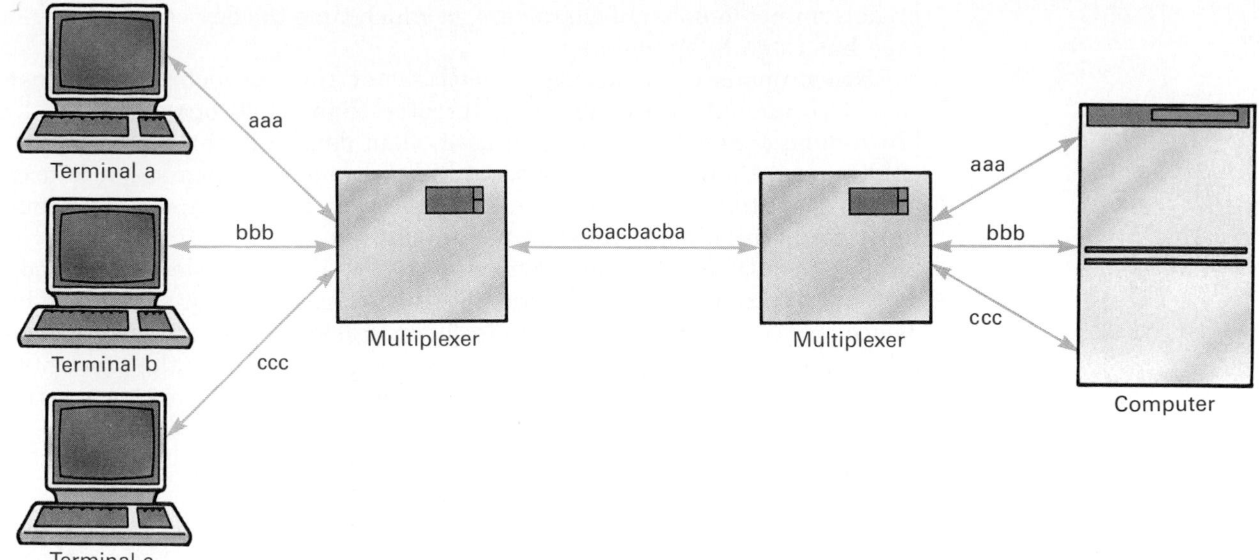

Figure 6.8
Multiplexers send a mixed stream of characters along one communication channel. A receiving multiplexer decodes the signal back into individual transmissions.

mitted over communication channels: (1) the bandwidth of the channel and (2) the method of data transmission—asynchronous or synchronous.

Channel Bandwidths

The **bandwidth,** or grade, of a communication channel determines the rate or speed that data can be transmitted over a channel. The term *bandwidth* is often shortened to *band.* There are three bands for communication channels: narrow band, voice band (also called voice grade), and broad band.

The slowest of these is the **narrow-band channel,** which transmits data at rates between 40 and 100 bits per second. A telegraph line is a narrow-band channel.

Voice-band channels can transmit data at rates between 110 and 9,600 bits per second. Telephone lines are voice-band channels.

The fastest of these channels is the **broad-band channel,** which can transmit data at rates up to several megabits per second. Advances in technology will soon allow data to be transmitted on some types of broad-band channels in the billions-of-bits-per-second range. Microwaves, coaxial cables, and fiber optics are broad-band channels.

Asynchronous and Synchronous Transmissions

Asynchronous transmission of data is a method in which one character is sent at a time. The transfer of data is controlled by start bits and stop bits. Each character is surrounded by bits that signal the beginning and end of the character. These characters allow the receiving terminal to synchronize itself with the receipt of data on a character-by-character basis.

Asynchronous transmission is the least expensive of the two methods. It is often used in low-speed transmission of data in conjunction with narrow-band channels and some slower speed (less than 1,200 bps) voice-band channels where the transmitting device operates manually or intermittently.

In **synchronous** transmission, blocks of characters are transmitted in timed sequences. Rather than using start and stop bits around each character, each block of characters is marked with synchronization characters. The receiving device accepts data until it detects a special ending character or a predetermined number of characters, at which time the device knows the message has come to an end.

Synchronous transmission is much faster than asynchronous transmission. It commonly uses the faster (greater than 1,200 bps) voice-band and broad-band channels and is often used when data transfer requirements exceed several thousand bits per second. Synchronous transmission is used in direct computer-to-computer communication for large computer systems because of the high data transfer speeds required.

Before data are transmitted, however, a set of traffic rules and procedures called **protocol** must be established. The same protocol must be followed by all devices participating in the communication session. These rules vary depending on the devices being used. Prearranged signals defining the protocol to be followed when transmitting and receiving data are sent between computers in an exchange called **handshaking.**

Modes of Transmission

The three modes in which the transfer of data over communication channels occurs are simplex, half-duplex, and full-duplex. In the **simplex** mode, data can be transmitted in only one direction (Figure 6.9a). A device using the simplex mode of transmission can either send or receive data, but it cannot do both. This mode might be used in a burglar alarm system whose source is in a building and whose destination is the local police station. The simplex mode does not allow any feedback that might ensure correct interpretation of the received signal. For example, police officers would have no way of knowing if the alarm was set off by a test, a malfunction, or by a burglar.

The **half-duplex** mode allows a device to send and receive data, but not at the same time. In other words, the transmission of data can occur in only one

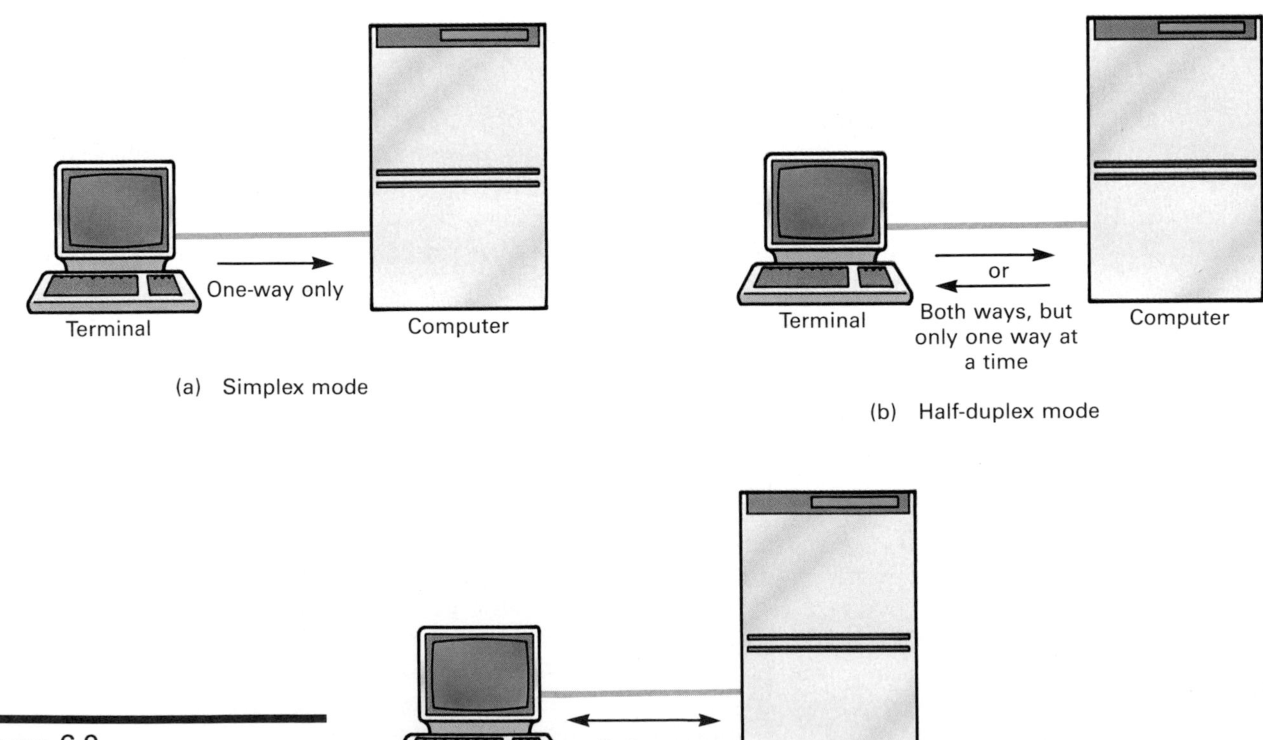

Figure 6.9
Data transmission takes place in one of three modes: simplex, half-duplex, or full-duplex.

direction at a time (Figure 6.9b). An example is a citizens band (CB) radio where the user must either talk or listen, but cannot do both at the same time.

The most sophisticated of these transmission modes is the **full-duplex** mode, which allows a device to receive and send data simultaneously (Figure 6.9c). For example, a telephone system using full-duplex mode allows the user to talk and listen at the same time. Telephone systems use either the half-duplex or full-duplex mode.

Micro-to-Micro Link

Microcomputers are often connected for data communication in a **micro-to-micro link,** so microcomputer users with incompatible data formats can share data. For example, data on an Apple Macintosh diskette can't be used by an IBM PS/2 diskette drive because the data are not saved on the disk in a format that the IBM computer can read. However, those data, provided they are in a standard format such as ASCII, can be sent via modem and telephone line to the IBM, saved on disk by the IBM, and then used in that format. The reverse, sending data from the IBM to the Apple computer, is also possible. If the two computers are located near each other, another option is to directly connect, or hard-wire, them using a null modem cable.

The **null modem cable** uses a different pin configuration from a modem cable and eliminates the need for a modem by directly matching the data transmit pin from one computer to the data receive pin on the other computer. The advantages of hard-wiring are that (1) it allows incompatible computers to transfer data; (2) it eliminates the need for modems at each computer; and (3) it allows data transfer to take place at speeds up to 9,600 bps. However, there are no error-detection capabilities with hard-wiring.

Micro-to-Mainframe Link

To share data and computing power, microcomputers can also be connected to large systems in a **micro-to-mainframe link.** As the number of microcomputers used in business increases, this connection is being used more frequently. As with micro-to-micro communication, micro-to-mainframe communication can be accomplished via modem and telephone lines or by hard-wiring.

However, the connection is not as simple because large systems use different formats for communication, and they handle data differently internally. To complicate the problem, the communication and data formats used among the various large systems also differ. Specialized hardware designed for the particular type of computer being used is usually needed to make the data compatible. For a microcomputer to communicate with a large system, three facts must be known: (1) the type of mainframe to be communicated with, (2) the mainframe's specific data format, and (3) the mainframe's specific communication protocols.

NETWORKS AND DISTRIBUTED DATA PROCESSING

A **computer network** is created when several computers are linked by data communication channels. Each computer in a network can have its own processing capabilities and can also share hardware, data files, and programs. The two basic types of networks are local area and wide area.

Wide Area Networks

A **wide area network** (WAN) consists of two or more computers that are geographically dispersed and linked by communication facilities such as the telephone system or microwave relays. This type of network is usually limited to use by large corporations and government agencies because of the high costs involved in building and maintaining it.

Local Area Networks

A **local area network** (LAN) consists of two or more computers directly linked within a small, well-defined area such as a room, building, or group of closely placed buildings (Figure 6.10). A LAN may be made up of only microcomputers or any combination of microcomputers and large computer systems.

The difference between a LAN and a multiuser microcomputer system is that a LAN is made up of stand-alone computers, whereas a multiuser microcomputer system typically has one computer that is shared among two or more terminals. A LAN usually has the following characteristics:

1. Two or more computers
2. Peripheral devices such as printers and hard-disk drives
3. Software to control the operation of the computers or other devices connected to the LAN
4. Special cables, usually coaxial or fiber optic, to connect the computers and other devices
5. A plug-in board to handle data transmissions

Figure 6.10
Wide area networks cover large access areas, whereas local area networks are generally confined to a single building or campus.

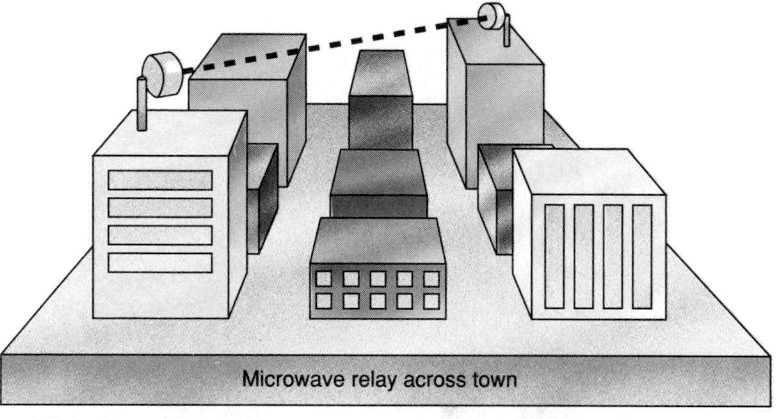

a. Wide Area Network

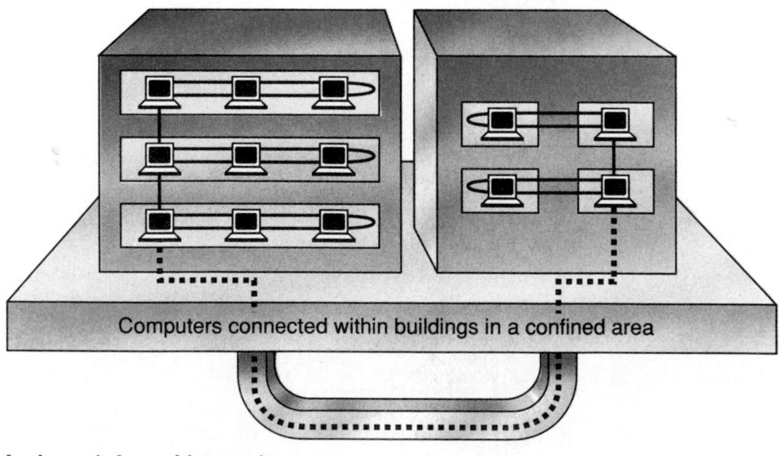

b. Local Area Network

One benefit of a LAN is lower hardware costs because several computers and users can share peripheral devices such as laser printers, hard-disk drives, color plotters, and modems. Another advantage is that the users can share data and programs.

Ensuring the security and privacy of data are two concerns of LAN users. The LAN must get the data to their destination, transmit the data correctly, and prevent unauthorized users from gaining access to those data. These tasks are accomplished through both hardware and software.

LANs vary in the type and number of computers that can be connected, the speed at which data can be transferred, and the type of software used to control the network. Some LANs require that all the computers be of a certain brand, whereas others allow a variety of brands to be connected. The number of computers in a LAN varies widely from smaller LANs that typically connect two to twenty-five computers, to larger LANs that can connect hundreds or thousands of computers.

The length of the cable connecting a computer to a LAN also varies depending on the LAN. Most LANs allow cables of about 1,000 feet, but some allow cables of several miles. Data transfer speeds range from several thousand bits per second to around 16 million bits per second, or up to 100 million bits per second for fiber optic network systems.

Programs that control the LANs, called **network operating systems,** also vary in the features they offer. Some programs allow the use of more than one operating system; others allow only one. On some LANs, file access is limited to one user at a time; on others, more than one user can access a file simultaneously.

Network Topology

Each computer or device in a network is called a **node.** How these nodes are connected is the network's **topology.** A network can be arranged in one of four different topologies: star network, ring network, tree network, or bus network.

Star Network

A **star network** consists of several devices connected to one centralized computer (Figure 6.11). All communication first goes through the centralized computer, which allows it to control the operation, work load, and resource allocation of the other computers in the network. For example, a bank with several branch offices would typically use a star network to control and coordinate those branches. The advantage is relative simplicity, but a problem can occur because of the single-point vulnerability of the network. If the central computer breaks down, the other computers cannot communicate with each other.

Ring Network

A **ring network** consists of several devices connected to each other in a closed loop by a single communication channel (Figure 6.12). There is no central, or predominant, computer in this network. The data must travel around the ring to each station in turn until it arrives at the desired station. A ring may be unidirectional or bidirectional. A **unidirectional ring** moves data in one direction only; a **bidirectional ring** moves data in both directions, but only one direction at a time. In a unidirectional ring, if one computer breaks down, special software is required to keep the network functional. When one node malfunctions in a bidirectional ring, a message can usually be sent in the opposite direction, still allowing the node to communicate with all the other active nodes in the network.

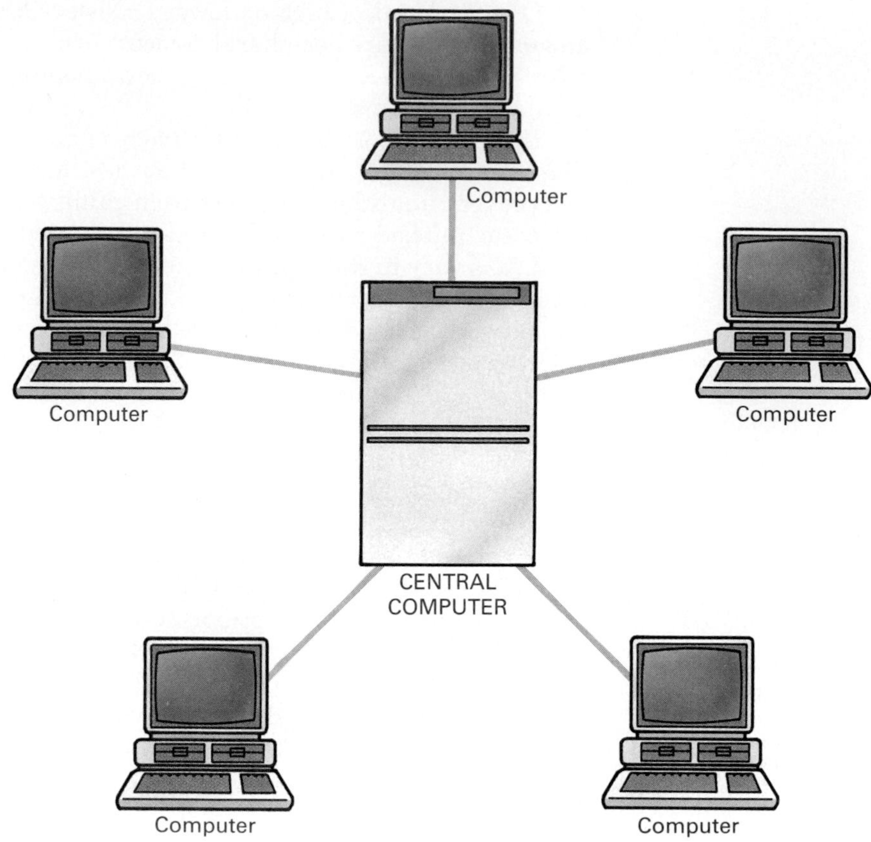

Figure 6.11
Star network.

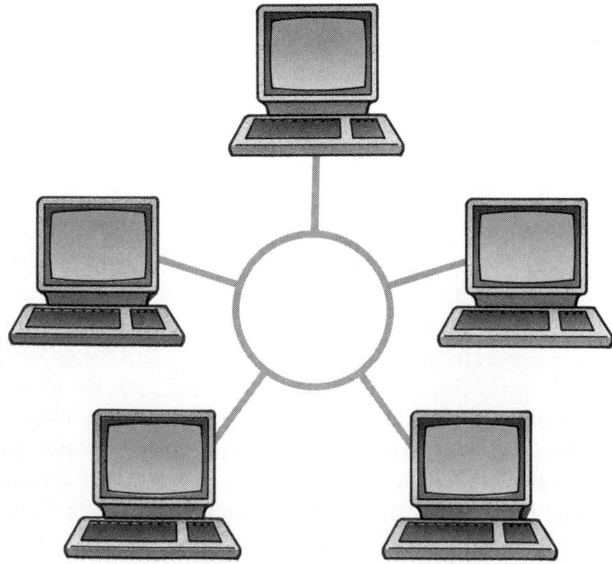

Figure 6.12
Ring network.

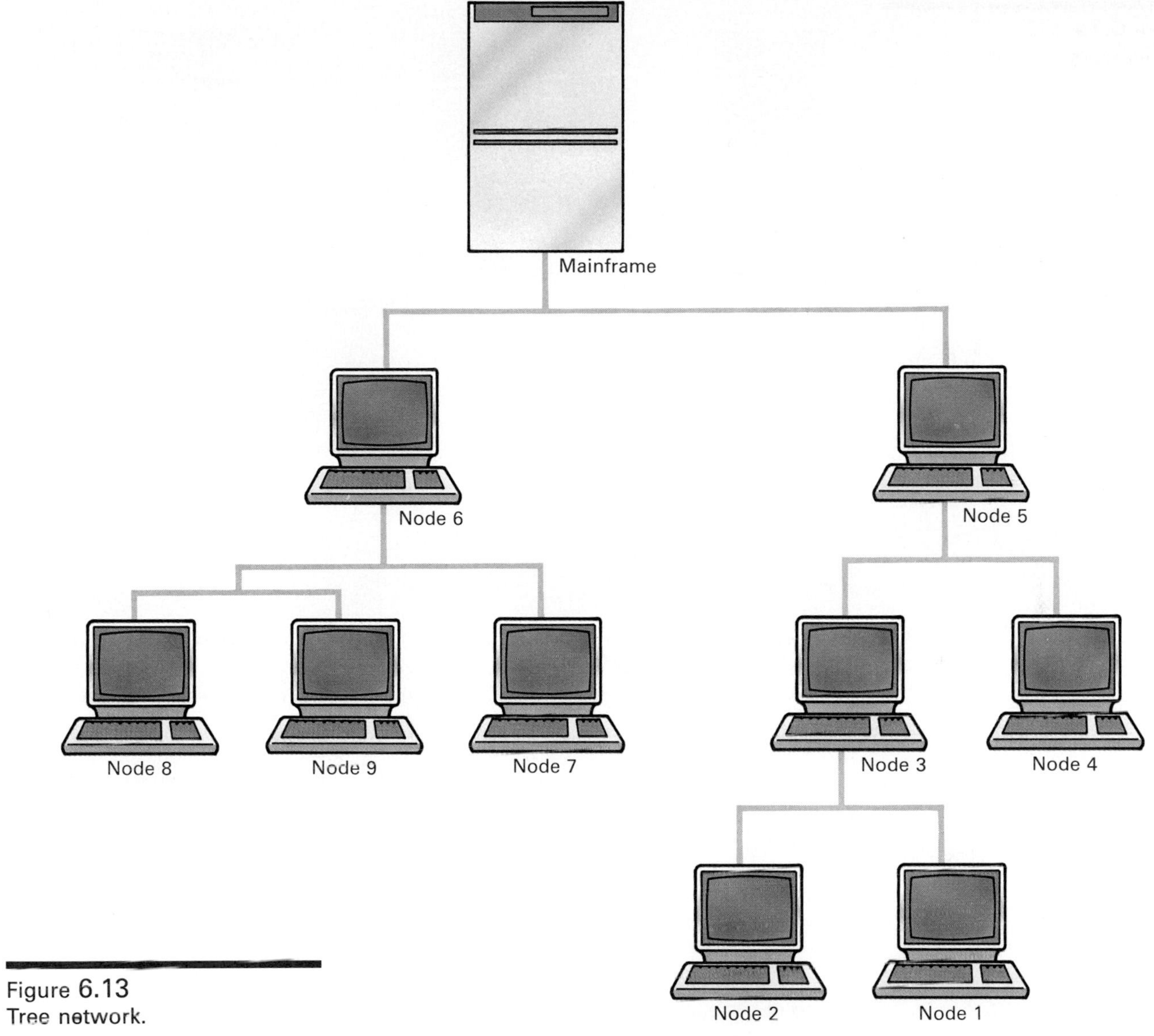

Figure 6.13
Tree network.

Tree Network

A **tree network** links computers in a hierarchical fashion and requires information to flow through the branches (Figure 6.13). To move from the computer at Node 1 in Figure 6.13 to Node 7, data would have to go through Nodes 3, 5, and 6 before arriving at 7.

An advantage of a tree structure is that functional groupings can be created. For example, one branch could contain all the general ledger terminals, another branch all the accounts receivable terminals, and so on. If one branch stops functioning, the other branches in a tree network are not affected. However, data movement through this network can be slow.

Bus Network

In a **bus network,** each computer is connected to a single communication cable via an interface; every computer can communicate directly with every other computer or device in the network (Figure 6.14). Each node is given an address. To access a particular node, a user just needs to know its address. This topology is frequently used with local area networks. Going through a hierarchy of nodes is not necessary here the way it is in a tree network.

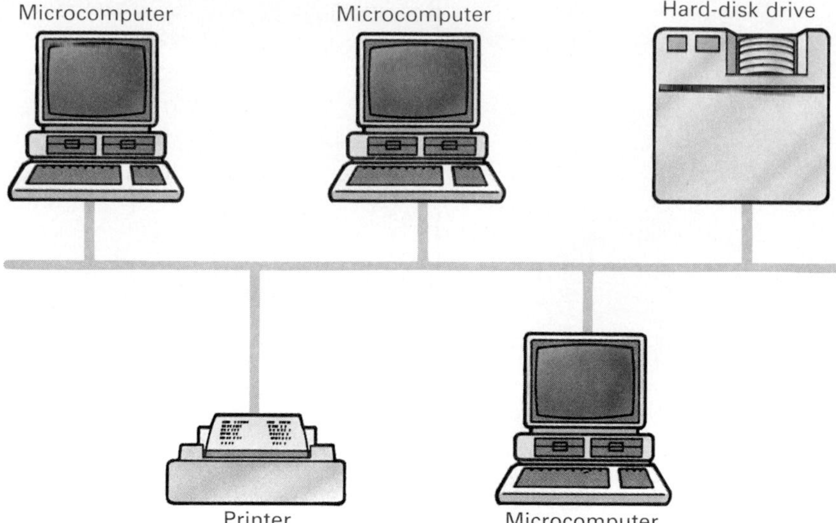

Figure 6.14
Bus network.

Popular Network Implementations

Two leading networking types are Ethernet and token-ring. **Ethernet** is a LAN design originally developed by Xerox in 1972. Ethernet uses a control method known as **carrier sense multiple access with collision detection** (CSMA/CD). In this access method, each node on the network "listens," or checks the circuit, to see if another node is sending a transmission. If the network is "quiet"—if no other station is sending a message—the node is able to transmit a message. The term *carrier sense* means that the node tests the circuit for a busy condition before transmitting.

As a message is transmitted over the network, it travels to all nodes and is examined by each of the nodes. If the address of the message matches the node, the station receives the message.

When two or more stations on the network attempt to communicate at the same time, a collision occurs. Following the collision, each station waits a period of time, then tries to retransmit. As long as the network traffic is fairly light, the network works quickly. When the traffic on the network becomes heavy, the time spent detecting collisions and resending messages can reduce network performance.

An alternative method of network implementation is **token ring.** In this system, an electronic message, called a **token,** is constantly circulated through the network. If the token is marked as free, meaning that no messages are being transmitted, then any station may attach a message to the token, marking it as busy, and send it to another address. The busy token is then passed from station to station until it reaches its destination address where the message is removed and the token is again made free to accept another message.

Token-ring systems have an advantage in being able to allow greater control over transmissions. Each station is guaranteed a chance to transmit a message within some period of time, and the system permits priorities to be set for various stations. The disadvantage of this system is that it is more complex than Ethernet and requires more computing resources to manage it.

Distributed Data Processing

Distributed data processing (DDP) is the concept of dispersing computers, devices, software, and data connected through communication channels into areas where they are used. The computers are organized functionally and geographically and work together as a cohesive system to support users' requirements.

This approach contrasts with a centralized system where all the data processing resources are located in one place. Typically, a centralized system has one large, general-purpose computer with many terminals attached to it. Although the centralized computer can do many tasks, it may not be the most efficient or cost-effective way to do many of them. A DDP system allows the use of many smaller, more specialized computers that can be tailored to complete a particular task or tasks efficiently and cost-effectively. DDP is not appropriate for all applications; large, centralized computing systems are still essential in some cases.

To ensure that it meets their needs, users should be integrally involved in the design of the DDP system. The success or failure of a DDP system ultimately depends on management's planning, commitment to, and control of the system as well as acceptance by users.

COMMUNICATION CHALLENGES

The use of electronic data communication is not without its challenges. Data sent over communication channels are subject to various kinds of interference, which may alter or destroy some of them. In addition to ensuring the security of the data, privacy of the data must be protected. Unauthorized access to data files can often be prevented by the use of passwords and access codes. To prevent highly sensitive data from being accessed and used from the communication channels, data are often **encrypted,** or scrambled, based on some code before being sent. Then the data are unscrambled using that same code after being received. One of the benefits of fiber optic cabling systems is that it is difficult to intercept the signal without detection.

HIGHLIGHT

The NYSE and Telecommunication

Most brokers and specialists use preprinted slips and pencils to note the deals they make on the floor of the New York Stock Exchange (NYSE). They keep track of details such as how much stock is involved, who the parties in the deal are, and what the price per share is.

The paper method, however, doesn't allow the traders the opportunity to review the details of the deal to make sure the broker wrote down and used the correct information. This paper method results in about 15 percent of trades being questionable.

Now, there is a push for computerized trading. The person who acts as the auctioneer uses an electronic workstation while the brokers use handheld terminals (a combination of laptop computer and telephone). The brokers enter the details of each deal on their terminals; the traders immediately see the transactions on the liquid-crystal display and lock them in or fix any mistakes. Besides eliminating the paper mess at the end of a day of trading, stockbrokers would like to see the percentage of questionable trades drop to near zero.

DATA COMMUNICATION AT WORK

Most of us deal with some business that uses some form of data communication every day. For example, many newspaper and magazine articles that you read are filed by journalists from remote locations using portable computers and data communication channels. Airlines and travel agencies receive and send information on flight schedules and reservations through data communication channels. The supermarket may have its cash registers linked to the store's large computer at a remote location to keep track of inventories.

Electronic funds transfer (EFT), the electronic movement of money among accounts, is a widely used data communication application. A large portion of money in the business and financial communities changes hands through EFT. A popular application of EFT is the automated teller machine.

In fact, the Society for Worldwide Interbank Financial Telecommunications (SWIFT), the most sophisticated private interbank system in the world, averages 750,000 transactions daily for 1,300 member banks in forty-six countries. After being upgraded, SWIFT's mainframe and communication network will process 1 million messages daily.

Some companies have adopted a method of employment, called **telecommuting,** where some personnel work at home and use their computers to communicate with the office computer.

Electronic mail is a system used by computers and communication channels to store and send messages. Many businesses use electronic mail systems to reduce paperwork and to save the time it takes for a message to reach its destination. At home, Bill Machrone, editor at *PC Magazine,* uses his Compaq Portable Plus microcomputer to write his "Editor's Notes" column, edit stories, and communicate with contributors through the MCI electronic mail service.

Information services and database services, such as CompuServe, The Source, Dow Jones News Retrieval, and Dialog, use data communication so their subscribers can access one or several large computers containing data banks on various topics. These services can be accessed easily from microcomputers equipped with the proper communication hardware and software.

Data communication has made the computer one of the most vital tools in our information-seeking society. It links two or more computers via telephone lines or direct cabling and enables users to send and receive electronic data without regard to the boundaries of time or distance.

Summary

- Data communication is the process of sending data from one point to another.
- The transmission of data takes one of two forms: analog or digital. Analog data transmission is the passage of data in a continuous wave form. Digital data transmission is the passage of data in distinct on and off electrical states.
- Modulation is the process of converting a digital signal into an analog signal. Demodulation is the process of converting the analog signal into a digital signal. A modem (modulator-demodulator) is the device that converts the signals.
- A communication channel is the pathway through which data are transmitted between devices.
- The baud rate of a communication channel is the number of bits per second (bps) that the signal being transmitted changes (modulates or demodulates).
- Asynchronous transmission transmits data one character at a time. Synchronous transmission transmits data as a block of characters in timed sequences.
- Data transfer can occur in three modes: simplex, half-duplex, and full-duplex.
- A computer network is created by linking several computers through the use of data communication channels. The two basic types of networks are local area networks and wide area networks.
- Ensuring the security and privacy of data are two important challenges facing users of data communication.

Key Terms

Data communication
Network
Telecommunication
Analog
Digital
Modem
Bit per second
Baud rate
Asynchronous
Synchronous
Protocol
Simplex
Half-duplex
Full-duplex
Wide area network
Local area network
Ethernet
Token ring
Distributed data processing

Review Questions

1. What is data communication?
2. Give the name for the process of using communication facilities such as the telephone system to transmit data.
3. Describe the difference between analog and digital data transmission.
4. Identify the process of converting an analog signal to a digital signal.
5. How does a modem function?
6. What two types of modems are generally used with microcomputers?
7. Describe the purpose of a communication channel.
8. Name the three basic types of communication channels.
9. Which type of communication channel transmits data in digital form?
10. Describe and sketch how a point-to-point channel configuration works.
11. What type of configuration has a number of terminals connected to the same communication channel?
12. How is the rate of data transmission measured?
13. What determines the rate of data transmission?
14. What are the three bandwidths for communication channels and how do they differ?
15. Describe asynchronous data transmission.
16. What type of transmission involves blocks of characters transmitted in timed sequences?
17. Describe protocol.
18. Describe the three modes in which the transfer of data can occur.
19. List three factors that must be known for a microcomputer to communicate with a large system computer.
20. What is a computer network?
21. Describe a local area network.
22. How does a wide area network differ from a local area network?
23. Name and describe the four different network topologies.
24. What is distributed data processing?
25. Differentiate between Ethernet and token-ring networks.

PROFILE

GRACE MURRAY HOPPER

(UPI/Bettmann)

Not many octogenarians make major career moves like this one, but in 1986, Grace Murray Hopper, at age seventy-nine, retired as a rear admiral in Naval Data Automation Command in the U.S. Navy, and now serves as senior consultant at Digital Equipment Corporation.

Admiral Hopper is widely known in the computer field for helping to develop early computers, and she is well known among students and members of the computer industry as a lecturer and spokesperson for innovation. During her presentations, she discusses data processing and the nature and importance of information.

Hopper, a native of New York City, attended Vassar College and went on to receive her master's degree and doctorate from Yale University. Her work in computer technology has been conducted in a mixed environment that includes the academic scene, the business world, and the military.

After joining the U.S. Naval Reserve in 1944, she worked with Howard Aiken to program the Mark I, the first sequence-controlled digital calculator. Besides teaching in colleges and universities, she was senior mathematician for Eckert-Mauchly Computer Corporation and worked for Sperry Corporation as a system engineer and later as a staff scientist in system programming. Part of this time Hopper was on military leave. She helped develop UNIVAC I, the first large, commercial computer, and she was instrumental in creating the COBOL programming language.

In 1966, she was retired at the age of sixty (the Navy thought she was too old) with the rank of commander in the U.S. Naval Reserve. Within seven months, however, Hopper was recalled to active duty. Much of her military service has been dedicated to helping run all the Navy's nonweapons computers and keeping the Navy at the leading edge of computer technology. Now, she has retired from the Naval Reserve a second time, once again moving into private industry.

Hopper has received world recognition and many honors as one of the outstanding contributors to the computer revolution. One unique honor was presented in 1969, when the Data Processing Management Association selected her as their first Computer Sciences "Man of the Year." There has been no higher award, she says, than that of the privilege and responsibility of service in the U.S. Navy.

When *Computerworld's* senior editor Janet Fiderio asked her if society has become too dependent on computers, she replied, "Well, we used to be dependent on paper. What difference does it make that our information is on computer or paper?" Fiderio answered, "Computers can fail." Hopper responded, "And paper can burn."

CHAPTER 7

INFORMATION SYSTEMS

IN THIS CHAPTER YOU WILL LEARN ABOUT

- **Business information systems**
- **The systems development life cycle**
- **Managerial uses for information systems**
- **Decision support and expert systems**

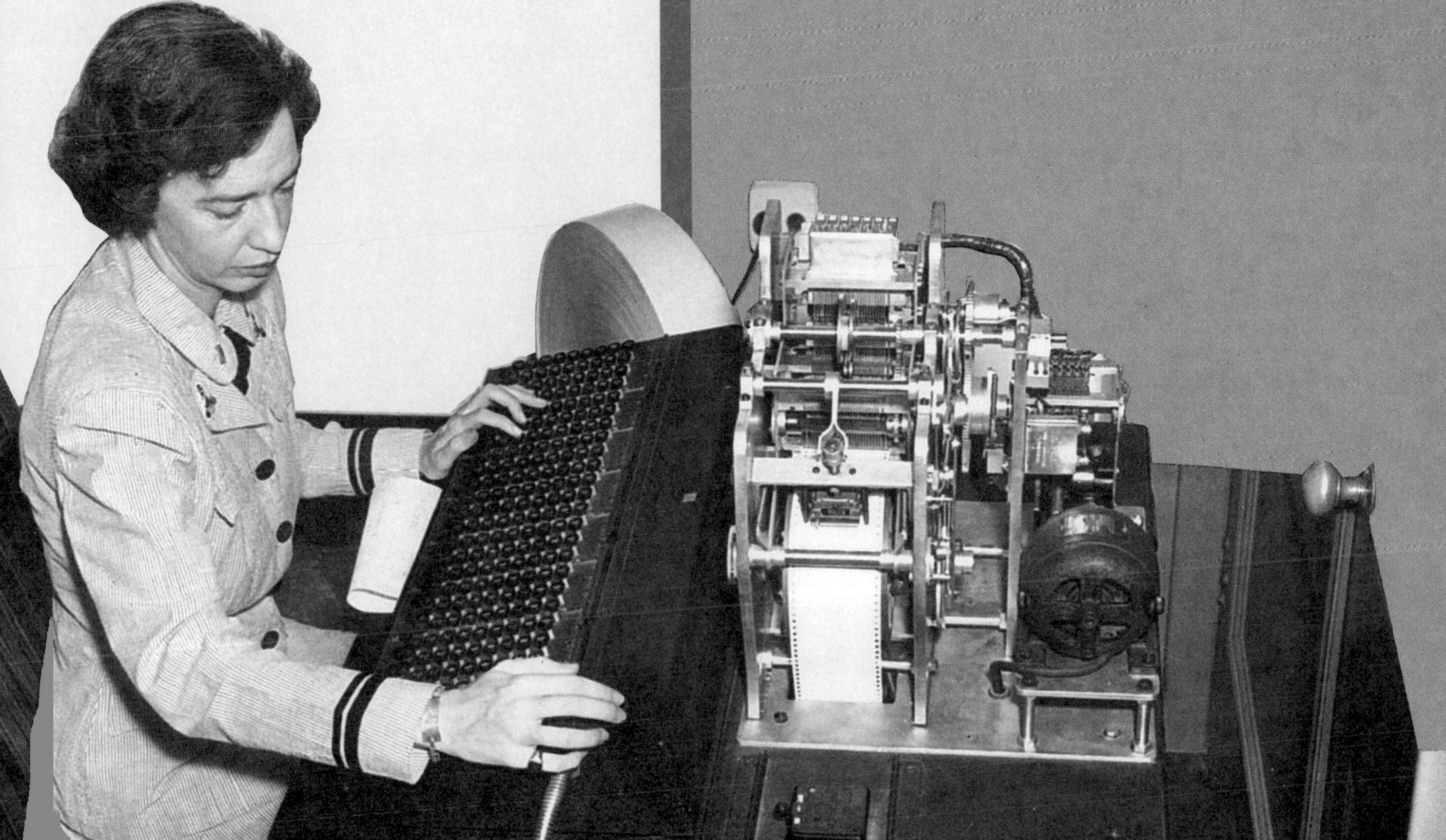

UPI/Bettmann

SYSTEMS FOR BUSINESS

In Chapter 1 you learned that an **information system** is the combination of people, data, and procedures used to create and distribute information throughout an organization (Figure 7.1). To operate, all businesses need an information system; but not all information systems include a computer. For many, however, the computer plays an integral part in the process. Simply buying a computer does not automatically solve the problem of converting data to information. An information system must be carefully developed through a systematic development process.

The first part of this chapter is an overview of the system life cycle. The information presented is general in nature and is designed to give you a basic understanding of the types of concerns that must be addressed when developing an information system. Later in the chapter, you'll learn about management information systems, a type of information system that supplies managers with the information they need.

SYSTEM LIFE CYCLE

For our purposes, a **system** is the combination of people, devices, and methods working together toward a common goal. Our focus is on organizational systems that use computers to reach the common goal of providing information.

An information system provides the data processing capabilities and information that an organization or business needs to be informed about various aspects of its operations. Because information is a valuable asset to any business or organization, it must be acquired and organized carefully. For a system to be useful and to have value, it must (1) provide accurate information, (2) provide timely information, and (3) be capable of communicating that information to the people in the organization who need it.

An organization can have one or more information systems in operation. Among other tasks, businesses use information systems for sales and order processing, administrative record keeping, and accounting and payroll applications. An oil company might use one information system to process and manage data about oil exploration, another system for refinery management, and yet another for customer accounts.

The **system life cycle** is the life span of an information system from its inception until it is removed or redesigned. It consists of five major stages as shown in Figure 7.2 on page C-129.

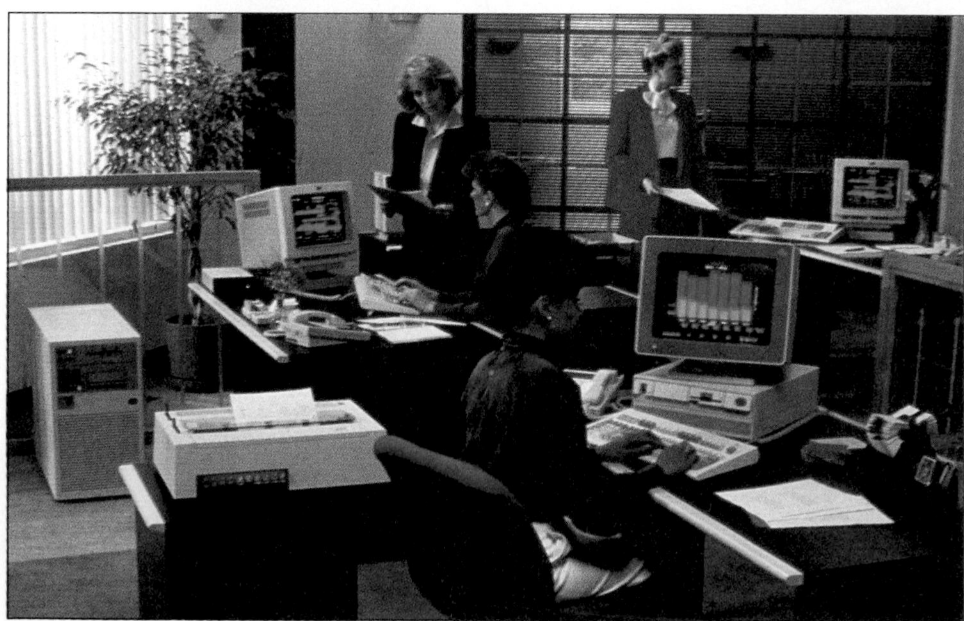

Figure 7.1
A system combines people, devices, and methods working together toward a common goal. In many information systems, the devices are the computers people use to convert data into information that can be distributed throughout an organization.

(Courtesy of International Business Machines, Inc.)

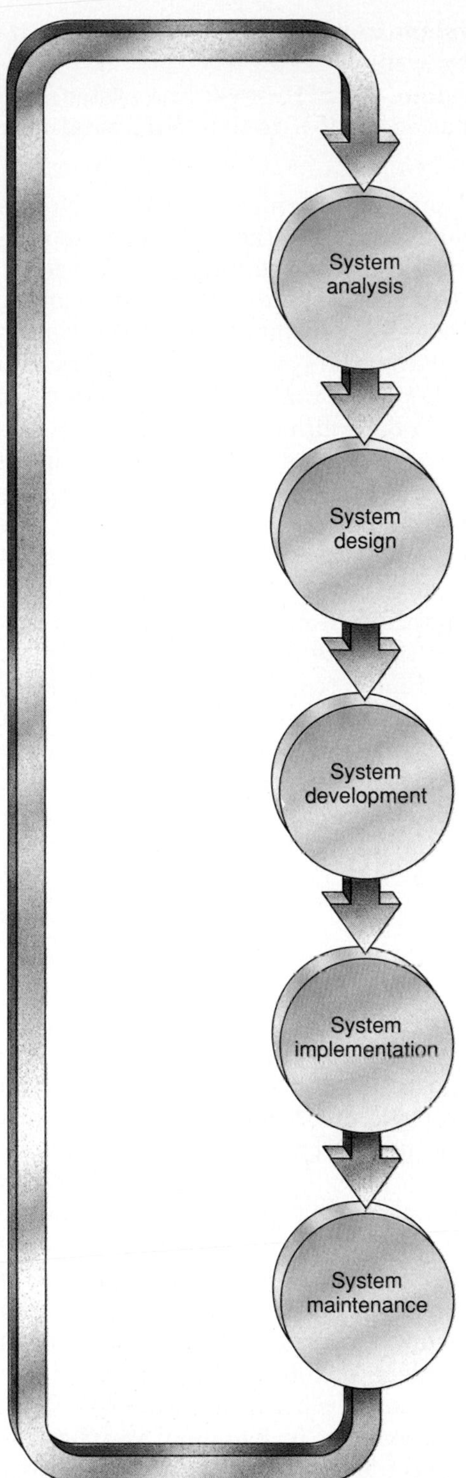

Figure 7.2
System life cycle.

1. **System analysis:** The current system is evaluated to determine if it should be modified or if a new system should be developed.
2. **System design:** A physical design of a proposed system is developed.
3. **System development:** The new information system is created from the physical design; the programs of the new or modified system are written.

4. **System implementation:** The organization installs and uses the new system.
5. **System maintenance:** The system is continually monitored and adjusted until it is time for a total reevaluation.

Developing an information system involves continual and clear communication among users and the system personnel who are responsible for designing and implementing the information system. The **user** is the person or persons who will use the information system once it's been installed. For example, users include the operators who run the computers and managers who request information from the system. **System personnel** include system analysts, system designers, and programmers. A **system analyst** is the person who works with users to determine their information needs. A **system designer** is the specialist who designs a system to fulfill the users' information needs. A **programmer** is the person who codes the instructions in a programming language so that they can be used by the computer. These positions are usually separate and distinct jobs; however, in some small organizations, one person may do all or several parts of these tasks.

An important means of communication throughout the system life cycle is provided by accurate and complete documentation. **Documentation** is the written or graphic record of the steps taken during the life cycle. Users and system personnel alike are responsible for accurately documenting each task they perform. This documentation forms the basis for understanding the nature of the system's operations and for correctly using its results.

The following sections explain each stage of the system life cycle and describe how you, as a user, and the system personnel go about the task of analyzing and solving a problem.

SYSTEM ANALYSIS

System analysis is the process of analyzing a system and trying to find a way to modify it or to create a new system to meet users' needs. The process is initiated when those who use the system recognize a problem or new opportunity that the current system cannot handle. As used here, the term *problem* means that the current system is not functioning properly for tasks it was designed to handle. The phrase *new opportunity* means that circumstances have arisen, such as a new product line, that the current system was not originally designed to handle. The distinction is made to show that an analysis is not always initiated in response to negative situations.

Under normal circumstances, the system analysis project is initiated by someone like you who uses the current information system and who recognizes the symptoms of a problem. Perhaps the information is not as timely as required; or maybe it is not as accurate as needed. Perhaps you have been doing some data processing in a manual way but now you would like to determine whether you could automate the work. Your first task is to try to clearly define the nature of your problem (Figure 7.3). Then you contact your system analyst to discuss your problem.

At this point, the system analyst is not looking for a solution so much as a clear understanding of the problem or new opportunity. After the area of concern has been recognized, the scope and purpose of the analysis should be communicated to all involved parties, including management, system personnel, and to you as one of the users. Once these parties have agreed on the scope and purpose, management must decide whether the system analyst should proceed with a feasibility study.

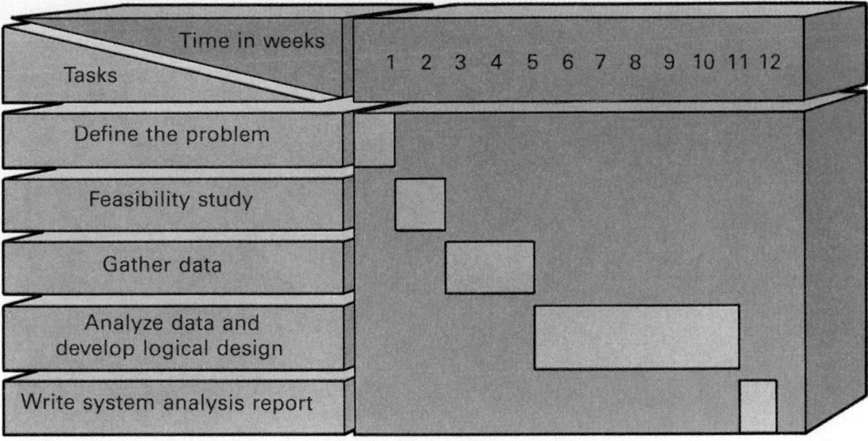

Figure 7.3
System analysis is carried out over a series of planned stages.

Feasibility Study

A **feasibility study** is a preliminary study to determine if the information system should be developed. Three questions need to be asked and answered:

1. Is the technology available to solve the problem or accommodate the new opportunity?
2. Would the system as proposed be accepted and used by the intended users?
3. Are the benefits of developing the appropriate information system greater than the costs?

The analyst must determine if the technology exists to create the desired system. The analyst doesn't need to be a technical expert, but he or she does need a general background and knowledge of sources where technological information can be obtained.

It is important for the analyst to design a system that fits the users' capabilities. A very technical and complex system may seem like the best solution to a problem, but it is worthless if the users cannot operate it, are intimidated by it, or are reluctant to use it.

A **cost-to-benefit study** is conducted by the analyst to identify the anticipated benefits, as well as any anticipated costs to the organization. The study determines how the system will be beneficial in terms of decreased costs or increased profits.

Data Gathering

If the project survives the feasibility study, the system analyst gathers data about the current system and the users' needs from both internal and external sources. External sources include trade journals, competing organizations, suppliers, and any other source outside the organization. Internal data sources include employees, managers, and any internally generated business documents such as operator's manuals, financial statements, and job descriptions.

Employees and managers may be personally interviewed or observed to determine how a job is really done. If you are involved in the analysis, you might be asked to keep a diary or to fill out a questionnaire. Although these can be effective data-gathering tools, there are dangers if they are used improperly. Observations can be incomplete or interpreted incorrectly. Diaries take a lot of time, and some may refuse to keep them or keep inadequate records that are of little use to the system analyst. Interviews require the analyst to have a high level of people-oriented skills, and questionnaires must be structured properly so they can be answered and so everyone interprets the questions the same way.

Data Analysis and Logical Design Development

After all pertinent data have been gathered by the system analyst, they are analyzed and the logical design of the system is developed. A **logical design,** which shows the flow of data through an information system, consists of two general steps: (1) determining the purpose and objectives of an information system and (2) determining the outputs, inputs, and processing requirements of the system from the users' points of view without concern for how the requirements will be physically accomplished. Any anticipated conditions that may cause changes later are also noted at this time.

The users and the analyst work together to determine the logical design of the new system. Each system requirement can be checked immediately to ensure that the users' needs are being met. You, as a representative user, would be an expert about the results the system must provide.

The analyst may use a flowchart to diagram the system's logical operations. A **flowchart** is a tool comprised of standardized symbols for showing the components of a system or the steps in solving a problem. System flowcharts and program flowcharts are the two basic types of flowcharts. A **system flowchart** graphically illustrates the types of hardware devices and storage media that are required to physically implement a logical design for an information system. System flowcharts use a set of standardized symbols (Figure 7.4). Figure 7.5 is an example of a system flowchart. **Program flowcharts,** discussed in the next chapter, illustrate the operations performed by the software.

Once the logical design is complete, a formal report with the analyst's recommendations is presented to management. This report is often accompa-

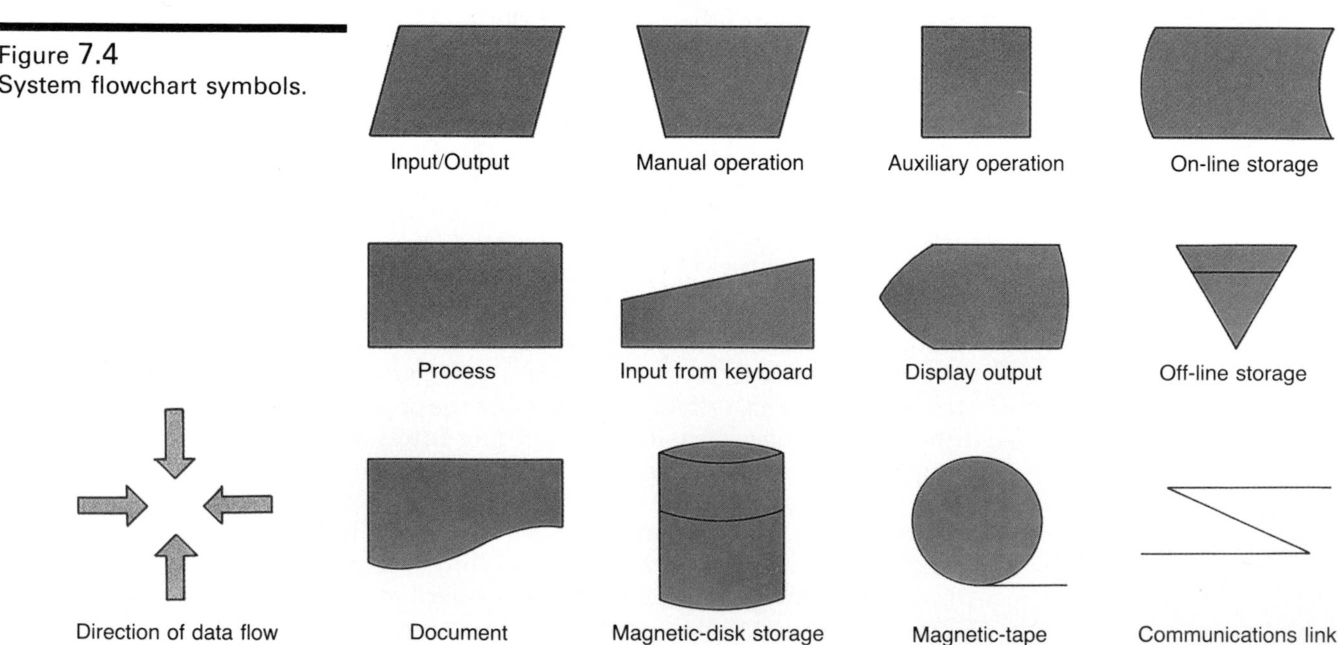

Figure 7.4
System flowchart symbols.

nied by an oral presentation to all involved parties. The report is reviewed by management in light of the feasibility study. Management then decides whether to (1) continue to the system design step, (2) repeat the system analysis step, or (3) terminate the project. If management decides to continue to the next step, the system analyst or system designer now proceeds with the system design.

SYSTEM DESIGN

System design involves the details of the physical design of the system; it is the *how* of the process. Once the logical design is outlined during system analysis, the analyst or a designer determines the physical design, which describes the hardware, the software, and the operating procedures required to make the system operational.

The analyst may develop a **prototype,** or stripped-down model, of the final system during this phase. The prototype does not contain the frills of the final version, but it allows the analyst or the users to evaluate the basic operation or suitability of the system.

The types of hardware and software needed to produce the output are identified and their costs are determined. For example, the analyst may decide that microcomputers rather than mainframes are appropriate, but specific brands or models are not identified until the system development stage.

Next, the inputs that were described in the system analysis are evaluated and appropriate corrections or changes are made. Once the input data have been verified, the designer works with the user to design the input screens, determine whether data will be entered in a batch mode or as source data, and design any paper forms that will be used to write on or code input data.

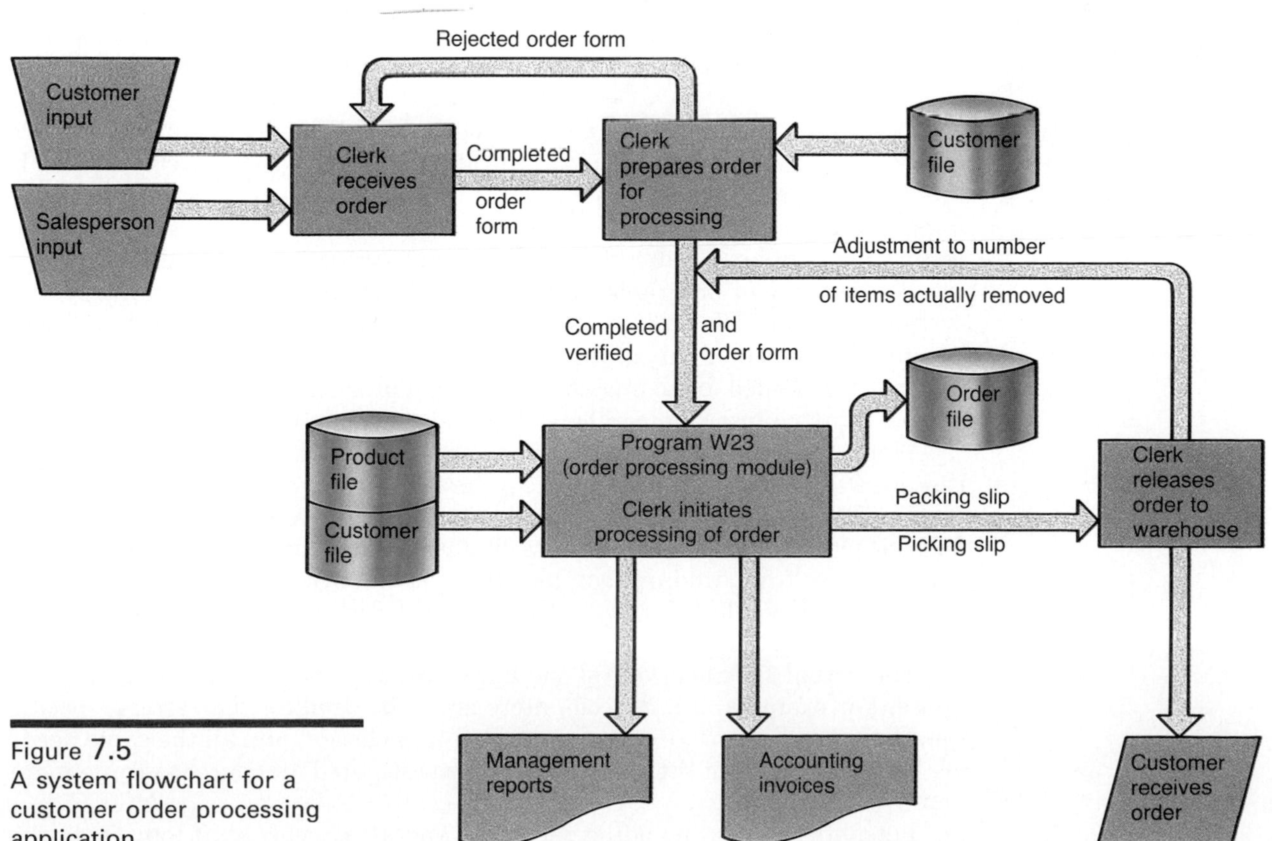

Figure 7.5
A system flowchart for a customer order processing application.

The designer then plans the required processing steps. These steps involve two basic tasks: developing the file design and the software design.

A **file design** shows the way data in the logical design are organized, stored, and controlled. The analyst consults users and system personnel to determine how data will be organized into fields, records, and files. The file design needs to reflect the specific needs of the system's users, but it also must consider the best way to make information available throughout the entire system when necessary. The designer also plans control procedures to protect against errors that may occur in the information system.

After the file design has been completed, the software design is developed. **Software design** involves designing the specific processing steps for programs to ensure that the available input will produce the desired output. The design should be easy to understand and maintain by others. Software development is discussed in more detail in the next chapter.

During this stage, work is also begun on the procedures to test the information system during the development and implementation steps. Procedures are established at this point because, later in the development and implementation steps, there is often a great deal of pressure to get a system installed and running as soon as possible. If testing procedures have not already been designed, they are often done haphazardly or not at all.

After the physical design of the system has been determined, a report containing all the system analysis and design work is submitted to management. This report is reviewed in light of the original feasibility study. Management may choose to (1) proceed to the system development phase, (2) redo the system analysis and/or system design, or (3) terminate the project.

SYSTEM DEVELOPMENT

System development refers to creating the new information system from the physical designs established in the preceding phase. The system analyst first determines if a suitable prewritten software package exists that can be purchased to implement the physical design, or if new programs must be developed.

Depending on the system design and the users' needs, packaged software may be available. Packaged software is usually general in nature because it is intended for a wide range of users. If this type of package is chosen, the analyst must make sure it completely fulfills the requirements of the users. Development time is greatly reduced if prewritten software can be used.

If a new set of programs must be written to implement the system, the system designer calls on a computer programmer to code the program. Documentation from the analysis and design stages gives the programmer all the information needed for coding. When coding a program, the programmer must ensure that the program can be easily understood and maintained.

When the programs are completed, they are tested using actual data from the users and test data from system personnel to test the extremes of the system. To be sure mistakes can be detected by the system, the tests are performed not only with accurate data, but also with data that contain errors. During these tests, and, in fact, anywhere in the system life cycle, modifications can be made to the design. However, the further into the cycle that the modification occurs, the more expensive and time consuming it's likely to be.

The actual specifications of the hardware are also developed during this phase. For example, if microcomputers are to be used for the system, specific types are selected now. Printers or plotters are chosen, and all the cable needs are finalized. Costs of the equipment are investigated and purchase orders are approved.

Personnel needs, including the users and all support staff to operate the information system, are also determined at this time.

Again, a report of recommendations is compiled and presented to management and users. After all the involved participants agree, the next stage—system implementation—can begin.

SYSTEM IMPLEMENTATION

System implementation involves installing the system in the users' computers, testing the installed system, converting from the old system to the new one, and training the users.

Testing

Testing actually should take place during each stage of system development. During system implementation, however, the system is tested as a whole rather than in parts. The hardware, software, and all other elements of the system must perform as well during normal, everyday processing as they did in the controlled tests.

The users evaluate the new system as they compare it with the old one. At this point, any minor flaws can still be detected and corrected. (For a brief historical footnote on testing, see Figure 7.6.) If the new system performs well and is accepted, the process of replacing the old system begins.

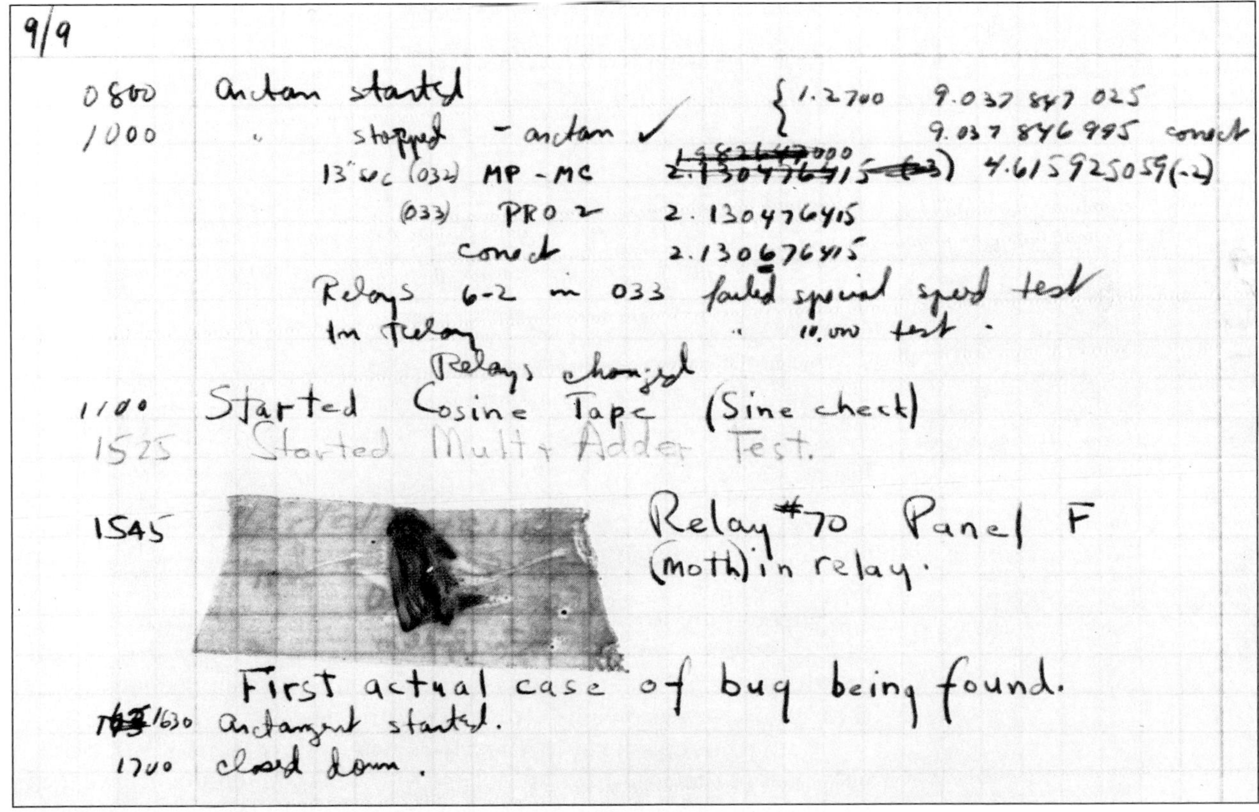

Figure 7.6
Grace Hopper relates the story that in 1945, she and a team of programmers were working on the Mark II when the computer simply quit. They couldn't determine what was wrong. Finally, they looked inside the computer and saw a large, dead moth in one of the signal relays. The moth, the first computer "bug," was removed and saved for posterity in a log book now located at the U.S. Naval Museum in Dahlgren, Virginia. After that incident, when naval officers checked on progress when a computer was not operating, the personnel advised that they were "debugging the program." (U.S. Navy photo)

Figure 7.7
Four conversion strategies for information systems.

Direct Conversion

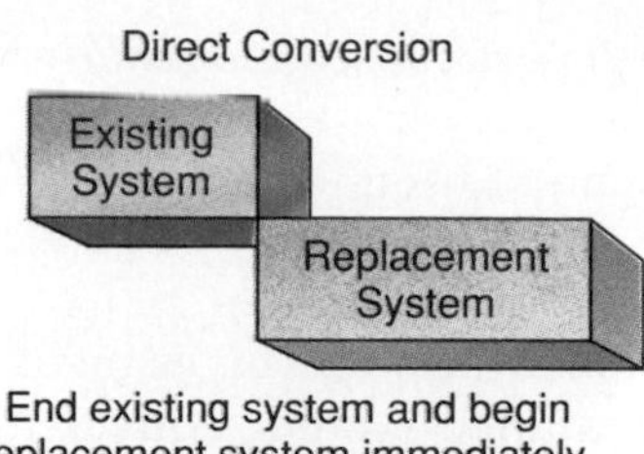

End existing system and begin replacement system immediately.

Pilot Conversion

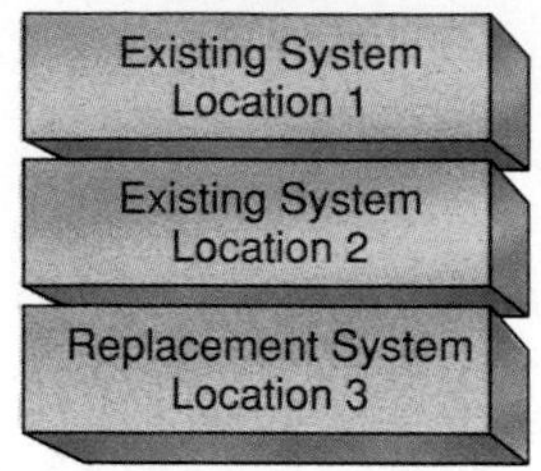

Replacement system is installed in one location and tried out before being installed in other locations.

Phased-In Conversion

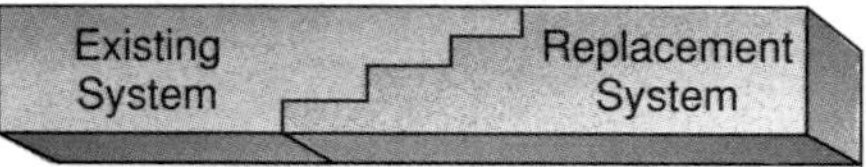

Gradually phase out existing system as replacement system is gradually phased in.

Parallel Conversion

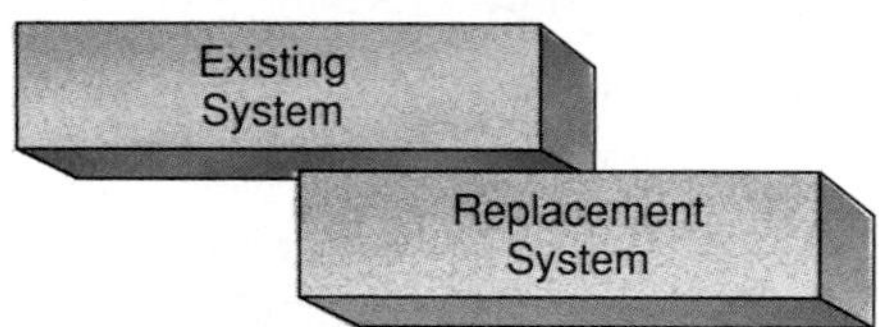

Existing system and replacement system are both run for a specified period of time and then the existing system is dropped.

Conversion

Conversion is the process of changing over from the old system to the new one. This changeover can take one of four basic forms: direct, pilot, phased, or parallel.

Direct conversion is the immediate changeover that results by dismantling the old system as soon as the new one starts operating (Figure 7.7). A disadvantage to this method is that there is no temporary backup in the event that unforeseen problems still exist with the new system.

With **pilot conversion,** the entire new system is installed, but it is used in only part of the organization's operation. This conversion allows users to fully evaluate the system and train employees while still operating the rest of the business or organization on the old system.

Phased conversion is the implementation of only part of the new system at one time. During phased conversion, the entire system is slowly introduced, piece by piece, over a period of time. This process of conversion takes longer but minimizes the risks of fully committing to a new system.

Parallel conversion is the operation of the old system and the new system alongside each other. The cost of running two systems simultaneously may be high, but this type of conversion allows for direct comparison, and the users do not have to worry about shutdowns if the new system fails to perform.

Training

Even the most highly developed system will not benefit the users if no one can operate it. Training programs and manuals should address all levels of personnel involved with the new system. Managers should learn what the system can do for them and their organization. Operators need training in how to enter data, how to retrieve data stored in files, and even how to fix a paper jam in a printer.

Once the system is installed and operating, it enters the system maintenance stage of the system life cycle.

SYSTEM MAINTENANCE

System maintenance is the ongoing process of monitoring and evaluating the new system. Computer technology and business and organizational needs are constantly changing; therefore, an information system may need to be updated periodically to keep it current and ensure that it continues to meet the users' needs.

System maintenance involves identifying the need for change in the current system and making the appropriate changes. Even the best-designed system may some day need to be replaced. When a problem or new opportunity is discovered, the system analysis phase of the system life cycle begins again.

MANAGEMENT INFORMATION SYSTEMS

To run a successful business or organization, the people in charge must continually make decisions based not only on current information about their organization but also on information about the rest of the world. Managers often use an information system to help them plan, organize, and direct their organization. If information is wrong, late, lengthy, or confusing, their decisions might be in error or not be made at all. Such blunders could cause a business to lose profits or fail altogether.

With the use of computers, information can be produced and disseminated faster than ever before. However, managers don't have time to sort through every piece of paper that comes into their offices.

An information system that supplies information specifically to help managers make better decisions is called a **management information system** (MIS). Each element is part of a total concept of integrated resources used by an organization to reach its goals and objectives. In the past, an MIS was simply a system in which managers talked, discussed, and shared information about their departments to help them make decisions. A modern MIS uses computers to generate reports from data stored about the organization's daily activities and provides them to managers in a timely fashion. The computer itself does not make the decisions; however, by using an MIS, a manager can access information more readily and make informed decisions faster.

The data used in an MIS must be stored in an organized way. If data are unorganized, they become impossible to retrieve and use in an efficient and timely manner, rendering the MIS virtually useless. To ensure that data retrieval is uncomplicated and timely, data may be stored in a database.

MANAGERS AND INFORMATION NEEDS

In an organization, decisions are made at all levels of management. Each level has its own needs for specific types of information to handle its own unique problems.

A manager is responsible for using available resources, including people, materials, and money, to achieve an organizational goal. For example, the overall organizational goal in business is usually to increase profits or reduce expenses. A manager works toward this goal through the four major functions of planning, organizing, directing, and controlling resources.

Planning is the process of developing courses of action to meet short- and long-term goals of the organization. **Organizing** involves assembling people, materials, and money, and providing a structure in which personnel are responsible and accountable in working toward the organizational goal. Supplying leadership in supervising personnel through communication and motivation is the process of **directing,** and **controlling** involves making sure the organization is moving toward its goal. Evaluations are made of the organization's performance, and if needed, plans are provided for modifications.

Management Levels

Management is divided into three levels: top-level managers, middle-level managers, and low-level managers (Figure 7.8). Each level is involved to varying degrees in each of the four management functions and each requires different types of information to reach its goals. Let's look at the types of decisions and at some of the information needs of each level of management. Note that the amount of detail required by a manager increases from the top level downward. The higher the level of manager, the broader and less detailed the information needs to be.

Top-Level Managers

Top-level managers, or strategic managers, make decisions involving the long-range, or strategic, goals of the organization. Of the four major functions of a manager, top-level managers spend most of their time planning and organizing. They need summarized information covering past and present operations and information projecting the future. This information is drawn from internal and external sources.

Middle-Level Managers

Middle-level managers, or tactical managers, divide their time among all four general duties of management and are concerned with short-term, tactical

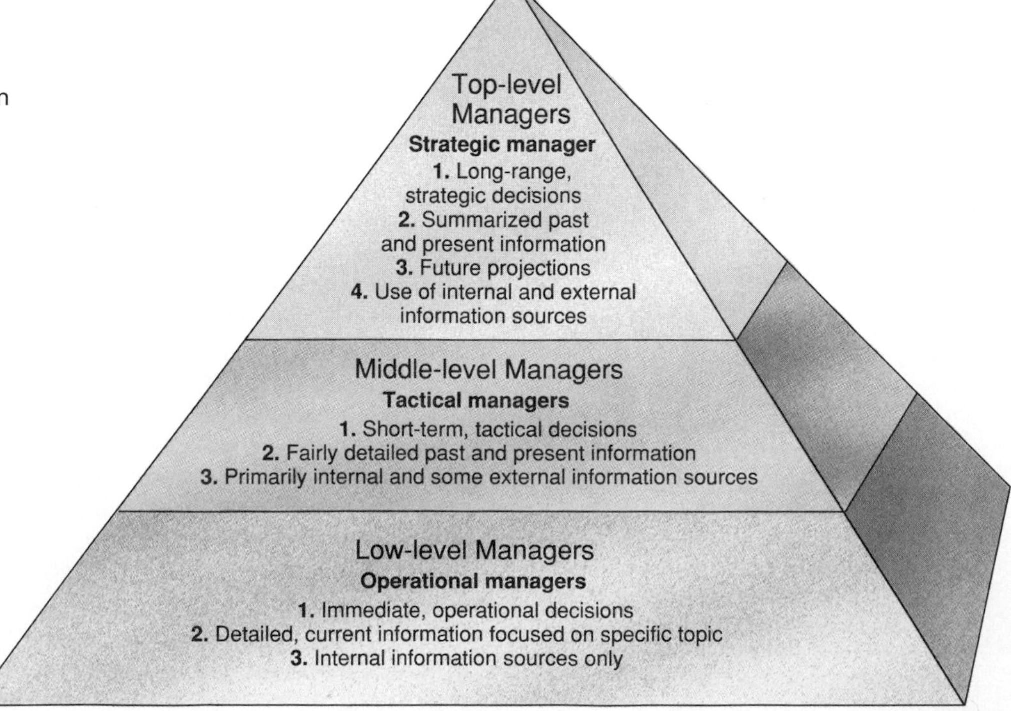

Figure 7.8
Management is divided into three levels, each of which requires different information to reach its goals. Higher managerial levels require broader, less detailed information than the lower level.

decisions. Their decisions are directed toward accomplishing the overall organizational goals established by top-level managers. Because they work on such tasks as budgets, schedules, and performance evaluations, they need information that is fairly detailed to compare present and past results and make adjustments where necessary. They mainly require internally generated information, but also use some external information.

Low-Level Managers

Low-level managers, or operational managers, are involved directly with the day-to-day operations of the business. They see that the tactical decisions of the middle-level managers are implemented by directing personnel at the operations level. Their information must be detailed, current, and focused on a specific topic. It comes from sources such as inventory lists, historical records, and procedures manuals.

Information Quality, Value, and Cost

Although all three levels of management work toward the organizational goals of the business, each requires different types of information, usually in the form of reports. Even when an MIS supplies a report, there is no guarantee it will be useful. For the document to have value in the decision-making process, the information must be timely, complete, free from inaccuracies, and communicated to the person who needs it. Reports from an MIS should be concise and contain only the information that the manager needs to make the decision. Too often, managers are flooded with reams of paper that only confuse the issue at hand.

As Grace Hopper points out in her lectures, in addition to the quality of information provided, the value and cost of keeping the information should be carefully evaluated. Hopper states that emphasis should be placed on examining the total information flow through an organization, activity, or company, and decisions should be made about which information is the most valuable. Then, the best equipment should be used with the most valuable information.

Hopper also states that information tends to lose its value over time, but the cost of storing and maintaining that information increases the longer it is kept. She suggests that users look more closely at information to see if it really needs to be stored; if not, get rid of it to reduce costs.

DECISION SUPPORT SYSTEMS

An MIS provides managers with primarily historical information in formats that were predefined at the time the system was originally created. A **decision support system** (DSS) is an extension of an MIS. It complements an MIS by allowing managers to determine what information they need, the processing to be done, and the format of the output. The emphasis is shifted from only supplying information about what has happened to allowing the manager to ask "what if" questions in order to predict what might happen in the future under certain circumstances. In other words, a DSS provides an information and planning model for managers (Figure 7.9).

A DSS can help middle- and top-level managers make decisions about nonroutine and unstructured problems; this is why computers are found on the desks of more and more executives. A DSS uses sophisticated software that simulates potential outcomes using analysis and modeling. Data can be drawn from the computer database, external sources, or both. The DSS does not actually make the decision, but it can help predict outcomes for given situations.

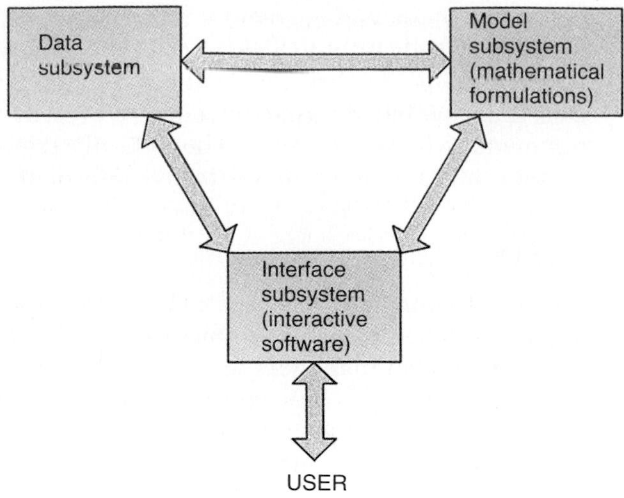

Figure 7.9
Relationship of components of a decision support system (DSS).

EXPERT SYSTEMS

A new type of support system being employed in business is the expert system. An outgrowth of studies in artificial intelligence, **expert systems** are based on the knowledge of a human expert. The person's expertise is put into the form of a program which a computer uses to mimic the human expert's ability to solve a particular type of problem.

An expert system has three parts: the user interface, an inference engine, and stored expertise. The **user interface** helps guide the user through the system's need for basic data and operations. The **inference engine** is actually the software that processes the commands and data; it performs the process that simulates the reasoning of a human expert. The reasoning may go on during the input process where input of some specific data or command causes the system to take one course of action versus another. To do this, the system

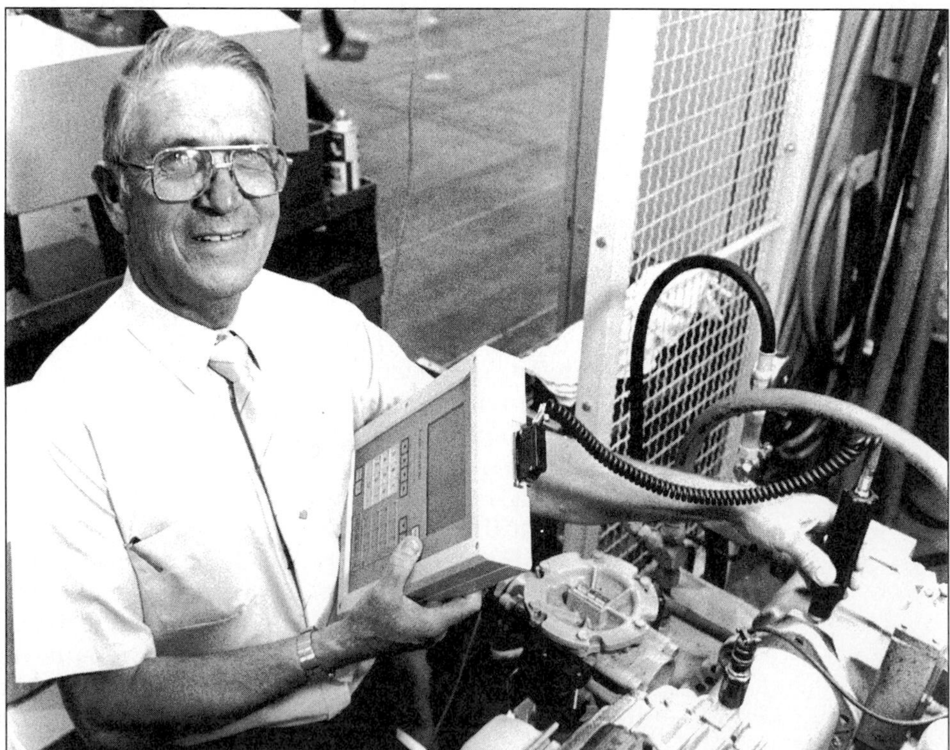

Figure 7.10
"Charlie" is General Motor's expert system for machine maintenance, named for the human expert whose knowledge the computer uses.

(Courtesy The Saginaw News)

relies on the **stored expertise,** which consists essentially of rules of behavior that capture some specific piece of knowledge and the way to deal with it.

There are many instances in which expert systems technology can help you to work more efficiently and accurately. Consumer loan processing, for example, can be done in large part by analyzing basic data supplied by a customer. If the customer's data fit a particular profile, the loan might be processed without further examination. Tax advice, which is certainly based on the application of rules to basic data, is another area where expert systems are being developed.

One interesting application of expert systems, called Charlie, was developed by General Motors. It seems that GM's top maintenance person, Charlie, was due to retire, but no one wanted to lose his years of valuable knowledge and expertise. So, for a period of time prior to retirement, system analysts followed Charlie on his rounds. Every time Charlie worked on a machine, they listed the logic he used, the tests he performed, and the nature of the problem he diagnosed. Eventually, the analysts were able to store Charlie's expertise and develop a computer-based system to help with machinery maintenance (Figure 7.10). So, though Charlie is now retired, his legacy remains in the form of an expert system that helps to keep GM running.

Summary

- An information system is a combination of people, data, and procedures needed to create and distribute information throughout an organization. Many information systems include a computer.
- A system life cycle is the life span of an information system; it consists of five stages: system analysis, system design, system development, system implementation, and system maintenance.
- Documentation, an important means of communication throughout the cycle, is the written or graphic record of the steps carried out during the life cycle of an information system.
- System analysis is the process of analyzing a system and trying to find a way to modify it or to create a new system to meet users' needs.
- A feasibility study is a preliminary study to determine if the information system should be developed. A cost-to-benefit study is conducted by the analyst to identify the anticipated benefits, as well as any anticipated costs, to the organization.
- A logical design shows the flow of data through an information system.
- A flowchart is a tool comprised of standardized symbols for showing the components of a system or the steps in solving a problem.
- System design involves the details of the physical design of the system; it is the *how* of the process.
- A prototype, or stripped-down model, of the final system does not contain the frills of the final version, but it allows the analyst or the users to evaluate the basic operation or suitability of the system.
- File design shows the way data in the logical design are organized, stored, and controlled.
- Software design involves designing the specific processing steps for programs to ensure that the available input will produce the desired output.
- System development refers to creating the new information system from the physical designs established in the software design phase.
- System implementation involves installing the system in the users' computers, testing the installed system, converting from the old system to the new one, and training the users.
- Testing is a process of testing the completed system design as a whole rather than in parts. The hardware, software, and all other elements of the system must perform as well during normal, everyday processing as they did in the controlled tests of each part of the system.
- Conversion is the process of changing over from the old system to the new one. This changeover can take one of four basic forms: direct, pilot, phased, or parallel.
- Direct conversion is the immediate changeover that results by dismantling the old system as soon as the new one starts operating.
- Pilot conversion defines a conversion where the entire new system is installed, but it is used in only part of the organization's operation.
- Phased conversion is the implementation of only part of the new system at one time. During phased conversion, the entire system is slowly introduced, piece by piece, over a period of time.

- Parallel conversion is the operation of the old system and the new system alongside each other.
- Training programs and manuals should address all levels of personnel involved with the new system.
- System maintenance is the ongoing process of monitoring and evaluating the new system.
- An information system that is used by top-level managers to make decisions about nonroutine and unstructured problems is a decision support system (DSS).
- Expert systems are based on the knowledge of a human expert. The person's expertise is put into the form of a program which a computer uses to mimic the human expert's ability to solve a particular type of problem.

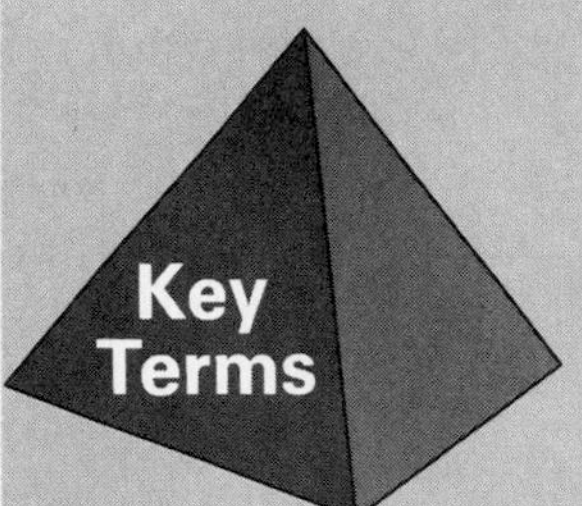

System life cycle
Programmer
Documentation
Feasibility study
Cost-to-benefit study
Logical design
Flowchart
Management information system
Decision support system
Expert system
User interface

Review Questions

1. What is a system? What is the purpose of an information system?
2. Describe the system life cycle.
3. What is documentation? Describe its function in the system life cycle.
4. What is the purpose of a system analysis?
5. Discuss the three concerns that are addressed during a feasibility study.
6. What are the two general steps in developing the logical design of an information system?
7. What happens during the system design stage?
8. What are prototypes and why are they developed?
9. Why should the testing procedures used in the development and implementation phases be designed during the system design stage?
10. What happens during the system development stage?
11. List the three steps involved in the system implementation stage.
12. List and discuss the four basic types of conversion.
13. Why is it important that users be involved in the system life cycle?
14. What is the purpose of system maintenance?
15. Describe a management information system.
16. Describe the role of a manager in an organization.
17. List the three levels of managers and discuss the types of decisions they make.
18. What are some of the factors that determine the quality of information and make it useful to management?
19. Why is it important to examine the quality and value of information generated by an MIS?
20. What is a decision support system and how is it related to a management information system?
21. Which is more appropriate for a manager who needs to make decisions that affect the future—an MIS or a DSS? Why?
22. Describe two ways microcomputers are being incorporated as part of an MIS or a DSS.
23. What is an expert system and how is it used?
24. Describe the three parts of an expert system.

PROFILE

EDSGER DIJKSTRA

(Photo and booklet courtesy of Edsger Dijkstra)

Since the days of the earliest programming efforts, programmers assumed that errors were something that they always had to contend with; some mistakes couldn't be discovered until the program was tested or put into actual use. Edsger Dijkstra (pronounced dike-stra) never had much sympathy for this viewpoint.

The Dutch scientist believes that programs should be written on a mathematical basis that increases the precision and reduces the randomness of results. His approach to the problem is called structured programming.

Born in 1930 in Rotterdam, Dijkstra is the son of a father who was a chemist and a mother who was a mathematician. After completing studies at the University of Leiden in 1948, Dijkstra planned to become a theoretical physicist. Fate intervened, however, when his father happened to see an advertisement in a science journal, *Nature,* for a summer school course on computing to be held in Cambridge, England.

The computer used for the class was the EDSAC, the first automatic electronic computer in Europe. At the time, Dijkstra did not know what an automatic electronic computer was. His curiosity and the thought that this invention might be something of interest to him as a theoretical physicist sent him to England. Although he eventually received his master's degree in physics, Dijkstra decided to pursue programming and became the Netherlands' first professional programmer.

During the late 1960s, when Dijkstra came under fire from his colleagues for his unconventional notions about programming, he started writing his "Notes on Structured Programming." He showed how programs can be structured to lessen their complexity. He advocated the creation of programs that did not rely on the use of unconditional branch instruction (the GOTO statement), and he argued that by using three programming structures—sequence, selection, and repetition—any program could be written without GOTO statements.

To disseminate his ideas, Dijkstra began writing and distributing a series of newsletters on his theories and observations to prominent members of the computing community throughout the world. Ultimately, the programming community at large began to discover the advantages of structured programming. Dijkstra had laid the foundation for turning programming into a science.

Dijkstra has since returned to the question that had originally prompted his programming research: Why not prove programs correct? He believes it is possible and continues to work on a method that would allow even a large, complex program to be proven error-free mathematically.

CHAPTER 8

PROGRAMMING CONCEPTS AND LANGUAGES

IN THIS CHAPTER YOU WILL LEARN ABOUT

- **Methods for designing good programs**
- **The process of developing a program**
- **The use of programming languages**
- **Examples of various programming languages**

GETTING TO THE NITTY-GRITTY

Programming can take place in the development phase of the system life cycle or at any other time a computer needs to be given instructions. Recall that a program, or software, is the series of instructions that directs the hardware to perform various tasks. In Chapter 2 you studied the two types of software—system and application—and learned that software can be purchased prewritten, or can be written by users or computer professionals.

This chapter explains *how* those instructions are developed using structured programming concepts and the program development process. In addition, programming languages, which provide instructions for a computer to perform specific operations, are described.

QUALITIES OF A GOOD PROGRAM

Several characteristics are essential for a program to be called good. A program must be correct; that is, it must do what it was designed to do in accordance with the specifications laid out when it was designed. A program should also be designed so that anyone who works with it finds its logic easy to understand, and so that program maintenance and updating can be done with relative ease. A program should run efficiently by executing instructions quickly and by using computer resources such as primary storage conservatively. Reliability is another important factor; a program must be able to operate under unforeseen circumstances, such as recovering from invalid data entries. Finally, a program needs to be flexible so it can operate with a wide range of legitimate input. For example, if a program requests a "yes" or "no" answer, it should be able to accept as valid entries any combination of capital and lowercase letters for the words *yes* and *no* in addition to the single letters Y, y, N, or n. Structured programming concepts can help a programmer achieve these qualities in a program.

STRUCTURED PROGRAMMING CONCEPTS

As uses for computers become more sophisticated, the software required to accomplish tasks becomes more complicated. Because of this complexity, a method to control the development of a program and assure its quality is essential.

Structured programming is a methodology that stresses the systematic design, development, and management of the program development process. The overall goals of structured programming can be separated into three elements:

1. Decrease development time by increasing programmer productivity and reducing the time to test and debug a program.
2. Decrease maintenance costs by reducing errors and by making programs easier to understand by making them less complex.
3. Improve the quality of software by providing programs with fewer errors.

Structured programming attempts to accomplish these goals by incorporating the following concepts:

1. Use of only the sequence, selection, and repetition control structures
2. Top-down design and use of modules
3. Management control

Control Structures

A **control structure** is a device in a programming language that determines the order of execution of statements in a program. Computer scientists suggest

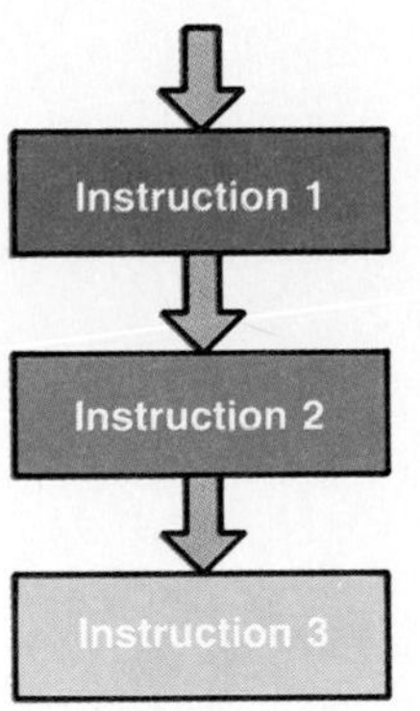

Figure 8.1
Sequence control structure.

that only three control structures are necessary for the design of any logical process: sequence, selection, and repetition.

A **sequence** control structure executes statements one after another in a linear fashion as illustrated in Figure 8.1. This is the sequence in which the computer will perform operations if no other directions are given.

A **selection,** or IF-THEN-ELSE, control structure presents two processing options. The option chosen depends on the result of the decision criterion, which is a relationship based on the comparison of data. The decision point is indicated by the diamond-shaped symbol, and it represents a question or comparison that can be answered either "true" or "false." Figure 8.2 depicts some variations of the selection control structure. In this structure, a "true" answer to the criterion results in action A, but a "false" answer results in action B.

A **repetition** control structure (also called **looping**) is used to execute an instruction or group of instructions more than once without the programmer having to recode them. The two basic variations of this type of structure are **DO WHILE** and **DO UNTIL.** The diamond-shaped decision criterion is similar to that used in the selection structure, and may be answered only "true" or "false."

If the decision criterion is placed before the statements to be repeated, then it is a DO WHILE loop as shown in Figure 8.3a. Figure 8.3b illustrates that a DO UNTIL loop places the decision criterion at the end of the statements to be repeated. In this structure, the statements are always executed at least once.

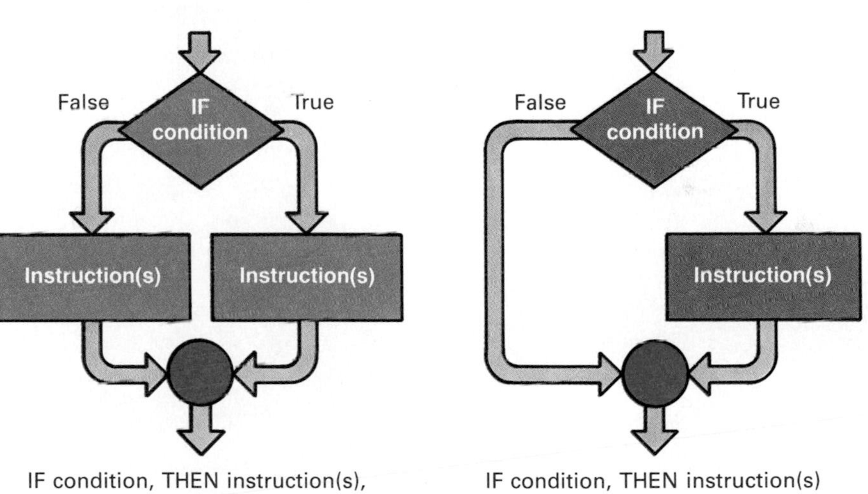

Figure 8.2
Selection, or IF-THEN-ELSE, structure.

Understanding Data Relationships

The selection and repetition structures you use in a program depend on your understanding of relationships of data. Data comparisons are based on equalities or inequalities (see Figure 8.4 on page C-149). If two data items are exactly the same, they are equal. It is easy to understand that if two fields contain the same number, they are equal. It is also true that two fields containing the letter "A" would be equal, but if one field contained "A" while another had "a," they would be unequal. You can also test for inequalities such as one field being greater than or less than another. These tests can be done for both numeric and non-numeric data; non-numeric data are evaluated based on the internal machine-language representation of the characters. For example, the space character has a lower value than the letter "A."

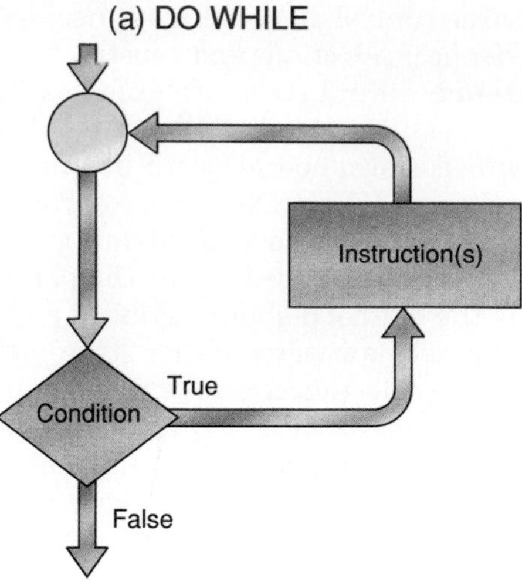

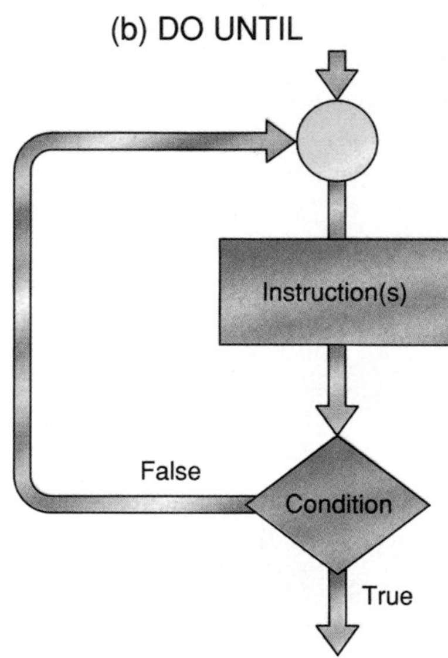

Figure 8.3
Repetition, or looping, structure.

Avoiding GOTOs

A fourth type of instruction that was often used in early programming was the unconditional branch. In many programming languages, this structure took the form of a GOTO statement, which allowed the execution of a program to jump indiscriminately to other points in the program. Programs designed with several of these unconditional branches were very confusing and difficult to follow, thereby earning them the name "spaghetti code."

The use of only the sequence, selection, and repetition (looping) structures and avoidance of unconditional branching are steps toward a structured programming methodology.

Top-Down Design and Modules

Top-down design is a concept by which the programmer starts with the major functions involved in a problem and divides them into subfunctions until the problem has been divided as much as possible. Top-down design involves three major steps:

Figure 8.4
Relational operators used in data relationships.

Operator	Relationship
=	Equality
< >	Inequality
<	Less than
>	Greater than
< =	Less than or equal to
> =	Greater than or equal to

1. Defining the output, input, and major processing steps required
2. Step-by-step refining of the major processing steps
3. Designing the algorithms

The first step involves three separate processes. First, the desired outputs are defined; second, the required inputs are determined; and finally, the major processing tasks are determined.

In the second step, each major processing task is broken down into smaller and smaller tasks until it cannot be broken down any further (Figure 8.5). This process forces an examination of all aspects of a problem at one level before starting on the next level. The programmer is left with **modules,** or groups, of processing instructions that are easy to write and understand. A program broken into smaller modules is easier to read, test, and maintain. Working from the top down (the general to the specific) rather than the bottom up (the specific to the general) avoids designing partial solutions that deal with only part of the problem.

The third step is designing the algorithm for each module. An algorithm is the finite set of step-by-step instructions that solve a problem.

In many cases, top-down design has resulted in a lower error rate and shorter program development time.

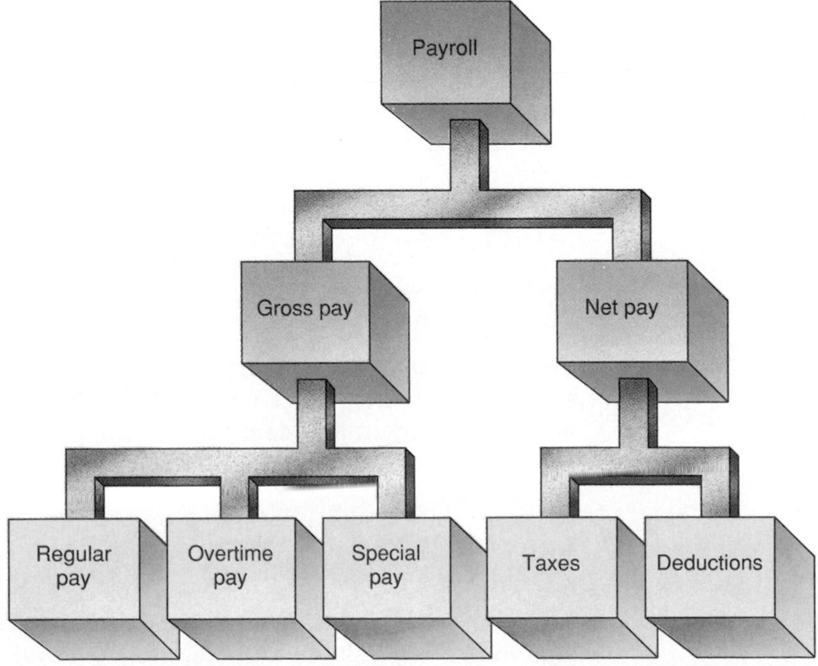

Figure 8.5
Top-down design is accomplished by breaking down major tasks into smaller, more manageable tasks.

Management Control

Management control is an essential part of the structured programming concept. Proper supervision of the programming process prevents the project from being sidetracked, keeps it on schedule, and assures that users' needs are being met.

When many people are involved with the design and development of a large program, different ideas and styles surface. To provide consistency and coordinate all work, a **chief programmer team** is established. The team consists of a number of specialized personnel to design and develop a program. The type of specialists may vary depending on the project. A typical team might consist of a chief programmer, assistant programmer, librarian, and other specialists as needed.

The chief programmer defines and assigns portions of the program development to various team members and takes responsibility for the project. He or she reviews each member's work, coordinates the integration of the work, and serves as liaison between management and the project. It is the chief programmer's responsibility to make sure appropriate personnel are on the team and to make changes or additions to the team as needed.

One technique the chief programmer team may use before beginning to code (write) a program is a **structured walkthrough**—a meeting of a system analyst, user(s), and possibly other system personnel. The system analyst discusses or "walks through" the program design with the other team members. The rationale behind the walkthrough is to "force" the analyst to explain the design to others with the expectation that errors will be caught and corrected before programming begins.

PROGRAM DEVELOPMENT PROCESS

The program development process is a recommended series of steps to follow when developing a program. The process consists of four steps:

1. Defining the problem
2. Designing the algorithm
3. Coding the program
4. Testing and debugging the program

This list does not include documentation as a separate step; however, documentation is an important requirement throughout all the steps. Documentation, as it relates to programming, is the text or graphics that provides specific instructions about, or records the purpose or function of, a particular step or instruction in a program. Although each step in the program development process is a separate and distinct process, the steps are all related; in actual practice, there may not be a clear separation between the steps.

Define the Problem

The first step in the program development process is to recognize that there is a problem, identify exactly what the problem is, determine the desired output and needed input, and determine if the problem can be solved by a computer. This is normally a part of the system analysis function described in the previous section.

Design the Algorithm

After the problem has been defined, an algorithm can be designed. Many design aids are available to assist programmers in designing and documenting an algorithm. Two common ones are flowcharts and pseudocode.

A flowchart uses standardized symbols to show the components of a system or the steps in solving a problem. System flowcharts, which were discussed in Chapter 7, and program flowcharts are the two basic types. A **program flowchart** graphically details the processing steps of a particular program. Figure 8.6 shows some standard programming flowchart symbols. A program flowchart has several purposes: (1) to clarify the program logic, (2) to identify alternate processing methods available, (3) to serve as a guide for program coding, and (4) to serve as documentation. Figure 8.7 is an example of a program flowchart constructed for a program that checks a client's payment record.

An alternative to flowcharts and another tool used to formulate the processing steps of a program is pseudocode. **Pseudocode** uses English phrases to describe the processing steps of a program or module. Often, the phrases resemble the programming language code, hence the name pseudocode.

Processing steps are expressed in a simple, straightforward manner so that the pseudocode can be easily converted to program code. Most programming departments establish rules and conventions to be followed when using pseudocode so that others will be able to read and interpret it. Figure 8.8 is an example of pseudocode as it might be written for the program in Figure 8.7.

Code the Program

After the solution has been clearly formulated, it is time to code (write) the program. **Coding** a program involves actually writing the instructions in a particular programming language that will tell the computer how to operate.

Test and Debug the Program

Now the program needs to be tested to ensure that it is correct and contains no errors. It is difficult, if not presently impossible, to test a complex program for every condition that may cause an error; however, sufficient tests can be made to be reasonably sure the program is correct and error-free.

Two types of program errors that may be encountered during the testing phase are syntax and logic errors. The syntax of a programming language is the set of rules and conventions to be followed when writing a program; these rules are similar to the grammatical rules of the English language. When these rules are violated, a **syntax error** occurs. All syntax errors must be found and corrected before a program will execute.

Figure 8.6
Program flowchart symbols.

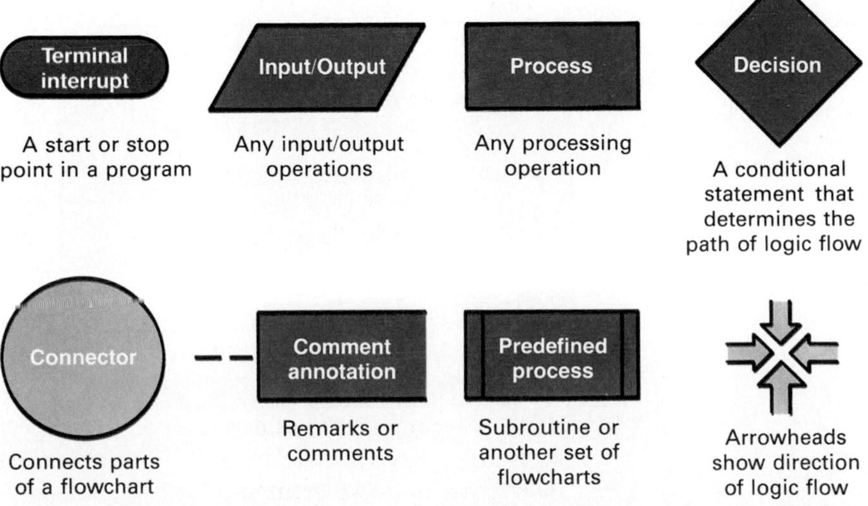

Figure 8.7
Program flowchart for checking a payment record.

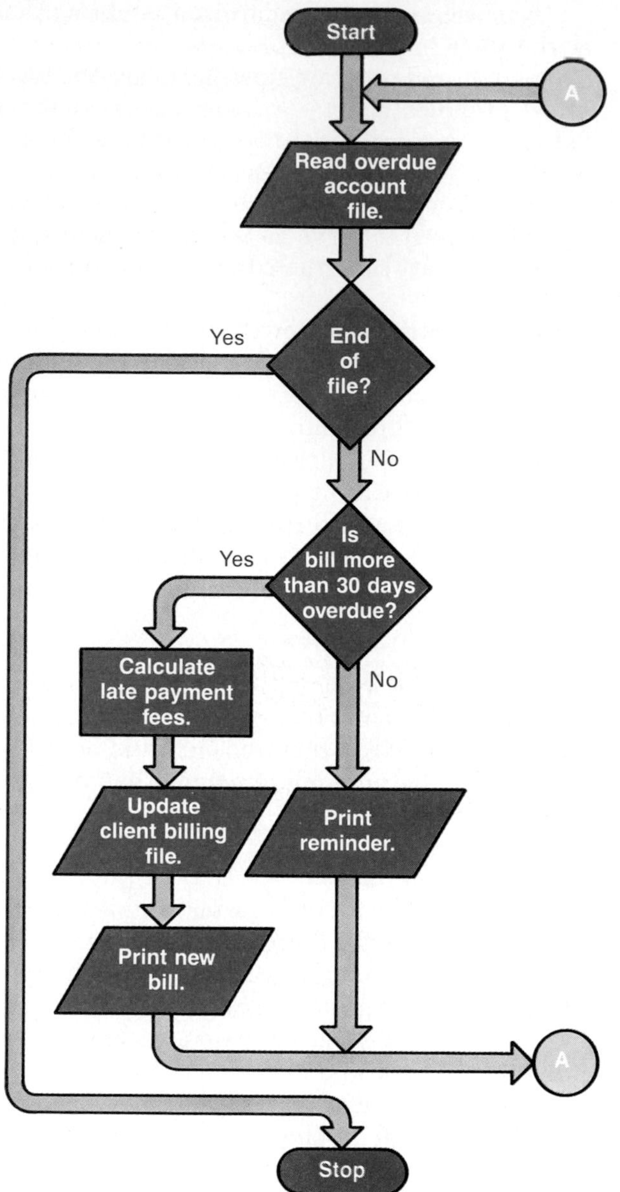

Figure 8.8
Pseudocode for the program shown in the flowchart in Figure 8.7.

```
Begin
  Read overdue billing file.
  DO WHILE not end of file
    IF bill more than 30 days overdue
      THEN
        Calculate late payment fees.
        Update billing file.
        Print new bill.
      ELSE
        Print payment reminder.
    End-if
    Read overdue billing file.
  End
```

The second type of error that may occur is a **logic error.** Perhaps invalid data were entered but the program did not anticipate that event. For example, if a program was set up to expect numeric data, and alphabetic data was entered instead, a poorly designed program would "crash," that is, stop executing. A properly written program would identify the problem, prompt the user with an error message, and permit the data to be reentered.

Another type of logic error, and the most difficult to find, is a logic error that does not stop the execution of the program; however, the results will not be accurate. With luck, the error will be obvious. Often, it is not. Here's a simple example: The problem is to add 2 apples to 4 apples and determine the total number of apples. The formula should be $2 + 4 = 6$. But, what if the wrong symbol, such as a multiplication sign, is typed while entering the program into the computer? Actually, $2 \times 4 = 8$. The answer of 8 is correct for the formula as entered, but not for this problem. Finding the logic error in this example is easy; however, finding a logic error in a complicated program can be like trying to find the proverbial needle in a haystack.

The process of finding any type of error and correcting it is called **debugging.** After a program is debugged, it can be installed and used.

PROGRAMMING LANGUAGES

People use languages such as English, French, German, and Spanish to communicate with one another. Each language consists of sounds and symbols and contains grammatical rules that govern its use. Programming languages are similar. A **programming language** is a set of written symbols that instruct the computer hardware to perform specified tasks. Use of these symbols is governed by a set of rules called syntax.

Of the hundreds of different programming languages available, all fit into one of several general categories: machine language, assembly language, high-level language, fourth-generation language, and object-oriented language.

Machine Language

Machine language is the only programming language that the computer can understand. It is a language made up entirely of 1s and 0s. There is not, however, one universal machine language. The arrangement of 1s and 0s to represent similar instructions, data, and memory locations differs among computers because of different hardware designs.

Machine-language programs have the advantage of very fast execution speeds and efficient use of primary storage. Using machine language to program, however, is tedious, difficult, and time consuming. Machine language is a low-level language. Since every detail of an operation must be indicated by the programmer, a low-level language requires that the programmer have specific knowledge of how the computer works. As you might imagine, it is easy to make an error and very difficult to debug a machine-language program.

Assembly Language

The next higher level of programming languages is assembly language. **Assembly languages** are also low-level languages because detailed knowledge of hardware specifics is still required. They use mnemonics in place of 1s and 0s to represent the operation codes (Figure 8.9). A **mnemonic** is an alphabetic abbreviation used as a memory aid. For example, instead of using a combina-

Assembler code (mnemonics)

```
sseg                  segment stack
                      db 256  dup (?)

sseg                  ends
dseg                  segment
data                  db "2 x 4 =  "

dseg         ends
cseg                  segment
assume       cs:cseg,ds:dseg,ss:sseg,es:nothing
start        proc far
                      push ds
                      mov ax,0
                      push ax
                      call main
start        endp

main                  proc near
                      cld
                      mov ax, dseg
                      mov ds, ax
                      mov ax, 0b000h
                      mov es, ax
                      mov dx, 0
                      mov bx, 0
                      lea si, data
                      mov di, 32848
                      mov al, 02h
                      mov bl, 04h
                      mul bl
                      or al, 30h
                      mov al, data+9
    msgsb:   mov cx,9
    lbl:              movsb
                      inc di
                      mov al, 135
                      mov [di], al
                      loop lbl
main                  endp
cseg                  ends
                      endstart
```

Machine-language instructions

```
0100
110010   100000  1111000  100000  110100  100000
111101   100000  100000
11110
10111000
1010000
11101000
11111100
10111000
10001110  11011000
10111000
10001110  11000000
10111010
10111011
10001101  110110
10111111
10110000  00000010
10110011  00000100
11110110  11100011
00001100  110000
10100000
10111001
10100100
1000111
10110000  10000111
10001000  00000101
11100010  1111000
```

Figure 8.9
Both assembly and machine-language programs can compute and print out the result of 2 × 4. Machine language uses only 1s and 0s; assembly language uses mnemonics.

tion of 1s and 0s to represent an addition operation, the mnemonic AD might be used.

Before they can be used by the computer, assembly languages must be translated into machine language. This conversion is done by a **language-translator program** called an **assembler.** Assembly languages provide an easier, more efficient way to program than machine languages and still maintain control over the internal functions of a computer at the most basic level. The advantages of programming with assembly languages are that they produce programs that are efficient, use less storage, and execute much faster than programs designed using high-level languages.

High-Level Language

High-level languages are languages whose instructions closely resemble human language and mathematical notation. High-level languages do not require the programmer to have detailed knowledge about the internal operations of a computer. Because of their close resemblance to human language, high-level languages are also much easier to learn and use than either machine or assembly languages. Typically, less time and effort are required to program in a high-level language because programming errors are easier to avoid and correct.

High-level languages must be translated into machine language before they can be used by a computer. One of two different language-translator programs is used to translate high-level languages: a compiler or an interpreter. A **compiler** translates a whole program of a high-level language, called the **source code,** at once into machine language before the program is executed. Once converted, the program is stored in machine-readable form, called the **object code.** The object code can be immediately executed anytime thereafter. The source code remains intact after the conversion and can be updated and changed as required, and then recompiled into the object code.

An **interpreter** translates a program into machine language one line at a time, executing each line of the program after it is translated. With most interpreters, the machine-readable form is not stored in primary storage or on secondary-storage media. Therefore, the program must be interpreted each time before it is executed.

Fourth-Generation Language

The different categories of languages are sometimes labeled by generations—from lowest to highest. Machine languages are considered first generation; assembly languages are second generation; and high-level languages are third generation. **Fourth-generation language** is a term that describes a variety of programming languages that allow users to create programs with much less effort than is required by even high-level languages. Fourth-generation languages have several objectives:

1. Increasing the speed with which programs are developed
2. Minimizing users' effort to obtain information from a computer
3. Decreasing the skill level required of users so that they can concentrate on the application rather than on the intricacies of coding, and thus solve their own problems without the aid of a professional programmer
4. Minimizing maintenance by reducing errors and making programs that are easy to change

Depending on the language, the sophistication of fourth-generation languages varies widely. These languages are usually used in conjunction with a database and its data dictionary and are often found as part of an MIS or DSS. Fourth-generation languages include database query languages, report generators, and application generators.

Recall that a database query language permits formulation of queries that relate to several records from one or more files. The appropriate records can then be printed or displayed in a suitable format.

A **report generator** allows data from a database to be extracted and formatted into reports. It also allows substantial arithmetic and logic operations to be performed on the data before they are displayed or printed.

An **application generator** allows data entry and permits the user to specify how the database will be updated, what calculations or logic operations will be performed, and what output will be created.

Object-Oriented Language

A new way of looking at programming, through **object-oriented languages,** views program design somewhat like looking into a box of interconnected parts. Some of the parts are unique to the particular problem being solved, whereas others may be more general in nature. So a library of common, general functions is created to be used as needed by various programs. For example, a general solution can be created which asks you to respond true or false by pressing certain keys. This general method of obtaining a response can then be used in a variety of particular ways—for example, to ask if you want to add a record to a file or to see if you want to exit a program. Similarly, you might construct general solutions for input or output functions, certain mathematical routines, and so on.

Your program thus would consist of a construction of various classes of predefined objects assembled together with an overall controlling logic that guides you through the solution of a particular problem. **Object-oriented programming** (OOP) is seen as a way of increasing programmer productivity while reducing errors.

PROCEDURAL VERSUS NONPROCEDURAL LANGUAGES

Programming languages are classified into two different types: procedural languages and nonprocedural languages. **Procedural languages** specify how something is accomplished. Common procedural languages are BASIC, Pascal, C, Ada, COBOL, and FORTRAN. **Nonprocedural languages** specify what is accomplished without going into the details of how. Database query languages and report generators are examples of nonprocedural languages.

The difference between procedural and nonprocedural languages can be illustrated with the analogy of giving directions to a taxi driver. Directions given using a procedural language approach might be: "Drive 600 yards forward. Turn right. Drive 350 yards forward. Turn left. Drive 500 yards forward. Stop." Using a nonprocedural language approach, you would simply tell the driver: "Take me to the Fairview Hotel."

MAJOR HIGH-LEVEL LANGUAGES

FORTRAN

FORTRAN (FORmula TRANslator) was introduced in 1957 and is the oldest high-level programming language. It was designed primarily for use by scientists, engineers, and mathematicians and is well suited for complex numerical calculations. Figure 8.10 is an example of a FORTRAN program.

COBOL

COBOL (COmmon Business-Oriented Language), developed in the late 1950s, is a widely used programming language for business data processing. It was specifically designed to manipulate the large data files typically encountered in business. Figure 8.11 is a COBOL program.

BASIC

BASIC (Beginner's All-purpose Symbolic Instruction Code) was developed at Dartmouth College in the mid-1960s to provide students with an easy-to-learn, interactive language on a time-sharing computer system. In an interactive language, each statement is translated into machine language and executed as soon as it is typed and entered into the computer. If there is an error in the statement entered, BASIC provides error messages immediately. Because it is easy to learn and use, BASIC became the most popular language for microcomputers and is available for most microcomputers in use today. Figure 8.12 shows a BASIC program.

Figure 8.10
A FORTRAN program that computes and prints the sum and average of ten numbers.

```
C    COMPUTE THE SUM AND AVERAGE OF 10 NUMBERS
C
           REAL NUM, SUM, AVG
           INTEGER TOTNUM, COUNTR
C
           SUM = 0.0
C    INITIALIZE LOOP CONTROL VARIABLE
           COUNTR = 0
           TOTNUM = 10
C
C    LOOP TO READ DATA AND ACCUMULATE SUM
     20 IF (COUNTR .GE. TOTNUM) GO TO 30
           READ, NUM
           SUM = SUM + NUM
C          UPDATE LOOP CONTROL VARIABLE
           COUNTR = COUNTR + 1
           GO TO 20
C    END OF LOOP - COMPUTE AVERAGE
     30 AVG = SUM / TOTNUM
C    PRINT RESULTS
           PRINT, SUM
           PRINT, AVG
           STOP
           END
```

Figure 8.11
This COBOL program performs the same task as the FORTRAN program in Figure 8.10—it computes and prints the sum and average of ten numbers.

```
Data Division.
Working-Storage Section.
01  Variable-Names.
    05  Counter           PIC 9(2)        Value 0.
    05  Total             PIC 9(3)        Value 0.
    05  AVERAGE           PIC 9(2)V9(2)   Value 0.
01  Output-Lines.
    05  Total-Line.
        10  Pic X(20) Value "The Total Amount is ".
        10  TOT-OUT PIC ZZ9.99.
    05  Average-Line.
        10  Pic X(20) Value "The Average amt. is ".
        10  AVG-OUT PIC Z9.99.

Procedure Division.
Main-Program.
    Perform with test after
        Varying Counter from 1 by 1
            Until Counter = 10
                Add 1 to Total
    End-Perform.

    Divide Total by Counter Giving Average Rounded.
    Move Total to TOT-OUT.
    Move Average to AVG-OUT.
    Display Total-Line.
    Display Average-Line.

    STOP RUN.
```

Figure 8.12
A BASIC program that computes and prints the sum and average of ten numbers.

```
10  REM COMPUTE SUM AND AVERAGE OF 10 NUMBERS
20  LET SUM = 0
30  FOR I = 1 TO 10
40    INPUT N(I)
50    LET SUM = SUM + N(I)
60  NEXT I
70  LET AVG = SUM / 10
80  PRINT "SUM = ",SUM
90  PRINT "AVERAGE = ",AVG
999 END
```

Pascal

Pascal, developed in the late 1960s by Niklaus Wirth of Zurich, was named for Blaise Pascal, the French mathematician and philosopher who invented the first practical, mechanical adding machine. It is suited for both scientific and file processing applications.

Pascal was originally designed to teach the concepts of structured programming and top-down design to students. Because of its structured nature, Pascal is often used in introductory programming classes. An example of a short Pascal program is shown in Figure 8.13.

Figure 8.13
A Pascal program that computes and prints the sum and average of ten numbers.

```
PROGRAM average(input, output);
{ Compute the sum and average of ten numbers }
VAR num, sum, avg : real;
    i : integer;

BEGIN
    sum:=0.0;
    FOR i := 1 TO 10 DO
    BEGIN
      read(num);
      sum:=sum + num;
    END;
    avg:=sum/10;
    writeln('Sum =',sum);
    writeln('Average =',avg);
END.
```

RPG

RPG (Report Program Generator) was developed in the mid-1960s. Since most people at that time had no programming experience, RPG was designed to be especially easy to learn and use. A programmer uses coding sheets to specify input, output, processing operations, and file specifications that are then entered into the computer for processing. Although it is easy to learn, RPG is limited in capabilities. It can produce reports and process files on tape or disk, but it is not well suited for mathematical or scientific applications.

C

The **C** programming language, developed at Bell Laboratories, incorporates many advantages of both low-level and high-level languages. Like assembly language, it enables the programmer to have extensive control over computer hardware. But because it uses English-like statements, which make it easy to read, it is often classified as a high-level language. C also incorporates sophisticated control and data structures, which make it a powerful but concise language. A variant of the C language, called C++, is used to create object-oriented programming applications.

C is a popular choice for developing system and application programs because of its power and structured nature. Figure 8.14 is an example of a C program.

Ada

The **Ada** programming language was developed in the late 1970s with the support of the U.S. Department of Defense. The goal was to build a very power-

Figure 8.14
A C program that computes and prints the sum and average of ten numbers.

```
#include <stdio.h>

main ()
    {
          int i, num;
          float sum;

          printf("Enter numbers \n");
          sum = 0;
          for (i = 0; i < 10; i++)
            {
               scanf("%d",&num);
               sum = sum + num;
            }
          printf("Sum = %3.1f\n",sum);
          printf("Average = %3.1f\n",sum / 10.0);
    }
```

Figure 8.15
An Ada program that computes and prints the sum and average of ten numbers.

```
PROCEDURE average number IS
    USE simple io;
    num, sum, avg: REAL;

BEGIN
    sum := 0;
    FORiIN 1...10 LOOP
      GET(num);
      sum:=sum + num;
    END LOOP;
    avg:=sum / 10;
    PUT("Sum ="); PUT(sum);
    PUT("Average ="); PUT(avg);
END average number;
```

ful, complete, and yet efficient structured language to be used in military applications, such as controlling weapon systems. Figure 8.15 is an example of an Ada program.

Which One Is "the Best"?

In truth, no one language is best for all computing needs. Each language was developed with a specific audience's needs in mind and each carries with it a particular style of use that reflects the language's original intent.

Because BASIC was originally designed to serve the needs of students in engineering or math-based courses, BASIC's instructions reflect the easy ability to form arithmetic expressions and to do somewhat complicated math. BASIC does not handle input and output very well, however.

COBOL, on the other hand, reflects the business world, where most processes are described by written procedures and the math is generally at a low level. With COBOL, filling all the boxes on a paycheck is somewhat easy, but solving a statistics problem using logarithms is not.

So how do you choose the right language? First, understand the nature of the problem to be solved. Then, choose a language that is best suited to the nature of the problem. Third, consider the type of hardware and software available and match the language chosen to the hardware. Yes, sometimes a compromise is necessary—you may write a program using BASIC because it was available, not necessarily because it was best for that application. But you should still have an idea of what that compromise costs in terms of program development.

Summary

- A program, or software, is the series of instructions that directs the hardware to perform various tasks.
- A good program is one that is correct, easy to understand, easy to maintain and update, efficient, reliable, and flexible.
- Structured programming is a programming methodology that involves systematic design, development, and management of the program development process.
- The program development process consists of the following series of steps: (1) define the problem; (2) design the algorithm; (3) code the program; and (4) test and debug the program.
- A program flowchart is a graphic representation of the steps of a program; standardized symbols are used. Pseudocode consists of English phrases to describe the processing steps in a program.
- Coding is the process of writing the algorithm in a specific programming language so it can be entered into the computer and executed. Once the algorithm is coded and entered, testing and debugging the program begins. Testing is the process of checking the correctness and identifying the errors in a program. Debugging is the process of finding and correcting any type of error in a program.

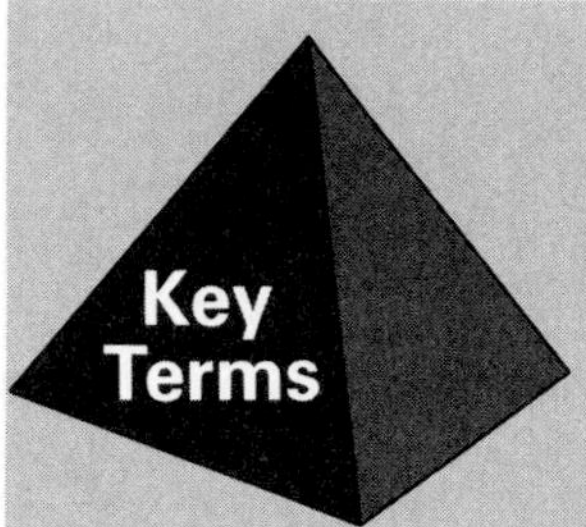

Sequence
Selection
Repetition
Top-down design
Pseudocode
Syntax error
Logic error
Debugging
Compiler
Interpreter
Object-oriented programming

Review Questions

1. List the six qualities of a good program and describe each.
2. Describe the three basic control structures used in structured programming.
3. Describe how the top-down approach to solving a problem works.
4. What is a module and how does the use of modules affect the development of a program?
5. Give the name for the finite set of step-by-step instructions used to solve a problem.
6. What is the function of a chief programmer team?
7. What happens in a structured walkthrough?
8. List and describe the steps in the program development process.
9. What is documentation and during what steps is it used?
10. List and discuss the types of program errors that may occur.
11. What is the process of finding and correcting errors in a program?
12. What does the term *syntax* mean in reference to programming?
13. Describe a programming language.
14. List and define the four general categories of programming languages.
15. What characterizes a low-level programming language?
16. Identify the language translator program that translates assembly language into machine language.
17. How does a compiler function?
18. How does an interpreter function?
19. What is the difference between a procedural and nonprocedural programming language?
20. Discuss some of the characteristics of major high-level programming languages.

PROFILE

YOU,
THE COMPUTER USER

(Kindra Clineff, The Picture Cube)

"The time has come," said the walrus, "for us to speak of cabbages and kings." Or for us to speak about your need to acquire a computing system to meet your needs.

You have learned, in these few pages, quite a bit about the world of computing and how it relates to you. Without any doubt, you are living in a computer-oriented society, and it will be increasingly difficult to go without this tool, especially if you decide to pursue a professional or technical occupation.

Perhaps you have now reached a decision to buy your own personal computer. It should not shock you to learn, upon reflection, that you have simply decided to "get a computer." No long analysis or hours of research, simply a feeling that you are ready to get your own system.

You may have already gone shopping for the computer at two or three computer stores or even a discount warehouse. Certainly, you have seen the many ads in the local newspaper and have compared the wide range of prices.

Friends are a great source of information, aren't they? Most of the time they will recommend what they have just bought, or would most likely get if money were no object. Often the recommendation will be, "This is what we use at work," or "They say that the R50-Turbo-M is the best one on the market." In other words, the evidence is hearsay and certainly not based on your personal needs or your own experience.

CHAPTER 9

BUYING YOUR OWN COMPUTER

You are making a major investment, and what you choose will have an impact on your ability to enjoy computing as a personal productivity tool. That being the case, shouldn't your decision be made on sound information? Well, let us then put you to work as an information processor. Your objective is to determine factually the best system—no, not the "best" as defined for a magazine article about the "ten best computers," but the best *for you,* for your needs and for your success.

IN THIS CHAPTER YOU WILL LEARN ABOUT

- **The process of selecting your own computer**
- **Defining your computing needs**
- **Finding the right software and hardware**
- **Things to consider when installing your system**
- **The compatibility issue**

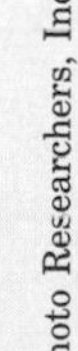

IDENTIFY YOUR NEEDS

First, you have to decide that you do indeed need a computer. Isn't that a somewhat silly question? Absolutely not, because a computer is not necessarily the right solution for everyone.

You have learned that an information system does not require a computer. If that is true, wouldn't there be a possibility that a computer is not for you? How would you know?

Remember the chapter about systems analysis and you'll know how to get started on your own analysis. First, determine what tasks you need to do—what problems you need to solve—and how those tasks might relate to computing. Make a list. For example, if you are a student who must write many term papers, a computer and word processing program might be useful. You might like to draw pictures, but unless you are a commercial designer you might be able to pass up having a computer-aided drawing program. But list it anyway, just so you have a complete picture of what you might be able to do with your computer. This is simply the problem definition phase of the acquisition process, not yet a time to go shopping.

ESTABLISH YOUR PRIORITIES

What is the most important problem you have to solve? That could be your highest priority use for the computer, if you had it. Take your listing of needs and rank those needs according to their importance to you.

Many computer buyers have vague reasons for buying a computer. Often they mention that they want to be able to play computer games. Would a video game or handheld game be less expensive than a computer costing several hundreds or thousands of dollars? Unless you have a serious reason to rank playing games high on your list, they probably will not sway your decision about the type of system you need. In contrast, the ability to keep the accounts for a business or to write the reports you need should influence your decision.

DETERMINE YOUR BUDGET

One of the important tasks faced by the system analyst was the feasibility study. You, too, must consider feasibility. For most of us, that relates directly to the amount of money we are able to invest in a new computer. You might consider alternatives such as paying over time (a loan) versus paying the full price at the time of purchase.

Another aspect of feasibility is time. If your need for a computer is urgent, then you will have to look at what is immediately available rather than what can be ordered for later delivery. Even here, though, there are alternatives: for example, you can rent a computer while waiting for yours to be delivered.

IDENTIFY ALTERNATIVE SOLUTIONS

There are many computers from which to choose, so which is going to be right for you? Actually, that is the wrong question to ask, but that is where many people concentrate their efforts. The right question to ask is, "Which *software* will get the job done best for me?"

Now, how will you arrive at that answer? Test software yourself, using typical work that you might like to do on the computer. For word processing, for example, take along a letter or report you need to do, and try using the software to get a feeling of how it will work for you. Many software dealers will let you try a demonstration of the software in the store.

If you are stuck trying to determine which programs to test, use references to help you create a list. Magazines, personal references, your instructor for this class—all are potential sources of data about the many available programs. Comparison articles in the computer press are especially good sources of data. The conclusion reached by a magazine may not be right for you, and you should read the article carefully to see if there is a particular bias, but the explanation of the choices is usually quite informative.

Do not concentrate on hardware, either. Just because you may have used one brand of computer in class does not make that automatically the preferred system for you. Try different models and different types of computers. Often, the same software is available for more than one type of machine. For example, WordPerfect can be run on both the Apple Macintosh and IBM PS/2 models. Try both alternatives and form your own opinion.

REMEMBER, SOFTWARE DEFINES HARDWARE

It is the software, after all, that will make the computer do the work you need to do, so choose the software that you find does the job best for you. Do not, however, ignore reality. You may need to have software that is the same as you would use in an office so you can work on projects at home as well as at the office. Perhaps you are going to be an engineering student or a computer science major; discover the specific software you might need to participate in those areas. In any case, software has a definite impact on the selection of the rest of your system, so carefully choose the programs you need.

As you select your software, you will need to pay attention to some important details. On the outside of most computer software packages (or at least in one of the manuals), there should be references to the type of hardware and operating systems required to run the program. So, the list of software you choose will help to complete a list of specifics that will eventually determine the computer you need. To get you started, use the form presented in Figure 9.1 as a guide. Figure 9.2 is an example of a completed form.

For the two programs shown in the filled-in form, Lotus 1-2-3 and WordPerfect, my computer would have to have a minimum of 1MB of RAM memory, but up to 4MB would be recommended for Lotus 1-2-3. At least 10MB of disk space is needed to hold the two programs, and an additional 2MB is required for the operating system—a total of at least 12MB of disk space. My system will not function unless DOS 3.0 or a later version is used; DOS 4.0 was selected. WordPerfect can use a mouse so that will be an option as will the math coprocessor that Lotus 1-2-3 can use. A color display can be supported by the software, and any printer can be used.

OK, IT'S TIME FOR HARDWARE

Now the fun part can begin. With a list in mind, you can choose the hardware that matches the software you have selected. Remember that the specifications for software define minimum configurations, for the most part, and options you might elect to include. There is really no upper limit, except the budget you set for yourself. Again, having a list might help; refer to Figure 9.3.

How do you fill in all of this information? Well, you will need to ask yourself a number of additional questions about the level of sophistication you require:

1. Will the computer stay in one place, or do I need it to be portable?
2. Does it have to be at least equal to some other computer I use—at work, home, or school?
3. Do I need to support software other than that in my list—such as software used at school, supplied by work, or to be acquired in the future?
4. Does the computer need to communicate with other computers either directly or linked by a modem?
5. Is it important to be able to display colors, graphic images, or multiple windows?

	Program Name	RAM (MB)	Disk (MB)	Operating System (Version)	Math (Copr)	Mouse	Display	Printer
1.								
2.								
3.								
4.								
5.								

Figure 9.1
Form for specifying software requirements.

	Program Name	RAM (MB)	Disk (MB)	Operating System (Version)	Math (Copr)	Mouse	Display	Printer
1.	Lotus 1-2-3 ver. 3.0	1MB to 4	3.5-5MB	DOS 3.0	if	no	color	any
2.	WordPerfect ver. 5.1	384KB min	to 5MB	DOS 3.0		yes	color	any
3.								
4.								
5.	DOS ver. 4.0	640KB min	2MB			yes	any	any

Figure 9.2
Filled-in form for specifying software requirements.

Figure 9.3
Form for specifying hardware requirements.

System Type: ______________________________

Model Number: ______________________________

Including:

Processor Type: ______________________________

Speed: ____________ MHz

RAM: ____________ MB

Math Coprocessor ______________________________

Diskette Type: ______________________________

Capacity: ______________________________

No. Drives ______________________________

Fixed Disk: ______________________________ MB

Adapter Cards:

____

____

____

Keyboard: ______________________________

Mouse: ______________________________

Display ______________________________

Modem: ______________________________

Printer: ______________________________

Other Devices: ______________________________

____

6. Will there be a need to store a great amount of data in addition to the room needed to store programs?
7. What about expansion and upgrades in the future? What types might these be and what limitations are imposed by the system I select?

PLANNING PAYS OFF

There is no easy way to buy a computer system; it takes research and careful planning. Sure, you could just go to the local computer store, pay your money, and carry home your new computer. But what would you be buying?

For many people, the answer is they are buying a lot of hardware and perhaps some boxes of programs with little or no idea of how to make it all work. The setup and installation of a computer is not hard, but it can be *made* difficult without careful planning. For example, what if you bought the latest IBM PS/2 model, only to discover later that the software you bought somewhere else came on a $5\frac{1}{4}$-inch disk, not the $3\frac{1}{2}$-inch version you need for your computer? You probably would be able to exchange the disks for the proper-size ones, but you would not be able to use the software until that was done.

KNOW YOUR SYSTEM

Consider this true story. Recently, a student took advantage of a special educational discount offered through school. IBM had a special "bundled" purchase—a computing system complete with a selection of software already installed and ready to go at a price about 55 percent of the normal retail price. One of the programs installed on the computer was a word processing program, Word for Windows from Microsoft.

To prepare better papers, the student then went to a software store and purchased a grammar-checker, a program that examines a word processing document to find irregular forms of grammar and makes suggestions to improve the writing. Grammar-checking programs can be a valuable asset, especially for the student who has many papers to write.

When the student followed the instructions to install the grammar-checking software, two problems arose. First, the student was unable to restart the computer; several error messages would appear on the screen, and the system would "die." After checking with the computer department at school, the student found that the instructions to install the software did not mention to be careful of some special operating system files that configure the system. When the software was loaded on the system's disk, it replaced the system file with another version under the same name, but without some critical instructions. When the system file was replaced, restoring the needed instructions, the computer operated perfectly.

Next, the student tried to use the grammar program. It didn't seem to work the way the instructions indicated or the way it worked in the store. Another student, who works in the school's computer center, volunteered to check out the problem. Quite simply, the problem was that the grammar-checking program was the wrong version for the word processing program. It would work with Microsoft Word, but not with the Word for Windows version.

Two common problems are demonstrated in this case. First, although software developers are trying to make it easy to use their software and to install it properly on a computer, installing and using are still tasks that require careful planning. Read the instructions carefully and get help if you are not certain about any step of the process.

Even an experienced computer user can run into problems. Sometimes the installation programs are just not as careful as they ought to be, and important files are altered or erased during the installation. For that reason, make copies of critical files before attempting to load software.

The second common problem was that the student failed to verify that the new program was compatible with the word processing program with which it would have to work. This is not at all surprising. Not only did the student fail to check if the new program would work with Word, but the student also did not realize that the Windows version was different from the other versions of the Word program.

A variation of the same problem is to forget the specific version of a program you are using. For example, this text is being written with a specific edition of WordPerfect, version 5.1. There are products on the market that will work with versions of WordPerfect. But because WordPerfect has added various new features and changed the file structure it uses to save files, a program that worked with WordPerfect version 4.2 or 5.0 may not be able to function with version 5.1.

COMPATIBILITY—A MAJOR ISSUE

One word often used to describe computers, software, and peripheral devices is *compatible*. It implies that the products are suitable for use together. For example, DOS is compatible with an IBM computer but not with a Macintosh.

The issue of compatibility is critical to your understanding of computing and to your success in using computers. It is both a subtle and a complex issue; but it is easy to understand if you just give it some thought.

A college computer lab installed some new computers. When the students tried to load BASIC to write programs, the BASIC program would appear to run, but the system would "freeze." Although the problem was not obvious, it was not difficult to solve. At the top of the BASIC screen is a notation of the version of BASIC being used. The screen noted that version A2.1 was loaded. The computer, however, was using DOS version 3.1, which has its own version of BASIC. The two versions were not compatible.

What had happened was that a student lab assistant, while installing some new computer equipment, decided to reload the computer with DOS, but had grabbed an old version. Even after this was pointed out, the student insisted that it made no difference—"all versions of BASIC are the same." Needless to say, replacing the old version with version A3.1 solved the problem and the system worked.

In the same lab, there is an instructor's system at the front of the room. This computer is not an IBM as are the students' computers, although it still uses the DOS operating system. BASIC will not run on the instructor's system because the version of BASIC distributed for an IBM system is unique to IBM hardware and will not function on the so-called compatible system.

Both of these issues involve compatibility of hardware and software. The example of the grammar-checker is also an issue of compatibility having to do with versions of specific programs. And there are many other variations of the compatibility theme. Remember that most of the problems can be avoided, or at least minimized, if you pay very careful attention to details.

Learn all you can about the particular type of computer you use or plan to use, how it operates, and what specific characteristics of the computer are important to remember when ordering new software or additional hardware. Read those boring manuals, especially where the installation or configuration instructions are given, to learn what basic facts you must know and which operations you must perform to keep your computer working efficiently for you.

GLOSSARY

Address The specific location in memory into which data are written or from which they can be read.

Algorithm A set of step-by-step instructions that solve a problem.

Alphabetic Data consisting only of the letters A through Z (either upper-case or lower-case) and the space character.

Alphanumeric Data represented by any allowable character the computer can store, including alphabetic characters, numeric digits, and symbols such as #, $, %, and so on.

Analog Transmission of data in a continuous wave form, such as a sound wave.

Application software Programs that solve problems and provide information.

Arithmetic and logic unit (ALU) The part of the CPU in which all mathematical and logical functions are performed. The basic mathematical functions include addition, subtraction, multiplication, and division. A logic function is one in which numbers or characters are compared with each other based on their relationships.

ASCII The American Standard Code for Information Interchange developed by the American National Standards Institute (ANSI) and used to represent characters in computer-readable form. See also *EBCDIC*.

Asynchronous A form of data transmission that sends data one character at a time. See also *Serial*.

Babbage, Charles P. Designer of the difference engine and the analytical engine. Babbage has been called "father of the computer" for the concepts these engines established. He described the functions of each of the computer's major components: input and output devices and a central processing unit containing a control unit, arithmetic and logic unit, and memory.

Baud rate A measure of the number of times per second the signal being transmitted changes (modulates or demodulates).

Binary A number system based on powers of 2 and consisting only of 1's and 0's, called *binary numbers*.

Binary logic Developed in the 1850s by George Boole. See *Boolean logic*.

Boolean logic The practice of reducing complex problems to a series of simple questions that can be answered only with Yes or No, reflected in the computer's 1 for on (Yes), and 0 for off (No).

Booting The process of loading operating system's control programs and the supervisor portion of the operating system into the computer's memory; this process occurs whenever the computer is turned on or restarted.

Buffers Temporary data holding areas built into either the CPU or the input or output devices.

Bus A common electrical pathway between the various components of the computer, connecting all parts of the CPU and the input and output devices.

Central processing unit (CPU) The combination of a control unit, arithmetic and logic unit (ALU), and memory.

Coding The process of writing the algorithm, or computer instructions, in a specific programming language so it can be entered into the computer and executed.

Common carriers Companies, such as the telephone company, that are licensed and regulated to transmit the data-communication property of others.

Communication channel The pathway through which data are transmitted between devices. There are three basic types of communication channels: wire cable, microwave, and fiber optics.

Computer A machine that can solve problems by accepting data, performing certain operations on those data, and presenting the results of those operations.

Computer literacy Having a general knowledge about computers, their use and functions, and how they affect individuals and society.

Computer programs The series of instructions the computer hardware must follow to complete an assigned task.

Computing system The combination of the computing hardware, software, data, procedures, and user, all working together to provide the benefits obtained by using the computer.

Control programs Operating system software that manages the computer hardware and resources. Three of the major functions of control programs are resource allocation, job management, and data management.

Control unit Part of the CPU and the computer's manager that receives instructions, interprets them, and directs other components to perform their activities. The control unit performs four activities: fetching, decoding, executing, and storing.

Coprocessor An additional processor that cooperates with the CPU in completing the computer's work by adding specialized processing capabilities. One of the most common coprocessors is the math coprocessor.

Cursor A special character or symbol that indicates the user's position on the screen or focuses attention to a specific area to allow communication and interaction between the user and the software.

Data The numbers, letters, symbols, words, or phrases that are input to the computer as raw facts during a data processing activity in order to be transformed into information.

Data communication The process of electronically sending data from one point to another.

Data integrity A term that means that the data are unimpaired and are accurate, timely, and useful.

Data managers Programs that store, organize, manipulate, retrieve, display, and print data.

Data processing Converting data into information as they flow through the computer in three steps: input, processing, and output.

Data storage hierarchy Bits, bytes, fields, records, files, and database.

Data validation The process of checking for erroneous data items.

Database An integrated collection of data items that is stored and retrieved under the control of a database management system.

Database management system (DBMS) A program, or system of programs, that creates an organization of data, often in multiple files.

Debugging The process of finding and correcting all errors in a program.

Decision support system (DSS) An information system used by top-level managers to make decisions about nonroutine and unstructured problems.

Decoding The control unit's act of translating program instructions into specific sequences of actions to be taken by the computer's other components.

Desktop publishing A concept that combines the use of a microcomputer with word processing, page-composition, and graphics software and high-quality laser printers to create newsletters, magazines, and other publications.

Digital Data represented in distinct on and off pulses, such as the computer's binary 0 and 1.

Digital computers Computers that use binary digits as their internal language. Most computers are digital computers.

Direct access A function that allows a record to be read directly from a disk without reading all preceding records.

Display See *Monitor*.

DOS prompt A very simple form of user interface on most machines using the MS-DOS or PC-DOS operating system. The interface is said to be character-based, or command-line oriented, because it indicates to the user to respond by typing in a series of characters to issue a command to the computer. The DOS prompt generally looks like C:/ > on the screen.

Dot-matrix printer A printer that uses print heads containing from nine to twenty-four pins to produce patterns of dots on the paper to form the individual characters.

Draft-quality print Print in which characters are formed with a minimum number of dots or lines for faster output than the standard quality characters but at the cost of a somewhat reduced quality.

Duplex Data transmission in two directions at the same time.

EBCDIC The Extended Binary Coded Decimal Interchange Code developed by IBM and used to represent characters in computer-readable form. See also *ASCII*.

Execute The control unit's action in carrying out the processing tasks required by a program.

Execution cycle The portion of the machine cycle during which the required operations are actually carried out and the new data resulting from the operation are stored in memory.

Expansion cards Accessory cards that can be inserted into slots inside the computer to expand the machine's capability or to add features.

Expert systems Computer application software based on the knowledge of a human expert wherein that person's expertise is put into the form of a program, using a computer to mimic the human expert's ability to solve a particular type of problem.

Feasibility study A preliminary study to determine whether the information system should be developed.

Fetching The act performed by the control unit in receiving instructions stored in the computer's memory.

Field Groups of characters representing a single fact.

File A collection of records related by their content and use.

Floppy diskette Also called a *diskette;* a small, flexible, mylar disk coated with iron oxide on which data can be stored.

Flowchart A pictorial representation using standardized symbols to show the components of a system or the steps in solving a problem.

GIGO (garbage-in, garbage-out) A term that indicates that the output is only as accurate as the input and the program that processes the data.

Graphics packages Applications software that will display data visually in the form of graphic images.

Half-duplex Two-way data transmission, but only one direction at a time.

Handshaking The exchange of prearranged signals defining the rules to be followed when transmitting and receiving data.

Hard copy Output in a relatively stable and permanent form, such as paper, that can be read immediately or stored and read later.

Hard disk A hard, inflexible platter made from materials such as aluminum and coated with magnetizable materials on which data can be stored.

Hoff, Ted The man who combined the ALU and the control unit on a single chip to form a microprocessor.

Icon A graphic symbol on the screen that represents a command or action.

Impact printer A printer that produces characters by using a hammer or pins to strike an ink ribbon, which in turn presses against a sheet of paper leaving an impression of the character on the paper. (An ordinary typewriter also works this way.)

Index A list of record addresses.

Indexed access Use of an index to locate records in a file, allowing both sequential and direct access to records stored on a disk.

Information Data that have been processed into a form that is accessible, useful, and meaningful to recipients.

Information processing cycle (IPOS) The four basic operations performed by a computer: input, processing, output, and storage.

Information system Any combination of people, data, and procedures used to create and distribute information throughout an organization.

Ink-jet printer A printer in which characters are formed on paper by spraying ink from tiny nozzles through an electrical field that arranges the charged ink particles into characters.

Input Collecting, verifying, and encoding data so the computer can read it.

Input device A peripheral device through which data are entered and transformed into machine-readable form.

Instruction cycle The portion of the machine cycle that includes the activity of fetching and decoding an instruction.

Integrated software Application software that allows several programs to share the same data more productively than if nonintegrated, individual programs were used. There are four types of integrated software: an integrated family of programs, the all-in-one integrated package, the integrated operating environment, and background integration.

Interface Hardware that connects the central processing system to peripheral devices; also called a *port.*

Kilobyte In the binary language of computers, one kilobyte equals 1,024 bytes.

Laser printer A printer in which images are produced on paper by directing a laser beam at a mirror, which bounces it onto a drum. The laser leaves a negative charge on the drum to which positively charged black toner powder will stick. As the paper rolls by the drum, the toner is transferred to the paper. A hot roller bonds the toner to the paper.

Letter-quality print Print made by fully formed (solid line) characters, as opposed to characters made up of dots or lines.

Local area network (LAN) A data communications network contained within a small geographical area, such as a room, building, or campus.

Machine cycle The cycle of operations performed by the control unit of the CPU. The machine cycle consists of two parts: the instruction cycle and the execution cycle.

Machine language The computer's internal language, comprising only the binary digits 0 and 1.

Magnetic disk A mylar or metallic platter on which electronic data can be stored.

Magnetic tape A one-half or one-fourth inch ribbon of mylar (a plastic-like material) coated with a thin layer of iron-oxide material; used to store data.

Main memory See *Primary storage unit.*

Mainframe computer A computer capable of controlling huge amounts of data storage and input and output devices, and of supporting many users who share the same computer.

Management information system (MIS) A system that aids managers in making decisions.

Megabyte 1,000 kilobytes, or 1,024,000 bytes.

Megahertz A term meaning millions of cycles per second; the measurement of how fast the computer is able to turn a circuit on and off.

Menu A type of user interface that consists of a list of alternative selections from which the user may choose the desired action or option.

Microcomputer A computer built with a microprocessor chip. It is generally used by only one person at a time. Also called a *personal computer.*

Minicomputer A computer that is less expensive and smaller than mainframe computers but is able to serve several users simultaneously.

Millions of instructions per second (MIPS) The number of machine instructions processed per second, often quoted as a performance statistic.

Modem (modulator–demodulator) A device that converts computer signals from digital to analog form or from analog to digital form. See also *Modulation.*

Modulation The process of converting a digital signal into an analog signal. *Demodulation* is the process of converting the analog signal into a digital signal.

Monitor A television-like device used to display data or information.

Near-letter-quality print Print achieved when the print head makes multiple passes over the same letters, filling in the spaces between the dots or lines.

Near-typeset-quality print Print similar in quality to that produced by a typesetting machine.

Numeric Data consisting only of the numeric digits 0 through 9, the plus or minus sign, and a decimal point.

Open architecture The ability to change the computer's components.

Operating system A set of programs that controls and supervises a computer system's hardware to allow the most efficient use of computer resources and to provide an interface between a user or an application program and the hardware.

Output Retrieving the results of processing and converting these results so the information can be used.

Output device A peripheral device that allows a computer to communicate with humans or another machine by accepting data from the computer and transforming them into a usable form.

Packaged software Software developed commercially by firms or groups who then sell the applications to the computer user.

Parallel An interface through which data are transferred either to or from the CPU and a peripheral device one byte at a time—i.e., eight bits at a time.

Peripheral Any hardware item, such as a disk drive, printer, or monitor, that is attached to the computer's CPU.

Personal computer See *Microcomputer.*

Picture element See *Pixel.*

Pirating Unauthorized copying and distribution of commercial software.

Pixel One picture element, or the image made to form one individual character or figure on the monitor.

Plotter A printer that produces high-quality graphics in one or more colors using pens that are attached to movable arms.

Port See *Interface.*

Presentation graphics Graphics software that assists in preparing materials for presentation purposes, such as slides and handouts for speakers or class lectures.

Primary storage unit The internal storage unit of the computer's CPU where programs and their data are stored during program execution. Also called *main memory.*

Printer A device that produces output on paper in the form of text or graphics.

Processing The creation of useful information from data by classifying, sorting, calculating, summarizing, and then storing the results.

Program The series of instructions that directs the hardware to perform various tasks.

Prompt A program-generated signal to the user, created by both application programs and operating systems, that indicates that the system is ready for an action. See also *DOS prompt.*

Protocol The set of rules and procedures defining the technical details for data transfer between two devices.

Pseudocode The use of English phrases to describe the processing steps in a program.

Public domain software Programs developed with public funds, such as government grants, or software for which the developer elects not to retain any rights, allowing for free distribution.

Random-access memory (RAM) That part of primary storage where data and program instructions are held temporarily while being manipulated or executed.

Read-only memory (ROM) Memory that can only be read; data cannot be written into it.

Reading The process of retrieving data from storage.

Record A collection of fields, each containing a unique fact but each field related to the other in some way.

Register A temporary memory storage location.

Resolution A measure of the number of picture elements, or pixels, that a screen contains.

Screen See *Monitor.*

SCSI (Small computer systems interface) A form of interface used for disk drives and other high-speed computer peripherals.

Sequential-access file A data file in which records are stored and accessed one after another.

Serial An interface used to transfer data either to or from the CPU and a peripheral device one bit at a time.

Service programs Operating system software that provides a service to the user or programmer of the computer system, such as FORMAT or SORT.

Shareware Software for which the developer owns the rights but allows it to be distributed free or for a nominal charge.

Simplex Data transmission in only one direction from the sending to the receiving unit.

Soft copy Usually a screen-displayed output that is a transient form and is lost when the computer is turned off.

Software See *Computer programs.*

Software license The right to use the software according to instructions contained within a packaged software product.

Source data entry Data entered directly into a computer system without manual transcription.

Spreadsheet program Software that displays, manipulates, and prints rows and columns of data.

Standard-quality print Print that is produced when characters composed of dots or lines are formed by a single pass of the print head.

Storage The nonvolatile data storage external to the computer's CPU, also called *secondary storage* or *auxiliary storage,* which may include magnetic tapes and magnetic disks.

Storing The control unit's task of moving the result of processing activities into the computer's memory.

Structured programming A programming method that involves systematic design, development, and management of the program development process.

Supercomputer The most expensive and powerful computers used, in which vast quantities of data are manipulated, primarily by government agencies, scientists, and large corporations.

Supervisor program A control program, also known in some operating systems as the *monitor, executive,* or *kernel,* that is responsible for controlling all the other operating system programs as well as other system and application programs.

Synchronous A form of data transmission that sends data as a block of characters in timed sequences.

Syntax The rules and conventions that must be followed when writing in a particular programming language.

System analysis The process of analyzing a system and trying to find a way to modify it or create a new system to meet the user's needs.

System life cycle The life span of an information system, consisting of five stages: system analysis, system design, system development, system implementation, and system maintenance.

Telecommunication See *Data communication.*

Terminal Monitors combined with keyboards so that input data can be viewed and checked as they are entered.

Testing The process of checking the correctness and identifying the errors in a program. Three types of errors or bugs may be encountered when testing: syntax, run-time, and logic.

Thermal-transfer printer A printer in which heat is used to transfer ink to paper.

Throughput A measure of the computer's ability to start and end a complete task.

Transcription A process of transferring from one recording and storage system into another. Transcription errors arise from mishandling data.

Transcription errors Data errors that arise from inaccurate copying of data from one format to another.

User-friendly A term that implies that the computer somehow assists the user, easing use by providing a better means by which the user can communicate his or her needs to the computer and by which it can guide the user when necessary.

User-written application packages Software designed and coded by the user, or written by developers according to the user's specifications.

Voice recognition The ability of the computer to understand spoken words or phrases.

Voice synthesis The process of electronically reproducing the human voice in recognizable patterns.

Volatile A term used to describe RAM memory's characteristic of being erased when the computer is turned off.

Wide area network (WAN) A data communications network that spans a large geographical area, such as a city.

Window A specifically defined area of the monitor in which may be displayed data, menus, program applications, icons, and other windows.

Word The number of adjacent bits that can be stored and manipulated as a unit.

Word processing software Software that enables the user to enter, edit, manipulate, save, and print text.

Writing The process of entering data into storage (primary or secondary).

PART 2

APPLICATION SOFTWARE

OUTLINE

WORDPERFECT VERSION 5.1

LOTUS 1-2-3 VERSION 2.2

dBASE III PLUS

DATA TRANSFER BETWEEN APPLICATIONS SOFTWARE

APPENDICES

Microsoft Word
THINK C
The Professional's Choice
WordPerfect
for IBM Personal Computers
and PC Networks
Lotus
123
Lotus 1-2-3
The world's most popular spreadsheet
GRAPHER

WORDPERFECT VERSION 5.1

INTRODUCTION

WordPerfect is an application software designed to do word processing. It allows the user to create text by typing characters on the microcomputer's keyboard. As the text is typed, it is entered into RAM. The microcomputer can then be used to manipulate the data. Manipulating text data is the primary function of word processing software. When the text has been manipulated into its finished form, the word processing software's commands can be used to print the text.

This module begins with a brief discussion of WordPerfect basics and file handling. It continues with a set of introductory tutorial lessons that presents the basic operations used to create, edit, format, and print a text file. The tutorial lessons then present the commands and techniques used in a set of time-saving procedures called *block operations*. Here the tutorial provides you with the opportunity to practice the word processing operations covered earlier. The introductory tutorial is followed by several short exercises and cases designed to introduce and reinforce the use of additional WordPerfect features, commands, and operations.

At the end of this module you will find a WordPerfect operation and command summary, which briefly describes WordPerfect's full range of commands and control key operations. You also will find a convenient WordPerfect quick reference command index, which lists the most commonly used WordPerfect commands.

As you progress through the material, you may notice slight differences between the menus and commands presented in the text and those shown on your monitor screen. The differences occur because of minor changes made to various versions of WordPerfect or differences among the types of hardware being used.

WORDPERFECT BASICS

Typing on Electronic Pages

WordPerfect is designed primarily to process text data. When you type the data on the keyboard, your words, sentences, and paragraphs appear on the monitor screen much as they would on a piece of paper in a typewriter. A small blinking cursor on the screen indicates where the next character that you type will appear.

As you continue to type, the lines of text begin to scroll on the monitor screen in the same way that paper feeds through a typewriter when the carriage return is pressed. When one screen's worth of text is complete, the text at the top of the screen scrolls up and disappears to make room at the bottom of the screen for new lines of text. Although the text disappears from view, the computer continues to hold it as part of the data in the file. You may use various WordPerfect commands to scroll text back and forth so that you can review text that is not currently displayed on the screen.

When you have typed a printed page's worth of text (default of 54 lines), WordPerfect displays a line of dashes across the screen (called a *page break*) to indicate that a new printed page is about to begin. The "electronic pages" of text are connected as new pages are added for every 54 lines of text typed.

WordPerfect refers to the text files you create in this manner as *documents* or document files.

Manipulating Text Data

As you enter text, you may move the cursor to edit any previously entered word, sentence, or paragraph. *Editing* a document involves either revising data by changing the written content of the text or formatting data by changing the appearance of the text. *Revising* includes operations such as deleting words, inserting words, moving paragraphs, and correcting misspellings. *Formatting* includes such operations as centering text, changing line spacing and margins, boldfacing, and underlining. WordPerfect's commands enable you to perform such text data manipulations.

WordPerfect Command Structure

WordPerfect provides menu commands to accomplish the revising and formatting operations. The command mode of WordPerfect is entered by typing certain keystrokes and keystroke combinations. The first keystroke in a menu command keystroke combination will be the **Ctrl**, **Shift**, or **Alt** key. The second keystroke in a keystroke combination will be a Function key (**F1** through **F10**.)

The Keyboard Command Template

WordPerfect provides a keyboard template to place over the Function keys on the keyboard. The template is essential to a beginning WordPerfect user because it lists the 40 main commands of WordPerfect; it can essentially be thought of as WordPerfect's main menu of commands. There are four such commands for each of the 10 Function keys. The four commands for each Function key are color coded to describe the keystroke or keystroke combination used to execute them:

Red = **Ctrl**
Green = **Shift**
Blue = **Alt**
Black = **Function keys**

To execute a command shown in red, green, or blue, you first press and hold the appropriate key (**Ctrl**, **Shift**, or **Alt**), and then press the Function key. To execute a command shown in black, you simply press the appropriate Function key.

WordPerfect Command Menus

When many of the WordPerfect commands are executed, they present menus of additional commands. The additional commands are selected by typing their number or letter. For instance, on the keyboard template next to Function key 8, the command "Format" is shown in green. If you press and hold the **Shift** key and then press the **F8** key, the following menu will be displayed on the screen:

```
Format

     1 - Line
             Hyphenation                        Line Spacing
             Justification                      Margins Left/Right
             Line Height                        Tab Set
             Line Numbering                     Widow/Orphan Protection

     2 - Page
             Center Page (top to bottom)        Page Numbering
             Force Odd/Even Page                Paper Size/Type
             Headers and Footers                Suppress
             Margins Top/Bottom

     3 - Document
             Display Pitch                      Redline Method
             Initial Codes/Font                 Summary

     4 - Other
             Advance                            Overstrike
             Conditional End of Page            Printer Functions
             Decimal Characters                 Underline Spaces/Tabs
             Language                           Border Options

Selection: 0
```

Here, there are four menu items (commands) listed to the left on the screen. Each command is preceded by a number and has one of its letters highlighted. You may select a command by typing either the command number or the highlighted letter in its name. In this example, if you type **1** or **L** (**L**ine), the following menu will appear:

```
Format: Line

     1 - Hyphenation                    No

     2 - Hyphenation Zone - Left        10%
                            Right       4%

     3 - Justification                  Full

     4 - Line Height                    Auto

     5 - Line Numbering                 No

     6 - Line Spacing                   1

     7 - Margins - Left                 1"
                   Right                1"

     8 - Tab Set                        Rel: -1", every 0.5"

     9 - Widow/Orphan Protection        No


Selection: 0
```

If your intention is to change the line spacing in the document, you next type **6** or **S** (Line **S**pacing).

Command Name Conventions

In this module, the full command used to complete an operation will be presented as the sequence (or path) of commands necessary to complete the operation. For instance, the full command to change line spacing will be stated in the form

Shift-F8 (Format),**L**ine,Line **S**pacing

Command Menu Trees

Later in the WordPerfect module, you will find command menu trees that graphically describe the command paths to a final completed operation. For instance, the small portion of the Format command tree that includes the operation of changing line spacing in a document will appear as follows:

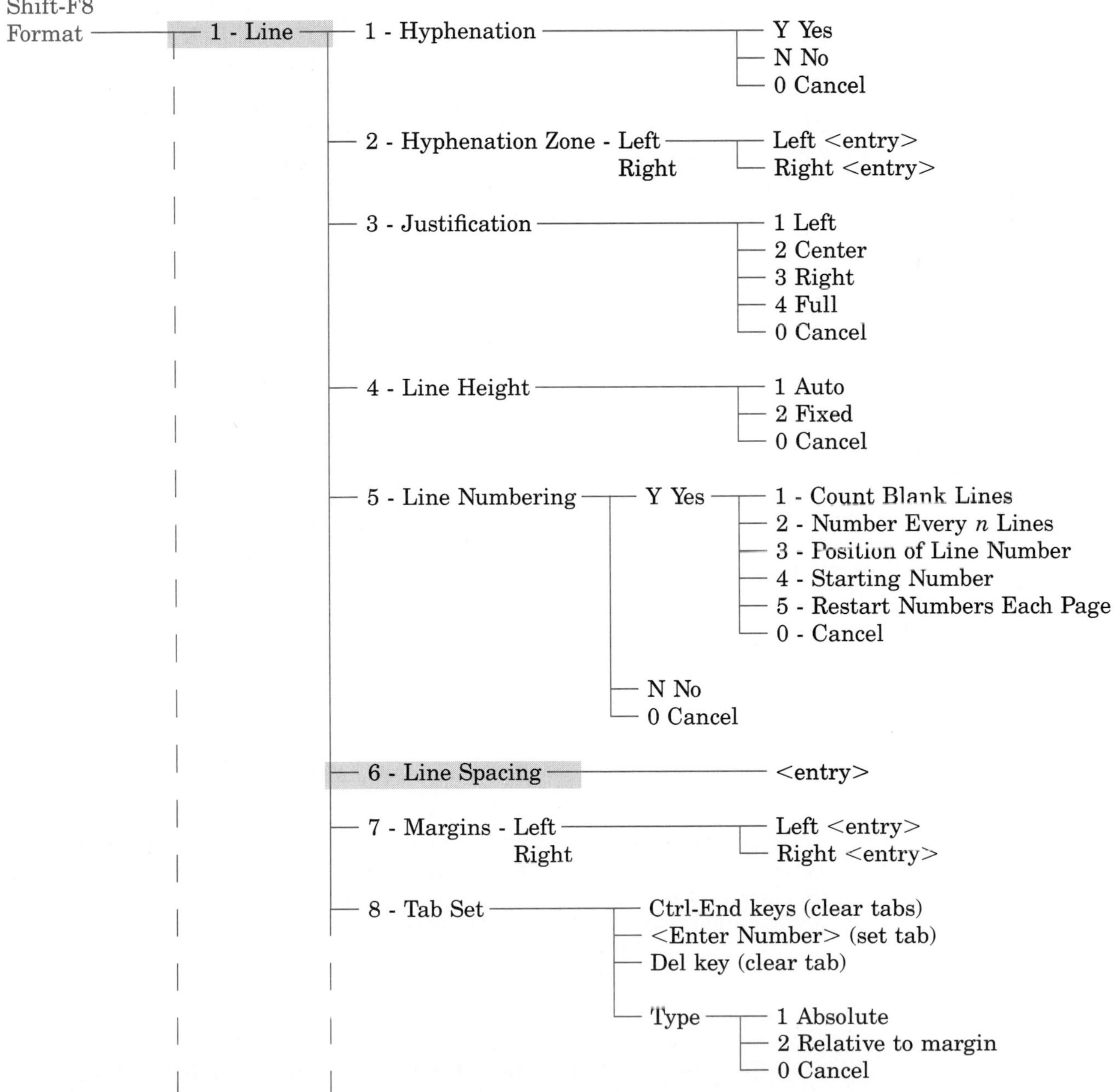

Command Index

The WordPerfect command summary also includes an index of completed operations. The index may be used to reference the appropriate command tree for further information, or simply to get you started toward successfully completing an operation while you are at the computer. An example of the index reference for line spacing appears as follows:

Italic Font	**Ctrl-F8** (Font)
Justification (on/off)	**Shift-F8,1** (Format),**Line**
Kerning	**Shift-F8,4** (Format),**O**ther
Keyboard Layout	**Shift-F1** (Setup)
Line	
Graphics	**Alt-F9** (Graphics)
Draw	**Ctrl-F3** (Screen)
Height	**Shift-F8,1** (Format),**Line**
Numbering	**Shift-F8,1** (Format),**Line**
Spacing	**Shift-F8,1** (Format),**Line**
Lists Feature	**Alt-F5** (Mark Text)

Command Keystroke Conventions

In this module, the keystrokes used to execute a command are shown with a dash (-) to indicate keystroke combinations. Commas are used to separate the keystrokes. For instance, in the last example the keystrokes used to change line spacing will be shown in the manual as **Shift-F8,1,6**.

WordPerfect's File Handling

WordPerfect, with all its features, is large enough to consume a considerable amount of RAM. In addition, as document files become several pages long, they rapidly use up RAM. WordPerfect circumvents the memory's size limits by keeping in RAM only the data currently needed. The rest of the data are maintained on disks and are brought into RAM as necessary.

How WordPerfect Is Loaded into RAM

To use the full extent of its commands, the WordPerfect software requires that eight floppy disks be available during editing. The floppy disks are labeled WordPerfect 1, WordPerfect 2, Speller, Thesaurus, Learning, Fonts/Graphics, PTR Program, and Conversion.

The basic word processing software of WordPerfect is kept on the WordPerfect 1 and WordPerfect 2 floppy disks. During normal editing operations, the WordPerfect 2 floppy disk must be kept in the disk drive. Software comprising other features of WordPerfect, such as its spelling checker, thesaurus, and graphics, are kept individually on the other floppy disks. To use other features of WordPerfect, the appropriate floppy disks must be inserted into the disk drive when needed.

Because of its total size, WordPerfect is best suited for computers having a hard disk. By copying all WordPerfect's software files onto the hard disk, you eliminate the need to change disks each time you use a special feature of the software.

How Document Files Are Loaded and Saved

When you first load WordPerfect into RAM, the software allows you to immediately begin entering text to create a document file. As you type, the data you enter begin to use up memory. When the memory of the computer becomes full, WordPerfect begins to save parts (blocks) of the document onto temporary files on the WordPerfect disk or directory. Once a block of data is copied onto a disk file, the space it has occupied in RAM may be erased to make room for new data.

If you move backwards in the text to correct errors or add data, and the section on which you want to work is not in RAM, WordPerfect copies what is in RAM onto the disk. It then reads the section on which you want to work into the memory space that was freed up. A current file being moved between RAM and disk storage in this fashion is called an *open file*.

When you are through creating and editing a document, you must use the appropriate WordPerfect commands to *close* the file. Closing a file causes all data in the document to be saved to your disk. The document will be saved under the name you give it at the time you save it.

Learning WordPerfect

WordPerfect is best learned by using it. Although you may be able to learn the fundamentals of creating and editing standard document files in just a few hours, the full set of WordPerfect commands and operations may take months to learn.

Getting Help

One WordPerfect command, **F3** (Help), provides an extensive on-line summary of information on the various commands of WordPerfect. To use the Help facility, you type **F3** (Help) and then follow the instructions shown to access various command topics. The data used to provide the Help facility are on the WordPerfect 1 floppy disk. You may need to reinsert the WordPerfect 1 floppy disk into the disk drive to use the **F3** (Help) command. When finished with the Help facility, you type the Space or ↵ key to return to the editing mode.

REQUIRED PREPARATION

The tutorials and exercises in this module will give you experience using the commands and features of WordPerfect. Before you begin the "hands-on" learning experience, however, you will need to complete a few initial steps to gain some preliminary information.

Initial Steps

1. Obtain a floppy disk appropriate for the microcomputer(s) you will be using to complete your course assignments. Your instructor or laboratory staff will be able to tell you which kind of disk to purchase.

Size: ____________________

Sides: ____________________

Density: ____________________

2. Format your disk to the specifications of the DOS and microcomputer hardware you will be using to complete your course assignments. Your instructor or laboratory staff will be able to tell you the steps to follow. **Caution:** Formatting a disk erases all files that may exist on that disk.

   Steps to Format a Disk: ________________________________

   ____

   ____

   ____

   ____

   ____

   ____

3. Each time you use the WordPerfect software, you will want to be sure that your text (data) files are saved on your disk. There will be certain steps to follow, either when you first load WordPerfect into RAM or immediately afterwards, to ensure that your files are automatically saved on your disk. Your instructor or laboratory staff will be able to tell you the steps to follow.

   Starting a WordPerfect Editing Session: ____________________

   ____

   ____

   ____

   ____

   ____

   ____

   ____

   ____

   ____

REQUIRED MATERIALS

1. An IBM DOS floppy disk (or hard-disk directory containing the DOS software)
2. A WordPerfect 1 and a WordPerfect 2 floppy disk (or hard-disk directory containing the software)
3. A formatted disk (your files disk)
4. A WordPerfect keyboard command template
5. This manual
6. Other ____________________

TUTORIAL CONVENTIONS

During the introductory WordPerfect tutorial you will create text files using various WordPerfect commands. The following are the conventions the tutorial's instructions will use.

↵	The bent arrow means to type the Enter key located on the right side of the keyboard.
Key-Key	Press and hold the first key, then type the next key shown.
Key, Key	Type the first key and then type the second key.
‖ ‖	Do not type the double brackets; type only what is inside them.

HOW TO GET OUT OF TROUBLE

If you want to:	*Then:*
■ Backspace and erase characters to the left of the cursor . . .	■ Type the Backspace key located on the right top side of keyboard.
■ Erase a line of text . . .	■ Move the cursor to the line to be erased and type Home,Home,Left,Ctrl-End.
■ Stop a command operation and return to editing the document . . .	■ Type **F1** (Cancel).
■ Leave the Reveal Codes screen to resume normal editing . . .	■ Type **Alt-F3** (Reveal Codes).
■ Stop the tutorial to continue later . . .	■ Type **F7** (Exit),**Y**,*drive*:WPTUT1 ↵,**Y**.
■ Continue with the tutorial after stopping . . .	■ After loading WordPerfect, type **Shift-F10** (Retrieve),*drive*:WPTUT1 ↵.

NOTE: Here drive *means type the letter (A, B, etc.) for the disk drive in which your files disk is kept.*

NOTE: As you complete the tutorial, you may see references made to screen positions that do not exactly match the positions displayed on your monitor. For instance, the text here may display a position of Ln 1.67" (line 1.67 inches) while your screen displays Ln 1.66" (line 1.66 inches). Such minor variations (1/100 of an inch) should be of no concern.

Throughout the tutorial lessons you will see the following symbol.

It indicates an opportune time to save your file(s) and quit the microcomputer session if you so desire.

GETTING STARTED

The proper "getting started" procedures require information specific to the hardware and software you are using. Refer to your notes in the preceding "Required Preparation" section for the specific information. The following is a general procedure for getting started; however, you may need to refer to Appendix A, "The Basics of DOS," to understand some of the terminology used here.

You will need to know in which disk drive (A: or B:) your files disk will be and where (disk drive and path) the WordPerfect software will be.

1. Load DOS from a floppy disk or hard disk, or return to the DOS operating level from the current software operating level.
2. Put the WordPerfect keyboard template over the Function keys on the keyboard.
3. Put your files floppy disk into the proper disk drive (drive name ___:).
4. When you see DOS's "*drive*:\ >" prompt on the screen, change the current disk drive to where your files disk is by typing *drive*: ↵.
5. If necessary, put the WordPerfect 1 disk in the proper disk drive (drive name___:).
6. Now enter the drive, path, and filename for WordPerfect by typing *drive*:*path*\\WP ↵.
7. If necessary, follow WordPerfect's instructions until the screen appears as follows.

```
_





                                        Doc 1 Pg 1 Ln 1" Pos 1"
```

LESSON 1
Creating a Document File

When WordPerfect is first loaded, you are presented with a blank screen onto which you may enter text. A blinking cursor should appear on the first position of the first line on the screen. At the bottom of the screen, a *status line* appears, which is used to display various messages about current editing operations. This is where many of WordPerfect's menus of commands will appear.

Entering Text

You are going to type part of a form letter prepared for prospective renters inquiring about units in a townhouse complex. As you enter the following text, be certain to type ↵ (Enter) only when the tutorial indicates that you are to do so. To correct typing errors as you go, use the Backspace key (top row, right side of keyboard) to backspace and erase characters you have typed. Also, use two spaces to separate sentences in the text.

1. Type ‖ ↵↵Thank you for your interest in Vista Ridge Townhouses. We feel that our one and two bedroom deluxe townhouse apartments offer adult living at its finest. ↵↵Each large unit has wall-to-wall carpeting, drapes, private patio and sun deck with a breathtaking view. In addition you will find the townhouse of your choice equipped with self-defrosting refrigerator, self-cleaning oven, dishwasher and garbage disposal unit.↵↵ ‖ .

At this point the screen should appear as

```
Thank you for your interest in Vista Ridge Townhouses.  We feel
that our one and two bedroom deluxe townhouse apartments offer
adult living at its finest.

Each large unit has wall-to-wall carpeting, drapes, private patio
and sun deck with a breathtaking view.  In addition you will find
the townhouse of your choice equipped with self-defrosting
refrigerator, self-cleaning oven, dishwasher and garbage disposal
unit.

-
```

How WordPerfect Manipulates Text as It Is Entered

As you enter text, WordPerfect's *word wrap* feature automatically begins a new line when the right margin of the current line is reached. If you want to begin a new line of text before you have reached the end of the previous line (such as when you want to begin a new paragraph), you must type ↵ (Enter). Typing ↵ stops the word wrap and moves the cursor forward to the next line.

Hard and Soft Returns

When a line is automatically wrapped to the next line by WordPerfect, the line is ended with what is known as a *soft return*. Groups of lines having soft return endings are considered by WordPerfect to be paragraphs of words. When a line is ended by typing ↵ (Enter), the line is ended by what is known as a *hard return*. A hard return separates paragraphs in WordPerfect.

Adding Text to a File

You will now finish the body of the text of the form letter.

2. Enter the text necessary to bring this document to the form shown in the following screen.

```
Thank you for your interest in Vista Ridge Townhouses.  We feel
that our one and two bedroom deluxe townhouse apartments offer
adult living at its finest.

Each large unit has wall-to-wall carpeting, drapes, private patio
and sun deck with a breathtaking view.  In addition you will find
the townhouse of your choice equipped with self-defrosting
refrigerator, self-cleaning oven, dishwasher and garbage disposal
unit.

Every tenant enjoys year-round swimming and sauna plus use of our
recreation room and tennis courts.

We are located in the South West Heights area, close to shopping,
city parks and University campus.  For an appointment to view one
of our fine townhouse apartments and a tour of the grounds, please
call Mr. Smith at (503) 244-7163.

_

                                   Doc 1 Pg 1 Ln 4.33" Pos 1"
```

LESSON 2 Basic Editing Operations

The basic editing operations of WordPerfect are revisional in nature. They allow you to change the content of the text by deleting and inserting characters, words, and larger units of text. To perform such operations, certain keystrokes are used. The general steps involved are

1. Move the cursor to the location where the change is to be made.
2. Use the appropriate keystrokes to make the change.

Moving the Cursor through a Document

The right side of the keyboard has a keypad that contains four keys with arrows on them. These keys (cursor control keys) may be used to move the cursor one character to the left or right and one line up or down by typing the key with the appropriate directional arrow on it. The printed page position of the cursor is displayed at the bottom of the screen in vertical (Ln) and horizontal (Pos) inches.

1. Use the cursor control keys to move the cursor to the *c* in *city* by following the path indicated in the following text.

```
We are located in the South West Heights area, close to shopping,
city parks and University campus.  For an appointment to view one
of our fine townhouse apartments and a tour of the grounds, please
call Mr. Smith at (503) 244-7163.

_
```

NOTE: If numbers appear on the screen at this time, type the Num Lock key once, and then use the Backspace key to erase the numbers and continue.

2. Watch the cursor move as you type the cursor left key (←) three or four times. Now type the cursor right key (→) five or six times.

Notice that when you attempt to move the cursor past the left or right margins of text, the cursor follows the word wrap path (either backwards or forwards) that was set when you entered the text.

Where the Cursor May Not Be Moved

WordPerfect's various cursor movement commands may be used to move the cursor anywhere on the screen where characters of text exist. The cursor may not be moved to areas where there are no text characters. As a demonstration, do the following.

3. Move the cursor to the *r* in *our* in the third paragraph.

```
Every tenant enjoys year-round swimming and sauna plus use of our
recreation room and tennis courts.

We are located in the South West Heights area, close to shopping,
```

4. Type the cursor down key (↓), then type it again.

Notice that the cursor jumped to the last character entered in the line to which it was being moved.

5. Now, with the cursor at 3.33" vertical (the status line displays the current cursor's (Ln) location), try to move the cursor to the right.

Since no characters are entered into the line, the cursor moves to the next line down following the word wrap.

When you want to move the cursor to an area of the screen where no characters exist, you may use the Space bar or Tab key to enter spaces or tabs (which are characters) into a line of text to move the cursor to the desired position (displayed as Pos on the status line).

WordPerfect Cursor Control Keys

Several keystrokes and keystroke combinations may be used to move the cursor around in a document. Although the WordPerfect keyboard template summarizes some of them, it is best to memorize the full list in order to use the word processing software most efficiently. To gain experience in some of the cursor control key operations, do the following:

6. Read the following table and practice using the cursor control keystrokes that are highlighted.

Cursor Movement	Keystrokes
Character Left	Left ←
Character Right	Right →
Line Up	Up ↑
Line Down	Down ↓
Word Left	Ctrl-←
Word Right	Ctrl-→
Forward to Character *a*	Ctrl-Home,*a*
Beginning of Line	Home,←
End of Line	Home,→
Top of File	Home,Home, ↑
Bottom of File	Home,Home, ↓
To Page *nn*	Ctrl-Home,*nn* ↵
Screen Up	− (Numeric Keypad)
Screen Down	+ (Numeric Keypad)
Page Up	Page Up (PgUp)
Page Down	Page Down (PgDn)
Previous Position	Ctrl-Home,Ctrl-Home

Revising a Paragraph of Text

Now that you are able to move the cursor throughout your document, you are ready to learn the basic word processing commands that allow you to revise text by inserting, deleting, or typing over characters, words, or lines of text.

Inserting or Typing over Text

On the right-hand side of the keyboard is a key marked "Ins" and/or one marked "Insert." These keys are used to switch WordPerfect between one of two editing modes, *Insert* or *Typeover*. The default mode is Insert.

7. If you see the "Typeover" message displayed on the left side of the status line, type the Ins or Insert key to switch WordPerfect back to the Insert mode.
8. Move the cursor to the first line of the second paragraph, and then to the *u* in *unit*.

```
Each large unit has wall-to-wall carpeting, drapes, private patio
and sun deck with a breathtaking view.  In addition you will find
the townhouse of your choice equipped with self-defrosting
refrigerator, self-cleaning oven, dishwasher and garbage disposal
unit.
```

9. Now type ||apartment||.

The paragraph now should appear as

```
Each large apartment unit has wall-to-wall carpeting, drapes, private patio
and sun deck with a breathtaking view.  In addition you will find
the townhouse of your choice equipped with self-defrosting
refrigerator, self-cleaning oven, dishwasher and garbage disposal
unit.
```

When the Insert mode is on, any characters that you type will be inserted into the text to the left of the cursor.

10. Now move the cursor with one of the cursor control keys.

```
Each large apartment unit has wall-to-wall carpeting, drapes,
private patio and sun deck with a breathtaking view.  In addition
you will find the townhouse of your choice equipped with self-
defrosting refrigerator, self-cleaning oven, dishwasher and garbage
disposal unit.
```

Notice that WordPerfect automatically rewraps the lines in a paragraph when revisions are made to it. This is referred to by WordPerfect as its *screen rewrite* feature.

11. Type the Ins key once.

Notice that the Typeover message appears on the left side of the status line.

12. Now move the cursor to the *a* in *apartment* and type ||townhouse||.

The paragraph now should appear as

```
Each large townhouse_unit has wall-to-wall carpeting, drapes,
private patio and sun deck with a breathtaking view.  In addition
you will find the townhouse of your choice equipped with self-
defrosting refrigerator, self-cleaning oven, dishwasher and garbage
disposal unit.
```

When the Typeover mode is on, any characters that you type will type over (overwrite) existing characters of text.

Deleting Text

There are several keystrokes and keystroke combinations that may be used to delete text from a document. The following table describes many of them.

Delete Operation	Keystroke(s)
Current Character	Delete (Del)
Previous Character	Backspace
Current Word	Ctrl-Backspace
Current Word Left	Home,Backspace
Current Word Right	Home,Delete (Del)
End of Line	Ctrl-End
End of Page	Ctrl-Page Down (PgDn)

Deleting Characters

13. Move the cursor down one line and to the *w* in *with.*

```
Each large townhouse unit has wall-to-wall carpeting, drapes,
private patio and sun deck with a breathtaking view.  In addition
you will find the townhouse of your choice equipped with self-
defrosting refrigerator, self-cleaning oven, dishwasher and garbage
disposal unit.
```

The Delete or Del key found on the right-hand side of the keyboard may be used to delete the character at the cursor position.

14. Type the Delete or Del key three times.

The Backspace key is used to delete the character to the immediate left of the cursor. If the Typeover mode is on, the characters are replaced with spaces. If the Insert mode is on, the characters are deleted from the text and the space is closed up.

15. Move the cursor four characters to the right (to the *b* in *breathtaking*). Use the Ins key to make sure the Insert mode is on, and then type the Backspace key four times.

Deleting Words

Another delete operation uses the keystroke combination Ctrl-Backspace to delete the word at the cursor location. A word is defined by WordPerfect to be a group of characters separated from other groups by spaces, or the group of spaces to the right of the cursor.

16. Move the cursor to any letter in the middle of the word *breathtaking* and type Ctrl-Backspace.

```
Each large townhouse unit has wall-to-wall carpeting, drapes,
private patio and sun deck view.  In addition you will
find the townhouse of your choice equipped with self-defrosting
refrigerator, self-cleaning oven, dishwasher and garbage disposal
unit.
```

Deleting Lines of Text

The final delete operation to be discussed here is one that deletes the line to the right of the cursor. The keystroke combination used is Ctrl-End. Although this lesson does not include a demonstration of the operation, you will find the keystroke combination to be very useful when you need to delete small sections of text.

The **F1** (Cancel) Command—WordPerfect's Panic Button

One of the first commands you should become familiar with is WordPerfect's **F1** (Cancel) command. The Cancel command may be used to abort and exit other WordPerfect commands. The Cancel command may also be used to recover any or all of the last three text deletions or Typeover text.

Recovering Deleted Text

To recover deleted text, you move the cursor to the position where you want the recovered text to appear and then type F1 (Cancel). The most recent deletion will appear on the screen at the cursor location. You may type **2** or **P** (Previous Deletion) to scroll continuously through the last three deletions, with each deletion appearing on the screen in order. When the appropriate deletion is displayed on the screen, you type **1** or **R** (**R**estore) to recover it, or type **F1** (Cancel) to abort the recovery operation.

17. Move the cursor to the *s* in *sun* (second paragraph, second line), and then type the **F1** (Cancel) command.

```
Thank you for your interest in Vista Ridge Townhouses.  We feel
that our one and two bedroom deluxe townhouse apartments offer
adult living at its finest.

Each large townhouse unit has wall-to-wall carpeting, drapes,
private patio and breathtaking sun deck view.  In addition you will
find the townhouse of your choice equipped with self-defrosting
refrigerator, self-cleaning oven, dishwasher and garbage disposal
unit.

Every tenant enjoys year-round swimming and sauna plus use of our
recreation room and tennis courts.

We are located in the South West Heights area, close to shopping,
city parks and University campus.  For an appointment to view one
of our fine townhouse apartments and a tour of the grounds, please
call Mr. Smith at (503) 244-7163.




Undelete: 1 Restore; 2 Previous Deletion: 0
```

At the bottom of the screen you will see the menu for the Cancel command.

18. Type **2** or **P** several times.

Notice how the last three sections of deleted text appear on the screen in the order they were deleted.

19. Continue typing **2** or **P** until the word *breathtaking* appears again, and then type **1** or **R** to restore the deleted text.

Practice Revisions

20. Use the methods of your choice to insert, overwrite, and/or delete the words in the paragraph so that it appears as follows.

```
Each spacious townhouse unit has wall-to-wall carpeting, drapes,
private patio and sun deck.  You will also find the townhouse of
your choice equipped with a completely modern kitchen including a
self-defrosting refrigerator, self-cleaning oven, dishwasher and
garbage disposal unit.
```

LESSON 3 Formatting Text

In the following steps you will gain experience at changing the appearance of a document. The operations here include changing left and right margins, changing line spacing, centering text, bolding text, and so on.

When WordPerfect commands and keystrokes are used to format text, codes are imbedded into the document. For instance, you learned earlier that WordPerfect inserts soft returns at the end of lines when it wraps text and that typing ↵(Enter) produces a hard return at the end of a line. To view WordPerfect codes on the monitor screen you may use the **Alt-F3** (Reveal Codes) command.

The **Alt-F3** (Reveal Codes) Command

The **Alt-F3** (Reveal Codes) command is an important WordPerfect command that allows you to edit your document while its imbedded codes are visible on the screen.

1. Move the cursor to the *E* in *Every* (first letter, third paragraph) and type the **Alt-F3** (Reveal Codes) command.

The screen will appear as follows.

```
Thank you for your interest in Vista Ridge Townhouses.  We feel
that our one and two bedroom deluxe townhouse apartments offer
adult living at its finest.

Each spacious townhouse unit has wall-to-wall carpeting, drapes,
private patio and sun deck.  You will also find the townhouse of
your choice equipped with a completely modern kitchen including a
self-defrosting refrigerator, self-cleaning oven, dishwasher and
garbage disposal unit.

Every tenant enjoys year-round swimming and sauna plus use of our
                                           Doc 1 Pg 1 Ln 3" Pos 1"
{  ▲   ▲   ▲   ▲   ▲   ▲   ▲   ▲   ▲   ▲   ▲   ▲   ▲   }   ▲   ▲
self[-]defrosting refrigerator, self[-]cleaning oven, dishwasher and[SRt]
garbage disposal unit.[HRt]
[HRt]
Every tenant enjoys year[-]round swimming and sauna plus use of our[SRt]
recreation room and tennis courts.[HRt]
[HRt]
We are located in the South West Heights area, close to shopping,[SRt]
city parks and University campus.  For an appointment to view one[SRt]
of our fine townhouse apartments and a tour of the grounds, please[SRt]
call Mr. Smith at (503) 244[-]7163.[HRt]

Press Reveal Codes to restore screen
```

The top portion of the Reveal Codes screen displays your document as it appears during normal editing. The bottom portion of the screen displays the same text with its imbedded codes. Such codes will be highlighted and enclosed in brackets. The code [SRt] indicates a soft return, and the code [HRt] indicates a hard return.

The cursors E and E appearing in the top and bottom portions of the screen may be moved at the same time (synchronously) using the cursor control keys. This feature allows you to move about and scroll through the text without leaving the Reveal Codes screen.

2. Watch the bottom portion of the screen and move the cursor left two characters.

The bottom cursor should now be on the [HRt] code at the end of the line ending with *unit.*

```
private patio and sun deck.  You will also find the townhouse of
your choice equipped with a completely modern kitchen including a
self-defrosting refrigerator, self-cleaning oven, dishwasher and
garbage disposal unit._

Every tenant enjoys year-round swimming and sauna plus use of our
                                        Doc 1 Pg 1 Ln 2.67" Pos 3.2"
{  ▲   ▲   ▲   ▲   ▲   ▲   ▲   ▲   ▲   ▲   ▲   ▲   ▲   }   ▲   ▲
private patio and sun deck.  You will also find the townhouse of[SRt]
your choice equipped with a completely modern kitchen including a[SRt]
self[-]defrosting refrigerator, self[-]cleaning oven, dishwasher and[SRt]
garbage disposal unit.[HRt]
[HRt]
Every tenant enjoys year[-]round swimming and sauna plus use of our[SRt]
recreation room and tennis courts.[HRt]
[HRt]
```

All of the editing and command features of WordPerfect are available to you while you are working with the Reveal Codes screen turned on. Since most of WordPerfect's formatting operations place hidden (imbedded) codes into the document, the Reveal Codes screen can be most useful for ensuring proper placement of such codes and for later finding and deleting unwanted codes from a document.

WordPerfect Format Codes

The codes that format text tend to fall into four general categories: hard codes and soft codes, format forward codes, line codes, and start and stop codes. The following section discusses each category as it presents the more important or most used formatting commands and keystrokes in WordPerfect.

Hard and Soft Codes

Soft codes are, for the most part, codes which WordPerfect generates and automatically inserts into a document. Hard codes are generated by the user. A soft code, such as the soft return, is flexible; it can be (and is) moved about when a paragraph or page is rewritten. A hard code, such as a hard return, is inflexible; WordPerfect will not automatically move or remove it from the document.

As mentioned, hard returns produced by typing the enter key may be used to separate paragraphs in a WordPerfect document.

3. With the cursor located on the [HRt] code following *unit*, type the Del key once. Then type it again.

```
Each spacious townhouse unit has wall-to-wall carpeting, drapes,
private patio and sun deck.  You will also find the townhouse of
your choice equipped with a completely modern kitchen including a
self-defrosting refrigerator, self-cleaning oven, dishwasher and
garbage disposal unit.Every tenant enjoys year-round swimming and
sauna plus use of our recreation room and tennis courts.

                                  Doc 1 Pg 1 Ln 2.67" Pos 3.2"
{  ▲  ▲  ▲  ▲  ▲  ▲  ▲  ▲  ▲  ▲  ▲  ▲  }  ▲  ▲
private patio and sun deck.  You will also find the townhouse of[SRt]
your choice equipped with a completely modern kitchen including a[SRt]
self[-]defrosting refrigerator, self[-]cleaning oven, dishwasher and[SRt]
garbage disposal unit.Every tenant enjoys year[-]round swimming and[SRt]
sauna plus use of our recreation room and tennis courts.[HRt]
[HRt]
```

By deleting the two hard returns ([HRt]s) that were separating the second and third paragraphs, you were able to combine them into one paragraph.

4. To gain experience in editing a document from the Reveal Codes screen, revise the second paragraph to read as in the following.

```
Each spacious townhouse unit has wall-to-wall carpeting, drapes,
private patio and sun deck.  You will find the townhouse of your
choice equipped with a completely modern kitchen including a self-
defrosting refrigerator, self-cleaning oven, dishwasher and garbage
disposal unit.  In addition, every Vista Ridge tenant enjoys year-
round swimming and sauna plus use of our recreation room and tennis
courts._

                                        Doc 1 Pg 1 Ln 3" Pos 1.7"
{  ▲  ▲  ▲  ▲  ▲  ▲  ▲  ▲  ▲  ▲  ▲  ▲  ▲  }  ▲  ▲
defrosting refrigerator, self[-]cleaning oven, dishwasher and garbage[SRt]
disposal unit.  In addition, every Vista Ridge tenant enjoys year[-]
round swimming and sauna plus use of our recreation room and tennis[SRt]
courts.[HRt]
[HRt]
```

5. When you are finished, type the **Alt-F3** (Reveal Codes) command to exit the Reveal Codes screen.

Other Hard and Soft Codes

Hard and Soft Page Breaks. WordPerfect generates soft page breaks ([SPg] code) every 54 lines of text. You can force a hard page break to occur by typing Ctrl-↵, thus inserting a [HPg] code into the text.

Hard Spaces and Hard Hyphens. If you do not want two or more words to be separated from each other when WordPerfect wraps a line in a paragraph, you can insert *hard spaces* between the words. Similarly, if you want a hyphenated word to remain whole, you can insert a *hard hyphen* into the word. To produce a hard space, you type the keys Home,Space. A [ ] code will be inserted into the text. To produce a hard hyphen, you type the keys Home,–. A hard hyphen appears in the text as simply a – (dash) in the Reveal Codes screen; a hyphen typed without the Home key appears as a [–] code in the Reveal Codes screen.

Deleting Hard Codes

All of the hard codes can be directly deleted with the Backspace or Del keys without using the Reveal Codes screen. This is not true for other types of codes.

Format Forward Codes

Many of the codes imbedded into a document by WordPerfect are format forward in nature. In general, the procedure is to first move the cursor to where you want the code to be placed in your document, and then execute the WordPerfect command that will generate the imbedded code. To demonstrate how such codes work, you will use a command to imbed a code that changes the left and right margins.

Changing Left and Right Margins

6. Move the cursor to the beginning of the second paragraph and then to the *E* in *Each*.
7. Type the **Shift-F8** (Format) command.

The following screen should appear:

```
Format

     1 - Line
              Hyphenation                    Line Spacing
              Justification                  Margins Left/Right
              Line Height                    Tab Set
              Line Numbering                 Widow/Orphan Protection

     2 - Page
              Center Page (top to bottom)    Page Numbering
              Force Odd/Even Page            Paper Size/Type
              Headers and Footers            Suppress
              Margins Top/Bottom

     3 - Document
              Display Pitch                  Redline Method
              Initial Codes/Font             Summary

     4 - Other
              Advance                        Overstrike
              Conditional End of Page        Printer Functions
              Decimal Characters             Underline Spaces/Tabs
              Language                       Border Options

Selection: 0
```

The **Shift-F8** (Format) command presents a menu of commands. The option to set Margins Left/Right can be found to the right of the menu command **1 - L**ine.

8. Type **1** or **L** to select the **Shift-F8** (Format),**L**ine command.

The following menu of commands should appear on the screen.

```
Format: Line

     1 - Hyphenation                    No

     2 - Hyphenation Zone - Left        10%
                            Right       4%

     3 - Justification                  Full

     4 - Line Height                    Auto

     5 - Line Numbering                 No

     6 - Line Spacing                   1

     7 - Margins - Left                 1"
                   Right                1"

     8 - Tab Set                        Rel: -1", every 0.5"

     9 - Widow/Orphan Protection        No


Selection: 0
```

Here you see that the **M**argins command is option **7** on the (Format),**L**ine command menu. You can see the current settings or values for each command on the menu to the right of the command.

9. Type **7** or **M** to select the **M**argins command.

By default, WordPerfect measures margins in printed page inches. In most cases the characters are printed in 10 pitch—that is, there are 10 characters per inch occurring on a printed line. This means that one inch of margin amounts to 10 characters.

10. Reset the current left and right margins by typing ||2↵2↵||.

In some cases, WordPerfect does not immediately return you to editing your document after a command has been executed. Here you have finished changing the margins for the document, but the Format,**L**ine command menu screen is still present. As a general rule, when a WordPerfect command puts a 0 (zero) over the menu selection cursor as it has here, typing ↵ will return you to the normal editing mode. At other times, the **F7** (Exit) command is used to return you to editing.

11. Type ||↵↵||, and then type the cursor down key once to cause WordPerfect to rewrite the screen.

```
Thank you for your interest in Vista Ridge Townhouses.  We feel
that our one and two bedroom deluxe townhouse apartments offer
adult living at its finest.

          Each spacious townhouse unit has wall-to-wall
          carpeting, drapes, private patio and sun deck.
          You will find the townhouse of your choice
          equipped with a completely modern kitchen
          including a self-defrosting refrigerator,
          self-cleaning oven, dishwasher and garbage
          disposal unit.  In addition, every Vista Ridge
          tenant enjoys year-round swimming and sauna
          plus use of our recreation room and tennis
          courts.

          We are located in the South West Heights area,
          close to shopping, city parks and University
          campus.  For an appointment to view one of our
          fine townhouse apartments and a tour of the
          grounds, please call Mr. Smith at (503) 244-
          7163.
                                      Doc 1 Pg 1 Ln 2.17" Pos 2"
```

When the **Shift-F8** (Format),**L**ine,**M**argins command was executed, WordPerfect inserted a [L/R Mar:2",2"] code into the document at the cursor location.

12. Type **Alt-F3** (Reveal Codes) to see the imbedded code. When finished, type **Alt-F3** (Reveal Codes) again to return to the normal editing screen.

Notice that all of the text following the [L/R Mar:2",2"] code was rewritten to fit the new left and right margins. A format forward code affects all of the following text up to the end of the document, or until another similar code, in this case another [L/R Mar:n",n"], is encountered.

13. Move the cursor to the *W* in *We* in the last paragraph and repeat the previous steps to set the margins Left = 1.5", Right = 1.5" (1 $\frac{1}{2}$ inches each). Type ||↵↵|| to return to editing, and then type the cursor down key to rewrite the screen.

```
Thank you for your interest in Vista Ridge Townhouses.  We feel
that our one and two bedroom deluxe townhouse apartments offer
adult living at its finest.

          Each spacious townhouse unit has wall-to-wall
          carpeting, drapes, private patio and sun deck.
          You will find the townhouse of your choice
          equipped with a completely modern kitchen
          including a self-defrosting refrigerator,
          self-cleaning oven, dishwasher and garbage
          disposal unit.  In addition, every Vista Ridge
          tenant enjoys year-round swimming and sauna
          plus use of our recreation room and tennis
          courts.

     We are located in the South West Heights area, close to
     shopping, city parks and University campus.  For an
     appointment to view one of our fine townhouse apartments
     and a tour of the grounds, please call Mr. Smith at (503)
     244-7163.

                                        Doc 1 Pg 1 Ln 4" Pos 1.5"
```

Deleting Format Forward Codes

You may use the Reveal Codes screen to delete codes that affect the document in a format forward manner, or you may often delete them using the Backspace or Del keys without entering the Reveal Codes screen.

14. Move the cursor to the *E* in *Each* in the second paragraph and type the Backspace key.

Notice the following message at the bottom of the screen.

"Delete [L/R Mar:2",2"]? **No** (**Y**es)

If you now type **Y**, the code will be deleted from the document. If you type any other key, the code will not be deleted.

15. Use the method of your choice to delete the two [L/R Mar:n",n"] codes that are in the document.
16. Now move to the top line on the screen (to the beginning of the document file) and use the **Shift-F8** (Format),**L**ine,**M**argins command to set the left margin to 1.5" and the right margin to 1.5". Remember that moving the cursor down will cause the screen to be rewritten for the new margins.

Changing Line Spacing

The **Shift-F8** (Format),**L**ine,Line **S**pacing command is another useful formatting command.

17. With the cursor at the top of the document, type the **Shift-F8** (Format),**L**ine,Line **S**pacing command.
18. Change the current line spacing to two by typing ‖2←┘‖. Then type ‖←┘←┘‖ to return to the normal editing mode.
19. Next use the Reveal Codes command to view the two format forward codes that are now imbedded at the beginning of your text.

```
     Thank you for your interest in Vista Ridge Townhouses.

     We feel that our one and two bedroom deluxe townhouse

     apartments offer adult living at its finest.

                                          Doc 1 Pg 1 Ln 1" Pos 1.5"
▲    {    ▲    ▲    ▲    ▲    ▲    ▲    ▲    ▲    ▲    ▲    }    ▲    ▲    ▲
[L/R Mar:1.5",1.5"][Ln Spacing:2][HRt]
[HRt]
Thank you for your interest in Vista Ridge Townhouses. [SRt]
We feel that our one and two bedroom deluxe townhouse[SRt]
apartments offer adult living at its finest.[HRt]
[HRt]
```

Line Codes

Line codes are codes that affect a line of text according to the current left and right margins or tab settings. When the Reveal Codes screen is on, the reverse video (highlighted) bar across the middle of the screen indicates where the current margins and tab stops occur. The { and } characters shown on the bar indicate where the current left and right margins are set. The ▲ characters indicate the locations of the various tab stops. (By default, tab stops are set every $\frac{1}{2}$ inch on a line. They can be changed, however, using the **Shift-F8**(Format),**L**ine,**T**ab Set command.)

Tabbing Text

The Tab key is used to move a line of text to the next tab stop, or to move the cursor to the next tab stop. If Insert is on, the Tab key generates a [Tab] code that moves the current line right to the next tab stop. If Typeover is on, the Tab key simply moves the cursor to the next tab stop on the current text line.

20. With the Reveal Codes screen on, move the cursor to the *T* in *Thank* in the first paragraph. Make sure that Insert is on, then type the Tab key (far left side of the keyboard). Next type the cursor down key to rewrite the screen so that it appears as follows.

```
          Thank you for your interest in Vista Ridge

     Townhouses.  We feel that our one and two bedroom deluxe

     townhouse apartments offer adult living at its finest.

                                          Doc 1 Pg 1 Ln 2" Pos 2"
▲    {    ▲    ▲    ▲    ▲    ▲    ▲    ▲    ▲    ▲    ▲    }    ▲    ▲    ▲
[L/R Mar:1.5",1.5"][Ln Spacing:2][HRt]
[HRt]
[Tab]Thank you for your interest in Vista Ridge[SRt]
Townhouses.  We feel that our one and two bedroom deluxe[SRt]
townhouse apartments offer adult living at its finest.[HRt]
[HRt]
```

Notice that the first line of text in the paragraph is now indented to the next tab stop (the first tab stop right of the left margin), and that a [Tab] code has been imbedded into the document.

Centering Text

WordPerfect's **Shift-F6** (Center) command inserts a [Center] line code into the document that centers the text between the left and right margins. To gain experience in using the command, do the following:

21. Use the Reveal Codes screen to move the cursor to the [Ln Spacing:2] code imbedded in the text.

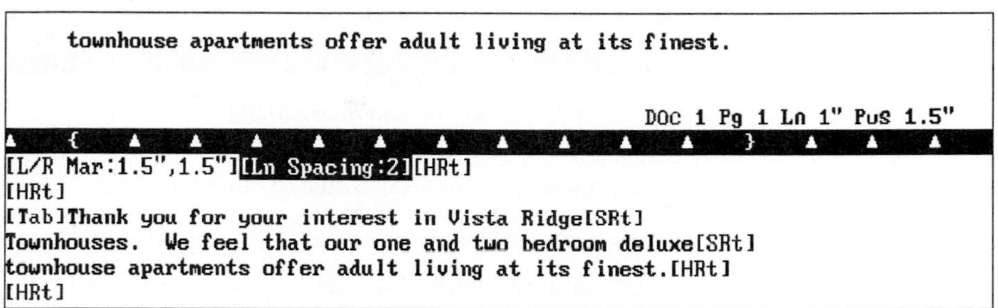

22. Type ‖↵↵‖ to insert one blank line between the [L/R Mar:1.5",1.5"] code and the [Ln Spacing:2] code. Then move the cursor to that blank line.

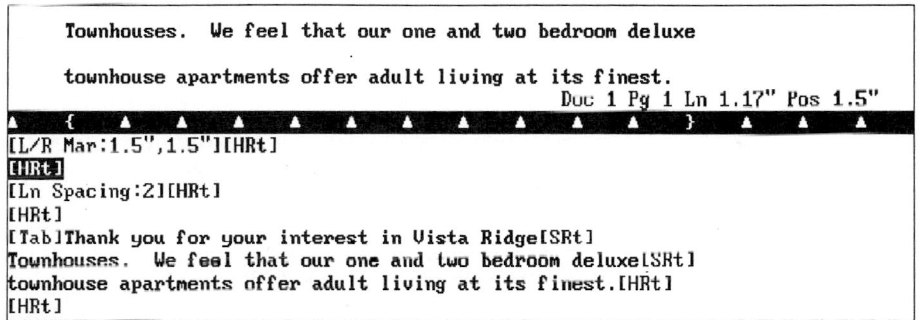

23. Next, type **Shift-F6** (Center) to place the [Center] code at the beginning of the line.

Text now typed on this line will appear centered between the current left and right margins.

24. Now type ‖Vista Ridge Townhouses‖.

```
                    Vista Ridge Townhouses



          Thank you for your interest in Vista Ridge

     Townhouses.  We feel that our one and two bedroom deluxe

     townhouse apartments offer adult living at its finest.
                                         Doc 1 Pg 1 Ln 1.17" Pos 5.35"
[L/R Mar:1.5",1.5"][HRt]
[Center]Vista Ridge Townhouses[HRt]
[Ln Spacing:2][HRt]
[HRt]
[Tab]Thank you for your interest in Vista Ridge[SRt]
Townhouses.  We feel that our one and two bedroom deluxe[SRt]
townhouse apartments offer adult living at its finest.[HRt]
[HRt]
Each spacious townhouse unit has wall[-]to[-]wall carpeting,[SRt]
drapes, private patio and sun deck.  You will find the[SRt]

Press Reveal Codes to restore screen
```

Deleting Line Codes

All of the line codes can be directly deleted with the Backspace or Del keys, without using the Reveal Codes screen, in the same manner that hard codes can be deleted.

Start and Stop Codes

Commands that generate start and stop codes imbed two codes into the document. The text between the two codes is the segment of text affected by the command's format.

Bolding and Underlining Text

Two commonly used WordPerfect commands that insert start and stop codes into the document are the **F6** (Bold) command, which is used to print text darker than normal, and the **F8** (Underline) command, which is used to underline text when it is printed. To gain experience using the WordPerfect commands that imbed start and stop codes into a document, do the following:

25. Make sure that the Reveal Codes screen is on, then move the cursor to the [Center] code in the second line of the document.

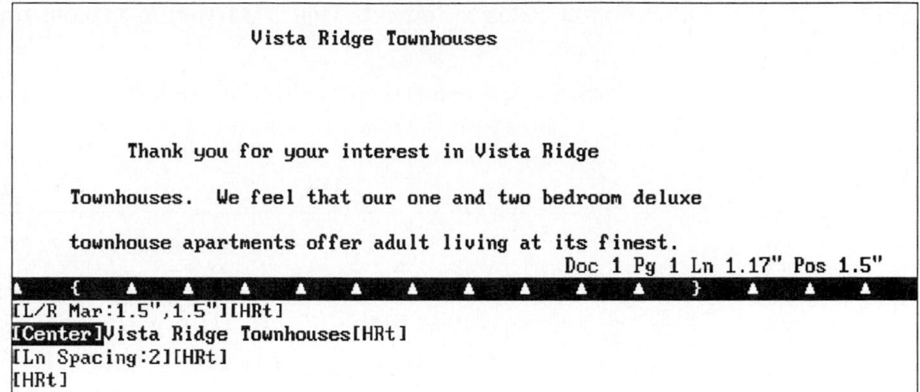

```
                    Vista Ridge Townhouses



          Thank you for your interest in Vista Ridge

     Townhouses.  We feel that our one and two bedroom deluxe

     townhouse apartments offer adult living at its finest.
                                          Doc 1 Pg 1 Ln 1.17" Pos 1.5"
[L/R Mar:1.5",1.5"][HRt]
[Center]Vista Ridge Townhouses[HRt]
[Ln Spacing:2][HRt]
[HRt]
```

26. Next type the delete keystrokes Ctrl-End to delete the [Center] code and the text on the line. Then type the **F6** (Bold) command.

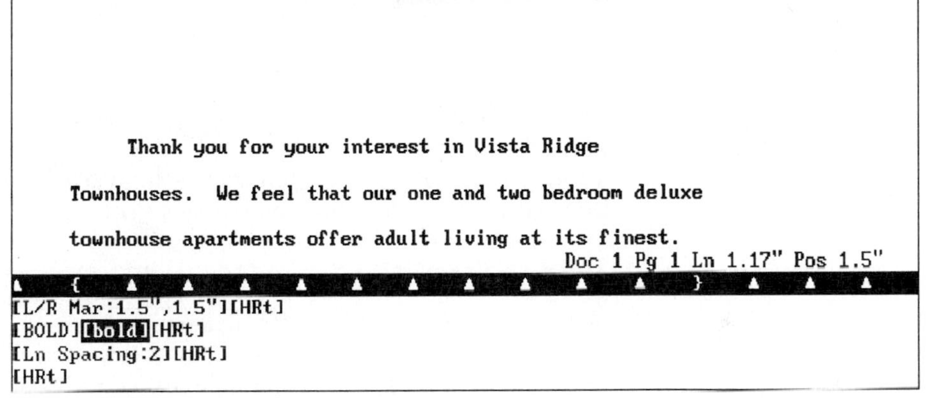

```
          Thank you for your interest in Vista Ridge

     Townhouses.  We feel that our one and two bedroom deluxe

     townhouse apartments offer adult living at its finest.
                                          Doc 1 Pg 1 Ln 1.17" Pos 1.5"
[L/R Mar:1.5",1.5"][HRt]
[BOLD][bold][HRt]
[Ln Spacing:2][HRt]
[HRt]
```

Notice that the **F6** (Bold) command inserted two codes, [BOLD] and [bold], into the document.

27. Continue by type ||Vista Ridge Townhouses||.

```
     Vista Ridge Townhouses



          Thank you for your interest in Vista Ridge

     Townhouses.  We feel that our one and two bedroom deluxe

     townhouse apartments offer adult living at its finest.
                                          Doc 1 Pg 1 Ln 1.17" Pos 3.7"
[L/R Mar:1.5",1.5"][HRt]
[BOLD]Vista Ridge Townhouses[bold][HRt]
[Ln Spacing:2][HRt]
[HRt]
```

Notice that the bolded text appears highlighted in the upper portion of the screen. WordPerfect often changes the display of text inclosed in start and stop codes to indicate that a particular type of format is in effect for that segment of text.

28. Now move the cursor to the far left position on the line and type the **Shift-F6** (Center) command. Then type the cursor down key to rewrite the screen.

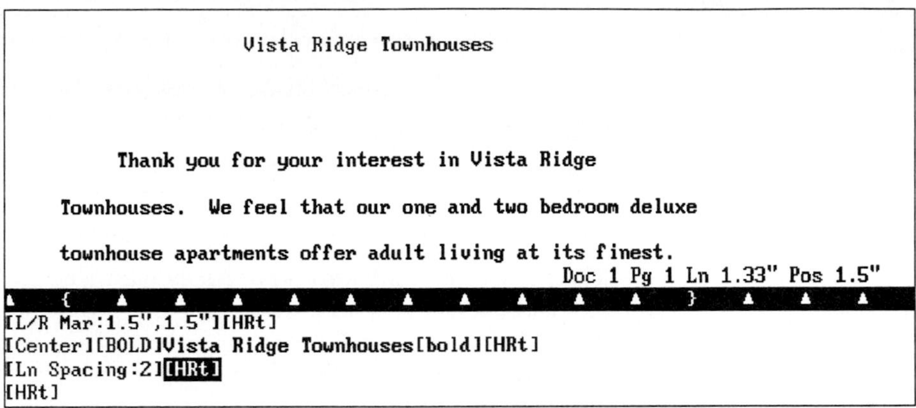

The **F8** (Underline) command inserts [UND] and [und] codes into a document, but otherwise works in the same manner as the **F6** (Bold) command. To stop bolding text, underlining text, or affecting text with any WordPerfect start/stop codes, you simply move the cursor out from between the codes.

Deleting Start and Stop Codes

You may delete start and stop codes in the same manner as you delete format forward codes, with or without the Reveal Codes screen. However, with start and stop codes, only one of the two codes need be deleted; the other will automatically be deleted.

Practice Reformatting the Document

Use the commands and operations discussed so far to complete the following steps.

29. Set the left margin to 1.25" and the right margin to 1.25" for the entire document.
30. Complete the centered letterhead as shown here:

Vista Ridge Townhouses

1800 S.W. Sunset View Avenue
Portland, OR 97207

31. Indent the first line of each paragraph to the first tab stop right of the left margin.
32. Keep the line spacing at 1 for the letterhead and 2 for the rest of the document.
33. Underline the phone number. Note that the underlined text will appear underlined and/or highlighted on the screen and will print underlined.

34. Use a hard space (Home,Space) and a hard hyphen (Home,-) to prevent WordPerfect from separating the area code, prefix, and phone number when it wraps the last line of the last paragraph.
35. Delete all unnecessary codes from your document.

The document should now appear as follows.

```
                    Vista Ridge Townhouses

                1800 S.W. Sunset View Avenue
                    Portland, OR 97207


     Thank you for your interest in Vista Ridge Townhouses.

We feel that our one and two bedroom deluxe townhouse

apartments offer adult living at its finest.


     Each spacious townhouse unit has wall-to-wall carpeting,

drapes, private patio and sun deck.  You will find the

townhouse of your choice equipped with a completely modern

kitchen including a self-defrosting refrigerator, self-

cleaning oven, dishwasher and garbage disposal unit.  In

addition, every Vista Ridge tenant enjoys year-round swimming

and sauna plus use of our recreation room and tennis courts.


     We are located in the South West Heights area, close to

shopping, city parks and University campus.  For an

appointment to view one of our fine townhouse apartments and

a tour of the grounds, please call Mr. Smith at

(503) 244-7163.

                                   Doc 1 Pg 1 Ln 7.83" Pos 1.25"
```

LESSON 4
WordPerfect Block Operations

An important feature of word processing is its ability to deal with segments, or blocks, of a document (sentences, paragraphs, etc.) independent from the rest of the document. The process involves two steps: (1) the segment of text is defined and (2) a WordPerfect command is used to affect that segment of text.

In the following lesson you will create a second page for the document you have been working on that describes four townhouse apartments immediately available for occupancy. While you create the page, several WordPerfect block operations will be introduced.

Formatting Blocks of Text

The **Alt-F4** (Block) command is used to define a portion of text to be subsequently affected by another WordPerfect command. To block (define) a portion of text, you move the cursor to the beginning of the text and type **Alt-F4** (Block). A blinking "Block on" message will appear on the status line at the bottom of the screen. You then move the cursor to the end of the text. The text being blocked will be displayed on the screen in reverse video. If you decide to abort the block operation, you may type **F1** (Cancel) to turn off the block. The last step to a block operation is to type the command keystroke or keystroke combination to affect the block of text. To demonstrate, do the following.

1. Move the cursor to the immediate right of the period in the last line of text.
2. Use the **Alt-F3** (Reveal Codes) screen and the Del or Delete key to delete any text or codes that may have been inadvertently placed in the document beyond this point.

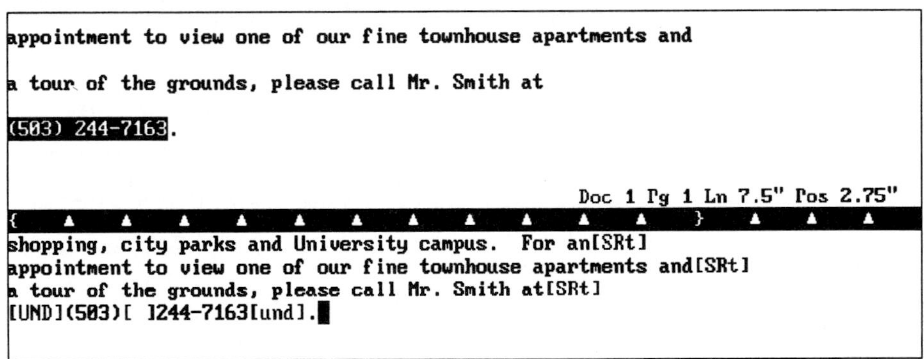
appointment to view one of our fine townhouse apartments and
a tour of the grounds, please call Mr. Smith at
(503) 244-7163.
Doc 1 Pg 1 Ln 7.5" Pos 2.75"
shopping, city parks and University campus. For an[SRt]
appointment to view one of our fine townhouse apartments and[SRt]
a tour of the grounds, please call Mr. Smith at[SRt]
[UND](503)[ ]244-7163[und].

3. Exit the Reveal Codes screen by typing **Alt-F3**. Then type ‖↵‖ 10 times.

A dotted horizontal line should appear on the screen. The line is generated by a [HRt—SPg] (Hard Return-Soft Page code) which indicates that a new printed page will begin at this point.

4. With the cursor at line (Ln) 1.33" use the **Shift-F8** (Format),**Line**,**Line Spacing** command to set the line spacing for the second page to single spacing. Before exiting the (Format),**Line** command menu screen, use the **7** (Margins) command to set the left and right margins to 1" each for the second page. Finally, type ‖ ↵↵ ‖ to return from the **Shift-F8** (Format),**Line** menu to normal editing.
5. Next type ↵ twice, then beginning on Ln 1.67", enter the following text:

```
Vista Ridge Townhouses
======================

Units Available
For Immediate Occupancy
```

6. Move the cursor to the *V* in *Vista* (Ln 1.67" Pos 1") and type **Alt-F4** (Block).

A blinking "Block on" message should appear at the bottom of the screen.

7. Now move the cursor down five lines to Ln 2.5".

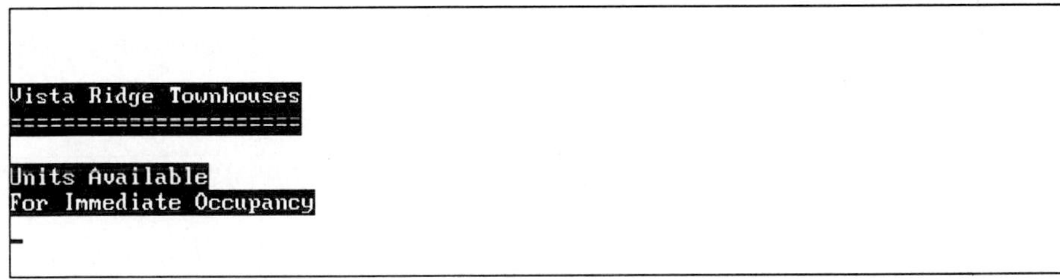

8. Now type the **Shift-F6** (Center) command.

At the bottom of the screen you should see the prompt:

"[Just:Cntr]? **No** (**Yes**)."

9. Type **Y** to center the document heading.

Since many people prefer to format their text after it has been entered, the ability to **Alt-F4** (Block) existing text and then **Shift-F6** (Center), **F8** (Underline), or **F6** (Bold) the blocked text is a useful feature.

Several other commands that may be used to format a block of text may be found on the Block/**Ctrl-F8** (Block/Font) menu of commands. To use the Block/Font commands, you first block the text to be affected, type **Ctrl-F8** (Font), select **1** Size or **2** Appearance, and then select the desired font size or appearance for the blocked portion of text. The complete Block/Font menu can be shown graphically as follows.

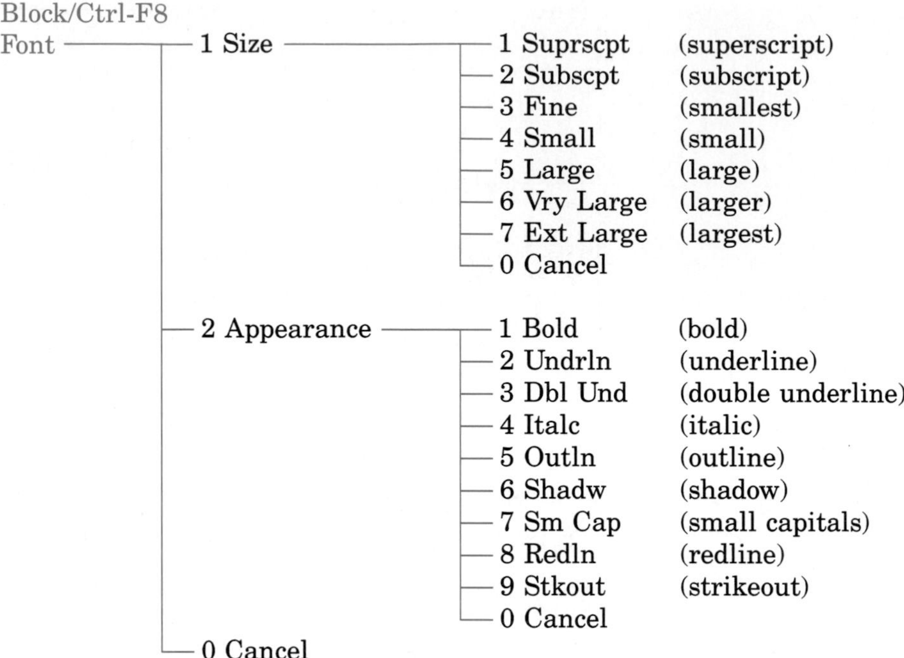

You should note, however, that printers vary in their ability to support the full range of styles and sizes for printed characters that the Font command offers.

Cut-and-Paste Operations

The term *cut-and-paste* refers to the ability to move, copy, or delete blocks of text. WordPerfect provides several ways in which you may perform cut-and-paste operations.

10. Move the cursor to Ln 3.17" Pos 1" by typing ||↵|| four times.
11. Now type ||# 12 - 1850 Square Feet, 3 Bedrooms, 2 Baths||.
12. Next type the **Alt-F6** (Flush Right) command.

The **Alt-F6** (Flush Right) command inserts a line code ([Flsh Rgt]) into the document that aligns the following text on the line against the right margin.

13. Type ||$480.00/Month ↵↵||.
14. Continue by typing in the remaining text shown in the following [use the Tab key to indent the lines of text].

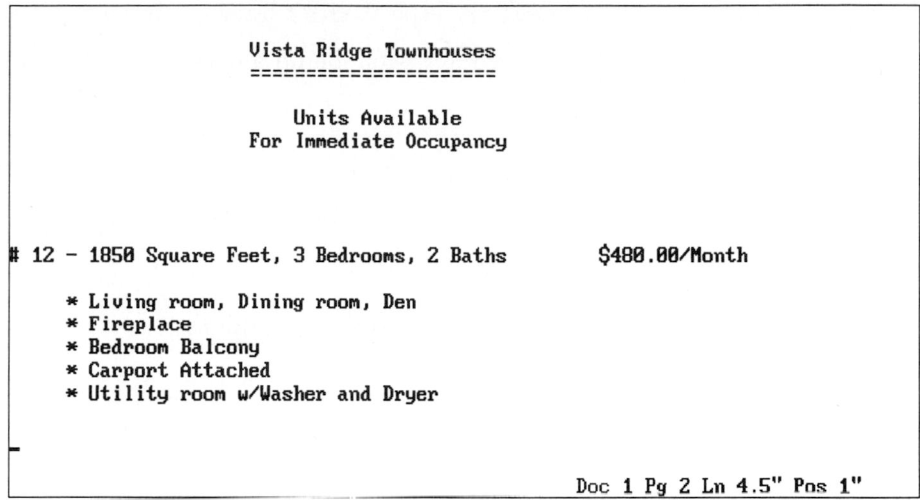

Vista Ridge Townhouses
======================

Units Available
For Immediate Occupancy

12 - 1850 Square Feet, 3 Bedrooms, 2 Baths $480.00/Month

* Living room, Dining room, Den
* Fireplace
* Bedroom Balcony
* Carport Attached
* Utility room w/Washer and Dryer

Doc 1 Pg 2 Ln 4.5" Pos 1"

Using the Block/**Ctrl-F4** (Move) Command

The Block/Move command may be used to move, copy, or delete a block of text. When the **Ctrl-F4**(Move) command is used to perform such operations, a copy of the blocked text is made and placed into what is known as the *Move Block buffer*. WordPerfect then treats the copy of text in the Move Block buffer as a separate file. Once a copy of blocked text has been placed into the Move Block buffer, it remains there until another Block/Move command causes another blocked section of text to replace it.

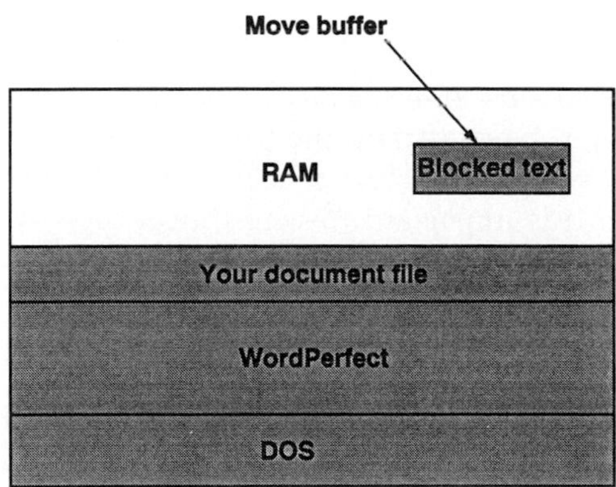

The Block/**Ctrl-F4** (Move),**B**lock,**M**ove Command

To gain experience at using the Block/Move command, you will first use the command to move the last feature listed to become the second feature listed.

15. Move the cursor to Ln 3.67" Pos 1" (beginning of the line with * *Fireplace* on it) and type ||←|| to create a blank line there.

16. Now move the cursor to the beginning of the line starting with * *Utility room* (Ln 4.33" Pos 1") and type **Alt-F4** (Block),Home,End to block the line of text.

17. Next type the **Ctrl-F4** (Move) command.

The following menu should appear at the bottom of the screen:

```
# 12 - 1850 Square Feet, 3 Bedrooms, 2 Baths         $480.00/Month

     * Living room, Dining room, Den

     * Fireplace
     * Bedroom Balcony
     * Carport Attached
     * Utility room w/Washer and Dryer


Move: 1 Block; 2 Tabular Column; 3 Rectangle: 0
```

18. Type **1** or **B** to specify **B**lock.

The next menu to appear is

```
1 Move; 2 Copy; 3 Delete; 4 Append: 0
```

19. Now select **1** or **M** to **M**ove.

When you selected **1** or **M** to move the block of text, WordPerfect first made a copy of the block of text and placed it into the Move Block buffer. It then erased the block of text from the screen.

The prompt at the bottom of the screen (Move cursor; press **Enter** to retrieve) indicates what you are to do next.

20. Move the cursor to the beginning of the blank line you created in step 15 (Ln 3.67" Pos 1") and type ||↵||.

In the second part of executing the Block/**Ctrl-F4** (Move),**B**lock,**M**ove command, a copy of the text in the Move Block buffer is inserted (regardless of the current Typeover/Insert mode) into the document at the location of the cursor. It is important to note that a copy of the text still remains in the Move Block buffer.

21. Use the cursor down key (and ↵key (if necessary) to move the cursor to Ln 4.5" Pos 1".

```
     * Living room, Dining room, Den
     * Utility room w/Washer and Dryer
     * Fireplace
     * Bedroom Balcony
     * Carport Attached



                                        Doc 1 Pg 2 Ln 4.5" Pos 1"
```

The **Ctrl-F4** (Move),**R**etrieve,**B**lock Command

The **Ctrl-F4** (Move),**R**etrieve,**B**lock command may be used to copy the text currently in the Move Block buffer into the document at the location of the cursor.

22. Now type **Ctrl-F4** (Move), then **4** or **R** (Retrieve), and then **1** or **B** (**B**lock) to retrieve the Move Block buffer text.
23. Now repeat the last step (**Ctrl-F4,4,1**) two more times.

```
     * Living room, Dining room, Den
     * Utility room w/Washer and Dryer
     * Fireplace
     * Bedroom Balcony
     * Carport Attached

     * Utility room w/Washer and Dryer  * Utility room w/Washer and
Dryer     * Utility room w/Washer and Dryer
                                                  Doc 1 Pg 2 Ln 4.5" Pos 1"
```

The Block/**Ctrl-F4** (Move),**B**lock,**C**opy Command

To copy a block of text, the Block/**Ctrl-F4** (Move), **B**lock,**C**opy command is used in the same manner as the Block/**Ctrl-F4** (Move),**B**lock,**M**ove command. The only difference between the two commands is that moving text causes the original block of text to be erased from the screen and copying text does not erase the original block of text.

The Block/**Ctrl-F4** (Move),**B**lock,**M**ove and Block/**Ctrl-F4** (Move),**B**lock,**Copy** commands both work by placing a copy of blocked text into the Move Block buffer where it can be retrieved later with the **Ctrl-F4**(Move),**R**etrieve,**B**lock command. However, only the most recently moved or copied text will be in the Move Block buffer at any point in time.

The Block/(Move),**B**lock,**D**elete Command

To continue, do the following.

24. Use the **Alt-F4** (Block) command and cursor keys to block the last two lines in the document, and then type **Ctrl-F4,1** (Move),**B**lock.

```
     * Living room, Dining room, Den
     * Utility room w/Washer and Dryer
     * Fireplace
     * Bedroom Balcony
     * Carport Attached

     * Utility room w/Washer and Dryer  * Utility room w/Washer and
Dryer     * Utility room w/Washer and Dryer
1 Move; 2 Copy; 3 Delete; 4 Append: 0
```

25. Now type **3** or **D** (**D**elete) to delete the block of text.
26. Next type the **F1** (Cancel) command.

The block of text just deleted with the Block/**Ctrl-F4** (Move),**B**lock,**D**elete command will appear on the screen.

As mentioned earlier, the **F1** (Cancel) command may be used to recover (Undelete) text that has been previously typed over or deleted. The **F1** (Cancel) command works in a manner similar to the Move command. The **F1** (Cancel) command maintains three buffers, called *Undelete buffers*, into which typed-over or deleted text is automatically copied at the time the event occurs. The last typeover or deletion is kept in the first buffer; the previous two typeovers or deletions are kept in the second and third buffers.

Unlike the Block/(Move),**B**lock,**M**ove and Block/(Move),**B**lock,**C**opy commands, the Block/(Move),**B**lock,**D**elete command does not place the blocked text into the Move Block buffer. Instead, it places it in the first buffer of the three Undelete buffers.

27. Now type **F1** (Cancel) or ||↵|| to exit from the Cancel command and return to normal editing.

Block/Backspace or Block/Del

A much faster method to delete a block of text is to first block the text with **Alt-F4** (Block) and then simply type the Backspace or Del key. The prompt "Delete Block? **N**o (**Y**es)" will appear at the bottom of the screen. To complete the deletion, type **Y**. The end result of Block/Backspace or Block/Del is exactly the same as Block/(Move),**B**lock,**D**elete.

Using the Undelete Buffers to Perform Move and Copy Operations

It might occur to you that one could delete text and then later undelete text to perform various move and copy operations—that is, use the Undelete buffers rather than the Move Block buffer to hold the text. One advantage to this approach is that considerably fewer keystrokes are required.

In fact, using the Cancel command is another way to perform cut-and-paste operations. However, if you do this, you need to keep in mind that the text in the Undelete buffers is easily and automatically replaced each time a typeover or deletion occurs.

Using the Block/**F10** (Save) Command to Perform Move and Copy Operations

The last method of performing cut-and-paste operations with WordPerfect involves saving a block of text onto the disk as a separate file and then later reading the file into the current document. To give you experience performing such cut-and-paste operations, do the following.

28. Move the cursor to the # character (Ln 3.17" Pos 1"), and then block the text which describes the available townhouse unit.

```
# 12 - 1850 Square Feet, 3 Bedrooms, 2 Baths          $480.00/Month

      * Living room, Dining room, Den
      * Utility room w/Washer and Dryer
      * Fireplace
      * Bedroom Balcony
      * Carport Attached_
```

29. Now type the **F10** (Save) command. At the bottom of the screen the message "Block name:" should appear.

NOTE: In the next steps, drive *means type the letter (A, B, etc.) for the disk drive in which your files disk is kept.*

30. Type ||*drive*:T12↵|| (for townhouse #12).

31. Next, move the cursor to Ln 4.5" Pos 1" and type **Shift-F10** (Retrieve). Answer the prompt "Document to be retrieved:" by typing ||*drive*:T12↵||.

Saving a block of text as a separate file and then reading the block into a document has several advantages over the other cut-and-paste operations discussed here. There are relatively few keystrokes involved, and the saved block will only be replaced on the disk if another block or document is saved with the same filename. The method also provides a simple means to copy blocks of text from one document file to one or more other document files. The biggest disadvantage of the approach is the possible accumulation over time of several small files on your disk.

Finishing the Document

32. Use the commands of your choice to bring the second page of the document to the form shown on the following page.

```
                    Vista Ridge Townhouses
                    ======================

                        Units Available
                    For Immediate Occupancy



# 12 - 1850 Square Feet, 3 Bedrooms, 2 Baths         $480.00/Month

     * Living room, Dining room, Den
     * Utility room w/Washer and Dryer
     * Fireplace
     * Bedroom Balcony
     * Carport Attached

# 27 - 1600 Square Feet, 3 Bedrooms, 1 1/2 Baths     $430.00/Month

     * Living room, Dining room, Den
     * Utility room w/Washer and Dryer Hookups
     * Fireplace
     * Carport Attached

# 44 - 1050 Square Feet, 3 Bedrooms, 2 Baths         $465.00/Month

     * Living room, Dining room, Den
     * Utility room w/Washer and Dryer
     * Fireplace
     * Bedroom Balcony

# 53 - 1200 Square Feet, 2 Bedrooms, 1 Bath          $380.00/Month

     * Living room, Dining room
     * Utility room w/Washer and Dryer
     * Fireplace

Typeover                                Doc 1 Pg 2 Ln 7.67" Pos 1"
```

LESSON 5
Basic File Operations

The remainder of the tutorial deals with the WordPerfect commands used to perform simple file management operations (deleting files, copying files, and so forth), saving document files, printing documents, and exiting the WordPerfect software.

Using the **F5** (List) Command

The **F5** (List) command may be used to change the default disk drive and perform several file management operations from within WordPerfect. The screen presented by the List command displays the files on the current disk or directory. To demonstrate some of the List command features, do the following.

1. Type the **F5** (List) command.

At the bottom of the screen you will see a message similar to

```
Dir A:\*.*                                    (Type = to change default Dir)
```

Changing the Default Disk Drive/Directory

The current default disk drive and directory appears on the left side of the status line. The information displayed there should describe where your files are currently located. To change WordPerfect's default disk drive and directory, you may type =, then enter the appropriate drive and directory.

2. If the drive and directory displayed on the left side of the message do not describe where your files are currently located, change the default disk drive and then type ||↵↵|| to view the List screen. Otherwise, type ||↵|| to view the List screen.

The **F5** (List) Command Screen

A screen similar to the following will appear.

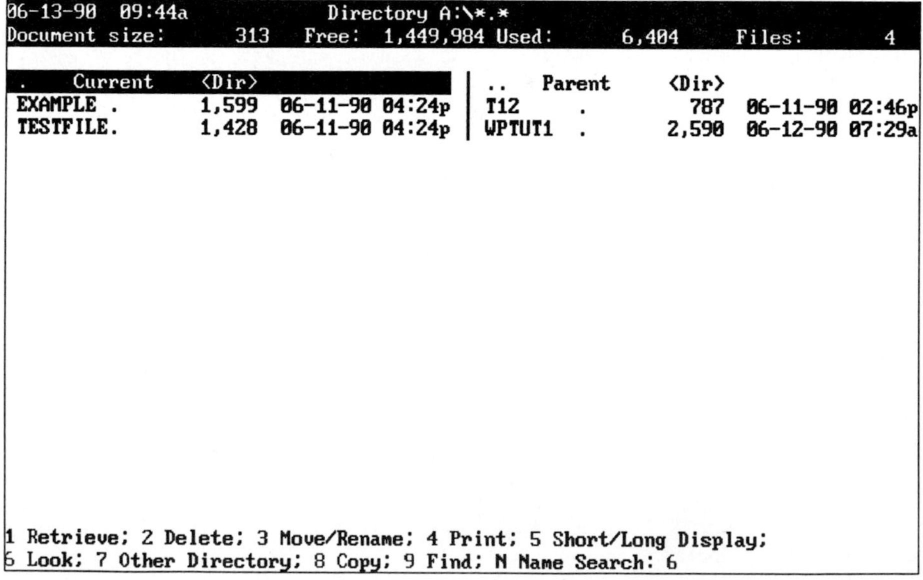

The reverse video bar shown in the top left corner of the screen is the List cursor. The cursor may be moved around the screen with the cursor control keys. In general, to use the **F5** (List) commands, you first move the cursor to a file listed on the screen, and then type the number or letter of the command you wish to execute, as in the following steps.

3. Move the cursor to the file named T12, and then type **2** or **D** (**D**elete).

The message "Delete *drive*:\ T12? **No Yes**" will appear at the bottom of the screen.

4. Next type **Y** to complete the Delete File operation.

The file you created for the purpose of making copies of text should now be erased from the disk.

5. Next type **F1** (Cancel) or **F7** (Exit) to leave the List screen and return to normal editing of the document.

Saving a Document

You may save a document file onto your disk by using the **F10** (Save) command.

6. Type **F10** (Save) to begin the save operation.

The message "Document to be saved:" will appear at the bottom of the screen on the status line.

7. Now type ||WPTUT1↵||.

WPTUT1 stands for WordPerfect tutorial #1 and is simply a filename that conforms to the rules for filenames.

Notice that when the Insert mode is on, the filename now appears on the left side of the status line. If you save the document again, the procedure will be slightly different. After you type **F10** (Save), WordPerfect will respond with the prompt "Document to be saved: *drive*:\ WPTUT1." If you type ↵, WordPerfect assumes you want to save the document under the same name. The message "Replace *drive*:\WPTUT1? **No** (**Yes**)" appears on the status line as a precaution against accidentally replacing the file on the disk with the file in memory. You must type **Y** to complete the resave operation.

While you create and edit your documents it is highly recommended that you use the **F10** (Save) command about every 15 minutes or so.

Printing a Document

You are now ready to print the document. To print a document currently in memory, you use the **Shift-F7** (Print) command.

8. Make sure the printer is on, on-line, and connected to your computer. (Your lab may have a shared device control switch. If so, you will need to select your computer as the one currently connected to the printer.)
9. Advance the paper in the printer to the top of the next page.
10. Now type the **Shift-F7** (Print) command

The following menu will appear on the screen.

```
Print

     1 - Full Document
     2 - Page
     3 - Document on Disk
     4 - Control Printer
     5 - Multiple Pages
     6 - View Document
     7 - Initialize Printer

Options

     S - Select Printer                 Epson FX-86e
     B - Binding Offset                 0"
     N - Number of Copies               1
     U - Multiple Copies Generated by   WordPerfect
     G - Graphics Quality               Medium
     T - Text Quality                   High

Selection: 0
```

11. Type **1** or **F** to select the **Shift-F7** (Print),**F**ull Document command.

The printer should respond by printing the document complete with margins, centered text, and underlining. Notice that the printed text is left and right justified to the margins. To print text with a ragged right margin, the type of justification you see on the screen, you must change justification to **L**eft with the **Shift-F8,1,3** (Format),**L**ine,**J**ustification command.

Exiting WordPerfect

The WordPerfect **F7** (Exit) command may be used to properly exit from many WordPerfect commands, or to erase your document file from memory and return to DOS (erase your document and WordPerfect from memory). The Exit command is the only proper way to quit WordPerfect. Any other method may result in lost data. To conclude the tutorial, do the following.

12. Type the **F7** (Exit) command.
13. Answer the prompt "Save document? **Y**es (**N**o)" by typing **N**. You have already just saved the document with the **F10** (Save) command.
14. Answer the next prompt "Exit WP? **N**o (**Y**es)" by typing **Y**.

Vista Ridge Townhouses

1800 S.W. Sunset View Avenue
Portland, OR 97207

Thank you for your interest in Vista Ridge Townhouses. We feel that our one and two bedroom deluxe townhouse apartments offer adult living at its finest.

Each spacious townhouse unit has wall-to-wall carpeting, drapes, private patio and sun deck. You will find the townhouse of your choice equipped with a completely modern kitchen including a self-defrosting refrigerator, self-cleaning oven, dishwasher and garbage disposal unit. In addition, every Vista Ridge tenant enjoys year-round swimming and sauna plus use of our recreation room and tennis courts.

We are located in the South West Heights area, close to shopping, city parks and University campus. For an appointment to view one of our fine townhouse apartments and a tour of the grounds, please call Mr. Smith at (503) 244-7163.

Vista Ridge Townhouses

Units Available
For Immediate Occupancy

12 - 1850 Square Feet, 3 Bedrooms, 2 Baths $480.00/Month

* Living room, Dining room, Den
* Utility room w/Washer and Dryer
* Fireplace
* Bedroom Balcony
* Carport Attached

27 - 1600 Square Feet, 3 Bedrooms, 1 1/2 Baths $430.00/Month

* Living room, Dining room, Den
* Utility room w/Washer and Dryer Hookups
* Fireplace
* Carport Attached

44 - 1050 Square Feet, 3 Bedrooms, 2 Baths $465.00/Month

* Living room, Dining room, Den
* Utility room w/Washer and Dryer
* Fireplace
* Bedroom Balcony

53 - 1200 Square Feet, 2 Bedrooms, 1 Bath $380.00/Month

* Living room, Dining room
* Utility room w/Washer and Dryer
* Fireplace

EXERCISES

EXERCISE 1
Printer Fonts

Required Preparation

Study the use of the **Ctrl-F8** (Font), **S**ize and **A**ppearance commands and the **Shift-F7** (Print) **V**iew Document command presented in the WordPerfect Command Summary.

Exercise Steps

1. Load WordPerfect into memory.
2. Type ‖This is an EXAMPLE‖, **Alt-F6** (Flush Right), ‖of Size:↵‖.
3. Next type ‖This is an EXAMPLE‖, **Alt-F6** (Flush Right), ‖of Appearance:↵‖.

The two lines should appear as follows.

```
This is an EXAMPLE                                of Size:
This is an EXAMPLE                          of Appearance:
```

4. Make six copies of the first line and eight copies of the second line, and then edit the lines so they appear as in the following.

```
This is an EXAMPLE                     of Size:Superscript
This is an EXAMPLE                       of Size:Subscript
This is an EXAMPLE                            of Size:Fine
This is an EXAMPLE                           of Size:Small
This is an EXAMPLE                           of Size:Large
This is an EXAMPLE                      of Size:Very Large
This is an EXAMPLE                     of Size:Extra Large

This is an EXAMPLE                      of Appearance:Bold
This is an EXAMPLE                 of Appearance:Underline
This is an EXAMPLE          of Appearance:Double Underline
This is an EXAMPLE                    of Appearance:Italic
This is an EXAMPLE                   of Appearance:Outline
This is an EXAMPLE                    of Appearance:Shadow
This is an EXAMPLE            of Appearance:Small Capitals
This is an EXAMPLE                   of Appearance:Redline
This is an EXAMPLE                 of Appearance:Strikeout




                                 Doc 1 Pg 1 Ln 3.83" Pos 1"
```

5. On each line use the **Alt-F4** (Block) command to first block the text, "This is an EXAMPLE". Then select **Ctrl-F8** (Font),**S**ize or **Ctrl-F8** (Font),**A**ppearance and select the appropriate font option for that line (the appropriate option is indicated on the flush right side of the line).
6. Set the line spacing to 2 (double) for the entire document.

7. Use the **Shift-F6** (Center) command, and enter your brand of printer where "Make/Model" is indicated in the following heading:

WordPerfect Fonts
Ctrl-F8 (Font) - Size:/Appearance:
Printer - Make/Model

8. Use the **Shift-F7** (Print), **V**iew Document commands to preview the page before you print it. The screen should appear similar to the following.

```
                    WordPerfect Fonts
           Ctrl-F8 (Font) - Size:/Appearance:
                Printer - Epson/FX-86e

This is an EXAMPLE                      of Size:Superscript
This is an EXAMPLE                        of Size:Subscript
This is an EXAMPLE                             of Size:Fine
This is an EXAMPLE                            of Size:Small
This is an EXAMPLE                            of Size:Large
This is an EXAMPLE                       of Size:Very Large
This is an EXAMPLE                      of Size:Extra Large

This is an EXAMPLE                       of Appearance:Bold
This is an EXAMPLE                  of Appearance:Underline
This is an EXAMPLE           of Appearance:Double Underline
1 100%  2 200%  3 Full Page  4 Facing Pages: 1     Doc 1 Pg 1
```

9. Print the document.

The appearance of the printed document will vary depending on the make and model of printer being used. Few printers support all of the available **Ctrl-F8** (Font) command formats.

10. Use the information obtained from the first page of the document to create a second page showing combined formats in a similar manner. For instance, show what a segment of large, bold, italic printed text looks like. Produce four such combinations.
11. Print two copies of the finished document and keep one copy with your WordPerfect documentation for future reference.
12. Save the document file under the name MYFONT and then exit WordPerfect.

EXERCISE 2
Personal Résumé

The following is a classic exercise that uses many basic word processing skills while providing the opportunity to create an important personal document.

Required Preparation

Study the use of the **F4** (▶Indent) and **Ctrl-F8** (Font) commands presented in the WordPerfect Command Summary.

Exercise Steps

1. Load WordPerfect into memory.
2. Using the following example, create your own résumé (or a résumé for someone else) in the same or similar form.
3. On a separate page, list the commands you used to format the document with the codes that the commands imbedded into the résumé.
4. Print the résumé and summary of commands/codes, and then save the file under the name RESUME.
5. Exit WordPerfect.

JEROME C. FAIRFAX

P.O. Box 198 Portland, OR 97207
(503) 244-8733 H (503) 229-2724 W

EDUCATION

Bachelor of Arts, Business Administration - Marketing
Bachelor of Arts, Spanish
Certificate of International Business Studies
PORTLAND STATE UNIVERSITY, Portland, OR June 1990

EXPERIENCE

Front Desk/Public Relations
Center Court Athletic Club, Portland, OR. Greet and register members and guests. Conduct tours of facility and explain benefits. Attend to members' needs, serve snack bar items and make reservations. Promote club programs, answer telephone inquiries, collect and process payments on accounts. (September 1988 to present)

Manager
Coffee House Juice Bar, Portland, OR. Directed set-up and closing procedures. Planned for special events. Presented and promoted product line. Screened and interviewed applicants. Oriented and trained new employees. Supervised five employees. Managed and supervised a food booth at the Artquake Festival with a crew of 20. Controlled cash flow. (June 1985 to September 1988)

Order Desk/Billing Clerk
Ruston Wholesale Glassware, Portland, OR. Assisted customers with glassware selections. Handled telephone orders, explained shipping policies to customers and invoiced the previous day's orders. Represented company at Oregon Restaurant Association Convention. (September 1984 to June 1985)

ORGANIZATIONS

AIESEC Association Internationale des Etudiants en Sciences Economiques et Commerciales .. International Association of Students in Economics and Commerce.

- Chapter Vice-President, 1987 - 1988
- Chairperson, Fundraising Committee 1986 - 1988

INTERESTS

Racquetball, white-water rafting, fishing and boating.

Excellent References Available

EXERCISE 3
Search and Replace

Required Preparation

Study the use of the F2 (▶Search), Shift-F2 (◀Search), and Alt-F2 (Replace) commands presented in the WordPerfect Command Summary.

Exercise Steps

1. Load WordPerfect and then retrieve the document you created in the introductory tutorial (WPTUT1).
2. Start at the top of the file and use the **F2** (▶Search) command to find the first occurrence of *Mr. Smith.* Edit the text to read *Mr. Jennings.*
3. Type Home,Home,Up to move the cursor to the top of the file. Turn on the Reveal Codes screen and then use the **F2** (▶Search) command to find the next five occurrences of a [Tab] code. When finished, return the screen to normal editing.
4. Type Home,Home,Up to move the cursor to the top of the file, and then use the **Alt-F2** (Replace) command to replace all occurrences of *townhouse* with *condominium.* Make sure that the replace operation is performed with Confirm as **Y** for *Yes.*
5. Next use the **Alt-F2** (Replace) command to delete all occurrences of the word *apartments.* Conduct the search backwards through the file and make sure that Confirm is **Y**es.
6. Edit the document so that it appears as it does on the following two pages.
7. Save the file under the name WPTUT1B, and then print the document and exit WordPerfect.

Vista Ridge Condominiums

1800 S.W. Sunset View Avenue
Portland, OR 97207

Thank you for your interest in Vista Ridge Condominiums. We feel that our one and two bedroom deluxe condominiums offer adult living at its finest.

Each spacious condominium unit has wall-to-wall carpeting, drapes, private patio and sun deck. You will find the condominium of your choice equipped with a completely modern kitchen including a self-defrosting refrigerator, self-cleaning oven, dishwasher and garbage disposal unit. In addition, every Vista Ridge owner enjoys year-round swimming and sauna plus use of our recreation room and tennis courts.

We are located in the South West Heights area, close to shopping, city parks and University campus. For an appointment to view one of our fine condominiums and a tour of the grounds, please call Mr. Jennings at (503) 244-7163.

Vista Ridge Condominiums

Units Available

12 - 1850 Square Feet, 3 Bedrooms, 2 Baths $44,250

* Living room, Dining room, Den
* Utility room w/Washer and Dryer
* Fireplace
* Bedroom Balcony
* Carport Attached

27 - 1600 Square Feet, 3 Bedrooms, 1 1/2 Baths $38,500

* Living room, Dining room, Den
* Utility room w/Washer and Dryer Hookups
* Fireplace
* Carport Attached

44 - 1050 Square Feet, 3 Bedrooms, 2 Baths $40,650

* Living room, Dining room, Den
* Utility room w/Washer and Dryer
* Fireplace
* Bedroom Balcony

53 - 1200 Square Feet, 2 Bedrooms, 1 Bath $24,450

* Living room, Dining room
* Utility room w/Washer and Dryer
* Fireplace

EXERCISE 4
Tabular Columns

Required Preparation

Study the use of the **Shift-F8** (Format),**L**ine,**T**ab Set and Block/**Ctrl-F4** (Move) commands presented in the WordPerfect Command Summary.

Exercise Steps

1. Load WordPerfect into memory.

In this exercise, you will specify tab stop settings and use the Tab key to produce the following document.

```
Paper Product      Descr.    Units Per     Average       Cost/Case
   Items                       Case       Sales/Week

Take-Out Cups

  Paper            8 oz        250          400. . . . . . $15.00
                   12 oz       250          800. . . . . . $17.00
                   16 oz       150          300. . . . . . $12.50

  Styrofoam        8 oz         75         1200. . . . . . .$3.50
                   12 oz        75          600. . . . . . .$4.25

Sandwich Wrap

  Wax Paper        Plain      5000         4000. . . . . . $50.75
                   Printed    5000         2500. . . . . . $75.30
  Aluminum         Printed    5000          900. . . . . .$125.00

Take-Out Utensils

  Forks            Plastic     500          350. . . . . . .$7.50
  Spoons           Plastic     500          275. . . . . . .$6.00
  Knives           Plastic     750           75. . . . . . .$9.00
                                                    Doc 1 Pg 1 Ln 1" Pos 1"
```

On Line 1" at Pos 1" you will insert a [Tab Set:] code into the document. The tabs are designed for centering the table headings to the tab stops in the first two lines of text. When you are finished specifying the appropriate tab stops, the **T**ab Set screen will appear as follows.

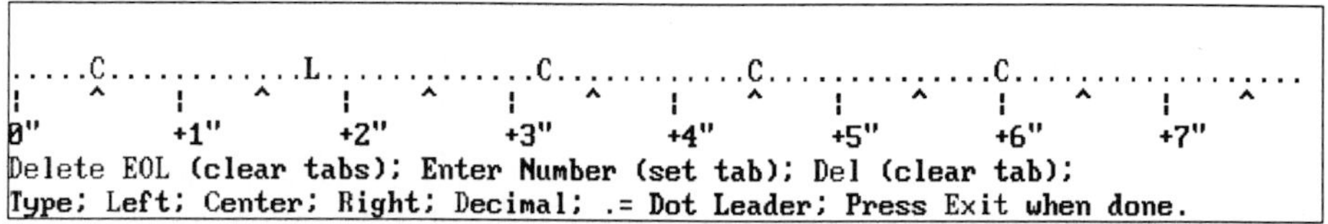

```
....C...........L............C...........C..............C..................
:    ^    :    ^    :    ^    :    ^    :    ^    :    ^    :    ^    :    ^
0"       +1"       +2"       +3"       +4"       +5"       +6"       +7"
Delete EOL (clear tabs); Enter Number (set tab); Del (clear tab);
Type; Left; Center; Right; Decimal; .= Dot Leader; Press Exit when done.
```

2. Move the cursor to the appropriate Ln"/Pos" screen position, and then use the **Shift-F8** (Format),**L**ine,**T**ab Set command to set the correct tab stop types at the positions shown.

3. Enter the first two lines of text, being sure to use the Tab key to move the cursor to the next heading position. End each line with a [HRt] (↵). When finished, use the Reveal Codes screen to ensure that only text characters, [Cntr Tab] codes, and [Tab] codes occur in the two lines.

On the line beneath the headings (Ln 1.33" Pos 1") occurs another [Tab Set:] code designed to align the items in the table to their respective tab stops in a variety of ways. When you are finished specifying the appropriate tab stops for the second [Tab Set:] code, the **T**ab Set screen will appear as follows.

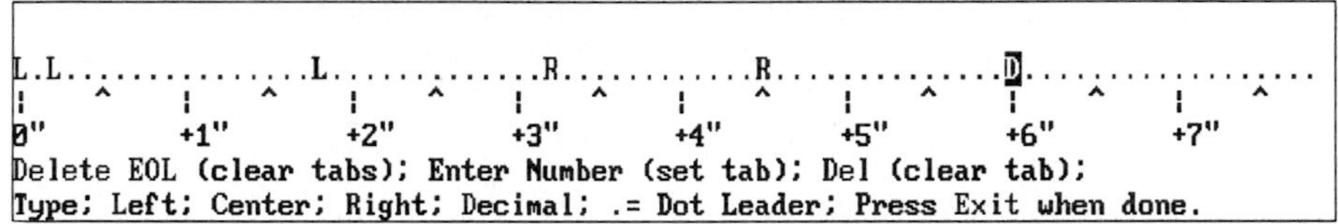

Notice that the last tab stop is **D**ecimal type with a Dot Leader.

4. Move the cursor to the appropriate Ln"/Pos" screen position, and then use the **Shift-F8** (Format),**L**ine,**T**ab Set command to set the correct tab stop types at the positions shown for the second [Tab Set:] code.
5. Enter the lines of text that comprise the table of items, numbers, and costs. Again, be sure to use the Tab key to move the cursor to the next entry position on a line and use a ↵ to end each line. Use the Reveal Codes screen to ensure that only text characters and [Tab] codes occur in the table.
6. Now save the file under the name TABCOLS.

In the next steps of this exercise, you will move the column labeled "Average Sales/Week" one column to the left. To do so, you will need to use the Block/**Ctrl-F4** (Move),Tabular **C**olumn,**M**ove command.

7. Review the steps required to perform a Tabular **C**olumn,**M**ove operation in the WordPerfect Command Summary.

If the following does not work as expected, use the **F7** (Exit) command to clear the screen (**F7**,n,↵) and then retrieve "TABCOLS" and try again.

8. Use the command to move the "Average Sales/Week" column (with its label) one column to the left.

```
Paper Product       Descr.     Average      Units Per      Cost/Case
  Items                       Sales/Week      Case

Take-Out Cups

  Paper             8 oz        400          250. . . . . . $15.00
                    12 oz       800          250. . . . . . $17.00
                    16 oz       300          150. . . . . . $12.50

  Styrofoam         8 oz        1200          75. . . . . . .$3.50
                    12 oz       600           75. . . . . . .$4.25

Sandwich Wrap

  Wax Paper         Plain       4000        5000. . . . . . $50.75
                    Printed     2500        5000. . . . . . $75.30
  Aluminum          Printed     900         5000. . . . . .$125.00

Take-Out Utensils

  Forks             Plastic     350          500. . . . . . .$7.50
  Spoons            Plastic     275          500. . . . . . .$6.00
  Knives            Plastic      75          750. . . . . . .$9.00
                                                    Doc 1 Pg 1 Ln 1" Pos 1"
```

9. Save the document under the name TABCOLS2, and then print the document.

To gain further experience, it is recommended that you practice copying and moving other columns in the table using the Block/**Ctrl-F4** (Move),Tabular **C**olumn commands.

10. When finished, exit WordPerfect.

EXERCISE 5
Formal Reports

Required Preparation

Study the use of the **Ctrl-2** (Spell), **Alt-F1** (Thesaurus), **Shift-F8** (Format), **P**age,**H**eader, **Shift-F7** (Print),**V**iew Document, and **Ctrl-F7** (Footnote) commands presented in the WordPerfect Command Summary.

Exercise Steps

1. Load WordPerfect into memory.
2. To begin the exercise, type the following text. The misspelled words in the text are intentional, so take care to enter the text exactly as it is shown here. Begin the heading "Introduction" six lines down from the top of the document (at Ln 2.16").

Introduction

Word Processing has longe been an intregal part of many business organizations. Webster difines Word Processing as "the production of typewriten documents (as business letters) with automated and usually computerized typing and text-editing equipment." The equipment may range from typewriters with memory, correction, and mag card features to dedicated word processing equipment to general perpuse computers using specalized word processing software.

Until recently, the the expanse of word processing equipment and software made it a viable option only to document-intense businesses that could justify the cost. Many businesses with lower volume needs turned to outside service organizations specalizing in Word Processing to provide this function. With the apperance of the microcomputer, however, even small businesses could afford to computerize many business functions, and soon thereafter word processing software became available and afordable to anyone with even minimal word processing requirements.

With the recent development and proliferation of word processing software for the desktop microcomputer comes a wide array of choices. Software prices now range from under fifty to several hundred dollars, with a coresponding range of features and capapilities. Its role in business has also changed, as word processing has become recognized as a useful and versitile tool for people at various organizational levels.

3. Use the **Ctrl-F2** (Spell) command to perform a spelling check on the entire document. Using WordPerfect's Spell feature, correct any misspelled words and remove any unnecessary double words from the document. The following is a list of correct spellings for the words upon which the spelling check should stop.

   long
   integral (use the Look Up command to find the proper spelling for this word)
   defines
   typewritten
   purpose
   specialized
   specializing
   appearance
   affordable
   desktop (the spell check will stop on any word not in its dictionary files; if it stops on desktop, use the Skip command, since this word is spelled correctly.)
   corresponding
   capabilities
   versatile

Notice that the spell checker did not catch the misspelling of the word *expense*, located in the first line of the second paragraph. The misspelled word expanse is itself a correctly spelled word. The word was included in the exercise to demonstrate that spell checking is no substitute for proofreading.

4. Edit the word expanse to reflect the correct spelling of the word *expense*.

5. Next use **Alt-F1** (Thesaurus) to find suitable synonyms for the following words.

    viable
    justify
    outside
    available
    useful

6. Now use the **Shift-F8** (Format) command to add a *Page Header A* to be printed on every page of the document. The header should be aligned flush right and should include the words "Word Processing Page #" followed by the code that will print the current page number in the header.
7. Next set the line spacing to 2 for the entire document. Then use the **Shift-F7** (Print),**V**iew Document command to ensure that the header will be properly printed.
8. Now move the cursor to the right of the word *dedicated*, found in the first paragraph, and enter a footnote containing the following text: ||Dedicated refers to hardware designed for one specific function.||
9. Move the cursor to the space following the second word in the first paragraph, *Processing*, and enter another footnote containing the text: ||Also referred to as Text Processing, a term deemed more appropriate by some.||
10. Use the **Shift-F7** (Print),**V**iew Document command to see that the two footnotes will be properly printed.
11. Save the document under the name "REPORT", print the document, and then exit WordPerfect.

EXERCISE 6 Boiler Plate Contracts

Many situations require a standard form or document (general text) that must be "filled" in with specific information. When this is the case, it is often possible to automatically merge the specific information into the general text to produce the desired finished document.

This exercise is designed to demonstrate the use of merge codes used in a procedure called *boiler plating*. In boiler plating, the general text is called the *primary file* and is the document in which the merge codes are placed. The specific information is either typed in by the user or is kept in other related files. In this exercise, the following merge codes will be used.

{DOCUMENT}*filename*˜

The {DOCUMENT}*filename*˜ merge code may be used to retrieve and insert the specified document file into the primary file at the location of the {DOCUMENT} code.

{INPUT}*message*˜

The {INPUT} merge code pauses a merge so text may be entered from the keyboard. When the {INPUT} code is selected from the **M**ore menu of merge codes, the prompt "Enter Message" appears on the status line. The message entered will be displayed on the status line when the code is encountered during a merge operation. The merge will then pause for the user to type the appropriate text. When finished, the user must type **F9** (End Field) to proceed with the merge operation.

{KEYBOARD}

The {KEYBOARD} code is similar to the {INPUT} code because it pauses the merge operation for the user to enter data from the keyboard. However, with the {KEYBOARD} code, a message is not displayed on the status line for the reader to view. When finished entering the text allowed by the {KEYBOARD} code, the user must type **F9** (End Field) to proceed with the merge operation.

{TEXT}*var˜ message˜*

The {TEXT} code may be used to prompt the user for a response, and then store the response in a variable for later use. To merge data contained in a WordPerfect variable, the {VARIABLE}*var˜* code is used.

{VARIABLE}*var˜*

The {VARIABLE} code is used to insert the contents of the specified variable into the document at the location of the code.

The above merge codes are placed into the primary file with the **Shift-F9** (Merge Codes),**M**ore command. After typing **Shift-F9** (Merge Codes),**M**ore, move the **M**ore menu bar to the code you desire and type ↵.

Required Preparation

Study the use of the **Ctrl-F9** (Merge/Sort),**M**erge commands, the **Shift-F9** (Merge Codes) command, and the **F9** (End Field) command presented in the WordPerfect Command Summary.

Exercise Steps

To begin, you will create the primary file for a rental contract. Here the merge codes have been shaded to make the text easier to read. The merge codes on your monitor screen will probably not be shaded.

1. Begin by entering the text as it is shown in the following. Be sure to use the **Shift-F6** (Center) command to center the contract heading.

```
                    Vista Ridge Townhouses
                       Rental Agreement
                    ======================

This rental agreement made and entered into this _
```

In the next step you will use the **Shift-F9** (Merge Codes),**M**ore command to insert a {KEYBOARD} merge code into the document at the location of the cursor.

2. Type **Shift-F9**, **6** or **M** for (Merge Codes),**M**ore, and then select the {KEYBOARD} code from the menu presented by the command.
3. Continue by typing ‖ day of ‖, and then insert another {KEYBOARD} merge code into the document.
4. Next type ‖ 1992, by and between Vista Ridge Townhouses, hereinafter called the lessor, and ‖.

The screen should now appear as follows.

```
                    Vista Ridge Townhouses
                       Rental Agreement
                    ======================

This rental agreement made and entered into this {KEYBOARD} day of {KEYBOARD} 19
and between Vista Ridge Townhouses, hereinafter called the lessor,
and _
```

Notice that WordPerfect will wrap text in a paragraph as though merge codes do not exist. In this case, the first line of text will not wrap until it has extended beyond the right border of the screen.

5. Now use the **Shift-F9** (Merge Codes),**M**ore command to select an {INPUT} merge code. Answer the "Enter Message:" prompt by typing ||Enter lesee's first and last names.↵||.
6. Continue by entering the text necessary to bring the contract to the form shown in the following.

```
                    Vista Ridge Townhouses
                       Rental Agreement
                    ======================

This rental agreement made and entered into this {KEYBOARD} day of {KEYBOARD} 19
and between Vista Ridge Townhouses, hereinafter called the lessor,
and {INPUT}Enter lessee's first and last names.~ hereinafter called
lessee,

In consideration of the covenants and stipulations herein contained
on the part of the lessee to be paid, kept and faithfully
performed, the lessor does hereby lease, demise, and let unto said
lessee those certain premises, for the stated payments in lawful
money, known and described as follows:
```

Notice that when a merge code has associated text, such as the message following the {INPUT} code, the text is treated (with respect for word wrap) as being characters of text in the line.

At this point in the contract, the primary document will be designed to merge the description for a specific townhouse unit. The various possible descriptions will be kept in separate disk files, each of which will have a filename that begins with the character "T" and ends with the number of the townhouse unit. For instance, the description for townhouse #44 will be kept in the file named "T44."

To accomplish this merge operation, a {TEXT} merge code will first be used to prompt the user to enter the number of the townhouse to which the contract pertains. The {TEXT} code will assign the user entry to the variable named "number." A {DOCUMENT} and {VARIABLE} code combination will then be used to merge the appropriate description into the document.

7. Move the cursor to Ln 3.67", Pos 1", and then use the Merge Codes command to select a {TEXT} code.
8. Answer the "Enter Variable:" prompt by typing ||number←||.
9. Next answer the "Enter Message:" prompt by typing ||Enter the number of the townhouse unit.←||.
10. Now move the cursor down one line, to Ln 3.83", and select the {DOCUMENT} merge code.
11. Answer the "Enter Filename:" prompt by typing ||T←||.
12. Now move the cursor left one character, under the ˜ (tilde) character.

The two merge codes should now appear on the screen in the following form.

```
{TEXT}number~Enter the number of the townhouse unit.~
{DOCUMENT}T~
```

13. Now, making sure that the Insert mode is on, use the Merge Codes command to select a {VARIABLE} code. Answer the "Enter Variable:" prompt by typing ||number ←||.

The codes should now appear on the screen as follows.

```
{TEXT}number~Enter the number of the townhouse unit.~
{DOCUMENT}T{VARIABLE}number~~
```

If, for any reason, only one tilde (˜) is at the end of the {DOCUMENT} {VARIABLE} code combination, enter (type) the second ˜ character into the appropriate place at this time.

The codes you just entered into the document will perform the following actions during a merge operation. First, prompt the user to enter the unit number of the townhouse, and then store that answer in the variable named "number" ({TEXT}number˜ Enter the number of the townhouse unit.˜). Next, insert the document named "T," plus the characters held in the variable named "number," into the document ({DOCUMENT} T{VARIABLE}number˜ ˜).

To complete the primary document, you will next enter three additional merge code combinations that will operate in a similar manner. The first such combination will merge either the file named LOCKY or the file named LOCKN. The second combination will merge either the file named CLEAN1 or the file named CLEAN2, and the third combination will merge either the file named PETY or the file named PETN.

14. Enter the necessary codes and text required to bring the primary file to the form shown on the following page. Note that the dollar signs in the contract occur at Pos 6.1".

```
                    Vista Ridge Townhouses
                       Rental Agreement
                    ======================

This rental agreement made and entered into this {KEYBOARD} day of {KEYBOARD} 19
and between Vista Ridge Townhouses, hereinafter called the lessor,
and {INPUT}Enter lessee's first and last names.~ hereinafter called
lessee,

In consideration of the covenants and stipulations herein contained
on the part of the lessee to be paid, kept and faithfully
performed, the lessor does hereby lease, demise, and let unto said
lessee those certain premises, for the stated payments in lawful
money, known and described as follows:

{TEXT}number~Enter the number of the townhouse unit.~
{DOCUMENT}T{VARIABLE}number~~

Additional monthly fees:
{TEXT}answer~Locker storage? (Y/N)~
{DOCUMENT}LOCK{VARIABLE}answer~~

                                Total Monthly Rent $

Deposits:
{TEXT}answer~Cleaning fee: 1 Small, 2 Large~
{DOCUMENT}CLEAN{VARIABLE}answer~~
{TEXT}answer~Pet Deposit? (Y/N)~
{DOCUMENT}PET{VARIABLE}answer~~

                                    Total Deposits $

                                  Payment Received $

Signed: _________________________ Lessor

        _________________________ Lessee
```

15. When finished, check that all codes have the proper number and placement of tildes (~), and then save the file under the name "RNTCNT" (for rental contract).
16. Now, use the **F7** (Exit) command to clear the screen (**F7**,n,↵).

The next steps in the exercise involve creating three separate files, each of which will contain a description for a different townhouse unit.

17. Noting that the dollar sign occurs at 6.1", type the text as shown in the following.

```
Townhouse # 12 - 1850 Square Feet, 3 Bedrooms, 2 Baths.  Includes
drapes, carpets, kitchen appliances, washer and dryer.

Address: 9110 S.W. Sunset Ave.  Portland, OR 97207

Rental Fee ...................................... $480.00/Month
```

18. Now make two copies of the townhouse description and edit the copied text to match the following.

```
Townhouse # 12 - 1850 Square Feet, 3 Bedrooms, 2 Baths.  Includes
drapes, carpets, kitchen appliances, washer and dryer.

Address: 9110 S.W. Sunset Ave.  Portland, OR 97207

Rental Fee .................................... $480.00/Month

Townhouse # 27 - 1600 Square Feet, 3 Bedrooms, 1 1/2 Baths.
Includes drapes, carpets, kitchen appliances, washer and dryer.

Address: 9157 S.W. Sunset Ave.  Portland, OR 97207

Rental Fee .................................... $430.00/Month

Townhouse # 44 - 1750 Square Feet, 3 Bedrooms, 2 Baths.  Includes
drapes, carpets, kitchen appliances, washer and dryer.

Address: 9167 S.W. Sunset Ave.  Portland, OR 97207

Rental Fee .................................... $465.00/Month

Typeover                                 Doc 1 Pg 1 Ln 2.5" Pos 2.3"
```

19. Use the Block/**F10** (Save) command to first block, and then save each of the townhouse descriptions. Save the blocks under the filenames T12, T27, and T44 for the townhouse descriptions, top to bottom on the screen respectively.
20. Again clear the screen with the **F7** (Exit) command (**F7**,n,↵).
21. Now type the following five lines of text, noting that the lines begin at Pos 1.5" and that the dollar signs occur at Pos 6.1".

```
    Cleaning Fee Non-Refundable ................ $ 35.00

    Cleaning Fee Non-Refundable ................ $ 55.00

    Pet Deposit ................................ $ 50.00/pet

    No Pet Deposit Made

    Locker Storage ............................. $ 25.00/month
```

22. Next block and save each line under the filename indicated in the following.

	Filenames
Cleaning Fee Non-Refundable .... $ 35.00	CLEAN1
Cleaning Fee Non-Refundable .... $ 55.00	CLEAN2
Pet Deposit .... $ 50.00/pet	PETY
No Pet Deposit Made	PETN
Locker Storage .... $ 25.00/month	LOCKY

23. Now block a single space character and save it under the filename LOCKN.

During a merge operation, WordPerfect must find all related files to be merged with the primary file. The file LOCKN (consisting of one space character) will be merged into the contract should the user answer "N" to the "Locker Storage? (Y/N)" prompt.

24. Next, use the **F7** (Exit) command to clear the screen.

You are now ready to perform a boiler plate type merge. The contract you will produce is for the following situation. The date is July 29th. The new renters are John and Lisa Livingston. They will be renting townhouse #27, which is a small unit requiring the $35 cleaning deposit. They have a Siamese cat and will need locker storage for their belongings.

25. Make sure the screen is clear, and then type **Ctrl-F9,1** (Merge/Sort),**M**erge.
26. Answer the "Primary file:" prompt by typing ||RNTCNT↵||. Answer the next prompt "Secondary file:" by typing ||↵||.

Secondary files are not normally used during this type of boiler plate merge operation.

A copy of the primary file, RNTCNT, should appear on the screen with the cursor stopped where the first {KEYBOARD} code occurred in the file. To continue, do the following.

27. Type ||29th||, and then type the **F9** (End Field) command.
28. When the cursor stops at the next {KEYBOARD} code, type ||July||, then type the **F9** (End Field) command.

The next merge code encountered:

{INPUT} Enter lessee's first and last names.~

should present the {INPUT} merge code message on the status line, then pause for the user to type an entry. Notice the message at the bottom of the screen.

29. Type ||John and Lisa Livingston||, then type the **F9** (End Field) command.

The remaining four sets of merge codes all perform similarly. They present a message at the bottom of the screen requesting a particular response from the user. The responses to the messages (27, Y, 1, etc.) then are used as the last part of the filename (T27, LOCKY, CLEAN1, etc.) to specify the particular document file to be merged into the primary file.

30. Continue by typing ||27|| and then the **F9** (End Field) command. Now answer the remaining three prompts appropriately. Be sure to end each entry by typing **F9** (End Field).
31. Save the finished contract under the name "LIVICNT", and then print the document. Next clear the screen with the **F7** (Exit) command, retrieve RNTCNT, and print the primary file. Finally, exit WordPerfect.

Vista Ridge Townhouses
Rental Agreement

This rental agreement made and entered into this 29th day of July 1992, by and between Vista Ridge Townhouses hereinafter called the lessor, and John and Lisa Livingston hereinafter called lessee,

In consideration of the covenants and stipulations herein contained on the part of the lessee to be paid, kept and faithfully performed, the lessor does hereby lease, demise, and let unto said lessee those certain premises, for the stated payments in lawful money, known and described as follows:

Townhouse # 27 - 1600 Square Feet, 3 Bedrooms, 1 1/2 Baths. Includes drapes, carpets, kitchen appliances, washer and dryer.

Address: 9157 S.W. Sunset Ave. Portland, OR 97207

Rental Fee $430.00/Month

Additional monthly fees:

Locker Storage .... $ 25.00/month

Total Monthly Rent $

Deposits:

Cleaning Fee Non-Refundable .... $ 35.00

Pet Deposit .... $ 50.00/pet

Total Deposits $

Payment Received $

Signed: ____________________________ Lessor

____________________________ Lessee

Vista Ridge Townhouses
Rental Agreement

This rental agreement made and entered into this day of 1992, by and between Vista Ridge Townhouses, hereinafter called the lessor, and Enter lessee's first and last names.˜ hereinafter called lessee,

In consideration of the covenants and stipulations herein contained on the part of the lessee to be paid, kept and faithfully performed, the lessor does hereby lease, demise, and let unto said lessee those certain premises, for the stated payments in lawful money, known and described as follows:

number˜Enter the number of the townhouse unit.˜
Tnumber˜˜

Additional monthly fees:
answer˜Locker storage? (Y/N)˜
LOCKanswer˜˜

Total Monthly Rent $

Deposits:
answer˜Cleaning fee: 1 Small, 2 Large˜
CLEANanswer˜˜
answer˜Pet Deposit? (Y/N)˜
PETanswer˜˜

Total Deposits $

Payment Received $

Signed: ____________________________ Lessor

____________________________ Lessee

EXERCISE 7
Business Form Letters–Part A

This exercise concerns a "frequent flyers" club that rewards its members with free air travel based on the number of miles they have traveled with a particular airline. In the exercise, you will create a small database (secondary file) to store information about club members. There are 12 fields of data for each member in the database. The first field contains the member's account number. Fields two through nine contain the member's title, first name, middle initial (if any), last name, address, city, state, and ZIP code. The last three fields in the record contain the air miles logged by the member in the years 1990, 1991, and 1992, respectively.

Required Preparation

Study the **Ctrl-F9** (Merge/Sort),**Merge** commands presented in the WordPerfect Command Summary.

Exercise Steps

1. Load WordPerfect and begin the exercise by creating a secondary file that contains the following fields of record data. When finished, save the file under the name MEMDAT1.

									(Miles Traveled)		
Acct	**T**	**First**	**M**	**Last**	**Address**	**City**	**St**	**Zip**	**1990**	**1991**	**1992**
1117	Ms.	Robin	R.	Nichols	1680 Rio Lindo	Portland	OR	97206	27,904	28,941	12,444
2014	Mr.	Richard	L.	Dehen	9215 Lincoln Drive	Portland	OR	97221	57,906	64,852	83,352
2021	Dr.	Michael	S.	Brown	1025 SW Jenkins Road	Beaverton	OR	97005	40,912	45,815	58,836
2037	Mr.	Mark	A.	Egger	1017 Molalla Avenue	Oregon City	OR	97045	119,899	110,506	112,716
2042	Mr.	Stewart		Matsura	140 South Spruce	Portland	OR	97256	50,825	68,432	10,256
2054	Ms.	Joanna	D.	Rowe	1800 River Drive	Eugene	OR	97401	98,803	110,647	142,128
2057	Mr.	John	J.	Corrida	1091 Tuckman Road	Hood River	OR	97031	285,005	263,755	255,000
2075	Dr.	Leslie	C.	Walther	1400 NW Garden Blvd.	Roseburg	OR	97470	137,886	143,423	66,444
5110	Mr.	Kevin	W.	McAdams	3770 Commercial SE	Salem	OR	97302	30,126	1,012	2,598
2111	Ms.	Paula		Hart	Box 2880	Portland	OR	97212	329,490	304,826	295,968

With the cursor at the top of the file, the screen should now appear as follows.

```
1117{END FIELD}
Ms.{END FIELD}
Robin{END FIELD}
R.{END FIELD}
Nichols{END FIELD}
1680 Rio Lindo{END FIELD}
Portland{END FIELD}
OR{END FIELD}
97206{END FIELD}
27,904{END FIELD}
28,941{END FIELD}
12,444{END FIELD}
{END RECORD}
================================================================================
2014{END FIELD}
Mr.{END FIELD}
Richard{END FIELD}
L.{END FIELD}
Dehen{END FIELD}
9215 Lincoln Drive{END FIELD}
Portland{END FIELD}
OR{END FIELD}
97221{END FIELD}
57,906{END FIELD}
                                                Doc 1 Pg 1 Ln 1" Pos 1"
```

2. Make sure the file has been properly saved, and then clear the screen.

You will now create a form letter that will serve as the primary file for the merge operation. The primary file, when merged with the secondary file, will produce the following document for the first record in the database.

```
                    Trans Continental Airways
                      Super Travellers Club

    Air England - French Airways - Asian Pacific - Bundesluft

Account No:  1117                               October 15, 1992

Robin R. Nichols
1680 Rio Lindo
Portland, OR 97206

Dear Ms. Nichols:

It is now easier than ever to find out your current mileage balance
with our new automated phone service.  Our toll free number for
account information is 1-800-445-7036.

When calling for information, you will be instructed to press the
buttons on your touch tone phone to enter your account number and
request information.  Of course, if you are not at a touch tone
phone or would like other information, simply stay on the line and
your call will be answered by a service representative.  We hope
you find this new system to be fast and convenient.

                                                Doc 1 Pg 1 Ln 1" Pos 1"
```

3. Enter the appropriate merge codes and text to create the primary file. When finished, save the file under the name FORMLET and clear the screen.
4. Now perform the merge operation that will produce a form letter for each record in the member database. After the merge operation has

been completed, print the first three merged form letters, a copy of the primary file used, and the first three records in the secondary file. Then exit WordPerfect.

EXERCISE 8
Business Form Letters–Part B

This exercise uses the small database of club member information created in Exercise 7.

Required Preparation

Study the **Ctrl-F9** (Merge/Sort) commands presented in the WordPerfect Command Summary.

Exercise Steps

To begin the exercise, you will create a small file containing the text and merge codes that will later serve as the *header record* for the secondary file MEMDAT1.

1. Load WordPerfect into memory and then create a header record for the database MEMDAT1 that uses the following field names.

   Field 1 – ACCTNO
   Field 2 – TITLE
   Field 3 – FIRST
   Field 4 – MI
   Field 5 – LAST
   Field 6 – ADDRESS
   Field 7 – CITY
   Field 8 – STATE
   Field 9 – ZIP
   Field 10 – M90
   Field 11 – M91
   Field 12 – M92

2. When finished, save the file under the name MEMHEAD and then clear the screen.
3. Next, create the primary file that would produce the following form letter if merged with the first record of the member database (assuming the header record is present.)

```
                    Trans Continental Airways
                      Super Travellers Club

    Air England - French Airways - Asian Pacific - Bundesluft

Account No:  1117                                October 15, 1992

Robin R. Nichols
1680 Rio Lindo
Portland, OR 97206

Dear Ms. Nichols:

Congratulations!

Because your mileage balance is now over 100,000 miles for the
year, you have earned your Silver Wings, making you one of our most
valued customers.  Full details of the Silver Wings membership
privileges will be in your mail soon.

Super Travelers Club
Silver Wings Department

                                        Doc 1 Pg 1 Ln 4.83" Pos 1"
```

4. Save the document under the name SILVER and then clear the screen.
5. Now use the **Ctrl-F9** (Merge/Sort) commands to select (copy) from the disk file MEMDAT1 to the screen those member records where the 1992 air mileage is greater than 100,000 miles but less than 200,000 miles.
6. Next, move the cursor to the top of the selected records file and retrieve the file named MEMHEAD (the header record file). Then save the selected records under the name MEMSILV and clear the screen.
7. Use the **Ctrl-F9** (Merge/Sort) commands to merge the primary file SILVER with the secondary file MEMSILV and print the two resulting form letters. Then exit WordPerfect.

EXERCISE 9 Keyboard Macros

WordPerfect's Macro feature may be used to save a series of frequently used keystrokes. The same keystrokes then may be executed at any time.

Required Preparation

Before beginning the exercise, read about the **Ctrl-F10** (Macro Define) and **Alt-F10** (Macro) commands in the WordPerfect Command Summary.

Exercise Steps

Before defining your own macros, you will reset the default directory for macro files with the **Shift-F1** (Setup) command. You should make a note of the currently defined directory for macro files in order to change it back upon completion of the exercise.

1. Type **Shift-F1**,**6**,**2** (Setup),**L**ocation of Files,**K**eyboard/Macro Files; write down the entry displayed; then change it to the location (drive and directory) of your tutorial files disk/directory; and use the ↵ key to return to normal editing.

Suppose that you often change from single-spaced to double-spaced text, and vice versa. You would like a macro to perform the necessary keystrokes. The steps to change line formatting to double spacing are as follows.

1. Type **Shift-F8,1,s** (Format),**L**ine,Line **S**pacing
2. Type ||2↵||
3. Type **F7** (Exit)

2. Define a macro named ALT-D to change to double spacing.
3. Test the macro by executing it with the **Alt-F3** (Reveal Codes) screen on.
4. Type **Ctrl-F10**,Alt-D,**2** (Macro Define),{*name*},**E**dit to check the macro against the example that follows the exercise. With the Macro Define screen displayed, type **Shift-Print Screen** (Shift-PrtScr) to print the screen.

The steps to change line formatting to single spacing are:

1. Type **Shift-F8,1,s** (Format),**L**ine,Line **S**pacing
2. Type ||1↵||
3. Type **F7** (Exit)

5. Define and test a macro named ALT-S to change to single spacing.

Now suppose that you often call out specific words in a document with both double underlining and bolding. With the cursor at the beginning of a word within a sentence, the following steps could be used for double underlining and bolding the word would be:

1. **Alt-F4** (Block)
2. Ctrl-→ (Word right)
3. ← (Cursor left)
4. **Ctrl-F8,2,3** (Font),**A**ppearance,**D**bl Und
5. **Alt-F4** (Block)
6. Ctrl-← (Word left)
7. **F6** (Bold)

6. Define and test a macro named ALT-U to hold the keystrokes for double underlining and bolding a word.
7. The following are suggestions for relatively simple macros. Now define and test a macro to perform an operation (execute keystrokes). The macro may be based upon the suggestions here or may be a macro of your choice.

1. Write a macro to type the headings for a memo, with lines for DATE:, TO:, FROM:, SUBJECT:, and so forth.
2. Write a macro to set left and right margins to two inches and to set left tabs every inch.
3. Read about the **Shift-F5** (Date/Outline) commands in the WordPerfect Command Summary, then write a macro to place date text in the format: Friday, 6 January 1992, 3:02 pm.

8. Before exiting WordPerfect, use the **Shift-F1** (Setup) command to change the default drive/directory for macro files to its original drive/directory as noted in Step 1.

Example Macros

```
Macro: Action

    File            ALTD.WPM

    Description     Double Space Text

    {DISPLAY OFF}{Format}1s2{Enter}
    {Exit}
```

```
Macro: Action

    File            ALTS.WPM

    Description     Single Space Text

    {DISPLAY OFF}{Format}1s1{Enter}
    {Exit}
```

```
Macro: Action

    File            ALTU.WPM

    Description     Double Underline & Bold

    {DISPLAY OFF}{Block}{Word Right}{Left}{Font}23{Block}{Word Left}{Bold}
```

CASES

CASE 1
Los Baez, Mexican Restaurant

Burke Wilson is the new owner of the Los Baez, a Mexican restaurant located near a large university in Seattle, Washington. The restaurant's main business is serving lunch and dinner to college students and faculty. Burke bought the restaurant knowing that it had several regular customers who enjoyed the quiet hacienda atmosphere and high-quality food available there.

The restaurant seats about 85 people, with most of the tables seating four to six customers. After several months of operating the restaurant, Burke noticed that during the lunch and dinner rushes many of the tables had only one or two people seated at them. In talking with customers, he found that often there were more people who would have joined the party for lunch but didn't because they didn't care for Mexican food.

Burke decided to offer a non-Mexican meal special during rush hours to encourage new customers to join their friends. Burke and the cook decided that a different non-menu meal special would be offered every day. After a few weeks of serving the specials, Burke noted in a conversation with the cook that the customers were taking advantage of the new special offerings: "Not only are new customers coming in, but regular customers are ordering the specials for a change of pace. The lasagna you made for today sold out before 2:00 PM. We should double the amount of meat loaf planned for tomorrow. I've noticed that very few customers can see the daily special chalkboard from their seats. What we really need is some way to include the daily special in our regular menu. If I had a nicely laid-out master copy, I could have it copied for about four cents a page. Besides making selecting from the menu more convenient for the customer, "disposable" menus might save us money over time because typesetting and laminating menus, like we do now, costs quite a bit."

Item Name	Item Description	Item Price	½ Order Price
Cheese nacho	cheddar cheese, white cheese, taco chips	$3.95	$2.95
Nacho grande	cheddar cheese, meat sauce, spiced meat	$4.95	$3.95
The mini nacho	cheddar cheese, meat sauce, spiced meat, sour cream, guacamole	$3.25	
(Include somewhere on menu: All nachos are topped with green onions, tomatoes, and black olives;also that sour cream or guacamole may be added for an additional $1.25.)			
Chips and salsa		$1.50	
Chips and bean dip		$1.95	
Chips and guacamole		$2.75	
Chili con carne		(bowl) $2.25	(cup) $1.95
All beef chili		(bowl) $3.75	(cup) $2.75
Texicana hot chili		(bowl) $3.00	(cup) $2.50
(Include somewhere on menu: All chili topped with cheese and onions)			
Dinner salad	topped with cheese and tomatoes	$1.50	
Chili and salad		$4.00	
Taco salad	a bed of lettuce topped with spiced meat, cheese, sour cream, guacamole, tomatoes, green onions, black olives, and a ring of taco chips	$3.95	
On the menu, the following items should be included in section titled SOUTH OF THE BORDER; they are all served with taco chips, but rice and beans may be added for an additional $1.25			
Taco	A soft flour tortilla, cheese, lettuce, tomatoes, spiced meat.	(2 Tacos) $2.95	(1 Taco) $1.75
Cheese enchilada	A corn tortilla, cheese, sour cream, enchilada sauce, topped with green onions	$3.25	
Beef enchilada	Same as cheese enchilada with spiced meat, refried beans, topped with green onions and olives	$3.75	

(continued)

Item Name	Item Description	Item Price	$\frac{1}{2}$ Order Price
Bean burrito	A flour tortilla filled with refried beans, cheese and sauce	$3.25	
Beef burrito	Same as a bean burrito with spiced meat	$3.75	
Bean tostada	A corn tortilla topped with refried beans, shredded lettuce, cheese and tomatoes	$3.25	
Beef tostada	Same as a bean tostada with spiced meat	$3.75	
Combination platter	Choice of any two of the above dishes served with rice and beans	$6.25	

On the menu, the following items should be listed as side orders.

Refried Beans	$.75
Rice	$.75
Sour Cream	$.50
Guacamole	$.75
Flour Tortilla	$.50
Corn Tortilla	$.50

On the menu, the following items should be listed as beverages.

Coffee/decaf	$.50
Assorted Teas	$.50
Hot Spiced Cider	$.50
Iced Tea	$.50
Milk	$.75
Sodas	$.50

The restaurant's name, address, and phone should be prominently displayed on the menu as follows:

The Los Baez
1939 S.W. 6th Ave
Seattle, Washington
(206) 365-7741

CASE 2A
Lakeside Limousine Service–Part A

Laura Gauge is the senior operations manager for a limousine service based in Chicago, Illinois. The firm, Lakeside Limousine Service, has been in business since early 1984. In its initial years, the company acquired several regular clients. Throughout the operating year, most requests for limousine services are for transportation to and from the busy O'Hare Airport in Chicago. In reviewing past records, Laura has reached the conclusion that Lakeside's airport business is growing at a fairly constant rate of 8 percent per year and that competition in the area is quite high. She has decided that future growth for the company must come from promoting services in areas having less competitive market conditions.

During the coming holiday season, Lakeside's marketing department plans to release an advertising campaign aimed at generating new clients. The company intends to promote the use of its services for transportation to and from Christmas and New Year celebrations, emphasizing the offer of reduced rates to keep drunk drivers off the road for a safer holiday season. Part of the planned campaign involves distributing informational brochures through the local Restaurant and Bar Association.

In a recent conversation with William Blake, head of the marketing department, Laura was heard to say, "Bill, your holiday season promotion idea seems to be worth trying, but we have never tried to tap this market before. We'll have to keep advertising costs down and try this idea on a trial basis this year. If it works out the way you think, next year we'll add radio and newspaper spots to the promotion. Let's see if we can use that new microcomputer to produce a presentable brochure, and then go ahead with our plans to distribute it through the Restaurant and Bar Association."

Lakeside Limousine Service
11015 Lake Shore Drive
(312) 446-7785

Limousine Service - $55.00 per hour, plus $3.85/mile traveled
$5.00/hour for each additional passenger

Limousine Features - Cellular Phone, VCR, Color TV, AM/FM Cassette
Stereo, Intercom, Sunroof, Privacy Windows

Campaign Slogan (key words) - Safe with Style

Discounts - Half Price Between 10:00 PM and 12:00 Midnight

CASE 2B
Lakeside Limousine Service–Part B

The Lakeside Limousine Service plans to institute a "Mileage Plus" program for regular clients who have been using its services for more than one year. The program will provide regular customers with a 15 percent mileage bonus for miles they have traveled in the current year.

To kick off the new program, form letters announcing the discounts and terms are to be mailed to clients who already qualify for bonus miles. The first mailing will be followed by a second mailing to new customers informing them of the program and their current mileage status. In addressing the marketing department, Laura stated, "As senior operations manager, it is my job to keep an eye on costs while maintaining a profitable operation. When the company was first getting started, it was important to keep costs as low as possible to get us on our feet. Everything from creating brochures to typing letters for our clients was done manually. With the onset of new microcomputer software, however, I have decided it is a good time to start to automate the processes."

Partial Customer Listing

Name	Address	City	ZIP	Date of First Use	Accrued Mileage
Keebler Ernie	7718 Ironwood Ct.	Glenview	60727	01/02/85	40
Chandler Michael	2500 Lakeview Ave.	Plainfield	60103	new client	18
Westward Grace	565 Naper Blvd.	Chicago	60163	11/12/88	120
Goodman Susan	11718 Roosevelt Rd.	Woodridge	60126	06/10/84	240
Martin Tad	9211 S. Lake	Villa Park	60223	new client	35
Walter Barbara	138 Woodland Ave.	Chicago	60111	09/15/89	76
Jordan Paul	6059 Drexel Rd.	Addison	60156	04/12/84	210
Baldwin Bradley	709 Briston Ave.	Glenview	60727	04/04/86	104
Cortland Lisa	820 Kimberly	Chicago	60163	11/01/85	86
Patton Walter	1800 79th Ct.	Addison	60156	new client	50
Carpetti George	561 Lorraine	Hillside	60150	commercial	NA
Smith Rose	11788 Holly Court	Northlake	60180	new client	15

CASE 3
Children's Hospital

Dr. Alan Rollins has been the Chief of Staff for more than 27 years at a small, non-profit children's hospital located in New Hampshire. Over the years, the hospital has produced all of its correspondence through the use of conventional typewriters and handwritten documents.

Last year, Dr. Kyle Saunders came to the hospital to fill the position of Chief Cardiologist. When he arrived, he was surprised at the lack of modern office equipment available for staff and doctors to use. Without informing Dr. Rollins about his plans, Dr. Saunders wrote a grant proposal requesting $25,000 from a local businessmen's foundation. The proposal specified that the funds were to be used to purchase microcomputers and word processing software for the hospital. Dr. Saunders was not in his office the day that the check for $25,000 arrived at the hospital. The following day, however, Dr. Rollins had a few words for Dr. Saunders: "Kyle, what is this microcomputer business all about? Nobody here knows how to use them and I certainly don't know anything about computers. Now I'm expected to go out and spend $25,000, given to this hospital in good faith, without knowing what to buy. What a mess."

Dr. Saunders left the office thinking, "What Alan needs is a brief report that compares the two best-selling word processing software on the market today and a rough price schedule for the hardware we will need to purchase. The report should probably include footnotes for terms he won't understand and endnotes describing where the information in the report came from."

Potential Periodical References

Byte
Info World
PC
PC Digest (hardware)
PC Week
PC World
Personal Computing
Software Digest
Software News

Other Sources of Information

Microcomputer Retail Stores
Office Equipment Trade Shows

CASE 4
Carousel Products, Inc.

John Hayes is the owner of Carousel Products, Inc., a company that distributes a variety of high-quality gifts and homeware exclusively through direct mail orders. To gain new customers, John contracts with other companies to enclose a color leaflet in their monthly billings to customers. The leaflet advertises a special product at an introductory price and includes a postage-paid order envelope. This method has proven very successful in attracting first-time buyers, and the sales generated have more than covered the expenses involved.

Unsure of why the amount of repeat business has been lower than expected, John conducted a telephone survey of these first-time buyers. He contacted them approximately six weeks after they received their introductory product. By this time they had received a form letter thanking them for their purchase, and had been added to the mailing list and been receiving regular mailings.

He found that although most customers were very happy with their purchases, they did not remember the name "Carousel," and subsequent mailings, including the form letter, had probably been discarded as junk mail. John feels that if the thank-you letter were more personalized and included a mention of the product ordered, customers would be more likely to remember the name of the company when they received further product information.

Although the data processing firm that manages John's database of customers can provide him with personalized form letters, the cost is too high and the quality is poor. John thinks that he might be able to produce the thank-you letters himself on his office microcomputer. Ideally, the letters would address the new customer by name and would somehow include a paragraph mentioning and describing the introductory product purchased. But the introductory product changes each month, and he's not sure how this can be handled.

Partial listing of recent first-time buyers

Name and Address			Month of Purchase
Beth Anderson	1218 S. Crestview	Glendale, UT 84052	January
David J. Kelly	112 W. Pine St.	Junction City, UT 84023	January
Eve Newman	2455 SE Ash	Cedar Grove, UT 84055	February
A.L. Strom	256 Windomere Way	Ogden, UT 84032	February
Judith Wendt	1645 S. Alberta Ave.	Orem, UT 84057	January

January's Introductory Product—Mini Wine Cellar

The Mini Wine Cellar is a solid oak cabinet that stores up to 40 bottles of wine under ideal conditions. The proper temperature and humidity are maintained through the exclusive design. Its classic design and fine craftsmanship make it an exquisite accessory for the dining room, living room, office, or den. Its outer door is made of beautifully molded hardwood, and its inner gate of polished stainless steel, with deadbolt lock, provides both elegance and security.

February's Introductory Product—Royale Towel and Bathroom Accessory Set

The set comes with a 16-piece towel ensemble that includes four king-size and four large bath towels, four handtowels, and four washcloths. The special weave of 100% cotton provides the ultimate in durability and softness. The accessories are in a rich wickerwood design that fits with any bathroom decor. The adjustable shelving unit is designed to make use of wall space over the toilet. Also included are a tissue holder, waste receptacle, two sizes of bathroom mats, and both a large and a small clothes hamper.

CASE 5 Westridge Paint Company

Ann Bender was recently promoted to the position of Controller for Westridge Paint Company, which manufactures and distributes a complete line of house paint. Westridge Paint is sold and delivered primarily to construction companies and contractors who buy in large quantities. As telephone orders are taken in the sales department, they are entered directly into the minicomputer and the company's accounting software generates invoices which include the appropriate pricing and quantity discounts for each client.

At the last sales meeting, Jerry Blackwell, the company's Sales Manager, said that he felt a substantial amount of sales could be realized if smaller quantities of paint could be sold to local contractors who would pick up their orders at the warehouse. Ann knew that this had been a point of contention between Jerry and Roger Kincaid, the company's previous controller and her former boss. Roger had been unbending on the issue, and she could recall his terse comments: "We tried it once. It didn't work. The invoices had to be handwritten by the warehouse employees and they were always wrong. They could never get the right pricing down. They couldn't even calculate the sales tax right! It's just not worth it!"

Although Ann knew that there was some basis to Roger's arguments, she felt that a simple invoicing system might be implemented in the warehouse. She also thought that this issue might have been one of the reasons Roger had been asked to leave the company. She suggested that sales from the warehouse could be most easily handled if a single price list could be used there. Everyone agreed that the warehouse employees should not be expected to deal with a complicated pricing structure. Jerry Blackwell said that he could come up with a price list for the warehouse, but that the 3 percent sales tax should be shown as a separate item on the invoices.

Ann called the warehouse foreman the next day and found that he had a microcomputer that he used only periodically for an inventory spreadsheet. He would be glad to make it available for invoice printing during regular business hours. Ann is sure that a simple invoice document could be designed in which only a quantity, product description, and price would need to be typed in, and the calculations for taxes, net price, and totals could be performed automatically. She hopes to present a workable solution at the next sales meeting.

Invoices should have columns for the following items, which should be presented in this order:

Quantity	Description	Unit Price	Total Price	Tax	Net Price

The Tax should be calculated as "3 percent of the Total Price," and the Net Price is equal to the Total Price plus the Tax. The columns for Total Price, Tax, and Net Price should be totaled at the bottom of the invoice. An example line of the invoice might be entered as follows.

Quantity	Description	Unit Price	Total Price	Tax	Net Price
5	5 gal Ivory	76.25	381.25	11.44	392.69

CASE 6
Steve Workman, Inventor

Steve Workman owns and operates a small electronics repair shop. In his spare time, however, he has developed a home security system which he hopes to make a commercial success. He has sold several of them already and has been able to produce enough to keep some inventory on hand. With the help of his broker, he is seeking venture capital in order to mass produce and market the product nationally.

Steve is going to attend a major electronics trade show in several weeks, and wants to have some promotional material about his security system to distribute at the show. However, it also will be several weeks before he will know whether any financing will be available for his product, and that will determine how much he can afford to spend on advertising. Because of the unknowns, Steve thinks his best strategy is to come up with a solution that will work whether or not the financing comes through.

Steve's plan is to produce a brochure that will serve two purposes. In addition to distributing them at the trade show, he will be mailing several hundred copies to potential customers. He has talked with a local advertising agency and come up with some ideas for the brochure, one being a single sheet of standard-size paper folded to produce a brochure with an address area on the outside. If he has the agency do the work, he can include a color photograph and have it printed in three colors. If, on the other hand, he must produce them on his microcomputer, he can substitute for the photo a graph representing performance comparisons of his system against other similar systems.

The advertising agency assured Steve that if he develops the layout and ad copy with a standard type size (10, 12, or 18 pitch), they will be able to produce a high-quality brochure within two days. Now he needs to decide on a name for his product and come up with the text for the brochure.

The home security system Steve has developed has many features and options that make it a superb system. The base unit is small and may be placed in any room in the house. It can be used with door sensors, window sensors, room motion detectors, and heat and smoke alarms. It may be set to turn on indoor or outdoor lights or to activate a siren or silent alarm at the first sign of intrusion.

When connected to a telephone line, it can be set to dial any telephone number and play a recorded message repeatedly as soon as the call is answered. It can store up to three telephone numbers, and if one is busy or does not answer within a specified time, it may be set to dial another. It also may be set with up to three recorded messages, using a different telephone number and message depending upon the type of emergency situation detected.

When away from home, you may program it to turn on any electric device, such as a television, radio, or room light at predetermined or random times of the day. If you have a television, VCR, or stereo system with remote control, it also may be programmed to change channels, stations, volume, and so forth.

You may preset a specific amount of time in which the system may be deactivated before alarms are issued, and it may be deactivated with a personal code known only to authorized persons. A separate backup unit system will be activated should any tampering be detected at the base unit.

HINTS AND HAZARDS

FILE OPERATIONS

HINT Save or resave your data every 15 minutes or so. You may want to purchase another disk to use as a backup disk for important files.

HAZARD Be careful about your keystrokes when saving your documents. You could easily miss a keystroke, which would result in saving a file named "Y" onto your disk. The keystrokes used to resave a file with the **F10** (Save) command are **F10**,↵,Y. The keystrokes used to resave a file during an exit from WordPerfect with the **F7** (Exit) command are **F7**,↵,↵,Y. To avoid confusion, it is suggested that you use the **F10** (Save) command liberally while editing and just prior to exiting WordPerfect. You should not use the **F7** (Exit) command to resave your file.

HAZARD Much literature about WordPerfect suggests that you use the space allocated to the filename extension for part of the name you give the document. For instance, you might name a memo ACCT1887.MEM to indicate that it is a memo concerning account #1887. This is poor advice because doing this might lead to a variety of complex problems. It is best not to use the extension space. Restrict your filenames to eight characters or less, begin the filename with a letter, and include no special characters or spaces in the filename.

HINT Files can be merged by simply retrieving one file into another. When a file is retrieved, it will be inserted into any existing text at the location of the editing cursor.

HAZARD Many applications software automatically erase the current file from RAM when another file is retrieved. As explained in the Hint above, this is not the case with WordPerfect. Experience has shown that beginning WordPerfect users, particularly if they have used other software, become confused when they retrieve a file without first erasing the current file from RAM.

BLOCK OPERATIONS

HINT Most of the basic cut-and-paste operations can be done using the Undelete file buffer instead of the Move buffer as long as you are careful not to inadvertently delete or typeover text while doing so. Using the Undelete buffer requires fewer keystrokes and the Undelete buffers are able to hold three blocks of text.

HINT If you accidentally unblock a block of text, you can immediately reblock it by typing **Alt-F4**,Ctrl-Home,Ctrl-Home ((Block),Previous position). The technique will not work correctly if the cursor has been moved after the unblocking event.

HAZARD There is only one set of Undelete buffers and one Move buffer. Two documents being edited concurrently (see the **Shift-F3** (Switch) command) share the buffers.

HINT Blocks of text can be copied or moved between Doc 1 and Doc 2 (see the **Shift-F3** (Switch) command for information on editing two files concurrently). If you want to copy a block of text from a file on the disk into the current file, use the (Switch) command to go to the other document screen, retrieve the disk file, and block the text. Then use either the **Ctrl-F4** (Move),**B**lock,**C**opy command to copy the block into the move buffer, or use the Backspace or

Delete key to copy the block into the undelete buffer. After returning to the original document (Doc 1) with the **Shift-F3** (Switch) command or the **F7** (Exit) command, complete the copy operation by retrieving the block from the buffer into which it was copied.

EDITING TEXT

HINT To produce a hanging paragraph (one in which the text resides offset to the right of a heading), type the heading and then type **F4** or **Shift-F4** (►Indent or ►Indent ◄) and then enter the text.

HAZARD The default answer to the (Replace) command's "w/confirm" prompt is "No." This is surprising since experience shows that global replace operations without confirmation can often have unanticipated results that are difficult to rectify. If using a text editor's (Replace) command is new to you, be sure to specify Y for "Yes" when the "w/confirm" prompt appears.

HINT When working on a large document over a period of time, it is often desirable to return to where you left off editing when you later retrieve a file. To do so, you may invent a place marker by using keyboard characters (such as - = -) and place the marker at the file location to which you want to return. Then you save the file. When you later retrieve the file, you can use the **F2** (►Search) command to find the marker.

HINT To view the current tab stops on the screen while editing, type **Ctrl-F3**,**1**,↑,↵((Screen),Window,Up,Enter). To turn off the tab stop display, type **Ctrl-F3**,**1**↓,↵((Screen),Window,Down,Enter).

HINT The Esc key may be used to repeat a keystroke or keystroke combination *n* number of times. For instance, to produce a row of asterisks across the document (64 asterisks), move the cursor to the left margin and type Esc,64,*.

WORDPERFECT CODES

HAZARD Be sure to develop the habit of deleting unnecessary codes from your document. Such codes will cause a document file to become cluttered and difficult to read in the Reveal Codes screen.

HINT You can quickly locate imbedded codes in your document with the ►Search and ◄Search commands. Type **F2** or **Shift-F2** (Search forward or Search backward) and then type the initial keystroke combinations that created the code for which you are searching. The screen will display a menu of commands that would generate the imbedded codes. Select the appropriate command from the menu, and then type **F2** or **Shift-F2** again.

HINT You can quickly delete all occurrences of a particular code with the Replace command. Move the cursor to the top of the document and type **Alt-F2** (Replace). Answer Y to the "w/confirm" prompt and answer the "= >Srch:" prompt by typing the initial keystroke combination that created the code. The screen will display a menu of commands that would generate the imbedded codes. Select the appropriate command from the menu and then type **Alt-F2** again. Answer the "Replace with:" prompt by typing **Alt-F2** once more.

HINT Be systematic about where you place your codes. If you often change line spacing or margins for paragraphs, consistently put the codes in the same place (just above the paragraph, just before the first letter, etc.) for each paragraph you reformat. If you have a favorite format of margins, line spacing, page numbering, and so on, create a small file of the necessary codes and save it under a filename like HEADER. Then when you are ready to create a new document, you can simply retrieve HEADER as the first step in creating the document.

HAZARD Some codes must occur at the top of a page in order to have the desired effect. Codes that set new page numbers, change headers or footers, or affect the top margin are some examples. You may want to place a hard page break in your document above such codes to keep them from being forced down on a page by rewrites occurring above them.

PRINTING FILES

HINT There are several ways to print a file or portion of a file. To print the current page of the current document or the entire current document, use the **Shift-F7**,**1** or **2** (Print),**F**ull Document or **P**age command. To print a block of text, block the text and then type **Shift-7**,Y (Print),Yes. To print certain pages of the current file, use the **Shift-F7**,**5** (Print),**M**ultiple Pages command.

HINT If your microcomputer has WordPerfect set up for printing on an Epson printer and you use it to create a document file, the file is saved with unseen data specifying that the file is to be printed with an Epson printer. If you bring a disk holding such a file to another microcomputer set up for another printer, WordPerfect may present an error message when the file is loaded for editing. The error message simply indicates that WordPerfect detects a discrepancy between the file's data and the system being used. WordPerfect will correct the file for the current system's printer.

SPECIAL FEATURES

HINT To modify the text of page headers or footers midway through a document, place a new [Header] or [Footer] code. For instance, to create a new header A printed on every page, type **Shift-F8,3,1,2**(Format),**P**age,**H**eaders,Header **A**,Every **P**age. The command **Shift-F8,3,1,5**(Format),**P**age,**H**eaders,Header **A**,Edit will not place a new header code, but will return you to the position of the original header code and allow you to modify its text and codes.

HAZARD Header A and Header B will both begin on the same line. To avoid overwriting one header with another, you may use one header on even pages and the other on odd pages. You may also use both headers on the same page if you design them so that they will not print in the same area of the page (use the Print,**V**iew Document command to test placement). The same hazard applies to footers.

HINT You can greatly speed up a spell check operation by not waiting for WordPerfect to display all the words its dictionary found when it stops on an unknown word. For instance, if you can see on the screen that the word is one that you want to skip, type 1 or 2 as soon as WordPerfect stops on the word. WordPerfect will immediately continue its search for unknown words.

HAZARD When you use WordPerfect to automatically generate tables of contents, lists, and indexes, the tables it produces are heavily formatted with [▶Indent◀], [▶Indent], [◀Margin Rel], and [Flsh Rgt] format codes. While the text of the table can be edited, it can be quite confusing to try to do so. Also, if the command to generate tables is executed again, any editing changes will be overwritten.

If you must edit a table after it has been generated, you may block and save the table, use the Switch command to change documents, retrieve the table, and resave it in DOS Text File Format with the Text In/Out command. The Text In/Out, Save DOS Text File Format command will leave the table intact and strip the WordPerfect codes from it. You then may use the Switch command to return to the original document and retrieve the table into the current document for editing.

HINT If you decide to insert a portion of newspaper-style columnar text into an existing document, first create the portion as a separate file and make sure it ends with a [Col Off] code. Then retrieve it into the document.

STUDY QUESTIONS

1. What is the main difference between word processing and typing? What is the resulting advantage for word processing?

   ____

2. What keystrokes are used to enter WordPerfect's command mode?

   ____

3. There are places in a document where the cursor may not be moved with the cursor control keys. Describe the areas and the method that one might use to move the cursor to them.

   ____

4. If the Cursor Left key is tapped again and again, what path will the cursor follow?

   ____

5. How does WordPerfect define a paragraph?

   ____

6. Name the four general categories of format codes.

   ____

   ____

   ____

   ____

7. The codes generated by the **F6** (Bold) command belong to which of the four categories of format codes?

   ____

8. The codes generated by WordPerfect when it produces a page break after 54 lines belong to which of the four categories of format codes?

   ____

9. The codes generated by the **Shift-F8**,**1**,**6** (Format),**L**ine,Line **S**pacing command belong to which of the four categories of format codes?

   ____

10. Describe two differences between hard returns and soft returns.

    ____

    ____

11. What keystrokes can be used to delete a soft page break?

    ____

12. What is a hard page and when would you want to use one in your document?

    ____

    ____

13. How can you keep WordPerfect from separating two or more words at the end of a line when it rewrites a paragraph?

14. If the format forward code [L/R Mar:] (left and right margins) is entered at the top of a document, will it stop affecting text when it reaches the format forward code [Ln Spacing:]?

15. What can be done to underline, boldface, or center text after it has been entered?

16. The term *Cut-and-paste* refers to your ability to perform three basic operations on a block of text. Name the three operations.

17. How does WordPerfect treat text held in its editing buffers, such as the Move and Undelete buffers?

18. How many blocks of text can be held in the Move buffer at one time?

19. How many blocks of text can be held in the Undelete buffers at one time?

20. If a block of text is undeleted with the **F1** (Cancel) command, does a copy of the block remain in the Undelete buffer?

21. Describe three ways in which text may be copied or moved in a document.

WORDPERFECT KEY TERMS GLOSSARY

Block operations Ability to deal with segments of a document independent from the rest of the document.

Boiler plating Procedure to automatically merge specific information into a standard form or document.

Buffer A portion of RAM used to temporarily store text that is moved, copied, or deleted.

Close file All data in the document is saved to a disk using software commands.

Cut and paste Ability to move, copy, or delete blocks of text.

Document Text file created with word processing software.

Editing Either revising data by changing the written content of the text or formatting data by changing the appearance of the text.

Filename extension Composed of three characters that follow the filename; usually reserved for the applications software's use.

Font Describes the appearance (type face) and size of printed characters. Font size is measured in characters per inch (cpi) for fixed width fonts and in point size for proportional fonts. Examples are Prestige Elite — 12 cpi and Roman Italic — 12 point.

Format forward codes Codes which affect all of the following text until another similar code or the end of the document is reached.

Formatting Changing the appearance of text.

Hard codes Codes generated by the user.

Hard hyphens Cause a hyphenated word to remain whole.

Hard return Indicates the end of a line that was placed by the user typing the Enter key. Separates paragraphs of text.

Hard spaces Prevent two or more words from being separated from each other when text wraps to the next line.

Header record Used in a secondary file to assign names to each of the data fields; allows field references in a primary file to be designated by field name instead of field number.

Insert Any characters typed are inserted into the text to the left of the cursor.

Justification Aligns sentences of paragraphs against the left margin only, both the left and right margin, or centers sentences horizontally on the page.

Line codes Codes that affect a line of text according to the current left and right margins and tab stop settings.

Macro A sequence of keystrokes recorded and saved on the disk that can be executed at any time.

Open file Current file that is moved between RAM and disk storage as changes are made.

Page break A line of dashes across the computer screen that indicates a new page is about to begin. Soft page breaks are generated by WordPerfect and hard page breaks are generated by the user.

Primary file Standard document with merge codes.

Revising Changing the written content of text.

Screen rewrite Feature that automatically rewraps the lines in a paragraph when revisions are made to it.

Secondary file Contains specific information to be merged into a primary file.

Soft codes Codes WordPerfect generates and automatically inserts into a document.

Soft return Indicates the end of the line that was automatically wrapped to the next line.

Start and stop codes Only text between the codes is affected.

Status line Used to display messages about current software operations.

Typeover Any characters typed will overwrite existing characters of text.

Word wrap Feature that automatically begins a new line when the right margin of the current line is reached.

WORDPERFECT OPERATION AND COMMAND SUMMARY

WORDPERFECT CONTROL KEYS

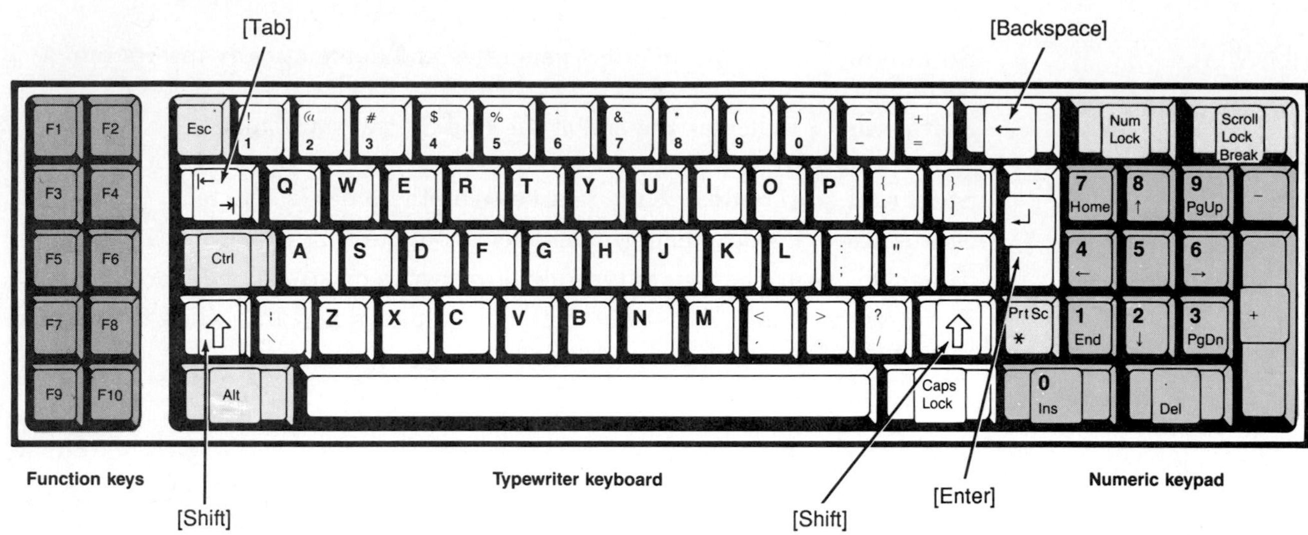

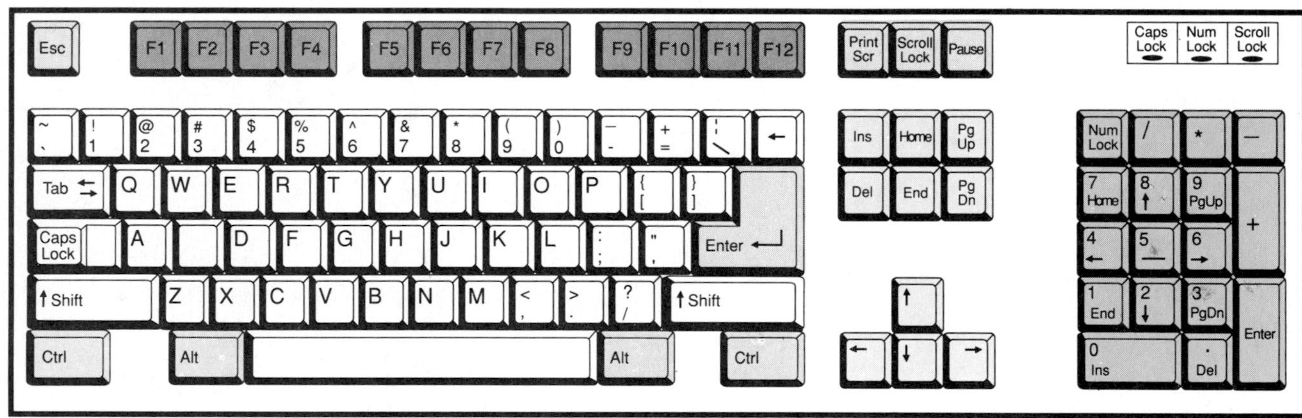

Normal Typewriter Keys

Control Keys

Function Keys

Numeric Keypad/Cursor Movement Keys

Cursor Movement Keys Only

NOTE: There are two or more keyboards in use. They are significantly different from each other.

CONTROL KEYS

Alt-letter Key Executes a keystroke macro named with the Alt key.

Ctrl-↵ Inserts a hard page break [HPg] code into the document.

Enter Key (↵) Inserts a hard return [HRt] code into the document.

Esc Key May be used to execute the following keystroke *n* number of times. Type Esc, a number, and then type the keystroke or keystroke combination to repeat.

Home,- Inserts a hard hyphen into the document.

Home,Space Inserts a hard space [ ] code into the document.

Ins Key Toggles between Insert and Typeover editing modes.

Num Lock Key Toggles 10-key numeric keypad to cursor control keys. The shift key may be used to temporarily shift this keypad to the opposite mode.

Shift-Tab Key Inserts a [◀Mar Rel] code into the text, releases the left margin, and moves the cursor to the previous tab stop.

Tab Key Inserts a [Tab] code into the document and tabs the cursor to the next tab stop.

WORDPERFECT CURSOR CONTROL KEYS

Cursor Movement	Keystrokes
Character Left	Left ←
Character Right	Right →
Line Up	Up ↑
Line Down	Down ↓
Word Left	Ctrl-Left
Word Right	Ctrl-Right
Beginning of Line	Home,Left
End of Line	Home,Right
Top of File	Home,Home,Up
Bottom of File	Home,Home,Down
Screen Up	− (Numeric Keypad)
Screen Down	+ (Numeric Keypad)
Page Up	Page Up (PgUp)
Page Down	Page Down (PgDn)
Previous Position	Ctrl-Home,Ctrl-Home
Forward to Character *a*	Ctrl-Home,*a*
To Page *nn*	Ctrl-Home,*nn* ↵

WORDPERFECT DELETE KEYS

Delete Operation	Keystrokes
Current Character	Delete (Del)
Previous Character	Backspace
Current Word	Ctrl-Backspace
Current Word Left	Home,Backspace
Current Word Right	Home,Delete (Del)
End of Line	Ctrl-End
End of Page	Ctrl-Page Down (PgDn)

WORDPERFECT KEYBOARD TEMPLATE COMMANDS

Command	Keystrokes
Block	**Alt-F4**
Bold	**F6**
Cancel	**F1**
Center	**Shift-F6**
Columns/Table	**Alt-F7**
Date/Outline	**Shift-F5**
End Field	**F9**
Exit	**F7**
Flush Right	**Alt-F6**
Font	**Ctrl-F8**
Footnote	**Ctrl-F7**
Format	**Shift-F8**
Graphics	**Alt-F9**
Help	**F3**
►Indent	**F4**
►Indent ◄	**Shift-F4**
List	**F5**
Macro	**Alt-F10**
Macro Define	**Ctrl-F10**
Mark Text	**Alt-F5**
Merge Codes	**Shift-F9**
Merge/Sort	**Ctrl-F9**
Move	**Ctrl-F4**
Print	**Shift-F7**
Replace	**Alt-F2**
Retrieve	**Shift-F10**
Reveal Codes	**Alt-F3**
Save	**F10**
Screen	**Ctrl-F3**
◄Search	**Shift-F2**
►Search	**F2**
Setup	**Shift-F1**
Shell	**Ctrl-F1**
Spell	**Ctrl-F2**
Style	**Alt-F8**
Switch	**Shift-F3**
Tab Align	**Ctrl-F6**
Text In/Out	**Ctrl-F5**
Thesaurus	**Alt-F1**
Underline	**F8**

WORDPERFECT COMMAND INDEX

Command	Keystroke
Align Character	**Shift-F8,4** (Format),**O**ther
Align Text to Tab	**Ctrl-F6** (Tab Align)
All Capitals Font	**Ctrl-F8** (Font)
Automatic References	**Alt-F5** (Mark Text)
Backup Documents	**Shift-F1** (Setup)
Base Font	**Ctrl-F8** (Font)
Block Text	**Alt-F4** (Block)
Bold Text	**F6** (Bold)
Cancel a Command	**F1** (Cancel)
Center	
Page (Top to Bottom)	**Shift-F8,2** (Format),**P**age
Text	**Shift-F6** (Center)
Clear Screen	**F7** (Exit)
Columnar Text Feature	**Alt-F7** (Columns/Table)
Comments in Document	**Ctrl-F5** (Text In/Out)
Compressed Font	**Ctrl-F8** (Font)
Copy	
Block of Text	**Ctrl-F4** (Move)
Rectangular Column of Text	Block/**Ctrl-F4** (Move)
Cursor Speed	**Shift-F1** (Setup)
Date	**Shift-F5** (Date/Outline)
Delete	
Block of Text	Block/BackSpace
Rectangular Column of Text	Block/**Ctrl-F4** (Move)
Directory (Change)	**F5** (List)
Disk Files	
Copy	**F5** (List)
Delete	**F5** (List)
Look	**F5** (List)
Move/Rename	**F5** (List)
Name Search	**F5** (List)
Print	**Shift-F7** (Print)
Display Pitch	**Shift-F8,3** (Format),**D**ocument
Document 2	**Shift-F3** (Switch)
Endnotes	**Ctrl-F7** (Footnote)
Enlarged Font	**Ctrl-F8** (Font)
Fast Save (unformatted)	**Shift-F1** (Setup)
Flush Right Text	**Alt-F6** (Flush Right)
Font Stop Code	**Ctrl-F8** (Font)
Footers	**Shift-F8,2** (Format),**P**age
Footnotes	**Ctrl-F7** (Footnote)
Force Page Number (odd/even)	**Shift-F8,2** (Format),**P**age
Graphics Boxes	**Alt-F9** (Graphics)
Headers	**Shift-F8,2** (Format),**P**age
Help Screens	**F3** (Help)
Hyphenation Feature	**Shift-F8,1** (Format),**L**ine
Indent (Left)	**F4** (▶Indent)
Indent (Left and Right)	**Shift-F4** (▶Indent◀)
Index Feature	**Alt-F5** (Mark Text)
Initial	
Codes	**Shift-F8,3** (Format),**D**ocument
Font	**Shift-F8,3** (Format),**D**ocument
Settings	**Shift-F1** (Setup)
Italic Font	**Ctrl-F8** (Font)
Justification (on/off)	**Shift-F8,1** (Format),**L**ine
Kerning	**Shift-F8,4** (Format),**O**ther
Keyboard Layout	**Shift-F1** (Setup)

Command	Keystroke
Line	
Draw	**Ctrl-F3** (Screen)
Graphics	**Alt-F9** (Graphics)
Height	**Shift-F8,1** (Format),**Line**
Numbering	**Shift-F8,1** (Format),**Line**
Spacing	**Shift-F8,1** (Format),**Line**
Lists Feature	**Alt-F5** (Mark Text)
Location of Auxiliary Files	**Shift-F1** (Setup)
Macro	
Create	**Ctrl-F10** (Macro Define)
Execute	**Alt-F10** (Macro)
Margins	
Left/Right	**Shift-F8,1** (Format),**Line**
Top/Bottom	**Shift-F8,2** (Format),**Page**
Master/Subdocuments Feature	**Alt-F5** (Mark Text)
Math Feature	**Alt-F7** (Columns/Table)
Merge	
Codes	**Shift-F9** (Merge Codes)
Feature	**Ctrl-F9** (Merge/Sort)
Move	
Block of Text	**Ctrl-F4** (Move)
Rectangular Column of Text	Block/**Ctrl-F4** (Move)
Outline Font	**Ctrl-F8** (Font)
Outline Numbers	**Shift-F5** (Date/Outline)
Overstrike Text	**Shift-F8,4** (Format),**O**ther
Page Number	
New	**Shift-F8,2** (Format),**Page**
Placement	**Shift-F8,2** (Format),**Page**
Paper Size/Type	**Shift-F8,2** (Format),**Page**
Paragraph Numbers	**Shift-F5** (Date/Outline)
Password Protection	**Ctrl-F5** (Text In/Out)
Print	
Adjust Pitch	**Shift-F8,4** (Format),**O**ther
Advance to Position	**Shift-F8,4** (Format),**O**ther
Block	**Shift-F7** (Print)
Colors	**Ctrl-F8** (Font)
Current Page	**Shift-F7** (Print)
Full Document	**Shift-F7** (Print)
Multiple Copies	**Shift-F7** (Print)
Quality	**Shift-F7** (Print)
Select Printer	**Shift-F7** (Print)
Send Printer Control Code	**Shift-F8,4** (Format),**O**ther
Stop	**Shift-F7** (Print)
View Printed Document on Screen	**Shift-F7** (Print)
Protect from Page Breaks	
Block of Text	Block/**Shift-F8** (Format)
Conditional End of Page	**Shift-F8,4** (Format),**O**ther
Widow/Orphan	**Shift-F8,1** (Format),**Line**
Redline	
Add to Document (Delete Strikeout)	**Alt-F5** (Mark Text)
Method	**Shift-F8,3** (Format),**D**ocument
Text	**Ctrl-F8** (Font)
Retrieve	
ASCII File	**Ctrl-F5** (Text In/Out)
Document	**Shift-F10** (Retrieve)
File from List	**F5** (List)
Reveal Codes	**Alt-F3** (Reveal Codes)

Command	Keystroke
Save	
Append Block to Disk File	Block/**Ctrl-F4** (Move)
Block of Text	Block/**F10** (Save)
Document	**F10** (Save)
Document and Exit WordPerfect	**F7** (Exit)
Document in ASCII Format	**Ctrl-F5** (Text In/Out)
Document in WordPerfect 4.2, 5.0 Format	**Ctrl-F5** (Text In/Out)
Screen Displays	**Shift-F1** (Setup)
Search	
Backward	**Shift-F2** (◀Search)
Forward	**F2** (▶Search)
And Replace	**Alt-F2** (Replace)
Shadow Font	**Ctrl-F8** (Font)
Shell to DOS	**Ctrl-F1** (Shell)
Sort Feature	**Ctrl-F9** (Merge/Sort)
Spell Check Feature	**Ctrl-F2** (Spell)
Split Screen	**Ctrl-F3** (Screen)
Strikeout Text	**Ctrl-F8** (Font)
Style Feature	**Alt-F8** (Style)
Summary in Document	**Shift-F8,3** (Format),**Document**
Superscript/Subscript	**Ctrl-F8** (Font)
Suppress Formatting (page only)	**Shift-F8,2** (Format),**Page**
Tab Set	**Shift-F8,1** (Format),**Line**
Table of Contents Feature	**Alt-F5** (Mark Text)
Thesaurus Feature	**Alt-F1** (Thesaurus)
Undelete Text	**F1** (Cancel)
Underline	
Double	**Ctrl-F8** (Font)
Spaces and Tabs	**Shift-F8,4** (Format),**Other**
Text	**F8** (Underline)
Units of Measure	**Shift-F1** (Setup)
UPPER/lower Case (Convert)	Block/**Shift-F3** (Switch)

```
F1
Cancel ──────── Undelete: ──────┬─ 1 Restore
                                ├─ 2 Previous Deletion
                                └─ 0 Cancel
```

F1 CANCEL

The **F1** (Cancel) command may be used to exit a WordPerfect menu or message, or recover up to three levels of deleted text from the Undelete buffers.

The **F1** (Cancel) command may be used to abort many WordPerfect menu or command operations. The command may also be used to recover any or all of the last three text deletions or typed-over text. To recover text, move the cursor to the position where you want the recovered text to appear and then type **F1** (Cancel). The most recent deletion will appear on the screen at the cursor location. The **P**revious Deletion command may be used to continuously scroll through the last three deletions, with each deletion appearing on the screen in order. When the appropriate deletion is displayed on the screen, type **1** or **R** (**R**estore) to recover it. Type **F1** (Cancel) or ↵ to abort the recovery operation.

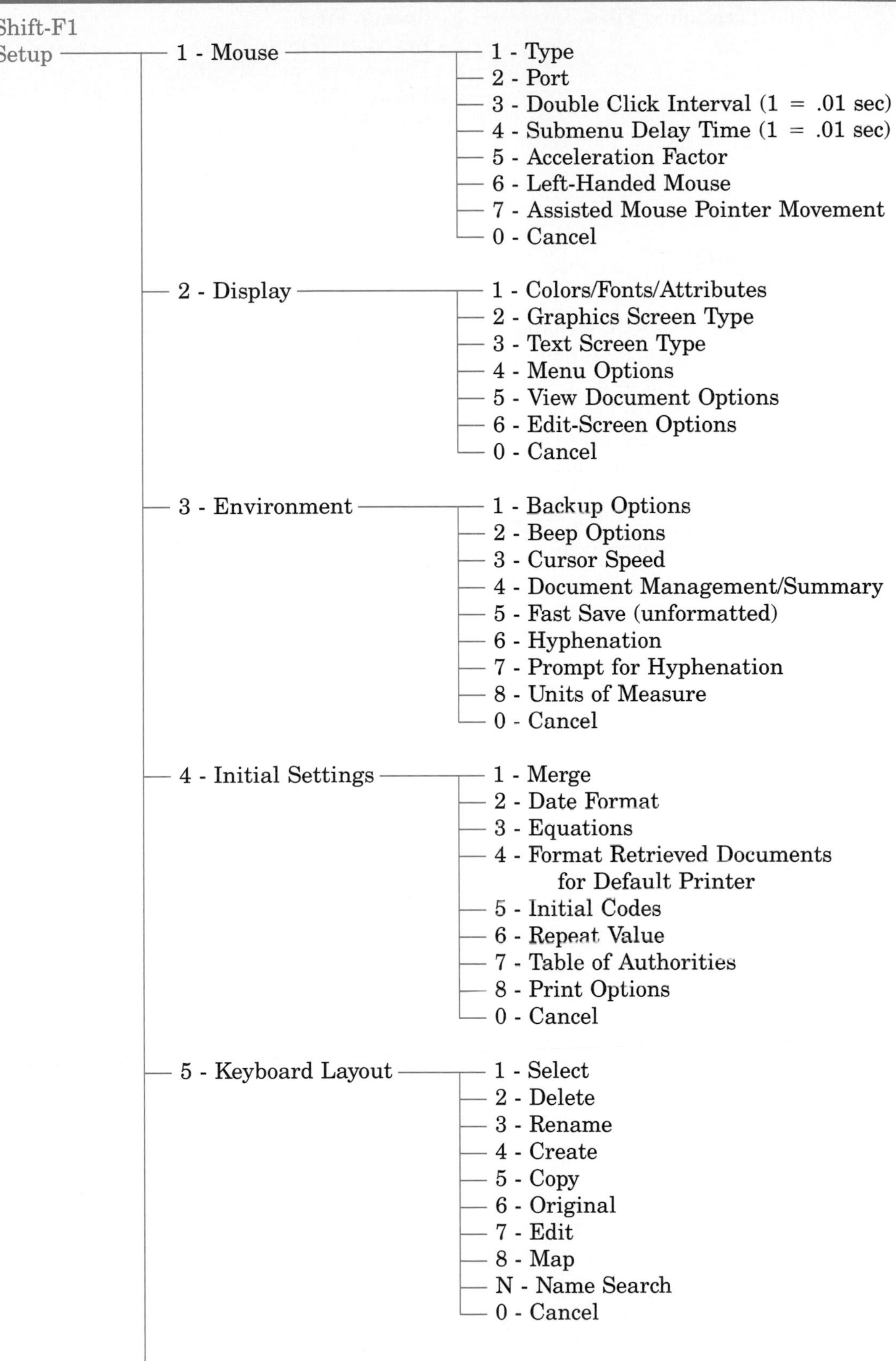
Shift-F1
Setup
1 - Mouse
1 - Type
2 - Port
3 - Double Click Interval (1 = .01 sec)
4 - Submenu Delay Time (1 = .01 sec)
5 - Acceleration Factor
6 - Left-Handed Mouse
7 - Assisted Mouse Pointer Movement
0 - Cancel
2 - Display
1 - Colors/Fonts/Attributes
2 - Graphics Screen Type
3 - Text Screen Type
4 - Menu Options
5 - View Document Options
6 - Edit-Screen Options
0 - Cancel
3 - Environment
1 - Backup Options
2 - Beep Options
3 - Cursor Speed
4 - Document Management/Summary
5 - Fast Save (unformatted)
6 - Hyphenation
7 - Prompt for Hyphenation
8 - Units of Measure
0 - Cancel
4 - Initial Settings
1 - Merge
2 - Date Format
3 - Equations
4 - Format Retrieved Documents for Default Printer
5 - Initial Codes
6 - Repeat Value
7 - Table of Authorities
8 - Print Options
0 - Cancel
5 - Keyboard Layout
1 - Select
2 - Delete
3 - Rename
4 - Create
5 - Copy
6 - Original
7 - Edit
8 - Map
N - Name Search
0 - Cancel

CONTINUED

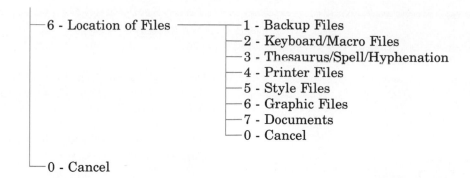

- 6 - Location of Files
  - 1 - Backup Files
  - 2 - Keyboard/Macro Files
  - 3 - Thesaurus/Spell/Hyphenation
  - 4 - Printer Files
  - 5 - Style Files
  - 6 - Graphic Files
  - 7 - Documents
  - 0 - Cancel
- 0 - Cancel

SHIFT-F1 SETUP

The **Shift-F1** (Setup) command alters or redefines the default settings for many WordPerfect commands and operations. The Setup command saves any new specifications onto the disk directory where WordPerfect resides. The specifications are kept on the disk in a file named WP{WP}.SET. WordPerfect reads the file and uses the specifications found there each time it is loaded. That is, the Setup command configures WordPerfect's environment.

NOTE: In a Microcomputing Laboratory, you should never attempt to change any of the WordPerfect settings with the **Shift-F1** *(Setup) command without the explicit approval of your instructor or laboratory staff.*

When a Setup command listed here has either a "Yes" or "No" setting, type Y or N, respectively, to change it.

Mouse

The **M**ouse command has a number of options that may be used to change the way a mouse device will operate while editing a document. See the WordPerfect manual or help screens for more information on the (Setup),**M**ouse commands. Also, see *Mouse Support* on p. W-244 for more information on using a mouse device with WordPerfect.

Display

The **D**isplay command sets the screen display characteristics for many WordPerfect operations.

Colors/Fonts/Attributes

The **C**olors/Fonts/Attributes command is used to change the screen colors or shades for color or monochrome monitors. When the **C**olors/Fonts/Attributes command is selected, another menu will appear. At this point the procedure varies depending on the video display card and monitor being used.

For instance, if your computer has an EGA or a VGA monitor card, you may see the following selection appear.

Setup:Colors/Fonts
- 1 - Screen Colors
- 2 - Italics Font, 8 Foreground Colors
- 3 - Underline Font, 8 Foreground Colors
- 4 - Small Caps Font, 8 Foreground Colors
- 5 - 512 Characters, 8 Foreground Colors
- 6 - Normal Font Only, 16 Foreground Colors
- 0 - Cancel

In most cases, you will select **S**creen Colors to set the display attributes for your monitor. The **S**creen Colors menu allows you to change the background/foreground colors for the various text attributes (bold, underline, etc.). The menu is largely self-explanatory.

When screen colors are changed, they affect the current document screen only (Doc 1 or Doc 2). To view the current screen colors for the other document screen, type **Shift-F3** (Switch) while viewing the Screen Colors menu. To copy the other document's screen colors to the current document screen, type **Ctrl-F4** (Move) while viewing the **S**creen Colors menu. (See **Shift-F3** (Switch) for an explanation of document screens 1 and 2.) Use **F7** (Exit) to properly exit the **S**creen Colors menu.

Graphics Screen Type — Text Screen Type

WordPerfect automatically selects the proper graphics or text screen driver for the graphics card and monitor type being used when it is loaded.

Menu Options

To change the screen appearance of the menu letter, pull-down menu display, or menu bars that are presented on the screen while in a WordPerfect command mode, you may use the **M**enuOptions command to select (Font),**S**ize and/or (Font),**A**ppearance for the display. The affected display then will appear on the screen as its font appears in the document's screen text (see **Ctrl-F8** (Font)).

View Document Options

The **V**iew Document Options command may be used to change the screen displays presented by the **Shift-F7** (Print),**V**iew Document command.

Edit-Screen Options

The **E**dit-Screen Options is a command that has several submenu commands:

```
├─ 6 - Edit Screen Options ──┬─ 1 - Automatically Format and Rewrite
                             ├─ 2 - Comments Display
                             ├─ 3 - Filename on the Status Line
                             ├─ 4 - Hard Return Display Character
                             ├─ 5 - Merge Codes Display
                             ├─ 6 - Reveal Codes Window Size
                             ├─ 7 - Side-by-side Columns Display
                             └─ 0 - Cancel
```

Automatically Format and Rewrite

Default — Yes

When **A**utomatically Format and Rewrite is "Yes," WordPerfect reformats the entire remaining document at the time a format forward code is inserted into it. When "No" is specified for the command, reformatting occurs as the cursor is moved through the document.

Comments Display

Default — Yes

You may include comments (text that will not be printed) in a document by using the **Ctrl-F5** (Text In/Out),Comment command. When **D**isplay Document Comments is "Yes," comments are displayed on the screen where they occur in the document. If **D**isplay Document Comments is changed to "No," the comments are not displayed on the screen.

Filename on the Status Line

Default — Yes

"Yes" causes the filename to be displayed on the Status line. "No" suppresses the display of the filename on the Status line.

Hard Return Display Character
Default — Space character
To make hard returns visible on the screen, you may use the **H**ard Return Display Character command to enter the character that you wish to be displayed on the screen where a hard return occurs in the document. The < character is often used for this purpose.

Merge Codes Display
Default — Yes
The **M**erge Codes Display command may be used to display, or not display, merge codes included in a document. (See **Ctrl-F9** (Merge/Sort) for more information on the display of merge codes.)

Reveal Codes Window Size
Default — 10 lines
The **R**eveal Codes Window Size command may be used to change the number of Reveal screen lines displayed by the **Alt-F3** (Reveal Codes) command.

Side-by-Side Columns Display
Default — Yes
When **S**ide-by-Side Columns Display is "Yes," columns generated by the **Alt-F7** (Columns/Table) command appear on the screen as they will be printed. To speed editing of such columns, you may change **S**ide-by-Side Columns Display to "No."

Environment

The **E**nvironment command has several submenu commands that affect various operational features of WordPerfect.

Backup Options

Default — Timed, Every 30 minutes
WordPerfect provides a backup feature to maintain backup files for your documents. The backup files may be of two types, **T**imed or **O**riginal.

Timed
Timed backup files are produced every ***n*** number of minutes (30 by default). When you specify **T**imed backup, you may also specify the number of minutes between the automatic backup operations. **T**imed backup files are given the filename and extension WP{WP}.BK1 or WP{WP}.BK2 (for Document 1 or 2, respectively — see the **Shift-F3** (Switch) command) and are kept in the directory specified with the **Shift-F1** (Setup),**L**ocation of Files,**B**ackup Files command.

If the **T**imed backup feature is being used and the system is shut off before exiting WordPerfect properly with the **F7** (Exit) command, WordPerfect will prompt "Old backup file exists **1 R**ename; **2 D**elete:" the next time WordPerfect is loaded. At this point you may rename the WP{WP}.BK*n* file, then retrieve it for editing with the **Shift-F10** (Retrieve) command, or you may delete the **T**imed Backup file.

To retrieve a file you have renamed using the backup feature, you must remember to specify the appropriate directory for the file.

Original
Original backup files are first created the second time a document file is saved. **O**riginal backup files have the same filename, but are given a .BK! extension by WordPerfect. The document file with no extension is the last

saved version; the document file with the .BK! extension is the next-to-the-last saved version. An **O**riginal backup file is kept in the same directory as the file it is backing up, regardless of the directory specified in the **Shift-F1** (Setup),**L**ocation of Files,**B**ackup Files command.

Beep Options

The Beep Options command has the following submenu of commands:

		Default
Setup:Beep Options	1 - Beep on Error	No
	2 - Beep on Hyphenation	Yes
	3 - Beep on Search Failure	No
	0 - Cancel	

Cursor Speed

Default–50 characters per second
Sets the speed at which any key will repeat when held down (including cursor movement keys). Options include 15, 20, 30, 40, and 50 characters per second or **N**ormal. **N**ormal is about 11 characters per second for most microcomputers.

Document Management/Summary

The **D**ocument Management/Summary command has the following submenu of commands:

		Default
Setup:Document Management/Summary	1 - Create Summary on Save/Exit	No
	2 - Subject Search Text	RE:
	3 - Long Document Names	No
	4 - Default Document Type	
	0 - Cancel	

The **D**ocument Management/Summary command may be used so WordPerfect automatically creates a document Summary when a file is saved. (See **Shift-F8** (Format),**D**ocument,**S**ummary for more information on document summaries).

The **L**ong Document Names command has either a "No" (default) or "Yes" setting. If **L**ong Document Names is set to "Yes," WordPerfect will prompt "Long Document Name" and "Long Document Type" each time a document is saved. The additional information entered becomes part of the file data and may be viewed using the **F5** (List),**S**hort/Long Display,**L**ong Display command. See **F5** (List) for more information.

See the WordPerfect manual or help screens for more information on the remaining **D**ocument Management/Summary commands.

Fast Save (Unformatted)

Default—Yes
When **F**ast Save (Unformatted) is "Yes," WordPerfect saves the document in an unformatted manner. An unformatted document will usually take longer to be printed from the disk.

Hyphenation/Prompt for Hyphenation

See the WordPerfect manual or help screens for more information on the Hyphenation and **P**rompt for Hyphenation commands.

Units of Measure

Default—"(inches)

Units of measure refers to the scale WordPerfect uses when it references document positions. The default scale is inches ("). The (Setup),**U**nits of Measure command may be used to change the default scale to any one of the following:

i = inches
c = centimeters
p = points (1/72 of an inch)
w = 1200ths of an inch
u = WordPerfect 4.2 Units (Lines/Columns)

Initial Settings

The **I**nitial Settings command is used to change the following:

Merge

The **M**erge command may be used to change the field and record delimiters that WordPerfect will recognize when a DOS text file is used as a primary file in a merge operation. See the WordPerfect manual or help screens for more information on merging DOS text (ASCII) files.

Date Format

Default—3 1,4 (Example—December 15, 1990)

Setup:Date Format
- 1 - Day of the Month
- 2 - Month (number)
- 3 - Month (word)
- 4 - Year (all four digits)
- 5 - Year (last two digits)
- 6 - Day of the Week (word)
- 7 - Hour (24-hour clock)
- 8 - Hour (12-hour clock)
- 9 - Minute
- 0 - am / pm
- %,$ - Leading zeros or spaces, abbreviation

See **Shift-F5** (Date/Outline) for more information.

Equations

The (Setup) command **I**nitial Settings,**E**quations may be used to redefine the default settings for the **Alt-F9** (Graphics),**E**quation,**C**reate or **E**dit command. Refer to these commands for more information.

Format Retrieved Documents For Default Printer

Default—No

When a document is saved, the current printer definition (set with the **Shift-F7** (Print),**S**elect Printer command) is saved with the file. If "Yes" is specified, a file later retrieved into a document area having a different current printer will cause WordPerfect to reformat the file to the current printer specifications.

Initial Codes

(See **Shift-F8** (Format),**D**ocument,Initial **C**odes.)

Repeat Value

Default—8

Changes the repeat value for the Esc key.

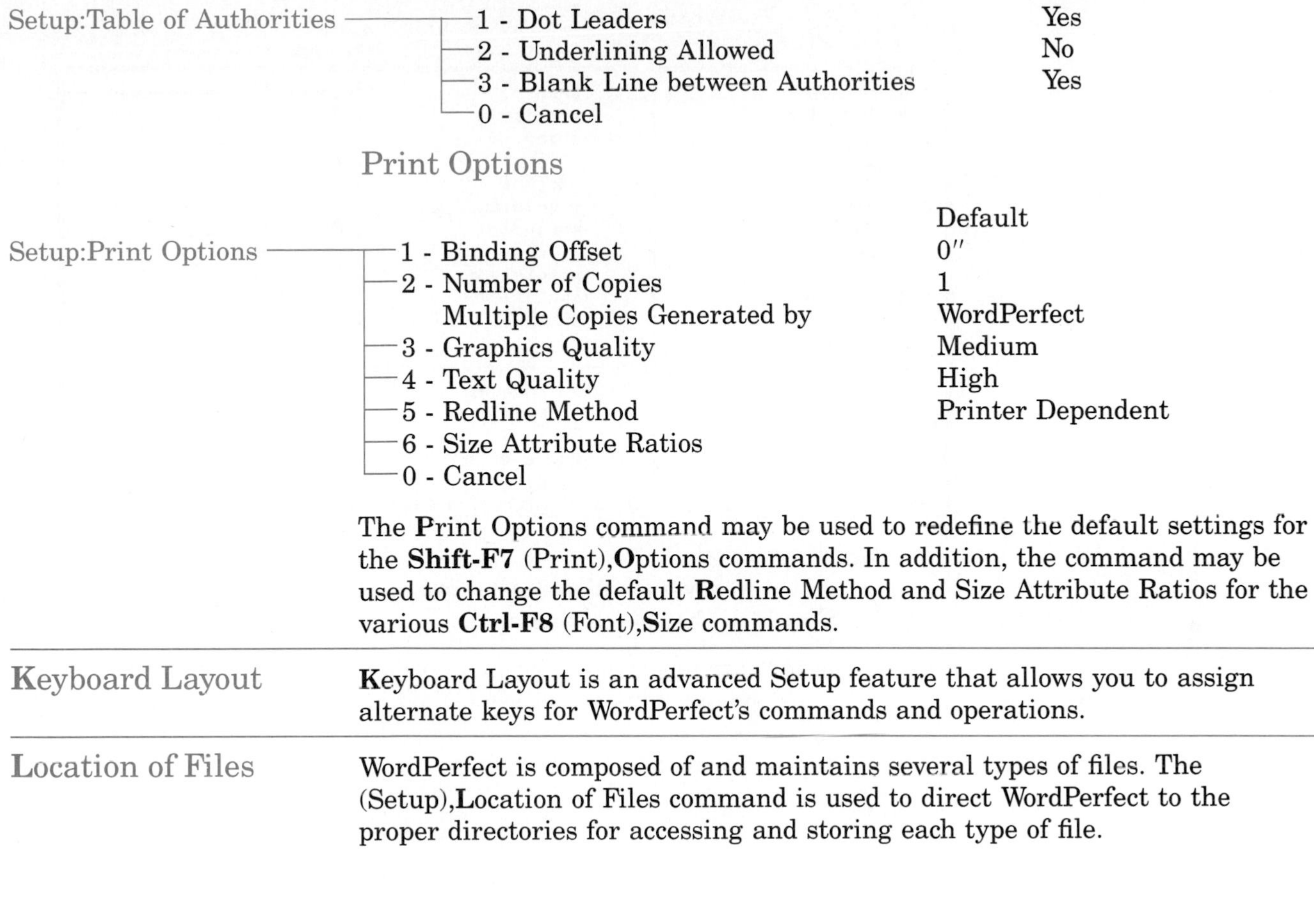

Table of Authorities

Setup:Table of Authorities		Default
	1 - Dot Leaders	Yes
	2 - Underlining Allowed	No
	3 - Blank Line between Authorities	Yes
	0 - Cancel	

Print Options

Setup:Print Options		Default
	1 - Binding Offset	0″
	2 - Number of Copies	1
	Multiple Copies Generated by	WordPerfect
	3 - Graphics Quality	Medium
	4 - Text Quality	High
	5 - Redline Method	Printer Dependent
	6 - Size Attribute Ratios	
	0 - Cancel	

The **P**rint Options command may be used to redefine the default settings for the **Shift-F7** (Print),**O**ptions commands. In addition, the command may be used to change the default **R**edline Method and Size Attribute Ratios for the various **Ctrl-F8** (Font),**S**ize commands.

Keyboard Layout

Keyboard Layout is an advanced Setup feature that allows you to assign alternate keys for WordPerfect's commands and operations.

Location of Files

WordPerfect is composed of and maintains several types of files. The (Setup),**L**ocation of Files command is used to direct WordPerfect to the proper directories for accessing and storing each type of file.

Alt-F1
Thesaurus —— [Word:<entry>] ——
- 1 Replace Word —— Press letter for word
- 2 View Doc
- 3 Look Up Word —— Word:<entry>
- 4 Clear Column
- 0 Cancel

ALT-F1 THESAURUS

WordPerfect comes with a thesaurus feature that displays synonyms and antonyms for words. The data through which WordPerfect searches to find synonyms and antonyms are kept on a separate disk. If you are using a computer with two floppy disk drives, you will need to insert the Thesaurus disk into the B: drive each time it is needed. If you have a hard disk drive, the Thesaurus disk may be copied into the same subdirectory as WordPerfect.

To cause WordPerfect to display synonyms and antonyms for a word in your document, move the cursor under the word and then type **Alt-F1** (Thesaurus). If the word is a "headword," a word that can be looked up by WordPerfect, the screen will appear similar to the following.

```
          campus.  For an appointment to view one of our fine
          townhouse apartments and a tour of the


fine=(a)=
 1 A ·choice            | 5    ·keen             |fine-(v)
   B ·splendid          |      ·precise          | 9    ·charge
   C ·superb            |      ·sharp            |      ·penalize
   D ·superior          |                        |      ·tax
                        | 6    ·elegant          |
 2 E ·average           |      ·exquisite        |fine-(ant)
   F ·fair              |      ·refined          |10    ·inferior
   G ·mediocre          |                        |      ·terrible
                        | 7    ·minute           |      ·thick
 3 H ·fragile           |      ·small            |      ·coarse
   I ·narrow            |      ·subtle           |      ·blunt
   J ·slender           |                        |      ·crude
   K ·thin              |fine-(n)                |      ·obvious
                        | 8    ·assessment       |
 4 L ·delicate          |      ·charge           |
   M ·gossamer          |      ·fee              |
   N  silky             |      ·forfeit          |
                        |      ·penalty          |
1 Replace Word; 2 View Doc; 3 Look Up Word; 4 Clear Column: 0
```

The word shown in reverse video in the text at the top of the screen is the headword for which the search was made.

Beneath the text are displayed reference words organized into word-type categories: synonymous adjectives (a), nouns (n), and verbs (v); and antonyms (ant). Reference words within a word-type category are organized into subgroups according to connotation.

The column with capital letters next to reference words is referred to as the current column. The current column may be changed with the cursor right and cursor left keys. The reference words displayed with a bullet (small dot to the left) are themselves headwords for which other reference words may be displayed. There may be more than one headword's list of reference words displayed on the screen. If there are, the headwords and reference word lists are displayed in separate columns.

There may be more reference words found than can be displayed on the screen. If this is the case, the cursor up and cursor down keys (also PgUp and PgDn keys) may be used to scroll through them.

Note that the following commands can only be executed by typing the command number.

1 Replace Word

A reference word may be selected to replace the headword in the text. To do so, you type **1** and then the letter displayed to the left of the appropriate reference word. If a letter is not displayed next to the reference word of your choice, you may change the current column by typing the cursor left or cursor right keys before entering the Replace Word command.

2 View Doc

The View Doc command allows you to move the cursor through the text at the top of the screen without leaving the (Thesaurus) command. You may not edit the text; however, you may scroll through it to view text not currently displayed.

If you wish to select another headword from the text, you may move the cursor under it and type **Alt-F1** (Thesaurus) again. If you do not want to select another headword, you may type **F7** (Exit) to return to the Thesaurus.

3 Look Up Word	The Look Up Word command allows you to directly type in a headword for which WordPerfect will search.
4 Clear Column	The Clear Column command erases the current column's headword and reference word list from the screen.

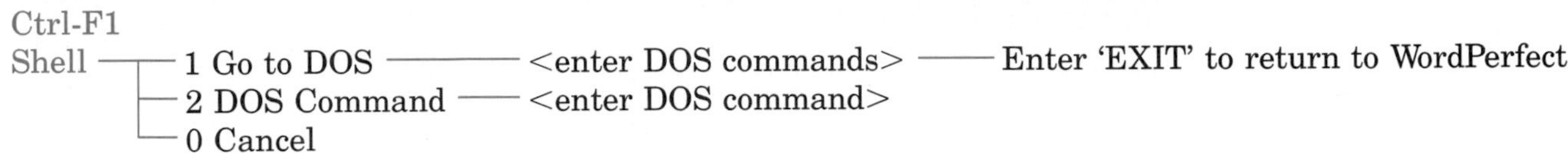

CTRL-F1 SHELL

The **Ctrl-F1** (Shell) command allows you to temporarily exit WordPerfect to DOS if the computer has enough RAM to accommodate the operation, or enter a single DOS command to be executed without leaving WordPerfect.

To exit WordPerfect to DOS, type **Ctrl-F1** (Shell),**1** or **G** for **G**o to DOS. To return to WordPerfect from DOS, type ||EXIT↵||. To execute a single DOS command from within WordPerfect, type **Ctrl-F1** (Shell),**2** or **C** for DOS **C**ommand, and then enter the DOS command.

If you choose to Go to DOS through the Shell command, you should always return to WordPerfect and exit WordPerfect properly by typing **F7** (Exit) before turning off the computer.

F2
►Search —— <entry> —— F2 —— {If found, cursor moves to next occurrence of entry}
└ Cancel key

F2 ►SEARCH

The **F2** (►Search) command is used to move the cursor forward to occurrences of specific words, phrases, and/or WordPerfect codes. To use the ►Search command, type **F2** (►Search). The prompt "->Srch:" will be displayed on the screen by the command. At this point, type the word/code pattern for which to search. You may type any keyboard characters, and you may include many WordPerfect codes by typing the keystroke combinations that would normally generate the command menus for the codes. For instance, to search for a line margins code [L/R Mar] you would type **F2** (►Search), and then type **Shift-F8,1,6** (Format),**L**ine,**M**argins.

When you have finished typing the search word/code pattern, type **F2** (►Search) again and the search operation will commence. When the specified word/code pattern is found, the search will halt and the cursor will be moved to the location where the word/code pattern occurs in the document. To continue the search for the same word pattern, type **F2**,**F2** (►Search, ►Search).

Lowercase search characters will match upper and lowercase characters in the document. Uppercase search characters will only match uppercase characters.

To search for stop codes such as [bold], type the command keystroke sequence twice, and then delete the start code from the "->Srch:" entry.

An extended search (one in which headers, footers, footnotes, and endnotes are also searched) may be performed by typing the Home key before typing **F2** (▶Search).

Block/▶Search

The ▶Search command may be used to expand (contract) a blocked portion of text up to the found word/code pattern.

The **F2** (▶Search), **Shift-F2** (◀Search), and **Alt-F2** (Replace) commands are highly interrelated commands.

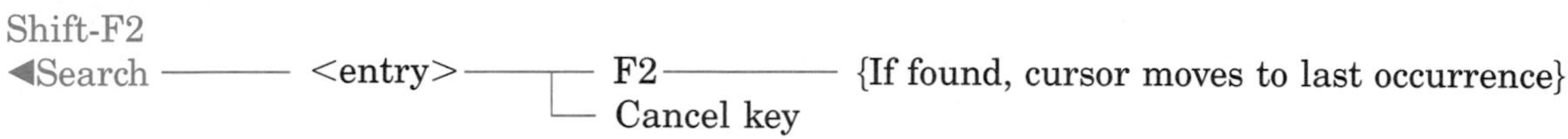

SHIFT-F2 ◀SEARCH

The (◀Search) command is used to move the cursor backwards to occurrences of specific words, phrases, or WordPerfect codes. The ◀Search command works in the same manner as the ▶Search command. See **F2** (▶Search) for more information on the Search operation.

Block/◀Search

The ◀Search command may be used to expand (contract) a blocked portion of text back to the found word/code pattern.

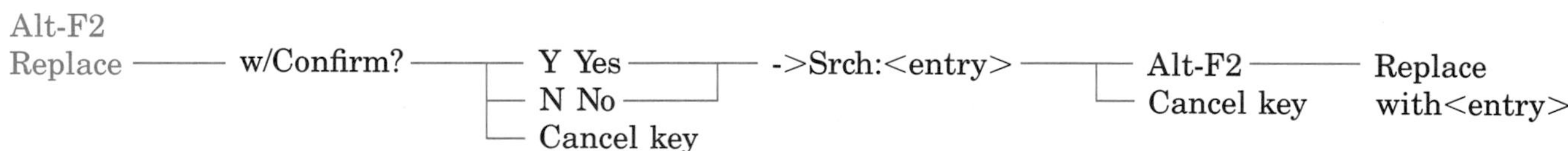

ALT-F2 REPLACE

The **Alt-F2** (Replace) command is used to search the document for occurrences of specific words, phrases, or WordPerfect codes and replace them with other words, phrases, or codes. To use the Replace command, begin by typing Alt-F2 (Replace).

The prompt "w/Confirm? **N**o (**Y**es)" will appear on the screen. If you type Y, WordPerfect will stop on each word pattern for which it is searching and will prompt "Confirm? **N**o (**Y**es)." You then may type Y to replace the word pattern, or N or ↵ to skip over the word pattern and continue searching.

It is recommended that you type Y at the initial "w/Confirm" prompt. If you type N or ↵ at the initial "w/Confirm" prompt, WordPerfect will automatically replace all of the occurrences of the word/code pattern in the document with the replacement word/code pattern.

The next prompt displayed by the Replace command is "->Srch:". WordPerfect normally searches for word/code patterns from the current cursor position forward in the document. To cause a search backwards in the document, type the cursor up key when you see the "->Srch:" prompt and the prompt will change to "<-Srch:". (Typing the cursor down key returns the search to forward.)

You next type the word pattern for which to search. You may type any keyboard characters or specify WordPerfect codes by typing the keystroke combinations that would normally generate the command menus for the codes. When finished type the **Alt-F2** (Replace) command again.

The next prompt "Replace with:" is answered by typing the word pattern you want the search word pattern to be replaced with. You may answer this prompt in the same manner as you answer the "->Srch:" prompt. When you have finished typing the replacement word pattern, type **Alt-F2** (Replace) once more, and the search and replace operation will commence.

Lowercase search characters will match upper and lower-case characters in the document; upper-case search characters will only match uppercase characters. An extended search (one in which headers, footers, footnotes, and endnotes are also searched) may be done by typing the Home key before typing **Alt-F2** (Replace).

Block/Replace

The Replace command operation may be done on a block of text by blocking the text to be searched before typing **Alt-F2** (Replace).

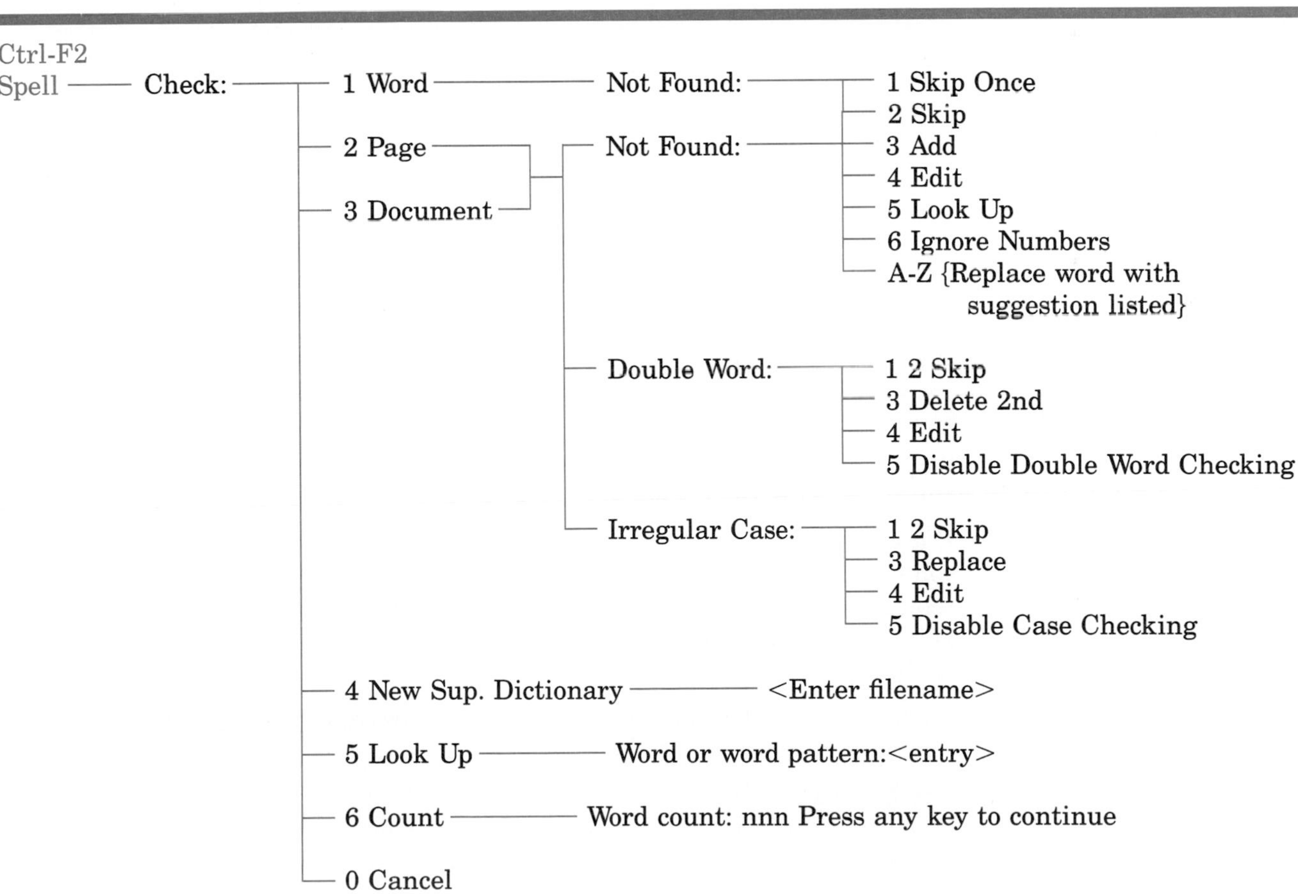

CTRL-F2 SPELL

WordPerfect comes with a spell checking feature that will search a document for words not found in its dictionary. The dictionary data are kept on a separate disk. If you are using a computer with two floppy disk drives, you will need to insert the Speller disk into the B: drive each time it is needed. If you have a hard-disk drive, the Speller diskette files may be copied into the same subdirectory as WordPerfect.

Check: Word — Page — Document

The spelling feature may be used to check the current word, page, or document. Each is similar in how WordPerfect checks for spelling errors.

WordPerfect will move to the start of the word, page, or document and begin comparing the words found there with the words in its dictionary. When it finds a word not listed in its dictionary, it stops and presents a screen similar to the following:

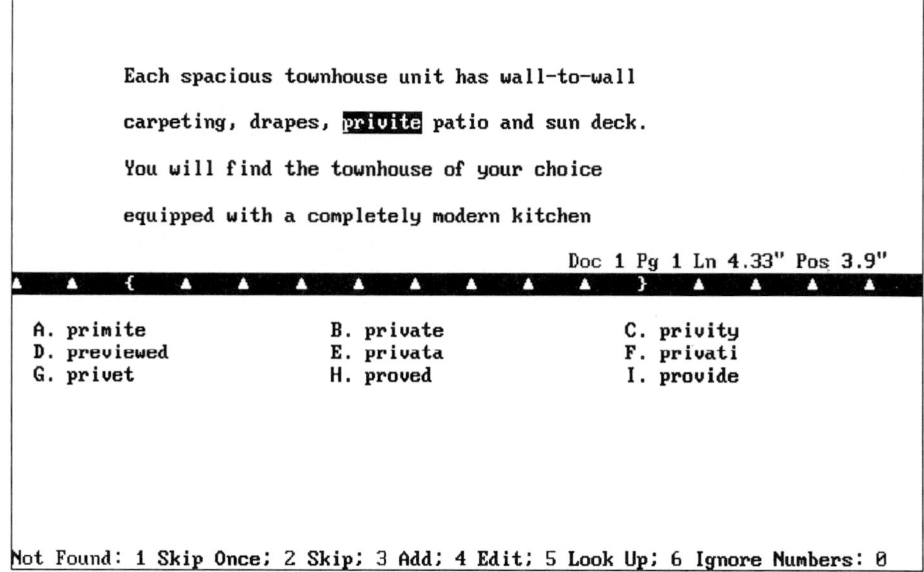

Not Found

At the top of the screen is the portion of the document where WordPerfect found an unknown word. Beneath is a list of words WordPerfect did find in its dictionary that may be the correct spelling for the unknown word. At the bottom of the screen is the Spell menu of commands.

If the correct spelling for the word appears in the middle of the screen, you may type the letter preceding it (A., B., etc.) to cause WordPerfect to replace the unknown word with a correctly spelled word. WordPerfect will automatically capitalize the replacement word if the word being replaced is capitalized.

Note that the following commands can only be executed by typing the command number.

1 Skip Once

If you type **1** (Skip Once), WordPerfect will continue its search and, if it encounters the word again, it will stop for you to correct it.

2 Skip

If you type **2** (Skip), WordPerfect will continue its search and ignore the word if it occurs again.

3 Add
You may use the Add command to cause WordPerfect to add the current word to a supplemental dictionary.

4 Edit
You may use the Edit command to edit the word. When you have finished editing, type the Enter key. If the edited word is found in the dictionary, WordPerfect will continue.

5 Look Up
You may use the Look Up command to look up words that match a pattern. The pattern is described by using the wild card characters ? and *. *Ca?e* will return *cafe*, *cage*, *cake*, etc. *Ca*e* will return *cabbage*, *cable*, *caboose*, etc.

6 Ignore Numbers
Use the Ignore Numbers command to cause WordPerfect to skip over all words containing a number.

Double Word

During its spelling check, WordPerfect also will stop on occurrences of double words. You are given the options to:**1** or **2** Skip, **3** Delete the 2nd word, **4** Edit the text, or **5** Disable Double Word Checking.

Irregular Case

The spell checking feature also checks for certain errors in capitalization. When WordPerfect locates a word in which such an error occurs, you are given the options: to **1** or **2** Skip (skips the word once), **3** Replace (replaces the word with the case defined by WordPerfect's internal set of rules), **4** Edit (allows editing of the word; type **F7** (Exit) to continue), and **5** Disable Case Checking (stops WordPerfect from checking for irregular case).

New Sup. Dictionary — The **N**ew Supplemental Dictionary command may be used to create a personal dictionary for use in a spelling check.

Look Up — The (Spell),**L**ook Up command is the same as the (Spell),Not Found,**5** Look Up command. You may use the (Spell),**L**ook Up command to look up words without starting a spell checking operation.

Count — When it has finished spell checking the document, WordPerfect will display the total number of words it checked during the spell check operation. Use the **C**ount command to count the number of words in a document without performing the spell checking operation.

Block/Spell — You can conduct a spell check operation on a block of text by using the Block/(Spell) command.

F3
Help ———— {Press Enter or Space bar to exit Help}

F3 HELP

The **F3** (Help) command provides an extensive set of on-line documentation for the user. The documentation is kept on the WordPerfect 1 disk. If you are using a computer with two floppy disk drives, you will need to insert the disk into the disk drive to use the **F3** (Help) command.

The **F3** (Help) command is a "context sensitive" command. That is, the **F3** (Help) command may be typed at any time while using WordPerfect, and the command will provide information on the current editing or command operation. For instance, if you type **Shift-F8,1,8** (Format),**L**ine,**T**ab Set, and then type **F3** (Help), the help screen will display information on setting tab stops with WordPerfect. Another approach is to first type **F3** (Help), and then type the keystrokes that will lead to the command on which you want further information.

To exit the (Help) command screens, type Space or ↵.

Shift-F3
Switch ———— {Press Switch key to return to original document}

SHIFT-F3 SWITCH

WordPerfect allows editing of two text files at the same time. When WordPerfect is first loaded, the default file for editing is Document 1 (displayed as "Doc 1" on the status line). To begin editing Document 2, type **Shift-F3**. Editing and file operations are treated as separate operations between the two documents. You must exit both documents with the **F7** (Exit) command to properly exit WordPerfect.

The two documents share the same Move buffer and Undelete buffers. You may copy text from one file to the other by using these buffers and the appropriate commands.

You may view both Document 1 and Document 2 at the same time by using the **Ctrl-F3,1** (Screen),**W**indow command.

Block/Switch

You may use the Block/(Switch) command to convert letters in a block of text to all uppercase or all lowercase letters.

Block/Shift-F3
Switch
- 1 Uppercase
- 2 Lowercase
- 0 Cancel

To convert lowercase letters to uppercase, block the text, then type the **Shift-F3,1** (Switch),**U**ppercase command. To convert uppercase letters to lowercase, block the text, then type the **Shift-F3,2** (Switch),**L**owercase command.

Alt-F3
Reveal Codes ———— {Press Reveal Codes key to restore screen}

ALT-F3 REVEAL CODES

The **Alt-F3** (Reveal Codes) command splits the screen and reveals imbedded WordPerfect codes. Cursor control keys synchronously move top and bottom cursors (cursors in the text and code screens). All editing and command operations are available while the Reveal Codes screen is on. Type **Alt-F3** (Reveal Codes) again to return to normal editing.

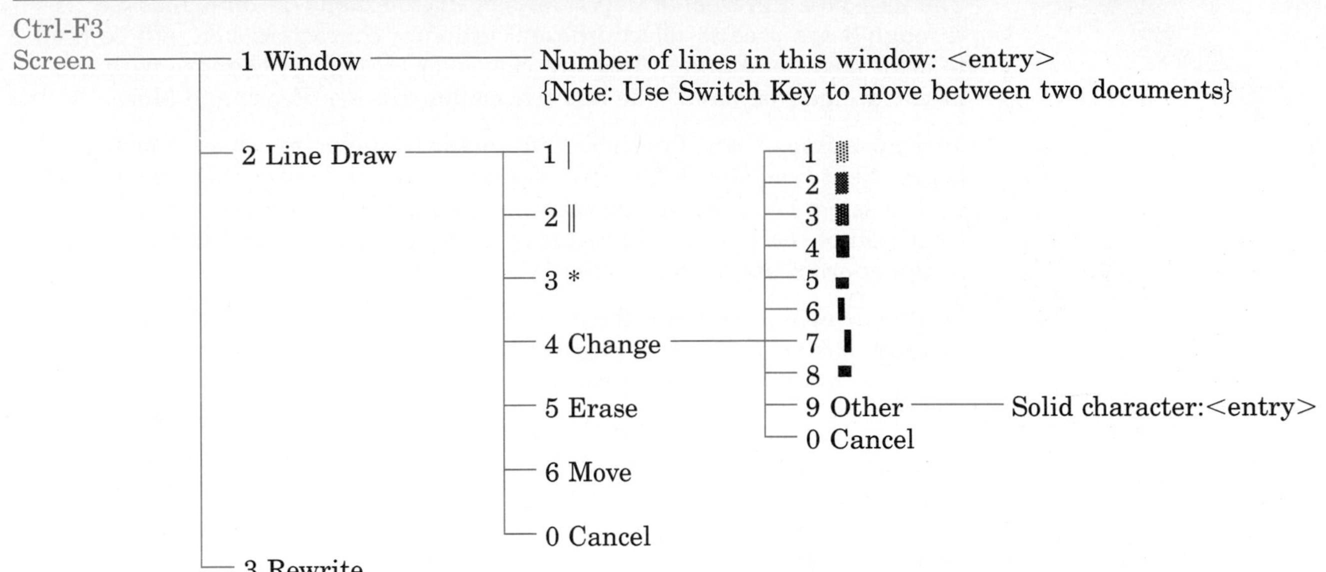

CTRL-F3 SCREEN

The **Ctrl-F3** (Screen) command may be used to rewrite the document for new format forward codes placed to split the screen in order to view Documents 1 and 2 simultaneously (see the **Shift-F3** (Switch) command) or to create various lines and boxes to be included in the current document.

Window

The **W**indow command may be used to split the screen horizontally to view Documents 1 and 2 at the same time (see **Shift-F3** (Switch)). Type **Ctrl-F3,1** and then enter the number of screen lines to be displayed for the current document. Typing 11 will split the screen in half (two equal windows). Typing 24 will return the screen to the normal one-screen mode. Screens may not be split into windows of less than two lines.

Use the **Shift-F3** (Switch) command to move the cursor from one window to the other.

Line Draw

The **Line Draw** command is used for drawing boxes and lines in the current text file. It provides screen graphic characters and commands that allow shapes to be drawn on the screen by using the cursor control keys. However, some printers do not support the screen graphics characters used by the **Line Draw** command, and printing a file with such characters in it may lead to unpredictable results.

The **Line Draw** command is composed of two menus. The relationship of the menus may be graphically represented as follows:

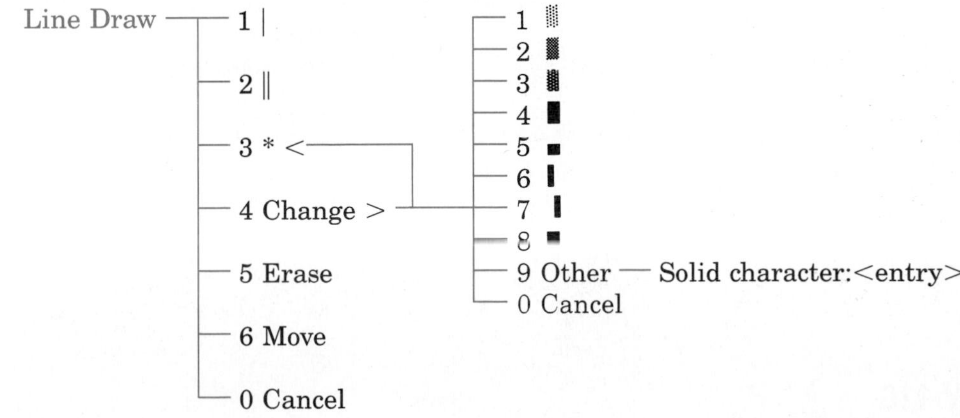

The first menu presented (left side) has six commands. Commands **1** through **3** are used to select different graphics characters that will be used to draw boxes and lines. The third character (*) may be changed with the next **C**hange command. The last two commands are **E**rase and **M**ove.

To draw a line or box, first move the cursor to the point where drawing is to begin. Next type **Ctrl-F3,2** (Screen),**L**ine Draw, and enter the number **1**, **2**, or **3** to select the graphics character of your choice. You may now draw lines composed of the selected character by using the cursor control keys to move in the appropriate draw direction.

To stop drawing and move the cursor to a new location, type **6** or **M** (**M**ove). To erase characters on the screen, type **5** or **E** (**E**rase) and then move the cursor across the characters you wish to erase.

The third graphics character shown on the **L**ine Draw menu, *, can be changed to any one of the characters shown on the right (1 through 8). Type **4** or **C** (**C**hange) and then type the number of the desired graphics character on the second **L**ine Draw menu. **9** or **O** (**O**ther) may be used to define a keyboard character to use in drawing lines.

It is generally recommended that you enter **L**ine Draw characters into an area of document text that has single line spacing (see **Shift-F8,1,6** (Format),**L**ine,Line **S**pacing) and that no [►Indent], [►Indent ◄], [Tab], or [◄Mar Rel] codes occur within the area. It also is recommended that each line of text in the area end with a hard return [HRt] code.

Rewrite

The **R**ewrite command may be used to rewrite the screen after the **Shift-F1,2,6,1** (Setup),**D**isplay,**E**dit Screen Options,**A**utomatically Format and Rewrite command has been changed to "No" (see the **Shift-F1** (Setup) command). Type **Ctrl-F3,3** or **Ctrl-F3,**↵ to rewrite the screen.

F4
Indent ———————— {Places indent code [►Indent] and moves cursor to next tab stop}

F4 ►INDENT
CODE = [►Indent]

The **F4** (►Indent) command indents subsequent text in a paragraph to the next tab stop. See the **Shift-F8** (Format),**L**ine,**T**ab Set command for information on setting tab stops.

To create a "hanging" paragraph (one that is indented to the right of a heading) type the heading, **F4** (►Indent), and then type the paragraph.

Heading: This is an example of a "hanging" paragraph produced with the **F4** (►Indent) command.

Shift-F4
Indent —————— {Places indent code [▶Indent ◀] and moves cursor to next tab stop}

SHIFT-F4
▶INDENT ◀
CODE =
[▶INDENT ◀]

The **Shift-F4** (▶Indent ◀) command causes subsequent text in a paragraph to be indented an equal number of tab stops from both the left and right margins. The next tab stop to the right of the cursor position determines the number of tab stops to be used for indentation. If the cursor position is to the right of half of the tab stops set, the [▶Indent ◀] code will not be placed. See the **Shift-F8** (Format), **L**ine,**T**ab Set command for information on setting tab stops.

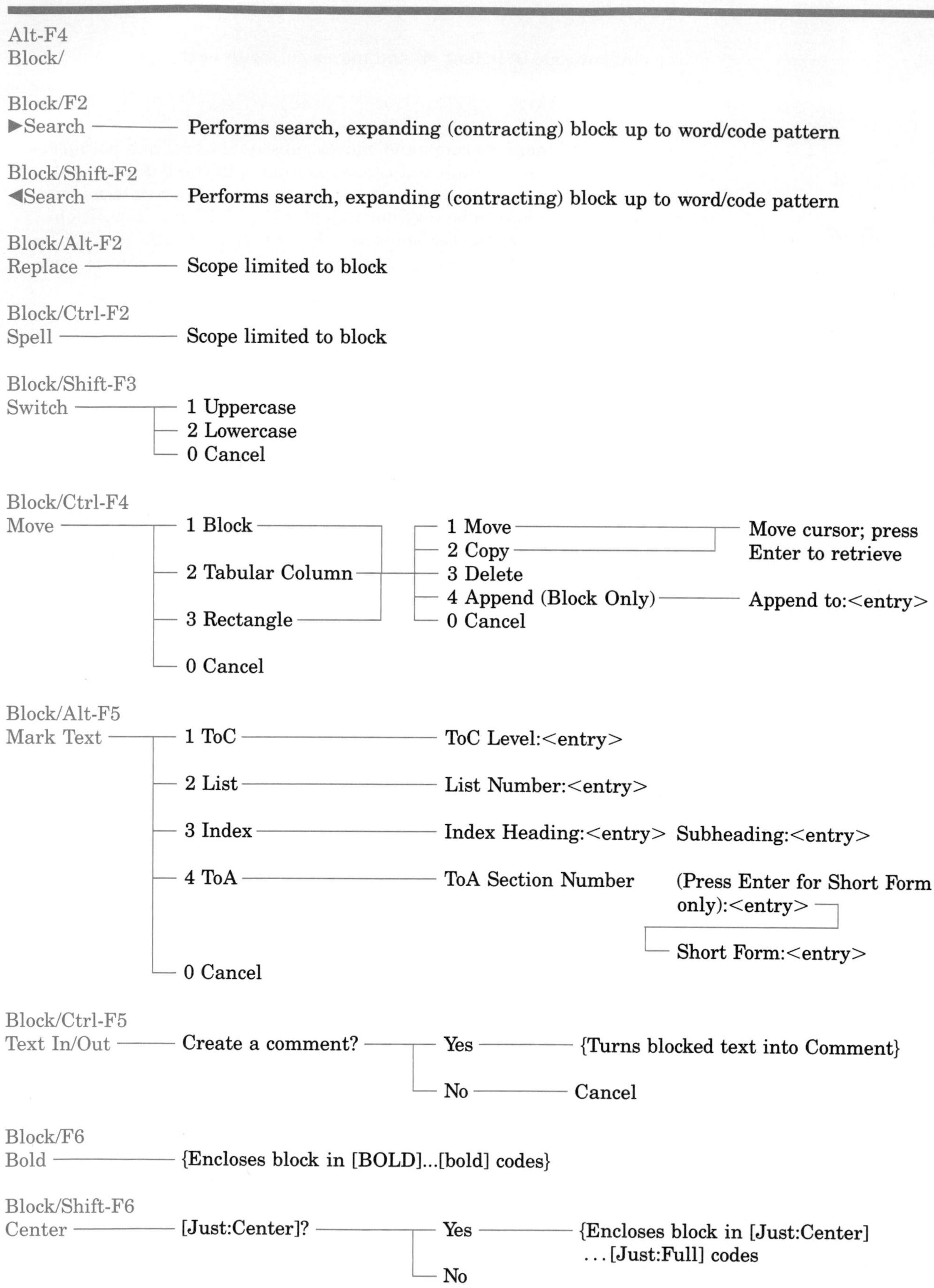
Alt-F4
Block/
Block/F2
►Search
Performs search, expanding (contracting) block up to word/code pattern
Block/Shift-F2
◄Search
Performs search, expanding (contracting) block up to word/code pattern
Block/Alt-F2
Replace
Scope limited to block
Block/Ctrl-F2
Spell
Scope limited to block
Block/Shift-F3
Switch
1 Uppercase
2 Lowercase
0 Cancel
Block/Ctrl-F4
Move
1 Block
2 Tabular Column
3 Rectangle
0 Cancel
1 Move
2 Copy
3 Delete
4 Append (Block Only)
0 Cancel
Move cursor; press Enter to retrieve
Append to:<entry>
Block/Alt-F5
Mark Text
1 ToC
ToC Level:<entry>
2 List
List Number:<entry>
3 Index
Index Heading:<entry>
Subheading:<entry>
4 ToA
ToA Section Number
(Press Enter for Short Form only):<entry>
Short Form:<entry>
0 Cancel
Block/Ctrl-F5
Text In/Out
Create a comment?
Yes
{Turns blocked text into Comment}
No
Cancel
Block/F6
Bold
{Encloses block in [BOLD]...[bold] codes}
Block/Shift-F6
Center
[Just:Center]?
Yes
{Encloses block in [Just:Center] ... [Just:Full] codes
No

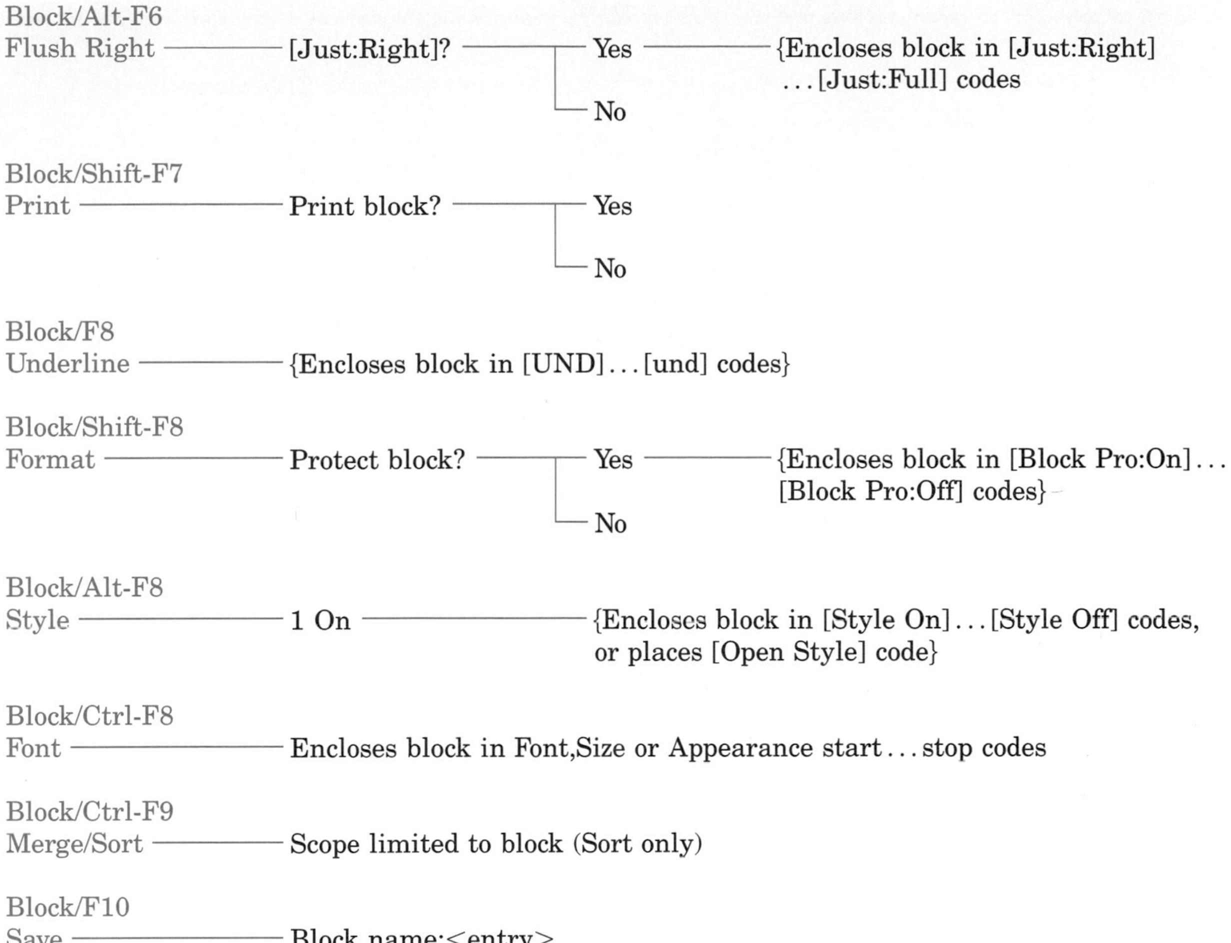

ALT-F4 BLOCK CODE = [Block]

The **Alt-F4** (Block) command is used to define a portion of text to be subsequently affected by another WordPerfect command. To block a portion of text, move the cursor to the beginning of the text to be blocked and type **Alt-F4** (Block). A blinking "Block on" message will appear at the bottom of the screen. Next, move the cursor to the end of the text to be blocked. Note that while Block is on, typing a character will automatically move the cursor forward to the character and typing ↵ will move the cursor forward to the next hard return [HRt] code. The blocked text will be displayed on the screen in reverse video.

The **Alt-F4** (Block) command trees describe which commands may be used to affect a section of blocked text. For more information on the Block/command operations, refer to the appropriate command menu.

To turn a Block off, type **F1** (Cancel) or **Alt-F4** (Block).

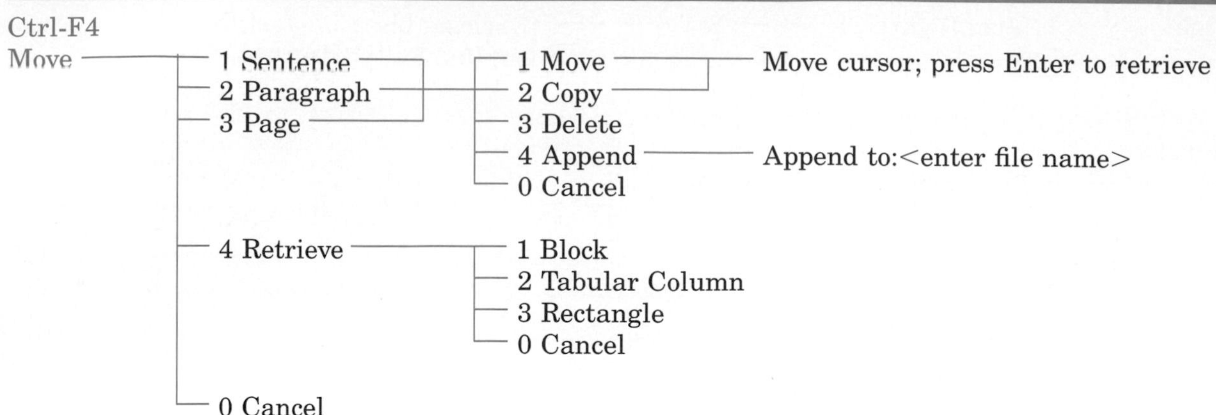

CTRL-F4 MOVE

The **Ctrl-F4** (Move) command is used to perform cut-and-paste operations. The operations include moving a section of text to another location, copying a section of text to another location, and deleting a section of text from the document.

The text being moved or copied is temporarily held during and after the operation in what is called a Move buffer. When text is deleted, it is held in an Undelete buffer. Once a cut-and-paste operation is completed, a copy of the text remains in the buffer. The copy of text in the buffer will be replaced by a subsequent Move or Delete operation. (See the introductory tutorial for more information on Move and Undelete buffers.)

The Move and Block/(Move) commands are highly related. Both are designed to facilitate the cutting and pasting of various sizes and shapes of text. The following discusses each of the commands and the type of text for which they are designed.

Move: **S**entence — **P**aragraph — **Pa**ge

The (Move) **S**entence, **P**aragraph, and **Pa**ge commands differ only in the number of lines of text they are designed to cut, copy, or delete. A sentence is defined by WordPerfect to be that text that occurs between periods and/or hard returns. A paragraph is defined by WordPerfect to be that text that occurs between hard returns. A page is defined by WordPerfect to be that text that occurs between soft or hard page breaks.

To perform a cut-and-paste operation on such sections of text, position the cursor on the sentence, paragraph, or page to be affected and type **Ctrl-F4** (Move). Next select the appropriate text definition (**S**entence, **P**aragraph, or **Pa**ge) by typing the command number or letter. The sentence, paragraph, or page of text will become highlighted on the screen (automatically blocked). The next menu that appears includes the options to **M**ove, **C**opy, **D**elete, or **A**ppend the blocked section of text.

Move

Use **M**ove to erase the blocked section from the screen and prepare to retrieve it from the Move buffer into another location in the text. To complete the **M**ove operation, move the cursor to where the text is to be retrieved and type ↵. You may type **F1** (Cancel) to interrupt the **M**ove operation and use the **Ctrl-F4,4,1** (Move),**R**etrieve,**B**lock command at a later time to retrieve the block of text. (See the **Ctrl-F4** (Move),**R**etrieve command.)

Copy

Use **Copy** to prepare to retrieve a copy of the blocked section of text from the Move buffer and place it in another location in the text. To complete the **Copy** operation, move the cursor to where the copied text is to be retrieved and type ↵. You may type **F1** (Cancel) to interrupt the **Copy** operation and use the **Ctrl-F4,4,1** (Move),**R**etrieve,**B**lock command at a later time to retrieve the block of text. (See the **Ctrl-F4** (Move),**R**etrieve command.)

Delete

Use **D**elete to delete the text from the document. A copy of the deleted text will be placed into the first Undelete buffer.

Append

Use the **A**ppend command to add the blocked text to the bottom of a document file stored on the disk. When **A**ppend is used, WordPerfect will prompt "Append to:". Enter the filename for the file to which you want the blocked text appended.

Retrieve

As previously mentioned, the Move and Block/(Move) commands are highly interrelated. In fact, the (Move),**S**entence, (Move),**P**aragraph, and (Move),P**a**ge commands simply provide the feature of automatically blocking the section of text before proceeding with the cut-and-paste operation. When the Move or Block/(Move),**B**lock commands are used to perform a copy or move operation, the blocked text is copied to the Move buffer and may later be retrieved with the (Move),**R**etrieve,**B**lock command.

The (Move),**R**etrieve command, however, has two other options besides **B**lock. The additional options are Tabular **C**olumn and **R**ectangle. The two other options are used to retrieve text from another Move buffer (the column buffer)—a buffer into which text may only be placed using the Block/(Move),Tabular **C**olumns or the Block/(Move),**R**ectangle commands.

Block/Move

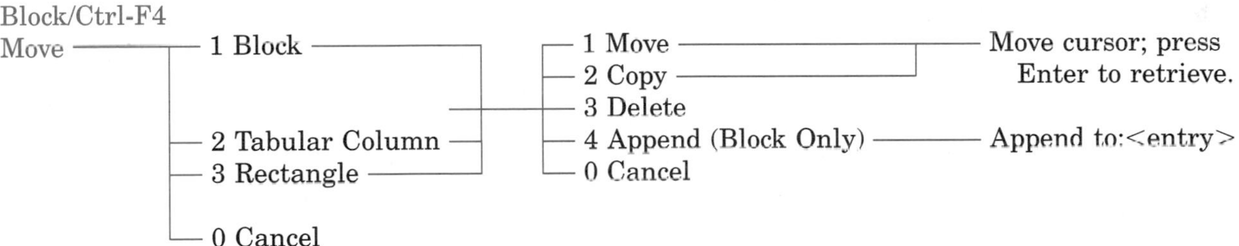

The Block/(Move) command may be used to perform cut-and-paste operations on two different shapes of text, block, or column.

Block

Block/(Move),**B**lock is used to perform cut-and-paste operations on text that can be described as being left to right, top to bottom in nature. Sentences, paragraphs, pages, or portions thereof, are Block shaped. Block the text to be affected and type **Ctrl-F4,1** (Move),**B**lock. Next select **M**ove, **C**opy, **D**elete, or **A**ppend. Finally, if the operation is to move or copy the column of text, move the cursor to where you want the column of text to appear and type ↵. You may type **F1** (Cancel) to interrupt the copy operation and use the **Ctrl-F4** (Move),**R**etrieve,**B**lock command at a later time to retrieve the block of text.

Tabular **C**olumn

Block/(Move),Tabular **C**olumn is used to perform cut-and-paste operations on a column of text defined by tabs, tab aligns, indents, or hard returns. Move the cursor to the top of the column of text you want to move, copy, or delete, and then turn Block on by typing **Alt-F4** (Block). Next move the cursor to the bottom of the column. The entire block will be highlighted at this point. Then type **Ctrl-F4,2** (Move),Tabular **C**olumn. Now only the column in which the cursor is located will be highlighted. Next select **M**ove, **C**opy, **D**elete, or **A**ppend. Finally, if the operation is to move or copy the column of text, move the cursor to where you want the column of text to appear and type ↵. You may type **F1** (Cancel) to interrupt the copy operation and use the **Ctrl-F4,4,2** (Move),**R**etrieve,Tabular **C**olumn command at a later time to retrieve the block of text.

Rectangle

The Block/(Move),**R**ectangle command is used to perform cut-and-paste operations on a rectangular segment of text. Move the cursor to the top left corner of the rectangle of text you want to move, copy, or delete, and then turn Block on by typing **Alt-F4** (Block). Move the cursor next to the bottom right corner of the rectangle. The entire block will be highlighted at this point. Then type **Ctrl-F4,3** (Move),**R**ectangle. Now only the rectangle described by its top left and bottom right corners will be highlighted. Next select **M**ove, **C**opy, **D**elete, or **A**ppend. Finally, if the operation is to move or copy the rectangle of text, move the cursor to the place you want the rectangle to appear and type ↵. You may type **F1** (Cancel) to interrupt the copy operation and use the **Ctrl-F4,4,3** (Move),**R**etrieve,**R**ectangle command at a later time to retrieve the block of text.

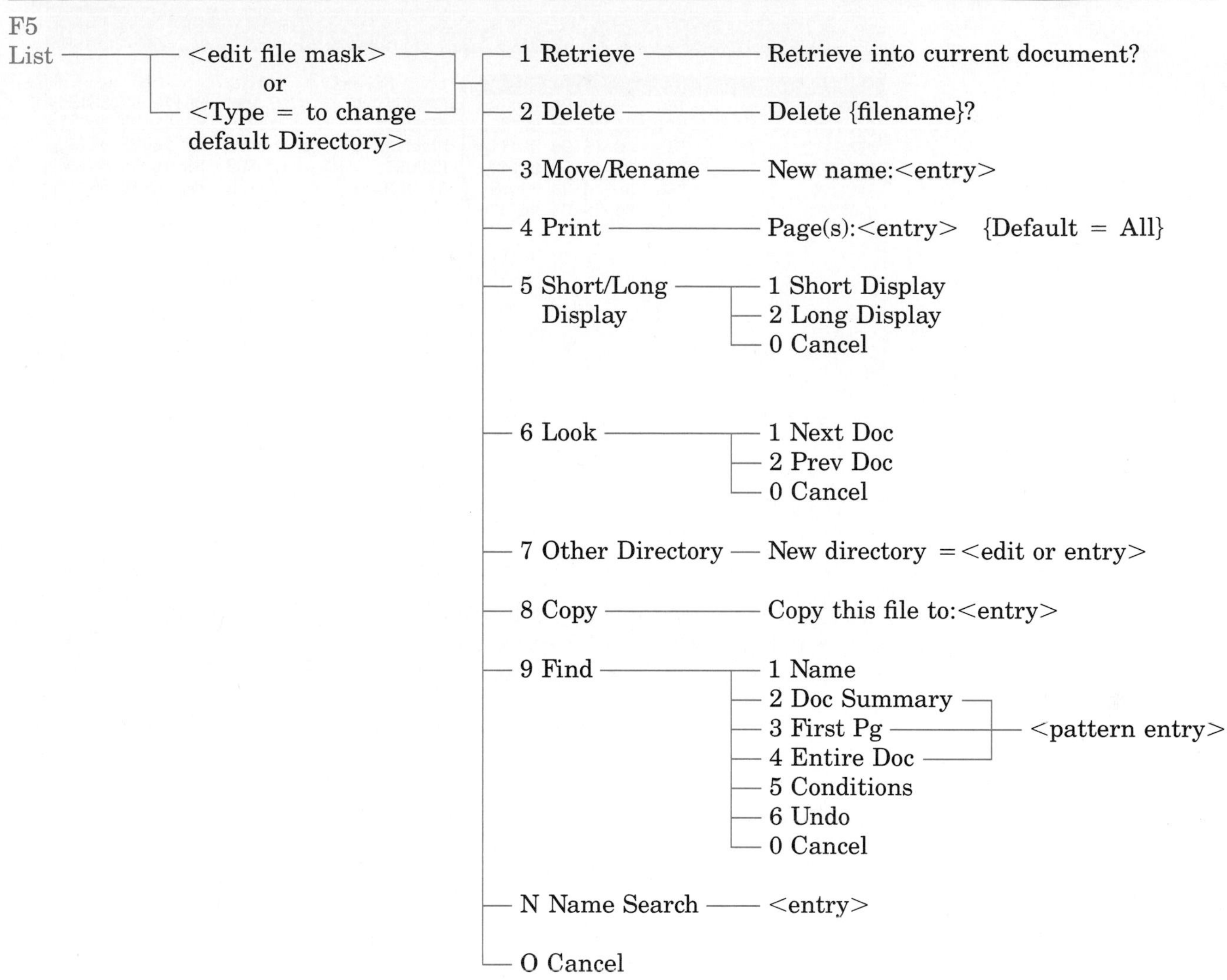

F5 LIST

The **F5** (List) command provides commands to change the default disk drive, perform basic file maintenance operations, and search through files for word pattern occurrences.

Changing the Default Disk Drive

When the **F5** (List) command is typed, a message:

Dir A:*.* (Type = to change default Dir)

appears on the screen. The A:*.* part of the message indicates which drive is the current drive. To cause WordPerfect to automatically look to another drive or directory for your word processing files, type = ↵ and then enter the drive name and/or path for the appropriate subdirectory. (See **F5,7** (List),**O**ther Directory for another method of changing the default drive.)

The List Screen

When the correct directory is displayed, type ↵ to cause WordPerfect to display the (List) screen. The screen will appear similar to the following:

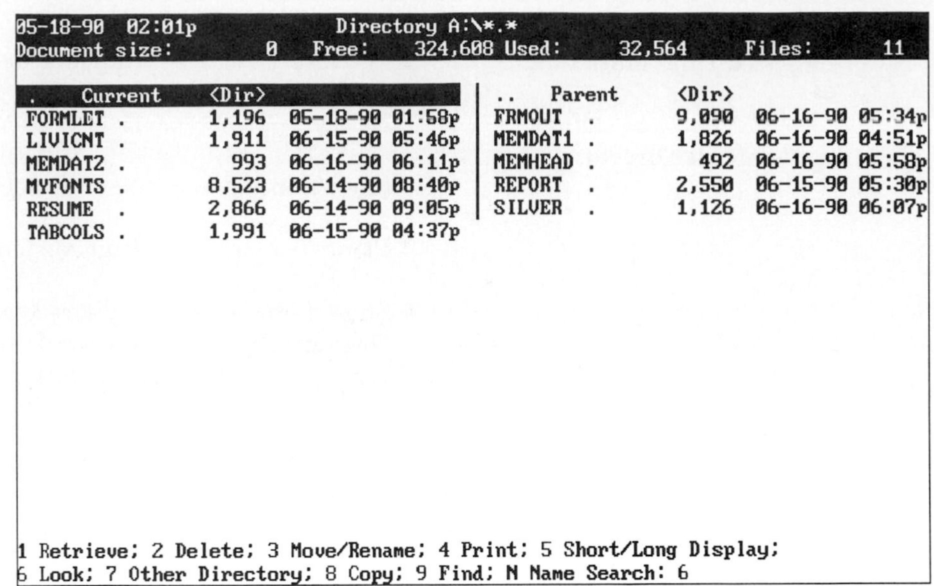

The top of the screen displays a header with information about the DOS system date and time, the size of the document currently being edited, the current directory, disk space available, and the number of files on the disk.

List File Maintenance Commands

The first eight commands on the (List) screen are commands associated with file maintenance. The inverted screen appearing at the top of the list of filenames is a cursor. The cursor may be moved with the cursor control keys to any one of the files displayed on the screen. The PgUp and PgDn keys may also be used to move the cursor. To execute the file maintenance commands, you first move the cursor to the appropriate filename and then type the number or letter of the command you wish to execute.

Retrieve

The **R**etrieve command loads a document into memory for editing or printing. The retrieved document will be inserted at the editing cursor location into any document that may already be in memory. Move the List cursor to the file to be retrieved, and then type **1** or **R** (**R**etrieve). (See **Shift-F10** (Retrieve) for another method of retrieving document files.)

Delete

Erases a file from the disk. Move the List cursor to the file to be deleted, and then type **2** or **D** (**D**elete). The message "Delete *filename*? **N**o (**Y**es)" will appear at the bottom of the screen. Type "Y" to complete the file deletion operation. When a file is deleted, it is permanently erased from the disk.

Move/Rename

The **M**ove/Rename command may be used to move a file to another disk or directory or rename a file. Move the List cursor to the file to be affected and then type **3** or **M** (**M**ove/Rename). To move the file, type the full directory specification for where the file is to be moved (drive/path). To rename the file, type a new filename. To move and rename the file, type the full file directory specification followed by the new filename.

Print

To print a file from the disk, move the List cursor to the file to be printed and type **4** or **P** (**P**rint). WordPerfect will respond with the prompt "Page(s): (All)". If you want the whole document to be printed, type ↵. You may, however, specify that only certain pages be printed. To specify certain pages you may enter one of the following:

N	Print page number *N*
N-	Print from page number *N* to end of document
N-n	Print pages *N* through *n* inclusive
-N	Print from beginning of document through page *N*
N,n	Print pages *N* and *n*
N-n,M	Print pages *N* through *n*, inclusive, and *M*

Page numbers must be entered in the way they appear on the printed document. (See **Shift-F7** (Print) for another method of printing certain pages of a disk file.)

To cancel a print job that has already started printing, use the **Shift-F7,4,1** ↵ (Print),**C**ontrol Printer,**C**ancel Job(s) command.

Short/Long Display

WordPerfect displays the List screen in one of two formats: **S**hort Display, which is the default format, and **L**ong Display, which lists the files' long document names and types (see **Shift-F1** (Setup),**E**nvironment,**D**ocument Management/Summary for information on entering long document names and types). The **L**ong Display lists only files created with WordPerfect and will alphabetize the listing by the long document name rather than by filename.

Look

The **L**ook command allows you to view a file on the disk without retrieving it. **L**ook is the default command on the List screen. If you move the List cursor to a filename and type ↵, the contents of the file will be displayed on the screen, but the file will not be retrieved. The **N**ext Doc and **P**rev Doc commands may be used to view the next or last previous document listed on the List screen.

Other Directory

The **O**ther Directory command may be used to change the default disk drive and/or subdirectory after the List screen has been presented. (See **F5** (List), "Changing the Default Disk Drive" for another method of changing the default drive.)

Copy

The **C**opy command is used to make a copy of a file. Move the List cursor to the file to be copied, and then type **8** or **C** (**C**opy). Then enter the file specification for the copied file.

List Search Commands

Find

The **F5** (List),**F**ind command is designed to search for occurrences of a word pattern in the files of the current disk and/or subdirectory. The size of the word pattern is limited to 39 characters. When the search is completed, the List screen will display only those files having the specified word pattern within them on the screen.

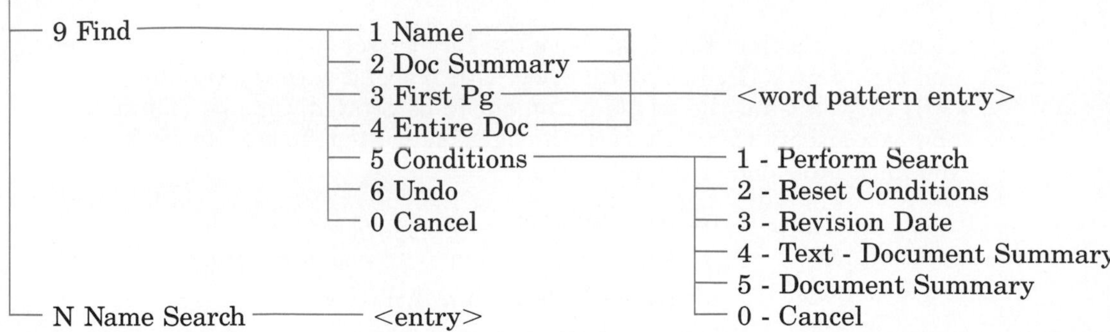

To use the **F**ind command, you first specify the scope of the search. The options include search **D**oc(ument) Summaries only (see **Shift-F8,3,5** (Format),**D**ocument,**S**ummary for information on Document Summaries), search First **P**age only (first 4,000 bytes of the file), or search the **E**ntire Doc(ument) for the word pattern. After you have selected the scope of the search you enter the word pattern for which to search.

You may use the **C**onditions command to bring up a different menu screen that may be used to set various additional criteria for the search.

Word Patterns

It is recommended that you enclose the word pattern to be searched for with quotes. Upper and lowercase characters are treated the same when a word search is performed.

The wild card characters ? and * may be used in the word pattern. The ? (question mark) has the effect of saying "accept any character here." For example, if the word pattern to search for is entered as: "April ?, 1988" all files with dates entered as text that match the word pattern, except for the middle character, will be displayed on the (List) screen. That is, files dated "April 2, 1988," "April 3, 1988," and so on, will be displayed.

The * (asterisk) has the effect of saying "accept any characters from this point on." For example, if the word pattern to search for is entered as: "Water*" all files having words such as "Waterville," "Waterdale," and so on, will be displayed.

Logical operators may be effected with the ; (semicolon) for AND and , (comma) for OR. The order of logical operator execution is from left to right. For example, "Bill";"product review" will display all files with the word patterns "Bill" and "product review" within them.

"Bill","Larry";"product review" will display all files with the word patterns "Bill" or "Larry" that also have the pattern "product review"—that is, ("Bill" OR "Larry") AND "product review."

Name Search

If you type **N** (**N**ame Search), the **N**ame Search command will begin execution. With **N**ame Search, you begin to type the filename of a file and the cursor will jump to the first filename with matching characters for the keystroke(s) you type. To end **N**ame Search, type **F1** (Cancel) or ↵.

Marking Files

You can Delete, Print, Copy, or Word Search several files at once by marking the files with an asterisk. Move the List cursor to the file(s) you want to erase, copy, print, or search, and then type an * (asterisk). When all of the appropriate files are marked, select the command you want executed from the (List) menu.

To "unmark" a file, move the List cursor to the file and type an * (asterisk) again.

Shift-F5
Date/Outline

- 1 Date Text — {Places today's system date as text}
- 2 Date Code — {Places code which always reflects computer's current system date}
- 3 Date Format
  - 1 - Day of the Month
  - 2 - Month (number)
  - 3 - Month (word)
  - 4 - Year (all four digits)
  - 5 - Year (last two digits)
  - 6 - Day of the Week (word)
  - 7 - Hour (24-hour clock)
  - 8 - Hour (12-hour clock)
  - 9 - Minute
  - 0 - am / pm
  - %,$ - Leading zeros or spaces, abbreviation
- 4 Outline
  - 1 On
  - 2 Off
  - 3 Move Family
  - 4 Copy Family
  - 5 Delete Family
  - 0 Cancel
- 5 Para Num — Paragraph Level (Press Enter for Automatic):<entry>
- 6 Define
  - 1 - Starting Paragraph Number
  - 2 - Paragraph
  - 3 - Outline
  - 4 - Legal (1.1.1)
  - 5 - Bullets
  - 6 - User-defined
    - Current Definition
    - Attach Previous Level
  - 7 - Enter Inserts Paragraph Number
  - 8 - Automatically Adjust to Current Level
  - 9 - Outline Style Name
  - 0 - Cancel
- 0 Cancel

SHIFT-F5 DATE/OUTLINE

The **Shift-F5** (Date/Outline) command may be used to insert (in a variety of formats) the current DOS system date and/or time into a document or to generate automatic outline and paragraph numbering.

Date Text

The Date **T**ext command inserts the system date/time as text at the current cursor location.

Date Code
Code = [Date:*format*]

Inserts the date/time as a WordPerfect code. The code will display the current DOS date and/or time each time the document is opened for editing or printing. The display will be in the current date format.

Date Format

Default—3 1,4 **Example—December 15, 1989**

Date Format
- 1 - Day of the Month
- 2 - Month (number)
- 3 - Month (word)
- 4 - Year (all four digits)
- 5 - Year (last two digits)
- 6 - Day of the Week (word)
- 7 - Hour (24-hour clock)
- 8 - Hour (12-hour clock)
- 9 - Minute
- 0 - am / pm
- %,$ - Leading zeros or spaces, abbreviation

The Date **F**ormat command allows the date/time format to be changed for the document. The menu of format options is largely self-explanatory. When the Date **F**ormat command is used to reset the display of dates in a document, all subsequent date text or date codes inserted into the file during the editing session will reflect the changed date format. To change the date format for all subsequent editing sessions, use **Shift-F1** (Setup),**I**nitial Settings,**D**ate Format.

Outline
Code = [Par Num:Auto]

WordPerfect provides a feature that automatically inserts and maintains outline numbers. The numbers are generated by codes that are inserted into the text when the **O**utline feature is on and the Enter key is typed.

On — Off

To turn the **O**utline feature on, type **Shift-F5,4,1** (Date/Outline),**O**utline,**O**n. The message "Outline" will appear on the status line. To turn the **O**utline feature off, type **Shift-F5,4,2** (Date/Outline),**O**utline,**O**ff.

The nature of the number displayed by an Outline code depends on the code's position on the screen—it changes according to the tab stop (see **Shift-F8** (Format),**L**ine,**T**ab Set) upon which the code occurs or follows.

It is generally easier to insert [Tab]s or [►Indent]s before a code to ensure that it is moved to a current tab stop. The following shows the various default number type displays and the [Tab]s required to generate them.

I.	No [Tab]s
[Tab] A.	1 [Tab]
[Tab] [Tab] 1.	2 [Tab]s
[Tab] [Tab] [Tab] a.	3 [Tab]s
[Tab] [Tab] [Tab] [Tab] (1)	4 [Tab]s
[Tab] [Tab] [Tab] [Tab] [Tab] (a)	5 [Tab]s
[Tab] [Tab] [Tab] [Tab] [Tab] [Tab] i)	6 [Tab]s

To use the **O**utline command it is recommended that you turn the **O**utline feature on, then generate several outline codes by typing Enter, Space, Enter, Space, Enter, and so on, until the screen appears:

I.

II.

III.

IV.

V.

VI.

VII.

VIII.

IX.

X.

Next turn off the **O**utline feature and edit the text into an outline form using the Tab key or **F4** (▶Indent) command to insert [Tab]s or [▶Indent] codes before the [Par Num:] outline codes. Renumbering of the displayed numbers will be automatic. The following is an example of how the text will appear after editing:

I. Introduction
  A. History of Company
    1. Founding Father
    2. Beginning Era
      a. First Product Line
    3. The Expansion Years
      a. New Product Lines
      b. New Markets
        (1) Foreign Sales
          (a) Japan
          (b) England
      c. Growth in Earnings
II.

To begin another outline in the same document, type **Shift-F5,6,1,** ↵(Date/Outline),**D**efine,**S**tarting Paragraph Number.

Move Family — Copy Family — Delete Family

The **O**utline command has three options: **M**ove Family, **C**opy Family, and **D**elete Family. An outline "family" is defined by WordPerfect as being the paragraph number and text on the line where the cursor currently resides, and all subsequent paragraph numbers and text of subordinate outline levels. The following illustration describes two examples of outline families:

1 I. Introduction
2 II. History of Word Processing
3 A. Word Processing as an Industry
4 B. In-House Word Processing Departments
5 C. Dedicated Word Processing Systems
6 III. Word Processing and Microcomputers
7 A. The Advent of the Microcomputer
8 1. A Multipurpose Tool for the Office
9 2. The Real Costs and Benefits of Microcomputing
10 B. The New Users of Word Processors
11 1. Today's Office Environment
12 2. High End vs. Low End Users
13 3. Assessment of Word Processing Needs
14 IV. Word Processing Software for Microcomputers

In the example, if the cursor is on line 2 when the **O**utline command is executed, then lines *2* through *5* comprise the outline family. If the cursor is on line *10* when the **O**utline command is executed, then lines *10* through *13* comprise the outline family.

To perform a cut-and-paste operation on an outline family, move the cursor to the top line of the family and type **Shift-F5,4** (Date/Outline),**O**utline and select either the **M**ove Family, **C**opy Family, or **D**elete Family command. To move or copy an outline family to another place in the document, you next move the cursor to a new location and type ↵. If an outline family is moved or copied, a copy of the text is held in the Move Block buffer and may be retrieved by using the **Ctrl-F4** (Move),**R**etrieve,**B**lock command. If the outline family is deleted, a copy of the text is held in the **F1** (Cancel) Undelete buffer and may be retrieved using the **F1** (Cancel),**R**estore command.

Para Num
Code =
[Par Num:Auto]—
[Par Num:*n*]

The **P**ara Num command is very similar to the **O**utline command. The differences are that only one code is inserted into the text each time the command is typed and you are able to override the automatic level number type.

To fix the displayed level number type, you may enter the desired level when you see the "Paragraph Level (Press Enter for Automatic):" prompt. For instance, if you type 2 when you see the message, the paragraph number will appear in the default form A. A fixed level paragraph number will not change its form when it is indented or tabbed to the right on the screen. It will change its value, however, if preceding codes of the same level are deleted or inserted (i.e., renumbering stays in effect).

To insert a [Par Num:Auto] code when the **Para** Num command is executed, type ↵ in answer to the "Paragraph Level (Press Enter for Automatic):" prompt.

Define
Code =
[Par Num Def:]

The **D**efine command is used to reset paragraph numbering within a document or change the style and punctuation used in automatic paragraph and outline numbering. When the **D**efine command is typed, the following screen appears:

```
Paragraph Number Definition

     1 - Starting Paragraph Number                  1
          (in legal style)
                                                   Levels
                                1      2      3      4      5      6      7      8
     2 - Paragraph              1.     a.     i.    (1)    (a)    (i)    1)     a)
     3 - Outline                I.     A.     1.     a.    (1)    (a)    i)     a)
     4 - Legal (1.1.1)          1      .1     .1     .1     .1     .1     .1     .1
     5 - Bullets                •      o      -      ■      *      +      ·      x
     6 - User-defined

     Current Definition         I.     A.     1.     a.    (1)    (a)    i)     a)
     Attach Previous Level             No     No     No     No     No     No     No

     7 - Enter Inserts Paragraph Number             Yes

     8 - Automatically Adjust to Current Level      Yes

     9 - Outline Style Name



Selection: 0
```

Starting Paragraph
Number

Use the **S**tarting Paragraph Number command to reset outline/paragraph numbering within a document. A [Par Num Def:] code will be inserted into the text that will affect all subsequent outline or paragraph codes.

Paragraph — **O**utline — **L**egal — **B**ullets — **U**ser-Defined

At the top of the screen presented by the **D**efine command, there are four predefined numbering styles, any one of which you may select by typing **2**, **3**, **4**, **5** or **P**, **O**, **L**, **B**. The Current Definition (selection) will be displayed beneath the predefined sets. To create your own style, type **6** or **U** (User-Defined) and then edit the set of levels to reflect your choices.

Attach Previous Level

Default — No
The **U**ser-defined command includes an additional line beneath the Current definition labeled "Attach Previous Level." Changing a level's command to "Yes" causes WordPerfect to produce level numbers that combine the current level with the previous level (for example, 1, 2, 2a, 2b, 2c, 3, 3a, 3b, etc.)

Enter Inserts Paragraph Number

Default — Yes
Changing this command to "No" stops WordPerfect from automatically generating paragraph numbers each time the Enter key is pressed while **O**utline is **O**n. It is generally recommended that this command is left as "Yes."

Automatically Adjust to Current Level

Default — Yes

WordPerfect previously generated a paragraph number, placed one line down and on the left margin, each time the ↵ key was typed while **O**utline was **O**n. By default, WordPerfect places the next paragraph number one line down, then adds enough [Tab] codes before it to move the number to the same tab stop as the last previous paragraph number. Entering "No" to the **A**utomatically Adjust to Current Level command causes the next generated paragraph number to be located on the left margin.

Outline Style Name

This command may be used to select a previously defined Outline style. See **Alt-F8** (Style), for more information on creating an Outline style. The Outline Style Name command may also be used to create or edit an Outline style. When **9** or **N** for Outline Style **N**ame is typed, WordPerfect presents a screen very similar to the **Alt-F8** (Style) screen. To select an Outline style from the screen, move the menu bar to the desired style and type **1** or **l** for Se**l**ect. The remaining commands shown on the status line function in the same manner as the commands shown on the **Alt-F8** (Style) screen.

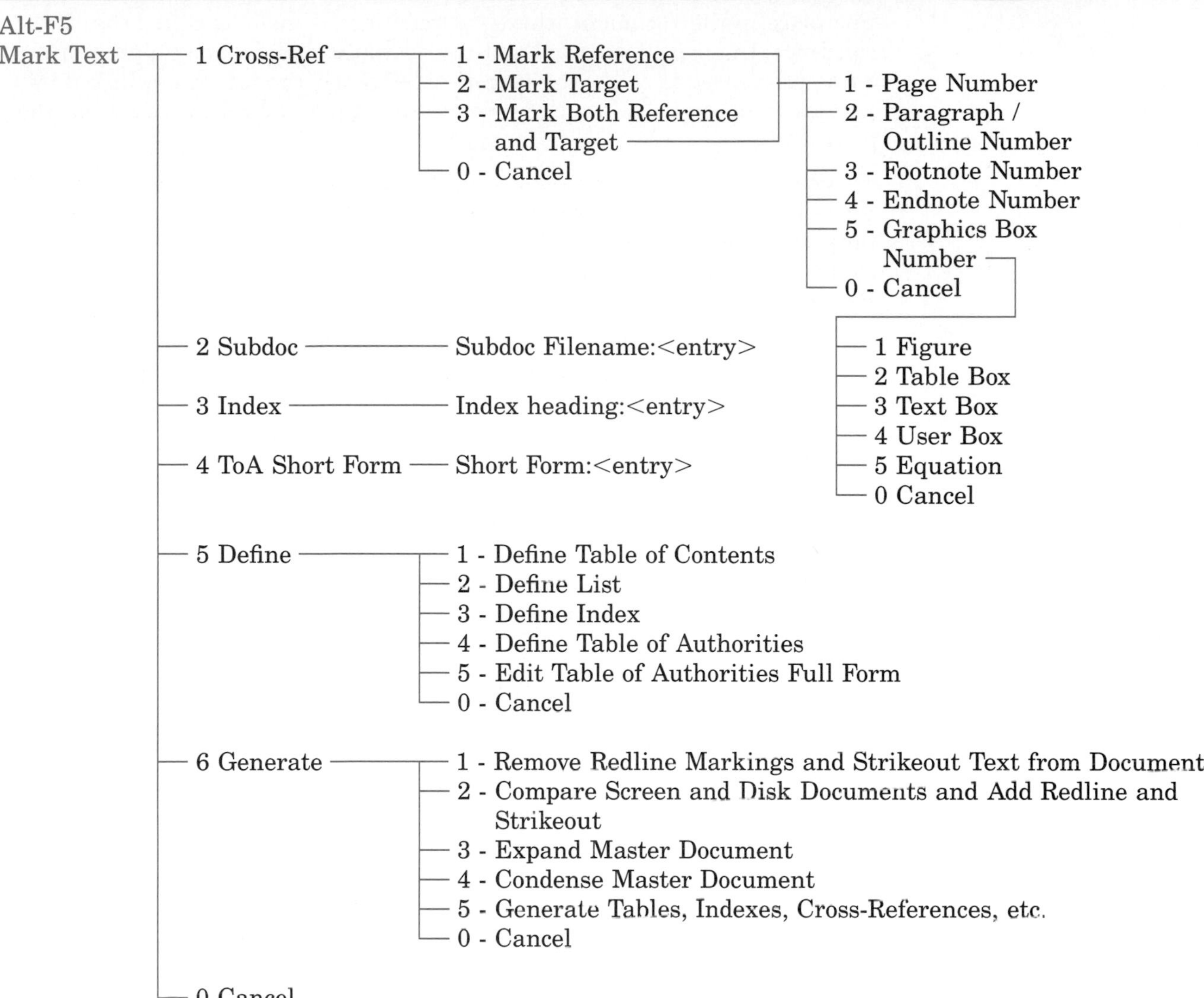

ALT-F5 MARK TEXT

The Mark Text command is used to insert automatic cross references to other locations in a document, to create, expand, and contract a master document, and to automatically produce tables of contents, lists, and indexes. The Block/(Mark Text) command is highly related to the Mark Text command.

Cross-**R**ef

The Cross-**R**ef (Cross Reference) command is used to insert a code where a reference to another part of the document is made, such as "see Contract Provisions, page 12." The reference number used, in this case the page number, will be automatically maintained for changes that may occur to the document. For instance, if page 10 in the document is later deleted, the reference to page 12 will become a reference to page 11. It is necessary, however, to use the (Mark Text),**G**enerate,**G**enerate Tables, Indexes, Cross-References, etc. command to cause the references to become updated for such editing changes to the document. See **Alt-F5,6** (Mark Text),**G**enerate, for more information.

The place in the document where the reference is made is called the reference; the page, paragraph/outline, footnote, endnote, or graphics box being referenced is called the target. A reference and target are linked by a name that you enter when you create the automatic reference within the document.

To create a single reference to a single target, you first move to where the reference is to occur and type the reference text up to the point where the target number is to appear. For instance, you might type ||(see Contract Provisions, page||. Next, you type **Alt-F5,1,3** (Mark Text),**C**ross-Ref,**B**oth Reference and Target.

The next command menu presented allows you to select one of several different types of numbers for the reference: **P**age Number, Paragraph/**O**utline number, **F**ootnote Number, **E**ndnote Number, or **G**raphics Box Number. In the example here, you would select **P**age Number by typing **1** or **P**. The next step is to move the cursor to the target. In the case where text (a sentence, paragraph, etc.) is the target, you will want to place the cursor at the beginning of the target text. When the cursor is properly located, you type ↵. The message "Target Name:" will appear on the status line. The final step in creating an automatic reference is to type and enter a name for the reference and its target.

Mark **R**eference Code = [Ref(*name*):Type #]

When you plan to later create a target for a reference, or will have many references to one target, use the Mark **R**eference command to create a reference with the intended target name. A ? will appear in the document at the reference position until a target with a matching name is created and the **Alt-F5,6** (Mark Text),**G**enerate command is used.

Mark **T**arget Code = [Target(*name*)]

If you have a target without a reference, or intend to have one target referenced more than once, use the Mark **T**arget command to name the target with the same name as its matching reference(s).

Mark **B**oth Reference and Target Code = [Ref(*name*):Type #] [Target(*name*)]

Use the Mark **B**oth Reference and Target command to name the reference and target in one operation.

Marking Footnote Targets

To mark a footnote as a target, move the cursor to where the footnote number appears in the text and type **Ctrl-F7,1,2**↵(Footnote),**F**ootnote,**E**dit. When the editing screen appears, place the target mark in the footnote itself.

Marking Graphics Box Targets

To mark a graphics box as a target (see **Alt-F9** (Graphics) for information on graphic box types) move the cursor immediately after the graphics box code to mark it as a target. A reference to a graphics box will be displayed as "*box type n*" (e.g., Figure 2).

Subdoc
Code = [Subdoc:*filename*]

The **S**ubdoc (Subdocument) command places a code in the document that includes the filename of a disk file. It is used in a boiler plate operation, where subdocuments (plates) can be automatically merged into a master document (creating a boiler). See **Alt-F5** (Mark Text),**G**enerate,**E**xpand Master Document for more information.

Creating Tables of Contents, Lists, Indexes, and Tables of Authorities

Each of the following procedures produces a table of references with or without associated page numbers. The table is either alphabetized by reference (as in an index) or ordered by appearance (as in a table of contents). The sorting and generating of page numbers (if any) are both done automatically by WordPerfect. The overall process for producing any of the tables involves the following steps.

1. Mark the words, phrases, or topics within the document to which the table will refer.
2. Select the page position and format for the table.
3. Generate the table.

Marking Text for Tables

The following discusses the various table types and how you may mark text to be included in them. For information on how to position, format, and generate the various tables, refer to the Mark Text command section "Defining and Generating Tables." Note that the Block/(Mark Text) commands are necessary for marking certain text for tables and are discussed here rather than at the end of the command explanations. The remaining Mark Text commands are discussed later.

Block/Mark Text

The Block/(Mark Text) command is used to mark text that will be included in a Table of Contents (ToC), List, Index, or Table of Authorities (ToA).

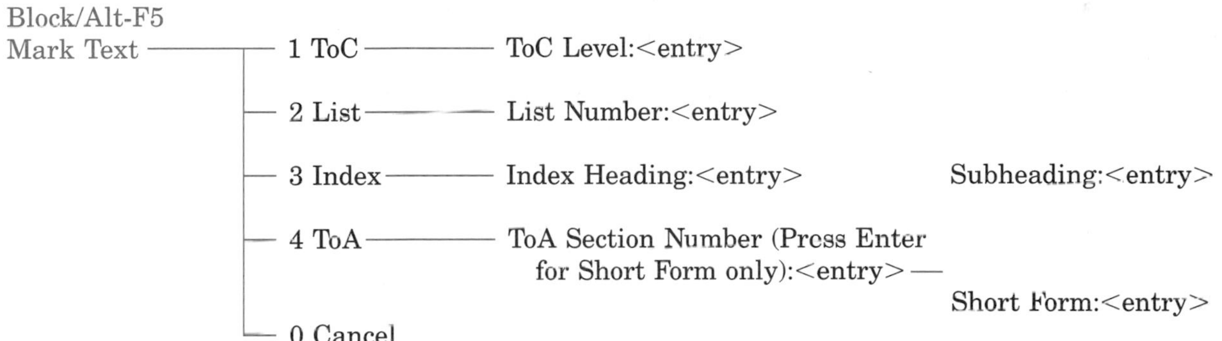

Block/Mark Text:ToC

Code = [Mark:ToC,*n*] *heading text* [EndMark:ToC,*n*]

The Block/(Mark Text),**ToC** command is used to mark text to be included in a table of contents. To mark the text, block the topic heading to be included in the table of contents and type **Alt-F5,1** Block/(Mark Text),**ToC**.

Up to five levels of headings may be included in a table of contents. When you mark a portion of text to be included in a table of contents, you must specify which ToC level (1 to 5) the heading is to be. The headings in the finished table of contents will appear indented to their appropriate level.

```
First Level ..................... nn
     Second Level ............... nn
     Second Level ............... nn
     Second Level ............... nn
          Third Level ........... nn
          Third Level ........... nn
     Second Level ............... nn
First Level ..................... nn
```

Block/Mark Text,**L**ist Code = [Mark:List,*n*] *list text* [EndMark:List,*n*]

The Block/(Mark Text),**L**ist command is used to mark text that will be included in a list. To mark the text, block the word, phrase, or heading, and then type **Alt-F5,2** Block/(Mark Text),**L**ist.

Up to 10 lists (1 to 10) may be generated per document. When you mark a block of text to be included in a list, you must specify in which list (1 to 10) the text is to be included. While all entries must be blocked and marked for Lists 1–5, if Graphics boxes are included in the document, some entries for Lists 6–10 may also be defined automatically by WordPerfect as follows: List 6 will include captions of Figures, List 7 will include captions of Tables, List 8 will include captions of Text Boxes, List 9 will include captions of User-defined Boxes, and List 10 will include captions of Equation Boxes. (See **Alt-F9** (Graphics) for more information on Graphics boxes.)

Mark Text,**I**ndex Code = [Index:*heading*]

There are several ways in which you may mark words or phrases to be included in an index. The general procedure is to move the cursor to the location in the text where the desired subject for the index occurs. You next type **Alt-F5,3** (Mark Text),**I**ndex. At this point you will be prompted to enter a heading.

Index Headings

Items marked for inclusion in an index may have either a single heading or a heading and a subheading, which are entered at the time the item is marked. If only a heading is entered, the item appears in the index by itself. If a heading and a subheading are entered, all items having the same heading will appear under the heading with their own subheading, as shown in the following example.

Almond 15
Apples
    Crab 23
    Delicious 34
    Gravenstein 5
    McIntosh 12
    Newton 16
Artichoke 36

Here, the subjects Almond and Artichoke were marked in the text with only a heading. The varieties of apples were all marked with the heading "Apples" and the appropriate variety type subheading.

Methods of Entering Index Headings

To enter the index heading(s) for a subject, you do one of the following.

1. Move the cursor to a key word in the text and type **Alt-F5,3** (Mark Text),**I**ndex. The word at the cursor location will be displayed with the heading prompt at the bottom of the screen, and typing ↵ will cause the word to become the heading. If the word does not appear how you want the heading to appear, you may type and enter a different heading.
2. Block the word or phrase in the text and type **Alt-F5,3** Block/(Mark Text),**I**ndex. The blocked text will be displayed with the heading prompt, and typing ↵ will cause it to become the heading.

3. Create a Concordance file. A Concordance file may be used to save time when an index reference is made to a subject that occurs in several places. A Concordance file is simply a user-created WordPerfect document that contains a list of words or phrases separated by hard returns [HRt]s. The file is used by WordPerfect to search the document for the words and phrases and to generate index references for them. The words and phrases within a Concordance file may be used in conjunction with words or phrases marked otherwise throughout the text to generate the index. The generation of an index will take less time if the words and phrases within the Concordance file are sorted.

Mark Text,To**A** and Block/Mark Text,To**A**

These two commands are used to mark text for a table of authorities. A table of authorities is a list of citations for a legal brief. See the WordPerfect manual or Help screens for more information on the subject.

Defining and Generating Tables

The final two (Mark Text) commands are **D**efine and **G**enerate.

Define

The (Mark Text),**D**efine command is used to define the location and format for tables.

- 1 - Define Table of Contents
  - 1 - Number of Levels
  - 2 - Display Last Level in Wrapped Format
  - 3 - Page Numbering
    - Level 1
    - Level 2
    - Level 3
    - Level 4
    - Level 5
      - 1 - None
      - 2 - Pg # Follows
      - 3 - (Pg #) Follows
      - 4 - Flush Rt
      - 5 - Flush Rt with Leader
      - 0 - Cancel
  - 0 - Cancel
- 2 - Define List—List Number (1 – 10)
  - List n Definition
    - 1 - No Page Numbers
    - 2 - Page Numbers Follow Entries
    - 3 - (Page Numbers) Follow Entries
    - 4 - Flush Right Page Numbers
    - 5 - Flush Right Page Numbers with Leaders
    - 0 - Cancel
- 3 - Define Index—Concordance Filename
  - 1 - No Page Numbers
  - 2 - Page Numbers Follow Entries
  - 3 - (Page Numbers) Follow Entries
  - 4 - Flush Right Page Numbers
  - 5 - Flush Right Page Numbers with Leaders
  - 0 - Cancel

Define Table of Contents — Define List — Define Index

The three commands discussed here are used to determine the position and format of the tables that will be subsequently generated. The commands here differ only slightly in their form. The Define Table of Contents command will prompt for the number of heading levels you desire, the Define List command will prompt for the number (1 to 10) of the list you are currently defining, and the Define Index command will prompt you for a Concordance file filename (if any).

To define a table of contents, list, or index, you first move the cursor to the page and location where you want the table to appear when it is generated. You next type **Alt-F5,5** (Mark Text),**D**efine and select the number for the type of table you are defining. After answering the initial prompts, you must specify the format for the table. The options and examples of each follow.

1 No Page Numbers	Example
2 Page Numbers Follow Entries	Example 47
3 (Page Numbers) Follow Entries	Example (47)
4 Flush Right Page Numbers	Example 47
5 Flush Right Page Numbers with Leaders	Example 47

After defining the table, a [Def Mark:ToC], [Def Mark:List *n*], or [Def Mark:Index] code will be inserted into the document at the cursor location. If you later wish to reposition, redefine, or regenerate a table, you should first remove the existing [Def Mark] code from the document.

Define/Edit Table of Authorities Full Form

These two commands are used to define location and format for a Table of Authorities. A Table of Authorities is a list of citations for a legal brief. See the WordPerfect manual or Help screens for more information on the subject.

Generate

The (Mark Text),**G**enerate command is used to remove all redline markings and strikeout text from the document, expand and condense master documents, generate tables of contents, lists, and indexes, and update cross-references for the document.

Remove Redline Markings and Strikeout Text from Document

This command removes all [REDLN][redln] codes from the document and deletes all text currently marked as (Font),Strikeout. See **Ctrl-F8,2,8** and **9** (Font),**A**ppearance,**R**edln and **S**tkout for more information.

Compare Screen and Disk Documents and Add Redline and Strikeout

This command compares a document on the disk with the document in memory. The comparison is made phrase by phrase. A phrase is defined by WordPerfect as text occurring between phrase markers, which may be periods, hard returns, and so forth. Differences between the two files are marked in the current file (the file in memory). Text existing in the disk file but not in the current file is added to the current file formatted as Strikeout. Text existing in the current file but not in the disk file is formatted as Redline in the current file. Text that has been moved in the current file is displayed with a message "Text Moved." See **Ctrl-F8,2,8** and **9** (Font),**A**ppearance,**R**edln and **S**tkout for more information.

Expand Master Document

A Master document is a document in which subdocument codes have been placed by the (Mark Text),**S**ubdoc command. Subdocuments are disk files to be included in a master document. To place a subdocument code into a master document you type **Alt-F5,2,***filename*↵(Mark Text),**S**ubdoc. A nonprinting message similar to the following will appear on the screen.

```
Subdoc: CHAPT11
```

When the **E**xpand Master Document command is used, the files referenced by the subdocument codes are retrieved and inserted into the Master document.

Condense Master Document

The C**o**ndense Master Document command deletes subdocument text from a Master document. See **E**xpand Master Document above.

Generate Tables, Indexes, Cross-References etc.

The **G**enerate Tables, Indexes, Cross-References etc. command is used to generate tables of contents, lists, and indexes as well as to update cross-references within the document. For tables with [Mark Def] codes in the document, the command inserts an [End Def] code at the bottom of the generated table.

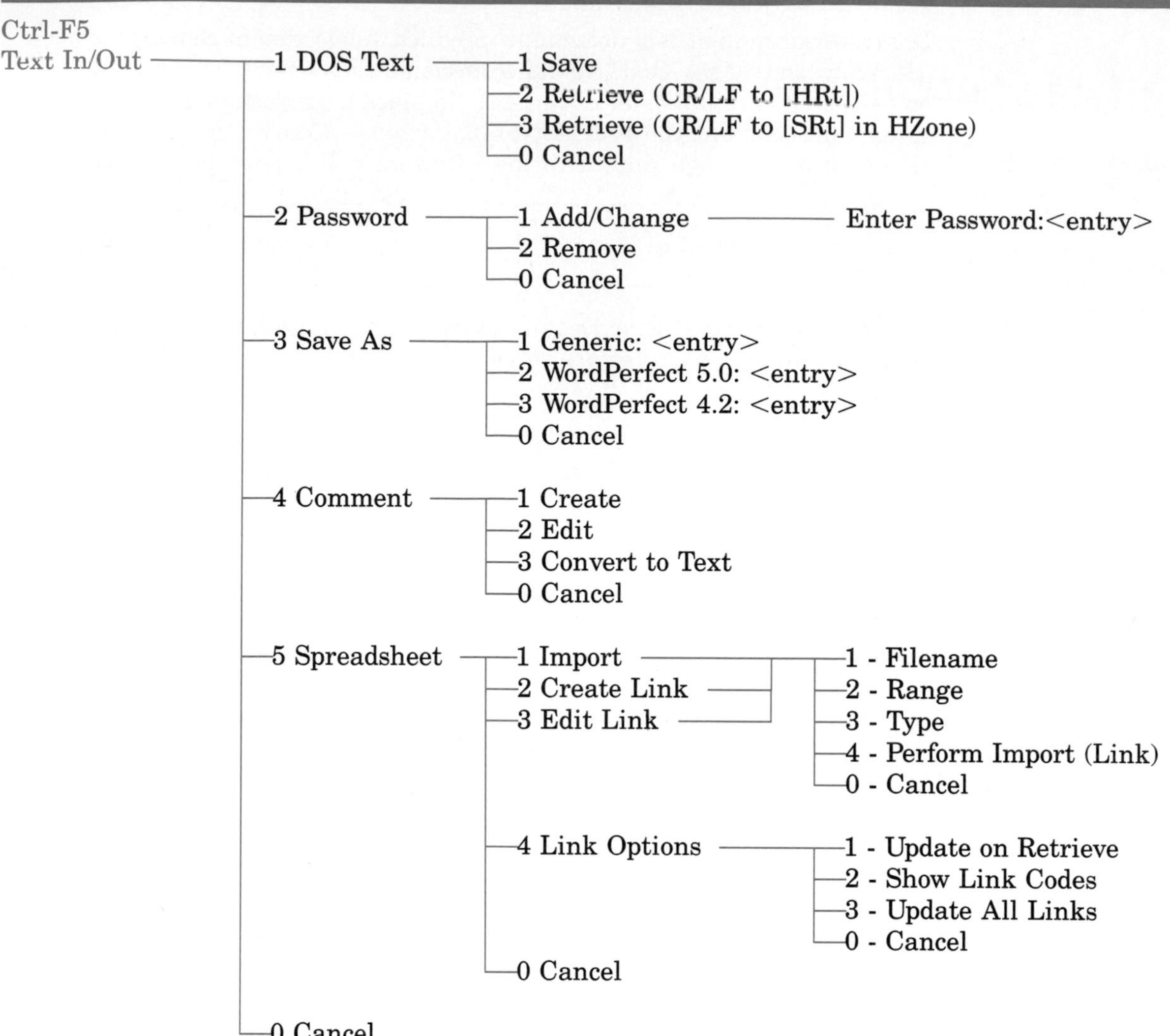

CTRL-F5 TEXT IN/OUT

The Text In/Out command is used to convert file formats for transfer between different software, to protect files from being viewed or printed by others, and to create or edit text comments.

DOS Text

WordPerfect refers to ASCII files as being DOS text. When you intend to transfer a file into another software such as DOS, Lotus 1-2-3, WordStar, etc., to process a WordPerfect document file, you will first need to convert the document file into ASCII using the DOS **T**ext,**S**ave command.

Save

The DOS **T**ext,**S**ave command saves the current document in ASCII format and removes all imbedded WordPerfect codes. All soft returns are converted to hard returns. CHR(13)s and [Tab]s are converted to spaces, CHR(32)s. Spaces are used to pad Center, Indent, and Flush Right text. See **Shift-F7** (Print),**S**elect Printers for information on creating DOS text (ASCII) files that include the printer control codes.

Retrieve (CR/LF to [HRt])

To retrieve an ASCII file created by another software, the **R**etrieve command may be used. Hard returns and line feeds in the file become hard returns in WordPerfect.

Retrieve (CR/LF to [SRt] in H-Zone)

If R**e**trieve is used, hard returns in the file become Soft Returns in WordPerfect if they occur between the current left and right margins. Two or more sequential hard returns in the file become hard returns in WordPerfect.

Password

WordPerfect allows a document to be locked with a password. However, if you forget the password, you will not be able to retrieve the file.

Add/Change

To lock the current text file, type **Ctrl-F5,2,1** (Text In/Out),**P**assword,**A**dd/Change. WordPerfect will respond with the message: "Enter password:" The password you type will not be displayed on the screen. Instead, WordPerfect will prompt you to: "Re-Enter Password:" so it may check for correct duplication of keystrokes. A password may be up to 24 characters long.

Once the password has been verified, you may save the document. From that point on, the password will be needed to retrieve the file.

Remove

To unlock a locked document, it is necessary to use the (Text In/Out), **P**assword,**R**emove command. Retrieve the file, and then type **Ctrl-F5,2,2** (Text In/Out),**P**assword,**R**emove to remove the password. Then save the file under its original name.

Save As

The Save **A**s command may be used to save a document in a form that can be read by previous versions of WordPerfect.

The options of the command include: **G**eneric (removes all WordPerfect codes except [Tab]s and [Indent]s), **W**ordPerfect 5.0 (removes all WordPerfect codes specific to version 5.1), and Word**P**erfect 4.2 (removes all WordPerfect codes specific to versions 5.0 and 5.1).

Comment Code = [Comment]

WordPerfect provides a means to provide documentation for your documents by inserting comments that will not be printed. Such internal documentation is done through the **Ctrl-F5** (Text In/Out),**C**omment command.

Create

The **C**reate comment command provides room for characters to be entered into the text at the current cursor location. Text formatting within the Comment screen is limited. When done, the comment will be displayed on the screen enclosed in a double-line box, as shown in the following example.

The following information should be revised each spring.

To remove the display of comments on the screen, use the **Shift-F1,2,6,2** (Setup),**D**isplay, **E**dit-Screen Options,**C**omments Display command. To delete a comment, move the cursor to the place where the comment occurs and use **Alt-F3** (Reveal Codes) to find the imbedded [Comment] code. Then, use the Backspace or Del key to erase it.

Edit

The **Edit** command may be used to modify an existing comment. Type **Ctrl-F5,4,2** (Text In/Out),**C**omment,**E**dit to begin editing. WordPerfect will find the comment for editing by searching backwards through the file. Therefore, if there is more than one comment in the file, you must move the cursor past the comment you wish to edit and then execute the **E**dit command.

Convert to Text

To convert a comment into text, move the cursor past the comment, and then type **Ctrl-F5,4,3** (Text In/Out),**C**omment,Convert to **T**ext.

Spreadsheet

The (Text In/Out),**S**preadsheet command allows data contained in a file created with a spreadsheet software (such as Lotus 1-2-3) to be included in a WordPerfect document. While the command has certain limitations, it can be useful in cases where a final document will include both spreadsheet and word processed type information.

The (Text In/Out),**S**preadsheet command is able to directly read files created with Lotus versions 1.0 through 2.2. Spreadsheets created with Lotus version 3.0 must first be saved in 2.2 format before they can be accessed by the **S**preadsheet command.

The following discusses the various **S**preadsheet commands using an example spreadsheet created with Lotus 1-2-3 Version 2.2.

A1: READY

	A	B	C	D	E	F
1						
2						
3			Forecasted	Cost of Goods	Net Profit	
4			Sales	Sold		
5		----------	----------	----------	----------	
6		January	$100,000.00	$65,000.00	$35,000.00	
7		February	$105,000.00	$68,250.00	$36,750.00	
8		March	$110,250.00	$71,662.50	$38,587.50	
9		April	$115,762.50	$75,245.63	$40,516.88	
10		May	$121,550.63	$79,007.91	$42,542.72	
11		June	$127,628.16	$82,958.30	$44,669.85	
12		==========	==========	==========	==========	
13			$680,191.29	$442,124.34	$238,066.95	
14						
15						
16						
17						
18						
19						
20						

08-Apr-90 08:40 AM UNDO

Import—Create Link

The **S**preadsheet command has two different commands (**I**mport and **C**reate **L**ink) that may be used to include spreadsheet data in a WordPerfect document. Both commands copy the specified spreadsheet data from the disk and insert it into the document at the location of the cursor.

The **I**mport command performs the operation on a "one point in time" basis. That is, when the spreadsheet data are merged into the document, they simply become part of the text data in the WordPerfect file. Any subsequent changes to the spreadsheet file that generated the merged data will not automatically be reflected in the WordPerfect file.

The **C**reate Link command, however, merges the spreadsheet data into the document and establishes a "link" to the spreadsheet file from which the merged data was copied. The advantage of the link is that subsequent changes to the spreadsheet file may easily be included in the WordPerfect file.

After the **I**mport or **C**reate Link command is executed, a screen similar to the following will appear:

```
Spreadsheet: Create Link

     1 - Filename

     2 - Range

     3 - Type                          Table

     4 - Perform Link
```

Filename

The first option on the screen, **F**ilename, is used to enter the filename for the spreadsheet file from which the spreadsheet data are to be copied. You must include the filename extension (e.g., .WK1). If the file is somewhere other than the current WordPerfect directory, you must include its path.

```
Spreadsheet: Create Link

     1 - Filename                      A:\FORECAST.WK1

     2 - Range                         <Spreadsheet>          A1..E13

     3 - Type                          Table

     4 - Perform Link
```

Range

The next option, **R**ange, is used to enter the range of cells in the spreadsheet to merge into the WordPerfect document. Once the filename of the spreadsheet has been specified, the default range to merge becomes all cells in the spreadsheet file (shown here as A1..E13). To enter a different range, type **2** or **R** for Range, and then type the cell address of the upper left cell in the range, a period, and then the cell address of the lower right cell in the range. You may also specify a range by using a range name previously assigned to a group of cells by using the spreadsheet software's command (e.g., /**R**ange,**N**ame,**C**reate).

Type

The spreadsheet data may be merged into the document as either **T**ext or as data in a WordPerfect T**a**ble. (See **Alt-F7** (Columns/Table) for more information on document tables.)

If **T**ext is selected, the maximum number of spreadsheet columns that can be merged into a document (in a single operation) is 20 columns. When merging spreadsheet data as text type, WordPerfect first generates a [Tab Set] code that approximates the column width formats of the spreadsheet range. It then merges the spreadsheet data into the document, inserting [TAB] codes between the data items in each row. Finally, at the bottom of the merged data, WordPerfect generates another [Tab Set] code that returns the tab stops to their original settings.

If Table (the default type) is selected the maximum number of spreadsheet columns that can be merged into a document (in a single operation) is 32 columns. When merging data as table type, WordPerfect first creates a document table that approximates the column width formats of the spreadsheet range. It then merges the spreadsheet data into the document table, putting the data of each spreadsheet cell into its comparable document table cell.

Perform Link—Perform Import

The final step required to merge spreadsheet data into a document is to execute the **P**erform Link command (shown as "**P**erform Import" if the **I**mport command was initially selected). In the example here, the spreadsheet data from cells B3 through E13 were merged from the spreadsheet file named "FORECAST. WK1" into a document as text, using the **C**reate Link command. When finished, the screen appeared:

```
Link:   A:\FORECAST.WK1

          Forecasted      Cost of Goods   Net Profit
          Sales           Sold
--------  --------------  --------------  --------------
January      $100,000.00      $65,000.00      $35,000.00
February     $105,000.00      $68,250.00      $36,750.00
March        $110,250.00      $71,662.50      $38,587.50
April        $115,762.50      $75,245.63      $40,516.88
May          $121,550.63      $79,007.91      $42,542.72
June         $127,628.16      $82,958.30      $44,669.85
========  ==============  ==============  ==============
             $680,191.29     $442,124.34     $238,066.95

Link End
```

The Link: and Link End comment codes, shown at the beginning and end of the merged data, appear on the screen when the **C**reate Link option is used to merge spreadsheet data. They do not appear in the document when the **I**mport option is used to merge spreadsheet data. The codes appear as a reminder that linked data occurs in the document. They will not be printed with the document nor will they appear on the **Shift-F7** (Print),**V**iew Document screen.

Edit Link

The **E**dit Link command may be used to alter the previously specified filename, range, or type (text or table) for a link area. To change the specifications for a link, position the cursor in the document after the location of the link and type **Ctrl-F5** (Text In/Out),**S**preadsheet,**E**dit Link.

After making changes to the link specifications, you may execute the **P**erform Link command again to re-merge the spreadsheet data with the changed specifications.

Link Options

There are three options available on the **L**ink Options menu.

Update on **R**etrieve
Default–No
Changing this option to "Yes" causes WordPerfect to update the spreadsheet data in existing link areas for any changes that may have been made to the source spreadsheet files, each time the document is retrieved into WordPerfect. This feature is most useful when it is important that the document's data accurately reflect the most recent changes to the spreadsheet file(s).

Show Link Codes
Default—Yes
Changing this option to "No" causes WordPerfect not to display the Link: and Link End comment codes on the editing screen.

Update All Links
The **U**pdate All Links command may be used to update all links in a document to reflect the most recent changes made to the source spreadsheet file.

Comments

The **C**reate Link command is the recommended method for merging spreadsheet data into a document. It produces the same results as the **I**mport command with the additional feature of easy updating for any changes that might be made to the spreadsheet file.

When creating links within a document, do not place one link area within another link area.

The portion of a spreadsheet (in columns) that can be merged into a document is rather small. In most cases, the absolute limitations of 20 spreadsheet columns for text type merges, and 32 columns for table type merges, will be further restricted by the document's left and right margins. If excessively wide spreadsheet data are merged as table type, the resulting table will extend beyond the document's right margin. However, the extended columns of data will not be printed with the document. If excessively wide spreadsheet data are merged as text, the results can be considerably less predictable. You will, therefore, want to consider the margin constraints of the intended WordPerfect document when designing the spreadsheet.

When merging spreadsheet data into a document, WordPerfect attempts to retain the spreadsheet appearance of the data. However, testing has shown that most merges will alter the appearance of the data in some manner. For instance, in the example here, the original spreadsheet had both rows of column labels centered over the columns. After the merge, the labels were left justified over the columns. The spreadsheet data can be edited in a normal fashion after it has been merged into a document. However, using the **U**pdate All Links command, subsequent to editing a link area, will result in the replacement of the edited text with the newly merged spreadsheet data.

Block/Text In/Out

To convert a section of text into a comment, first block the text, and then type **Ctrl-F5** (Text In/Out). Next type Y in response to the "Create a comment? No (Yes)" prompt.

F6
Bold —— {Places Bold Start Code [BOLD]} —— <enter text> —— Bold key {Places Bold Stop Code [bold]}

F6 BOLD
CODE = [BOLD]
bold text [Bold]

The Bold command is used to print text in boldface type (darker than normal). Typing **F6** (Bold) inserts [BOLD] and [bold] codes into text. Text typed afterwards is entered between the codes and is displayed on the screen in highlight. To stop bolding text, type **F6** (Bold) again.

Block/Bold

To boldface existing text, block the text and then type **F6** (Bold).

Shift-F6
Center —— {Places Center Start Code [Center]} —— <enter text> —— Center key {Places dot leader}
Enter key {Stops centering text}

SHIFT-F6 CENTER
CODE =
[CENTER]
centered text
[HRt]

The (Center) command is used to center text between the current left and right margins. Typing **Shift-F6** (Center) inserts a [Center] code into the text. Text typed afterwards appears centered on the line.

Centering of text is stopped when the Enter key ↵ is typed. Typing **Shift-F6** (Center) again (before typing ↵ to stop centering) produces a dot leader that extends leftward from the centered text.

You can center text in an existing line that ends with a [HRt] by moving the cursor to the line and typing **Shift-F6** (Center).

Block/Center
Code =
[Just:Center]
centered text
[Just:*type*]

To center several lines of existing text, block the text and then type **Shift-F6** (Center). Next answer "Y" to the "[Just:Center]? **N**o (**Y**es)" prompt. Centering text in this manner places a [Just:Center] code at the beginning of the centered text, and a [Just:*type*] code (where *type* is the currently selected line justification) at the end of the centered text. (See **Shift-F8** (Format),**Line**,**Justification** for more information).

Alt-F6
Flush Right —— {Places Flush Right Start Code [Flsh Rgt]} —— <enter text> —— Flush Right key {Places dot leader}
Enter key {Stops flush right text}

ALT-F6 FLUSH RIGHT
CODE =
[Flsh Rgt]
text [HRt]

The Flush Right command is used to align text flush against the right margin. Typing **Alt-F6** (Flush Right) inserts a [Flsh Rgt] code into the text and moves the cursor to the right margin. Text typed afterwards is entered between the right margin and the code and appears right justified as it is typed. Right justifying of text is stopped when the Enter key is typed. Typing **Alt-F6** (Flush Right) again (before typing ↵ to stop flush right text) produces a dot leader that extends leftward from the flush right text.

You can flush right text in an existing line that ends with a [HRt] by moving the cursor to the line and typing **Alt-F6** (Flush Right).

To right justify text at tab stops, see the **Ctrl-F6** (Tab Align) command.

Block/Flush Right
Code =
[Just:Right]
flush right text
[Just:*type*]

To flush right several lines of existing text, block the text and then type **Alt-F6** (Flush Right). Next type Y to the "[Just:Right]? **N**o (**Y**es)" prompt. Centering text in this manner places a [Just:Right] code at the beginning of the centered text, and a [Just:*type*] code (where *type* is the currently selected line justification) at the end of the flush right text. (See **Shift-F8** (Format),**L**ine,**J**ustification for more information).

Ctrl-F6
Tab Align ———— {Places [DEC TAB] Code} ———— <enter text>

CTRL-F6 TAB ALIGN CODE = [DEC TAB]

The Tab Align command is used to tab the cursor to the next tab stop and align the text typed afterwards flush right to the tab stop. (See **Shift-F8** (Format),**L**ine,**T**ab Set for information on setting tab stops.)

The Tab Align command may be used to produce right aligned columns of text. In the following example, the (Tab Align) command was used to move the cursor to the tab stop, the name was typed, and then the Enter key was pressed.

```
            tab stop
                |
  Richard Alden
     Kathey Dole
    Jerry Calvin
         Jo Hays
```

The Tab key and Tab Align command may be used together to produce right and left justified columns of text. In the following example, the Tab key was used to move the cursor to the first tab stop, the role was entered, and then the Tab Align command was used to move the cursor to the second tab stop where the name was entered. The Enter key was used to move to the next line.

```
tab stop                         tab stop
    |                                |
    Leading Man        Richard Alden
    Leading Woman        Kathey Dole
    Actor 1             Jerry Calvin
    Actor 2                  Jo Hays
```

The Tab Align command uses an align character to align text first flush right to the tab stop until the align character is typed, then left of the tab stop. The default align character is the period (.). The feature is most useful for entering dollar amounts. In the following example, the **Ctrl-F6** (Tab Align) command was used to move the cursor to the tab stop. A dollar amount was then typed, followed by a period (the current align character).

Finally the cent amount was typed and the Enter key was typed to move to the next line.

tab stop

$ 1,250.73
$ 15.00
$ 0.00
$ 116,000.35

The align character may be changed with the **Shift-F8** (Format),**O**ther,**D**ecimal/Align Character command.

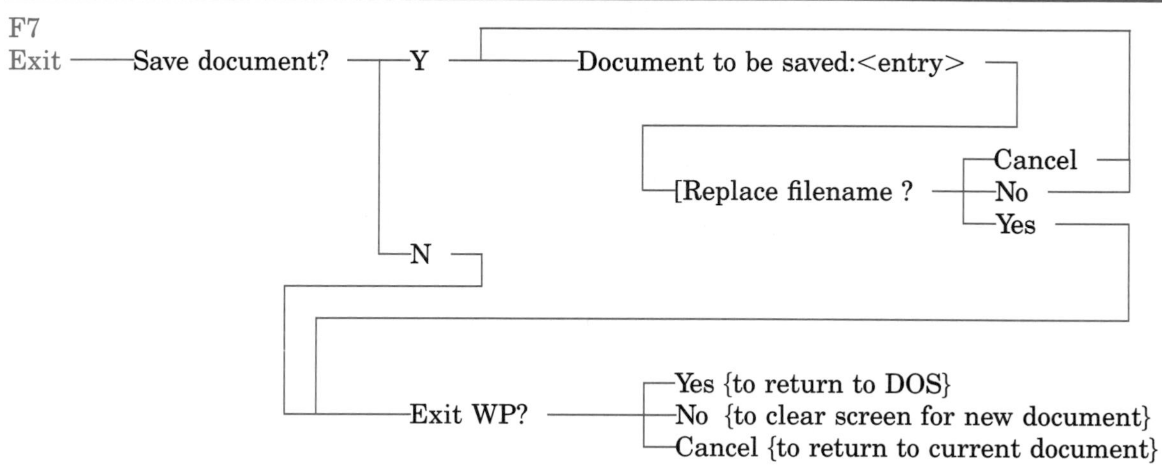

F7 EXIT

The Exit command is used to save the current document and exit WordPerfect. It also is used to exit many WordPerfect commands or operations.

In order to assure that your documents are saved correctly, you should always quit WordPerfect with the **F7** (Exit) command. Type **F7** (Exit), and then either save or do not save your file (type Y or N, respectively). Next type Y in answer to the "Exit WP? (Y/N)" prompt.

To remove the current document from RAM without leaving WordPerfect, you type N in answer to the "Exit WP? (Y/N)" prompt.

If you are editing two documents (see the **Shift-F3** (Switch) command), you will need to exit from each before returning to DOS.

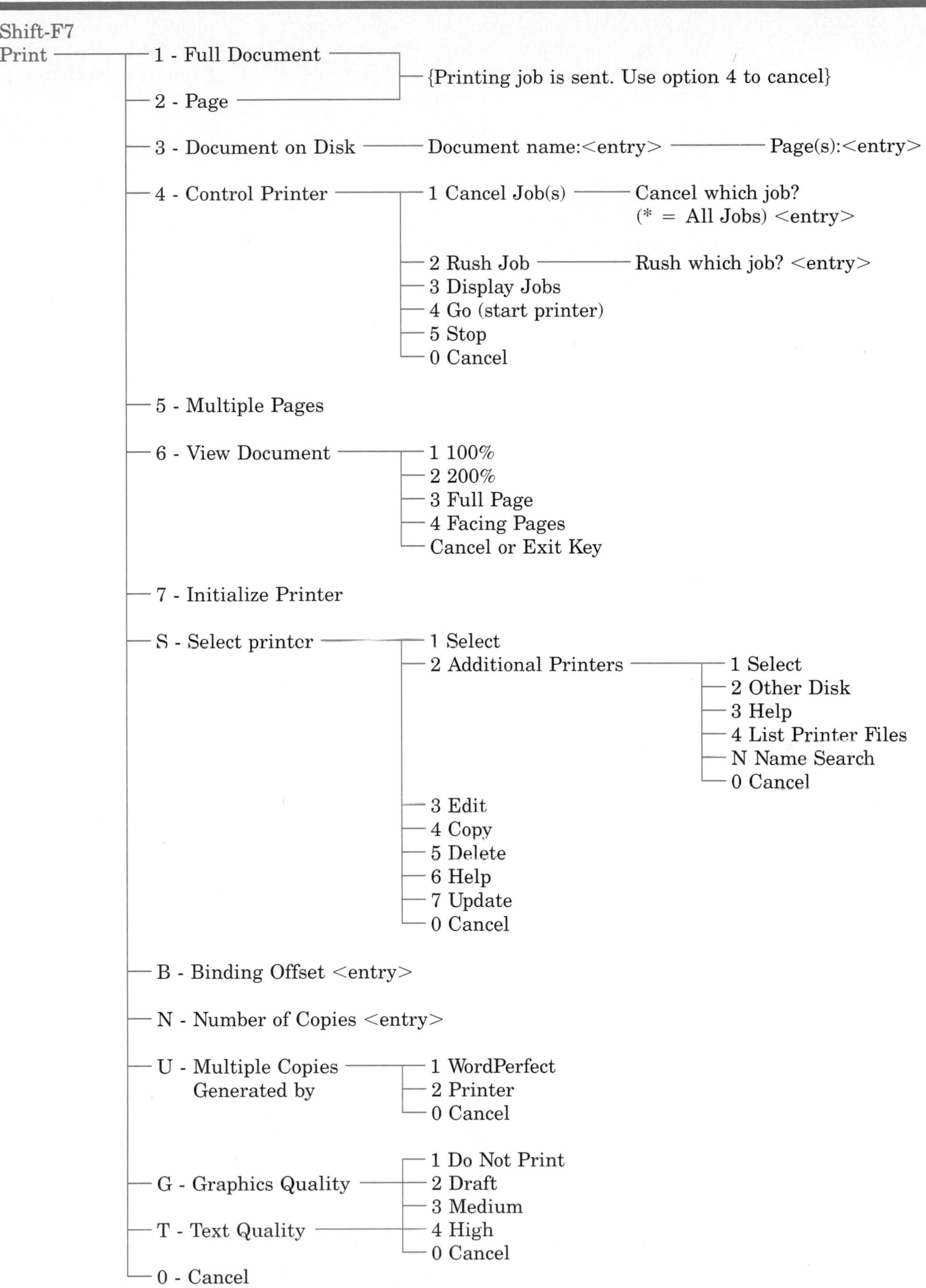
Shift-F7
Print
1 - Full Document
2 - Page
{Printing job is sent. Use option 4 to cancel}
3 - Document on Disk
Document name:<entry>
Page(s):<entry>
4 - Control Printer
1 Cancel Job(s)
Cancel which job?
(* = All Jobs) <entry>
2 Rush Job
Rush which job? <entry>
3 Display Jobs
4 Go (start printer)
5 Stop
0 Cancel
5 - Multiple Pages
6 - View Document
1 100%
2 200%
3 Full Page
4 Facing Pages
Cancel or Exit Key
7 - Initialize Printer
S - Select printer
1 Select
2 Additional Printers
1 Select
2 Other Disk
3 Help
4 List Printer Files
N Name Search
0 Cancel
3 Edit
4 Copy
5 Delete
6 Help
7 Update
0 Cancel
B - Binding Offset <entry>
N - Number of Copies <entry>
U - Multiple Copies
Generated by
1 WordPerfect
2 Printer
0 Cancel
G - Graphics Quality
T - Text Quality
1 Do Not Print
2 Draft
3 Medium
4 High
0 Cancel
0 - Cancel

SHIFT-F7 PRINT

The **Shift-F7** (Print) command is used to print a document either in full or by page, to control the current print operation, to preview the printed pages of a document on the screen, to select printer types, and to select certain print options.

Full Document

Type **Shift-F7,1** (Print),**F**ull Document to print the entire current document. To print a document from the disk, see the **Shift-F7** (Print),**D**ocument on Disk command or the **F5** (List),**P**rint command. To cancel a print operation, see the **Shift-F7** (Print),**C**ontrol Printer,**C**ancel Job(s) command.

Page

Type **Shift-F7,2** (Print),**P**age to print only the current page of the current document (the page where the editing cursor is located). To print multiple pages, see the commands **Shift-F7** (Print),**M**ultiple Pages, **Shift-F7** (Print),**D**ocument on Disk, or F5 (List),**P**rint.

Document on Disk

Use the **D**ocument on Disk command to print all or part of a document on the disk. After you type **Shift-F7,3** (Print),**D**ocument on Disk, WordPerfect will prompt "Document name:". Enter the name of the document to print. WordPerfect will next respond with the prompt "Page(s): (All)". If you want the entire document to be printed, type ↵. You may, however, specify that only certain pages be printed. To specify certain pages you may enter one of the following.

N	Print page number *N*
N-	Print from page number *N* to end of document
N-*n*	Print pages *N* through *n* inclusive
-*N*	Print from beginning of document through page *N*
N, *n*	Print the specified pages
N-*n*,*M*	Print pages *N* through *n* inclusive, and page *M*

Page numbers must be entered in the way they appear on the printed document.

Control Printer

The **C**ontrol Printer command is used to monitor and control ongoing print operations. The **C**ontrol Printer command screen appears as follows.

```
Print: Control Printer

Current Job

Job Number: 2                                   Page Number:  1
Status:     Printing                            Current Copy: 1 of 1
Message:    None
Paper:      Standard 8.5" x 11"
Location:   Continuous feed
Action:     None


Job List

Job  Document         Destination          Print Options
 2   (Screen)         LPT 1


Additional Jobs Not Shown: 0



1 Cancel Job(s); 2 Rush Job; 3 Display Jobs; 4 Go (start printer); 5 Stop: 0
```

In this example, the current document (Screen) is being printed. When a document on a disk is being printed, "(Disk File)" will be displayed under the Document heading. The Job Number is listed as 2 (the second time something has been printed during the editing session). At the bottom of the screen appears the (Print),Control Printer Menu.

Cancel Job(s)

The **C**ancel Job(s) command may be used to stop printing. Type **Shift-F7,4,1** (Print),Control Printer,**C**ancel Job(s). WordPerfect will respond with the message "Cancel which job? (* = All Jobs)." To cancel all print jobs type *, then type Y at the "Cancel all print jobs?" prompt. To cancel the current print job type ↵ instead of *.

Rush Job

When more than one print job is being sent to the printer, the **R**ush Job command may be used to move a document waiting to be printed to the head of the printing queue.

Display Jobs

The **D**isplay Jobs command may be used to produce a list of all documents waiting to be printed. The Control Printer screen will normally display only the next three jobs.

Go (start printer)

Resumes printing a document after the printer has been stopped.

Stop

Stops the printer without cancelling the print jobs. Use (Print),Control Printer,**G**o (start printer) to resume printing.

Multiple Pages

The **M**ultiple Pages command may be used to print only certain pages of the current document. When the **M**ultiple Pages command is selected, WordPerfect prompts "Page(s):". To specify certain pages, you may enter one of the following:

N	Print page number *N*
N-	Print from page number *N* to end of document
N-*n*	Print pages *N* through *n* inclusive
-*N*	Print from beginning of document through page *N*
N, *n*	Print the specified pages
N-*n*,*M*	Print pages *N* through *n* inclusive, and page *M*

Page numbers must be entered in the way they appear in the printed document.

View Document

The **V**iew Document command creates a temporary file for you to view on the screen. The file is designed to most closely resemble the document as it will be printed, and includes footnotes, headers, page numbers, etc. The command is useful for discovering formatting problems caused by errant codes.

To preview a document, type **Shift-F7,6** (Print),**V**iew Document. In a few moments, the screen will display the current page of the document as it will appear when printed. You cannot edit the text displayed by the **V**iew Document screen. You may, however, view different portions of the text by using the cursor control keys ↑, ↓, PgUp and PgDn. The options of the

View Document command include: (1) 100% (actual size); (2) 200% (enlarge the text on the screen); (3) Full page (reduce the text to fit a full page on the screen, the default size for the text on the screen); and (4) Facing Pages (display two full pages on the screen at once). Note that there is no command letter available for these commands. When you are finished with viewing the file, type **F7** (Exit).

Initialize Printer

This command is used to download soft fonts to the printer. See the WordPerfect Help screens or manual for more information.

Select Printer

Printers vary in their capabilities and in the ASCII codes that cause them to do what they do. Therefore, WordPerfect needs to know what printer(s) it will be using. With WordPerfect come several disks labeled *Printer Disk 1*, *Printer Disk 2*, and so forth. On these disks are files that describe a particular printer. When WordPerfect is installed on a computer, these disks must be available. However, after the printer types have been selected during the install process, the specific printer information for the selected printers is saved with the WordPerfect software and need not be specified again. When one, two, or more types of printers are selected during the install procedure, the selected printers can be thought of as "available" printers for WordPerfect.

Select

The **S**elect command is used to choose one of the available printer definitions for use in printing a document. Information on the selected printer is saved with the document file. The default printer for the **S**elect command is the first available printer specified or the last available printer selected. To select a printer, move the **S**elect Printer cursor to the appropriate printer and type **1** or **S** (**S**elect).

Additional Printers

The **A**dditional Printers command is used to add to the list of current printer definitions. To add an additional printer to the current list of available printer definitions, type **Shift-F7,S,2** (Print),**S**elect Printer,**A**dditional Printers. WordPerfect will present a list of all the supported printers. Move the **A**dditional Printers menu bar to the desired printer and type **1** or **S** to (**S**elect).

WordPerfect will display the filename for the file which contains the specific information for the printer you have selected; in most cases you will type ↵ at this point. If WordPerfect is able to access the appropriate file, it will respond by presenting a "filename.PRS" prompt on the status line. At this point you should type ↵. WordPerfect will next present a screen labeled "Helps and Hints," which provides information about the printer being selected. In most cases, you will type **F7** (Exit) to exit the Helps and Hints screen. The next screen presented will be a screen that allows you to edit the printer information (see **E**dit below); in most cases you will simply type ↵ to exit this screen. The final screen presented will be the **S**elect Printer screen.

Edit

The **E**dit command allows you to edit information about the available printer upon which the **S**elect Printer cursor is currently located. The command has the extended tree structure:

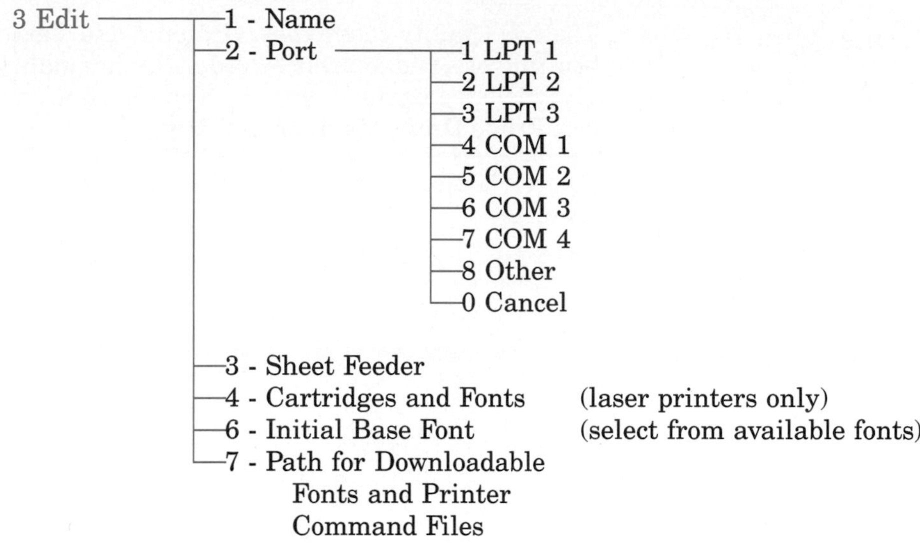

While an explanation of all menu commands found here is beyond the scope of this text, there is one useful procedure associated with the **E**dit command menu that involves creating an ASCII text file with printer control codes included in it.

To create such a file, type **Shift-F7,S** (Print),**S**elect Printer. Next move the **S**elect Printer cursor to the appropriate printer listed and, if necessary, type **1** or **S** (**S**elect) to make it the current printer. Then type **3** or **E** to present the **E**dit menu. Next type **2** or **P** (**P**ort) and make a note as to what the current port is. Type **8** or **O** (**O**ther) and then enter a path and filename for the ASCII file. The next step is to return to the **Shift-F7** (Print) menu by typing the **F7** (Exit) key twice and then print the full document or page(s) desired. You will need to use the **S**elect Printer,**E**dit command to reset the original port for the printer when finished.

Copy — Delete — Help — Update

The next four commands are used to perform maintenance routines on the available printers. The **C**opy command makes a copy of the highlighted printer making two of them available, one of which you may want to edit. **D**elete deletes the highlighted printer driver. **H**elp provides the "Helps and Hints" screen for the highlighted printer driver. **U**pdate saves any editing changes made to the highlighted printers.

Binding Offset

The **B**inding Offset command offsets printing by the specified inches on odd and even pages for binding two-sided copies. Text is shifted to the right on odd-numbered pages and to the left on even-numbered pages.

Number of Copies

The **N**umber of Copies command is used to print multiple copies of a file. Type **Shift-F7,N** (Print),**N**umber of Copies, enter the number desired, and then continue with the print command operation.

Multiple Copies Generated by

When the **Shift-F7,N** (Print),**N**umber of Copies command is used to print more than one copy of a document, the **U**,**Mu**ltiple Copies Generated by command allows the copies to be produced by either WordPerfect or the printer. If **W**ordPerfect is selected, the copies of the document (print job) are printed in their entirety, one after another. If **P**rinter is selected, multiple copies of each page of the document are printed sequentially.

Graphics Quality — Text Quality	The two Quality commands, **G**raphics and **T**ext, may be used to speed up printing of a rough draft by reducing the quality of either the graphics or text included in the document. The selections for both commands include Do **N**ot Print, **D**raft, **M**edium, and **H**igh.
Block/Print	To print a block of text, block the text to be printed and then type **Shift-F7** (Print).

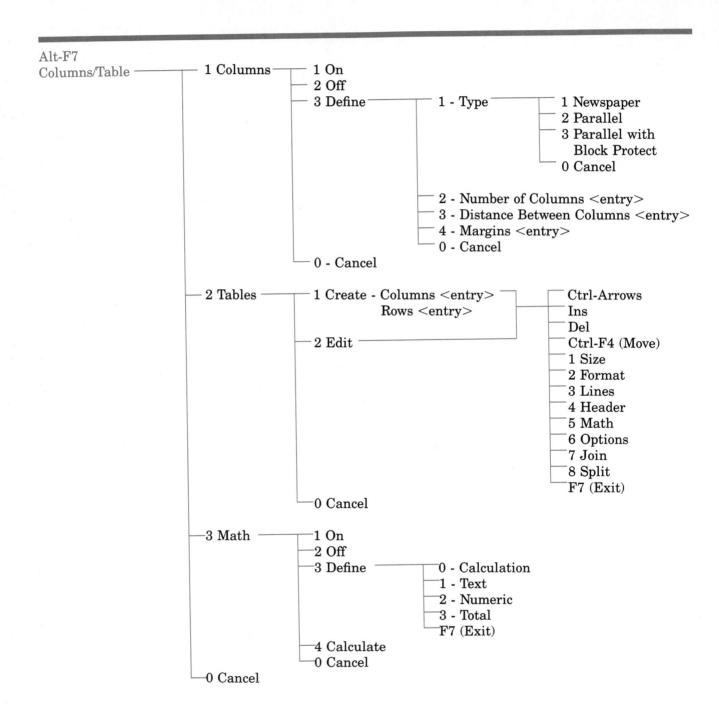

Alt-F7 Columns/Table

- 1 Columns
  - 1 On
  - 2 Off
  - 3 Define
    - 1 - Type
      - 1 Newspaper
      - 2 Parallel
      - 3 Parallel with Block Protect
      - 0 Cancel
    - 2 - Number of Columns <entry>
    - 3 - Distance Between Columns <entry>
    - 4 - Margins <entry>
    - 0 - Cancel
  - 0 - Cancel
- 2 Tables
  - 1 Create - Columns <entry>
    Rows <entry>
  - 2 Edit
    - (1 Create and 2 Edit both lead to:)
    - Ctrl-Arrows
    - Ins
    - Del
    - Ctrl-F4 (Move)
    - 1 Size
    - 2 Format
    - 3 Lines
    - 4 Header
    - 5 Math
    - 6 Options
    - 7 Join
    - 8 Split
    - F7 (Exit)
  - 0 Cancel
- 3 Math
  - 1 On
  - 2 Off
  - 3 Define
    - 0 - Calculation
    - 1 - Text
    - 2 - Numeric
    - 3 - Total
    - F7 (Exit)
  - 4 Calculate
  - 0 Cancel
- 0 Cancel

ALT-F7 (Columns/Table)

ALT-F7 COLUMNS/ TABLE

The **Alt-F7** (Columns/Table) command is used to create areas in a document that separate text into columns on a page, into rows and columns in a table, or to create areas in which certain math operations may be performed. The Columns/Table command is divided into three major commands. The **Alt-F7** (Columns/Table),**C**olumns command is used strictly for creating areas of columnar text. The **Alt-F7** (Columns/Table),**M**ath command is used to create areas in which math operations may be performed. The **Alt-F7** (Columns/Table),**T**ables command is used to create tables, which are spreadsheet-like in nature and incorporate elements of both columnar text and math operations.

Alt-F7 (Columns/ Table),**C**olumns

The **C**olumns feature is used to produce text that is columnar in format. The two basic styles of columnar text are Newspaper Type, where text continuously runs through columns on a page, and Parallel Type, where text is more table-like in nature. The following discusses how to use the **C**olumns command in light of the steps used to create columns in a document.

Steps in Creating Text Columns

There are four basic steps involved when using the **C**olumns command to create a document with a columnar text area.

1. Define the type and left/right margins for the columns.
2. Turn Columns On.
3. Enter the text.
4. Turn Columns Off.

The following discusses the various column commands in conjunction with other steps required to create text columns.

Define the Columns — Columns,**D**efine Code = [Col Def:]

The **D**efine command presents a screen that is used to define the style and margins for text columns. When the **D**efine screen is exited, a [Col Def:] code is inserted into the text at the cursor location. The style and margins for columns stay in effect for the rest of the document or until another [Col Def:] code is encountered. The **D**efine command screen appears similar to the following.

```
Text Column Definition

     1 - Type                                   Newspaper

     2 - Number of Columns                      2

     3 - Distance Between Columns

     4 - Margins

     Column     Left       Right      Column     Left       Right
       1:       1"         4"         13:
       2:       4.5"       7.5"       14:
       3:                             15:
       4:                             16:
       5:                             17:
       6:                             18:
       7:                             19:
       8:                             20:
       9:                             21:
      10:                             22:
      11:                             23:
      12:                             24:

Selection: 0
```

Type The **T**ype command is used to specify either Newspaper or Parallel column style.

Newspaper Newspaper type is when text flows from the last line in a column on a page to the first line of the next column on the page. The following screen shows an example of Newspaper style.

```
                         Vista Ridge June Newsletter


-Rec Remodeled-           toddlers area, a          events, see Mr.
The recreation room       new indoor bar-b-         Smith in the
in Harris Commons         que (with all the         managers office,
will be closed for        accessories), and a       Building A.
remodeling until          spacious cedar sun
July 17th.                deck facing the           -Welcome Newcomers-
                          pool.                     Vista Ridge is
When completed, the                                 pleased to welcome
newly remodeled           To reserve rental         two new families
facility will pro-        time for your late        this month.
vide a large              summer social
```

Parallel With **P**arallel type, text is entered into columns in a horizontal fashion. It is used when the text is record-like in structure and where items within the records have varying line lengths. The following screen shows an example of Parallel style.

```
             Vista Ridge Cleaning/Occupancy Journal
             --------------------------------------


Unit                      Style                     Comments
----                      -----                     --------

Apartment #14             3 bedroom, 2              Available for
                          floors, 1 and 1/2         occupancy August
                          baths.                    23rd.  Replace
                                                    living room carpet,
                                                    paint throughout.

Apartment #32             1 bedroom, 1 bath         Vacant.  Repaper
                                                    walls in kitchen,
                                                    repair front steps.
```

Parallel with Block Protect A third column style, Parallel with **B**lock Protect, may be specified to create parallel columns in which the records of data are protected against being separated by soft page breaks. See Block/(Format) (Block/**Shift-F8**) for more information on protecting blocks of text.

Number of Columns The **N**umber of Columns command is used to specify the number of columns you want to appear on a page. In the examples above, three columns were specified.

Distance Between Columns The **D**istance Between Columns command is used by WordPerfect when it sets automatic left and right margins for each column. The margins may, however, be changed after they are generated.

Margins The last specifications made to define columns are the left and right margins for each column. WordPerfect will compute a set of margins and allow you to edit them. When the margins are all correctly specified, type **F7** (Exit) to exit the Text Column Definition.

Turn Columns On – **C**olumns,**O**n Code = [Col On]
The next step in creating text columns is to define the portion of the document in which the columnar format is to occur.

A note of caution is in order here. When you turn columns on within a document, the remainder of the document becomes formatted into the defined columns. If you are creating a columnar portion of text anywhere other than at the end of a document, it is recommended that you create the columnar portion in Document 2 (see **Shift-F3** (Switch)) then copy the portion (including the [Col Def:], [Col On], and [Col Off] codes) into Document 1.

To format a portion of text into Text Columns, move the cursor to where the columns are to begin and type **Alt-F7,1,1** (Columns/Table),**C**olumns,**O**n. The command will insert a [Col On] code into the text.

Enter the Text
With the type of columns defined and the [Col On] code placed in the document, you are ready to enter the columnar text. The manner in which you enter the text depends on the type of columns you have defined.

Newspaper Type If the type of columns is newspaper, you simply enter the text as you would during normal editing. When the first column on a page is filled (the bottom of the page is reached), WordPerfect will move to the top of the second column for you to continue entering text.

If you want to begin the next column before the bottom of the page is reached, you may do so by entering a hard page (Ctrl-↵) in front of the line that you want moved to the next column.

Parallel Style If the style of columns is Parallel, you begin by entering the text for the first record item into the first column. When done, you type Ctrl-↵(Hard Page) to move the cursor to the second column to enter the second item for the record.

The Hard Page keystroke in Parallel column text mode causes [Col Off] and [Col On] codes to be imbedded in the document at the end of each record's data (after the last column). The codes are used by WordPerfect to maintain the horizontal structure of the record-type data. Care must be taken to avoid deleting these codes.

Editing in Columnar Text Modes To move from one column to the next, the following keystrokes may be used:

Ctrl-Home,→	Jump one column right
Ctrl-Home,←	Jump one column left
Ctrl-Home,Home,→	Jump to last column
Ctrl-Home,Home,←	Jump to first column

You must block text to cut or copy it within a column. You may speed up scrolling and screen rewriting by using the **Shift-F1,2,6,7**

(Setup),**D**isplay,**E**dit screen Options,**S**ide-by-side Columns Display command to display each column on a separate page while editing.

Turn Columns Off—Columns,Off Code = [Col Off]

The final step in creating text columns is to turn Columns Off. Move the cursor to where columnar text is to end and type **Alt-F7,1,2** (Columns/Table),**C**olumns,**O**ff. The command inserts a [Col Off] code into the document.

Alt-F7 (Columns/Table),**T**ables

Tables is a rather extensive command that allows the user to create areas within a document in which text may be organized into rows and columns and/or in which math operations (addition, subtraction, division, and multiplication) may be performed. In past versions of WordPerfect, these areas were created using the **Alt-F7** (Columns/Table),Column **D**efine,**P**arallel and **Alt-F7** (Columns/Table),**M**ath commands. While the two older commands remain intact with version 5.1, they have become somewhat obsolete with the introduction of the **T**ables command. The **T**ables command is usually easier to use and more versatile.

The following command tree further describes the **Alt-F7** (Columns/Table), **T**ables command menu of options.

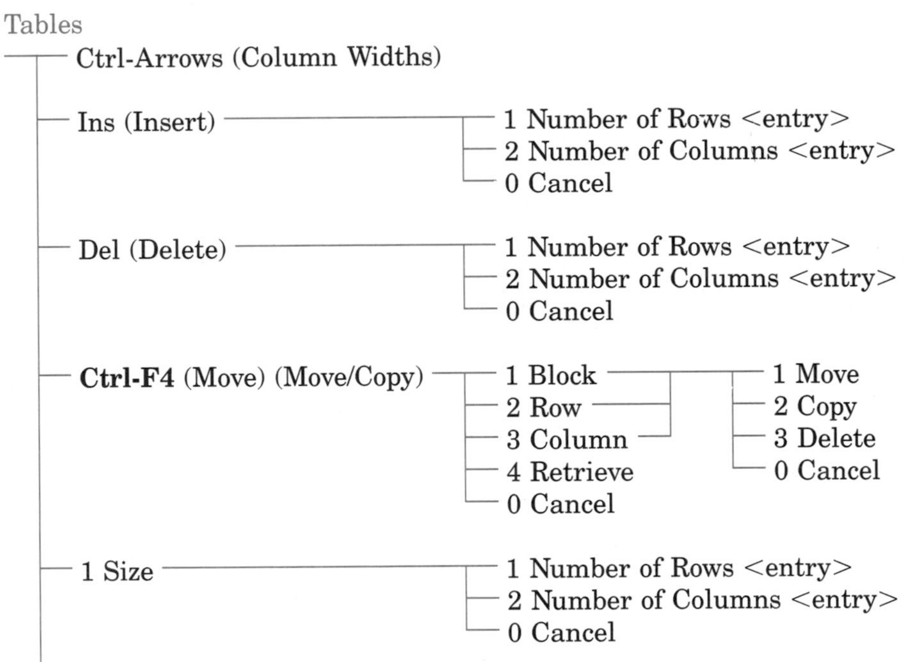

CONTINUED

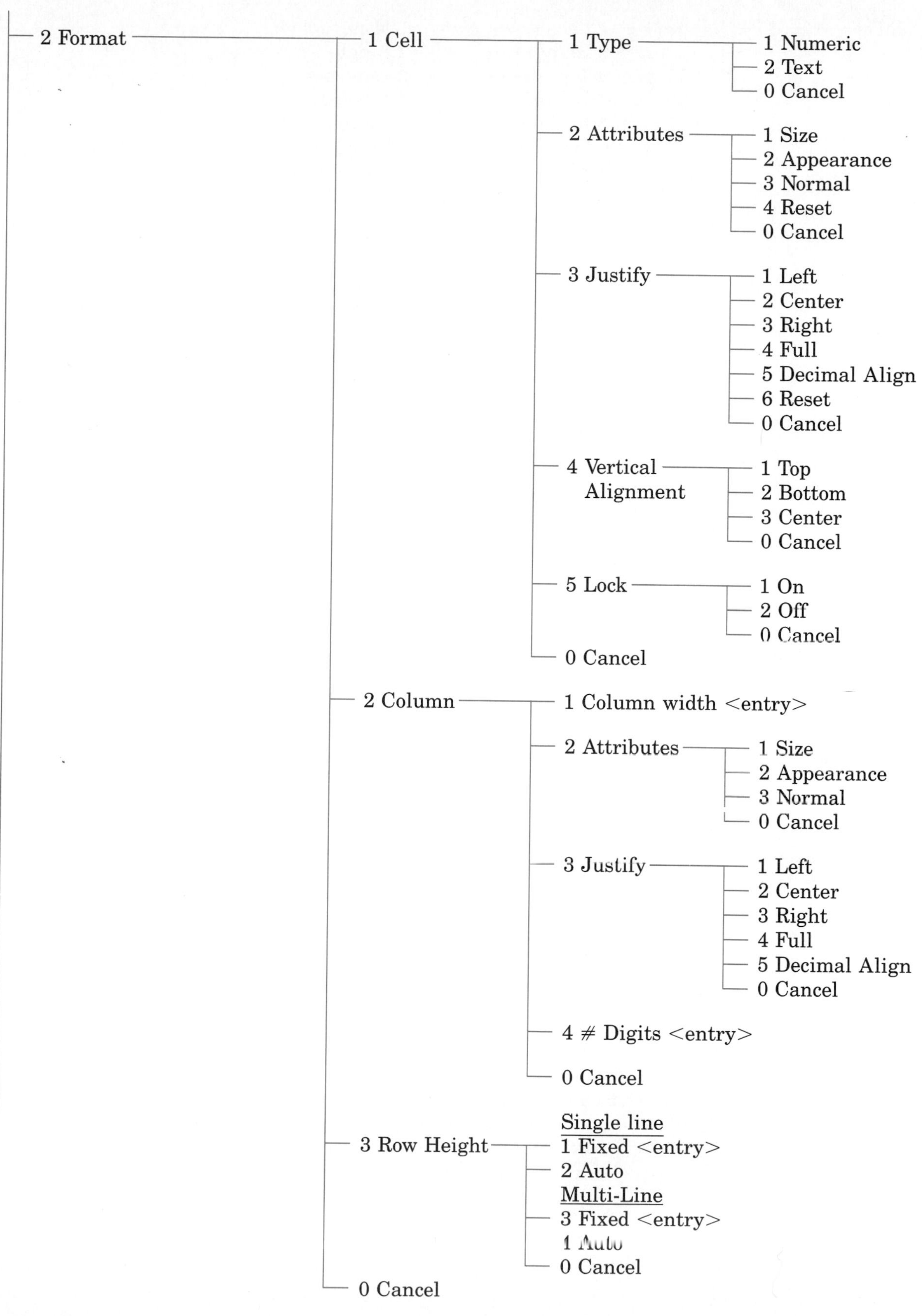

CONTINUED

W-153

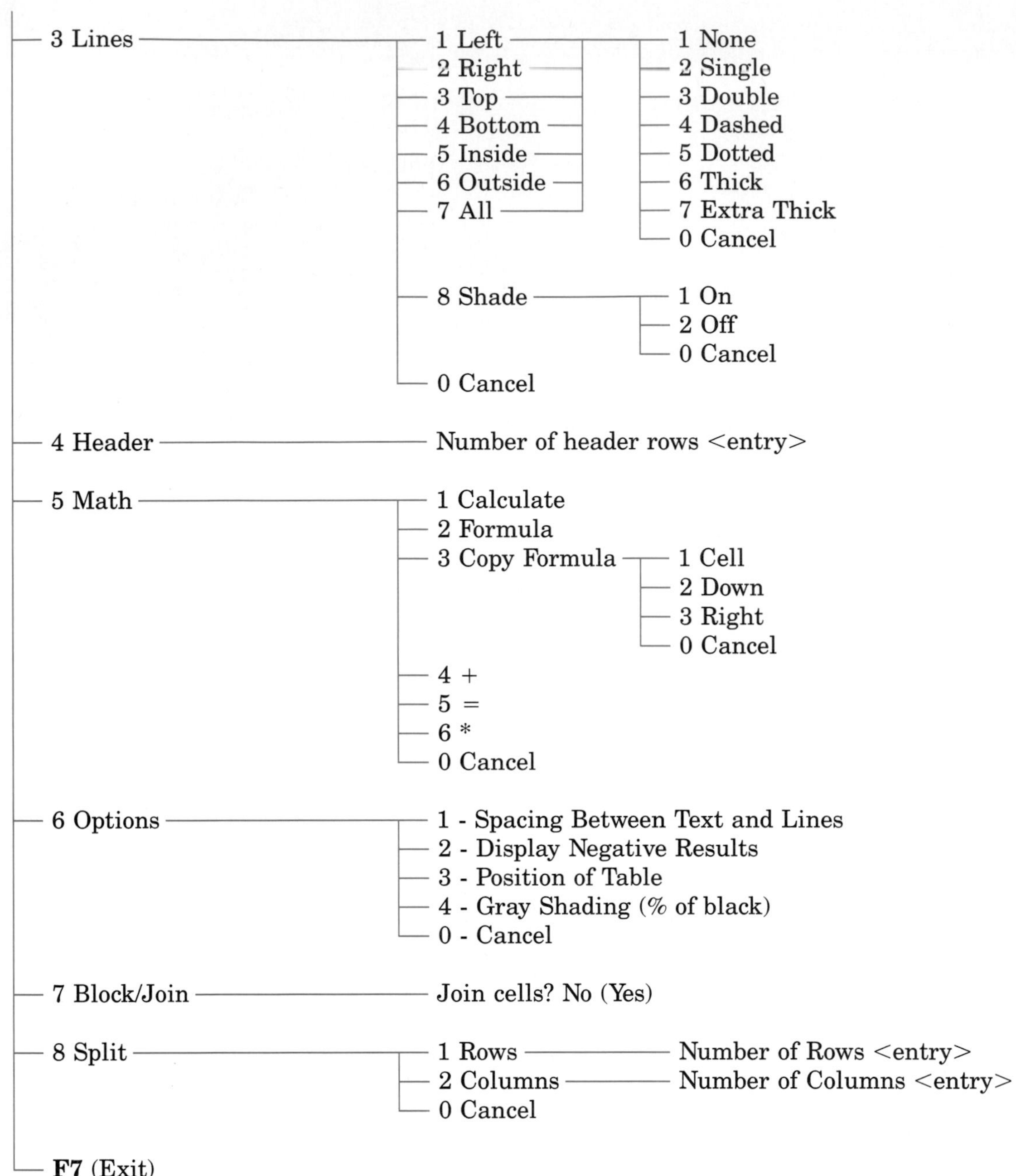

The essential benefit of using the **T**ables command is that it divides a portion of the document into separate areas, called cells, into which data may be entered and edited in an independent manner. This allows for documents in which adjacent columns may be used to organize text. For instance, the following screen illustrates one form of text organization within a table area.

```
          Vista Ridge Cleaning/Occupancy Journal
          --------------------------------------

Unit                Style                     Comments
```

Apartment #14	3 bedroom, 2 floors, 1 and 1/2 baths.	Available for occupancy August 23rd. Replace living room carpet, paint throughout.
Apartment #32	1 bedroom, 1 bath	Vacant. Repaper walls in kitchen, repair front steps.

Steps Used to Produce a Table

The following steps are used to produce a table area within a document. Note that the steps here are not necessarily shown in the order that they are executed.

1. Create the table
2. Format the table
3. Enter the table data
4. Format the table data

Creating a Simple Table

To create a table within a document, you begin by using the **Alt-F7** (columns/Table),**T**ables,**C**reate command. First move the cursor to the area in which the table is to occur, and then type **Alt-F7,2,1**. The initial default format for a table is one row divided into three columns. The **T**ables,**C**reate command, however, prompts you to enter the desired number of columns and rows. In the example above, the default value of three columns was used, and the number of rows was then specified as being three. Once the number of columns and rows is specified, the table will appear on the screen, as in the following example.


```
Table Edit:  Press Exit when done        Cell A1 Doc 1 Pg 1 Ln 1.81" Pos 1.12"
Ctrl-Arrows Column Widths; Ins Insert; Del Delete; Move Move/Copy;
1 Size; 2 Format; 3 Lines; 4 Header; 5 Math; 6 Options; 7 Join; 8 Split: 0
```

At the bottom of the screen appears the Table Edit menu. The commands on the menu are used to change the appearance of the table and/or the appearance of the data contained in the table. You may not, however, directly enter text into the table while in the Table Edit mode (while the

Table Edit menu appears on the screen). To enter text into cells of the table, you may type **F7** (exit) to return to the normal editing mode.

Table Codes In the normal editing mode, the **Alt-F3** (Reveal Codes) command shows where the table definition begin and end codes, [Tbl Def:] and [Tbl Off], have been imbedded into the document. Between these codes are a series of [Row][Cell][Cell][Cell] codes.

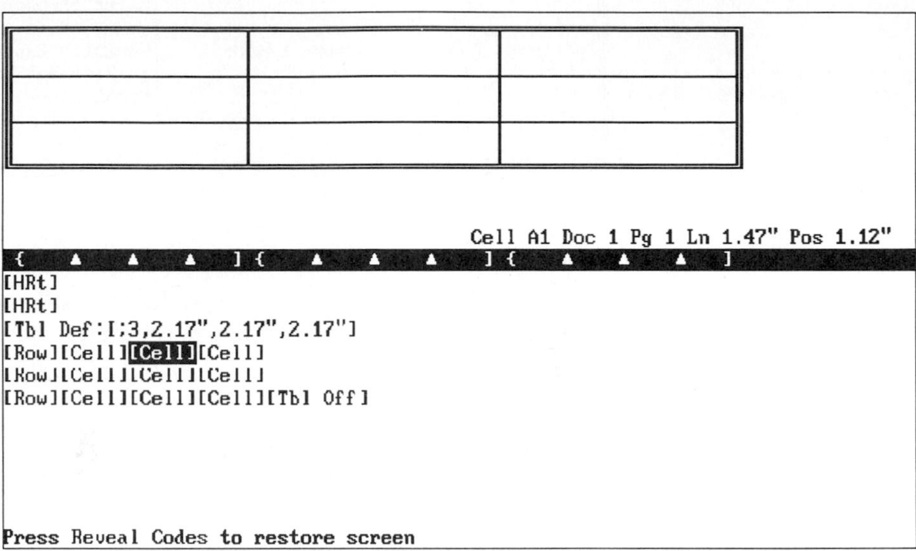

During normal editing, the [Row][Cell][Cell] and [Tbl Off] codes cannot be individually deleated from the document. Only the [Tbl Def:] code can be deleted, and doing so deletes the table (but not the data that may be in the table) from the document. Also, when a [Tbl Def:] code is deleted, all of its associated table coes are deleted, and none of the codes are copied into the Undelete buffer. It is therefore impossible to use the **F1** (Cancel) command to recover a deleted table if the table was deleted by removing the [Tbl Def:] code from the document. If an entire table, including all table codes, is deleted as a block, it may be recovered with the **F1** (Cancel) command.

Table Cell Addresses Each cell in a table is assigned a unique address (which can be thought of as a name). The address or name of the cell depends on its column/row location in the table. The columns in a table are lettered alphabetically from left to right. So if there are three columns in a row, they will be lettered A, B, and C, with column A on the far left. Similarly, the rows in a table are numbered from top to bottom. A particular cell's address is obtained by combining the column letter and row number of its table location. For example, the top-left cell in a table always has the address A1 (first column, first row). If there is a cell adjacent to cell A1 in the same row, its address will be B1.

A table may have a maximum of 32 columns and 32,765 rows. The address of the current cell (the cell in which the editing cursor is currently located) is displayed on the status line along with the “Doc,” “Ln,” and “Pos” information.

Entering Text Into a Table To enter text into a table, you may move the cursor to the appropriate cell and then type the desired text. By default, text entered into a cell will word-wrap according to the left and right boundaries of the cell, and all cells in a row will automatically expand to the same number of lines as the cell in the row that contains the most lines. For example, in the following screen, each cell in the first row has expanded to the size of the last cell in the row.

Apartment #14	3 bedroom, 2 floors, 1 and 1/2 baths.	Available for occupancy August 23rd. Replace living room carpet, paint throughout._

Commands that justify text on a line (such as center, flush right, indent, and so forth), affect the text in a cell with respect ot the boundaries of the cell. For example, the **Shifjt-F6** (Center) command will center a line of text within a cell, rather than within the current left and right margins of the document.

Two exceptions to the justification rule are the Tab and Margin Release (Shift-Tab) keystrokes, which have special meanings while editing text in a table. See "Table Area Cursor Movement and Editing Keystrokes" below, for more information on these two keystrokes.

Table Area Cursor Movement and Editing Keystrokes During normal editing and when the cursor is located within a table area, there are several additional cursor movement and editing keystrokes that may be used.

Cursor Movement	**Keystrokes**
Cell Right	Tab
Cell Left	Shift-Tab
Cell Up	↑
Cell Down	↓
Beginning of Text in a Cell	Ctrl-Home,↑
Last Line of Text in a Cell	Ctrl-Home,↓
First Cell in a Column	Ctrl-Home,Home,↑
Last Cell in a Column	Ctrl-Home,Home,↓
First Cell in a Row	Ctrl-Home,Home,←
Last Cell in a Row	Ctrl-Home,Home,→
First Cell in a Table (A1)	Ctrl-Home,Home,Home,↑
Last Cell in a Table	Ctrl-Home,Home,Home,↓

Insert	**Keystrokes**
New Row Above Cursor Location	Ctrl-Ins

Delete	**Keystrokes**
Current Row	Ctrl-Del,Y
End of Text Line, Current Cell Only	Ctrl-End
Remaining Text in Current Cell*	Ctrl-PgDn,Y

*The WordPerfect manual states that Ctrl-PgDn does not delete across cell boundaries. However, this is not true in the version being used to produce this text (updated April 1990). It is suggested that appropriate precautions are taken (save your file) before using the Ctrl-PgDn keystrokes.

If you want to include a [Tab] code in a cell, type Ctrl-v,Tab; if you want to include a Margin Release [◄Mar Rel] code in a cell, type Ctrl-v,Shift-Tab.

Commands to Format a Table

To change the appearance of a table, the **Alt-F7** (Columns/Table),**T**ables,**E**dit command may be used. The easiest way to use the command is to first move the cursor to a location in the table you wish to edit, then type **Alt-F7** (Columns/Table). The Table Edit menu will then appear on the screen, and you will again be in the Table Edit mode. If the cursor is not located in a table area when **Alt-F7** is typed, you may continue by typing **2** or **T** for **T**ables, then **2** or **E** for **E**dit. WordPerfect will then conduct a search backwards through the document to find a table to edit. If no table is found, WordPerfect will proceed to search forward in the document for a table to edit. If a table is found, the Table Edit menu will appear on the screen.

Apartment #14	3 bedrooms, 2 floors, 1 and 1/2 baths.	Available for occupancy August 23rd. Replace living room carpet, paint throughout.
Apartment #32	1 bedroom, 1 bath	Vacant. Repaper walls in kitchen, repair front steps.

Table Edit: Press Exit when done Cell A1 Doc 1 Pg 1 Ln 1.47" Pos 1.12"

Ctrl-Arrows Column Widths; Ins Insert; Del Delete; Move Move/Copy;
1 Size; 2 Format; 3 Lines; 4 Header; 5 Math; 6 Options; 7 Join; 8 Split: 0

When the Table Edit menu is on the screen, the entire current cell is displayed in reverse video (highlighted). To help simplify matters, the reverse video display will be called the edit cursor. The following keystrokes may be used to move the edit cursor from cell to cell.

Edit Cursor Movement	**Keystroke(s)**
Cell Right	→
Cell Left	←
Cell Up	↑
Cell Down	↓
First Cell in a Column	Home,↑
Last Cell in a Column	Home,↓
First Cell in a Row	Home,←
Last Cell in a Row	Home,→
First Cell in a Table (A1)	Home,Home,↑
Last Cell in a Table	Home,Home,↓

The following Table Edit menu commands are used to change the appearance and/or structure of a WordPerfect table.

Changing Column Widths

To change the width of a column in the table, you may move the edit cursor to the appropriate column, and then type either Ctrl-← or Ctrl-→. Typing Ctrl-← shrinks the column one character at a time, while typing Ctrl-→ expands the column one character at a time.

Inserting Rows or Columns Into a Table

To insert rows or columns, you may move the edit cursor to where the rows or columns are to be inserted, and then type the Ins key (rows will be inserted directly above the edit cursor location, and columns will be inserted directly to the left of the edit cursor). After you type the Ins key, WordPerfect will prompt "Insert: **1 R**ows; **2 C**olumns:". Type **1** ↵ or **2** ↵ to specify rows or columns. The next prompt displayed by WordPerfect will be "Number of Rows:" or "Number of columns:". At this point, you may enter the number of rows or columns you wish to have inserted into the table.

Rows or columns inserted into a table will have the same attributes, justification, and width settings as the row or column in which the edit cursor resided when the Ins key was typed. Cell data will not be copied to the inserted rows or columns.

Another method of inserting rows or columns is to block the number of rows or columns you wish to have inserted, and then type the Ins key. When this method is used, it is not necessary to enter the number of rows or columns you want inserted; the number of blocked rows or columns will be the number inserted into the table.

Deleting Rows or Columns From a Table

To delete rows or columns, you may move the edit cursor to where the rows or columns are to be deleted, and then type the Del key (rows will be deleted at, and directly below, the edit cursor location, and columns will be deleted at, and directly to the right of, the edit cursor). After you type the Del key, WordPerfect will prompt "Delete: **1 R**ows; **2 C**olumns:". Type **1**↵ or **2**↵ to specify rows or columns. The next prompt displayed by WordPerfect will be "Number of Rows:" or "Number of Columns:". At this point you may enter the number of rows or columns you wish to have deleted from the table.

Another method is to block several rows or columns to be deleted, and then type the Del key. WordPerfect will prompt "Delete: **1 R**ows: **2 C**olumns:". Type **1**↵ or **2**↵ to delete the highlighted rows or columns, respectively. Rows or columns deleted from a table may be recovered by typing **F1** (Cancel) while in the Table Edit mode.

Ctrl-F4 (Move)

While in the Table Edit mode, the **Ctrl-F4** (Move) command may be used to move, copy, or delete a block, row, or column of the table.

Block/**M**ove, **C**opy, and **D**elete One way to perform cut-and-paste operations within a table area is to first block two or more cells, and then type the **Ctrl-F4** (Move) command and select **1 B**lock. WordPerfect then presents the **1 M**ove, **2 C**opy, **3 D**elete menu. If you choose to move or copy the block data to another area in the table, any data that may exist in the area being copied or moved to will be overwritten (replaced) by the blocked data. If you choose to delete the block, only the data in the block is deleted; the row/column cells in the block remain intact. To move copy, or delete a single cell, simply move the cursor to the appropriate cell, and then type **Ctrl-F4** (Move), then **1** or **B** for **B**lock.

Row or Column—Move, Copy, or Delete Another way to perform cut-and-paste operations within a table area is to move the edit cursor to the appropriate place in the table, and then type **Ctrl-F4** (Move) and select either **2 R**ow or **3 C**olumn. WordPerfect then presents the **1 M**ove, **2 C**opy, **3 D**elete menu. If you choose to move or copy the current row or column, both the data and the current row or column will be inserted into the new location. If you choose to delete the row or column, both the data and the row or column will be deleted from the table.

Retrieve—Block, Row, or Column The Retrieve command may be used to retrieve the last block, row, or column that was moved or copied with the **Ctrl-F4** (Move) command. The buffer that holds this data is independent of the normal Move buffers and may only be accessed by the **Re**trieve command while in the Table Edit mode.

F1 (Cancel)
While in the Table Edit mode, the **F1** (Cancel) key may be used to undelete the last block, row, or column deleted. There is only one undelete buffer in the Table Edit mode, and the buffer is independent of the three Undelete buffers used by the **F1** (Cancel) command in the normal editing mode.

Size
The **S**ize command may be used to add or delete rows or columns from a table. When the command is executed, WordPerfect will prompt "Table Size: **1 R**ows; **2 C**olumns:". At this point you may select to change either the number of rows or the number of columns in the table. After selecting rows or columns, WordPerfect will prompt "Number of Rows:" or "Number of Columns:". The number of rows or columns currently included in the table will appear after the prompt. You may change the number by simply entering the desired figure.

The **S**ize command will add or delete rows at the bottom of the table, regardless of the edit cursor's location when the command is executed. Similarly, the command will add or delete columns at the far right of the table, regardless of the location of the edit cursor when the command is executed.

Format,**C**olumn,**W**idth
The **W**idth command may be used to change the width of the current column or several blocked columns. At the "Column width:" prompt, you type the desired column width in inches (or in the current unit of measure, if other than inches). For information on changing the width of the current column in character units, see "Changing Column Widths."

Format,**R**ow Height
By default, WordPerfect will adjust the height of a row according to the greatest number of lines of wrapped text in a single cell of the row. WordPerfect will also automatically adjust the row's height to accommodate the largest font size that may exist in the row. (See **Ctrl-F8** (Font,**S**ize). The **F**ormat,**R**ow Height command may be used to override the automatic adjustment of row heights. To use the command, you may move the edit cursor to the row to be affected, and then type **2** or **F**, **3** or **R** for **F**ormat,**R**ow Height. The following menu will appear on the screen.

```
Row Height -- Single line: 1 Fixed; 2 Auto;  Multi-line: 3 Fixed; 4 Auto: 4
```

To fix the height of the current row so that it will accept only one line of text, type **1** or **F** (Single line: **1 F**ixed), and then enter the height (in inches) that will accommodate the size of type which will be entered into the row. To fix the height of the current row so that it will accept multiple lines of wrapped text, type **3** or **x** (Multi-line: **3** Fi**x**ed), and then enter the desired height of the row in inches.

To return a row to the default automatic variable height, type either **2** or **4** (depending on whether the row was previously fixed as single line or multi-line) for Auto.

When a row's height is fixed, there is a limit to the amount of text that can be entered into any cell in the row. If that limit is exceeded, the additional text will not be displayed on the screen, nor will it be printed. The additional text, however, is retained as part of the table's data. If the row is later changed to automatic height or a fixed height of a size large enough to display the text, the "hidden" text will appear on the screen and will be printed with the table.

Block/Lines

The **L**ines command is used to change the appearance of the lines that border the table and the cells within the table. The command may also be used to shade the table area. To change the appearance of the table lines, you first block the area to be affected by the command then type **3** or **L** for **L**ines.

WordPerfect will next present a menu that includes the options: **L**eft, **R**ight, **T**op, **B**ottom, **I**nside, **O**utside, or **A**ll. The menu items refer to the times in the table that are positioned relative to the blocked area. That is, **R**ight refers to the lines that border the blocked area on the right, **I**nside refers to the lines inside the blocked area, and **O**utside refers to all lines that border the blocked area.

After you have selected the lines to be affected, WordPerfect will present a menu with the options **N**one (no lines), **S**ingle, **D**ouble, Da**s**hed, D**o**tted, **T**hick, or **E**xtra Thick. From this menu you may select the style of line you desire. To shade a table area, you first block the area to be shaded, type **3** or **L** for Lines, **8** or **S** for **S**hade, and then **1** or **O** for **O**n. See the **O**ptions,Gray Shading command, below, for more information on changing table shading.

The following table has the bottom line in each row formatted to a different style line and has column C shaded. You should note that different printers will produce different results when printing the lines and shades included in a table.

None Single		Shaded Column
Double		
Dashed		
Dotted		
Thick		
Extra Thick		

Header

The **H**eader command may be useful when a table includes column labels in its cells and spans two or more pages. The command is used to reprint *n* number of rows at the top of each page on which the table occurs. To use the command you type **4** or **H** for **H**eader, and then enter the number of rows (starting from the top of the table) that you want reprinted on each page. An asterisk will be displayed on the status line next to the cell address when the edit cursor is moved to a row marked as a header row. To remove headers from a table, use the **H**eader command to specify 0 as the number of header rows.

Options

The **O**ptions command may be used to change several miscellaneous formats for all cells in a table.

Spacing Between Text and Lines This command lets you specify the distance between the lines that border the table's cells and the text within the cells.

Display Negative Results When a table includes math data (see "Math Operations in a Table"), this command may be used to display the negative results of a calculation either with a minus sign, e.g. −300.75, or with parentheses, e.g. (300.75).

Position of Table By default, WordPerfect positions a table against the current left margin in the document. This position can be changed by using the **P**osition of Table command. The choices offered by the command are **L**eft, **R**ight, **C**enter, **F**ull, and **S**et Position. The **L**eft, **R**ight, and **C**enter commands all position the table relative to the current left and right margins. These commands will only make a difference in table position if the table is smaller in width than the distance between the two margins. The **F**ull command expands the table to the full width between left and right margins, and the **S**et Position command allows you to enter the table's exact distance from the left edge of the paper.

Gray Shading (% of black) The **G**ray Shading command may be used to adjust the percentage of gray that is printed when cells of the table are shaded. The default value is 10% of black. See "Block/Lines", above, for more information on shading cells in a table.

Join—Split

The **J**oin and S**p**lit commands are used to combine or divide cells in a table. These two commands allow for tables that are not symmetrical in nature—a common design feature of many business forms.

<table>
<tr><td colspan="3">Vista Ridge Townhouses
Lease/Credit Application</td></tr>
<tr><td colspan="2">Name:</td><td>Phone:</td></tr>
<tr><td colspan="3">Current Address:</td></tr>
<tr><td>City:</td><td>State:</td><td>Zip:</td></tr>
</table>

The **J**oin command is used to combine two or more cells into one. To use the command, you block the cells to be joined and then type **7** or **J** for **J**oin. WordPerfect will next prompt "Join cells?" Typing Y will complete the join operation.

The **Split** command may be used to divide one cell into two or more cells. To divide a single cell into multiple cells, first move the edit cursor to the cell you want to divide, and then type **8** or **p** for **Split**. WordPerfect will prompt "Split: **1 Rows**; **2 Columns**;". Select **Rows** if you want the cell divided horizontally or select **Columns** if you want the cell divided vertically. WordPerfect will next prompt "Number of Rows:" or "Number of Columns:". Enter the number of cells into which you want the current cell split. You can split several cells at once by first blocking the cells then following the steps above.

Commands to Format Data in a Table

The Tables Edit menu's **2 Format** command may be used to change the appearance of text data entered into certain cells or columns of cells in a table. After selecting **2 Format**, you may select **1 Cell** to format the current cell or the currently blocked range of cells, or **2 Column** to format the current column or the currently blocked range of columns.

Attributes and Justify

The **Format**,**Cell** and **Format**,**Column** commands both have submenus that include the commands **2 Attributes** and **3 Justify**. The **Attributes** command includes many of the same formatting options (**Size**, **Appearance**, and **Normal**) available during normal editing with the **CTRL-F8** (Font) command. The **Justify** command includes the same options available during normal editing with the **Shift-F8** (Format),**1 Line**,**3 Justification** command.

When an attribute (such as underline or large) or a justification (such as right justified or centered) is desired of the text in a cell, there are two ways the changes can be made.

One approach is to format the text in the normal editing mode. For example, if you want the text in cell B2 to be bold, you may move the cursor to cell B2, type the text, block the text and then type the **F6** (Bold) command. If you want the text in cell B2 to be centered in the cell, enter the text into the cell, and then move the cursor to the top of the cell and type the **Shift-F8** (Format),**L**ine,**J**ustification,**C**enter command. (When included in a table area, a [Just:] code will only affect text in the current cell.)

The other approach is to use the Table Edit menu's **F**ormat command to select an attribute or justification for a particular cell, column, or a block of cells or columns. For example, if you want the text in cell B2 to be bold, you move the edit cursor to cell B2 and type the **F**ormat,**C**ell,**A**ttributes,**A**ppearance,**B**old command. If you want the text in column B to be centered, you move the edit cursor to a cell in column B and type the **F**ormat,C**o**lumn,**J**ustify,**C**enter command.

In the examples here, either method will produce the same printed results. There are, however, several important differences between the two approaches. To help simplify the following discussion, the first approach will be called the Normal Editing approach, and the second approach will be called the Table Edit approach.

First, the Normal Editing approach can be used to affect only a portion of the text in a cell, such as a word or phrase. The Table Edit approach, however, affects all text in the specified cells or columns. You cannot, for example, use the Table Edit approach to underline one word in a cell or to center only the first line in each cell of a column.

Second, the Normal Editing approach inserts the appropriate codes (such as [BOLD]... [bold]) into the cell where they are visible with Reveal Codes. The Table Edit approach inserts no codes into the table, and the fact that certain cells or columns have been formatted in a particular way can often be somewhat difficult to discern.

Third, since the Normal Editing approach inserts codes into the cell, it is relatively simple matter to remove a particular attribute or justification from the cell. You simply use the Reveal Codes screen to find the appropriate code and then delete it from the cell. With the Table Edit approach you must type **F**ormat,**C**ell or Co**l**umn, and then use the **A**ttribute,**R**eset or the **J**ustify,**R**eset command. In both cases, there are several more keystrokes involved than in the Normal Editing approach.

In addition, you cannot use the Table Edit approach to remove just one of many possible attributes that may have been given to a cell or column. So to remove only the bold attribute from a cell that has been given the attributes of large, italic, bold, and underlined, you must reset the cell (which results in no attributes for the cell), and then execute the commands necessary to assign each of the other attributes (large, italic, and underlined) back to the cell. When the Normal Editing approach, you would simply leave the other codes in place and delete the [BOLD] or [bold] code from the cell.

The Table Edit approach's biggest advantages are that cells in a table can be preformatted and that the assigned formats are not easily changed or altered. This makes the approach most useful when tables are being prepared for use by individuals who are less knowledgeable in the use of the software.

Format

In addition to the commands used to assign attributes and justifications to cells or columns in a table, the **F**ormat command offers other menu items that may be used to affect the display of data in a table. The following discusses the remaining **F**ormat commands.

Cell To use the following commands, move the edit cursor to the appropriate cell and then type **F**ormat,**C**ell. If you wish to affect several adjacent cells in a single operation, block the appropriate cells and then type **F**ormat,**C**ell.

Type The **T**ype command provides the options **1 N**umeric, and **2 T**ext. By default, WordPerfect treats all cells in a table as being **N**umeric type cells. Numeric cells are able to hold data that will be used a mathematical operations within a table (see "Math Operations in a Table" on p. W-165 for more information).

A Numeric type cell may hold text data. However, according to the WordPerfect manual, if the cell is referenced in a math formula, the cell will be assigned the value of 0 (zero) in the calculation of the formula. A Text type cell that holds a number and is referenced by a math formula will generate an error (shown as "??" in the cell containing the formula).

Vertical Alignment The WordPerfect manual states that the **V**ertical Alignment command may be used to adjust the up and down printed position of data in cells. The options of the command are **T**op, **B**ottom, and **C**enter.

Lock The **L**ock command may be used to prevent the contents of cells from being edited. The feature is most useful when tables are being prepared for use by individuals who are less knowledgeable in the use of the software. The options of the command are **1 O**n and **2** O**ff**. To protect a cell, type **1** or **O** for **O**n; to unprotect a cell, type **2** or **f** for Of**f**.

Column To use the following commands, move the edit cursor to the appropriate column and then type **F**ormat,**C**olumn. If you wish to affect several adjacent columns in a single operation, block the appropriate columns, and then type **F**ormat,**C**olumn.

 # Digits The # **D**igits command may be used to specify the number of places to the right of the decimal point that a calculated math result will display. The default number is two decimal places. However, you may specify up to 15 places of accuracy (see "Math Operations in a Table" following, for more information).

Math Operations in a Table

The cells in a table area may be used to calculate simple math operations (addition, subtraction, multiplication, and division). The calculations are based on numbers and formulas that are entered into the table. In general, numbers are entered into the table during normal editing, while formulas are entered into the table using the Table Edit menu's **M**ath command. A simple example of entering numbers and formulas into a table might include the following steps.

First a table that is created with three columns and one row. The user exits the Table Edit mode by typing **F7** (Exit), and then proceeds (in the normal editing mode) to enter the number 12 into cell A1, and the number 2 into cell B1.

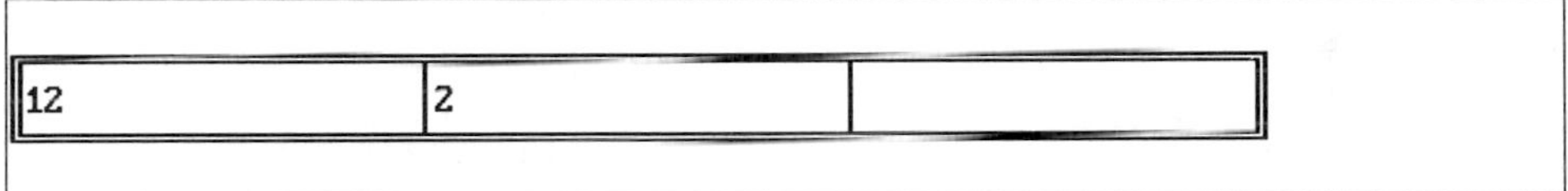

The user next types **Alt-F7** (Columns/Table) to again enter the Table Edit mode, and then moves the edit cursor to the cell C1.

```
12                     2

Table Edit:  Press Exit when done        Cell C1 Doc 1 Pg 1 Ln 4.47" Pos 5.43"
Ctrl-Arrows Column Widths; Ins Insert; Del Delete; Move Move/Copy;
1 Size; 2 Format; 3 Lines; 4 Header; 5 Math; 6 Options; 7 Join; 8 Split: 0
```

At this point the user is ready to enter a formula into the current cell (C1). To do so, the user types the **M**ath,**F**ormula command, and the prompt "Enter formula:" appears at the bottom of the screen. It is the user's intention to enter a formula that will multiply the contents of cell A1 by the contents of cell B1. To do so, the user now enters the formula A1*B1. The screen returns to the display of the Table Edit menu, and the cell C1 now displays a calculated results of the entered formula. Notice that when the current cell contains a formula, the formula is displayed on the far left side of the status line.

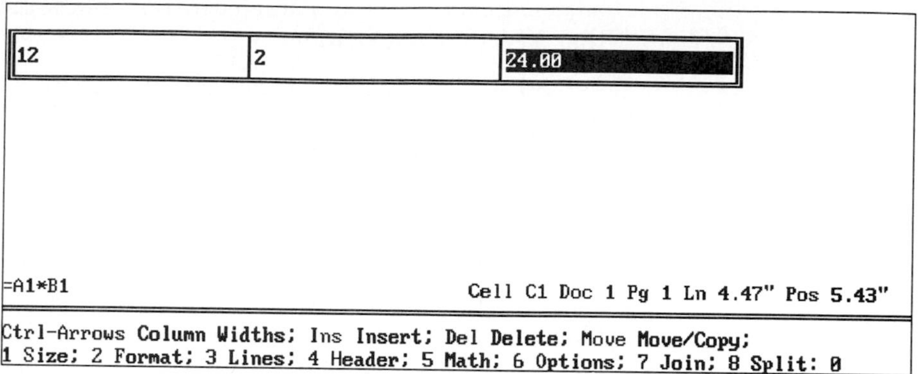

This simple example describes the basic elements involved in creating a table in which math calculations will be performed. First, certain cells contain only numbers. These numbers are the values that will ultimately be used to produce one or more calculated results. For this reason, such numbers are called *key values*. Second, some cells in the table contain mathematical expressions (called formulas) that reference other cells in the table. In this example, the formula in cell C1 was composed of a reference to cell A1 multiplied (*) by a reference to cell B1 (A1*B1). The data types of 1) numbers, which are the beginning values for subsequent calculations, and 2) formulas, which produce the calculated results, form the basis for performing any math calculations in a table area.

Entering Numbers into Table Cells

The numbers which serve as key values normally are (and usually should be) entered into table cells during normal editing. There are a few important rules and guidelines to follow when making such entries.

Do not include text (letters) in the cell holding the number. The WordPerfect manual states "Cells with letters are not considered valid numbers." While testing shows that text included in the cell has no effect whatsoever on the calculated results, it is still very poor technique to include string and numeric data in the same cell when that cell is to be used in a math calculation.

Enter only one number into one line in a cell. Two or more numbers entered on the same line will cause WordPerfect to combine them into one number; another number on other line will cause WordPerfect to use the number closest to the bottom of the cell.

Be sure that the cell into which the number is entered has not been formatted as text (see **F**ormat,**C**ell,**T**ype above).

Finally, when you change the key values in a table, the formulas in the table will not automatically recalculate the correct values. After changing key values in a table, you must use the **M**ath,**C**alculate command to cause the table to recalculate and display the correct values for formulas. See "Calculating Math in a Table," for more information.

The following examples use the same example table developed earlier. Cells A1 and B1 are used to hold the key values; cell C1 holds the formula A1*B1.

12	2	24.00

(12 * 2 = 24)

Reg $12, On Sale $5	2	250.00

(125 * 2 = 250)

12 15	2	30.00

(15 * 2 = 30)

12	2	??

(Cell A1 has been formatted as text.)

Entering Formulas into Table Cells

Formulas may contain cell references, numbers, and mathematical operators. It is generally a good idea, however, to keep number in their own cells and refer to those cells in the formula, rather than include the numbers directly in the formula.

The cell references in a formula do not necessarily need to reference cells containing key values. They may instead reference cells in which other formulas are entered. When such a reference is made, the calculated value of the cell being referenced will be the value used by the referencing cell. For instance:

Item	Qty	Price	Total	(Discount)	Invoice
10857-X	16	2.50	40.00	.15	34.00
	16	*2.50*	*B2*C2*	*.15*	*D2−(D2*E2)*

In the previous example, both numbers and formulas are entered into the second row. Cells B2, C2 and E2 all hold numbers (key values). Cell D2 holds a formula that is used to multiply Quantity by Price to produce a Total amount. Cell F2, however, references the Total amount (a calculated value) and the Discount amount (a key value) to produce an Invoice amount, or final price.

Mathematical Operators

The operators used to perform mathematical calculations in the table are:

+	Addition
−	Subtraction
*	Multiplication
/	Division

When two or more operators are included in a formula, WordPerfect evaluates the formula from left to right. This order can be changed by placing operations inside of parentheses, which will cause them to be evaluated first.

Math Functions Other options available with the Table Edit menu's **Math** command are **4**+, **5** =, and **6**∗, which are used to enter math functions into a table.* A function can be thought of as a special type of formula that may be entered into a cell.

The three math functions perform the following calculations:

+	Subtotal	Adds all values (key and calculated) in the same column up to the last previous Subtotal.
=	Total	Adds all Subtotals in the same column up to the last previous total.
∗	Grand Total	Adds all Totals in the same column up to the last previous Grand Total.

To enter a math function into a table cell, first move the edit cursor to the cell and type of **Math** command, and then select the function that you desire. The following table provides an example of how such functions may be used:

Category 1	Group 1	Item 1	100.00	
		Item 2	200.00	
		Subtotal	300.00	(+)
	Group 2	Item 1	300.00	
		Item 2	400.00	
		Subtotal	700.00	(+)
		Total	1,000.00	(=)
Category 2	Group 1	Item 1	50.00	
		Item 2	150.00	
		Subtotal	200.00	(+)
	Group 2	Item 1	250.00	
		Item 2	350.00	
		Subtotal	600.00	(+)
		Total	800.00	(=)
		Grand Total	1,800.00	(∗)

One way to erase a function from a cell is to use the Table Edit mode's **Ctrl-F4** (Move),**B**lock,**C**opy command to copy a blank cell to the cell where an undesired function occurs.

*It in important to note that the characters + and ∗, when they are entered into a cell using the Math command, have entirely different meanings than the mathematical operators + and ∗, which must be entered from the keyboard.

Copying Formulas

The Table Edit menu's **M**ath command also includes the option **3** Co**p**y Formula, which is specifically designed for copying a single formula into several cells in a table. The Copy Formula command is most useful in situations similar to the following:

Item	Qty	Price	Total
10857-X	16	2.50	40.00
10557-N	8	1.10	
10834-N	10	1.15	
10330-Y	3	6.00	
10325-R	7	2.75	
10778-X	5	3.30	

*B2*C2*

In the table above, columns B and C contain key values, and cell D2 contains a formula that multiplies the contents of cell B2 by the contents of cell C2. To complete the table, the user may continue to enter formulas into the cells of column D, making sure that each formula references the two adjacent cells to the left. The other alternative is to copy the formulas into the remaining cells using the commands of the Table Edit menu. When formulas are copied with the Table Edit mode's **Ctrl-F4** (Move) command or **M**ath,Co**p**y Formula command, the formulas are copied in what is called a *relative* fashion.

Perhaps the easiest way to understand what relative means when copying formulas in a table is to consider a formula as being a positionally dependent statement. That is, instead of thinking of the formula here as saying "the contents of cell B2 times the contents of the cell C2," think of the formula as saying "the contents of the cell that is two cells to the left, times the contents of the cell that is one cell to the left." It is with respect to this positional nature that WordPerfect will copy formulas.

To copy a formula into one or more cells in a table, move the edit cursor to the cell in which the formula is entered, and then type the **M**ath,Co**p**y Formula command. WordPerfect will then present the menu, "Copy Formula To: **1** **C**ell; **2** **D**own; **3** **R**ight." To copy the formula to a single cell, type **1** or **C** for **C**ell, and then move the edit cursor to the cell into which you want the formula copied and type ↵. To copy the formula into two or more cells directly below or to the right of the original formula, type **2** **D**own or **3** **R**ight, then enter the number of cells into which you want the formula copied.

For example, to complete the table shown above, the edit cursor is moved to cell D2, and then the **M**ath,Co**p**y Formula,**D**own command is typed. The number of cells into which copies of the formula are to be placed is then entered as 5. After the commands are executed, the table would appear as shown in the following.

Item	Qty	Price	Total	
10857-X	16	2.50	40.00	*B2*C2*
10557-N	8	1.10	8.80	*B3*C3*
10834-N	10	1.15	11.50	*B4*C4*
10330-Y	3	6.00	18.00	*B5*C5*
10325-R	7	2.75	19.25	*B6*C6*
10778-X	5	3.30	16.50	*B7*C7*

Calculating Math in a Table

The final option of the **M**ath command to be discussed here is **1 C**alculate. The command is an important one since formulas do not automatically recalculate their values when changes are made to the key values in the table. Furthermore, WordPerfect does not indicate that a table needs to be recalculated in order to display correct values. Therefore, it is important to remember to calculate any math areas in the table before printing the document. To calculate formulas in a table, type **M**ath,**C**alculate while in the Table Edit mode.

Alt-F7 (Columns/Table),**M**ath

WordPerfect provides a math feature for doing automatic calculations within a document. In most cases, you will find that the **Alt-F7** (Columns/Table),**T**ables command provides an easier method for creating an area within a document where math calculations are performed.

There are several steps involved in preparing a document to include math calculations. When the steps are completed, the document will include a portion of text that has been structured for doing math calculations. The structured portion of text may be represented as:

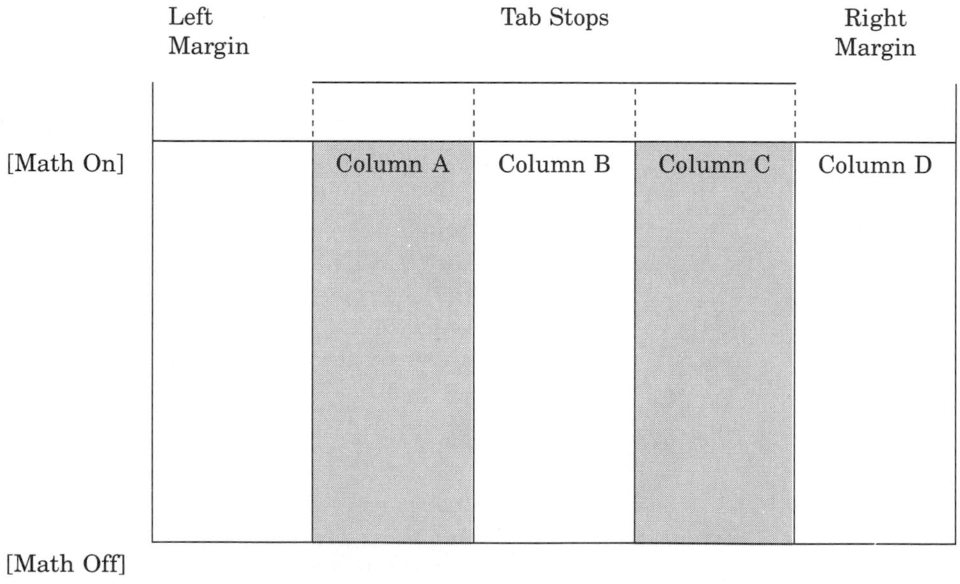

Left Margin | Tab Stops | Right Margin

[Math On] | Column A | Column B | Column C | Column D

[Math Off]

The area of a document defined for math operations is set apart with [Math On] and [Math Off] codes imbedded into the text. Within the math area, various columns are defined by the current tab stops (see **Shift-F8** (Format),**L**ine,**T**ab Set for information on setting tab stops).

The area between the left margin and the first tab stop to the right of the left margin may be used to enter text. The columns labeled A, B, C, and so on, may be defined for one of four different data types. If you want the column to contain Subtotals, Totals, and Grand Totals, you specify the column to be Numeric. Numeric is the default definition of all columns. If you want the column to contain text, you specify the column to be Text. If you want the column to display totals obtained from the column to the immediate left, you specify the column to be Total. Finally, if you want the column to display the results of formulas referring to values obtained from other columns, you specify the column to be Calculation.

Steps in Creating a Math Area

There are five basic steps in creating a math area within a document.

1. Set the appropriate tab stops.
2. Define the columns for math data type.
3. Turn Math On and Math Off for the math area.
4. Enter the math data.
5. Calculate.

The following discusses the various Math commands in conjunction with other steps required to create a math area in a document.

Set the Tab Stops

The first step in creating a math area within a document is to set tab stops for the math portion that coincide with the planned format. Note that a [Tab Set:] code will be imbedded in the text at the current cursor location and will affect only the text following it.

Define the Columns — Code = [Math Def]

To define the columns for the type of math data they will be holding, the **Alt-F7** (Columns/Table),**M**ath,**D**efine command is used. When the **D**efine command is executed, the screen appears as follows:

```
Math Definition             Use arrow keys to position cursor

Columns                     A B C D E F G H I J K L M N O P Q R S T U V W X

Type                        2 2 2 2 2 2 2 2 2 2 2 2 2 2 2 2 2 2 2 2 2 2 2 2

Negative Numbers            ( ( ( ( ( ( ( ( ( ( ( ( ( ( ( ( ( ( ( ( ( ( ( (

Number of Digits to         2 2 2 2 2 2 2 2 2 2 2 2 2 2 2 2 2 2 2 2 2 2 2 2
  the Right (0-4)

Calculation   1
  Formulas    2
              3
              4

Type of Column:
      0 = Calculation    1 = Text     2 = Numeric    3 = Total

Negative Numbers
      ( = Parentheses (50.00)        - = Minus Sign  -50.00


Press Exit when done
```

The various columns (A through X) are displayed at the top of the screen. Column A corresponds to the first tab stop, column B to the second, and so on. Beneath each column letter are three specifications that can be changed for the column by using the Math Definition screen: the column type, how negative numbers will be displayed (in parentheses or with negative signs), and how many digits will be displayed to the right of the decimal.

Initially, all columns are set to Numeric type, with negatives in parentheses, and a display of two decimal places. The following briefly discusses the different column types available and the operations associated with them.

(1) Text Defining a column as Text allows you to enter labels, headings, descriptions, and so on, into the column. The area from the left margin to the first tab stop is always Text in nature. Columns after the first tab stop should be defined for text if they are to contain text.

(2) Numeric Columns defined as Numeric are designed to contain numbers and WordPerfect operators for subtotals, extra subtotals, totals, extra totals, and grand totals. The following describes the operators used by WordPerfect and the order in which they should appear within a column.

Order	Operator	Meaning
1st	+	Subtotal (totals the numbers up to the last subtotal above it)
2nd	t	Extra subtotal (used for a single entry subtotal)
3rd	=	Total (totals the subtotals up to the last total above it)
4th	T	Extra total (used for a single entry total)
5th	*	Grand total (totals the totals up to the last grand total above it)

A sixth operator, N, may be used in conjunction with the other operators listed to produce a negative subtotal. For example, the operator N+ will produce a Subtotal that will be subtracted, rather than added, in a subsequent Total or Grand total.

(3) Total Columns defined as Total are most often used to display totals obtained from the column to the immediate left. The operators used in Total columns are the same as those used in Numeric columns.

It is important to note that subtotals, totals, and grand totals in a Total column will obtain their displayed values from both the column to the left and from the same column. That is, a Total (=) entered into a Total column will display the sum amount for all subtotals occurring above it in both the Total column and in the column to the left.

(0) Calculation A column defined as Calculation may be used to enter formulas into the document. A maximum of four columns may be defined as Calculation in nature. One formula may be entered into a Calculation column. The formula then is used to compute values from numbers found across the rows in the math area. When you tab the cursor to a Calculation column, WordPerfect displays an ! (exclamation point) at the cursor location. The ! indicates that the formula will be used to compute a value for that row (line).

You enter a Calculation formula into the Math Definition screen at the time you specify the column to be Calculation type. An example of a formula designed to display 20 percent of the value found on the same line in the A column would be ".2*A." Totals across rows in the A, B, and C columns could be obtained with the formula "A+B+C."

All formulas are evaluated from left to right (there is no operator precedence), and nested parentheses are not allowed.

Four WordPerfect specific operators are available; however, they must be used independently of one another and other formulas. The operators are:

+	Add numbers in the Numeric columns
+/	Average numbers in the Numeric columns
=	Add numbers in the Total columns
= /	Average numbers in the Total columns

Turn Math On and Math Off — Codes = [Math On] [Math Off]

The next step in creating a math area in the document is to insert a [Math On] code at the top of the area and a [Math Off] code at the bottom of the area.

To insert a [Math On] code into the document, move the cursor to the top of the math area and type **Alt-F7,3,1** (Columns/Table),**Math,On**. Executing the **Math,On** command inserts a [Math On] code into the document. When the cursor is moved past a [Math On] code, the message "Math" appears on the status line. To insert a [Math Off] code into the document, move the cursor to the bottom of the math area and type **Alt-F7,3,2** (Columns/Table),**Math,Off**.

Enter the Math Data

The next step involves entering the text and math data for the math area. To do so you enter text into the columns defined as text and use the tab key to move the cursor to the appropriate places in other type columns to enter numbers and appropriate WordPerfect operators. A typical math portion having one Numeric column and using the area between the left margin and first tab stop for labels might appear as:

```
April 1991
                       Sales
Purchases
   Item A               100.00
   Item B               200.00
   Item C               300.00
      Subtotal               +

   Item 1                50.00
   Item 2               100.00
   Item 3               150.00
      Subtotal               +

   Other               t200.00

Returns
   Item A                10.00
   Item B                20.00
   Item C                30.00
      Subtotal              N+

Month End Total              =

Math                                        Doc 1 Pg 1 Ln 1" Pos 1"
```

As you enter the math data, numbers will align flush right to their tab stops, and the period (.) key will be used for alignment. Numbers that overlap into the previous column will cause incorrect calculations.

Calculate the Math Area

The final step in creating a math document is to calculate the math area. To calculate a math area in a document, type **Alt-F7,3,4** (Columns/Table), **M**ath,**C**alculate. In the example, the calculated portion of the document would appear as follows.

```
April 1991
                    Sales
Purchases
   Item A            100.00
   Item B            200.00
   Item C            300.00
      Subtotal       600.00+

   Item 1             50.00
   Item 2            100.00
   Item 3            150.00
      Subtotal       300.00+

   Other            t200.00

Returns
   Item A             10.00
   Item B             20.00
   Item C             30.00
      Subtotal        60.00N+

Month End Total    1,040.00=

Math                                                  Doc 1 Pg 1 Ln 1" Pos 1"
```

Although the screen displays the WordPerfect math operators next to the calculated values, they will not be printed.

Once a math portion of a document has been created, you may move the cursor to the area and change the numbers within it. Care must be taken to maintain the original alignment of numbers to their tab stops. It is generally easier to delete a number and its preceding alignment codes with the Backspace key and then retab to the column and enter a new number. You then must use the **Alt-F7** (Columns/Table),**M**ath,**C**alculate command to recalculate the area for the new values.

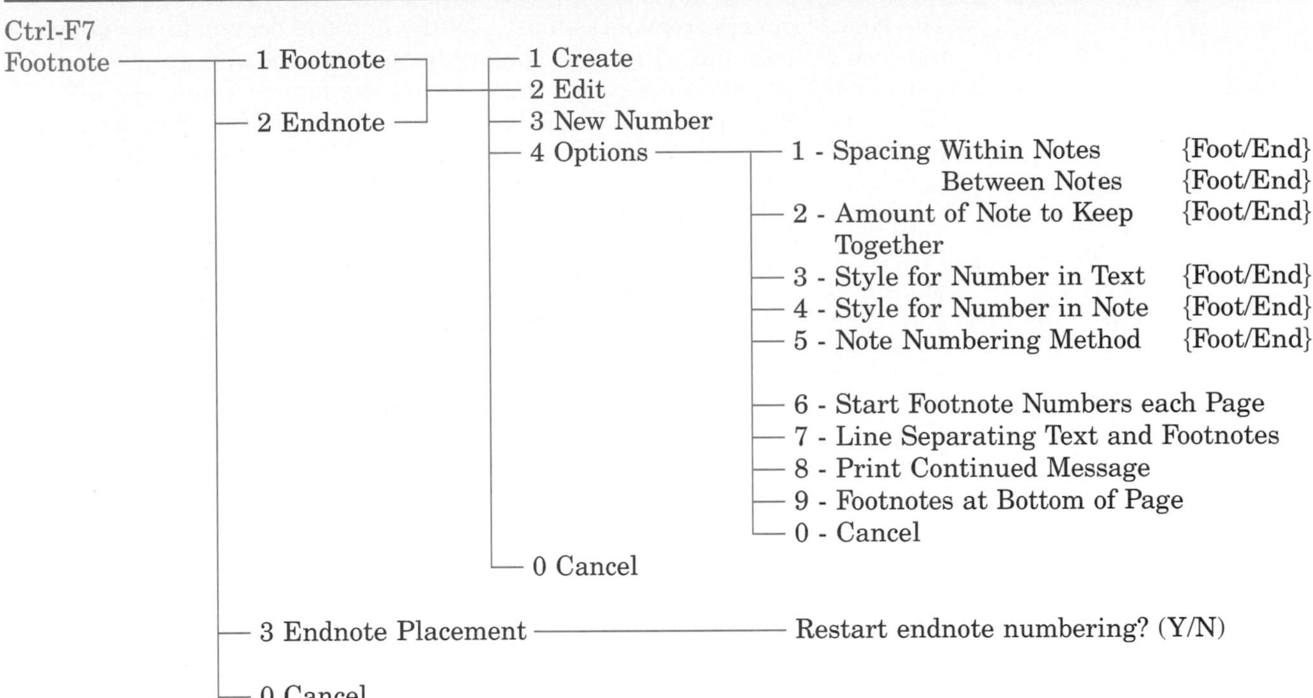

CTRL-F7 FOOTNOTE

WordPerfect provides for footnotes and endnotes to be included in a document in a variety of standard formats. The numbering of the notes is maintained automatically by WordPerfect.

Footnotes and Endnotes

The procedure for creating footnotes or endnotes is straightforward. Move the cursor to the word, sentence, or paragraph that the footnote will reference, and then where you want the note number to appear in the text. Then type **Ctrl-F7** (Footnote) and select either the **F**ootnote or **E**ndnote command from the menu. Next, enter the note text on a blank screen provided by the command. When finished, you type **F7** (Exit) and a note number appears on the document screen at the cursor position.

Footnotes will be printed at the bottom of the page containing the text they reference, while endnotes will be printed on pages where endnote placement codes occur in the document. Endnotes are generated with the **Alt-F5** (Mark Text),**G**enerate,**G**enerate Tables,Indexes,CrossReferences, etc. command before they may be printed. **Alt-F3** (Reveal Codes) may be used to view the first 50 characters of a note imbedded in a document.

Create

Code = [Footnote:n;[Note Num]*text*]
[Endnote:n;[Note Num]*text*]

The **C**reate command is used to create footnotes and endnotes. Move the cursor to the place where the note number is to appear and type **Ctrl-F7,1,1** or **2,1** (Footnote),**F**ootnote,**C**reate or **E**ndnote,**C**reate. Next, enter the text for the footnote on the blank screen provided by the command, and then type **F7** (Exit).

Edit

The **E**dit command is used to edit existing footnotes or endnotes. Type **Ctrl-F7,1,2** or **2,2** (Footnote),**F**ootnote,**E**dit or **E**ndnote,**E**dit, and then enter the number of the note you want to edit. Type **F7** (Exit) when done.

New Number Code = [New Ftn Num:*n*] [New End Num:*n*]

The **N**ew Number command is most useful when one document is divided into two or more files. To resume proper footnote or endnote numbering in the next file, move the cursor to the left of the first note number in the file and type **Ctrl-F7,1,3** or **2,3** (Footnote),**F**ootnote,**N**ew Number or **E**ndnote,**N**ew Number. Then, enter the appropriate starting number for the footnotes or endnotes in the file. All subsequent notes in the file will be automatically renumbered.

Options Code = [Ftn Opt] [End Opt]

The **O**ptions command provides several formatting styles for footnotes and endnotes. When a default option setting is changed with the **O**ptions command, a [Ftn Opt] or [End Opt] code is inserted into the text at the cursor location. The formatting change then affects the footnotes or endnotes in the subsequent text. The **O**ptions menu screen differs slightly for footnotes and endnotes. The first five options discussed here may be selected for footnotes and/or endnotes; the remaining four options are for footnotes only.

The following briefly describes of the format styles and their default values.

Spacing Within Notes/Between Notes

Default—1 line/0.167″ (inches, normally 1 line)
Sets the line spacing for text within footnotes or endnotes at 1, 1.5, 2 lines, and so forth, and/or the spacing between separate footnotes or endnotes. Enter the "Between Notes" number as the number of inches that you desire between notes.

Amount of Note to Keep Together

Default—0.5″ (normally 3 lines)
Forces WordPerfect to keep *n* inches of footnote and/or endnote text within a note together if the note needs to be split onto two pages.

Style for Number in Text

Default— [SUPRSCPT][Note Num][suprscpt]
You may redefine the display of a number by including characters, or any of the (Font),**S**ize or **A**ppearance attributes (see **Ctrl-F8** (Font)). The codes necessary for the new display are obtained from typing command keys. For example, to add parentheses to the footnote numbers appearing in the text, you would type **Ctrl-F7,1,4** (Footnote),**F**ootnote,**O**ptions, and type **3** or **T** (Style for Number in **T**ext).

The message "Replace with: [SUPRSCPT][Note Num][suprscpt]" will appear on the screen. You then type **Ctrl-F8,1,1**,(,**Ctrl-F7,1,2**,),**Ctrl-F8,1,1**↵, which reads: **S**ize,Su**p**erscript,Left parenthesis,**F**ootnote,Number **C**ode,Right parenthesis,**S**ize,Su**p**erscript(end). The status line will display

[SUPRSCPT]([Note Num])[suprscpt]

and the number appearing in the text for a footnote will be printed as $^{(2)}$.

Style for Number in Note

Default— [SUPRSCPT][Note Num][suprscpt](five preceding spaces)
This command is the same as Style for Number in **T**ext, except it affects the display of the number in the note itself rather than how the number appears in the text.

Note Numbering Method
Default—Numbers
Options include the following.

1 Numbers	(1, 2, 3, etc.)
2 Letters	(a, b, c, etc.)
3 Characters	(*, **, ***, etc.)

The next four commands appear only on the (Footnote),**O**ptions screen.

Start Footnote Number each Page
Default—No
Typing Y causes footnote numbers to start at 1, a, or * for each page.

Line Separating Text and Footnotes
Default—2-inch Line
Before printing footnotes on a page, WordPerfect prints a solid line to separate them from the text. This option is used to define what type of line will be printed. The following choices are available.

1 No Line
2 2-inch Line
3 Margin to Margin

Print Continued Message
Default—No
Typing Y causes the message "(Continued)" to be printed if the footnote is broken up by a soft page break.

Footnotes at Bottom of Page
Default—Yes
Typing N causes footnotes to immediately follow the text on a page.

Endnote **P**lacement
Code =
[Endnote Placement]

The Endnote **P**lacement command inserts a code into the text that will cause WordPerfect to print the endnotes at the code's location. While placing the code, the message "Restart endnote numbering? No (Yes)" will appear. To restart numbering after the placement code, type Y. WordPerfect will place the [Endnote Placement] code, followed by a Hard Page [HPg] code, into the text. The following message will appear on the screen.

> Endnote Placement
> It is not known how much space endnotes will occupy here.
> Generate to determine.

= =

To determine the amount of space the endnotes will occupy type **Alt-F5,6,5** (Mark Text),**G**enerate,**G**enerate Tables, Indexes, Cross-References, etc. The endnote placement message will indicate the area to be occupied by endnotes when the document is printed.

F8
Underline ——— {Places Underline Start Code [UND]} — <enter text> ——— Underline key {Places Underline Stop Code [und]}

F8 UNDERLINE
CODE = [UND]
underlined text
[und]

The Underline command is used to underline printed text. Typing **F8** (Underline) inserts [UND] and [und] codes into the text. Text typed afterwards is entered between the codes and is displayed on the screen as underlined. To stop underlining text, type **F8** (Underline) again.

To double underline text, see **Ctrl-F8,2** (Font),**A**ppearance. To stop underlining spaces or to underline tabs, see **Shift-F8,4**(Format),**O**ther.

Block/Underline

To underline a block of text, block the text, and then type **F8** (Underline).

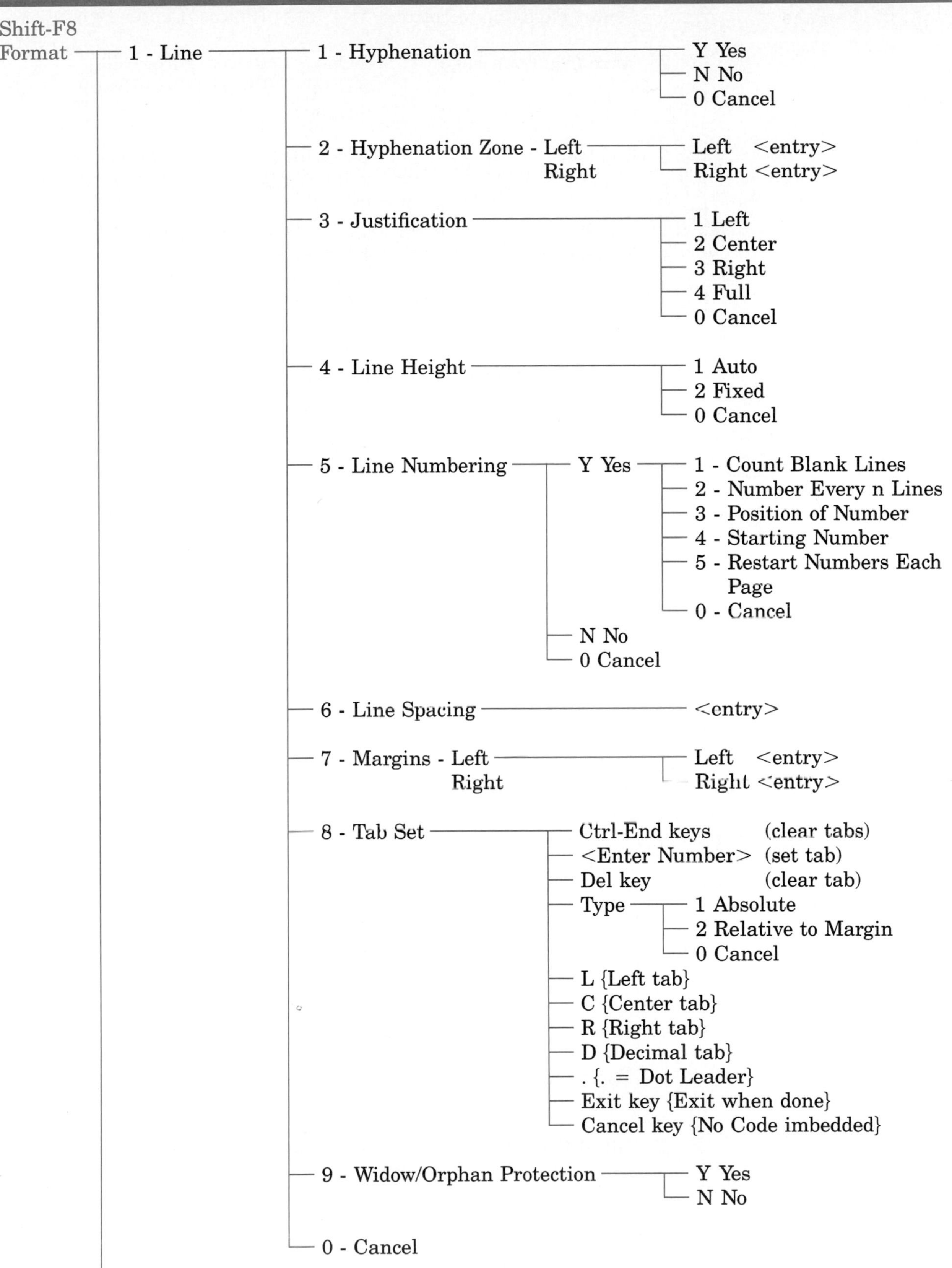
Shift-F8
Format
1 - Line
1 - Hyphenation
Y Yes
N No
0 Cancel
2 - Hyphenation Zone - Left
Right
Left <entry>
Right <entry>
3 - Justification
1 Left
2 Center
3 Right
4 Full
0 Cancel
4 - Line Height
1 Auto
2 Fixed
0 Cancel
5 - Line Numbering
Y Yes
1 - Count Blank Lines
2 - Number Every n Lines
3 - Position of Number
4 - Starting Number
5 - Restart Numbers Each Page
0 - Cancel
N No
0 Cancel
6 - Line Spacing
<entry>
7 - Margins - Left
Right
Left <entry>
Right <entry>
8 - Tab Set
Ctrl-End keys (clear tabs)
<Enter Number> (set tab)
Del key (clear tab)
Type
1 Absolute
2 Relative to Margin
0 Cancel
L {Left tab}
C {Center tab}
R {Right tab}
D {Decimal tab}
. {. = Dot Leader}
Exit key {Exit when done}
Cancel key {No Code imbedded}
9 - Widow/Orphan Protection
Y Yes
N No
0 - Cancel

CONTINUED

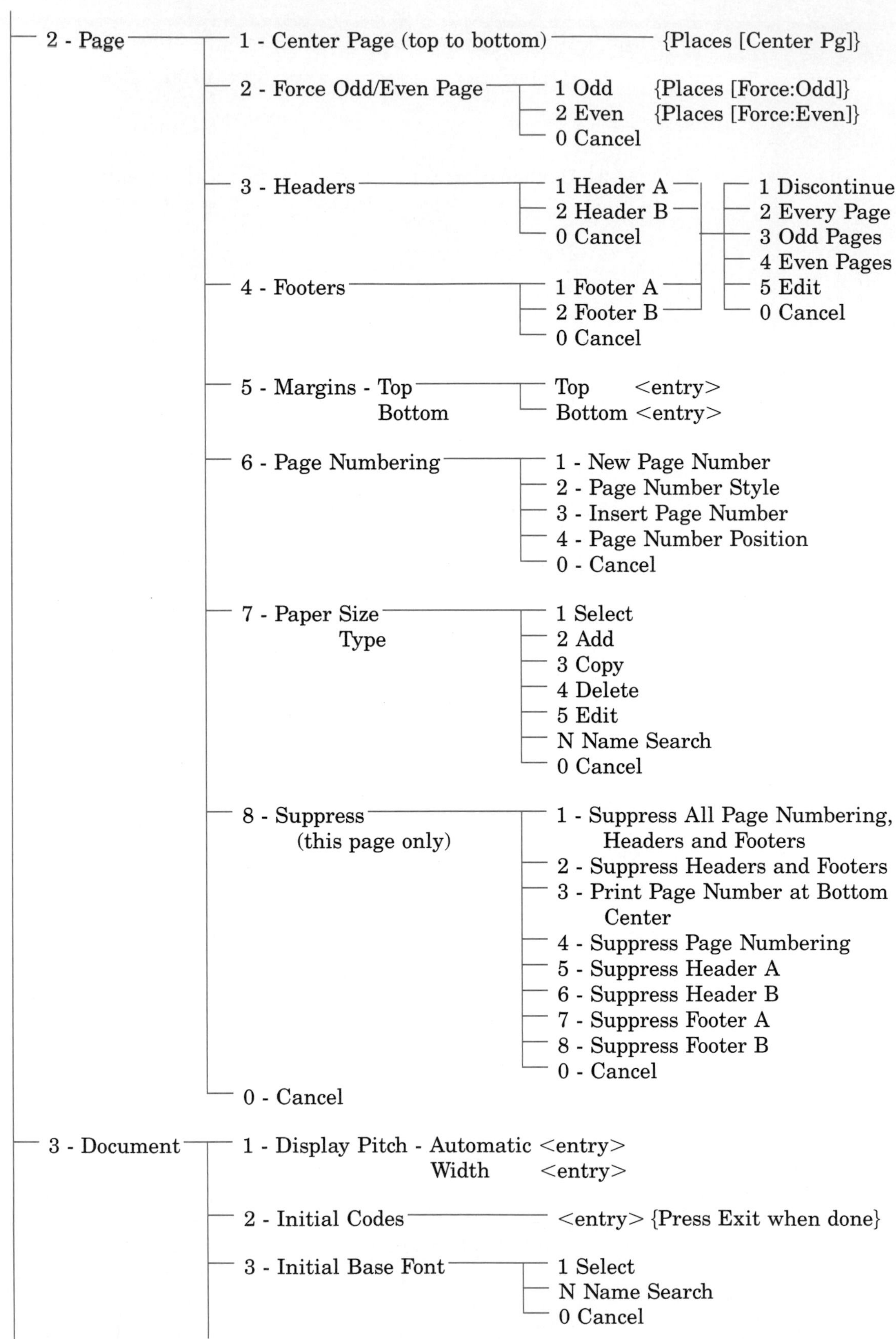
2 - Page
1 - Center Page (top to bottom)
{Places [Center Pg]}
2 - Force Odd/Even Page
1 Odd {Places [Force:Odd]}
2 Even {Places [Force:Even]}
0 Cancel
3 - Headers
1 Header A
2 Header B
0 Cancel
1 Discontinue
2 Every Page
3 Odd Pages
4 Even Pages
5 Edit
0 Cancel
4 - Footers
1 Footer A
2 Footer B
0 Cancel
5 - Margins - Top
Bottom
Top <entry>
Bottom <entry>
6 - Page Numbering
1 - New Page Number
2 - Page Number Style
3 - Insert Page Number
4 - Page Number Position
0 - Cancel
7 - Paper Size
Type
1 Select
2 Add
3 Copy
4 Delete
5 Edit
N Name Search
0 Cancel
8 - Suppress
(this page only)
1 - Suppress All Page Numbering, Headers and Footers
2 - Suppress Headers and Footers
3 - Print Page Number at Bottom Center
4 - Suppress Page Numbering
5 - Suppress Header A
6 - Suppress Header B
7 - Suppress Footer A
8 - Suppress Footer B
0 - Cancel
0 - Cancel
3 - Document
1 - Display Pitch - Automatic <entry>
Width <entry>
2 - Initial Codes
<entry> {Press Exit when done}
3 - Initial Base Font
1 Select
N Name Search
0 Cancel

CONTINUED

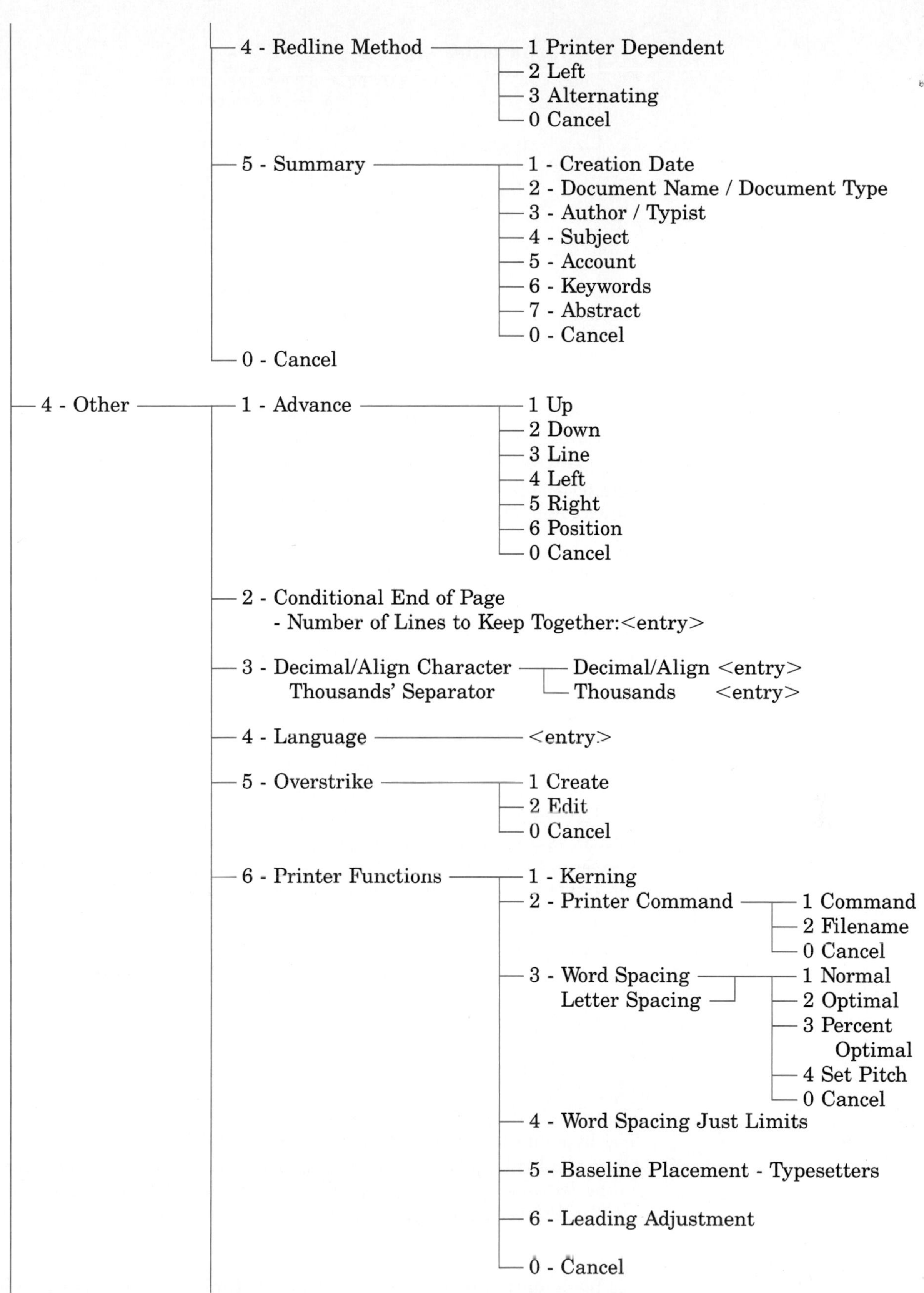

4 - Redline Method
1 Printer Dependent
2 Left
3 Alternating
0 Cancel
5 - Summary
1 - Creation Date
2 - Document Name / Document Type
3 - Author / Typist
4 - Subject
5 - Account
6 - Keywords
7 - Abstract
0 - Cancel
0 - Cancel
4 - Other
1 - Advance
1 Up
2 Down
3 Line
4 Left
5 Right
6 Position
0 Cancel
2 - Conditional End of Page
- Number of Lines to Keep Together:<entry>
3 - Decimal/Align Character
Thousands' Separator
Decimal/Align <entry>
Thousands <entry>
4 - Language
<entry>
5 - Overstrike
1 Create
2 Edit
0 Cancel
6 - Printer Functions
1 - Kerning
2 - Printer Command
1 Command
2 Filename
0 Cancel
3 - Word Spacing
Letter Spacing
1 Normal
2 Optimal
3 Percent Optimal
4 Set Pitch
0 Cancel
4 - Word Spacing Just Limits
5 - Baseline Placement - Typesetters
6 - Leading Adjustment
0 - Cancel

CONTINUED

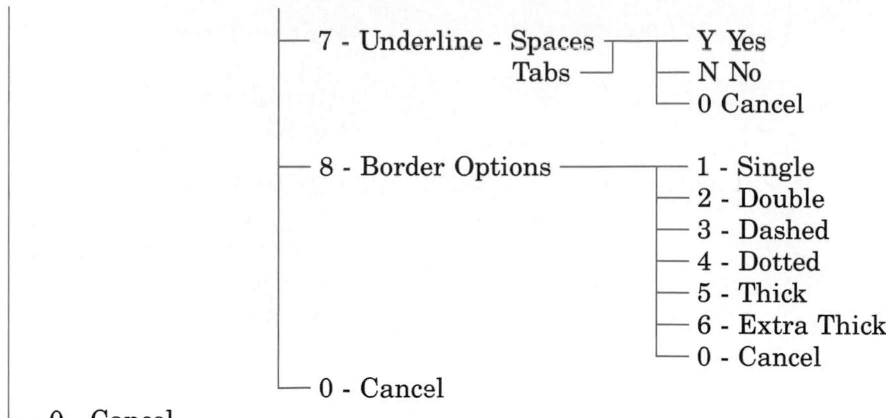

SHIFT-F8 FORMAT

The **Shift-F8** (Format) command has a rather extensive command tree associated with it. In general, the Format commands are designed to control the appearance of the finished document. The various Format commands are categorized by the relative size of document text they are designed to affect: **L**ine, **P**age, **D**ocument, and **O**ther.

Line

The **Shift-F8** (Format),**L**ine commands affect the appearance and/or WordPerfect's treatment of the lines of text within a document. The following discusses the default values and uses for each **Shift-F8,1** (Format),**L**ine command.

Hyphenation — Code = [Hyph On] [Hyph Off]

Default—No
By default, WordPerfect will not pause to hyphenate words when it word wraps a sentence. If this feature is turned on by specifying Yes with this command, WordPerfect will hyphenate words based on three considerations: the Hyphenation Zone (see **Shift-F8** (Format),**L**ine,Hyphenation **Z**one), the Hyphenation Dictionary (which contains a set of rules for hyphenating words), and the Hyphenation prompt (which can be changed with the **Shift-F1** (Setup) command). See the WordPerfect manual or Help screens for more information on the Hyphenation Dictionary and Hyphenation prompt.

Hyphens inserted into a word by the Hyphenation feature are soft hyphens, hyphens that will only be displayed or printed when they occur at the end of a line. Undisplayed soft hyphens may be viewed with the (Reveal Codes) command. You may enter soft hyphens into a document without the Hyphenation feature by typing Ctrl-*hyphen* (press and hold the Ctrl key and then type the hyphen (-) key.)

Hyphenation **Z**one — Code = [HZone:]

Default—Left = 10%, Right = 4%
The hyphenation zone is what determines which words will be hyphenated when the hyphenation feature is on. The zone is an area measured in inches to the left and right of the current right margin. The default zone used by WordPerfect is 10% of the current line length (the distance between the left and right margins) to the left of the right margin, and 4% of the current line length to the right of the right margin. The setting causes the hyphenation feature to stop on words that begin at a position equal to or greater than 90% of the current line length and extend 4% or more of the current line length to the right of the right margin. You may use the Hyphenation **Z**one command to change the percentages.

Justification Code = [Just:*type*]

Default—Full

The **J**ustification command includes four different styles of line justification. The default is **F**ull, which justifies the printed text to both left and right margins. The other three options are **L**eft (justifies text to the left margin), **R**ight (justifies text to the right margin), and **C**enter (centers text between the left and right margins).

To view justified text on the screen, you must use the **Shift-F7,6** (Print),**V**iew Document command. The **L**ine,**J**ustification command imbeds a [Just:*type*] code into the document that affects all subsequent text in the document.

Line Height Code = [Ln Height:*nn*″] [Ln Height:Auto]

Default—Auto

The Line **H**eight command is used to change the number of lines printed in a vertical inch on the page. The two possible settings are **A**uto and **F**ixed. With **A**uto, WordPerfect automatically maintains the appropriate line height for the font in use (see **Ctrl-F8,1** (Font),**S**ize for more information on fonts). Specifying **F**ixed allows you to enter a fixed height in inches for the printed lines. However, specifying **F**ixed for any line height other than 0.17″ (six lines per inch) may cause problems with some printers. See **Shift-F8,1,6** (Format),**L**ine,Line **S**pacing for information on changing line spacing.

Line Numbering Code = [Ln Num:On] [Ln Num:Off]

Default—No (Off)

The Line **N**umbering command is used to automatically number each line in a document. Move the cursor to where you want line numbering to begin, and then type **Shift-F8,1,5,Y** (Format),**L**ine,Line **N**umbering,**Y**es. A small, self-explanatory menu concerning ways of numbering will be presented on the screen. To turn off the line numbering, move the cursor to the place where numbering is to end and type **Shift-F8,1,5,N** (Format),**L**ine,Line **N**umbering,**N**o.

Line Spacing Code = [Ln Spacing:*n.n*]

Default—1 (single spacing)

The Line **S**pacing command is used to set the spacing between lines in the document. When the command is executed, a [Ln Spacing:] code is inserted into the document. Line spacing then will stay in effect for the rest of the document or until another [Ln Spacing:] code is encountered.

Spacing may be set at line and half-line intervals. For example, 2 specifies double spacing and 1.5 specifies $1\frac{1}{2}$ lines between text lines. Finer adjustments may be made by entering values such as 1.1, 1.05, etc.; however, not all printers are able to support the finer adjustments. The normal editing screen will display the nearest whole number of line spaces for the current line spacing.

Margins Left/Right Code = [L/R Mar:*n.nn*″,*n.nn*″]

Default—Left = 1″, Right = 1″

The **M**argins command is used to set the left and right margins within a document. When the **M**argins command is executed, a [L/R Mar:] code is inserted into the document, and the margins will stay in effect for the rest of the document or until another [L/R Mar:] code is encountered. To change margins, type **Shift-F8,1,7** (Format),**L**ine,**M**argins, and then enter the new left and right margins in inches. (To set top/bottom page margins see **Shift-F8,2,5** (Format),**P**age,**M**argins.)

Tab Set   Code = [Tab Set:*type*:*stops*]

Default—Type = **R**elative, Stops = **L**eft every 0.5″

The **T**ab Set command is used to set tab stops within a document. When tab stops are set with the **T**ab Set command, a [Tab Set:] code is inserted into the text, and it stays in effect for the rest of the document or until another [Tab Set:] code is encountered. When the **T**ab Set command is executed, the following lines appear at the bottom of the screen:

```
L....L....L....L....L....L....L....L....L....L....L....L....L....L....L....L...
!    ^    !    ^    !    ^    !    ^    !    ^    !    ^    !    ^    !    ^
0"        +1"       +2"       +3"       +4"       +5"       +6"       +7"
Delete EOL (clear tabs); Enter Number (set tab); Del (clear tab);
Type; Left; Center; Right; Decimal; .= Dot Leader; Press Exit when done.
```

The top line indicates the tab position of the current tab stops. By default, WordPerfect automatically sets Left tabs every ½ inch. A cursor will be displayed on the line. The cursor may be moved left and right with the cursor control keys.

Type

The first option of the **T**ab Set command is **T**ype. The two types of tab stops that may be set are **A**bsolute and **R**elative to Margin. If **A**bsolute is selected, the tab stops are set as fixed measurements (in inches) from the left edge of the page and will not change their position when the left margin is changed. When **R**elative to Margin (the default setting) is selected, the tab stops are set as fixed measurements (in inches) from the left margin. Relative tab stops will adjust their positions on the page accordingly to changes in the left margin.

Left—**C**enter—**R**ight—**D**ecimal—.Dot Leader

In total, seven different types of tab stops may be specified with the **T**ab Set command. Each type affects the manner in which data will be oriented to the tab stop after the Tab key is used to move the cursor there. The type also affects the type of Tab code that is imbedded into the document. The following describes the tab stop types and provides examples of how they affect text.

	Tab Stop
L Left justify	Left Justify
C Center	Center text
R Right justify	Right Justify
D Decimal align	123.00
Left justify w/dot leader	............................Left w/leader
Right justify w/dot leader	...........Right w/leader
Decimal align w/dot leader	....123.00

Deleting Tab Stops To delete an existing tab stop, you may move the cursor to the tab position and type the Del key. To delete all tab stops to the right of the cursor, you may type Ctrl-End.

Setting Tab Stops There are two ways in which you may set new tab stops. One is to enter the position number for the tab stop. When a number is typed and entered, WordPerfect automatically puts an L (Left tab stop) at the position number. You also may set multiple tab stops in this way by typing the first tab stop position, a comma, and then the interval between tab stops that you desire. For instance, typing || 1,0.5↵ || will set Left tabs, beginning at position 1″, and occuring every ½ inch thereafter.

The other method of setting tab stops is to move the cursor to the appropriate place on the tab line and enter the letter of the type of tab stop you want to occur there. If you want the tab stop to have a preceding dot leader, you type the letter and then a period (.).

When finished specifying tab stops, you type **F7** (Exit) to quit the **T**ab Set command.

Widow/Orphan Protection Code = [W/O On] [W/O Off]

Default—No (Off)
A widow is the last line of a paragraph appearing on the first line of a page, and an orphan is the first line of a paragraph appearing on the last line of a page. To prevent such last and first lines from being separated from their paragraphs, type **Shift-F8,1,9,Y** (Format),**L**ine,**W**idow/Orphan Protection,**Y**es. A [W/O On] code will be inserted at the cursor location, and the following text will be protected against widows and orphans. To turn off widow/orphan protection, move the cursor to where protection is to end and type **Shift-F8,1,9,N** (Format),**L**ine,**W**idow/Orphan Protection,**N**o.

Page

The **Shift-F8** (Format),**P**age commands affect the appearance of and/or WordPerfect's treatment of the pages within a document. The following discusses the default values (if any) and uses for each **Shift-F8,2** (Format),**P**age command.

Center Page (top to bottom) Code = [Center Pg]

Default—No
The Center Page command is used to vertically center a page of text. Move the cursor to the top of the page (before any imbedded codes) and type **Shift-F8,2,1,Y** (Format),**P**age,**C**enter **P**age,**Y**es.

Force Odd/Even Page Code = [Force:Odd] [Force:Even]

The F**o**rce Odd/Even Page command forces the page number to be either odd or even. If the page number does not need to be changed, it will remain the same. If the page number needs to be changed, it will be increased by 1.

Headers and Footers Codes = [Header:*text*] and [Footer:*text*]

Headers or footers may be included in a document by using the **P**age,**H**eaders or **P**age,**F**ooters command. Up to two headers (A and B) and two footers (A and B) may be included on the pages in a document.

To create a header or footer, move the cursor to the beginning of the page and type **Shift-F8,2,3** or **4** (Format),**P**age,**H**eaders or **F**ooters. Continue by selecting the header or footer you want to create (A or B), and then select **2** Every **P**age, **3 O**dd Pages, or **4 E**ven Pages to determine on which pages the header or footer will be printed. An editing screen will then appear for you to enter the header or footer text. Most of WordPerfect's (Font) commands (underline, flush right, bold, etc.) are available when entering the text for a header or footer.

When finished, type **F7** (Exit) to save the data and return to the (Format),**P**age menu. A [Header:] or [Footer:] code will be inserted into the text where the header or footer is created.

Other options that appear after you have typed **Shift-F8** (Format),**P**age, **H**eaders or **F**ooters, then **A** or **B** are **1 D**iscontinue (to discontinue a previously defined header or footer) and **5 E**dit (to edit a previously defined header or footer). When you select **5 E**dit, WordPerfect will search backwards through the file for the most recent [Header:] or [Footer:] code of the type specified (A or B) and allow you to edit its text.

You may include a page number in a header or footer by typing Ctrl-B at the location within the header or footer where you want the page number to occur.

Margins Top/Bottom — Code = [T/B Mar:]

Default—Top = 1″, Bottom = 1″
The **P**age,**M**argins command is used to set the top and bottom page margins within a document. When the **M**argins command is executed, a [T/B Mar:] code is inserted into the document, causing the margins to stay in effect for the rest of the document or until another [T/B Mar:] code is encountered. To change margins, move the cursor to the top of the page and type **Shift-F8,2,5** (Format),**P**age,**M**argins. Next enter the new top and bottom margins in inches. (To set left/right margins, see the **Shift-F8,1,7** (Format),**L**ine,**M**argins command.)

Page Numbering

The Page Numbering command includes options for various formats of automatic page numbering. When the Page **N**umbering command is typed, a screen similar to the following appears:

```
Format: Page Numbering

     1 - New Page Number       1

     2 - Page Number Style     ^B

     3 - Insert Page Number

     4 - Page Number Position No page numbering
```

New Page Number — Code = [Pg Num:n]

The New Page Number command may be used to set a new beginning page number within a document. Move the cursor to the top of the page where new numbering is to begin, and then type **Shift-F8,2,6,1** (Format),**P**age,Page **N**umbering,**N**ew Page Number. Page numbers may be entered and subsequently printed as Arabic Numbers (1, 2, 3, . . .), lower case Roman Numerals (i, ii, iii, iv, . . .) or uppercase Roman Numerals (I, II, III, IV, . . .).

Page Number Style — Code = [Pg Num Style:]

Default—^B
The Page Number **S**tyle command may be used to customize the appearance of the page number. The ^ B character shown on the line next to the command is the control character that will generate the page number and must be present in the command's entry. You may, however, use the Page Number **S**tyle command to add text or other characters to the printed page

number. For example, in a paper concerned with the topic of word processing, you may want the pages numbered in the style "Word Processing/Page #1" (for page 1). The appropriate entry for such a style of page numbering would be || Word Processing/Page #^ B↵ ||.

Insert Page Number

Code = [Insert Pg Num:]

You may include a page's number anywhere on the page by moving the cursor to the desired location and typing Ctrl-B. The keystroke produces the control character ^ B, which is seen in the entry of the Page Number **S**tyle command. To include the page number and a style that has been specified with the page Number **S**tyle command into the document, move the cursor to the desired location on the page and type the **Shift-F8** (Format),**P**age,Page **N**umbering,**I**nsert Page Number command.

Page Number **P**osition

Code = [Pg Numbering:*placement*]

Default—No page numbering

The Page Number Position command may be used to begin or discontinue printed page numbering and to specify printing of page numbers in one of eight different page positions. The Page Number **P**osition command presents the following screen.

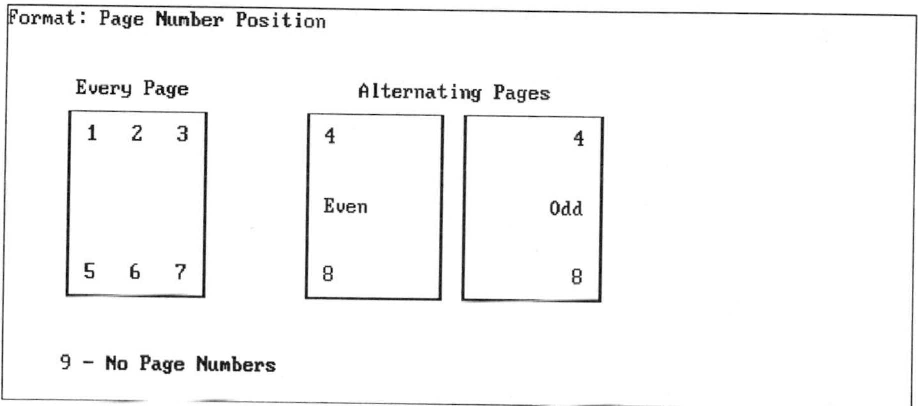

The page number placements include: (1) Top Left of every page; (2) Top Center of every page; (3) Top Right of every page; (4) Top Alternating left and right pages; (5) Bottom Left of every page; (6) Bottom Center of every page; (7) Bottom Right of every page; and (8) Bottom Alternating left and right pages. Option (9) **N**o Page Numbers may be used to discontinue printing of page numbers.

Paper **S**ize/Type

Code = [Paper Sz/Typ:]

Default—8.5″ x 11″ / Standard

This command may be used when using a printer that has more than one location for forms (different sizes of paper or orientations of text). The various forms that the printer supports are defined for WordPerfect using the **Shift-F7,S,3** (Print),**S**elect Printer,**E**dit command. For more information, see the WordPerfect manual or Help screens.

Suppress (this page only)

Code = [Suppress:]

The **S**uppress command is used to suppress various page format options for the current page. The command is self-explanatory.

Document

The **Shift-F8** (Format),**D**ocument commands affect the appearance and/or WordPerfect's treatment of the entire document. The following discusses the default values (if any) and uses for each **Shift-F8,3** (Format),**D**ocument command.

Display Pitch

Default—Automatic = Yes, Width = 0.1″
The **D**isplay Pitch command may be used to expand or contract the screen display widths of absolute measured characters such as tabs, indents, etc. The higher the Width setting, the less screen space is displayed for such characters.

Initial Codes

The Initial **C**odes command provides a method to override many of WordPerfect's default command settings for a document. The command presents a screen similar to the **Alt-F3** (Reveal Codes) screen. To change the default setting for a document, type **Shift-F8,3,2** (Format),**D**ocument,Initial **C**odes. When the Initial Codes screen is presented, you next type the keystrokes which would normally change a command's default setting. For example, to change the default line spacing from one to two (double spacing), you would type **Shift-F8,1,6,2** (Format),**L**ine,Line **S**pacing,2. A [Ln Spacing:2] code will appear in the bottom portion of the Initial **C**odes screen. You may continue to enter such codes into the Initial Codes screen until all of the default settings you desire are made. You then type **F7** (Exit) to properly exit the command.

The Initial **C**odes command does not place a visible code into the document; however, the Initial **C**odes settings are saved with the document. You may edit a document's initial codes by again executing the Initial **C**odes command and using the same editing keystrokes that are used in the (Reveal Codes) screen. (To change the initial codes for all documents, see **Shift-F1,5,4** (Setup),**I**nitial Settings,**I**nitial Codes.)

Initial Base Font

Most printers are capable of printing in more than one font. When the **Shift-F7,S,2** (Print),**S**elect Printer,**A**dditional Printers command is used, WordPerfect automatically selects one of the printer's fonts as the default font. You may use the Initial Base **F**ont command to change the default printer font for a document. See **Ctrl-F8,4** (Font),Base **F**ont for another method to change the default font for a document.

Redline Method

Default—Printer Dependent
The **R**edline Method command is used to select how redlined text is printed. The choices include **P**rinter Dependent (determined by WordPerfect's printer definition file), **L**eft (prints redline text with a horizontal bar printed in the left margin), and **A**lternating (prints redlined text with horizontal bars alternating between left and right margins for facing pages). See **Ctrl-F8,2,8** (Font),**A**ppearance,**R**edln for more information on redlined text.

Summary

WordPerfect provides a means for you to provide documentation for your documents. In other words, you are able to insert text into a document that will not be printed. Such internal documentation may be done through the **S**ummary command.

The command provides a screen for entry of the following information: Creation **D**ate, Document **N**ame and Type, Au**t**hor and Typist, **S**ubject, Acc**o**unt, and **K**eywords for use with the **F5** (List),**F**ind command. In addition, up to 780 characters of text may be included in the summary by using the **A**bstract command.

Other

The **Shift-F8** (Format),**O**ther commands are the final group of Format commands. The following discusses the default values (if any) and uses for each **Shift-F8,4** (Format),**O**ther command.

Advance — Code = [Adv:]

The **A**dvance command imbeds a code that causes the printer to adjust its printing position for the text following the code. The options of the **A**dvance command include **U**p, **D**own, L**i**ne, **L**eft, **R**ight, and **P**osition.

To cause all following characters to be printed above or below the normal line, use the **U**p or **D**own commands. To cause all following characters to be printed to the left or right of the normal position, use the **L**eft or **R**ight commands. The **U**p, **D**own, **L**eft, and **R**ight commands all require a relative position in inches to be entered. For example, to cause the following text to be printed one-half line higher than the preceding text, you would use the **U**p command and enter the distance as being .08 (assuming 6 lines per inch, .167″ per line). The L**i**ne and **P**osition commands require that an absolute position be entered, the same position you would see on the status line (Ln ″ or Pos ″) if you were to move the cursor there.

To readjust printing to the previous position, use the **A**dvance command to move in the opposite direction for the same distance.

NOTE: Many printers do not support the Advance feature.

Conditional End of Page — Code = [Cndl EOP:*n*]

The Conditional End of Page command is used to keep a certain number of lines in a document from being separated by a soft page break.

Move the cursor to the line above the first line in the document to be protected and type **Shift-F8,4,2** (Format),**O**ther,**C**onditional End of Page, and then enter the number of lines to protect.

Decimal/Align Character — Code = [Decml/Align Char:]

Default—. / ,
The **D**ecimal/Align Character command is used to change the character that WordPerfect uses to align text at tab stops. The default Align Character is the period (.). The command also is used to change the character that WordPerfect uses to separate the thousands used in numbers within a math portion of text. The default Thousands' separator is the comma (,).

Language — Code = [Lang:]

Default—US
The **L**anguage command is used to change the language used with the Spell Check, Thesaurus, and hyphenation features. Separate disks must be purchased to perform the other language operations.

Overstrike — Code = [Ovrstk:]

The **O**verstrike command causes one character to be overstruck by one or more following characters. To overstrike characters, type **Shift-F8,4,5** (Format),**O**ther,**O**verstrike. The **O**verstrike options include **C**reate and **E**dit. You next select the **C**reate command and enter the text to be overstruck.

For example, to produce a not-equal sign, type **Shift-F8** (Format),**O**ther, **O**verstrike,**C**reate, and then type || =/↵ || as the entry. The normal editing screen will display only the / character; however, the printer will print ≠ and the Reveal Codes screen will show the code [Ovrstk:=/]. To edit an overstrike code, type **Shift-F8,4,5,2** (Format),**O**ther,**O**verstrike,**E**dit.

Printer Functions

The **P**rinter Functions command is used for specialized control over the printing of a document.

Kerning — Code = [Kern:On] [Kern:Off]

Default—No (Off)
Kerning reduces the space between the letters in a word by eliminating unneeded space for certain letter combinations. For instance, the letters WA will be printed closer together since they "fit" each other. Not all printers or fonts support the kerning feature.

Printer Command — Code = [Ptr Cmd:]

The **P**rinter Command is used to insert a printer control code into a document. Control codes must be obtained from the printer's manual. When entering the control code into a document, characters less than ASCII 32 or greater than ASCII 126 must be entered as decimal numbers in angle brackets (for example, <27> = Esc). All keyboard characters may be entered directly, or as decimal numbers, in angle brackets (for example, M or <77>).

Command Use **C**ommand to enter a printer code that will reside within the document.

Filename Use the **F**ilename command to specify a file in which the desired printer codes reside.

Word Spacing/Letter Spacing — Code = [Wrd/Ltr Spacing:]

Default—Optimal/Optimal
The **W**ord Spacing/Letter Spacing command is used to change the printed spacing of the letters and words within a document. The choices include **N**ormal (the printer manufacturer's settings), **O**ptimal (WordPerfect's settings), **P**ercent of Optimal (user-defined setting), and **S**et Pitch (user-defined characters per inch).

Word Spacing **J**ustification Limits — Code = [Just Lim:]

Default—Compressed 60% / Expanded 400%
When justification is on (the default mode), WordPerfect expands and compresses spaces between words to right justify lines of text as it prints a document. The Word Spacing **J**ustification Limits command may be used to alter the way in which WordPerfect treats the expansion/contraction of spaces. See the WordPerfect manual or **F3** (Help) screens for more information.

Baseline Placement for Typesetters and **L**eading Adjustment

The **B**aseline Placement for Typesetters command provides a means for more precise placement of text on a line, and the **L**eading Adjustment command allows different line spacing amounts to be assigned to Soft and Hard Return codes. See the WordPerfect manual or Help screens for more information.

Underline — Code = [Underln:Spaces/Tabs]

Default—Spaces Yes, Tabs No
The **U**nderline command may be used to stop WordPerfect from underlining spaces or to cause WordPerfect to start underlining tabs in a document.

Border Options

Code = [Brdr Opt]

The **B**order Options command may be used to change the printed appearance of the various graphics box borders and table lines. (See **Alt-F9** (Graphics) for more information on graphics box border styles; see **Alt-F7** (Columns/Table) for more information on table lines.) The command allows the thickness, shading, and other factors affecting appearance to be changed for each of the six border/line styles. The command inserts a [Brdr Opt] code which affects all subsequent graphics borders or table lines in the document.

Block/Format
Code =
[Block Pro:On]
[Block Pro:Off]

To protect a block of text from being separated by soft page breaks, first block the text to be protected and then type **Shift-F8** (Format). Next, type Y in response to the "Protect block? No (Yes)" prompt.

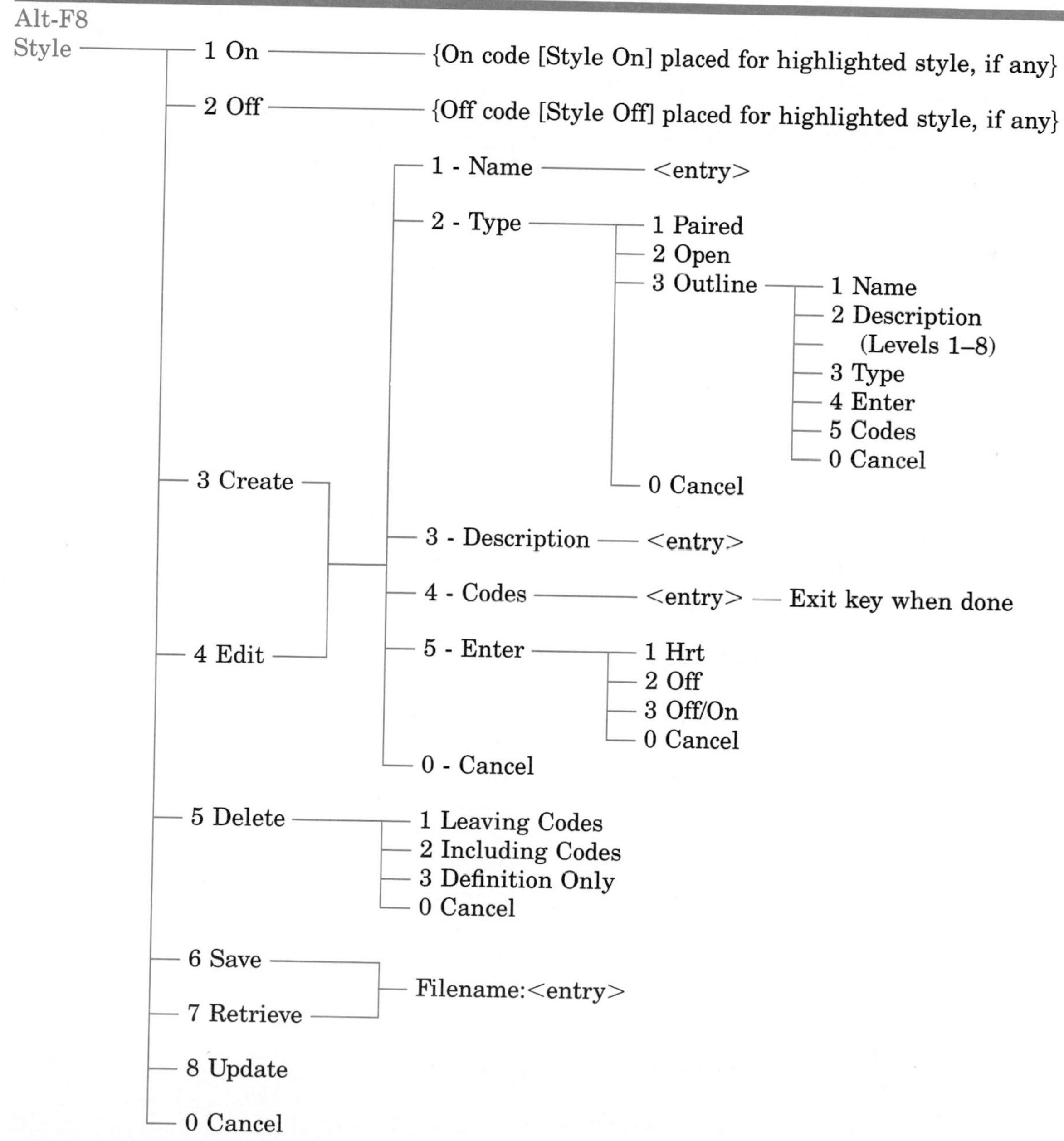

During the creation and editing of a document, you will often find that certain combinations of codes and/or text are repeated throughout the text. When this occurs, a Style containing the combination of codes/text may be created once using the **Alt-F8** (Style) command. The Style (combination of codes/text) can then be inserted into the text at the appropriate places. The **Alt-F8** (Style) command is most useful when code combinations are included in the recurring event.

There are three types of Styles: Paired, Open, and Outline. A Paired Style contains codes that are start and stop in nature (such as [BOLD] [bold]). A Paired Style type inserts a [Style On:] and [Style Off:] code into the document. Text typed afterwards is inserted between the two codes and becomes affected by the start and stop codes included in the Style. To stop affecting the Style on the text being entered, the **Alt-F8** (Style) command is executed again.

An Open Style may or may not contain start and stop codes; however, it does not pause for the user to enter text between them if it does have such codes. An Open Style is primarily used to contain codes that are format forward in nature (such as [L/R Mar:]). An Open Style inserts a [Open Style:] code into the document that contains the Style's codes and text. Format forward codes in an Open Style stay in effect until another code of the same type is encountered (in another [Open Style:] code or singularly).

An Outline style may be used to produce individual Paired or Open styles for each of the eight levels included in a paragraph or outline numbered section of a document. (See **Shift-F5** (Date/Outline), for more information on automatic paragraph/outline numbering.)

Styles created with the **Alt-F8** (Style) command are saved with the document. You may, however, save Styles in their own files in order to later retrieve them into another document.

When the **Alt-F8** (Style) command is executed a screen similar to the following appears.

```
Styles

 Name          Type      Description

 Blund         Paired    Bold and Double underline
 Headings      Paired    Very large, bold for title headings
 Quote         Open      Single spaced, indented margins for citations
 Text          Open      Double spaced, normal margins for text
 Title         Open      Centered page for title page















1 On; 2 Off; 3 Create; 4 Edit; 5 Delete; 6 Save; 7 Retrieve; 8 Update: 1
```

Here, five styles (two Paired and three Open) have been previously created. The inverted bar across the screen is the Style screen cursor. The cursor may be moved with the cursor control keys ↑ and ↓.

At the bottom of the screen appears the Style menu of commands. In general, the procedure to execute a command is to first move the cursor to the appropriate Style shown on the screen, and then type the number or letter of a command. For example, to delete the Style named Title, you would move the cursor to the last Style shown on the screen, and then type **5** (**D**elete).

On—Off
Codes =
[Style On:]
[Style Off:]

Once a Style has been created (see **Alt-F8** Style,Create), the **O**n and **O**ff commands are used to insert the Style codes into the document for the current Style (the Style upon which the Style cursor is currently located).

If the Style is Paired, the **O**n command is used to begin the insert operation. After the text to be affected has been entered, the **Alt-F8,2** (Style),**O**ff command is executed to end the operation. A set of Paired Style codes (On/Off) may also be placed around existing text by first blocking the text in the document and then typing **Alt-F8,1** (Style),**O**n. The [Style On:] code will be placed at the beginning of the block, and the [Style Off:] code will be placed at the end. If the Style is Open, only the **O**n command is used.

To turn an Outline style on, move the cursor to the area in the document where outline or paragraph numbered text is to occur and type **Shift-F5** (Date/Outline),**D**efine. Next, type **9** or **N** for Outline Style **N**ame, and enter the name you gave the style when it was created (see **C**reate below). You will probably find it useful to change the **O**utline,**D**efine,**A**utomatically Adjust to Current Level command to "No" when using an Outline Style. Next, use the **Shift-F5** (Date/Outline),**O**utline or **P**ara Num commands to generate the automatic numbering for the text area.

Create and Edit

The **C**reate command is used to create a new Style, and the **E**dit command is used to edit the current Style. Both commands present the same screens. The first screen presented allows you to enter the following information.

Name

You may create a name for the Style, preferably eight characters or less in length. If you do not name the style, it will be assigned a number (1, 2, 3, . . .).

Type

The Type is either **P**aired, **O**pen, or Ou**t**line and is selected from a menu on the status line. When the type of style is specified as Outline, WordPerfect will first prompt "Name:". To proceed, you must enter the name for the Outline style. WordPerfect will next prompt "Level Number (1-8):". If there are any codes currently defined in the style, these codes will become the style codes for the level you enter. Once you have entered the level number, the screen will appear similar to the following.

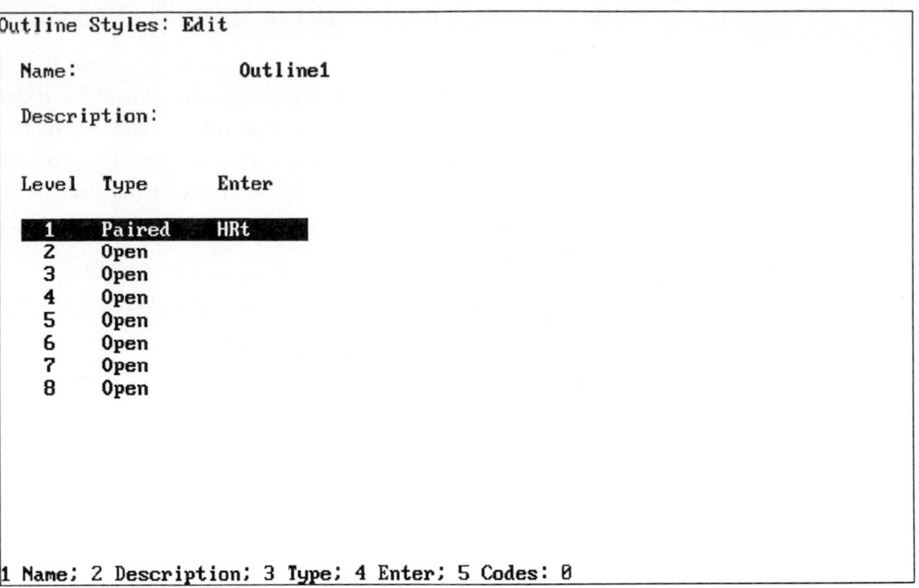

A highlighted cursor will appear on the first level number. The cursor may be moved up and down to different levels with the ↑ and ↓ keys. To define a style for a particular paragraph or outline level, you first move the cursor to the appropriate level. You may then specify the **T**ype (Paired or Open), **E**nter key definition, and enter any **C**odes for the level's style by selecting the appropriate commands from the status line.

Although they appear on a different menu, the commands used to define a style for a paragraph or outline level (**D**escription, **T**ype, **E**nter, and **C**odes) are the same commands used to define the other two types of style, Paired and Open. (See the explanation for the Style definition commands below.)

Description

Room is available for you to enter a full description of what the Style is intended for (approximately 50 characters).

Codes

The **C**odes command presents a screen similar to the **Alt-F3** (Reveal Codes) screen. When the (Style),**C**odes screen is presented, you type the keystrokes which would normally cause a command code to be generated.

For example, to change the line spacing from one to two (double spacing), you would type **Shift-F8,1,6,2**↵(Format),**L**ine,Line **S**pacing,2. A [Ln Spacing:2] code will appear in the bottom portion of the (Style),**C**odes screen. You may continue to enter such codes or text into the (Style),**C**odes screen until all of the desired codes/text appear there. You next type **F7** (Exit) to properly exit the Style editing screen.

If the Style being created is a Paired Style, the codes screen will display a [Comment] code with the message:

Place Style On Codes above, and Style Off Codes below.

Codes entered before the [Comment] code affect the text following the [Style On:] code in the document. However, text in the document that follows the

Style's [Style Off:] code are usually not affected by the codes placed either before or after the [Comment] code.

For example, if the line spacing for a Style is changed to 2 by placing a [Ln Spacing: 2] code before the [Comment] code, it is not necessary to place another [Ln Spacing:] code after the comment to return the line spacing to the document's normal line spacing. The [Style Off:] code automatically returns to the document's current line spacing regardless of any codes that may follow the [Comment] code in the Style.

The exceptions to the rule include the codes found in the **Shift-F8** (Format),**P**age menu. If the (Format),**P**age codes are meant to affect only the text included between the [Style On:] and [Style Off:] codes, they must be reset with the codes that follow the [Comment] code.

Enter

The **E**nter command is used for Paired Styles only. The command may be used to define the use of the Enter key during the text entering portion of the insert [Style:] code operation. The choices are **H**rt (hard return, the normal use), **Off** (have the keystroke turn the Style off), and **Off/On** (have the keystroke turn the Style off then back on again).

Delete

The **Alt-F8** (Style),**D**elete command has three options. The **L**eaving Codes command deletes the style from the Style screen and deletes the associated style codes from the document. However, the codes that were contained in the style codes are left in place. The **I**ncluding Codes command deletes the style from the Style screen and all associated style codes (with their contained codes) from the document. The **D**efinition Only command deletes the style from the Style screen and leaves all style codes in the document intact.

Save

The **S**ave command may be used to save the current styles to a file. Move the Style screen cursor to the appropriate Style and type **6** or **S** (Save), and then enter a filename to save the styles.

Retrieve

The **R**etrieve command may be used to retrieve styles that have been saved in a file.

Update

You can create a library of Styles (a file of Styles that may be retrieved into the Style screen). If a style library has been created, the **U**pdate command may be used to retrieve the file into the Style screen. See the WordPerfect manual or **F3** (Help) screens for more information.

Block/Style

A set of Paired Style codes (On/Off) can be placed around existing text by blocking the text in the document, and then typing **Alt-F8,1** (Style),**O**n. The [Style On:] code will be placed at the beginning of the block, the [Style Off:] code will be placed at the end.

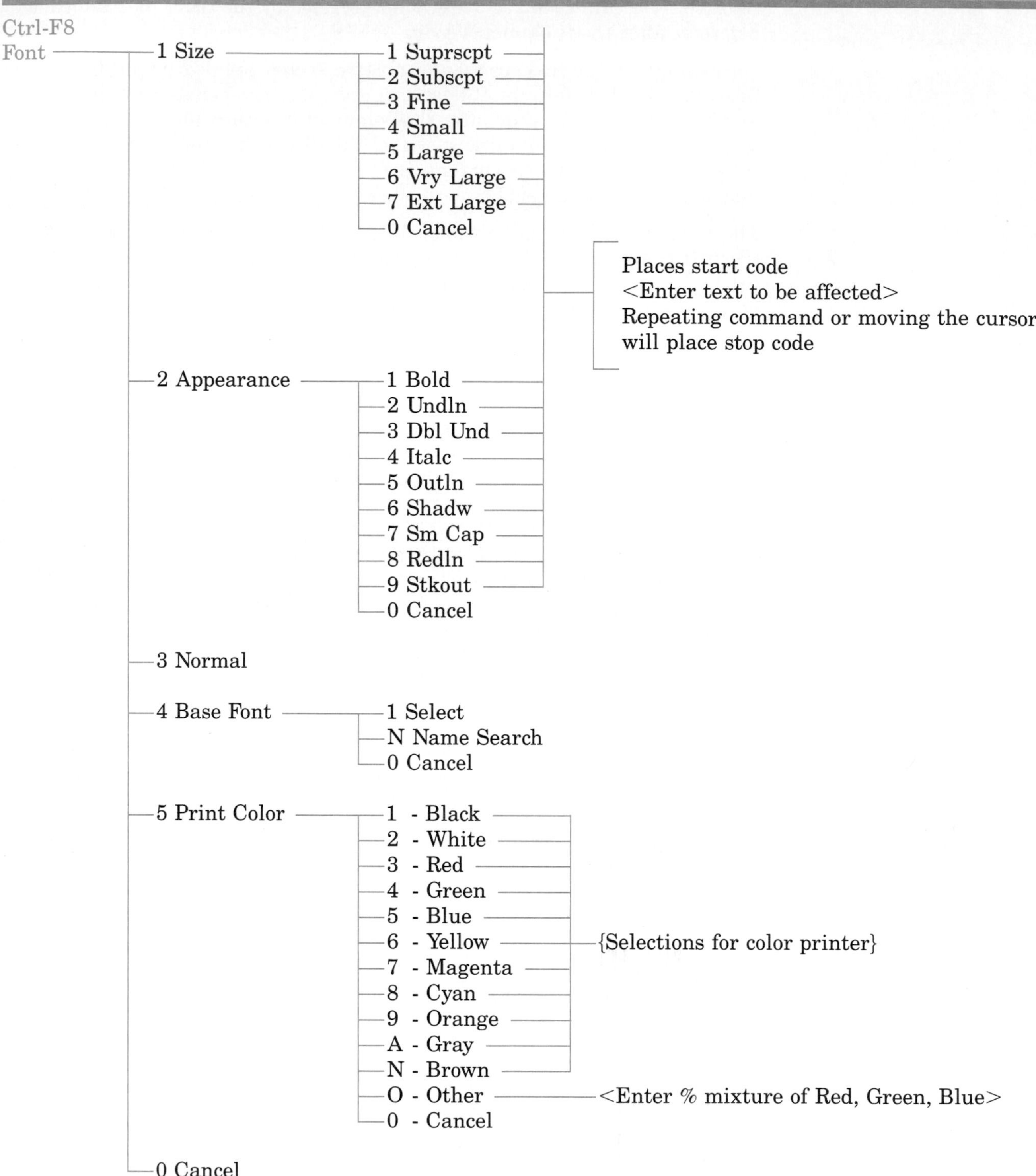

CTRL-F8 FONT

The **Ctrl-F8** (Font) command is used to select various sizes and styles of printed characters. *Font* is a term that describes a set of printed characters that have the same size and style.

Size refers to the height and width of the characters within a font. Two terms used to describe different sizes of types are *point* and *pitch*. Point is a measurement of height for characters in a font. One point is approximately 1/72 of an inch in height. Pitch is a measurement of width for characters in a font. Pitch describes the number of characters that occur in a printed inch of text. In other words, 10 pitch equals 10 characters per inch (CPI).

Proportional is a term that describes a font that does not have a fixed pitch. In a proportional font, the number of printed characters in an inch varies, depending on the width of the specific characters. That is, the characters *il* will be printed in less space than the characters *LO* in a proportional font.

Style refers to the appearance of the printed character. Italic, Roman, and Helvetica are all proper names for different styles of type. The proper name for a style is often used with other terms (such as *Bold*) to further describe the style.

In many cases, the printer you are using will print in the default font *San Serif* or *Pica*, 12 point, 10 pitch.

The following **Ctrl-F8** (Font) commands all deal with changing the size and appearance of printed characters in a document. The commands, however, are highly printer dependent and should be tested before including them in your documents.

Size

In general, the **S**ize commands are used to alter the point and pitch for printed characters. The **S**ize commands all generate start and stop codes to effect the change in font. To use the commands, you may begin by typing the appropriate **S**ize command, and then entering the text to be affected by the command. To stop the **S**ize effect on text being entered, move the cursor past the stop code in the document, or type **Ctrl-F8,3** (Font),**N**ormal to insert a new stop code into the document to the left of the cursor location. To change the size of existing text, block the text, and then type the appropriate **S**ize command.

Su**p**rscpt — Code = [SUPRSCPT] [suprscpt]

The Su**p**rscpt (Superscript) command causes characters of text to be printed above the normal line or be reduced to Fine size and printed at the top margin of the current line.

Su**b**scpt — Code = [SUBSCPT] [subscpt]

The Su**b**scpt (Subscript) command causes characters of text to be printed below the normal line or to be reduced to Fine size and printed at the bottom margin of the current line.

Fine — Code = [FINE] [fine]

The **F**ine command reduces the size of print to the smallest size available with the **S**ize commands (often to 17 pitch).

Small — Code = [SMALL] [small]

The **S**mall command reduces the size of print (often to 12 pitch).

Large — Code = [LARGE] [large]

The **L**arge command enlarges the print (often to 8.5 pitch).

Vry Large — Code = [VRY LARGE] [vry large]

The **V**ry Large (Very Large) command enlarges the print (often to 5 pitch).

Ext Large — Code = [EXT LARGE] [ext large]

The **E**xt Large (Extra Large) command enlarges the print (often the same as **V**ery Large).

Appearance

The **A**ppearance commands are used to alter the style of printed characters. The **A**ppearance commands all generate start and stop codes and insert them into the text in order to effect the change in font. To use the commands, you may begin by typing the appropriate **A**ppearance command, and then entering the text to be affected by the command. To stop the **A**ppearance effect on text being entered, move the cursor past the stop code in the document, or type **Ctrl-F8,3** (Font),**N**ormal to insert a new stop code into the document to the left of the cursor location. To change the style of existing text, block the text, and then type the appropriate **A**ppearance command.

Bold and **U**ndln Codes = [BOLD] [bold]—[UND] [und]

The **Ctrl-F8** (Font),**A**ppearance,**B**old command is the same as the **F6** (Bold) command. The **Ctrl-F8** (Font),**A**ppearance,**U**ndrln command is the same as the **F8** (Underline) command.

Dbl Und Code = [DBL UND] [dbl und]

The **D**bl Und (Double Underline) command produces a double underline for text in a document.

Italc Code = [ITALC] [italc]

The **I**talc command changes the font of the text in a document to italic.

Outln and Sh**a**dw Codes = [OUTLN] [outln]—[SHADW] [shadw]

The **O**utln (Outline) and Sh**a**dw (Shadow) commands offset and reprint text to create a double image effect.

Sm **C**ap Code = [SM CAP] [sm cap]

The Sm **C**ap (Small Capitals) command prints lower-case letters as smaller upper-case letters.

Redln and **S**tkout Codes = [REDLN] [redln]—[STKOUT] [stkout]

When two or more people are involved in revising text, it is often desirable to "call out," or identify, certain segments of text as being text for proposed changes. The **R**edln (Redline) command is designed to help identify text being suggested for addition to a document. The **S**tkout (Strikeout) command is designed to help identify text being suggested for deletion from a document. Different printers mark such text in different ways. See **Shift-F8,3,4** (Format),**D**ocument,**R**edline Method for information on changing the way in which redlined text is marked.

To remove all redline codes and delete all strikeout text from a document, use the **Alt-F5,6,1** (Mark Text),**G**enerate,**R**emove Redline Markings and Strikeout Text From Document command.

Normal

The **N**ormal command may be used to insert **Ctrl-F8** (Font) stop code(s) into a document. The command may be used to exit the Font code procedure used to change the size or appearance of text or to edit previously formatted text. The **N**ormal command generates stop codes for all unmatched Font start codes preceding the current cursor location.

Base **F**ont
Code = [Font:]

The Base **F**ont command may be used to change the normal printer font used in printing a document. The command presents a screen of all the fonts your printer supports. To select a different printer font, move the screen's cursor to the appropriate font, and type ↵.

Print **C**olor
Code = [Color:]

The Print **C**olor command is used to change the colors for text printed on a printer capable of using colors. See the WordPerfect manual or **F3** (Help) screens for more information.

F9
End Field — Places [Mrg:END FIELD][HRt] codes; {END FIELD} appears in text.

F9 END FIELD

The **F9** (End Field) command inserts a [Mrg:END FIELD] code and a hard return [HRt] into a document. The command may be used to separate fields within records in a secondary merge file. For more information on merge operations, see **Ctrl-F9** (Merge/Sort).

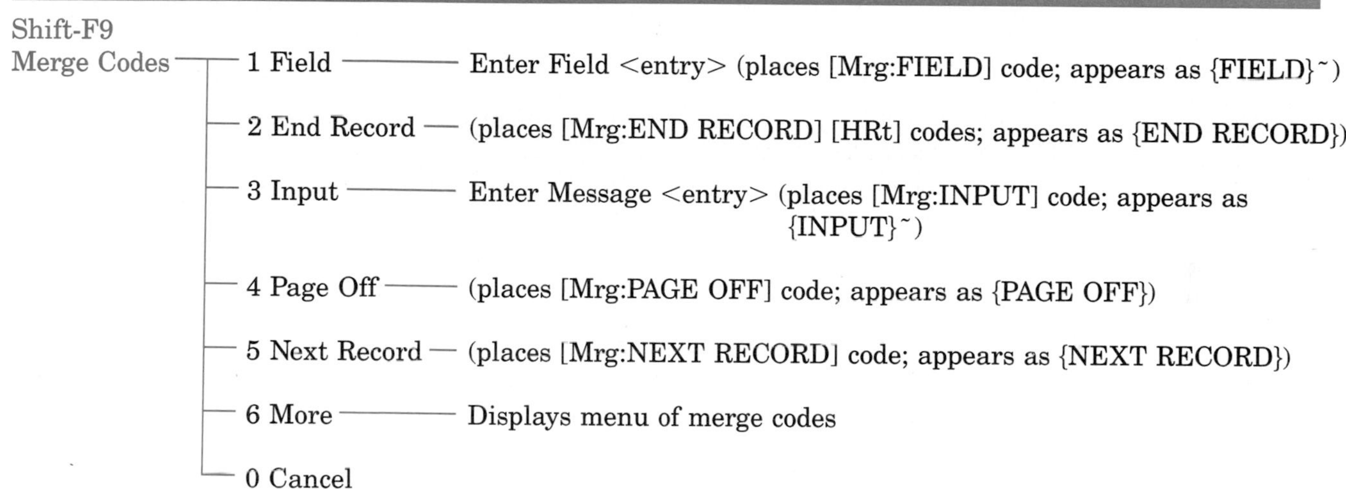

SHIFT-F9 MERGE CODES

The **Shift-F9** (Merge Codes) command provides a menu of merge codes used in merge text operations. A merge code selected from the menu is inserted into the document at the current cursor location. For more information on merge operations, see **Ctrl-F9** (Merge/Sort).

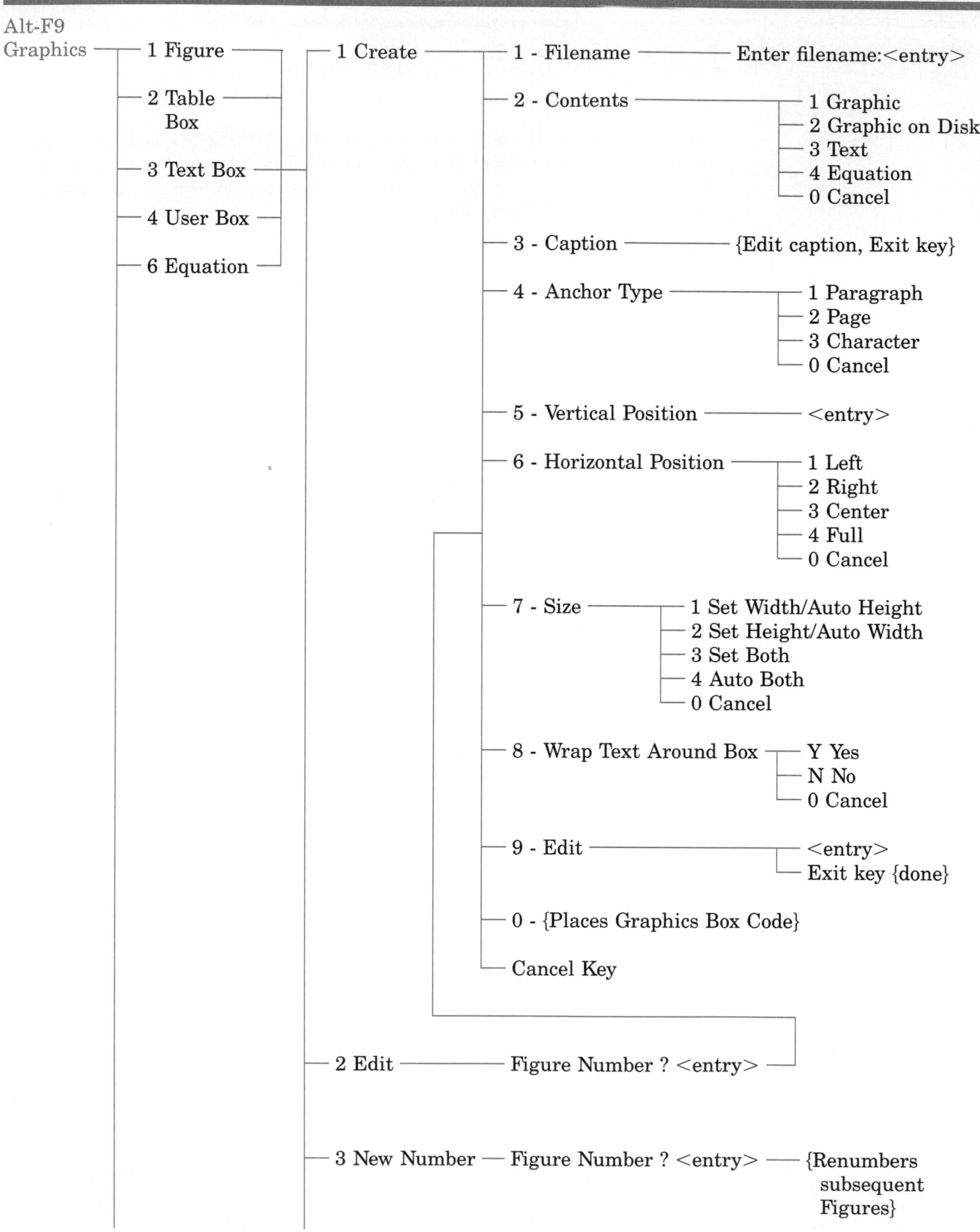
Alt-F9
Graphics
1 Figure
2 Table Box
3 Text Box
4 User Box
6 Equation
1 Create
1 - Filename
Enter filename:<entry>
2 - Contents
1 Graphic
2 Graphic on Disk
3 Text
4 Equation
0 Cancel
3 - Caption
{Edit caption, Exit key}
4 - Anchor Type
1 Paragraph
2 Page
3 Character
0 Cancel
5 - Vertical Position
<entry>
6 - Horizontal Position
1 Left
2 Right
3 Center
4 Full
0 Cancel
7 - Size
1 Set Width/Auto Height
2 Set Height/Auto Width
3 Set Both
4 Auto Both
0 Cancel
8 - Wrap Text Around Box
Y Yes
N No
0 Cancel
9 - Edit
<entry>
Exit key {done}
0 - {Places Graphics Box Code}
Cancel Key
2 Edit
Figure Number ? <entry>
3 New Number
Figure Number ? <entry>
{Renumbers subsequent Figures}

CONTINUED

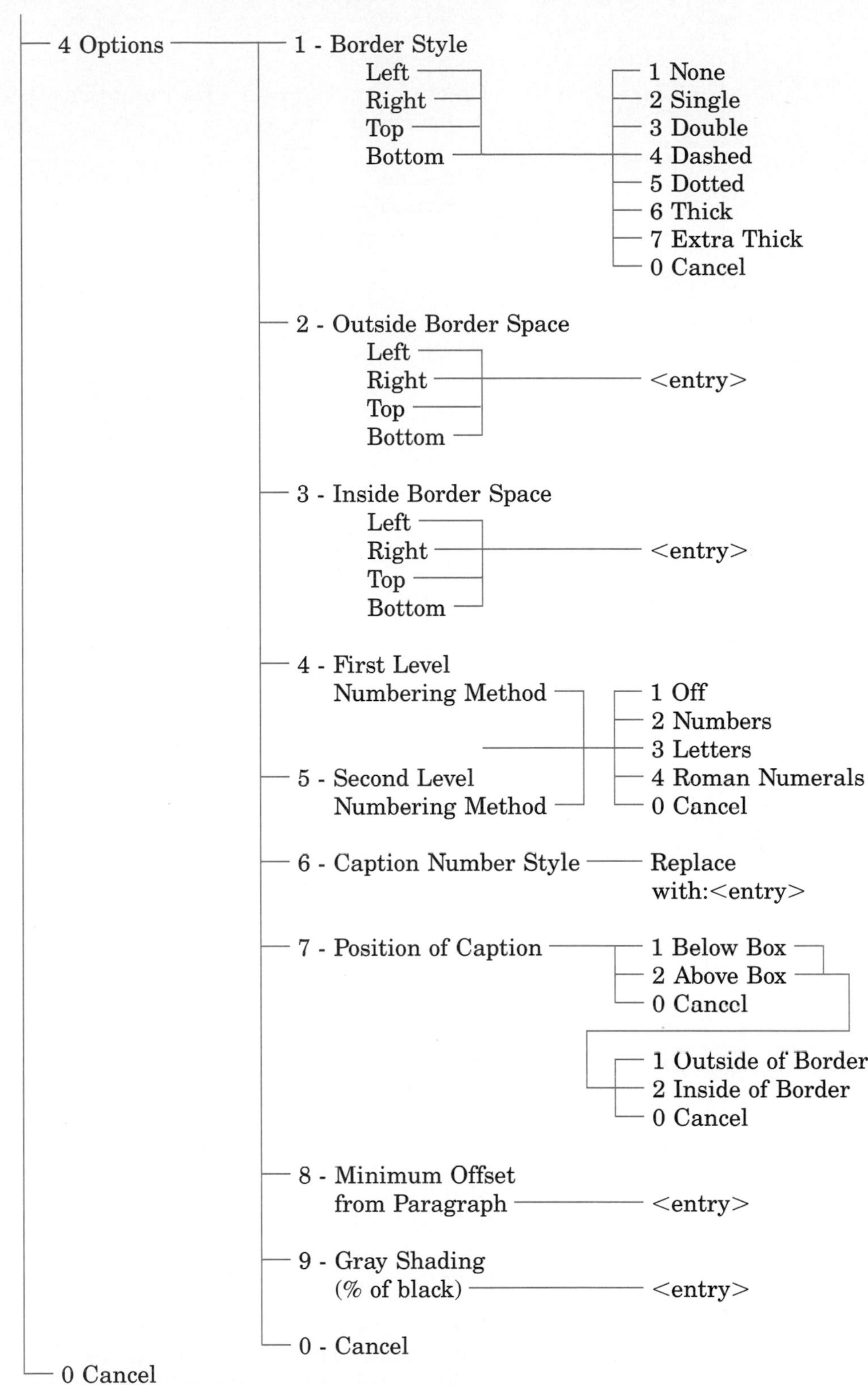
4 Options
1 - Border Style
Left
Right
Top
Bottom
1 None
2 Single
3 Double
4 Dashed
5 Dotted
6 Thick
7 Extra Thick
0 Cancel
2 - Outside Border Space
Left
Right
Top
Bottom
<entry>
3 - Inside Border Space
Left
Right
Top
Bottom
<entry>
4 - First Level
Numbering Method
5 - Second Level
Numbering Method
1 Off
2 Numbers
3 Letters
4 Roman Numerals
0 Cancel
6 - Caption Number Style
Replace
with:<entry>
7 - Position of Caption
1 Below Box
2 Above Box
0 Cancel
1 Outside of Border
2 Inside of Border
0 Cancel
8 - Minimum Offset
from Paragraph
<entry>
9 - Gray Shading
(% of black)
<entry>
0 - Cancel
0 Cancel

CONTINUED

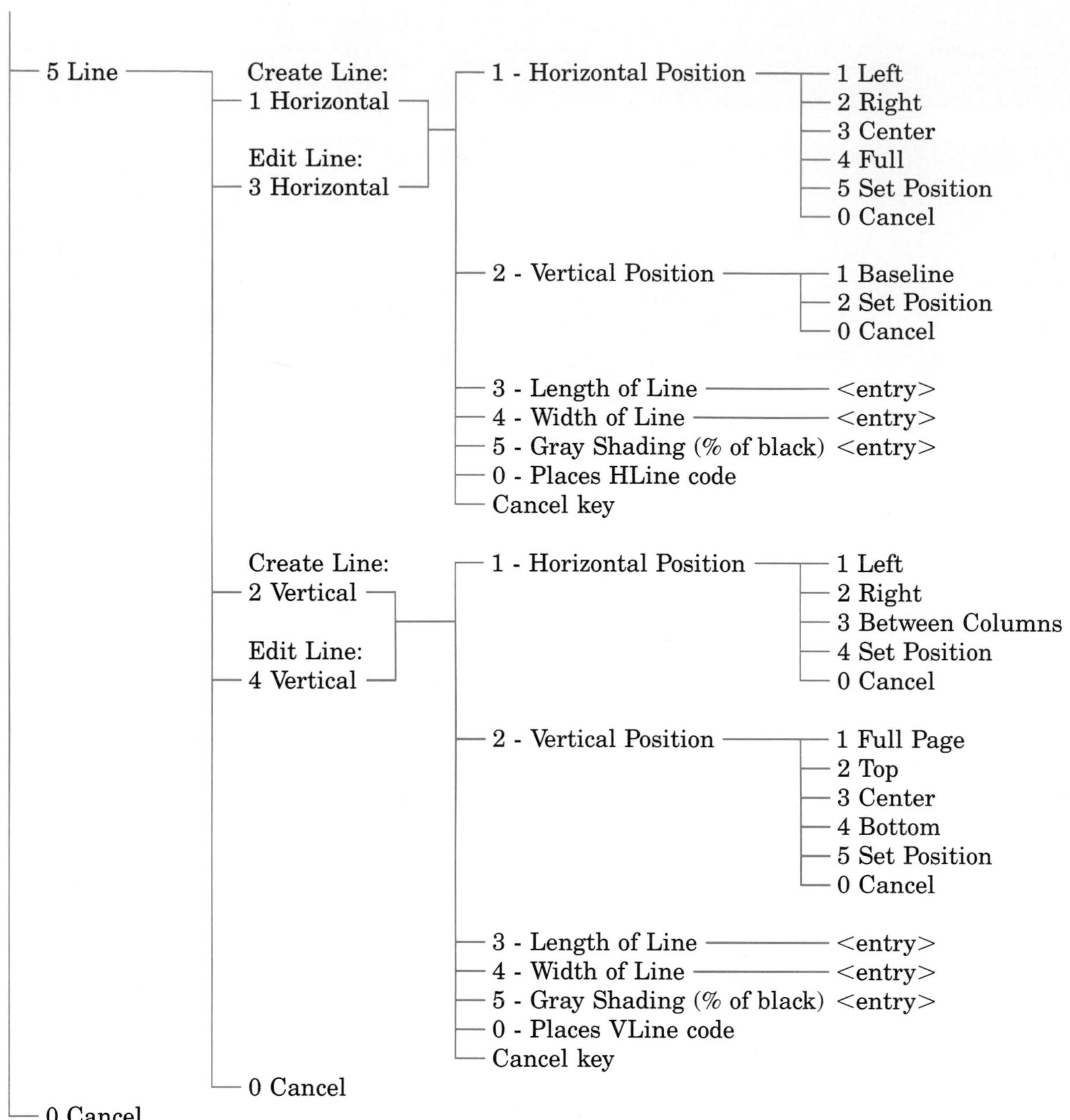

ALT-F9 GRAPHICS

The **Alt-F9** (Graphics) command allows you to present "boxes" of data (often obtained from other files) on the printed pages of a document file and to print various types of lines in a document. The five categories of graphics boxes are Figure, Table, Text, Equation, and User.

Figure Boxes

Figure boxes may be used to display graphics obtained from files generated by software other than WordPerfect. Lotus 1-2-3 .PIC files are one such type of file. Other well-known software graphics directly supported by WordPerfect include Dr. Halo, GEM, Enable, PC Paint Plus, PC Paintbrush, and Symphony.

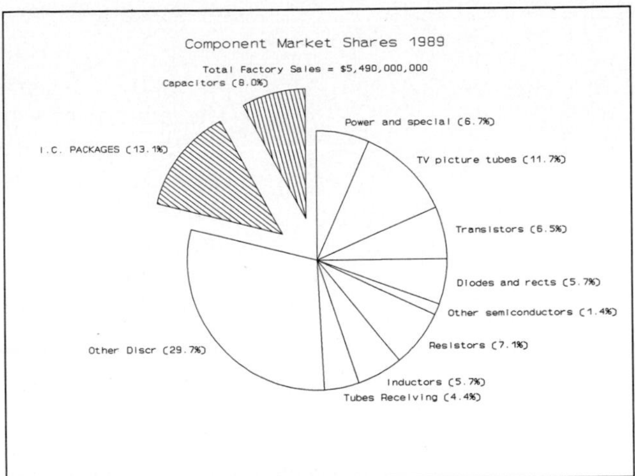

Figure 1 Western States

Table Boxes

Table boxes may be used to place tables of numbers, statistics, and so forth into a document. Tables may be obtained from files created by WordPerfect or from ASCII files generated by other software and subsequently edited by WordPerfect. Edited Lotus .PRN files are one type of ASCII file that may be included in table boxes.

Table I Western States

Capacitor Markets by Material Type	1989	1990
Aluminum	19.60%	16.90%
All other, fixed	2.90%	1.80%
Ceramic	16.00%	15.40%
Mica	4.90%	4.10%
Variable	4.60%	2.40%
Paper & film	32.10%	30.50%
Tantalum	21.20%	20.90%

Text Boxes

Text boxes may be used to display cameos, side bars, quotes, or other special text that you want set off from the rest of the document. The text for a Text box may be obtained from files created by WordPerfect or from ASCII files generated by other software and subsequently edited by WordPerfect.

Historical Note

The advent of Integrated Circuits occurring in the early 1970s began to impact capacitor industry sales by the mid 1980s. Market shares for paper, film, and aluminum material capacitors dropped sharply, while mica capacitors maintained a constant 5% of total market share in units.

1 Industry Cameo

Equation Boxes

Equation boxes may be used to create WordPerfect equations to be included in a document.

$$x = \frac{-b \pm \sqrt{b^2 - 4ac}}{2}a$$

User Boxes

User boxes may be used to present data that is neither figure, table, text, nor equation in nature.

Box Labels and Numbers

In general, the different box types have nothing to do with the data displayed within them. Table boxes may be used to display graphics, and Figure boxes may be used to display tables. The box types are used by WordPerfect because it automatically labels and numbers the boxes in a document. Figure boxes are automatically labeled "Figure 1," "Figure 2," etc., and Table boxes are automatically labeled "Table I," "Table II," etc. Specifying certain boxes as Figures and other boxes as Tables allows for such things as having box "Figure 6" displayed on the same page as box "Table IV." The exception is equation boxes, which must be specified as being equation type in order to display a WordPerfect equation.

The graphics box number may be referenced with an automatic Cross-Reference within the document (see **Alt-F5**,**1** (Mark Text),Cross-**R**ef).

Creating a Graphics Box

There are four basic steps involved in creating a Graphics box.

1. Select the box type—Figure, Table, Text, User, or Equation.
2. Use the **C**reate command to specify the filename (if any) for the data to be included in the box and to specify various settings such as size, position, labels, etc.
3. Exit the (Graphics) command with the **F7** (Exit) command and use the **Shift-F7**,**6** (Print),**V**iew Document command to preview the page.
4. Continue by editing the graphics box and/or graphics box file and viewing the document page until the desired result is achieved.

Figure—**T**able—Text **B**ox—**U**ser—**E**quation

These five **Alt-F9** (Graphics) commands allow you to specify the type of Graphics box that you desire to create or edit.

Create — Code =[*Type* Box:n;;]

The **C**reate command produces a screen of commands used to set various specifications for the graphics box being created. Once a graphics box has been created, a graphics box code is inserted into the document. A graphics box outline (screen display), which indicates where the box will be printed, can be viewed on the screen during normal editing. To view the appearance of the page without printing it, you may use the **Shift-F7,6** (Print),**V**iew Document command. To change the box type of a graphics box (Figure, Table, etc.), you can type **Alt-F9** while the Create menu is on the screen, and then re-enter the box type specification. To properly exit the **C**reate command, you should type ↵ or **F7** (Exit). Typing **F1** (Cancel) aborts the (Graphics),**C**reate operation. The following options are available on the **C**reate menu.

Filename

Use the **F**ilename command to specify the file in which the graphics box's data resides (the source file). Be sure to specify the filename extension if any. When the **F**ilename command is used, the data in the source file is copied into the document's graphics box. If you later edit or change the data in the source file, you will need to edit the graphics box and again enter the filename to ensure that the last edited version of the source file is displayed in the document. You may create an "empty" graphics box by not specifying a filename. An empty graphics box can have text directly entered into it by using the **Alt-F9** (Graphics),**C**reate,**E**dit command. It is generally easier to directly enter text into the graphics box when the type is Text in nature.

Contents

The C**o**ntents command may be used to specify the type of data that will be included in the graphics box. If the **F**ilename command is used to specify a file before typing the C**o**ntents command, WordPerfect will determine the contents type based on the type of data found in the file. The four types of contents that can be specified with the C**o**ntents command are: **G**raphic, Graphic on **D**isk, **T**ext, and **E**quation. Specify **G**raphic if you want the graphics data to become part of the data included in the document. Specify Graphic on **D**isk if you want the graphics data to be kept separate from the data in the document. **T**ext should be specified when the data are word-processed text, and **E**quation must be specified when the data are to be in the form of a WordPerfect Equation.

Caption

The **C**aption command is used to provide a label for the graphics box. The label will automatically include the box type and the number that is generated by a [Box Num] code. You may add to the label by typing text onto the screen presented by the **C**aption command and/or delete the automatic label by backspacing over the [Box Num] code.

The position of the label relative to the graphics box is determined by the type of graphics box being created. To change the position of the label, use the **Alt-F9** (Graphics),**O**ptions,**P**osition of Caption command.

Anchor Type

Default—Paragraph

The Anchor **T**ype command is used to determine how the graphics box will maintain its position in the document.

If **P**aragraph is selected, the graphics box code is placed at the beginning of the current paragraph (the paragraph in which the editing cursor is currently located). The normal editing screen will display an outline of the box's top side located at the line position where the editing cursor was located when the box was created. A Paragraph type graphics box will move up and down in the document along with its associated text (the text in the paragraph that begins with the graphics box code).

If **P**age is selected, the graphics box code is inserted at the current cursor location. The command prompts "Number of pages to skip:", which provides an opportunity for you to have the graphics box printed *n* number of pages following the placement of the code. A Page type graphics box will remain fixed in its position when the text around it is moved up or down. The **P**age command should be executed before any text has been entered around the graphics box.

If **C**haracter is selected, a graphics box code is inserted at the current cursor location; however, the graphics box outline displayed on the screen will only be one character in size (regardless of the actual size of the graphics box). A Character type graphics box moves about in a text as its box code moves (during normal editing, the code is treated like a single character of data).

Vertical Position

The **V**ertical Position command is used to adjust the placement of the graphics box vertically on the page. The options for the command depend on the Type (Paragraph, Page, or Character) currently specified for the graphics box.

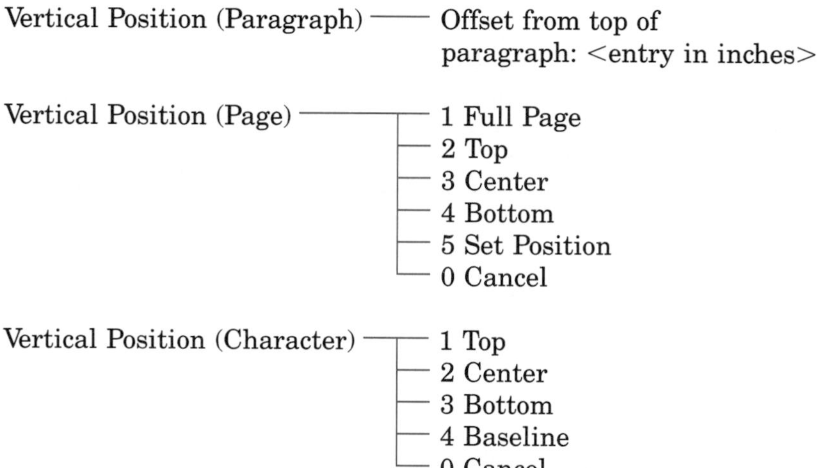

If the graphics box Anchor **T**ype is Paragraph, you may enter a positive number of inches to position the box below the line on which the graphics box code resides. 0″ positions the top of the graphics box on the same line as its code.

If the graphics box Anchor **T**ype is Page, you can align the graphics box against the **T**op line, **B**ottom, **C**enter of the page of text, or you can **S**et Position as being *n*″ below the top of the page. The option "**F**ull Page" produces a graphics box that fills the page area within the current margins. A **F**ull Page position box code should be placed on a page by itself.

If the graphics box Anchor **T**ype is Character, you can position the box so that the text of the line on which the code resides aligns to the **T**op, **C**enter, or **B**ottom of the Box. **B**aseline is used to align the baseline of the data in a graphics box with the baseline of the text.

Horizontal Position

The **H**orizontal Position command is used to adjust the placement of the graphics box horizontally on the page. The options for the command depend on the Type (Paragraph or Page) that has been specified for the graphics box. Character type boxes may not be positioned with the **H**orizontal Position command.

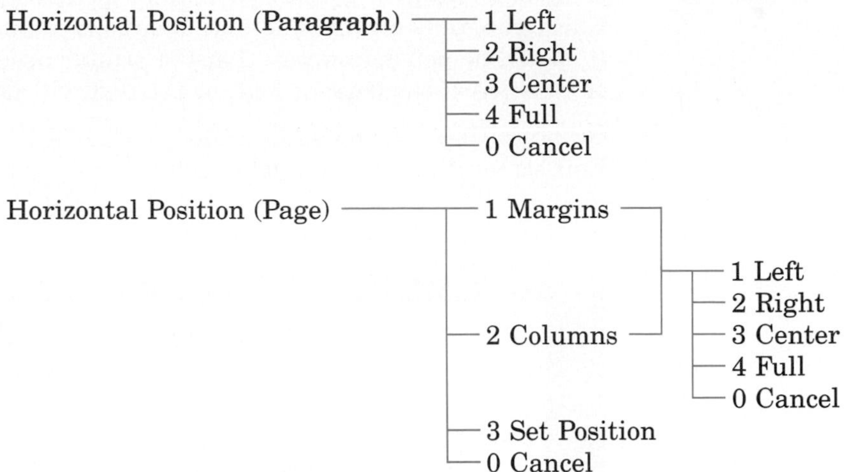

If the graphics box Anchor **T**ype is Paragraph, the **H**orizontal Position command may be used to align the box with the current **L**eft or **R**ight margins or horizontally **C**enter the box between the current left and right margins. The option **F**ull expands the box to fill the area between the left and right margins.

If the graphics box Anchor **T**ype is Page, the **H**orizontal Position command may be used to align the box with the current **M**argins in the same manner as a Paragraph type box is aligned. The **C**olumns command may be used to align the box (**L**eft, **R**ight, **C**enter, or **F**ull) inside of a column included in a columnar portion of text (see **Alt-F7** (/Table/Columns) for more information on creating columnar text). The Set Position command may be used to offset the box from the left edge of the page by *n* number of inches.

Size

The **S**ize command may be used to enlarge or shrink a graphics box by specifying the box's dimensions (in inches). The **S**ize options include Set **W**idth/Auto Height, Set **H**eight/Auto Width, Set **B**oth and **A**uto Both.

With graphic boxes containing graphics data, the first two options allow you to change the size of the box without altering the aspect (shape) of the graphics in the box. In other words, if the Set **W**idth/Auto Height command is used to change the width of the graphics box, WordPerfect will automatically compute the height necessary to maintain the original shape of the graphics in the box. If the box contains only text, the lines of text will be re-wrapped within the box to conform to the box's new dimensions.

Wrap Text Around Box

Default–Yes
When the **W**rap Text Around Box command is changed to "No," the text in the document overwrites the data in the graphics box when the document is printed. The box outline screen display is turned off when the command is changed to "No."

Edit

The **E**dit command may be used to alter the appearance of the data in a graphics box.

Text Data If the data in the box are Text in nature, or if no filename has been entered with the Create command, the screen presented by the **Edit** command allows you to enter and/or edit the text in the box. You also are allowed to rotate the graphics box relative to the page on which it will be printed. To rotate a graphics box, you type **Alt-F9** (Graphics) while in the **E**dit command's screen. The Rotate options include 0°, 90°, 180°, and 270°. It should be noted, however, that the printer used must support the rotated orientation of the current font, or the text will not be printed.

Graphics Data If the data in the graphics box is Graphic in nature, an **E**dit screen similar to the following will be presented:

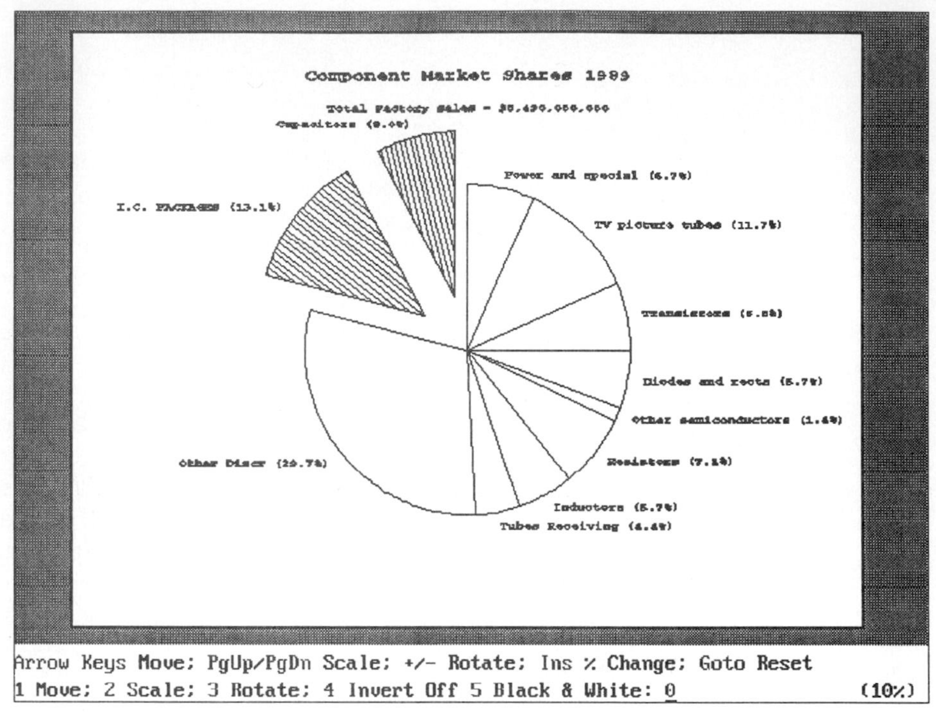

Two menus, one above the other, will appear on the status line. The menus have similar functions.

The message "Arrow Keys **M**ove" will appear on the top menu. To move the graphics within the box, you may type the cursor keys ↑, ↓, →, or ←. By default, typing a direction key will move the graphics image approximately 1/6 of the graphics box's horizontal or vertical dimension. The command option "**M**ove" will appear on the bottom menu. The **M**ove command may be used to enter the precise distance in inches (positive or negative) to move the graphics image horizontally and/or vertically within the graphics box.

The message "PgUp/PgDn **Scale**" will appear on the top menu. To expand the graphics image in the box, you may type the PgUp key. To contract the size of the graphics image in the box, you may type the PgDn key. By default, typing the PgUp or PgDn keys adjusts the size of the image by 10%. The command option "**S**cale" will appear on the bottom menu. The **S**cale command may be used to expand the image horizontally (Scale X) and/or vertically (Scale Y) by entering a precise percentage of the original size for each dimension.

On the top menu will appear the message "+/− Rotate." To rotate the graphics image 36° counter-clockwise, you may type the + (plus) key. Typing the − (minus) key rotates the image 36° in the opposite direction. The command option “**R**otate” will appear on the bottom menu. The Rotate command may be used to rotate the image to an absolute orientation ranging in degrees from 0° to 360°.

“Ins % Change” will appear on the top menu. You may change the default placement values of the top menu by typing the Ins key. The current value (10% by default) is shown in the bottom right hand corner of the **E**dit screen. Typing the Ins key presents (in order) the other possible percentage options: 5%, 1%, and 25%. Type the Ins key until the desired percentage is displayed.

Also on the top menu appears the message “Goto Reset.” Typing the Ctrl-Home (Goto) keys while in the Graphics,**E**dit screen causes the image to return to its original form.

The **I**nvert command on the bottom menu may be used to reverse the colors (black and white) of the image in the graphics box, and the **B**lack and White command may be used to change the screen display from color to black and white.

Equation Data In order for a graphics box to contain a WordPerfect generated equation, the contents of the box (**2** Contents) must be specified as being “Equation.” When the contents are specified Equation and the **E**dit command (**9** **E**dit) is selected, the following screen will appear.

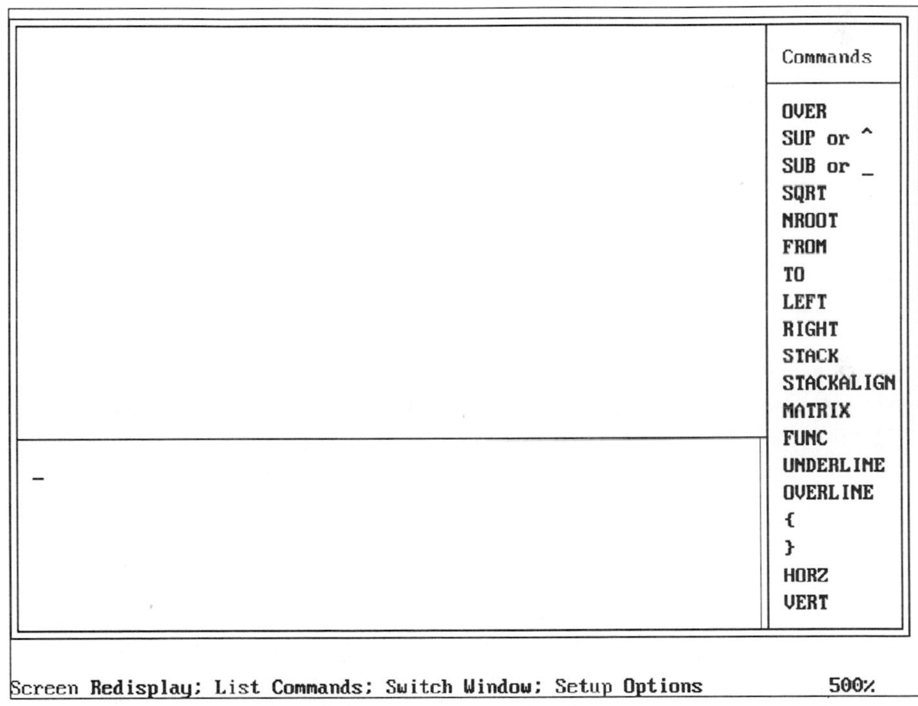

The Equation Editing Screen The editing screen, used to create or edit equations, is divided into three parts. At the bottom of the screen, on the left side, is an area called the *Editing Window,* which may be used to enter the data necessary to create an equation. On the right appears what is called the *Equation Palette,* which may be used to generate certain items of the data necessary to create the equation in the Editing Window. Finally, in the top left portion of the editing screen, there is an area called the *Display Window* that may be used to produce a graphics image of the equation as it will appear in the document.

The Editing Window When the editing screen is first presented, a cursor appears in the Editing Window and the user may begin to enter the data required to produce an equation. The data entered into the editing window is comprised of equation *commands, symbols, variables,* and numbers. Equation commands are used to construct various formats for the equation. For example, the command **OVER** can be used to display the fractional form when it is used as an editing window entry. For example, the result of entering *x OVER y* in the editing window will produce the equation:

$$\frac{x}{y}$$

Equation symbols are used to produce characters not found on the keyboard. For example, characters such as those used to designate "less than or equal to" and "divided by" can be included in an editing window entry by typing: *x <= y DIV z*. The result of such an entry will be:

$$x \leq y \div z$$

An equation variable is defined as any character, or group of characters, that begins with a letter and is not recognized as being an equation command or symbol name. Such an entry in the equation will be in the same form as it appears in the editing window. In the preceding examples, x, y, and z were all entered as variables.

Numbers are similar to variables because they will appear in the equation in the same form as they are entered into the editing window. For example, the editing window entry: *1 OVER x,* will produce the equation:

$$\frac{1}{x}$$

The Equation Palette Equation commands and symbols selected for use in the data of the Editing Window can be found in the Equation Palette. The user may switch to the menu by typing **F5**(List), which, on the editing screen, is shown on the status line as the **List** Commands command. When the **F5** key is pressed, a selection cursor (reverse video display) appears within the Equation Palette. To select a command or symbol from the Equation Palette, the cursor control keys, ↑ and ↓, may be used to move the cursor to the desired menu item, then the ↵ key is pressed.

For example, to produce the equation that represents the formula y equals one over the square root of n, the user could begin by typing: *y = 1 OVER*. The user could then type **F5** to switch to the Equation Palette, then move the cursor to the selection "SQRT." With the SQRT menu option highlighted, the user can type ↵. Typing ↵ causes the highlighted command to be automatically inserted into the Editing Window at the location of the cursor and returns the user to the Editing Window in order to finish entering the equation data, as in the following. (In this case, the user would complete the data by simply typing the variable "n.")

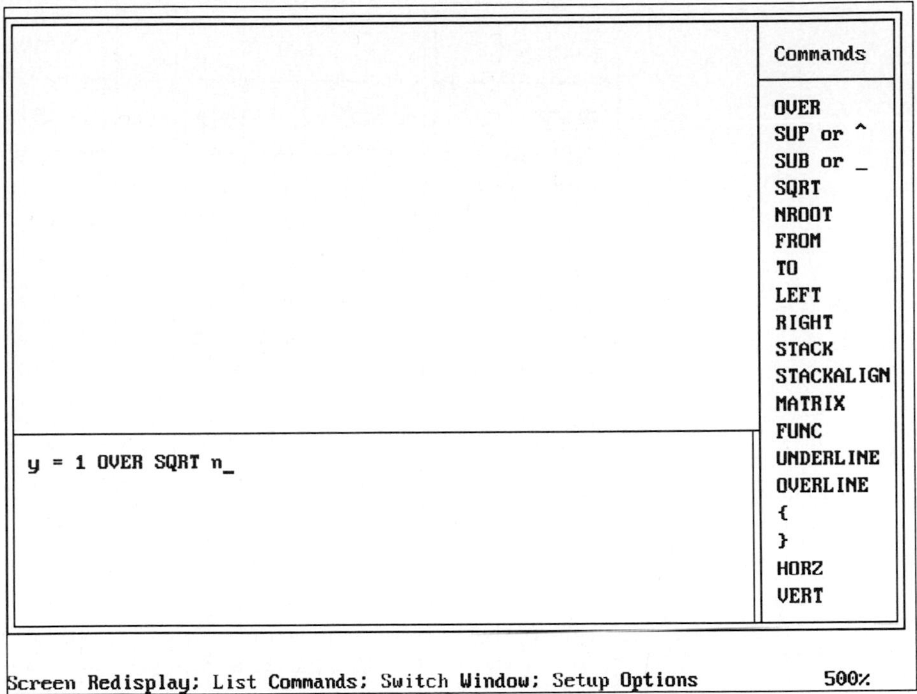

It is not necessary to use the Equation Palette to enter commands and symbols if the user knows the appropriate word to enter. So in this example, the user could have simply typed "SQRT" at the appropriate place in the Equation Window line.

The Equation Palette consists of several different menus that can be accessed by typing either the PgUp (Page Up) or PgDn (Page Down) keys after the user has switched to the palette by typing the **F5** (**List** Commands) command. The following show each of the menus as they appear on the editing screen.

Commands
OVER
SUP or ^
SUB or _
SQRT
NROOT
FROM
TO
LEFT
RIGHT
STACK
STACKALIGN
MATRIX
FUNC
UNDERLINE
OVERLINE
{
}
HORZ
VERT

Large

Symbols					
/	//	///	∞	∂	∇
×	÷	±	∓	·	⊻
≤	≥	≪	≫	≪	≫
≠	¬	<	>	≼	≽
≡	≢	~	≃	≈	≅
∝	≐	∥	⊥	∀	∃
∴	∵	∷	∔	≟	≒
≓	≎	≉	≍	≭	⌣
⌢	≬	≀	⊤	⊦	⊣
⊨	∠	∡	∢	⊾	∘

Greek					
α	β	γ	δ	ε	ϵ
ζ	η	θ	ϑ	ι	κ
λ	μ	ν	ξ	ο	π
ϖ	ρ	ϱ	σ	ς	τ
υ	ϕ	φ	χ	ψ	ω
Α	Β	Γ	Δ	Ε	Ζ
Η	Θ	Ι	Κ	Λ	Μ
Ν	Ξ	Ο	Π	Ρ	Σ
Τ	Υ	Φ	Χ	Ψ	Ω

Arrows					
←	→	↑	↓	↔	↕
⇇	⇉	⇆	⇄	⇐	⇒
⇑	⇓	⇔	⇕	↗	↘
↙	↖	↝	↼	↽	⇀
⇁	⇋	⇌	↿	↾	⇃
⇂	↩	↪	↦	◀	▶
▵	▿	◃	▹	△	▽
◂	▸	▴	▾	≜	≙
⋈	⋆	★	◇	◆	⋄
○	○	∘	•	□	■

Sets

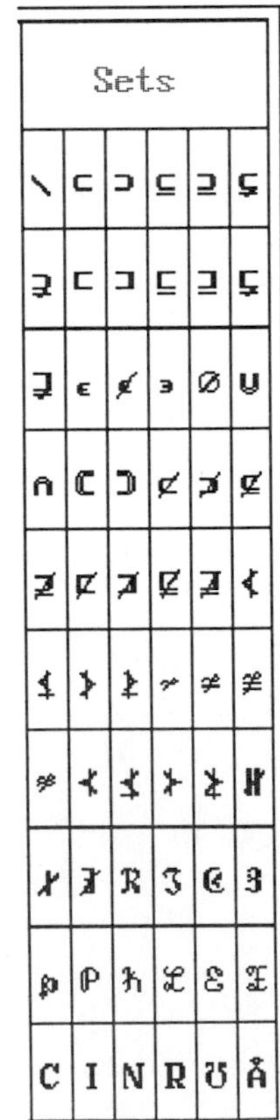

Other

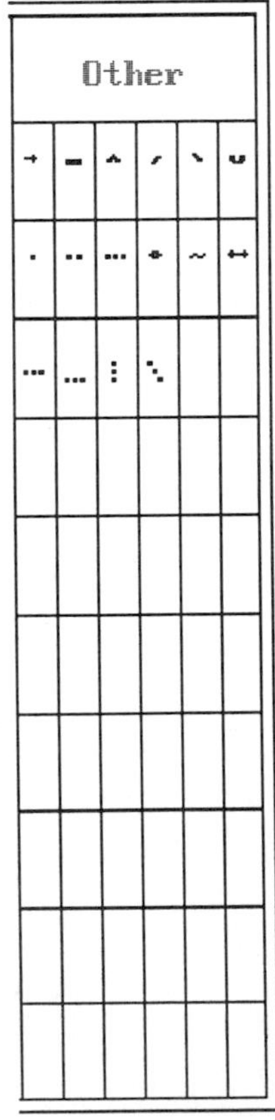

Functions
cos
sin
tan
arccos
arcsin
arctan
cosh
sinh
tanh
cot
coth
sec
cosec
exp
log
ln
lim
liminf
limsup

ALT-F9 (Graphics)

When an Equation Palette menu has more selections than can be displayed on the screen, typing the ↓ key (cursor down) will scroll the items up onto the screen where they may then be viewed and selected.

The Display Window The last area of the editing screen to discuss, the Display Window, may be used to view a graphics image of the equation that is currently described in the Editing Window. To do so, the **Ctrl-F3** (Screen) command, shown as "**Screen** Redisplay" on the status line, may be used. Using the last example, if the **Ctrl-F3** keystrokes are used, the editing screen will appear as follows.

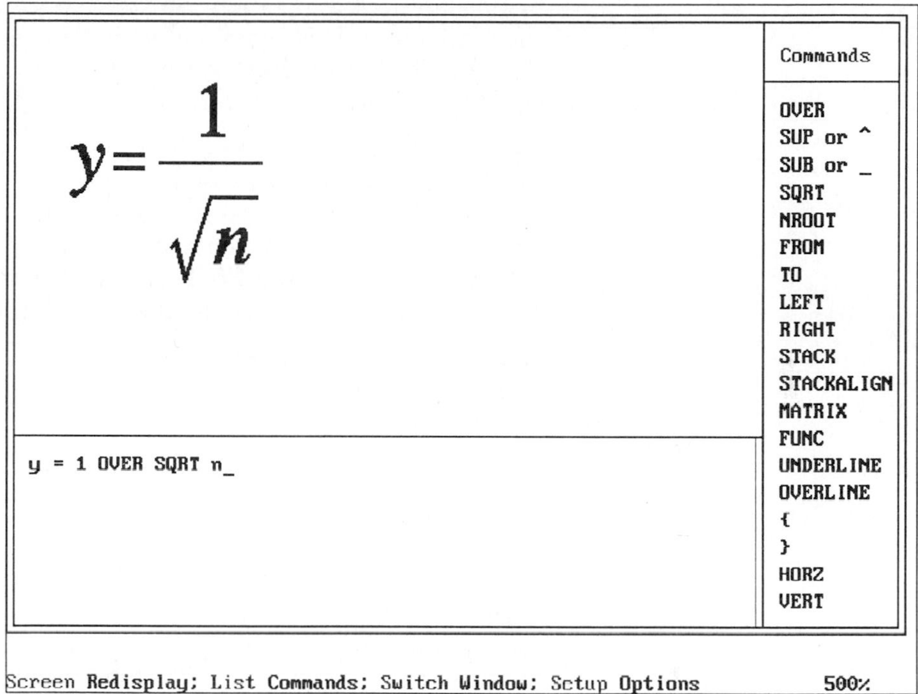

The equation shown here will be printed in the document as:

$$y = \frac{1}{\sqrt{n}}$$

Switch Window Command The graphics image in the Display Window can be adjusted in various ways by using the **Shift-F3** (Switch) command, shown as "**Switch** Window" on the status line. When **Shift-F3** is typed, the following menu appears on the status line.

```
Arrow Keys Move; PgUp/PgDn Scale; Goto Reset; Switch Window          500%
```

Arrow Keys Move The graphics image in the Display Window may be moved horizontally or vertically by typing the cursor control keys ←, →, ↑, and ↓. Moving the image in the Display Window does not affect the placement of the equation in the document; the command merely moves the graphics image so that it is more easily viewed.

PgUp/PgDn Scale Typing the PgUp or PgDn keys adjusts the size of the graphics image up or down. Shown on the far right of the status line, the default size is 500% of the size of the equation as it will appear in the document. The size of the image can be adjusted from 25% to 1000%.

Goto Reset Typing Ctrl-Home (shown as **Goto** Reset on the status line) resets the position and size of the graphics image to the original default settings.

Switch Window The **Shift-F3** (Switch) command (shown as **Switch** Window on the status line) may be used to return to the Editing Window.

Setup Options The last menu item on the Editing Window menu of commands is selected by typing **Shift-F1** (Setup) shown as **Setup** Options on the status line. This command provides a menu that allows you to print the equation as graphics or not, set the graphical font size, and position the equation horizontally or vertically within the graphics box.

Saving an Equation You can save an equation's definition by typing **F10** (Save) *filename* while in the Editing Window. Similarly, a previously saved equation definition can be retrieved by typing **Shift-F10** (Retrieve) *filename* while in the Editing Window. When retrieving a previously saved equation definition, you can type **F5** (List) directly after typing **Shift-F10**,(Retrieve), and then use the (List) screen to retrieve the equation definition.

Equation Command Syntax The following describes some general rules and provides certain command/symbol words that may be used when defining an equation in the Editing Window.

In many cases, the items contained in an equation definition must be separated from each other. It is a good general rule to separate items from each other by including a space between them.

Spaces included in an equation definition are not included in the printed equation. To include a space in the printed equation, insert a ˜ (tilde) into the definition where the space is to occur. A ` (backward accent) may be used to create a "thin space" (1/4 of a full space).

The \ (backslash) may be used to create a literal out of what would otherwise be recognized as an equation command or symbol. For instance, to include a ˜ in an equation, you can enter \ ˜. The backslash prevents Word Perfect form interpreting the tilde as meaning "insert a space here."

Certain operators that occur on the keyboard must be typed. For instance +,=,−,/,<,>, and * are all operators that occur on the keyboard and are not included in the Equation Palette.

Braces { } are used to group items in an equation definition. For example:

y = 1 OVER SQRT n − 1	$y = \frac{1}{\sqrt{n}} - 1$
y = 1 OVER {SQRT n − 1}	$y = \frac{1}{\sqrt{n} - 1}$
y = 1 OVER SQRT {n − 1}	$y = \frac{1}{\sqrt{n - 1}}$

More than 360 different commands and symbols are available with the Equation feature. The following table presents a few examples of commands and how they might be used.

Command	Editing Window Entry	Equation Produced
SUP or ^ (Superscript)	X^n	X^n
SUB or _ (Subscript)	X SUB n	X_n
LONGDIV (Long Division)	x~LONGDIV {~y + x^2}	$x\overline{)y + x^2}$
OVER (Fraction)	x OVER { y−1}	$\frac{x}{y-1}$
SQRT (Square root)	y = SQRT { x−1 OVER n}	$y = \sqrt{x - \frac{1}{n}}$
NROOT (Nth root)	y = NROOT 3 {{ x−1} OVER n}	$y = \sqrt[3]{x - \frac{1}{n}}$
BINOM (Binomial)	BINOM x y	$\binom{x}{y}$
FROM TO (limits)	SUM FROM { n = 1} TO 30	$\sum_{n=1}^{30}$
BOLD (Bold)	BOLD x OVER y	$\frac{\mathbf{x}}{\mathbf{y}}$
ITAL (Italic)	ITAL { x OVER y}	$\frac{x}{y}$

For more information on equations, refer to the WordPerfect manual or Help screens.

New Number Code = [New *box type* Num: *n*]

The **New** Number command is used to restart graphics box numbering within a document. To use the command, you move the cursor to where renumbering is to begin, and then type **Alt-F9** (Graphics). Next, select the type box (Figure, Table, Text, User, or Equation) for the new numbering to affect, type **3** or **N** for **New** Number, and then enter the beginning number to use in the renumbering.

Options Code = [*Box type* Opt]

The **O**ptions commands are designed to customize the appearance of the graphics box borders and captions for the Figure, Table, Text or User-defined boxes occurring in the text. The **O**ptions command inserts [Fig Opt], [Tbl Opt], [Txt Opt], [Usr Opt], or [Equ Opt] codes into the document. These codes will affect the four types of graphic boxes occurring in the rest of the document. To use the **O**ptions command, you first type **Alt-F9** (Graphics), and then select the type of graphics box for which the changes are intended. You then type **4** or **O** (**O**ptions). When the **O**ptions command is selected, a menu similar to the following is presented:

```
Options: Figure

     1 - Border Style
              Left                          Single
              Right                         Single
              Top                           Single
              Bottom                        Single
     2 - Outside Border Space
              Left                          0.167"
              Right                         0.167"
              Top                           0.167"
              Bottom                        0.167"
     3 - Inside Border Space
              Left                          0"
              Right                         0"
              Top                           0"
              Bottom                        0"
     4 - First Level Numbering Method       Numbers
     5 - Second Level Numbering Method      Off
     6 - Caption Number Style               [BOLD]Figure 1[bold]
     7 - Position of Caption                Below box, Outside borders
     8 - Minimum Offset from Paragraph      0"
     9 - Gray Shading (% of black)          0%

Selection: 0
```

Border Style

The **B**order Style command allows you to change the appearance of the Left, Right, Top and/or Bottom sides of the box surrounding the Figure, Table, Text, or User-defined graphics data. The **B**order Style options include **N**one and the following.

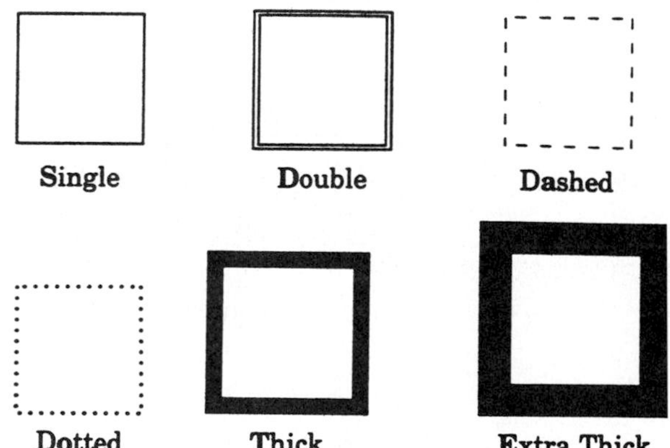

To change the Border Style, type **1** or **B,** and then enter the appropriate command number or letter to set the border style for each side of the graphics box. See **Shift-F8** (Format),**O**ther,**B**order Options for information on changing the appearance of borders around graphics boxes and tables.

Outside Border Space

The **O**utside Border Space command allows you to adjust the amount of space (margin) that occurs between text wrapped around a box and the box's Left, Right, Top, and Bottom sides.

Inside Border Space

The **I**nside Border Space command allows you to adjust the amount of space (margin) that occurs between the graphics data within a graphics box and the box's Left, Right, Top, and Bottom sides.

First Level Numbering Method

The **F**irst Level Numbering Method command may be used to change the appearance of the graphics box number generated by the **C**aption command's [Box Num] code. The choices include **O**ff (no number), **N**umbers (1, 2, 3), **L**etters (A, B, C), and **R**oman Numerals (I, II, III).

Second Level Numbering Method
A second level of Caption numbering may be used to allow for automatic box numbers such as "Figure 1a." To print the extended box number with the graphics box, you will need to use the Caption Number Style command below.

The **S**econd Level Numbering Method command may be used in the same manner as the First Level Numbering Method command. Letters and Roman numerals in the second level are lower case (a, b, c and i, ii, iii).

Caption Number Style
The **Caption** Number Style allows you to change the printed appearance of the caption generated by the **C**aption command's [Box Num] code. When the **C**aption Number Style command is used, the current style is placed on the status line for you to edit. You may change the label used (for instance, change "Figure" to "Graph" or change "Table" to "Chart"). Format codes from the (Font),**A**ppearance menu (Bold, Underline, Italic, etc.) may be included in the caption by typing the command keystrokes that would normally produce the codes. To produce a stop code for such format codes, move the editing cursor to where the stop code is to be inserted and type the appropriate command keystrokes again. To print the first level number, type a "1" where you want the automatic number to appear. To print a second level number, type a "2" where you want the number to appear.

Position of Caption
The **P**osition of Caption command may be used to locate the graphic box's caption. The choices are **B**elow Box or **A**bove Box and then **O**utside of Border or **I**nside of Border.

Minimum Offset from Paragraph
For Paragraph type boxes, WordPerfect will reduce the offset from the top line if the paragraph is too close to the bottom of the page for the box to fit on the page. The **M**inimum Offset from Paragraph command may be used to set a minimum distance from the top of the paragraph for WordPerfect to use when it starts to reduce the offset amount.

Gray Shading (% of Black)
The **G**ray Shading command may be used to shade the contents of graphics boxes in the document. The shading factor is entered as a percentage of black (100% = totally black, 0% = no shading).

Line

The **Alt-F9,5** (Graphics),**L**ine command allows you to create and/or edit horizontal and vertical lines that will be printed with your document. The lines cannot be viewed on the screen during normal editing; however, they may be viewed on the screen using the **Shift-F7,6** (Print),**V**iew Document command.

The **L**ine command allows you to either create or edit a horizontal or vertical graphics line. To create a line in the document, move the cursor to the appropriate place in the document and type **Alt-F9** (Graphics),**L**ine, and then select Create Line: either **H**orizontal or **V**ertical. To edit a graphics line, move the cursor past the location of the line code and type **Alt-F9** (Graphics),**L**ine, and then select Edit Line: either H**o**rizontal or V**e**rtical.

Create—Edit, Horizontal — Code = [Hline:]

The two Horizontal commands produce a screen of commands used to define the type of horizontal line you wish to create or change (edit). To create a horizontal line, move the editing cursor to the position where the line is to appear, and then type **Alt-F9,5,1** (Graphics),**L**ine,Create Line:**H**orizontal.

Horizontal Position

Default— Full

The **H**orizontal Position command may be used to position the line **L**eft (against the left margin), **R**ight (against the right margin), **C**enter (centered between the left and right margins), **F**ull (extending from the left margin to the right margin), or at a **S**et position (starting at a specified number of inches in from the left of the page and extending right).

Vertical Position

Default—Baseline

The **V**ertical Position command may be used to align the bottom of the horizontal graphics line with the baseline of the text line that contains the [HLine:] code or to set the position of the line *n* number of inches from the top of the page.

Length of Line

If the **H**orizontal Position is anything other than **F**ull, you may use the **L**ength of Line command to enter the length of the line in inches.

Width of Line

The **W**idth of Line command may be used to set the thickness of the line. The default value is .013″ wide.

Gray Shading (% of Black)

Default—100%

The **G**ray Shading command may be used to shade the line in the document. The shading factor is entered as a percentage of black (100% = totally black, 0% = no shading).

Create—Edit, Vertical Code=[Vline:]

The two Vertical commands produce a screen of commands used to define the type of vertical line you wish to create or change (edit). With a vertical line, both the horizontal and vertical positions on the page are specified.

Horizontal Position

Default—Left Margin

The **H**orizontal Position command may be used to position the line **L**eft (against the left margin), **R**ight (against the right margin), **B**etween Columns (centered between columns in columnar text), or at a **S**et position (a specified number of inches in from the left side of the page).

Vertical Position

Default—Full Page

The **V**ertical Position command may be used to position the line **F**ull Page (extending from the top margin to the bottom margin), **T**op (against the top margin), **C**enter (centered between the top and bottom margins), **B**ottom (against the bottom margin), or at a **S**et position (a specified number of inches down from the top margin).

Length of Line

If the **V**ertical Position is anything other than **F**ull Page, you may use the **L**ength of Line command to enter the length in inches.

Width of Line

The **W**idth of Line command may be used to set the thickness of the line. The default value is .013″ wide.

Gray Shading (% of Black)

Default—100%

The **G**ray Shading command may be used to shade the line in the document. The shading factor is entered as a percentage of black (100% = totally black, 0% = no shading).

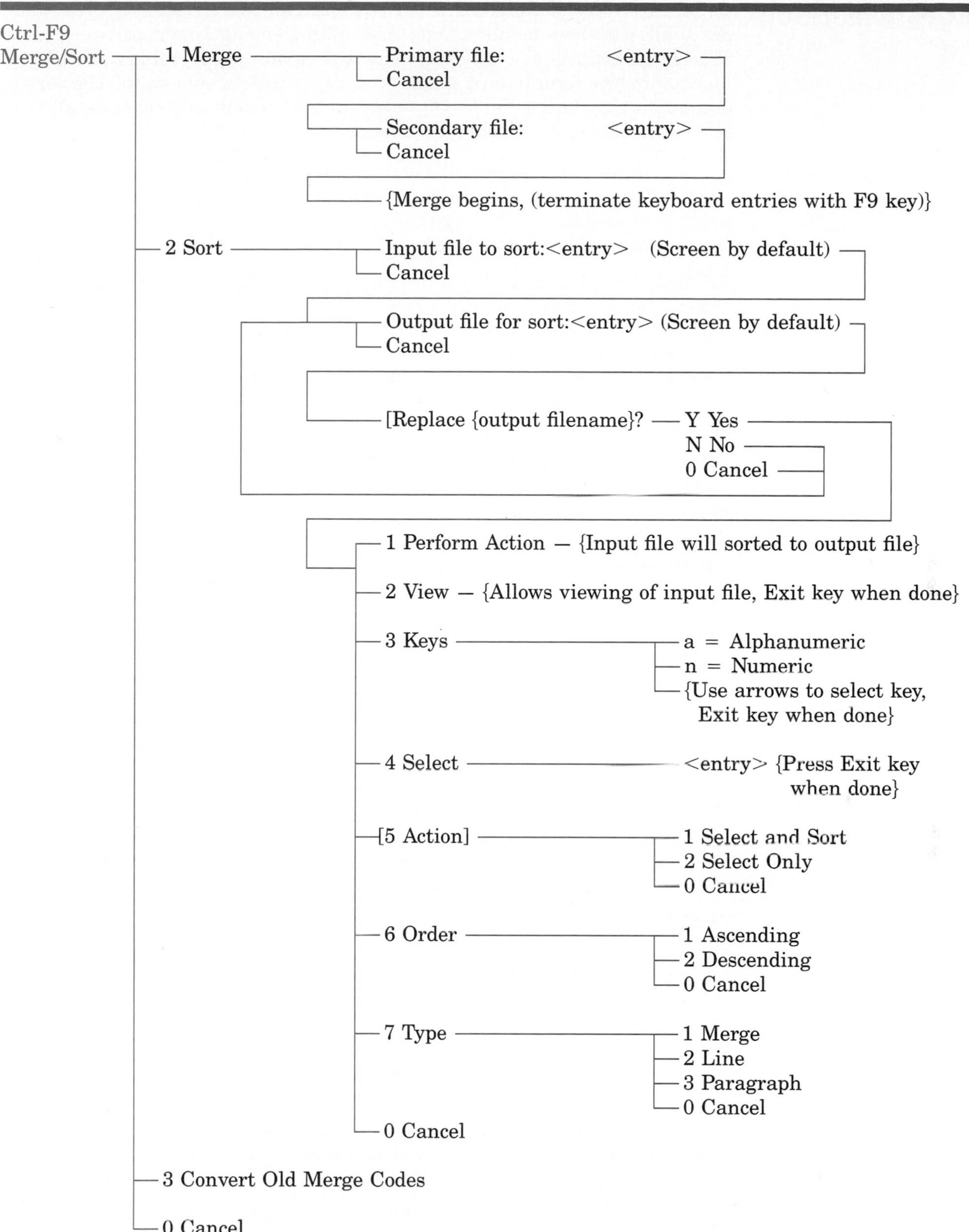
Ctrl-F9
Merge/Sort
1 Merge
Primary file: <entry>
Cancel
Secondary file: <entry>
Cancel
{Merge begins, (terminate keyboard entries with F9 key)}
2 Sort
Input file to sort:<entry> (Screen by default)
Cancel
Output file for sort:<entry> (Screen by default)
Cancel
[Replace {output filename}? — Y Yes
N No
0 Cancel
1 Perform Action — {Input file will sorted to output file}
2 View — {Allows viewing of input file, Exit key when done}
3 Keys
a = Alphanumeric
n = Numeric
{Use arrows to select key,
Exit key when done}
4 Select
<entry> {Press Exit key
when done}
[5 Action]
1 Select and Sort
2 Select Only
0 Cancel
6 Order
1 Ascending
2 Descending
0 Cancel
7 Type
1 Merge
2 Line
3 Paragraph
0 Cancel
0 Cancel
3 Convert Old Merge Codes
0 Cancel

CTRL-F9 MERGE/SORT

The **Ctrl-F9** (Merge/Sort) command provides two WordPerfect features that are similar to those found in Data Base Management System software. The merge feature includes operations that combine text from two or more files to produce form letters, mailing labels, contracts, and so on. The sort operations may be used to sort text within a document and conditionally select and extract text from a document.

Merge Operations—Merge

Certain situations exist where a standard form or document (general text) needs to be filled in with specific information. When this is the case, it is possible to automatically merge the specific information into the general text to produce the desired finished document.

All merge operations require a primary file (the file containing the general text) and may require a secondary file (a file containing specific information). Specific information may be entered from the keyboard or obtained from document files during the merge operation. Merge codes are placed into the primary file. It is the Merge codes that cause WordPerfect to look to the secondary file, keyboard, or document file for specific information. When a merge is completed, the appropriate specific information will be merged with the general text, and the finished document(s) will be ready to print.

The following discusses the steps and merge codes involved in completing a merge operation. It begins with an example of a simple merge used to create a form letter.

Simple Merges

The most common use of merge operations is to provide inside addresses and salutations for form letters. In this case, the general text (primary file) is the letter, and the specific information (names and addresses of people to be included in the letter) is kept in a secondary file.

Creating a Secondary File

In the example, the first step will be to create the secondary file. The information in the secondary file will include the first name, last name, phone number, and complete address of three people. The information in the secondary file is organized like data in a database. Together, the four separate information items for each person (first and last names, phone number, and address) constitute a record of data.

Fields in a Secondary File The separate information items for each record (first and last names, phone number, and so forth) are entered into fields within the record and are separated from each other with a [Mrg:END FIELD] code and a hard return [HRt]. The **F9** (End Field) command inserts the two codes into the file. The [Mrg:END FIELD] code causes WordPerfect to display {END FIELD} on the screen where the code occurs. See **F9** (End Field) for more information on the **F9** (End Field) command.

In this example, the first record of data will be for a Mr. David Cupra, and the first field of data in the record will contain the salutation title "Mr." To enter the first field of data, the title is typed, and then the **F9** (End Field) command is typed. With Reveal Codes on, the screen appears as follows.

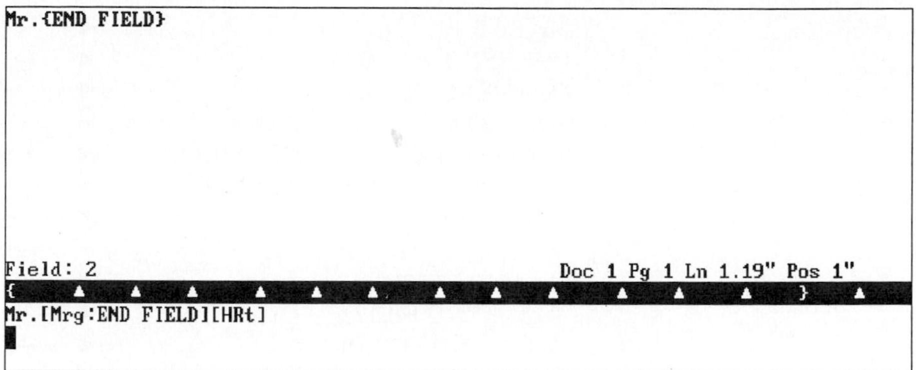

Records in a Secondary File Records in a secondary file are separated from each other with a [Mrg:END RECORD] merge code and a hard page [HPg] code. The **Shift-F9,2** (Merge Codes),**E**nd Record command inserts both codes into the file. The [Mrg:END RECORD] code causes WordPerfect to display {END RECORD} on the screen where the code occurs. See **Shift-F9** (Merge Codes) for more information on the Merge Codes command.

In the example here, the remaining fields of data have been entered for Mr. Cupra. At the end of the field data, the **Shift-F9** (Merge Codes),**E**nd Record command was executed to insert a [Mrg:END RECORD] code and [HPg]code into the document. When finished, the screen appears as follows (with Reveal Codes on).

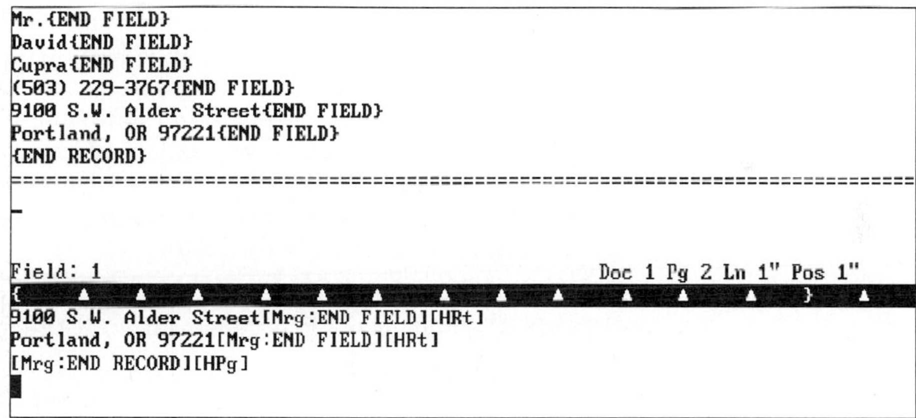

When finished entering the data for all three records, the secondary file has the following form.

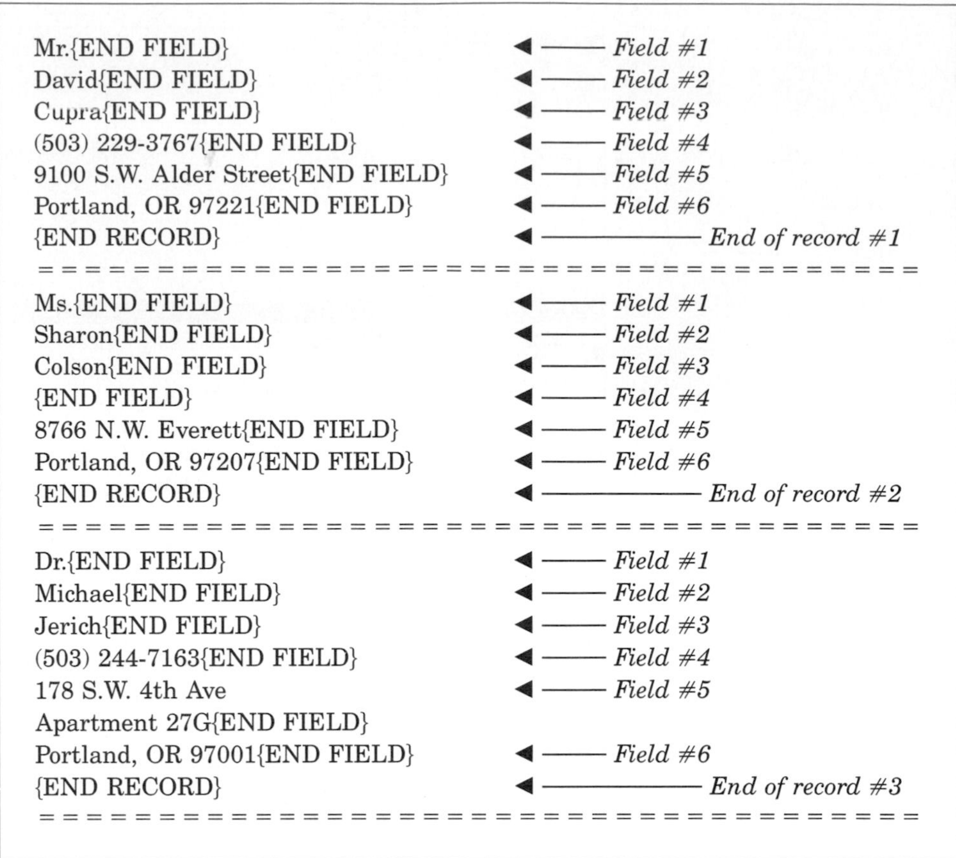

```
Mr.{END FIELD}                          ◄—— Field #1
David{END FIELD}                        ◄—— Field #2
Cupra{END FIELD}                        ◄—— Field #3
(503) 229-3767{END FIELD}               ◄—— Field #4
9100 S.W. Alder Street{END FIELD}       ◄—— Field #5
Portland, OR 97221{END FIELD}           ◄—— Field #6
{END RECORD}                            ◄———————— End of record #1
======================================
Ms.{END FIELD}                          ◄—— Field #1
Sharon{END FIELD}                       ◄—— Field #2
Colson{END FIELD}                       ◄—— Field #3
{END FIELD}                             ◄—— Field #4
8766 N.W. Everett{END FIELD}            ◄—— Field #5
Portland, OR 97207{END FIELD}           ◄—— Field #6
{END RECORD}                            ◄———————— End of record #2
======================================
Dr.{END FIELD}                          ◄—— Field #1
Michael{END FIELD}                      ◄—— Field #2
Jerich{END FIELD}                       ◄—— Field #3
(503) 244-7163{END FIELD}               ◄—— Field #4
178 S.W. 4th Ave                        ◄—— Field #5
Apartment 27G{END FIELD}
Portland, OR 97001{END FIELD}           ◄—— Field #6
{END RECORD}                            ◄———————— End of record #3
======================================
```

The fields in the secondary file may be referred to by their number. Notice that Field #3 is the field that holds the last name for every person (each record) in the file. The Field#–item relationship must be maintained in the secondary file. If an item is not available for a given record, such as Ms. Colson's phone number (Field #4, record #2), an empty field must be entered there. However, the fields may be variable in length, such as the address (Field #5) for Dr. Jerich (record #3).

The next step in the example is to save the file under the filename PROSPCTS and clear the document from RAM with the **F7** (Exit) command.

Creating a Primary File

The primary file in the example will be the form letter into which the names and addresses from the secondary file will be merged. Fields of data from the secondary file are inserted into the primary file at the locations where [Mrg:FIELD] merge codes (shown as {FIELD}*n*˜ on the normal editing screen) appear. The {FIELD} indicates a field of data will be merged, and the *n*˜ indicates the field number for the field that will be merged. For example, placing the merge code {FIELD}3˜ into the primary file will cause the last names in the sample secondary file to be inserted at the position where the {FIELD}3˜ merge code occurs.

The {FIELD}*n*˜ codes are generated by moving the cursor to the appropriate location in the primary file and typing **Shift-F9,1** or **F** (Merge Codes),**F**ield. You then answer the "Enter Field:" prompt by entering the appropriate field number.

If you want to avoid blank lines in the finished document caused by empty fields in the secondary file, you may answer the "Enter Field:" prompt by typing the field number and then a ? (question mark). The code will display {FIELD}*n*?~.

When the primary file is finished it might appear something like the following.

```
                  Vista Ridge Townhouses

{FIELD}1~ {FIELD}2~ {FIELD}3~
{FIELD}5~
{FIELD}6~

Dear {FIELD}2~,

Thank you, {FIELD}2~, for your recent visit and tour of the grounds at
Vista Ridge Townhouses.

We have reviewed your references and are pleased to inform you that
we are able to offer any of our available units for your immediate
occupancy.

We appreciate your patience and look forward to meeting you again.
If you have any questions we can answer at this time, please call
me.

Sincerely,


Jerome Smith
Manager
                                          Doc 1 Pg 1 Ln 1" Pos 1"
```

Once the primary file is created, it is saved onto the disk (under the filename ACCEPTED in this example) and the document screen is cleared with the **F7** (Exit) command.

The final step in completing the simple merge is to type **Ctrl-F9,1** (Merge/Sort),**M**erge, and then answer the "Primary file:" prompt by entering ACCEPTED and the "Secondary file:" prompt by entering PROSPCTS.

When the merge operation is completed, a document will appear on the screen consisting of three form letters, each separated by hard page codes automatically inserted by the merge feature. Each letter will have a different inside address and salutation. The first such letter appears as follows.

```
                        Vista Ridge Townhouses

Mr. David Cupra
9100 S.W. Alder Street
Portland, OR 97221

Dear David,

Thank you, David, for your recent visit and tour of the grounds at
Vista Ridge Townhouses.

We have reviewed your references and are pleased to inform you that
we are able to offer any of our available units for your immediate
occupancy.

We appreciate your patience and look forward to meeting you again.
If you have any questions we can answer at this time, please call
me.

Sincerely,


Jerome Smith
Manager
                                                Doc 1 Pg 1 Ln 1" Pos 1"
```

The file may then be printed.

Other Merge Codes

There are several different merge codes available with WordPerfect. Some of the codes, such as {END FIELD}, {END RECORD} and {FIELD}n~, are found on the initial **Shift-F9** (Merge Codes) command menu. The remaining merge codes may be accessed by typing the **Shift-F9** (Merge Codes),**M**ore command. The **M**ore command presents an alphabetical list of all remaining merge codes on the screen. A cursor (reverse video display) may be moved up and down the list by typing the ↑ and ↓ keys. When the desired merge code is highlighted with the cursor, typing ↵ will select the code for insertion into the document at the current editing cursor location.

Many of the merge codes require that certain data is entered at the time the code is placed in the document. For example, the {INPUT} merge code is designed to pause a merge operation, present the user with a message, and then wait until the user has typed the desired information before continuing the merge operation. The full form of the code is {INPUT}*message*~. When the code is selected from the **M**ore menu, WordPerfect presents the prompt "Enter Message:" on the status line. At this point, you may enter the message you want to present to the user during the merge operation. Such a message might be "Enter the day of the week."

When the code is placed in the document, it appears on the screen as

{INPUT}Enter the day of the week~

Merge codes are different from the other WordPerfect codes. Their presence is indicated in a document by the display of the merge code name (enclosed in braces) on the screen during normal editing. Although the merge code is displayed on the screen, it is given a length of 0 (zero) characters when WordPerfect determines word wrap or Pos cursor position.

However, any additional data, such as messages, variable names, and/or filenames (along with the~s (tildes) that are displayed with the merge code) are inserted into the document as normal text. As such, they can be edited in a normal fashion after a merge code has been inserted into the document.

Editing such data will subsequently change the message, variable name, and/or filename acted upon by the code during a merge operation. It is important to note that the tildes used with merge codes act as delimiters and must remain intact for the merge code to work properly during a merge operation.

The following includes a list of the merge codes found on the **M**ore command.

WordPerfect Merge Codes

{ASSIGN}*var* ~ *expr* ~
{BELL}
{BREAK}
{CALL}*label* ~
{CANCEL OFF}
{CANCEL ON}
{CASE}*expr* ~ *cs1* ~ *lbl* ~ . . . *csN* ~ *lbn* ~~
{CASE CALL}*expr* ~ *csl* ~ *lbl* ~ . . . *csN* ~ *lbn* ~~
{CHAIN MACRO}*macroname* ~
{CHAIN PRIMARY}*filename* ~
{CHAIN SECONDARY}*filename* ~
{CHAR}*var* ~ *message* ~
{COMMENT}*comment* ~
{CTON}*character* ~
{DATE}
{DOCUMENT}*filename* ~
{ELSE}
{END FIELD}
{END FOR}
{END IF}
{END RECORD}
{END WHILE}
{FIELD}*field* ~
{FIELD NAMES}*name1* ~ . . . *nameN* ~~
{FOR}*var* ~ *start* ~ *stop* ~ *step* ~
{GO}*label* ~
{IF}*expr* ~
{IF BLANK}*field* ~
{IF EXISTS}*var* ~
{IF NOT BLANK}*field* ~
{INPUT}*message* ~
{KEYBOARD}
{LABEL}*label* ~
{LEN}*expr* ~
{LOCAL}*var* ~ *expr* ~
{LOOK}*var* ~
{MID}*expr* ~ *offset* ~ *count* ~
{MRG CMND}*codes*{MRG CMND}
{NEST MACRO}*macroname* ~
{NEST PRIMARY}*filename* ~
{NEST SECONDARY}*filename* ~
{NEXT}
{NEXT RECORD}
{NTOC}*number* ~
{ON CANCEL}*action* ~
{ON ERROR}*action* ~
{PAGE OFF}
{PAGE ON}
{PRINT}
{PROCESS}*codes*{PROCESS}
{PROMPT}*message* ~
{QUIT}
{RETURN}
{RETURN CANCEL}
{RETURN ERROR}
{REWRITE}
{STATUS PROMPT}*message* ~
{STEP OFF}
{STEP ON}
{STOP}
{SUBST PRIMARY}*filename* ~
{SUBST SECONDARY}*filename* ~
{SYSTEM}*sysvar* ~
{TEXT}*var* ~ *message* ~
{VARIABLE}*var* ~
{WAIT}*10ths second* ~
{WHILE}*expr* ~

For a complete description of all merge codes, see the WordPerfect manual. The following discusses some of the more often used merge codes.

{BELL}

The {BELL} merge code causes the computer to beep. It may be used in conjunction with merge codes that present a message for the user to respond to. An example might be

{BELL}{INPUT}Enter the day of the week.~

Here, the {BELL} code causes the computer to beep, then the {INPUT} code presents the message on the status line and pauses the merge operation for the user to enter the desired data.

{CANCEL OFF}—{CANCEL ON}

The {CANCEL OFF} code may be used to disable the **F1** (Cancel) key during a merge operation. The {CANCEL ON} code may be used to enable the **F1** (Cancel) key after it has been disabled with a {CANCEL OFF} code.

{CHAR}*var˜ message˜*

Similar to the {TEXT}*var˜ message˜* code, the {CHAR}*var˜message˜* code pauses the merge operation and presents a message on the status line. The {CHAR} code, however, only accepts a single character entry by the user and does not require the **F9** (End Field) keystroke to terminate the entry. The character typed by the user is stored in the variable (var) specified in the merge code.

{COMMENT}*comment˜*

The {COMMENT} code may be used to place user messages or other documentation in a primary file. {COMMENT} codes do not cause the merge operation to pause.

{DATE}

The {DATE} merge code may be placed in the primary file to automatically insert the current DOS system date into the text. The date will be inserted as text in the current date format (see **Shift-F5** (Date/Outline) for information on setting date formats).

{DOCUMENT}*filename˜*

The {DOCUMENT} *filename˜* merge code may be used to retrieve and insert the specified document file into the primary file at the location of the {DOCUMENT} code.

The {DOCUMENT} code may be used in conjunction with a {VARIABLE}*var˜* code to selectively retrieve a file. For example, suppose there were four different paragraphs held in separate files on the disk with the filenames PARA1, PARA2, PARA3, and PARA4. During the merge operation, you want the user to be able to select one of the paragraphs to insert into the primary file.

To do so, you may first use a merge code to ask the user which paragraph to merge. Two examples of such codes might be

{TEXT}number˜Enter the appropriate paragraph number; 1, 2, 3, or 4˜

{CHAR}number˜Enter the appropriate paragraph number; 1, 2, 3, or 4˜

In both cases, whatever the user enters in response to the message, "Enter the appropriate paragraph number; 1, 2, 3 or 4," will be stored in the variable named "number."

The next step is to include (in the primary file below the code that requests the paragraph's number) a {DOCUMENT} code in the form: {DOCUMENT} PARA˜. This is done by typing PARA↵ in response to the "Enter Filename:" prompt when the code is selected from the **M**ore menu. The final step is to move the cursor to the immediate right of the filename included in the {DOCUMENT} code and select the {VARIABLE} merge code from the **M**ore menu. In this example, you would type number↵ in response to the "Enter Variable:" prompt presented when the {VARIABLE} code is selected.

The results of following the steps described here will be

{DOCUMENT}PARA{VARIABLE}number˜˜

This combination of codes will cause WordPerfect to merge the file whose filename begins with PARA and that ends with the characters held in the variable named "number." Notice that there are two tildes required at the end of the code combination. If Typeover mode is on when the {VARIABLE} code is inserted into the document, one of the tildes will be deleted. You may either retype the tilde in the appropriate place or make sure that Insert is on when the {VARIABLE} code is selected.

{END FIELD}
The {END FIELD} merge code is used to indicate the end of a field of data in a secondary file. See *Simple Merges* above for more information on the {END FIELD} code.

{END RECORD}
The {END RECORD} merge code is used to indicate the end of a record of data in a secondary file. See *Simple Merges* above for more information on the {END RECORD} code

{FIELD}*field~*
The {FIELD} *field~* merge code is used to specify a field of data in a secondary file for insertion into a primary file. See *Simple Merges* on p. W-220 for more information on the {FIELD} *field~* code.

{FIELD NAMES}*name1~... nameN~~*
The {FIELD NAMES} code is used to create a unique record (called a "*header*" record) in a secondary file. See *Simple Merges* for more information on fields in a secondary file. The {FIELD NAMES} code assigns names to the fields in the database. The header record containing the {FIELD NAMES} code must be the first record in the secondary file.

To insert a {FIELD NAMES} code into a secondary file, move the cursor to the top of the file, type **Shift-F9** (Merge Codes),**6** or **M** for **M**ore, and then select the {FIELD NAMES} code from the menu. WordPerfect will next prompt "Enter Field 1:". Type and enter the name you wish to give the first field in each record. WordPerfect will continue prompting "Enter Field 2:", "Enter Field 3:", and so on. When you have finished naming each field in the record, type **F7** (Exit). The **F7** keystroke places the {FIELD NAMES} code and an {END RECORD} code into the file.

A header record for the previous example database might appear as follows.

```
{FIELD NAMES}title~first~last~phone~address~city~~{END RECORD}
===========================================================================
Mr.{END FIELD}
David{END FIELD}
Cupra{END FIELD}
(503) 229-3767{END FIELD}
9100 S.W. Alder Street{END FIELD}
Portland, OR 97221{END FIELD}
{END RECORD}
===========================================================================
```

Including a {FIELD NAMES} code in the secondary file allows you to reference fields from the primary file by specifying field names, instead of field numbers, when selecting {FIELD}*field~* codes. For example, the text in a primary file may have the inside address and salutation in the following form.

```
                    Vista Ridge Townhouses

{FIELD}title~ {FIELD}first~ {FIELD}last~
{FIELD}address~
{FIELD}city~

Dear {FIELD}first~,

Thank you, {FIELD}first~, for your recent visit and tour of the grounds at
Vista Ridge Townhouses.
```

{INPUT}*message*~
The {INPUT} merge code pauses a merge to allow text to be entered from the keyboard. When the {INPUT} code is selected from the **M**ore menu of merge codes, the prompt "Enter Message:" appears on the status line. The message entered will be displayed on the status line when the code is encountered during a merge operation. The merge will then pause for the user to type the appropriate text. When finished, the user must type **F9** (End Field) to proceed with the merge operation.

{KEYBOARD}
The {KEYBOARD} code is similar to the {INPUT} code because it pauses the merge operation for the user to enter data from the keyboard. The {KEYBOARD} code does not, however, provide for a message to be displayed on the status line for the user to view. When finished entering the text allowed for by the {KEYBOARD} code, the user must type **F9**(End Field) to proceed with the merge operation.

{NEST PRIMARY}*filename* ~
The {NEST PRIMARY} code is similar to the {DOCUMENT} code because it inserts a specified document file into the primary file at the location of the code. The {NEST PRIMARY} code, however, will subsequently search the merged data for occurrences of additional merge codes and will execute the codes if they are found. The {DOCUMENT} code does not search the merged data for codes.

{PRINT}
Used in the primary file, the {PRINT} code sends all previously merged text to the printer. The text occurring before the {PRINT} code is then deleted from the merged file.

{PROMPT}*message* ~
The {PROMPT} code presents a message on the status line for the user to view. It does not, however, pause the merge operation. A {PAUSE}*message*~ {WAIT}*10ths second* ~ code combination may be used to present a message, then pause for *n* 10ths of a second while the user reads the message.

{TEXT}*var* ~ *message* ~
The {TEXT} code may be used to prompt the user for a response, and then store the response in a variable for later use. To merge data contained in a WordPerfect variable, the {VARIABLE}*var* ~ code is used. One example of how the two codes may be used together might involve a type of form letter in which a single variable phrase or word (such as "married couples," "single people," or "retired citizens") occurs one or more times. In such cases a {TEXT}*var* ~ *message* ~ code may be used to obtain, from the user, the appropriate phrase for the document. Such a code might appear as

{TEXT}type ~ Enter the type of tenant making the inquiry~

In the remainder of the primary file, {VARIABLE}type ~ codes may be used to insert the phrase where it is desired. For example,

> Here at Vista Ridge, {VARIABLE}type ~ enjoy year-round swimming and sauna, plus use of our recreation room and tennis courts.

{VARIABLE}*var*~
The {VARIABLE} code is used to insert the contents of the specified variable into the document at the location of the code. See the {CHAR}, {DOCUMENT}, and {TEXT} codes for more information on storing data to WordPerfect variables, and for examples on using the {VARIABLE} code.

{WAIT}*10ths second*~
The {WAIT} code may be used to pause the merge operation for *n* 10ths of a second. See the {PROMPT}*message* ~ code for one example on how the {WAIT} code may be used.

Sort/Select Operations—Sort

The **Ctrl-F9** (Merge/Sort) command may be used to sort text or conditionally extract (select) text from a document. When text is sorted, it appears ascending or descending in alphabetical or numeric order. When text is selected, only certain text (text that passes a condition) will appear.

Input/Output Files

When sorting or selecting text, WordPerfect uses the following approach.

input file ⟶ process ⟶ output file

The text to be sorted or selected from exists in the input file. During the sort or select operation, a copy of the data in the input file is made first. The copy then is sorted and/or selected (processed), and the processed data are saved to the output file. If the output file is specified as being the same as the input file, the original data in the input file will be overwritten by the processed data.

When the data to be processed exists as a portion of text within a larger document, the recommended procedure is as follows: 1) retrieve the file; 2) block the portion of text to be processed; 3) type **Ctrl-F9,2** (Merge/Sort),**S**ort to begin the sort or select operation. The block of text is treated as both the input and output file by the **S**ort command.

Because of the overwriting nature of the process, it is highly recommended that you save or back up your files before attempting to complete a sort or select operation.

Sort/Select Keys

Keys are the data items upon which WordPerfect sorts text, or they are the data items used in logical expressions upon which WordPerfect selects text. Keys are specified by their location in the text and by their data type, string or numeric (WordPerfect refers to string data as being "alphanumeric").

There are three different text formats that may be sorted or selected: Line, Merge, and Paragraph, In each case, the text is organized into records (the units that will be sorted or selected).

Line Format

In Line format text, the records to sort or select are arranged on lines with fields of data (data items) occurring at tab stops (see **Shift-F8,1,8** (Format),**L**ine,**T**ab Set for more information on setting tab stops). Each line of data is considered to be a record, and each data item is considered to be a field of data. The data items are entered by using the Tab key or **F4** (Indent) command to separate them from each other.

Field 1	Field 2	Field 3	Field 4	Field 5	Field 6
Pratt John	225-1234	M	06/22/82	1949.00	200.00
Smoller Ellen	225-3212	F	09/15/83	1650.00	300.00
Jones David	292-3832	M	06/15/82	1550.00	25.00
Sill Sally	224-4321	F	02/15/84	1507.00	0.00
	↑	↑	↑	↑	↑
	L	**L**	**L**	**D**	**D**

In the example above, Left and Decimal tab stops were set, and the data items for name, phone, gender, date, salary, and account were entered with the Tab key used to align the data items at the appropriate tab stops.

The keys for Line format text are defined by data type (string or numeric), the field number where they occur, and the word number within the field where they occur. For example, if you wanted to sort or select the example line text by salary, you would define the appropriate key as numeric, field #5, word #1. If you wanted to sort or select the text by first names, you would specify the key as alphanumeric, field #1, word #2.

Merge Format

With Merge format text, records are in a secondary merge file format in which each record is ended with an {END RECORD} merge code and a hard page [HPg] code, and each field within a record is ended with an {END FIELD} merge code and a hard return [HRt] code. See **Ctrl-F9** (Merge/Sort),Merge Operations for more information on secondary merge files. The following is an example of a secondary merge file's format.

```
Mr.{END FIELD}                         ◄—— Field #1
David{END FIELD}                       ◄—— Field #2
Cupra{END FIELD}                       ◄—— Field #3
(503) 229-3767{END FIELD}              ◄—— Field #4
9100 S.W. Alder Street{END FIELD}      ◄—— Field #5
Portland, OR 97221{END FIELD}          ◄—— Field #6
{END RECORD}                           ◄———————— End of record #1
=====================================
Ms.{END FIELD}                         ◄—— Field #1
Sharon{END FIELD}                      ◄—— Field #2
Colson{END FIELD}                      ◄—— Field #3
{END FIELD}                            ◄—— Field #4
8766 N.W. Everett{END FIELD}           ◄—— Field #5
Portland, OR 97207{END FIELD}          ◄—— Field #6
{END RECORD}                           ◄———————— End of record #2
=====================================
```

The keys for Merge format text are defined by data type (string or numeric), the field number where they occur, and the word number within the field where they occur. For instance, if you wanted to sort or select the example merge text by last name, you would define the appropriate key as alphanumeric, field #3, word #1. If you wanted to sort or select the text by ZIP codes, you would specify the key as alphanumeric, field #6, word #3.

Paragraph Format

In Paragraph format text, the record is considered to be the text occurring between two or more hard returns ([HRt]s). The keys used to sort or select paragraphs are defined by the line in which they occur, the field in which they occur (if Tabs or Indents are used they define fields such as Field #1 at [Tab] or [Indent] #1 and so on) and the word number in the line or field of the paragraph where they occur. For instance, if you wanted to sort or select paragraphs by the first word of the first line in each paragraph, and the first line of each paragraph is indented, you would specify the key as alphanumeric, line #1, field # 2, word # 1.

Sorting/Selecting Text

You begin to sort or select text by making sure that there are current backup copies of the text available. You then decide if the text needs to be blocked. If so, you block the text. You then type **Ctrl-F9** (Merge/Sort). If text is blocked, the **S**ort command menu screen will appear next.

If text is not blocked, you will need to type **2** or (**S**ort), and then answer the Input file/Output file prompts by entering the filenames or typing ↵ for Screen. Selecting Screen is the same as specifying the current document as the input and/or output file. After completing the steps, the **S**ort command menu screen will appear. In the following examples, a line format blocked portion of text will be used. The records to sort and/or select from are employee records, with the fields last name/first name, phone number, date hired, salary, and amount on personal account with the company. The **S**ort command menu screen appears as follows.

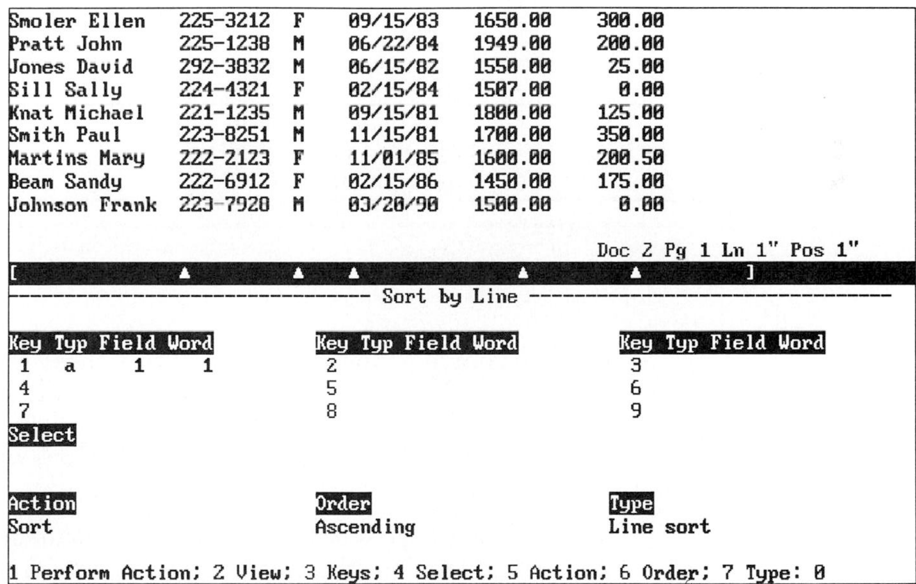

A portion of the blocked text is displayed at the top of the screen. The **S**ort command menu screen begins with a ruler line which displays the current tab stops. Beneath the ruler line is an area used to define keys, and four descriptions of current **S**ort screen settings: Select, Action, Order, and Type (of Sort). At the bottom of the screen appears the **S**ort command menu.

Perform Action

The **P**erform Action command is used to execute the sort or select operation after all of the appropriate sort/select settings have been made.

View

The **V**iew command may be used to scroll through the text at the top of the screen without leaving the **S**ort menu screen. The **F7** (Exit) command is used to exit the **V**iew command.

Keys

The **K**eys command is used to define the keys to be used in a sort or select operation. When the **K**eys command is executed, the cursor jumps to the key definition area of the **S**ort menu screen, and you are allowed to edit the key definition displayed there. The first Sort key is, by default, defined as alphanumeric, field #1, word #1.

There are nine key definitions available. If the action for which the keys are being defined is **S**ort, the sort order will be primary sort on key #1, secondary sort on key #2, and so on. In the example here, if you wanted the records to be sorted first by Male/Female and then by salary amounts within those two categories, you would set key #1 to a, 3, 1 (alphanumeric, field #3, word #1) and key #2 to n, 5, 1 (numeric, field #5, word #1).

Select

The **S**elect command is used to extract records of text that meet certain criteria. When the select process is over, only those records meeting the criteria will appear in the Output file or on the screen. To select records, you must first define all keys that will be used in the criteria. You then type **4** or **S** (**S**elect) and enter the logical expression to be used as the select criteria. The WordPerfect operators for such expressions include the following:

Relational

=	Equal
<	Less than
>	Greater than
<=	Less than or equal to
>=	Greater than or equal to
<>	Not equal to

Logical

+	OR
*	AND

In the example, if you wanted to extract those records for men with salaries greater than or equal to $1650.00, you would first define the two keys for gender and salary. Here, key #8 will be defined for gender as a, 3, 1 (alphanumeric, field #3, word #1) and key #9 will be defined for salary as n, 5, 1 (numeric, field # 5, word #1).

You then may type **4** or **S** (**S**elect), and the cursor will jump to the Select description area on the screen for you to enter the criteria. The criteria is entered in the form

key8 = M * key9 >= 1650

Once the **S**elect command has been used to enter the criteria, the action to perform automatically becomes Select rather than Sort. To return to sorting, you must type **4** or **S** (**S**elect) and delete the criteria shown on the screen (use the Del key, Backspace key, or Ctrl-End keys to complete the deletion).

Action
When a select criteria exists, the **A**ction command may be used to **S**elect and Sort or Select **O**nly. With **S**elect and Sort, the extracted records are sorted on the currently defined keys. With Select **O**nly, the records are only extracted.

Order
The **O**rder command may be used to set the sort order to **A**scending or **D**escending.

Type
The **T**ype command is used to specify the format type, **M**erge, **L**ine, or **P**aragraph for the data being sorted or selected. The current type is displayed under the ruler line of the **S**ort menu screen.

Convert Old Merge Codes

The **Ctrl-F9** (Merge/Sort),Convert Old Merge Codes command may be used to convert merge codes created with an earlier version of WordPerfect into 5.1 format. Retrieve the file in which the older merge codes exist and type **Ctrl-F9** (Merge/Sort),**3** or **C** for **C**onvert Old Merge Codes

---

F10
Save — Document to be saved:<entry> — {Document saved}
Replace {filename}? — Y Yes
N No
Cancel Key

F10 SAVE

The **F10** (Save) command may be used to save a document without clearing the screen or returning to DOS. It is recommended that you use the **F10** (Save) command frequently while you are editing. If the document is one that has not been previously saved, you must next enter a filename under which to save it. If the file has been previously saved, WordPerfect will display the original filename as the default answer to the "Document to be saved:" prompt. Type ↵ if you want to save the document under the same name (replace the copy on the disk). Type a new name if you do not want to replace the file on the disk. If you use an existing filename, WordPerfect will pause and prompt "Replace *filename*? No (Yes)." Type Y to replace the file on the disk or type N or ↵ to reenter the filename.

Block/Save

You may save a block of text by blocking the text before you type **F10** (Save).

Shift-F10
Retrieve — Document to be retrieved:<entry> — {file will be retrieved into current document}
Cancel key

SHIFT-F10 RETRIEVE

The **Shift-F10** (Retrieve) command may be used to retrieve a document file onto a clear screen or into a current document at the cursor location. Type **Shift-F10** (Retrieve), and then enter the filename of the file you wish to retrieve.

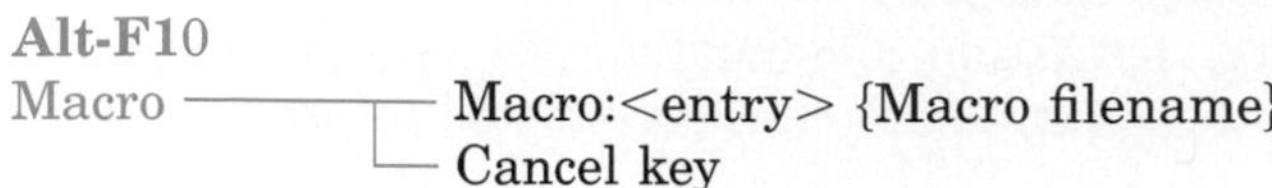

ALT-F10 MACRO

The (Macro) command is used to load and execute a keystroke macro that was named with ↵ or characters at the time it was created. See **Ctrl-F10** (Macro Define) for more information on creating, saving, and executing keystroke macros.

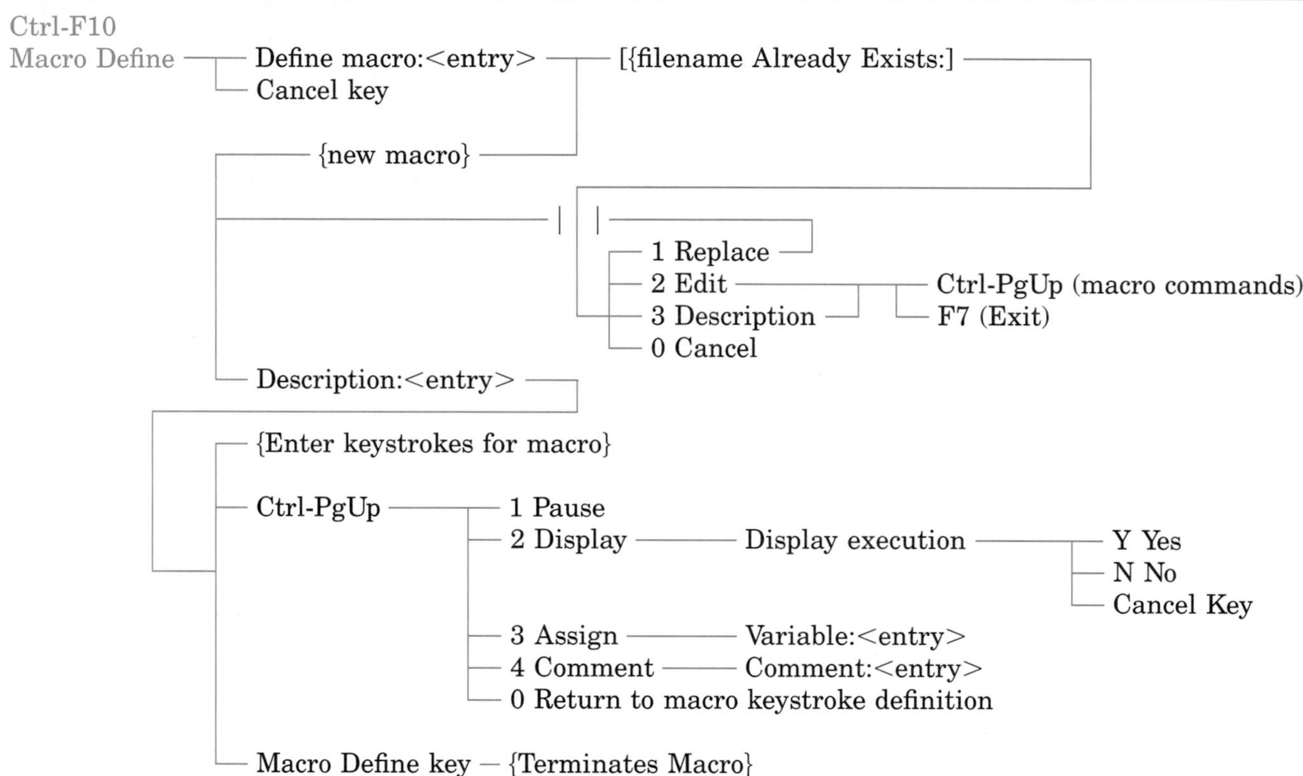

CTRL-F10 MACRO DEFINE

When using WordPerfect, you use three basic types of keystrokes: character keystrokes, which enter text into the document; keystroke commands, which perform certain operations (such as Ctrl-End to delete the line right); and menu keystrokes, which invoke WordPerfect's command mode.

A macro is a collection of keystrokes, saved by WordPerfect, that may be executed (automatically retyped) at any time. The keystrokes in the macro may be character, keystroke command, and/or command menu in nature. Macros are a time-saving feature of WordPerfect.

To explain how keystroke macros may be created, suppose that you have created a document within which there are several key words you now wish to italicize. To italicize the words in the document, you have been using the following steps.

1. Move the cursor to the beginning of the word and type **Alt-F4** (Block).
2. Type Ctrl-Right (to jump the cursor to the other side of the word, thus blocking the word).
3. Type **Ctrl-F8,2,4** (Font),**A**ppearance,**I**talc (the set of keystrokes used to insert the start and stop codes for italics, [ITALC] and [italc]).

Notice that, except for the keystrokes used to move the cursor to the word in step 1, all other keystrokes are exactly the same for any word you may want to italicize. In other words, the remaining keystrokes are systematic. Large groups of systematic keystrokes are prime candidates for becoming keystroke macros.

Steps in Creating and Using Keystroke Macros

There are four basic steps required to create a keystroke macro.

1. Begin defining the macro by typing **Ctrl-F10** (Macro Define).
2. Enter a name and description for the macro.
3. Type the keystrokes you want saved in the macro.
4. End defining the macro by typing **Ctrl-F10** (Macro Define) again.

How you may execute a macro (cause WordPerfect to automatically retype the keystrokes within it) depends on the name you give the macro in step 2 of the steps required to create a macro.

Naming and Using a Macro

One to Eight Characters

If you enter a name consisting of up to eight characters, the macro is saved on the disk in the Keyboard/Macro Files subdirectory (see **Shift-F1,6** (Setup),**L**ocation of Files for more information) with a .WPM filename extension. To execute the macro you type **Alt-F10** (Macro) and then enter the filename of the macro.

Alt-Letter

If you name the macro by holding down the Alt key and typing a letter key (A to Z), the macro is saved on the disk in the Keyboard/Macro Files subdirectory under the filename ALT*letter* with a .WPM extension. To execute the macro, you simply type Alt-letter. For example, if you named the macro Alt-A, you would later type **Alt-A** to execute it.

Enter Key

If you name the macro by typing ↵, the macro is saved on the disk in the Keyboard/Macro Files subdirectory under the filename and extension WP{WP}.WPM. Only one such macro may be in the current Keyboard/Macro Files subdirectory at one time. To execute the macro, you type **Alt-F10** (Macro) and then ↵.

Defining a Macro

To begin defining a macro, you type **Ctrl-F10** (Macro Define). A "Define macro:" prompt will appear on the status line. At this point you enter the macro name of your choice (see *Naming and Using a Macro* above). If the macro name entered is not the current name for another macro, the prompt "Description:" will next appear on the status line. Here you are allowed to enter a short (39 character) description (documentation) for the macro. After the description is entered, a blinking "Macro Def" prompt appears on the status line. At this point subsequent keystrokes become the keystrokes included in the macro.

Entering the Keystrokes For a Macro

To enter the keystrokes for a macro, you simply type them as you would during normal editing. For example, to enter the keystrokes to italicize the current word you would type

Alt-F4,Ctrl-Right,**Ctrl-F8,2,4** (Block,Word Right,(Font),**A**ppearance,**I**talc)

The Ctrl-PgUp Keystroke

While entering the keystrokes for a macro in the above fashion, the Ctrl-PgUp keystroke may be used to present a menu of optional changes that may be made to the macro. If you are in the normal editing mode, the Ctrl-PgUp keystroke presents a menu consisting of **P**ause, **D**isplay, **A**ssign, and **C**omment. If you are in a command mode, the menu consists of **P**ause and **D**isplay.

Pause The **P**ause command may be used to cause the macro to temporarily stop its execution so that you may enter text or move the cursor. A pause in a macro is ended when the user types ↵.

In the example, if you wanted to create a macro that could be used to italicize either a word, a letter in a word, or a paragraph, you could enter a pause after the **Alt-F4** (Block) keystroke in the macro. That is, the keystrokes to enter into the macro would become

Alt-F4,Ctrl-PgUp,**1,Ctrl-F8,2,4** (Block,**P**ause,(Font),**A**ppearance,**I**talc)

To use the macro, you move the cursor to the beginning of the text you want to italicize, and then begin the execution of the macro. After the macro starts the block operation (types **Atl-F4** (Block)) it pauses for you to move the cursor, thus expanding the block to cover whatever text you want to italicize. When the appropriate text is blocked, you type ↵, and the remaining keystrokes in the macro are executed.

Display
Default—No (Off)
The **D**isplay command may be used to cause WordPerfect to display all menus and other items that would normally be displayed during the execution of the macro's keystrokes.

Assign The **A**ssign command may be used to pause the macro for the user to assign a value to a WordPerfect variable. The command is related to a group of commands collectively referred to by WordPerfect as being "Advanced Macro" commands. See the WordPerfect manual or Help screens for more information.

Comment The **C**omment command allows keystrokes that will not be executed to be included in the macro. The command is most useful for entering short sections of documentation into the macro.

Finishing the Macro's Definition

Once all of the keystrokes have been entered into the macro, you type **Ctrl-F10** (Macro Define) again to stop defining the macro.

Editing a Macro

WordPerfect provides a means to edit the keystrokes in a macro. To edit a macro, you type **Ctrl-F10** (Macro Define), and then enter the name of the macro you wish to edit. When the (Macro Define) command is used to define a macro that already exists, WordPerfect will prompt "*macro name.* WPM Already Exists: 1 **R**eplace; 2 **E**dit; 3 **D**escription:." To change the description for the macro, you type **3** or **D** (**D**escription), and then edit the current description. To edit the keystrokes in the macro, you type **2** or **E** (**E**dit). The **Ctrl-F10** (Macro Define), **E**dit command will present a screen similar to the following.

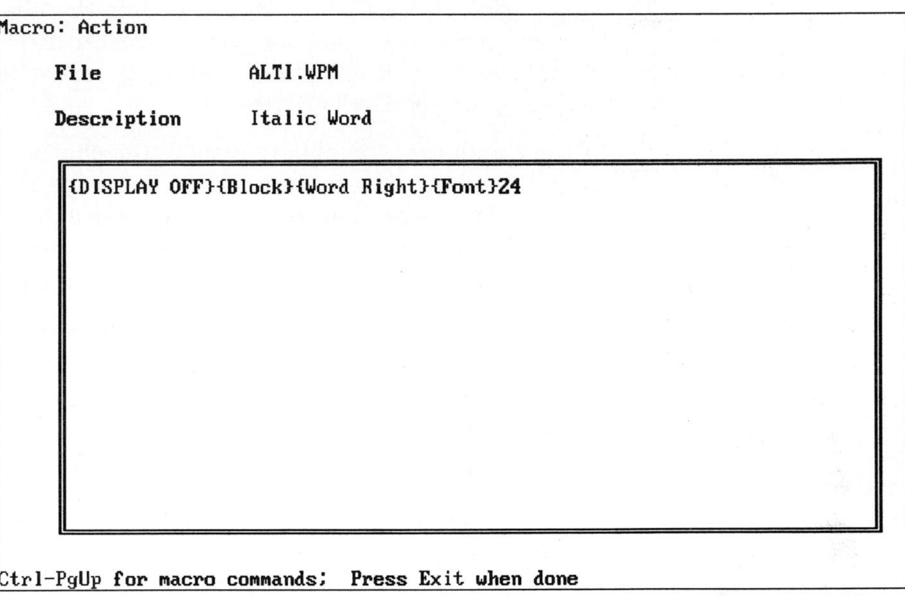

Macro: Action
File ALTI.WPM
Description Italic Word
{DISPLAY OFF}{Block}{Word Right}{Font}24
Ctrl-PgUp for macro commands; Press Exit when done

An editing cursor will appear in the box holding the macro keystrokes. To delete a keystroke, you may use the Backspace or Del keys in the same manner as during normal editing.

To insert keyboard characters such as "1" or "F," you may move the cursor to where the characters are to be inserted and then type the characters.

To insert non-printable keystrokes such as {Left} and {Enter} (← and ↵), you move the cursor to where the keystrokes are to appear in the macro, and then type **Ctrl-F10**. You next type the keystrokes to be inserted in the macro. When finished, type **Ctrl-10** again to return to normal editing of the macro. To produce a list of extended macro commands from which a selection may be made, you may type Ctrl-PgUp. See the WordPerfect manual or Help screens for more information on such commands.

When finished editing the macro, type **F7** (Exit) to return to normal document editing.

WordPerfect has a feature called "Compose" that allows you to include nonstandard characters in your document. The additional characters are organized into 11 different tables (called "character maps"). To include a compose character in your document, you type **Ctrl-v**. A "Key =" prompt will appear on the status line. You next type the appropriate map number, a comma, the appropriate compose character number, ↵. For instance, to include a cent mark (¢), which is found in character map four, under the number 19, you type **Ctrl-v**,4,19,↵.

If the computer is unable to display the character on the monitor screen, it will display instead a small box where the character will appear in the printed document. You may increase or decrease the size of the printed compose character by using the **Ctrl-F8** (Font),**S**ize commands. See **Ctrl-F8** (Font),**S**ize for more information on changing font sizes.

The following tables describe the definitions of the various character maps and show the associated compose numbers for the characters included in them.

CHARACTER MAP 0 (ASCII)

	0										1									
	0	1	2	3	4	5	6	7	8	9	0	1	2	3	4	5	6	7	8	9
30				!	"	#	$	%	&	'	(	)	*	+	,	-	.	/	0	1
50	2	3	4	5	6	7	8	9	:	;	<	=	>	?	@	A	B	C	D	E
70	F	G	H	I	J	K	L	M	N	O	P	Q	R	S	T	U	V	W	X	Y
90	Z	[	\	]	^	_	`	a	b	c	d	e	f	g	h	i	j	k	l	m
110	n	o	p	q	r	s	t	u	v	w	x	y	z	{	|	}	~			

CHARACTER MAP 1 (MULTINATIONAL 1)

	0										1									
	0	1	2	3	4	5	6	7	8	9	0	1	2	3	4	5	6	7	8	9
0	`	˙	˜	ˆ	_	/	´	¨	¯	'	'	'	¸	'	°		˛	.	.	˘
20	ˏ	¯	˘	ß	ı	ȷ	Á	á	Â	â	Ä	ä	À	à	Å	å	Æ	æ	Ç	ç
40	É	é	Ê	ê	Ë	ë	È	è	Í	í	Î	î	Ï	ï	Ì	ì	Ñ	ñ	Ó	ó
60	Ô	ô	Ö	ö	Ò	ò	Ú	ú	Û	û	Ü	ü	Ù	ù	Ÿ	ÿ	Ã	ã	Đ	đ
80	Ø	ø	Õ	õ	Ý	ý	Đ	đ	Þ	þ	Ă	ă	Ā	ā	Ą	ą	Ć	ć	Č	č
100	Ĉ	ĉ	C	c	Ď	ď	Ě	ě	E	e	Ē	ē	Ę	ę	Ǵ	ǵ	Ğ	ğ	Ǧ	ǧ
120	Ģ	ģ	Ĝ	ĝ	G	g	Ĥ	ĥ	Ħ	ħ	I	i	Ī	ī	Į	į	Ĩ	ĩ	Ĳ	ĳ
140	Ĵ	ĵ	Ķ	ķ	Ĺ	ĺ	Ľ	ľ	Ļ	ļ	Ŀ	ŀ	Ł	ł	Ń	ń	'N	ŉ	Ň	ň
160	Ņ	ņ	Ő	ő	Ō	ō	Œ	œ	Ŕ	ŕ	Ř	ř	Ŗ	ŗ	Ś	ś	Š	š	Ş	ş
180	Ŝ	ŝ	Ť	ť	Ţ	ţ	Ŧ	ŧ	Ŭ	ŭ	Ű	ű	Ū	ū	Ų	ų	Ů	ů	Ũ	ũ
200	Ŵ	ŵ	Ŷ	ŷ	Ź	ź	Ž	ž	Z	z	Ŋ	ŋ	D̄	d̄	L̄	l̄	N̄	n̄	R̀	r̀
220	S̄	s̄	T̄	t̄	Y̆	y̆	Ỳ	ỳ	D̓	d̓	O̓	o̓	U̓	u̓						

CHARACTER MAP 2 (MULTINATIONAL 2)

	0	1	2	3	4	5	6	7	8	9	10	11	12	13	14	15	16	17	18	19
0	˙	¨	˚	˳	ʼ	^	=	–	K	˘	'	'	'	,	‹	ˍ	˩	ʟ	'	'
20	,	˘	'	'	ˇ	˅	⁄	˝												

CHARACTER MAP 3 (BOX DRAWING)

	0	1	2	3	4	5	6	7	8	9	10	11	12	13	14	15	16	17	18	19
0	░	▒	▓	█	▌	▀	▐	▄	─	│	┌	┐	┘	└	├	┬	┤	┴	┼	═
20	║	╔	╗	╝	╚	╠	╦	╣	╩	╬	╒	╕	╛	╘	╓	╖	╜	╙	╞	╥
40	╡	╨	╟	╤	╢	╧	╫	╪	╴	╵	╶	╷	╸	╹	╺	╻	╼	╾	╽	╿
60	┞	┟	┡	┢	┭	┮	┯	┰	┥	┦	┧	┩	┵	┶	┷	┸	┽	┾	┿	╀
80	╁	╂	╃	╄	╅	╆	╇	╈												

CHARACTER MAP 4 (TYPOGRAPHICAL SYMBOLS)

	0	1	2	3	4	5	6	7	8	9	10	11	12	13	14	15	16	17	18	19
0	●	○	■	•	⋆	¶	§	¡	¿	«	»	£	¥	₧	ƒ	ª	º	½	¼	¢
20	²	ⁿ	®	©	¤	¾	³	‛	’	‘	‟	”	“	–	—	‹	›	○	□	†
40	‡	™	℠	℞	●	∘	■	▪	□	▫	‒	ﬀ	ﬃ	ﬄ	ﬁ	ﬂ	…	$	₣	₢
60	₠	₤	‚	„	⅓	⅔	⅛	⅜	⅝	⅞	☻	⊕	☻	%	℅	‰	№	–	¹	

CHARACTER MAP 5 (ICONIC SYMBOLS)

	0	1	2	3	4	5	6	7	8	9	10	11	12	13	14	15	16	17	18	19
0	♥	♦	♣	♠	♂	♀	☼	☺	☻	♪	♫	▬	⌂	‼	√	↨	⌐	⌙	◘	◙
20	←	☛	☚	✓	☐	☒	☹	♯	♭	♮	☎	⌚	⌛	¢	␣					

CHARACTER MAP 6 (MATH/SCIENTIFIC)

	0	1	2	3	4	5	6	7	8	9	10	11	12	13	14	15	16	17	18	19
0	−	±	≤	≥	∝	/	∕	\	÷	∣	⟨	⟩	∼	≈	≡	∈	∩	∥	∑	∞
20	¬	→	←	↑	↓	↔	↕	▸	◂	▴	▾	·	·	∘	•	Å	°	µ	‾	×
40	∫	∏	∓	∇	∂	′	″	→	ℯ	ℓ	ℏ	ℑ	ℜ	℘	⇄	⇆	➡	⬅	⬆	⬇
60	⬌	⬍	↗	↘	↖	↙	∪	⊂	⊃	⊆	⊇	∍	∅	⌈	⌉	⌊	⌋	≪	≫	∠
80	⊗	⊕	⊖	⊕	⊙	∧	∨	⊻	⊤	⊥	⌒	⊢	⊣	□	■	◇	◆	⟦	⟧	≠
100	≢	∵	∴	∷	∮	ℒ	ℭ	ℨ	℘	○	△	◇	★	‴	∐	≃	≅	≺	≼	≻
120	≽	∃	∀	≪	≫	⊎	⊊	⊋	⊓	⊔	⊏	⊑	⋤	⊐	⊒	⋥	▵	▿	◃	▹
140	⋈	⌣	⌢	◯	→	↩	↪	↦	↼	↽	⇀	⇁	⇌	⇋	↿	↾	⇃	⇂	⇉	⇇
160	⌣	⌢	(	)	⊛	⊛	⊝	Ʊ	∡	∢	◁	▷	△	▽	∔	≐	≒	≓	⋄	×
180	⊨	▲	⋮	⌉	★	≮	≰	≯	≱	≁	≉	≢	≄	⊀	⋠	⊁	⋡	⊄	⊅	⊈
200	⊉	⊄	⊅	⊈	⊉	∦	∤	∗	∄	∉	∌	ℰ	ℱ	ℂ	ℐ	ℕ	ℝ	²	⊾	∋
220	⋯	…	⋮	⋱	‾	↔	+	−	=	∗										

CHARACTER MAP 7 (MATH/SCEINTIFIC EXTENSION)

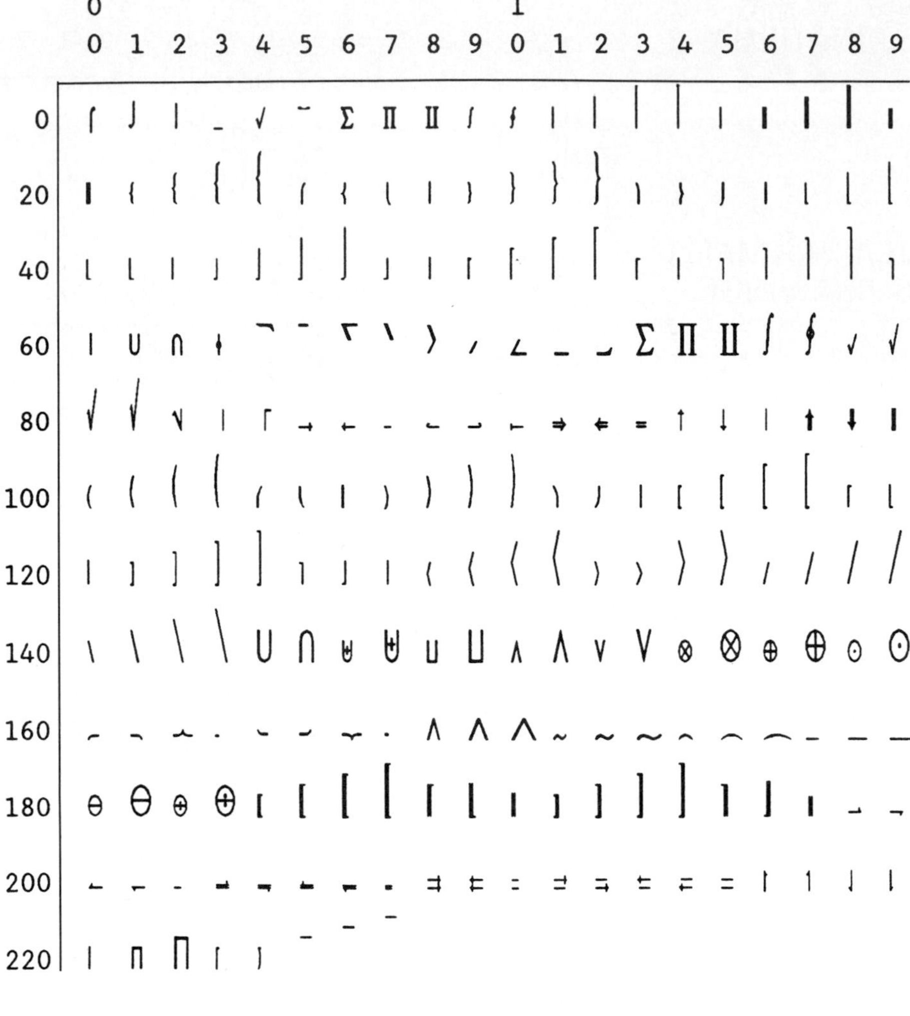

CHARACTER MAP 8 (GREEK)

	00	01	02	03	04	05	06	07	08	09	10	11	12	13	14	15	16	17	18	19
0	Α	α	Β	β	Β	ϐ	Γ	γ	Δ	δ	Ε	ϵ	Ζ	ζ	Η	η	Θ	θ	Ι	ι
20	Κ	κ	Λ	λ	Μ	μ	Ν	ν	Ξ	ξ	Ο	ο	Π	π	Ρ	ρ	Σ	σ	Σ	ς
40	Τ	τ	Υ	υ	Φ	φ	Χ	χ	Ψ	ψ	Ω	ω	ά	έ	ή	ί	ϊ	ό	ύ	ῡ
60	ώ	ε	ϑ	ϰ	ϖ	ϱ	ϒ	φ	ϖ	;	·	´	¯	᾿	῾	`	^	·	·	.
80	῎	῞	῏	῟	᾿	῾	΄̣	`̣	^̣	·̣	·̣	῎̣	῞̣	῏̣	῟̣	᾿̣	῾̣	ὰ	ᾶ	ᾳ
100	ᾴ	ᾷ	ἀ	ἄ	ἆ	ἁ	ᾀ	ᾄ	ᾁ	ἀ	ἄ	ἆ	ἁ	ᾀ	ᾄ	ᾁ	ὲ	ἐ	ἔ	ἕ
120	ἐ	ἔ	ἕ	ὴ	ῆ	ῃ	ῄ	ῂ	ῇ	ἠ	ἤ	ἦ	ἡ	ᾐ	ᾔ	ᾑ	ἠ	ἤ	ἦ	ἡ
140	ᾐ	ᾔ	ᾑ	ὶ	ῖ	ἰ	ἴ	ἰ	ἴ	ἶ	ἱ	ἰ	ἴ	ἶ	ἱ	ὸ	ὀ	ὄ	ὅ	ὁ
160	ὄ	ὅ	ὺ	ῦ	ὐ	ὔ	ὐ	ὔ	ὖ	ὑ	ὐ	ὔ	ὖ	ὑ	ὼ	ῶ	ῳ	ῴ	ῲ	ῷ
180	ὠ	ὤ	ὦ	ὡ	ᾠ	ᾤ	ᾡ	ὠ	ὤ	ὦ	ὡ	ᾠ	ᾤ	ᾡ	ʹ	͵	ϛ	ϝ	ϙ	ϡ

CHARACTER MAP 9 (HEBREW)

	0										1									
	0	1	2	3	4	5	6	7	8	9	0	1	2	3	4	5	6	7	8	9
0	א	ב	ג	ד	ה	ו	ז	ח	ט	י	ך	כ	ל	ם	מ	ן	נ	ס	ע	ף
20	פ	ץ	צ	ק	ר	שׁ	שׂ	ת	בּ	כּ	פּ	◌ִ	◌ֵ	◌ֶ	◌ֻ	◌ָ	◌ַ	◌ְ	◌ֲ	◌ֱ
40	◌ֳ		◌ֹ	◌ּ																

CHARACTER MAP 10 (CYRILLIC)

	0										1									
	0	1	2	3	4	5	6	7	8	9	0	1	2	3	4	5	6	7	8	9
0	А	а	Б	б	В	в	Г	г	Д	д	Е	е	Ё	ё	Ж	ж	З	з	И	и
20	Й	й	К	к	Л	л	М	м	Н	н	О	о	П	п	Р	р	С	с	Т	т
40	У	у	Ф	ф	Х	х	Ц	ц	Ч	ч	Ш	ш	Щ	щ	Ъ	ъ	Ы	ы	Ь	ь
60	Э	э	Ю	ю	Я	я	Ґ	ґ	Ђ	ђ	Ѓ	ѓ	Є	є	Ѕ	ѕ	І	і	Ї	ї
80	Ј	ј	Љ	љ	Њ	њ	Ћ	ћ	Ќ	ќ	Ў	ў	Џ	џ	Ѣ	ѣ	Ѳ	ѳ	Ѵ	ѵ
100	Ѫ	ѫ	Ӡ	ӡ	Ш	ш	Ɨ	ɨ	Ѧ	ѧ	А́	а́	Е́	е́	И́	и́	О́	о́	У́	у́
120	Ы́	ы́	Э́	э́	Ю́	ю́	Я́	я́	À	à	È	è	Ѐ	ѐ	Ѝ	ѝ	Ò	ò	Ỳ	ỳ
140	Ы̀	ы̀	Э̀	э̀	Ю̀	ю̀	Я̀	я̀	□	□										

CHARACTER MAP 11 (HIRAGANA AND KATAKANA)

	0										1									
	0	1	2	3	4	5	6	7	8	9	0	1	2	3	4	5	6	7	8	9
0	ぁ	ぃ	ぅ	ぇ	ぉ	っ	ゃ	ゅ	ょ	ゔ	ゕ	ゖ	あ	い	う	え	お	か	き	く
20	け	こ	が	ぎ	ぐ	げ	ご	さ	し	す	せ	そ	ざ	じ	ず	ぜ	ぞ	た	ち	つ
40	て	と	だ	ぢ	づ	で	ど	な	に	ぬ	ね	の	は	ひ	ふ	へ	ほ	ば	び	ぶ
60	べ	ぼ	ぱ	ぴ	ぷ	ぺ	ぽ	ま	み	む	め	も	や	ゆ	よ	ら	り	る	れ	ろ
80	わ	を	ん	〔	〕	[	]	「	」	「	」	.	。	、	ゝ	ゞ	〃	ー	`	・
100	ァ	ィ	ゥ	ェ	ォ	ッ	ャ	ュ	ョ	ヴ	ヵ	ヶ	ア	イ	ウ	エ	オ	カ	キ	ク
120	ケ	コ	ガ	ギ	グ	ゲ	ゴ	サ	シ	ス	セ	ソ	ザ	ジ	ズ	ゼ	ゾ	タ	チ	ツ
140	テ	ト	ダ	ヂ	ヅ	デ	ド	ナ	ニ	ヌ	ネ	ノ	ハ	ヒ	フ	ヘ	ホ	バ	ビ	ブ
160	ベ	ボ	パ	ピ	プ	ペ	ポ	マ	ミ	ム	メ	モ	ヤ	ユ	ヨ	ラ	リ	ル	レ	ロ
180	ワ	ヲ	ン	ヽ	ヾ															

CODES.WPM

The WordPerfect 5.1 software includes a WordPerfect macro named CODES.WPM that is designed to produce a printed copy of a document that contains the imbedded codes included in the document.

The WordPerfect macro actually consists of four macros: CODES.WPM, the main "calling" macro; and REVEALCO.WPM, REVEALTX.WPM, and REVEALBX.WPM, three second-level ("chained" or "nested") macros. In order for the macro to work properly, the three nested macros must be located in the directory specified with the **Shift-F1** (Setup),**L**ocation of Files,**K**eyboard/Macro Files command. If this directory has been specified as the drive where your files are kept, you will need to copy the macro files onto your disk.

Ask your microcomputing laboratory staff for directions on what to do. Do not copy any files onto your disk without their explicit approval.

To use the CODES.WPM macro, you may use the following steps:

1. Make sure you have a backup copy of the file on which you plan to execute the macro.
2. Retrieve the file into WordPerfect and make sure there is not another document in the other Document area. (See **Shift-F3** (Switch), for more information on the two document areas).
3. Type **Alt-F10** (Macro), and then answer the "Macro:" prompt by typing ‖ CODES↵ ‖.

The following *pull-down* menu will appear on the screen as follows.

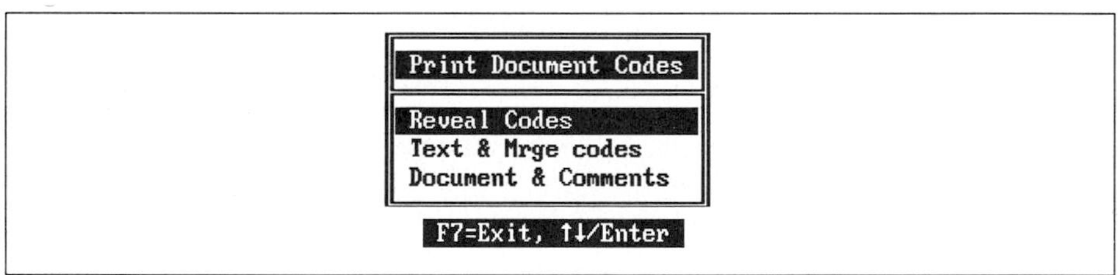

A highlighted cursor (menu bar) will appear on the "Reveal Codes" option of the menu. The menu bar may be moved up and down with the ↑ and ↓ keys. To make a selection from the menu, you may move the menu bar to the desired option and type ↵. To exit the macro, you may type **F7** (Exit). The three options on the pull-down menu are used to do the following.

REVEAL CODES

The **R**eveal Codes option produces a printed copy of the document as it appears in the Reveal Codes screen. All imbedded codes are printed with the text included in the document.

TEXT & MRGE CODES

The **T**ext & mrge codes option produces a printed copy of the document as it appears on the normal editing screen. Merge codes on the screen, displayed in the form {MERGE CODE}, are printed with the text in the document. This command is useful for printing secondary files because it does not eject a page each time an {END RECORD} code is reached. (See **Ctrl-F9** (Merge/Sort) for more information on merge codes).

DOCUMENT & COMMENTS

The Document & Comments option produces a printed copy of the document as it appears in the normal editing screen. Comments, displayed on the screen in the form:

This is an example

are printed with the text in the document. (See **Ctrl-F5** (Text In/Out),Comment for more information on document comments).

After you have selected the type of document codes you want printed, a second pull-down menu, like the one that follows, will appear.

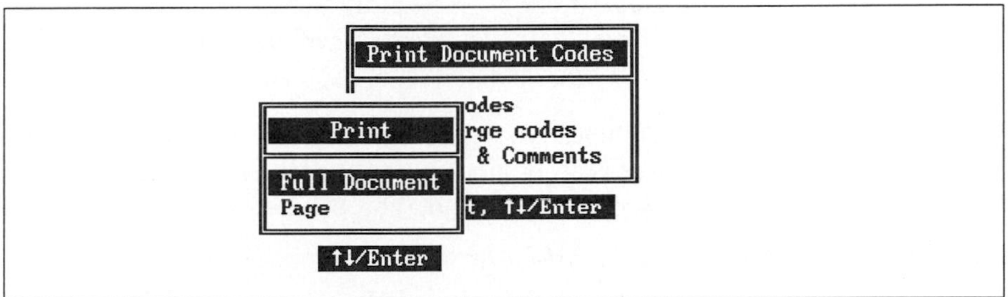

From the second menu you may choose to either print the entire document or print only the current page. Before making this selection, however, you should make sure that the printer for your microcomputer is turned on and on-line.

The macro works by making a copy of the current document and placing the copy in the other Document area. As the copy operation proceeds, the codes in the original document are replaced with text equivalents in the copied file, thus creating a "codes" document in the other Document area.

After the macro prints the codes document, it presents the prompt "Save codes Document Yes (No)" on the status line. Typing N causes the macro to erase the codes document from the other Document area, and return to the original document. Typing Y causes the macro to save the codes document (under a name that you give it) before it ereases it from the other Document area, and returns to the original document.

MOUSE SUPPORT

A *mouse* is a hardware device that connects to the computer and may be used to perform "screen-oriented" operations with certain software. With WordPerfect, a mouse may be used to block text, move the editing cursor on the screen, and access WordPerfect commands.

The mouse device usually has two buttons (left and right) and rides on a roller ball. When a mouse is in use, a mouse *pointer* appears on the monitor screen. With WordPerfect, the mouse pointer appears as a small rectangular character (▮). The following terms are used when discussing mouse operations:

Click	Press a mouse button.
Double-click	Rapidly press a mouse button twice.
Drag	Press and hold a mouse button then move the mouse.

BLOCKING TEXT

To block text with a mouse, first move the mouse pointer to where blocking is to begin, press the left mouse button, then drag the mouse to where blocking is to end. The blocked text will appear highlighted on the screen.

CURSOR MOVEMENT

To reposition the editing cursor on the screen, move the mouse pointer to the desired location and click the left mouse button. The cursor may only be moved to areas on the screen where characters have been entered.

MOUSE MENUS

To access WordPerfect's commands, the mouse uses a *pull-down* menu system. To view the mouse menu, click the right mouse button. To remove the mouse menu from the screen you may click the right mouse button again. The mouse menu first appears on the screen in a form similar to the following.

```
File Edit Search Layout Mark Tools Font Graphics Help
```

The menu contains nine command menu items. A menu bar (reverse video) will be displayed on the "File" option. To select a menu item from this menu you may move the mouse pointer to the desired command and click the left mouse button; or you may use the ← or → cursor movement keys to move the menu bar to the desired command and then type ↵; or type the highlighted letter that appears in the desired command's name. When a command is selected from the menu, a pull-down menu will appear on the screen below the selected command, as shown in the following.

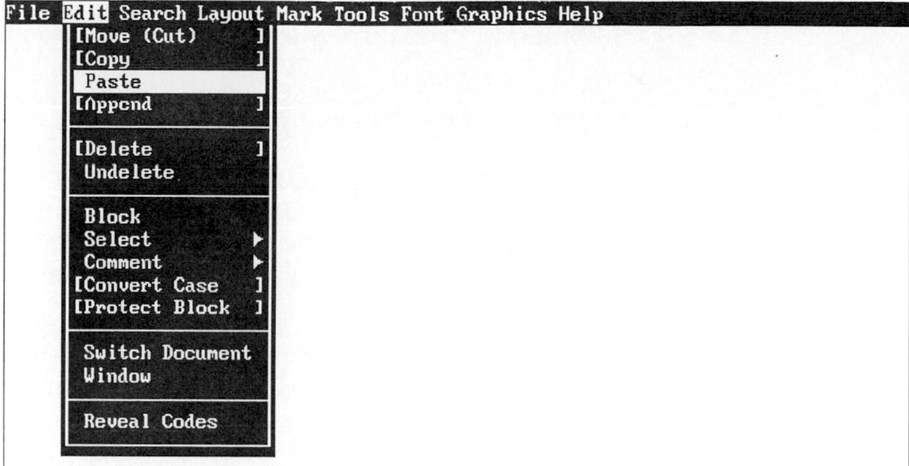

Commands may be selected from the pull-down menu in the same manner as in the first menu. That is, use the mouse pointer, move the menu bar with the ↑ or ↓ keys and then type ↵, or type the highlighted letter in the command name.

When a pull-down menu command is enclosed in brackets, such as [Convert Case], it means the command cannot currently be selected. This usually means that text must be blocked before the command may be selected from the pull-down menu.

When a pull-down menu command has a ▶ character displayed to the right, such as Select, it means the command has further pull-down sub-menus from which selections may be made.

When the final pull-down menu command is selected, WordPerfect enters its conventional command mode at a particular level. For example, if the Select command is selected from the Edit pull-down menu, WordPerfect presents the following pull-down sub-menu.

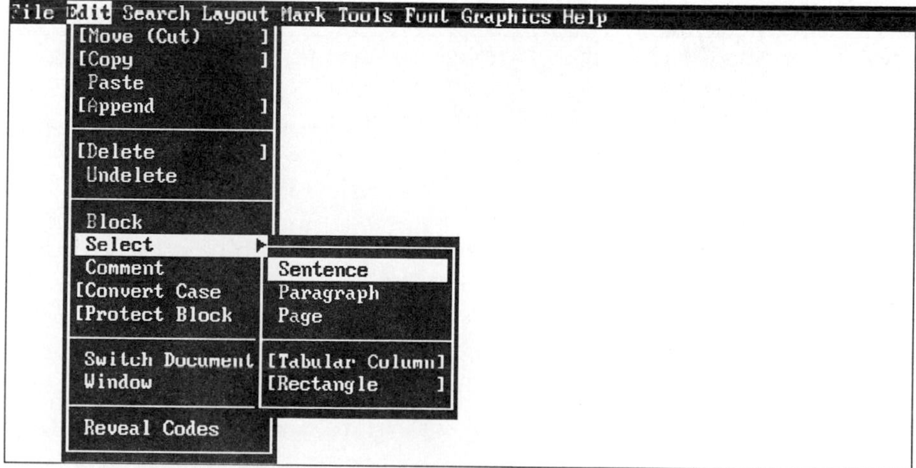

If the Sentence command is then selected from the second pull-down menu, WordPerfect will display the following menu on the status line.

```
1 Move; 2 Copy; 3 Delete; 4 Append: 0
```

This is the same menu presented when the **Ctrl-F4** (Move),**S**entence command is typed. Once WordPerfect has entered its conventional command menu mode, you may select commands by either typing the command number or letter, or you may move the mouse pointer to the command and click the left mouse button.

When a WordPerfect command presents a menu screen in which a menu bar (reverse video) is displayed, such as the menu bar of the List Files screen, a double click of the left mouse button has the effect of moving the menu bar to the mouse pointer location then typing ↵.

Pressing the left mouse button and then clicking the right mouse button has the same effect as typing the **F1** (Cancel) command. With a three-button mouse, the center button may be used for **F1** (Cancel).

MOUSE MENU COMMAND TREES

The following command tree structures describe each of the nine main pull-down menu commands in terms of the equivalent conventional command keystrokes that would be required to execute the pull-down command or that would be required to bring WordPerfect to the point where it leaves the pull-down menu and enters the conventional command mode.

File

Retrieve — **Shift-F10** (Retrieve)

Save — **F10** (Save)

Text In — **Ctrl-F5** (Text In/Out)
- 1 DOS Text
  - 2 Retrieve (CR/LF to [HRt])
  - 3 Retrieve (CR/LF to [SRt] in HZone)
- 5 Spreadsheet
  - 1 Import
  - 2 Create Link
  - 3 Edit Link
  - 4 Link Options

Text Out — **Ctrl-F5** (Text In/Out)
- 1 DOS Text
  - 1 Save
- 3 Save As
  - 1 Generic
  - 2 WordPerfect 5.0
  - 3 WordPerfect 4.2

Password — **Ctrl-F5** (Text In/Out) — 2 Password

List Files — **F5** (List)

Summary — **Shift-F8** (Format) — 3 Document — 5 Summary

Print — **Shift-F7** (Print)

Setup — **Shift-F1** (Setup)

Go to DOS — **Ctrl-F1** (Shell) — 1 Go to DOS

Exit — **F7** (Exit)

Edit

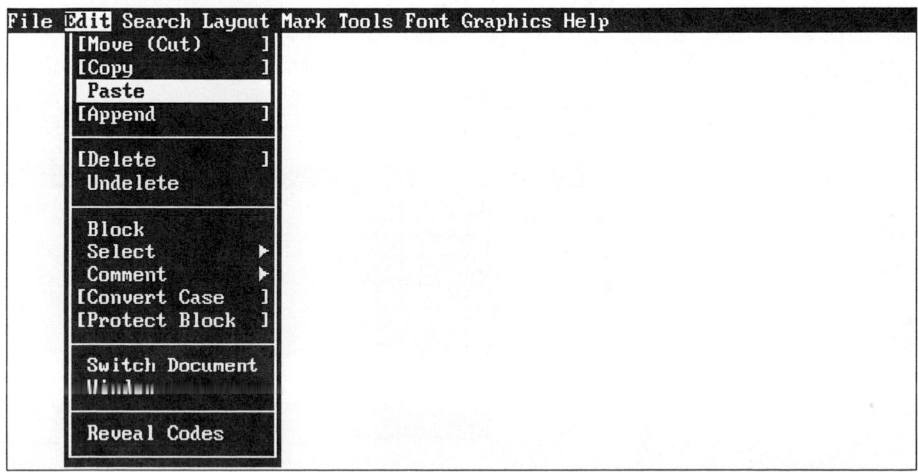

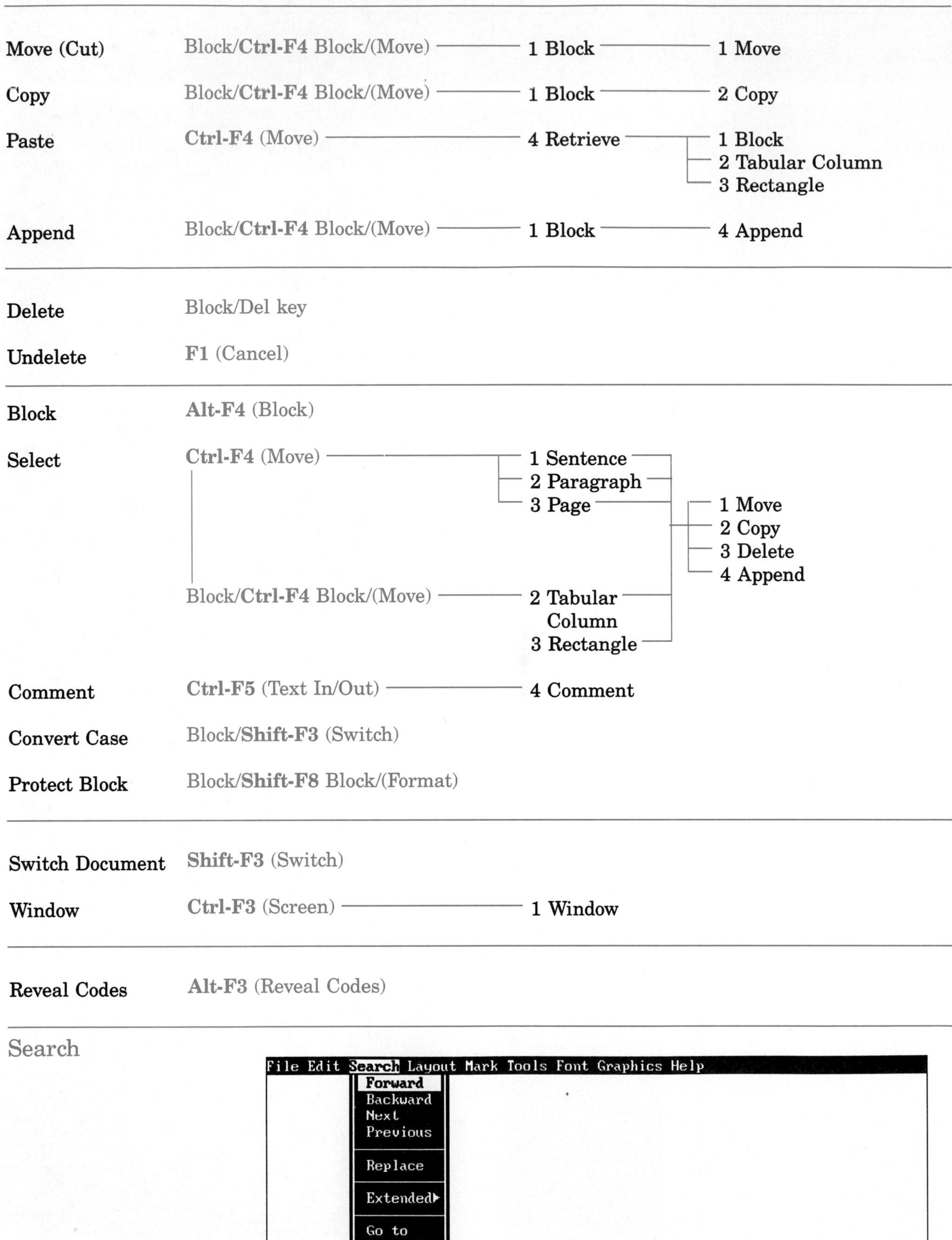

Function	Keystrokes	Menu option	Sub-option
Move (Cut)	Block/**Ctrl-F4** Block/(Move)	1 Block	1 Move
Copy	Block/**Ctrl-F4** Block/(Move)	1 Block	2 Copy
Paste	**Ctrl-F4** (Move)	4 Retrieve	1 Block 2 Tabular Column 3 Rectangle
Append	Block/**Ctrl-F4** Block/(Move)	1 Block	4 Append
Delete	Block/Del key		
Undelete	**F1** (Cancel)		
Block	**Alt-F4** (Block)		
Select	**Ctrl-F4** (Move)	1 Sentence 2 Paragraph 3 Page	1 Move 2 Copy 3 Delete 4 Append
	Block/**Ctrl-F4** Block/(Move)	2 Tabular Column 3 Rectangle	
Comment	**Ctrl-F5** (Text In/Out)	4 Comment	
Convert Case	Block/**Shift-F3** (Switch)		
Protect Block	Block/**Shift-F8** Block/(Format)		
Switch Document	**Shift-F3** (Switch)		
Window	**Ctrl-F3** (Screen)	1 Window	
Reveal Codes	**Alt-F3** (Reveal Codes)		

Search

Forward	**F2** (▶Search)
Backward	**Shift-F2** (◀Search)
Next	**F2**, **F2** (▶Search), (▶Search) (search forward for last search string)
Previous	**Shift-F2**, **Shift-F2** (◀Search), (◀Search) (search backward for last search string)
Replace	**Alt-F2** (Replace)
Extended	Home — F2 (▶Search) — Shift-F2 (◀Search) — F2, F2 (▶Search), (▶Search) — Shift-F2, Shift-F2 (◀Search), (◀Search) — Alt-F2 (Replace)
Go to	Ctrl-Home

Layout

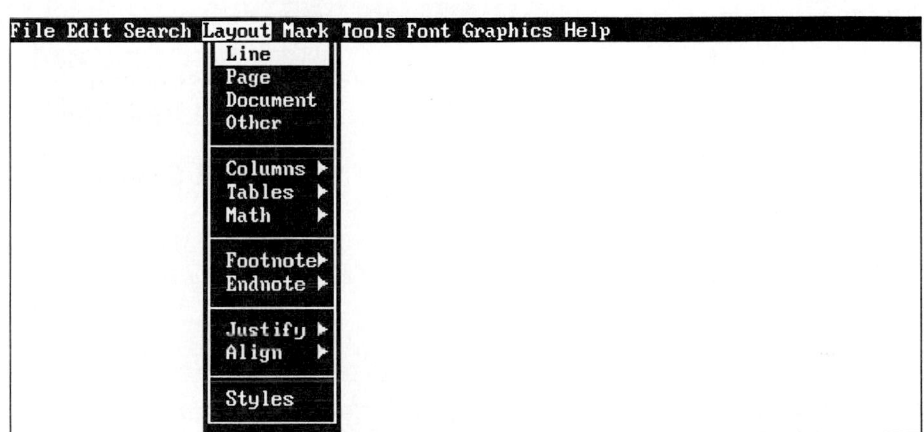

Line	**Shift-F8** (Format) — 1 Line
Page	**Shift-F8** (Format) — 2 Page
Document	**Shift-F8** (Format) — 3 Document
Other	**Shift-F8** (Format) — 4 Other
Columns	**Alt-F7** (Columns/Table) — 1 Columns
Tables	**Alt-F7** (Columns/Table) — 2 Tables
Math	**Alt-F7** (Columns/Table) — 3 Math

Footnote	**Ctrl-F7** (Footnote)	1 Footnote	
Endnote	**Ctrl-F7** (Footnote)	2 Endnote 3 Endnote Placement	

Justify	**Shift-F8** (Format)	1 Line	3 Justification
Align	**F4** (▶Indent) **Shift-F4** (▶Indent◀) **Shift-Tab** [◀Mar Rel] **Shift-F6** (Center) **Alt-F6** (Flush Right) **Ctrl-F6** (Tab Align) **Ctrl-**↵[HPg]		

Styles	**Alt-F8** (Style)

Mark

Index	**Alt-F5** (Mark Text)	3 Index
Table of Contents	Block/**Alt-F5** Block/(Mark Text)	1 ToC
List	Block/**Alt-F5** Block/(Mark Text)	2 List
Cross-Reference	**Alt-F5** (Mark Text)	1 Cross-Ref
Table of Authorities	**Alt-F5** (Mark Text)	4 ToA Short Form

Define	**Alt-F5** (Mark Text)	5 Define

Generate	**Alt-F5** (Mark Text)	6 Generate	
Master Documents	**Alt-F5** (Mark Text)	6 Generate	3 Expand Master Document 4 Condense Master Document
Subdocument	**Alt-F5** (Mark Text)	2 Subdocument	

Document Compare	**Alt-F5** (Mark Text)	6 Generate	1 Remove Redline Markings and Strikeout Text from Document 2 Compare Screen and Disk Documents and Add Redline and Strikeout

Tools

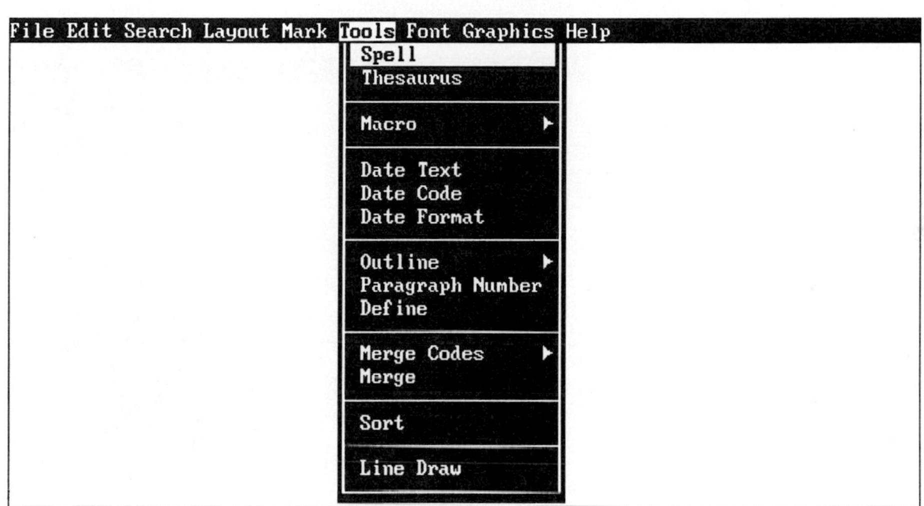

Spell	**Ctrl-F2** (Spell)
Thesaurus	**Alt-F1** (Thesaurus)

Macro	**Ctrl-F10** (Macro Define) **Alt-F10** (Macro)

Date Text	**Shift-F5** (Date/Outline)	1 Date Text
Date Code	**Shift-F5** (Date/Outline)	2 Date Code
Date Format	**Shift-F5** (Date/Outline)	3 Date Format
Outline	**Shift-F5** (Date/Outline)	4 Outline

Paragraph Number	**Shift-F5** (Date/Outline)	5 Para Num	
Define	**Shift-F5** (Date/Outline)	6 Define	

Merge Codes	**Shift-F9** (Merge Codes)		
Merge	**Ctrl-F9** (Merge/Sort)	1 Merge	

Sort	**Ctrl-F9** (Merge/Sort)	2 Sort	

Line Draw	**Ctrl-F3** (Screen)	2 Line Draw	

Font

```
File Edit Search Layout Mark Tools Font Graphics Help
                                   Base Font

                                   Normal
                                   Appearance ►
                                   Superscript
                                   Subscript
                                   Fine
                                   Small
                                   Large
                                   Very Large
                                   Extra Large

                                   Print Color

                                   Characters
```

Base Font	**Ctrl-F8** (Font)	4 Base Font	

Normal	**Ctrl-F8** (Font)	3 Normal	
Appearance	**Ctrl-F8** (Font)	2 Appearance	
Superscript	**Ctrl-F8** (Font)	1 Size	1 Suprscpt
Subscript	**Ctrl-F8** (Font)	1 Size	2 Subscpt
Fine	**Ctrl-F8** (Font)	1 Size	3 Fine
Small	**Ctrl-F8** (Font)	1 Size	4 Small
Large	**Ctrl-F8** (Font)	1 Size	5 Large
Very Large	**Ctrl-F8** (Font)	1 Size	6 Vry Large

Extra Large	**Ctrl-F8** (Font) ——— 1 Size ——— 7 Ex Large
Print Color	**Ctrl-F8** (Font) ——— 5 Print Color
Characters	**Ctrl-v**(Compose)

Graphics

```
File Edit Search Layout Mark Tools Font Graphics Help
                                        Figure    ▸
                                        Table Box  Create
                                        Text Box   Edit
                                        User Box   New Number
                                        Equation   Options

                                        Line      ▸
```

Figure	**Alt-F9** (Graphics) ——— 1 Figure
Table Box	**Alt-F9** (Graphics) ——— 2 Table Box
Text Box	**Alt-F9** (Graphics) ——— 3 Text Box
User Box	**Alt-F9** (Graphics) ——— 4 User Box
Equation	**Alt-F9** (Graphics) ——— 6 Equation
Line	**Alt-F9** (Graphics) ——— 5 Line

Help

```
File Edit Search Layout Mark Tools Font Graphics Help
                                                 Help
                                                 Index
                                                 Template
```

Help	**F3** (Help)
Index	**F3** (Help) A–Z
Template	**F3** (Help), **F3** (Help)

WORDPERFECT CODES

The following is a list of WordPerfect codes that may appear on the (Reveal Codes) screen:

[ ]	Hard Space
[-]	Hyphen
-	Soft Hyphen
[/]	Cancel Hyphenation
[Adv]	Advance
[BLine]	Baseline Placement
[Block]	Beginning of Block
[Block Pro]	Block Protection
[Bold]	Bold
[Box Num]	Caption in Graphics Box
[Cell]	Table Cell
[Center]	Center Line
[Center Pg]	Center Page Top to Bottom
[Cndl EOP]	Conditional End of Page
[Cntr Tab]	Centered Tab
[CNTR TAB]	Hard Centered Tab
[Col Def]	Column Definition
[Col Off]	End of Text Columns
[Col On]	Beginning of Text Columns
[Color]	Print Color
[Comment]	Document Comment
[Date]	Date/Time function
[Dbl Und]	Double Underline
[Dec Tab]	Decimal Aligned Tab
[DEC TAB]	Hard Decimal Aligned Tab
[Decml/Algn Char]	Decimal Character/Thousands' Separator
[Def Mark:Index]	Index Definition
[Def Mark:List]	List Definition
[Def Mark:ToC]	Table of Contents Definition
[End Def]	End of Index, List, or Table of Contents
[End Mark]	End of Marked Text
[End Opt]	Endnote Options
[Endnote]	Endnote
[Endnote Placement]	Endnote Placement
[Equ Box]	Equation Box
[Equ Opt]	Equation Box Options
[Ext Large]	Extra Large Print
[Fig Box]	Figure Box
[Fig Opt]	Figure Box Options
[Fine]	Fine Print
[Flsh Rgt]	Flush Right
[Font]	Base Font
[Footer]	Footer
[Footnote]	Footnote
[Force]	Force Odd/Even Page
[Ftn Opt]	Footnote/Endnote Options
[Full Form]	Table of Authorities, Full Form
[Header]	Header
[HLine]	Horizontal Line

[HPg]	Hard Page Break
[HRt]	Hard Return
[HRt-SPg]	Hard Return - Soft Page
[Hyph Off]	Hyphenation Off
[Hyph On]	Hyphenation On
[HZone]	Hyphenation Zone
[>Indent]	Indent
[>Indent<]	Left/Right Indent
[Index]	Index Entry
[ISRt]	Invisible Soft Return
[Italc]	Italics
[Just]	Line Justification
[Just Lim]	Word/Letter Spacing Justification Limits
[Kern]	Kerning
[L/R Mar]	Left and Right Margins
[Lang]	Language
[Large]	Large Print
[Leading Adj]	Leading Adjustment
[Link]	Spreadsheet Link
[Link End]	Spreadsheet Link End
[Ln Height]	Line Height
[Ln Num]	Line Numbering
[Ln Spacing]	Line Spacing
[<Mar Rel]	Left Margin Release
[Mark:List]	List Entry
[Mark:ToA]	Table of Authorities Entry
[Mark:ToC]	Table of Contents Entry
[Math Def]	Definition of Math Columns
[Math Off]	End of Math
[Math On]	Beginning of Math
[!]	Formula Calculation
[t]	Subtotal Entry
[+]	Calculate Subtotal
[T]	Total Entry
[=]	Calculate Total
[*]	Calculate Grand Total
[N]	Negative
[New End Num]	New Endnote Number
[New Equ Num]	New Equation Box Number
[New Fig Num]	New Figure Box Number
[New Ftn Num]	New Footnote Number
[New Tbl Num]	New Table Box Number
[New Txt Num]	New Text Box Number
[New Usr Num]	New User Box Number
[Note Num]	Footnote/Endnote Reference
[Outline Lvl]	Outline Style
[Outline Off]	Outline Off
[Outline On]	Outline On
[Outln]	Outline (attribute)
[Ovrstk]	Overstrike
[Paper Sz/Typ]	Paper Size and Type
[Par Num]	Paragraph Number

[Par Num Def]	Paragraph Numbering Definition
[Pg Num]	New Page Number
[Pg Numbering]	Page Number Position
[Ptr Cmnd]	Printer Command
[RedLn]	Redline
[Ref]	Reference (Automatic Reference)
[Rgt Tab]	Right Aligned Tab
[RGT TAB]	Hard Right Aligned Tab
[Row]	Table Row
[Shadw]	Shadow
[Sm Cap]	Small Caps
[Small]	Small Print
[SPg]	Soft Page Break
[SRt]	Soft Return
[StkOut]	Strikeout
[Style Off]	Style Off
[Style On]	Style On
[Subdoc]	Subdocument (Master Documents)
[Subdoc Start]	Beginning of Subdocument
[Subdoc End]	End of Subdocument
[SubScrpt]	Subscript
[Suppress]	Suppress Page Format
[SuprScrpt]	Superscript
[T/B Mar]	Top and Bottom Margins
[Tab]	Left Aligned Tab
[TAB]	Hard Left Aligned Tab
[Tab Set]	Tab Set
[Target]	Target (Cross-Reference)
[Tbl Box]	Table Box
[Tbl Def]	Table Definition
[Tbl Off]	Table Off
[Tabl Opt]	Table Box Options
[Text Box]	Text Box
[Txt Opt]	Text Box Options
[Und]	Underlining
[Undrln]	Underline Spaces/Tabs
[Usr Box]	User-Defined Box
[Usr Opt]	User-Defined Box Options
[VLine]	Vertical Line
[Vry Large]	Very Large Print
[W/O Off]	Widow/Orphan Off
[W/O On]	Widow/Orphan On
[Wrd/Ltr Spacing]	Word and Letter Spacing

LOTUS 1-2-3 VERSION 2.2

INTRODUCTION

Lotus 1-2-3® is an applications software designed for creating formula-based models called *spreadsheets*. In addition to its spreadsheet features, Lotus 1-2-3 has features that provide the user with the ability to create graphs and perform basic database management operations. It also has software that incorporates a built-in programming language whose programs are called *macros*. Lotus 1-2-3 has some word processing capabilities.

This module begins with a brief discussion of Lotus 1-2-3's basic spreadsheet concepts. It continues with a set of introductory tutorial lessons that present the basic operations used to create, format, and print a Lotus spreadsheet. The initial tutorial lessons focus on the essential concepts and operations involved in creating and using an electronic spreadsheet. The remaining tutorial lessons expose you to techniques, commands, and operations that will enhance your spreadsheet skills.

The introductory tutorial lessons are followed by discussions of spreadsheet design, mixed cell references, and Lotus 1-2-3 functions. These discussions conclude the module's materials that relate directly to Lotus 1-2-3's spreadsheet feature. Three remaining discussions address other Lotus features—graphics, databases, and macros. Each discussion includes several specific examples of how to perform the various operations.

The discussions of Lotus features are followed by several short exercises and cases designed to introduce and reinforce the use of additional Lotus 1-2-3 features, commands, and operations.

At the end of the module you will find a Lotus 1-2-3 operation and command summary that briefly describes the full range of commands and control keys available with Lotus 1-2-3. Each major set of command descriptions is prefaced with a tree-style graphic representation of the command's structure. Here you also will find a quick reference command index that may be used to initiate several common spreadsheet operations.

SPREADSHEET BASICS

Spreadsheet Layout

In the Lotus 1-2-3 spreadsheet, letters are used to designate columns and numbers are used to designate rows. You specify a particular position (or cell) in the spreadsheet by column letter and row number. For example, the cell G3 is located in column G, row 3. Lotus calls this combination of letter and number the *cell address*. (Note that the actual Lotus spreadsheet does not display the lines that designate cell locations as they are shown here.)

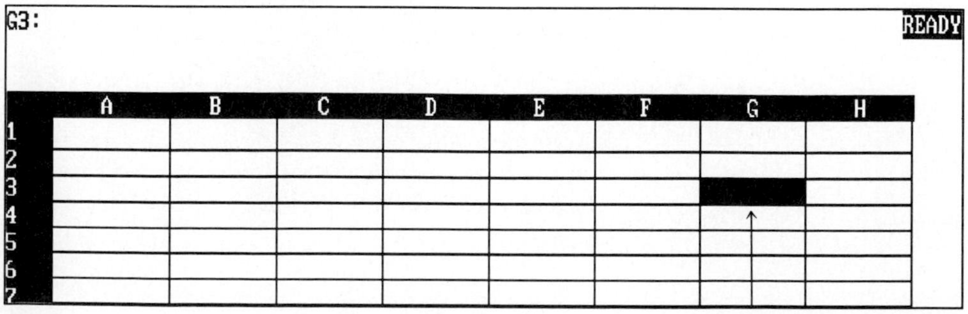

G3: READY

	A	B	C	D	E	F	G	H
1								
2								
3								
4								
5								
6								
7								

Cell G3

Entering Data into a Spreadsheet

The reverse video screen display shown at cell position G3 is called the *spreadsheet pointer.* The pointer may be moved about the spreadsheet by typing the keyboard cursor control keys. To directly enter data into a spreadsheet cell, you first move the pointer to the appropriate cell and then type your entry. When entering data in this manner, you normally have the option of entering either a string expression or a numeric expression into the cell. Lotus refers to string expressions as being *labels* and numeric expressions as being *values.* Here, a cell entry that must be string data is referred to as being a label, string value, or simply *string.* An entry that must be numeric data is referred to as being a numeric value or simply *numeric.* On occasions where the entry may be either string or numeric, it is referred to here as being simply a value.

When you make a cell entry, Lotus 1-2-3 automatically determines which of the two data types (string or numeric) is being entered into a cell at the first keystroke of the data entry operation. If the first keystroke is any of the following, Lotus 1-2-3 assumes you are entering a numeric value into the cell.

0 1 2 3 4 5 6 7 8 9 + − . (@ # $

If the first keystroke is any other keyboard character, Lotus 1-2-3 assumes you are entering a string value (label) into the cell.

The following example spreadsheet shows some string and numeric values that have been entered into cells. Notice that labels automatically justify to the left side of the cell and that numeric values automatically justify to the right side. The numerics in this case are constants, the number 1200. Numeric values also may take the more complex form of spreadsheet formulas.

A10: READY

	A	B	C	D	E	F	G	H
1		JAN	FEB	MARCH	APRIL			
2	INCOME	1200	1200	1200	1200			
3	TAXES							
4	NET PAY							
5								
6								
7								

Spreadsheet Formulas

To determine taxes and net pay in the example, the user may enter formulas into each of the cells within rows 3 and 4. For instance, if a 28% tax rate is assumed, the formula .28*B2 may be entered as the numeric value for January's tax amount (into cell B3) and the formula +B2−B3 may be entered into cell B4 for January's net pay.

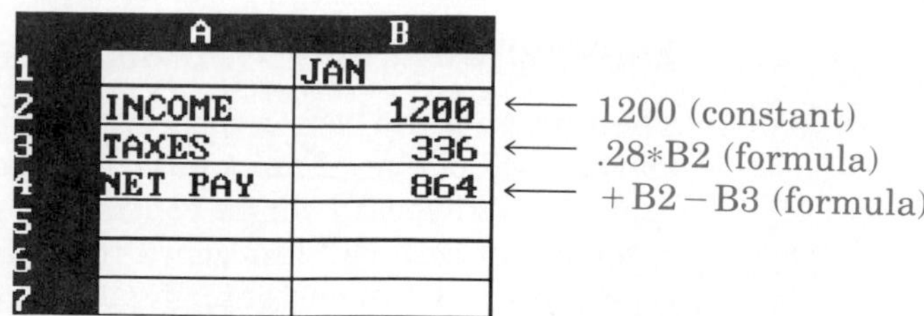

Although formulas become the contents of cells B3 and B4, Lotus 1-2-3 will display 336 and 864 (the evaluations of the expressions). If you later change January's income (cell B2), the values displayed for January's taxes (cell B3) and net pay (cell B4) will change automatically.

	A	B	
1		JAN	
2	INCOME	1400	← New INCOME entered
3	TAXES	392	← New TAXES displayed
4	NET PAY	1008	← New NET PAY displayed
5			
6			
7			

Window Lines

Lotus 1-2-3 reserves three lines (called *window lines* or, collectively, the *control panel*) at the top of the monitor screen to display information about current operations. The lines indicate the cell where the spreadsheet pointer is currently located (called the current cell). The area to the right of the current cell display indicates the cell's actual contents (as opposed to its displayed contents). The lines also are used to display command menu options, messages, and prompts for the various Lotus command operations.

Lotus Command Structure

When you use Lotus 1-2-3, you are either directly entering data (labels or numeric values) into the spreadsheet's cells or you are executing a Lotus 1-2-3 command.

To manipulate the data in a spreadsheet, Lotus 1-2-3 provides *menus* from which you may select commands. The menus often are connected in a layered fashion: one menu command providing (calling) another submenu of commands. Sometimes a final command operation will require that you pass through several preliminary menus to reach the desired one.

Calling the Main Menu

When you type the Slash key (/), you enter Lotus 1-2-3's command mode by calling the Main menu.

```
B2: 1400                                                                    MENU
Worksheet  Range  Copy  Move  File  Print  Graph  Data  System  Add-In  Quit
```

The menu is displayed on the middle line of the control panel at the top of the screen. To select a Lotus command, you may either type the first letter of the command word or move the *command pointer* (shown here located on **W**orksheet) to the desired command and press the Enter key. (When a Lotus command is referred to in this module, the first letter of the command—the portion you would need to type to execute the command—appears in bold type.)

The bottom window line displays a listing of the submenu (or a brief explanation) for the command upon which the command pointer is currently located (the current command). In this example, with the command pointer on **W**orksheet, its submenu of commands would appear on the line below it as follows.

```
B2: 1400                                                                MENU
Worksheet  Range  Copy  Move  File  Print  Graph  Data  System  Quit
Global, Insert, Delete, Column, Erase, Titles, Window, Status, Page
       A        B        C        D        E        F        G        H
1               JAN      FEB      MARCH    APRIL
2  INCOME       1400     1200     1200     1200
3  TAXES         392
4  NET PAY      1008
```

Working through Command Submenus

If you select **W**orksheet from the Main menu, its submenu of commands moves to the middle (menu) line and becomes the active menu from which you may select a command. The first command of the menu, **G**lobal, will then be highlighted, and its submenu of commands will appear on the line below it.

```
B2: 1400                                                                MENU
Global  Insert  Delete  Column  Erase  Titles  Window  Status  Page
Set worksheet settings
       A        B        C        D        E        F        G        H
1               JAN      FEB      MARCH    APRIL
2  INCOME       1400     1200     1200     1200
3  TAXES         392
4  NET PAY      1008
```

If the command pointer is next moved one command to the right, a brief explanation of the **I**nsert command appears as follows.

```
B2: 1400                                                                MENU
Global  Insert  Delete  Column  Erase  Titles  Window  Status  Page
Insert blank column(s) or row(s)
       A        B        C        D        E        F        G        H
1               JAN      FEB      MARCH    APRIL
2  INCOME       1400     1200     1200     1200
3  TAXES         392
4  NET PAY      1008
```

If you now select the **I**nsert command, a third menu that allows you the option of inserting a column or a row into the spreadsheet appears on the menu line and becomes the menu from which to select.

```
B2: 1400                                                        MENU
Column  Row
Insert one or more blank columns to the left of the cell pointer
       A         B         C         D         E         F         G         H
1               JAN       FEB      MARCH     APRIL
2  INCOME        1400      1200      1200      1200
3  TAXES          392
4  NET PAY       1008
```

Finally, if you elect to insert a row into the spreadsheet, the row is inserted and you are left in the data entry (READY) mode.

```
B2:                                                             READY


       A         B         C         D         E         F         G         H
1               JAN       FEB      MARCH     APRIL
2
3  INCOME        1400      1200      1200      1200
4  TAXES          392
5  NET PAY       1008
```

This process of working through submenus often requires a series of steps progressing toward the end command operation. The series of steps may be viewed in a tree structure format as follows.

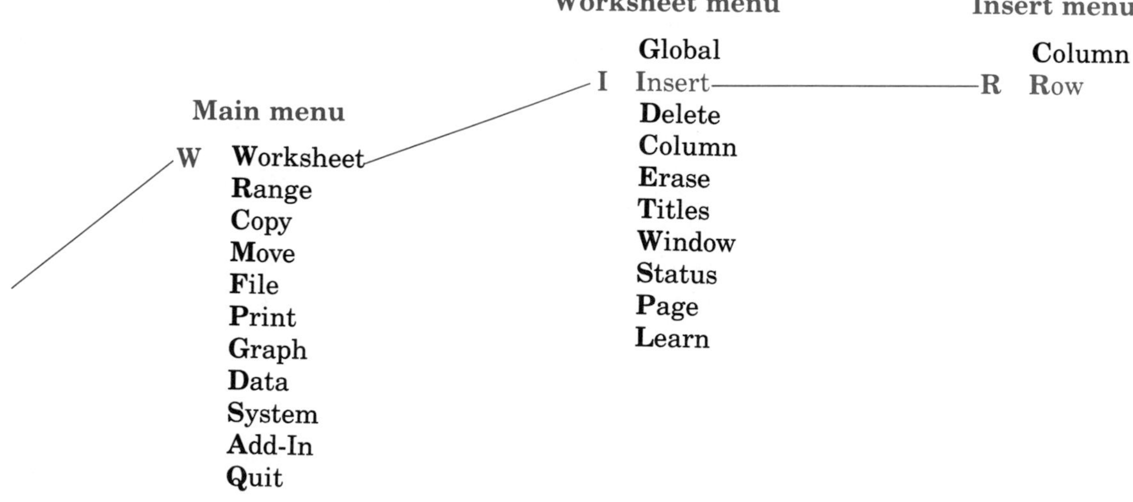

Backing Up or Aborting a Command Operation

When executing a final command operation involves several steps, it is useful to know that typing the Esc key will cause Lotus 1-2-3 to back up one menu or command operation. Pressing the key marked Ctrl and then typing the key marked Scroll Lock (or Break) will abort a command operation and return you to the data entry (READY) mode.

Learning Lotus 1-2-3

Lotus 1-2-3 often requires the completion of a number of steps in specific order to perform a particular command operation. As you use this applications software, you will become familiar with the steps involved. Careful study of the tree diagrams and command summaries will help you master the command sequences.

Getting Help

Lotus 1-2-3 also has an on-line help facility that tries to anticipate your questions and provides a screen of information about the command(s) you are trying to use. You can gain access to a *help screen* at any time by typing the F1 Function key. Each help screen provides information and a selection of other help screens from which to choose. You can select other help screens by using the pointer control keys to move the pointer to highlight the subject of your choice. You then type the Enter key to view that help screen. Typing the Esc key exits you from the help screen mode and returns you to where you left off.

REQUIRED PREPARATION

The tutorial lessons and exercises in this module will give you experience using the commands and features of Lotus 1-2-3. Before you begin the "hands-on" learning experience, however, you will need to complete a few initial steps and gain some preliminary information in order to be adequately prepared.

Initial Steps

1. Obtain a floppy disk appropriate for the microcomputer you will be using to complete your course assignments. Your instructor or laboratory staff will be able to tell you which kind of disk to purchase.

   Size: ______________________

   Sides: ______________________

   Density: ______________________

2. Format your disk to the specifications of the DOS and microcomputer hardware you will be using to complete your course assignments. Your instructor or laboratory staff will be able to tell you the steps to follow. ***Caution: Formatting a disk will erase all files that may exist on that disk.***

   Steps to Format a Disk: ______________________________________

   ____

   ____

   ____

   ____

   ____

   ____

3. Each time you use the Lotus 1-2-3 software, you will want to be sure that your spreadsheet files are saved on your disk. There will be certain steps to follow, either when you first load Lotus into RAM or immediately afterwards, to ensure that your files are automatically saved on your disk. Your instructor or laboratory staff will be able to tell you the steps to follow.

Starting a Lotus 1-2-3 Spreadsheet Session: ____________________

____

____

____

____

____

____

____

____

____

TUTORIAL LESSONS

REQUIRED MATERIALS

1. An IBM DOS floppy disk (or hard-disk directory containing the DOS software).
2. A Lotus system disk (or hard-disk directory containing the software).
3. A formatted disk (your files disk).
4. This manual.
5. Other ________________________________

TUTORIAL CONVENTIONS

During the introductory Lotus tutorial you will create a spreadsheet file using various Lotus 1-2-3 commands. The following are the conventions the tutorial's instructions will use.

↵	The bent arrow means to type the Enter key located on the right side of the keyboard.
Key-Key	Key combinations using a hyphen indicate that you should press and hold the first key and then type the next key shown.
Key,Key	Key combinations using a comma indicate that you should type the first key and then type the second key.
‖ ‖	Do not type the double lines; type only what is inside them.

HOW TO GET OUT OF TROUBLE

If you want to:	*Then:*
■ Erase characters before you have entered them into a cell. . .	■ Type the Backspace key located on the right top side of keyboard.
■ Erase the existing contents of a cell. . .	■ Move the pointer to the cell to be erased and type ‖ /**R,E,** ↵ ‖ .
■ Back up one command operation or menu. . .	■ Type the Esc key once (the Esc key is located on the top row, far left side).
■ Stop any command operation and return to the data entry mode. . .	■ Press and hold the Ctrl key (left side) and then type the Break key (top right side).
■ Stop the tutorial to continue later. . .	■ Type ‖ /**F,S,***filename,* ↵ ‖ . Watch the disk drive light to make sure the spreadsheet has been saved. Then type ‖ /**Q,Y** ‖ to quit Lotus 1-2-3.
■ Continue with the tutorial after stopping. . .	■ Load Lotus 1-2-3 into memory and then type ‖ /**F,R,***filename,* ↵ ‖ .

Throughout the tutorial lessons you will see the following symbol.

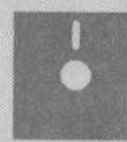

It indicates an opportune time to save your file(s) and quit the microcomputer session if you so desire.

GETTING STARTED

The proper "getting started" procedures require information specific to the hardware and software you are using. Refer to your notes in the preceding Required Preparation section for the specific information. The following is a general procedure for getting started; however, you may need to refer to Appendix A, "The Basics of DOS," to understand some of the terminology used here.

You will need to know in which disk drive (A: or B:) your files disk will be and where (disk drive and path) the Lotus 1-2-3 software will be.

NOTE: Here drive *means type the letter (A, B, etc.) for the disk drive in which your files disk is kept.*

1. Load DOS from a floppy disk or hard disk, or return to the DOS operating level from the current software operating level.
2. Put your files disk into the proper disk drive (drive name _______:).
3. If necessary, put the Lotus System disk in the proper disk drive (drive name _______:).
4. Now make the drive\directory for the Lotus software the current directory by typing *drive:*,**CD***path*↵.
5. Type ‖ LOTUS↵ ‖ .

The Lotus Access System

Lotus 1-2-3 is comprised of several different programs which come on different disks when the software is purchased. LOTUS is the filename for the 1-2-3 Access System, the software selection program that helps the user select which Lotus program to load into RAM.

You should now see the Access System commands at the top of the monitor screen.

```
1-2-3  PrintGraph  Translate  Install  Exit
Use 1-2-3

                        1-2-3 Access System
                      Copyright  1986, 1989
                  Lotus Development Corporation
                       All Rights Reserved
                           Release 2.2

The Access system lets you choose 1-2-3, PrintGraph, the Translate utility,
and the Install program, from the menu at the top of this screen.  If
you're using a two-diskette system, the Access system may prompt you to
change disks.  Follow the instructions below to start a program.

o  Use → or ← to move the menu pointer (the highlighted rectangle
   at the top of the screen) to the program you want to use.

o  Press ENTER to start the program.

You can also start a program by typing the first character of its name.

Press HELP (F1) for more information.
```

Different versions of Lotus have different commands and screens associated with the Access System. Take a moment to note which version of Lotus 1-2-3 you are using.

LESSON 1 Loading the Lotus 1-2-3 Spreadsheet Software

Using the Command Pointer

The reverse video display around the command 1-2-3 is Lotus 1-2-3's command pointer. On the far right side of the keyboard is a numeric keypad which contains four keys with arrows on them. Lotus 1-2-3 has programmed the arrow keys to move its pointers.

1. Use the → and ← arrow keys to move the pointer across the command menu.

A short explanation of each menu command appears below the menu of commands as the pointer moves across it. Two methods allow you to select a command from a Lotus menu. You can move the pointer to the desired command and then type the Enter key, or you can type the first letter or character of the desired command. 1-2-3 is the command that will erase the Access System program from RAM and then load the Lotus spreadsheet software into memory.

2. Move the pointer to the 1-2-3 command and type ↵. Depending on the version of Lotus you are using, you next may need to type a keyboard key to remove the Lotus copyright notice or emblem from the screen.

The screen should now appear similar to the following.

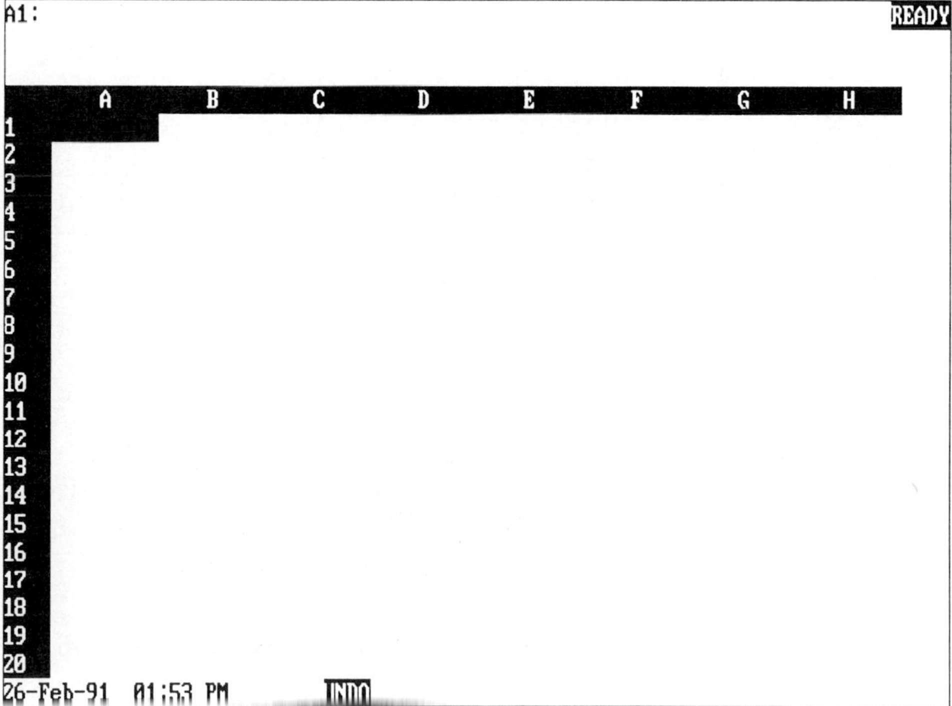

LESSON 2
Viewing the Spreadsheet

What you now see on the screen is one small part of a large matrix or spreadsheet.

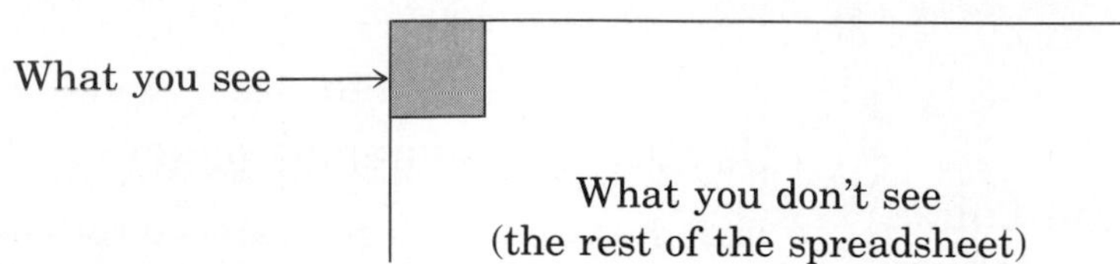

The reverse video display at cell A1 is the Lotus spreadsheet pointer.

1. Move the spreadsheet pointer by using the four arrow (pointer control) keys to your right. If, instead of moving the pointer, the arrowed keys cause numbers to appear at the top left of the screen, type the Esc key and then the Num Lock key.

What happens when you keep moving the pointer to the right or keep moving the pointer down? Notice that the pointer may be used to "push" the monitor screen around on the spreadsheet.

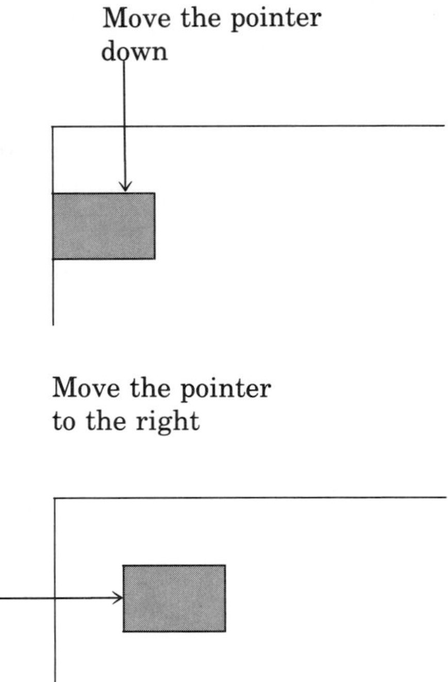

Typing the Home key (found on the numeric keypad) will send the spreadsheet pointer to the A1 (top left) cell.

2. Type the Home key.

On the far left of the keyboard (or across the top) are ten keys marked F1 through F10. These are Function keys. Each is programmed to perform a particular operation.

3. Type the key marked F5 and read the prompt shown at the top of the screen.

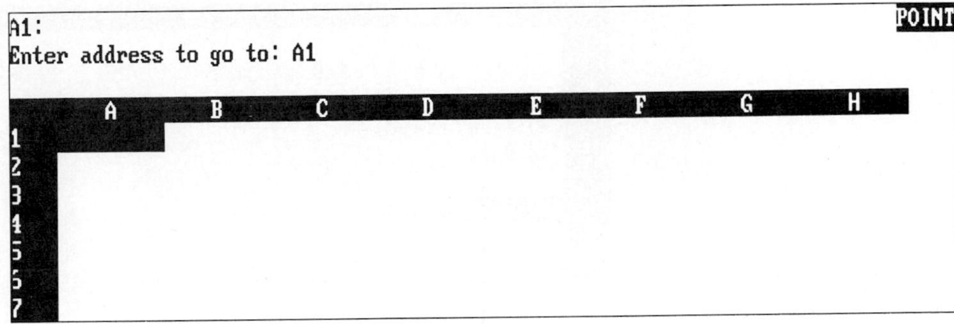

4. Now type ‖ G57↵ ‖ .

Notice where the pointer is located now. The F5 key may be used to send the pointer wherever you wish on the spreadsheet.

5. Press the Home key to return the pointer to cell A1.

LESSON 3
Entering Labels into a Spreadsheet

1. Move the pointer to cell B2.

In the upper left corner of the screen you will see the letter-number coordinate for the current pointer position.

2. Type ‖JAN‖ and then move the pointer to the right one cell (C2).
3. Type ‖FEB‖. Keep going until you reach ‖DEC‖ (M2).
4. Type the Home key.

The screen should appear as follows.

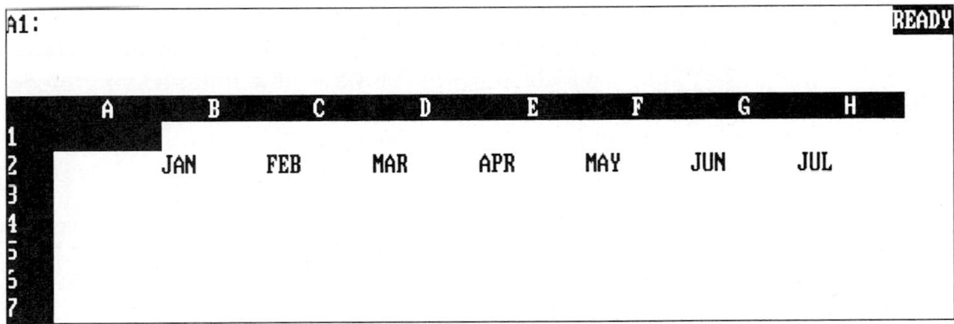

You have just labeled the spreadsheet's columns and now you are going to label its rows. As you continue, watch the control panel at the top of the monitor screen to keep track of what Lotus 1-2-3 is doing.

5. Move the pointer to cell A4 and type ‖GROSS PAY AMOUNT‖.
6. Move the pointer to cell A5 and type ‖TAX RATE‖.
7. Move the pointer to cell A7 (two cells down) and type ‖FED & STATE TAXES ↵‖.

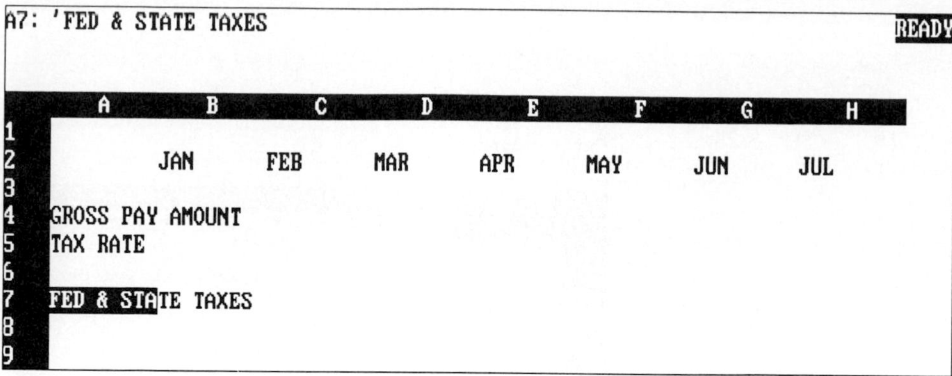

Editing the Contents of a Cell

Once a cell entry has been made, you may edit the entry by using the F2 (EDIT) Function key.

8. Move the pointer to cell A4 and then type the F2 Function key.

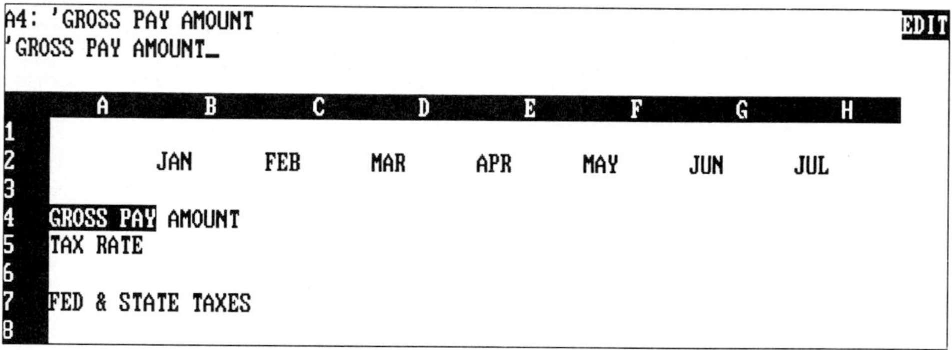

On the middle line of the control panel at the top of the screen you will see a blinking *edit cue* or cursor. To the right you will see the message "EDIT" which indicates you are now in an editing mode. While in the editing mode, the keystrokes listed in the following tables may be used to change the contents of the current cell.

Cursor Movement	Keystrokes
Character Left	Left ←
Character Right	Right →
Beginning of Cell	Home
End of Cell	End

Delete Operation	Keystrokes
Current Character	Del
Preceding Character	Backspace
Typeover Text	Ins (toggles between Insert and Typeover modes)

9. Use the available editing keystrokes to change the label in A4 to read GROSS INCOME and then type Enter.

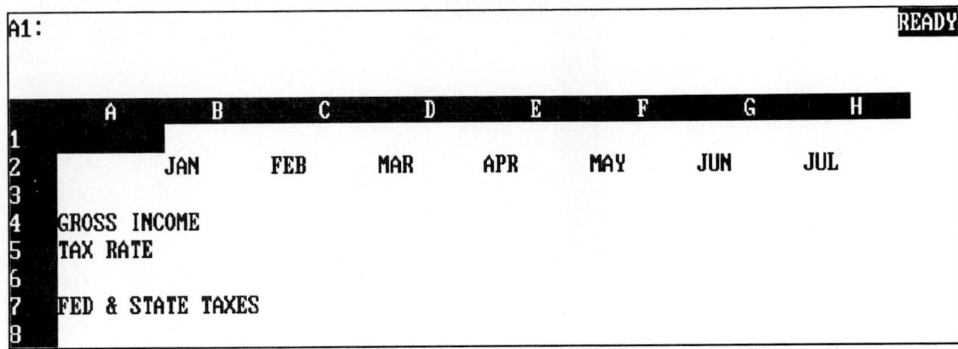

The Undo Feature

Lotus 1-2-3's Undo feature allows you to undo the last change made to a spreadsheet, whether it resulted from a cell being edited or from a command operation being performed. To undo the last change, you type Alt-F4 (hold down the Alt key, and then type F4).

NOTE: The Undo feature is not available with version 2.01. If you are using version 2.01, skip the following step.

10. Watch what happens to the label in cell A4 as you type Alt-F4 once to undo the last change, and then type Alt-F4 again to restore the cell's label to read GROSS INCOME.

Using Label Prefixes

To make the next label entry into the spreadsheet you will use one of Lotus 1-2-3's label-prefixes. The prefixes are used to format labels in their cells. The following table lists each prefix and its effect.

Character	Effect
Single quote (')	Left justifies label (default)
Caret (^)	Centers label
Double quote (")	Right justifies label
Backslash (\)	Repeats label in cell

The label prefix you will use is \, the *repeating label* prefix, which is most useful for creating underlines in spreadsheets.

11. Move the pointer to cell A8 and then type ‖ \-↵ ‖. (Be sure to use the backslash key.)

Cell A8 now should be filled with dashes.

Finishing the Row Labels

Enter the rest of the spreadsheet's row labels. After you have typed row labels A4 through A22 your spreadsheet should appear as follows.

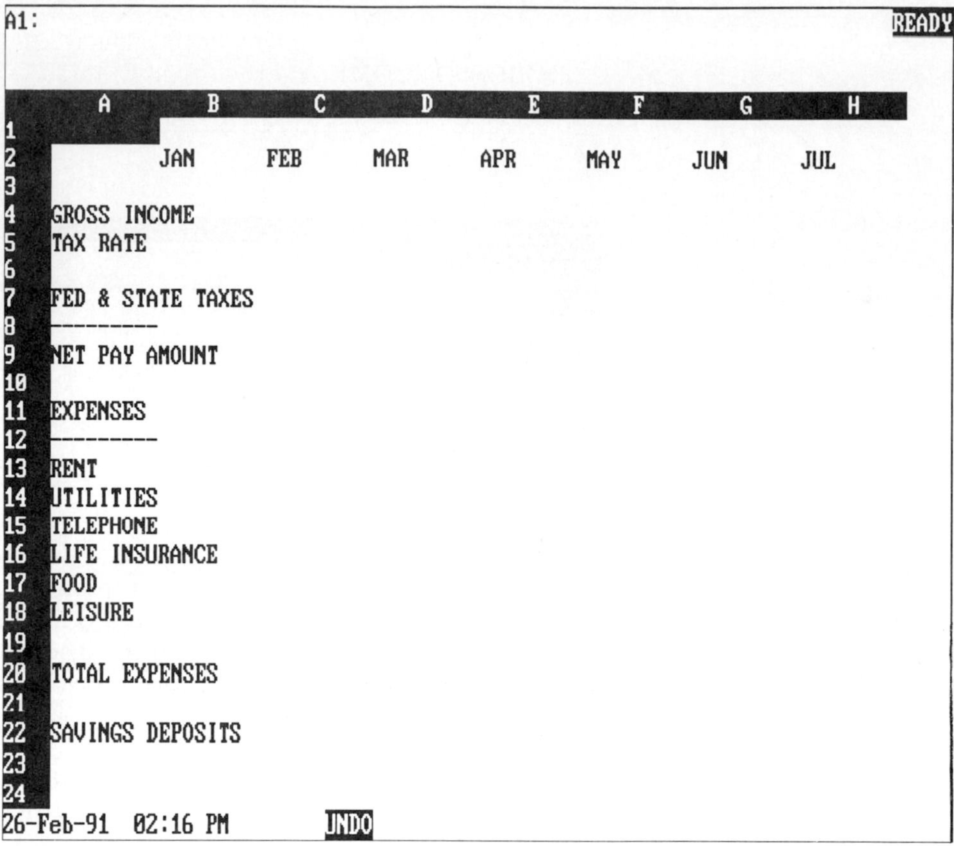

Changing a Column's Width

Many of the row labels you have entered extend into column B. Lotus 1-2-3 allows a label to extend into the next cell if the cell into which it is extending is blank. The default column width setting is 9.

1. Move the pointer to column A (the pointer needs to be in the column whose width you are changing).
2. Type ‖ / ‖.

The / keystroke will call Lotus 1-2-3's Main menu. In the row of submenu commands for the current Main menu command (/**W**orksheet), you should see the command **C**olumn. This is the command you want to use. To access this submenu command you first must select the /**W**orksheet command of the Main menu.

Calling the /**W**orksheet Submenu

3. Type ‖ **W** ‖ (or ↵) to select the /**W**orksheet commands.

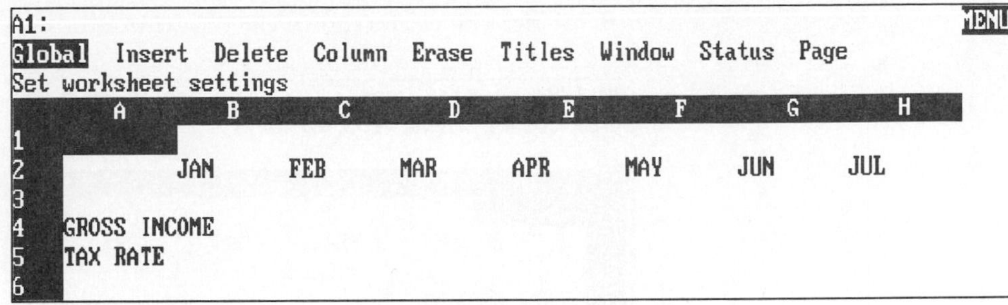

Now the /Worksheet submenu has become the menu from which you are choosing, and the line under it shows the submenu for the currently highlighted **G**lobal command.

4. Move the menu pointer to the **C**olumn command to see the submenu of commands that appears below it.

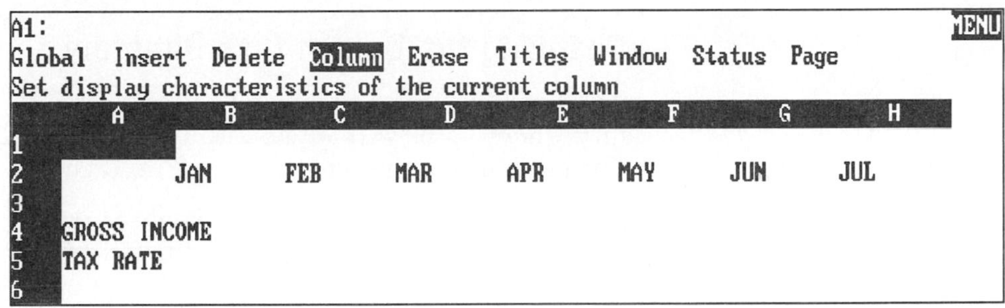

5. Type ↵ to select the **C**olumn command.

Setting the New Column Width

With the **S**et-Width command highlighted, the following message should now appear below it.

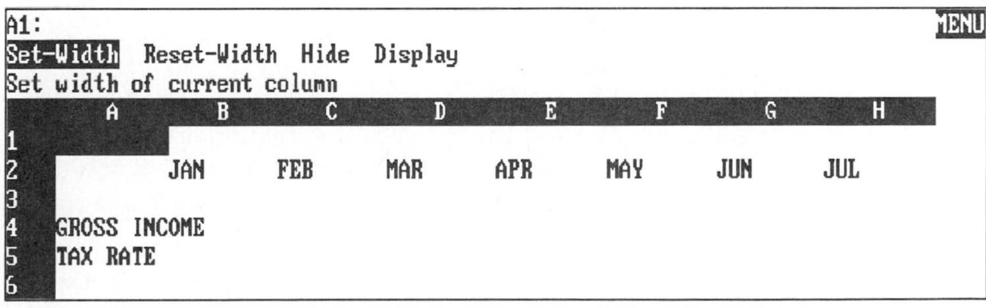

6. Select the command to Set-Width and answer the next prompt

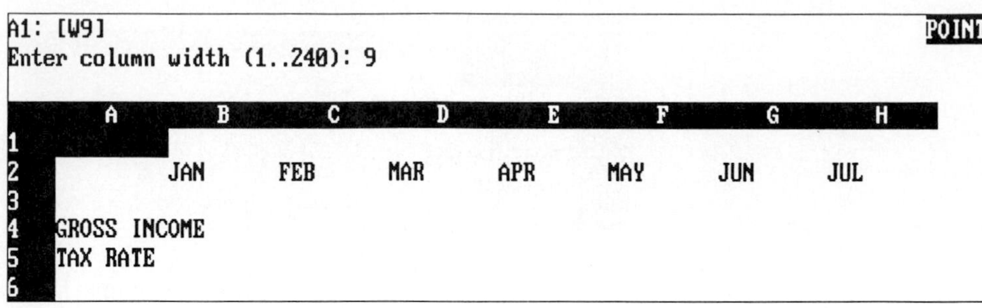

by typing ‖ 18↵ ‖ .

Column A should now be twice as wide as the other columns in the spreadsheet. Notice that the column width indicator at the top left of the screen has changed to [W18].

Changing the Default Disk Directory

Another Lotus command may be used to change the current default directory where Lotus will automatically look to read and write spreadsheet files. The sequence of the commands is /**F**ile,**D**irectory.

7. Use the proper command sequence to reach the point where the top of the screen appears similar to the following.

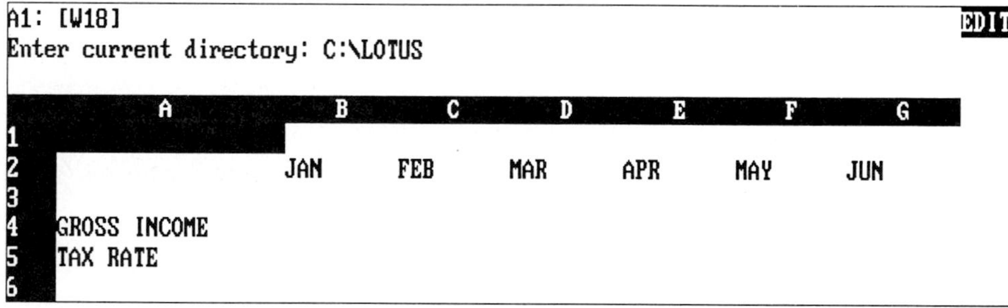

8. If the current default drive and directory (shown here as C:\LOTUS) is not the same as the location of your files disk, enter the drive and directory describing where your files disk is located. (In many cases, A:↵ or B:↵ will be the appropriate entry.) If the default directory does not need to be changed, simply type ↵.

If the Lotus software you are using does not automatically save its spreadsheet files to the location of your files disk, you will want to use the /**F**ile,**D**irectory command in this manner each time you begin a spreadsheet session.

Using the /File,Save Command

The next command presented here will be used to save a copy of the spreadsheet work you have completed so far. The sequence of the commands is /**F**ile,**S**ave.

9. Use the proper command sequence to reach the point where the top of the screen appears similar to the following.

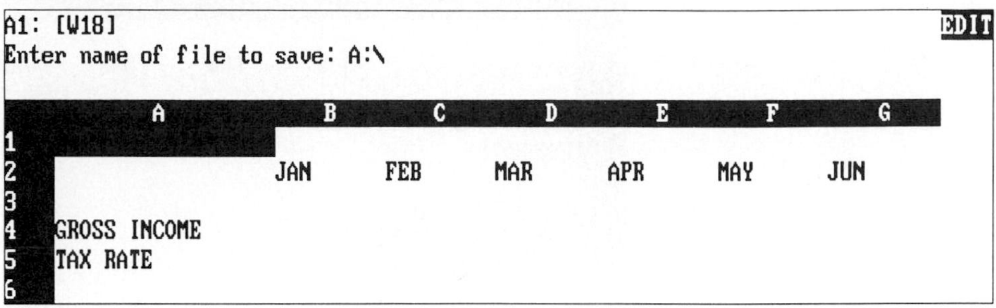

10. Next type ||LOTUT↵ || to cause Lotus to save the partially completed spreadsheet under the name LOTUT (for Lotus Tutorial).

LESSON 5 Ranges of Cells

A *range* of cells may be a single cell, a row of cells, a column of cells, or any rectangular block of cells. In this section of the tutorial lessons you will be dealing with ranges composed of single cells or rows of cells. Many of Lotus's commands act on ranges of cells, so you should develop a thorough understanding of their use. This lesson will introduce you to ranges by using the /Copy command.

Specifying Ranges in the /**C**opy Command

You now will use the Main menu command /Copy, which is designed to copy the contents of a cell or group of cells into another cell or group of cells. The cells from which data are copied are referred to as the "FROM range" of cells; the cells into which data are copied are referred to as the "TO range" of cells.

1. Move the pointer to A8 (------------------) and type || / || to call the Main menu.
2. Now select the **C**opy command from this menu.

Default Range Specifications

When you look at the top of the screen you will see that Lotus 1-2-3 is asking for the FROM range. Your object is to copy the set of dashes (in cell A8) into the rest of the cells in that row.

Since you will copy from cell A8, that single cell is the FROM range. Lotus 1-2-3 anticipates that this may be the case and has put the range A8..A8 (cell A8 to cell A8) as the default answer to its own prompt.

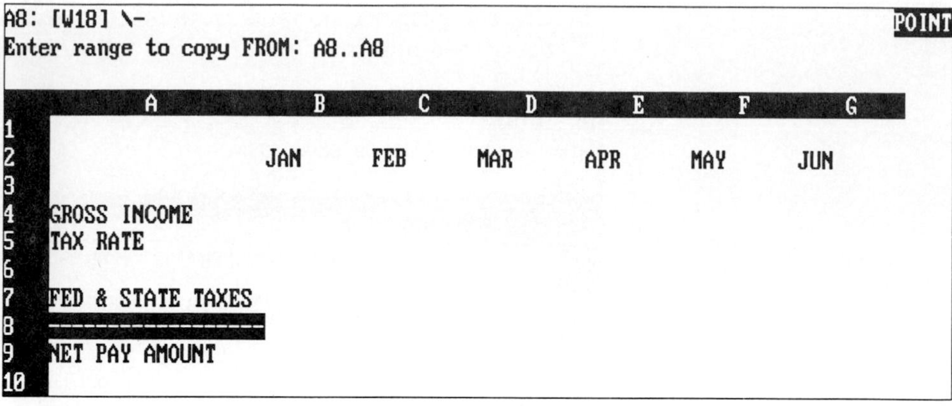

3. Type ↵ to accept cells A8..A8 as the range from which you want to copy.

Now Lotus 1-2-3 wants to know the range of cells into which you want the data copied. Since you are going to underline across the rest of the spreadsheet (up to cell M8), the TO range is the row of cells from B8 through M8 (B8..M8). The default answer (now cell A8), however, is not the correct TO range.

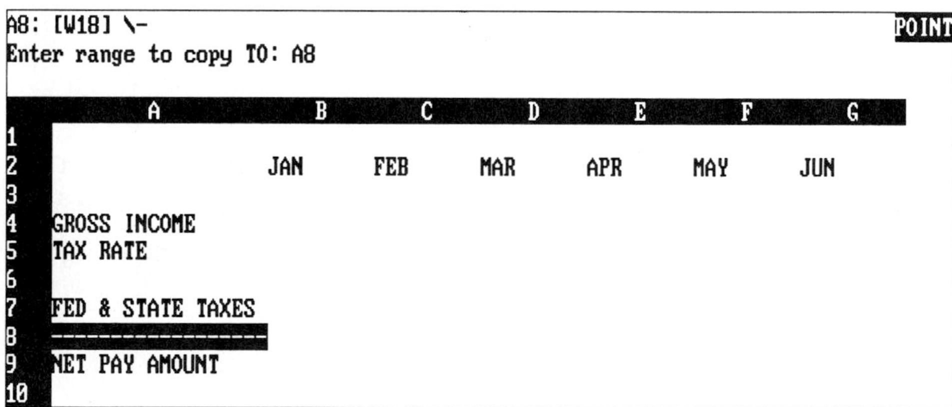

Typing in a Range Specification

You can change a default range specification by typing and entering the desired range from the keyboard. When typing in a range specification, the entry is made in the following order: top left cell, period, bottom right cell.

4. Type ‖ B8.M8 ↵ ‖. Then make sure that this row has indeed been copied as you directed.

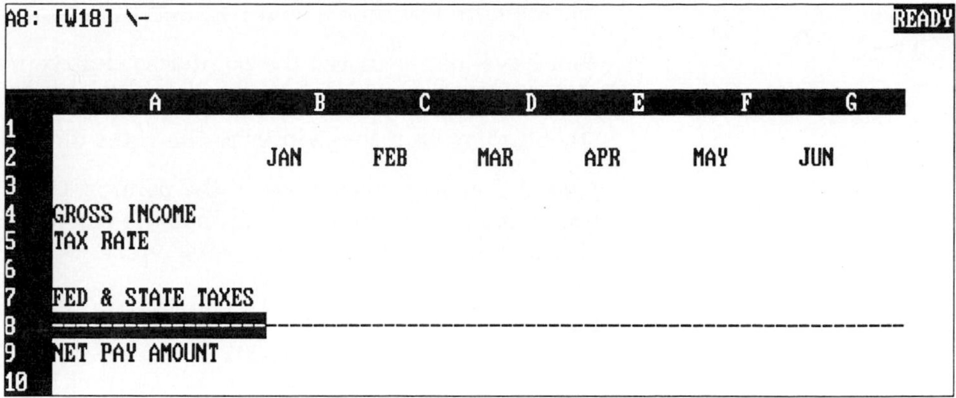

Pointing to a Range Specification

Another very useful way to specify a range while using a command such as /Copy is to point to the range with the spreadsheet pointer. When you use the pointer to specify a range of cells, you first move the pointer to the beginning cell of that range, type the period key to *anchor* the pointer to that cell, and then move the pointer to the ending cell of the range and press the Enter key. You may use the Esc key to "unanchor" the pointer at any time.

To give you experience in pointing to a range, you will use the /Copy command to copy the contents of cell A12 into the rest of the cells in that row (B12..M12).

5. Move the pointer to cell A12 and type || /**C** || to call the Main menu and select the /**C**opy command.

The top of the screen should appear as follows.

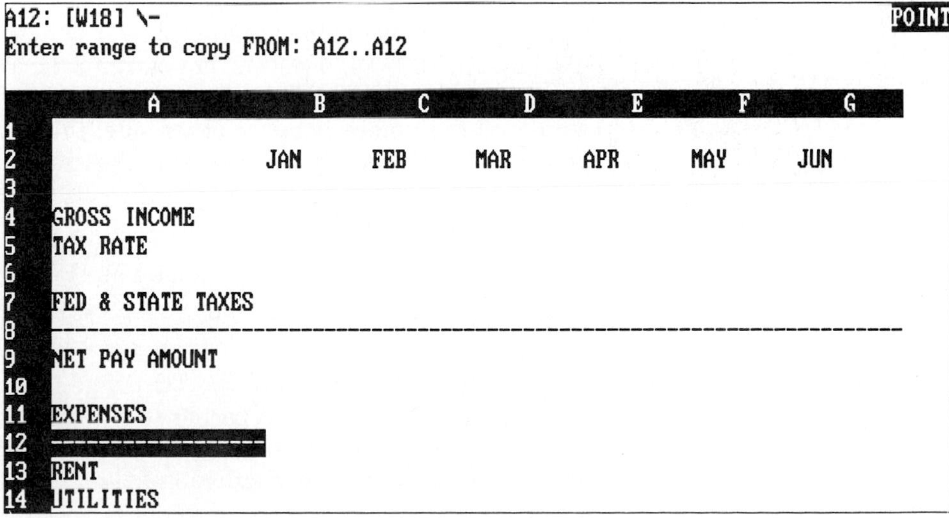

6. Type the Enter key to accept the current default FROM range.
7. Now move the pointer around on the spreadsheet and watch the "Enter range to copy TO:" prompt's default answer change.

The default answer changes with every move of the pointer. Lotus is waiting for you to move to the beginning of the TO range.

8. Move the pointer to cell B12 and then type the period key.

You have just anchored the pointer so that you may now point to the range you are specifying.

9. Start moving the pointer to the right along row 12.

Notice that with each move of the pointer, the TO range specification at the top of the screen changes, and that the range being pointed to on the spreadsheet is displayed in reverse video.

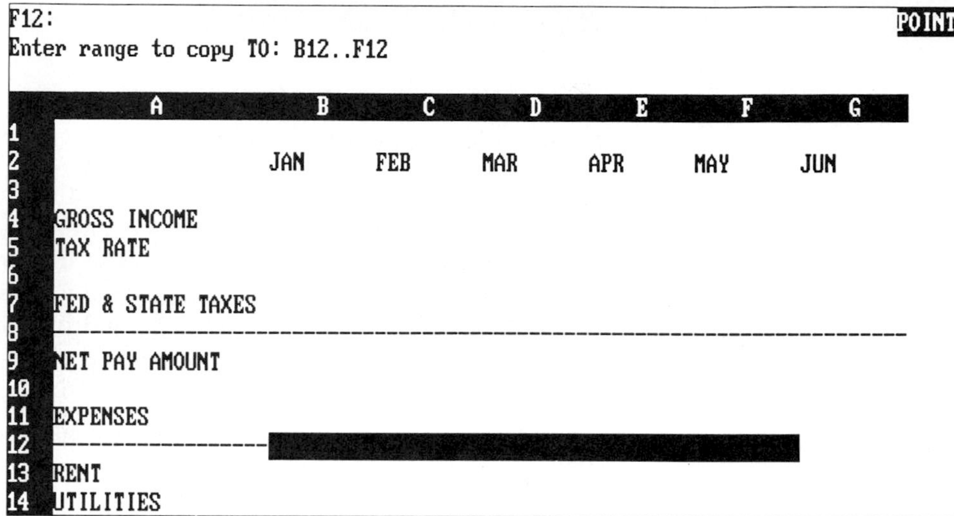

10. Move the pointer to cell M12; again look at the TO range prompt at the top of the screen (B12..M12). Then type the Enter key to accept the range B12..M12 as the appropriate TO range for the copy operation.

Pointing to a range rather than typing it is most useful when you are not sure how far the range goes or how large it is. When you need to see what the range includes, simply anchor the pointer to the top left corner of the range and then move it to the other side, the bottom right corner. You type the Enter key to specify the range as the area displayed in reverse video.

Naming a Specified Range

A third method of specifying a range uses Lotus 1-2-3's ability to name a range and later specify the range by using its name.

In completing the next steps, it is useful to know that when the FROM range is larger than one cell, the TO range may be specified as the single cell located in the upper left corner of the TO range. The FROM range then will be copied to the TO range with the upper left cell of the FROM range corresponding to the upper left cell of the TO range.

*The /**R**ange,**N**ame,**C**reate Command*

11. Type || / || to call the Main menu. Then progress through the sequence of commands **R**ange,**N**ame,**C**reate.

The prompt "Enter name:" will appear at the top of the screen. Lotus 1-2-3 is waiting for you to name the range you will specify in the next step of using this command. Range names may be up to 14 characters long and must not have spaces or special characters in them.

12. Name the range by typing ‖ undrl ↵ ‖ (for underline).

Next, Lotus 1-2-3 will prompt for the range specification of cells you want named "undrl."

13. Answer the "Enter range:" prompt by typing ‖ A8.M8 ↵ ‖.

Now that you have named the range of cells (the row of underlines from cell A8 through cell M8) you may refer to the range by its name in any Lotus command requesting a range specification.

Using a Named Range in a Command

14. Move the pointer to cell A19 and type ‖ /C ‖ to begin executing the /Copy command.
15. This time answer the FROM range prompt by typing ‖ undrl ↵ ‖ .

The TO range begins at cell A19 and goes through cell M19. Using the rule for copying more than one cell to a range, the uppermost left cell of the TO range is cell A19. The default destination displayed is A19. If you press the period key the default destination will change to A19..A19. Either A19 or A19..A19 will work.

16. Answer the "TO" prompt by typing ↵.
17. Finally, repeat this last process to underline the last row in the spreadsheet (under SAVINGS DEPOSITS).

Summary on Ranges and Using the /**C**opy Command

Your understanding of the concept of ranges and their use may be highly instrumental in determining how you can best design your spreadsheets. Ranges always have the form of a rectangle. They may be defined by: a) pointing to them; b) typing in their coordinates; or 3) using a name you have previously given them. Your choice of range specification method will depend on how you plan to use the range.

The rule for copying ranges of more than one cell into other ranges illustrates how experimentation can teach you a great deal about how Lotus 1-2-3 behaves. Try copying a row of cells into a column of cells, or vice versa. Although you may not get what you expect, you will learn something that could be useful later.

Resaving a Spreadsheet

Now is a good time to update the copy of LOTUT on your disk with the copy in RAM. The process of resaving a spreadsheet is slightly different than that of saving one.

18. Start the resave operation by typing the /File,Save command. The top of the screen should appear similar to the following.

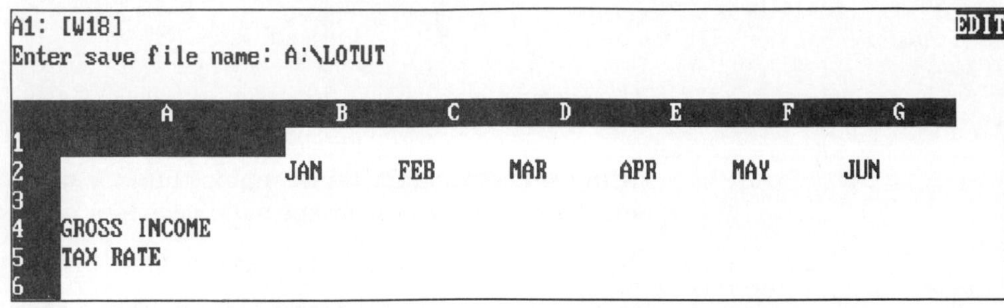

When a spreadsheet is being resaved, Lotus places its original name after the "Enter save file name:" prompt as a default answer.

19. Type ↵ to save the spreadsheet under the same name used previously.

The next menu of commands is displayed when you are resaving a spreadsheet with a filename that already exists on the disk. The **C**ancel command aborts the current save operation, leaving the file on the disk intact. The **R**eplace command completes the save operation by replacing the file on the disk with the current spreadsheet. The **B**ackup command is used to rename the file on the disk with a .BAK extension, and then save the current spreadsheet under the original filename with a .WK1 extension. By consistently using the **B**ackup command, you can always maintain the two most recent versions of a spreadsheet.

NOTE: The Backup command is not available in version 2.01.

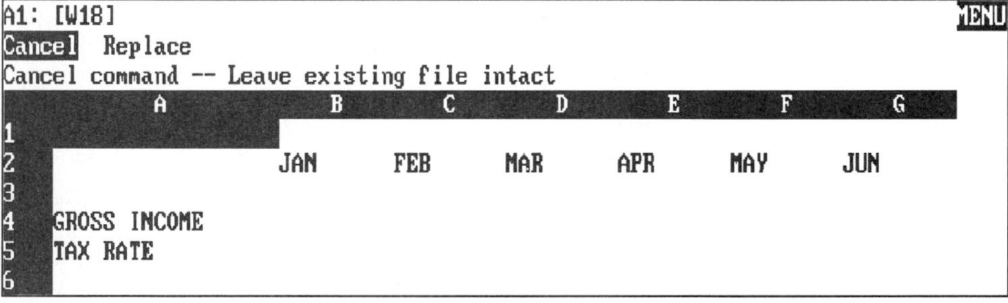

20. Select the **R**eplace command to complete the resave operation.

LESSON 6
Relative vs. Absolute Cell References

Copying Formulas

When the /**C**opy command is used to copy formulas, a new dimension of spreadsheet design is introduced. To show you how the /**C**opy command affects how you enter formulas into the spreadsheet, and how those formulas later derive their values, you will begin to fill in the spreadsheet's numeric data.

Entering and Copying a Simple Formula

1. Move the pointer to January's gross income (B4) and type ‖ 1855 ‖ .

2. Now move to cell C4 and type ‖ +B4 ↵ ‖ .

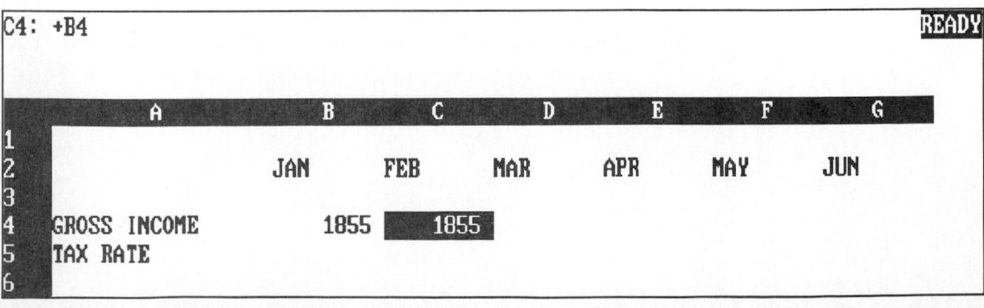

For copying purposes, this simple formula effectively says "the value in cell C4 is to be the same value found one cell to the left (cell B4)."

3. With the pointer on cell C4, type ‖ /C ‖ to call the /Copy command.

You next will copy the formula into the entire year's gross income amounts.

4. Specify the single cell C4..C4 as the FROM range by typing ↵.
5. Specify the TO range as cells D4 through M4, ‖ D4.M4 ↵ ‖ .

The formula will be copied into the appropriate range of cells, and all months should show a gross income of 1855.

Relative References

Move the pointer along the row labeled GROSS INCOME and watch the window line with the current cell information at the top of the screen. Notice that the formula was copied in a *relative* fashion. That is, each cell formula says "the value in this cell is to be the same value found one cell to the left."

```
C4: +B4                                                              READY

         A            B         C         D         E         F         G
1
2                    JAN       FEB       MAR       APR       MAY       JUN
3
4  GROSS INCOME      1855      1855      1855      1855      1855      1855
5  TAX RATE
6                              +B4       +C4       +D4       +E4       +F4
7  FED & STATE TAXES
```

When you use a formula to compute a value for a cell to display, the formula will usually contain *cell references* (Lotus refers to them as cell addresses). The single cell reference in the original formula for this example was +B4.

When the formula was copied, it was copied in a relative fashion. That is, as the cell into which the formula was being copied moved to the right one position, the cell reference in the formula shifted to the right one position.

Absolute References

It is possible, and often desirable, to have one or more cell references in a formula remain the same (not change) when the formula is copied into one or more cells. Lotus refers to such a reference as an *absolute cell address* or absolute cell reference. To produce an absolute cell reference within a formula, you include a dollar sign ($) before the column letter and row number in the cell reference. For instance, if you wanted all of the copied formulas in cells C4 through M4 to reference the starting gross income amount, you would enter the original formula as +$B$4. The result of copying the absolute formula into the same range as before would be as shown in the following screen.

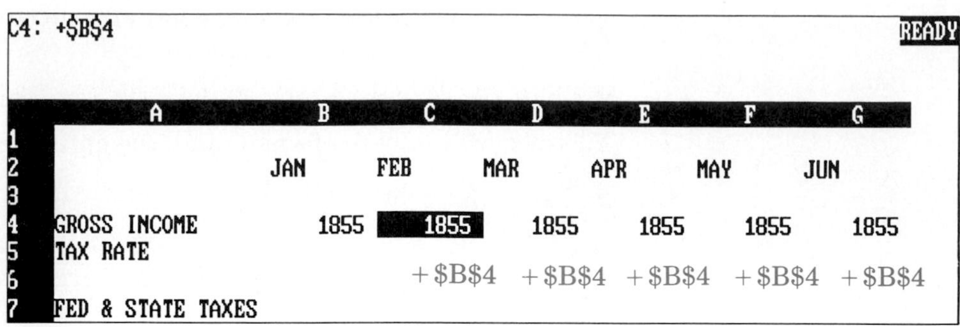

Although the cells would still display the number 1855, the amount would be derived in a different manner. The copied formulas now all say, in effect, "display the same value here as is displayed in cell B4" (the month of January).

The Difference between Relative and Absolute References

To demonstrate the difference between copying a formula with a relative reference and copying a formula with an absolute reference into a range of cells, assume that the year's gross income will be the same for four months. After four months you will receive a raise of $200 per month.

6. Move the pointer to May's gross income (F4) and type F2 (EDIT). Then type ‖ +200 ↵ ‖. The formula in cell F4 should now read +E4+200.

If you received a raise in May, that raise probably would stay in effect for the rest of the year. When you create an original formula to be copied into other cells, whether you enter the cell references for that formula as relative or absolute determines an important element of your spreadsheet's design.

Entering and Copying a Formula with an Absolute Reference

In the following steps you will create a formula that must have one of its cell references remain absolute when it is copied into the rest of the row's cells. This formula will be used to compute the federal and state taxes for the spreadsheet.

7. Move the pointer to cell A6 and type ‖ .23 ↵ ‖.

This figure represents the effective yearly tax rate you expect to pay. The formula to compute your federal and state taxes will multiply the tax rate (23%) times your gross pay amount for each month. The formula for the month of January could be typed as +A6*B4.

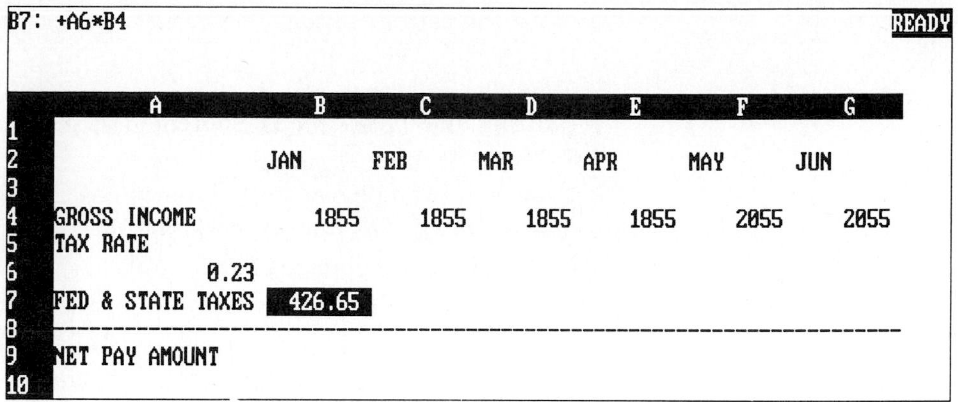

```
B7: +A6*B4                                                        READY

           A             B        C        D        E        F        G
 1
 2                      JAN      FEB      MAR      APR      MAY      JUN
 3
 4  GROSS INCOME         1855     1855     1855     1855     2055     2055
 5  TAX RATE
 6              0.23
 7  FED & STATE TAXES  426.65
 8  ---------------------------------------------------------------------
 9  NET PAY AMOUNT
10
```

If this formula then was copied into the rest of the cells in the row, the results would be as follows.

```
B7: +A6*B4                                                        READY

           A             B        C        D        E        F        G
 1
 2                      JAN      FEB      MAR      APR      MAY      JUN
 3
 4  GROSS INCOME         1855     1855     1855     1855     2055     2055
 5  TAX RATE
 6              0.23
 7  FED & STATE TAXES  426.65        0        0        0        0        0
 8  ---------------------------------------------------------------------
 9  NET PAY AMOUNT
10                     +A6*B4   +B6*C4   +C6*D4   +D6*E4   +E6*F4   +F6*G4
```

The formulas are copied with both cell references adjusting relative to the cell into which the formula is being copied.

Although the formula works for January's federal and state taxes, it has not been entered to copy correctly to the rest of the cells in the row. To make each formula in the row refer to cell A6 for the tax rate by which that month's pay amount will be multiplied, the original formula should be entered as either $A6*B4 or $A$6*B4. That is, the cell reference for the tax rate in this formula must be kept absolute.

8. Enter the correct formula for cell B7 and then copy that formula into the range of cells for the row.
9. Now move the pointer along the row and observe how the formulas differ from each other.

LESSON 7 Using the Pointer to Enter a Formula

When you enter a formula you can use the pointer to identify cell references for that formula. You may use this feature to reduce the chance of incorrect cell references being entered into a formula.

The formula for the net pay amount in the month of January is +B4−B7. To enter this formula, do the following.

1. Move the pointer to cell B9 (the cell in which to enter the formula) and type ‖ + ‖ .
2. Move the pointer to cell B4 (January's GROSS INCOME). Look at the control panel at the top of the screen. It indicates the formula you are entering into cell B9.
3. Type ‖ − ‖ and move the pointer to cell B7. The finished formula should appear on the edit line as +B4−B7.
4. Type ↵ to finish entering the formula.
5. Copy the formula into the range of cells C9 through M9.
6. Once more, move the pointer along the ninth row and look at the window line at the top of the screen to see how the cell references changed for each cell when the formula was copied.

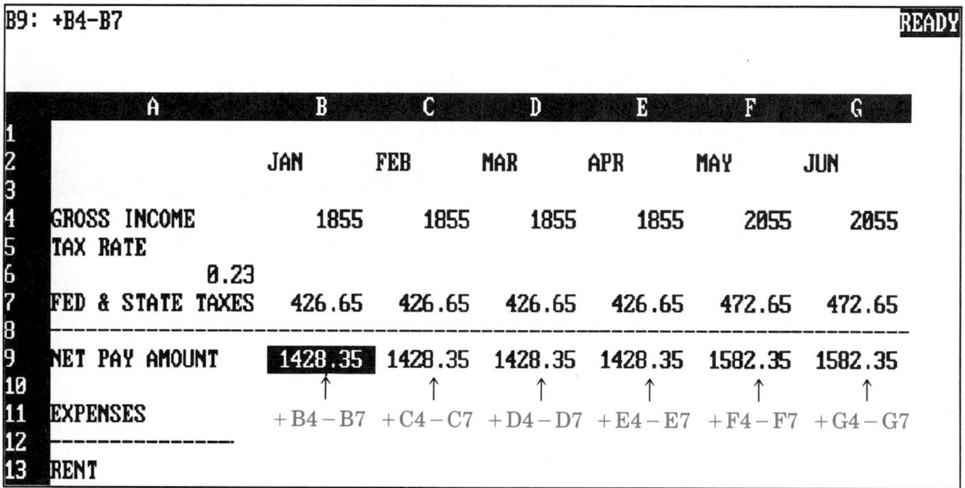

Both cell references were copied as relative references, as they should have been.

LESSON 8 Rejustifying a Range of Labels

You may have noticed that the month labels are not lined up very well with the numeric values you are entering into the spreadsheet. To demonstrate one of the /**R**ange commands and to make the spreadsheet more readable, do the following.

Using the /**R**ange,**L**abel Command

1. Type ‖ /**R**‖ to call the /**R**ange commands, and then select the command **L**abel.
2. Choose the command that will "Right-align labels in cells." Then define the range of labels to be right-aligned as B2..M2 (the row of month labels).
3. Type the Home key. The following shows what you should see.

```
A1: [W18]                                                    READY

         A            B        C        D        E        F        G
1
2                    JAN      FEB      MAR      APR      MAY      JUN
3
4  GROSS INCOME      1855     1855     1855     1855     2055     2055
5  TAX RATE
6            0.23
7  FED & STATE TAXES 426.65   426.65   426.65   426.65   472.65   472.65
8  ----------------------------------------------------------------------
9  NET PAY AMOUNT    1428.35  1428.35  1428.35  1428.35  1582.35  1582.35
10
11 EXPENSES
12 ----------------------------------------------------------------------
13 RENT
14 UTILITIES
15 TELEPHONE
16 LIFE INSURANCE
17 FOOD
18 LEISURE
19 ----------------------------------------------------------------------
20 TOTAL EXPENSES
26-Feb-91  03:10 PM        UNDO
```

LESSON 9
Adding Data to the Spreadsheet

Finish the next expense amounts in the spreadsheet by entering the following numeric values in the same manner as you entered the year's gross income amounts. For instance, for the first item, RENT, enter the number 375 into cell B13 and the formula +B13 into cell C13, and then copy the formula into the rest of the year's rent row.

1. RENT is 375 per month all year.
2. UTILITIES are 100 per month all year.
3. TELEPHONE is 18 per month all year.
4. LIFE INSURANCE is 28.65 per month all year.

Enter the remaining expense items by using a formula to compute the amounts. For instance, the formula to enter into cell B17 (JAN's FOOD expense) is .30*B9.

5. FOOD is 30% of NET PAY AMOUNT all year.
6. LEISURE is 15% of NET PAY AMOUNT all year.

This is what your spreadsheet should look like at this point.

A1: [W18] READY

	A	B	C	D	E	F	G
1							
2		JAN	FEB	MAR	APR	MAY	JUN
3							
4	GROSS INCOME	1855	1855	1855	1855	2055	2055
5	TAX RATE						
6	0.23						
7	FED & STATE TAXES	426.65	426.65	426.65	426.65	472.65	472.65
8	------------------	----------	----------	----------	----------	----------	----------
9	NET PAY AMOUNT	1428.35	1428.35	1428.35	1428.35	1582.35	1582.35
10							
11	EXPENSES						
12	------------------	----------	----------	----------	----------	----------	----------
13	RENT	375	375	375	375	375	375
14	UTILITIES	100	100	100	100	100	100
15	TELEPHONE	18	18	18	18	18	18
16	LIFE INSURANCE	28.65	28.65	28.65	28.65	28.65	28.65
17	FOOD	428.505	428.505	428.505	428.505	474.705	474.705
18	LEISURE	214.2525	214.2525	214.2525	214.2525	237.3525	237.3525
19	------------------	----------	----------	----------	----------	----------	----------
20	TOTAL EXPENSES						

26-Feb-91 03:13 PM UNDO

LESSON 10 Introduction to Functions

Total expenses could be expressed in a formula as +B13+B14+B15+B16+B17+B18 for the month of January. Instead, you will use one of Lotus 1-2-3's spreadsheet functions. The general form of a *function* is **@XYZ** (argument). The @ sign tells Lotus 1-2-3 that you are entering a function into a cell. The XYZ represents the function's name, and the *arguments* in the parentheses are composed of cell references, ranges, values, or formulas for the function to act upon.

Using the **@SUM** Function

1. Move the pointer to cell B20 and type ‖ **@SUM**(B13.B18) ↵ ‖ .

The formula **@SUM**(B13..B18) will sum the cell contents of the cells in the range specified in the function's argument.

2. Now copy the function into cells C20 through M20. Notice that the cell references in the function also were copied in a relative fashion.

LESSON 11 Finishing the Spreadsheet

Entering Savings Deposits

The label SAVINGS DEPOSITS represents money left to deposit in your bank account.

1. Enter the appropriate formula into cell B22 and copy it into the rest of the cells in the spreadsheet row.

Now the bottom lines of your spreadsheet should look like this.

```
20  TOTAL EXPENSES    1164.407 1164.407 1164.407 1164.407 1233.707 1233.707
21
22  SAVINGS DEPOSIT   263.9425 263.9425 263.9425 263.9425 348.6425 348.6425
23  -----------------------------------------------------------------------
24
26-Feb-91  03:16 PM         UNDO
```

A Running Savings Account Balance

You have one more row of values to add to the spreadsheet. This row will be labeled SAVINGS ACCOUNT and will reflect the total savings you expect after each month's deposit, with *x* amount of yearly interest, compounded monthly.

2. Move the pointer to cell A24 and type ‖ SAVINGS ACCOUNT ‖ .
3. Now move to cell A25 and type ‖ INTEREST RATE= ‖ .
4. Move to cell B25 and type ‖ .0525 ‖ (the yearly rate of interest, 5 1/4%).
5. Move to cell A26. Type ‖ \=↵ ‖ . Now copy this repeating label underline through to DEC (M26).
6. Move the pointer to cell A27 and type ‖ BEGINNING BALANCE ‖ .
7. Move to cell B27 and type in ‖ 0 ↵ ‖ (zero), the beginning balance for the savings account.

Entering a More Complicated Formula

You are ready to enter the formula for computing a running total of the savings account for the year. The formula will multiply the previous month's balance by 1 plus the monthly interest rate (add that month's interest earned). Then it will add the deposit made at the end of the previous month to derive the beginning balance for the current month. The general form of the formula for the month of FEB is +B27*(1+B25/12)+B22. The order in which the formula will be computed is as follows.

1. Take the yearly interest rate, B25, and divide it by 12 to determine the monthly interest rate.

   B25/12

2. Add 1 to this, giving the correct multiplier for determining the balance with interest added to it.

   (1+B25/12)

3. Take what you already have in the bank, B27, and multiply it by the multiplier to give principal plus interest earned for the month.

   +B27*(1+B25/12)

4. Finally, add the deposit you will make from the money you had (after expenses) from the month before.

   +B27*(1+B25/12)+B22

After entering this formula into February's beginning balance, you will copy it into the appropriate cells for the rest of the year. However, one of the cell references in the formula must be copied with an absolute cell reference. All cells in the row will refer to this specific cell in their formulas. This cell reference will need to be typed with a $ sign preceding its column letter. The other two references in the formula will be relative to the particular month into which they are being copied.

To test your understanding of relative and absolute cell addresses, the following step requires you to decide which cell addresses to enter as relative and which as absolute. Refer to the previous discussions on relative and absolute cell addresses of formulas if necessary.

8. Type the correct formula for the month of FEB and copy it into the range of cells for BEGINNING BALANCE (set the TO range as D27..M27).

The bottom lines of your spreadsheet should look like the following if you have typed the original formula correctly.

```
19 --------------------------------------------------------------------------
20 TOTAL EXPENSES     1164.407 1164.407 1164.407 1164.407 1233.707 1233.707
21
22 SAVINGS DEPOSIT    263.9425 263.9425 263.9425 263.9425 348.6425 348.6425
23 --------------------------------------------------------------------------
24 SAVINGS ACCOUNT
25 INTEREST RATE=       0.0525
26 ==========================================================================
27 BEGINNING BALANCE           0 263.9425 529.0397 795.2967 1062.718 1416.010
28
26-Feb-91  03:35 PM          UNDO                                    CAPS
```

Causing the Spreadsheet to Recalculate

Now that the spreadsheet is functionally complete, you can test its ability to recalculate automatically for any changes you enter into it.

Assume your boss gives you a $100.00 raise immediately (in January) and another $150.00 raise in May in lieu of the $200.00 raise in May.

9. Change your spreadsheet to accommodate the changed salary.

Assume that taxes are cut this year and your estimated effective federal and state tax rate will drop to 18%.

10. Enter the new tax rate to see how it affects your home budget spreadsheet.

Suppose you receive a notice from your landlord informing you rent will be increased $20.00 per month beginning in March.

11. Enter the change into your spreadsheet.

Assume UTILITIES will be $125.00 JAN through MAR; $100.00 APRIL through AUGUST; $130.00 SEPT through DEC.

12. Change your spreadsheet to accommodate these expectations.

Your spreadsheet should look like this.

A1: [W18] READY

	A	B	C	D	E	F	G
1							
2		JAN	FEB	MAR	APR	MAY	JUN
3							
4	GROSS INCOME	1955	1955	1955	1955	2105	2105
5	TAX RATE						
6	0.18						
7	FED & STATE TAXES	351.9	351.9	351.9	351.9	378.9	378.9
8	------------------	----------	----------	----------	----------	----------	----------
9	NET PAY AMOUNT	1603.1	1603.1	1603.1	1603.1	1726.1	1726.1
10							
11	EXPENSES						
12	------------------	----------	----------	----------	----------	----------	----------
13	RENT	375	375	395	395	395	395
14	UTILITIES	125	125	125	100	100	100
15	TELEPHONE	18	18	18	18	18	18
16	LIFE INSURANCE	28.65	28.65	28.65	28.65	28.65	28.65
17	FOOD	480.93	480.93	480.93	480.93	517.83	517.83
18	LEISURE	240.465	240.465	240.465	240.465	258.915	258.915
19	------------------	----------	----------	----------	----------	----------	----------
20	TOTAL EXPENSES	1268.045	1268.045	1288.045	1263.045	1318.395	1318.395
21							
22	SAVINGS DEPOSIT	335.055	335.055	315.055	340.055	407.705	407.705
23	------------------	----------	----------	----------	----------	----------	----------
24	SAVINGS ACCOUNT						
25	INTEREST RATE=	0.0525					
26	==================	==========	==========	==========	==========	==========	==========
27	BEGINNING BALANCE	0	335.055	671.5758	989.5690	1333.953	1747.494
28							

O20: READY

	H	I	J	K	L	M	N	O
1								
2	JUL	AUG	SEP	OCT	NOV	DEC		
3								
4	2105	2105	2105	2105	2105	2105		
5								
6								
7	378.9	378.9	378.9	378.9	378.9	378.9		
8	----------	----------	----------	----------	----------	----------		
9	1726.1	1726.1	1726.1	1726.1	1726.1	1726.1		
10								
11								
12	----------	----------	----------	----------	----------	----------		
13	395	395	395	395	395	395		
14	100	100	130	130	130	130		
15	18	18	18	18	18	18		
16	28.65	28.65	28.65	28.65	28.65	28.65		
17	517.83	517.83	517.83	517.83	517.83	517.83		
18	258.915	258.915	258.915	258.915	258.915	258.915		
19	----------	----------	----------	----------	----------	----------		
20	1318.395	1318.395	1348.395	1348.395	1348.395	1348.395		
21								
22	407.705	407.705	377.705	377.705	377.705	377.705		
23	----------	----------	----------	----------	----------	----------		
24								
25								
26	==========	==========	==========	==========	==========	==========		
27	2162.844	2580.012	2999.004	3389.830	3782.365	4176.618		
28								

13. Now is a good time to resave your work. Use the /**F**ile,**S**ave command to update the copy of LOTUT on the disk.

LESSON 12 Stopping and Restarting a Lotus Session

This lesson marks the halfway point in the tutorial lessons. To give you experience in using two important commands, and to provide an opportunity to quit the tutorial and resume later, do the following.

Erasing a Spreadsheet from RAM

1. Make sure the spreadsheet is saved on your disk and then type the /**W**orksheet,**E**rase command.

The /**W**orksheet,**E**rase command is used to erase the current spreadsheet from RAM, which allows you to begin creating a new spreadsheet. The prompt at the top of the screen is a precautionary step designed to prevent you from erasing the spreadsheet from RAM before you have saved it on the disk.

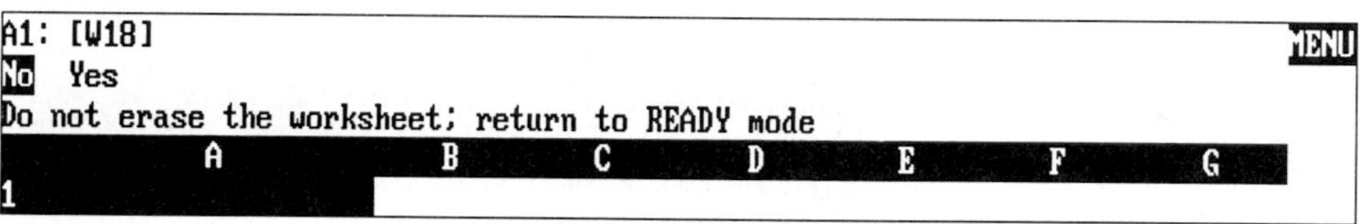

2. Answer **Y**es to the prompt. The screen should now be cleared.

The /Quit Command

The /**Q**uit command is used to erase the Lotus spreadsheet software from RAM. If it is your intention to stop the tutorial now and continue at a later time, do the following.

3. Type the /**Q**uit command and answer **Y**es to the precautionary **N**o **Y**es prompt that appears.
4. Use the **E**xit command of the Access System to return to the DOS operating level. You will need to repeat the Getting Started section of the tutorial lessons when you are ready to resume.

The /File,Retrieve Command

When you are ready to resume work on a spreadsheet file you have previously saved on your disk, the /**F**ile,**R**etrieve command is used to copy the file from the disk into RAM.

5. Type the /**F**ile,**R**etrieve command. A screen similar to the following should appear.

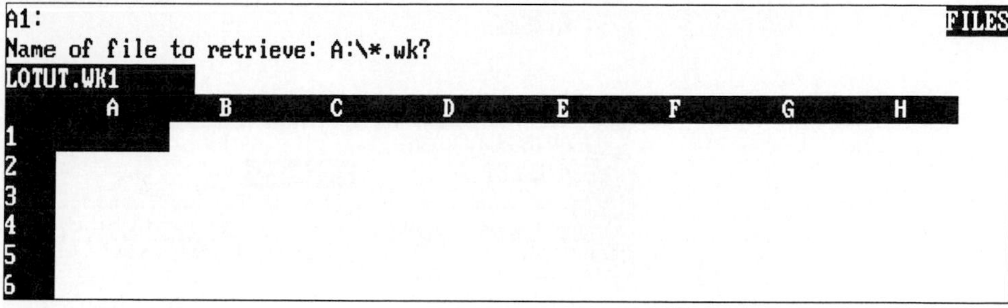

Lotus begins the process of retrieving a spreadsheet file by reading the current disk directory and placing the names of all spreadsheet files (files having a WK1 extension) on the bottom line of the control panel. You then may retrieve a particular spreadsheet by moving the pointer on that line to the appropriate spreadsheet filename and typing ↵.

6. Retrieve the LOTUT spreadsheet into RAM.

LESSON 13 Formatting a Spreadsheet

Formatting Ranges of Cells

The command to call a set of /**R**ange commands is on the Main menu. You used one of these commands to assign a label prefix (/**R**ange,**L**abel) for the row of month labels to align them more precisely with the numeric values in the spreadsheet. You also used the /**R**ange commands to name a range, and then later used the name to specify the range. The /**R**ange commands include the following.

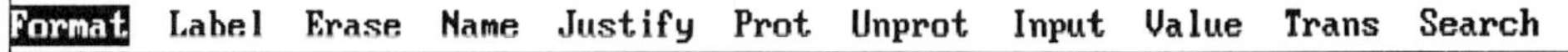

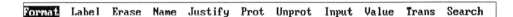

The first item in the /**R**ange submenu is the **F**ormat command, which is used for formatting ranges of cells. The submenu of /**R**ange,**F**ormat commands includes

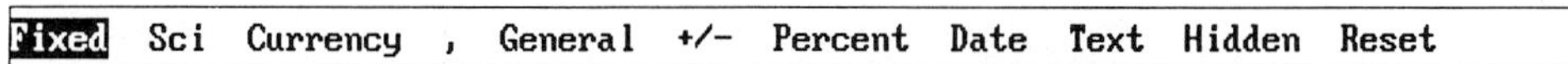

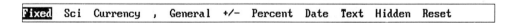

1. Move the pointer to cell B25 (the yearly interest rate on savings).

You will use the /**R**ange,**F**ormat commands to format this single cell to display its data in percent notation.

2. Type the /**R**ange,**F**ormat command, and then find and select the command to format as a **P**ercent.

The number of decimal places will be two (2). Since 2 is the default value shown with the prompt, you can simply type ↵.

3. Type ↵.
4. Type ↵ to enter B25..B25 as the appropriate range to format.

BEFORE:

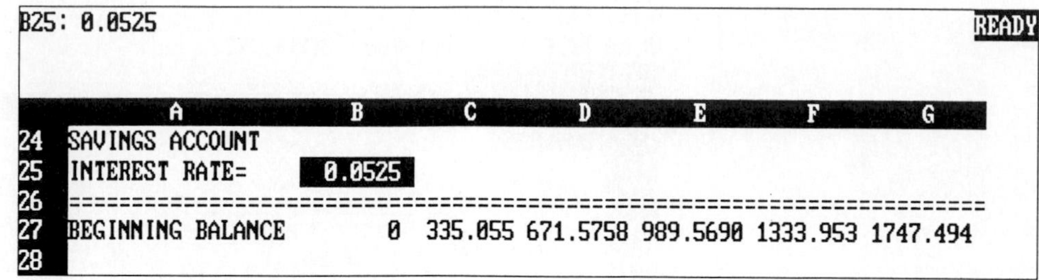

STEPS: /**RFP** (/**R**ange,**F**ormat,**P**ercent)
Enter number of decimal places (0..15): 2↵
Enter range to format: B25..B25↵

AFTER:

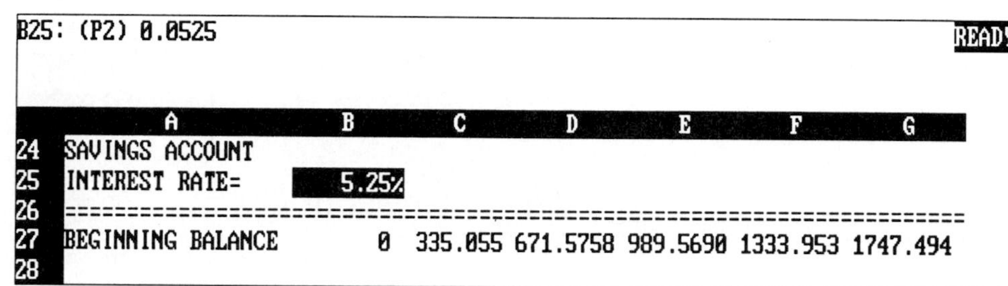

Notice that the value shown at the top of the screen remains 0.0525; however, for purposes of viewing the spreadsheet, the value in the cell B25 now is shown as 5.25%. The (P2) shown at the top of the screen with the cell's value indicates the cell now is formatted to display as a percentage with two decimal places.

5. Repeat the last step to format the tax rate (the 0.18 in cell A6) to display as a percent with zero decimal places.
6. Move the pointer to B22 (SAVINGS DEPOSITS row) and type the /**R**ange,**F**ormat. Select **C**urrency with 2 decimal places. Set the range to format as B22 through M22.

BEFORE:

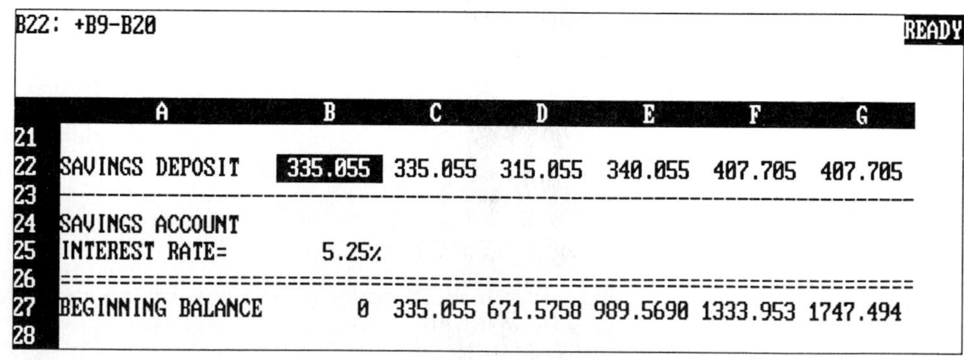

STEPS: /**RFC** (/**R**ange,**F**ormat,**C**urrency)
Enter number of decimal places (0..15): 2 ↵
Enter range to format: B22..M22 ↵

AFTER:

```
B22: (C2) +B9-B20                                                    READY

              A              B         C         D         E         F         G
21
22 SAVINGS DEPOSIT      $335.06   $335.06   $315.06   $340.06   $407.71   $407.71
23 ------------------------------------------------------------------------------
24 SAVINGS ACCOUNT
25 INTEREST RATE=         5.25%
26 ==============================================================================
27 BEGINNING BALANCE           0  335.055  671.5758  989.5690  1333.953  1747.494
28
```

If you use the **Currency** format, cells with values in them display their values in standard currency notation. The partial cents that were shown before have been rounded just for display purposes. They remain part of the value held in the cell and will be used in any formula referring to that cell.

7. Repeat the last step selecting the **T**ext command instead of the **C**urrency command for this range of cells.

BEFORE:

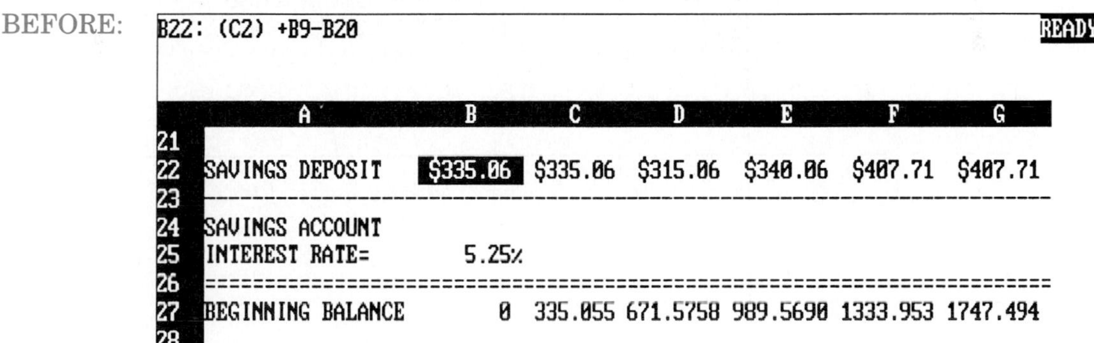

```
B22: (C2) +B9-B20                                                    READY

              A              B         C         D         E         F         G
21
22 SAVINGS DEPOSIT      $335.06   $335.06   $315.06   $340.06   $407.71   $407.71
23 ------------------------------------------------------------------------------
24 SAVINGS ACCOUNT
25 INTEREST RATE=         5.25%
26 ==============================================================================
27 BEGINNING BALANCE           0  335.055  671.5758  989.5690  1333.953  1747.494
28
```

STEPS: /RFT (/**R**ange,**F**ormat,**T**ext)
Enter range to format: B22..M22 ↵

AFTER:

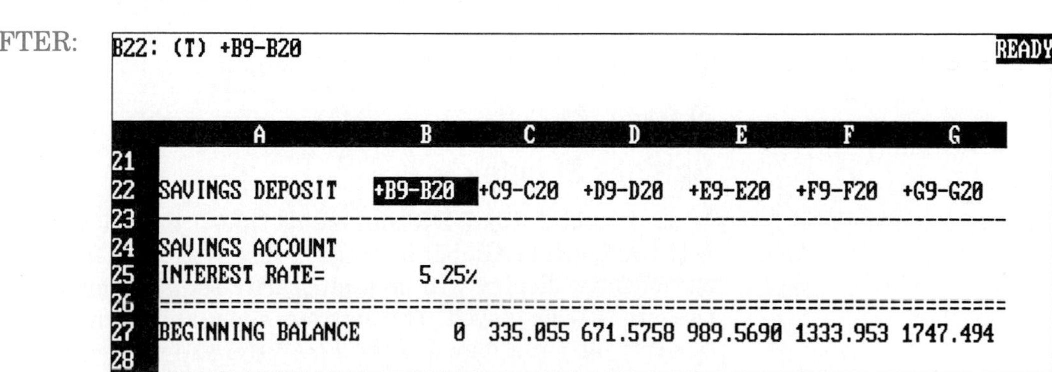

```
B22: (T) +B9-B20                                                     READY

              A              B         C         D         E         F         G
21
22 SAVINGS DEPOSIT      +B9-B20   +C9-C20   +D9-D20   +E9-E20   +F9-F20   +G9-G20
23 ------------------------------------------------------------------------------
24 SAVINGS ACCOUNT
25 INTEREST RATE=         5.25%
26 ==============================================================================
27 BEGINNING BALANCE           0  335.055  671.5758  989.5690  1333.953  1747.494
28
```

The **Text** formatting command will display the formulas used in a range of cells.

8. Finally, use the /**R**ange,**F**ormat,**R**eset command to return the row of cells B22..M22 back to the default spreadsheet format (General).

Global Formatting Commands

When the term *global* is used in computers, it generally means "in effect or affecting the entire set of data." The term *default* means "automatically in effect." For instance, the default global label-prefix for Lotus 1-2-3 is the single quote (') (left justified). Unless you specify otherwise, any label you enter into a cell will automatically be justified to the left in that cell. When you do specify otherwise, such as when you used the /**R**ange,**L**abel,**R**ight command to right justify the month labels in their cells, you are overriding the default global setting.

Lotus 1-2-3 allows you to change certain global settings through the /**W**orksheet,**G**lobal commands. These commands are as follows.

9. Use the /**W**orksheet,**G**lobal command to see the global settings that you may change.

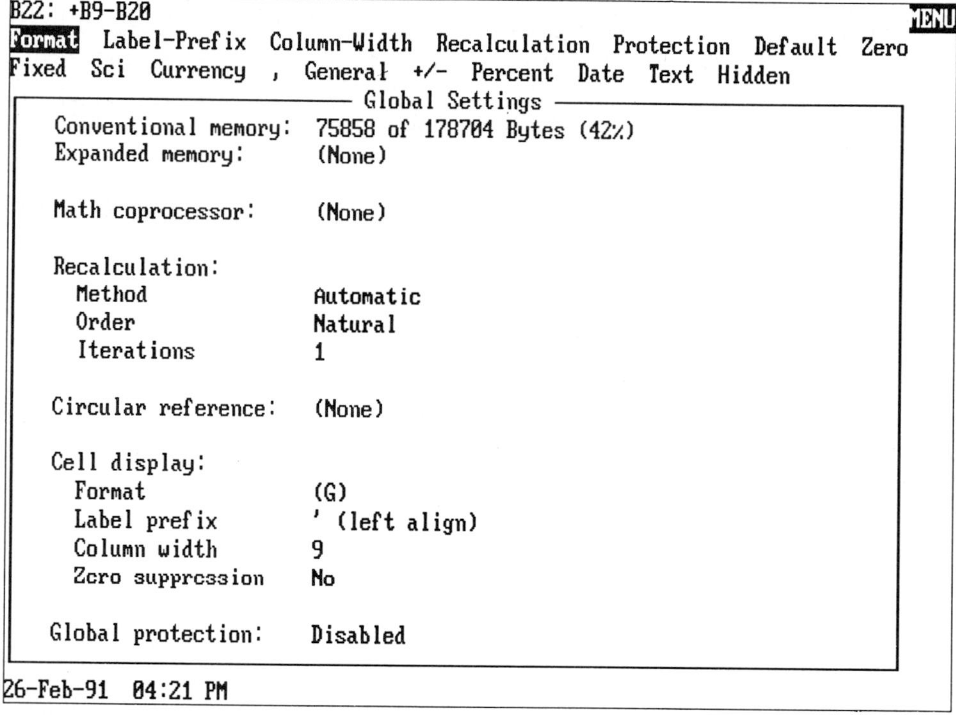

Settings Sheets

With several Lotus 1-2-3 commands that are used to modify certain types of settings (such as Global settings, Print settings, Graph settings, etc.), the spreadsheet display will be temporarily replaced by a settings sheet such as the one now displayed. The settings sheet shows the current status of various settings. You may use the F6 (WINDOW) Function key to turn the display of the settings sheet on or off as desired.

NOTE: Settings sheets are not displayed with version 2.01.

Lotus 1-2-3 allows you to define a global format for the entire spreadsheet through the /**W**orksheet,**G**lobal,**F**ormat commands. The available formatting commands are the same as with the /**R**ange,**F**ormat commands, except that the entire spreadsheet rather than just a specified range is affected.

10. Now select the **F**ormat command, and then select **C**urrency and specify two decimal places.

```
B22: +B9-B20                                                          READY

               A              B        C        D        E        F        G
10
11 EXPENSES
12 ------------------------------------------------------------------------
13 RENT                    $375.00  $375.00  $395.00  $395.00  $395.00  $395.00
14 UTILITIES               $125.00  $125.00  $125.00  $100.00  $100.00  $100.00
15 TELEPHONE                $18.00   $18.00   $18.00   $18.00   $18.00   $18.00
16 LIFE INSURANCE           $28.65   $28.65   $28.65   $28.65   $28.65   $28.65
17 FOOD                    $480.93  $480.93  $480.93  $480.93  $517.83  $517.83
18 LEISURE                 $240.47  $240.47  $240.47  $240.47  $258.92  $258.92
19 ------------------------------------------------------------------------
20 TOTAL EXPENSES        ******************************************************
21
22 SAVINGS DEPOSIT         $335.06  $335.06  $315.06  $340.06  $407.71  $407.71
23 ------------------------------------------------------------------------
24 SAVINGS ACCOUNT
25 INTEREST RATE=            5.25%
26 ========================================================================
27 BEGINNING BALANCE         $0.00  $335.06  $671.58  $989.57 ******************
28
29
26-Feb-91  04:23 PM          UNDO
```

Notice that when a value becomes too large to display in a cell (in this case because of the addition of $ signs and commas), Lotus 1-2-3 indicates the situation by putting asterisks in the affected cell.

LESSON 14 Global Change of Column Widths

One solution to the problem of numeric entries that are too large to display in their cells is to enlarge the display width of the cell. One /Worksheet,Global command allows you to change the default global column width of nine characters to any width size between 1 and 240 characters.

1. Type the /**W**orksheet,**G**lobal,**C**olumn-Width command and enter the new global column width as 12.

```
A30: [W18]                                                            READY

               A                B              C              D              E
19 -------------------------------------------------------------------------
20 TOTAL EXPENSES       $1,268.05     $1,268.05     $1,288.05     $1,263.05
21
22 SAVINGS DEPOSIT        $335.06       $335.06       $315.06       $340.06
23 -------------------------------------------------------------------------
24 SAVINGS ACCOUNT
25 INTEREST RATE=           5.25%
26 =========================================================================
27 BEGINNING BALANCE        $0.00       $335.06       $671.58       $989.57
28
```

LESSON 15 Altering the Spreadsheet

Suppose you neglected an expense item (or acquired a new one) and needed to include it in your spreadsheet. The following steps will show you how to add it to your spreadsheet.

Inserting a Spreadsheet Row or Column

1. Move the pointer to anywhere in row 14 (UTILITIES) and type the /**W**orksheet,**I**nsert,**R**ow command.

The command to insert rows allows you to insert one row or more at once by specifying a range of rows to insert. In this case you will insert only one row, so the default range shown is correct.

2. Type ↵ to insert the single row.
3. Move the pointer to any month's total expense amount.

Notice that Lotus automatically adjusts existing cell references in its formulas and functions to accommodate an alteration (such as an inserted or deleted row) of the spreadsheet. For instance, the formula for January's total expenses @**SUM**(B13..B18) in row 21 automatically has been changed to @**SUM**(B13..B19) to accommodate the row inserted into the range. Similarly, the formula +B9−B20 for January's savings deposits has been changed to +B9−B21.

4. Move the spreadsheet pointer to A14 and label the new row PARKING since it will be the row for parking fees paid for three-month parking permits.
5. Now move to the months January, April, July, and October to enter the amount of $75.00 into these cells for the PARKING spreadsheet row.

Moving a Spreadsheet Row or Column

What if you decide parking expenses should be located below utilities rather than below rent?

6. Move the pointer to row 16 for telephone expenses and insert a single row there.
7. Move the pointer to A14 and type the /**M**ove command.
8. Enter the range to /**M**ove FROM as A14..M14 and the TO range as A16 (the uppermost left cell of the row you just inserted).

Deleting a Spreadsheet Row or Column

9. Move the pointer back to row 14, where PARKING used to be. Type the /**W**orksheet commands, find the **D**elete command, and then use the command to delete that single row.

LESSON 16 More on Viewing the Spreadsheet

The spreadsheet you have created is so large that only a portion of it may be viewed on the screen at a time. The portion to the top left should appear as follows.

```
A1: [W18]                                                        READY

           A               B           C           D           E
1
2                          JAN         FEB         MAR         APR
3
4  GROSS INCOME      $1,955.00   $1,955.00   $1,955.00   $1,955.00
5  TAX RATE
6               18%
7  FED & STATE TAXES   $351.90     $351.90     $351.90     $351.90
8  ----------------------------------------------------------------
9  NET PAY AMOUNT    $1,603.10   $1,603.10   $1,603.10   $1,603.10
10
11 EXPENSES
12 ----------------------------------------------------------------
13 RENT                $375.00     $375.00     $395.00     $395.00
14 UTILITIES           $125.00     $125.00     $125.00     $100.00
15 PARKING              $75.00                              $75.00
16 TELEPHONE            $18.00      $18.00      $18.00      $18.00
17 LIFE INSURANCE       $28.65      $28.65      $28.65      $28.65
18 FOOD                $480.93     $480.93     $480.93     $480.93
19 LEISURE             $240.47     $240.47     $240.47     $240.47
20 ----------------------------------------------------------------
26-Feb-91  04:33 PM      UNDO
```

To view the last eight columns of the spreadsheet you need to use the pointer to "push" or *scroll* the screen across. Lotus 1-2-3 provides several ways to use the pointer to move the screen about on a large spreadsheet.

Moving Quickly about the Spreadsheet

You already have used Function key F5 to "GOTO" a particular cell and have used the Home key to move quickly back to cell A1. To see the other ways that you can move quickly about the spreadsheet, do the following.

1. Type the Home key to send the pointer to cell A1. Next type the PgDn key on the numeric keypad. Then type the PgUp key found on the same keypad.

The PgDn and PgUp keys move the pointer and the screen one "page" (one screen's worth of spreadsheet) up or down at a time.

Next, find the Tab key on the left side of the keyboard marked with two arrows. It is just above the key marked Ctrl.

2. Type the Tab key once or twice.

The lower case of this key moves the pointer and the screen one page (one screen) to the right. Shift to the upper case of the key to move the pointer and screen one page to the left.

3. Type the Home key to send the pointer to cell A1.
4. Now move the pointer to A8 and type the key marked End on the numeric keypad.

Notice the indicator at the bottom of the spreadsheet showing the END mode is turned on.

5. Type the Pointer Right key (→).
6. Type the End key. Then type the Pointer Left key (←).
7. Now type the End key/Pointer Down key (↓) combination three times in a row.
8. Type the End key/Pointer Up key (↑) combination four times in a row.

The End key turns on a mode that, when used with the pointer control keys, moves in the direction indicated by the pointer control key until the pointer reaches the last nonblank cell in the spreadsheet, if the pointer was originally on a nonblank cell. The pointer will move to the cell following the last blank cell if it was originally on a blank cell.

9. Type the End key and then the Home key.

This End key combination sends the pointer to the lowest right cell of the rectangle defined by the spreadsheet (the effective opposite of Home).

These methods of moving the pointer are extremely useful when pointing to ranges at the time they are being specified, or when pointing to cell references in a formula when a formula is being created.

Freezing Titles

Lotus 1-2-3 has the ability to let you "freeze" rows, columns, or both when viewing large spreadsheets. This is particularly useful when row or column labels disappear from view because the screen is pushed to another section of the spreadsheet. For instance, when you want to view the row labeled BEGINNING BALANCE, the month labels for the row disappear off the top of the screen.

10. Move the pointer to row 4. Type the /**W**orksheet command and select the **T**itles command.

You want to freeze the row of month labels that is horizontal in the spreadsheet.

11. Select the **H**orizontal command of this menu.
12. Now use the pointer to push the screen down the spreadsheet until the last rows appear for viewing.

Notice that the rows above the pointer's position at the time the titles were frozen do not scroll off the screen.

13. Use the pointer to push the screen to the right until the month of December is showing.

The month labels scroll with the rest of the spreadsheet, but now the row labels have disappeared.

14. Type the Home key, move the pointer to cell B4, and then use the **T**itles command to set both horizontal and vertical title freeze.
15. Scroll the screen to the right and then down. Both the row labels and column labels now are frozen.
16. Type the Home key.

Notice that when titles are frozen you are unable to move the pointer to them with the pointer control keys. Home now is defined as the upper left corner of the unfrozen spreadsheet. To move the pointer into a frozen area, press Function key F5 (GOTO) and then the address of a cell within the frozen area.

The /**W**orksheet,**T**itles,**C**lear command unfreezes all fixed titles.

17. Use this command to unfreeze the titles on your spreadsheet.

The next portion of the tutorial introduces a concept called modeling and also will demonstrate techniques for dealing with large spreadsheets.

LESSON 17 Modeling with a Spreadsheet

Modeling allows you to ask "What if?" and then use the rapid recalculation power of the spreadsheet to obtain the answer quickly. To take you through a lesson on how you can model with the spreadsheet, you will add another value to the spreadsheet.

Adding a Summary for Interest Earned

1. Move to cell L30 and type ‖ INTEREST EARNED = ‖ . (5 spaces)
2. Next move to cell N26 and type ‖ ENDING BALANCE ‖ .
3. Copy the formula in cell M28 to cell N28.

This area of the spreadsheet should now look like the following.

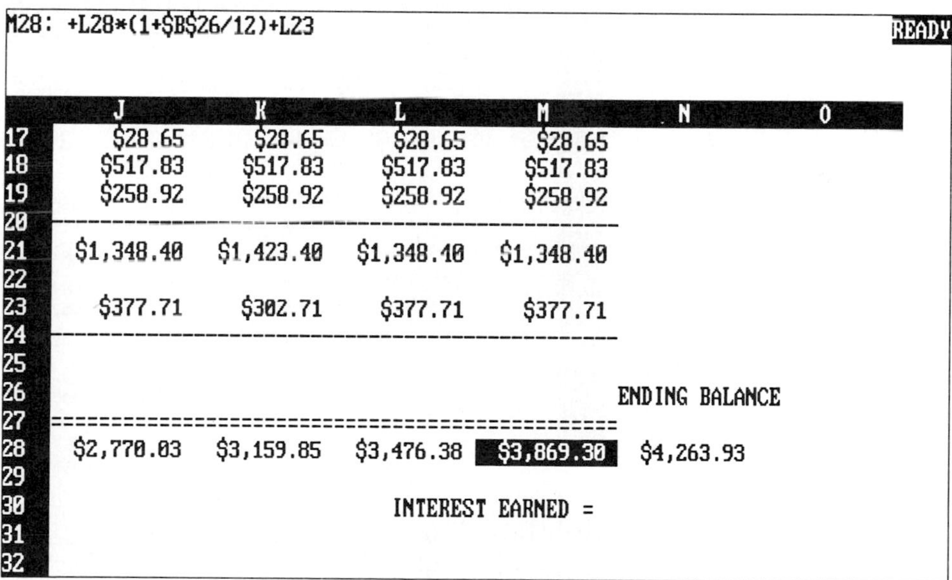

M28: +L28*(1+$B$26/12)+L23 READY

	J	K	L	M	N	O
17	$28.65	$28.65	$28.65	$28.65		
18	$517.83	$517.83	$517.83	$517.83		
19	$258.92	$258.92	$258.92	$258.92		
20	----------	----------	----------	----------		
21	$1,348.40	$1,423.40	$1,348.40	$1,348.40		
22						
23	$377.71	$302.71	$377.71	$377.71		
24	----------	----------	----------	----------		
25						
26					ENDING BALANCE	
27	==========	==========	==========	==========		
28	$2,770.03	$3,159.85	$3,476.38	$3,869.30	$4,263.93	
29						
30			INTEREST EARNED =			
31						
32						

Advantages of Pointing to Enter a Formula

In cell N30 you will enter the formula that will give the total interest earned on your savings for the year. The formula will subtract the beginning balance and all deposits from the ending balance to determine its answer. Since cell references for the formula are located in several areas of the spreadsheet, you will use the pointing method to enter the formula into the appropriate spreadsheet cell. As you move about the spreadsheet to point to various cell references, try using the rapid methods of moving the pointer.

4. With the pointer on cell N30 type ‖ + ‖ to indicate that you are starting to enter a numeric value into this cell.
5. Move the pointer to the year's ending balance amount. Look at the edit line at the top of the screen to see that the formula is being entered.
6. Type ‖ − ‖ (minus).

The pointer will return to N30 and the edit line should show +N28−.

7. Move the pointer to the beginning balance amount for January and type ‖ − ‖ again.

The pointer will return again to N30 and the formula continues to grow.

8. Now type ‖ **@SUM**(‖ and then move the pointer to the beginning of the savings deposits values.
9. Press the period key to set the anchor for the range you are going to sum.
10. Move the pointer to the end of the savings deposits row and type ‖) ‖ .

The formula is complete: +N28−B28−**@SUM**(B23..M23).

11. Now type ↵ to enter the formula.

```
N30: +N28-B28-@SUM(B23..M23)                                         READY

        J           K           L           M           N           O
17    $28.65      $28.65      $28.65      $28.65
18   $517.83     $517.83     $517.83     $517.83
19   $258.92     $258.92     $258.92     $258.92
20 ------------------------------------------------
21 $1,348.40   $1,423.40   $1,348.40   $1,348.40
22
23   $377.71     $302.71     $377.71     $377.71
24 ------------------------------------------------
25
26                                              ENDING BALANCE
27 ================================================
28 $2,770.03   $3,159.85   $3,476.38   $3,869.30   $4,263.93
29
30                         INTEREST EARNED =         $97.07
31
32
```

Splitting the Window on the Spreadsheet

With deposits given, two factors will affect interest earned—the interest rate and the beginning balance. You can find both values in the B column, and you can find the interest earned to the far right (out of view) in the N column. To view these columns at the same time and access them with the pointer, you may use the /**W**orksheet,**W**indow set of commands.

12. Move the pointer anywhere in the C column and type the /**W**orksheet,**W**indow,**V**ertical command.

```
B1:                                                                    READY

              A              B                  C           D           E
1                                  1
2                           JAN    2           FEB         MAR         APR
3                                  3
4  GROSS INCOME          $1,955.00 4     $1,955.00   $1,955.00   $1,955.00
5  TAX RATE                        5
6                 18%              6
7  FED & STATE TAXES       $351.90 7       $351.90     $351.90     $351.90
8  ------------------------------- 8  ------------------------------------
9  NET PAY AMOUNT        $1,603.10 9     $1,603.10   $1,603.10   $1,603.10
10                                 10
11 EXPENSES                        11
12 ------------------------------- 12 ------------------------------------
13 RENT                    $375.00 13      $375.00     $395.00     $395.00
14 UTILITIES               $125.00 14      $125.00     $125.00     $100.00
15 PARKING                  $75.00 15                               $75.00
16 TELEPHONE                $18.00 16       $18.00      $18.00      $18.00
17 LIFE INSURANCE           $28.65 17       $28.65      $28.65      $28.65
18 FOOD                    $480.93 18      $480.93     $480.93     $480.93
19 LEISURE                 $240.47 19      $240.47     $240.47     $240.47
20 ------------------------------- 20 ------------------------------------
26-Feb-91  04:43 PM       UNDO
```

The **W**indow commands **H**orizontal and **V**ertical split the screen into separate windows through which you can view the spreadsheet. Each window may be used to scroll the spreadsheet.

The pointer can reside in only one window at any given time, but it may be moved from one window to the other by typing Function key F6.

13. Type Function key F6 several times. Then move the pointer to the window on the left.

14. Try moving the pointer to the right six columns.

You can scroll the spreadsheet in this window with the pointer in the same manner as you previously scrolled the spreadsheet.

15. Type the Home key and then use the pointer to scroll up the spreadsheet until the bottom three rows are located in about the middle of the screen.

Notice that the spreadsheet on the right also scrolls. The term for such scrolling is *synchronized scrolling* and the /**W**orksheet,**W**indow commands include the commands to **S**ynchronize and **U**nsynchronize the scrolling of spreadsheets being viewed through the windows.

16. Type the F6 key to move to the right window and scroll it to the left until you can see the last three columns (L, M, and N).

17. Now move to the left window by typing F6.

```
B36:                                                              READY

              A                 B            L          M           N
17 LIFE INSURANCE          $28.65 17     $28.65     $28.65
18 FOOD                   $480.93 18    $517.83    $517.83
19 LEISURE                $240.47 19    $258.92    $258.92
20 -------------------------------20 -----------------------
21 TOTAL EXPENSES       $1,343.05 21  $1,348.40  $1,348.40
22                                22
23 SAVINGS DEPOSIT        $260.06 23    $377.71    $377.71
24 -------------------------------24 -----------------------
25 SAVINGS ACCOUNT                25
26 INTEREST RATE=           5.25%26                      ENDING BALANCE
27 ===============================27 =======================
28 BEGINNING BALANCE        $0.00 28  $3,476.38  $3,869.30  $4,263.93
29                                29
30                                30    INTEREST EARNED =      $97.07
31                                31
32                                32
33                                33
34                                34
35                                35
36                                36
26-Feb-91  04:46 PM         UNDO
```

You may move the pointer in the left window to change the interest rate, beginning balance, or both, and you can see the effect the changes have on interest earned for the year in the window to the right.

Test Your Understanding: Using the Spreadsheet to Model

Suppose you actually had $1500.00 in the account at the beginning of the year. Where would you enter this figure in your spreadsheet and by how much does this change affect the year's interest earned?

18. Make the change to the spreadsheet.

Assume you hear about a "sure thing" investment and are considering it as an alternative to putting your money in the savings and loan. The investment offers a 28% return instead of the 5.25% you currently receive. What effect would this investment have on the year's interest earned?

19. Enter the change in interest rate and observe the effect on interest earned.

Removing a Split Screen Display

20. Type the /**W**orksheet,**W**indow command and select the command to **C**lear.

The **C**lear command returns the screen to one window and to its normal appearance.

LESSON 18 Other Yearly Summaries

To complete the spreadsheet you will add a final column of summary information of total amounts for various income and expense items.

1. Move to cell N2 and type ‖ "TOTALS↵ ‖ .

NOTE: We've used the label prefix " to right justify the label in the cell.

2. Move to cell N4 and type ‖ @**SUM**(B4.M4)↵ ‖ .
3. Now copy the formula into the range N5..N23.

Notice that several cells in this column now display $0.00. It is important to note that cells containing labels, when included in a numeric entry such as an @**SUM** function, are assigned a numeric value of zero.

4. Use the /**R**ange,**E**rase command to erase the cells that tried to sum a range holding nothing except labels.

Turning Off Automatic Recalculation

Depending on the type of hardware you are using, you may note an increasing wait (the pointer disappears) after you make a cell entry or change a cell's contents. This is because Lotus 1-2-3 (by default) automatically recalculates the entire spreadsheet every time a cell's contents are changed. The larger the spreadsheet is, the longer the wait becomes. To stop automatic recalculation you may use the /**W**orksheet,**G**lobal,**R**ecalculation,**M**anual command. To turn automatic calculation back on, you use the /**W**orksheet,**G**lobal,**R**ecalculation,**A**utomatic command.

While **R**ecalculation is in the **M**anual mode, you need to type the F9 (CALCULATE) Function key to cause a recalculation of the spreadsheet.

LESSON 19 Printing a Spreadsheet

Using the /Print Commands

You now are ready to set up the spreadsheet to be printed. It is far too wide to fit on an 8½″ × 11″ piece of paper; however, Lotus 1-2-3 compensates by printing it on additional pieces of paper. You also can choose to condense the spreadsheet as it is printed if your printer has that feature.

1. To begin, type the /**P**rint,**P**rinter command.

A settings sheet will now display those Print Settings that are currently defined. The first setting that you will define is the range of cells you want printed.

2. Select the **R**ange command and set the range for printing to be the entire year's budget spreadsheet (A1..O30).

Sticky Menus

Notice that you were not returned to the data entry mode after the **R**ange command was finished. Instead, the /**P**rint,**P**rinter submenu still appeared on the screen. Lotus refers to command menus that do not immediately return you to the data entry mode as being *"sticky menus."* Such menus often have the option to **Q**uit included in them. The **Q**uit command usually may be used to return to the data entry mode.

Completing the Print Operation

Once you have specified the range to print, the specification becomes part of the spreadsheet's data (as do all of the options and specifications you select for a particular spreadsheet). So, if you save the spreadsheet after you have set your print range, you need not specify that range again in order to print the same portion of the spreadsheet later.

3. Make sure the printer is turned on, on-line, and connected to your computer.

NOTE: Your lab may have a shared device control switch. You will need to select your computer as the one currently connected to the printer.

4. Advance the paper in the printer to the top of the next page.
5. Select and enter the **A**lign command of the /**P**rint,**P**rinter menu to tell Lotus 1-2-3 that the printer is at the top of a page.

*NOTE: Selecting **A**lign does not produce a visible reaction from Lotus 1-2-3.*

6. Now select the **G**o command of the menu to begin printing the specified range. After it has been printed, select the **P**age command to advance the paper in the printer to the top of the next page.

Notice that Lotus 1-2-3 will print (by default) the number of columns it can fit in 72 characters across the page, and then advance a page and begin printing columns where it left off. Lotus 1-2-3 also will automatically "page" its printing for spreadsheets that have too many rows to fit in its default page length of 66 lines per page.

Default widths and lengths for printing (as well as several other default settings) can be changed by using the /**P**rint,**P**rinter,**O**ptions commands.

```
Header  Footer  Margins  Borders  Setup  Pg-Length  Other  Quit
```

Using Print Options

To gain experience using three very useful print **O**ptions available, do the following.

7. Select the **O**ptions command of the /**P**rint,**P**rinter menu.
8. Set the **B**orders to be "**C**olumns" A1.

With Lotus 1-2-3 you may choose certain columns and/or rows to be automatically included in each page of the printed spreadsheet.

9. Next select the **S**etup command.

The **S**etup command sends special control codes to the printer to alter its normal printing. One of the most useful control codes with spreadsheet applications causes the printer to print in condensed mode. If your printer is able to print in this mode, you must send it the correct code. Since the correct codes vary from printer to printer, your answer to the "Enter Setup String:" prompt on the screen will vary depending on the brand of printer you are using. However, with such major manufacturers as Epson, Gemini, IBM, and Okidata, the code is \027\015.

10. Type and enter the appropriate code for your printer.
11. Now select the **M**argins command and set the **R**ight margin to 132.

With condensed print, the number of characters you can fit across a standard 8½″ × 11″ sheet of paper is 132. You do, however, need to extend the right margin setting to tell Lotus 1-2-3 to start paging its spreadsheet at 132 characters rather than 72.

12. Select the **Q**uit command of the **O**ption commands to return you to the /**P**rint, **P**rinter commands.
13. Finally, respecify the **R**ange to be printed as B1..O30.

The A column in the spreadsheet has been specified as a border and will be printed automatically with each page printed.

14. Now select the **G**o command to again print the spreadsheet.
15. After it is printed, select the **P**age command to advance the paper. Now turn the printer off and then back on again to return it to its default print settings (normal-sized type).
16. When you return to your computer, type the **Q**uit command to exit the /**P**rint,**P**rinter commands.

LESSON 20 Finishing the Tutorial Lessons

To conclude the tutorial lessons, do the following.

1. Use the /**F**ile command to resave the spreadsheet under its original name LOTUT.
2. Use the /**Q**uit command to exit the spreadsheet software, and then use the Access System's **E**xit command to return to the DOS operating level.

SPREADSHEET DESIGN

Only a few specific rules exist to help you design your spreadsheet. These rules may, however, prove useful in helping you design spreadsheets that avoid the problems that beginning users are likely to experience.

SEPARATE KINDS OF DATA IN SEPARATE SPREADSHEET AREAS

The Spreadsheet's Keys

In the introductory tutorial you created a spreadsheet that incorporated elements of poor spreadsheet design. The most serious design flaw was the way in which constants (real numbers) were included within the calculating body of the spreadsheet. Below is a portion of the spreadsheet you created in the tutorial section with the contents of the cells shown. The constants are shown in gray.

```
A1: [W18]                                                         READY

           A               B          C          D          E
1
2                         JAN        FEB        MAR        APR
3
4  GROSS INCOME           1955        +B4        +C4        +D4
5  TAX RATE
6              0.18
7  FED & STATE TAXES  +$A$6*B4   +$A$6*C4   +$A$6*D4   +$A$6*E4
8  ----------------------------------------------------------------
9  NET PAY AMOUNT        +B4-B7     +C4-C7     +D4-D7     +E4-E7
10
11 EXPENSES
12 ----------------------------------------------------------------
13 RENT                    375       +B13     +C13+20       +D13
14 UTILITIES               125       +B14       +C14         100
15 PARKING                  75                                75
16 TELEPHONE                18       +B16       +C16        +D16
17 LIFE INSURANCE        28.65       +B17       +C17        +D17
18 FOOD                 0.3*B9     0.3*C9     0.3*D9      0.3*E9
19 LEISURE             0.15*B9    0.15*C9    0.15*D9     0.15*E9
20 ----------------------------------------------------------------
26-Feb-91  05:10 PM        UNDO
```

Such constants are called the *spreadsheet's keys*. They are the primary source of all values displayed in the spreadsheet. If you retrace the references of the formulas you will find that they ultimately refer to a cell holding a spreadsheet key.

As you look at the spreadsheet on the screen, however, it is difficult to tell which cells are holding formulas and which are holding keys. Even using the /**W**orksheet,**G**lobal,**F**ormat,**T**ext command will not always result in the display of a formula where a formula actually exists (such as when a cell has previously been /**R**ange,**F**ormatted).

Keys in Their Own Area

It is an accepted rule of spreadsheet design that, whenever possible, all keys should be kept in a separate, identifiable area of the spreadsheet. The calculating area should contain either formulas referring *directly* to the keys or referring *back* to them through a series of formulas. The spreadsheet should have been initially designed in two parts.

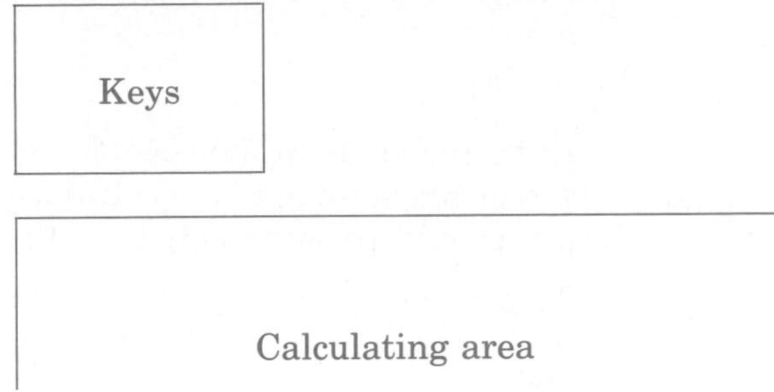

Cell references should refer directly to a given key

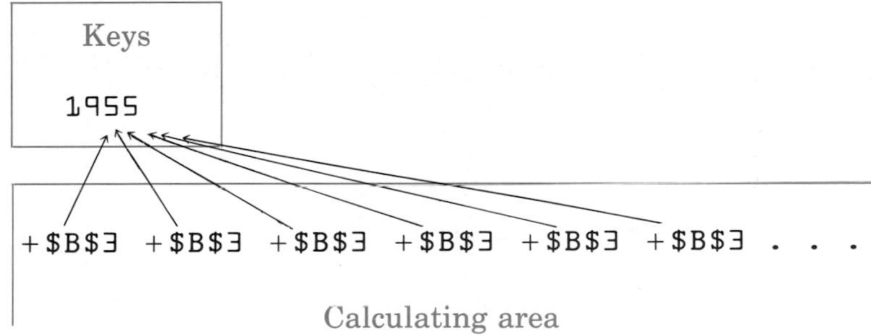

or, they should refer to a key indirectly through a series of formulas.

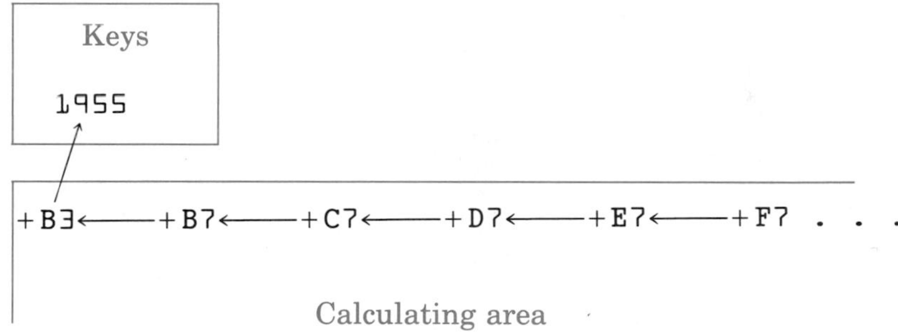

They also might use a variation.

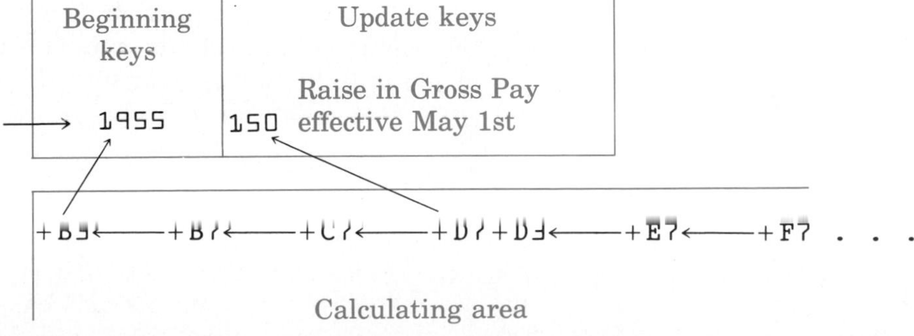

In the last example the keys have been separated into two types, beginning amounts and updates. In this spreadsheet a third type of key, percentage rates, could be included in a separate area within the spreadsheet's keys area.

SPREADSHEET DOCUMENTATION

Each key value in the spreadsheet should have its own label to explain its use and relevance to the calculating portion of the spreadsheet. That is, the key should be documented.

Along with separating the keys into their own area(s) and thoroughly documenting them, you should have an area set aside for additional documentation of the spreadsheet. This area could include things such as remarks and comments about the assumptions and relationships built into the spreadsheet, the date it was last updated, its filename, current print settings and more.

MAPPING OUT THE SPREADSHEET

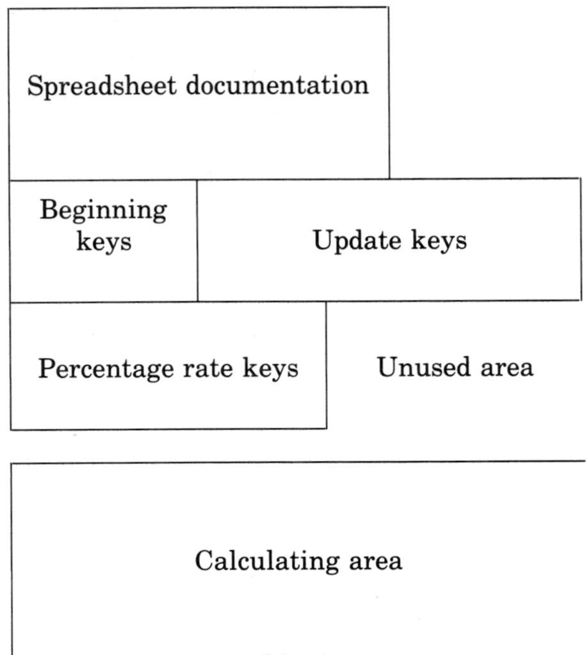

As you create more complex spreadsheets using more advanced features of Lotus 1-2-3, you will recognize that the spreadsheet should be mapped out with a pencil and piece of paper before it is created on the computer. A question such as "What happens to my key area if I need to use the /**W**orksheet command to insert a column or a row into my calculating area?" may lead you initially to map your spreadsheet as follows.

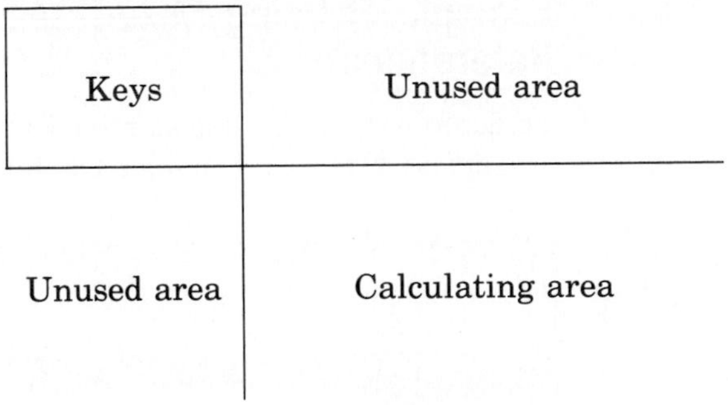

Keys	Unused area
Unused area	Calculating area

Such a plan may help you avoid disruption of spreadsheet areas later.

SPREADSHEET TEMPLATES

You may want to design a spreadsheet that is to be used more than once. For example, a spreadsheet designed to track expenditures against a departmental budget may be needed periodically. In a case like this, you can create a spreadsheet that acts as a master copy, or in spreadsheet jargon, as a *template*. The purpose of having a spreadsheet template is to avoid having to recreate the spreadsheet each time it is needed. The procedure for creating a spreadsheet template is as follows.

Once you have mapped out the spreadsheet, enter and test the labels, formulas, and keys to ensure the spreadsheet is reliable in its answers. Add any necessary documentation.

After the spreadsheet is operationally complete, set all relevant keys (those constants that may change from period to period) to zero by entering zeros in the cells that contain them. Save the spreadsheet on the diskette in its template form. To save a template it is customary to use a name such as "Master" to indicate that it is the master copy.

Once you have created and saved the template, you need to: a) load that spreadsheet into RAM; b) enter the appropriate key values for that period; and c) save that period's finished spreadsheet on the diskette under a different name. The original template remains on the diskette in its original form for the next time it is needed.

MIXED CELL REFERENCES

The cell references you have used so far have been either totally relative (as in +A5) or totally absolute (as in +$A$5). These are the two most common forms of cell references used in formulas destined to be copied into other cells.

Lotus 1-2-3 calls variations from these two forms *mixed references*. Although they are used less frequently, mixed references can be the desirable form for copying formulas into other cells. Using the example reference of cell A5, the variations are

+$A5 copies the formula with the references to the A column as absolute, but with the references to the fifth row as relative.

+A$5 copies the formula with the references to the A column as relative, but with the references to the fifth row as absolute.

Example of Using Mixed Cell References

To demonstrate the use of mixed references and their implication for spreadsheet design, consider the following situation.

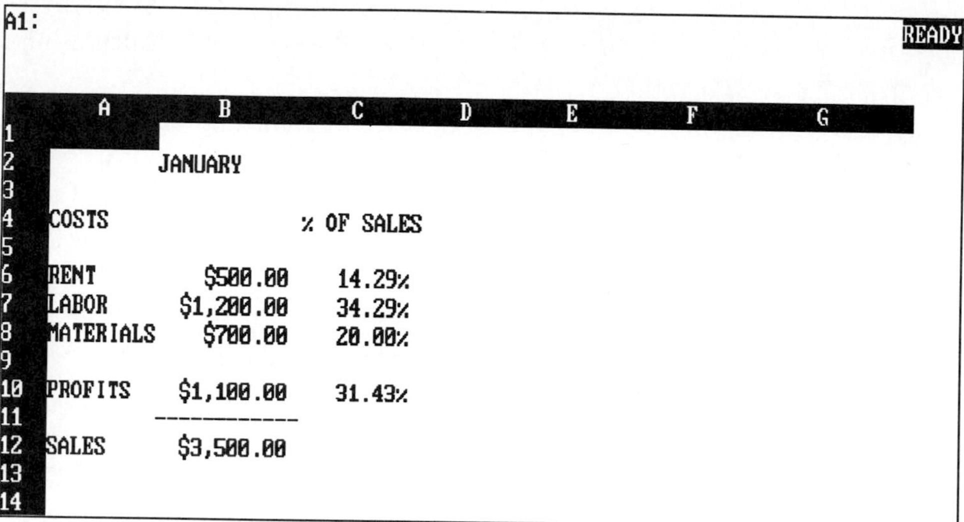

A1: READY

	A	B	C	D	E	F	G
1							
2		JANUARY					
3							
4	COSTS		% OF SALES				
5							
6	RENT	$500.00	14.29%				
7	LABOR	$1,200.00	34.29%				
8	MATERIALS	$700.00	20.00%				
9							
10	PROFITS	$1,100.00	31.43%				
11		------------					
12	SALES	$3,500.00					
13							
14							

In this spreadsheet all values in the B column (the dollar figures) are spreadsheet keys. Values in the C column are derived by formulas.

The designer of this spreadsheet intended to copy the rectangular range of labels, keys, and formulas of the spreadsheet into the area on the right side for the next month's figures.

	A	B	C	D	E	F	G
1							
2		JANUARY				JANUARY	
3							
4	COSTS		% OF SALES		COSTS		% OF SALES
5							
6	RENT	$500.00	14.29%		RENT	$500.00	14.29%
7	LABOR	$1,200.00	34.29%		LABOR	$1,200.00	34.29%
8	MATERIALS	$700.00	20.00%		MATERIALS	$700.00	20.00%
9							
10	PROFITS	$1,100.00	31.43%		PROFITS	$1,100.00	31.43%
11		------------				------------	
12	SALES	$3,500.00			SALES	$3,500.00	
13							
14		FROM : range				TO : range	
15							

After copying the range of cells the designer can change the label JANUARY to FEBRUARY, enter new keys, and have the formulas compute the correct percent of sales figures for that month.

In constructing the original portion of the spreadsheet the formula for rent as a percent of sales would be entered and copied into the rest of the appropriate cells for that column. To be copied correctly during this first copy operation, the formula would need to keep the reference to sales (B12) as absolute. But, for the next copy operation (creating February's report) the reference for the cell must be able to shift to the right in a relative fashion (to cell F12).

The solution to the problem is to keep the reference to the SALES row absolute so it does not shift down (in a relative fashion) in the first copy operation, and leave the reference to the SALES column as relative so it will shift to the right in the second copy operation. To do this, the original formula would be entered as

+B6/B$12

First: The original formula is entered.

	A	B	C	D	E	F	G
1							
2		JANUARY					
3							
4	COSTS		% OF SALES				
5							
6	RENT	$500.00	+B6/B$12				
7	LABOR	$1,200.00					
8	MATERIALS	$700.00					
9							
10	PROFITS	$1,100.00					
11		------------					
12	SALES	$3,500.00					
13							
14							

Second: The formula is copied into that column.

	A	B	C	D	E	F	G
1							
2		JANUARY					
3							
4	COSTS		% OF SALES				
5							
6	RENT	$500.00	+B6/B$12				
7	LABOR	$1,200.00	+B7/B$12				
8	MATERIALS	$700.00	+B8/B$12				
9							
10	PROFITS	$1,100.00	+B10/B$12				
11		------------					
12	SALES	$3,500.00					
13							
14							

Third: The second copy operation is completed.

	A	B	C	D	E	F	G
1							
2		JANUARY				JANUARY	
3							
4	COSTS		% OF SALES		COSTS		% OF SALES
5							
6	RENT	$500.00	+B6/B$12		RENT	$500.00	+F6/F$12
7	LABOR	$1,200.00	+B7/B$12		LABOR	$1,200.00	+F7/F$12
8	MATERIALS	$700.00	+B8/B$12		MATERIALS	$700.00	+F8/F$12
9							
10	PROFITS	$1,100.00	+B10/B$12		PROFITS	$1,100.00	+F10/F$12
11		------------				------------	
12	SALES	$3,500.00			SALES	$3,500.00	
13							
14							

Fourth: The month label and keys are changed, and the spreadsheet computes the correct figures for FEBRUARY.

	A	B	C	D	E	F	G
1							
2		JANUARY				FEBRUARY	
3							
4	COSTS		% OF SALES		COSTS		% OF SALES
5							
6	RENT	$500.00	14.29%		RENT	$500.00	11.76%
7	LABOR	$1,200.00	34.29%		LABOR	$1,500.00	35.29%
8	MATERIALS	$700.00	20.00%		MATERIALS	$950.00	22.35%
9							
10	PROFITS	$1,100.00	31.43%		PROFITS	$1,300.00	30.59%
11		------------				------------	
12	SALES	$3,500.00			SALES	$4,250.00	
13							
14							

LOTUS 1-2-3 FUNCTIONS

A *spreadsheet function* can be described as a shorthand method of accomplishing a specific task. The general formats for Lotus functions are

@**XYZ**(argument)
@**XYZ**(argument1,argument2,..argumentN)
@**XYZ**

Functions always begin with the @ sign and the function name. Arguments then are placed within parentheses. Some functions require only one argument, some require several arguments, and some require no arguments at all. When more than one argument is specified, the arguments must be separated by commas.

When referring to a function, one says that the function returns a value based upon the function's argument(s), if any. For example, the @**SUM** function returns the sum of the cells specified by its argument(s). If entered as @**SUM**(B13..B18), all cells within the range B13..B18 will be summed. If entered as @**SUM**(B13..B18,G12..J12), all cells within both ranges B13..B18 and G12..J12 will be summed.

Depending upon the function, arguments may be specified as follows.

Specification	Example
A single cell	@**ABS**(G12)
A range of cells (with coordinates)	@**SUM**(B13..B18)
A named range	@**SUM**(totals)
A constant numeric value	@**SQRT**(1250)
A constant string value	@**LENGTH**("Net Pay")
A condition or formula	@**IF**(A6>7,A6*1000,A6*B2)

Lotus 1-2-3 functions may be divided into the following basic categories.

1. Mathematical functions
2. Statistical functions
3. Financial functions
4. Date and Time functions
5. String functions
6. Logical and Special functions
7. Engineering functions

In the subsequent discussions, the most important or most often used functions in each of these categories are covered.

MATHEMATICAL FUNCTIONS

@**ABS**(value)	Returns the absolute value of the value argument.
@**INT**(value)	Returns the integer portion of a value.
@**MOD**(value, modulo)	Returns the remainder of a division operation. The value is divided by the modulo and the function returns the remainder (the modulus).

@**RAND**	Generates a random number. The function has no argument and the value returned changes each time the spreadsheet is reealculated.
@**ROUND**(value,places)	Returns the value rounded to the specified number of decimal places.
@**SQRT**(value)	Returns the square root of the value.

Most mathematical functions are fairly straightforward. Their arguments consist of single values, such as constants, cell references, or the computed results of formulas.

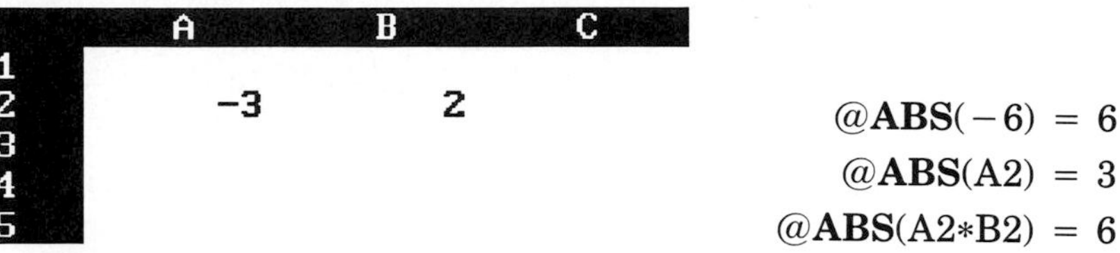

@**ABS**(−6) = 6
@**ABS**(A2) = 3
@**ABS**(A2*B2) = 6

@**ROUND**(value,places)

The @**ROUND** function is important for financial and other business-related spreadsheets. It is important because the values you see displayed on the monitor screen are formatted for display purposes only. All values are actually stored in RAM and are accurate to about 15 decimal places. The stored values are used in all of Lotus's computations. The results of the computations can often be confusing to beginning users who are trying to figure out why the spreadsheet does not agree with their calculators.

A solution for avoiding discrepancies in accuracy is to use the @**ROUND** function to return the rounded value (to the desired number of decimal places) for all values of concern. As an example, the internal results become

10/3 = 3.333333333333333
@**ROUND**(10/3,2) = 3.330000000000000

(Actually, the last two or three decimal places are undependable; however, this seldom interferes with the practical use of a spreadsheet.)

Negative "places" may be used in the @**ROUND** function to round numbers to the left of the decimal.

@**ROUND**(10000/3,2) = 3333.33
@**ROUND**(10000/3, −2) = 3300

@**INT**(value)

The Integer function is useful when decimal parts of a value are not desired and rounding is unnecessary, such as in some production models where a fraction of a unit will not be produced. With Lotus the value returned is the true integer portion of the argument with the remainder truncated for both positive and negative numbers.

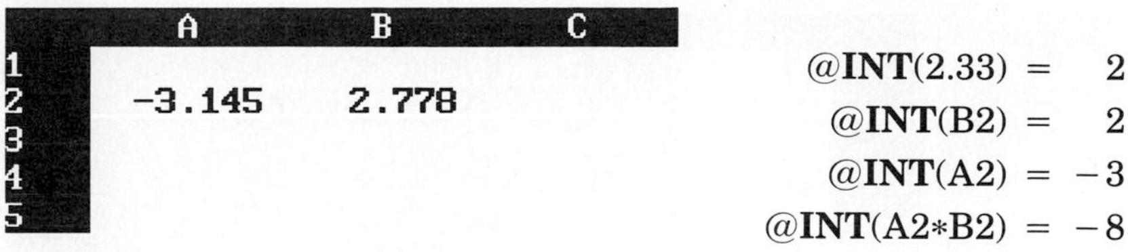

@**INT**(2.33) = 2
@**INT**(B2) = 2
@**INT**(A2) = −3
@**INT**(A2*B2) = −8

@MOD(value,modulo)

The @**MOD** function returns the modulus of the value divided by the modulo. In longhand division it looks like this:

$$\begin{array}{r} 12 \\ \text{Modulo} \longrightarrow 3\overline{)38} \longleftarrow \text{Value} \\ \underline{30} \\ 08 \\ \underline{6} \\ 2 \longleftarrow \text{Modulus} \end{array}$$

The modulus is the numerator of the fractional remainder, 2/3, to the answer for this problem, 12 ⅔. The @**MOD** function can be useful in determining if partial batches or even/odd situations exist.

STATISTICAL FUNCTIONS

@**AVG**(list)	Returns the average value of all nonblank cells specified.
@**COUNT**(list)	Returns the number of nonblank cells in the specified list.
@**MAX**(list)	Returns the highest single value found in the specified list.
@**MIN**(list)	Returns the lowest single value found in the specified list.
@**STD**(list)	Returns the standard deviation from the mean for the nonblank cells in the specified list.
@**SUM**(list)	Returns the sum of all cells in the specified list.
@**VAR**(list)	Returns the variance of the values for the nonblank cells in the specified list.

Since all of these functions are important in business and are similar in form, they will be discussed as a group. The statistical functions are fairly straightforward, but are designed to deal with several values rather than the single value used by the mathematical functions.

The values may be cell references, ranges of cells, constants, or any combination of these, separated by commas in a list.

	A	B	C
1			
2	2	5	7
3	4		
4	6		
5	8	12	

@SUM(6,8,1) = 15
@SUM(A2..A5) = 20
@SUM(A2..A5,B2) = 25
@SUM(A2..A5,A2..C2,B5,10) = 56

Note that Lotus assigns all labels the value of 0 (zero) and uses the zeros in computing the value returned by a function. Lotus does not, however, use blank (empty) cells in computing the value returned. With most of the statistical functions, if cells with labels in them are included in the function's argument(s), an incorrect value will be returned by the function for the group of values of concern. Blank cells are ignored in calculations, and thus do not interfere with the results.

In the following example, for instance, within the range A1..A6 are the values of concern 2, 4, and 6; two cells with labels in them (A3 and A5); and the blank cell A1. Notice the results of using this range as the argument for the statistical functions.

	A	B
1		
2	2	
3	-------	
4	4	
5	-------	
6	6	
7		
8		
9		
10		

@SUM(A1..A6)	=	12	correct
@COUNT(A1..A6)	=	5	incorrect
@AVG(A1..A6)	=	2.4	incorrect
@MAX(A1..A6)	=	6	correct
@MIN(A1..A6)	=	0	incorrect
@STD(A1..A6)	=	2.332380	incorrect
@VAR(A1..A6)	=	5.44	incorrect

To illustrate how statistical functions may be used, study the following example spreadsheet and the table below it.

	A	B	C	D
1				
2	SALES	1984	1985	1986
3		------------	------------	------------
4	JAN	1250	1310	1340
5	FEB	1115	1170	1195
6	MAR	1320	1390	1420
7	APR	1405	1485	1515
8	MAY	1380	1450	1480
9	JUN	1550	1630	
10	JUL	1575	1655	
11	AUG	1525	1600	
12	SEP	1515	1590	
13	OCT	1490	1565	
14	NOV	1385	1450	
15	DEC	1320	1390	
16				

Measurement	Function Used	Returned Value
Total 1985 sales	@**SUM**(C4..C15)	17685
1984 top month's sales	@**MAX**(B4..B15)	1575
1985 low month's sales	@**MIN**(C4..C15)	1170
Average January sales	@**AVG**(B4..D4)	1300
Average 1st quarter sales	@**AVG**(B4..D6)	1278.888
Average 1st & last quarter sales	@**AVG**(B4..D6,B13..D15)	1340.666
Total sales entered to date	@**SUM**(B4..B15,C4..C15, D4..D15) or @**SUM**(B4..D15)	41465
Total data entries to date	@**COUNT**(B4..D15)	29
Standard Deviation of total monthly sales	@**STD**(B4..D15)	136.6816
Variance of total monthly sales	@**VAR**(B4..D15)	18681.86

FINANCIAL FUNCTIONS

@**CTERM**(int,fv,pv)	Returns the number of periods needed for a present value investment (pv) to grow to a given future value (fv) at a given periodic interest rate (int).
@**DDB**(cost,salvage, life,period)	Returns the calculated depreciation on an asset using the double-declining balance method.
@**FV**(pmt,int,n)	Returns the future value of a stream of equal annuity payments (pmt) at a given periodic interest rate (int) over a given number of periods (n).
@**IRR**(guess, range)	Returns the approximate internal rate of return for a range of cash flows, given the help of a guess to start the computation.
@**NPV**(rate,range)	Returns the net present value of a stream of cash flows at a given discount rate.
@**PMT**(pv,int,n)	Returns the amount of a stream of equal annuity payments given a present value investment (pv), an interest rate (int), and number of periods (n).
@**PV**(pmt,int,n)	Returns the present value of a stream of equal annuity payments (pmt) for a given number of periods (n) at a given periodic interest rate (int).
@**RATE**(fv,pv,n)	Returns the required rate of interest for a present value investment (pv) to grow to a specified future value (fv) in a given number of periods (n).
@**SLN**(cost, salvage,life)	Returns the depreciation on an asset for a single period using the straight-line method.

@**SYD**(cost,salvage, life,period)	Returns the depreciation on an asset for a specified period using the sum-of-the-years'-digits method.
@**TERM**(pmt,int,fv)	Returns the number of periods required for a stream of equal annuity payments (pmt) to grow to a given future value (fv) at a given interest rate (int).

The financial functions are related to the time value of money and depreciation of assets. The time value of money functions, which will be covered in this section, are frequently used in business applications. Each function requires more than one argument in order to return the correct answer.

Compounding Interest Formula

When an investment is made at a fixed interest rate, the interest is compounded over the time of the investment. For instance, if $1,000 is invested for three years, earning 10% interest compounded annually, the balance at the end of the three years (fv) would be $1,331, which could be calculated as follows.

	Year 1	Year 2	Year 3
Beginning Balance	$1,000	$1,100	$1,210
+Interest Earned	$ 100	$ 110	$ 121
Ending Balance	$1,100	$1,210	$1,331

If you are interested in only the balance at the end of the last period (fv), you could use a formula to calculate the future value. The formula for computing this future value (fv) for any present value investment (pv), periodic interest rate (int), and number of periods (n) is

$$fv = pv * (1+int)^\wedge n$$

Thus, if you wanted to know the future value of $5,000 invested for 7 years at 5.25% (.0525) interest compounded annually, you could enter the formula into a spreadsheet as follows.

	A	B	C	D	E
1					
2		Present Value (pv)	$5,000		
3					
4		Interest Rate (int)	0.0525		
5					
6		Number of Periods (n)	7		
7		------------------------------	----------	----------	----------
8		Future Value (fv) =	+C2*(1+C4)^C6	=	$7,153.601
9					

On the other hand, if you knew the future value you wished to earn, but needed the present value investment required given the interest rate and number of periods, the formula for present value would be used.

pv = fv * 1/(1+int)^n

For example, if you wanted to know the investment needed today (pv) to earn $7,500 (fv) in 7 years at 5.25% interest compounded annually, you could enter the formula into a spreadsheet as follows.

```
     A          B                        C           D        E
1
2          Future Value (fv)          $7,500
3
4          Interest Rate (int)        0.0525
5
6          Number of Periods (n)           7
7          -----------------------------------------------------------
8          Present Value (pv) =     +C2*1/(1+C4)^C6   =   $5,242.114
9
```

All of the Lotus functions concerned with the time value of money derive their computations from these basic interest compounding formulas. Note, however, that interest is often compounded for periods other than a year. When this is the case, you must specify both interest rate (int) and number of periods (n) using the same type of time period. For instance, if interest were to be compounded monthly in the last example, the interest should be entered as .004375 (.0525/12) and the number of periods should be entered as 84 (7*12).

@**CTERM**(int,fv,pv) and @**RATE**(fv,pv,n)

The **@CTERM** and **@RATE** functions are designed to provide either the number of periods (n) or the periodic interest rate (int) when the other variables in the equation are given. In the following example, a present value of $5,000 and a future value of $7,500 are used. When the interest rate (.0525) is given, **@CTERM** returns the exact number of periods required. When the number of periods (5) is given, **@RATE** returns the exact interest rate required.

```
     A          B                           C              D        E
1
2          Present Value (pv)             5,000
3          Future Value (fv)              7,500
4
5          ----------------------------------------------------------
6          Interest Rate (int)          0.0525
7          Number of Periods (n) =    @CTERM(C6,C3,C2) = 7.924148
8          ----------------------------------------------------------
9
10         ----------------------------------------------------------
11         Number of Periods (n)              5
12         Interest Rate (int) =      @RATE(C3,C2,C11) = .084471
13         ----------------------------------------------------------
```

Annuity Functions @**FV**, @**PV**, @ **PMT**, and @**TERM**

The functions discussed in the previous section deal with a lump sum investment earning compounded interest. When an investment involves equal payments to be made or received for every period involved, it is called an annuity. Annuities may be viewed in terms of the future value that will be produced by some number of equal annuity payments, or in terms of the present value required to produce a stream of equal annuity payments.

@**FV**(pmt,int,n)

The @**FV** function returns the future value, given an annuity payment (pmt), interest rate (int), and number of periods (n). For example, if you wanted to know the future value of $125 annuity payments invested every month for 3 years (36 periods), and earning .4375% (.004375) interest compounded monthly (5.25% annual percentage rate/12 months), you could use the @**FV** function.

	A	B	C	D	E
1					
2		Payment (pmt)	$125		
3		Interest (int)	0.004375		
4		Number of Periods (n)	36		
5		------------------------	------------------------	--------	--------
6		Future Value (fv) =	@FV(C2,C3,C4)	=	$4,862.248
7					

@**PV**(pmt,int,n)

The @**PV** function returns the present value (pv) of a stream of annuity payments (pmt), given the interest rate (int) and number of periods (n). If the above example were restated so that you wanted to know how much to invest today in order to provide an annuity of $125 per month for 36 months (given the same monthly interest rate of .4375% compounded monthly) you could use the @**PV** function.

	A	B	C	D	E
1					
2		Payment (pmt)	$125		
3		Interest (int)	0.004375		
4		Number of Periods (n)	36		
5		------------------------	------------------------	--------	--------
6		Present Value (pv) =	@PV(C2,C3,C4)	=	$4,155.133
7					

@**PMT**(pv,int,n)

The @**PMT** function returns the amount of an annuity payment, given a present value (pv), interest rate (int) and number of periods (n). For instance, if you wanted to make a $3,000 purchase today financing it by obtaining a loan to be repaid over three years at a 1.25% monthly percentage rate, you could determine the amount of your installment payments as shown in the following example.

	A	B	C	D	E
1					
2		Present Value (pv)	$3,000		
3		Interest (int)	0.0125		
4		Number of Periods (n)	36		
5		------------------------------			
6		Payment (pmt) =	@PMT(C2,C3,C4)	=	$103.9959
7					

@**TERM**(pmt,int,fv)

The @**TERM** function returns the number of periods (n) required to reach a given future value (fv), given the amount of annuity payments (pmt) and the interest rate (int). For example, if you wanted to know the length of time it would take to accumulate $50,000 (fv), given annuity payments of $6,500 per year earning an annual percentage rate of 7.5% (.075), you could use the @**TERM** function.

	A	B	C	D	E
1					
2		Future Value (fv)	$50,000		
3		Interest (int)	0.075		
4		Payment (pmt)	$6,500		
5		------------------------------			
6		Number of Periods (n) =	@TERM(C4,C3,C2)	=	6.298
7					

@**NPV**(rate,range) and @**IRR**(guess,range)

While the annuity functions deal with streams of equal payments, the @**NPV** and @**IRR** functions deal with streams of unequal cash flows. The stream of cash flows is represented by a range of values entered in the spreadsheet. Negative values are treated as cash outflows and positive values as cash inflows.

The net present value function @**NPV** returns the present value of a range of cash flows discounted at an opportunity cost determined at an alternate rate (called the discount rate) for the same flows. The periods are assumed to be equal in time and the rate used is a periodic discount rate. Note that with the @**NPV** function, the first cash flow in the range of cash flows is treated as occurring at the end of the first period. Subsequent cash flows are treated as occurring at the end of their periods.

The range in the argument must be a single row or column of cells. Blank cells and cells with labels within the range are counted as cash flows of 0 for the period. The rate argument used in the function is the periodic discount rate. Since it is usually the case (for valuation purposes) that the first cash flow is to occur at time 0 (zero), the use of the @**NPV** function often takes the following form.

First cash flow + @**NPV**(discount rate,subsequent cash flows)

The following example uses this formula with a periodic discount rate of 5.25%, an initial cash outflow of $500, and subsequent cash inflows of $200, $175, $150, and $125.

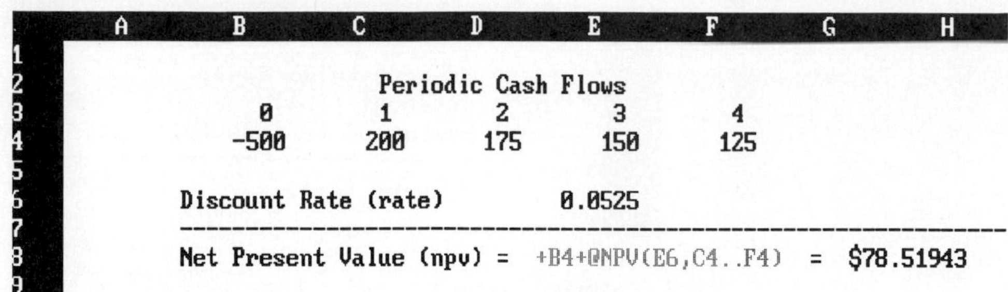

The **@IRR** function returns an approximate internal rate of return for a series of cash flows in which the IRR is defined as the rate at which those cash flows have a zero net present value. The periods are assumed to be equal in time. The guess argument of the **@IRR** function serves as a starting point for the iterative process that the function uses to determine the IRR. If the guess is too far off the actual IRR, the function will return ERR. Guesses between 0.0 and 1.0 usually will yield a calculated IRR. Sometimes there is more than one IRR possible for a series of cash flows, so different guesses may result in different values.

The guess rate is entered as a decimal and the range in the argument must be a single row or column of cells. Blank cells and cells with labels within the range are counted as cash flows of 0 for that period. Note also that the IRR is a periodic rate, so if the cash flows are yearly, the value returned by the function will be an annual rate. The following example calculates an IRR using 14% (.14) as the guess, an initial cash outflow of $500, and subsequent cash inflows of $200, $175, $150, and $125.

```
     A     B      C      D      E      F      G      H
1
2                  Periodic Cash Flows
3          0      1      2      3      4
4        -500    200    175    150    125
5
6    Estimated Rate (guess)      0.14
7    ---------------------------------------------------
8    Internal Rate of Return =  @IRR(E6,B4..F4)  =  0.124414
9
```

DATE AND TIME FUNCTIONS

@DATE(year, month, day)	Returns the serial number date value for the year, month, and day.
@DATEVALUE(date string)	Returns the serial number date value for a date string that is in a valid Lotus date format.
@DAY(serial date value)	Returns the day of the month (1–31) for a serial date value.
@HOUR(serial date value)	Returns the hour (0–23) for the fractional portion (time value) of a serial date value.
@MINUTE(serial date value)	Returns the minute (0–59) for the fractional portion (time value) of a serial date value.

@**MONTH**(serial date value)	Returns the month number (1–12) for a serial date value.
@**NOW**	Returns the current date and time as a serial date/time value.
@**SECOND**(serial date value)	Returns the seconds (0–59) for the fractional portion (time value) of a serial date value.
@**TIME**(hr,min,sec)	Returns the fractional portion (time value) of a serial date value for the specified hour, minute, and second value arguments.
@**TIMEVALUE**(time string)	Returns the fractional portion (time value) for a time string that is in a valid Lotus time format.
@**TODAY**	Returns @**INT**(@**NOW**), the integer portion of the function @**NOW.**
@**YEAR**(serial date value)	Returns the year for a serial date value.

Date and Time functions have many business-related spreadsheet applications. Lotus 1-2-3 maintains an internal calendar that extends from January 1, 1900 to December 31, 2099. Lotus has assigned a number to each day in this period. The numbers are serial: the date January 1, 1900 has been assigned the value 1; January 2, 1900 the number 2; and so on up to December 31, 2099, which has been assigned the value 73050.

With each date assigned a serial number in this manner, the computer can perform "date arithmetic."

	Date	Serial Number	Arithmetic	
Date #1	4/17/91	33345	−33345	
Date #2	12/25/91	33597	+33597	
			252	Shopping days until Christmas

If a decimal portion is added to a serial date value, it is used to represent a fractional part of a day and may be used as a Lotus time value. For example, .25 represents 1/4 of a day or 6 hours. Therefore, the serial date value 33597.25 would represent both the date 12/25/91 and the time 6:00 AM.

@**DATE**(year,month,day) and @**TIME**(hr,min,sec)

The @**DATE** and @**TIME** functions allow you to enter dates and times in a format to which you are accustomed, returning the appropriate serial date/time value.

	A	B	C
1			
2		@DATE(91,4,17) =	33345
3			
4		@TIME(8,30,0) =	0.3541666667
5			
6		@DATE(91,4,17)+@TIME(8,30,0) =	33345.354167
7			

If a year beyond 1999 is to be used in the @**DATE** function, it must be specified by adding 100 to the last two digits of the year. For example, April 17, 2000 would be entered as @**DATE**(100,4,17) and April 17, 2010 as @**DATE**(110,4,17)

Once a serial date/time value has been entered, either directly or with the @**DATE** or @**TIME** functions, the /**R**ange,**F**ormat,**D**ate command may be used to format the cell to display the value in a date or time format.

```
   A                B                        C              D        E
1
2    @DATE(91,4,17)+@TIME(8,30,0) = 33345.354167   <-- Format General
3
4    @DATE(91,4,17)+@TIME(8,30,0) =    17-Apr-91   <-- Format D1
5    @DATE(91,4,17)+@TIME(8,30,0) =       17-Apr   <-- Format D2
6    @DATE(91,4,17)+@TIME(8,30,0) =       Apr-91   <-- Format D3
7    @DATE(91,4,17)+@TIME(8,30,0) =     04/17/91   <-- Format D4
8    @DATE(91,4,17)+@TIME(8,30,0) =        04/17   <-- Format D5
9    @DATE(91,4,17)+@TIME(8,30,0) =  08:30:00 AM   <-- Format D6
10   @DATE(91,4,17)+@TIME(8,30,0) =     08:30 AM   <-- Format D7
11   @DATE(91,4,17)+@TIME(8,30,0) =     08:30:00   <-- Format D8
12   @DATE(91,4,17)+@TIME(8,30,0) =        08:30   <-- Format D9
13
```

Remember that the displayed contents of a cell formatted with /**R**ange,**F**ormat,**D**ate are not the actual contents of the cell. The cell holds, or has returned, a number that can be used in, or derived by, a formula.

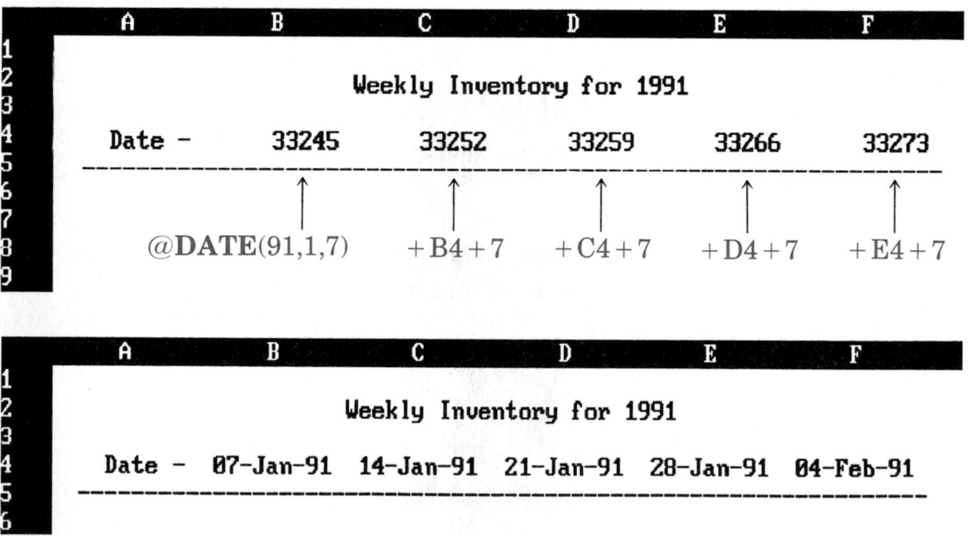

```
   A          B          C          D          E          F
1
2                  Weekly Inventory for 1991
3
4    Date -     33245      33252      33259      33266      33273
5  ------------------------------------------------------------------
6                 ↑          ↑          ↑          ↑          ↑
7                 |          |          |          |          |
8          @DATE(91,1,7)  +B4+7      +C4+7      +D4+7      +E4+7
9
```

```
   A          B          C          D          E          F
1
2                  Weekly Inventory for 1991
3
4    Date -  07-Jan-91  14-Jan-91  21-Jan-91  28-Jan-91  04-Feb-91
5  ------------------------------------------------------------------
6
```

@DAY @MONTH @YEAR @HOUR @MINUTE @SECOND

Once a serial date/time value has been entered into the spreadsheet, certain elements of the date or time such as the month number (1–12) or the hour number (0–23) may be returned by a function that uses a serial date value as its argument.

	A	B	C	D	E	F
1						
2		@DATE(91,4,17) =	33345		@DAY(C6) =	17
3					@MONTH(C6) =	4
4		@TIME(8,30,0) =	0.3541666667		@YEAR(C6) =	91
5						
6		+B2+B4 =	33345.354167		@HOUR(C6) =	8
7					@MINUTE(C6) =	30
8					@SECOND(C6) =	0
9						

STRING FUNCTIONS

@**CHAR**(number)	Returns the corresponding ASCII character. The number argument must be between 1 and 255; otherwise, the function will return ERR.
@**CLEAN**(string)	Removes nonprintable characters from strings imported with the /**F**ile,**I**mport command.
@**CODE**(string)	Returns a number representing the ASCII value of the first character in the string. If the argument is an empty cell or a cell containing a value, @**CODE** will return ERR.
@**EXACT**(string1, string2)	Compares two strings to test if the strings are exactly the same. Returns 1 (true) if the strings match exactly and 0 (false) if the strings do not match exactly.
@**FIND**(string1,string2, n)	Returns the location of string1 (substring) in string2, with the search beginning at the *n*th position of string2. The first character of string2 is considered position 0.
@**LEFT**(string,n)	Returns the left-most n characters in a string.
@**LENGTH**(string)	Returns the number of characters in a string.
@**LOWER**(string)	Returns the same string, with all letters converted to lower case.
@**MID**(string,start,n)	Returns an extracted substring from a larger string. The start argument determines the position in the string where the substring is to begin (the first character is position 0), and the n argument determines the length of the substring.
@**N**(range)	Returns the value of a number or a formula found in the top left cell of the specified range. If the cell is empty or contains a label, @**N** returns the value 0. @**N** always returns a numeric value.
@**PROPER**(string)	Returns the same string, with all first letters of words converted to upper case and subsequent letters converted to lower case.
@**REPEAT**(string,n)	Returns a string with the specified string argument repeated n times.

@**REPLACE**(string1, start,n,string2)	Returns a string in which a certain portion of string1 has been replaced by string2. The start argument specifies the position in string1 to begin the replacement (first position is 0), and the n argument determines how many characters will be replaced in string1. The entire string2 will be inserted into string1, regardless of the n argument.
@**RIGHT**(string,n)	Returns the right-most n characters in a string.
@**S**(range)	Returns the string value of the top left cell of the range. If the cell is empty or contains a numeric value, @**S** returns an empty (null) string. @**S** always returns a string value.
@**STRING**(n,decimals)	Returns the string of a numeric value n, rounded to the number of places specified by the decimal's argument.
@**TRIM**(string)	Removes trailing spaces from a string. Will change the value returned by the @**LENGTH** function.
@**UPPER**(string)	Returns the same string, with all letters converted to upper case.
@**VALUE**(string)	Returns a numeric value from a number that has been entered as a label or string value. The string may contain only number characters (0–9), a currency sign ($), thousand's separators (,), a decimal indicator (.), and leading or trailing spaces; otherwise, the function will return ERR.

The Lotus String functions provide a method of performing a number of common string manipulations. These functions may be useful when data has been imported with the /**F**ile,**I**mport command, when a spreadsheet contains much text, and when macros are being executed. The following is an example of the values returned by some of the String functions.

```
     A    B    C    D    E    F    G    H
1
2       Trouble brings experience, and experience brings wisdom.
3  ------------------------------------------------------------
4  @FIND("experience",B2,0)  =          15
5  @FIND("experience",B2,16) =          31
6  @LENGTH(B2)               =          56
7
8  @LEFT(B2,14) =         Trouble brings
9  @RIGHT(B2,7) =         wisdom.
10 @MID(B2,8,5) =         bring
11
12 @LOWER(B2)  = trouble brings experience, and experience brings wisdom.
13 @PROPER(B2) = Trouble Brings Experience, And Experience Brings Wisdom.
14 @UPPER(B2)  = TROUBLE BRINGS EXPERIENCE, AND EXPERIENCE BRINGS WISDOM.
15
16 @REPLACE(B2,0,7,"Adversity") = ─┐
17   ┌─────────────────────────────┘
18   └→Adversity brings experience, and experience brings wisdom.
19
```

LOGICAL AND SPECIAL FUNCTIONS

@@(cell address)	When the cell address argument specifies a cell containing a label which, in turn, is another cell's address (e.g., A1), the function returns the contents of the cell referenced by the label. For example, if cell A1 = 15 and cell B2 = A1, then @@(B2) returns 15.
@**CELL**(attribute, range)	Returns the specified attribute of the cell in the upper left corner of the specified range. The result of the function is updated whenever the spreadsheet is recalculated.
@**CELLPOINTER** (attribute)	Returns the specified attribute of the cell in which the pointer is located. @**CELLPOINTER** functions will only display new values when the spreadsheet is recalculated.
@**CHOOSE**(valueX, value0, value1, ...valueN)	Returns one value from a list of possible values, based on the index (valueX). If valueX = 0, then value0 is returned; if valueX = 1, value1 is returned, and so forth. If valueX is not within the range of choices (value0...valueN), the function will return ERR.
@**COLS**(range)	Returns the number of columns in a range.
@**ERR**	Returns ERR (error).
@**FALSE**	Returns the value 0 (false).
@**HLOOKUP**(valueX, range,offset)	Returns the contents of some cell in a table. The location of the table is specified by the range argument. The column of the lookup cell is determined by comparing the valueX argument to ascending values found in the top row of the table. The row of the lookup cell is determined by the offset argument, which speci-

	fies some number of rows below the top row of the table.
@**IF**(condition,true value,false value)	Returns one of two values—the true value if the condition tests true or the false value if the condition tests false.
@**INDEX**(range,column, row)	Returns the contents of the cell found in the specified range at the intersection of the column and row arguments specified. The first column is column 0 and the first row is row 0. If the column or row specified does not fall within the specified range, the function will return ERR.
@**ISERR**(cell address)	Returns 1 (true) if the cell specified by the cell address argument contains ERR; otherwise, returns 0 (false).
@**ISNA**(cell address)	Returns 1 (true) if the cell specified by the cell address argument contains NA; otherwise, returns 0 (false).
@**ISNUMBER**(cell address)	Returns 1 (true) if the cell specified by the cell address argument contains a numeric value or is empty; otherwise, returns 0 (false).
@**ISSTRING**(cell address)	Returns 1 (true) if the cell specified by the cell address argument contains a label (string); otherwise, returns 0 (false).
@**NA**	Returns NA (not available).
@**ROWS**(range)	Returns the number of rows in a range.
@**TRUE**	Returns the value 1 (true).
@**VLOOKUP**(valueX, range,offset)	Returns the contents of some cell in a table. The location of the table is specified by the range argument. The row of the lookup cell is determined by comparing the valueX argument to ascending values found in the left-most column of the table. The column of the lookup cell is determined by the offset argument, which specifies some number of columns to the right of the left-most column of the table.

The Logical and Special functions allow the spreadsheet designer to incorporate some decision-making capabilities into a spreadsheet, and to trap for some possible error occurrences when building a spreadsheet template.

@**IF**(condition,true value,false value)

@**IF** is the true conditional function of Lotus. The first part of its argument is a logical expression using the relational operators <, >, and =. It also may include the logical operators #NOT#, #AND#, and #OR#. The computer evaluates the condition as either TRUE (equal to 1) or FALSE (equal to 0). Based on this evaluation, the @**IF** function returns either the true value or the false value argument. The following example spreadsheets demonstrate the use of the @**IF** function. Some rules of spreadsheet design will be set aside in order to help make the example easier to read and more understandable.

Simple Condition, Single @IF

The following spreadsheet computes the gross pay for salespersons working for a particular firm. Each salesperson receives a base pay per month of $1200.00 and an additional 10% commission on sales greater than $10000.

	A	B	C	D	E
1					GROSS
2	DATE HIRED	SALESPERSON	TERR	SALES	PAY
3					
4	05-Dec-79	Speakerman, Larry	1	15050	1705
5	15-Feb-76	Adams, Deborah	1	9050	1200
6	10-Jun-82	Edwards, Carl	1	7500	1200
7	25-Apr-84	Parsons, Shelly	2	16050	1805
8	01-Aug-67	Russell, Bob	2	14000	1600
9	31-Oct-77	Carlson, Richard	2	9050	1200
10	20-Mar-84	Hart, Nelson	3	11000	1300
11	05-May-84	Martin, Cathy	3	8750	1200
12	01-Jan-85	Hunter, Carol	3	7800	1200
13	25-Aug-78	Jackson, Steve	3	7650	1200
14					

The function originally entered into cell E4 (Larry Speakerman's gross pay) was

@**IF**(D4>10000,1200+0.1*(D4−10000),1200)

The function says

If the value in cell D4 is greater than 10000
return the value 1200 + 10% of the difference between the value in cell D4 and 10000.
Otherwise, return the value 1200.

The @**IF** function then was copied into the other cells in that column.

Simple Condition, Nested @IFs

Each salesperson is to receive a bonus based on the performance of all salespersons in their territory. Salespersons in territory #1 will receive a $50.00 bonus; those in territory #2, a $75.00 bonus; and those in territory #3, a $25.00 bonus.

	A	B	C	D	E	F
1					GROSS	
2	DATE HIRED	SALESPERSON	TERR	SALES	PAY	BONUS
3						
4	05-Dec-79	Speakerman, Larry	1	15050	1705	50
5	15-Feb-76	Adams, Deborah	1	9050	1200	50
6	10-Jun-82	Edwards, Carl	1	7500	1200	50
7	25-Apr-84	Parsons, Shelly	2	16050	1805	75
8	01-Aug-67	Russell, Bob	2	14000	1600	75
9	31-Oct-77	Carlson, Richard	2	9050	1200	75
10	20-Mar-84	Hart, Nelson	3	11000	1300	25
11	05-May-84	Martin, Cathy	3	8750	1200	25
12	01-Jan-85	Hunter, Carol	3	7800	1200	25
13	25-Aug-78	Jackson, Steve	3	7650	1200	25
14						

The function originally entered into cell F4 (Larry Speakerman's bonus) was

@**IF**(C4 = 1,50,@**IF**(C4 = 2,75,25))

In the example, the false value of the first @**IF** is another @**IF** function.

@**IF**(cond,true value,@**IF**(cond,true value,false value))

The total nested function says:

If the value in C4 equals 1,
  return the value 50.
Otherwise,
  if the value in C4 equals 2,
    return the value 75.
  Otherwise, return the value 25.

Complex Condition, Single @IF

In the final example, complex conditions using logical operators will be used in a single @**IF** function.

In addition to receiving gross pay with commissions and the territory performance bonus, any salesperson who was hired after May 1, 1984 and has sales greater than $7,500, or any salesperson who was hired after May 1, 1982 and has sales greater than $10,000, will receive an additional bonus of $15.00.

	A	B	C	D	E	F	G
1					GROSS		ADDED
2	DATE HIRED	SALESPERSON	TERR	SALES	PAY	BONUS	BONUS
3							
4	05-Dec-79	Speakerman, Larry	1	15050	1705	50	0
5	15-Feb-76	Adams, Deborah	1	9050	1200	50	0
6	10-Jun-82	Edwards, Carl	1	7500	1200	50	0
7	25-Apr-84	Parsons, Shelly	2	16050	1805	75	15
8	01-Aug-67	Russell, Bob	2	14000	1600	75	0
9	31-Oct-77	Carlson, Richard	2	9050	1200	75	0
10	20-Mar-84	Hart, Nelson	3	11000	1300	25	15
11	05-May-84	Martin, Cathy	3	8750	1200	25	15
12	01-Jan-85	Hunter, Carol	3	7800	1200	25	15
13	25-Aug-78	Jackson, Steve	3	7650	1200	25	0
14							

The @**IF** function originally entered into cell G4 was

@**IF**((A4>@**DATE**(84,5,1)#AND#D4>7500)#OR#(A4>@**DATE**(82,5,1) #AND#D4>10000),15,0)

Here Lotus's normal order of precedence for logical operators #AND# and #OR# (evaluation left to right) is overridden by including parentheses in the complex condition of the form

(cond AND cond) or (cond AND cond)

If the total condition is evaluated as being true, this @**IF** function will return the value 15; if false, the value 0 will be returned.

@**CHOOSE**(valueX,value0,value1,value2,...valueN)

The @**CHOOSE** function uses an index (the integer valueX) to select a value to return from a list of values (value0...valueN). For example, if valueX equals 0, the first value of the list is returned; if valueX equals 1, the second value of the list is returned. If valueX is greater than the number of values in the list, the value ERR is returned.

In the following example, the @**CHOOSE** function is used to return values for a summary report for any one of three different divisions within a firm. The Summary Report area of the spreadsheet uses the value held in cell D3 as the index for its two @**CHOOSE** functions. To change the Summary Report, the user need only change the value in the cell D3.

```
    A    B                  C           D          E          F          G
1
2    -------------------------------------------------------------
3    SUMMARY REPORT  Division #        3
4
5    Sales/Salesperson  $9,680 <— @CHOOSE(D3,@NA,C12/C14,E12/E14,G12/G14)
6
7    Sales/Advertising   10.24 <— @CHOOSE(D3,@NA,C12/C16,E12/E16,G12/G16)
8    dollar
9    =============================================================
10                  Divison #1        Division #2        Division #3
11
12   SALES...........$150,900          $135,500            $96,800
13
14   # Salespersons...       12                16                 10
15
16   Advertising cost. $13,240           $21,275             $9,450
17
```

Based on the value in cell D3, the @**CHOOSE** functions will return the appropriate values for Sales/Salesperson and Sales/Advertising dollar for divisions 1, 2, or 3. Notice that the @**NA** function is listed as the zero index list value. This is one method of compensating for the awkward zero index that Lotus uses in this function.

@**VLOOKUP**(valueX,range,offset)

The @**VLOOKUP** function uses a table of values through which to search and from which to return an appropriate value. The search is based on the valueX argument. A classic example of the usefulness of the @**VLOOKUP** function is in looking up the appropriate tax amount for a given individual. The search through the table is based on the individual's taxable income and the value returned from the table is based on the filing status of the individual.

Using a small portion of the actual tax table that would be used, the following spreadsheet lets the user enter the taxable amount (from $24,000 to $24,400) into cell G2 and his or her filing status (1 through 4) into cell G4. The spreadsheet then uses an @**VLOOKUP** function in cell G7 to return the appropriate tax amount from the table found in range A12..E20.

```
        A        B        C        D        E        F        G
 1           Filing Status
 2   Single......................1   TAXABLE INCOME -->     24,256
 3   Married, filing jointly.......2
 4   Married, filing separately....3   FILING STATUS  -->          2
 5   Head of household............4
 6                                     TAX AMOUNT
 7                                     FROM TAX TABLE -->      3,394
 8                                                               ↑
 9   Taxable          Married  Married   Head of                 |
10    Income  Single    Joint Separate    House @VLOOKUP(G2,$TAXTABLE,G4)
11   ------- -------- ------- -------- --------
12    24,000   4,273    3,339    5,314    3,953
13    24,050   4,288    3,350    5,333    3,967
14    24,100   4,303    3,361    5,352    3,981
15    24,150   4,318    3,372    5,371    3,995
16    24,200   4,333    3,383    5,390    4,009
17    24,250   4,348    3,394    5,409    4,023
18    24,300   4,363    3,405    5,428    4,037
19    24,350   4,378    3,416    5,447    4,051
20    24,400   4,393    3,427    5,466    4,065
```

The @**VLOOKUP** function in cell G7 was entered as @**VLOOKUP** (G2,$TAXTABLE,G4). Before the function can be evaluated, the range of cells A12..E20 must have been named TAXTABLE. The $ sign keeps the range reference absolute if the function is copied into other cells at a later time.

When the computer evaluates the @**VLOOKUP** function it moves to the top left cell of the range named TAXTABLE (cell A12) and compares the value there (24,000) to the first value in its argument (24,256). It then continues down that column, comparing each value with 24,256 (in this case until it reaches cell A18, 24,300). It then backs up one cell (to A17) and uses the offset argument (in this case, 2) to move that number of cells (2) to the right. There it finds the value 3,394 and returns it as the appropriate value for the function.

The values in the first column of the table (the values used to look up) must be in ascending order with no duplicates. If the first value in this column is larger than the value being looked up, or if the offset (the third argument) is greater than the width of the table range in columns, the result will be ERR. The offset for the first column is 0 (zero).

The @**VLOOKUP** function gets its name from the direction in which it looks up values—(V)ertically down the first column on the left side of a table. The @**HLOOKUP** function performs the same operations, but looks up its values (H)orizontally across the top row of a table, with its offset being the number of rows down from the first row.

@**CELL**(attribute,range) and @**CELLPOINTER**

The functions **@CELL** and **@CELLPOINTER** return information about an attribute of a cell in the spreadsheet. The attributes that may be returned are listed in the following table.

Attribute	Return Value	Example	
Address	Cell Address	$B$3	
Row	Row Number	3	
Col	Column Number	2	(column B)
Contents	Cell Contents	1225	
Type	Type of data 1,v,b	v	(label, value, blank)
Prefix	Label Prefix ',",^, none	'	
Protect	Protection Status 1,0	1	(1 = Protected)
Width	Column Width	12	
Format	Cell Format Abbreviation	C2	(currency, 2 decimals)

The returned value for the specified attribute will be updated whenever the spreadsheet is recalculated, either automatically or manually with the F9 (CALC) key. The **@CELL** function returns the specified attribute of the top left cell in the specified range. The **@CELLPOINTER** function returns the specified attribute of the cell in which the pointer is located when a spreadsheet recalculation occurs.

The following is an example of each of the attributes that may be returned by the **@CELL** and **@CELLPOINTER** functions. In the **@CELL** function, the range was specified as NET, which is the named range B5..B5, and the pointer was located at cell A3 when the CALC key (F9) was pressed.

A3: [W24] 'Taxes

```
              A                 B       C          D                       E
1
2  Gross Income               $40,000
3  Taxes                      $14,800
4  ===============================
5  Net Income                 $25,200
6
7
8  @CELL("address",NET)  = $B$5       | @CELLPOINTER("address")  = $A$3
9  @CELL("row",NET)      =        5   | @CELLPOINTER("row")      =        3
10 @CELL("col",NET)      =        2   | @CELLPOINTER("col")      =        1
11 @CELL("contents",NET) =    25200   | @CELLPOINTER("contents") = Taxes
12 @CELL("type",NET)     = v          | @CELLPOINTER("type")     = l
13 @CELL("prefix",NET)   =            | @CELLPOINTER("prefix")   = '
14 @CELL("protect",NET)  =        1   | @CELLPOINTER("protect")  =        1
15 @CELL("width",NET)    =        9   | @CELLPOINTER("width")    =       24
16 @CELL("format",NET)   = C0         | @CELLPOINTER("format")   = G
17
```

ENGINEERING FUNCTIONS

@**ACOS**(value)	Returns the arc cosine.
@**ASIN**(value)	Returns the arc sine.
@**ATAN**(value)	Returns the arc tangent.
@**ATAN2**(value1,value2)	Returns the 4-quadrant arc tangent.
@**COS**(value)	Returns the cosine.
@**EXP**(value)	Returns the exponential.
@**LN**(value)	Returns the log base e.
@**LOG**(value)	Returns the log base 10.
@**PI**	Returns pi (3.141592653589794).
@**SIN**(value)	Returns the sine.
@**TAN**(value)	Returns the tangent.

Engineering functions actually are mathematical functions, but are treated separately because they are used less often in business-related spreadsheets.

LOTUS 1-2-3 GRAPHICS

Businesses frequently use graphics to aid in understanding data. Lotus 1-2-3 gives you the capability of presenting your spreadsheet's data in a variety of graphic forms.

LOTUS GRAPHICS OVERVIEW

To create a graph using Lotus, use the Main menu's /Graph commands. They are as follows.

```
Type  X  A  B  C  D  E  F  Reset  View  Save  Options  Name  Group  Quit
```

Types of Graphs

You usually begin the process of creating a graph by selecting the type of graph to produce. Your options are **L**ine graph, **B**ar graph, **XY** graph, **S**tacked-Bar graph, and **P**ie chart.

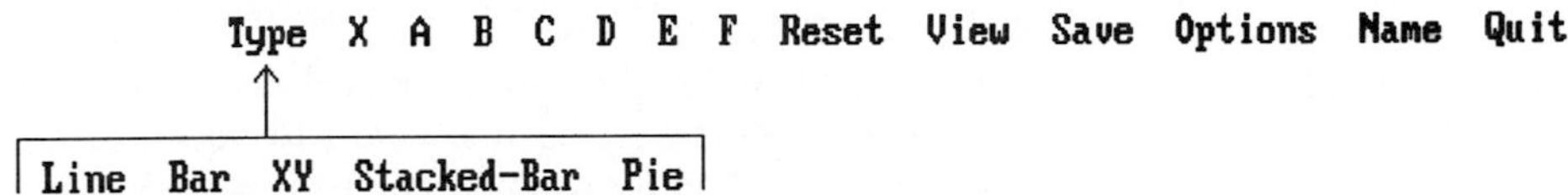

Specifying Data to be Graphed

After selecting the type of graph, you may select the range(s) of numeric data you want graphically represented. As many as six different ranges of data may be graphically displayed. The ranges are specified as the **A** (first), **B** (second), **C** (third), **D** (fourth), **E** (fifth), and **F** (sixth) data ranges of the /**G**raph commands. The **X** range is an additional data range for an XY type graph; for all other graph types, it specifies a range of cells holding data to be displayed as titles. The **G**roup command is used to set all data ranges in a single operation.

NOTE: The **G**roup *command is not available with version 2.01.*

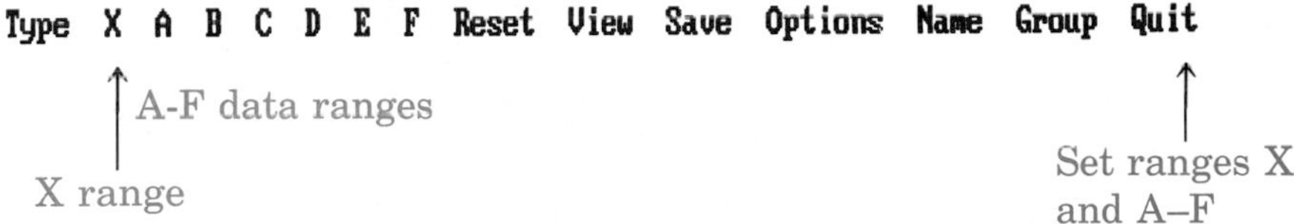

Viewing the Graph

After you have specified the data ranges, you may view the graph on the monitor screen by selecting the **V**iew command of the /Graph commands. The graph will be displayed in its basic form.

```
Type  X  A  B  C  D  E  F  Reset  View  Save  Options  Name  Group  Quit
```

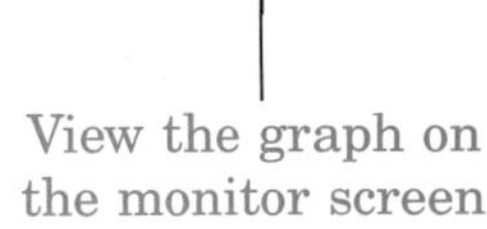

Adding Options

Typing any key will return you from viewing the graph to the /Graph menu of commands. There you may use the **O**ptions command to add **T**itles, **L**egends, **D**ata-Labels, **G**rids, and more to the graphics display. As you make changes or additions, you may use the **V**iew command to again look at the graph.

```
Type  X  A  B  C  D  E  F  Reset  View  Save  Options  Name  Group  Quit
                                                 ↑
```

Add labels and format the graph

Using the GRAPH (F10) Function Key

When you are satisfied with the appearance of the graph, you may exit the /Graph commands by using the /**G**raph,**Q**uit command. You then can change the data in your spreadsheet and observe how those changes affect the graph by tapping the F10 (GRAPH) Function key. This key serves as a substitute for typing the command key sequence /**G**raph,**V**iew,any key,**Q**uit that would otherwise be necessary to accomplish the same operation. After you use the F10 key to view the graph, tap any key to return to the spreadsheet display (READY mode).

Erasing the Graph Settings

When you are ready to create another graph for the spreadsheet, you may use the **R**eset command of the /Graph commands to erase all or some of the settings for the current graph.

```
Type  X  A  B  C  D  E  F  Reset  View  Save  Options  Name  Group  Quit
                            ↑
```

Erases all or some of the graph settings

Naming a Graph

If you want to produce another graph for the same spreadsheet and do not want to lose the current graph's settings (data ranges, titles, etc.) you must use the /**G**raph,**N**ame,**C**reate command to name the current graph. When you name the graph, its settings are stored with the spreadsheet's data under the name you have given them. You then may make specifications for another graph and view them as you set it up.

```
Type  X  A  B  C  D  E  F  Reset  View  Save  Options  Name  Group  Quit
                                                        ↑
```

Makes current /Graph settings a permanent part of the spreadsheet's data

Printing a Graph

When you are ready to print the current graph on the printer, you must first use the **S**ave command of the /**G**raph commands to save the screen output of the current graph to its own file on the diskette. The file is given a .PIC extension by Lotus to identify it as a Lotus "Picture" file.

```
Type  X  A  B  C  D  E  F  Reset  View  Save  Options  Name  Group  Quit
```

Saves the current graph's screen output to a separate file

The next step in printing a graph is to /**Q**uit the Lotus spreadsheet program and use the PrintGraph program to print the finished graph on the printer. The PrintGraph program is available on a separate diskette or as a separate program file on a hard-disk system.

CREATING THE FIVE BASIC GRAPH TYPES

The following spreadsheet will be used to illustrate how each of the five basic graph types may be produced.

	A	B	C	D	E	F	G	H
1								
2		* * Quarterly	Sales	Figures	* *	Totals	Adv $/	
3						1990	Sales	
4	SALES REGION	#1	#2	#3	#4	-------	-----	
5								
6	California	20,769	25,487	16,037	36,043	98,336	7.8%	
7	Washington	18,753	23,065	19,250	29,610	90,678	5.1%	
8	Oregon	19,250	22,400	17,374	28,525	87,549	4.2%	
9	Idaho	14,070	19,376	14,126	25,200	72,772	2.9%	
10	Alaska	13,230	14,070	10,780	14,000	52,080	2.1%	
11								

Pie Charts

In many ways, a Lotus pie chart is the simplest form of graph to produce. A pie chart uses only one data range whose sum constitutes the pie to be divided among the data elements of the range. Each slice of the pie is displayed graphically as a computed percent of the whole. Labels describing each piece of the pie may be specified in an X range. The labels in the X range should correspond to the data elements in the A data range.

	A	B	C	D	E	F	G	H
1								
2		* * Quarterly Sales Figures * *				Totals	Adv $/	
3						1990	Sales	
4	SALES REGION	#1	#2	#3	#4	-------	-----	
5								
6	California	20,769	25,487	16,037	36,043	98,336	7.8%	
7	Washington	18,753	23,065	19,250	29,610	90,678	5.1%	
8	Oregon	19,250	22,400	17,374	28,525	87,549	4.2%	
9	Idaho	14,070	19,376	14,126	25,200	72,772	2.9%	
10	Alaska	13,230	14,070	10,780	14,000	52,080	2.1%	
11								
12								
13								

X range A6..A10

A data range F6..F10

```
Type          = Pie
A data range  = F6..F10
X range       = A6..A10
View
```

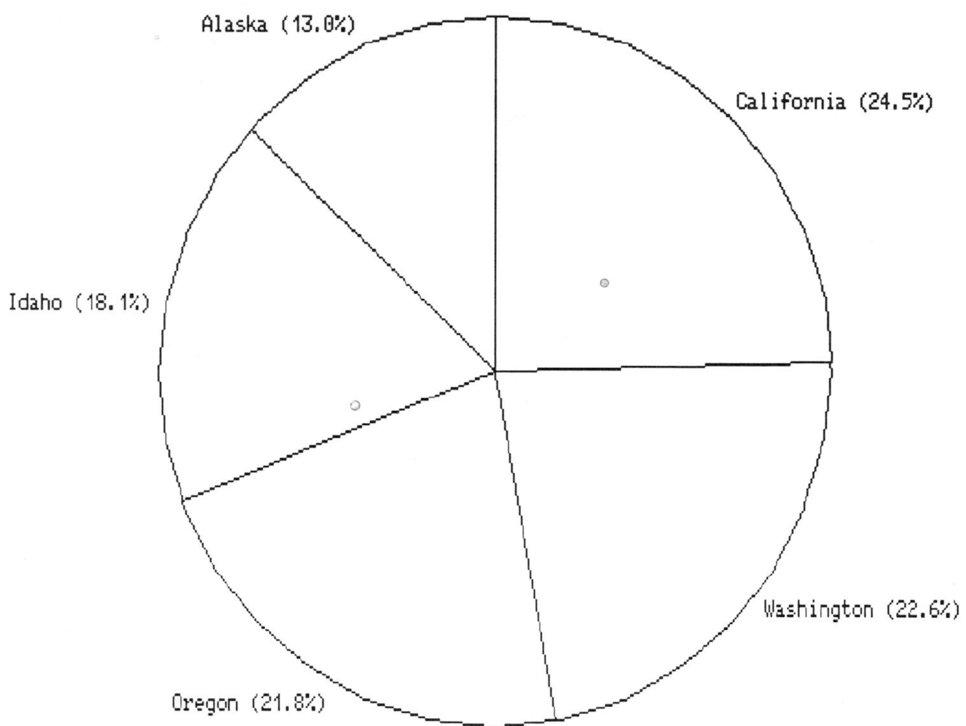

While the pie chart uses only a single data range (the A range) to create the graph, a second data range (the B range) may be used to effect shading patterns and to "explode" the pie by offsetting one or more slices. The numeric values 1–7 may be used to designate shading patterns, and the numeric values used 0 or 8 to designate no shading. Adding 100 to any of these values will cause the corresponding pie slice to be offset from the rest of the pie. Like the X range for labels, the B data range for shading should be set to correspond to the A data range.

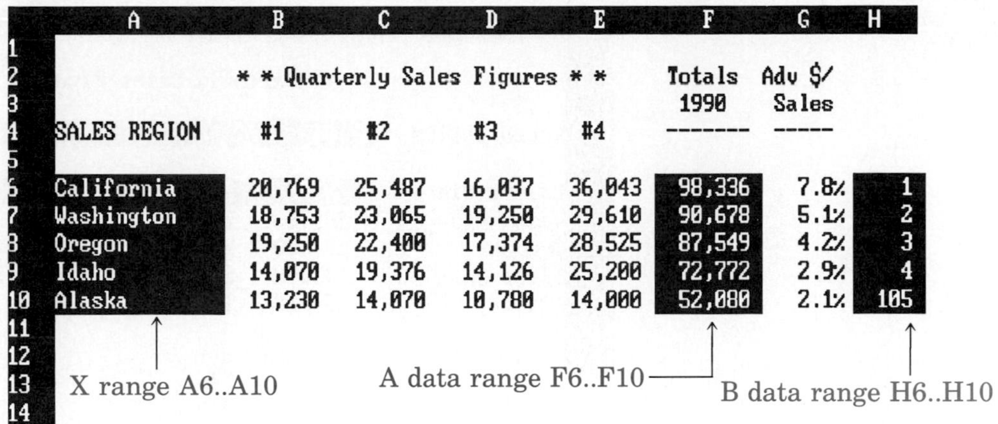

	A	B	C	D	E	F	G	H
1								
2		* * Quarterly Sales Figures * *				Totals	Adv $/	
3						1990	Sales	
4	SALES REGION	#1	#2	#3	#4	-------	-----	
5								
6	California	20,769	25,487	16,037	36,043	98,336	7.8%	1
7	Washington	18,753	23,065	19,250	29,610	90,678	5.1%	2
8	Oregon	19,250	22,400	17,374	28,525	87,549	4.2%	3
9	Idaho	14,070	19,376	14,126	25,200	72,772	2.9%	4
10	Alaska	13,230	14,070	10,780	14,000	52,080	2.1%	105
11								
12								
13								
14								


```
Type          = Pie
A data range  = F6..F10
B data range  = H6..H10
X range       = A6..A10
View
```

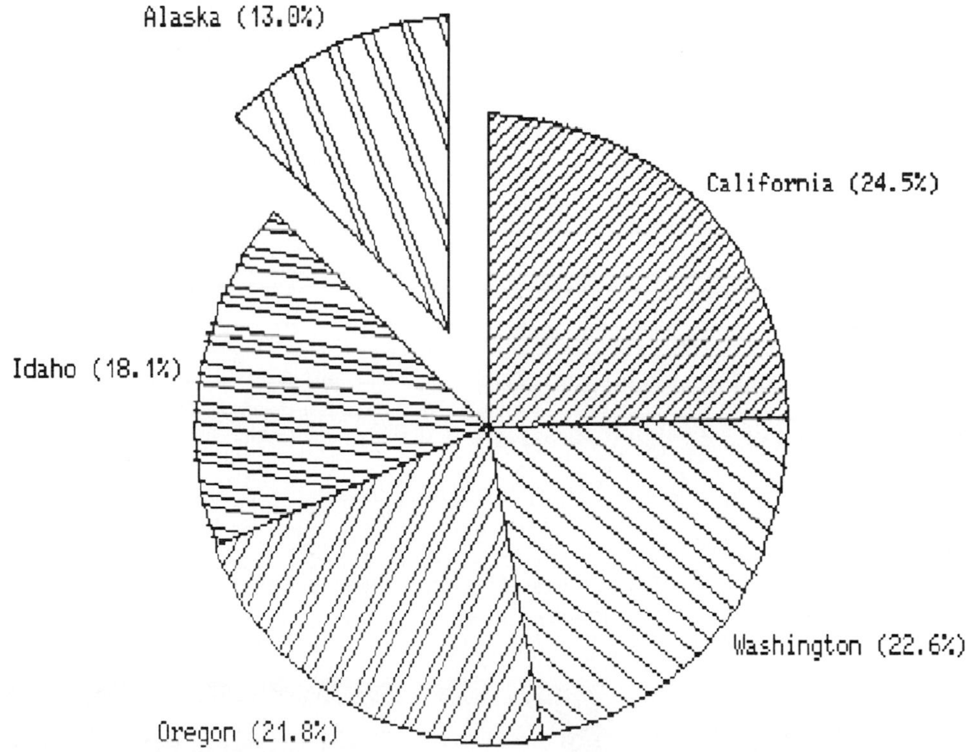

Line Graphs

Line graphs may include up to six data ranges that are plotted with the X range used to label the X axis of the graph. The first example plots quarterly sales for the California sales region.

	A	B	C	D	E	F	G
1							
2		* * Quarterly Sales Figures * *				Totals	Adv $/
3						1990	Sales
4	SALES REGION	#1	#2	#3	#4	-------	-------
5							
6	California	20,769	25,487	16,037	36,043	98,336	7.8%
7	Washington	18,753	23,065	19,250	29,610	90,678	5.1%
8	Oregon	19,250	22,400	17,374	28,525	87,549	4.2%
9	Idaho	14,070	19,376	14,126	25,200	72,772	2.9%
10	Alaska	13,230	14,070	10,780	14,000	52,080	2.1%
11							
12	X-range	A data range					

```
Type          = Line
A data range  = B6..E6
X range       = B4..E4
View
```

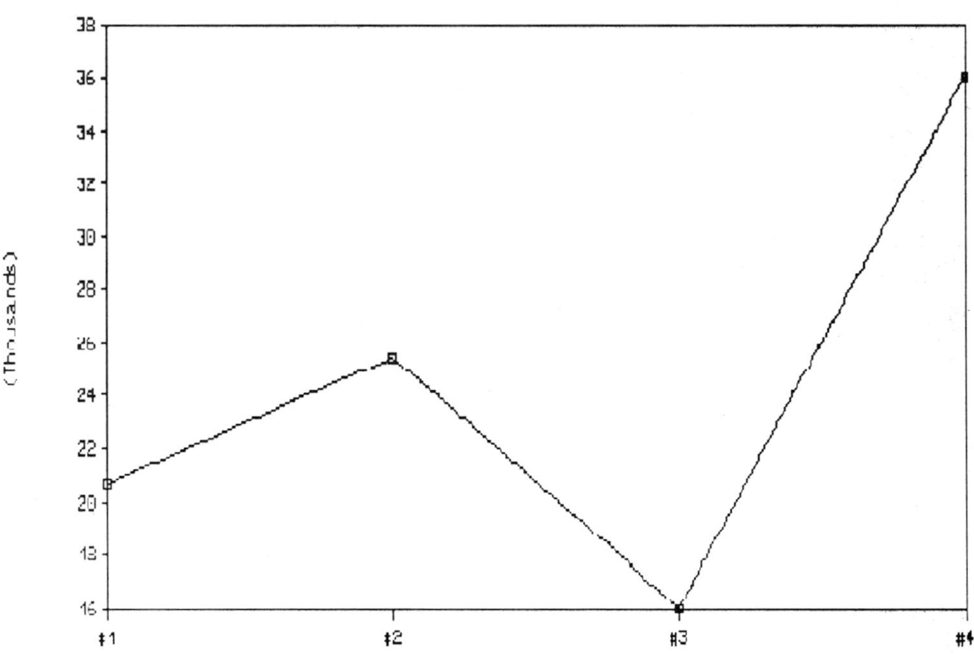

The next example uses several data ranges (A through E) to produce a line graph.

	A	B	C	D	E	F	G
1							
2		* * Quarterly Sales Figures * *				Totals	Adv $/
3						1990	Sales
4	SAL X range ⟶	#1	#2	#3	#4	-------	-------
5							
6	Cal A range ⟶	20,769	25,487	16,037	36,043	98,336	7.8%
7	Was B range ⟶	18,753	23,065	19,250	29,610	90,678	5.1%
8	Ore C range ⟶	19,250	22,400	17,374	28,525	87,549	4.2%
9	Ida D range ⟶	14,070	19,376	14,126	25,200	72,772	2.9%
10	Ala E range ⟶	13,230	14,070	10,780	14,000	52,080	2.1%
11							

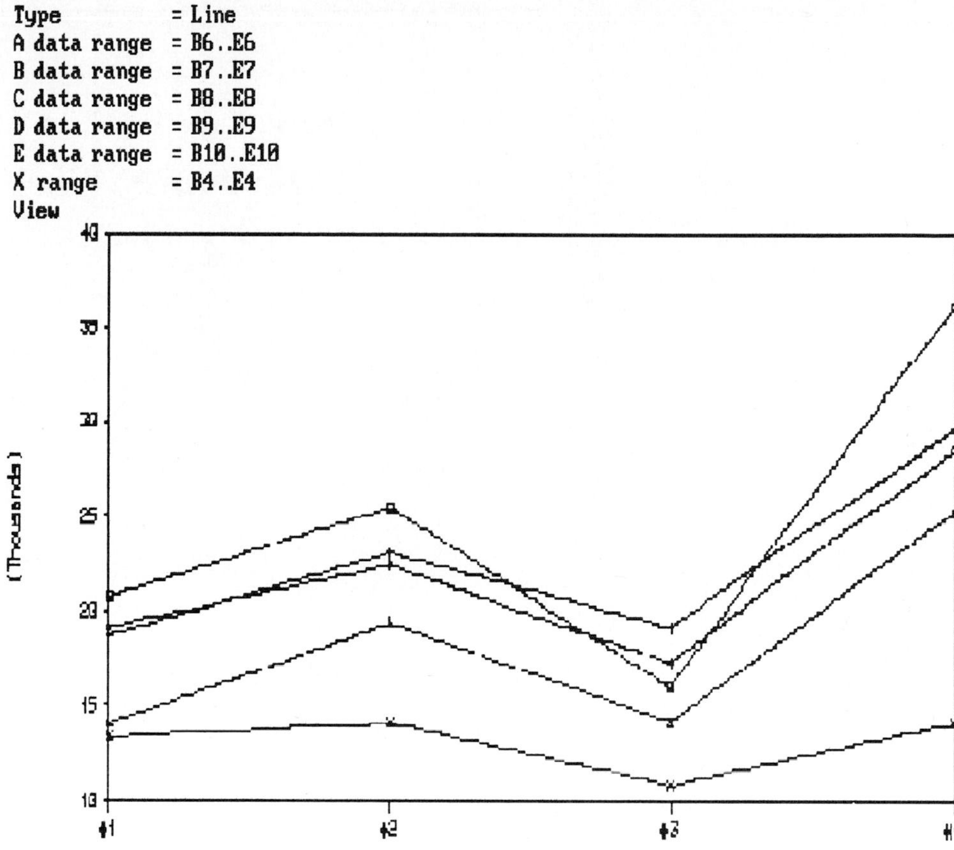

Bar Graphs

The following examples change the two preceding line graphs to bar graphs (/**G**raph,**T**ype,**B**ar). All other settings for the graphs remain the same.

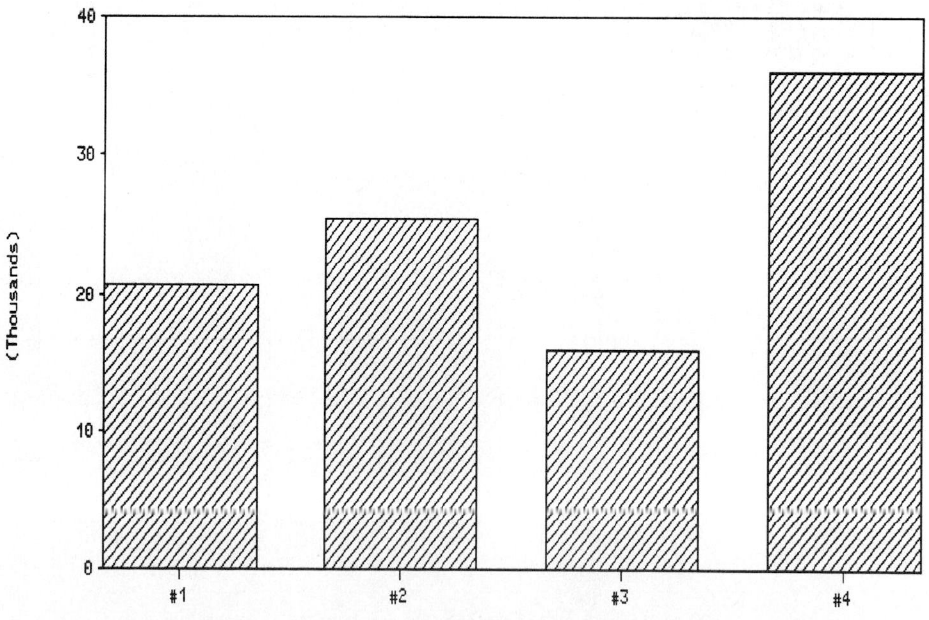

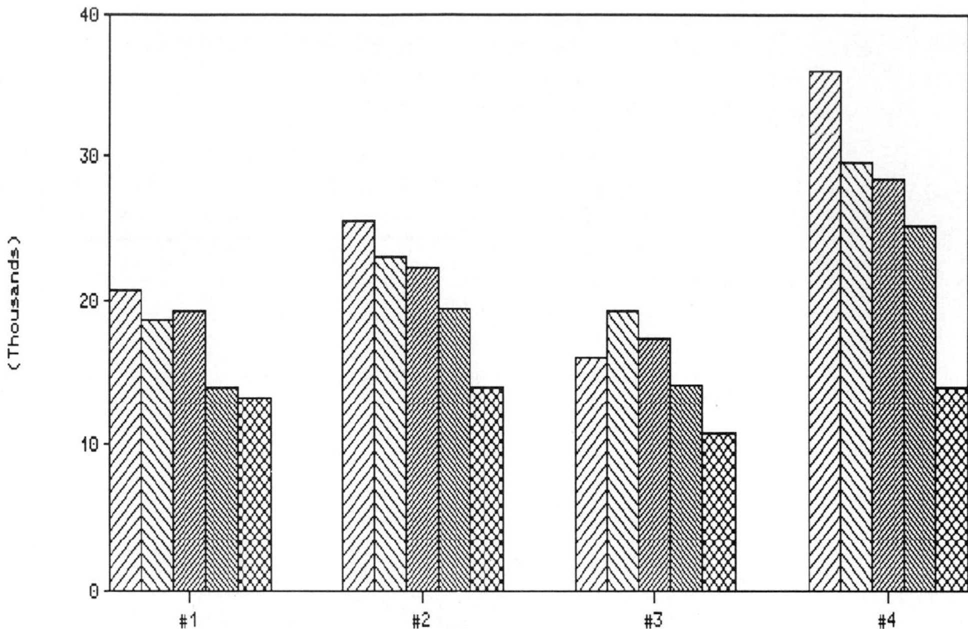

Notice that the bars for each data range are automatically assigned a different shading pattern (the patterns shown on your screen may vary somewhat from the illustrations shown here).

Stacked Bar Graphs

Stacked bar graphs vary from bar graphs in that they show the elements in the data ranges as distinct contributors to the total height of a bar. All settings except **Type** (used in the preceding bar graph) are the same for the stacked bar graph.

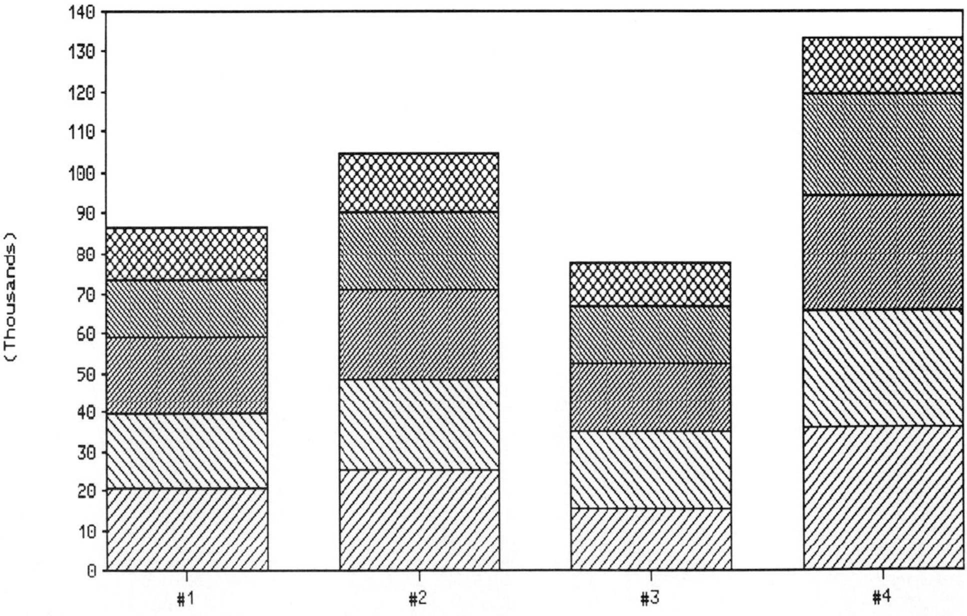

XY Graphs

XY graphs differ from the other types of graphs in that the X range is used not for labels, but for a data range containing values to be used as the X axis scale. The Y axis scale reflects values in the A–F data ranges. For each value in the A–F ranges, a data point appears on the graph at the appropriate intersection of the two axes. This type of graph may be used to show correlations or relationships between two types of data.

In the following example, the X range is specified as the range of cells containing the advertising-dollars-to-sales-dollars ratio expressed as a percent. The single A data range is specified as the total yearly sales for each region. The resulting XY graph indicates that sales increase with an increase in advertising expenditures, but that the rate of increase diminishes as advertising expenditures continue to rise.

	A	B	C	D	E	F	G
1							
2		* * Quarterly Sales Figures * *				Totals	Adv $/
3						1990	Sales
4	SALES REGION	#1	#2	#3	#4	-------	------
5							
6	California	20,769	25,487	16,037	36,043	98,336	7.8%
7	Washington	18,753	23,065	19,250	29,610	90,678	5.1%
8	Oregon	19,250	22,400	17,374	28,525	87,549	4.2%
9	Idaho	14,070	19,376	14,126	25,200	72,772	2.9%
10	Alaska	13,230	14,070	10,780	14,000	52,080	2.1%
11							
12							
13							
14							

A data range F6..F10
X range G6..G10

Type = XY
A data range = F6..F10
X range = G6..G10
View

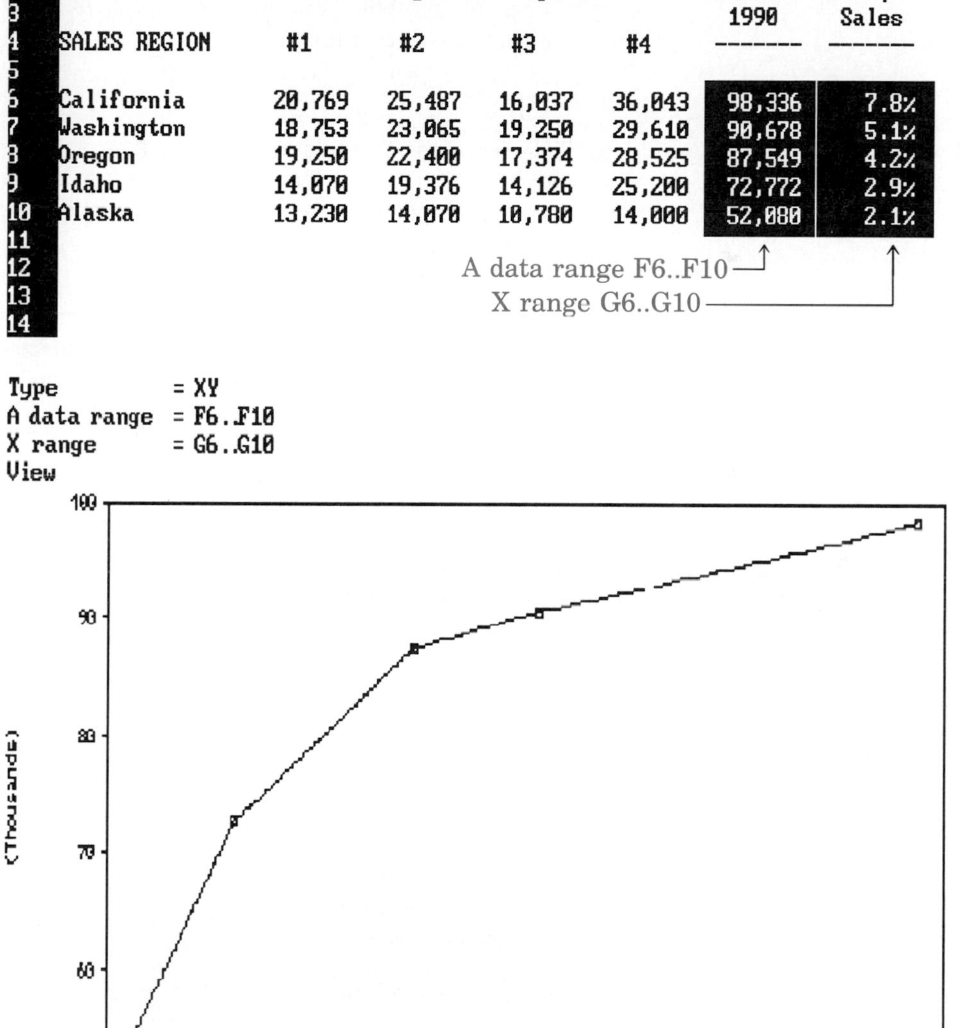

The line connecting the data points may or may not be displayed with the graph.

ADDING OPTIONS TO A GRAPH

Several **O**ptions commands are available with the /**G**raph commands. They may be used to enhance and/or alter the appearance of a graph. The options tend to fall into two general categories: those used to add labels to the graph and those used to change the display format of the graph.

Adding Labeling Options

The **L**egend, **T**itles, and **D**ata-Labels commands of the **O**ptions commands are all used to add labeling to the current graph.

Legends

A legend identifies the various lines on a line graph, the bars on a bar graph, or the points on an XY graph. Legend labels are entered for the data ranges used to produce a graph. The legend is displayed at the bottom of the graph with the symbols, shading, or color used in the line, XY point, or bar displayed for the data range.

Titles

The **T**itles command labels an entire graph with a first graph title line and a second graph title line. These two titles are centered and displayed at the top of the graph. Titles also may be put on the X axis and the Y axis of graphs having these two axes.

Data-Labels

Data-Labels are entered as a range of labels corresponding to the data elements in a data range. The specification of Data-Labels is very similar to the specification of an X range used to label an X axis. Specified Data-Labels, however, are displayed within the graph. They may be centered, or may be to the left, right, above, or below the corresponding data point in the graph. Data-Labels are always centered when they are used in bar graphs.

The following graph demonstrates how legends, titles, and Data-Labels may be included in a graph.

```
Type          = Bar
A data range  = B6..E6
B data range  = B7..E7
C data range  = B8..E8
D data range  = B9..E9
E data range  = B10..E10
X range       = B4..E4
Options
  Legend
    A range = California
    B range = Washington
    C range = Oregon
    D range = Idaho
    E range = Alaska
  Titles
    First  = Comparative Quarterly Sales
    Second = California Sales Figures Displayed
    X-Axis = QUARTERS
    Y-Axis = DOLLAR SALES
  Data-Labels
    A range = B6..E6
    Center
View
```

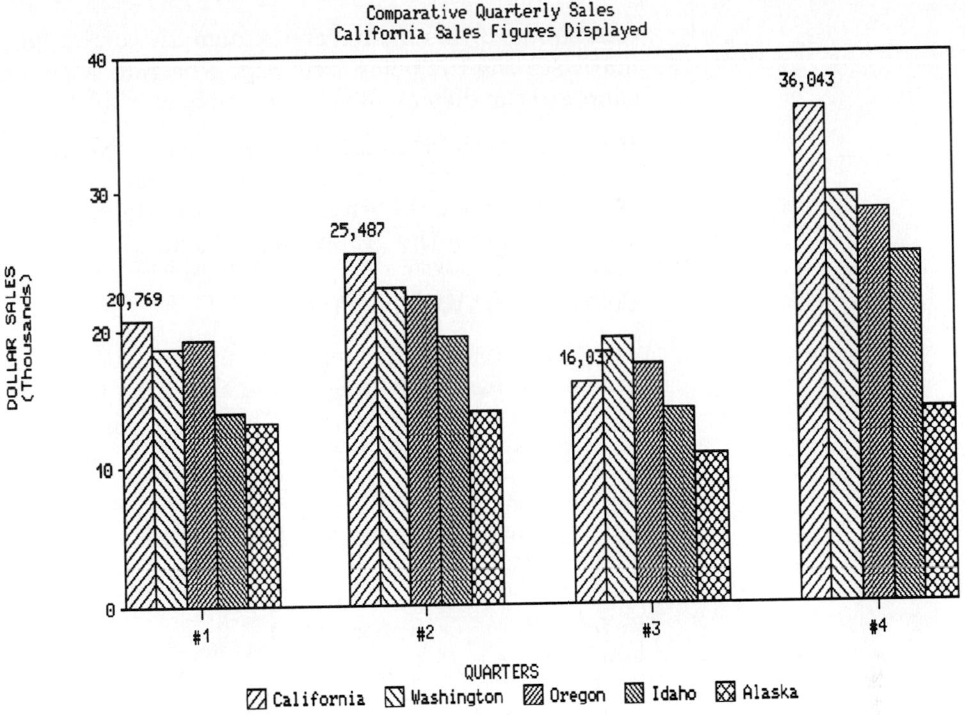

Changing Graph Formats

The **F**ormat, **G**rid, **S**cale, **C**olor, and **B**&W commands of the **O**ptions commands are used to format the display of the current graph.

Format Commands

The **F**ormat command is used for line and XY graphs. It allows the graph to display only lines, only symbols, both lines and symbols (the default setting), or neither lines nor symbols. The display can be for the entire graph or for any of the data ranges A through F.

Grid Commands

A **G**rid within a graph may be displayed as horizontal lines corresponding to the ticks (perpendicular hash marks) on the Y axis, vertical lines corresponding to the ticks on the X axis, both (a true grid display), or cleared from the graph after having been set. The default setting is **C**lear (no grid lines).

Scale Commands

The **S**cale command may be used to override Lotus's automatic scaling of the Y axis or the X axis, or to skip the display of every *n*th label in an X range used to label the X axis. If you select **S**cale, then either **Y**-scale or **X**-scale, the following options are displayed.

Automatic Manual Lower Upper Format Indicator Quit

Manual turns off the automatic scaling and must be selected before you view a graph with upper and/or lower limits set with the **U**pper or **L**ower commands of this menu. The **A**utomatic command returns Lotus to automatic scaling (its default setting). The **I**ndicator command allows you to suppress the display of the scale indicator on the graph.

If you select the **F**ormat command, the menu of options presented will be similar to those presented with the /**R**ange,**F**ormat or /**W**orksheet,**G**lobal,**F**ormat commands. Here, however, it is used to format the numbers on the graph's X or Y axis.

Color and B&W Commands

The **C**olor and **B**&W commands are mutually exclusive and, when selected, provide no further menus. If you select the **C**olor command, the graph will be displayed in color. If you select **B**&W (the default setting), the graph will be displayed in black and white.

The last bar graph example will now be further enhanced to demonstrate some of the formatting **O**ption commands. The following settings have been added to it.

```
Grid          = Horizontal
Scale
   Skip       = 2
   Y Scale
      Manual
      Upper   = 60000
      Format  = Currency, 0 decimals
```

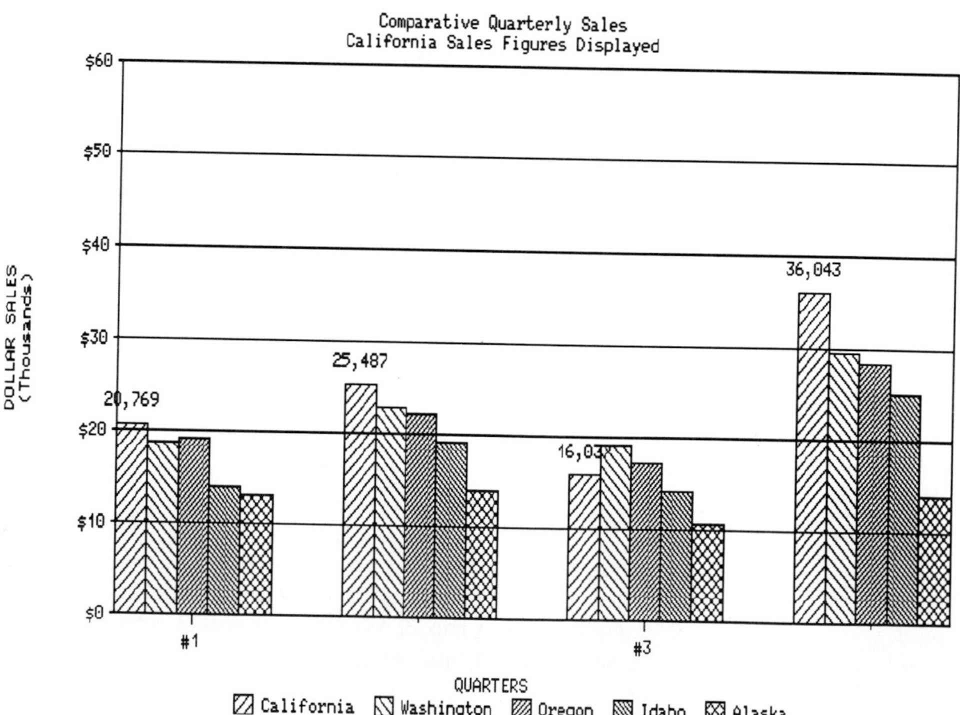

PRINTING A GRAPH

Saving a Picture File

Before you print a Lotus 1-2-3 graph, you must save the screen output of that graph to its own file on the diskette by using Lotus's /**G**raph,**S**ave command. Once you have saved it, you must exit the spreadsheet with the /**Q**uit command, returning to the Lotus Access System or to DOS.

Accessing the PrintGraph Program

You may either select the **P**rintGraph command of the Lotus Access System, or you may load this software directly from the DOS operating level by typing in its filename PGRAPH.EXE (or simply PGRAPH). First be sure that the diskette with the PGRAPH.EXE file on it is in the current default disk drive or that it is available and will be accessed on your network or hard drive.

After the software has been loaded into RAM, the following screen will be displayed with the menu of **P**rintGraph commands at the top of the screen and current settings at the bottom.

```
Copyright 1986, 1989 Lotus Development Corp.  All Rights Reserved. V2.2    MENU

Select graphs to print or preview
Image-Select  Settings  Go  Align  Page  Exit

   GRAPHS    IMAGE SETTINGS                       HARDWARE SETTINGS
   TO PRINT   Size               Range colors      Graphs directory
               Top        .395   X                   A:\
               Left       .750   A                 Fonts directory
               Width     6.500   B                   A:\
               Height    4.691   C                 Interface
               Rotation   .000   D                   Parallel 1
                                 E                 Printer
              Font               F
               1  BLOCK1                           Paper size
               2  BLOCK1                             Width       8.500
                                                     Length     11.000

                                                  ACTION SETTINGS
                                                   Pause  No   Eject  No
```

The tree structure of the **P**rintGraph command menus and explanations of the **P**rintGraph commands follow.

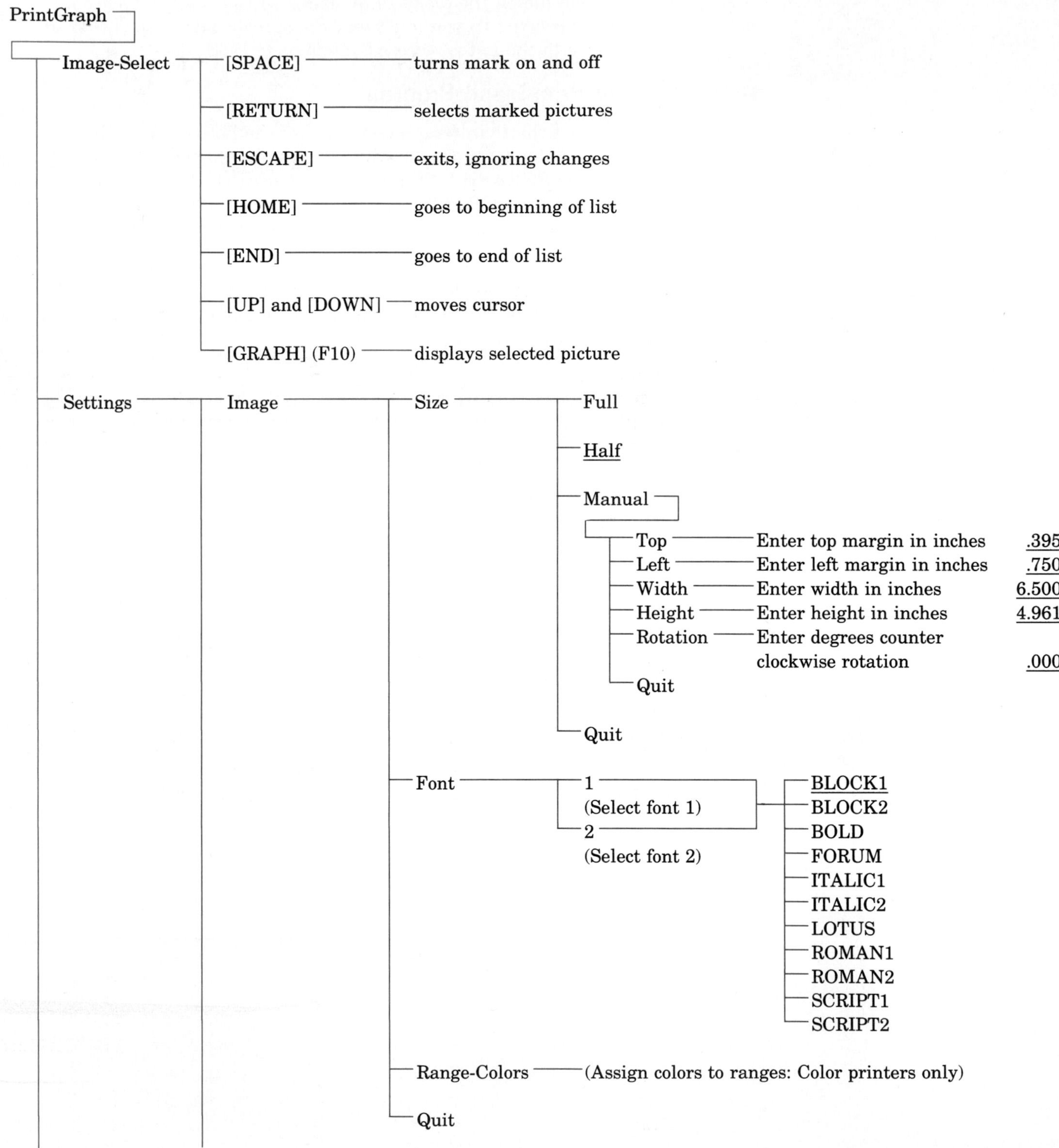

CONTINUED

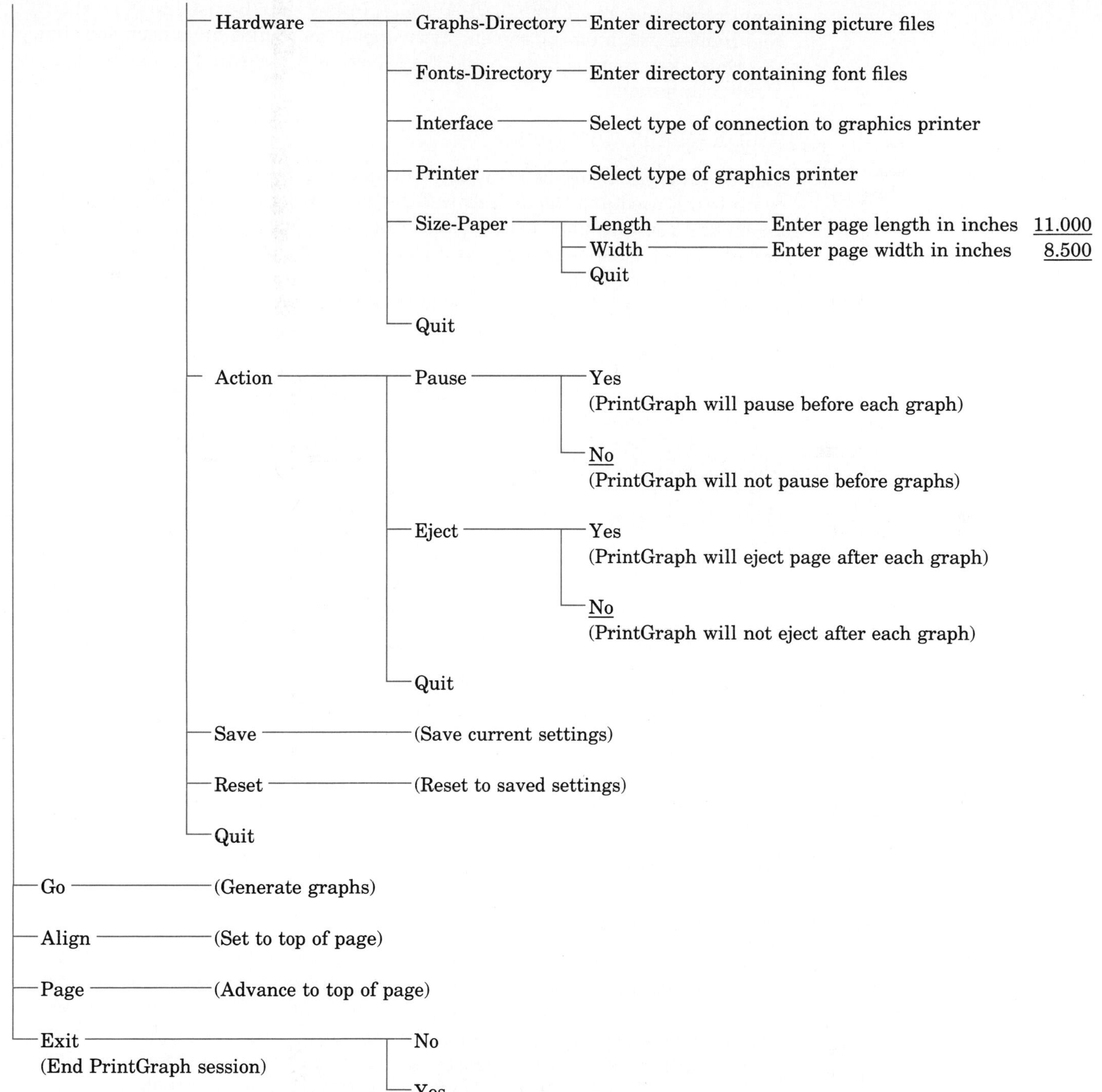

The Image-Select Command

The graph(s) to be printed must first be selected by using the **I**mage-Select command of the **P**rintGraph menu. When the command is used, the screen displays a listing of the .PIC files on your disk. If no files appear, you may need to designate another drive/directory for .PIC files (see the **S**ettings command). A pointer used to highlight files in the list may be moved up and down with the cursor control keys. The space bar marks (or unmarks) the highlighted file. The F10 (GRAPH) function key may be used to view the highlighted graph on the screen. After one or more files have been selected, the Enter key may be used to end the selection process and return to the **P**rintGraph menu.

The **S**ettings Command

Before your graph can be printed, you must specify the type of printer hardware being used and the disk drive/directories where the needed files may be found. You also may specify various options concerning how graphs are to be printed, such as margins and placement on the page. Once you have specified this information, it may be saved in its own file. The **P**rintGraph program will use these settings each time the program is loaded.

The **G**o Command

Once you have selected the appropriate printer, directories, and options with the **S**ettings command and have selected the .PIC file(s) to be printed with the **I**mage-Select command, the **G**o command may be used to begin printing the graph(s).

The **A**lign and **P**age Commands

The **A**lign and **P**age commands work in the same way as their counterparts in the spreadsheet /**P**rint commands. **A**lign tells the computer that the paper in the printer is at the top of a page; **P**age causes the computer to advance the paper in the printer to the top of the next page.

Configuring PrintGraph with the Settings Command

The **S**ettings commands of the PrintGraph program provide Lotus with information about how graphs are to be printed. After the **S**ettings command is selected, the following options are available.

```
Image   Hardware   Action   Save   Reset   Quit
```

Image Commands

The **S**ettings,**I**mage,**S**ize command is used to select automatic or manual placement of the graph on the page when printed. Automatic placement selections are **F**ull to print the graph on a full page and rotated 90 degrees or **H**alf to print the graph on the top half of a page with no rotation. **H**alf is the default setting. Manual placement may be selected to change the **T**op margin, **L**eft margin, **W**idth, **H**eight, and **R**otation of the graph.

The **S**ettings,**I**mage,**F**ont command may be used to select one of several PrintGraph fonts (styles of lettering) to be used for titles and labels on the printed graph. Two different fonts may be used on the graph. Font **1** is used for the first title line. Font **2** is used for all other titles and labels on the graph. The directory where font files are located must be selected with the **S**ettings,**H**ardware,**F**onts-Directory command before fonts may be selected.

The **S**ettings,**I**mage,**R**ange-Colors command is used only in conjunction with a color printer. The colors for the graph's X range and A–F data ranges may be set to the desired colors.

Hardware Commands

The **S**ettings,**H**ardware commands are used to specify directories where files needed by PrintGraph are located, the printer being used, and how commands should be sent to the printer. In a microlab, the hardware specifications will probably have been set and saved previously, and you will not need to change them. If they have not, you may need to use the following **H**ardware commands.

The **S**ettings,**H**ardware,**G**raphs-Directory command is used to specify the location of your .PIC files. The **S**ettings,**H**ardware,**F**onts-Directory command is used to specify the location of PrintGraph font files. These directories must be set before .PIC files or fonts may be selected.

The **S**ettings,**H**ardware,**I**nterface command is used to specify the printer port to which your graphics printer is connected. The interface may be either a parallel or serial port on your computer.

The **S**ettings,**H**ardware,**P**rinter command is used to select the type of printer you have and the density (high or low) in which graphs are to be printed. If high density is selected, the graph quality will be higher, but the graph will take longer to print. The printers that appear on the list for selection will include only those previously selected through the Lotus Install program.

The **S**ettings,**H**ardware,**S**ize-Paper command may be used to specify the height and width of your printer's paper. Default settings are for standard size 8½″ by 11″ paper.

Action Commands

The **S**ettings,**A**ction,Pause command may be used to cause PrintGraph to pause before printing each graph selected. **P**ause may be set to **Y**es or **N**o. **N**o is the default, but **Y**es may be selected if you are using your printer's single sheet feed option.

The **S**ettings,**A**ction,**E**ject command is used to determine whether or not the printer should advance to the top of a new page automatically after each graph is printed. The default is **N**o eject.

Save and Reset Commands

The **S**ettings,**S**ave command is used to save the currently defined settings in a configuration file so that these settings will become the defaults the next time PrintGraph is used. The **S**ettings,**R**eset command may be used to restore all settings to the default values found in the configuration file.

/DATA,SORT, /DATA,QUERY, AND DATABASE FUNCTIONS

Lotus 1-2-3 has two specialized commands for database operations, /**D**ata,**S**ort and /**D**ata,**Q**uery, as well as some special database functions. These data commands and functions are designed to deal with spreadsheet data similar to the way a database management system (DBMS) deals with data. Although Lotus is not a DBMS, some of the terminology and concepts of database management will be used in discussing how the spreadsheet database commands and functions work.

DATABASE STRUCTURE AND TERMINOLOGY

The /**D**ata,**S**ort commands are used to sort data and the /**D**ata,**Q**uery commands are used to search through data and find cases evaluated as true for a given condition. Like the /**D**ata,**Q**uery commands, the database functions search for occurrences of a condition in a set of data and then return summary values based upon only instances for which the condition is true. The spreadsheet's data must be organized in a particular way for these commands and functions.

Related data items are entered in adjacent cells of a row in the spreadsheet. Each data item is called a *field* of data. A single row of related data is called a *record,* and the rectangular range of records is called the *database.* When you use the /**D**ata,**Q**uery commands or data functions, you must have an additional row of *field names* occupying the top row of the database.

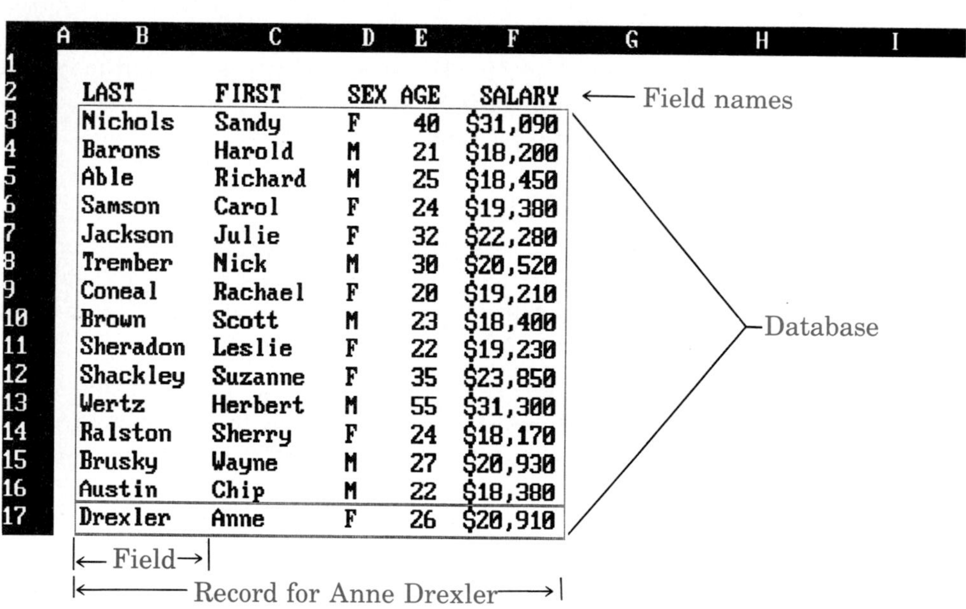

	B	C	D	E	F
1					
2	LAST	FIRST	SEX	AGE	SALARY
3	Nichols	Sandy	F	40	$31,090
4	Barons	Harold	M	21	$18,200
5	Able	Richard	M	25	$18,450
6	Samson	Carol	F	24	$19,380
7	Jackson	Julie	F	32	$22,280
8	Trember	Nick	M	30	$20,520
9	Coneal	Rachael	F	20	$19,210
10	Brown	Scott	M	23	$18,400
11	Sheradon	Leslie	F	22	$19,230
12	Shackley	Suzanne	F	35	$23,850
13	Wertz	Herbert	M	55	$31,300
14	Ralston	Sherry	F	24	$18,170
15	Brusky	Wayne	M	27	$20,930
16	Austin	Chip	M	22	$18,380
17	Drexler	Anne	F	26	$20,910

THE /DATA,SORT COMMANDS

The /**D**ata,**S**ort commands are straightforward and require only three steps to sort spreadsheet data which are organized in a database form. The menu of /**D**ata,**S**ort commands consists of the following.

Data-Range Primary-Key Secondary-Key Reset Go Quit

Setting the Data-Range to Sort

The first step in sorting spreadsheet data is to define the range of data to be sorted by using the **D**ata-Range command. The range includes only the actual records of the database to be sorted. Using the previous example, an appropriate range to sort would be B3..F17.

	A	B	C	D	E	F	G	H	I
1									
2		LAST	FIRST	SEX	AGE	SALARY			
3		Nichols	Sandy	F	40	$31,090			
4		Barons	Harold	M	21	$18,200			
5		Able	Richard	M	25	$18,450			
6		Samson	Carol	F	24	$19,380			
7		Jackson	Julie	F	32	$22,280			
8		Trember	Nick	M	30	$20,520			
9		Coneal	Rachael	F	20	$19,210			
10		Brown	Scott	M	23	$18,400			
11		Sheradon	Leslie	F	22	$19,230			
12		Shackley	Suzanne	F	35	$23,850			
13		Wertz	Herbert	M	55	$31,300			
14		Ralston	Sherry	F	24	$18,170			
15		Brusky	Wayne	M	27	$20,930			
16		Austin	Chip	M	22	$18,380			
17		Drexler	Anne	F	26	$20,910			

Data-Range

Setting Sort Keys

The next step is to define the sort key(s). A key is any cell address in the column of data on which the database is to be sorted. Up to two fields may be specified as keys on which to sort: one is called the Primary-Key and the other is called the Secondary-Key.

The field specified as the Primary-Key has the highest precedence for sorting. The Primary-Key is the only sort key required. If a Secondary-Key is specified, the database also will be sorted on that field, but it will take a lower precedence. When a sort key is selected, you are provided a choice of either ascending or descending sort order.

Sorting the Database

Once the data range, sort key(s), and the sort order for each key have been specified, the **G**o command of the /**D**ata,**S**ort commands causes the data in the data range to be sorted. The following example uses the field named SEX as the Primary-Key and the field named SALARY as the Secondary-Key for a data sort operation.

```
/Data,Sort,Data-Range     - Enter Data-Range: B3..F17
          Primary-Key     - Primary sort key: D2
                            Sort order (A or D): A
          Secondary-Key   - Secondary sort key: F2
                            Sort order (A or D): D
          Go
```

	A	B	C	D	E	F	G	H	I
1									
2		LAST	FIRST	SEX	AGE	SALARY			
3		Nichols	Sandy	F	40	$31,090			
4		Shackley	Suzanne	F	35	$23,850			
5		Jackson	Julie	F	32	$22,280			
6		Drexler	Anne	F	26	$20,910			
7		Samson	Carol	F	24	$19,380			
8		Sheradon	Leslie	F	22	$19,230			
9		Coneal	Rachael	F	20	$19,210			
10		Ralston	Sherry	F	24	$18,170			
11		Wertz	Herbert	M	55	$31,300			
12		Brusky	Wayne	M	27	$20,930			
13		Trember	Nick	M	30	$20,520			
14		Able	Richard	M	25	$18,450			
15		Brown	Scott	M	23	$18,400			
16		Austin	Chip	M	22	$18,380			
17		Barons	Harold	M	21	$18,200			

THE /**D**ATA,**Q**UERY COMMANDS

The /**D**ata,**Q**uery commands locate records in the database. The variation of /**D**ata,**Q**uery discussed here searches the database for records that meet certain conditions (criteria). It also copies the data in certain fields of the records to another place in the spreadsheet. This process is called *extracting data from the database.*

The Three Ranges Required to Extract Data

1. The Input range includes the database and its row of field names. It is the range in which Lotus searches for records. It is specified with the **I**nput command of the /**D**ata,**Q**uery commands.
2. The Criterion range holds logical expressions that determine which records will be extracted from the Input range. It is usually a small range and is specified by using the **C**riterion command of the /**D**ata,**Q**uery commands.
3. The Output range, specified with the **O**utput command of the /**D**ata,**Q**uery commands, determines which fields of the records will be extracted and the location of the copied data. Data from records in the Input range that meet the condition(s) in the Criterion range will be copied to the Output range only for those fields included in the Output range.

To use the /**D**ata,**Q**uery commands effectively, you need to understand how the three ranges relate to each other and how the conditions in the criterion range work. The following example will show how the ranges are defined for an extract operation.

An Example of Extracting Data

Using the same database used in the /**D**ata,**S**ort example, you want to extract the last names, ages, and salaries of all employees over age 30.

The first step is to define the Input range as B2..F17, which includes the row of field names and all records in the database. The field names must be included in the Input range; however, if you were only interested in searching through the first ten records, you should define the Input range to include only the row of field names and those ten records.

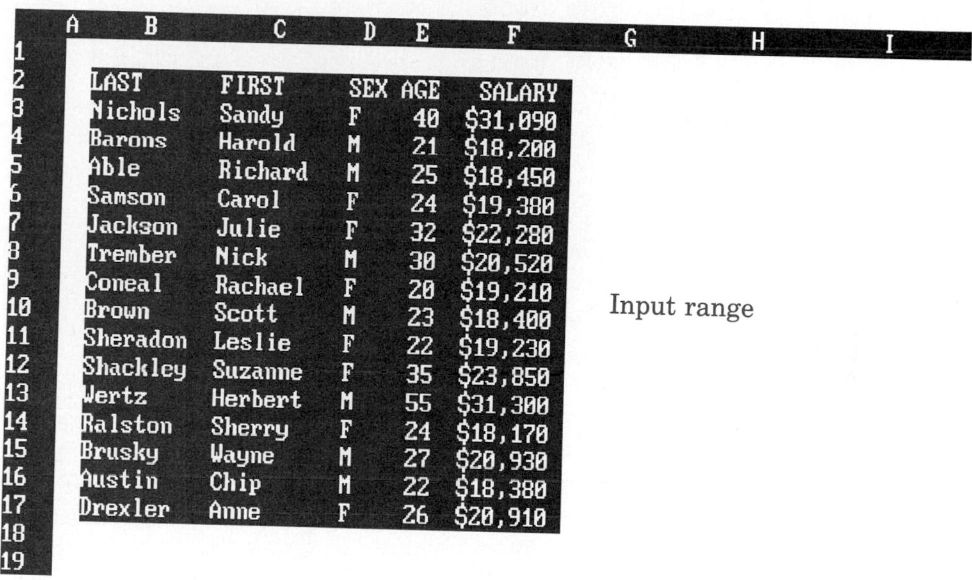

	B	C	D	E	F
1					
2	LAST	FIRST	SEX	AGE	SALARY
3	Nichols	Sandy	F	40	$31,090
4	Barons	Harold	M	21	$18,200
5	Able	Richard	M	25	$18,450
6	Samson	Carol	F	24	$19,380
7	Jackson	Julie	F	32	$22,280
8	Tremher	Nick	M	30	$20,520
9	Coneal	Rachael	F	20	$19,210
10	Brown	Scott	M	23	$18,400
11	Sheradon	Leslie	F	22	$19,230
12	Shackley	Suzanne	F	35	$23,850
13	Wertz	Herbert	M	55	$31,300
14	Ralston	Sherry	F	24	$18,170
15	Brusky	Wayne	M	27	$20,930
16	Austin	Chip	M	22	$18,380
17	Drexler	Anne	F	26	$20,910
18					
19					

The next step is to define the Output range, the area into which the records meeting the criteria will be copied. The first row of the Output range contains the field names for the fields to be copied from the Input range. Since you want to copy into the Output range only the last names, ages, and salaries for records meeting the criterion (all employees over age 30), the corresponding field names should be entered into another area of the spreadsheet, which will then be defined as the Output range. The **O**utput command of the /**D**ata,**Q**uery commands then is used to specify the range by its location. Here it would be H2..J17.

NOTE: The field names used in the Output range must exactly match the spelling of the field names in the Input range; however, case (upper or lower) and label prefixes used may be different.

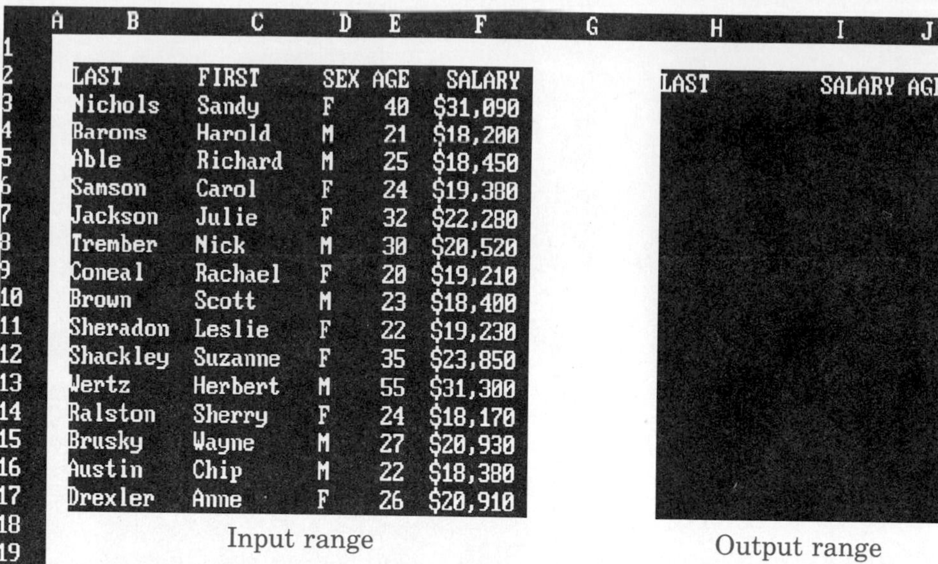

	A	B	C	D	E	F	G	H	I	J
1										
2		LAST	FIRST	SEX	AGE	SALARY		LAST		SALARY AGE
3		Nichols	Sandy	F	40	$31,090				
4		Barons	Harold	M	21	$18,200				
5		Able	Richard	M	25	$18,450				
6		Samson	Carol	F	24	$19,380				
7		Jackson	Julie	F	32	$22,280				
8		Trember	Nick	M	30	$20,520				
9		Coneal	Rachael	F	20	$19,210				
10		Brown	Scott	M	23	$18,400				
11		Sheradon	Leslie	F	22	$19,230				
12		Shackley	Suzanne	F	35	$23,850				
13		Wertz	Herbert	M	55	$31,300				
14		Ralston	Sherry	F	24	$18,170				
15		Brusky	Wayne	M	27	$20,930				
16		Austin	Chip	M	22	$18,380				
17		Drexler	Anne	F	26	$20,910				
18										
19										

Input range Output range

The last range that must be defined to complete a /**D**ata,**Q**uery,**E**xtract operation is the Criterion range. This is where the logical expression equivalent to "Age > 30" will be entered. The smallest possible Criterion range consists of two cells, one above the other. The top cell must hold a field name and the bottom cell normally holds a logical expression. The expression should reference a cell in the first record of the database, normally the same field as the field name entered above it. Here an appropriate criterion would be

The next step is to move to a third area of the spreadsheet and enter into one cell the label AGE and to enter into the cell below it the expression +E3>30. The two cells into which this data is entered will display

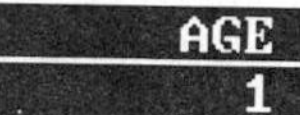

The 1 displayed in the second cell is the result of the computer's evaluation of the logical expression +E3>30. The value in E3 is greater than 30, so the computer evaluates it as true and displays the numeric value 1 (true). If the value in E3 were not greater than 30, the numeric value displayed would be 0 (false). To make the expressions in a Criterion range readable, cells holding logical expressions often are formatted as Text with the /**R**ange,**F**ormat,**T**ext command.

Once the Criterion range data have been entered into cells, the **C**riterion command of the /**D**ata,**Q**uery commands is used to specify the cells comprising the Criterion range.

The final step in the extract operation is to use the **E**xtract command of the /**D**ata,**Q**uery commands to begin the data extraction. When this is done, the last names, salaries, and ages of every Input range record for a person over age 30 will appear in the Output range.

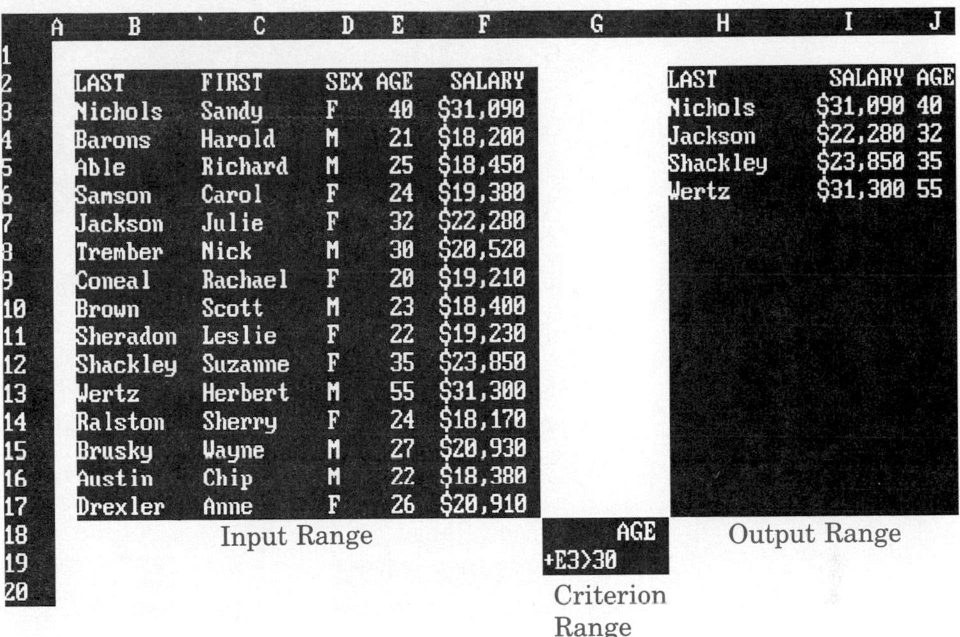

LAST	FIRST	SEX	AGE	SALARY
Nichols	Sandy	F	40	$31,090
Barons	Harold	M	21	$18,200
Able	Richard	M	25	$18,450
Samson	Carol	F	24	$19,380
Jackson	Julie	F	32	$22,280
Trember	Nick	M	30	$20,520
Coneal	Rachael	F	20	$19,210
Brown	Scott	M	23	$18,400
Sheradon	Leslie	F	22	$19,230
Shackley	Suzanne	F	35	$23,850
Wertz	Herbert	M	55	$31,300
Ralston	Sherry	F	24	$18,170
Brusky	Wayne	M	27	$20,930
Austin	Chip	M	22	$18,380
Drexler	Anne	F	26	$20,910

AGE
+E3>30

LAST	SALARY	AGE
Nichols	$31,090	40
Jackson	$22,280	32
Shackley	$23,850	35
Wertz	$31,300	55

Criterion Range Conditions

The way that you structure your field name labels and logical expressions within a Criterion range determines the character of the records evaluated as true for the criteria (conditions) in the range. To demonstrate the alternatives, several different Criterion ranges relating to this database will be discussed.

A Criterion Range with No Condition

The simplest criterion is no criterion at all. If two blank cells are defined as the Criterion range, all records are evaluated as true for the criterion, and the appropriate fields will be copied to the Output range.

Simple Criterion Range/Simple Condition

The example used to extract records for employees older than age 30 showed a simple Criterion range (two cells) and a simple numeric condition. A simple Criterion range also could hold a string condition using the relational operators =, >, <, >=, <=, and < >. For example, to extract all records for employees whose last name begins with *M* or greater, the condition *last name* >= *"M"* would be entered in the Criterion range.

Criterion Range

Output Range

LAST	SALARY	AGE
Nichols	$31,090	40
Samson	$19,380	24
Tremher	$20,520	30
Sheradon	$19,230	22
Shackley	$23,850	35
Wertz	$31,300	55
Ralston	$18,170	24

Simple Criterion Range/Complex Condition

It is possible to include a complex condition in a simple Criterion range (two cells) by using the logical operators #AND# and #OR#. For example, if you want to extract records for employees who are both over age 30 *and* who are female, the complex condition would be entered using the #AND# operator.

Criterion Range

Output Range

LAST	SALARY	AGE
Nichols	$31,090	40
Jackson	$22,280	32
Shackley	$23,850	35

If you want to extract records for employees who are either over age 30 *or* who are female, the complex condition would be entered using the #OR# operator.

Criterion Range

Output Range

LAST	SALARY	AGE
Nichols	$31,090	40
Samson	$19,380	24
Jackson	$22,280	32
Coneal	$19,210	20
Sheradon	$19,230	22
Shackley	$23,850	35
Wertz	$31,300	55
Ralston	$18,170	24
Drexler	$20,910	26

Notice that when cell references are used to enter the condition expression, the actual field name used in the Criterion range need not be related to the condition. It must, however, be a valid field name from the Input range. For instance, in the last two examples the field name LAST was used; however, the condition +E3>30 references the field AGE and the condition D3="F" references the field SEX.

Wild Card Characters

Special string expressions in the Criterion range also may produce partial comparisons in a data search by including "wild card" characters in the expression. The two wild card characters are the asterisk (*), which means "any other characters remaining," and the question mark (?), which means "any character located here."

When wild card characters are used, no cell references or relational operators are included in the condition expression. In this case, therefore, the field name used in the Criterion range must be that field for which the comparison is to be made.

For example, the following Criterion ranges will produce the output shown in the Output ranges, given the same Input range used in the preceding examples.

Criterion Ranges

LAST
Sh*

Output Range

LAST	SALARY	AGE
Sheradon	$19,230	22
Shackley	$23,850	35

LAST
S*

LAST	SALARY	AGE
Samson	$19,380	24
Sheradon	$19,230	22
Shackley	$23,850	35

LAST
?r*

LAST	SALARY	AGE
Trember	$20,520	30
Brown	$18,400	23
Brusky	$20,930	27
Drexler	$20,910	26

LAST
?r???er

LAST	SALARY	AGE
Trember	$20,520	30
Drexler	$20,910	26

Complex Criterion Range/Simple Conditions

When you need to combine string conditions that include wild card characters with other numeric or string conditions, the Criterion range needs to be enlarged. The logical operators connecting the different conditions become implicit by the expressions' positioning in the Criterion range.

For example, if you want to extract records for all employees whose last name begins with *S and* whose salary is less than $20,000, the appropriate logical operator would be AND. The equivalent of the logical operator #AND# in a complex Criterion range is achieved by entering field names and condition expressions side by side in the Criterion range.

LAST	SALARY
S*	+F3<20000

If, on the other hand, you want to extract records for all employees whose last name begins with *S or* whose salary is less than $20,000, the appropriate logical operator would be OR. The equivalent of the logical operator #OR# in a complex Criterion range is achieved by entering field names side by side, but entering the condition expressions in separate rows in the Criterion range.

LAST	SALARY
S*	
	+F3<20000

When complex Criterion ranges are used to extract data, it is useful to think of the Criterion range as a filter through which the record must pass to reach the Output range. Records can be thought of as starting at the left of the Criterion range and attempting to move through the filter to the Output range on the right.

In a complex Criterion range with an implicit AND (condition AND condition), conditions are located side by side in the same row. Records are first tested against the left-most condition. Those that fail the condition drop out. Those that pass the condition then are tested against the next condition to the right. Only records evaluated as true for all conditions pass to the Output range.

In the preceding example of the complex Criterion range with the implicit AND, the records would attempt to pass the two conditions as shown in the following. Notice that only records for Samson, Sheradon, and Shackley pass the first condition, and of those, only records for Samson and Sheradon pass the second condition.

LAST	SALARY
S*	+F3<20000

LAST	FIRST	SEX	AGE	SALARY
Nichols	Sandy	F	40	$31,090
Barons	Harold	M	21	$18,200
Able	Richard	M	25	$18,450
Samson	Carol	F	24	$19,380
Jackson	Julie	F	32	$22,280
Trember	Nick	M	30	$20,520
Coneal	Rachael	F	20	$19,210
Brown	Scott	M	23	$18,400
Sheradon	Leslie	F	22	$19,230
Shackley	Suzanne	F	35	$23,850
Wertz	Herbert	M	55	$31,300

When a complex Criterion range has condition expressions entered into separate rows (condition OR condition), the record may pass through the Criterion range via any of the condition rows. Records that pass the condition(s) in the upper-most condition row pass directly to the Output range. Those that fail drop to the next condition row down and are tested against the condition(s) there. Only records that fail to pass all condition rows drop out. All others are copied to the Output range.

In the preceding example of the complex Criterion range with the implicit OR, the records would attempt to pass the Criterion range conditions as shown. Notice that while the records for Barons and Able fail the first condition, they pass the second. Since the record for Samson passes the first condition, it is not even tested against the second condition, but passes directly to the Output range.

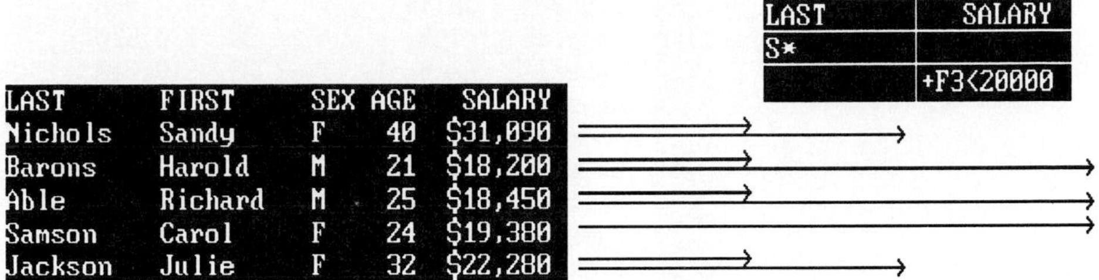

LAST	SALARY
S*	
	+F3<20000

LAST	FIRST	SEX	AGE	SALARY
Nichols	Sandy	F	40	$31,090
Barons	Harold	M	21	$18,200
Able	Richard	M	25	$18,450
Samson	Carol	F	24	$19,380
Jackson	Julie	F	32	$22,280

Database Functions

The statistical functions of Lotus have counterparts designed specifically for dealing with database spreadsheet data. These functions are as follows.

@DCOUNT **@DMIN** **@DSTD** **@DAVG**
@DSUM **@DMAX** **@DVAR**

The purpose of database functions is to return a computed value (such as an average) from a range of cells (such as the column of salaries in a database) based only upon records that meet a Criterion (such as all males in the database). A database function's general form is

@DFUNCT(Input range,offset,Criterion range)

The Input range and Criterion range arguments are specified in the same way as specified for the /**D**ata,**Q**uery commands. The offset argument is used to specify the column (field) in the database for which the computation is to be made. Since offset means "how many columns to the right of the first column," an offset value of 0 specifies the first column, an offset value of 1 specifies the second column, and so forth.

Example of Using Database Functions

Like the statistical functions, the database functions are very similar to each other in form and use. To demonstrate how the data functions may be used, in the following example two **@DAVG** functions are used to return the average salaries for all males and females in the employee database.

	A	B	C	D	E	F	G	H	I	J
1										
2		LAST	FIRST	SEX	AGE	SALARY		Averages		
3		Nichols	Sandy	F	40	$31,090		------------------------------		
4		Barons	Harold	M	21	$18,200		Male Salaries	=	$20,883
5		Able	Richard	M	25	$18,450				
6		Samson	Carol	F	24	$19,380		@DAVG(B2..F17,4,H18..H19)		
7		Jackson	Julie	F	32	$22,280				
8		Tember	Nick	M	30	$20,520				
9		Coneal	Rachael	F	20	$19,210		Female Salaries	=	$21,765
10		Brown	Scott	M	23	$18,400				
11		Sheradon	Leslie	F	22	$19,230		@DAVG(B2..F17,4,I18..I19)		
12		Shackley	Suzanne	F	35	$23,850				
13		Wertz	Herbert	M	55	$31,300				
14		Ralston	Sherry	F	24	$18,170				
15		Brusky	Wayne	M	27	$20,930				
16		Austin	Chip	M	22	$18,380		Criterion Ranges		
17		Drexler	Anne	F	26	$20,910		------------------------------		
18			Input Range					SEX	SEX	
19								M	F	
20										

WHAT IS A MACRO?

In its simplest form, a macro is a collection of keystrokes entered as labels into a cell or range of cells. The top cell of the range is then named using the /**R**ange,**N**ame,**C**reate command. The name given to a range that holds a macro must begin with a backslash (\) followed by a single letter of the alphabet. Once the macro has been entered and named, Lotus will sequentially execute the keystrokes represented in it whenever the Alt key is held down and the letter of the macro's name is typed.

STEPS REQUIRED TO CREATE A MACRO

The following example will show the steps involved in creating a macro.

Assessing the Problem

Macros are created to solve problems or to save time. Let's suppose that you have a spreadsheet file that you have been working on for several days. Your routine is always the same. After each session you save the spreadsheet under its original name to update the file on the disk, and you then exit 1-2-3. Eight keystrokes are required to accomplish your save-and-exit routine. A macro can accomplish the task faster and in one keystroke combination.

Coding the Macro

To create a macro you record the exact sequence of keystrokes required for your regular routine. With paper and a pencil you write down the keys that you press when you complete the save-and-exit steps manually. The keystrokes and commands that you use are as follows.

Keystrokes	Actions and Prompts
/	Call the Main Menu.
F	Select the **F**ile command.
S	Select the **S**ave command.
	Lotus presents the prompt
	`Enter save file name: A:\ASSGN1.WK1`
	The name shown is the one with which you loaded the file (its original name) and is the default prompt of the /**F**ile,**S**ave command.
↵	Type the Enter key to enter this as the correct filename.
	Next you see the prompt
	`Cancel  Replace`
R	Select **R**eplace to update the file.
	Lotus returns to the READY mode.
/	Call the Main Menu again.
Q	Select the **Q**uit command.
	Next you see the prompt
	`No  Yes`
Y	Select **Y**es to complete the Quit operation.

After you systematically record the keystrokes as **/FS**↵ **R/QY** on a piece of paper, you are ready to create the macro that, when executed, will complete these eight keystrokes.

Locating the Macro

Following the rules of spreadsheet design, you move the pointer to an area set off from any current or foreseeable spreadsheet overlap or interference. You next document the area by entering the label "Spreadsheet Macros." You then are ready to type in the macro. Note this very important fact, however—the keystroke ↵ (Enter) is represented in a macro with a tilde (~) character.

Entering the Macro

You begin entering into a cell the keystrokes you have written down for the macro. Since your keystrokes must be entered as labels, you begin your entry by typing in a label prefix (', ", or ^). When it is complete, your macro should look like this.

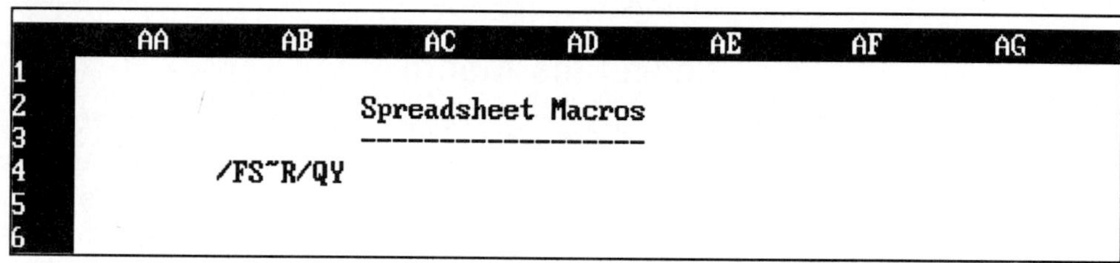

Naming a Macro

Your next step is to use the /**R**ange,**N**ame,**C**reate command to name the single cell AB4..AB4 with an appropriate macro name. Since "D" might be a good name for "Done," you specify the range name as \D.

Enter name: \D

Lotus recognizes a named range as being a macro by the backslash in its name. To complete documentation of the macro, you enter the macro name as a label into the AA column and a short description of the macro's function into the AC column.

Invoking a Macro

Now that the macro has been entered and named, the next time you are ready to save-and-exit you simply press and hold the Alt key and then type the D key. Lotus then will begin to execute, in order, the keystrokes in the macro named \D. The result is that the save-and-exit routine is completed with one keystroke combination rather than eight keystrokes, saving you valuable time.

CAUTIONS ABOUT MACROS

Although macros can be useful, they also have some drawbacks. The keystrokes in them are executed so fast that there is seldom time to stop a rampaging macro before it has done substantial damage to your spreadsheet.

Even in the very simple macro used in the example, if a C or ~ character is accidentally placed where the R character should be (/**FS**~**R**/**QY**), the macro would not replace the file on the disk. It would, however, execute the /**Q**uit,**Y**es command, causing you to lose all of the work you had completed during the current editing session.

Safeguards Against Macro Catastrophes

1. Always save your spreadsheet prior to testing a new macro.
2. The Alt-F2 key combination turns on and off (toggles) a STEP mode. When the STEP mode is on, Lotus executes each keystroke in the macro only after you have typed a keyboard key. Thus, execution of the macro is slowed down, allowing you to observe the results of each keystroke in it.
3. While a macro is being executed, an indicator at the bottom of the screen will show CMD. If you want to stop the execution of the macro before it is completed, the Ctrl-Break key combination will interrupt the execution of the macro.

REPRESENTING SPECIAL KEYSTROKES IN A MACRO

As you will recall, the tilde character (~) is used in macros to represent the Enter key keystroke. This is one example of how a substitute entry may be used in a macro to represent the actual keystroke used. Other special keystrokes are represented in a macro by entering the key's name or function enclosed in braces. For instance, if you want to create a macro to copy a single cell into the cell below it, your macro would look like /**C**~{**DOWN**}~. The macro duplicates the following steps.

1. After you have moved to the cell from which to copy you would type /**C** to call the **C**opy command.
2. The default FROM range shown would be that single cell, so the Enter key would be pressed (~).
3. The default TO range next shown also would be that cell, but it can be changed by pointing to the appropriate TO range. To do so you would type the "down" pointer control key once. To represent the keystroke in a macro, you enter {**DOWN**}.
4. The default TO range shown then would be the cell that the pointer indicates (the cell below the original cell), so the Enter key would be pressed (~).

The following table lists the macro commands for special keystrokes and the keyboard equivalents which they represent within a macro. The pointer movement commands and editing commands also may include a number indicating that the command is to be repeated several times. For example, {**DOWN 3**} would be equivalent to {**DOWN**} {**DOWN**} {**DOWN**}.

Macro Keyboard Equivalent Commands

Command	Keyboard Equivalent
Function Keys	
{**EDIT**}	F2
{**NAME**}	F3
{**ABS**}	F4
{**GOTO**}	F5
{**WINDOW**}	F6
{**QUERY**}	F7
{**TABLE**}	F8
{**CALC**}	F9
{**GRAPH**}	F10
Pointer Movement Keys	
{**UP**}	↑
{**DOWN**}	↓
{**LEFT**}	←
{**RIGHT**}	→
{**PGUP**}	PgUp
{**PGDN**}	PgDn
{**BIGLEFT**}	Shift-Tab
{**BIGRIGHT**}	Tab
{**HOME**}	Home
{**END**}	End
Editing Keys	
{**DEL**} or {**DELETE**}	Del
{**ESC**} or {**ESCAPE**}	Esc
{**BS**} or {**BACKSPACE**}	Backspace key
~	Enter key ↵
{~}	Tilde character
{{ } and { }}	Brace characters

Interactive Macros

{**?**} is a unique macro command. It may be used to suspend the execution of a macro in order to allow the user to type in spreadsheet data, to answer command prompts, or to move the spreadsheet pointer. In the following example, a macro has been designed to /**R**ange,**F**ormat any range of cells to display Currency format with two decimal places.

```
/RFC2~{?}~
```

To use the macro you first move to the beginning of the range to be formatted, and then invoke the macro with the Alt-letter key combination. The macro calls the /**R**ange,**F**ormat,**C**urrency command and specifies 2 decimal places. The pointer is automatically anchored. The {**?**} command then suspends the execution of the macro to let you move the pointer to the end of the range to be formatted (point to the range). When you are finished, you type the Enter key to signal your completion. The macro will continue executing where it left off. The final ~ in the macro is used to Enter the range you have pointed to.

BUILDING A MACRO LIBRARY

The macros discussed here so far are simple, general purpose macros that could be useful in any spreadsheet. As you continue to use Lotus you will identify sets of keystrokes that you use often, and you may want to create a library or collection of macros to use in each of your spreadsheets. The following procedure may be used to create a single set of general purpose macros, which may then be combined into any of your spreadsheets.

You begin by creating and testing your set of macros within an existing spreadsheet. In the following example, five macros have been put in a well-documented area of a spreadsheet.

```
     AA          AB                    AC          AD         AE          AF
1
2          Spreadsheet Macros
3   ---------------------------------------------------------------------------
4   Name Macro                        Description
5
6    \D  /FS~R/QY                     Save/update spreadsheet and exit 1-2-3
7
8    \C  /C~{?}~                      Copy current cell into any cell by
9                                     pointing
10
11   \M  /RFC2~{?}~                   Format $xx,xxx.xx range beginning
12                                    at current cell
13
14   \B  /RE~                         Erase the current cell
15
16   \P  /PPOML10~~R132~S\015~QQ      Print macro -
17                                    Set Margins Left = 10, Right = 132
18                                    Setup string - condensed (Epson)
19
```

The macro names have been entered as labels into the AA column; the actual macros have been entered into the AB column; and a short description of each macro has been entered in the AC column. The macros in the AB column must be separated from each other by blank cells.

Using the /File,Xtract Command

Once you have entered and documented this area of the spreadsheet (AA2..AC18), it may be saved as its own file by using the /**F**ile,**X**tract command. In the example, the spreadsheet macro area might be saved under the name MACLIB. The command would be

/**F**ile,**X**tract,**F**ormulas or **V**alues
    Enter xtract file name: A:\MACLIB
    Enter xtract range: AA2..AC18

NOTE: An Xtracted file may have its formulas converted to constants (Values) or left intact (Formulas). Since this area of the spreadsheet is all labels, it doesn't matter which option is selected.

When the **X**tract operation is complete, the macro area of the spreadsheet will be saved on the disk in its own .WK1 file.

Using the /**F**ile,**C**ombine Command

When you start a new spreadsheet or when you want to have your library of macros available within an existing spreadsheet, you may use the /**F**ile,**C**ombine command to read the macro library file (MACLIB.WK1) into the current spreadsheet. The command will copy it into any location you desire. Here the macros will be read into the current spreadsheet at the cell address A100.

The first step in combining a .WK1 file from the disk into a current file is to move the spreadsheet pointer to the upper left corner of the desired range location for the incoming spreadsheet data. In the example the pointer would be moved to cell A100. The command then would be

/**F**ile,**C**ombine,**C**opy,**E**ntire-File
Enter name of file to combine: A:\MACLIB

When the operation is complete, the MACLIB spreadsheet will be combined with the current spreadsheet and its location will be A100..C116.

```
        A         B         C         D         E         F         G         H
99
100          Spreadsheet Macros
101  ---------------------------
102  Name    Macro     Description
103
104   \D     /FS~R/QY  Save/update spreadsheet and exit 1-2-3
105
106   \C     /C~{?}~   Copy current cell into any cell by
107                    pointing
108
109   \M     /RFC2~{?}Format $xx,xxx.xx range beginning
110                    at current cell
111
112   \B     /RE~      Erase the current cell
113
114   \P     /PPOML10~Print macro -
115                    Set Margins Left = 10, Right = 132
116                    Setup string - condensed (Epson)
117
```

Any range names that may have existed in the file being combined no longer exist after the **C**ombine operation. After combining your macro library into a spreadsheet, you need to again name each macro range in order for it to be used in the new spreadsheet.

Using the /**R**ange,**N**ame,**L**abels,**R**ight Command

If the macro names have been entered as labels into cells to the left of all macros, as in this example, the /**R**ange,**N**ame,**L**abels,**R**ight command may be used to name the macro cells. With the pointer located at cell A104, the top label, the command would be executed as follows.

/**R**ange,**N**ame,**L**abels,**R**ight
Enter label range: A104..A114

After this command has been executed, each of the labels in the range A104..A114 will be used to name the cell to its right.

A Macro to Name Macros

If the macros in your library are laid out differently, you may find it more convenient to include in your macro library a macro that, when executed, will name each of the other macros. You will still need to name this macro before it may be executed.

Several different designs for this macro exist. The macro shown at the bottom of this macro library works if the spreadsheet pointer is on the cell indicated when the macro is invoked. The manual steps required to name and then execute the macro have been included in the description area.

```
       A       B        C         D         E         F         G         H
102   Name    Macro    Description
103
104    \D     /FS~R/QY Save/update spreadsheet and exit 1-2-3
105
106    \C     /C~{?}~  Copy current cell into any cell by pointing
107
108    \M     /RFC2~{?}Format $xx,xxx.xx range beginning at current cell
109
110    \B     /RE~     Erase the current cell
111
112    \P     /PPOML10~~R132~S\015~QQ
113                    Print macro -
114                    Set Margins Left = 10, Right = 132
115                    Setup string - condensed (Epson)
116 pointer->  HERE
117    \S     {UP 4}/RNC\P~~     Macro to Name Ranges for Macros in Library
118           {UP 2}/RNC\B~~     1) Name the first cell in this macro \S
119           {UP 2}/RNC\M~~     2) Move the pointer to the cell marked HERE
120           {UP 2}/RNC\C~~     3) Type Alt-S
121           {UP 2}/RNC\D~~
```

HOW LOTUS EXECUTES A MACRO

Notice that the macro to name macros is several cells deep and that its range name names only the top cell of the macro. When a macro is invoked, Lotus begins executing the keystrokes in the named cell from left to right. When all the keystrokes in a cell have been executed, Lotus looks to the next cell down for further macro keystrokes. This continues until a blank cell (or the {**QUIT**} command) is encountered, causing execution of the macro to stop. An interesting implication of this is that a cell within a macro can also be named as a different macro, which can then be used to execute only the portion of the larger macro from that cell down (a macro within a macro).

A MENU OF MACROS—THE {**MENUBRANCH**} COMMAND

One of Lotus's special macro commands, the {**MENUBRANCH**} command, allows one macro to display a menu of eight different macros. Any of the macros in the menu then may be invoked through a menu selection process almost identical to Lotus's command selection process. To demonstrate the use of the {**MENUBRANCH**} command, the separate macros used so far will be incorporated into a menu.

The Structure of a Menu Range

The overall design of a menu range is as follows.

row 1 →	first selection	second selection	third selection
row 2 →	first description	second description	third description
row 3 →	commands	commands	commands

The menu range may be defined to include all selections, descriptions, and commands. It also may be defined as only the cell containing the first selection. Lotus then will automatically use up to seven additional cells to the right of the first until a blank cell is encountered. The cell immediately below each menu selection is used for a longer label describing the menu selection. The cell below each description is where the commands for that selection begin.

An Example of a Menu Macro

To demonstrate the basic menu range structure, a macro named \M (cell B103) will hold the single command {**MENUBRANCH** MENU1} which tells Lotus to present the menu located at the range named MENU1 (cell B107).

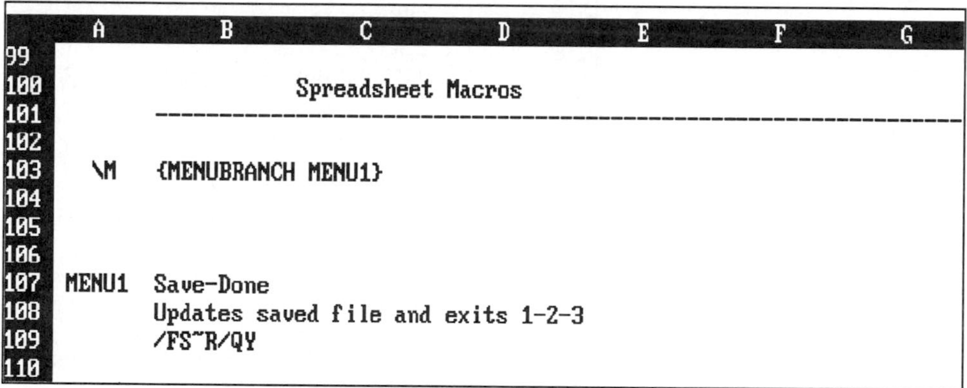

Invoking the Menu Macro

When the \M macro is executed from anywhere in the spreadsheet, the top of the screen now will display the Macro Menu named MENU1 as follows.

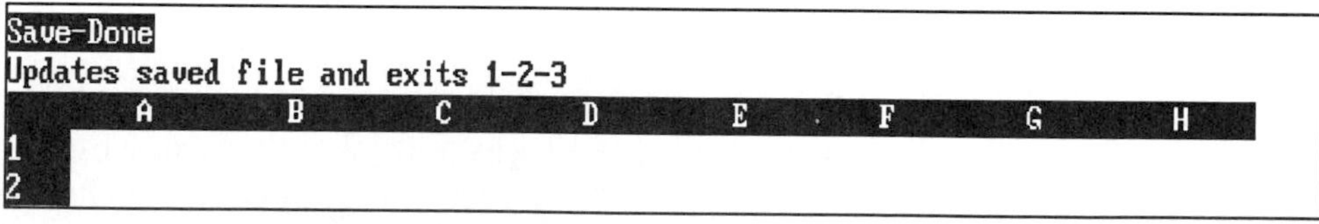

If you press the Enter key or the first letter of the menu selection, **S,** the macro keystrokes /**FS**~**R**/**QY** will be executed.

Adding Menu Options

To expand the example, the macro commands to copy a single cell into any location (previously \C) will be added to the menu range.

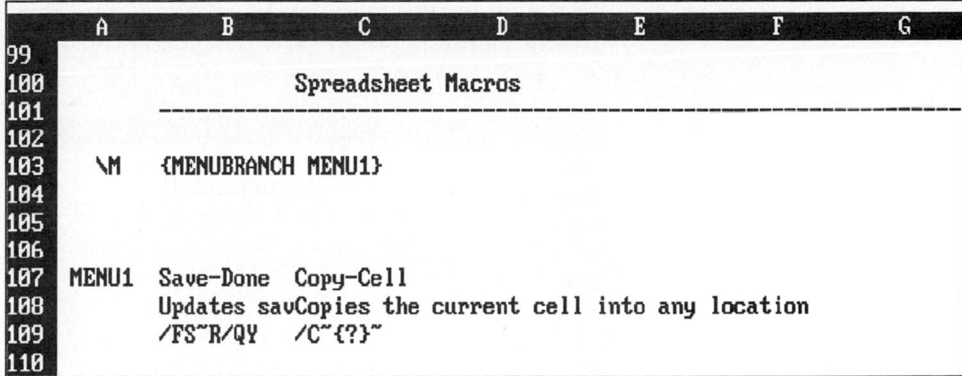

Entering the description for the new command stops the description for the first command from extending into that cell's area. If you wanted to view the first description again, you could move the pointer to that cell and the description would be displayed at the top of the screen.

Now when the \M macro is invoked, the first and second prompt lines of the spreadsheet will display

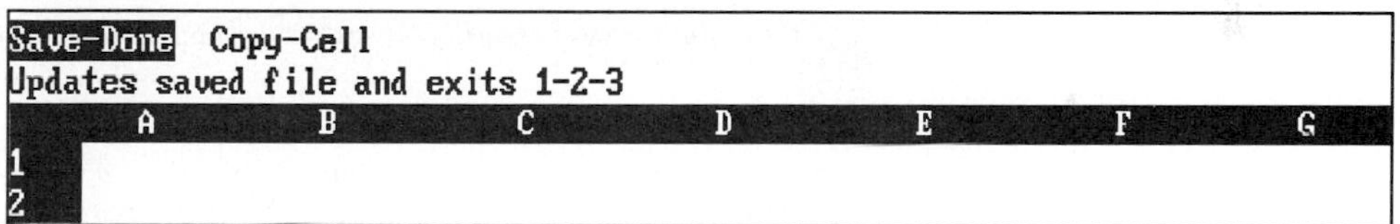

If you move the command pointer to the right it will display

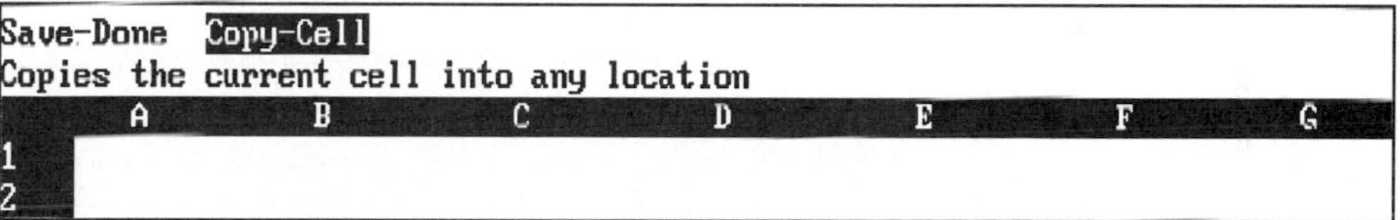

You now may select from the menu the macro commands to execute—either those to save and exit or those to copy a cell into any location. To select, either use the pointer and type the Enter key, or type the first character (**S** or **C**) of a selection. Since the first character may be typed, each menu selection should begin with a different character. The Ctrl-Break key combination may be used to return to the READY mode.

To complete the example, the entire macro library will be put into the following menu macro.

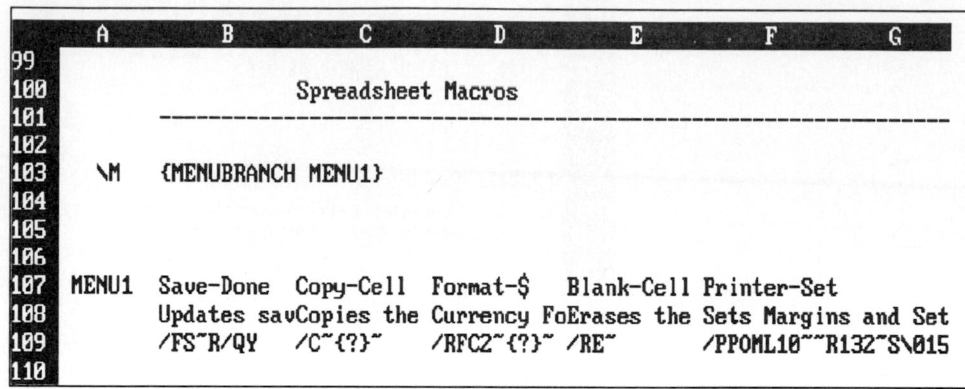

```
      A       B          C          D          E          F          G
99
100                         Spreadsheet Macros
101           ------------------------------------------------------------
102
103    \M     {MENUBRANCH MENU1}
104
105
106
107   MENU1   Save-Done  Copy-Cell  Format-$   Blank-Cell Printer-Set
108           Updates savCopies the Currency FoErases the Sets Margins and Set
109           /FS~R/QY   /C~{?}~    /RFC2~{?}~ /RE~       /PPOML10~~R132~S\015
110
```

Now when the Alt-M keys are typed, the screen displays

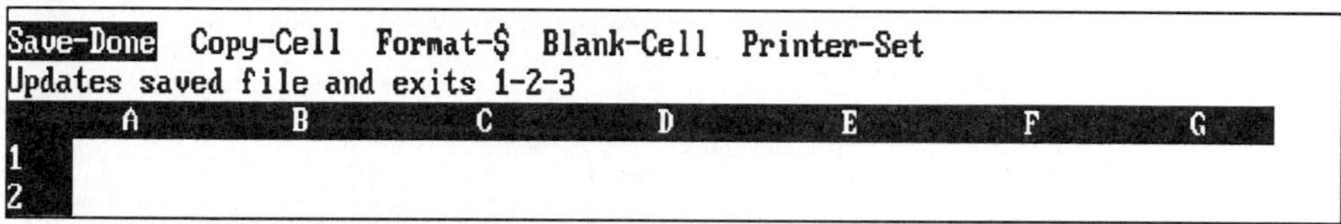

```
Save-Done  Copy-Cell  Format-$  Blank-Cell  Printer-Set
Updates saved file and exits 1-2-3
      A       B          C          D          E          F          G
1
2
```

You have created your own Lotus menu, complete with explanations for each command in it. It operates just like a spreadsheet menu of commands: each command shown invokes a macro you have written.

The {**MENUCALL**} Command

Both the {**MENUBRANCH**} and {**MENUCALL**} commands pass control to the menu found in the location specified by the command. If {**MENUBRANCH**} is used to call the menu, macro execution will not return to the calling macro unless another command directs it to do so. However, if {**MENUCALL**} is used to call a menu, after the menu selection is made and its commands have been executed, macro execution will return to the macro that called the menu, beginning with the command following the {**MENUCALL**} command.

The following is an example of using {**MENUCALL**} for the same menu as in the previous example.

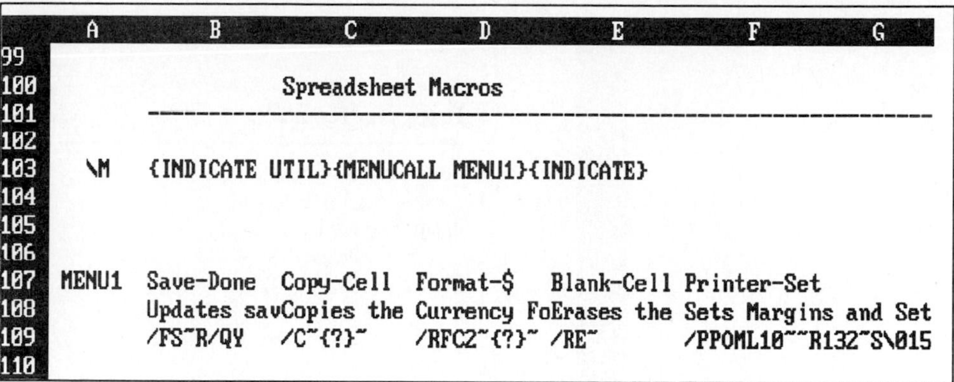

In the macro shown here, the {**INDICATE** UTIL} command is used before executing the menu to cause the indicator in the top right corner of the screen to display UTIL (for utilities) while the menu is being displayed. This might be useful to differentiate menus you have created from the normal Lotus menus. However, once executed, the indicator will continue to display UTIL until another command is executed to change it.

To return the indicator to its normal displays (READY, MENU, POINT, etc.), the {**INDICATE**} command must be executed without a string argument. As an alternative to placing this command at the end of each set of macro commands in the menu, it is placed after the {**MENUCALL**} command. This causes the command to be executed after the menu has been called, regardless of which menu option is selected.

ADVANCED MACRO COMMANDS

If you have computer programming experience, you may have noticed similarities between the macros discussed so far and writing programs using a programming language such as BASIC. In fact, macros are a type of spreadsheet programming language and the similarities become more apparent when advanced macro commands are discussed.

The macro commands discussed in this section are treated as advanced commands since their use requires some understanding of the principles of programming. The commands will be presented by using an example macro that will be built up as new commands are discussed. The macro will be designed to assist in data entry for the following spreadsheet area.

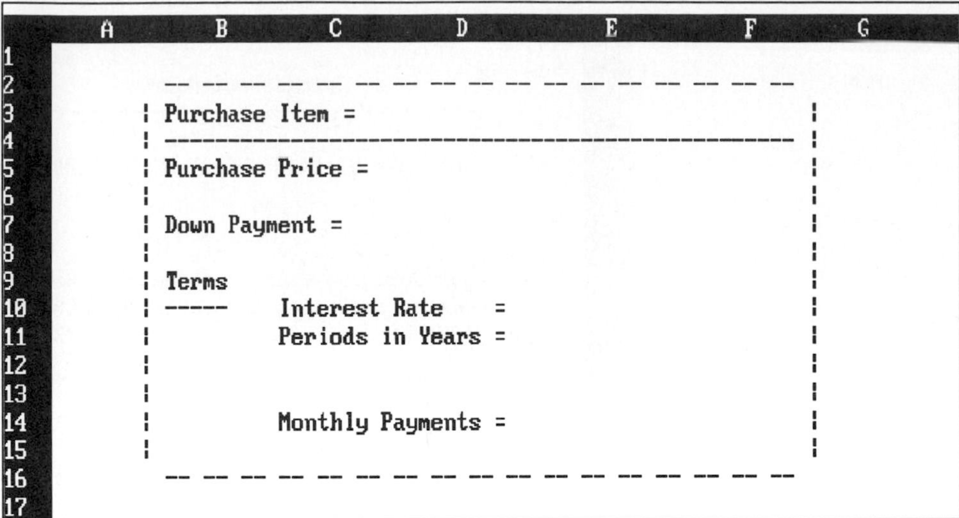

In a separate portion of the spreadsheet, the following macro will be created.

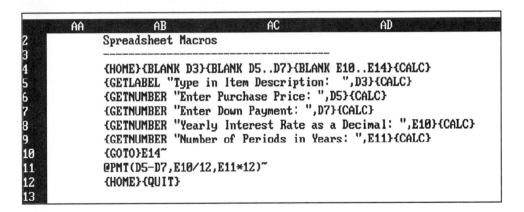

```
      AA      AB                         AC                        AD
2             Spreadsheet Macros
3             ------------------------------------
4             {HOME}{BLANK D3}{BLANK D5..D7}{BLANK E10..E14}{CALC}
5             {GETLABEL "Type in Item Description:  ",D3}{CALC}
6             {GETNUMBER "Enter Purchase Price: ",D5}{CALC}
7             {GETNUMBER "Enter Down Payment: ",D7}{CALC}
8             {GETNUMBER "Yearly Interest Rate as a Decimal: ",E10}{CALC}
9             {GETNUMBER "Number of Periods in Years: ",E11}{CALC}
10            {GOTO}E14~
11            @PMT(D5-D7,E10/12,E11*12)~
12            {HOME}{QUIT}
13
```

The {**BLANK**} Command

The macro begins by moving the pointer to the Home position and erasing all of the data entry cells it will use when it is executed (which is essentially the same as initializing variables in a BASIC program). The {**BLANK**} command is used to perform a /**R**ange,**E**rase without having to move the cursor. After the {**HOME**} command is used to move the pointer to the Home position, the {**BLANK** range} command is used to erase the ranges where new data is to be entered.

The {**GETNUMBER**} and {**GETLABEL**} Commands

The {**GETNUMBER** "message",range} and {**GETLABEL** "message",range} commands are used to display a message (prompt) on the first prompt line of the spreadsheet. They then wait for the user to enter a response, and the response is copied into the cell at the upper left corner of the range specified in the command. If the response is intended to be a string value, the {**GET-LABEL**} command is used; if it is intended to be a numeric value, the {**GETNUMBER**} command is used.

When the {**GETLABEL**} command is executed, its prompt is presented at the top prompt line of the spreadsheet.

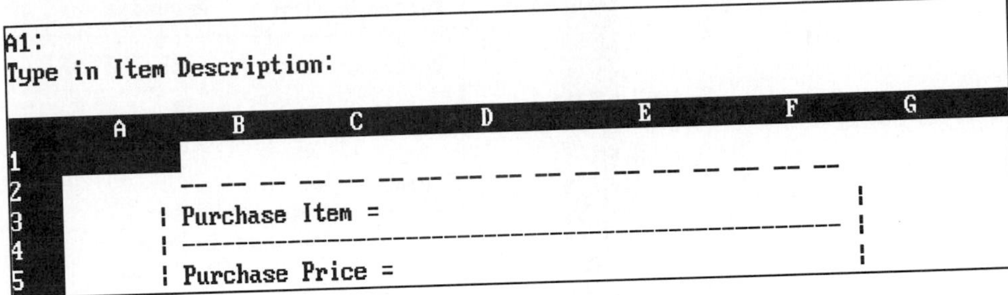

A label describing the item being considered for purchase is then typed in. After the Enter key is pressed, the label is copied into the cell D3. The commands {**GETLABEL**} and {**GETNUMBER**} must be followed by the {**CALC**} command in order for entries to appear while the macro is being executed. The next command, {**GETNUMBER** "Enter Purchase Price: ",D5}, is then executed.

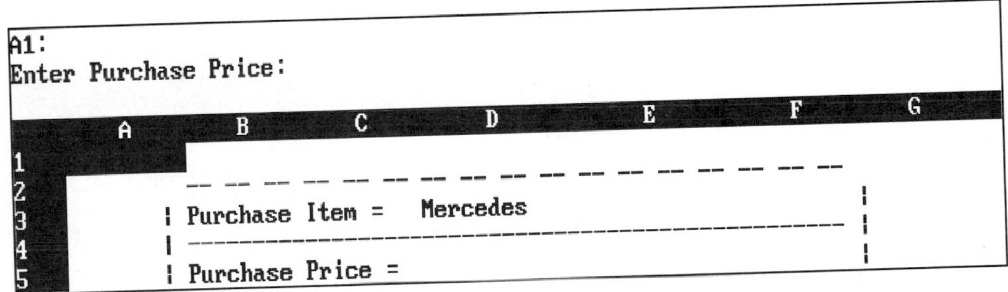

The macro continues to present prompts, accept data, and copy that data to the appropriate cells until the command {**GOTO**}E14~@**PMT**(D5-D7,E10/12,E11*12)~ is reached. This command causes the pointer to move to cell E14 and enter the @**PMT** function to calculate monthly payments, given the data provided by the user.

The {**QUIT**} Command

The {**QUIT**} command is used to stop execution of a macro. This command will be included in the example at various points in the macro's development.

When execution of the macro is completed, the spreadsheet will appear similar to the following.

```
       A        B         C          D          E          F          G
1
2             -- -- -- -- -- -- -- -- -- -- -- -- -- -- -- -- --
3          ! Purchase Item =   Mercedes                              !
4          ! ----------------------------------------------------    !
5          ! Purchase Price =   $45,000.00                           !
6          !                                                         !
7          ! Down Payment =     $10,000.00                           !
8          !                                                         !
9          ! Terms                                                   !
10         ! -----      Interest Rate    =          18.00%           !
11         !            Periods in Years =               4           !
12         !                                                         !
13         !                                                         !
14         !            Monthly Payments =       $1,028.12           !
15         !                                                         !
16            -- -- -- -- -- -- -- -- -- -- -- -- -- -- -- -- --
17
```

The example macro now will be expanded to include conditional execution of a subroutine if the monthly payment calculated is greater than $200. The modified macro is shown here.

```
        AA          AB                      AC                     AD
2                Spreadsheet Macros
3                ------------------------------------
4                {HOME}{BLANK D3}{BLANK D5..D7}{BLANK E10..E14}{CALC}
5                {GETLABEL "Type in Item Description:  ",D3}{CALC}
6                {GETNUMBER "Enter Purchase Price: ",D5}{CALC}
7                {GETNUMBER "Enter Down Payment: ",D7}{CALC}
8                {GETNUMBER "Yearly Interest Rate as a Decimal: ",E10}{CALC}
9                {GETNUMBER "Number of Periods in Years: ",E11}{CALC}
10               {GOTO}E14~
11               @PMT(D5-D7,E10/12,E11*12)~
12               {IF E14>200}{EXCESS}
13               {HOME}{QUIT}
14
15      EXCESS   {GOTO}C17~EXCESSIVE PAYMENT~
16               {GETLABEL "Press Enter to continue",C17}{BLANK C17}
17
```

The {**IF**} Command

The {**IF** condition} command is the conditional macro command. When Lotus encounters the {**IF**} command, it evaluates the logical expression specified as the command's condition. If the condition is evaluated as true, the rest of the commands in the same cell are executed. If the condition is evaluated as false, execution of the macro resumes at the next cell down.

In the example, cell AB12 holds the command {**IF** E14>200}. When the command is executed, if the expression E14>200 is evaluated as true, the subroutine EXCESS is called with the {routine-name} command found in the same cell; otherwise, execution continues with the {**HOME**} {**QUIT**} commands in the next cell down.

The {routine-name} Command

The {routine-name} command is used to execute a subroutine. A subroutine is simply another range where macro commands are located. The range is named with the /**R**ange,**N**ame,**C**reate command. During macro execution, when the range name is encountered in a {routine-name} command, the commands in the subroutine will be executed before subsequent commands in the calling macro are executed.

In the example, cell AB15 has been given the range name EXCESS, and the commands beginning there are executed if the {**IF** condition} in the calling macro is evaluated as true. The subroutine displays a message indicating that the payment is too high and then erases the message when the Enter key is pressed. Now if the same values used in the previous example are entered, the screen will appear as follows after the payment is calculated.

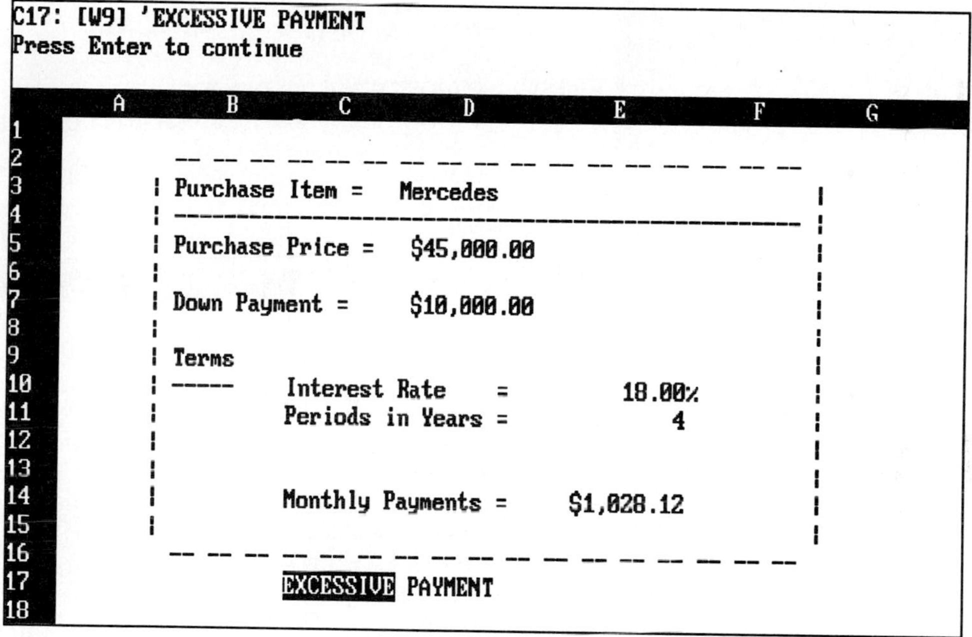

The last modification to the macro will be to include options to repeat the process for another set of values, to print the form, or to quit. The modified macro appears as follows.

```
AD13:                                                              READY

       AA          AB                  AC                AD
2              Spreadsheet Macros
3              ---------------------------------------
4              {HOME}{BLANK D3}{BLANK D5..D7}{BLANK E10..E14}{CALC}
5              {GETLABEL "Type in Item Description:  ",D3}{CALC}
6              {GETNUMBER "Enter Purchase Price: ",D5}{CALC}
7              {GETNUMBER "Enter Down Payment: ",D7}{CALC}
8              {GETNUMBER "Yearly Interest Rate as a Decimal: ",E10}{CALC}
9              {GETNUMBER "Number of Periods in Years: ",E11}{CALC}
10             {GOTO}E14~
11             @PMT(D5-D7,E10/12,E11*12)~
12             {IF E14>200}{EXCESS}
13             {MENUBRANCH CONT}
14
15    EXCESS   {GOTO}C17~EXCESSIVE PAYMENT~
16             {GETLABEL "Press Enter to continue",C17}{BLANK C17}
17
18     CONT    Continue            Print form          Quit
19             Enter another set   Print the form shoDone entering data
20             {BRANCH AB4}        /PPRA1..G17~AGQ     {HOME}{QUIT}
21                                 {MENUBRANCH CONT}
```

The {**BRANCH**} and {**MENUBRANCH**} Commands

The {**MENUBRANCH**} command at the end of the original macro (cell AB13) is used to send macro execution to the menu located at cell AB18 (range name CONT). The menu has three options: Continue, Print form, and Quit. If Continue is selected, the {**BRANCH**} command is used to send control back to the beginning of the original macro (cell AB4). If Print form is selected, keystrokes to print the range comprising the data entry form are executed and then another {**MENUBRANCH**} command is executed to repeat the same menu. If the Quit option is selected, the commands to end the macro are executed.

When the macro is executed, and all the values have been entered, the screen will appear as follows.

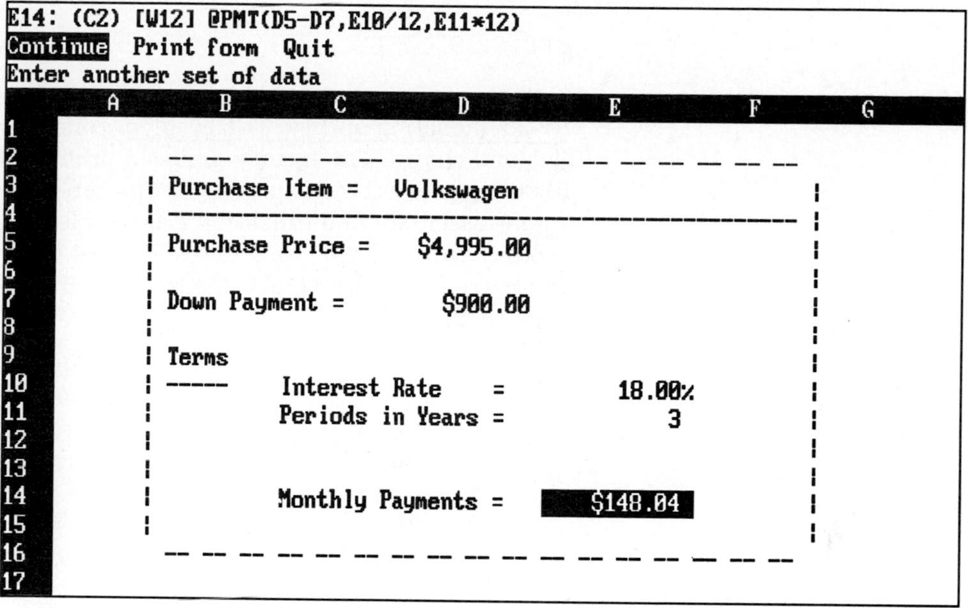
```
E14: (C2) [W12] @PMT(D5-D7,E10/12,E11*12)
Continue  Print form  Quit
Enter another set of data
        A        B         C          D           E          F         G
1
2            -- -- -- -- -- -- -- -- -- -- -- -- -- -- -- -- --
3          | Purchase Item =   Volkswagen                         |
4          | -------------------------------------------------   |
5          | Purchase Price =    $4,995.00                        |
6          |                                                      |
7          | Down Payment =        $900.00                        |
8          |                                                      |
9          | Terms                                                |
10         | -----      Interest Rate    =          18.00%        |
11         |            Periods in Years =              3         |
12         |                                                      |
13         |                                                      |
14         |            Monthly Payments =      $148.04           |
15         |                                                      |
16           -- -- -- -- -- -- -- -- -- -- -- -- -- -- -- -- --
17
```

EXERCISES

EXERCISE 1
What If?

Required Preparation

Study the section titled *Spreadsheet Design* (pages L-50–L-56).

Exercise Steps

A classic management problem will be used here to demonstrate Lotus 1-2-3's modeling ability. The problem concerns a factory that produces tables and chairs. The factory makes a profit of $8.00 for every table and $6.00 for every chair it produces. The production process involves two operations—assembly and finishing. Each table takes 4 hours to assemble and 2 hours to finish. Each chair takes 2 hours to assemble and 4 hours to finish. There are 60 total assembly hours and 48 total finishing hours available per week in the factory.

1. Design a spreadsheet to determine how many tables and chairs per week the company should make to maximize profits. The spreadsheet should contain two cells (one for tables and one for chairs) into which you will enter "best guess" numbers (the number of tables and number of chairs, respectively, that should be produced each week). The rest of the spreadsheet should display the number of assembly and finishing hours left available in the week, and the dollar profits expected, based on the two current best guess numbers. Be sure to separate all key values from formulas in the spreadsheet.
2. Load Lotus 1-2-3 and then create the spreadsheet to determine the solution to the problem posed in part 1. Note that the number of assembly and/or finishing hours left available in the week cannot be negative.

Management is considering a change in production of its tables that would increase the assembly time to 6 hours per table. However, the change also would increase profits to $10.00 per table. Write down the answers to the following questions.

3. To maximize profits, should management make the change to the production of its tables?
4. How much profit must management make per table to achieve the same profits as before?
5. What impact would the change have on the efficient use of the available assembly and finishing times per week?
6. Return the spreadsheet to the original set of assumptions (4 hours assembly, $8.00 profit per table).

Another suggestion has been made that would increase the total assembly time to 68 hours and the total finishing time to 58 hours per week. However, the changes would cost $.50 in profits for both tables and chairs (profits/table = $7.50, profits/chair = $5.50).

7. Under the assumptions above, how many tables and chairs should be manufactured per week in order to maximize profits?
8. Do the changes to assembly and finishing times increase net profits for the factory?
9. What impact would the change have on the efficient use of the available assembly and finishing times per week?

10. Save the spreadsheet under the name PRODMOD (production model), print the spreadsheet, and then exit the spreadsheet software with the /Quit command.

EXERCISE 2 Meat and Cheese Portions

Required Preparation

Study the section titled *Spreadsheet Design* (pages L-50–L-56).

Exercise Steps

This exercise concerns a fast-food restaurant that specializes in Mexican-American food. One element of cost/quality control in such a restaurant involves the amount of meat and cheese used when a food item is assembled by kitchen employees (food portioning). The following table describes the various food items and the amounts of meat and cheese that should be included in them.

Item	Meat	Cheese	Price
Taco	2 oz	.5 oz	.89
Burrito	4 oz	1.0 oz	1.89
Enchilada	3 oz	.75 oz	1.29
Tostado	2 oz	.5 oz	.89
Tamale	3 oz	.75 oz	1.39

The restaurant uses a point-of-sale cash register that produces a tape at the end of the week listing the total units sold of each item. Management takes a physical inventory at the beginning of each week and keeps track of any meat or cheese shipments that arrive during the week. By comparing the weekly inventories, management is able to determine how much meat and cheese were actually used. The register tape and portion tables are used to determine how much meat and cheese should have been used. The management wants the total cost of the meat used in a week to amount to 16.5% of item sales for the week. Similarly, it wants the cost of cheese to be close to 6.5% of sales. At the end of each week, management wants a report that shows the actual pounds of meat and cheese used compared against the amounts that should have been used, with the difference (variance) in pounds shown. It also wants the report to include the actual meat/cheese cost percentages for the week shown. The following information may be used to create and test the spreadsheet.

Meat Information

Cost	$1.19/lb
Beginning Amount	550 lbs
Shipments:	
Tuesday	350 lbs
Thursday	295 lbs
Ending Amount	500 lbs

Cheese Information

Cost	$1.87/lb
Beginning Amount	215 lb
Shipments:	
Wednesday	290 lbs
Ending Amount	305 lbs

Sales Information

Item	Units Sold
Tacos	2067
Burritos	789
Enchiladas	507
Tostados	150
Tamales	308

1. Use paper and pencil to map out (design) a spreadsheet template for the restaurant.
2. Load Lotus 1-2-3 and then enter the data and commands necessary to create the spreadsheet template.
3. Save the template under the name "FOODCOST" and then print the spreadsheet.
4. Enter the week's sample data and then print the spreadsheet again.
5. Save the spreadsheet again under the name "WEEK1" and then exit the spreadsheet software with the /**Q**uit command.

EXERCISE 3 Payment Schedules

Required Preparation

Study the @**PMT** function in the section on Financial functions (pages L-61–L-64) and the @**CHOOSE** function in the section on Logical and Special functions (page L-75). See also the explanation of mixed references on page L-53, and the /**D**ata,**F**ill command in the Lotus Command Summary.

Exercise Steps

In this exercise you will create a table of monthly payments for a retail store that offers financing to its customers. The salespeople would like to have a printed copy of the tables to carry with them as they help customers in the showroom. Although they will have to calculate the payment for the exact price of an item, they would like a quick reference that gives the monthly payments their customers could expect, given a ballpark price within $50 to $100 of the actual price. Prices of merchandise that may be financed range from $200 to $10,000. Since the company changes its interest rates based upon a fluctuating prime rate, these schedules will have to be updated and reprinted periodically.

1. Leaving several rows for key entries at the top of a new spreadsheet, enter labels for the payment table with columns for financing periods of 12 months, 24 months, 36 months, and 48 months.

The table area should look similar to the following.

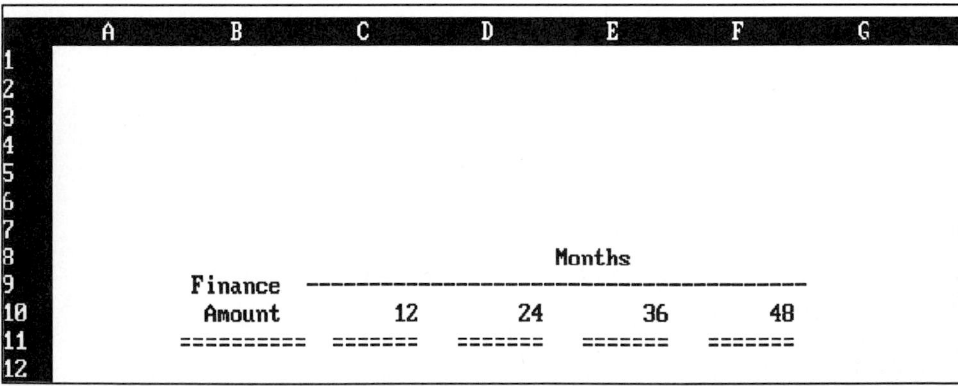

2. Use the /**D**ata,**F**ill command to create a list of finance amounts in the appropriately labeled column of the spreadsheet. The amounts from $200 to $1,000 should be listed at $50 intervals and those from $1,000 to $10,000 at $100 intervals.
3. Format the finance amounts to display as currency with 0 decimal places.
4. In the key area above the table, enter labels for the interest rate, stated as a monthly rate and an annual rate.
5. Enter the annual rate as 18% (.18) and the monthly rate as 1.5% (.015), and format these cells to display percentages with 2 decimal places.

The spreadsheet now should appear similar to the following.

	A	B	C	D	E	F	G
1							
2		Interest Rate					
3		==========	==========				
4		Monthly	Annual				
5		1.50%	18.00%				
6							
7							
8					Months		
9		Finance	----------	----------	----------	----------	
10		Amount	12	24	36	48	
11		==========	=======	=======	=======	=======	
12		$200					
13		$250					
14		$300					
15		$350					
16		$400					
17		$450					
18		$500					
19		$550					
20		$600					

By using an absolute reference and two mixed references in the arguments of the @PMT function, you should be able to enter the function into one cell in such a way that it then may be copied to all other cells in the table.

6. Now enter the **@PMT** function to calculate the payment for the upper left corner of the table ($200 financed for 12 months) using the appropriate interest rate.
7. Copy the cell with the **@PMT** function to all cells in the table area, and then format these cells to display currency with 2 decimal places.

The last two steps should result in a table displaying the following payment values.

	A	B	C	D	E	F	G
1							
2		Interest Rate					
3		====================					
4		Monthly	Annual				
5		1.50%	18.00%				
6							
7							
8					Months		
9		Finance	------------	------------	------------	------------	
10		Amount	12	24	36	48	
11		==========	=======	=======	=======	=======	
12		$200	$18.34	$9.98	$7.23	$5.87	
13		$250	$22.92	$12.48	$9.04	$7.34	
14		$300	$27.50	$14.98	$10.85	$8.81	
15		$350	$32.09	$17.47	$12.65	$10.28	
16		$400	$36.67	$19.97	$14.46	$11.75	
17		$450	$41.26	$22.47	$16.27	$13.22	
18		$500	$45.84	$24.96	$18.08	$14.69	
19		$550	$50.42	$27.46	$19.88	$16.16	
20		$600	$55.01	$29.95	$21.69	$17.62	

The key area now will be modified so that one of four different interest rates may be selected for the table. The annual interest rates are 15%, 18%, 21% and 24%. Someone using this spreadsheet should be able to enter a number from 1 to 4, respectively, to select one of these interest rates and then print a new rate schedule.

8. Modify the key area to include an @**CHOOSE** function so that one of the four interest rates may be selected.
9. Set the appropriate print range, add any special print formatting desired such as border rows or columns, and print the spreadsheet.
10. Save the spreadsheet under the name PMTSCHED.

EXERCISE 4 Employees Payroll

Required Preparation

Study the section titled Lotus 1-2-3 Functions (pages L-57–L-78).

Exercise Steps

In the following exercise several of the more commonly used functions will be introduced. The exercise concerns a small group of half-time and full-time employees who work at varying rates of pay.

1. Begin the exercise by entering the following data into the spreadsheet. Note that the labels across the top have been centered with the /**R**ange,**L**abel,**C**enter command, and that the dollar amounts in column E are formatted as currency with two decimal places. Also, use the

/Worksheet,Column,Set-Width command to make column D six characters wide and column E 11 characters wide.

A1: READY

	A	B	C	D	E	F	G	H
1								
2								
3	EMPLOYEE	LAST	FIRST	ALLOW	PAY			
4	STATUS	NAME	NAME	ANCES	RATES			
5								
6	HALF	Adams	Eric	0	$7.00			
7	FULL	Edwards	Carol	2	$12.65			
8	FULL	Hill	Bob	0	$7.50			
9	HALF	Johnson	Janet	1	$17.52			
10	FULL	Martin	Rebecca	0	$8.29			
11	FULL	Miller	Nancy	1	$8.01			
12	HALF	Parkison	Mark		$9.50			
13	FULL	Parsons	Larry	2	$7.86			
14	HALF	Randall	Cathy	1	$21.52			
15	HALF	Russell	Wesley	0	$16.83			
16	HALF	Smith	Jennie		$12.35			
17	FULL	Williams	Laurie	1	$8.90			
18								
19								
20								

17-May-90 09:51 PM

2. Now move the pointer to row 6 and fix the horizontal titles using the /Worksheet,Titles,Horizontal command.
3. Move the pointer to cell A20 and enter the following labels.

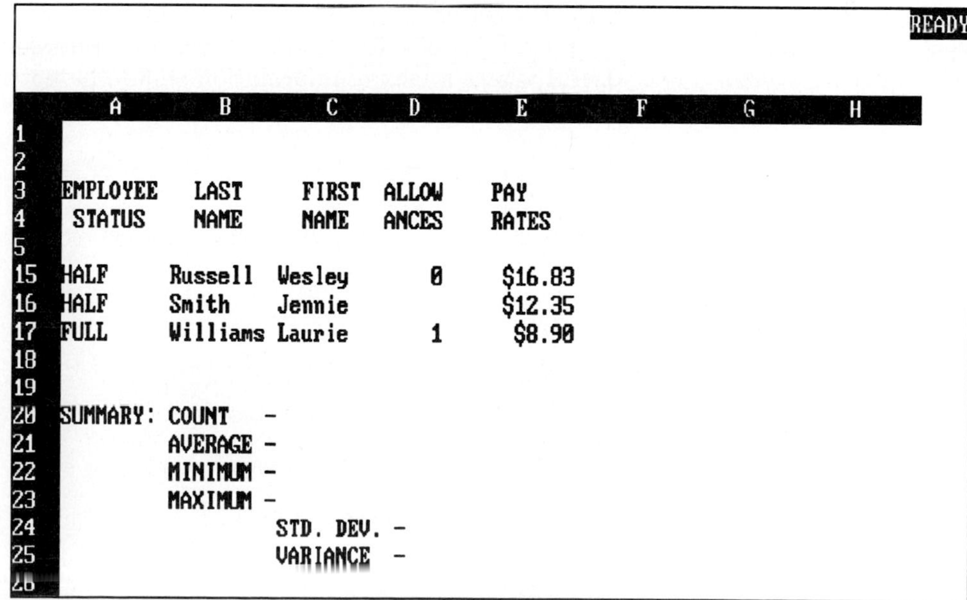

4. Move the pointer to cell C20 and enter an @**COUNT** function to count the number of employees (first names) contained in that column. Next copy the function into the next two cells to the right.

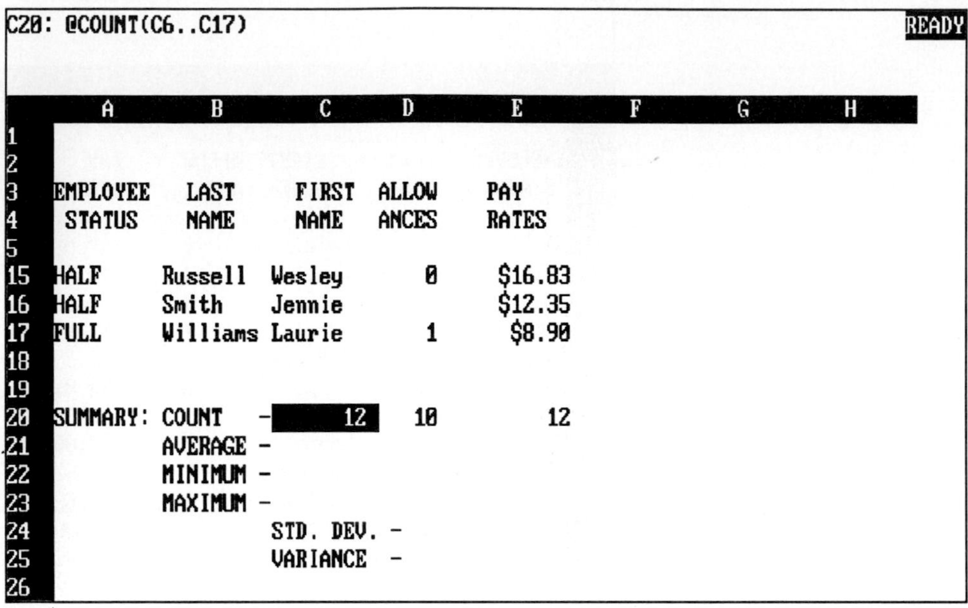

C20: @COUNT(C6..C17)
READY
A B C D E F G H
EMPLOYEE STATUS
LAST NAME
FIRST NAME
ALLOW ANCES
PAY RATES
HALF Russell Wesley 0 $16.83
HALF Smith Jennie $12.35
FULL Williams Laurie 1 $8.90
SUMMARY: COUNT - 12 10 12
AVERAGE -
MINIMUM -
MAXIMUM -
STD. DEV. -
VARIANCE -

Notice that the ALLOWANCES column shows a total of 10 entries, while the others show 12 each. The @**COUNT** function counts only the nonblank cells in the specified range.

5. Move to the lower of the two blank cells in the ALLOWANCES column and type ||@**NA**↵||.

Notice that the count for this column is now 11 and that cell D16 now contains the letters NA—which stands for "not available." The @**NA** function is an example of a function that uses no argument. This type of function is useful where a lack of information should be noted whenever the cell is referenced by a spreadsheet formula.

6. Move to the other blank cell in this column across from the name Mark Parkison and enter another @**NA** function. The SUMMARY area of the spreadsheet should now appear as follows.

```
D12: (G) [W6] @NA                                                  READY

      A        B         C       D        E        F        G        H
1
2
3  EMPLOYEE   LAST      FIRST   ALLOW     PAY
4   STATUS    NAME      NAME    ANCES     RATES
5
12 HALF      Parkison Mark         NA      $9.50
13 FULL      Parsons  Larry         2      $7.86
14 HALF      Randall  Cathy         1     $21.52
15 HALF      Russell  Wesley        0     $16.83
16 HALF      Smith    Jennie       NA     $12.35
17 FULL      Williams Laurie        1      $8.90
18
19
20 SUMMARY:  COUNT   -       12    12         12
21           AVERAGE -
22           MINIMUM -
23           MAXIMUM -
24                    STD. DEV. -
25                    VARIANCE  -
26
17-May-90   10:50 PM
```

You will be entering a number of functions which will use the pay rates found in column E, so it will save time if you now name that range.

7. Use the /**R**ange,**N**ame,**C**reate command to name this range (E6..E17) RATES, and then move to cell E21 and type ||@**AVG**(RATES)↵||.

The average pay rate of 11.4941666 should now appear in this cell.

8. To keep the spreadsheet easy to read, format the range D21..E25 to be fixed with 2 decimal places.
9. Now copy the @**AVG** function in cell E21 to cell D21.

You need to take note of two things: (1) when copied, the formula changed to read @**AVG**(D6..D17) (was copied in a relative fashion), and (2) the cell for average allowances now displays NA. Since one or more cells in the referenced range (D6..D17) contain an @**NA** function, the cell making the reference will display NA. This prevents the referencing cell from displaying possibly inaccurate information.

10. Now use the @**MIN**, @**MAX**, @**STD**, and @**VAR** functions to complete the SUMMARY portion of the spreadsheet. When finished, the area should appear as follows.

```
E25: (F2) [W11] @VAR(RATES)                                         READY

      A          B         C       D        E         F        G        H
1
2
3  EMPLOYEE    LAST      FIRST   ALLOW     PAY
4   STATUS     NAME      NAME    ANCES    RATES
5
20 SUMMARY: COUNT   -       12      12        12
21          AVERAGE -               NA     11.49
22          MINIMUM -               NA      7.00
23          MAXIMUM -               NA     21.52
24                    STD. DEV. -           4.56
25                    VARIANCE  -          20.82
26
```

11. Type the Home key and remove (clear) the titles fix. Next move the pointer to cell F4 and complete the following column labels. Note that the labels all use the ^ (Center) label prefix.

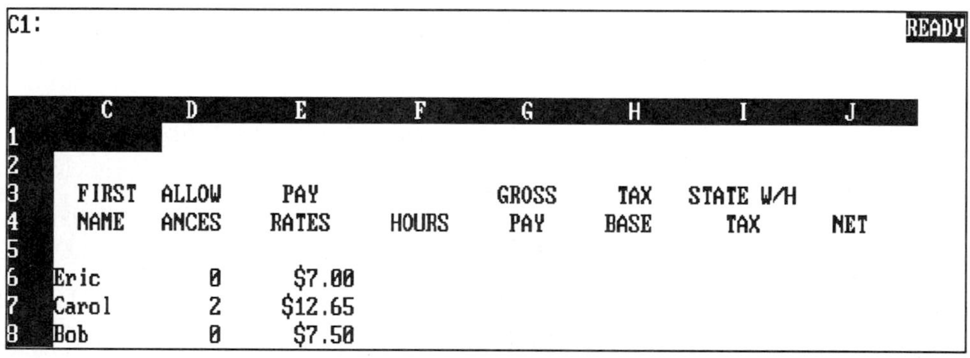

```
C1:                                                                  READY

      C        D        E        F        G        H         I        J
1
2
3   FIRST    ALLOW     PAY              GROSS     TAX    STATE W/H
4   NAME     ANCES    RATES    HOURS     PAY     BASE       TAX      NET
5
6  Eric         0     $7.00
7  Carol        2    $12.65
8  Bob          0     $7.50
```

Here all employees with a STATUS of HALF are half-time employees, and all others are full-time. A two-week payroll is being prepared, and all full-time employees have worked 80 hours, while half-time employees have worked 40 hours. To complete the HOURS column in the spreadsheet, the @**IF** function will be used.

The @**IF** function is used to evaluate a condition, and then return one value in the cell if the condition is true and another value if the condition is false. The @**IF** function has the form

@**IF**(condition, true value, false value)

The condition in the function may be any expression which can be evaluated as either true or false. An expression might be D6>1, D6=D10, or C3="FIRST". If the expression is evaluated as true, the true value will be displayed in the cell. If it is evaluated as false, the false value will appear in the cell.

12. Move to cell F6 and enter the @**IF** function that will test if the employee is half-time or not, and then return the number 40 if the em-

ployee is half-time or the number 80 if not. Next copy the formula into the remaining rows of the HOURS column.

A1: READY

	A	B	C	D	E	F	G	H
1								
2								
3	EMPLOYEE	LAST	FIRST	ALLOW	PAY		GROSS	TAX
4	STATUS	NAME	NAME	ANCES	RATES	HOURS	PAY	BASE
5								
6	HALF	Adams	Eric	0	$7.00	40		
7	FULL	Edwards	Carol	2	$12.65	80		
8	FULL	Hill	Bob	0	$7.50	80		
9	HALF	Johnson	Janet	1	$17.52	40		
10	FULL	Martin	Rebecca	0	$8.29	80		
11	FULL	Miller	Nancy	1	$8.01	80		
12	HALF	Parkison	Mark	NA	$9.50	40		
13	FULL	Parsons	Larry	2	$7.86	80		
14	HALF	Randall	Cathy	1	$21.52	40		
15	HALF	Russell	Wesley	0	$16.83	40		
16	HALF	Smith	Jennie	NA	$12.35	40		
17	FULL	Williams	Laurie	1	$8.90	80		
18								

13. Move to column G under the title GROSS PAY. Calculate the gross pay for the first employee and copy this formula (rate*hours) for the rest of the employees.

The next column (TAX BASE) will be calculated by using the following formula

$$\text{tax base} = \text{gross pay} - (42 * \text{number of allowances})$$

14. Move to cell H6 and enter the appropriate formula. Then copy it to the rest of the cells in the column.

A1: READY

	A	B	C	D	E	F	G	H
1								
2								
3	EMPLOYEE	LAST	FIRST	ALLOW	PAY		GROSS	TAX
4	STATUS	NAME	NAME	ANCES	RATES	HOURS	PAY	BASE
5								
6	HALF	Adams	Eric	0	$7.00	40	280	280
7	FULL	Edwards	Carol	2	$12.65	80	1012	928
8	FULL	Hill	Bob	0	$7.50	80	600	600
9	HALF	Johnson	Janet	1	$17.52	40	700.8	658.8
10	FULL	Martin	Rebecca	0	$8.29	80	663.2	663.2
11	FULL	Miller	Nancy	1	$8.01	80	640.8	598.8
12	HALF	Parkison	Mark	NA	$9.50	40	380	NA
13	FULL	Parsons	Larry	2	$7.86	80	628.8	544.8
14	HALF	Randall	Cathy	1	$21.52	40	860.8	818.8
15	HALF	Russell	Wesley	0	$16.83	40	673.2	673.2
16	HALF	Smith	Jennie	NA	$12.35	40	494	NA
17	FULL	Williams	Laurie	1	$8.90	80	712	670
18								

You next will use one of the LOOKUP functions, which are used for looking up values in a table. The function you will be using is **@VLOOKUP,** the vertical LOOKUP function. The format is

@VLOOKUP(valueX,range,offset)

where valueX is a number or string to be looked up in the first column of a table, the range is the location of the table itself, and the offset is the number of columns to the right of the first column in the table where the function finds the value to return.

15. Move to cell A34 and enter the appropriate labels and numbers for the area. Note that the values in column C have been formatted to display percentage notation with one decimal place.

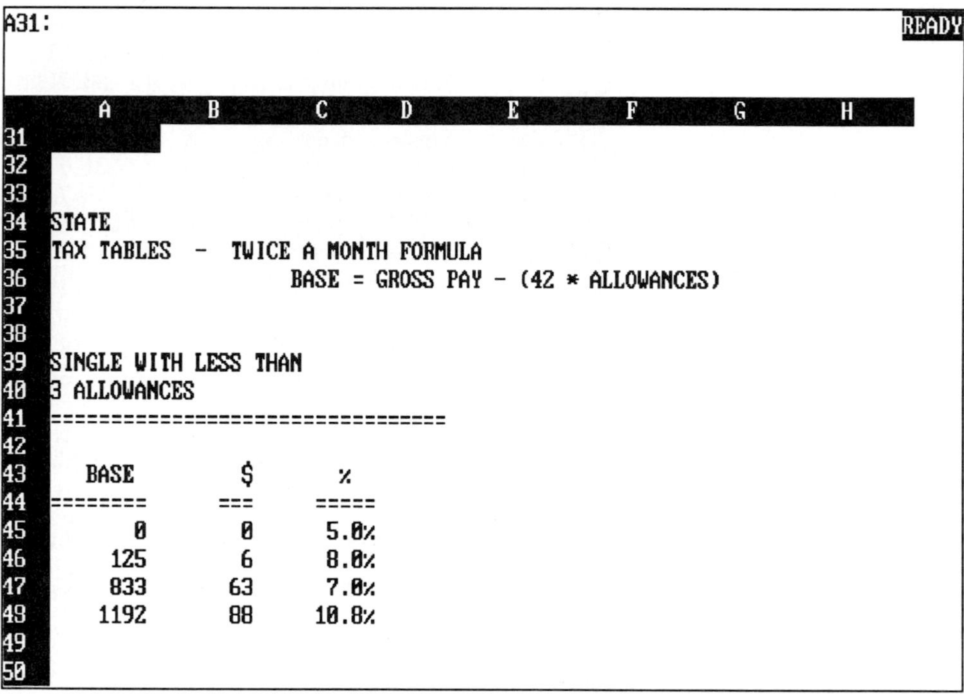

```
A31:                                                        READY
       A         B         C       D        E        F        G        H
31
32
33
34 STATE
35 TAX TABLES  -  TWICE A MONTH FORMULA
36                        BASE = GROSS PAY - (42 * ALLOWANCES)
37
38
39 SINGLE WITH LESS THAN
40 3 ALLOWANCES
41 ================================
42
43   BASE        $        %
44 ========     ===     =====
45        0       0      5.0%
46      125       6      8.0%
47      833      63      7.0%
48     1192      88     10.0%
49
50
```

16. Use the /**R**ange,**N**ame,**C**reate command to give the range A45..C48 the name TABLE.

The formula for computing an employee's state withholding tax will use the values from this table, based upon the tax base.

Consider the following example

@VLOOKUP(130,$TABLE,2)

There the **@VLOOKUP** function begins by looking up the value 130 in the right-most column of TABLE. Since the formula ultimately will be copied into other cells, the reference to TABLE has been made absolute by preceding the name with a dollar sign. The look up operation results in row 46 being identified as the appropriate row in the table from which to return a value. The final argument in the function (2) tells it to move 2 columns to the right and return the value found there. The displayed value of the example function here will be 8.0%.

The general formula for calculating the state withholding tax in this spreadsheet is

$ column + % column * (TAX BASE − BASE column)

You will use the **@VLOOKUP** function to return the appropriate values from the table in this formula, so the actual formula in your spreadsheet will have the following format.

@VLOOKUP(x,range,offset) + **@VLOOKUP**(x,range,offset)*(x − **@VLOOKUP**(x,range,offset))

In this formula the x value and the range will remain the same for all three functions. The offset, however, will change with each function. The x value you will be using is the employee's TAX BASE. The range will be $TABLE, where the $ designates the range as an absolute range so that it may be copied. The offsets must be entered so that the appropriate values from the table are placed in the formula.

17. Move to cell I6 under the label STATE W/H TAX. Type in the formula to calculate tax, according to the model above. (It may be helpful to split the screen into 2 windows with the /**W**orksheet,**W**indow,**H**orizontal command, and to set the windows to unsynchronized scrolling.)

The tax for the first employee should come to 18.4. If you don't get this answer, check your offset values against the table again. Once the formula has been correctly entered, copy it to the rest of the cells in this column.

C1: READY

	C	D	E	F	G	H	I	J
1								
2								
3	FIRST	ALLOW	PAY		GROSS	TAX	STATE W/H	
4	NAME	ANCES	RATES	HOURS	PAY	BASE	TAX	NET
5								
6	Eric	0	$7.00	40	280	280	18.4	
7	Carol	2	$12.65	80	1012	928	69.65	
8	Bob	0	$7.50	80	600	600	44	
9	Janet	1	$17.52	40	700.8	658.8	48.704	
10	Rebecca	0	$8.29	80	663.2	663.2	49.056	
11	Nancy	1	$8.01	80	640.8	598.8	43.904	
12	Mark	NA	$9.50	40	380	NA	NA	
13	Larry	2	$7.86	80	628.8	544.8	39.584	
14	Cathy	1	$21.52	40	860.8	818.8	61.504	
15	Wesley	0	$16.83	40	673.2	673.2	49.856	
16	Jennie	NA	$12.35	40	494	NA	NA	
17	Laurie	1	$8.90	80	712	670	49.6	
18								

The last column to be added to this worksheet will be the net pay amount. For the purposes of this example, the state tax will be the only deduction from gross pay. You may have noticed that some of the tax figures came out to three decimal places. When deducting this from gross pay, however, you will want to have this rounded off to a dollars and cents figure with just two decimal places. You will use the **@ROUND** function to do this. Its format is

@ROUND(value,places)

18. Move to cell J6 and enter a formula which will subtract the rounded tax figure from the gross pay. Copy this formula to the rest of the cells in the J column.

The final addition to this spreadsheet will be to add some dates. The function for entering a date value has the following format

@DATE(year,month,day)

For example, the date December 25, 1990 would be entered as @DATE(90,12,25)

19. Move the pointer to cell A1 and enter the label DATE:. Move to cell B1 and enter the **@DATE** function with the year, month, and date values for today's date.

A number should now appear in this cell; however, it will not look much like a date. The number is called a serial date and represents the number of days from December 31, 1899.

20. Change the format for this cell with the /**R**ange,**F**ormat,**D**ate command, and select the (DD-MMM) date format.
21. Move to cell D1 and type ||WEEK 1 ENDING:||, and then move to cell D2 and enter the label ||WEEK 2 ENDING:||. (Assume that the week-ending dates are always Fridays.)
22. In cell F2 enter a formula to calculate the date for the most recent Friday. This should be the value in cell B1 minus some number of days. After doing that, enter a formula in cell F1 that subtracts 7 days from the value in cell F2. Then use the /**R**ange,**F**ormat,**D**ate command to format both cells as (DD-MMM).
23. Save the spreadsheet under the name "PAYROLL," and then print the spreadsheet using condensed print. Then exit the spreadsheet software using the /**Q**uit command.

EXERCISE 5 Bar Graphs and Pie Charts

Required Preparation

Study the section titled Lotus 1-2-3 Graphics (pages L-79–L-95) and the /Graph commands presented in the Lotus 1-2-3 Command Summary.

Exercise Steps

1. Load Lotus 1-2-3, and then enter the data and commands necessary to create the following spreadsheet.

A1: [W12] READY

	A	B	C	D	E	F	G
1							
2		WESTERN REGIONAL SALES (Dollars in '000s)					
3							
4			1986	1987	1988	1989	1990
5							
6	TRUCKS	Units	362	420	504	601	632
7		Dollars	$5,068	$6,510	$8,568	$12,020	$13,904
8							
9	VANS	Units	120	166	132	110	94
10		Dollars	$1,680	$2,407	$1,980	$1,733	$1,551
11							
12	FULL SIZE	Units	140	231	350	475	550
13		Dollars	$2,030	$3,581	$6,300	$9,500	$12,650
14							
15	MID SIZE	Units	675	800	1,104	1,307	1,445
16		Dollars	$683	$7,600	$13,248	$18,298	$22,398
17							
18	COMPACTS	Units	1,685	1,469	1,046	918	1,005
19		Dollars	$7,583	$8,080	$6,276	$6,059	$7,035
20							

26-Apr-90 05:27 AM

You will next create a bar graph that displays the number of vehicle units sold for each category (TRUCKS through COMPACTS) over the years 1986 to 1990.

2. Use Lotus to create the following graph.

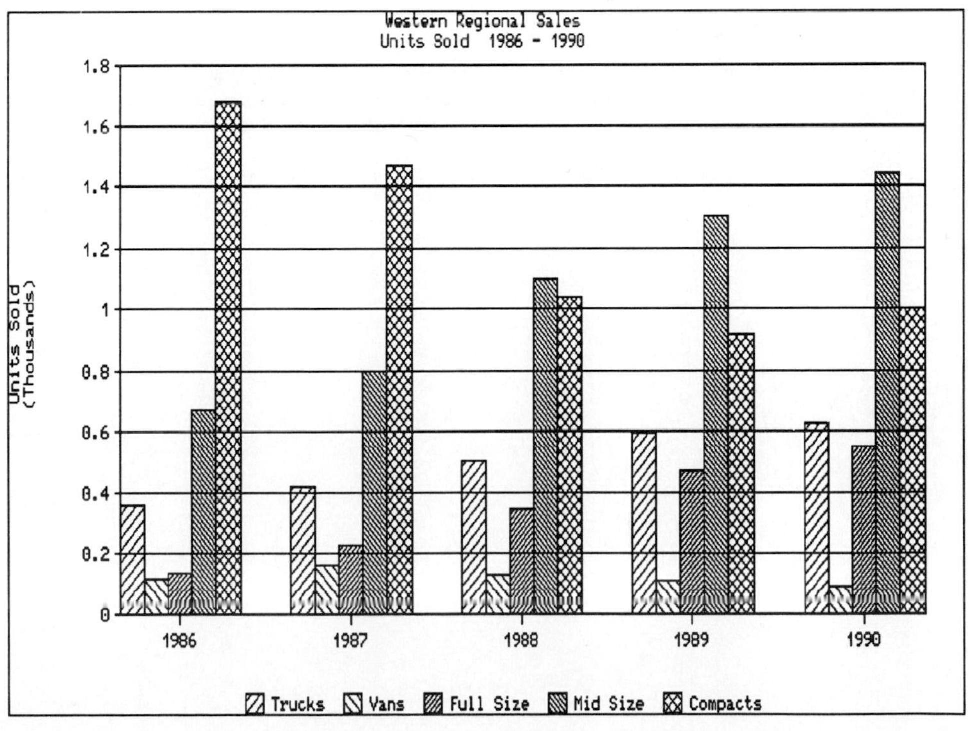

3. Use the /**G**raph,**N**ame command to create the name "UNITS" for the graph. Then use the /**G**raph,**R**eset command to reset all graph settings.

You next will create two pie charts designed to demonstrate the increase in sales for mid-size passenger automobiles for the period from 1986 to 1990. Before you set the data ranges to graph, however, you will need to modify the spreadsheet. Copy the necessary ranges of data to another place in the spreadsheet and make your modifications to the copied data.

4. Use Lotus to create the following pie chart.

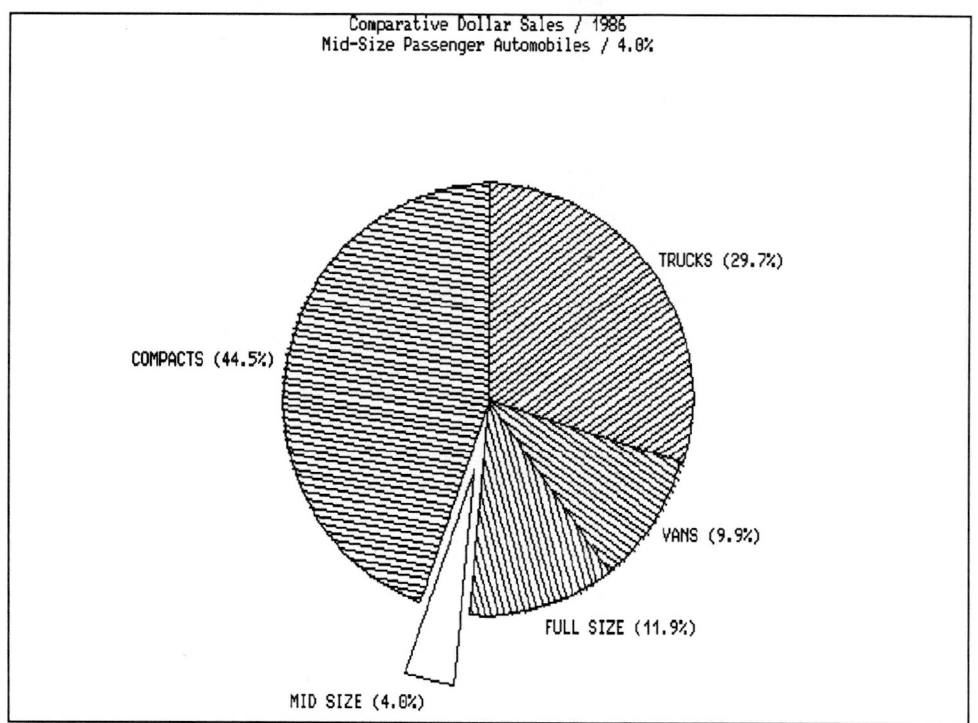

5. Name the graph “PIE1” and then create the next pie chart as shown here.

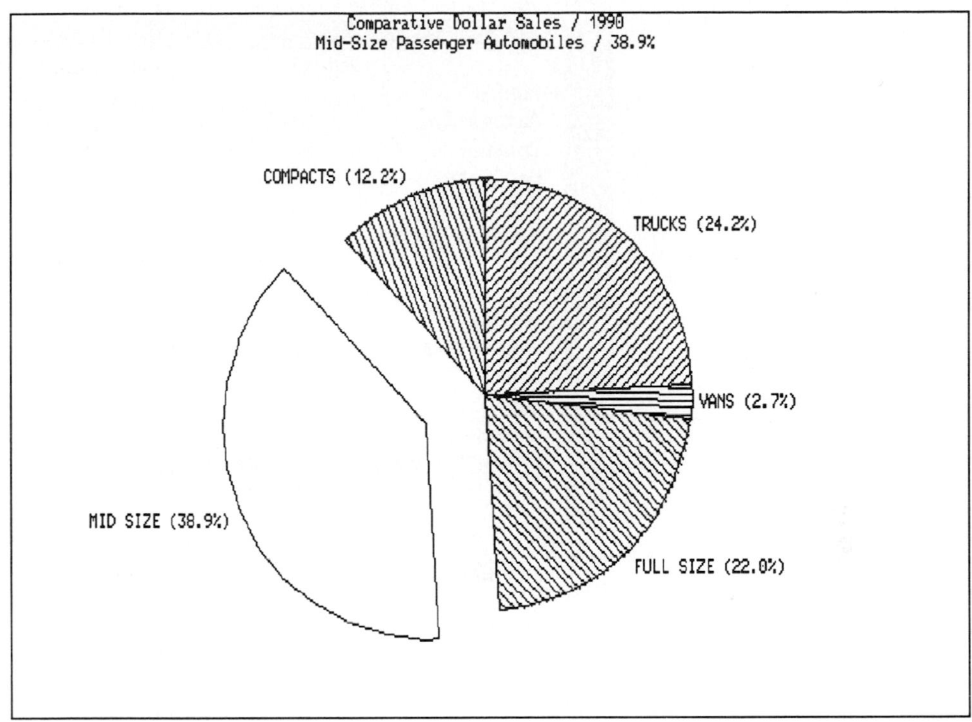

6. Name the second pie chart “PIE2” and then use the /**G**raph,**S**ave command to save each graph under the same name you used when you previously named them.
7. Save the spreadsheet under the name “GRAPH1” and then use the /**Q**uit command to exit the spreadsheet software.
8. Load the PGRAPH (PrintGraph) software and use its commands to print out each graph.

EXERCISE 6 Monthly Sales Projections

Required Preparation

Study the /**F**ile,**X**tract and /**F**ile,**C**ombine commands in the Lotus Command Summary. Also review the /**R**ange,**N**ame,**C**reate and /**R**ange,**N**ame,**D**elete commands.

Exercise Steps

In this exercise you will gain experience using Lotus's /**F**ile commands to extract and combine portions of a spreadsheet. This exercise involves a department store that projects sales on a monthly basis, and then compares the projected sales to actual sales. Management is concerned with the wide variances that occur monthly using their current method of projecting sales. It would like to review the figures for January, February, and March, as well as year-to-date figures for the end of February and March.

The following spreadsheet layout will be used for calculating variances for the three months for each of the five departments shown.

	A	B	C	D	E	F
1			Actual Sales	Projected	Variance ($)	Variance (%)
2	JANUARY					
3		Automotive	$101,519	$120,506		
4		General	$354,660	$326,417		
5		Hardware	$74,827	$76,250		
6		Housewares	$506,125	$575,064		
7		Plant & Garden	$55,965	$34,700		
8			----------	----------	----------	----------
9						
10	FEBRUARY					
11		Automotive	$126,898	$140,995		
12		General	$336,927	$408,021		
13		Hardware	$66,596	$70,912		
14		Housewares	$683,268	$661,319		
15		Plant & Garden	$41,973	$41,640		
16			----------	----------	----------	----------
17						
18	MARCH					
19		Automotive	$184,002	$184,278		
20		General	$411,405	$396,596		
21		Hardware	$87,906	$83,906		
22		Housewares	$611,524	$550,548		
23		Plant & Garden	$39,033	$48,580		
24			----------	----------	----------	----------

1. Begin by setting a global column width of 14 for the spreadsheet and a global format of Currency with 0 decimal places.
2. Set the width of column A to 2 characters.
3. Type in the labels and numeric sales figures as shown in the example.

The formulas for the two variance columns are as follows.

Dollar Variance = Actual Sales − Projected Sales
Percent Variance = Dollar Variance/Actual Sales

4. Enter the appropriate formulas to calculate the two variance values for the January automotive department sales figures. Then copy these formulas for all departments and months.
5. Now change the format for cells holding a percent variance to display as a percentage with 2 decimal places.
6. Enter the word "Total" as a right-aligned label in cells B9, B17, and B25.
7. Enter the appropriate function to calculate monthly totals of actual sales, projected sales, and dollar variances for all departments.

The total percentage variance for all departments is not a sum of the individual departments' percentage variances, but is calculated using the same formula that was used for the individual departments.

8. Enter or copy the appropriate formula for the monthly total percentage variances.

The spreadsheet should now appear as follows.

	A	B	C	D	E	F
1			Actual Sales	Projected	Variance ($)	Variance (%)
2	JANUARY					
3		Automotive	$101,519	$120,506	($18,987)	-18.70%
4		General	$354,660	$326,417	$28,243	7.96%
5		Hardware	$74,827	$76,250	($1,423)	-1.90%
6		Housewares	$506,125	$575,064	($68,939)	-13.62%
7		Plant & Garden	$55,965	$34,700	$21,265	38.00%
8			----------	----------	----------	----------
9		Total	$1,093,096	$1,132,937	($39,841)	-3.64%
10	FEBRUARY					
11		Automotive	$126,898	$140,995	($14,097)	-11.11%
12		General	$336,927	$408,021	($71,094)	-21.10%
13		Hardware	$66,596	$70,912	($4,316)	-6.48%
14		Housewares	$683,268	$661,319	$21,949	3.21%
15		Plant & Garden	$41,973	$41,640	$333	0.79%
16			----------	----------	----------	----------
17		Total	$1,255,662	$1,322,887	($67,225)	-5.35%
18	MARCH					
19		Automotive	$184,002	$184,278	($276)	-0.15%
20		General	$411,405	$396,596	$14,809	3.60%
21		Hardware	$87,906	$83,906	$4,000	4.55%
22		Housewares	$611,524	$550,548	$60,976	9.97%
23		Plant & Garden	$39,033	$48,580	($9,547)	-24.46%
24			----------	----------	----------	----------
25		Total	$1,333,870	$1,263,908	$69,962	5.25%
26						

9. Make any corrections necessary in your spreadsheet. Then save it under the filename PROJQTR1.

In the next steps you will extract the data for each of the three months, creating three new spreadsheet files. Before extracting the data, you will name the three data ranges for the monthly sales and the range of titles in row 1 of the spreadsheet.

10. Use the /**R**ange,**N**ame,**C**reate command to name ranges as follows: range A2..F9 JANUARY; range A10..F17 FEBRUARY; the range A18..F25 MARCH; and the range C1..F1 TITLES.
11. Save the file again under the name PROJQTR1 so that the saved copy will include the range names.

The /**F**ile,**X**tract command is used to save a portion of a spreadsheet file to another spreadsheet file (extension .WK1). The extracted portion may be saved with all of its formulas kept intact, or with all cells converted into their numeric or string values in the new spreadsheet file.

12. With the cursor located at cell A1, type the /**F**ile,**X**tract,**F**ormulas command and at the prompt "Enter xtract file name:," type ‖JANPROJ↵‖.
13. When the prompt "Enter xtract range: A1..A1" appears, use the pointer control keys to expand the range to include cells A1..F9. Then type the Enter key.

When the ranges to be extracted have been named, you may use the range name instead of pointing to the range to be extracted with the /**F**ile,**X**tract command.

14. Leaving the cursor at cell A1, repeat the /**F**ile,**X**tract,**F**ormulas command. At the prompt "Enter xtract file name:," type ||FEBPROJ←|| and at the prompt "Enter xtract range: A1..A1," type ||FEBRUARY←|| to specify the range named FEBRUARY as the range to be extracted.
15. Repeat the /**F**ile,**X**tract,**F**ormulas command again. At the prompt "Enter xtract file name:," type ||MARPROJ←||. This time at the prompt "Enter xtract range: A1..A1," type the F3 (NAME) key to see a list of named ranges at the top of the screen. Use the pointer control keys to point to the name MARCH, and then type the Enter key.
16. Use the /**F**ile,**R**etrieve command to retrieve the first extracted file JANPROJ.

The screen should now appear as follows.

	A	B	C	D	E	F
1			Actual Sales	Projected	Variance ($)	Variance (%)
2	JANUARY					
3		Automotive	$101,519	$120,506	($18,987)	-18.70%
4		General	$354,660	$326,417	$28,243	7.96%
5		Hardware	$74,827	$76,250	($1,423)	-1.90%
6		Housewares	$506,125	$575,064	($68,939)	-13.62%
7		Plant & Garden	$55,965	$34,700	$21,265	38.00%
8			----------	----------	----------	----------
9		Total	$1,093,096	$1,132,937	($39,841)	-3.64%
10						

17. Type the F5 (GOTO) key, and then type the F3 (NAME) key to see a list of named ranges in this extracted spreadsheet. Move the pointer to select MARCH as the named range to go to. Then type the Enter key.

Notice that although the range extracted from the PROJQTR1 file only included the ranges named JANUARY and TITLES, all range name definitions were kept in the extracted file. Since the ranges named FEBRUARY and MARCH have no data in this spreadsheet, these names should be deleted.

18. Use the /**R**ange,**N**ame,**D**elete command to delete the range names FEBRUARY and MARCH.
19. Print the spreadsheet, and then resave the file under the name JANPROJ and retrieve the file FEBPROJ.

The screen should now appear as follows.

	A	B	C	D	E	F
1	FEBRUARY					
2		Automotive	$126,898	$140,995	($14,097)	-11.11%
3		General	$336,927	$408,021	($71,094)	-21.10%
4		Hardware	$66,596	$70,912	($4,316)	-6.48%
5		Housewares	$683,268	$661,319	$21,949	3.21%
6		Plant & Garden	$41,973	$41,640	$333	0.79%
7			----------	----------	----------	----------
8		Total	$1,255,662	$1,322,887	($67,225)	-5.35%
9						

Notice that although February data extracted from the file PROJQTR1 was in the range A10..F17 in the original file, it begins at cell A1 in the extracted file.

20. Use the F5 (GOTO) and F3 (NAME) keys to move the pointer to the various named ranges and see how Lotus has adjusted the location of the ranges in this file.
21. Delete the unnecessary range names, and then resave the file under the name FEBPROJ.

The /**F**ile,**C**ombine command is used to combine data from a file saved on the disk with the file currently in RAM (on the screen). It includes options to copy, add, or subtract the incoming data, and to include the entire file specified or only a range of data from that file.

You will first use the **C**opy option to add titles to the current spreadsheet. The incoming data is copied into the spreadsheet beginning at the current pointer location and overwrites any data located there.

22. Move the pointer to row 1 and use the /**W**orksheet,**I**nsert,**R**ow command to insert a blank row at the top of the spreadsheet for titles.
23. Move the cursor to cell C1 and execute the command /**F**ile,**C**ombine,**C**opy,**N**amed/Specified-Range. At the prompt "Enter range name or coordinates:," type ||TITLES←||.
24. Then at the prompt "Name of file to combine:," either point to the file PROJQTR1 and type the Enter key or type ||PROJQTR1←||.
25. Resave this file under the name FEBPROJ.

The **A**dd option of the /**F**ile,**C**ombine command is used to add incoming values to the values in the current spreadsheet. Labels and cells containing formulas are not overwritten by incoming data; only cells containing values or blank cells will have incoming values added. You now will use this command to add the January values in the JANPROJ file to the February values on the screen, resulting in cumulative year-to-date figures for the end of February.

26. Change the label in cell A2 to "FEBRUARY YTD."
27. With the pointer still located at cell A2, execute the command /**F**ile,**C**ombine,**A**dd,**N**amed/Specified-Range. Specify JANUARY as the range name and JANPROJ as the filename.

The spreadsheet on the screen should now display as follows.

	A B	C	D	E	F
1		Actual Sales	Projected	Variance ($)	Variance (%)
2	FEBRUARY YTD				
3	Automotive	$228,417	$261,501	($33,084)	-14.48%
4	General	$691,587	$734,438	($42,851)	-6.20%
5	Hardware	$141,423	$147,162	($5,739)	-4.06%
6	Housewares	$1,189,393	$1,236,383	($46,990)	-3.95%
7	Plant & Garden	$97,938	$76,340	$21,598	22.05%
8		----------	----------	----------	----------
9	Total	$2,348,758	$2,455,824	($107,066)	-4.56%
10					

28. Print the spreadsheet, and then save it under the filename FEBYTD.
29. Now change the label in cell A2 to read MARCH YTD. Then execute the appropriate command to add the March values to the spreadsheet.

The March year-to-date values should appear as follows.

	A B	C	D	E	F
1		Actual Sales	Projected	Variance ($)	Variance (%)
2	MARCH YTD				
3	Automotive	$412,419	$445,779	($33,360)	-8.09%
4	General	$1,102,992	$1,131,034	($28,042)	-2.54%
5	Hardware	$229,329	$231,068	($1,739)	-0.76%
6	Housewares	$1,800,917	$1,786,931	$13,986	0.78%
7	Plant & Garden	$136,971	$124,920	$12,051	8.80%
8		----------	----------	----------	----------
9	Total	$3,682,628	$3,719,732	($37,104)	-1.01%
10					

30. Print the spreadsheet. Then save it under the name MARYTD and exit Lotus.

EXERCISE 7 Customer Information

Required Preparation

Study the section titled /**D**ata,**S**ort, /**D**ata,**Q**uery, and Database Functions, (pages L-96–L-106), the **@DATE** function found in the section titled Lotus 1-2-3 Functions (pages L-66), and the /**D**ata commands presented in the Lotus 1-2-3 Command Summary.

Exercise Steps

1. Load Lotus 1-2-3 and then change the spreadsheet's column widths to the following: Column A—18 characters; column E—3 characters; and columns F and G—both 11 characters.
2. Enter the following data. Note the following: (1) the column labels all begin with the ^ (Center) label prefix (except TERRITORY); (2) column F is formatted as currency with 2 decimal places; (3) and the dates in column G are entered with **@DATE** functions and are formatted as (DD-MMM-YY).

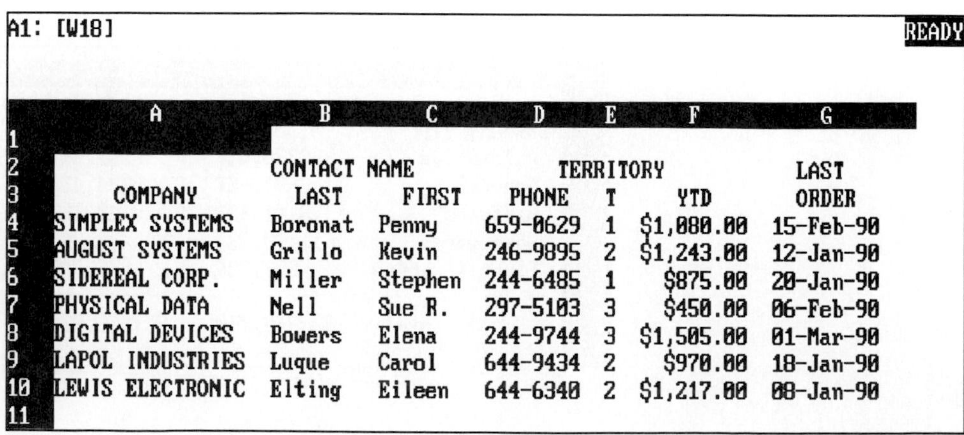
A1: [W18] READY

	A	B	C	D	E	F	G
1							
2		CONTACT NAME			TERRITORY		LAST
3	COMPANY	LAST	FIRST	PHONE	T	YTD	ORDER
4	SIMPLEX SYSTEMS	Boronat	Penny	659-0629	1	$1,080.00	15-Feb-90
5	AUGUST SYSTEMS	Grillo	Kevin	246-9895	2	$1,243.00	12-Jan-90
6	SIDEREAL CORP.	Miller	Stephen	244-6485	1	$875.00	20-Jan-90
7	PHYSICAL DATA	Nell	Sue R.	297-5103	3	$450.00	06-Feb-90
8	DIGITAL DEVICES	Bowers	Elena	244-9744	3	$1,505.00	01-Mar-90
9	LAPOL INDUSTRIES	Luque	Carol	644-9434	2	$970.00	10-Jan-90
10	LEWIS ELECTRONIC	Elting	Eileen	644-6340	2	$1,217.00	08-Jan-90
11							

The database here is meant to represent a partial list of corporate customers who make purchases throughout the year. The field names and their descriptions are as follows.

Field Names	Explanation
COMPANY	The name of the customer
LAST	Purchasing individual's last name
FIRST	Purchasing individual's first name
PHONE	Telephone number
T	Customer's sales territory
YTD	Customer purchases for the year-to-date
ORDER	Date of the last order made by the customer

3. Sort the range of records in ascending order on the company's name.

A1: [W18] READY

	A	B	C	D	E	F	G
1							
2		CONTACT NAME			TERRITORY		LAST
3	COMPANY	LAST	FIRST	PHONE	T	YTD	ORDER
4	AUGUST SYSTEMS	Grillo	Kevin	246-9895	2	$1,243.00	12-Jan-90
5	DIGITAL DEVICES	Bowers	Elena	244-9744	3	$1,505.00	01-Mar-90
6	LAPOL INDUSTRIES	Luque	Carol	644-9434	2	$970.00	18-Jan-90
7	LEWIS ELECTRONIC	Elting	Eileen	644-6340	2	$1,217.00	08-Jan-90
8	PHYSICAL DATA	Nell	Sue R.	297-5103	3	$450.00	06-Feb-90
9	SIDEREAL CORP.	Miller	Stephen	244-6485	1	$875.00	20-Jan-90
10	SIMPLEX SYSTEMS	Boronat	Penny	659-0629	1	$1,080.00	15-Feb-90
11							

4. Print the sorted database.
5. Sort the records according to territory (ascending) and year-to-date sales within each territory (descending). Then print the database again.

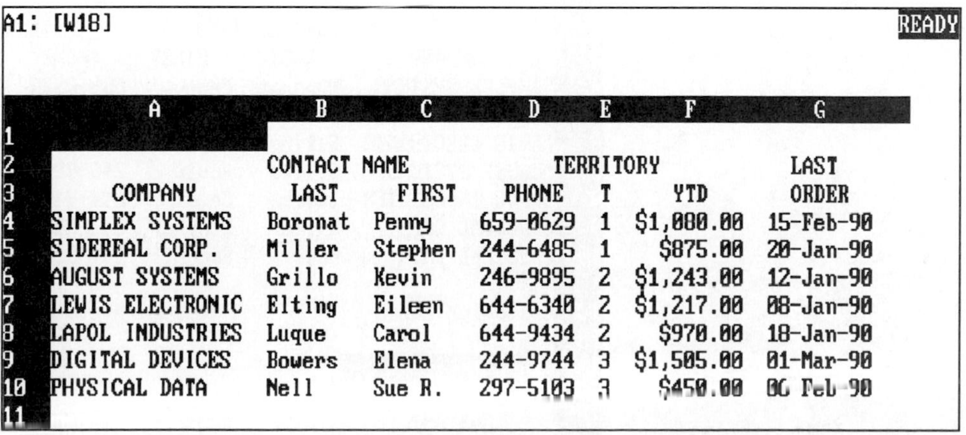

A1: [W18] READY

	A	B	C	D	E	F	G
1							
2		CONTACT NAME			TERRITORY		LAST
3	COMPANY	LAST	FIRST	PHONE	T	YTD	ORDER
4	SIMPLEX SYSTEMS	Boronat	Penny	659-0629	1	$1,080.00	15-Feb-90
5	SIDEREAL CORP.	Miller	Stephen	244-6485	1	$875.00	20-Jan-90
6	AUGUST SYSTEMS	Grillo	Kevin	246-9895	2	$1,243.00	12-Jan-90
7	LEWIS ELECTRONIC	Elting	Eileen	644-6340	2	$1,217.00	08-Jan-90
8	LAPOL INDUSTRIES	Luque	Carol	644-9434	2	$970.00	18-Jan-90
9	DIGITAL DEVICES	Bowers	Elena	244-9744	3	$1,505.00	01-Mar-90
10	PHYSICAL DATA	Nell	Sue R.	297-5103	3	$450.00	06-Feb-90
11							

6. Use the /**D**ata,**Q**uery commands to specify the database (with field names included) as being the Input range, the cells A13..A14 as the Criterion range (format cell A14 to display Text), and cells A16..E16 as the Output range.

7. Finish the necessary steps to extract the company name, first and last names of the purchaser, phone number, and territory number for all records in territory 2. Organize the Input range so that the extracted data is sorted by the last name of the purchaser.

```
A1: [W18]                                                          READY

   A                  B          C         D         E  F          G
1
2                     CONTACT NAME               TERRITORY         LAST
3       COMPANY         LAST       FIRST     PHONE    T    YTD       ORDER
4  SIMPLEX SYSTEMS    Boronat    Penny     659-0629  1  $1,080.00  15-Feb-90
5  DIGITAL DEVICES    Bowers     Elena     244-9744  3  $1,505.00  01-Mar-90
6  LEWIS ELECTRONIC   Elting     Eileen    644-6340  2  $1,217.00  08-Jan-90
7  AUGUST SYSTEMS     Grillo     Kevin     246-9895  2  $1,243.00  12-Jan-90
8  LAPOL INDUSTRIES   Luque      Carol     644-9434  2    $970.00  18-Jan-90
9  SIDEREAL CORP.     Miller     Stephen   244-6485  1    $875.00  20-Jan-90
10 PHYSICAL DATA      Nell       Sue R.    297-5103  3    $450.00  06-Feb-90
11
12 Criterion Range
13        T
14 +E4=2
15
16      COMPANY         FIRST      LAST      PHONE    T
17 LEWIS ELECTRONIC   Eileen     Elting    644-6340  2
18 AUGUST SYSTEMS     Kevin      Grillo    246-9895  2
19 LAPOL INDUSTRIES   Carol      Luque     644-9434  2
20
```

8. Change the Output range to include the company name, year-to-date sales, last order date, and territory number. Then perform a /**D**ata,**Q**uery,**E**xtract again.

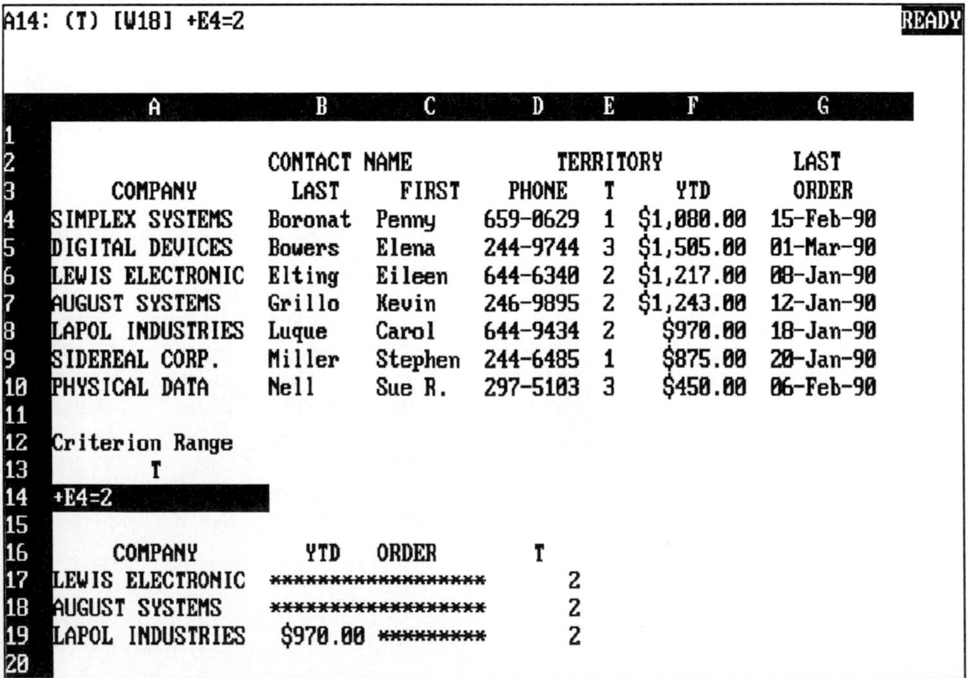

```
A14: (T) [W18] +E4=2                                               READY

   A                  B          C         D         E  F          G
1
2                     CONTACT NAME               TERRITORY         LAST
3       COMPANY         LAST       FIRST     PHONE    T    YTD       ORDER
4  SIMPLEX SYSTEMS    Boronat    Penny     659-0629  1  $1,080.00  15-Feb-90
5  DIGITAL DEVICES    Bowers     Elena     244-9744  3  $1,505.00  01-Mar-90
6  LEWIS ELECTRONIC   Elting     Eileen    644-6340  2  $1,217.00  08-Jan-90
7  AUGUST SYSTEMS     Grillo     Kevin     246-9895  2  $1,243.00  12-Jan-90
8  LAPOL INDUSTRIES   Luque      Carol     644-9434  2    $970.00  18-Jan-90
9  SIDEREAL CORP.     Miller     Stephen   244-6485  1    $875.00  20-Jan-90
10 PHYSICAL DATA      Nell       Sue R.    297-5103  3    $450.00  06-Feb-90
11
12 Criterion Range
13        T
14 +E4=2
15
16      COMPANY          YTD    ORDER           T
17 LEWIS ELECTRONIC   ******************          2
18 AUGUST SYSTEMS     ******************          2
19 LAPOL INDUSTRIES    $970.00 *********          2
20
```

Notice that the column widths here are not wide enough to display the numeric values that were extracted. You can increase the widths of the two columns to view or print the extracted data.

In completing the next steps, you will find the following information helpful. The order of the field names occurring in the Output range does not have to be the same order that they occur in the Input range. However, you may need to increase the width of columns in order to print the extracted data in the spreadsheet. You may include columns in an Output range that have no field name at the top. In such cases the column will be left blank. If you increase (lengthen) an Output range by adding a field name to it, you must respecify the size of the Output range by using the /**D**ata,**Q**uery,**O**utput command.

9. Change the Output range to include the company name, first and last names of the purchaser, and the phone number. Next change the Criterion range to extract the data for all companies whose name begins with "LAPO." Extract the data and print the entire spreadsheet.
10. Change the Output range to include the company name, territory number, and year-to-date sales. Then change the Criterion range to extract the data for all companies in territory 2 with sales greater than $1000.00. Extract the data and print the entire spreadsheet.
11. Change the Output range to include the company name, last order date and year-to-date sales. Then change the Criterion range to extract the data for all companies in territory 1 whose last order was in January. Extract the data and then move the pointer to cell A14. Type F2 (EDIT) and then type the Home key. Next type a label prefix (′," or ^) and then type ↵. (The last steps simply change the condition into a label so that it can be entirely printed). Print the entire spreadsheet.
12. Erase the data in the Criterion range and then use the @**DSUM** and @**DAVG** functions (in cells F13 and F14) along with the appropriate labels to produce the following summary added to the spreadsheet. Note that the Criterion range for the functions is found in cells B13 and B14, and that the criterion references a cell (E12) for the territory number. When such a reference is made in a criterion, it must be entered as absolute.

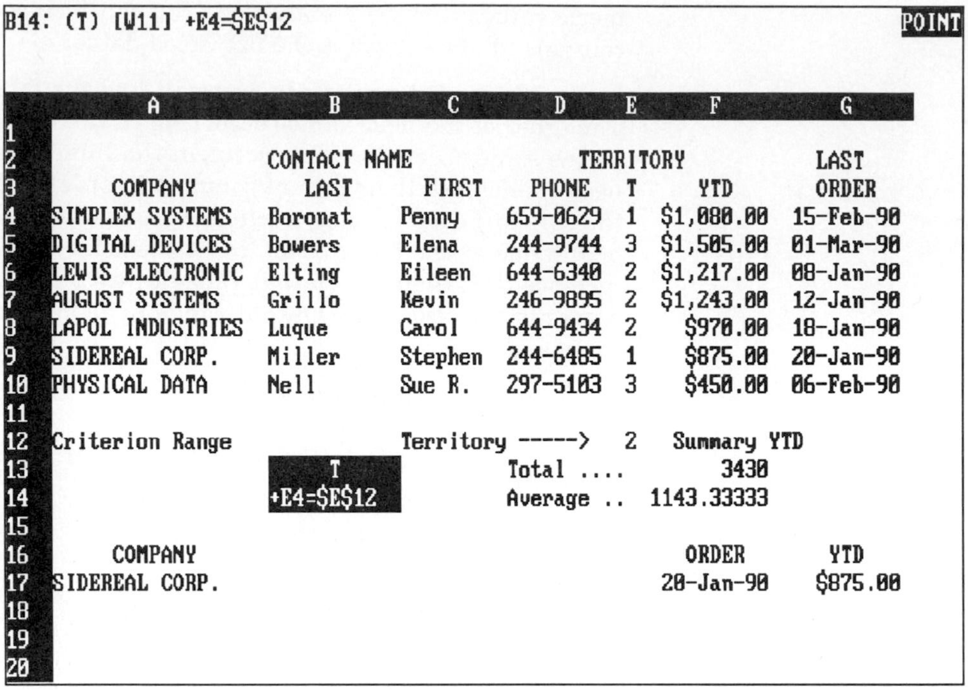

```
B14: (T) [W11] +E4=$E$12                                              POINT

          A              B          C          D        E     F            G
 1
 2                  CONTACT NAME                    TERRITORY              LAST
 3       COMPANY         LAST       FIRST      PHONE    T     YTD          ORDER
 4  SIMPLEX SYSTEMS    Boronat     Penny      659-0629  1  $1,080.00   15-Feb-90
 5  DIGITAL DEVICES    Bowers      Elena      244-9744  3  $1,505.00   01-Mar-90
 6  LEWIS ELECTRONIC   Elting      Eileen     644-6340  2  $1,217.00   08-Jan-90
 7  AUGUST SYSTEMS     Grillo      Kevin      246-9895  2  $1,243.00   12-Jan-90
 8  LAPOL INDUSTRIES   Luque       Carol      644-9434  2    $970.00   10-Jan-90
 9  SIDEREAL CORP.     Miller      Stephen    244-6485  1    $875.00   20-Jan-90
10  PHYSICAL DATA      Nell        Sue R.     297-5103  3    $450.00   06-Feb-90
11
12  Criterion Range               Territory -----> 2    Summary YTD
13                         T                 Total ....        3430
14                     +E4=$E$12             Average ..  1143.33333
15
16       COMPANY                                             ORDER        YTD
17  SIDEREAL CORP.                                         20-Jan-90    $875.00
18
19
20
```

13. Save the spreadsheet under the name CUSTOMER and then print the spreadsheet. Next exit the spreadsheet software by using the /**Q**uit command.

EXERCISE 8
A Basic Macro Library

Required Preparation

Study the section titled Lotus 1-2-3 Macros up to the section titled *Advanced Macros* (pages L-107–L-117). Also review the @**ROUND,** @**UPPER** , @**LOWER,** and @**PROPER** functions found in the section titled Lotus 1-2-3 Functions (pages L-57–L-105), and the /**R**ange,**N**ame,**L**abels command presented in the Lotus 1-2-3 Command Summary.

Exercise Steps

The @**ROUND** function forces Lotus to keep a cell's value at a certain level of accuracy. In the following steps you will create a macro that will both edit a cell containing a value and properly insert an @**ROUND** function into it.

1. Load Lotus 1-2-3 and then move the pointer to any cell and enter the formula 10/3.

The value 3.333333 should be displayed in the cell.

2. With the pointer on the cell, type the following keystrokes: F2,Home. Then type ‖ @**ROUND**(‖ . Next type the keys End,comma,2,),↵.

The contents of the cell should appear as @**ROUND**(10/3,2) and the cell should display the value 3.33. You should note that the keystrokes used in this example were general purpose in nature. That is, the same keystrokes will produce the same results when used on any cell containing a value.

3. Use the /**R**ange,**E**rase command to erase the cell containing the **@ROUND** function. Then use the /**W**orksheet,**G**lobal,**C**olumn-Width command to set all columns in the spreadsheet to a width of 12. Next use the /**W**orksheet,**C**olumn command to set the A column to a width of 4.
4. Move to cell A7 and type ‖ '\R↵ ‖ . The label "\R" should now appear in the cell. Next move to cell B7 and enter the following label: {EDIT}{HOME}@**ROUND**({END},2)~{QUIT}

The {QUIT} command is used to end the execution of a macro and should be the final command that occurs in a macro.

5. Now use the /**R**ange,**N**ame command to give the name \R to the cell containing the macro.
6. Save the spreadsheet under the name MACLIB. Then enter a fraction, such as 4/7, into a blank cell in the spreadsheet. With the pointer on the cell containing the fraction, type Alt-R to test the macro you have just created.

The **@LOWER, @PROPER,** and **@UPPER** functions are used to change the displayed case of the string (Label) contents of a spreadsheet cell. The set of keystrokes used to insert any one of these String functions into a cell are very similar to those used to insert an **@ROUND** function into a cell.

To create the next three macros, use the following procedure.

a. Enter into column A the label that describes the macro's name. Be sure to start the entry with the left justify Label-Prefix (').

b. Into a blank cell enter an appropriate label from which the intended function will return a value (this will be a test cell).

c. Type the keystrokes necessary to insert the function into the test cell. Record (write down) the keystrokes used.

d. Into the cell to the immediate right of the cell containing the macro's name, enter the keystrokes recorded above in their proper order and macro syntax. Be sure to end the macro with a {QUIT} command.

e. When finished entering the macro, use the /**R**ange,**N**ame command to name the cell containing the macro the same name that appears to its left (the name in column A).

f. Save the spreadsheet and then test the macro on a test cell.

7. Into cell A8 enter the label "\L." Then enter a macro into cell B8 that will insert an **@LOWER** function into the current spreadsheet cell.
8. Into cell A9 enter the label "\P." Then enter a macro into cell B9 that will insert an **@PROPER** function into the current spreadsheet cell.
9. Into cell A10 enter the label "\U." Then enter a macro into cell B10 that will insert an **@UPPER** function into the current spreadsheet cell.

In the next steps you will create macros designed to remove **@ROUND, @LOWER, @PROPER,** and **@UPPER** functions from a spreadsheet cell without removing their data arguments.

10. Move the pointer to a blank cell in the spreadsheet and enter the formula 10/3.

The value 3.333333 should be displayed in the cell.

11. Use the Alt-R macro to insert an @**ROUND** function into the cell.
12. With the pointer on the cell, type the keystrokes F2,Home. Then type the Del key 7 times. Next type the End key and then type the Backspace key 3 times. Typing ↵ will finish the editing of the cell.
13. Move to cell A17 and type ‖ '\X↵ ‖ . The label "\X" should now appear in the cell. Next move to cell B17 and enter the following label: {EDIT} {HOME} {DEL 7} {END} {BS 3}~{QUIT}.
14. Use the /**R**ange,**N**ame command to give the name \X to the cell containing the macro designed to remove an @**ROUND** function from a cell.

To create the next two macros, use the same procedures as you used before.

15. Into cell A18 enter the label "\Y." Then enter a macro into cell B18 that will remove an @**LOWER** or @**UPPER** function from the current spreadsheet cell.
16. Into cell A19 enter the label "\Z." Then enter a macro into cell B19 that will remove an @**PROPER** function from the current spreadsheet cell.

You next will create a menu macro designed to access the three macros contained in cells B17 through B19.

17. Move to cell A12 and enter the label "\E." Then move to cell B12 and enter the label {MENUBRANCH B13}. Next give the range name \E to the cell B12.
18. Now enter the following labels into the range B13..D15.

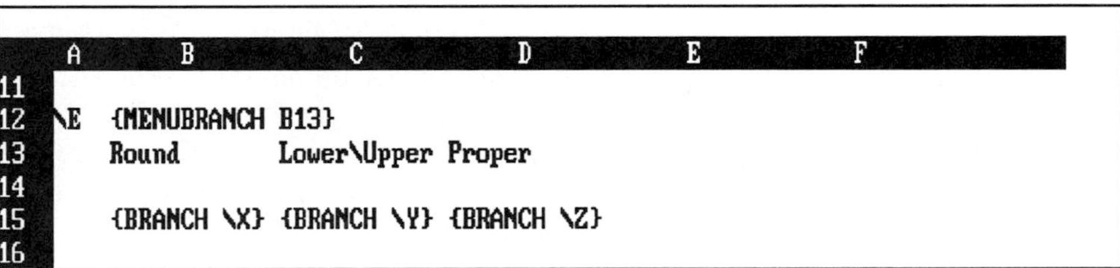

19. Now enter the following labels into the cells in row 14.

B14	Erase @**ROUND** function
C14	Erase @**LOWER** or @**UPPER** function
D14	Erase @**PROPER** function

The screen should now appear as follows.

```
     A     B            C            D            E            F
11
12  \E  {MENUBRANCH B13}
13      Round        Lower\Upper  Proper
14      Erase @ROUNDErase @LOWERErase @PROPER function
15      {BRANCH \X} {BRANCH \Y} {BRANCH \Z}
16
```

20. Save the spreadsheet. Then create three or four test cells to test the menu macro. Next test the macro by moving the pointer to one of the test cells and typing Alt-E.

In the final steps of the exercise you will create another menu macro named \M that will access the macros to insert functions into cells and access the \E menu macro if desired.

21. Move to cell A2 and enter the following labels into the range A2..F3.

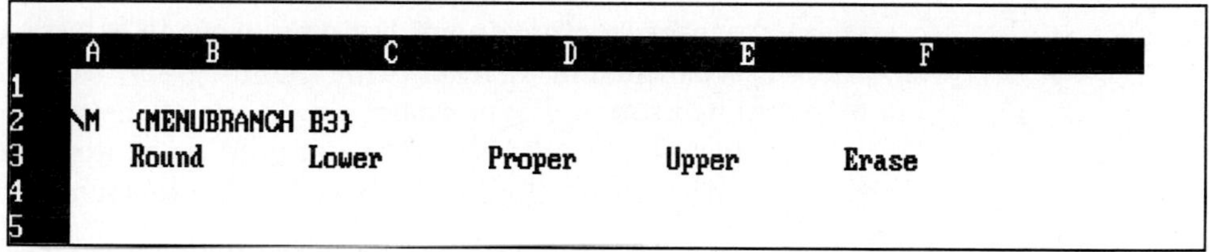

	A	B	C	D	E	F
1						
2	\M	{MENUBRANCH B3}				
3		Round	Lower	Proper	Upper	Erase
4						
5						

22. Complete the menu macro by entering suitable descriptions for each macro into row 4 and by entering the appropriate {BRANCH} commands into row 5.

23. Name the new menu macro. Then save the spreadsheet and thoroughly test the Alt-M menu macro. Print the spreadsheet and then exit Lotus 1-2-3 by using the /Quit command.

CASES

CASE 1
SIMS, Inc.

Sharon Albright is a project manager for Specialized Inventory Management Systems, Inc. (SIMS), a company that does customized software installations throughout the world. She manages about ten teams of two to eight analysts each, who are sent to client organizations to install systems. Although the people under her direction submit progress reports weekly, they submit their expense reports whenever they get around to it, and many times she has found it hard to read the handwritten entries. This has been a constant source of annoyance for Sharon, since she must take time to decipher and double check the reports before submitting the information to accounting.

Sharon has tried everything from cajoling to threatening not to pay expenses in order to get her employees to submit their reports weekly and to type them or at least print them legibly. But the Vice-President in charge of Operations, Roger Anderson, is one of the worst offenders. Because the analysts know this, they haven't paid much attention to Sharon's requests. But now Sharon thinks she may be able to solve this problem.

About nine months ago Roger Anderson talked the company into purchasing personal laptop computers for every analyst in the company. Top management disagreed about whether having these laptop computers would really be useful. Knowing that Roger now must prove that his suggestion is benefitting the company, Sharon approached him with the idea of having expense reports entered on the laptop computers, to be submitted weekly from anywhere in the world by using the computers' modems. Roger jumped at the idea and asked her to design a spreadsheet for this purpose as soon as possible.

Sharon feels that the existing expense report form needs revision since no one seems to fill it out in the same way. She would design it so that the beginning and ending date for the one-week period (Sunday through Saturday) would appear at the top of the form. Also, a place for the name of the person submitting the report and a mailing address to which the check is to be sent would appear near the top of the form. Below it would give space for daily expenses, including hotel room charges and a per diem of $30–$55 depending on the country. Also included in the report would be car rental expenses or a $0.32 per mile auto allowance if a personal car is used, in which case beginning and ending odometer readings would be given. If other transportation expenses such as round-trip airfare, cab fares and road tolls were incurred, they would also be listed in the report. All other expenses would be treated as miscellaneous expenses, but ample space would be provided for a description.

CASE 2
Westport Pet Supplies

Jim Southland has founded a new company called Westport Pet Supplies. The company's main business will be mixing and packaging a variety of premium canned pet foods. Jim's initial plans are to produce two product lines of cat food, adult and kitten mixes. The adult mix will provide $0.16 profit per 7 oz. can, while the kitten mix will provide $0.07 profit per 4 oz. can. Both mixes are made from the same ingredients—meat by-products that provide protein and a moist premixed cereal blend that provides fiber, carbohydrates, and nine essential vitamins. Both ingredients must be constantly and individually refrigerated prior to the mixing/canning process.

When building the production facility, Jim installed two large refrigeration units, one which holds 700 lbs. of meat by-products and one which holds 500 lbs. of premixed cereal. In the production process the refrigerated bins must be completely emptied and then sanitized before they can be refilled with new ingredients.

A can of adult cat food contains 4 oz. of meat by-products and 3 oz. of cereal. The kitten mix requires 3 oz. of meat by-products and 1 oz. of cereal per can.

In a recent conversation with his soon-to-be production manager, Stan Thomas, Jim was overheard to say, "Look, Stan, this thing is complicated. In order to get the price break we need to stay in business, I had to guarantee the supplier that we would order 700 lbs. of meat and 500 lbs. of cereal in the same shipment twice a week. That means we need to produce just the right number of cans of each cat food from each shipment so that we aren't wasting ingredients and are maximizing our profits. You know we need to make at least $375 on each shipment of ingredients to cover our operating costs. I'm not certain, but I'm beginning to think we may need to raise our prices or build larger refrigeration units to make a reasonable profit. I wish there was some way to put all these factors together in one place so that we could see how these kinds of changes would affect our operation."

CASE 3
Paint Contract Bids

Larry Scott is a self-employed house painter who has become quite successful through word-of-mouth advertising and referrals from several local paint stores. Larry's typical job begins with a visit to a house to interview the homeowner. The visit provides Larry with information about the size of the job, type and color of paint desired, the amount of trim work involved, and the extent of preparation (washing and/or scraping) required before painting can begin.

Following the visit, Larry returns home to prepare a bid for the job. The bid takes into account the cost of paint used, the estimated number of hours of labor involved (Larry employs two assistants to help him on the job), and any incidentals that may need to be included (such as replacing broken panes of glass). Normally the bid is itemized so the potential customer can see what he/she is paying for.

In a recent conversation with one of his assistants, Larry was heard to say, "Kevin, how are your evening classes going at the college? Robin tells me the two of you are taking a computer course. I don't know anything about computers, but it sounds like I might be able to use one to help me prepare the bids for our jobs. Business has gotten to the point where I'm spending hours in the evening doing calculations and paperwork. If I could see exactly how the computer could help, I might be tempted to take some of this summer's profits and buy one."

Note that several of the prices here are calculated prices based on the square footage of the area to paint.

Preparation	Bid Price
Pressure Washing	$150.00 per house
Scraping	$100.00 per day (each man working)
Priming	$0.25/1 sq. ft.
Materials	10% of total preparation price

Painting	Bid Price
If Latex	$15.00/400 sq. ft.
If Stain	$12.00/450 sq. ft.
If Oil	$22.00/400 sq. ft.
Painting Labor	$0.25/1 sq. ft.
If second coat	65% of total first coat price

Finishing

Trim Openings (doors, windows, etc.) $30.00 each

Other

Add 15% for three story (or otherwise difficult) structure

CASE 4 College Financial Plan

Jake Williams is a sophomore at Mt. Scott Community College. He plans to transfer to the nearby state university next year, and is in the process of determining how he will finance next year's tuition since it is higher at the university than at the community college. So far, he's been able to work part time to pay most of his college expenses, and financial aid has helped pay for the rest. He will be eligible to receive more aid next year since he is now independent of his parents.

Jake has obtained the information he needs to start planning his budget for next year, but there are a few things he hasn't decided. For instance, he's not sure whether he wants to live on campus or remain in his present apartment, which requires a 30-minute commute to the university. If he stays where he is, his rent will be $320 per month, his board (food and sundry items) will be $160 per month, and his transportation costs will be $70 per month. The university is located downtown, where prices are much higher. If he moves on campus, his board will be $200 per month, but his rent will be only $275 per month and transportation only $25 per month.

Jake's also not sure whether he wants to work next year, because he expects his courses at the university to require more time than he puts in now. If he doesn't work, he will have to obtain more money in loans, and he's concerned about how much debt he should incur during his college years. If he stays in his apartment off campus, he can keep his current job and net about $400 per month. On campus jobs are extremely scarce, and he would have to take a work-study position as part of his financial aid package if he wants to work on campus. The work-study job would net him only $200 per month. If he lives on campus he cannot keep his current job, and if he lives off campus he cannot take a work-study job. His other option is to not work at all, but he doesn't know if this is even feasible.

He can obtain three types of financial aid: a grant, which does not have to be paid back; a university loan at 5% interest; and a bank loan at 8% interest. Loan interest does not begin accruing until he graduates. He may repay the university loan over 10 years, and interest on the bank loan will go up to 10% after the first four years of repayment.

Since the grant is dependent on the amount of money he earns during the year, he will receive nothing if he works off campus, $300 each term if he takes the work-study job, and $600 each term if he doesn't work at all. The amount available as a lower interest university loan also will depend upon his income. He may receive $800 per term if he works off campus, $1,000 each term if he takes the work-study job, and $1,335 per term if he doesn't work at all. The 8% bank loan may be used to pay the rest of his expenses up to a limit of $2,000 for the year (not $2,000 per term). The 8% bank loan amount may not exceed the amount needed to meet his total expenses after any earned income, grant, and university loan monies have been determined.

Aside from his room, board, and transportation expenses, Jake's cost of attending the university will be $561 per term, which will cover his tuition, fees, and books. The tuition expenses and financial aid payments occur in October, January, and April. His income from an off-campus job or a work-study job, as well as his room, board, and transportation expenses, occur on a monthly basis for the full year, October to September, even though he will not be attending summer term (July through September).

Jake wants to determine what his full year's budget (October to September) will be given his various alternatives. He needs to know what alternatives are possible in terms of living on campus or off campus and working or not working, and the impact each would have on the amount of grant money he may receive and the amount he would have to borrow under the two loan programs. He also would like to determine his expected monthly cash flow situation given the expenses and income for the various alternatives. Jake has heard a friend talk about a spreadsheet program that is useful for "what if?" situations like his, and he wonders if it could be used to help him sort out his alternatives.

CASE 5 C & B Foods Company

C & B Foods is a food processing company that produces a line of freeze-dried camping and backpacking products. As product manager, Steve McGrath has been asked to research and evaluate the feasibility of adding a new product. Steve has identified freeze-dried eggs with chili peppers as a likely new product. This new product could be used to make Mexican omelets and other spicy egg dishes. The company does not produce any freeze-dried egg products because of poor consumer acceptance. However, Steve thinks the added flavor of chili peppers could help eliminate the usual complaint that freeze-dried eggs taste like sulfur.

Steve had some initial market research done and found that in addition to the expected market of campers and backpackers, there is also a potential market among busy consumers who want a quick and easy breakfast product. The new freeze-dried egg product will be sold in eight ounce packages. Steve has developed the following estimates from the market research figures concerning potential sales for the new product and the probability of achieving different sales levels.

First Year Sales:	250,000 units	20% chance (worst case)
	500,000 units	50% chance (likely case)
	750,000 units	30% chance (best case)

To determine the feasibility of introducing the new product, Steve decided to forecast potential sales for 15 periods (years). Steve predicts that the sales growth rate will be approximately 10 percent per year for years one through three, 15 percent per year for the next five years, and about 8 percent per year thereafter. Market indicators show that the total market for freeze-dried egg products of all types should be about 5 million units annually by the beginning of year six.

Steve must develop a sales forecast for each of the potential first-year sales levels (worst case, likely case, and best case scenarios). Since the first year's sales, the sales growth rates, and the total market size are predictions, Steve wants a model that will allow him to change these factors as new information becomes available.

Bob Kane, the sales manager, will want to know potential sales levels and the market share the company can expect given each scenario. Steve will make a formal presentation of his product idea and research findings at the next product development meeting, and he hopes to use graphs to make his information easy to understand. He plans to use a microcomputer during his presentation, with his spreadsheet model projected onto a screen so that he can easily respond to comments and opinions of the people in the meeting by adjusting the key values in his model, if necessary.

CASE 6
Prescott Stoneware, Inc.

Mark Prescott is a craftsman who makes and sells stoneware planters, lamps, and various other items. He has earned a good reputation at art festivals and craft shows where he displays and sells his products. He also has begun selling his stoneware items to a few giftware shops in the area, and demand for his products is growing. A few months ago he built on to his home, adding a small retail shop, office, and inventory storage room. About a year ago he purchased a microcomputer, and he does some of the accounting for his business using a spreadsheet program.

Sales from his home shop have been good, and he thinks that they will continue to grow. He has developed a spreadsheet for entering and printing invoices as orders are taken. The invoice portion of his spreadsheet, with a sample invoice entered, follows.

	A	B	C	D	E	F	G	H	I
1									
2	SOLD TO:		Adams Gift Gallery			SHIP TO:	Adams Gift Gallery		
3			1202 SW Fifth Ave.				1202 SW Fifth Ave.		
4			James Lake, MA 02156				James Lake, MA 02156		
5									
6		QTY	PROD NO	DESCRIPTION		PRICE	TOTAL	DSCNT	NET
7	1	6	L2015	Lamp 15", 2-tone		$5.50	$33.00	8.50%	$30.20
8	2	10	P2010	Planter 10"		$6.00	$60.00	7.50%	$55.50
9	3	4	P2014	Planter 14"		$12.00	$48.00		$48.00
10	4								
11	5								
12	6								
13	7								
14	8								
15	9								
16	10								
17								SUBTOTAL	$133.70
18								3% SALES TAX	$4.01
19								FREIGHT	$25.00
20								INVOICE TOTAL	$162.71

The name and address next to the label SOLD TO: indicates where the invoice is to be sent. This is usually the same as the SHIP TO: name and address, though sometimes it is different. Mark's invoice has space for ten products, and he has decided that, for now, if anyone should order more than that, he will simply create another invoice. He has developed a set of product codes with associated descriptions, prices, and discount percentages for orders of more than five products. He maintains his product list in another portion of the spreadsheet, as follows.

	J	K	L	M	N	O
1						
2						
3						
4		PROD	DESCRIPTION	PRICE	DSCNT	
5		L2015	Lamp 15", 2-tone	$5.50	8.50%	
6		L2024	Lamp 24", 2-tone	$7.50	8.50%	
7		L2036	Lamp 36", 2-tone	$10.00	10.00%	
8		L3015	Lamp 15", designed	$7.00	7.50%	
9		L3024	Lamp 24", designed	$10.00	7.50%	
10		L3030	Lamp 30", designed	$15.50	8.00%	
11		L3036	Lamp 36", designed	$18.00	8.00%	
12		P2004	Planter 4"	$2.00	6.50%	
13		P2006	Planter 6"	$3.00	6.50%	
14		P2008	Planter 8"	$4.50	7.50%	
15		P2010	Planter 10"	$6.00	7.50%	
16		P2012	Planter 12"	$9.00	8.50%	
17		P2014	Planter 14"	$12.00	8.50%	
18						

Mark has found that he can use the @**VLOOKUP** function to automatically enter the description, unit price, and discount percentage into the invoice after the product code has been entered. To do this, he first named the range that holds his product list PRODUCTS. He specified the range as K5..N18 to include one row beyond the last product so that a blank invoice line would look up the blank cells K18..N18. He also used the global zero suppression feature of the spreadsheet software so that the @**VLOOKUP** functions could be entered into his invoice template without displaying a full invoice of zeros.

The function he used for the first description entry was

@**VLOOKUP**(C7,$PRODUCTS,1)

He copied this function to all the cells in the D column, and entered and copied similar functions in the F and H columns. The total column is calculated as quantity * price, and the net column subtracts the discount percentage if the quantity was over five. The subtotal and sales tax cells hold formulas, but the freight cell is a manual entry because the amount depends on how each customer wants his/her order shipped.

So far, Mark is the only one who has been entering and printing invoices, so he's very familiar with the operation of his spreadsheet. He would like to turn over more of these responsibilities to his wife, Sally, who has been helping run the business. Sally, however, is not very familiar with the computer and is somewhat apprehensive about taking on this responsibility. She told Mark that he has to make it "idiot-proof," so that she can enter and print the invoices without having to type much or make a lot of calculations. The last time she tried to enter an invoice, she accidentally typed over some of the formulas he had in the spreadsheet.

Mark knows that there is a way of protecting cells so that they cannot be overwritten, but he's never used this feature before. He has to decide which areas of the spreadsheet he would leave unprotected for Sally to enter invoice information. He also would like to make certain procedures more automatic, such as copying the SOLD TO: name and address to the SHIP TO: area when it is the same, printing the invoice, and blanking out the invoice after it has been printed and saved. He wants to modify the invoice spreadsheet to make it an easy to use template.

HINTS AND HAZARDS

DATA ENTRY

HINT When you enter data into cells, watch the LABEL/VALUE indicator at the top right of the screen. Based on your first keystroke, Lotus makes an assumption about the type of data you are entering into a cell. String data beginning with a numeric character, such as 4th Street, must be entered by first typing a label prefix ', ", or ^. Numeric data beginning with an alphabetic character, such as a cell reference, must be preceded by a numeric character 0 through 9, +, −, ., (, @, #, or $.

HAZARD If a formula displays an incorrect value that could be attributable to a cell reference value equal to zero (0), check the cells to which the formula refers to see if a number accidentally was entered as a label. If one of the cells has its data left-justified, it may well be an incorrectly entered cell. Remember that, by default, values are automatically justified to the right and labels are automatically justified to the left.

HINT Use the pointing method of entering formulas for faster and more accurate results.

HINT The keys on the numeric keypad at the right side of the keyboard toggle between a numeric mode and a pointer control mode when you type the Num Lock key. However, they also shift to the opposite mode if you hold down the Shift key. When you are entering several cells worth of numeric data, it is useful to leave the keypad in the pointer control mode. When you are ready to enter data into a cell, shift with your left hand and enter the data with the ten-key pad. When you are done, release the Shift key and move the pointer to the next cell.

HINT You may use the F2 (EDIT) key to edit the current cell. In the EDIT mode, the cell's data are displayed at the second prompt line. You can use the pointer control keys (←, →) to move a cursor across the data. The Home key jumps the cursor to the far left of the data; the End key jumps the cursor to the far right of the data.

Any characters that you type are inserted to the left of the cursor. The Ins key may be used to toggle the overwrite mode (indicator OVR) on or off. The Del or Backspace keys delete characters. When you are done editing, press the Enter key.

HINT Formulas and numbers may be converted to string data by using the EDIT mode to insert a label prefix as the first character.

HINT Pressing the F2 key (EDIT) and then the F9 key (CALC) converts the contents of the current cell from a formula or string expression into a constant value on the editing line. If the Enter key is typed, the change becomes permanent; if the Esc key is typed, the cell will retain its original contents. To convert several cells to constant values, use the /**R**ange,**V**alue command.

HAZARD Beginners often find that the spreadsheet's computed answers do not agree with answers they have gotten on a calculator or by hand. The reason is that Lotus holds all numeric data to fifteen places of accuracy. To control Lotus's level of accuracy, use the @**INT** or @**ROUND** functions. For more information, refer to @**ROUND** in the "Spreadsheet Functions" section and see the next Hint.

HINT The following macro, when invoked, will edit the current cell to include the **@ROUND** function, with two decimal places of accuracy for the value that the cell computes or holds.

{**EDIT**} {**HOME**}**@ROUND**({**END**},2)~

HINT In larger spreadsheets, automatic recalculation of the entire spreadsheet will slow down data entry. You may turn off the automatic recalculation with the /**W**orksheet,**G**lobal,**R**ecalculation, **M**anual command. When you turn it off, the spreadsheet only recalculates when the F9 (CALC) key is pressed. (See next Hazard.)

HAZARD When recalculation is manual, a CALC indicator at the bottom of the screen will tell you that your spreadsheet needs to be recalculated. Even so, it is an easy point to forget. To return Lotus to automatic recalculation, use the /**W**orksheet,**G**lobal,**R**ecalculation, **A**utomatic command.

RANGES

HINT When specifying a range by pointing to it, the period key may be used to shift the pointer's anchor from corner to corner. The blinking cursor indicates the free cell, the cell at the corner opposite the anchored cell. The anchor cell and free cell will shift each time the period key is pressed.

HINT You can use the /**R**ange,**N**ame,**C**reate command to name areas of the spreadsheet to facilitate rapid movement about the spreadsheet with the F5 (GOTO) key. First, name a cell in a specified area of the spreadsheet with a range name. When you are ready to move to the area, type the F5 (GOTO) key and answer its "Enter address to go to:" prompt by typing the F3 (NAME) key. The named ranges in the spreadsheet will be displayed in a menu at the top of the screen. You may use the pointer control keys to enter the name of your choice as the answer to the prompt.

HAZARD When naming ranges, you often may want to use abbreviated names to identify the ranges. Care must be taken, however, not to use a legal cell address as a range name. For example, a range holding an income statement for the 4th quarter might be named INC4, but should not be named IS4 since this is also a cell address. In such a case, Lotus always would recognize the name as a cell address, even if selected from a list of range names as described in the previous Hint.

HINT The top left cell of any range is the key cell for the range. The F5 (GOTO) key will send the pointer to the top left cell of a named range as the address to GOTO. The top left cell is specified as the TO range for a copy or move operation.

HINT If a range has been named, both the top left and bottom right corner cells are key cells for identifying the range by name. If either of these cells is deleted with the /**W**orksheet,**D**elete command, or if either is replaced with the /**M**ove command, the range becomes undefined even though its name remains intact. Any formulas referencing the range name will display ERR.

CELL REFERENCES

HINT When pointing to cells while entering a formula, the F4 (ABS) key may be used to automatically insert dollar signs ($) into the cell reference for the cell that the pointer is currently pointing to.

HINT Moving a cell or range of cells with the /**M**ove command does not cause a change in cell references in the same manner as copying a cell or range of cells with the /**C**opy command. With the /**M**ove command, all cells with references to cells in the moved range have their references updated in a relative fashion. The updating occurs even if the references were originally entered as absolute. References in the moved range are updated only if they are references to other cells in the moved range.

HINT You may keep a reference to a named range absolute by inserting a dollar sign ($) in front of the range's name. For example, if the range B5..B20 were named EXPENSES, the name in a function such as @**SUM**($EXPENSES) would be interpreted by Lotus as @**SUM**($B$5..$B$20). If range names are specified in a formula without the dollar sign, any copy operation involving the range reference will adjust the range's location in a relative fashion.

HAZARD It is possible to create a cell reference that is circular. By tracking the cell references, you find that they lead back to the original cell, thus forming a circle of references with every cell's displayed value dependent on that of the next. In a few esoteric applications, you may do this intentionally. Usually, however, it indicates that an error has been made. Circular references are detected by Lotus and when one occurs, a CIRC indicator is displayed at the bottom of the screen.

ALTERING THE SPREADSHEET

HAZARD Avoid using the commands /**W**orksheet,**I**nsert and /**W**orksheet,**D**elete to expand or contract areas of the spreadsheet by inserting and deleting rows and columns. When possible, use the /**M**ove command instead to avoid accidentally inserting or deleting rows or columns important to other areas of the spreadsheet. For instance, when a row is deleted, it is deleted from the entire spreadsheet.

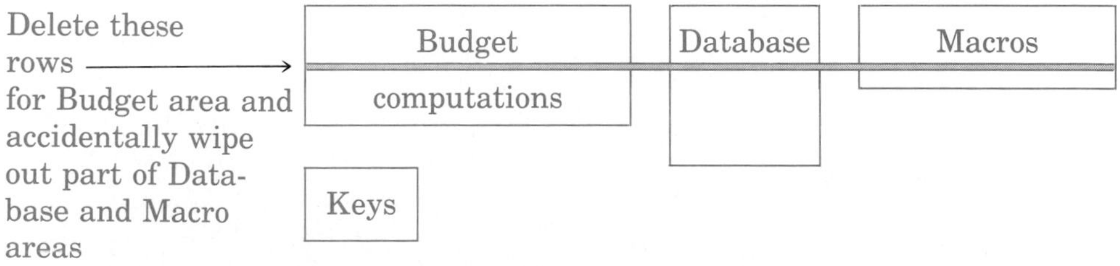

By using the /**M**ove command, you overcome the problem. Here you would move the FROM range indicated to the TO range indicated.

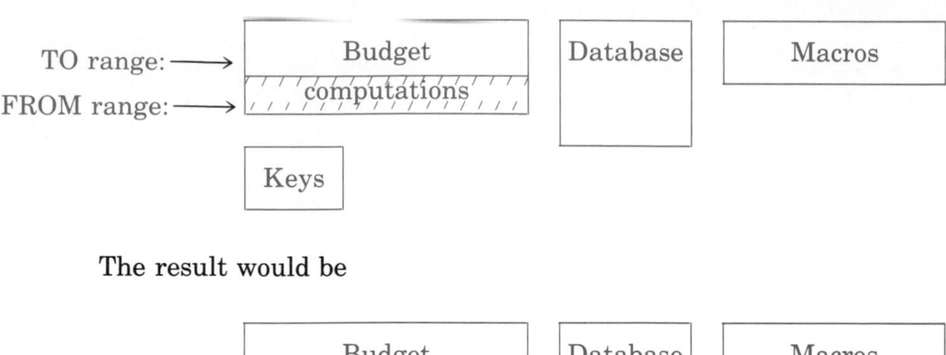

The result would be

HINT Any spreadsheet data that are arranged in columns may be sorted with the /**D**ata,**S**ort command. This can be useful for setting up or restructuring **@VLOOKUP** tables.

HAZARD When you use the /**D**ata,**S**ort commands, if one or more columns are accidentally omitted from the data range to sort, the entire set of data will probably be irreparably altered. When several sorting operations must be done on the same data range, it is a good idea to use the /**R**ange,**N**ame,**C**reate command to name the range, and then use its range name to specify it as the range to sort with the /**D**ata,**S**ort,**D**ata-Range command.

SPREADSHEET DESIGN

HINT The amount of RAM that a spreadsheet uses is dependent on the size of its active area. The active area is defined as the rectangle encompassing all of the cells into which data have been entered. For example:

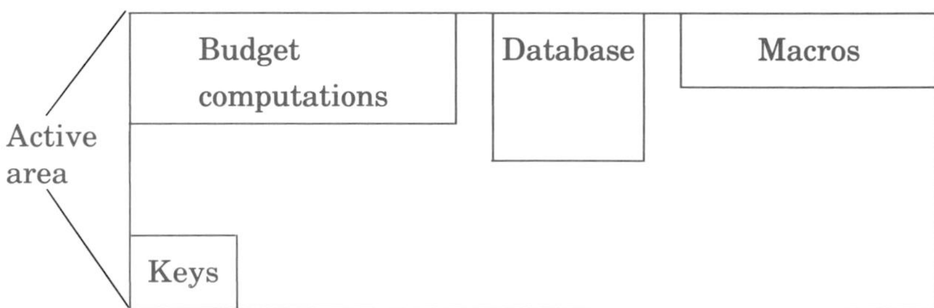

Here the active area is much larger than the area necessary to hold the spreadsheet's data, and the difference in size uses up RAM. Although rules of good spreadsheet design may require that some areas of the spreadsheet be left blank, you also will want to consider RAM limitations when you map out a large spreadsheet.

HINT If you move data, delete rows and/or columns, or erase a range of cells in a spreadsheet to make more RAM available, the active area of the current spreadsheet remains the same and you have no immediate gain. The End,Home keystroke sequence may be used to verify the position of the right-most and bottom-most cell in the active area. To decrease the active area and make more RAM available, use the /**F**ile,**X**tract,**F**ormulas command to save the range that now encompasses all spreadsheet entries to disk. Then retrieve the Xtracted file with the /**F**ile,**R**etrieve command.

PHANTOM SPACE CHARACTERS

HAZARD When a space character is inadvertently added to the end of a character string, you may experience errors that are difficult to detect. When entering range names, field names for a database, or macro keystroke cells, use particular care that unwanted spaces do not occur at the end of an entry. For example, if a macro that is supposed to round the contents of a cell to two decimal places is entered as

‖ {**EDIT**} {**HOME**}@**ROUND**({**END**},2)~ ↵ ‖

when the macro is executed a space will be entered into the current cell as soon as the pointer is moved upon completion of the macro, and the original cell entry will be lost.

A database field name or range name with a trailing space will not match the same name without the trailing space. If a /**D**ata,**Q**uery operation is not working properly, check for phantom spaces at the end of field names in the Input, Output, and Criterion ranges. If an error message occurs indicating that a range name you have used does not exist, check that you have not added a trailing space.

STUDY QUESTIONS

1. With thc spreadsheet pointer on cell D2, the screen appears as

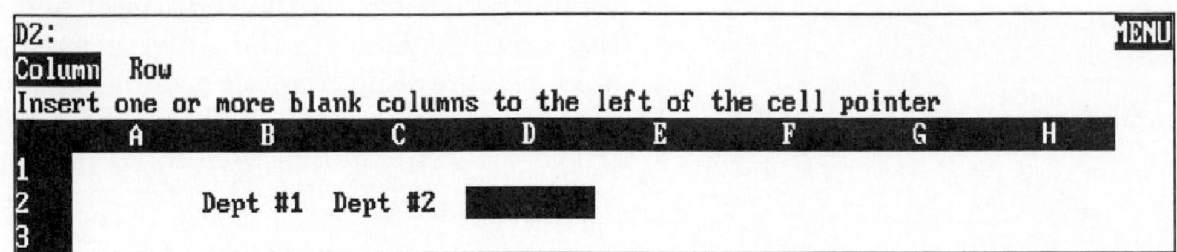

You try entering "Dept #3" into cell D2, but instead of seeing the date being entered you hear several beeps. What is the problem?

____

2. The spreadsheet pointer is on cell B2. You are trying to enter a row of column labels. You type ‖1st Quarter‖ to enter the first cell's data and the screen appears as

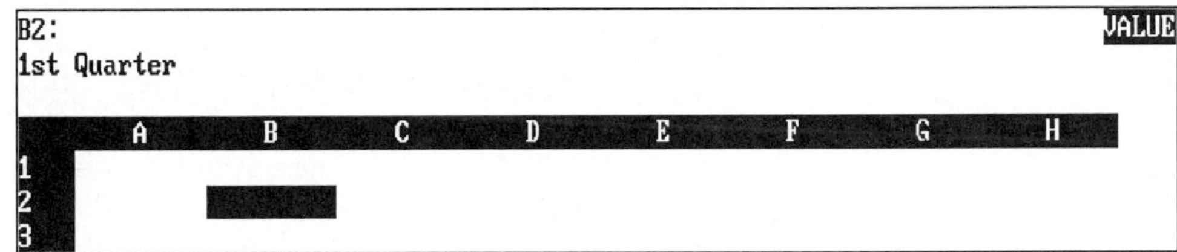

When you type the Enter key to enter the data into B2, the computer beeps. What is the problem and how can it be solved?

____

____

____

3. The following spreadsheet is used for a simple break-even model.

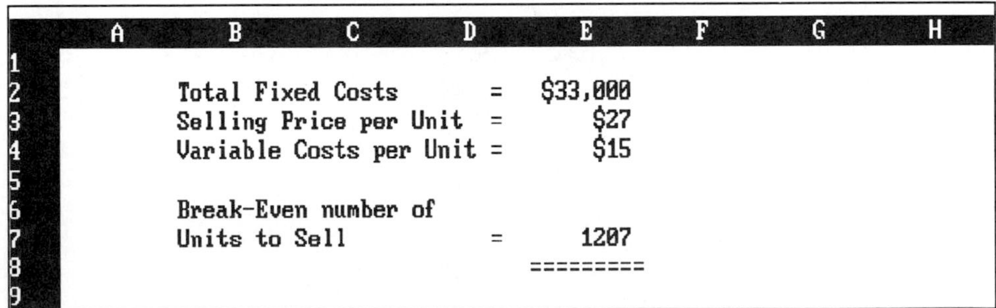

a. The difference between a unit's selling price and its variable cost is the contribution margin. You determine break-even sales in units by dividing total fixed costs by a unit's contribution margin. The formula in cell E7 has been entered as +E2/E3−E4. The resulting answer of 1207, however, is incorrect. The actual answer should be derived by Price − Variable Cost = $12, and $33,000/$12 = $2750. What is the problem and how can it be solved?

b. Another way of mathematically "saying" the same thing as the formula in the last question is "the reciprocal of the contribution margin times fixed cost, or 1/contribution margin * fixed cost." What would be an appropriate formula, using this alternate form of the equation, to enter into cell E7?

4. The following spreadsheet is designed to provide a simple financial forecast. The keys for the spreadsheet are a beginning sales figure of $65,000 for January; an expected growth in sales of 1.00% per month for the year; and the cost of goods sold as a percent of sales equal to 65.00%. The cells showing percent figures hold numeric constants formatted with the /**R**ange,**F**ormat,**P**ercent command. All other cells holding numeric data have been formatted with the /**R**ange,**F**ormat,**C**urrency command (0 decimal places).

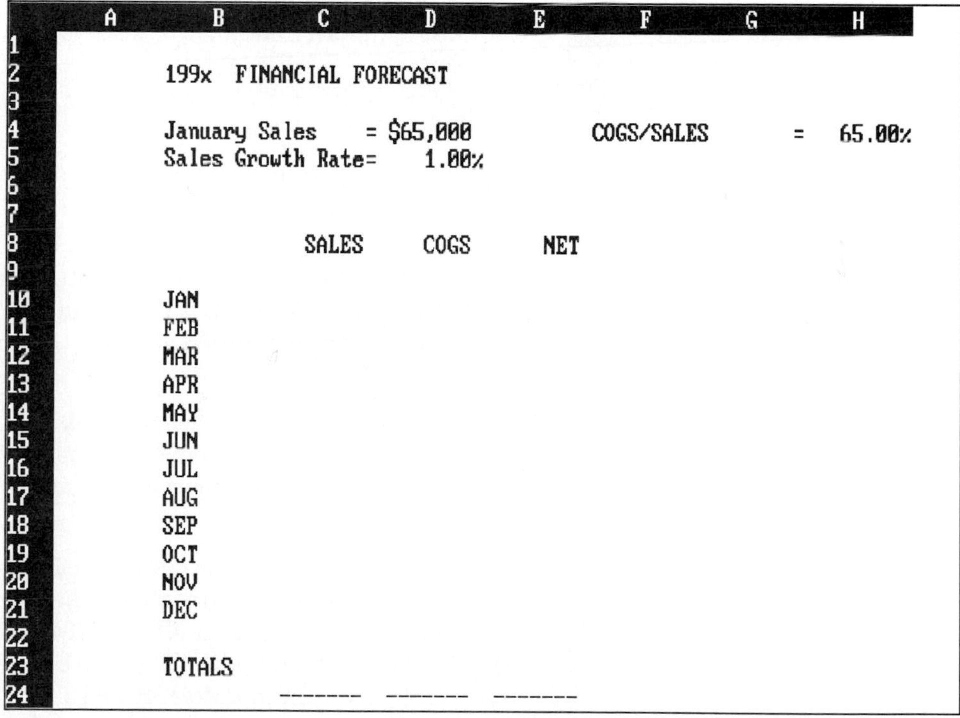

	A	B	C	D	E	F	G	H
1								
2		199x FINANCIAL FORECAST						
3								
4		January Sales =		$65,000		COGS/SALES	=	65.00%
5		Sales Growth Rate=		1.00%				
6								
7								
8			SALES	COGS	NET			
9								
10		JAN						
11		FEB						
12		MAR						
13		APR						
14		MAY						
15		JUN						
16		JUL						
17		AUG						
18		SEP						
19		OCT						
20		NOV						
21		DEC						
22								
23		TOTALS						
24			-------	-------	-------			

a. The first formula you enter will be the formula to display January's sales figure. What would be an appropriate formula to enter into cell C10?

b. You will enter the next formula into C11. It will be the formula to display February's sales figure. The formula will be copied into the rest of the month cells in column C (C12..C21) with the /Copy command. What would be an appropriate formula to enter into cell C11?

____

```
      A         B         C         D         E         F         G         H
1
2          199x  FINANCIAL FORECAST
3
4          January Sales     = $65,000            COGS/SALES        =    65.00%
5          Sales Growth Rate=     1.00%
6
7
8                     SALES      COGS      NET
9
10         JAN       $65,000
11         FEB       $65,650
12         MAR       $66,307
13         APR       $66,970
14         MAY       $67,639
15         JUN       $68,316
16         JUL       $68,999
17         AUG       $69,689
18         SEP       $70,386
19         OCT       $71,090
20         NOV       $71,800
21         DEC       $72,518
22
23         TOTALS
24                   -------   -------   -------
```

c. Next enter the formula to total the C column into cell C23. Use a spreadsheet function. Once you enter the function, it will be copied into the two cells in row 23 (D23 and E23). What would be an appropriate entry for cell C23?

____

d. Next enter the formula for January's COGS into D10. The formula will be copied into the remaining cells in the column (D11..D21). What would be an appropriate formula to enter into cell D10?

____

e. NET is the difference between SALES and COGS for each month. The next steps in creating this forecasting spreadsheet are to enter a formula into January's NET (E10) and to copy that formula into the rest of the months' NET cells (E11..E21). What would be an appropriate formula to enter into E10?

____

f. Checking the spreadsheet with your calculator, you find the SALES TOTALS (C23) to be off by a dollar. Why the discrepancy? How can it be remedied?

____

____

5. The next five questions refer to the following spreadsheet. The constants and formulas that are entered in column D are shown here documented to the right on the same row in which they occur.

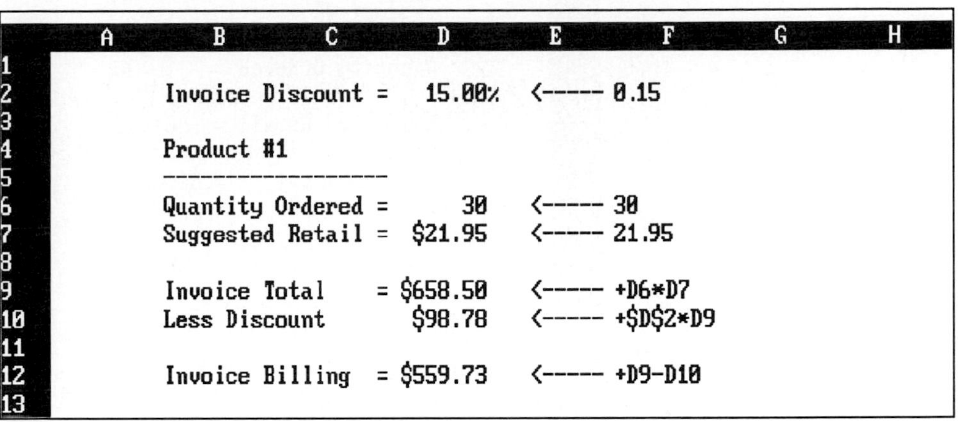

```
     A    B    C    D      E    F    G    H
1
2         Invoice Discount =  15.00%   <----- 0.15
3
4         Product #1
5         ------------------
6         Quantity Ordered =     30    <----- 30
7         Suggested Retail = $21.95    <----- 21.95
8
9         Invoice Total    = $658.50   <----- +D6*D7
10        Less Discount       $98.78   <----- +$D$2*D9
11
12        Invoice Billing  = $559.73   <----- +D9-D10
13
```

a. If the formula in cell D10 were copied into the second cell to its right, F10, what would be the formula in cell F10 after the copy operation?

____

b. If the formula in cell D12 were copied into cell D14, what would be the formula in cell D14 after the copy operation?

____

c. If the formula in cell D12 were copied into cell F9, what would be the formula in cell F9 after the copy operation?

____

d. If the /Move command were used to move the formula in cell D9 to the right two cells (to F9), what would be the formulas in cells D10, D12, and F9 after the move operation?

____

____

____

e. If a single row were inserted with the pointer on the seventh row, as shown in the following screen, what would be the formulas in cells D10, D11, and D13 after the insertion?

____

____

____

```
       A      B       C       D       E       F       G       H
1
2          Invoice Discount =   15.00%
3
4          Product #1
5          ------------------
6          Quantity Ordered =       30
7
8          Suggested Retail =  $21.95
9
10         Invoice Total    = $658.50
11         Less Discount       $98.78
12
13         Invoice Billing  = $559.73
14
```

6. The default global column width for a spreadsheet is nine characters. If you use the /**W**orksheet,**C**olumn,**S**et-Width command to set column C to 12 characters wide, and then use the /**W**orksheet,**G**lobal,**C**olumn-Width command to set the spreadsheet's columns one character wider (ten characters each), what is the effect on the width of column C?

____

7. A range of cells is formatted to display currency format with zero (0) decimal places with the /**R**ange,**F**ormat,**C**urrency command. The spreadsheet then is globally formatted to display currency format with two decimal places with the /**W**orksheet,**G**lobal,**F**ormat,**C**urrency command. What is the effect on the previously formatted range?

____

8. The following spreadsheet is designed to provide budget information for a monthly period. Projected sales are compared to actual sales. A budgeted labor cost based on 17.5% of actual sales is compared to an actual labor cost, and a budgeted cost of goods sold based on 55% of actual sales is compared against actual COGS. The formulas and constants used in the spreadsheet are documented on the same line in which they occur. How might the spreadsheet have been better designed?

____

____

```
       A      B       C       D       E       F       G       H
1
2          Monthly Report    DECEMBER             1990
3          ----------------------------------------------
4          Projected Sales           =   4,500 <----- 4500
5          Actual Sales              =   5,200 <----- 5200
6          Over (Under) Projected    =     700 <----- +E5-E4
7          Budgeted Labor Cost       =     910 <----- 0.175*E5
8          Actual Labor Cost         =   1,200 <----- 1200
9          Over (Under) Budget       =     290 <----- +E8-E7
10         Budgeted COGS             =   2,860 <----- 0.55*E5
11         Actual COGS               =   2,750 <----- 2750
12         Over (Under) Budget       =   (110) <----- +E11-E10
13
```

9. Describe the steps involved in making the preceding example a spreadsheet template to be used each month.

10. Use the following inventory spreadsheet for the next five questions.

	A	B	C	D	E	F	G
1		Item Part	Quantity	Per Unit		Extensions	
2		Number	On Hand	Cost	Price	Cost	Price
3		19165	35	$1.21	$1.65	$42.35	$57.75
4		19166	46	$0.35	$0.49	$16.10	$22.54
5		19167	89	$3.55	$4.80	$315.95	$427.20
6		19168	12	$2.67	$3.60	$32.04	$43.20
7		19169	53	$2.25	$3.00	$119.25	$159.00
8		19170	6	$1.95	$2.65	$11.70	$15.90
9		19171	22	$1.55	$2.10	$34.10	$46.20
10		19172	31	$5.50	$7.45	$170.50	$230.95
11		19173	100	$3.95	$5.35	$395.00	$535.00
12		19174	19	$4.25	$5.75	$80.75	$109.25
13		19175	77	$0.65	$0.85	$50.05	$65.45
14		19176	33	$1.19	$1.60	$39.27	$52.80
15							
16		INVENTORY LEVELS					
17		Maximum Quantity =		100			
18		Minimum Quantity =		6			
19		Average Quantity =		44			
20							
21		INVENTORY VALUATION					
22		Total Value of Inventory (Cost)				$1,307.06	
23		Avg. Value of Inventory per Item (Cost)				$108.92	
24							

a. In cell D17 a formula using a spreadsheet function has been entered. It returns the highest value found in its argument(s) and is used here to indicate the highest inventory quantity on hand for a single item. What is an appropriate form for the function entered into cell D17?

b. A similar formula has been entered into cell D18. It returns the lowest value found in its argument(s) and is used here to indicate the lowest inventory quantity on hand for a single item. What is an appropriate form for the function entered into cell D18?

c. The next cell entry (D19) is a formula using a function to return the mean average quantity on hand. This value (43.583333) has, in turn, been rounded by another function in the formula to return the final value of 44. What is an appropriate form for the functions entered in cell D19?

d. The extensions shown are dollar values of inventory based on per unit cost or selling price times quantity on hand. Cell F22, under the label INVENTORY VALUATION, contains a function returning the total inventory dollar amount of the cost extensions. What would be an appropriate formula for cell F22?

____

e. The final formula, in cell F23, computes the average inventory value for all items inventoried. What would be an appropriate formula to enter into cell F22?

____

LOTUS 1-2-3 KEY TERM GLOSSARY

Absolute Cell Reference A form of cell reference in a formula that keeps the referenced cell the same regardless of the location to which the formula is copied.

Anchor To specify the first cell of a range when pointing to a range.

Arguments References, ranges, values, or formulas for a function to act upon.

Cell Address The location of a cell in the spreadsheet, expressed as a combination of a letter (column) and a number (row).

Cell Reference See *Cell Address.*

Command Pointer Highlighted area of the control panel which displays the current choice in a menu.

Control Panel The top three lines of the monitor where Lotus displays menus, prompts, and commands.

Database Data arranged in groups of records, each record consisting of one or more fields.

Default A term used to define a setting that is used by Lotus when not specified by the user.

Edit Cue Blinking highlighted word EDIT which appears at the upper right corner of the monitor to indicate Lotus is in its edit mode.

Extracting Data from the Database Copying selected information from the database to another part of the spreadsheet based upon criteria designated by the user.

Field Name The name of a column where similar information is stored in each record of a database.

Function Precoded routines that perform a series of operations or calculations quickly. Functions are often shortcuts to accomplish what would otherwise require long numeric expressions.

Global An operation that is performed throughout the spreadsheet in all applicable cases.

Help Screen A screen containing information about a command, operation, and so forth, which is accessed by typing the **F1** (Help) key.

Label A string expression that is entered into a cell.

Macro A collection of keystrokes that is automatically executed when the macro is invoked.

Menus Displays of commands on the control panel at the top of the screen from which you may select.

Mixed References Cell references that are partly relative and partly absolute.

Numeric A cell entry that evaluates numeric data.

Range One cell, or any rectangular group of cells.

Record A set of related information in a database, comprised of one or more fields.

Relative A form of cell reference in a formula that allows the referenced cell to change when the formula is copied to another location.

Repeating Label Prefix The backslash (\) symbol which will cause the next characters entered in a cell to be repeated for the entire width of the cell.

Scroll To move the area of the spreadsheet visible on the monitor to another section of the spreadsheet.

Settings Sheet Information about spreadsheet settings, displayed in place of the normal spreadsheet when certain commands are executed.

Spreadsheet A software designed for entering data and performing calculations using columns and rows.

Spreadsheet Keys Constants that are the source of all values displayed in the spreadsheet.

Spreadsheet Pointer A highlighted indicator which shows which cell, or group of cells, is currently being referenced.

Sticky Menus Menus that do not immediately return the user to the data entry mode.

String A cell entry that must be a label (i.e., non-numeric expression).

Synchronized Scrolling Scrolling two separate spreadsheets as they appear in two different windows.

Template A master copy of a spreadsheet that is designed to be used more than once with new data entered and with formulas that obtain values.

Value A cell entry that may be either numeric or a string.

Window Lines The top three lines of the monitor which Lotus reserves for the Control Panel.

LOTUS 1-2-3 OPERATION AND COMMAND SUMMARY

LOTUS CONTROL KEYS

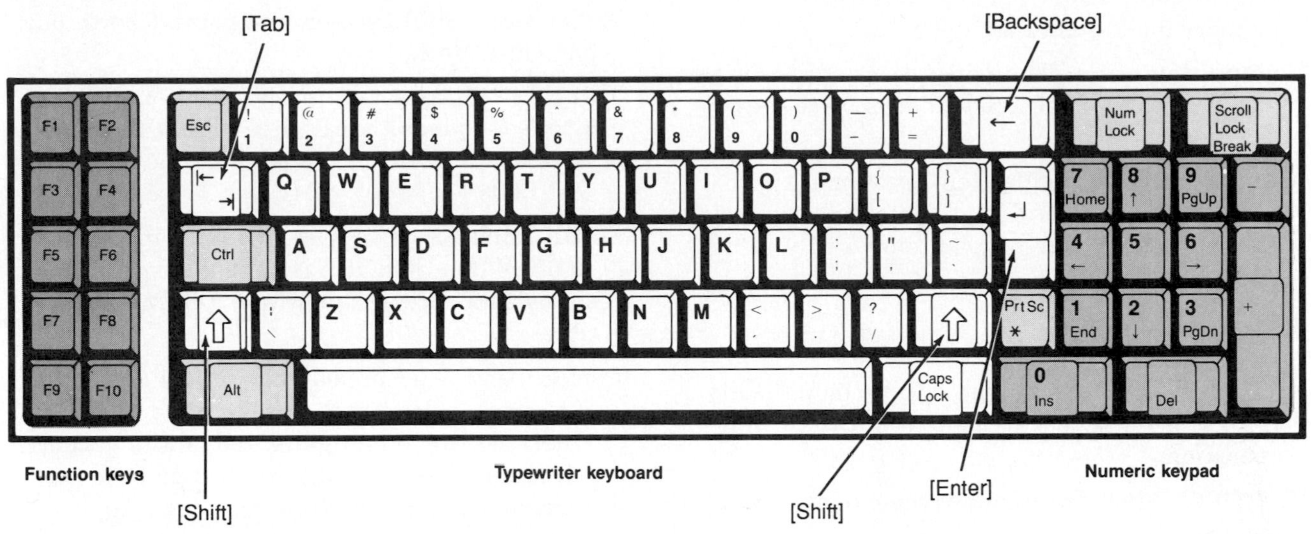

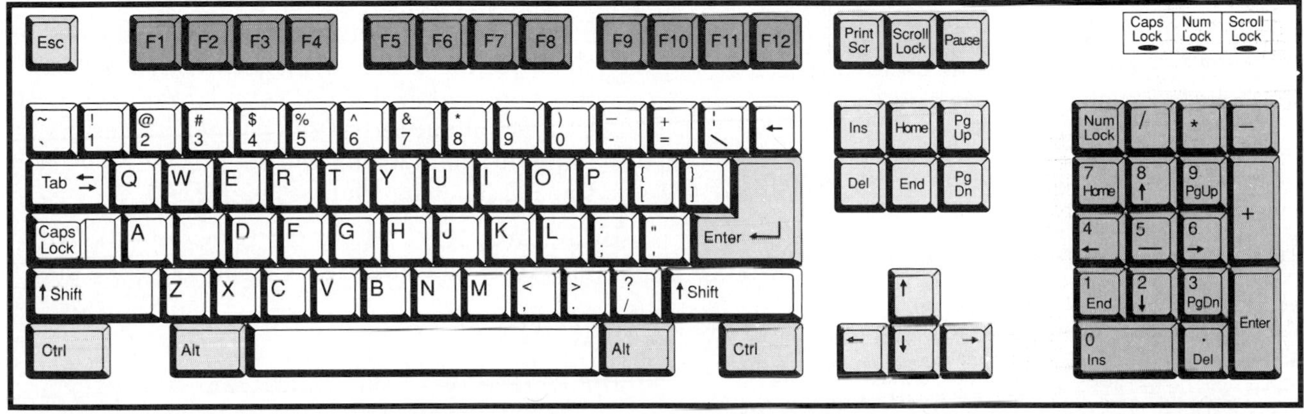

Normal Typewriter Keys

Control Keys

Function Keys

Numeric Keypad/Cursor Movement Keys

Cursor Movement Keys Only

KEY COMBINATIONS

Ctrl-Break Cancels any Lotus 1-2-3 command operation. Returns the spreadsheet to the READY mode.

Alt-Alpha Key Used with alphabetic keys to invoke keyboard macros.

Alt-F1 COMPOSE Used to compose international characters by entering a combination of standard keyboard characters.

Alt-F2 STEP Turns STEP mode on/off. The STEP mode is used during execution of macros. Lotus waits for a keystroke before executing each step of the macro.

Alt-F3 RUN Allows you to execute a macro by selecting the named range from a list of all named ranges.

Alt-F4 UNDO Cancels the last change made to the spreadsheet.

Alt-F5 LEARN Turns the macro learn mode on and off. Used to automatically enter keystrokes as macro commands in range specified with /Worksheet,Learn command.

OTHER CONTROL KEYS

Slash Key (/) Calls the spreadsheet's Main menu of commands.

Enter Key ↵ Enters the current line into memory for Lotus to act upon.

Escape Key Cancels an operation when editing a cell. In the MENU mode, backs up to previous menu level.

Num Lock Key Toggles ten-key numeric keypad to pointer control keys. The Shift key may be used to shift this keypad temporarily to the opposite mode.

FUNCTION KEYS 1–10

F1 HELP Accesses Lotus's on-line help facility. Help screens appear in context of the current operation.

F2 EDIT Allows contents of the current cell to be edited.

F3 NAME Displays the list of current range names while in the POINT mode.

F4 ABS Facilitates defining cell references as absolute or relative when in the POINT, VALUE, or EDIT mode.

F5 GOTO Moves the pointer to the specified cell or range name.

F6 WINDOW Moves the pointer from one window to the other.

F7 QUERY Repeats the last /**D**ata,**Q**uery operation.

F8 TABLE Repeats the last /**D**ata,**T**able operation.

F9 CALC Recalculates the spreadsheet.

F10 GRAPH Displays the currently defined graph.

POINTER CONTROL KEYS

Arrow Keys Move pointer one cell at a time in the direction of the arrows.

Home Key Moves pointer to top left corner of spreadsheet (A1) in the READY or POINT modes. In EDIT mode, moves cursor to beginning of cell entry.

PgUp Key Shifts screen and pointer up one page at a time.

PgDn Key Shifts screen and pointer down one page at a time.

Tab Key Shifts screen to the right one page at a time (same as Ctrl-Right). Shift-Tab shifts screen to the left one page at a time (same as Ctrl-Left).

Scroll Lock Key Toggles SCROLL indicator on/off. When SCROLL is on, scrolling of the spreadsheet occurs one row or column at a time.

Period Key Anchors current cell as one corner of a range, allowing the range to be expanded. When the range is highlighted, shifts anchor cell and free cell to allow the range to be expanded or contracted from another corner.

POINTER KEY COMBINATIONS

End-Arrow Key Causes the pointer to move in the direction of the arrow until it reaches the last nonblank cell if the pointer was originally on a nonblank cell. If the pointer was originally on a blank cell, the pointer will move to the cell following the last blank cell.

End-Home Key Moves the pointer to the bottom right cell in the spreadsheet's active area.

EDITING KEYS

Backspace Key Backspaces and erases the character to the left of the cursor when entering data into a cell or when editing a cell or command parameter.

Del Key Erases the character at the cursor location when editing a cell or command parameter.

Ins Key Toggles OVR indicator (overwrite) on and off. When in the EDIT mode, characters are inserted unless OVR is toggled on. At completion of the entry, OVR is turned off automatically.

LOTUS 1-2-3 COMMAND INDEX

Command	Keystroke
Absolute References	F4 (ABS)
Absolute value	@**ABS**
Clear Graph Settings	/**G**raph,**R**eset
Clear Print Settings	/**P**rint,**P**rinter,**C**lear
Clear Titles	/**W**orksheet,**T**itles,**C**lear

Clear Window	/Worksheet,Window,Clear
Clear Worksheet	/Worksheet,Erase
Date Calculations	@DAY, @MONTH, @YEAR
Date Display	/Range,Format,Date
Date Entry Function	@DATE
Date System Date/Time	@NOW
Decimal Places Calculation	@ROUND,@INT
Decimal Places Display	/Range,Format
Delete Cell Contents	/Range,Erase
Delete Character	F2 (EDIT)
Delete Column or Row	/Worksheet,Delete
Delete File	/File,Erase
Delete Range Name, single	/Range,Name,Delete
Delete Range Names, all	/Range,Name,Reset
Delete Records	/Data,Query,Delete
Erase	See Delete
Format, Default	/Worksheet,Global,Format
Format, Range	/Range,Format
Formulas, Removing	/Range,Value
Formulas, Displaying on Screen	/Range,Format,Text
Formulas, Printing	/Print,Printer,Options,Other,Cell-Formulas
Hide Cell	/Range,Format,Hidden
Hide Column	/Worksheet,Column,Hide
Insert Character	F2 (EDIT)
Insert Column or Row	/Worksheet,Insert
Justify Labels, Default	/Worksheet,Global,Label-Prefix
Justify Labels in Range	/Range,Label
Justify Text	/Range,Justify
Move Range	/Move
Numbering, Automatic	/Data,Fill
Page Breaks, Printing	/Worksheet,Page
Password, File Protection	/File,Save
Print Graphs	/Graph,Save; PrintGraph
Printer Control Codes	/Print,Printer,Options,Setup
Printer Control Codes	/Worksheet,Global,Default,Printer,Setup
Printer Selection	/Worksheet,Global,Default,Printer,Name
Protect Range of Cells On/Off	/Range,Protect; /Range,Unprotect
Protection of Cells On/Off	/Worksheet,Global,Protection
Protection On, Data Entry	/Range,Input
Ranges, Listing Named Ranges	/Range,Name,Table
Ranges, Locating Named Ranges	F5 (GOTO); F3 (NAME)
Ranges, Naming	/Range,Name,Create
Recalculation Method	/Worksheet,Global,Recalculation
Recalculation, Manual	F9 (CALC)
Regression Analysis	/Data,Regression
Save Graph for Printing	/Graph,Save
Save Graph Settings	/Graph,Name
Save Range as File	/File,Xtract
Save Worksheet	/File,Save
Sorting	/Data,Sort
Table, Listing Named Ranges	/Range,Name,Table
Tables, Transpose Columns and Rows	/Range,Transpose
Time Calculation	@HOUR, @MINUTE, @SECOND
Time Entry	@TIME
Time Format	/Range,Format,Date,Time
Width of Column, single	/Worksheet,Column,Set-Width
Width of Columns, default	/Worksheet,Global,Column-Width
Windows, Moving Cursor	F6 (WINDOW)
Zero Display	/Worksheet,Global,Zero

/WORKSHEET COMMANDS

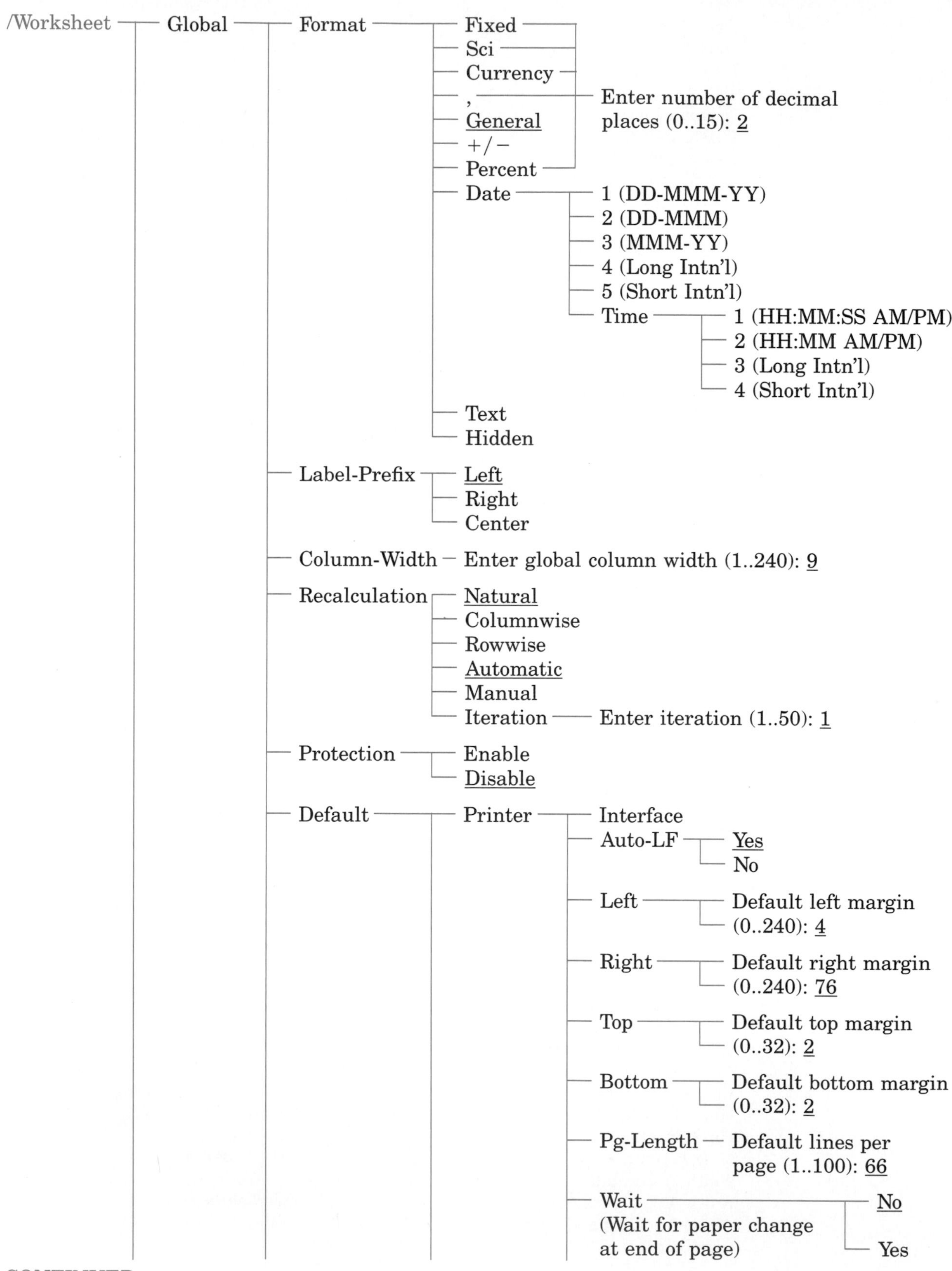

NOTE: Shaded commands shown here were added to Lotus 1-2-3 with Version 2.2. If you are using Version 2.01, you will not see these commands on your screen.

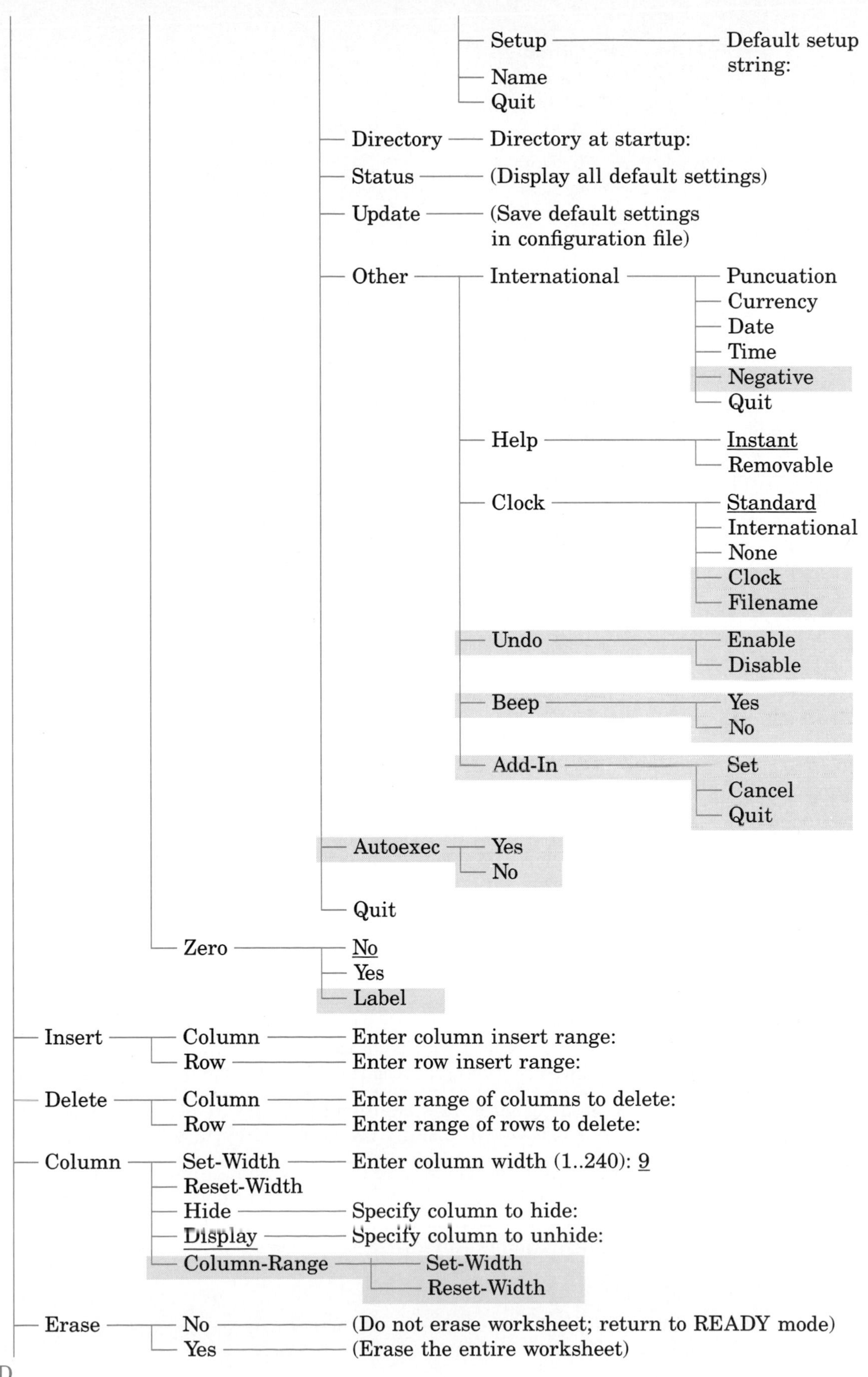

Setup
Default setup string:
Name
Quit
Directory
Directory at startup:
Status
(Display all default settings)
Update
(Save default settings in configuration file)
Other
International
Puncuation
Currency
Date
Time
Negative
Quit
Help
Instant
Removable
Clock
Standard
International
None
Clock
Filename
Undo
Enable
Disable
Beep
Yes
No
Add-In
Set
Cancel
Quit
Autoexec
Yes
No
Quit
Zero
No
Yes
Label
Insert
Column
Enter column insert range:
Row
Enter row insert range:
Delete
Column
Enter range of columns to delete:
Row
Enter range of rows to delete:
Column
Set-Width
Enter column width (1..240): 9
Reset-Width
Hide
Specify column to hide:
Display
Specify column to unhide:
Column-Range
Set-Width
Reset-Width
Erase
No
(Do not erase worksheet; return to READY mode)
Yes
(Erase the entire worksheet)

CONTINUED

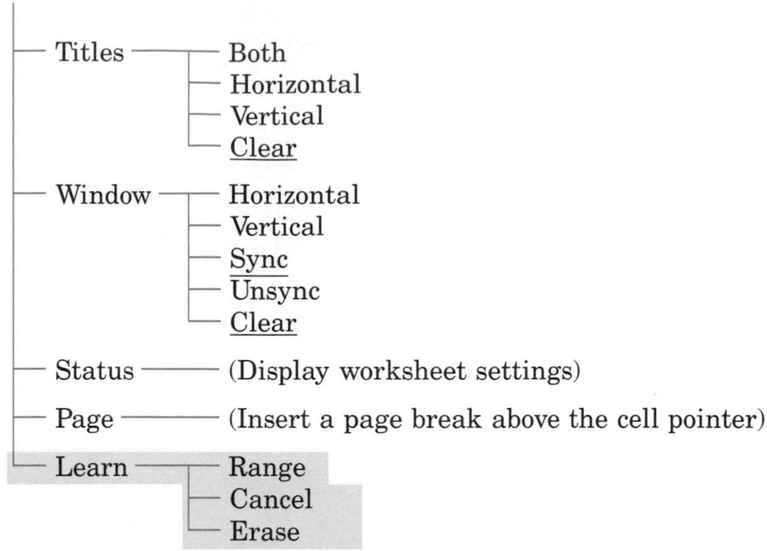

/**W**orksheet **G**lobal **F**ormat **F**ixed **S**ci **C**urrency **,** **G**eneral **+**/– **P**ercent **D**ate **T**ime **T**ext **H**idden	Sets global format for display of values. **F**ixed specifies the number of decimal places and **S**ci displays scientific notation. **C**urrency displays values with a currency sign (a preceding $ by default), commas separating thousands, and negative values in parentheses. **,** (comma) displays values with commas separating thousands and negative values in parentheses. **G**eneral (default) displays values with the maximum precision allowed by the column width. **+**/– displays a number of + or – signs in the cell, + signs for positive values and – signs for negative values. **P**ercent displays the value as a percentage, followed by the % sign. **D**ate provides a further menu of various date and **T**ime formats. **T**ext displays the actual cell contents, including formulas and functions. **H**idden suppresses the display of cell contents for all cells in the spreadsheet set to the default format.
/**W**orksheet **G**lobal **L**abel-Prefix **L**eft **R**ight **C**enter	Sets global alignment of labels. **L**eft (default) justifies labels from the left side of the cells. **R**ight justifies labels from the right side of the cells. **C**enter centers labels in cells.
/**W**orksheet **G**lobal **C**olumn-Width	Sets global column width. Default is nine characters. To see the effect of changing column widths on the spreadsheet, you may increase the width displayed by typing cursor right or decrease it by typing cursor left.
/**W**orksheet **G**lobal **R**ecalculation **N**atural **C**olumnwise **R**owwise **A**utomatic **M**anual **I**teration	Sets the order of recalculation to **N**atural, **C**olumnwise, or **R**owwise. Default order is **N**atural (usually the most appropriate for recalculation). **R**ecalculation also may be set either to **A**utomatic or **M**anual. When **M**anual is selected, automatic recalculation is turned off and the CALC Function key (F9) must be used to recalculate the spreadsheet. Default recalculation is **A**utomatic.

/**W**orksheet **G**lobal **P**rotection **E**nable **D**isable	Sets global protection status of spreadsheet. Selections are **E**nable to turn protection on and **D**isable to turn protection off. Default status is off. With protection on, spreadsheet cells may not be edited unless they are within an unprotected range. (See **R**ange commands **/R,P** and **/R,U**.)
/**W**orksheet **G**lobal **D**efault **P**rinter **D**irectory **S**tatus **U**pdate **O**ther **I**ntn'l **H**elp **C**lock **U**ndo **B**eep **A**dd-In **A**utoexec	May be used to redefine default printer, default disk drive, and directory. Status displays current default settings. Default settings are held in a configuration file on the system disk and **U**pdate causes any changes made to be written to the file. **O**ther,**I**nternational allows you to redefine the punctuation used in entry and display of decimal places, thousands separators, function argument separators, currency, times, and negative numeric values. **O**ther,**H**elp determines access to the Lotus Help feature. **I**nstant causes the Help file to remain open during the entire session. The disk containing the Help file may not be removed. Use **I**nstant when Help is on a fixed disk. When **R**emovable is selected, the Help file is closed when you exit the Help feature. The disk may be removed. Use **R**emovable when the Help file is on a removable disk. **O**ther,**C**lock determines the date and time formats used for the time indicator in the lower left corner of the screen. **S**tandard sets the date format to Lotus standard long format and the time format to Lotus standard short format. **I**nternational sets the formats to those selected with the **/W,G,D,O**ther,**I**nternational command. **N**one suppresses display of the date and time indicator. **C**lock and **F**ilename are used, respectively, to change the indicator to either display the current date and time or the current filename. **O**ther,**U**ndo is used to turn the Undo feature on or off. When Undo is on, the most recent change made to a spreadsheet can be undone by typing Alt-F4. **O**ther,**B**eep is used to determine whether a beep or tone will be sounded when an error occurs. **O**ther,**A**dd-In is used to specify special add-in applications that should be loaded automatically whenever you begin a 1-2-3 work session. **A**utoexec is used to determine whether autoexec macros (those named \0) will begin executing when a spreadsheet is first loaded.
/**W**orksheet **G**lobal **Z**ero	Determines whether cells containing values equal to zero are displayed. **Y**es suppresses display of zero values. **N**o, the default setting, displays zero values. **L**abel allows you to specify text to appear in any numeric cell with a zero value.
/**W**orksheet **I**nsert **R**ow **C**olumn	Inserts one or more rows or columns in the spreadsheet. Rows are inserted just above the pointer; columns are inserted just to the left of the pointer. To insert more than one row or column, define the range of rows or columns to be inserted.

Command	Description
/Worksheet Delete Row Column	Deletes one or more rows or columns in the spreadsheets. A single row or column is deleted where the pointer is located. To delete more than one row or column, define the range of rows or columns to be deleted.
/Worksheet Column Set-Width Reset-Width Hide Display Column-Range Set-Width Reset-Width	Set-Width and Reset-Width are used to change the width of the column in which the pointer is currently located. Set-Width allows you to enter a new column width. To see the effect of the changing column width on the spreadsheet, you may increase the width by typing cursor right, or decrease it by typing cursor left. Reset-Width sets the column width to the current Global,Column-Width. Hide suppresses the display of columns while retaining the data contained in hidden columns. Display redisplays hidden columns. Columns that were hidden are marked with asterisks. Column-Range,Set-Width and Column-Range,Reset-Width are used to set or reset the width of several adjacent columns in a single operation.
/Worksheet Erase Yes No	Erases the current spreadsheet from the computer's RAM and displays a blank spreadsheet. Before the spreadsheet is erased, you must select Yes. Selecting No will cancel the Erase command. This precaution ensures that the spreadsheet is not inadvertently erased without being saved.
/Worksheet Titles Both Horizontal Vertical Clear	Freezes either rows, columns, or both as titles that will remain on the screen even if the pointer is moved to other locations on the spreadsheet. If Horizontal is selected, rows just above the pointer become titles. If Vertical is selected, columns just to the left of the pointer become titles. Both will produce both title rows and columns. Clear will unfreeze all titles. When titles are in use, the title rows and/or columns may only be accessed when in the POINT mode.
/Worksheet Window Horizontal Vertical Sync Unsync Clear	Creates two windows on the spreadsheet by splitting the screen either horizontally or vertically, allowing two separate portions of the spreadsheet to be viewed at the same time. Either area may be accessed, and the WINDOW Function key (F6) is used to move from one window to the other. Spreadsheet settings such as Formats and Titles may be defined differently for the two windows. Scrolling may be Synchronized or Unsynchronized. Clear will return the screen to just one window; the settings from the upper or left window will be retained.
/Worksheet Status	Displays current global settings, protection status, and amount of system memory (RAM) still available.
/Worksheet Page	Inserts a new row into the spreadsheet with a double colon (::) marking the page break in the current column of the new row. A new printed page will begin at the row below the page break row. Nothing else entered in the page break row will be printed.
/Worksheet Learn Range Cancel Erase	Used with the Alt-F5 Learn key to have macro keystrokes automatically recorded in a range of cells (the Learn Range) as they are typed on the keyboard. Learn is used to specify the Learn range, and Cancel is used to cancel any existing specification. Erase is used to erase all cells in the currently specified Learn range.

/RANGE COMMANDS

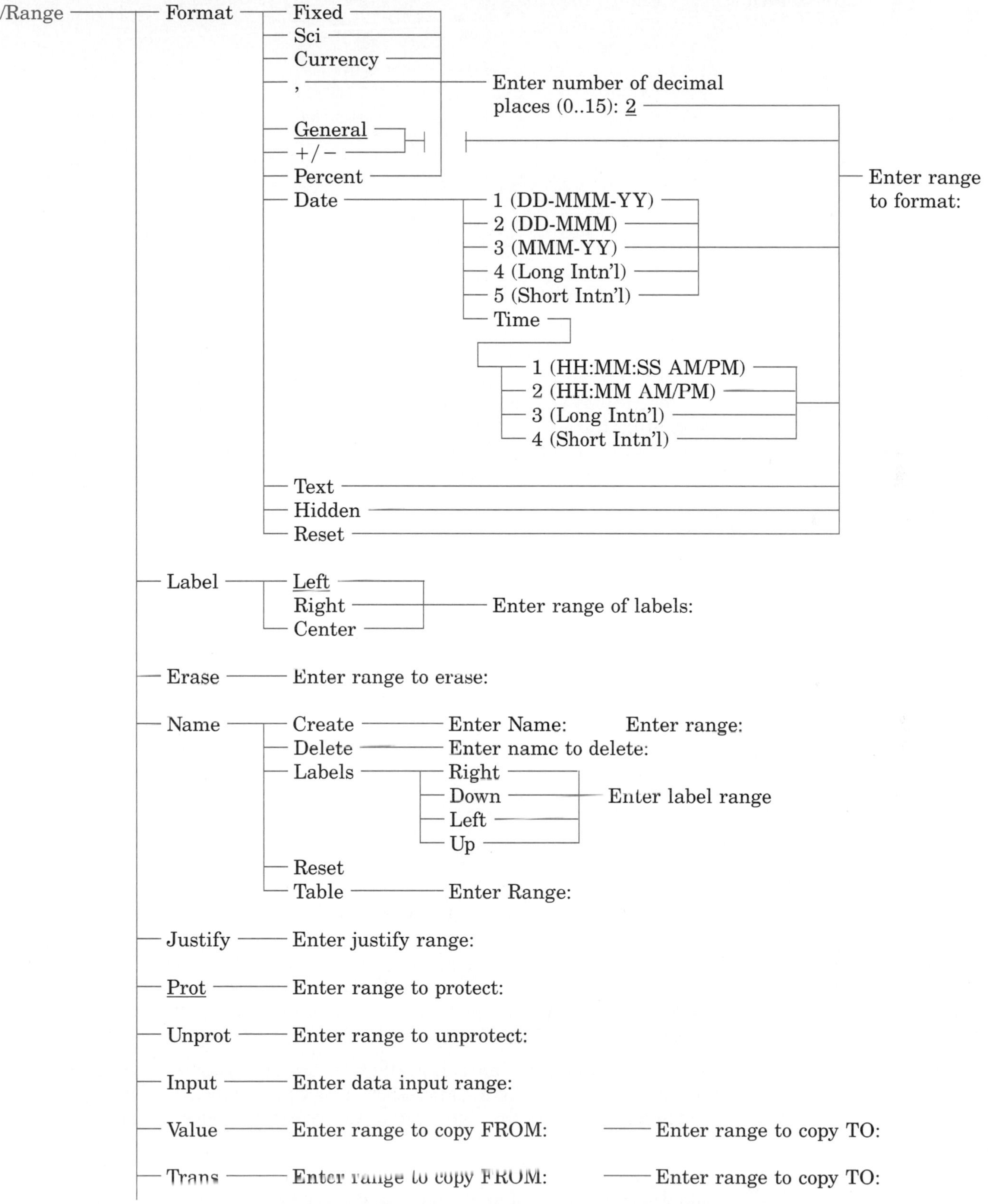

CONTINUED

NOTE: Shaded commands shown here were added to Lotus 1-2-3 with Version 2.2. If you are using Version 2.01, you will not see these commands on your screen.

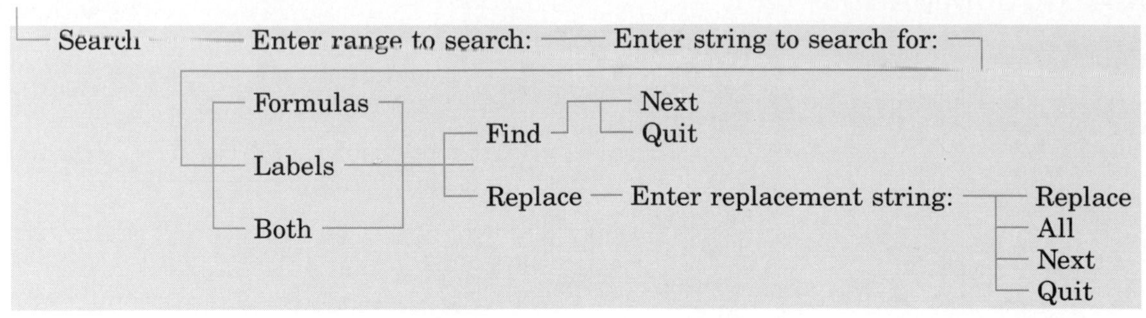

/Copy — Enter range to copy FROM: — Enter range to copy TO:

/Move — Enter range to move FROM: — Enter range to move TO:

/**R**ange **F**ormat **F**ixed **S**ci **C**urrency **,** **G**eneral **+**/− **P**ercent **D**ate **T**ime **T**ext **H**idden **R**eset	Sets format for display of values in specified range. **F**ixed specifies the number of decimal places and **S**ci displays scientific notation. **C**urrency displays values with a currency sign (a preceding $ by default), commas separating thousands, and negative values in parentheses. **,** (comma) displays values with commas separating thousands and negative values in parentheses. **G**eneral (default) displays values with the maximum precision allowed by the column width. **+**/− displays a number of + or − signs in the cell, + signs for positive values and − signs for negative values. **P**ercent displays the value as a percentage, followed by the % sign. **D**ate provides a further menu of various date and **T**ime formats. **T**ext displays the actual cell contents, including formulas and functions. **H**idden suppresses the display of cell contents in the range. **R**eset sets format to the currently selected **G**lobal,**D**efault,**F**ormat.
/**R**ange **L**abel **L**eft **R**ight **C**enter	Sets alignment of labels in the specified range. **L**eft (default) justifies labels from the left side of the cells. **R**ight justifies labels from the right side of the cells. **C**enter centers labels in cells.
/**R**ange **E**rase	Erases the contents of all cells in the specified range.
/**R**ange **N**ame **C**reate **D**elete **L**abels **R**ight **D**own **L**eft **U**p **R**eset **T**able	**C**reate allows a range to be named. Range names may be up to fifteen characters long. The name then may be used to specify the range in any function or command calling for a range. **D**elete is used to delete a single range name. **R**eset will delete all range names. Deleting cells at the upper left or lower right corner of a named range by deleting rows or columns (/**W**,**D**) will cause the range name to become undefined, and any cells referencing that range will display ERR. **L**abels may be used to automatically name ranges from cells containing labels. Options are **R**ight, **D**own, **L**eft, and **U**p to name, respectively, the single cell ranges to the right, below, to the left, or above a range of cells containing labels. **T**able alphabetically lists all existing range names and corresponding addresses in a two-column table. Locate the **T**able in an empty portion of the spreadsheet to avoid writing over existing data.

Command	Description
/**R**ange **J**ustify	Rearranges the contents of cells containing labels to fit within margins set by the specified range.
/**R**ange **P**rot **U**nprot **I**nput	By default, all cells in the spreadsheet are protected, but Global Protection is turned off. When Global Protection is turned on with the /**W**orksheet,**G**lobal,**P**rotection,**E**nable command, the corresponding /**R**ange commands are used as follows. **U**nprot is used to specify a range of cells to be unprotected, which allows editing of the cells. **P**rot is used to specify a range of cells to be protected, which prevents editing of the cells. **I**nput is used to specify a range of cells for data input, but pointer movement will be restricted to only the unprotected cells in the range. The data input operation continues until you type the Enter key without making any change to the current cell.
/**R**ange **V**alue	Copies a range of cells, converting formulas in the FROM range to values in the TO range. Locate TO range in an empty portion of the spreadsheet if you do not want the values to replace existing data in your spreadsheet.
/**R**ange **T**ranspose	Copies a range of cells, transposing columns and rows. For example, a range of 2 rows by 5 columns specified as the FROM range will be copied to the TO range occupying 5 rows by 2 columns.
/**R**ange **S**earch **F**ormulas **L**abels **B**oth **F**ind **R**eplace	Used to search for a sequence of characters (the search string) within a specified range of cells and optionally to replace the search string with another sequence of characters (the replacement string). You may specify that cells to be searched should be only **F**ormulas (values), only **L**abels, or **B**oth values and labels. **F**ind is used to locate cells containing the search string. If such a cell is located, the pointer stops on the cell and the occurrence of the search string is highlighted. Options are then **N**ext to find the next occurrence of the search string or **Q**uit to discontinue the search. **R**eplace is used to specify a replacement string before the search begins. When the search string is found, the following options are available: **R**eplace to replace the currently highlighted occurrence of the search string, and then continue the search; **A**ll to automatically replace what is currently highlighted and all subsequent occurrences of the search string; **N**ext to leave the highlighted occurrence of the search string intact and continue the search; and **Q**uit to discontinue the search.
/**C**opy	Copies the contents of a cell or range of cells to another cell or range of cells. Cell references in formulas will be adjusted unless they are specified as absolute references before the **C**opy command is used. The TO range coordinate is specified as the uppermost left corner of the range.
/**M**ove	While the **C**opy command causes duplication of a cell or range, the **M**ove command is used to physically move a cell or range of cells to another location on the spreadsheet. After defining the range to be moved, place the pointer at the upper left corner of the area to which the range is to be moved. All formulas referencing cells in a moved range are changed to reflect the new positions of those cells. Formulas within the moved range change only if their references are to other cells in the range.

/FILE COMMANDS

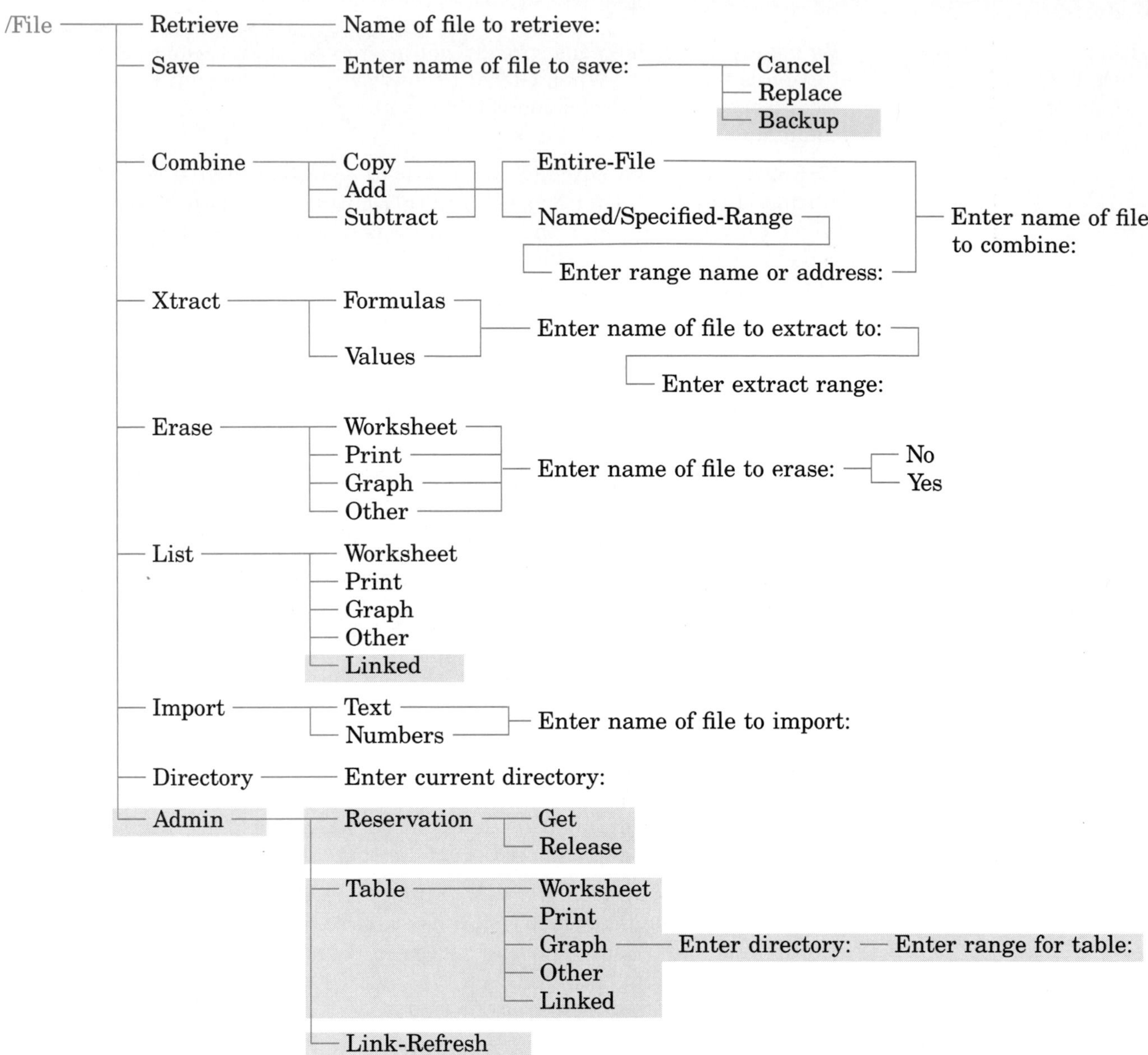

NOTE: Shaded commands shown here were added to Lotus 1-2-3 with Version 2.2. If you are using Version 2.01, you will not see these commands on your screen.

/**F**ile **R**etrieve	Erases the current spreadsheet and loads a new spreadsheet (.WK1) file from the diskette. Spreadsheet files on the current disk or directory appear on bottom menu line. The file to be loaded may be pointed to or typed in.
/**F**ile **S**ave *filename* *filename* P *password* **C**ancel **R**eplace **B**ackup	Saves the current spreadsheet on the diskette. If the spreadsheet originally was loaded into RAM with the **/F,R** command, the filename used to load it will appear on the prompt line. The diskette file copy may be replaced with the current spreadsheet, or a new filename may be entered. To create a password for a file, type the filename, a space, and the letter *P* before typing the Enter key. You will be prompted to enter a password and then reenter it for verification. A password may be up to fifteen characters long and a differentiation is made between upper- and lower-case letters. The same password then must be used when the file is retrieved (**/F,R**).

To delete a password, use the /**F**ile,**S**ave command. When the [PASSWORD PROTECTED] indicator appears next to the filename, type the Backspace or Escape key to remove the indicator, and then continue with the **S**ave procedure. To change a password, use the same procedure used to create a password.

If the file being saved already exists on the disk, you are given the options **C**ancel to cancel the save operation, **R**eplace to replace the existing file with the current spreadsheet, or **B**ackup to give the existing disk file the extension .BAK, and then save the current spreadsheet with the normal extension .WK1.

/**F**ile **C**ombine **C**opy **A**dd **S**ubtract	Combines all (Entire File) or part (Named Range) of a spreadsheet file on the diskette with the current spreadsheet. The position of the pointer in the current spreadsheet determines where incoming cells will be placed. Any overlaid cells below and to the right of the pointer will be replaced by the incoming cells. If the options **A**dd or **S**ubtract are selected, the combined spreadsheet will add to or subtract from the overlaid cells holding values.
/**F**ile **X**tract **F**ormulas **V**alues	Writes a portion of the current spreadsheet to a diskette file. If the option **F**ormulas is selected, the new spreadsheet file will retain the same formulas used in the current spreadsheet. Selecting **V**alues will cause only the currently displayed values of all formulas to be saved in the new spreadsheet file as constants.
/**F**ile **E**rase **W**orksheet **P**rint **G**raph **O**ther	Allows files to be erased from the diskette without exiting from the spreadsheet program. Selecting **W**orksheet, **P**rint, or **G**raph determines the type of files that will appear on the bottom menu line for selection. If **O**ther is selected, all files in the default directory will be displayed on the bottom menu line. The filename to be erased may be selected from the menu displayed or may be entered on the keyboard.
/**F**ile **L**ist **W**orksheet **P**rint **G**raph **O**ther **L**inked	Temporarily replaces the spreadsheet display with a display of files and the amount of space left on the diskette. Selecting **W**orksheet, **P**rint, or **G**raph determines the type of files that will be displayed. If **O**ther is selected, all files in the default directory will be displayed. **L**inked is used to list only .WK1 files that are linked to the current spreadsheet by means of a linked cell reference. A linked cell reference has the format + <<*filename*>>*cell address*.
/**F**ile **I**mport **T**ext **N**umbers	Reads data from any ASCII file into the current spreadsheet. Unless specified otherwise, only files with a .PRN extension will be displayed for selection. If **T**ext is selected, each line of the imported file will be entered into a single cell of the current spreadsheet, beginning with the current cell and moving down. If **N**umbers is selected, only values and strings delimited with legal **L**abel-Prefix characters (on both sides) in the ASCII file will be read into the current spreadsheet.
/**F**ile **D**irectory	Allows current disk drive and directory to be changed.
/**F**ile **A**dmin **R**eservation **T**able **L**ink Refresh	**R**eservation is used only on a network system to control updating of spreadsheet files that are shared by many users. **T**able is used to copy information about disk files (file names, sizes, date and time stamps) into a range of cells in the current spreadsheet. **L**ink-Refresh is needed only on a network system and only if the current spreadsheet has linked cell references to other files. If another network user has modified and resaved a linked file, **L**ink-Refresh may be needed to update current spreadsheet formulas.

/PRINT COMMANDS

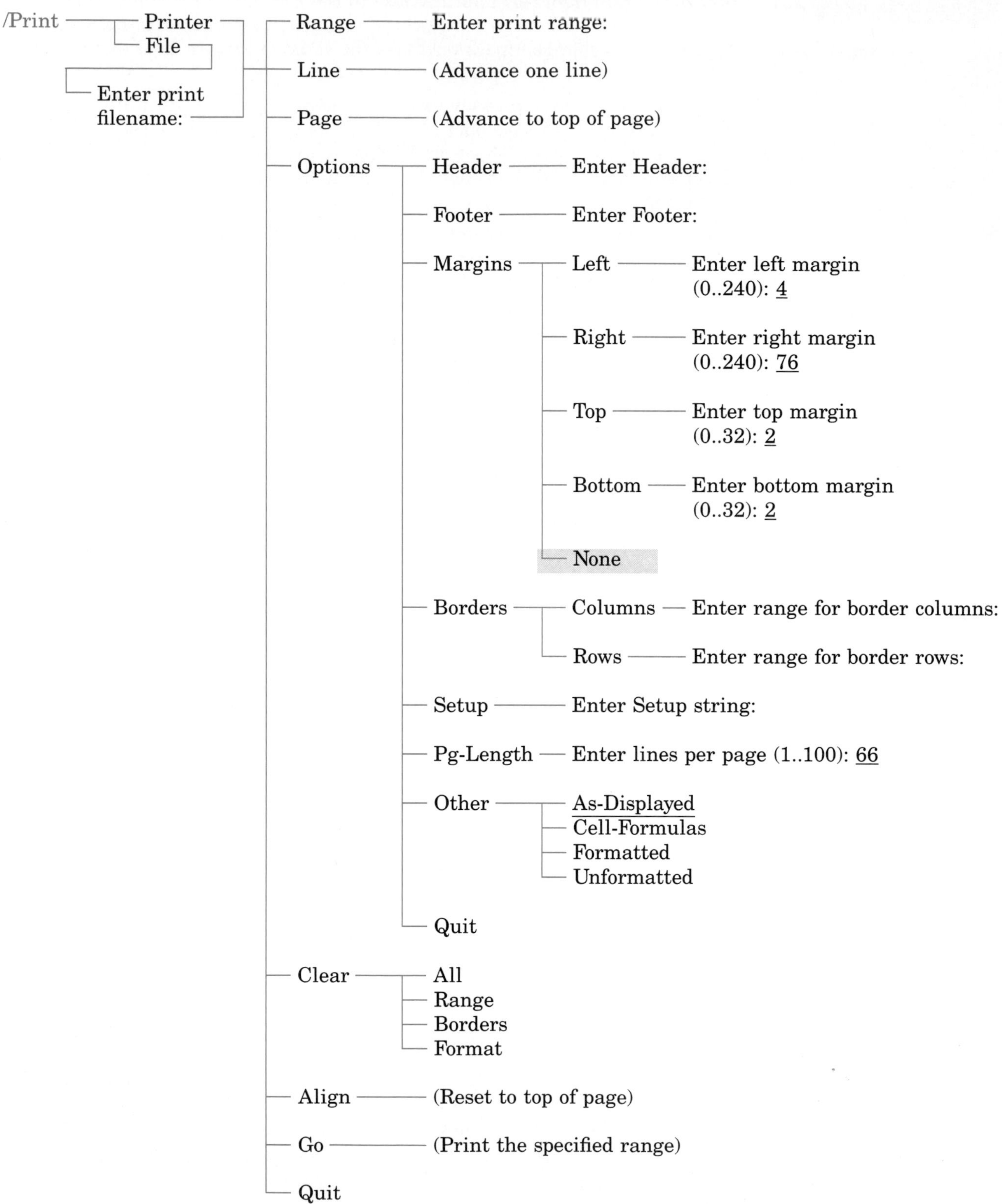

NOTE: Shaded commands shown here were added to Lotus 1-2-3 with Version 2.2. If you are using Version 2.01, you will not see these commands on your screen.

/**P**rint
  Printer
    Range
	Defines the range of the current spreadsheet to be printed. If print range previously has been defined, it will be displayed and may be undefined by using the Esc or Backspace key. When the /**P**rint,**P**rinter,**G**o command is given, the currently defined range is printed.

/**P**rint
  Printer
    Line
    Page
	Line advances the paper in the printer one line. **P**age advances paper to the top of the next page. After printing, paper will not advance to the top of next page unless **P**age is selected.

/**P**rint
  Printer
    Options
      Header
      Footer
      Margins
      Borders
      Setup
      Page-Length
      Other
      Quit
	Options is used to set various print parameters. **H**eaders and **F**ooters (top and bottom page labels) may be added to each page of printed output. **M**argins may be adjusted from their default settings. **B**orders for each page of printed output may be specified as particular columns or rows from within the spreadsheet. Printer control codes used to invoke such options as condensed printing and line spacing may be sent to the printer through the **S**etup command. **P**age-Length also may be adjusted. The **O**ther command allows the spreadsheet's cell-formulas and labels to be printed one per line, which is useful for hard-copy documentation of a spreadsheet.

/**P**rint
  Printer
    Clear
      All
      Range
      Borders
      Format
	Clears defined print settings or returns them to their default values. Options to **C**lear are **A**ll, **R**ange, **B**orders, and **F**ormat. **R**ange clears only the print range setting. **B**orders clears border columns and rows. **F**ormat returns margins, page length, and setup string to their default values. **A**ll clears the **R**ange, **B**orders, and **F**ormat.

/**P**rint
  Printer
    Align
	Align is selected to define the current printer position as the top of a page. Adjust paper in printer, and then select **A**lign.

/**P**rint
  Printer
    Go
	Begins printing of the spreadsheet. Before issuing the **G**o command, the print range must be defined. To assure proper pagination, use the **A**lign command to reset the top of page before printing.

/**P**rint **F**ile	Printing to a **F**ile uses the same commands as printing to the **P**rinter. In this case, however, all output is sent to a text file. Unless otherwise specified, the file is given the Lotus extension .PRN. .PRN files may be printed at a later time using other software or may be used to transfer spreadsheet data to other applications software.

/GRAPH COMMANDS

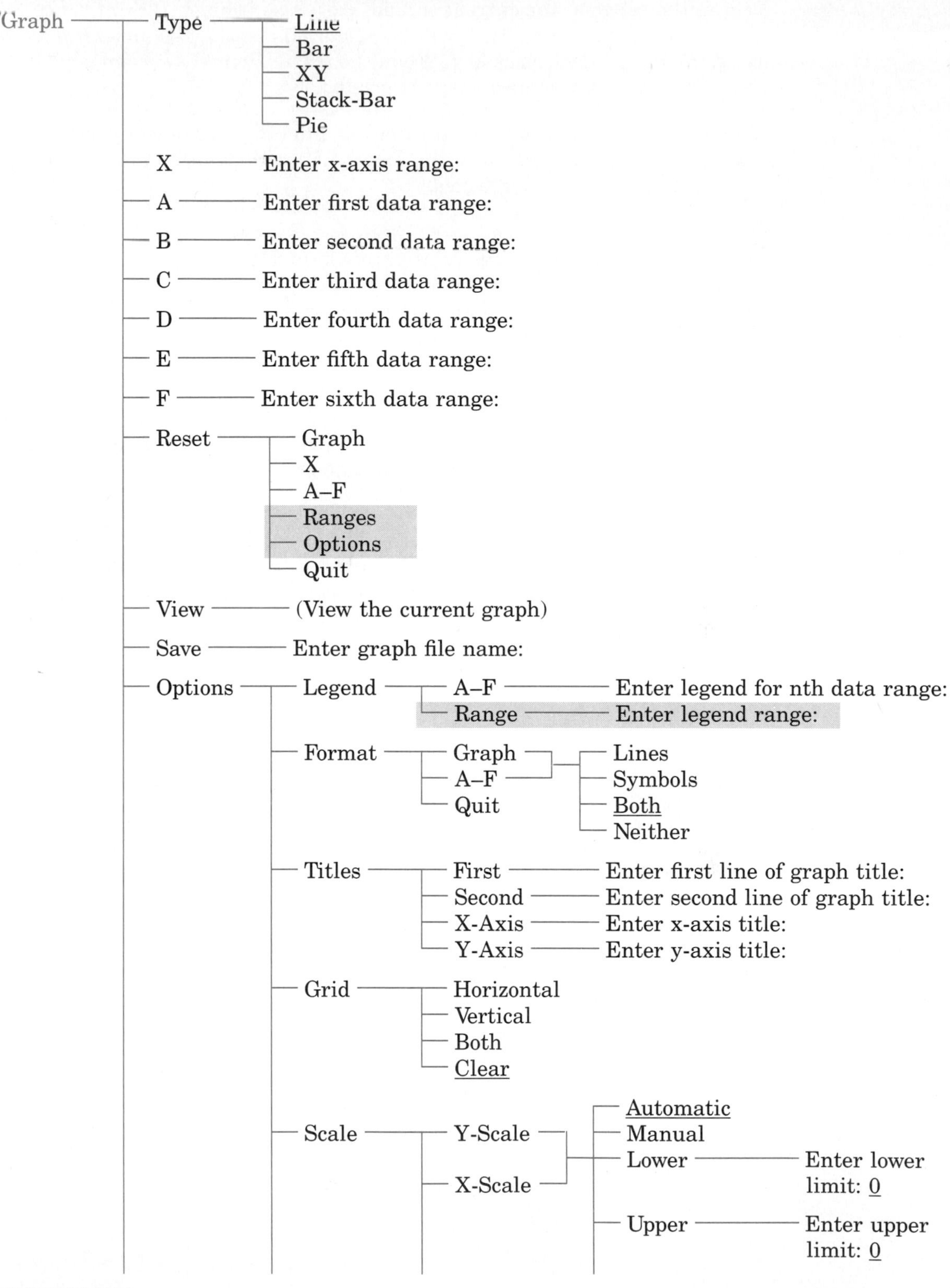

CONTINUED

NOTE: Shaded commands shown here were added to Lotus 1-2-3 with Version 2.2. If you are using Version 2.01, you will not see these commands on your screen.

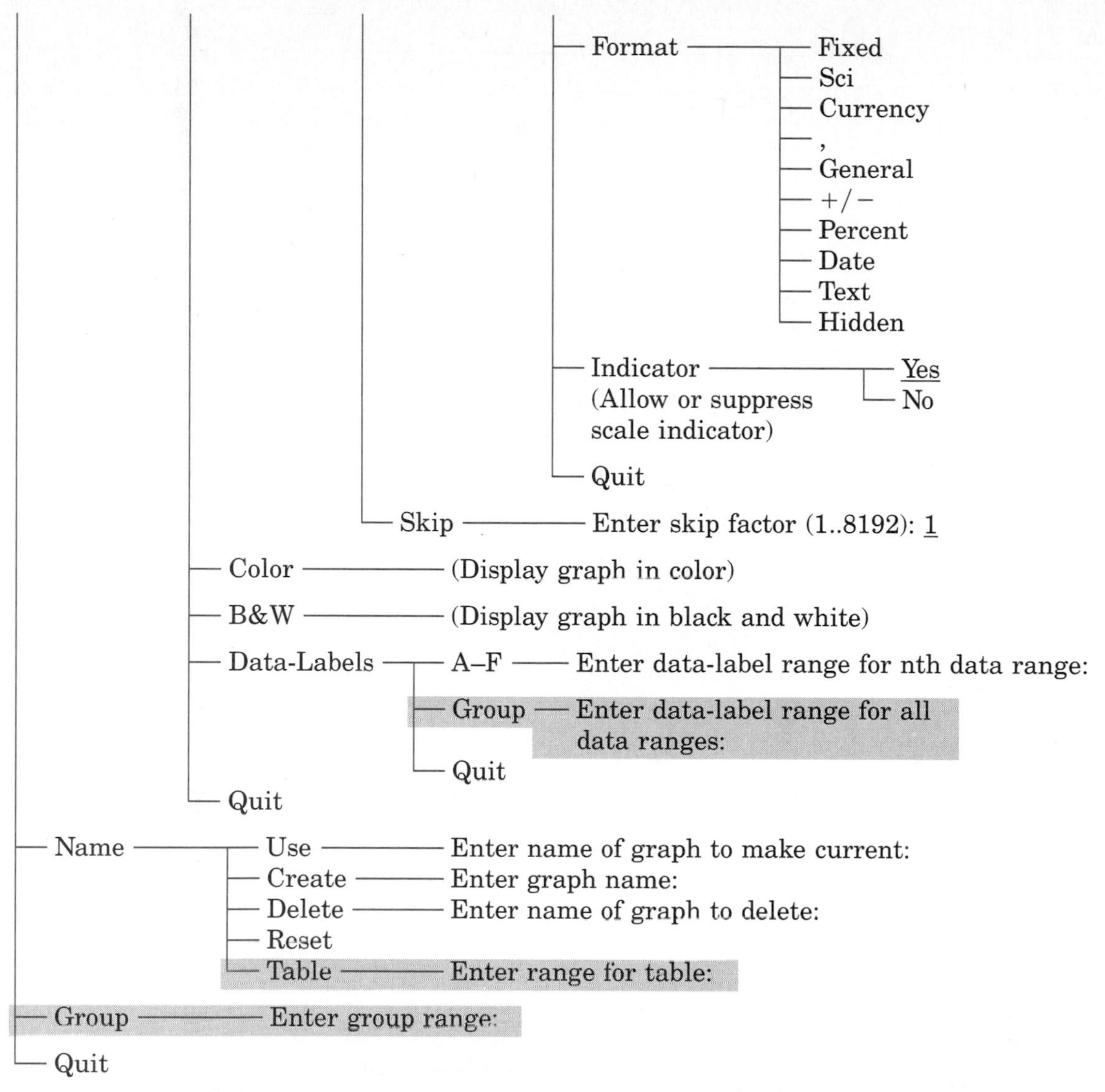

/Graph **T**ype **L**ine **B**ar **XY** **S**tack-Bar **P**ie	Selects one of the five graph types: **L**ine graph, **B**ar graph, **XY** graph, **S**tack-Bar graph, or **P**ie chart. Each type requires certain definitions of the spreadsheet data ranges to be used in creating the graph. The **B**ar, **S**tack-Bar, and **L**ine graphs all require at least one data range to graph, and will accept up to six data ranges. These ranges are identified as the /Graph data ranges **A–F**. An **X** range may also be defined. Values or labels in the **X** range appear as labels on the graph's X axis. Only the **A** data range is required to create a **P**ie chart, but the **B** data range and **X** range also may be defined. If defined, the **B** data range is used to determine coloring or shading patterns for the slices of the pie, and the **X** range is used to label the slices of the pie. The **XY** graph is somewhat different than any of the other graph types in that the **X** range must hold values. These values are scaled and placed along the X axis. Up to six data ranges (**A–F**) may be used, and at least one is required.
/Graph **X**	Sets the **X** range values for the **XY** graph, and also sets labels for all other graph types.

Command	Description
/**G**raph **A–F**	Sets each of the six data ranges to be graphed.
/**G**raph **R**eset **G**raph **X** **A–F** **R**anges **O**ption **Q**uit	Cancels some or all of the currently defined graph settings. To cancel all, select **G**raph. Selecting each setting individually will cancel only that setting. Select **Q**uit when finished cancelling settings.
/**G**raph **V**iew	Displays the currently defined graph on the monitor screen. If the appropriate data ranges for the graph have not been defined, the screen may be blank. Pressing any key will return the display of the spreadsheet with the **/G**raph commands as the current menu.
/**G**raph **S**ave	Saves the current graph in a file on the diskette (.PIC) to be printed later with the Lotus PrintGraph program.
/**G**raph **O**ptions **L**egend **F**ormat **T**itles **G**rid **S**cale **C**olor **B**&W **D**ata-Labels **Q**uit	Sets a number of options to enhance the display of the graph. **O**ptions include adding the following to a graph: a **L**egend to identify the data ranges; a **F**ormat for **L**ine and **XY**-type graphs; **T**itles for the graph and its X and Y axes; horizontal and/or vertical **G**rid lines; and data range **D**ata-Labels. The **S**cale option may be used to change the scale used on the X and Y axes and to set a format for the numeric values displayed on the axes. **C**olor or **B**&W (Black and White) may be selected for screen display of the graph. When done setting **O**ptions for the graph, select **Q**uit.
/**G**raph **N**ame **U**se **C**reate **D**elete **R**eset **T**able	This command, which is similar to using range names, allows you to give the current graph settings a name. **C**reate is used to name the settings. Selecting **U**se and entering a graph name will cause the named graph to become the current graph. **D**elete is used to delete a single graph name and **R**eset deletes all graph names. Named graph settings are saved along with the spreadsheet file.

You may also use the **T**able option to cause all named graphs and their types to be recorded in a specified range of the spreadsheet.

/DATA COMMANDS

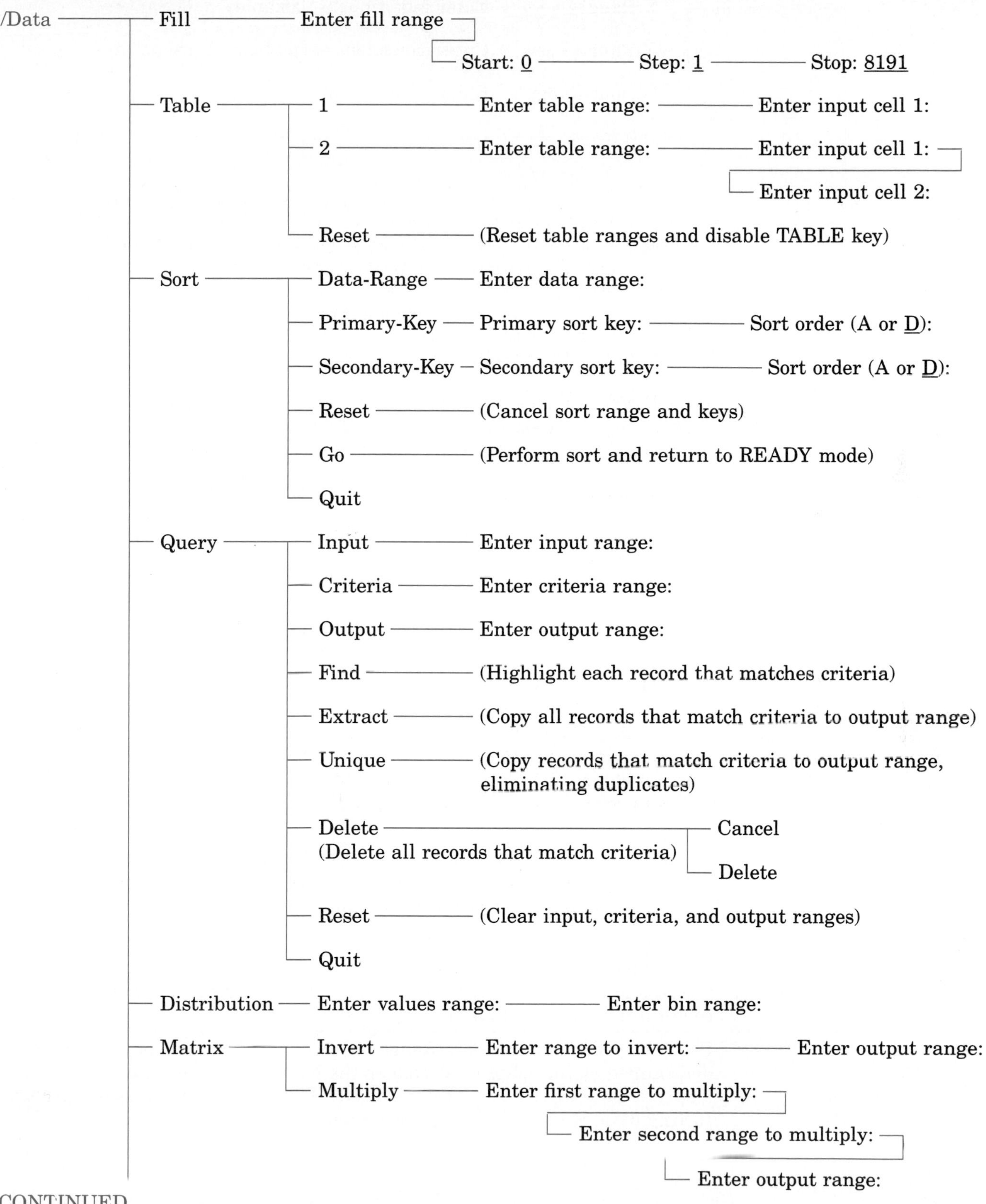

CONTINUED

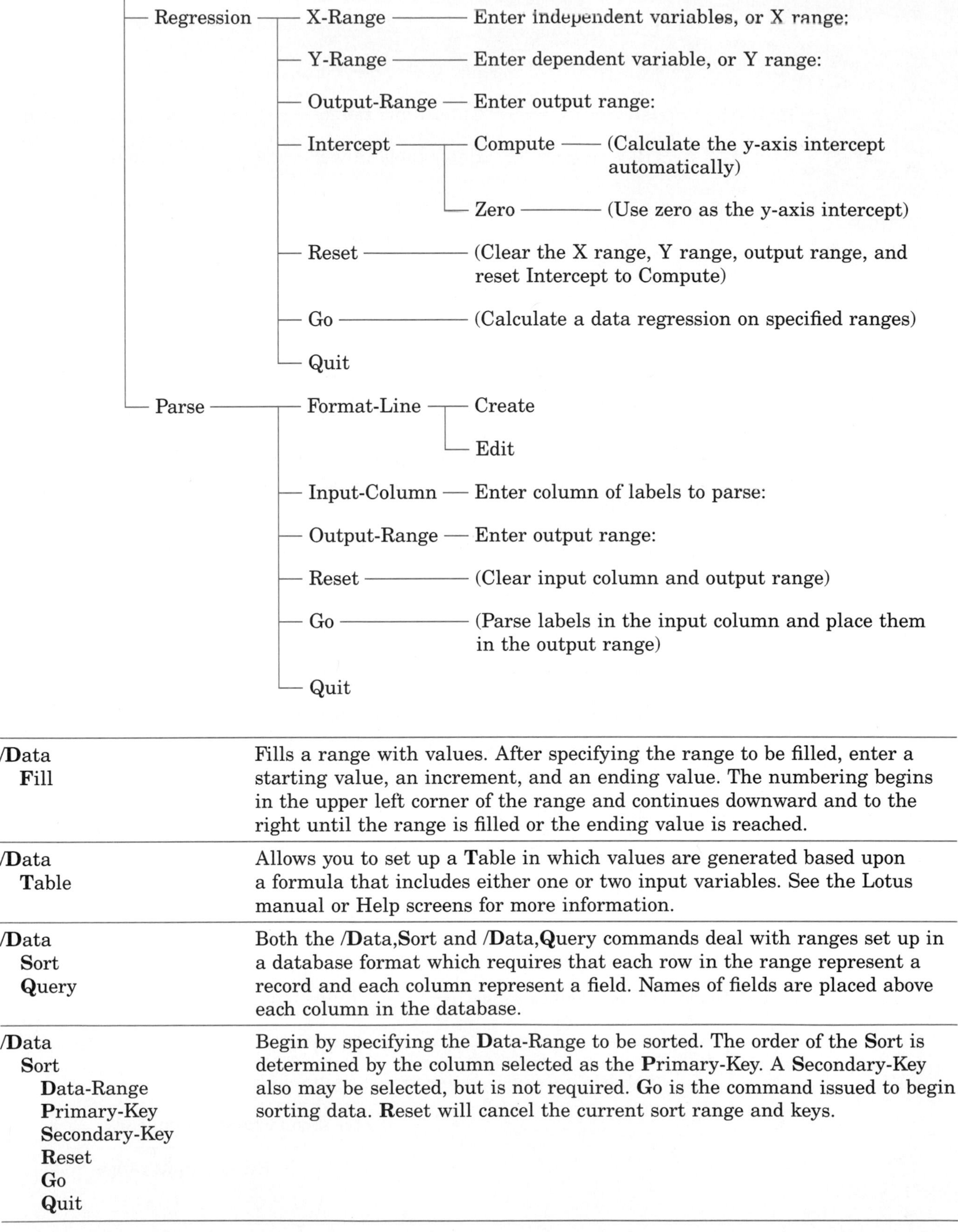

/**D**ata **F**ill	Fills a range with values. After specifying the range to be filled, enter a starting value, an increment, and an ending value. The numbering begins in the upper left corner of the range and continues downward and to the right until the range is filled or the ending value is reached.
/**D**ata **T**able	Allows you to set up a **T**able in which values are generated based upon a formula that includes either one or two input variables. See the Lotus manual or Help screens for more information.
/**D**ata **S**ort **Q**uery	Both the /**D**ata,**S**ort and /**D**ata,**Q**uery commands deal with ranges set up in a database format which requires that each row in the range represent a record and each column represent a field. Names of fields are placed above each column in the database.
/**D**ata **S**ort **D**ata-Range **P**rimary-Key **S**econdary-Key **R**eset **G**o **Q**uit	Begin by specifying the **D**ata-Range to be sorted. The order of the **S**ort is determined by the column selected as the **P**rimary-Key. A **S**econdary-Key also may be selected, but is not required. **G**o is the command issued to begin sorting data. **R**eset will cancel the current sort range and keys.

/**D**ata
Query
Input
Criterion
Output
Find
Extract
Unique
Delete
Reset
Quit

This command is used to search a database range for records meeting given criteria. Records found in the search may be highlighted (**F**ind), copied to another area of the spreadsheet (**E**xtract and **U**nique), or deleted from the spreadsheet (**D**elete). **D**elete and **F**ind require only **I**nput and **C**riterion range specifications. **E**xtract and **U**nique require specification of an **O**utput range as well. The field names at the top of each column must be included in these ranges. **R**eset cancels the **I**nput, **C**riterion, and **O**utput range specifications.

/**D**ata
Distribution

Calculates a frequency distribution for the values in a specified range.

/**D**ata
Matrix
Invert
Multiply

Multiplies or inverts matrices and copies resulting matrix into another portion of the spreadsheet. Matrices have a maximum size of 90 by 90.

Invert converts matrix to its inverse. The matrix to be inverted must be a square matrix. **M**ultiply is used to multiply two matrices, resulting in a product matrix. The number of columns in the first range and the number of rows in the second range must be equal.

Locate the Output range in an empty portion of the spreadsheet if you do not want the values to replace existing data in your spreadsheet.

/**D**ata
Regression
X-Range
Y-Range
Output-Range
Intercept
Compute
Zero
Reset
Go
Quit

Determines the relationship between a set of dependent variables and one or more sets of independent variables.

The **X**-Range is used to specify the range of independent variables. Data in the **X**-Range must be arranged in columns and a maximum of 16 independent variables may be specified. The **Y**-Range is used to specify the range of the dependent variable. Data in the **Y**-Range must be arranged in a single column. The number of rows in the X and Y ranges must be equal.

The **O**utput-Range specifies where the results of the regression analysis will be placed. Locate the **O**utput-Range in an empty portion of the spreadsheet if you do not want the information to replace existing data in your spreadsheet.

Intercept is used to calculate the intercept as a constant or to set the intercept at zero. **C**ompute is the default setting.

Reset cancels all ranges and the zero intercept option. **G**o calculates the regression results and copies them to the **O**utput-Range. The results of a regression analysis are

Constant
Std Err of Y Est
R Squared
No. of Observations
Degrees of Freedom
X Coefficients
Std Err of Coef.

/Data
Parse
Format-Line
Create
Edit
Input-Column
Output-Range
Reset
Go
Quit

Converts an imported ASCII text file into standard spreadsheet format by treating the text as a column of long labels and entering them into a single column of the spreadsheet which overflows into the adjacent columns. The data then may be parsed or decoded into individual cell entries.

Format-Line determines the decoding pattern for rows of labels below it and how that data will be parsed into cells. Format symbols are

L	first character of block = label
V	first character of block = value
D	first character of block = date
T	first character of block = time
S	skip the character for parse
>	continuation of block
*	undefined or blank space, may be used as wild card

Input-Column is used to specify the column of labels to be parsed plus the **F**ormat-Line. **O**utput-Range is used to specify the area in the spreadsheet where the parsed data will be copied (this may include the **I**nput-Column range or be a separate portion of the spreadsheet).

Reset cancels **I**nput-Column and **O**utput-Range settings. **G**o parses the data and copies the results to **O**utput-Range. Before parsing data, be sure the columns in the **O**utput-Range are wide enough to hold the entire block. Otherwise, the incoming data may be truncated.

/SYSTEM, /ADD-IN, AND /QUIT COMMANDS

/System —— (Type EXIT and press ENTER to return to 1-2-3)

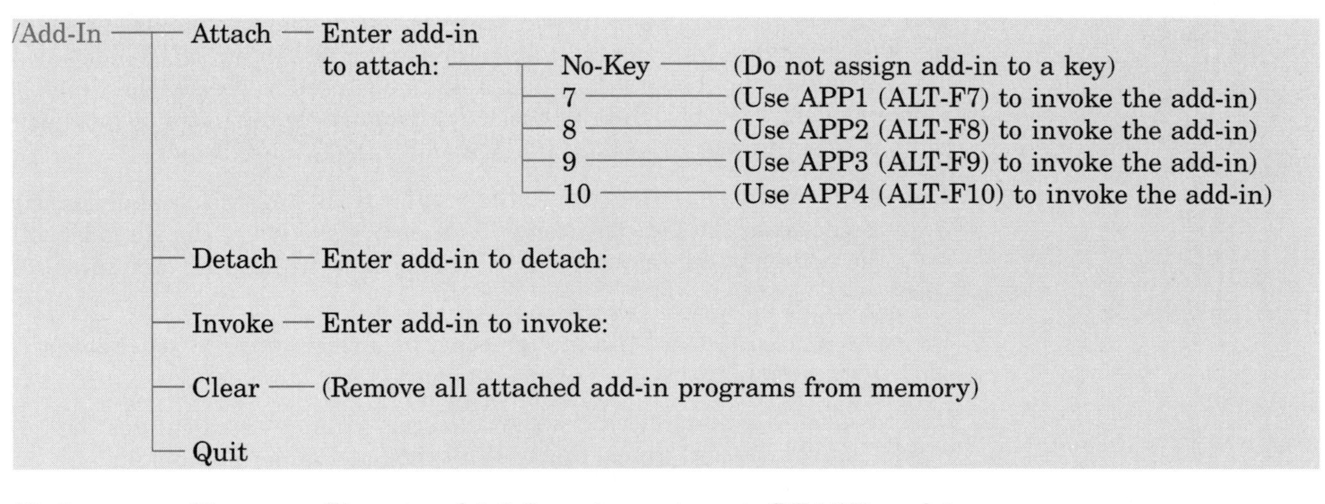

/Quit —— No —— (Do not end 1-2-3 session; return to READY mode)
—— Yes —— (End 1-2-3 session (Remember to save your worksheet first))

NOTE: Shaded commands shown here were added to Lotus 1-2-3 with Version 2.2. If you are using Version 2.01, you will not see these commands on your screen.

/System

Allows you to temporarily access the DOS level of operation while leaving the Lotus spreadsheet software in memory. At the DOS level, type EXIT to return to the spreadsheet.

/Add-In **A**ttach **D**etach **I**nvoke **C**lear **Q**uit	The /**A**dd-In commands are used to manage special software, called *Add-In* applications, that may be loaded into RAM at the same time you are using the 1-2-3 spreadsheet software. The **A**ttach command is used to load an Add-In into RAM. The **D**etach command is used to remove a single Add-In from RAM, and the Clear command is used to remove all Add-Ins from RAM. After an Add-In has been loaded, the **I**nvoke command is used to execute (begin running) the Add-In application. As an alternative, a function key, F7 through F10, may be assigned to an Add-In when it is first loaded with the **A**ttach command so that the Add-In may later be invoked by typing Alt-*function key*.
/**Q**uit **N**o **Y**es	Exits the Lotus spreadsheet software and removes it from memory, returning to the Lotus Access Menu or to the DOS level of operation. **Y**es must be selected to complete the command. If you have not saved your work, you may select **N**o and then use the /**F**ile,**S**ave command before exiting.

LOTUS 1-2-3 SPREADSHEET FUNCTIONS

@@(cell address) When the cell address argument specifies a cell containing a label which, in turn, is another cell's address (e.g., A1), the function returns the contents of the cell referenced by the label. For example, if cell A1 = 15 and cell B2 = "A1", then @@(B2) returns 15.

@**ABS**(value) Returns the absolute value.

@**ACOS**(value) Returns the arc cosine.

@**ASIN**(value) Returns the arc sine.

@**ATAN**(value) Returns the arc tangent.

@**ATAN2**(value1,value2) Returns the 4-quadrant arc tangent.

@**AVG**(list) Returns the average value of all cells in the specified list.

@**CELL**(attribute, range) Returns the specified attribute of the cell in the upper left corner of the specified range. The attribute to be returned by the function may be specified as "address," "row," "col," "contents," "type," "prefix," "protect," "width," or "format." The result of the function is updated only when the spreadsheet is recalculated either automatically or by pressing the CALC (F9) key.

@**CELLPOINTER**(attribute) Returns the specified attribute of the cell in which the pointer is located. @**CELLPOINTER** functions will only display new values when the spreadsheet is recalculated either automatically or by pressing the CALC (F9) key.

@**CHAR**(value) Returns the corresponding ASCII character. The value argument must be between 1 and 255 or the function will return ERR.

@**CHOOSE**(valueX,value0,value1,value2,... valueN) Returns one value from a list of possible values based on the index (valueX). If valueX = 0, then value0 is returned; if valueX = 1, value1 is returned, and so forth. If valueX is not within the range of choices (value1..valueN), the function will return ERR.

@**CLEAN**(string) Removes nonprintable characters from strings imported with the /**F**ile,**I**mport command.

@**CODE**(string) Returns a number representing the ASCII value of the first character in the string. If the argument is an empty cell or a cell containing a value, @**CODE** will return ERR.

@**COLS**(range) Returns the number of columns in a range.

@**COS**(value) Returns the cosine.

@**COUNT**(list) Returns the number of non-blank cells in the specified list.

@**CTERM**(int,fv,pv) Returns the number of periods needed for a present value investment (pv) to grow to a specified future value (fv) at a given periodic interest rate (int).

@**DATE**(year,month,day) Returns the serial number representing the date specified by the three arguments year, month, and day. For example, @**DATE**(90,12,25) = 33232. When formatted with the date format D1, this number displays as 25-Dec-90.

@**DATEVALUE**(date string) Returns the serial number representing the date of the date string argument. The date string must conform to one of the five date formats:

(D1) DD-MMM-YY	12-Dec-90
(D2) DD-MMM	12-Dec
(D3) MMM-YY	Dec-90
(D4) Long Intn'l	(as currently configured)
(D5) Short Intn'l	(as currently configured)

@**DAY**(serial date value) Returns the day of the month (1-31) for a serial date value.

@**DDB**(cost,salvage,life,period) Returns the calculated depreciation on an asset using the double-declining balance method.

@**ERR** Returns ERR (error).

@**EXACT**(string1,string2) Compares two strings to test if the strings are exactly the same. Returns 1 (true) if the strings match exactly. Returns 0 (false) if the strings do not match exactly.

@**EXP**(value) Returns the exponential.

@**FALSE** Returns the value 0 (false).

@**FIND**(string1,string2,n) Returns the location of stringl (substring) in string2, with the search beginning at the *n*th position of string2. The first character of string2 is considered position 0.

@**FV**(pmt,int,n) Returns the future value of a stream of annuity payments (pmt) at a periodic interest rate (int) over a specified number of periods (n).

@**HLOOKUP**(valueX,range,offset) Returns the contents of some cell in a table. The location of the table is specified by the range argument. The column of the lookup cell is determined by comparing the valueX argument to ascending values found in the top row of the table. The row of the lookup cell is determined by the offset argument, which specifies some number of rows below the top row of the table.

@**HOUR**(serial date/time value) Returns the hour value (0–23) from the fractional portion (time value) of a serial date value.

@**IF**(condition, true value,false value) Returns one of two values, the true value if the condition tests true, the false value if the condition tests false.

@**INDEX**(range,column,row) Returns the contents of the cell found in the specified range at the intersection of the column and row arguments specified. The first column is considered column 0 and the first row is considered row 0. If the column or row specified does not fall within the specified range, the function will return ERR.

@**INT**(value) Returns the integer portion of a value.

@**IRR**(guess,range) Returns the approximate internal rate of return for a range of cash flows, given the help of a guess to start the computation.

@**ISERR**(cell address) Returns 1 (true) if the cell specified by the cell address argument contains ERR; otherwise, returns 0 (false).

@**ISNA**(cell address) Returns 1 (true) if the cell specified by the cell address argument contains NA; otherwise, returns 0 (false).

@**ISNUMBER**(cell address) Returns 1 (true) if the cell specified by the cell address argument contains a numeric value or is empty; otherwise, returns 0 (false).

@**ISSTRING**(cell address) Returns 1 (true) if the cell specified by the cell address argument contains a label (string); otherwise, returns 0 (false).

@**LEFT**(string,n) Returns the left-most n characters in a string.

@**LENGTH**(string) Returns the number of characters in a string.

@**LN**(value) Returns the log base e.

@**LOG**(value) Returns the log base 10.

@**LOWER**(string) Returns the same string, with all letters converted to lower case.

@**MAX**(list) Returns the highest single value found in the specified list.

@**MID**(string,start,n) Returns an extracted substring from a larger string. The start argument determines the position in the string where the substring is to begin (the first character is position 0), and the n argument determines the length of the substring.

@MIN(list) Returns the lowest single value found in the specified list.

@MINUTE(serial date/time value) Returns the minute (0–59) value from the fractional portion (time value) of a serial date value.

@MOD(value,modulo) Returns the remainder of a division operation. The value is divided by the modulo and the function returns the remainder (the modulus).

@MONTH(serial date value) Returns the month number (1–12) for a serial date value.

@N(range) Returns the value of a number or a formula found in the top left cell of the specified range. If the cell is empty or contains a label, **@N** returns the value 0. **@N** always returns a numeric value.

@NA Returns NA (not available).

@NOW Returns the current date and time as a serial date/time value.

@NPV(rate,range) Returns the net present value of a stream of cash flows at a given discount rate.

@PI Returns pi (3.141592653589794).

@PMT(pv,int,n) Returns the amount of a stream of annuity payments given a present value investment (pv), an interest rate (int), and the number of periods (n).

@PROPER(string) Returns the same string, with all first letters of words converted to upper case and subsequent letters converted to lower case.

@PV(pmt,int,n) Returns the present value of a stream of equal annuity payments (pmt) for a given number of periods (n) at a given periodic interest rate (int).

@RAND Generates a random number. The function has no argument and the value returned changes each time the spreadsheet is recalculated.

@RATE(fv,pv,n) Returns the required rate of interest for a present value investment (pv) to grow to a specified future value (fv) in a given number of periods (n).

@REPEAT(string,n) Returns a string with the specified string argument repeated n times.

@REPLACE(string1,start,n,string2) Returns a string in which a certain portion of string1 has been replaced by string2. The start argument specifies the position in string1 to begin the replacement (first position is 0), and the n argument determines how many characters will be replaced in string1.

@RIGHT(string,n) Returns the right-most n characters in a string.

@ROUND(value,places) Returns the value rounded to the specified number of decimal places.

@ROWS(range) Returns the number of rows in a range.

@S(range) Returns the string value of the top left cell of the range. If the cell is empty or contains a numeric value, **@S** returns an empty (null) string. **@S** always returns a string value.

@SECOND(serial date/time value) Returns the seconds (0–59) from the fractional portion (time value) of a serial date value.

@SIN(value) Returns the sine.

@SLN(cost,salvage,life) Returns the depreciation on an asset for a single period using the straight-line method.

@SQRT(value) Returns the square root of the value.

@STD(list) Returns the standard deviation from the mean for the nonblank cells in the specified list.

@STRING(n,decimals) Returns the string of a numeric value n, rounded to the number of places specified by the decimals argument.

@SUM(list) Returns the sum of all cells in the specified list.

@SYD(cost,salvage,life,period) Returns the depreciation on an asset for a specified period using the sum-of-the-years'-digits method.

@TAN(value) Returns the tangent.

@TERM(pmt,int,fv) Returns the number of periods required for a stream of annuity payments (pmt) to grow to a given future value (fv) at a given interest rate (int).

@TIME(hr,min,sec) Returns the fractional portion (time value) of a serial date value for the specified hour, minute, and second value arguments.

@TIMEVALUE(time string) Returns the fractional portion (time value) for a time string that is in a valid Lotus time format.

@TODAY Returns **@INT(@NOW)**, the integer portion of the function **@NOW**.

@TRIM(string) Removes trailing spaces from a string. Will change the value returned by the **@LENGTH** function.

@TRUE Returns the value 1 (true).

@UPPER(string) Returns the same string, with all letters converted to upper case.

@VALUE(string) Returns a numeric value from a number that has been entered as a label or string value. The string may contain only number characters (0–9), a currency sign ($), thousand's separators (,), a decimal indicator (.), and leading or trailing spaces; otherwise, the function will return ERR.

@VAR(list) Returns the variance of the values for the nonblank cells in the specified list.

@VLOOKUP(valueX,range,offset) Returns the contents of some cell in a table. The location of the table is specified by the range argument. The row of the lookup cell is determined by comparing the valueX argument to ascending values found in the left-most column of the table. The column of the lookup cell is determined by the offset argument, which specifies some number of columns to the right of the left-most column of the table.

@YEAR(serial date value) Returns the year for a serial date value.

LOTUS 1-2-3 MACRO COMMANDS QUICK REFERENCE

Macro Keyboard Equivalent Commands

Command	Keyboard Equivalent
Function Keys	
{EDIT}	F2
{NAME}	F3
{ABS}	F4
{GOTO}	F5
{WINDOW}	F6
{QUERY}	F7
{TABLE}	F8
{CALC}	F9
{GRAPH}	F10
Pointer Movement Keys	
{UP}	↑
{DOWN}	↓
{LEFT}	←
{RIGHT}	→
{PGUP}	PgUp
{PGDN}	PgDn
{BIGLEFT}	Shift-Tab
{BIGRIGHT}	Tab
{HOME}	Home
{END}	End
Editing Keys	
{DEL} or {DELETE}	Del
{ESC} or {ESCAPE}	Esc
{BS} or {BACKSPACE}	Backspace key
~	Enter key ↵
{~}	Tilde character
{ { } and { } }	Brace characters

Macro Programming Commands

Macros may be used to develop programs or routines that will be used repeatedly, or to accomplish tasks that are program-like in nature. The following are the most commonly used commands for controlling program flow in a macro. For those with a knowledge of BASIC programming, the equivalent BASIC commands are shown as a reference.

Lotus Macro Command	BASIC Equivalent
{**IF** condition}	**IF...THEN**
{**BRANCH** range}	**GOTO**
{routine-name}	**GOSUB**
{**RETURN**}	**RETURN**
{**QUIT**}	**END**
{**GETLABEL** message,range}~	**INPUT** "prompt" A$
{**GETNUMBER** message,range}~	**INPUT** "prompt" A
{**MENUBRANCH** range}	none

Additional Macro Commands

Controlling Output

{**BEEP**}	Causes computer to sound a beep.
{**INDICATE** string}	Changes the mode indicator in the upper right corner to display the specified string (up to five characters only). A cell reference or range may not be used. To return to standard mode indicators, use {**INDICATE**}. To remove display of indicator mode, use {**INDICATE** ""}.
{**PANELOFF**}	Used to suppress output of the window lines (top 3 lines) to speed up execution of a macro.
{**PANELON**}	Restores the output of the window lines during macro execution.
{**WINDOWSOFF**}	Used to suppress output of the spreadsheet display to speed up execution of a macro and decrease user confusion.
{**WINDOWSON**}	Restores the output of the spreadsheet during macro execution.

Controlling Program Flow

{**BRANCH** range}	Passes control of macro execution to commands located in the specified range. Equivalent to BASIC's **GOTO** or **GO TO** command.
{**DEFINE** argument1:type, argument2:type, . . . argument N:type}	{**DEFINE**} is the first command in a subroutine that is to be called with arguments. The {**DEFINE**} command specifies where and how to store data being passed. Arguments 1 through N are cell references for the cells in which the passed values will be stored. Type refers to how Lotus will treat the cell contents, either as a **VALUE** or a **STRING**. Default type is **STRING**. When using **VALUE** as the type, a string, invalid number, or invalid formula will result in an error.
{**DISPATCH** location}	Indirect branch command. Will pass control to a destination contained in the location cell. When using a range name as the specified location, the named range must contain only one cell. {**DISPATCH**} works in essentially

	the same manner as BASIC's **GO TO** command when using a variable to specify the program line number (i.e., **GO TO** *n*).
{**FOR** counter-location, start-number,stop-number, step-number, start-location}	Controls looping process. Counter-location is where the value being incremented is stored. Start-location is the cell containing the first command of the macro subroutine containing the loop commands. Start, stop, and step numbers determine the number of executions in the loop. {**FOR**} is the macro equivalent to BASIC's **FOR/NEXT** loop structure.
{**FORBREAK**}	Interrupts the current {**FOR**} loop and continues execution of the macro with the command following the {**FOR**} command. {**FORBREAK**} may be used only in a subroutine called by a {**FOR**} command.
{**IF** condition} true command	Executes the commands on the same line and following the {**IF**} command if the condition evaluates as true. Equivalent to BASIC's **IF THEN** command.
{**ONERROR** branch-location, message-location}	If an error occurs during macro execution, control is passed to the specified branch location, and the optional error message is displayed in the message location cell. The {**ONERROR**} command should be located above the most likely place for the error to occur. Only one {**ONERROR**} command is in effect at one time. {**ONERROR**} will be activated if the CTRL-BREAK keys are pressed unless the {**BREAKOFF**} command has been executed.
{**QUIT**}	Ends macro execution and returns to READY mode.
{**RESTART**}	Used only in subroutines. When {**RESTART**} is encountered, the subroutine stack is eliminated. The subsequent commands in the current subroutine will be executed; however, when the {**RETURN**} command is encountered, instead of returning control to the calling routine, macro execution ends.
{**RETURN**}	Used in subroutines called with {routine-name} and {**MENUCALL**} commands. Returns control to the calling routine, beginning with the command immediately after the command that called the subroutine.
{routine-name}	Passes control to macro commands found in the named range specified as routine-name (subroutine). Control will be passed back to calling routine when {**RETURN**} command is encountered in subroutine. If subroutine begins with {**DEFINE**} command, the {routine-name} command must include argument specifications following the range name.

Command	Description
{**BREAKOFF**}	Disables the CTRL-BREAK key combination, preventing the user from being able to interrupt macro execution before its completion.
{**BREAKON**}	Reenables use of the CTRL-BREAK key combination to interrupt macro execution.
{**GET** location}	Pauses during macro execution to allow a single keystroke entry, and stores that entry in the specified location. The single keystroke may be any standard keyboard character, a Lotus function key, or pointer control key. {**GET**} does not provide for a control panel prompt. An alternative command is {**?**}.
{**GETLABEL** message, range}	Displays the message on the second window line, pauses for a user entry, and stores the entry as a label in the cell specified by range.
{**GETNUMBER** message,range}	Displays the message on the second window line, pauses for a user entry, and stores the entry as a number in the cell specified by range. If the entry is not a valid numeric entry, ERR will appear in the cell specified by range.
{**LOOK** location}	Allows test of the type-ahead buffer to see if any characters have been typed during macro execution. Any characters in the buffer are copied into the specified location. Macro execution is not suspended. Characters are left in the buffer for use in the {**GET**}, {**GETLABEL**}, or {**GETNUMBER**} commands.
{**MENUBRANCH** range} and {**MENUCALL** range}	Pass macro execution to macro menu commands located in specified range. After user makes menu selection, the appropriate commands as defined in the menu will be executed. After all commands for a menu selection have been executed, control will pass back to the command following {**MENUCALL**} in the calling routine if {**MENUCALL**} was used. If {**MENUBRANCH**} was used, macro execution will end unless control is passed explicitly to another routine by a {**BRANCH**} command. If Esc is passed instead of making a menu selection, control passes back to the calling routine, regardless of which command was used to call the menu. {**MENUBRANCH**} and {**MENUCALL**} override the {**PANELOFF**} command.
{**WAIT** serial date/time value}	Interrupts execution of the macro, displays the **WAIT** indicator until the specified time, and then continues with the macro execution The serial date/time value must contain both the date (integer portion) and time (decimal portion). CTRL-BREAK will interrupt the {**WAIT**} command unless the {**BREAKOFF**} command has been executed.

{**BLANK** range}	Erases cell contents in the specified range. Performs the same function as the /**R**ange,**E**rase command. Format and protection settings are unaffected.
{**CONTENTS** destination, source,width, format-code}	Copies string or numeric data from the source cell, converts in to string data, and enters it into the destination cell. If the specified destination or source location is a range, only the upper left cell of the range will be used. The optional width number causes Lotus to treat the source cell as if it had the specified column width, but does not actually change the column width. The optional format number causes Lotus to treat the source cell as if it had the corresponding format, but does not actually change the source cell's format. As a result, the destination cell may contain a left-aligned label that looks like a number having a different format and width than the numeric data contained in the source cell. The following table describes the various format codes available.

Code	Format	Decimals
0–15	Fixed	0–15
16–32	Scientific	0–15
33–47	Currency	0–15
48–63	Percentage	0–15
64–79	Comma	0–15
112	+/− Bar Graph	
113	General	
114	D1 (DD-MMM-YY)	
115	D2 (DD-MMM)	
116	D3 (MMM-YY)	
121	D4 (Long Intn'l)	
122	D5 (Short Intn'l)	
119	D6 (HH:MM:SS AM/PM)	
120	D7 (HH:MM AM/PM)	
123	D8 (Long Intn'l)	
124	D9 (Short Intn'l)	
117	Text Format	
118	Hidden Format	
127	Current Default Format	

{**LET** location:**VALUE**} and {**LET** location:**STRING**}	Stores an entry in a specified cell. If the specified location is a range name, only the upper left cell is used. **VALUE** or **STRING** determines the type of data that will be accepted into the location cell.

{**PUT** range,column-number, row-number,**NUMBER**} *and* {**PUT** range,column-number, row-number,**STRING**}	Stores an entry in a location that is specified by a row and column offset in the range. If the specified location is a single cell, an error will result unless row-number and column-number are specified as 0. A column or row number located outside the range results in an error that cannot be trapped with the {**ONERROR**} command. **NUMBER** or **STRING** determines the type of data that will be accepted into the location cell.
{**RECALCCOL** range,condition, iteration-number}	Recalculates the formulas in the specified range by columns. The optional condition will cause the range to be recalculated until the condition is true. The condition must be a logical expression or reference a cell in the range which contains a logical expression. The optional iteration argument specifies the number of recalculations performed on the range. Recalculations will be repeated until the condition is true or the iteration count is reached, whichever occurs first. The {**CALC**} command recalculates the entire spreadsheet. Use {**CALC**} at the end of a macro using {**RECALC**} to be sure that the current data is accurate.

Accessing Files

{**CLOSE**}	Closes a currently open file. If no file is open, the {**CLOSE**} command will be ignored and the next command in the macro will be executed. {**CLOSE**} should always be used before completion of a macro in which the {**OPEN**} command was used.
{**FILESIZE** location}	Determines the length of the currently open file in bytes and displays the value in the specified cell location. If no file is open, the {**FILESIZE**} command will be ignored.
{**GETPOS** range}	Records file pointer position in currently open file and displays the value in the upper left cell of the range. The first position in a file is 0. If no file is open, the {**GETPOS**} command will be ignored.
{**OPEN** filename, access-mode}	Opens an external file to read, write, or both. The filename specification must be a string that is a valid DOS filename (specification may include a path) or a cell containing a valid file specification string. The access-mode is a single character that specifies the type of file access. **R** Read only access to existing file. Use the {**READ**} and {**READLN**} commands. **W** Opens new file to access with {**WRITE**} and {**WRITELN**} commands. An existing

file with the same filename will be erased and replaced with the new file.

M Opens existing file for read/write access. Allows {**READ**}, {**READLN**}, {**WRITE**}, and {**WRITELN**} commands to be used.

{**READ** byte-count,range}
Reads a specified number of characters from the currently open file, beginning with the current file pointer location. The characters then are displayed as a long label in the first cell of the specified range. {**READ**} copies characters from a file to the spreadsheet. Byte-count must be a number between 0 and 240. {**READ**} should not be used with ASCII text files; use {**READLN**} for ASCII text files.

{**READLN** range}
Reads characters from the currently open file, beginning with the current file pointer location in the file. Characters are read and displayed in the specified range until the end of the line is encountered or 240 characters have been read.

{**SETPOS** file-position}
Sets position of the file pointer in the currently open file. The file-position specifies the number of bytes from the beginning of the file (byte 0). A pointer may inadvertently be set past the end of the file. The {**FILESIZE**} command will help determine the position of the last character in the file. If no file is open, the {**SETPOS**} command will be ignored.

{**WRITE** string}
Copies a string of characters from the spreadsheet to the currently open file, beginning at the current file pointer position, if a file has been opened with the {**OPEN**} command and either the **W**(rite) or **M**(odify) access mode. The string argument may be a string, a cell reference, a named range of a single cell, or an expression evaluating to a string value. {**WRITE**} may be used to concatenate characters on a line. If the file pointer is not at the end of the open file, the existing characters in the file will be overwritten. If the pointer is at the end of the file, the length of the file will be increased by the number of incoming characters. If the pointer is past the end of the file, the file length is increased to the sum of the current file pointer position plus the number of incoming characters.

{**WRITELN** string}
Copies a string of characters from the spreadsheet to the current file pointer location, if a file has been opened with the {**OPEN**} command and either the **W**(rite) or **M**(odify) access mode, adding a carriage return and line feed after the last character in the string. The string argument may be a string, a cell

reference, a named range of a single cell, or an expression evaluating to a string value. {**WRITELN**} may be used with an empty string to add a carriage return and line feed to the end of a line in the open file. If the pointer is not at the end of the open file, the existing characters in the file will be overwritten. If the pointer is at the end of the file, the length of the file will be increased by the number of incoming characters. If the pointer is past the end of the file, the file length is increased to the sum of the current file pointer position plus the number of incoming characters.

DBASE III PLUS

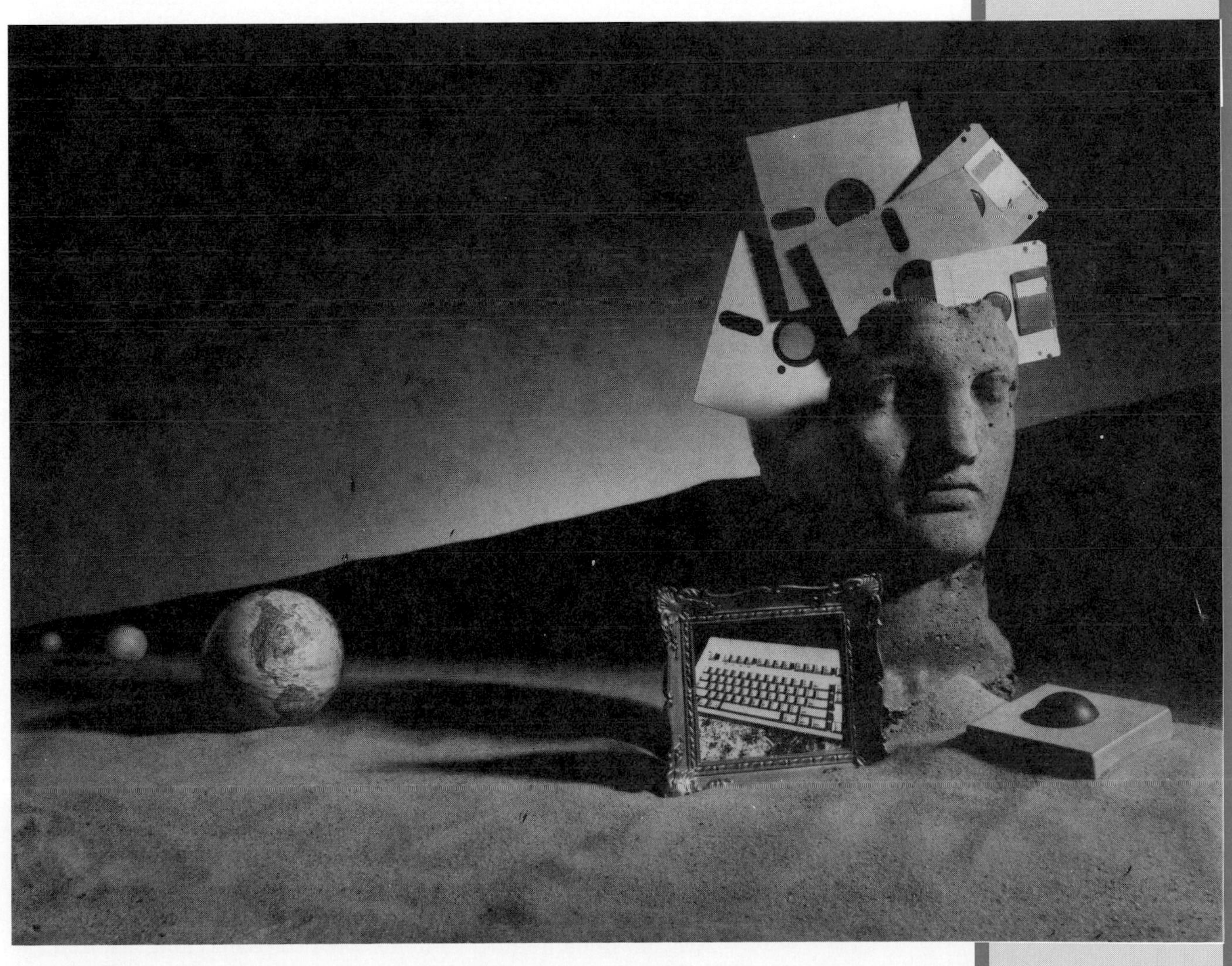

INTRODUCTION

dBASE III Plus® is a database management system (DBMS) software, the type of applications software that allows the user to create, maintain, and manipulate records of data. You may use dBASE III Plus commands in two separate ways: you may use one command at a time that dBASE executes in a direct mode as it is entered; or you may use several (a batch of) commands, held in a file that you create, that dBASE will execute as a group when you type the appropriate command.

The following section begins with a brief discussion of dBASE basics and dBASE III Plus file handling. It continues with a set of tutorial lessons that focuses on the fundamentals of using dBASE commands while in the direct mode. In the tutorial lessons you will create a database file of records; learn how to edit, append, and delete records from the database; sort and index records; search for particular records in the database; and produce dBASE reports. The tutorial lessons are followed by an extended discussion about how dBASE commands may be assembled in a file and then executed as a group. Several examples are presented in a step-by-step sequence, presenting new dBASE III Plus commands and concepts, using the database file created in the tutorial lessons. After this, several exercises and cases designed to introduce and reinforce the use of additional dBASE III Plus features, commands and operations are presented. At the end of the module, a dBASE III Plus operation and command summary briefly describes the full range of commands and control key operations available with dBASE III Plus.

DATABASE BASICS

The term *database* describes data organized in a manner that makes it possible to access specific information. In many computer applications, data in a database file are organized in records with fields holding related data items. When the data are arranged in this manner, the database is known as a *relational database.* In the following example, checkbook data are shown arranged as a small relational database file.

2160	03/03/90	Payless Drug Store	13.60	Medicine
2161	03/05/90	Vista Ridge Properties	325.00	Rent
2162	03&05/90	AT&T	13.50	Phone
2163	03/11/90	Albertson's Food	35.15	Grocery
2164	03/15/90	First Federal	160.00	Car payment

In this example, each record contains data on a check written against a personal checking account. The five fields of each record hold a check number, date, payee, amount, and purchase description, respectively.

Record Structure

Before data items such as those shown above can be entered into a database file, the structure of the records for the database must be defined. The record structure describes each field with a field name, the type of data it will hold, and the length of the field measured in characters. Once the record structure has been defined, all records entered or later added to the database file will have the same number of fields with the same lengths, and each field will hold the same type of data for that record.

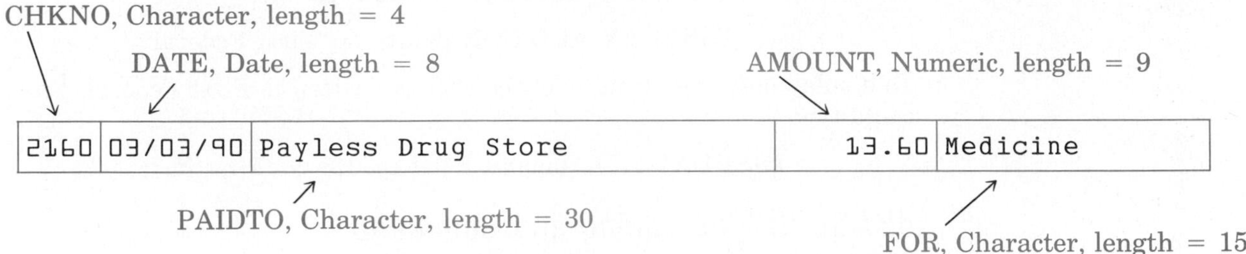

Here each field has been given a name (shown in capitals) and has been described by data type and length.

dBASE III Plus Data Types

In addition to the standard data types, string and numeric, dBASE III Plus allows date and logical data types to be entered into its variables and fields.

Date-Type Data

Date-type data are entered either into record fields whose structures have been prespecified to hold date-type data, or into variables by converting string-type data into date-type data with a dBASE function. All fields or variables holding date-type data are automatically eight characters long, and the default order of date-type data held in them is month/day/year.

03/15/90

Month Day Year

Logical-Type Data

Fields or variables holding logical-type data are automatically one character long. They hold a logical True or a logical False value. These can be directly entered into fields as T, t, Y, or y for True and F, f, N, or n for False, or entered indirectly into fields or variables as .T. or .t. for True and .F. or .f. for False. Once a logical field or variable has had data assigned to it, it may (as a single item) be used as a condition in an expression.

dBASE III Plus Command Structure

Command-Driven Software

dBASE III Plus may be used as either a menu-driven or command-driven software. *Menu-driven software* provide menus of commands from which the user selects. WordPerfect and Lotus 1-2-3 can be described as menu-driven software. *Command-driven software* respond to command words which are typed and entered. DOS, the software covered in appendix A, can be described as a command-driven software. In the following tutorial lessons, you will be given the steps to ensure you are left in dBASE's command mode, the primary use of dBASE III Plus. Entering the command **ASSIST** will put you into dBASE's menu-driven mode. While dBASE III Plus's menu-driven mode may help beginning users learn command syntax, its slow speed and limited uses make dBASE III Plus's command mode preferable.

Using dBASE's command mode requires that you memorize the dBASE command words. Fortunately, consistencies between dBASE commands make them relatively easy to memorize, and they tend to resemble standard

English terminology. For instance, to display all checks written to First Federal in the example database, you could type

DISPLAY ALL FOR paidto = "First Federal"

To display only the amounts of the checks written to First Federal, you could type

DISPLAY ALL amount **FOR** paidto = "First Federal"

dBASE III Plus Editing and Command Modes

Like other software, dBASE allows the direct entry of data while in an editing mode, and access to its commands while in a command mode. Unlike other software, however, dBASE has multiple editing and command modes.

dBASE Command Modes

The Dot (.) Prompt Command Mode

The most common method of entering dBASE commands is while in the dot (.) prompt mode. The dot (.) prompt mode is indicated when a period appears to the left of a cursor at the bottom of the screen.

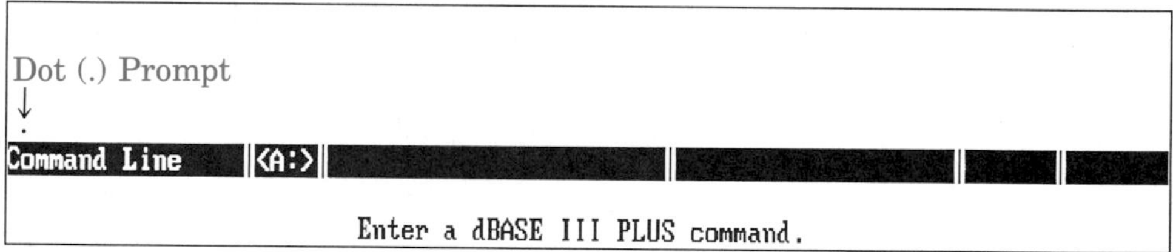

In the dot (.) prompt mode, you type and enter the dBASE command.

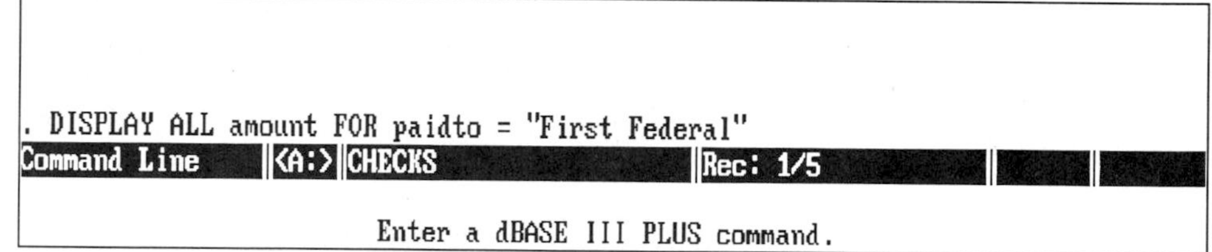

*The **ASSIST** Command Mode*

Another method of entering dBASE commands is through the use of command menus called *pull-down menus*. With such menus, the user moves a cursor across various menu options and selects a menu item by typing ↵. As menu items are selected, additional submenus often appear in order to complete a command operation. In the screen below, the **ASSIST** mode is being used to complete the same command previously entered in the dot (.) prompt mode. Notice that the dBASE command being entered appears at the bottom of the screen as the user constructs it from the pull-down menus.

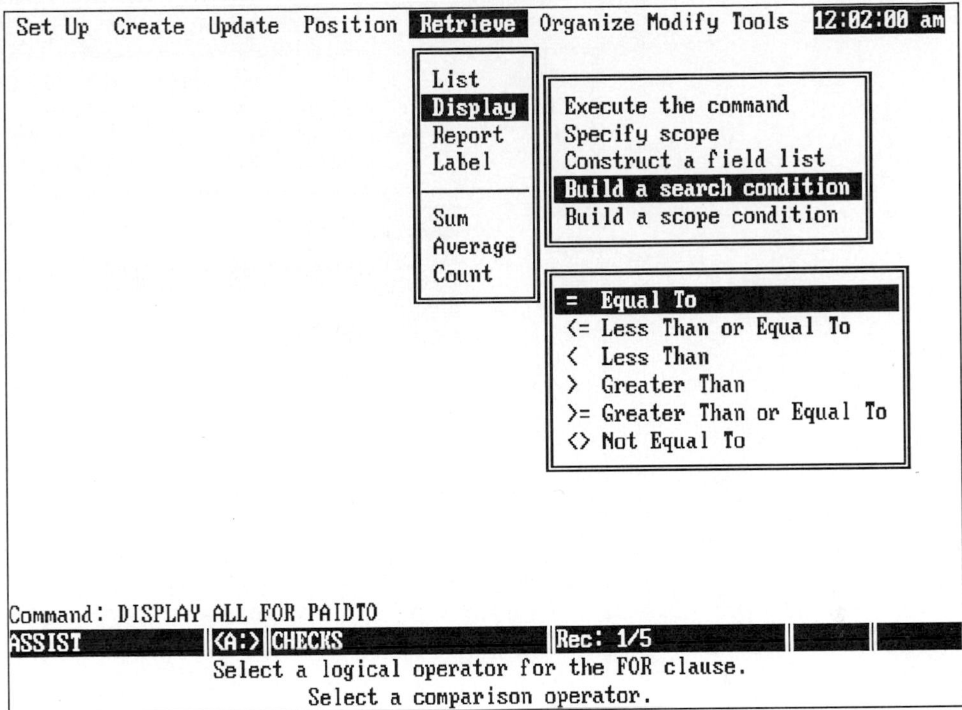

Some dBASE III Plus features provide only the pull-down menu mode for entering commands.

dBASE Editing Modes

Full-Screen Editing Mode

The full-screen editing mode is used when data held in fields or variables are to be directly entered or edited. The full-screen mode is indicated by a reverse video display of the fields or variables placed on the screen. A blinking cursor, located in one of the reverse video areas, indicates the data item currently being edited. In the following screen, the fields of the first record in the example database file have been placed on the screen in a full-screen editing mode. Notice that a menu of editing keystrokes appears at the top of the screen.

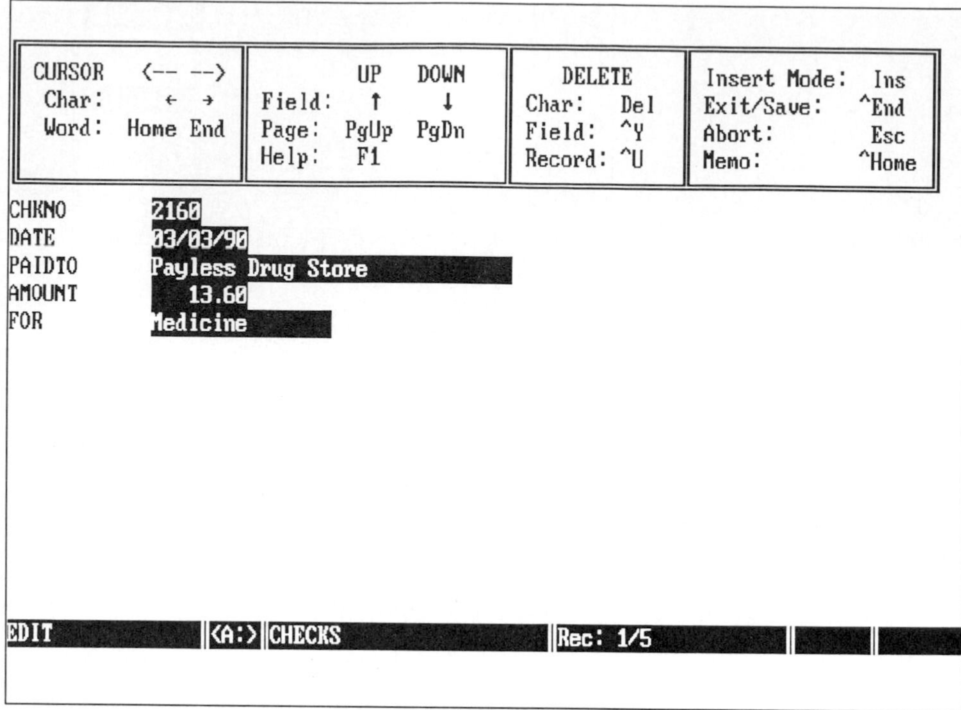

Text Editing Mode

Another dBASE editing mode is used to create the command files mentioned previously and to enter data into a .DBT file (see "dBASE's Other Files," page D-7–D-8, for more information on .DBT files). In this mode the screen appears much like a word processing screen, and keystrokes similar to those used in word processing are used to create the batch of dBASE commands contained in the file. For this reason, the editing mode is referred to here as being a text editing mode.

dBASE III Plus's File Handling

dBASE III Plus is a relatively large software which in its entirety would use up a considerable amount of RAM. In addition, as databases become several hundred records long, they would use up RAM rapidly. dBASE circumvents the RAM size limitations by keeping only data currently needed in RAM at any time. It maintains the rest of the data on the disk, bringing it into RAM as necessary.

How dBASE is Loaded into RAM

The set of instructions that makes up the dBASE III Plus software is kept in several separate program files. Using certain dBASE commands causes the disk drive holding the dBASE software to activate because such commands are not covered by the instructions currently in RAM, and the program file to execute the command needs to be read into RAM. Through software segmentation, dBASE is able to use less RAM space to accomplish its database operations. However, you must keep the appropriate dBASE programs available (in a disk drive or on a hard disk) at all times while you are using the software.

How a Database is Loaded and Saved

The first step in creating a database is to name the disk file that will hold the records of data. dBASE then creates a file on the disk, leaving it empty but structured so that data may be saved (copied) to it. A file left in this condition is said to be *open*.

dBASE then provides space in RAM to hold database record data. When you enter the data, it uses up the available RAM. When the space fills, dBASE begins to save parts (blocks) of the data into the file on the disk. Once a block of data is copied to the disk, the space it occupied in RAM may be erased to make room for new records to be entered.

When dBASE needs to process database data stored on the disk, the data are read into RAM, processed, and then written back out onto the disk file in processed form.

When you are done using dBASE, you type and enter dBASE's **QUIT** command, which causes any data left in RAM to be copied onto the disk file(s) so that all data are saved. **QUIT** is always the last command you type when using dBASE. It closes all dBASE files.

dBASE's Other Files

dBASE is able to create and maintain several types of files other than database files. These other files are typically used by dBASE to modify or support its processing of data in a database. dBASE III Plus may have several such files loaded into RAM or open at the same time. The following briefly describes the types of files dBASE III Plus can create and provides the filename extension that dBASE gives them.

.CAT *Catalog files* are created with the **SET CATALOG TO** command. A catalog file maintains an active list of related files which dBASE will treat as belonging to a particular group or set of files.

.DBF *Database files* are created in a full-screen editing mode. They hold the records and the record structure of a database.

.DBT *Database memo files* are used with a .DBF database file when the database file has fields in its record structure specified for memo-type data. A memo-type field in a .DBF file is used to store up to 4,000 characters of text related to the record. The memo text is actually stored in a .DBT file and the memo-type field in the .DBF file contains a ten-character address that tells dBASE where in the associated .DBT file the memo text may be found.

.FMT *Format files* contain dBASE commands used to customize the full-screen editing presentation of fields and/or variables.

.FRM *Report form files* are created with the **MODIFY REPORT** command (using pull-down menus). The report form files contain user-defined specifications for producing columnar-type reports from the data in a database.

.LBL *Label form files* are created with the **MODIFY LABEL** command (using pull-down menus). The label form files contain user-defined specifications for producing mailing or identification labels from the data in a database.

.MEM *Memory variable files* are created with the **SAVE TO** command. They hold the variable names and contents for variables current at the time the command was executed.

.NDX *Index files* are created with the **INDEX** command. .NDX files are used concurrently with a .DBF (database) file to cause dBASE to treat the database as though its records are sorted.

.PRG *Program files* (called *command files*) are created in a text editing mode with the **MODIFY COMMAND** command. Program files contain dBASE commands to be executed in sequence when the **DO** command is used. A dBASE .PRG file can be very similar to a program written in a programming language.

.QRY *Query files* are created with the **MODIFY QUERY** command (using pull-down menus). Query files contain user-defined conditions that cause dBASE to affect only certain records during its processing of a database.

.SCR *Screen files* are produced with the **MODIFY SCREEN** command (using pull-down menus). Screen files are source files used by dBASE to produce .FMT (format) files.

.TXT *Text files* may be created with several dBASE III Plus commands. They are ASCII data format files that can be processed by other software.

.VUE *View files* are created with the **MODIFY VIEW** command (using pull-down menus). View files contain the set of working relationships that exist between a group of related files.

LEARNING dBASE III PLUS

The dBASE III Plus commands for creation, maintenance, and basic processing of a database are fairly straightforward; however, the full range of commands available in dBASE makes it closer to being a programming language than an applications software. A knowledge of another programming language such as BASIC, COBOL, or Pascal is perhaps the greatest aid in learning to use dBASE III Plus to its fullest extent.

If you have not done so already, it is highly recommended that you study appendix C "Using Expressions" before continuing with the dBASE tutorial lessons.

As you progress through the material in this manual, you may notice slight differences between the screens displayed here and those on your monitor. These differences are due to minor changes made to the different versions of dBASE III Plus.

Getting Help

dBASE has a command, **HELP,** which will present information about specific dBASE commands and operations. To use the command, you type the command word **HELP** followed by a space, and then the command or operation for which you want information. If dBASE has the information, it will display it on the monitor screen.

REQUIRED PREPARATION

The tutorial lessons and exercises in this module will give you experience using the commands and features of dBASE III Plus. Before you begin the "hands-on" learning experience, however, you will need to complete a few initial steps and gain some preliminary information in order to be adequately prepared.

Initial Steps

1. Obtain a floppy disk appropriate for the microcomputer you will be using to complete your course assignments. Your instructor or laboratory staff will be able to tell you which kind of disk to purchase.

Size: ____________________

Sides: ____________________

Density: ____________________

2. Format your disk to the specifications of the DOS and microcomputer hardware that you will be using to complete your course assignments. Your instructor or laboratory staff will be able to tell you the steps to follow. ***Caution:*** **Formatting a disk erases all files that may exist on the disk.**

Steps to Format a Disk: ____________________

____

____

____

____

____

____

3. Each time you use the dBASE software, you will want to be sure that your data files are saved on your disk. There will be certain steps to follow, either when you first load dBASE into RAM or immediately afterwards to ensure that your files are automatically saved on your disk. Your instructor or laboratory staff will be able to tell you the steps to follow.

Starting a dBASE Session: ____________________

____

____

____

____

____

____

____

____

____

REQUIRED MATERIALS

1. An IBM DOS floppy disk (or hard-disk containing the DOS software).
2. A dBASE System 1 and a dBASE System 2 floppy disk (or hard-disk containing the software).
3. A formatted floppy disk (your files disk).
4. This manual.
5. Other ______________________________

TUTORIAL CONVENTIONS

During the introductory dBASE III Plus tutorial you will create various files using dBASE commands. The following are the conventions the tutorial's instructions will use.

↵	The bent arrow means to type the Enter key located on the right side of the keyboard.
^Key	Keys preceded by the ^ sign indicate that you should press and hold the Ctrl key and then type the next key shown.
Key,Key	Key combinations using a comma indicate that you should type the first key and then type the second key.
‖ ‖	Do not type the double lines; type only what is inside them.

HOW TO GET OUT OF TROUBLE

If you want to:	*Then:*
■ Erase characters being entered as a dBASE command or data. . .	■ Type the Backspace key located on the right top side of keyboard.
■ Stop any command operation and return to the dot (.) prompt. . .	■ Type the Esc key located on the top far-left side of the keyboard.
■ Stop any editing operation and return to the dot (.) prompt. . .	■ Press and hold the Ctrl key and then type the End key (convention is ^End).
■ Stop the tutorial to continue later. . .	■ Type ‖**QUIT**↵‖ at the dot (.) prompt.
■ Continue with the tutorial after stopping. . .	■ After loading dBASE into RAM, type ‖**SET DEFAULT TO** *drive:* ↵ **USE** empfile↵‖.

NOTE: Here drive *means type the letter (A, B, etc.) for the disk drive in which your files disk is kept.*

Throughout the tutorial lessons you will see the following symbol.

It indicates an opportune time to save your file(s) and quit the microcomputer session, if you so desire.

GETTING STARTED

The proper "getting started" procedures require information specific to the hardware and software you are using. Refer to your notes in the preceding Required Preparation section for the specific information. The following is a general procedure for getting started; however, you may need to refer to Appendix A, "The Basics of DOS," to understand some of the terminology used here.

You will need to know in which disk drive (A: or B:) your files disk will be, and where (disk drive and path) the dBASE III Plus software will be.

1. Load DOS from a floppy disk or hard disk, or return to the DOS operating level from the current software operating level.
2. Put your files floppy disk into the proper disk drive (drive name ______:).
3. If necessary, put the dBASE System disk 1 in the proper disk drive (drive name ______:).
4. When you see DOS's *drive:*\> prompt on the screen, change the current disk drive and path to where the dBASE III Plus software resides by typing ||*drive:*↵ **CD***path*↵||.
5. Now begin to load the dBASE software by typing ||dBASE↵||.
6. If necessary, follow dBASE's instructions to insert the System disk 2, and type ↵ when ready.

In a few moments dBASE III Plus will load into RAM. You will know dBASE is loaded when you see a dot (.) prompt appear next to a blinking cursor at the bottom of the screen.

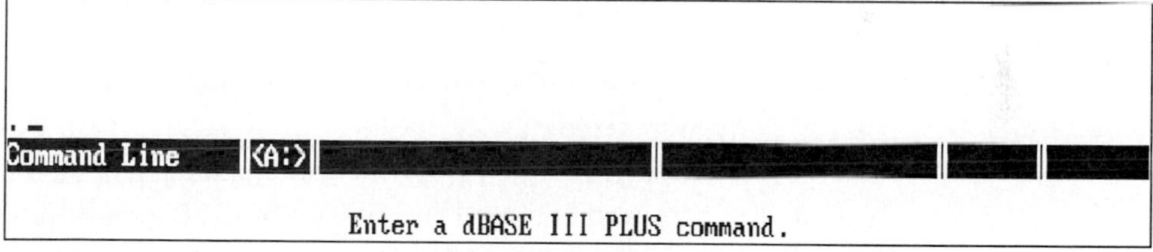

7. If you do not see the dot (.) prompt as shown here, type the Esc key.

In the next step, enter the drive letter for the drive where your files disk resides.

8. Now type ||**SET DEFAULT TO** *drive:*↵||.

This dBASE command causes dBASE to automatically address the specified drive for any file to which you later refer.

LESSON 1 Entering Commands in the Dot (.) Prompt Mode

The dot (.) appearing on the screen indicates that you are in a dBASE command mode. When the dot appears with the cursor next to it, anything that you type and enter is evaluated as a command by dBASE III Plus.

Syntax Errors

If you type an incorrect form of a dBASE command while you are in the command mode, dBASE will display a "syntax error" message, or, if the mistake is in the first word of the command, an "***Unrecognized command verb" message.

When dBASE III Plus detects a syntax error, it displays its error message and the command it was evaluating at the time on the screen with a question mark over the area where it stopped evaluating the command. For example, if in the last step of Getting Started you had typed

SET DFEAULT TO A:

dBASE would respond

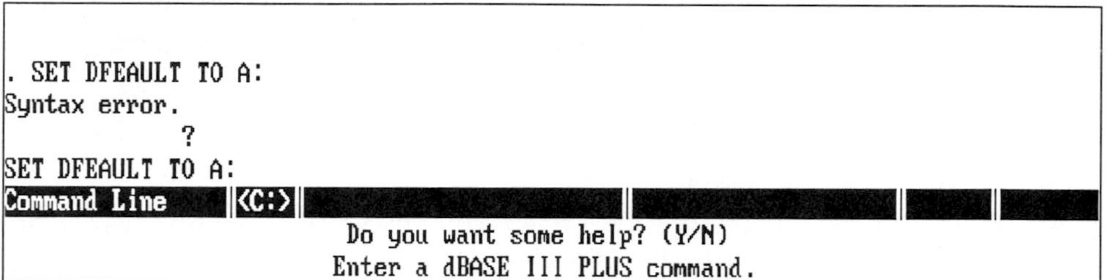
. SET DFEAULT TO A:
Syntax error.
?
SET DFEAULT TO A:
Command Line
<C:>
Do you want some help? (Y/N)
Enter a dBASE III PLUS command.

The message "Do you want some help? (Y/N)" appears at the bottom of the screen. Typing Y at this point will cause dBASE to display its **HELP** screen for the **SET** command.

Recovering from Syntax Errors

To recover from a command with a syntax error it is usually recommended that you first type any key except Y to answer the "Do you want some help?" message and then enter the command again, making sure the word **DEFAULT** and all other words are spelled correctly. However, to reenter the command, you do not need to type the entire command again.

The HISTORY Buffer

dBASE III Plus sets aside a small portion of RAM (a *buffer*) called HISTORY, into which it stores previously typed commands. The default number of commands stored in HISTORY is 20 commands. The buffer allows the user to back up, and then edit and reenter a previous command.

To display a previous command entered in the dot (.) prompt mode, the cursor up (↑) key is typed. Each time the key is typed, dBASE displays the last previous command (scrolls back through the commands in HISTORY). To scroll forward, the cursor down (↓) key is typed. When the desired command is displayed, the following keystrokes may be used to edit the command in a dBASE text editing mode.

Editing Operation	**Keystrokes**
Cursor Movement	
Character Left	Left ←
Character Right	Right →
Word Left	Home
Word Right	End
Insert/Overwrite	Ins
Delete Characters	
Current Character	Delete (Del)
Previous Character	Backspace
Word Right of Cursor	^T
Line Right of Cursor	^Y
Abort editing changes	Esc

When editing is completed, ↵ may be typed to reenter the command.

LESSON 2 Creating a Database

To continue the tutorial, you will create a small database of records. Each record's data concern an employee of a small retail shop where policy allows personal store purchases to be charged against the employee's store account.

Using the **CREATE** Command

To begin building the database, you will use the **CREATE** command. This command has the form **CREATE** [<filename>]. The filename you specify is used to name the database (.DBF) file.

1. Type ||**CREATE** empfile ↵||. (Empfile stands for employee file.)

The **CREATE** command causes dBASE to leave the dot (.) prompt mode and enter one of its full-screen editing modes. You can tell that you are in such a mode when the area of the screen at the cursor's location is displayed in reverse video. When you are in one of dBASE's editing modes, you do not enter dBASE commands since all characters that you type will be treated as data by dBASE. To save the data you have entered and exit from dBASE's editing modes (return to the dot (.) prompt command mode), you may type ^END.

Specifying a Database Record Structure

The following will appear on the screen.

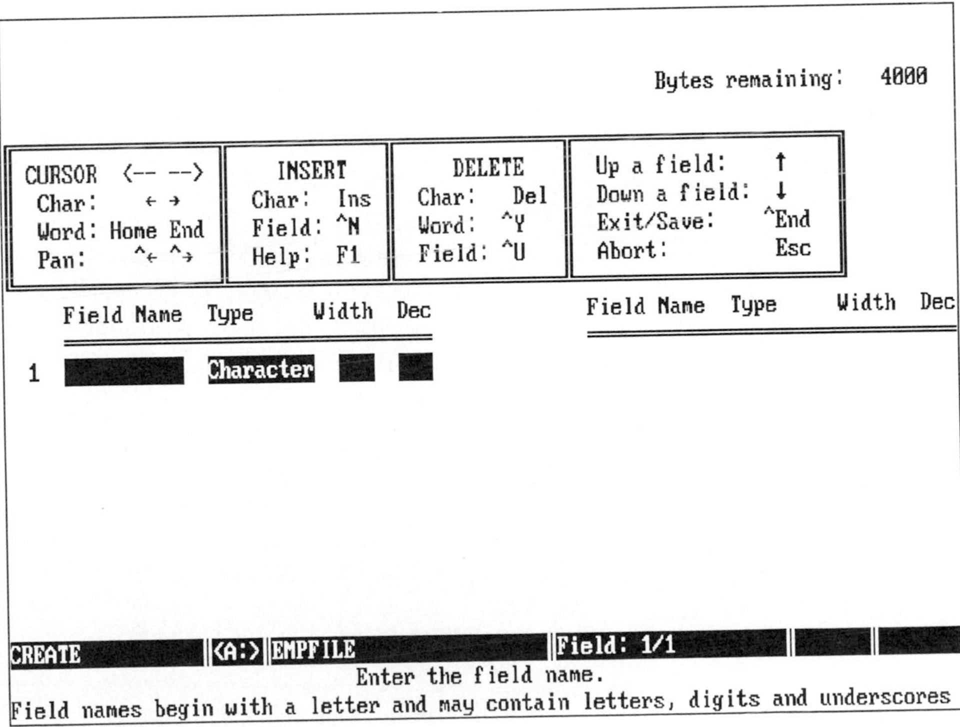

To specify the record structure, each field needs to be specified by field name; the type of data (Character, Numeric, or Date) it will hold; how many characters in width it will be; and finally, if the field is numeric, how many decimal places will be displayed.

2. Begin to specify the record structure by typing ||employee↵|| into the area under Field Name.

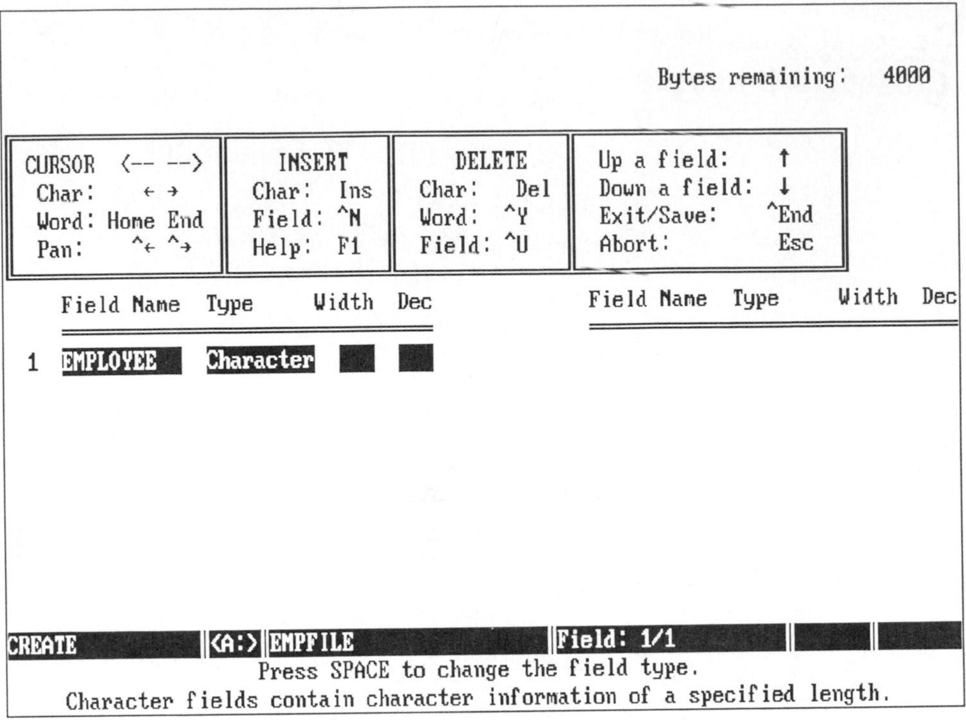

Next, you will enter the data type for the field named "EMPLOYEE." There are a total of five data types available, three of which are used in the tutorial. To select a data type for a field, you may either enter the first letter of the data type description (C = Character, N = Numeric, D = Date) or you may type the space bar to cause dBASE to display different data types in the area, and then tap the Enter key when the appropriate type is displayed.

3. Type the space bar several times to see the different data types displayed, and then type ||C|| to specify Character-type data.
4. Next type ||20↵|| into the area under Width to specify that the field named "EMPLOYEE" is to be 20 characters wide.

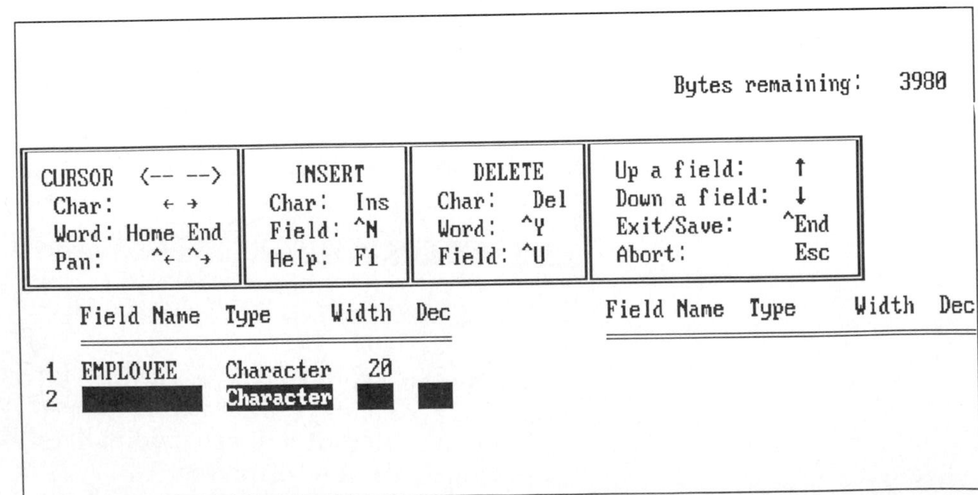

Notice that dBASE skipped over the decimal places (Dec), and the areas to specify the next field are presented. Two rules of field specification to remember are (1) only numeric fields have their decimal places specified and (2) all date fields have a width of eight characters.

In the next steps, you will finish specifying the record structure for the database empfile. Take care to enter all data exactly as shown. If you make an error entering data, try using the editing keystroke menu at the top of the screen to make your corrections. If you are unsuccessful editing the mistakes, type the Esc key twice to abort, and then start over by typing **CREATE** empfile↵.

5. Now finish specifying the record structure by entering the following data.

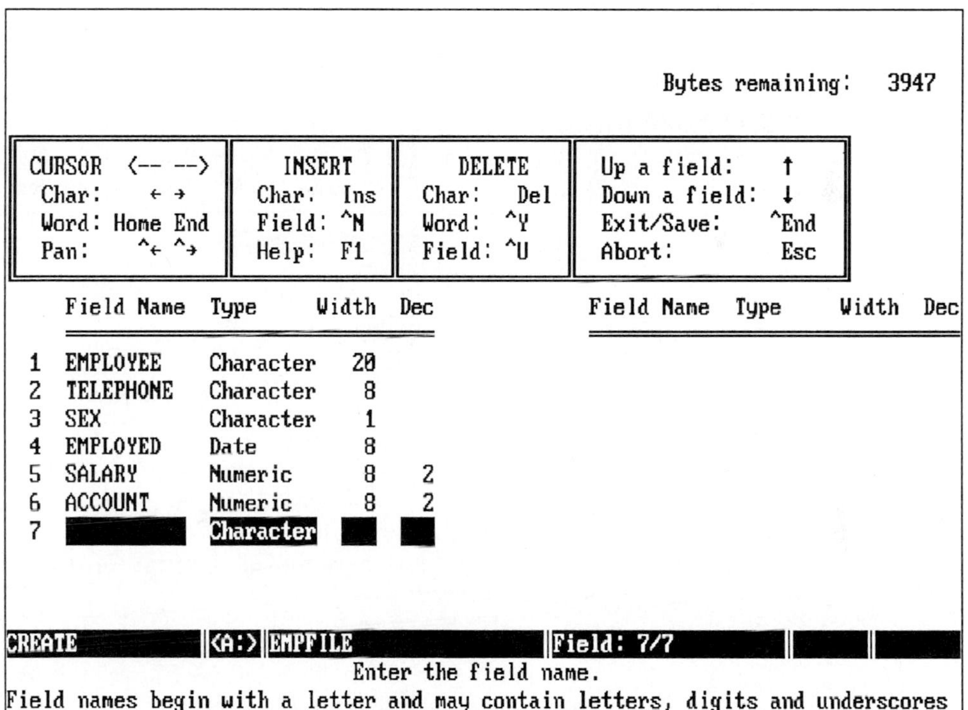

6. When dBASE presents field 7, type ↵ or ||^End||.

Typing ↵ when the last field is presented, or typing ^End, signals dBASE that you are ready to end specifying the record structure. The following message will appear at the bottom of the screen.

```
Press ENTER to confirm. Any other key to resume.
```

7. Type the Enter key.

Each Record's Structure

The record structure you have defined for the database named empfile includes six fields, three of which will hold characters, two of which will hold numeric data, and one of which will hold date-type data. Each field's length has been specified, so the total length of each record is known.

LESSON 3 Entering Records into a Database

NOTE: If you are continuing the tutorial after having used the **QUIT** *command, type* ||**USE** empfile↵ **APPEND**↵|| *to view the following record entry screen.*

Your next steps involve entering data into the records of the database. As you enter data into records, you will be in another dBASE full-screen editing mode. On the screen, you should now see the prompt

```
Input data records now? (Y/N)
```

1. Type ||Y||.

dBASE will begin by displaying the first record with empty fields (shown in reverse video) into which you can now enter data.

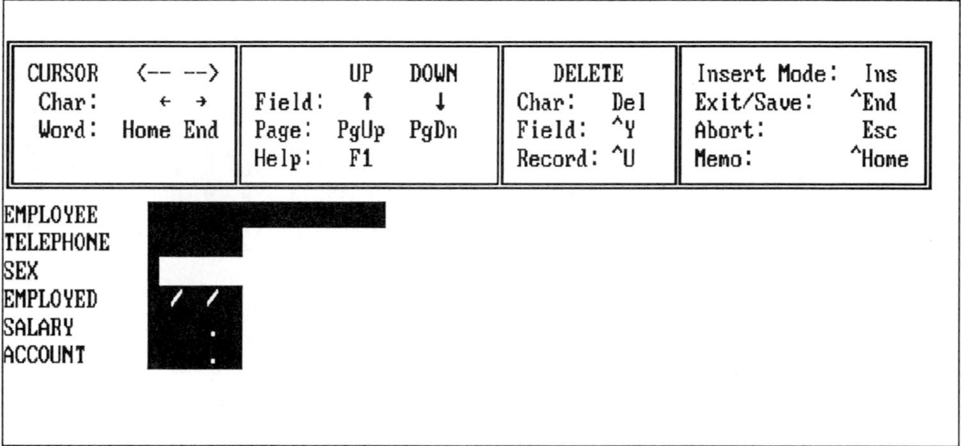

Each field's name is displayed to the left of the field. A cursor will be located at the first character of the first field to indicate where the data typed will be entered.

On the right side of the keyboard is a numeric keypad containing four keys with arrows on them. The arrowed keys *(cursor control keys)* may be used to move the cursor from field to field (↑ and ↓ keys) or from character to character within a field (← and → keys). If an attempt is made to move the cursor past the top field of the current record, the previous record is displayed.

dBASE presents the next record for data entry once the last field of the previous record has had data entered into it, or once an attempt has been made to move the cursor past the last field of the previous record.

Entering the Records Data

1. Enter the following data into each field of each record, 1 through 8, after you have read the following notes.

NOTE: (1) Make sure that you enter the upper-case/lower-case characters for the data, exactly as shown. (2) Type ||USE empfile↵ APPEND↵|| if you accidentally return to the dot (.) prompt before you are finished entering the record data. (3) If you make an error when you are entering data, don't worry. You will see later how to edit records, delete records, and make other changes. (4) A prompt that indicates which record is currently being entered appears at the bottom of the screen. It does so, however, by displaying the record number for the next previous record. That is, while the first record is being entered the prompt displays "Rec: None," while the second record is being entered the prompt displays "Rec: EOF/1." (The prompt means you are at the "End Of File" in empfile.DBF and that there is one record entered into the database file so far.)

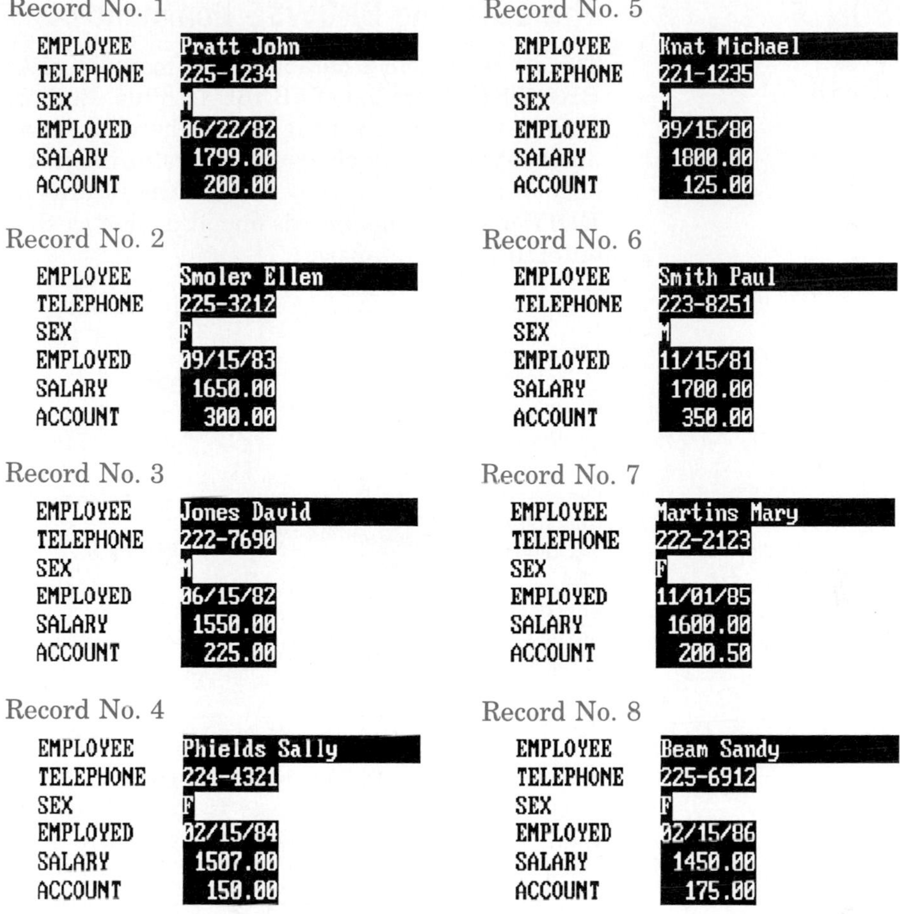

Record No. 1
EMPLOYEE Pratt John
TELEPHONE 225-1234
SEX M
EMPLOYED 06/22/82
SALARY 1799.00
ACCOUNT 200.00
Record No. 2
EMPLOYEE Smoler Ellen
TELEPHONE 225-3212
SEX F
EMPLOYED 09/15/83
SALARY 1650.00
ACCOUNT 300.00
Record No. 3
EMPLOYEE Jones David
TELEPHONE 222-7690
SEX M
EMPLOYED 06/15/82
SALARY 1550.00
ACCOUNT 225.00
Record No. 4
EMPLOYEE Phields Sally
TELEPHONE 224-4321
SEX F
EMPLOYED 02/15/84
SALARY 1507.00
ACCOUNT 150.00
Record No. 5
EMPLOYEE Knat Michael
TELEPHONE 221-1235
SEX M
EMPLOYED 09/15/80
SALARY 1800.00
ACCOUNT 125.00
Record No. 6
EMPLOYEE Smith Paul
TELEPHONE 223-8251
SEX M
EMPLOYED 11/15/81
SALARY 1700.00
ACCOUNT 350.00
Record No. 7
EMPLOYEE Martins Mary
TELEPHONE 222-2123
SEX F
EMPLOYED 11/01/85
SALARY 1600.00
ACCOUNT 200.50
Record No. 8
EMPLOYEE Beam Sandy
TELEPHONE 225-6912
SEX F
EMPLOYED 02/15/86
SALARY 1450.00
ACCOUNT 175.00

Ending Data Entry

2. When you are done entering the record data, type ↵ on the first field of the next blank record presented to save the data and return to dBASE's dot (.) prompt. When adding records to a database, the ↵ keystroke typed when a new record is presented signals dBASE to end the editing operation.

LESSON 4
Putting a Database into Use

The **USE** Command

Before you can process the records in a database with dBASE's commands, you first must specify the database file to use by typing the **USE** command.

1. Type ||**USE** empfile↵|| to cause dBASE to access (open) the database file you have created.

When a database is in use, the data in it are not constantly displayed on the screen as are other types of data with other applications software. Nonetheless, the entire database is present in RAM (or on the disk) and is now accessible to you through the commands of dBASE III Plus.

The **EDIT** and **BROWSE** Commands

To edit records in a database, you may use either the **EDIT** command or the **BROWSE** command of dBASE III Plus. Both commands cause dBASE to enter a full-screen editing mode where you can move to different fields of different records to change the data in them. **EDIT** and **BROWSE** differ only in the way that they present the records on the screen for viewing. **EDIT** presents the records one at a time in the same format as records are entered into a database.

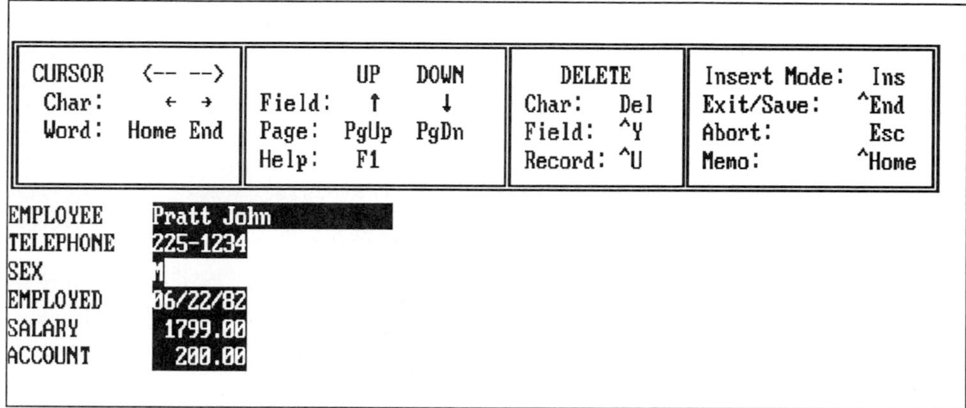

```
CURSOR    <-- -->  |          UP    DOWN  |    DELETE     | Insert Mode:  Ins
 Char:      ←  →   | Field:   ↑      ↓    | Char:    Del  | Exit/Save:   ^End
 Word:  Home End   | Page:  PgUp   PgDn   | Field:   ^Y   | Abort:        Esc
                   | Help:   F1           | Record:  ^U   | Memo:       ^Home

EMPLOYEE   Pratt John
TELEPHONE  225-1234
SEX        M
EMPLOYED   06/22/82
SALARY      1799.00
ACCOUNT      200.00
```

BROWSE presents the records horizontally in groups (one screen's worth at a time) in a form much closer to how you can visualize them represented in memory while dBASE is working with them.

```
CURSOR    <-- -->  |          UP    DOWN  |    DELETE     | Insert Mode:    Ins
 Char:      ←  →   | Record:  ↑      ↓    | Char:    Del  | Exit:          ^End
 Field: Home End   | Page:  PgUp   PgDn   | Field:   ^Y   | Abort:          Esc
 Pan:      ^←  ^→  | Help:   F1           | Record:  ^U   | Set Options: ^Home

EMPLOYEE------------ TELEPHONE SEX EMPLOYED SALARY-- ACCOUNT-
Pratt John           225-1234  M   06/22/82  1799.00   200.00
Smoler Ellen         225-3212  F   09/15/83  1650.00   300.00
Jones David          222-7690  M   06/15/82  1550.00   225.00
Phields Sally        224-4321  F   02/15/84  1507.00   150.00
Knat Michael         221-1235  M   09/15/80  1800.00   125.00
Smith Paul           223-8251  M   11/15/81  1700.00   350.00
Martins Mary         222-2123  F   11/01/85  1600.00   200.50
Beam Sandy           225-6912  F   02/15/86  1450.00   175.00
```

Editing Keystrokes

When using either **EDIT** or **BROWSE,** you may use keystrokes for such things as moving the cursor, scrolling the database, or deleting a record. The keystroke commands are executed by tapping keys found on the numeric keypad or by typing Ctrl-keystroke combinations. The following table gives a brief summary of the keystrokes to which you may refer while you complete the following steps.

Action Desired	Keystrokes
Cursor Movement	
Character Left	Left ←
Character Right	Right →
Field Right	End
Field Left	Home
Next Record	Down ↓
Previous Record	Up ↑
Scroll 18 Records Up	PgUp
Scroll 18 Records Down	PgDn
Insert/Overwrite	Ins
Delete Characters	
Current Character	Delete (Del)
Previous Character	Backspace
Word Right of Cursor	^T
Line Right of Cursor	^Y
Delete Current Record	^U
Save Updates and Exit	^End

Using **BROWSE** to Edit Records

1. Type ||**BROWSE**←||.

dBASE will display the small database on the screen. Notice that the first record in the database is displayed in reverse video.

Moving from One Record to Another

2. Type the cursor down key several times, and then type the cursor up several times.

The cursor up and down keystroke commands move the reverse video display from one record to another. The keystrokes demonstrate an important fundamental of database operations when they are used to move the reverse video display up and down through the database.

Introduction to the Database Record Pointer

While a database is in use, an unseen *record pointer* exists at all times. At any given moment the record pointer points to one particular record in the database, called the *current record.*

While in the **BROWSE** editing mode, the keys ↓ and ↑ move the record pointer one record down or up, and dBASE displays the current record in reverse video. In the command dot (.) prompt mode, there are commands that move the record pointer from one record to another, but it is seldom visually apparent that the pointer in fact has been moved.

Other Editing Keystroke Commands

Once you have moved the record pointer to the record to edit, you may move the cursor to the field to edit by typing the End key (forward one field) or Home key (back one field). When you have reached the field of concern, the ← and → keys may be used to move the cursor within the field. Any characters that you type will be written over the characters that exist in the field unless the Ins key is used to turn on the Insert mode. When the Insert mode is on, any characters that you type will be inserted into the field. The Del key may be used to delete the character above the cursor.

Updating the Records

3. Use the editing features of **BROWSE** to modify the database to reflect the following changes.
   a. David Jones has moved and his new phone number is 292-3832.
   b. Sally Phields is now married and her new last name is Sill.
   c. John Pratt has received a raise of $150.00 per month to bring his monthly salary to $1,949.00.
4. Correct any incorrect data that may have been entered when you created the database.

When you are finished the database should appear as follows.

```
CURSOR  <-- -->  |        UP    DOWN  |    DELETE     | Insert Mode:  Ins
 Char:    ←  →   | Record:  ↑     ↓   | Char:   Del   | Exit:        ^End
 Field: Home End | Page:  PgUp  PgDn  | Field:  ^Y    | Abort:        Esc
 Pan:     ^← ^→  | Help:   F1         | Record: ^U    | Set Options: ^Home

EMPLOYEE------------ TELEPHONE SEX EMPLOYED SALARY-- ACCOUNT-
Pratt John           225-1234  M   06/22/82 1949.00   200.00
Smoler Ellen         225-3212  F   09/15/83 1650.00   300.00
Jones David          292-3832  M   06/15/82 1550.00   225.00
Sill Sally           224-4321  F   02/15/84 1507.00   150.00
Knat Michael         221-1235  M   09/15/80 1800.00   125.00
Smith Paul           223-8251  M   11/15/81 1700.00   350.00
Martins Mary         222-2123  F   11/01/85 1600.00   200.50
Beam Sandy           225-6912  F   02/15/86 1450.00   175.00
```

Marking a Record for Deletion

In order to delete a record from the database, you must complete two steps. First, you mark the record for deletion. Then, you execute the dot (.) prompt command **PACK.** The **PACK** command physically removes the record from the database.

You may mark a record for deletion either in an editing mode or in the dot (.) prompt command mode. To execute the **PACK** command, you must be in the dot (.) prompt mode.

When you are in an editing mode, you mark a record for deletion by moving the record pointer to the appropriate record and typing ^U. The record still appears on the screen, but the message DEL is displayed at the bottom of the screen whenever that record becomes the current record. You may "un-mark" such a record by moving the record pointer to it and typing ^U again.

Finishing the Editing Session

5. If you have any unwanted records in the database, mark them for deletion now.

6. Type ||^End|| to save the changes made, end the editing session, and return to the dot (.) prompt command mode.
7. If you marked any records for deletion, type ||**PACK**↵|| to physically erase them from the database.

Adding Records to the Database

When you need to add records to an existing database, you may use the dBASE III Plus **APPEND** command. After you type **APPEND,** dBASE puts you in the same editing mode you were in when you last entered records. The **APPEND** command lets you add records, starting at the next available record number, until you execute the ^End (save and exit) keystroke command.

8. Type ||**APPEND**↵|| and add the following information into the blank record that dBASE will present.

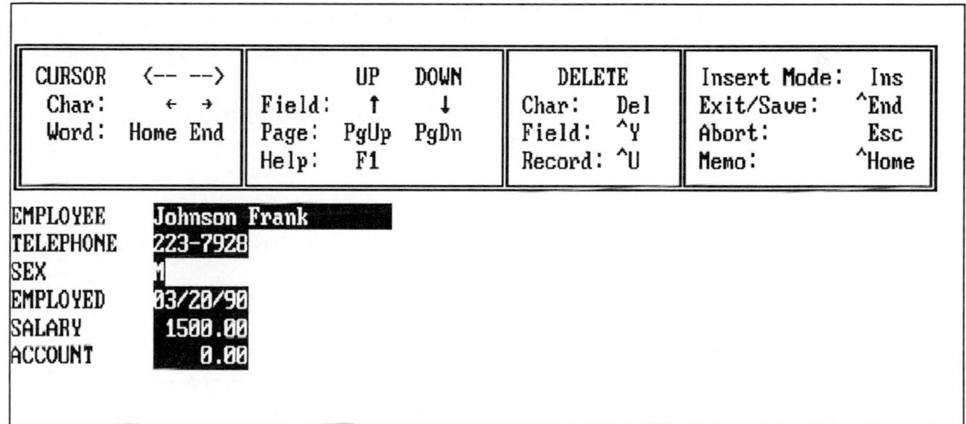

9. Type ↵ on the first field of the next record presented to quit appending records.

LESSON 6
dBASE III Plus Dot (.) Prompt Command Fundamentals

dBASE Command Conventions and Terminology

When you refer to the dBASE Operation and Command Summary in this manual or to the dBASE user's manual published by the software's developer, Ashton-Tate, you often will see the commands described in a form similar to

COMMAND [<scope>] [<expression list>] [**FOR** <condition>]

When commands are presented in the form shown above, the word(s) shown in upper case are dBASE command word(s). Although the convention uses upper case to indicate the word is a dBASE command, you may type the command in upper case or lower case when you are using it.

Command Parameters

The items following the command word(s) are called *command parameters.* Parameters may be defined as "additions to a command that affect the way the command will be executed." The types of parameters that are allowed for any particular command are described with lower-case words such as "scope." The < >s surrounding a parameter indicate that the data entered are user supplied. When a command's parameters are shown in brackets, e.g. [<scope>], they are optional—the command will work without them.

Using the **DISPLAY** Command to Explain Command Terminology

The next several steps are designed to illustrate the most important points of the command descriptions and the fundamentals of processing data using dBASE III Plus commands.

The Purpose and Form of the **DISPLAY** Command

The **DISPLAY** command may be used to display records of the database in a variety of ways. When you see the command listed in a reference, its form will be similar to

DISPLAY [<scope>] [<expression list>] [**FOR** <condition>]

Using the **DISPLAY** Command with No Parameters

1. Type ‖**DISPLAY↵**‖.

dBASE will respond by displaying a single record of the database.

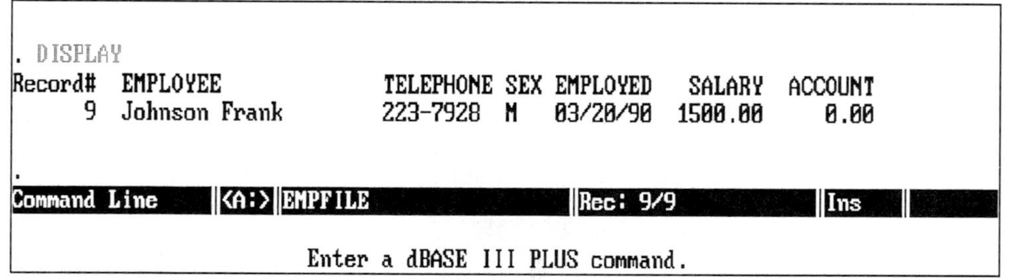

When the **DISPLAY** command is used with no parameters, it displays all of the fields of data for a single record. The record displayed will be the one to which the record pointer is pointing at the moment.

More on the Database Record Pointer

The **APPEND** command that you executed previously moved the record pointer to the last record in the database so that you could enter data into the record. Since then, the record pointer has not been moved. It can be considered as existing alongside the records in the database.

```
        Record#  EMPLOYEE              TELEPHONE SEX EMPLOYED   SALARY  ACCOUNT
              1  Pratt John            225-1234  M   06/22/82  1949.00   200.00
              2  Smoler Ellen          225-3212  F   09/15/83  1650.00   300.00
              3  Jones David           292-3832  M   06/15/82  1550.00   225.00
              4  Sill Sally            224-4321  F   02/15/84  1507.00   150.00
              5  Knat Michael          221-1235  M   09/15/80  1800.00   125.00
              6  Smith Paul            223-8251  M   11/15/81  1700.00   350.00
              7  Martins Mary          222-2123  F   11/01/85  1600.00   200.50
Record        8  Beam Sandy            225-6912  F   02/15/86  1450.00   175.00
pointer →     9  Johnson Frank         223-7928  M   03/20/90  1500.00     0.00
```

Moving the Record Pointer Several dBASE commands move the record pointer when they are executed, and some commands are designed specifically to move the pointer. The dBASE commands **SKIP** [<n>], **GO TOP, GO BOTTOM,** and **GOTO** <n> (where n is the number of records to skip or the record number to go to) are used to move the record pointer.

2. Type and enter the following commands (shown in gray). See how the record pointer is moved as you view the record displayed (shown in black type) by the **DISPLAY** command.

NOTE: dBASE commands may be typed in upper case or lower case. You need only type the first four letters of a dBASE command. For example, typing ||disp↵|| works as well as ||DISPLAY↵||.

```
. GO TOP
. DISPLAY
Record#  EMPLOYEE              TELEPHONE SEX EMPLOYED   SALARY  ACCOUNT
      1  Pratt John            225-1234  M   06/22/82  1949.00   200.00

. SKIP
Record No.      2
. DISPLAY
Record#  EMPLOYEE              TELEPHONE SEX EMPLOYED   SALARY  ACCOUNT
      2  Smoler Ellen          225-3212  F   09/15/83  1650.00   300.00

. SKIP 3
Record No.      5
. DISPLAY
Record#  EMPLOYEE              TELEPHONE SEX EMPLOYED   SALARY  ACCOUNT
      5  Knat Michael          221-1235  M   09/15/80  1800.00   125.00

. GO BOTTOM
. DISPLAY
Record#  EMPLOYEE              TELEPHONE SEX EMPLOYED   SALARY  ACCOUNT
      9  Johnson Frank         223-7928  M   03/20/90  1500.00     0.00

. GOTO 3
. DISPLAY
Record#  EMPLOYEE              TELEPHONE SEX EMPLOYED   SALARY  ACCOUNT
      3  Jones David           292-3832  M   06/15/82  1550.00   225.00
```

Using the **DISPLAY** Command with the <scope> Parameter

The Four Possible Scopes: ***ALL, RECORD*** *<n>,* ***NEXT*** *<n>,* ***and REST***

The first listed user-supplied parameter of the **DISPLAY** command is <scope>. The parameter is found in several dBASE commands and it affects the record pointer when it is used. The four possible <scope>s are **ALL, REST, NEXT** <n>, and **RECORD** <n>. The <n> describes a number of records or a specific record number that you supply.

3. Type ||**DISPLAY ALL**←||.

dBASE will respond by displaying the following.

```
. DISPLAY ALL
Record#  EMPLOYEE                 TELEPHONE SEX EMPLOYED   SALARY  ACCOUNT
      1  Pratt John               225-1234  M   06/22/82  1949.00   200.00
      2  Smoler Ellen             225-3212  F   09/15/83  1650.00   300.00
      3  Jones David              292-3832  M   06/15/82  1550.00   225.00
      4  Sill Sally               224-4321  F   02/15/84  1507.00   150.00
      5  Knat Michael             221-1235  M   09/15/80  1800.00   125.00
      6  Smith Paul               223-8251  M   11/15/81  1700.00   350.00
      7  Martins Mary             222-2123  F   11/01/85  1600.00   200.50
      8  Beam Sandy               225-6912  F   02/15/86  1450.00   175.00
      9  Johnson Frank            223-7928  M   03/20/90  1500.00     0.00

.
Command Line    ||<A:>||EMPFILE            ||Rec: EOF/9        ||Ins  ||

                    Enter a dBASE III PLUS command.
```

A <scope> of **ALL** changes the way in which the **DISPLAY** command is executed. It has the same effect as typing **GO TOP, DISPLAY, SKIP, DISPLAY, SKIP, DISPLAY,** continuing until you reach the end of the database.

4. Now type ||**DISPLAY**←||.

dBASE will display the following.

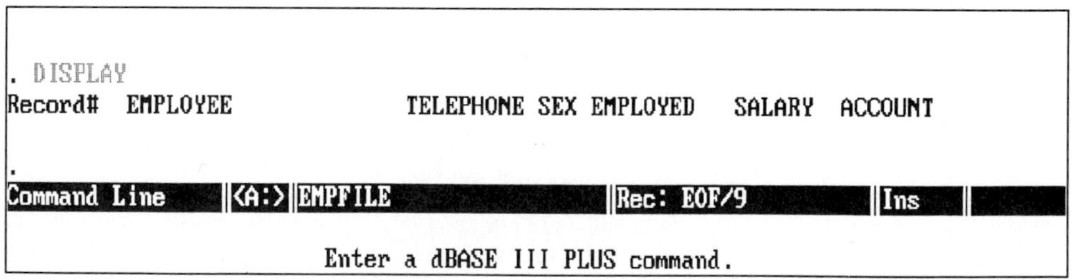

```
. DISPLAY
Record#  EMPLOYEE                 TELEPHONE SEX EMPLOYED   SALARY  ACCOUNT

.
Command Line    ||<A:>||EMPFILE            ||Rec: EOF/9        ||Ins  ||

                    Enter a dBASE III PLUS command.
```

The fact that no record data are displayed (including Record#) indicates that the record pointer currently resides past the bottom of the database (EOF/9).

5. Type ||**DISPLAY RECORD** 2↵||.

dBASE will display the following.

The <scope> **RECORD** <n> has the same effect as typing **GOTO** 2, **DISPLAY.** Notice that the pointer remains on record 2 (Rec: 2/9 shown at the bottom of the screen).

6. Now type ||**DISPLAY NEXT** 3↵||.

dBASE will respond by displaying the following.

```
. DISPLAY NEXT 3
Record#  EMPLOYEE            TELEPHONE SEX EMPLOYED  SALARY  ACCOUNT
      2  Smoler Ellen        225-3212  F   09/15/83 1650.00   300.00
      3  Jones David         292-3832  M   06/15/82 1550.00   225.00
      4  Sill Sally          224-4321  F   02/15/84 1507.00   150.00

.
Command Line     ||<A:>||EMPFILE              ||Rec: 4/9          ||Ins  ||

                   Enter a dBASE III PLUS command.
```

The <scope> **NEXT** <n> has the same effect as **DISPLAY, SKIP, DISPLAY** . . . <n> number of times. Notice that the record pointer is left on record 4 (Rec: 4/9).

7. Now type ||**DISPLAY REST**↵||.

```
. DISPLAY REST
Record#  EMPLOYEE            TELEPHONE SEX EMPLOYED  SALARY  ACCOUNT
      4  Sill Sally          224-4321  F   02/15/84 1507.00   150.00
      5  Knat Michael        221-1235  M   09/15/80 1800.00   125.00
      6  Smith Paul          223-8251  M   11/15/81 1700.00   350.00
      7  Martins Mary        222-2123  F   11/01/85 1600.00   200.50
      8  Beam Sandy          225-6912  F   02/15/86 1450.00   175.00
      9  Johnson Frank       223-7928  M   03/20/90 1500.00     0.00

.
Command Line     ||<A:>||EMPFILE              ||Rec: EOF/9        ||Ins  ||

                   Enter a dBASE III PLUS command.
```

The <scope> **REST** has the same effect as **DISPLAY, SKIP, DISPLAY, SKIP** . . . until the end of the database file (EOF/9) is reached.

Using the **DISPLAY** Command with the <expression list> Parameter

The second optional parameter of the **DISPLAY** command is <expression list>. An <expression> (<exp> for short) is an item or group of items with operators whose values can be determined by dBASE III Plus. An expression list is one or more expressions separated by commas.

The items in an expression may include constants, dBASE functions, memory variable names, and/or names used to describe the fields holding database data. The operators used in an expression may include the mathematical operators (^, *, /, +, −), the relational operators (<, >, =), and the logical operators (.NOT., .AND., .OR.). When an expression contains relational operators, dBASE will evaluate the expression as being either .T. for true or .F. for false. To give you experience using expression lists, do the following.

8. Type ‖**CLEAR**↵‖.

CLEAR is the dBASE III Plus command used to clear the screen.

9. Next type ‖**GOTO RECORD** 6↵ **DISPLAY** employee↵‖.

NOTE: "employee" is a field name, so it must be typed in its entirety. It may, however, be typed in upper case or lower case.

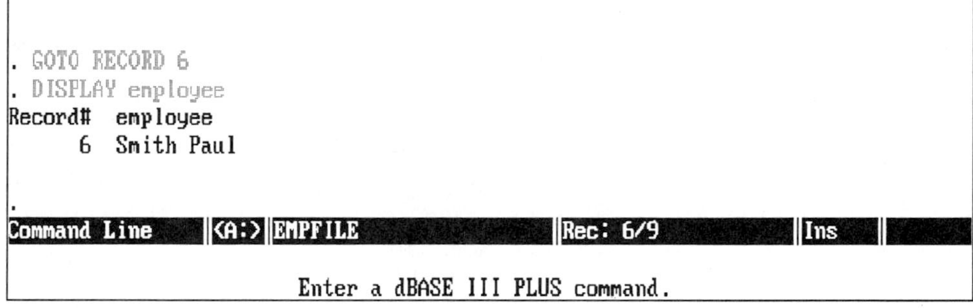

dBASE will display the record number and contents of the single field, employee, for the current record. Notice that the field label over the employee's name appears exactly as typed in the expression list of the **DISPLAY** command.

10. Continue by typing ||**DISPLAY ALL** employee, telephone←┘||.

dBASE will respond by displaying the following.

```
. DISPLAY ALL employee,telephone
Record#  employee               telephone
      1  Pratt John             225-1234
      2  Smoler Ellen           225-3212
      3  Jones David            292-3832
      4  Sill Sally             224-4321
      5  Knat Michael           221-1235
      6  Smith Paul             223-8251
      7  Martins Mary           222-2123
      8  Beam Sandy             225-6912
      9  Johnson Frank          223-7928

.
Command Line    ||<A:>||EMPFILE                  ||Rec: EOF/9        ||Ins ||

                       Enter a dBASE III PLUS command.
```

"employee, telephone" is an example of an expression list containing two expressions (field names) separated by commas.

To make the following examples more sensible, assume that management prefers its employees to keep their account amounts less than 15 percent of their monthly salaries.

11. Type ||**DISPLAY ALL** employee, "Limit =", .15 * salary←┘||.

dBASE will display the following.

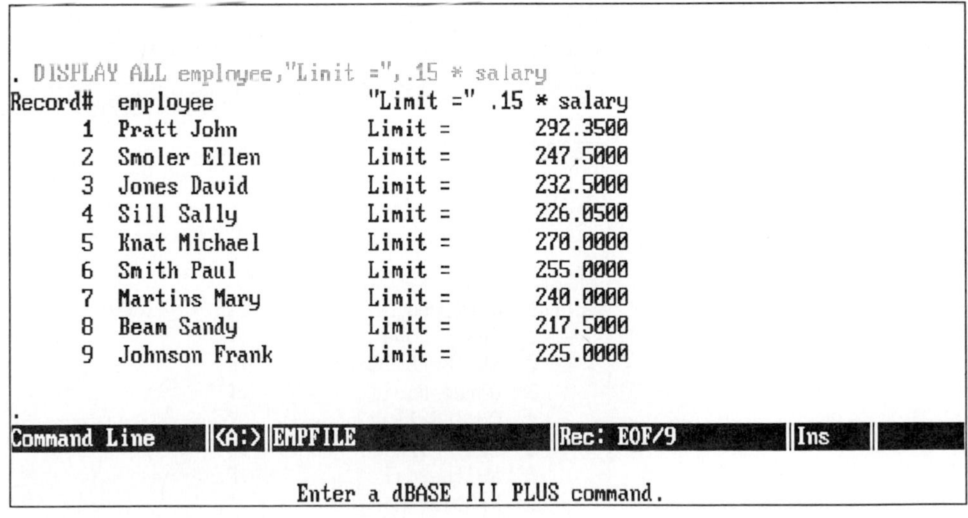

```
. DISPLAY ALL employee,"Limit =",.15 * salary
Record#  employee               "Limit =" .15 * salary
      1  Pratt John             Limit =        292.3500
      2  Smoler Ellen           Limit =        247.5000
      3  Jones David            Limit =        232.5000
      4  Sill Sally             Limit =        226.0500
      5  Knat Michael           Limit =        270.0000
      6  Smith Paul             Limit =        255.0000
      7  Martins Mary           Limit =        240.0000
      8  Beam Sandy             Limit =        217.5000
      9  Johnson Frank          Limit =        225.0000

.
Command Line    ||<A:>||EMPFILE                  ||Rec: EOF/9        ||Ins ||

                       Enter a dBASE III PLUS command.
```

"employee, "Limit =", .15 * salary" is an example of an expression list consisting of a field, a constant, and an expression with two items and an operator whose value can be determined.

12. Next type ||**DISPLAY ALL** employee, **INT**(.15 * salary), **INT**(.15 * salary − account) **OFF**←||.

dBASE will display the following.

```
. DISPLAY ALL employee,INT(.15 * salary),INT(.15 * salary - account) OFF
employee              INT(.15 * salary)  INT(.15 * salary - account)
Pratt John                          292                           92
Smoler Ellen                        247                          -52
Jones David                         232                            7
Sill Sally                          226                           76
Knat Michael                        270                          145
Smith Paul                          255                          -95
Martins Mary                        240                           39
Beam Sandy                          217                           42
Johnson Frank                       225                          225

.
Command Line    ||<A:>||EMPFILE            ||Rec: EOF/9          ||Ins  ||

                     Enter a dBASE III PLUS command.
```

In this example, the **INT** (Integer) function is used to remove trailing cents and zeros from the limit amount (**INT**(.15 * salary)) and from the amount the employee is currently under/over (−) that limit (**INT**(.15 * salary − account)).

Notice that a previously unmentioned **DISPLAY** parameter, **OFF,** may be used to stop the display of each record's record number. It also is possible to stop the display of the expression labels (first row of output) by typing the command **SET HEADING OFF.** To reestablish the display of expression labels, you type **SET HEADING ON.**

13. Now type ||**DISPLAY ALL** employee, .15 * salary − account > 0←||.

dBASE will display the following.

```
. DISPLAY ALL employee,.15 * salary - account > 0
Record#  employee             .15 * salary - account > 0
      1  Pratt John           .T.
      2  Smoler Ellen         .F.
      3  Jones David          .T.
      4  Sill Sally           .T.
      5  Knat Michael         .T.
      6  Smith Paul           .F.
      7  Martins Mary         .T.
      8  Beam Sandy           .T.
      9  Johnson Frank        .T.

.
Command Line    ||<A:>||EMPFILE            ||Rec: EOF/9          ||Ins  ||

                     Enter a dBASE III PLUS command.
```

Here the use of an expression containing a relational operator results in dBASE evaluating the expression as being either .T. for true or .F. for false for each record. Such an expression is referred to as being a condition.

Using the **DISPLAY** Command with the **FOR** <condition> Parameter

Using Conditions within a dBASE Command

The third parameter is [**FOR** <condition>], which allows selective execution of the command with which it is used. A <condition> is an expression that includes relational operators causing dBASE to evaluate it as either .T. for true or .F. for false. The items in the condition may include constants, dBASE functions, variable names, and/or names for the fields used to hold database data. The operators used in a condition may include the mathematical operators (^, *, /, +, −), the relational operators (<, >, =), and the logical operators (.NOT., .AND., .OR.).

A Change in Scope When the [**FOR** <condition>] parameter is used with a command, the default <scope> of the command becomes **ALL** records. The change in scope causes the record pointer to move to the top of the database, where the first record is evaluated for the fields of concern included in the **FOR** <condition>.

.T. and .F. The record at the top of the database will be evaluated as either .T. for true or .F. for false. If the value determined for the condition is .F., the command will not be executed for the record; dBASE will move the pointer to the next record and evaluate it.

Using Simple Conditions

14. Type and enter the following commands (printed in gray) to see how the optional parameter [**FOR** <condition>] affects the **DISPLAY** command's response (shown in black type).

```
. CLEAR
. DISPLAY FOR sex = "M"
Record#  EMPLOYEE                TELEPHONE SEX EMPLOYED   SALARY  ACCOUNT
      1  Pratt John              225-1234  M   06/22/82  1949.00   200.00
      3  Jones David             292-3832  M   06/15/82  1550.00   225.00
      5  Knat Michael            221-1235  M   09/15/80  1800.00   125.00
      6  Smith Paul              223-8251  M   11/15/81  1700.00   350.00
      9  Johnson Frank           223-7928  M   03/20/90  1500.00     0.00

. DISPLAY employee,telephone FOR sex = "F"
Record#  employee                telephone
      2  Smoler Ellen            225-3212
      4  Sill Sally              224-4321
      7  Martins Mary            222-2123
      8  Beam Sandy              [illegible]

. DISPLAY FOR sex = "f"
Record#  EMPLOYEE                TELEPHONE SEX EMPLOYED   SALARY  ACCOUNT
```

No records will be displayed since you entered the record data character "f" (lower case) into the field named sex. The "M" and "F" used in the command's [**FOR** <condition>] parameter are references to data items in your database. You must refer to such items precisely, and in the same case as they exist in their fields.

15. Continue by typing and entering the commands shown in gray below.

```
. DISPLAY FOR employee = "Smith Paul"
Record#  EMPLOYEE                    TELEPHONE SEX EMPLOYED   SALARY  ACCOUNT
      6  Smith Paul                  223-8251  M   11/15/81  1700.00   350.00

. DISPLAY FOR employee = "Smi"
Record#  EMPLOYEE                    TELEPHONE SEX EMPLOYED   SALARY  ACCOUNT
      6  Smith Paul                  223-8251  M   11/15/81  1700.00   350.00

. DISPLAY FOR employee = "Sm"
Record#  EMPLOYEE                    TELEPHONE SEX EMPLOYED   SALARY  ACCOUNT
      2  Smoler Ellen                225-3212  F   09/15/83  1650.00   300.00
      6  Smith Paul                  223-8251  M   11/15/81  1700.00   350.00

. DISPLAY FOR employee = "S"
Record#  EMPLOYEE                    TELEPHONE SEX EMPLOYED   SALARY  ACCOUNT
      2  Smoler Ellen                225-3212  F   09/15/83  1650.00   300.00
      4  Sill Sally                  224-4321  F   02/15/84  1507.00   150.00
      6  Smith Paul                  223-8251  M   11/15/81  1700.00   350.00
```

Although you must refer to the data items precisely, you may refer to character items in part, as long as the segment ("Smi", for instance) is meant to evaluate as .T.rue from the far left of the data field. In other words, the segment must begin at the beginning.

16. Next type

```
. DISPLAY FOR employee < "K"
Record#  EMPLOYEE                    TELEPHONE SEX EMPLOYED   SALARY  ACCOUNT
      3  Jones David                 292-3832  M   06/15/82  1550.00   225.00
      8  Beam Sandy                  225-6912  F   02/15/86  1450.00   175.00
      9  Johnson Frank               223-7928  M   03/20/90  1500.00     0.00
```

Character data inequalities also may be used in a condition.

```
. DISPLAY FOR salary * 12 <= 18000
Record#  EMPLOYEE                    TELEPHONE SEX EMPLOYED   SALARY  ACCOUNT
      8  Beam Sandy                  225-6912  F   02/15/86  1450.00   175.00
      9  Johnson Frank               223-7928  M   03/20/90  1500.00     0.00
```

You may use numeric expressions with mathematical operators as items in a condition.

Converting Data Types

The data items used within a simple condition must be of the same data type. You often may need to convert one data item into another data type for use in the **FOR** <condition> parameter. Data type conversion is accomplished through using dBASE functions. Two such functions are the **DTOC** (Date-to-Character) and **CTOD** (Character-to-Date) functions. To give you experience converting data types, do the following.

17. Type and enter the command shown in gray.

```
. DISPLAY FOR employed > CTOD("01/01/84")
Record#  EMPLOYEE                 TELEPHONE SEX EMPLOYED    SALARY  ACCOUNT
      4  Sill Sally               224-4321  F   02/15/84   1507.00   150.00
      7  Martins Mary             222-2123  F   11/01/85   1600.00   200.50
      8  Beam Sandy               225-6912  F   02/15/86   1450.00   175.00
      9  Johnson Frank            223-7928  M   03/20/90   1500.00     0.00
```

Here the character data "01/01/84" must be converted to date-type data with the **CTOD** (Character-to-Date) function in order to compare it with the data in the date-type field employed.

Using More Complex Conditions

Logical operators may be used with relational operators to test for more than one condition at a time.

18. Type and enter the commands shown in gray.

```
. DISPLAY FOR salary < 1600 .AND. sex = "F"
Record#  EMPLOYEE                 TELEPHONE SEX EMPLOYED    SALARY  ACCOUNT
      4  Sill Sally               224-4321  F   02/15/84   1507.00   150.00
      8  Beam Sandy               225-6912  F   02/15/86   1450.00   175.00

. DISPLAY employee,salary FOR salary < 1600 .OR. salary > 1800
Record#  employee                   salary
      1  Pratt John                1949.00
      3  Jones David               1550.00
      4  Sill Sally                1507.00
      8  Beam Sandy                1450.00
      9  Johnson Frank             1500.00
```

Displaying Certain Data with the **DISPLAY** Command

Use the **DISPLAY** command and its various parameters to display the described information from the database.

19. Display all fields of the second record.

```
Record#  EMPLOYEE                TELEPHONE SEX EMPLOYED   SALARY  ACCOUNT
      2  Smoler Ellen            225-3212  F   09/15/83  1650.00   300.00
```

20. Display only the employee's name and salary for all records.

```
Record#  employee                 salary
      1  Pratt John              1949.00
      2  Smoler Ellen            1650.00
      3  Jones David             1550.00
      4  Sill Sally              1507.00
      5  Knat Michael            1800.00
      6  Smith Paul              1700.00
      7  Martins Mary            1600.00
      8  Beam Sandy              1450.00
      9  Johnson Frank           1500.00
```

21. Display the name, gender, and date hired for all employees who make more than $1,600.00 per month.

```
Record#  employee                sex employed
      1  Pratt John              M   06/22/82
      2  Smoler Ellen            F   09/15/83
      5  Knat Michael            M   09/15/80
      6  Smith Paul              M   11/15/81
```

22. Display the name, date hired, and salary of all employees who were hired before May 30, 1984.

```
Record#  employee                employed   salary
      1  Pratt John              06/22/82  1949.00
      2  Smoler Ellen            09/15/83  1650.00
      3  Jones David             06/15/82  1550.00
      4  Sill Sally              02/15/84  1507.00
      5  Knat Michael            09/15/80  1800.00
      6  Smith Paul              11/15/81  1700.00
```

23. Display the name, date hired, and salary of all men who were hired on or before June 15, 1982.

```
Record#  employee             employed   salary
      3  Jones David          06/15/82  1550.00
      5  Knat Michael         09/15/80  1800.00
      6  Smith Paul           11/15/81  1700.00
```

LESSON 7
Other Important dBASE Dot (.) Prompt Commands

The **DELETE** and **RECALL** Commands

Marking and Unmarking Records for Deletion

The **DELETE** command may be used to mark a record for deletion when you are in the dot (.) prompt command mode. The form of the **DELETE** command is

DELETE [<scope>] [**FOR** <condition>]

To unmark a record marked for deletion, the **RECALL** command may be used. Its form is

RECALL [<scope>] [**FOR** <condition>]

1. To demonstrate using the two commands, type and enter the following commands shown in gray.

```
. GO TOP
. DELETE
      1 record deleted
. DISPLAY NEXT 3
Record#  EMPLOYEE             TELEPHONE SEX EMPLOYED   SALARY  ACCOUNT
      1 *Pratt John           225-1234  M   06/22/82  1949.00   200.00
      2  Smoler Ellen         225-3212  F   09/15/83  1650.00   300.00
      3  Jones David          292-3832  M   06/15/82  1550.00   225.00
```

Notice that Record #1 still appears, but there is an asterisk next to it. The asterisk indicates that the **DELETE** command marked the record for deletion, but did not physically remove it from the database. To unmark this record, you may use the **RECALL** command.

2. Continue by typing the following commands shown in gray.

```
. GOTO 1
. RECALL
      1 record recalled
. DISPLAY NEXT 3
Record#  EMPLOYEE             TELEPHONE SEX EMPLOYED   SALARY  ACCOUNT
      1  Pratt John           225-1234  M   06/22/82  1949.00   200.00
      2  Smoler Ellen         225-3212  F   09/15/83  1650.00   300.00
      3  Jones David          292-3832  M   06/15/82  1550.00   225.00
```

3. Next type

```
. GOTO 1
. DELETE FOR employee = "Jones Da"
     1 record deleted
. DISPLAY
Record#  EMPLOYEE              TELEPHONE SEX EMPLOYED   SALARY  ACCOUNT
```

(The record pointer is left at the bottom of the database.)

```
. GO TOP
. DISPLAY NEXT 3
Record#  EMPLOYEE              TELEPHONE SEX EMPLOYED   SALARY  ACCOUNT
      1  Pratt John            225-1234  M   06/22/82  1949.00   200.00
      2  Smoler Ellen          225-3212  F   09/15/83  1650.00   300.00
      3 *Jones David           292-3832  M   06/15/82  1550.00   225.00

. DELETE FOR salary > 1600
     4 records deleted
. DISPLAY ALL
Record#  EMPLOYEE              TELEPHONE SEX EMPLOYED   SALARY  ACCOUNT
      1 *Pratt John            225-1234  M   06/22/82  1949.00   200.00
      2 *Smoler Ellen          225-3212  F   09/15/83  1650.00   300.00
      3 *Jones David           292-3832  M   06/15/82  1550.00   225.00
      4  Sill Sally            224-4321  F   02/15/84  1507.00   150.00
      5 *Knat Michael          221-1235  M   09/15/80  1800.00   125.00
      6 *Smith Paul            223-8251  M   11/15/81  1700.00   350.00
      7  Martins Mary          222-2123  F   11/01/85  1600.00   200.50
      8  Beam Sandy            225-6912  F   02/15/86  1450.00   175.00
      9  Johnson Frank         223-7928  M   03/20/90  1500.00     0.00
```

4. Continue by typing and entering the commands shown in gray.

```
. RECALL ALL
     5 records recalled
. DISPLAY ALL
Record#  EMPLOYEE              TELEPHONE SEX EMPLOYED   SALARY  ACCOUNT
      1  Pratt John            225-1234  M   06/22/82  1949.00   200.00
      2  Smoler Ellen          225-3212  F   09/15/83  1650.00   300.00
      3  Jones David           292-3832  M   06/15/82  1550.00   225.00
      4  Sill Sally            224-4321  F   02/15/84  1507.00   150.00
      5  Knat Michael          221-1235  M   09/15/80  1800.00   125.00
      6  Smith Paul            223-8251  M   11/15/81  1700.00   350.00
      7  Martins Mary          222-2123  F   11/01/85  1600.00   200.50
      8  Beam Sandy            225-6912  F   02/15/86  1450.00   175.00
      9  Johnson Frank         223-7928  M   03/20/90  1500.00     0.00
```

The **PACK** Command

To physically delete all records marked for deletion you use the **PACK** command. The **PACK** command has no parameters—its form is simply **PACK.** Once it is executed, all records marked for deletion are permanently erased from the database.

The **COUNT, SUM,** and **AVERAGE** Commands

The **COUNT, SUM,** and **AVERAGE** commands are used to provide summary data for the database. Their forms are

COUNT [<scope>] [**FOR** <condition>] [**TO** <memvar>]
SUM [<expression list>] [<scope>] [**FOR** <condition>] [**TO** <memvar>]
AVERAGE [<expression list>] [<scope>] [**FOR** <condition>] [**TO** <memvar>]

Notice the introduction of a new type of command parameter, [**TO** <memvar>].

Memory Variables

When the **COUNT, SUM,** and **AVERAGE** commands are executed, dBASE will display a number on the monitor screen. For instance, typing **SUM** account↵ with empfile in use causes dBASE to display the following.

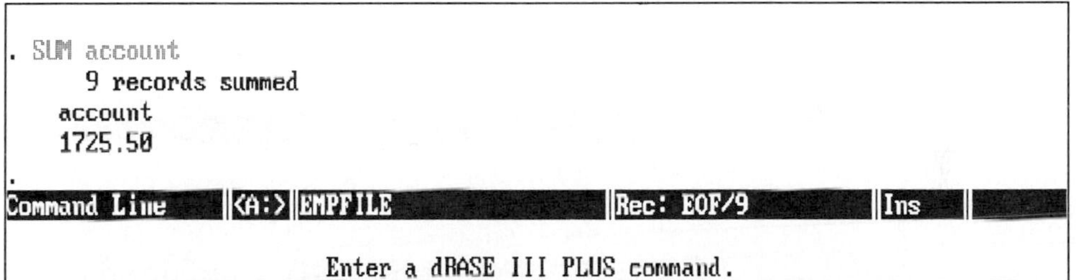

The number 1725.50 represents the sum of all account fields in the database. The [**TO** <memvar>] parameter of the three commands causes dBASE not only to display the number, but also to store the number in a memory location (variable) for later reference. You can consider a memory variable a single field with its own unique name, independent of the database, able to hold character-, numeric-, logical-, or date-type data. The variable's name is supplied by the user when the variable is created. Several dBASE commands use <memvar>s in their parameters.

*The **STORE TO** and = Commands*

The **STORE** command places data directly into a memory variable. Its form is

STORE <expression> **TO** <memvar>

Some examples of the **STORE** command would be

STORE 5 **TO** A
STORE 10 **TO** B
STORE A+B **TO** C
STORE "Hello There" **TO** D

Another method of directly placing data into a dBASE memory variable is to use the equal (=) sign. The dBASE commands above would then take the form

A = 5
B = 10
C = A+B
D = "Hello There"

Memory variable names must start with a letter and may be up to ten characters long. The additional characters can be letters or numbers, but no special characters or spaces should be included in the names.

The ? Command

The **?** command is used to display the contents of a memory variable, the contents of a field in the current record, an expression, and/or a string or numeric constant. As an example of how the **?** command works, assume the record pointer is on the first record of this database and type the following commands shown in gray.

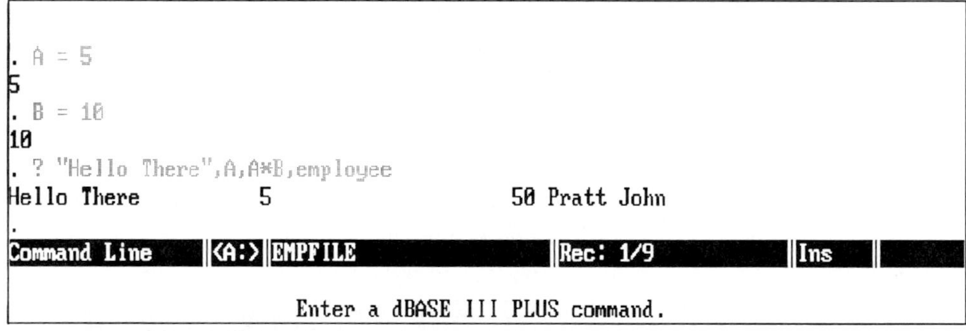
. A = 5
5
. B = 10
10
. ? "Hello There",A,A*B,employee
Hello There 5 50 Pratt John
.
Command Line <A:> EMPFILE Rec: 1/9 Ins
Enter a dBASE III PLUS command.

The **DISPLAY MEMORY** Command

The **DISPLAY MEMORY** command displays the name, type of data, and contents of all memory variables currently defined. With dBASE III Plus, 256 memory variables may be currently defined.

Using the **COUNT** and **SUM** Commands

5. Continue by typing and entering the following commands shown in gray.

```
. COUNT FOR sex = "M" TO x
      5 records
. COUNT FOR sex = "F" TO y
      4 records
. ? "Total men =",x
Total men =          5
. ? "Total women =",y
Total women =          4
. DISPLAY MEMORY
X           pub   N           5  (         5.00000000)
Y           pub   N           4  (         4.00000000)
   2 variables defined,       18 bytes used
 254 variables available,   5982 bytes available

.
Command Line    <A:> EMPFILE                Rec: EOF/9          Ins

                        Enter a dBASE III PLUS command.
```

```
. SUM salary FOR sex = "M" TO xpay
      5 records summed
     salary
   8499.00
. SUM salary FOR sex = "F" TO ypay
      4 records summed
     salary
   6207.00
. ? "Total male salaries = ",xpay
Total male salaries =        8499.00
. ? "Total female salaries = ",ypay
Total female salaries =        6207.00
.
Command Line    <A:> EMPFILE                Rec: EOF/9          Ins

                        Enter a dBASE III PLUS command.
```

```
. AVERAGE salary FOR sex = "M" TO xavg
      5 records averaged
  salary
 1699.80
. AVERAGE salary FOR sex = "F" TO yavg
      4 records averaged
  salary
 1551.75
. xprint = "Average male salary = "
Average male salary =
. yprint = "Average female salary = "
Average female salary =
. ? xprint,xavg
Average male salary =        1699.80
. ? yprint,yavg
Average female salary =        1551.75
.
Command Line    |<A:>|EMPFILE              |Rec: EOF/9        |Ins  |

                  Enter a dBASE III PLUS command.
```

```
. DISPLAY MEMORY
X          pub   N          5  (         5.00000000)
Y          pub   N          4  (         4.00000000)
XPAY       pub   N    8499.00  (      8499.00000000)
YPAY       pub   N    6207.00  (      6207.00000000)
XAVG       pub   N    1699.80  (      1699.80000000)
YAVG       pub   N    1551.75  (      1551.75000000)
XPRINT     pub   C  "Average male salary = "
YPRINT     pub   C  "Average female salary = "
    8 variables defined,      104 bytes used
  248 variables available,   5896 bytes available

.
Command Line    |<A:>|EMPFILE              |Rec: EOF/9        |Ins  |

                  Enter a dBASE III PLUS command.
```

The **REPLACE** Command

One highly useful dBASE command is **REPLACE,** which has the form

REPLACE [<scope>] <field> **WITH** <expression> [**FOR** <condition>]

The **REPLACE** command is most useful for making the same change to several records meeting a certain condition. For instance, to give all women in the database a 10 percent increase in salary, the command

REPLACE salary **WITH** salary + (salary * .10) **FOR** sex = "F"

could be entered. When executed, each of the female employees would receive a pay raise of 10 percent. The command says, in effect, "For each record, replace what is in the field named salary with what is there plus 10 percent of what is there, if "F" is found in the field named sex for that record."

The default <scope> is **ALL** since the **FOR** parameter is used; the <field> to replace is salary; the <expression> to replace the field salary with is "salary + (salary * .10)"; and the <condition> of the **FOR** parameter is "sex = "F"."

6. Type and enter the following commands shown in gray to see how dBASE's **REPLACE** command works.

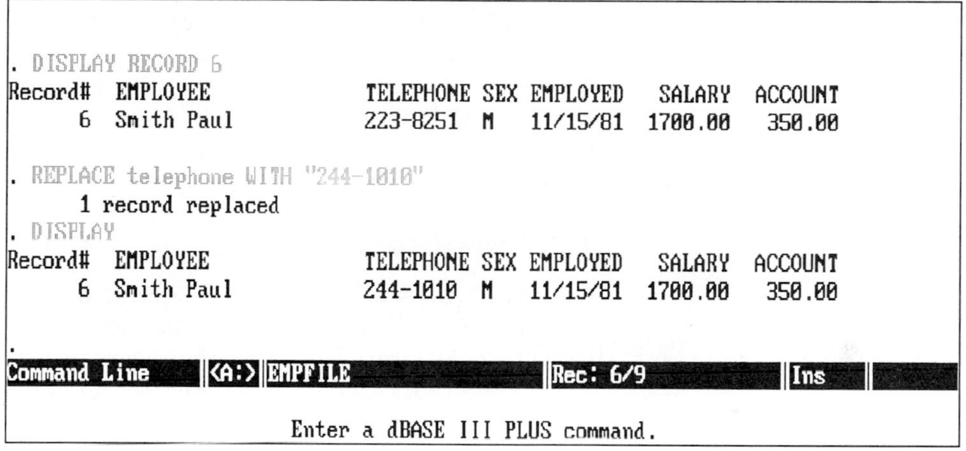

```
. DISPLAY RECORD 6
Record#  EMPLOYEE                TELEPHONE SEX EMPLOYED   SALARY  ACCOUNT
      6  Smith Paul              223-8251  M   11/15/81  1700.00   350.00

. REPLACE telephone WITH "244-1010"
      1 record replaced
. DISPLAY
Record#  EMPLOYEE                TELEPHONE SEX EMPLOYED   SALARY  ACCOUNT
      6  Smith Paul              244-1010  M   11/15/81  1700.00   350.00

.
Command Line    |<A:>|EMPFILE              |Rec: 6/9        |Ins |

                     Enter a dBASE III PLUS command.
```

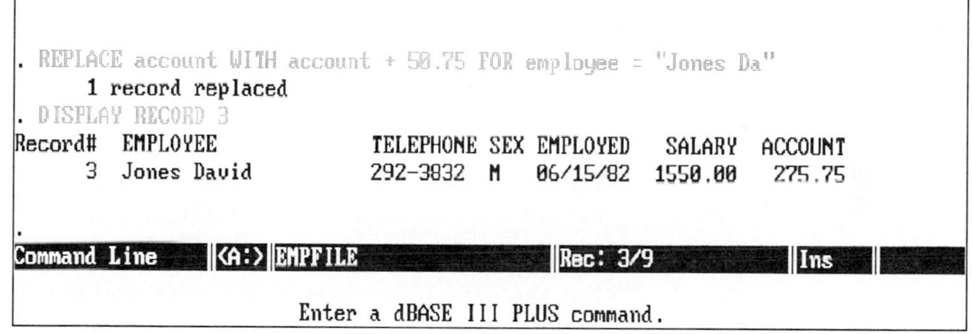

```
. REPLACE account WITH account + 50.75 FOR employee = "Jones Da"
      1 record replaced
. DISPLAY RECORD 3
Record#  EMPLOYEE                TELEPHONE SEX EMPLOYED   SALARY  ACCOUNT
      3  Jones David             292-3832  M   06/15/82  1550.00   275.75

.
Command Line    |<A:>|EMPFILE              |Rec: 3/9        |Ins |

                     Enter a dBASE III PLUS command.
```

NOTE: The account amount was $225.00 before the change.

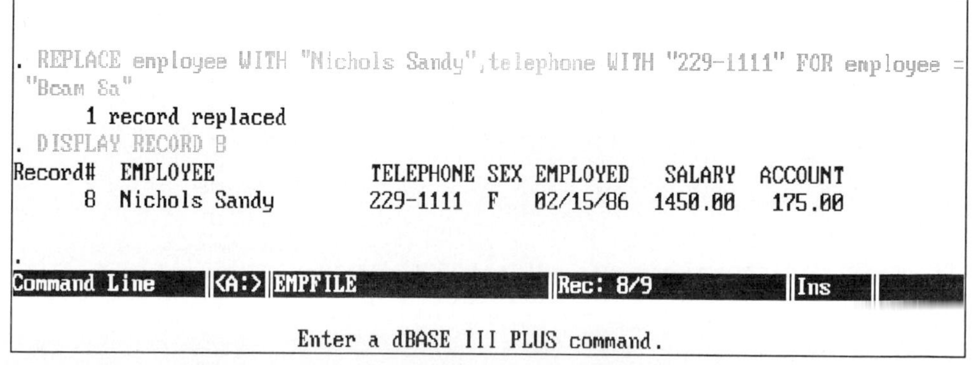

```
. REPLACE employee WITH "Nichols Sandy",telephone WITH "229-1111" FOR employee =
 "Bcam Sa"
      1 record replaced
. DISPLAY RECORD 8
Record#  EMPLOYEE                TELEPHONE SEX EMPLOYED   SALARY  ACCOUNT
      8  Nichols Sandy           229-1111  F   02/15/86  1450.00   175.00

.
Command Line    |<A:>|EMPFILE              |Rec: 8/9        |Ins |

                     Enter a dBASE III PLUS command.
```

Notice that when a command is longer than the screen line of 80 characters, dBASE automatically wraps it around to the next line when the command is executed. The maximum length of a dBASE III Plus command is 254 characters.

The **LOCATE** Command

The **LOCATE** command is used to move the record pointer to the first record in the database whose data evaluate as .T.rue for the command's **FOR** <condition>. The form of the **LOCATE** command is

LOCATE [<scope>] **FOR** <condition>

If the [<scope>] is omitted or is specified as **ALL,** the search for record(s) evaluating .T.rue begins at the top of the database and continues down, record after record (sequentially), until a record that satisfies the **FOR** condition is found or until the bottom of the database is reached. If a record that satisfies the **FOR** <condition> is found, dBASE stops the record pointer on it, making it the current record, and displays its record number on the screen.

The **CONTINUE** Command

Once the **LOCATE** command has found a record that satisfies its **FOR** <condition>, another dBASE command, **CONTINUE,** may be used to locate the next record in the database that satisfies the same **FOR** <condition>. The **CONTINUE** command has no parameters.

LESSON 8
Sorting a Database

The **SORT** Command

Two different methods exist for sorting the records in a dBASE III Plus database. One method uses the **SORT** command with the form

SORT TO <new file> **ON** <field list>

When the **SORT** command is executed, dBASE creates a second database file on the disk using the records and record structure from the current database file. You then have two database files from which to choose when you enter the **USE** command.

For example, if you type ||**SORT TO** payfile **ON** salary↵|| while empfile is in use, a second database (.DBF) file will be created under the name "payfile." If you then type ||**USE** payfile↵ **DISPLAY ALL**↵||, the database would be displayed as it exists, sorted according to salary with the records of the database renumbered.

NOTE: The following screens are for illustration only. Do not enter the commands shown.

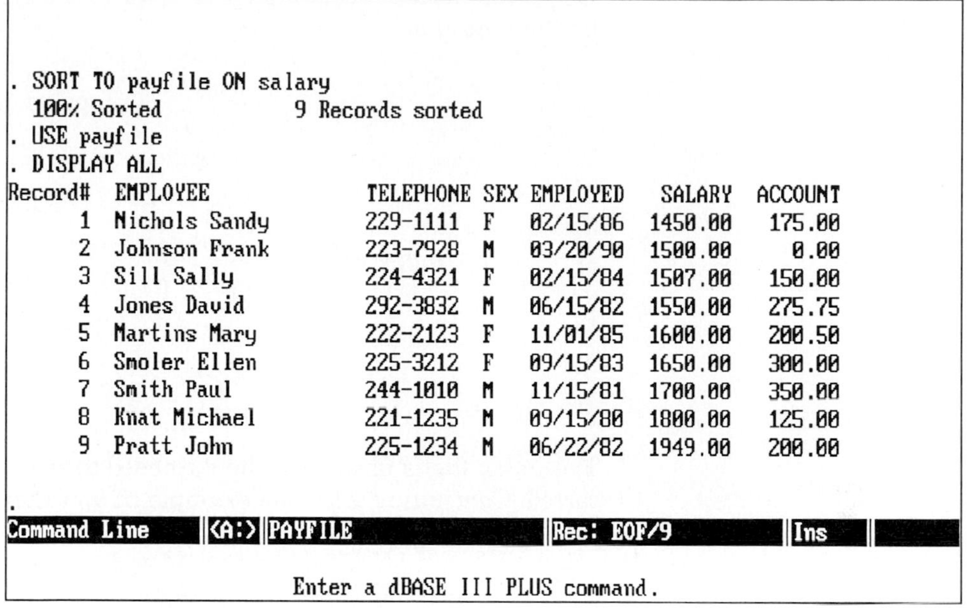

```
. SORT TO payfile ON salary
  100% Sorted           9 Records sorted
. USE payfile
. DISPLAY ALL
Record#  EMPLOYEE                TELEPHONE SEX EMPLOYED   SALARY  ACCOUNT
      1  Nichols Sandy           229-1111  F   02/15/86  1450.00   175.00
      2  Johnson Frank           223-7928  M   03/20/90  1500.00     0.00
      3  Sill Sally              224-4321  F   02/15/84  1507.00   150.00
      4  Jones David             292-3832  M   06/15/82  1550.00   275.75
      5  Martins Mary            222-2123  F   11/01/85  1600.00   200.50
      6  Smoler Ellen            225-3212  F   09/15/83  1650.00   300.00
      7  Smith Paul              244-1010  M   11/15/81  1700.00   350.00
      8  Knat Michael            221-1235  M   09/15/80  1800.00   125.00
      9  Pratt John              225-1234  M   06/22/82  1949.00   200.00

.
Command Line    <A:> PAYFILE           Rec: EOF/9          Ins

                     Enter a dBASE III PLUS command.
```

The **INDEX** Command

The other method of sorting records is with the **INDEX** command, which has the form

INDEX ON <expression> **TO** <index file>

The **INDEX** command, however, does not actually sort the records in the database nor does it create an entire new database file. Instead, it creates a smaller index file which is given an .NDX file extension when it is saved onto the disk.

An index file resides in RAM with its related database and is copied into RAM when the **USE** command is given with its **INDEX** parameter. For instance, if you type **INDEX ON** salary **TO** paydex ↵, an index (.NDX) file named paydex will be created on the disk.

If you then type **USE** empfile **INDEX** paydex↵, both the database (empfile.DBF) and index (paydex.NDX) file will be read into RAM.

An Index File in RAM

Using the model of computer RAM, an index file in use with a database can be thought of as

Computer Memory

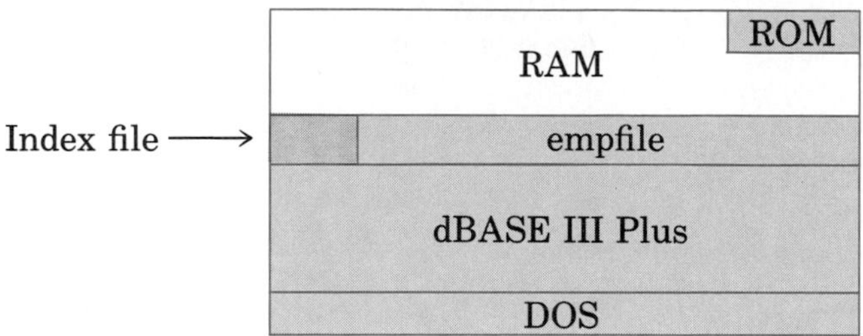

The index file is used with the database to treat the database as if it were sorted. Continuing with the example, if you then type **DISPLAY ALL↵**, the screen will display the following.

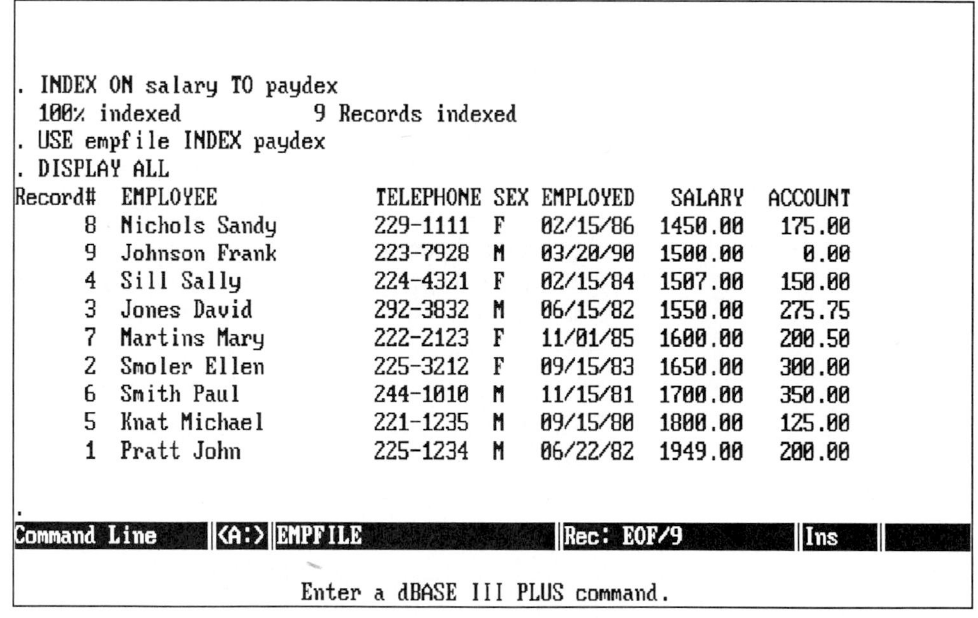

```
. INDEX ON salary TO paydex
  100% indexed          9 Records indexed
. USE empfile INDEX paydex
. DISPLAY ALL
Record#  EMPLOYEE             TELEPHONE SEX EMPLOYED   SALARY  ACCOUNT
      8  Nichols Sandy        229-1111  F   02/15/86  1450.00   175.00
      9  Johnson Frank        223-7928  M   03/20/90  1500.00     0.00
      4  Sill Sally           224-4321  F   02/15/84  1507.00   150.00
      3  Jones David          292-3832  M   06/15/82  1550.00   275.75
      7  Martins Mary         222-2123  F   11/01/85  1600.00   200.50
      2  Smoler Ellen         225-3212  F   09/15/83  1650.00   300.00
      6  Smith Paul           244-1010  M   11/15/81  1700.00   350.00
      5  Knat Michael         221-1235  M   09/15/80  1800.00   125.00
      1  Pratt John           225-1234  M   06/22/82  1949.00   200.00

.
Command Line     ||<A:>||EMPFILE              ||Rec: EOF/9        ||Ins  ||

                      Enter a dBASE III PLUS command.
```

Notice the record numbers have not changed; they are still in their original order in the database file empfile. An index file displays the database file *as though* it were sorted, while leaving records in their original order.

How an Index File Affects the Record Pointer

1. Type and enter the following commands shown in gray to see how dBASE's **INDEX** command works.

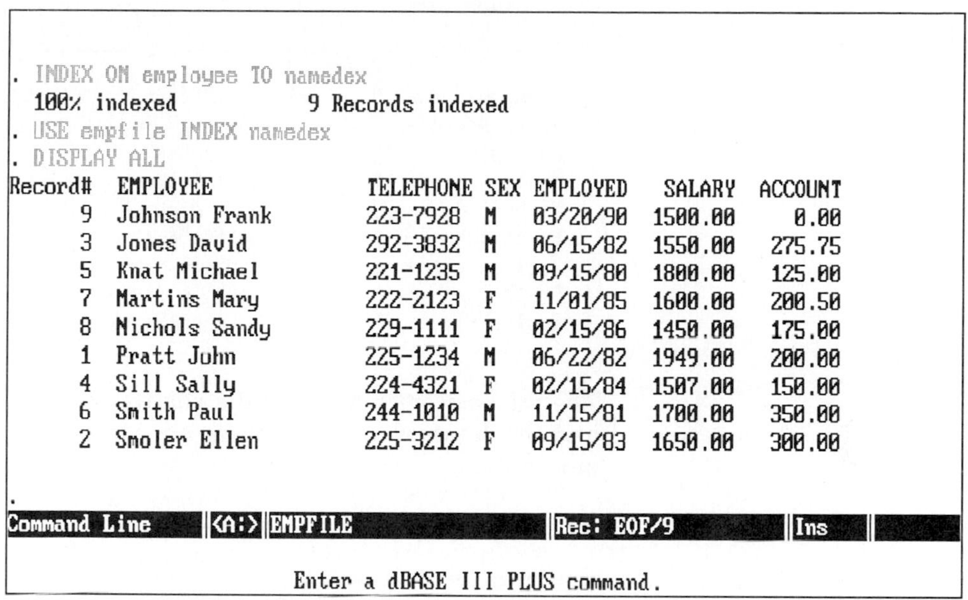

```
. INDEX ON employee TO namedex
  100% indexed          9 Records indexed
. USE empfile INDEX namedex
. DISPLAY ALL
Record#  EMPLOYEE               TELEPHONE SEX EMPLOYED  SALARY  ACCOUNT
      9  Johnson Frank          223-7928  M   03/20/90  1500.00    0.00
      3  Jones David            292-3832  M   06/15/82  1550.00  275.75
      5  Knat Michael           221-1235  M   09/15/80  1800.00  125.00
      7  Martins Mary           222-2123  F   11/01/85  1600.00  200.50
      8  Nichols Sandy          229-1111  F   02/15/86  1450.00  175.00
      1  Pratt John             225-1234  M   06/22/82  1949.00  200.00
      4  Sill Sally             224-4321  F   02/15/84  1507.00  150.00
      6  Smith Paul             244-1010  M   11/15/81  1700.00  350.00
      2  Smoler Ellen           225-3212  F   09/15/83  1650.00  300.00

.
Command Line  ||<A:>||EMPFILE          ||Rec: EOF/9        ||Ins ||

                  Enter a dBASE III PLUS command.
```

When you create an index file, you usually index on a <field>. This field becomes the index file's *key*. The keys in the index file are sorted and used with their corresponding record numbers to direct the record pointer to the database. It is useful to think of the record pointer as residing next to the index file, not next to the database, and the index file as being made up of a sorted list of key data with their associated record numbers.

Index File

	#
→ Johnson Frank	9
Jones David	3
Knat Michael	5
Martins Mary	7
Nichols Sandy	8
Pratt John	1
Sill Sally	4
Smith Paul	6
Smoler Ellen	2

Database File

#						
1	Pratt John	225-1234	M	06/22/82	1949.00	200.00
2	Smoler Ellen	225-3212	F	09/15/83	1650.00	300.00
3	Jones David	292-3832	M	06/15/82	1550.00	275.75
4	Sill Sally	224-4321	F	02/15/84	1507.00	150.00
5	Knat Michael	221-1235	M	09/15/80	1800.00	125.00
6	Smith Paul	244-1010	M	11/15/81	1700.00	350.00
7	Martins Mary	222-2123	F	11/01/85	1600.00	200.50
8	Nichols Sandy	229-1111	F	02/15/86	1450.00	175.00
9	Johnson Frank	223-7928	M	03/20/90	1500.00	0.00

With an index file in use with a database, a command such as **GO TOP** sends the record pointer to the top of the index file rather than to the top of the database. dBASE then uses the record number located there to determine which record to make the current record. So, if a command such as **DISPLAY** is executed while the record pointer is at the top of the index file, record #9 of the database file in the example will be displayed.

The result of using a command such as **DISPLAY ALL** is that the pointer goes to the top of the index file, and dBASE displays the database file record for the record number located there, moves the record pointer down one record in the index file (**SKIP**s), and displays the database file record for the record number found there.

Index File | Database File

Index File	#	#	Database File					
Johnson Frank	9	1	Pratt John	225-1234	M	06/22/82	1949.00	200.00
→ Jones David	3 →	2	Smoler Ellen	225-3212	F	09/15/83	1650.00	300.00
Knat Michael	5	3	Jones David	292-3832	M	06/15/82	1550.00	275.75
Martins Mary	7	4	Sill Sally	224-4321	F	02/15/84	1507.00	150.00
Nichols Sandy	8	5	Knat Michael	221-1235	M	09/15/80	1800.00	125.00
Pratt John	1	6	Smith Paul	244-1010	M	11/15/81	1700.00	350.00
Sill Sally	4	7	Martins Mary	222-2123	F	11/01/85	1600.00	200.50
Smith Paul	6	8	Nichols Sandy	229-1111	F	02/15/86	1450.00	175.00
Smoler Ellen	2	9	Johnson Frank	223-7928	M	03/20/90	1500.00	0.00

The process continues until the pointer reaches the bottom of the index file, and the database records appear on the screen as if they are sorted by employee name.

Indexing on More than One Field

You may create key data for an index file based on more than one field of record data as long as the data being used are characters or converted to characters. To do this, you type **INDEX ON** <field> + <field> **TO** <index file>.

2. To demonstrate, type and enter the following commands shown in gray.

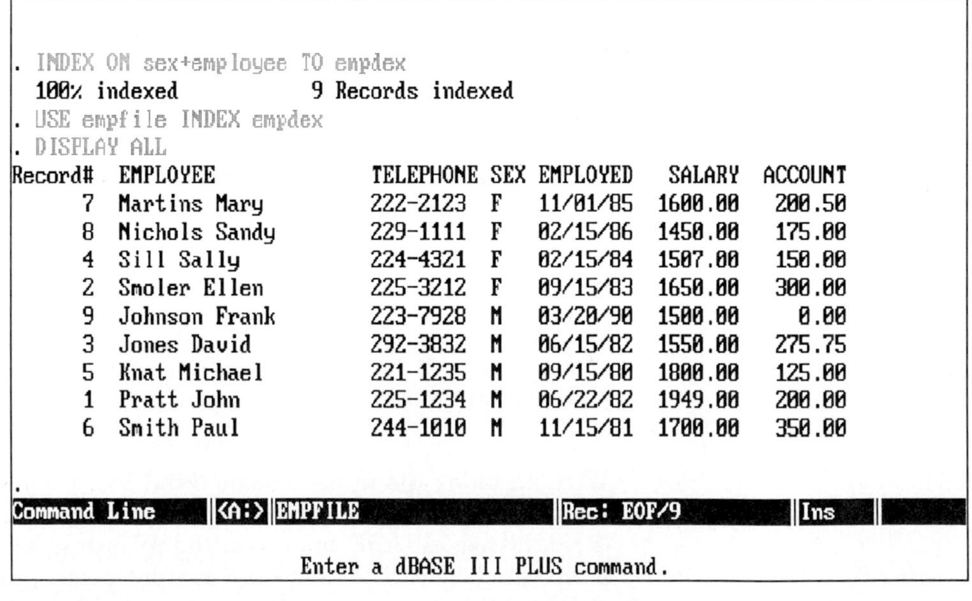

```
. INDEX ON sex+employee TO empdex
  100% indexed          9 Records indexed
. USE empfile INDEX empdex
. DISPLAY ALL
Record#  EMPLOYEE                 TELEPHONE SEX EMPLOYED   SALARY  ACCOUNT
      7  Martins Mary             222-2123  F   11/01/85  1600.00   200.50
      8  Nichols Sandy            229-1111  F   02/15/86  1450.00   175.00
      4  Sill Sally               224-4321  F   02/15/84  1507.00   150.00
      2  Smoler Ellen             225-3212  F   09/15/83  1650.00   300.00
      9  Johnson Frank            223-7928  M   03/20/90  1500.00     0.00
      3  Jones David              292-3832  M   06/15/82  1550.00   275.75
      5  Knat Michael             221-1235  M   09/15/80  1800.00   125.00
      1  Pratt John               225-1234  M   06/22/82  1949.00   200.00
      6  Smith Paul               244-1010  M   11/15/81  1700.00   350.00

.
Command Line    |<A:>|EMPFILE             |Rec: EOF/9          |Ins  |

                       Enter a dBASE III PLUS command.
```

Indexing on more than one field creates an index file with its key data sorted on characters found in the first field (in this case an M or F), followed by characters found in the second field (employee's name here).

Index File

```
FMartins Mary    7
FNichols Sandy   8
FSill Sally      4
FSmoler Ellen    2
MJohnson Frank   9
MJones David     3
MKnat Michael    5
MPratt John      1
MSmith Paul      6
```

Advantages of Indexing

Automatic Updating

Indexing a database is typically the more efficient method of sorting records in a database. One of its advantages is that an index file automatically is updated for records added, deleted, or edited when it is in use with its database.

Several index files may be put into use with the database by entering their names into a list, with each name separated by commas, when you type the **USE** command

USE empfile **INDEX** paydex,namedex, . . .

All index files in use will be updated for changes made to the database, and the first index file listed is the one where the record pointer will reside.

*Faster Record Search/The **SEEK** Command*

When the commands discussed so far cause dBASE to search through the database for records, the search is conducted sequentially from the top of the database to the bottom, with each record evaluated to see if it is .T.rue for the **FOR** <condition>. In large databases, the sequential process of searching can take considerable time.

When a database is in use with an index file, dBASE can find a record very rapidly if the data item for which it is searching is key data for the index. The faster search is done with the **SEEK** command

SEEK <key expression>

For instance, if using an index file with employee names as key data in use with the database empfile, you could move the pointer to Sandy Nichols' record by typing the command

SEEK "Nicho"

The reason that **SEEK** is so much faster at locating a record is because the data through which it is searching (the index file's key data) are sorted. With sorted data the search does not have to begin at the top of the data, but can begin anywhere in the list of key data items. If the first key data item evaluated is less than the one for which dBASE is searching, dBASE can jump the pointer down several data items to make another evaluation. If the record pointer overshoots (if the second key data item is greater than the one for which dBASE is searching), the bounds have been set for finding the sought-after key data item, and the search continues in the same up and down manner until dBASE finds the data item. The result is that fewer evaluations need to be made in order to find the key data item and its record number.

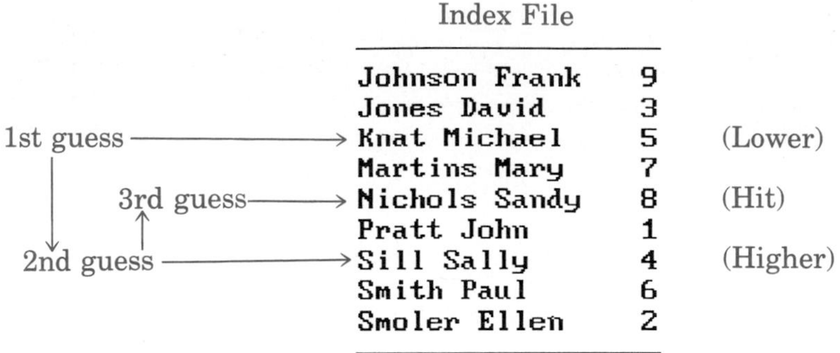

LESSON 9
Creating a dBASE III Plus Report

The **REPORT** Command

The **REPORT** command is used to generate list-type reports based on the fields of data in a database. Its form is

> **REPORT FORM** [<form file>] [<scope>] [**FOR** <condition>] [**HEADING** <character string>] [**TO PRINT**]

The default <scope> of the **REPORT** command is **ALL.** When executed, the **REPORT** command produces a report similar to the following.

```
        Page No.     1
        06/15/90
                              Employee Full Report
                              ====================

                                                      Current  Account
        Employee Name          Phone #  Hire Date      Salary  Balance
        -------------          -------  ---------     -------  -------


        Johnson Frank          223-7928 03/20/90      1500.00     0.00
        Jones David            292-3832 06/15/82      1550.00   275.75
        Knat Michael           221-1235 09/15/80      1800.00   125.00
        Martins Mary           222-2123 11/01/85      1600.00   200.50
        Nichols Sandy          229-1111 02/15/86      1450.00   175.00
        Pratt John             225-1234 06/22/82      1949.00   200.00
        Sill Sally             224-4321 02/15/84      1507.00   150.00
        Smith Paul             244-1010 11/15/81      1700.00   350.00
        Smoler Ellen           225-3212 09/15/83      1650.00   300.00
       *** Total ***
                                                     14706.00  1776.25

Command Line   |<A:>|EMPFILE                  |Rec: EOF/9   |    |

                         Enter a dBASE III PLUS command.
```

The report is columnar, with each column containing the evaluated results of an expression. The columns have column labels and the report has a report title. Totals and subtotals may or may not be included in the report. To produce such a report, the **REPORT** command requires that several specifications be made. A report's specifications are entered while in a dBASE full-screen, menu-driven mode, and are automatically saved by dBASE in a form file with an .FRM extension when the mode is exited by selecting the Exit menu option.

Creating a Report Form File—The **MODIFY REPORT** Command

The **MODIFY REPORT** command is used to enter the mode in which you make a report's specifications. The command's form is

MODIFY REPORT <form file>

To give you experience creating report form files for the **REPORT** command to use, you will first create the form file that produces the example report shown previously.

1. Type ||**USE** empfile **INDEX** namedex←||.

The database(s) whose data will be referred to in the report specifications must be in use prior to executing the **MODIFY REPORT** command.

2. Now type ||**MODIFY REPORT** fullrepo←||.

fullrepo will be the filename of the .FRM file for this report. The following will appear on the screen.

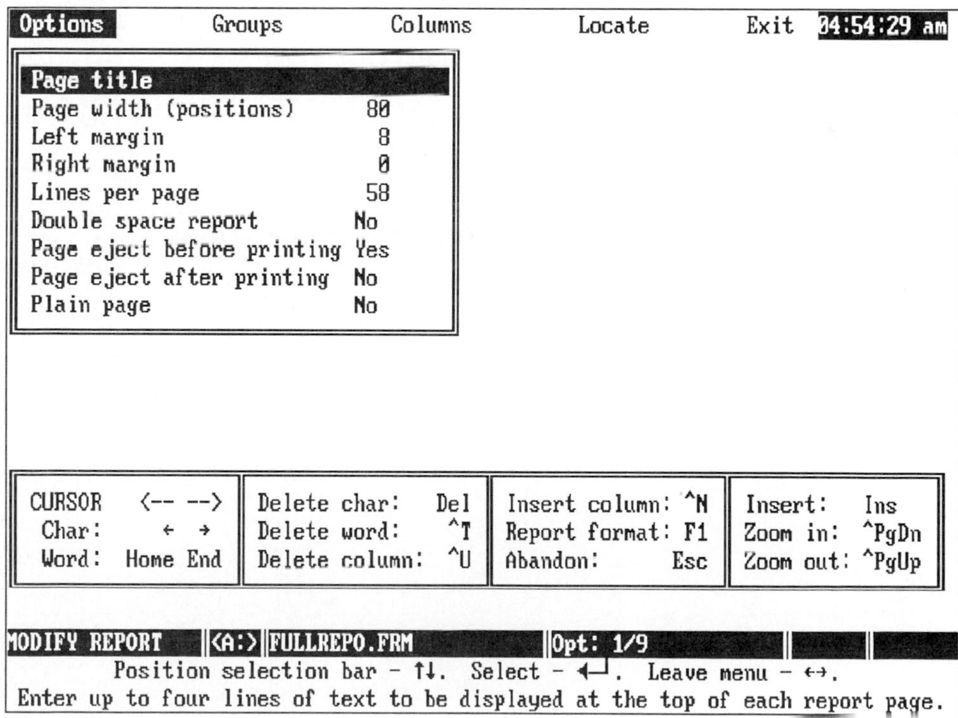

Navigating through dBASE III Plus Menus

Across the top of the screen appears a single line of menu options: Options; Groups; Columns; Locate; and Exit. This line is referred to as the menu bar. You will see one of the options highlighted with a reverse video display.

3. Press the cursor right (→) key two or three times.

Notice that as the highlight moves across the menu bar, dBASE presents a new screen below the highlighted option. The screen appearing below the menu bar option is called a pull-down menu, and is the current menu from which you may select.

To make a selection from a pull-down menu, the ↓ or ↑ keys may be used to move the highlight of the pull-down menu down or up. When the desired menu item is highlighted, the Enter key is pressed to invoke that menu operation. When a menu operation is invoked, you often are left in an editing mode for data entry. The following table of editing keystrokes may be referred to as you complete the next tutorial steps.

Action Desired	Keystrokes
Cursor Movement	
Character Left	Left ←
Character Right	Right →
Line Down	Down ↓
Line Up	Up ↑
Insert/Overwrite	Ins
Delete Characters	
Current Character	Delete (Del)
Previous Character	Backspace
Word Right of Cursor	^T
Line Right of Cursor	^Y
Save and Exit Editing Mode	^End
Columns Menu Bar Option Only	
Move to the Next Column	PgDn
Move to the Previous Column	PgUp
Delete Current Column	^U
Insert New Column	^N

Making Report Specifications

4. Move the menu bar highlight to Options and then select Page title from the pull-down menu by typing ↵.

Selecting Page title causes dBASE to provide an area on the screen into which you may enter the report title.

5. Enter the report title as shown in the following.

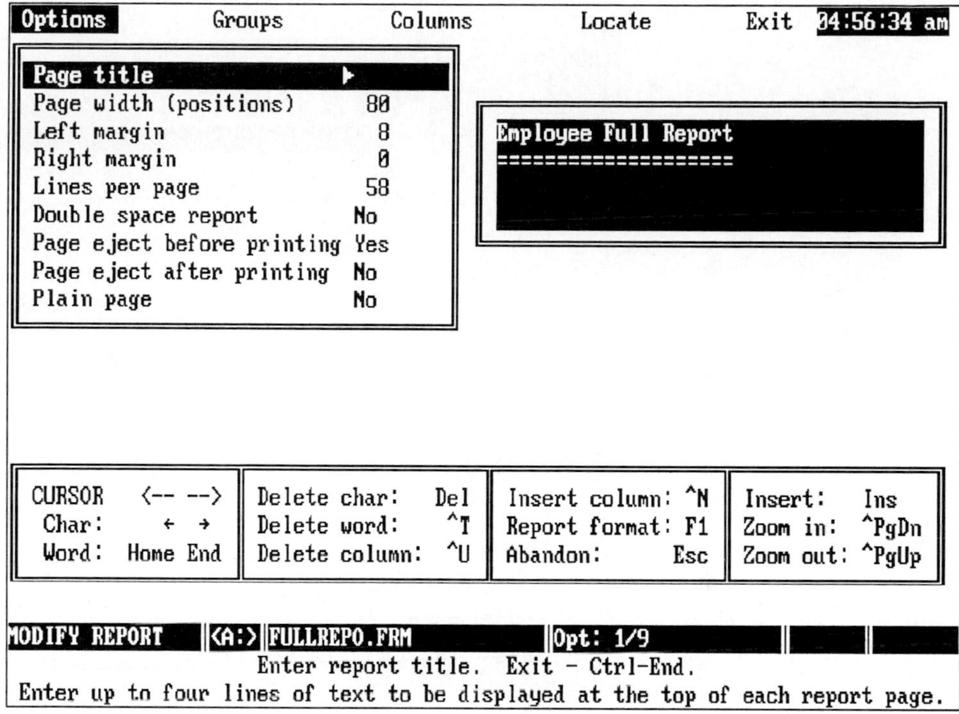

6. When done, type ||^End|| to save and exit the editing mode.
7. Move the pull-down highlight to the menu item marked "Page width (positions)" and select this item by typing ↵. Change the default answer of 80 characters to 72 characters by typing ||72↵||.

You now are ready to specify the contents of the report's columns. To do this you will use the pull-down menu provided by the Columns option of the menu bar.

8. Move the menu bar highlight to Columns.

The pull-down menu presented is for the first column of data in the report. Here you specify the contents of the column (Contents) and the column label to be used in the report (Heading).

9. Select the Contents menu item by typing ↵, and then enter the column contents of the first column by typing ||employee↵||.

Notice that the default value for Width changed from 0 to 20. Twenty characters is the field width of the field named "employee" in empfile.

When you enter the contents of a report column, dBASE checks to see if it is in the form of an expression it can evaluate. If field names are used, they must be fields found in the active database(s). If the expression is made up of a single field name, dBASE will automatically set the default width of the report column to the same width as the field to which it refers.

10. Next select the Heading item of the pull-down menu and enter the column heading as shown below.

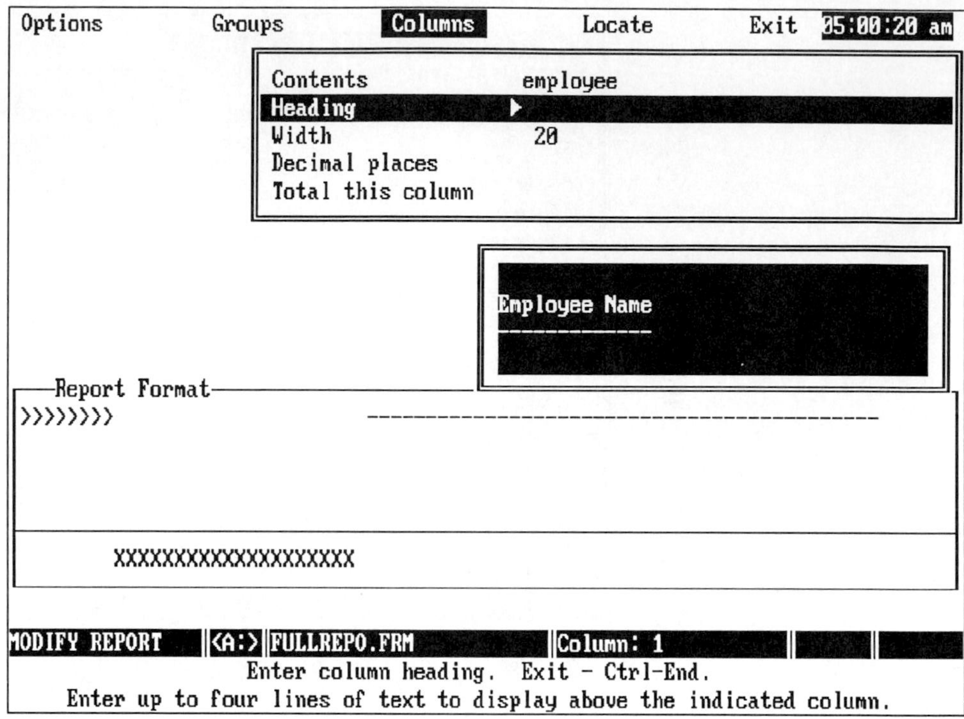

11. When done, type ||^End||.

When specifying the contents and headings of report columns, the PgDn key may be used to move to the next column and the PgUp key is used to move to a previous column.

12. Tap the PgDn key and complete the next column's specifications as shown. (Remember that you must select a menu item by typing ↵ before you enter the data.)

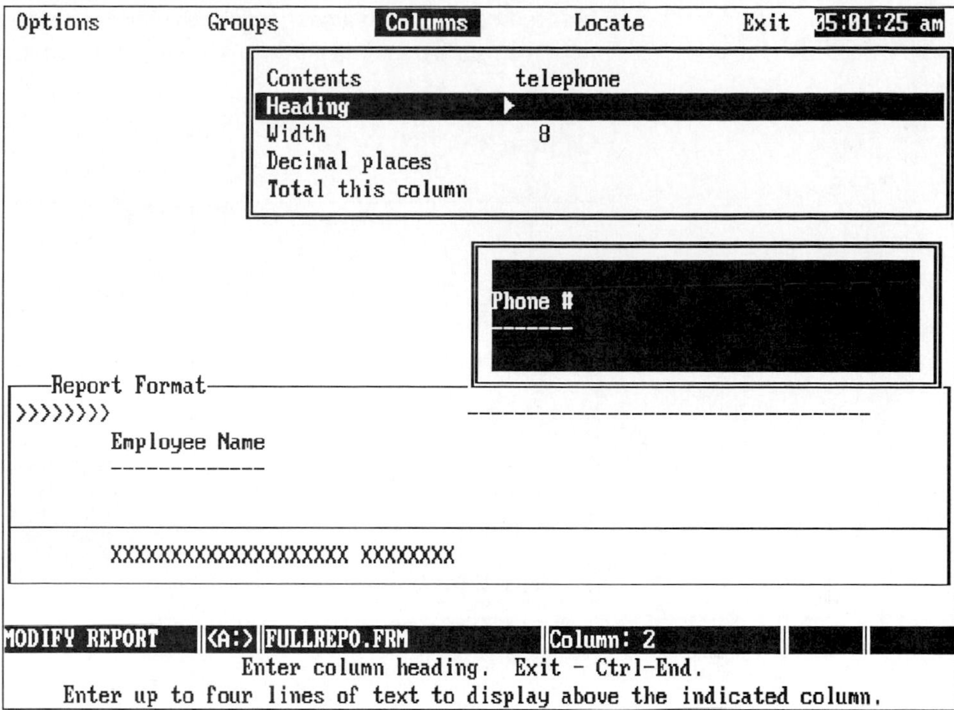

13. After entering the column heading, tap the PgDn key to move to the third column's specifications.

Before continuing, notice the area in the bottom half of the screen.

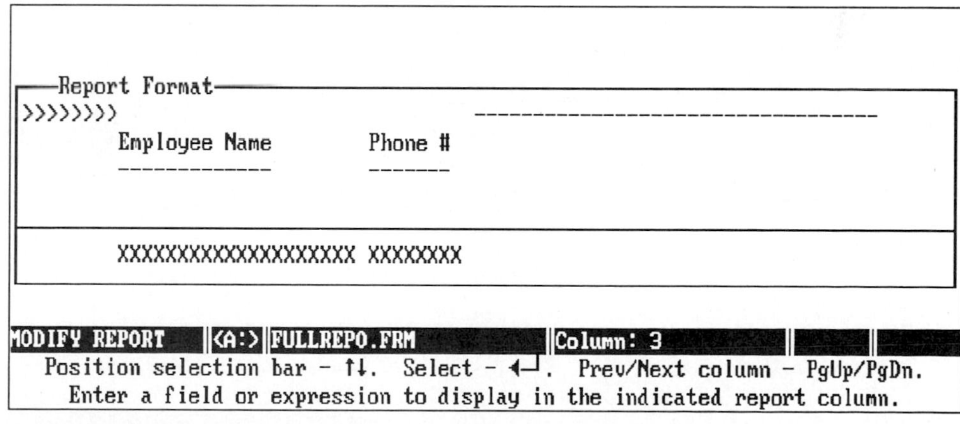

At the bottom of this area is a highlighted line (called the status bar) displaying information about the report you are creating, fullrepo, and the column you are currently on, Column 3. Over the status bar is an emerging picture representing what the finished report will look like. Shown here are the characters used by the left margin (>>>>>>>>), the specified column labels, and a mask for the characters of data included in the column.

The default width of each column in the report is based on the width of the field (or expression) specified as the contents of the column, or the width of the column heading, whichever is larger. The default value can be changed by entering a different value using the Width menu item. Within the printed report, character- or date-type data will be automatically left justified, while numeric-type data will be right justified.

14. Finish specifying the report's column contents with the following data.

Column 3:

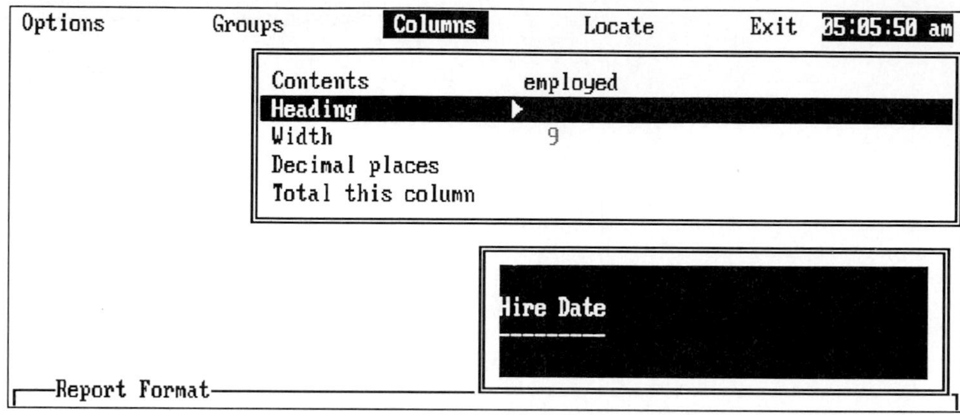

Column 4:

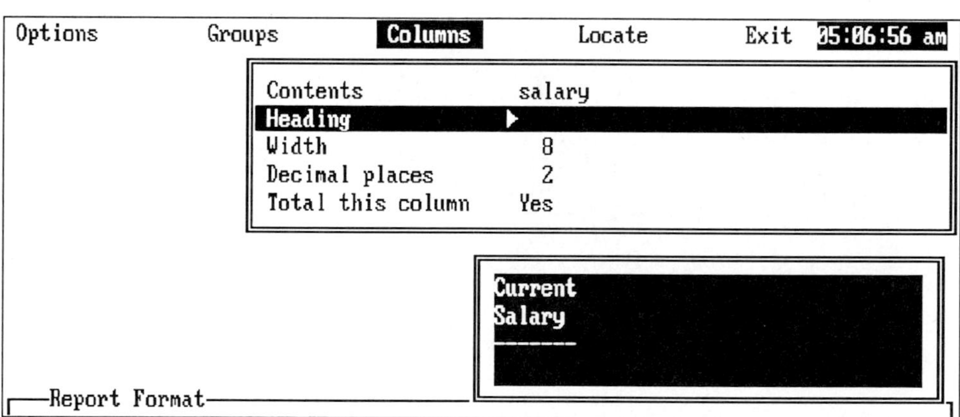

Column 5:

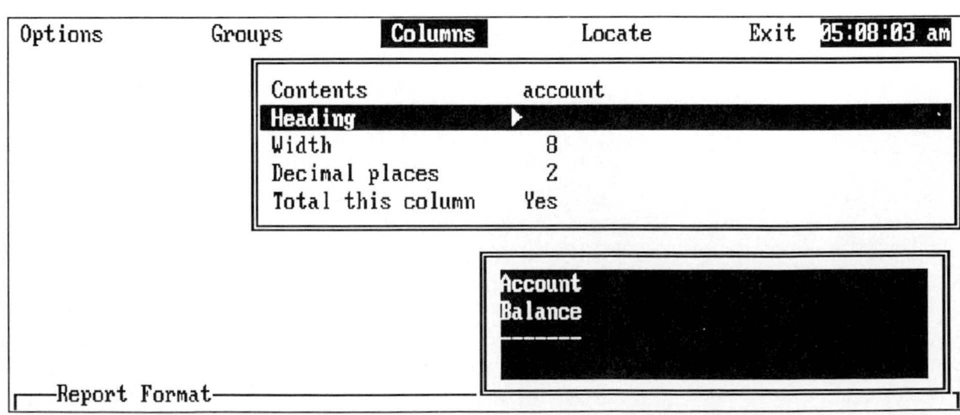

When finished entering the data for field 5, the screen should appear as follows.

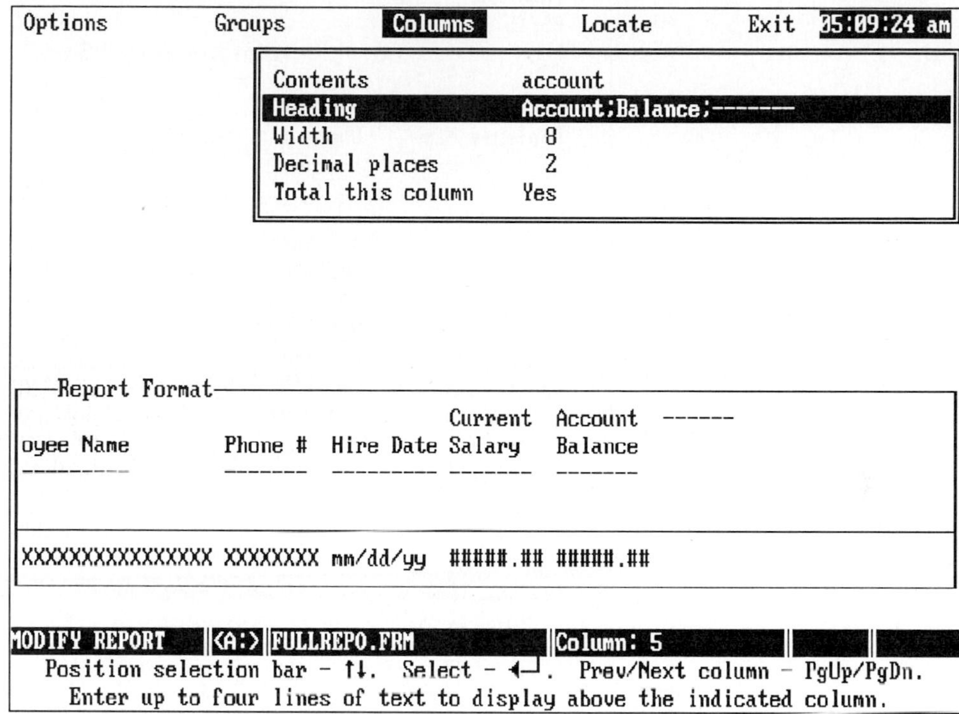

15. Move the menu bar highlight to Exit and select the Save option to save the report data and exit to the dot (.) prompt.

Running Reports

With the report specifications entered and saved in a form file, you are now able to produce the report using the **REPORT FORM** command.

16. Type ||**REPORT FORM** fullrepo↵||.

```
Page No.     1
06/15/90
                        Employee Full Report
                        ====================
                                             Current   Account   Account
Employee Name    Phone #    Hire Date    Salary     Limit   Balance
-------------    -------    ---------   -------   -------   -------



Johnson Frank    223-7928   03/20/90    1500.00    225.00      0.00
Jones David      292-3832   06/15/82    1550.00    232.00    275.75
Knat Michael     221-1235   09/15/80    1800.00    270.00    125.00
Martins Mary     222-2123   11/01/85    1600.00    240.00    200.50
Nichols Sandy    229-1111   02/15/86    1450.00    217.00    175.00
Pratt John       225-1234   06/22/82    1949.00    292.00    200.00
Sill Sally       224-4321   02/15/84    1507.00    226.00    150.00
Smith Paul       244-1010   11/15/81    1700.00    255.00    350.00
Smoler Ellen     225-3212   09/15/83    1650.00    255.00    350.00
*** Total ***
                                       14706.00   2204.00   1776.25

Command Line  |<A:>|EMPFILE            |Rec: EOF/9          |     |

                  Enter a dBASE III PLUS command.
```

Later you will see how to print a report on the printer.

Changing a Report's Specifications

A report's specifications may be altered by using the **MODIFY REPORT** command. To give you experience in using this command, as well as the full-screen, menu-driven mode it provides, do the following.

17. Type ||**MODIFY REPORT** fullrepo↵||.

*NOTE: Refer to the **MODIFY REPORT** editing keystrokes (see table, page D-48) to assist you in making the following changes.*

18. Make the following changes to the specifications in fullrepo.FRM.
    a. Change the report's Options/Left margin to 4.
    b. Reduce the width of the column containing employee names (Column 1) from 20 to 16.
    c. Increase the width of the telephone column (Column 2) to 10.
    d. Move to the account column (Column 5) and insert a new column into the report (type ^N to do this).
    e. Enter the following data into the new Column 5.

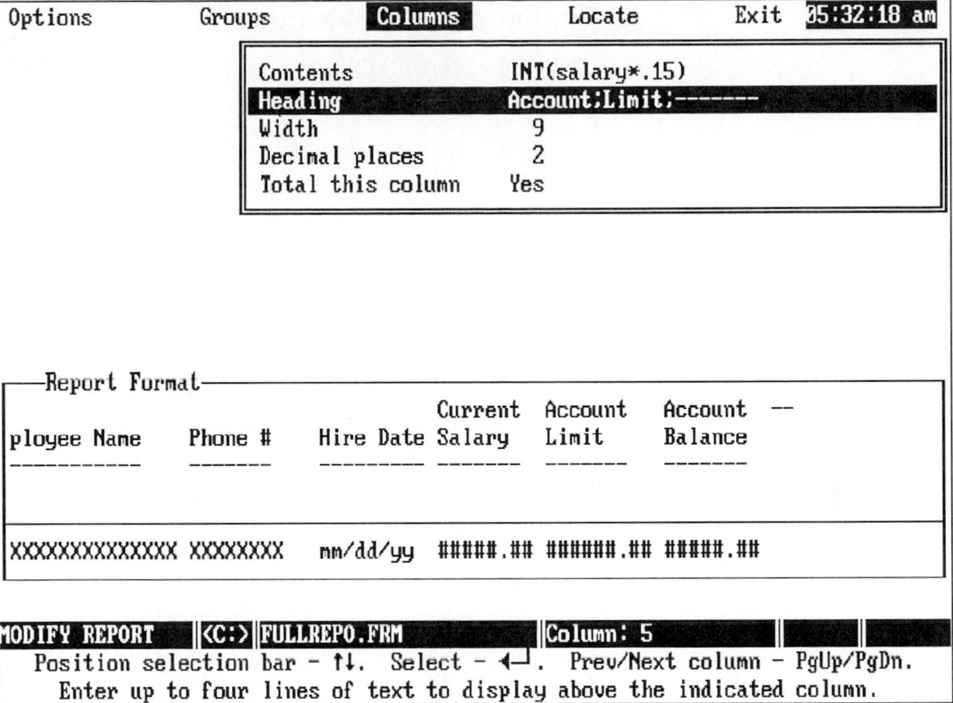
```
Options          Groups          Columns          Locate          Exit  05:32:18 am

                   Contents              INT(salary*.15)
                   Heading               Account;Limit;-------
                   Width                   9
                   Decimal places          2
                   Total this column     Yes

Report Format
                                         Current  Account      Account    --
ployee Name    Phone #    Hire Date      Salary   Limit        Balance
-----------    -------    ---------      -------  -------      -------

XXXXXXXXXXXXXX XXXXXXXX   mm/dd/yy  #####.## ######.## #####.##

MODIFY REPORT  |<C:>|FULLREPO.FRM          |Column: 5
 Position selection bar - ↑↓.  Select - ←┘.  Prev/Next column - PgUp/PgDn.
   Enter up to four lines of text to display above the indicated column.
```

19. Select the Save menu item of the Exit menu bar option to exit the **MODIFY REPORT** mode, and then type ‖**REPORT FORM** full-repo←┘‖.

The report produced should have the following form.

```
Page No.     1
06/15/90
                       Employee Full Report
                       ====================
                                             Current    Account   Account
Employee Name    Phone #     Hire Date       Salary      Limit    Balance
-------------    -------     ---------       -------    -------   -------


Johnson Frank    223-7928    03/20/90       1500.00     225.00      0.00
Jones David      292-3832    06/15/82       1550.00     232.00    275.75
Knat Michael     221-1235    09/15/80       1800.00     270.00    125.00
Martins Mary     222-2123    11/01/85       1600.00     240.00    200.50
Nichols Sandy    229-1111    02/15/86       1450.00     217.00    175.00
Pratt John       225-1234    06/22/82       1949.00     292.00    200.00
Sill Sally       224-4321    02/15/84       1507.00     226.00    150.00
Smith Paul       244-1010    11/15/81       1700.00     255.00    350.00
Smoler Ellen     225-3212    09/15/83       1650.00     255.00    350.00
Smoler Ellen     225-3212    09/15/83       1650.00     247.00    300.00
*** Total ***
                                           14706.00    2204.00   1776.25

Command Line   |<A:>|EMPFILE            |Rec: EOF/9

                     Enter a dBASE III PLUS command.
```

Running Selective Reports

dBASE's **REPORT** command lets you be selective with your reports through the use of the **FOR** <condition> parameter of the command.

20. Type the following commands shown in gray.

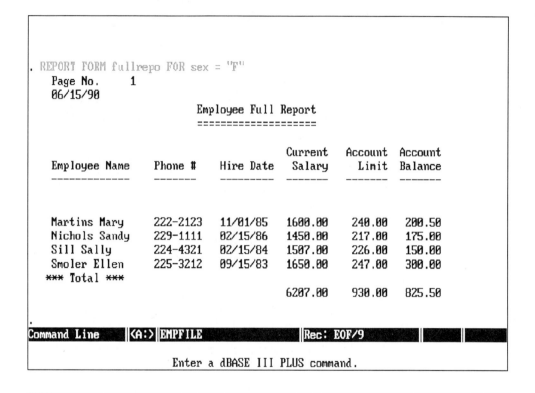

```
. REPORT FORM fullrepo FOR sex = "F"
   Page No.     1
   06/15/90
                          Employee Full Report
                          ====================

                                              Current   Account  Account
   Employee Name    Phone #    Hire Date    Salary     Limit   Balance
   -------------    -------    ---------    -------   -------  -------


   Martins Mary     222-2123   11/01/85    1600.00    240.00   200.50
   Nichols Sandy    229-1111   02/15/86    1450.00    217.00   175.00
   Sill Sally       224-4321   02/15/84    1507.00    226.00   150.00
   Smoler Ellen     225-3212   09/15/83    1650.00    247.00   300.00
  *** Total ***
                                           6207.00    930.00   825.50

.
Command Line     |<A:>|EMPFILE              |Rec: EOF/9        |    |

                     Enter a dBASE III PLUS command.
```

```
. REPORT FORM fullrepo FOR employed < CTOD("01/01/83")
   Page No.     1
   06/15/90
                          Employee Full Report
                          ====================

                                              Current   Account  Account
   Employee Name    Phone #    Hire Date    Salary     Limit   Balance
   -------------    -------    ---------    -------   -------  -------


   Jones David      292-3832   06/15/82    1550.00    232.00   275.75
   Knat Michael     221-1235   09/15/80    1800.00    270.00   125.00
   Pratt John       225-1234   06/22/82    1949.00    292.00   200.00
   Smith Paul       244-1010   11/15/81    1700.00    255.00   350.00
  *** Total ***
                                           6999.00   1049.00   950.75

.
Command Line     |<A:>|EMPFILE              |Rec: EOF/9        |    |

                     Enter a dBASE III PLUS command.
```

Adding a Report Heading

Another **REPORT** command parameter, **HEADING,** may be used to further describe the report being produced.

21. Type the following command shown in gray.

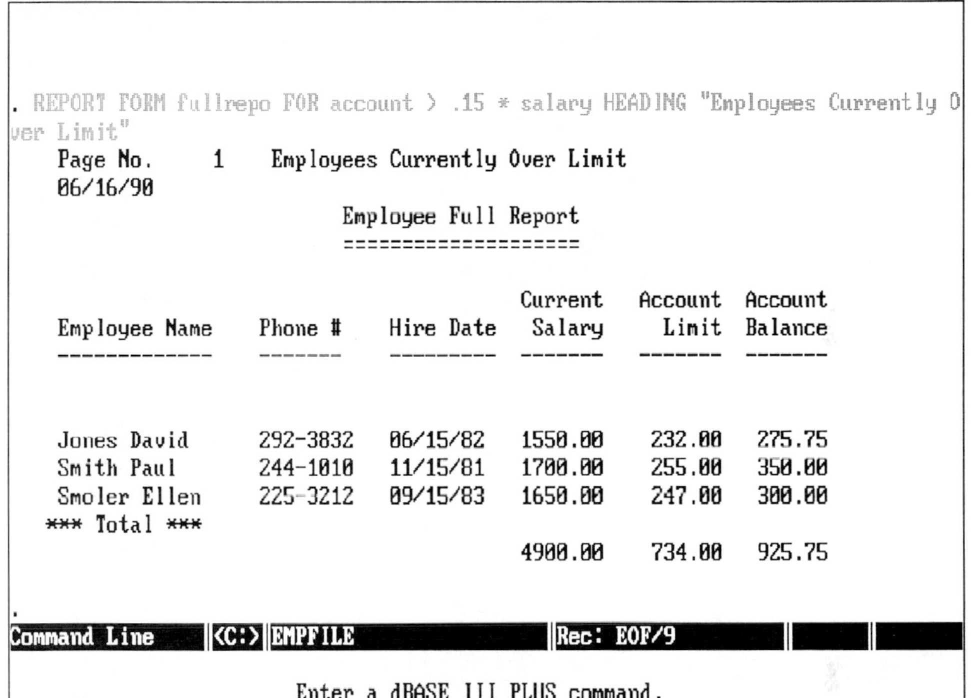

```
. REPORT FORM fullrepo FOR account > .15 * salary HEADING "Employees Currently O
ver Limit"
   Page No.     1    Employees Currently Over Limit
   06/16/90
                         Employee Full Report
                         ====================

                                               Current   Account  Account
   Employee Name    Phone #    Hire Date   Salary     Limit  Balance
   -------------    -------    ---------   -------   -------  -------


   Jones David      292-3832   06/15/82    1550.00    232.00   275.75
   Smith Paul       244-1010   11/15/81    1700.00    255.00   350.00
   Smoler Ellen     225-3212   09/15/83    1650.00    247.00   300.00
  *** Total ***
                                           4900.00    734.00   925.75

.
Command Line  ||<C:>||EMPFILE          ||Rec: EOF/9      ||    ||

                    Enter a dBASE III PLUS command.
```

Report Totals

When a column's contents are specified as numeric data, dBASE's **MODIFY REPORT** command defaults the column's "Total this column" menu item answer to "Yes." To remove report totals, you must move the pull-down menu highlight to the "Total this column" menu item and type ↵. When this is done, the answer toggles to "No" and report totals will not be printed for that column. Repeating the process will toggle the "Total this column" answer back to "Yes."

Subtotals in Reports

You can subtotal groups of data with the **REPORT** command if the database in use is currently indexed or sorted on the field(s) by which you wish to subtotal and the appropriate specifications have been made in the **MODIFY REPORT** editing mode. To give you experience with report subtotals, complete the following steps.

22. Type ||**USE** empfile **INDEX** empdex↵ **MODIFY REPORT** acctrepo↵||.

23. Use the Options menu bar option to enter the page title shown, change the page width to 65 positions, and set the left margin to 15 characters.

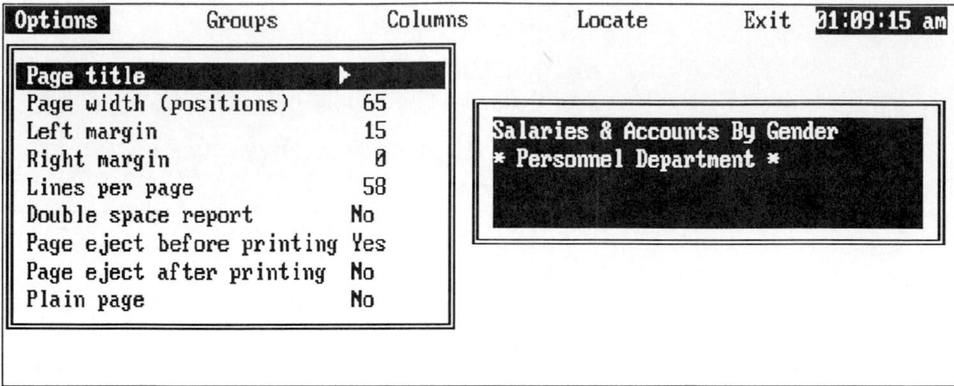

24. Move to the Groups option of the menu bar.
25. Complete this pull-down menu screen by entering the following data.

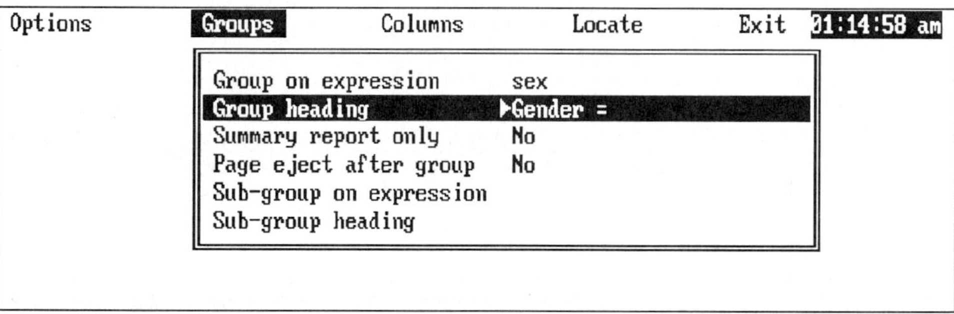

26. Move the menu bar highlight to Columns and complete the following column specifications as shown.

Column 1:

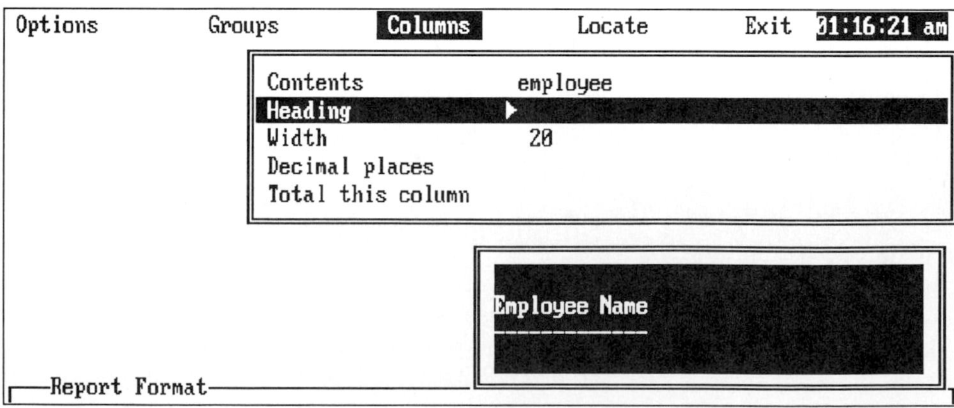

Column 2:

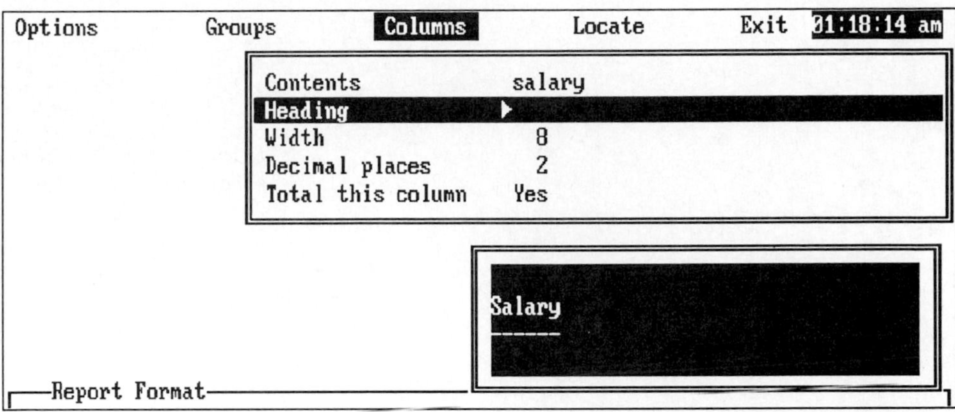

Column 3:

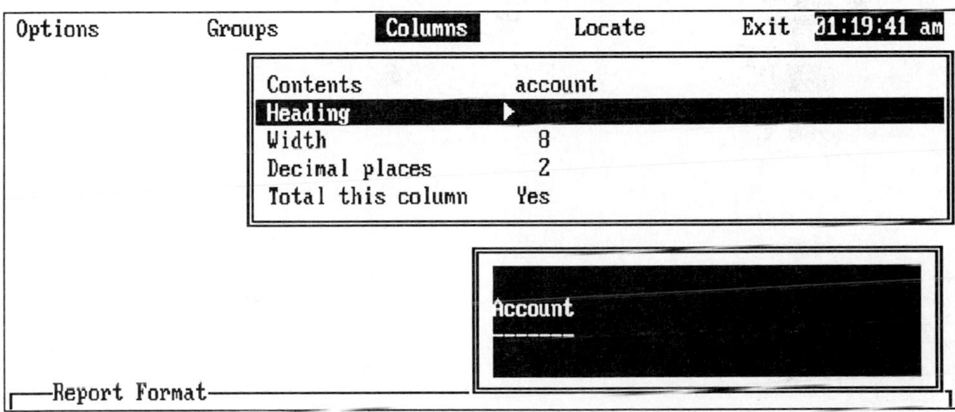

27. Save and exit the **MODIFY REPORT** mode, and then type ||**REPORT FORM** acctrepo↵|| to produce the following report.

```
          Page No.     1
          06/16/90
                   Salaries & Accounts By Gender
                      * Personnel Department *


          Employee Name          Salary  Account
          -------------          ------  -------


         ** Gender = F
          Martins Mary          1600.00   200.50
          Nichols Sandy         1450.00   175.00
          Sill Sally            1507.00   150.00
          Smoler Ellen          1650.00   300.00
         ** Subtotal **
                                6207.00   825.50

         ** Gender = M

          Johnson Frank         1500.00     0.00
          Jones David           1550.00   275.75
          Knat Michael          1800.00   125.00
          Pratt John            1949.00   200.00
          Smith Paul            1700.00   350.00
         ** Subtotal **
                                8499.00   950.75
         *** Total ***
                               14706.00  1776.25

.
Command Line    ||<A:>||EMPFILE          ||Rec: EOF/9      ||    ||

                     Enter a dBASE III PLUS command.
```

More on Column Contents

It is important to note that the contents of a report column can be any expression that dBASE is able to evaluate. In order to create such expressions, it often is necessary to convert data types within them through the use of dBASE functions.

Data Type Conversion Functions

You already have used the **CTOD** function to convert character-type data to date-type data in the tutorial. This was done so that a comparison of like data types could be made in a condition. Other dBASE functions used to convert data types include the following.

DTOC(<date variable>)

Date-to-Character-Function Converts date-type data to character-type data.

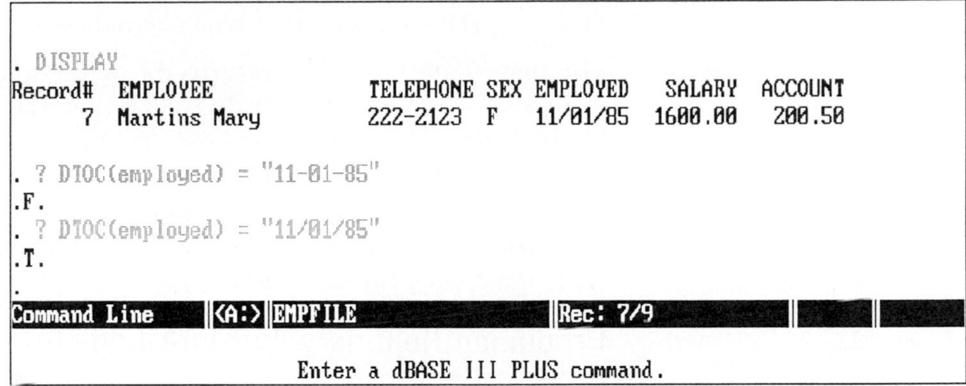

STR(<numeric data> [,<length>] [,<decimals>])

Numeric-to-String Function Returns a character string converted from a numeric expression. Most useful for deleting leading spaces in output of numeric data and/or forcing the display of desired decimal places.

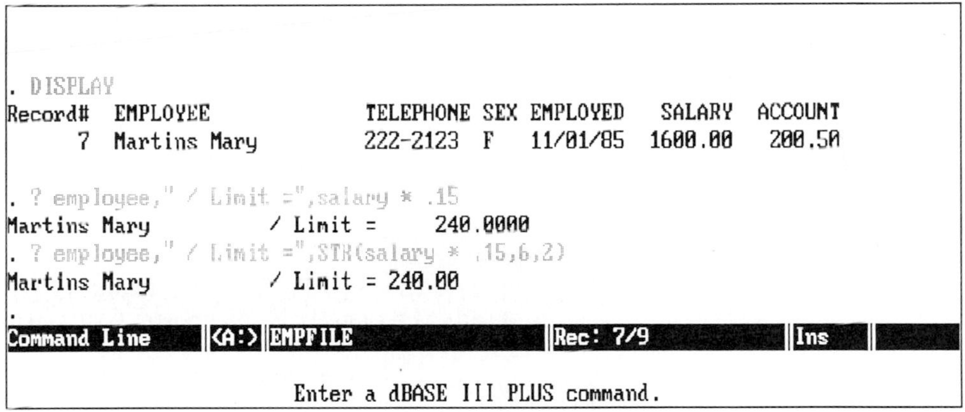

VAL(<character data>)

Character-to-Value Function Returns the numeric value of numbers held as strings beginning at the first character of <character data>.

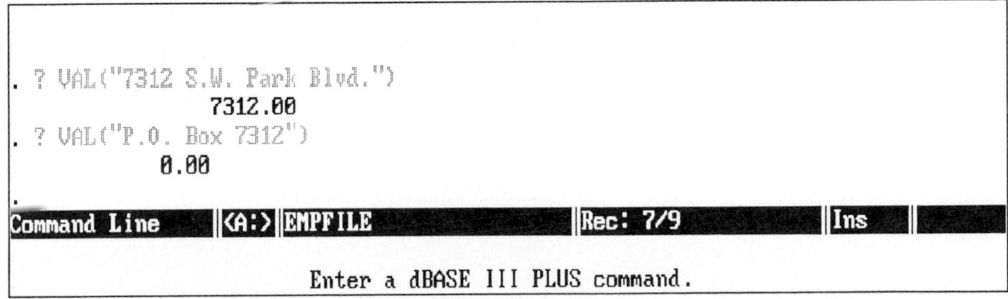

The Immediate If Function

A useful function available with dBASE III Plus is the Immediate If function. Its form is

IIF(<condition>,<true expression>,<false expression>)

The Immediate If function returns its <true expression> if its <condition> evaluates .T.rue and returns its <false expression> if its <condition> evaluates .F.alse. This function is most useful for including conditional column output in a dBASE III Plus report.

With the **IIF** function, the <true expression> and <false expression> may be character-, numeric-, logical-, or date-type data. However, both expressions must be of the same data type.

Producing Reports with More Complex Column Contents

To give you experience using more complex expressions in report column contents, complete the following steps.

28. Type ||**USE** empfile **INDEX** namedex←┘||.

29. Next type ||**AVERAGE** salary **TO** salavg←┘||.

30. Type ||date = **CTOD**("06/30/90")←┘||.

You may enter today's date here.
Use the format mm/dd/yy.

The last two steps create two memory variables: one numeric variable named "salavg," holding the average salary, and one date-type variable named "date," holding today's date. They are variables to which the finished report specifications will refer.

31. Type ||**MODIFY REPORT** salaries ←┘||.

32. Complete the report's Options, changing page width to 77, left margin to 3, and the page title, as shown.

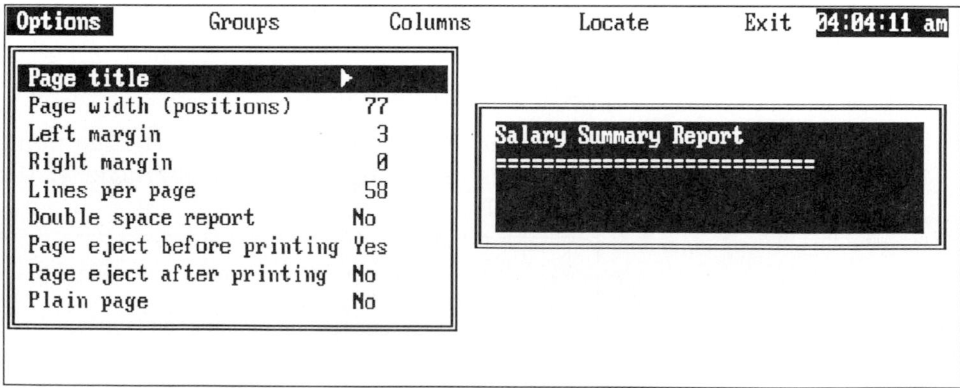

33. Move to the Columns option of the menu bar and enter the first column's data as follows.

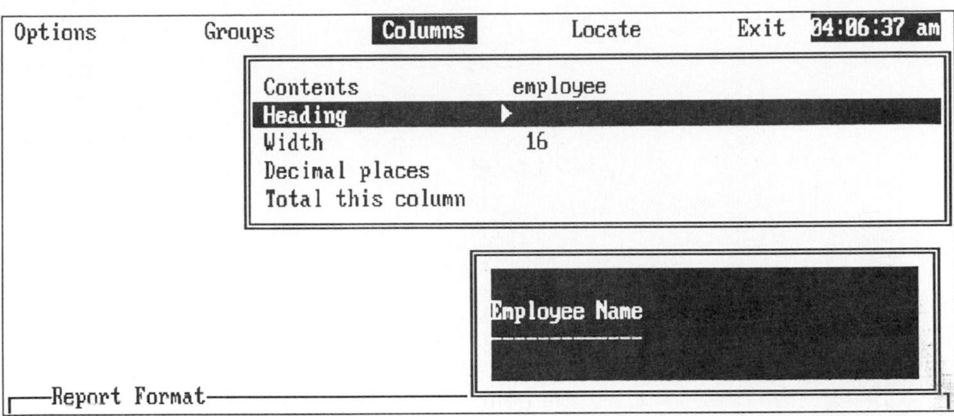

34. Type ||PgDn|| to move to the next column.

The next column's contents will be salary. This time, however, you are going to precede the displayed dollar amount (numeric data) with a dollar sign ($) (character data) in the column. To do so, you will use the **STR** function to convert salary into character data, and then concatenate (add) it to the string, "$".

35. Complete this column's data as shown.

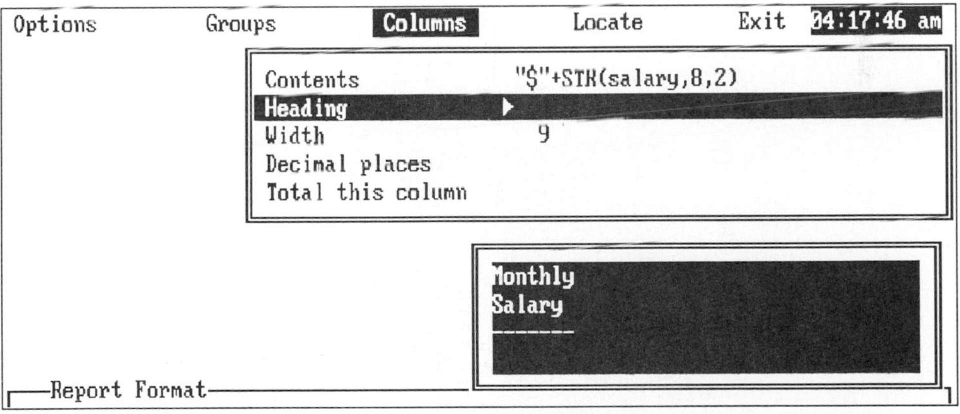

36. Type ||PgDn|| to move to the next column.

In this column (Column 3) you will enter the contents which will display the number of years each employee has worked for the company. To arrive at the final expression used, you must know that date-type data may be used in certain mathematical operations. The following are some examples of "date arithmetic."

```
. date1 = CTOD("06/15/90")
06/15/90
```

Place the date-type data for June 15, 1990 into the variable "date1."

```
. ? date1 + 90
09/13/90
```

Print date1 + 90. September 13, 1990 occurs 90 days after June 15, 1990.

```
. date2 = CTOD("08/14/90")
08/14/90
```

Place the date-type data for August 14, 1990 into the variable "date2."

```
. ? date2 - date1
        60
```

Print date2 minus date1. There are 60 days between June 15 and August 14, 1990.

By using the memory variable "date," which is holding today's date, and the date field "employed," which holds the hire date for each employee, along with some date arithmetic and display formatting using the **STR** function, you are able to enter the contents for Column 3.

37. Enter the column data as shown.

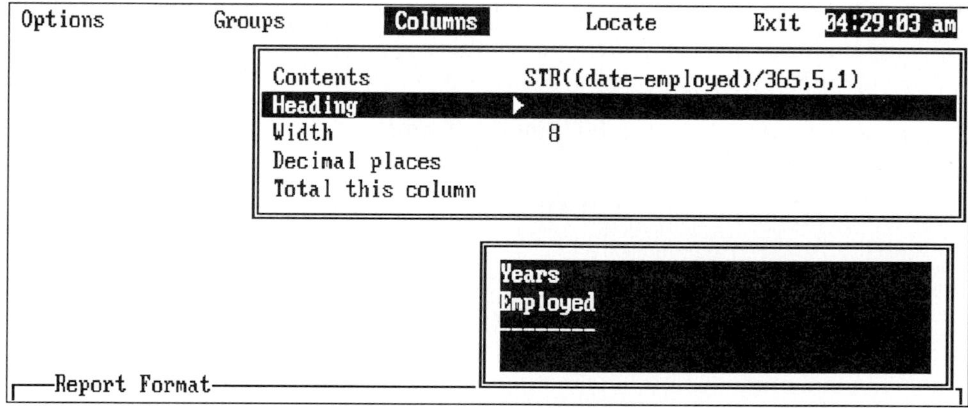

38. Type ||PgDn|| to move to Column 4.

You will enter a simple expression for column contents into column 4. Its purpose is to provide a vertical line through the report.

39. Enter the column contents as shown.

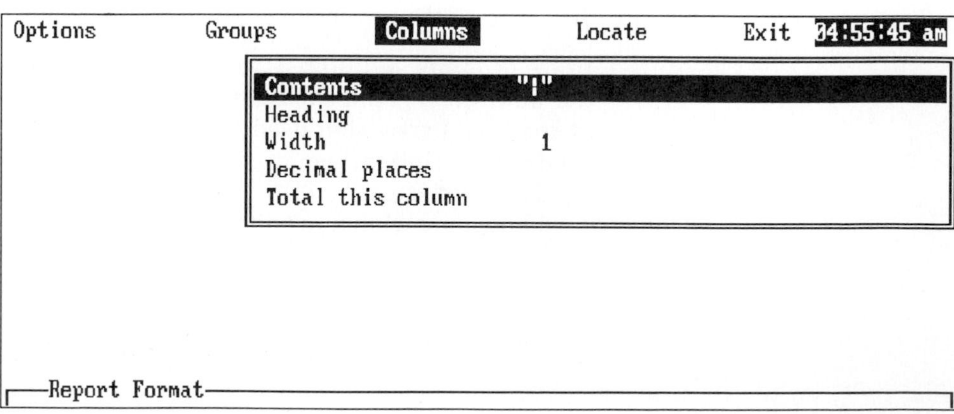

40. Type ||PgDn|| to move to the final column of the report, Column 5.

This column will have the heading "Comments" and its contents will produce the following: If the employee's salary is above or equal to the average salary, no data will be displayed in the column for that employee. However, if the employee's salary is below the average, the message "Under average salary" will be displayed in the column for that employee. The only way to produce such a column of data in a report is through using the **IIF** function.

41. Enter Column 5's contents data as

IIF(salary >= salavg, "", "Under average salary")

then enter the heading and width as shown.

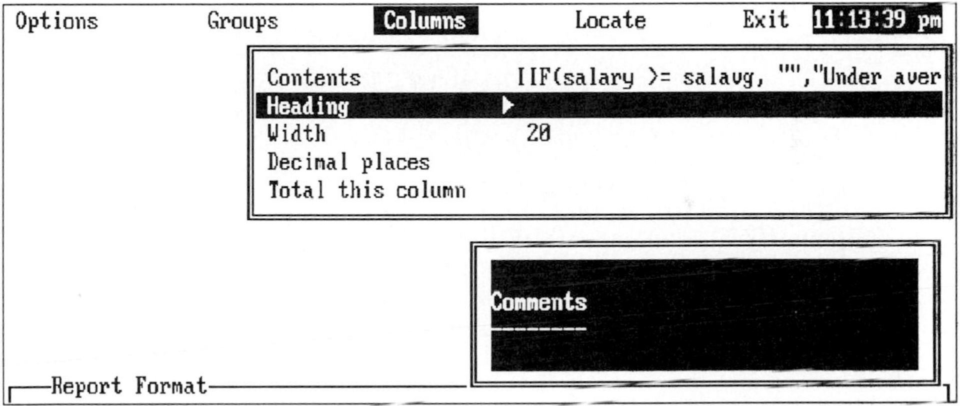

42. Save and exit the **MODIFY REPORT** mode, and then type ||**REPORT FORM** salaries↵|| to produce the following report. (Your report will not have the same figures for "Years Employed.")

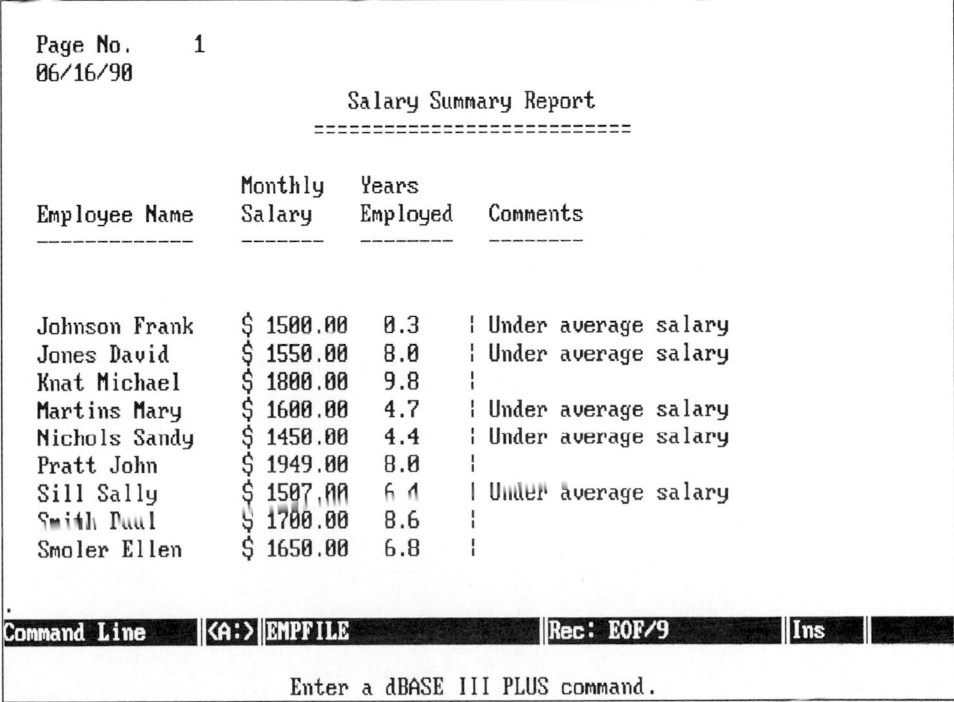

Page No. 1
06/16/90

Salary Summary Report

Employee Name	Monthly Salary	Years Employed	Comments
Johnson Frank	$ 1500.00	0.3	Under average salary
Jones David	$ 1550.00	8.0	Under average salary
Knat Michael	$ 1800.00	9.8	
Martins Mary	$ 1600.00	4.7	Under average salary
Nichols Sandy	$ 1450.00	4.4	Under average salary
Pratt John	$ 1949.00	8.0	
Sill Sally	$ 1507.00	6.4	Under average salary
Smith Paul	$ 1700.00	8.6	
Smoler Ellen	$ 1650.00	6.8	

Printing Out a Report

The **REPORT** command will print a report on the printer when you include the **TO PRINT** parameter in it.

43. Make sure the printer is turned on, on-line, and connected to your computer.

NOTE: Your lab may have a shared device control switch. You will need to select your computer as the one currently connected to the printer.

44. Type and enter the following **REPORT** commands.

||**REPORT FORM** fullrepo **TO PRINT**↵||

||**REPORT FORM** salaries **TO PRINT FOR** employed < CTOD("01/01/84")↵||

||**REPORT FORM** acctrepo **TO PRINT**↵||

||**REPORT FORM** fullrepo **TO PRINT FOR** sex= "M" .AND. employed >= **CTOD**("01/01/82") **HEADING** "All Male Employees Hired After 1981"↵||

LESSON 10 Quitting dBASE III Plus

To quit dBASE and return to the DOS operating level (A>), you use the **QUIT** command. The **QUIT** command is very important since it saves all new file data that may have been created during the session. It then closes all dBASE files that may be open at the time before returning to DOS. **QUIT** is always the last command you enter when you use dBASE III Plus.

1. Type ||**QUIT**↵|| to end this dBASE session.

AN OVERVIEW OF COMMAND FILES

In the dBASE tutorial, you used a number of dBASE commands to manipulate the data in the database empfile.DBF. You displayed records, replaced data in fields, used memory variables to store totals, created report forms, and performed other operations. dBASE executed all of the commands immediately after you entered them.

The direct mode of entering commands can be quite useful for extracting needed information or performing various operations quickly. However, as the commands to perform an operation become longer and more complex, or when certain commands or sets of commands are used repeatedly, typing and entering each command becomes a cumbersome way to accomplish tasks. At such times you may want to consider saving the command(s) in a command file.

Command files are similar to programs written in programming languages such as BASIC. A command file contains dBASE commands which dBASE will execute one after another. All of the commands you have used may be included in a command file, and several dBASE commands and command structures are normally used only in command files.

Creating a dBASE III Plus Command File

Command files are created in the Modify editing mode. To enter the Modify mode from the dot (.) prompt mode, you use the **MODIFY COMMAND** command, which has the form

MODIFY COMMAND <filename>

Command files that you create in this editing mode are stored on the disk under a filename that you supply. dBASE adds a .PRG file extension to the name to identify it as a dBASE program.

When you type the **MODIFY COMMAND** command, dBASE first looks to the default drive for a .PRG file with the same <filename> you specified. If one does not exist, it allocates space on the diskette for a new file under the name specified. If it does find a .PRG file with the specified name, it copies the file into RAM for you to edit.

Entering dBASE Commands into a Command File

When a new .PRG file is specified with the **MODIFY COMMAND** command, a blank screen is presented. Each command in the command file is typed on a single line and the Enter key ↵ is used to advance forward (down the screen) to enter the next command. Since you are in an editing mode, dBASE will not execute the commands when you enter them.

Previous lines may be edited using keystroke commands similar to the keystroke commands used in dBASE's other editing modes (**EDIT** or **BROWSE**, for example).

Saving a Command File

As with all of dBASE's editing modes, the keystroke command ^End is used to save the .PRG file onto the diskette and return you to the dot (.) prompt mode.

Executing the Commands in a Command File

dBASE will open the command file and begin to execute the commands in it when the **DO** command is typed from the dot (.) prompt mode. The **DO** command has the basic form

DO <filename>

When the **DO** command is entered, commands in the specified file will be executed in the order that they appear, top to bottom, until the last command is completed. dBASE then will return to the dot (.) prompt mode.

The Steps for Creating a Command File

In summary, the basic steps in creating a command file are

1. Type ||**MODIFY COMMAND** <filename>↵|| to begin editing.
2. Type each command on a separate line.
3. Type ||**^**End|| to save the file.
4. Type ||**DO** <filename>↵|| to execute the commands in the file.

Correcting the Commands in a Command File

If you have made mistakes, you may easily edit your command file by repeating steps 1 through 3 above and using the editing keystroke commands in the following table while in the editing mode to make the necessary changes.

Keystroke	Action
Cursor right key	Moves cursor right one character.
Cursor left key	Moves cursor left one character.
Home key	Moves cursor one word to the left.
End key	Moves cursor one word to the right.
Cursor down key	Moves cursor to the next line.
Cursor up key	Moves cursor to the previous line.
PgUp key	Scrolls the screen up 17 lines.
PgDn key	Scrolls the screen down 17 lines.
Ins key	Toggles between OVERWRITE and INSERT modes.
Enter key ↵	Terminates current line. In the INSERT mode, inserts a line below the current line.
Del key	Deletes character over cursor.
← (Backspace key)	Deletes character to left of cursor.
^T	Erases word to right of cursor.
^Y	Erases current line.
^KR	Reads and inserts another file into the current file.
^END	Saves changes and returns to dot (.) prompt.
Esc	Aborts all changes made and returns to dot (.) prompt.

dBASE III PLUS EXAMPLE COMMAND FILES

The following discussion will provide a general idea of how command files may be used in conjunction with databases. It will introduce you to some of the most often used programming commands and structures through a set of example programs.

Databases and Other Files Used

The first six example programs are written to be used with the database empfile.DBF created in the dBASE tutorial. The following shows the structure of empfile.DBF and a listing of its records.

```
Structure for database: B:empfile.dbf
Number of data records:        9
Date of last update    : 07/20/90
Field  Field Name  Type       Width    Dec
    1  EMPLOYEE    Character     20
    2  TELEPHONE   Character      8
    3  SEX         Character      1
    4  EMPLOYED    Date           8
    5  SALARY      Numeric        8      2
    6  ACCOUNT     Numeric        8      2
** Total **                      54
```

```
Record#  EMPLOYEE              TELEPHONE SEX EMPLOYED   SALARY  ACCOUNT
      1  Pratt John            225-1234  M   06/22/82  1949.00   200.00
      2  Smoler Ellen          225-3212  F   09/15/83  1650.00   300.00
      3  Jones David           292-3832  M   06/15/82  1550.00   275.75
      4  Sill Sally            224-4321  F   02/15/84  1507.00   150.00
      5  Knat Michael          221-1235  M   09/15/80  1800.00   125.00
      6  Smith Paul            244-1010  M   11/15/81  1700.00   350.00
      7  Martins Mary          222-2123  F   11/01/85  1600.00   200.50
      8  Nichols Sandy         229-1111  F   02/15/86  1450.00   175.00
      9  Johnson Frank         223-7928  M   03/20/90  1500.00     0.00
```

Program #6, raises.PRG, requires that another database file for historical salary information be created and have data appended into it from empfile.DBF. The steps for creating this second database are

1. Type ||**CREATE** salhist↵||.
2. Enter the structure as shown in the following.

```
   Field Name  Type       Width  Dec          Field Name  Type       Width  Dec
   ==============================             ==============================
1  EMPLOYEE    Character    20
2  DATEINCR    Date          8
3  SALARY      Numeric       8    2
```

3. Type ||**USE** salhist↵||.
4. Type ||**APPEND FROM** empfile↵||.
5. Type ||**REPLACE ALL** dateincr **WITH CTOD**("01/01/90")↵||.
6. Type ||**DISPLAY ALL**↵||.

For a more complete explanation, see **APPEND FROM** in the operation and command summary (page D-153).

The database salhist.DBF should appear as follows.

```
Record#  EMPLOYEE                 DATEINCR    SALARY
      1  Pratt John               01/01/90   1949.00
      2  Smoler Ellen             01/01/90   1650.00
      3  Jones David              01/01/90   1550.00
      4  Sill Sally               01/01/90   1507.00
      5  Knat Michael             01/01/90   1800.00
      6  Smith Paul               01/01/90   1700.00
      7  Martins Mary             01/01/90   1600.00
      8  Nichols Sandy            01/01/90   1450.00
      9  Johnson Frank            01/01/90   1500.00
```

Other files referred to and used in the example programs also are products of completing the dBASE tutorial. They include acctrepo.FRM, empdex.NDX, namedex.NDX, fullrepo.FRM, and salaries.FRM.

Example Program Formats

Each example program is presented in five parts.

1. A *program description* of the task that the program is designed to perform.
2. A listing with summary explanations of the *new commands and functions* used in the particular program.
3. A *program listing* of the command file.
4. Any *preliminary commands* required to execute the program successfully.
5. A *sample execution* showing what the output of that program may be.

The description prefacing each program includes an algorithm for the program. An *algorithm* is a step-by-step outline of the program's operation. Each step is described in words close to those used in everyday communication.

Example Program 1—payment.PRG

Program Description

The first sample program is designed to let the user post a payment to an employee's personal account. The intended database in use is empfile.DBF. The general algorithm for the program is

1. Present the user with the employee's name for the current record.
2. Ask the user for the amount of payment.
3. Replace the current record's "account" field with what is there minus the payment.
4. Display the new account balance and prompt the user to indicate when he/she is done viewing the screen.

New Commands and Functions Used

* <comment> dBASE considers any line beginning with an asterisk (*) a comment line and will ignore it during execution. Comments must be placed on lines separate from other commands. See **NOTE** in the operation and command summary, page D-174.

CLEAR The **CLEAR** command clears the screen at any point in a command file.

? [<exp1>[,<exp2>, . . .]] The **?** command displays "the value of" expressions which may include current fields, memory variables, and/or constants. If more than one expression follows the **?** command, the expressions must be separated by commas.

The plus (+) sign may be used to combine different character-type data items into a single character expression. The operation of combining character strings with the plus sign is called string *concatenation.*

INPUT [<expC>] **TO** <memvarN> **INPUT** pauses execution of the program after it displays a prompt defined by the character expression <expC>. The user then is allowed to type and enter a response to the prompt. The response is held in the <memvarN>. The **INPUT** command is used for numeric-type data responses.

ACCEPT [<expC>] **TO** <memvarC> **ACCEPT** is the counterpart of **INPUT.** It is used for character-type data input from the keyboard. The response will be held in the <memvarC> as a character string.

REPLACE <field1> **WITH** <exp1> [,<field2> **WITH** <exp2>, . . .] Replaces the contents of the current record's <field>s with the value of the corresponding expressions <exp>. An expression must evaluate to the same data type as the field being replaced.

RETURN Signals the end of the command file and returns control to the dot (.) prompt or program from which the program was called.

Program Listing

```
* PROGRAM:  Payment.PRG  -  to post payment to employee's account

CLEAR

?
? "       * * *  Payment to Employee Account  * * *  "
?
? "            Employee:  " + employee
? "            Acct Bal = ",account
?

INPUT "              Enter amount of payment:  " TO pmt
REPLACE account WITH account - pmt

?
?
? "            New Balance = ",account
?
ACCEPT "When finished viewing screen, press Enter key  " TO dummy
CLEAR
RETURN
```

Preliminary Commands

```
. USE empfile

. SET TALK OFF

. LOCATE FOR employee = "Jones"

. DO payment
```

Sample Execution

```
       * * *  Payment to Employee Account  * * *

            Employee:  Jones David
            Acct Bal =    275.75

            Enter amount of payment:  125.00


            New Balance =    150.75

When finished viewing screen, press Enter key
```

Example Program 2—purchase.PRG

Program Description

The second example program lets the user post a purchase to an employee's personal account. The intended database in use in empfile.DBF. The second program differs from the first in that it includes two **IF . . . ELSE . . . ENDIF** structures to check certain conditions before it posts any changes to the database. The general algorithm is

1. Present the user with the employee's name and account balance for the current record.
2. Ask the user for the amount of purchase.
3. If the purchase plus the balance on the account is more than 15 percent of that employee's salary, then
   - **A.** Ask the user if the purchase is authorized by credit.

   Otherwise,
   - **A.** The purchase is automatically authorized.

   End if.
4. If the purchase is authorized, then
   - **A.** Replace the current record's field "account" with what is there plus the purchase amount.
   - **B.** Display the employee's new account balance.

   Otherwise,
   - **A.** Display a message saying that the purchase is not authorized and has not been posted.

   End if.
5. Prompt the user to indicate when he/she is done viewing the screen.

New Commands and Functions Used

```
IF <condition>
  any commands
ELSE
  any commands
ENDIF
```

The <condition> parameter of the **IF** command is a logical expression that can be evaluated as true (.T.) or false (.F.). If the <condition> evaluates true, the commands between the **IF** and the **ELSE** will be executed. If the <condition> evaluates false, the commands between the **ELSE** and the **ENDIF** will be executed.

Every **IF** command must have a corresponding **ENDIF** command to signal the end of that command structure. The **ELSE** portion of the structure and the commands following it are optional. (If the **ELSE** clause is omitted, commands between the **IF** and **ENDIF** are executed if the <condition> evaluates as true; otherwise, they are ignored.)

STORE <expression> **TO** <memvar> Places the value of the <expression> into a memory variable <memvar>. The data type of <memvar> is determined by the type of the <expression> that is stored to it (numeric, character, date, or logical).

UPPER(<expC>) The **UPPER**(<expC>) function returns the upper-case equivalent of its character string argument. It often is useful for comparisons of character strings input by a user.

Program Listing

```
*  PROGRAM:  Purchase.PRG  -  to post employee purchases on account
CLEAR
?
?
? "        *  *  *  Employee Purchase on Account  *  *  *  "
?
? "             Employee:  " + employee
? "             Acct Bal = ",account
?
INPUT "            Enter amount of desired purchase:  " TO amt

IF account + amt > salary * .15
  ?
  ? "Employee's account will exceed 15% of salary with this purchase"
  ? "OK from Credit Manager required"
  ?
  ACCEPT "            OK received (y/n) ?  " TO ok
ELSE
  STORE "Y" TO ok
ENDIF
?
?

IF UPPER(ok) = "Y"
  REPLACE account WITH account + amt
  ? "             New Balance = ",account
ELSE
  ? "     Approval Denied  -  Purchase not Posted  "
ENDIF
?
ACCEPT "When finished viewing screen, press Enter key  " TO dummy
CLEAR
RETURN
```

Preliminary Commands

```
. USE empfile

. SET TALK OFF

. GOTO 6

. DO purchase
```

Sample Execution

```
      * * *  Employee Purchase on Account  * * *

           Employee:  Smith Paul
           Acct Bal =    350.00

           Enter amount of desired purchase:  700

Employee's account will exceed 15% of salary with this purchase
OK from Credit Manager required

           OK received (y/n) ?  y


           New Balance =   1050.00

When finished viewing screen, press Enter key
```

Example Program 3—transact.PRG

Program Description

Example program 3 is known as a calling program. It is designed to allow the user to access either program 1, payment.PRG, or program 2, purchase.PRG, through its execution. A graphic representation of the relationship might be

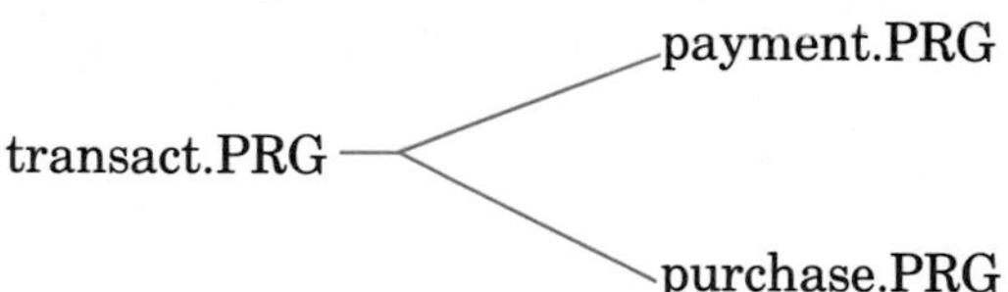

Within transact.PRG, the user is asked if the transaction to be posted is a payment or a purchase. Depending on the response, the command **DO** payment or **DO** purchase is executed. When either **DO** command is executed, dBASE starts executing the command file specified in it. When dBASE is finished with the called command file, it returns to transact.PRG and resumes execution where it left off. Example program 3 also introduces the idea of initializing the environment by including preliminary commands (to open the proper files and select a record) within the program.

Finally, transact.PRG incorporates a loop in which the posting of amounts to accounts is repeated until the user chooses to quit.

The general algorithm for program 3, transact.PRG, is

1. Initialize by setting **TALK OFF** and selecting empfile.DBF for use with its index file namedex.NDX.
2. Present the user with documentation of the program.
3. Set a <memvar> flag that will control loop processing to true.

4. Continue executing the following loop instructions until the flag is no longer true.
   - **A.** Present the user with a menu of selections to (1) Post a Purchase; (2) Post a Payment; or (3) Exit the Program.
   - **B.** Continue to prompt for a selection until a valid selection (1, 2, or 3) has been entered.
   - **C.** If the selection was either 1 or 2, then
     - **1.** Display a list of employee names in the database file.
     - **2.** Ask the user for the name of the employee of concern.
     - **3.** Search the file for the name entered and move the record pointer to that record.
     - **4.** If the name is not found or no name was entered, then
       - **a.** Ask if the user wants to continue the program.

       Otherwise,
       - **a.** If the menu selection was 1, then
         - **a1.** Execute purchase.PRG.

         Otherwise,
         - **a1.** Execute payment.PRG.

         End if.

       End if.

     Otherwise,
     - **1.** Change the <memvar> flag to no longer true.

     End if.
5. End of the loop instructions.
6. Close the files and clear the screen.

New Commands and Functions Used

SET TALK OFF and **SET STATUS OFF** Two of dBASE's **SET** commands that allow you to set features on or off. You will want to place the **SET TALK OFF** command at the beginning of your program to prevent dBASE's "talk" from cluttering up the screen. The **SET STATUS OFF** command suppresses display of the status bar at the bottom of the screen.

USE <filename> **INDEX** <index file list> Most programs will use a specific database file and sometimes a specific index file. Placing the appropriate **USE** command at the beginning of your command file ensures that the proper files are in use.

TEXT
  any data
ENDTEXT

This command structure allows you to print several lines of text without having to use a **?** command on each line.

DO WHILE <condition>
  any commands
ENDDO

This structure is used for creating loops. As long as the <condition> evaluates as true (.T.), the commands between the **DO WHILE** and **ENDDO** will be executed repeatedly, with the condition checked at the beginning of each iteration.

To end the execution of the loop, one or more items used in the <condition> must change to make the <condition> false. When this occurs, the next time the **DO WHILE** <condition> is evaluated execution of the program will resume with the command immediately following the loop's **ENDDO** command.

@ <x,y> **SAY** <exp> This command prints the evaluation of an expression <exp> starting at a specific location on the screen. The *x* value is the row number; the *y* value is the column number.

@ <x1,y1> **TO** <x2,y2> [**DOUBLE**] Draws a box on the screen with the upper-left corner defined by the <x1,y1> coordinate and the lower-right corner defined by the <x2,y2> coordinate. The box will be drawn with a single line unless the **DOUBLE** parameter is used to cause the box to be drawn with a double line.

@ <x,y> **SAY** <exp> **GET** <field / memvar> [**PICTURE** <expC>]
or
@ <x,y> **GET** <field / memvar> [**PICTURE** <expC>]

The @ **GET** command may be used alone or combined with the @ **SAY** command. It is used to input or edit the contents of a field or memory variable at a specified screen location. The @ **GET** commands are activated when the **READ** command is executed. In command files, @ **GET** is often preferable to **ACCEPT** or **INPUT** since it allows better control of screen appearance and data entry formats.

The **PICTURE** <expC> clause may be used to specify certain types of data which must be entered in the @ **GET**'s field or memory variable. In the example program, the **PICTURE** expressions use the template characters "9," "!," "X," and "Y." The "9" restricts input of character data to the characters 0 through 9, the "!" forces a character to be upper case, the "X" allows any character to be entered, and the "Y" is used with logical-type data to accept "Y" for .T. (true) and "N" for .F. (false).

READ @ **GET** commands are normally followed by a **READ** command, which causes the cursor to move to the first @ **GET** <field / memvar> for editing. The cursor may be moved to any of the active @ **GET** fields or variables. When data has been entered for all of the active @ **GET**s, execution resumes with the next command after the **READ** command.

$** (Relational Operator) The relational operator **$ is used to compare two string expressions and determine whether the first expression is a substring of the second. For example, the expression <memvarC> **$** "123" is true (.T.) if the value of <memvarC> is "1," "2," "3," "12," "23," or "123"; if it contains any other character string, the expression is false (.F.).

SEEK <exp> Searches the index file in use for the first index key that matches the expression <exp> and moves the record pointer to the corresponding record in the database file. If no index key is found for the expression, the record pointer is moved to the end of the file and the **EOF**( ) function returns .T. (true).

TRIM(<expC>) The **TRIM** function returns the character string argument with any trailing spaces removed.

EOF( ) The End-of-file function **EOF( )** is a dBASE function that returns the logical value .T. (true) when the record pointer is moved past the last record of the database file. It often is used after a search operation to determine if a record was found (end-of-file is false).

SPACE(<expN>) The **SPACE** function returns a character string of spaces with a length defined by the argument <expN>.

DO <filename> **DO** may be used to call another program from the current program. When a **RETURN** is encountered in the called program, the calling program resumes execution at the command following the **DO** <filename> command.

Program Listing

```
* PROGRAM:  Transact.PRG  -  calling program for purchase and payment programs

SET TALK OFF
SET STATUS OFF
USE empfile INDEX namedex

CLEAR
TEXT
    This program is for updating employees' personal accounts.  After
    selecting the type of transaction to post, a purchase on account or
    a payment, you will enter the name of an employee.

ENDTEXT
ACCEPT "    Press Enter to Begin " TO dummy

STORE .T. TO cont
DO WHILE cont
  CLEAR
  @  7,30 SAY "  Transaction Menu  "
  @  6,25 TO 8,55 DOUBLE
  @ 10,30 SAY " 1 - Post Purchase  "
  @ 11,30 SAY " 2 - Post Payment   "
  @ 12,30 SAY " 3 - Exit           "
  @  9,25 TO 15,55

  STORE " " TO choice
  DO WHILE .NOT. choice $ "123"
    @ 14,30 SAY " Enter Selection: " GET choice PICTURE "9"
    READ
  ENDDO

  IF choice $ "12"
    CLEAR
    ?
    ?
    DISPLAY ALL Employee OFF
    STORE SPACE(20) TO name
    @  3,30 SAY "Enter Name: " GET name PICTURE "!XXXXXXXXXXXXXXXXXXX"
    READ

    SEEK TRIM(name)
    IF EOF() .OR. name = SPACE(20)
      @ 5,30 SAY "Invalid Name Entered, Continue (Y/N) ? " GET cont PICT "Y"
      READ
    ELSE
      IF choice = "1"
        DO purchase
      ELSE
        DO payment
      ENDIF
    ENDIF
  ELSE
    STORE .F. TO cont
  ENDIF
ENDDO

USE
CLEAR
RETURN
```

Preliminary Commands

```
. DO transact
```

Sample Execution

```
This program is for updating employees' personal accounts.  After
selecting the type of transaction to post, a purchase on account or
a payment, you will enter the name of an employee.

Press Enter to Begin
```

```
                    Transaction Menu

                 1 - Post Purchase
                 2 - Post Payment
                 3 - Exit

                 Enter Selection:  1
```

```
Employee                      Enter Name:  Johnson
Johnson Frank
Jones David
Knat Michael
Martins Mary
Nichols Sandy
Pratt John
Sill Sally
Smith Paul
Smoler Ellen
```

```
      * * *  Employee Purchase on Account  * * *

          Employee:  Johnson Frank
          Acct Bal =        0.00

          Enter amount of desired purchase:  800.00

Employee's account will exceed 15% of salary with this purchase
OK from Credit Manager required

          OK received (y/n) ?  n


    Approval Denied  -  Purchase not Posted

When finished viewing screen, press Enter key
```

```
                    Transaction Menu

                    1 - Post Purchase
                    2 - Post Payment
                    3 - Exit

                    Enter Selection: 3
```

Example Programs 4 and 5—reports1.PRG and reports2.PRG

Program Description

The next two example programs also are connected to each other. Program 4, reports1.PRG, is the calling program, and program 5, reports2.PRG, is the program being called. Their relationship might be graphically depicted as

reports1.PRG⟶ reports2.PRG

Example program 4, reports1.PRG, allows the user to select the way a report will be displayed or output, and to select the report to be produced. It then conditionally initializes the appropriate output devices and calls reports2.PRG to produce the desired report. Both programs use the **DO CASE...ENDCASE** structure, which is similar to the **IF...ELSE...ENDIF** structure.

The general algorithm for example program 4, reports1.PRG, is

1. Initialize the environment by setting **TALK** and **STATUS OFF** and selecting empfile.DBF with its index file empdex.NDX as the database file for use.
2. Present the user with a menu numbered 1 through 3 with the options (1) displayed on screen, (2) sent to printer, and (3) written to a file.
3. Instruct the user to enter his/her answer.
4. Clear the screen and present to the user a second menu numbered 1 through 4 with the options (1) Salary Summary Report, (2) Salaries & Accounts by Gender, (3) Employee Full Report, and (4) All of the above.
5. Instruct the user to enter his/her answer.
6. Determine the Case for the output selection.
   - **A.** Case: the user answered "Sent to the printer."
     1. Initialize the printer for output.
     2. Do reports2.PRG.
     3. Reset the output device to the screen.
   - **B.** Case: the user answered "Written to a text file."
     1. Initialize a .TXT file.
     2. Do reports2.PRG.
     3. Close the .TXT file.
   - **C.** Otherwise: the user answered "Displayed on screen only."
     1. Do reports2.PRG. The output automatically will be sent to the screen.

   End Case.
7. Close the files.

The general algorithm for example program 5, reports2.PRG, is

1. Initialize environment for salaries.FRM.
   - **A.** Determine the average salary of all employees and store it to a memory variable.
   - **B.** Store the current system date to a memory variable.
2. Determine the Case for the report selection.
   - **A.** Case: the user selected "Salary Summary Report."
     1. Produce the report using the salaries.FRM file.
   - **B.** Case: the user selected "Salaries & Accounts by Gender."
     1. Produce the report using the acctrepo.FRM file.
   - **C.** Case: the user selected "Employee Full Report."
     1. Produce the report using the fullrepo.FRM file.
   - **D.** Otherwise: the user selected "All of the above reports."
     1. Produce the report using the salaries.FRM file, and then prompt to continue.
     2. Produce the report using the acctrepo.FRM file, and then prompt to continue.
     3. Produce the report using the fullrepo.FRM file, and then prompt to continue.

   End Case.
3. Return to the calling program reports1.PRG.

New Commands Used

DO CASE
  CASE <condition>
    <any commands>
  CASE <condition>
    <any commands>
  OTHERWISE
    <any commands>
ENDCASE

The **DO CASE...ENDCASE** command structure is useful when the <condition>s used are mutually exclusive. As soon as a <condition> is evaluated as .T. (true), only those commands following it, up to the next **CASE, OTHERWISE,** or **ENDCASE,** will be executed. Execution then resumes with the command following **ENDCASE.** The **OTHERWISE** is optional. If it is used, commands following **OTHERWISE** will be executed when none of the previous **CASE** <condition>s are evaluated as true.

DO <filename> **WITH** <expression list> The **WITH** <expression list> is used to pass values (expressions) to the program being called with the **DO** command. The receiving program must be designed to accept the values and store them to local memory variables through the **PARAMETERS** command.

PARAMETERS <memvar list> **PARAMETERS** is the command used to accept values being passed by a calling program. **PARAMETERS** must be the first executable command in the program being called.

SET PRINT ON The **SET PRINT ON** command sends the screen output to the printer. **SET PRINT OFF** is the reverse of this command.

SET ALTERNATE on / OFF and **SET ALTERNATE TO** <filename>
The **SET ALTERNATE ON** command is used to send screen output to a text file on the diskette, which is given a .TXT file extension. The text file may later be edited with a word processing software.

To create and open an alternate file, use the command **SET ALTERNATE TO** <filename>. To close the alternate file, use the command without a <filename> specified.

SET ALTERNATE ON must be executed before screen output will be sent to the alternate file. **SET ALTERNATE OFF** will suspend sending output to the current text file.

Reports2.PRG uses no new commands. It provides an example of a procedure that would only be called from another program which passes a value to the memory variable "reptno" as a parameter.

The commands in this program could have been included in reports1.PRG, but they would need to have been listed three times. In this case, it is more efficient to place the commands in their own file, reports2.PRG, and call this program from three places in reports1.PRG with the single command, **DO** reports2. In addition, any other program could call reports2.PRG as long as the necessary files are in use and a parameter is passed.

Program Listings

```
*  PROGRAM:  Reports1.PRG  - to print report forms

SET TALK OFF
SET STATUS OFF
USE empfile INDEX empdex
CLEAR

@  5,10 SAY "This program allows you to print a number of reports "

@  7,20 SAY "      These reports may be:      "
@  8,15 TO 16,60
@  9,20 SAY "1 - Displayed on the screen only "
@ 11,20 SAY "2 - Sent to the printer          "
@ 13,20 SAY "3 - Written to a text file       "
STORE " " TO mode
DO WHILE .NOT. mode $ "123"
  @ 15,20 SAY "Select 1, 2, or 3 " GET mode PICTURE "9"
  READ
ENDDO
CLEAR

@  6,10 SAY "Which of the following reports would you like to use ? "
@  8,15 TO 18,60
@  9,20 SAY "1 - Salary Summary Report          "
@ 11,20 SAY "2 - Salaries and Accounts by Gender "
@ 13,20 SAY "3 - Employee Full Report           "
@ 15,20 SAY "4 - All of the above reports       "
STORE " " TO choice
DO WHILE .NOT. choice $ "1234"
  @ 17,20 SAY "Select 1, 2, 3, or 4 " GET choice PICTURE "9"
  READ
ENDDO
CLEAR

DO CASE
   CASE mode = "2"
     SET PRINT ON
     DO reports2 WITH choice
     SET PRINT OFF

   CASE mode = "3"
     SET ALTERNATE TO reports.txt
     SET ALTERNATE ON
     DO reports2 WITH choice
     SET ALTERNATE OFF
     SET ALTERNATE TO

   OTHERWISE
     DO reports2 WITH choice

ENDCASE

USE
RETURN
```

```
* PROGRAM:  Reports2.PRG  -  called from Reports1.PRG

PARAMETERS reptno
AVERAGE ALL salary TO salavg
STORE DATE() TO date

DO CASE
   CASE reptno = "1"
     REPORT FORM salaries

   CASE reptno = "2"
     REPORT FORM acctrepo

   CASE reptno = "3"
     REPORT FORM fullrepo

   OTHERWISE
     REPORT FORM salaries
     ACCEPT "Press Enter for next report " TO dummy
     REPORT FORM acctrepo
     ACCEPT "Press Enter for next report " TO dummy
     REPORT FORM fullrepo
     ACCEPT "Press Enter to continue     " TO dummy
ENDCASE
RETURN
```

Preliminary Commands

```
. DO reports1
```

Sample Execution

```
          This program allows you to print a number of reports

                        These reports may be:

                 1 - Displayed on the screen only

                 2 - Sent to the printer

                 3 - Written to a text file

                 Select 1, 2, or 3  1
```

```
Which of the following reports would you like to use ?

        1 - Salary Summary Report

        2 - Salaries and Accounts by Gender

        3 - Employee Full Report

        4 - All of the above reports

        Select 1, 2, 3, or 4  3
```

```
Page No.     1
07/23/90
                       Employee Full Report
                       ====================

                                             Current   Account  Account
Employee Name    Phone #    Hire Date   Salary     Limit   Balance
-------------    -------    ---------   -------   -------  -------


Martins Mary     222-2123   11/01/85    1600.00    240.00   200.50
Nichols Sandy    229-1111   02/15/86    1450.00    217.00   175.00
Sill Sally       224-4321   02/15/84    1507.00    226.00   150.00
Smoler Ellen     225-3212   09/15/83    1650.00    247.00   300.00
Johnson Frank    223-7928   03/20/90    1500.00    225.00     0.00
Jones David      292-3832   06/15/82    1550.00    232.00   150.75
Knat Michael     221-1235   09/15/80    1800.00    270.00   125.00
Pratt John       225-1234   06/22/82    1949.00    292.00   200.00
Smith Paul       244-1010   11/15/81    1700.00    255.00  1050.00
*** Total ***
                                       14706.00   2204.00  2351.25
```

Example Program 6—raises.PRG

Program Description

This example program is designed to maintain a second database, salhist.DBF, which is used to keep records of each employee's raises over a period of time. Included in raises.PRG are the commands and parameters used when two or more databases are put into use at the same time.

The general algorithm for the example program 6, raises.PRG, is

1. Initialize the environment by setting **TALK** and **STATUS OFF.**
2. Select work area 2 and put salhist.DBF into use there.

3. Select work area 1 and put empfile.DBF into use with its index file namedex.NDX. Leave work area 1 the current work area.
4. Set a memory variable to true for control of a loop and continue executing the following loop instructions until the memory variable is set to false.
   - **A.** Initialize the memory variables to be used and display a program description.
   - **B.** Ask the user to enter the name of the employee of concern.
   - **C.** Move empfile's record pointer to the employee's record.
   - **D.** If the end of file is encountered (the name cannot be found) or no name has been entered, then
     - **1.** Ask if the user wants to continue the program.
     - **2.** Set the loop variable to the user's response.
   - **E.** Otherwise,
     - **1.** Present a screen for the user to input the date of the raise and the percent increase.
     - **2.** Compute and display the new salary on the screen.
     - **3.** Ask the user to confirm the new salary.
     - **4.** If it is confirmed, then
       - **a.** Replace the current record's salary field with the new salary.
       - **b.** Select work area 2, salhist.DBF.
       - **c.** Move salhist's record pointer to the first record whose field "employee" matches the field "employee" of the current record in empfile.
       - **d.** Insert a blank record immediately before the current record in salhist.
       - **e.** Fill the fields in the blank record with the appropriate data.
       - **f.** Display all data in salhist for that employee.
       - **g.** Select work area 1 empfile.

     End if.
     - **5.** Ask the user if there are more salary increases to enter.
     - **6.** Set the loop variable to the user's response.

   End if.

   End of the loop instruction.
5. Close the files.

New Commands Used

SELECT <work area / alias> Ten separate work areas are available, each capable of having one database file in use. To put more than one database file into use, first select the desired work area with the **SELECT** command, and then enter the **USE** command specifying the database file to open. Independent record pointers are maintained for each database in use. Field data may be read across work areas by using aliases (the filename or a letter A through J).

CTOD(<expC>) The Character-to-Date function is used to convert character-type data to date-type data. In "raises.PRG," the **CTOD** function converts a blank date string to a date-type memory variable to be used with an @ **GET** command.

@ <x,y> **CLEAR** Clears the screen from the row and column specified by the <x,y> coordinate, downward and to the right.

LOCATE FOR <condition> Sets the record pointer in the current database file to the first record which evaluates as true (.T.) for the condition. If no such record is found, the record pointer will be at the end of the file.

INSERT [BLANK] [BEFORE] The **INSERT BLANK** command adds a blank record to the database in use just after the current record. This is usually done so that a subsequent **REPLACE** command can be used to store data in the new record. The **[BEFORE]** parameter is used to place the blank record immediately before the current record.

Program Listing

```
*  PROGRAM:  Raises.PRG  -  to keep records of previous salary levels

SET TALK OFF
SET STATUS OFF
SELECT 2
USE salhist
SELECT 1
USE empfile INDEX namedex

STORE .T. TO cont
DO WHILE cont
  STORE CTOD("  /  /  ") TO effdate
  STORE SPACE(20)        TO name
  STORE 0                TO increase
  CLEAR
  @  5,15 SAY " *   *   *   Entering Salary Increases   *   *   *"
  @ 10,10 SAY "Name of Employee (Last First)  " GET name
  READ
  SEEK TRIM(name)
  IF EOF() .OR. name = SPACE(20)
    @ 15,10 SAY "Invalid name entry -- Continue (Y/N) ? " GET cont PICT "Y"
    READ
  ELSE
    @  8, 1 CLEAR
    @  8,15 SAY "EMPLOYEE"
    @  8,45 SAY "CURRENT SALARY"
    @ 10,15 SAY employee
    @ 10,45 SAY salary PICTURE "9,999.99"
    @ 15,15 SAY "Enter Effective Date (mm/dd/yy) "
    @ 15,50 GET effdate
    @ 17,15 SAY "Enter percent increase as decimal "
    @ 17,50 GET increase PICTURE "0.9999"
    READ
    @ 19,15 SAY "New Salary = "
    @ 19,30 SAY salary * (1 + increase) PICTURE "9,999.99"
    STORE " " TO ok
    DO WHILE .NOT. ok $ "YN"
      @ 19,45 SAY "Is this correct (Y/N) ? " GET ok PICTURE "!"
      READ
    ENDDO
    IF ok = "Y"
      REPLACE salary WITH salary * (1 + increase)
      SELECT 2
      LOCATE FOR employee = empfile->employee
      INSERT BLANK BEFORE
      REPLACE employee WITH empfile->employee, dateincr WITH effdate
      REPLACE salary WITH empfile->salary
      CLEAR
      @ 10,15 SAY "SALARY HISTORY"
      ?
      DISPLAY FOR employee = empfile->employee OFF
      SELECT 1
    ENDIF
    ?
    @ ROW(),15 SAY "More Salary Increases to Enter (Y/N) " GET cont PICT "Y"
    READ
  ENDIF
ENDDO
CLOSE DATABASES
RETURN
```

Preliminary Commands

```
. DO raises
```

Sample Execution

```
          *   *   *   Entering Salary Increases   *   *   *


   Name of Employee (Last First)   Sill
```

```
          *   *   *   Entering Salary Increases   *   *   *

          EMPLOYEE                      CURRENT SALARY

          Sill Sally                    1,507.00



          Enter Effective Date (mm/dd/yy)    06/15/91

          Enter percent increase as decimal  0.1000

          New Salary =   1,657.70       Is this correct (Y/N) ?  Y
```

```
          SALARY HISTORY

EMPLOYEE              DATEINCR   SALARY
Sill Sally            06/15/91  1657.70
Sill Sally            01/01/90  1507.00

          More Salary Increases to Enter (Y/N)  N
```

Example Program 7—menu.PRG

Program Description

The final example program, menu.PRG, has no new commands, structures, or functions to explain. It is the main calling program designed to allow the user to select which of the six previous sample programs he/she would like to access. It is the program that ties the other six into a system—a database management system—of programs. With it, the system can be graphically displayed as

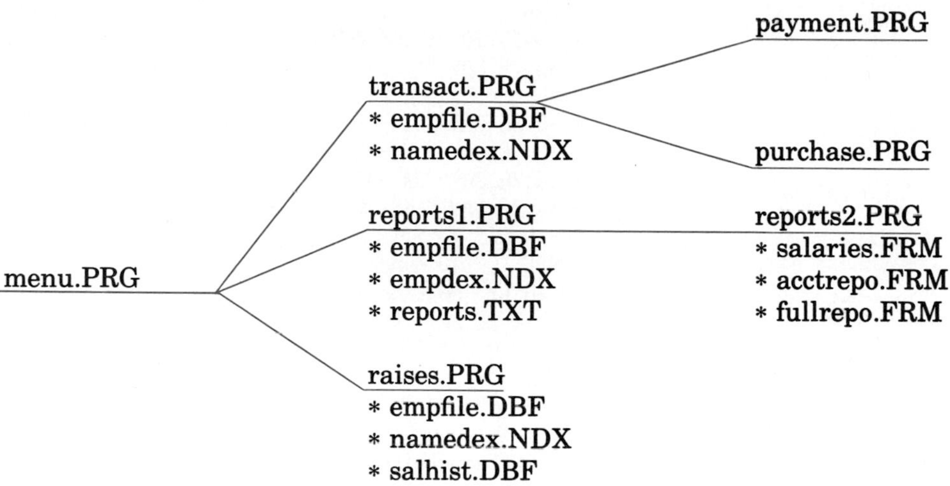

Program Listing

```
* PROGRAM:  Menu.PRG  -  main menu to call programs

SET TALK OFF
SET STATUS OFF
STORE .T. TO contmenu

DO WHILE contmenu
  CLEAR
  @  4,15 TO  18,60 DOUBLE
  @  5,20 SAY "     *  *  *  MAIN MENU  *  *  *   "

  @  8,20 SAY " 1 - Employee Account Transactions "
  @ 10,20 SAY " 2 - Reports                       "
  @ 12,20 SAY " 3 - Salary Increases              "
  @ 14,20 SAY " 4 - Quit                          "

  STORE " " TO menchoice
  DO WHILE .NOT. menchoice $ "1234"
    @ 17,25 SAY "ENTER SELECTION  " GET menchoice PICTURE "9"
    READ
  ENDDO

  DO CASE
     CASE menchoice = "1"
       DO transact
     CASE menchoice = "2"
       DO reports1
     CASE menchoice = "3"
       DO raises
     OTHERWISE
       STORE .F. TO contmenu
  ENDCASE
ENDDO

CLOSE ALL
CLEAR
SET TALK ON
SET STATUS ON

RETURN
```

Preliminary Commands

```
. DO menu
```

Sample Execution

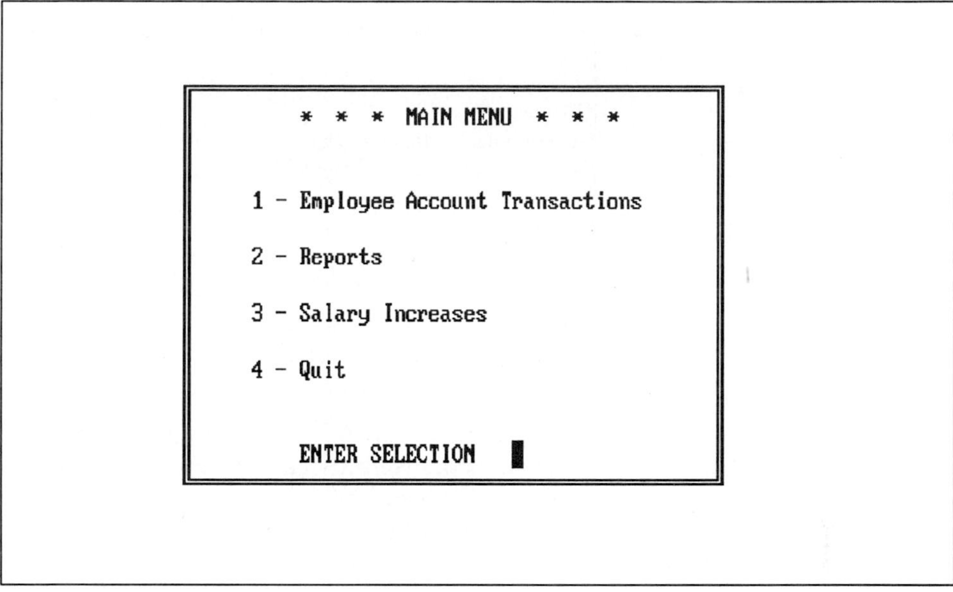

* * * MAIN MENU * * *
1 - Employee Account Transactions
2 - Reports
3 - Salary Increases
4 - Quit
ENTER SELECTION

PROGRAMMING TIPS

1. If you have a command that is longer than 65 characters, dBASE's text editor (**MODIFY COMMAND**) will automatically wrap the command down to the next line as you type it in. When dBASE wraps a command, the far right side of the editing screen will not display the normal "<" character. This indicates that the Enter key was not typed at the end of the line. dBASE stops evaluating a command when it encounters an Enter key character. To remove an Enter key character that is accidentally included in an extended command, move the cursor to the end of the line and type **^**T. Then type spaces until dBASE rewraps the line. dBASE command lines may actually be up to 254 characters long.
2. You may want to leave blank lines in your program to improve readability. Blank lines will not affect how the program runs; neither will indenting program lines. The practice of indenting command structures is invaluable to program debugging and readability, as demonstrated in the example dBASE command files.
3. The **MODIFY COMMAND** text editor can handle command files up to 4,096 bytes (characters) long. Files approaching this limit begin to show considerable delays in editing operations. Commands entered beyond this limit will be truncated from the file by dBASE.

dBASE is a procedural language, designed for creating interrelated programs to accomplish a processing task. The separate programs (procedures) are connected through structures of program calls and returns. This fundamental difference between dBASE and other programming languages, such as BASIC, requires that the programmer design systems that are subroutine in nature.

4. When dBASE encounters a syntax error in a program, it will display a message similar to:

```
Syntax error.
          ?
SET TALK TO OFF
Called from - A:menu.prg
Cancel, Ignore, or Suspend? (C, I, or S)
```

At this point, you may type “C” to cancel program execution and then use **MODIFY COMMAND** to open the file and correct the error. If the error is not going to have any serious effect on the rest of the program, you may type “I” to ignore the command line that produced the error and continue execution of the program.

You also may type “S” to suspend execution of the program. This allows you to execute commands from the dot (.) prompt and then continue the program. For example, you may want to view memory variable contents with the **DISPLAY MEMORY** command, store a value to a variable with the **STORE** command, or create an index file needed by the program.

When a program is suspended, memory variables created in the program will be in memory; if it is cancelled, the variables are lost. While a program is suspended, the file remains open and cannot be edited with **MODIFY COMMAND.** From the dot (.) prompt, you may type **RESUME** to continue execution of the suspended program or **CANCEL** to cancel execution and close the file.

SUSPEND is also a command that may be placed in a command file for debugging purposes. Use **SUSPEND** when you wish to check values of memory variables or the status of the environment at a certain point in the program. Other dBASE commands useful for debugging command files are **SET DEBUG on / OFF, SET ECHO on / OFF,** and **SET STEP on / OFF.**

EXERCISES

EXERCISE 1
Required Preliminary Exercise

Before completing the other dBASE III Plus exercises found in this module, you will need to create two small database files. This exercise will provide you with instructions on how to create the files.

Required Preparation

Study the explanations of the **APPEND FROM, BROWSE, CREATE, DISPLAY,** and **REPLACE** commands found in the dBASE III Plus Command Summary.

Exercise Steps

1. Load dBASE III Plus into memory.

In the tutorial lessons, you created a database that was kept intentionally simple. For instance, the data for the employees' first and last names were kept in the same field. Normally, first and last names would be placed in separate fields in the record. Additional fields for name titles (such as Mr., Ms., Ph.D, Dr., etc.), fields for middle initials, nicknames, and so on, might be considered for inclusion in the record structure. Telephone numbers often have extensions and/or area codes associated with them. In the following steps, you will create a new database file called "empinfo." The file will be used to hold address and phone information for the same group of employees. Each record also includes a special "key" field (named "empno") which is used to hold the company's employee number for that person.

2. Use the **CREATE** <filename> command to define the following record structure for the database file empinfo.

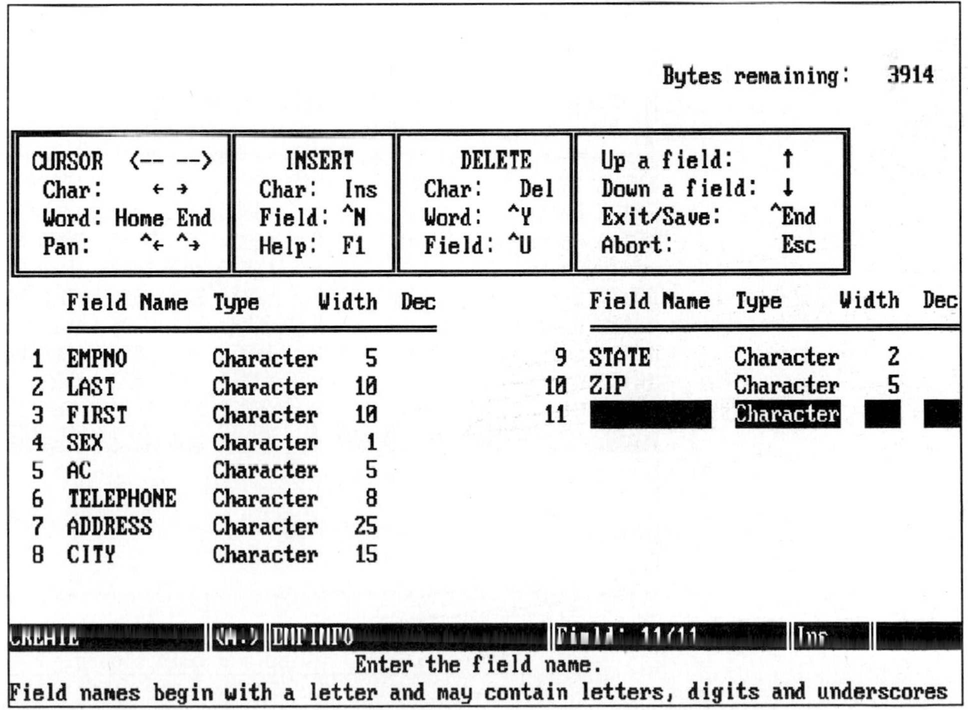

3. When finished, type ||^End,↵,N|| to complete the operation without inputting data records at this time.
4. Use the **USE** <filename> command to make empinfo the current database file. Then use the **APPEND FROM** <filename> to copy all fields having the same name in the file empfile to the current database file, empinfo.
5. Next type ||**GO TOP**||. Use the **BROWSE** command to see that the telephone numbers and gender data have been copied to empinfo.

```
EMPNO LAST------ FIRST----- SEX AC--- TELEPHONE ADDRESS-----------------
                            M         225-1234
                            F         225-3212
                            M         292-3832
                            F         224-4321
                            M         221-1235
                            M         244-1010
                            F         222-2123
                            F         229-1111
                            M         223-7928
```

6. Exit the **BROWSE** editing mode and then use the **REPLACE** [<scope>] <field> **WITH** <exp> command to replace all area code fields (ac) with the string data "(503)".
7. Use the **BROWSE** command to enter or edit the following fields of data. Notice that two of the area codes need to be changed to (206).

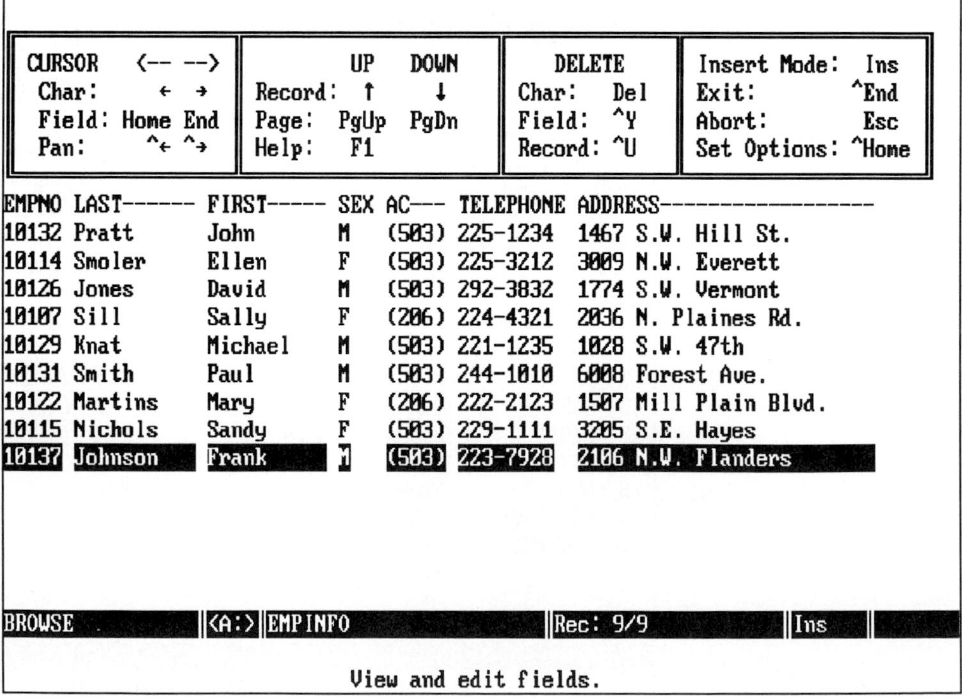

```
CURSOR    <-- -->        UP   DOWN       DELETE        Insert Mode:   Ins
 Char:     ←   →    Record:  ↑    ↓     Char:   Del    Exit:         ^End
 Field: Home End    Page:  PgUp  PgDn   Field:  ^Y     Abort:         Esc
 Pan:     ^←  ^→    Help:   F1          Record: ^U     Set Options: ^Home

EMPNO LAST------ FIRST----- SEX AC--- TELEPHONE ADDRESS-----------------
10132 Pratt      John       M   (503) 225-1234  1467 S.W. Hill St.
10114 Smoler     Ellen      F   (503) 225-3212  3009 N.W. Everett
10126 Jones      David      M   (503) 292-3832  1774 S.W. Vermont
10107 Sill       Sally      F   (206) 224-4321  2036 N. Plaines Rd.
10129 Knat       Michael    M   (503) 221-1235  1028 S.W. 47th
10131 Smith      Paul       M   (503) 244-1010  6008 Forest Ave.
10122 Martins    Mary       F   (206) 222-2123  1507 Mill Plain Blvd.
10115 Nichols    Sandy      F   (503) 229-1111  3205 S.E. Hayes
10137 Johnson    Frank      M   (503) 223-7928  2106 N.W. Flanders

BROWSE          <A:> EMPINFO              Rec: 9/9             Ins

                         View and edit fields.
```

8. Exit the **BROWSE** editing mode and use the **REPLACE** [<scope>] <field> **WITH** <exp> command to replace all city fields with the string data "Portland", all state fields with the string data "OR", and all ZIP code fields with the string data "972".
9. Now use the **BROWSE FIELDS** <field list> command to edit only the fields named first, last, city, state, and ZIP. Change the field data to reflect the following.

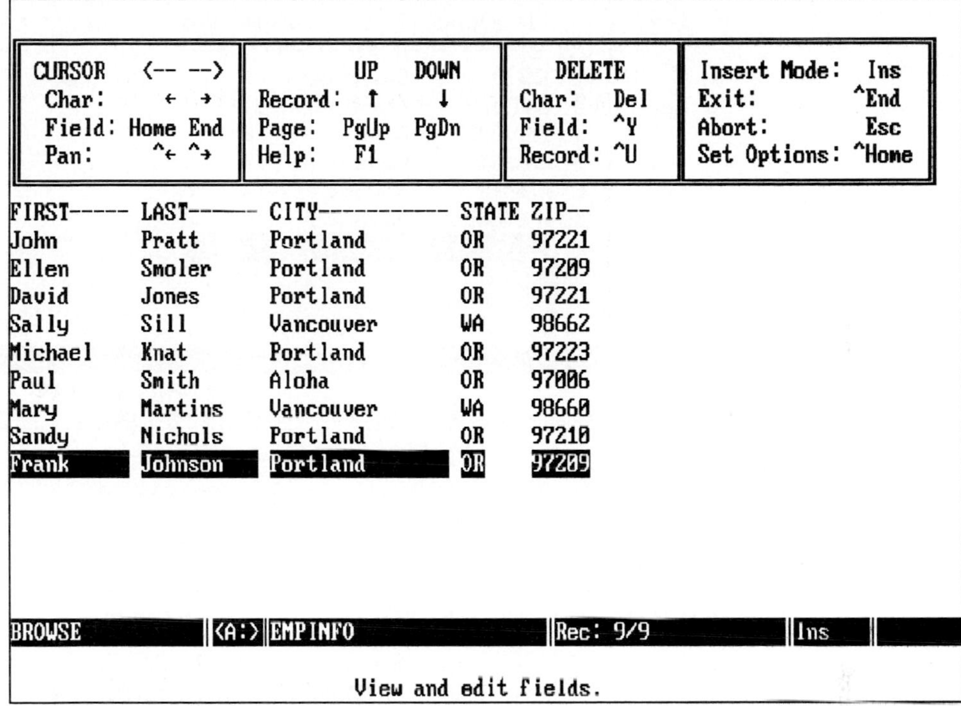

10. Exit the **BROWSE** editing mode and close the database file by typing ||**USE**↵||.
11. Now use the **CREATE** <filename> command to define the following record structure for the new database file empacct.

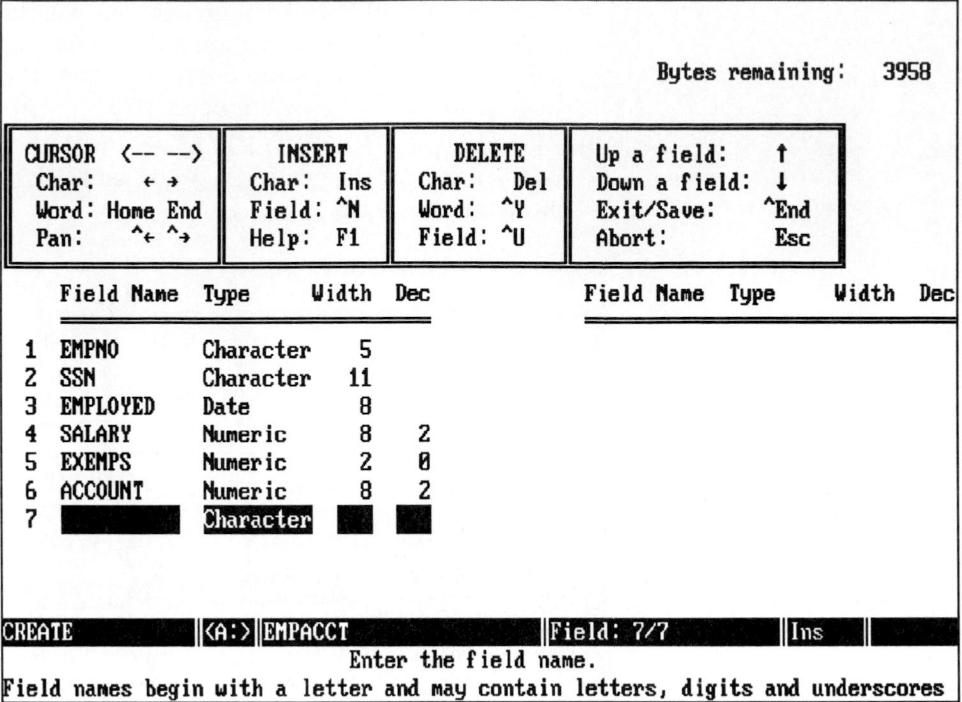

12. When finished type ‖^End,↵,N‖ to complete the operation without inputting data records.
13. Use the **USE** <filename> command to make empacct the current database file. Then use the **APPEND FROM** <filename> to copy all fields having the same name in the file empfile to the current database file empacct.
14. Now use the **BROWSE** editing mode to see that the fields employed, salary, and account have been copied to the new database file.

EMPNO	SSN--------	EMPLOYED	SALARY--	EXEMPS	ACCOUNT-
		06/22/82	1949.00		200.00
		09/15/83	1650.00		300.00
		06/15/82	1550.00		275.75
		02/15/84	1507.00		150.00
		09/15/80	1800.00		125.00
		11/15/81	1700.00		350.00
		11/01/85	1600.00		200.50
		02/15/86	1450.00		175.00
		03/20/90	1500.00		0.00

As a shortcut to data entry and a way to ensure that the employee numbers are exactly the same in each database, you will next put two database files into use at the same time, link the two record pointers by setting a relation to the record numbers found in each database, and then replace the empno fields in empacct with the empno fields found in empinfo. A complete explanation of the process is premature at this point; however, you may refer to the operation and command summary for more information on each of the commands used here if you desire.

15. Exit the **BROWSE** editing mode and then type the following commands.

    USE empacct↵
    SELECT 2↵
    USE empinfo↵
    SET RELATION TO RECNO() INTO empacct↵
    REPLACE ALL empacct->empno **WITH** empinfo->empno↵
    CLOSE ALL
    SELECT 1
    USE empacct

16. Now use the **BROWSE** editing mode to enter the remaining data for the empacct database file as shown here.

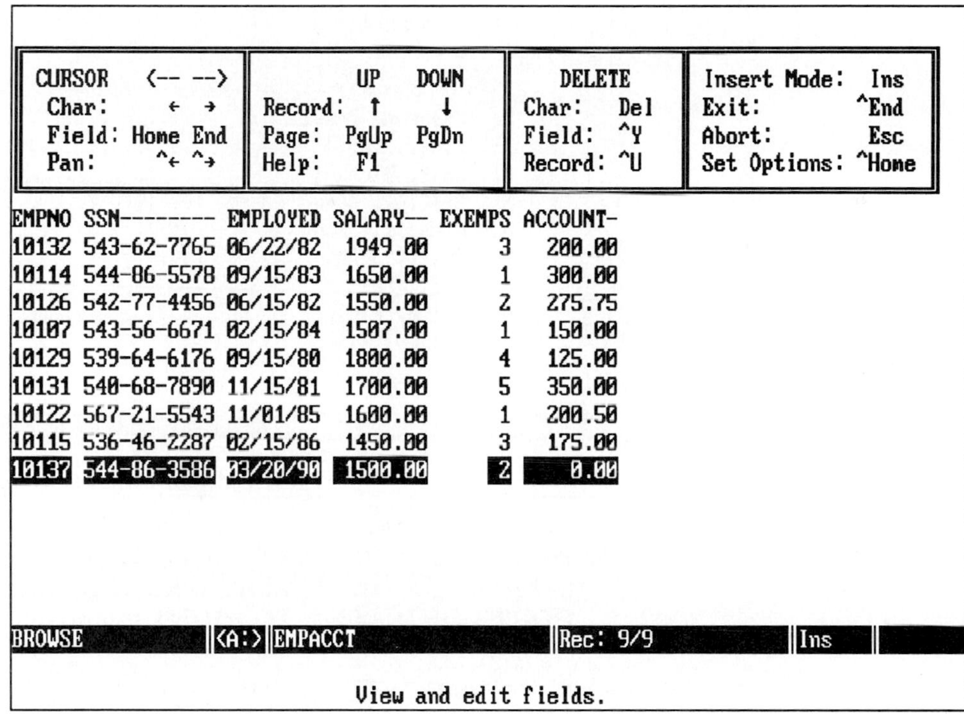

EMPNO	SSN--------	EMPLOYED	SALARY--	EXEMPS	ACCOUNT-
10132	543-62-7765	06/22/82	1949.00	3	200.00
10114	544-86-5578	09/15/83	1650.00	1	300.00
10126	542-77-4456	06/15/82	1550.00	2	275.75
10107	543-56-6671	02/15/84	1507.00	1	150.00
10129	539-64-6176	09/15/80	1800.00	4	125.00
10131	540-68-7890	11/15/81	1700.00	5	350.00
10122	567-21-5543	11/01/85	1600.00	1	200.50
10115	536-46-2287	02/15/86	1450.00	3	175.00
10137	544-86-3586	03/20/90	1500.00	2	0.00

17. Exit the **BROWSE** editing mode and then use the **DISPLAY** <scope> **TO PRINT** command to print out the contents of the database files empacct and empinfo.
18. Use the **QUIT** command to close all files and exit dBASE.

EXERCISE 2 Employee Phone Numbers

This exercise uses the empinfo database file to produce a list of employee telephone numbers that will be copied and mailed to each employee's home address.

Required Preparation

Study the explanations of the **MODIFY REPORT, MODIFY LABEL,** and **INDEX** commands as well as the **TRIM** and **IIF** functions found in the dBASE III Plus Operation and Command Summary.

Exercise Steps

1. Load dBASE III Plus into memory.
2. Use the appropriate dBASE commands to produce the following report from the indexed file empinfo.

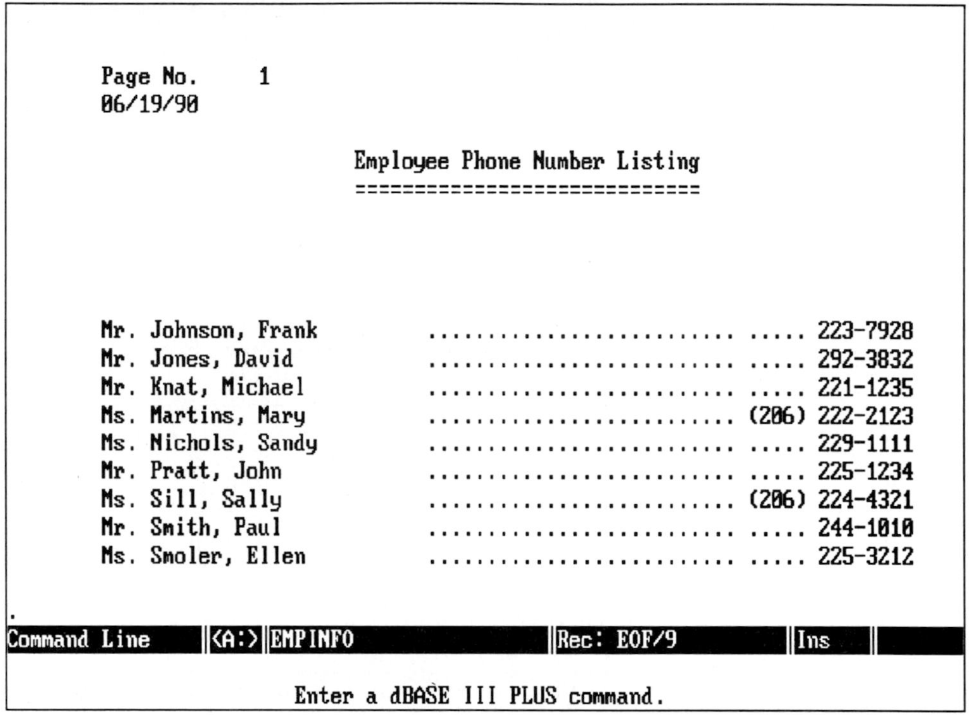

```
Page No.     1
06/19/90

                    Employee Phone Number Listing
                    =============================

Mr. Johnson, Frank      ......................... ..... 223-7928
Mr. Jones, David        ......................... ..... 292-3832
Mr. Knat, Michael       ......................... ..... 221-1235
Ms. Martins, Mary       ......................... (206) 222-2123
Ms. Nichols, Sandy      ......................... ..... 229-1111
Mr. Pratt, John         ......................... ..... 225-1234
Ms. Sill, Sally         ......................... (206) 224-4321
Mr. Smith, Paul         ......................... ..... 244-1010
Ms. Smoler, Ellen       ......................... ..... 225-3212

.
Command Line  ||<A:>||EMPINFO          ||Rec: EOF/9    ||Ins  ||

                    Enter a dBASE III PLUS command.
```

3. Write down the expressions you used for each column's contents and the name you gave the .FRM file when you created it. Then, use the **REPORT FORM** <file> **TO PRINT** command to produce a printed copy of the list.
4. Use the **MODIFY LABEL** command to produce a **LABEL FORM** that will generate the following type of address labels. (Do not change Options for the label form and use the first three lines of the label to enter your expressions.)

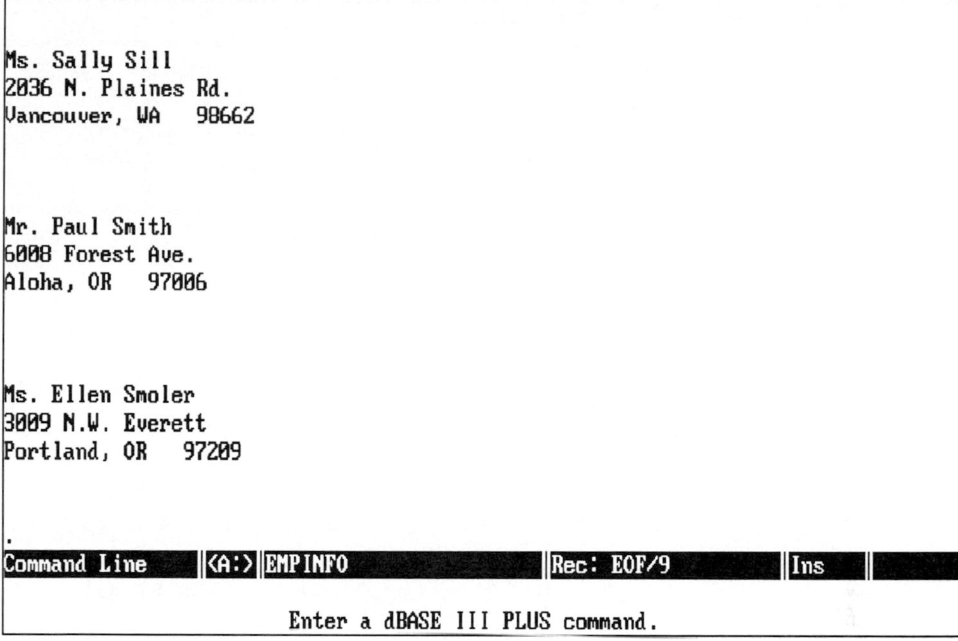
```
Ms. Sally Sill
2036 N. Plaines Rd.
Vancouver, WA   98662


Mr. Paul Smith
6008 Forest Ave.
Aloha, OR   97006


Ms. Ellen Smoler
3009 N.W. Everett
Portland, OR   97209

.
Command Line  ||<A:>||EMPINFO        ||Rec: EOF/9      ||Ins ||

                    Enter a dBASE III PLUS command.
```

5. Write down the expressions you used for each column's contents and the name you gave the .LBL file when you created it. Then, use the **LABEL FORM** <file> **TO PRINT** command to produce a printed copy of the list.
6. Use the **QUIT** command to close all files and exit dBASE.

EXERCISE 3 Data Entry Screens

This exercise produces a customized full-screen editing screen for use when adding or editing records of the empinfo database file.

Required Preparation

Study the explanations of the @ **SAY,** @ **GET, READ, MODIFY SCREEN,** and **SET FORMAT TO** commands found in the dBASE III Plus Operation and Command Summary.

Exercise Steps

1. Load dBASE III Plus into memory.

dBASE III Plus format (.FMT) files are used to create customized screens for data input and/or output. They contain @ **SAY,** @ **GET,** and **READ** commands only. They may be created in one of two ways: by entering the commands directly into the .FMT file through the use of dBASE's **MODIFY COMMAND** command or by using the **MODIFY SCREEN** command. In this exercise, you will first create a small test .FMT file through the use of the **MODIFY COMMAND** command.

2. Type ||**MODIFY COMMAND** test.FMT↵||. Then use the **MODIFY** text editing mode to enter the following commands.

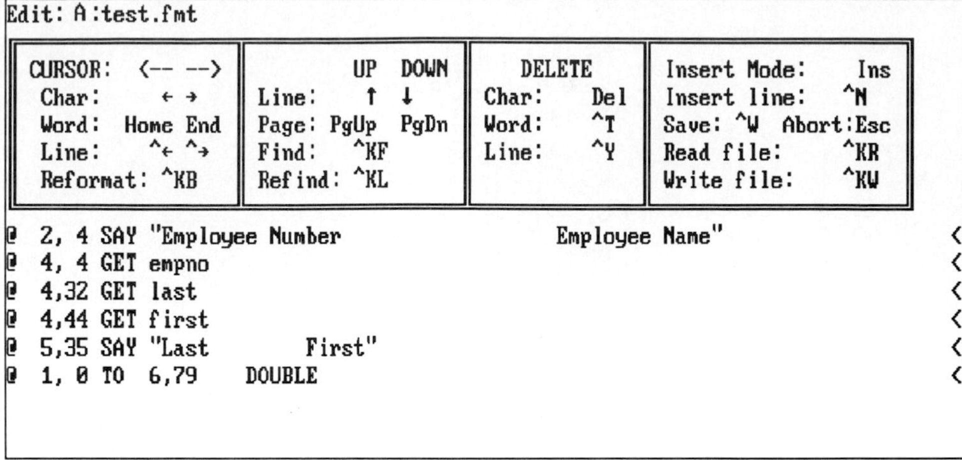

3. When finished type ||**^**End|| to save the file and exit the editing mode.
4. Use the **USE** <file> command to make empinfo the current database file. Then use the **SET FORMAT TO** <file> command to open the test.FMT file.

With empinfo in use and the format file in effect (open), the full-screen editing commands **EDIT, APPEND,** or **READ** will use the screen coordinates, text, and fields specified in the .FMT file to produce an editing screen.

5. Type ||**EDIT**←|| to view the screen produced by test.FMT.

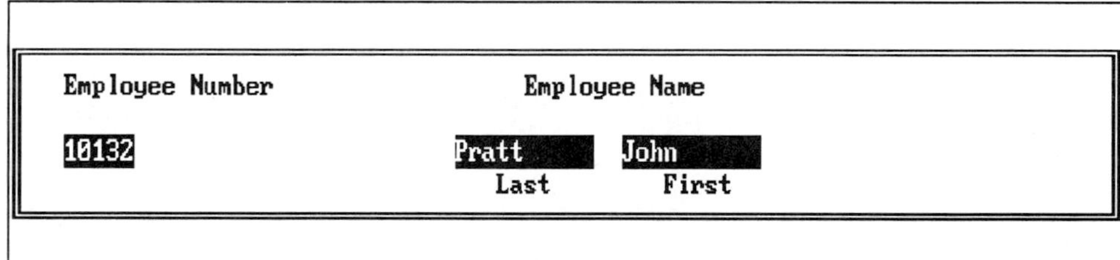

6. Type the PgDn key a few times to see the other records in the database file. Then type the Esc key to exit the editing mode.

When creating an .FMT file in this manner, you must calculate the screen coordinates for the @ **SAY** and @ **GET** commands manually, and then type them in. Another method of creating an .FMT file allows you to place text and fields on a screen and, when finished, the command used automatically generates an .FMT file with @ **SAY** and @ **GET** commands that accurately reflect the screen placement of the data.

7. Type ||**MODIFY SCREEN** empinpt←||. The following will appear on the screen.

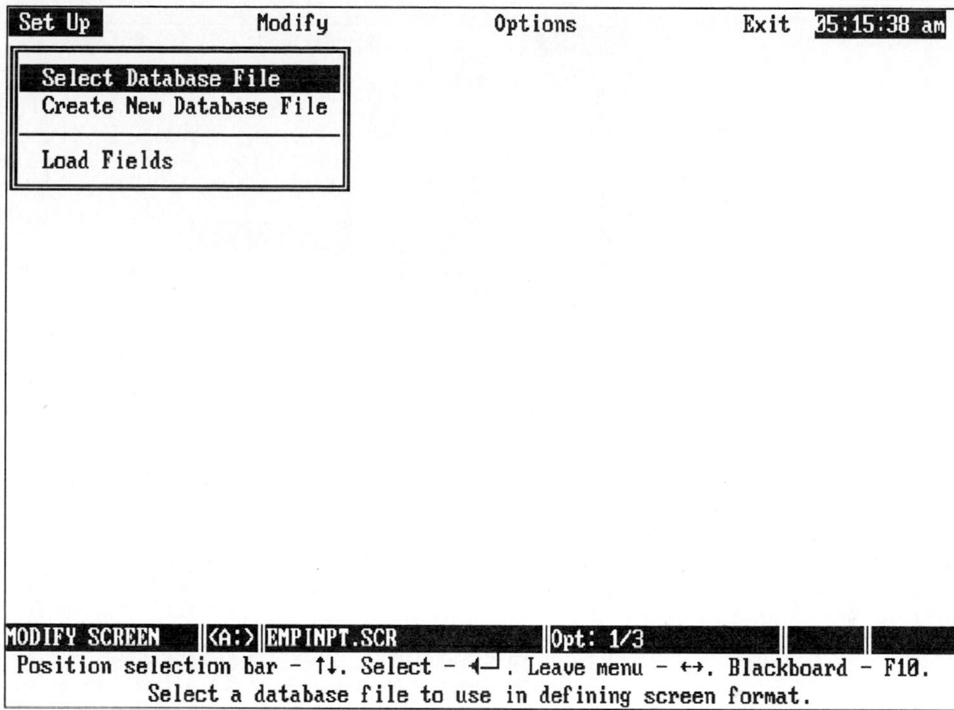

8. Type ↵ and select empinfo as the database file by moving the pull-down menu bar to its name and then typing ↵ again.
9. Use the "Load Fields" command to load all fields of the database by marking each one with ↵.

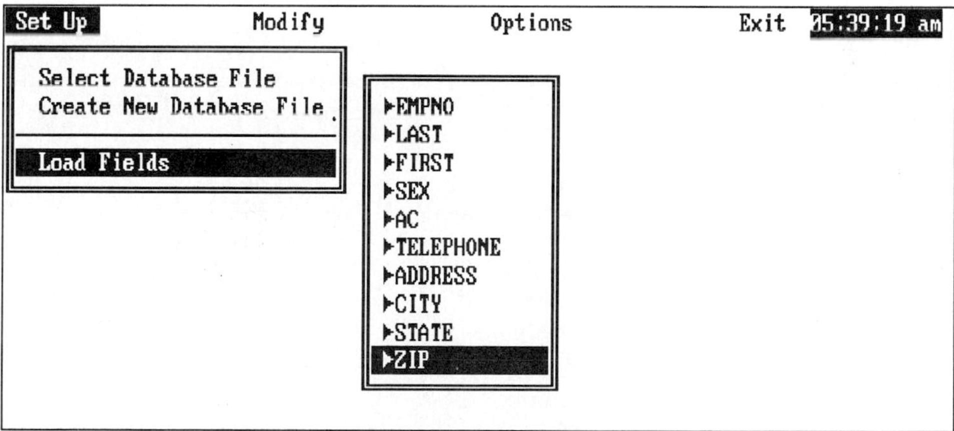

10. When finished, type ||^End|| to load the fields and automatically switch to the "blackboard" mode of the **MODIFY SCREEN** command.

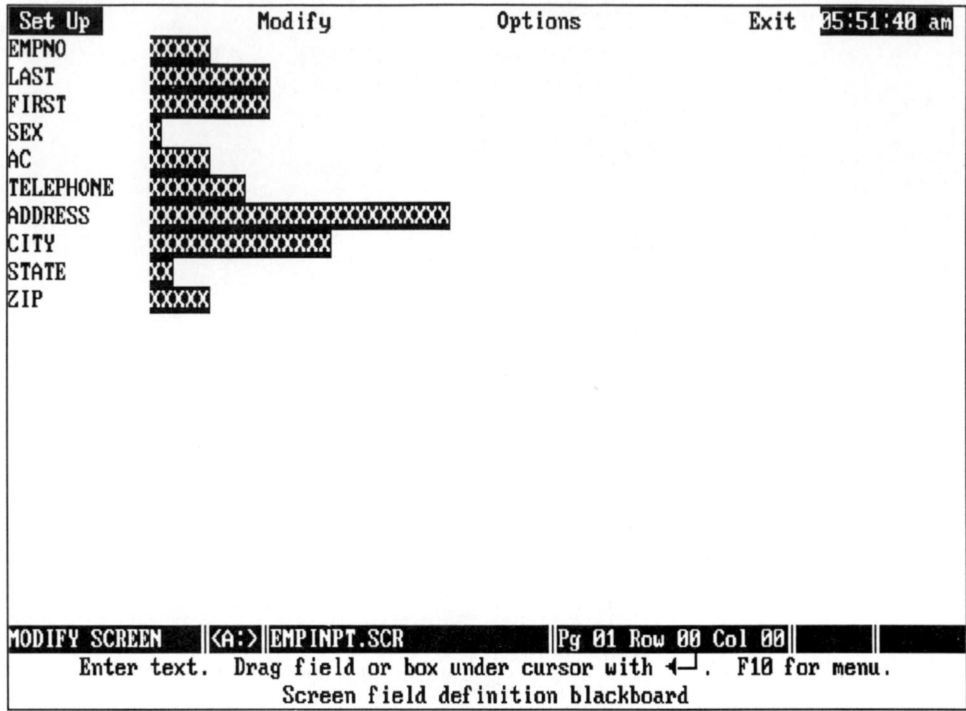

The areas on the screen shown in reverse video and filled with *X*s represent the fields that have been loaded onto the screen. dBASE places the field names next to them so that you can tell which field is which. You now are ready to begin composing the input screen. The following is a summary of editing operations available to you while in the **MODIFY SCREEN** blackboard mode.

Action Desired	Keystrokes
Cursor Movement	
Character Left	Left ←
Character Right	Right →
Field Right	End
Field Left	Home
Line Down	Down ↓
Line Up	Up ↑
Insert/Overwrite	Ins
Insert Line	^N (or ←┘ with Ins ON)
Delete Line	^Y
Delete Characters	
Current Character	Delete (Del)
Previous Character	Backspace
Word Right of Cursor	^T

To move a field on the screen—Move the cursor to the field and type ←┘. Then move the cursor to the new location and type ←┘ again.

To abort the **MODIFY SCREEN** operation—Type F10 and then select the "Exit, Abandon" command.

In completing the next exercise step, you may find the following hints helpful. Begin by inserting 8 or 9 lines at the top of the screen and then type a field label into the blank area. Next, move to the appropriate field for the label and move it next to the label. Next, move to the field name for that field and delete it from the screen.

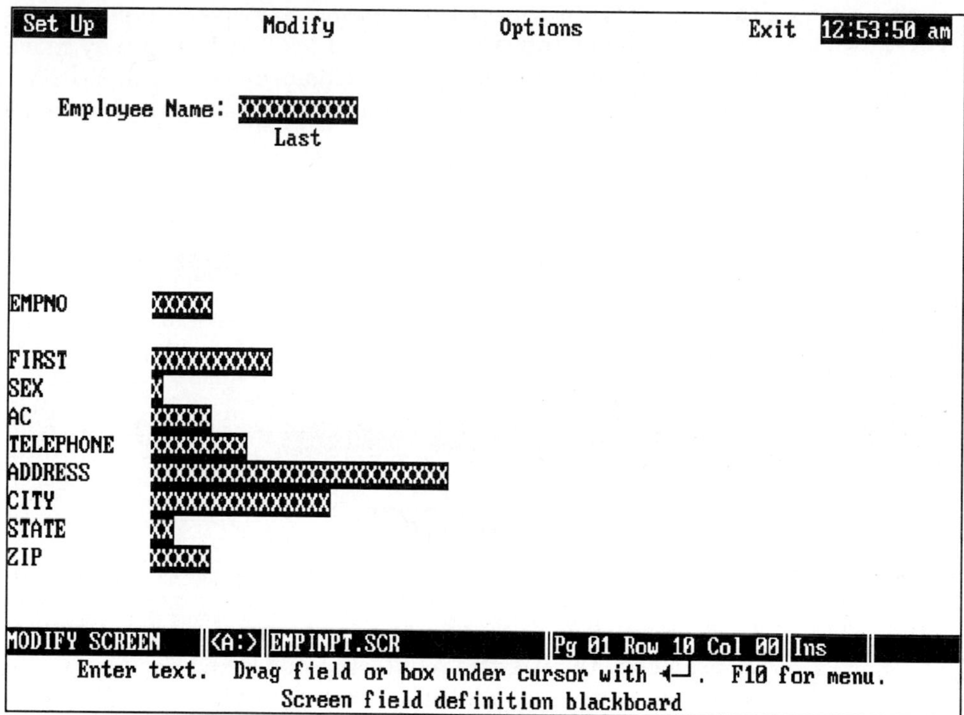

11. Use the blackboard mode of the **MODIFY SCREEN** command to compose an input screen similar to the following.

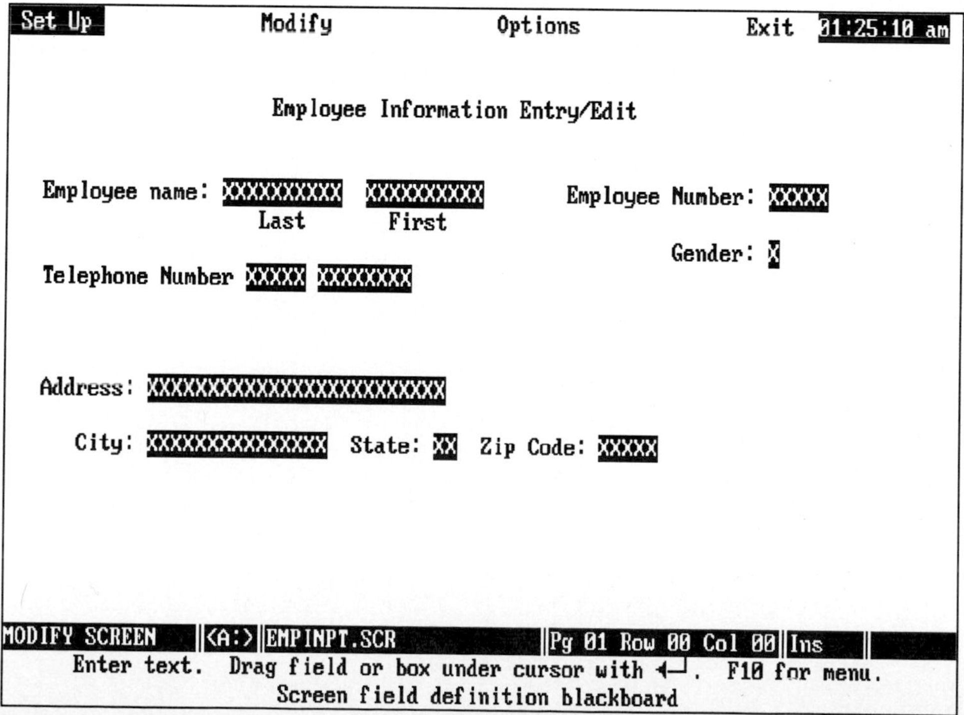

12. When finished, type F10 and then select the Options pull-down menu.

In the next step you will place a double-line box around the screen heading. To do so, you first select Option's Double bar menu item, which will automatically put you back into the blackboard mode. You then move the cursor to one corner of where you want the box drawn and type ↵. You then move the cursor to the diagonally opposite corner and type ↵ again. If you later want to change the size or shape of the block, you may move the cursor to where the box needs adjustment (somewhere on the box itself), type ↵, then move the cursor in the desired direction. When the box appears as you want it to appear, type ↵ again.

13. Place a double bar box around the heading as shown here.

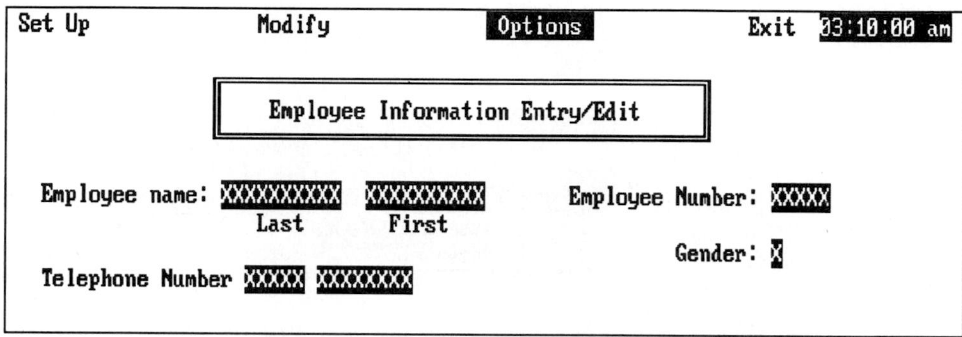

In the next steps you will add *picture clauses* to the .FMT file. A picture clause keeps the user from entering undesired data into a field when the .FMT file is used to present a screen for data entry. For instance, specifying a picture of "99999" for the employee number field will prevent the user from entering any non-number character into the field (such as typing a lower-case "l" for a number 1).

14. Move the cursor to the field for employee number and then type F10 to return to the **MODIFY SCREEN** menus. Select the "Picture Template" option of the "Modify" command and then enter five 9s into the "Picture value" area at the bottom of the screen.

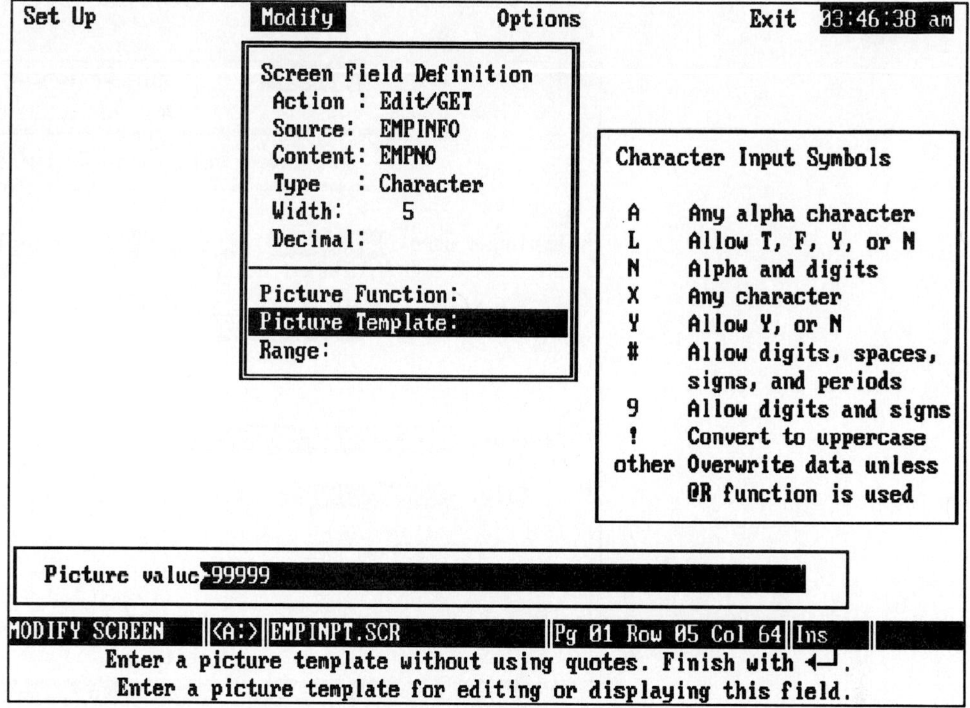

Take a moment to read the "Character Input Symbols" explanation shown on the screen. Each character in a picture clause restricts data entry in a different manner. You may notice that the character *X* allows any characters to be entered and that *X* is the default picture character used by the **MODIFY SCREEN** command.

15. Now type ||↵,F10|| to return to the blackboard mode and repeat the last steps to make the following restrictions on data entry.
    a. Make the ZIP code field numbers only (99999).
    b. Make the Gender and State fields convert to upper case (!) and (!!).
    c. Include parentheses in the area code field ((999)).
    d. Make the telephone field three numbers, a dash, then four more numbers (999–9999).

When finished, the blackboard screen should appear as follows.

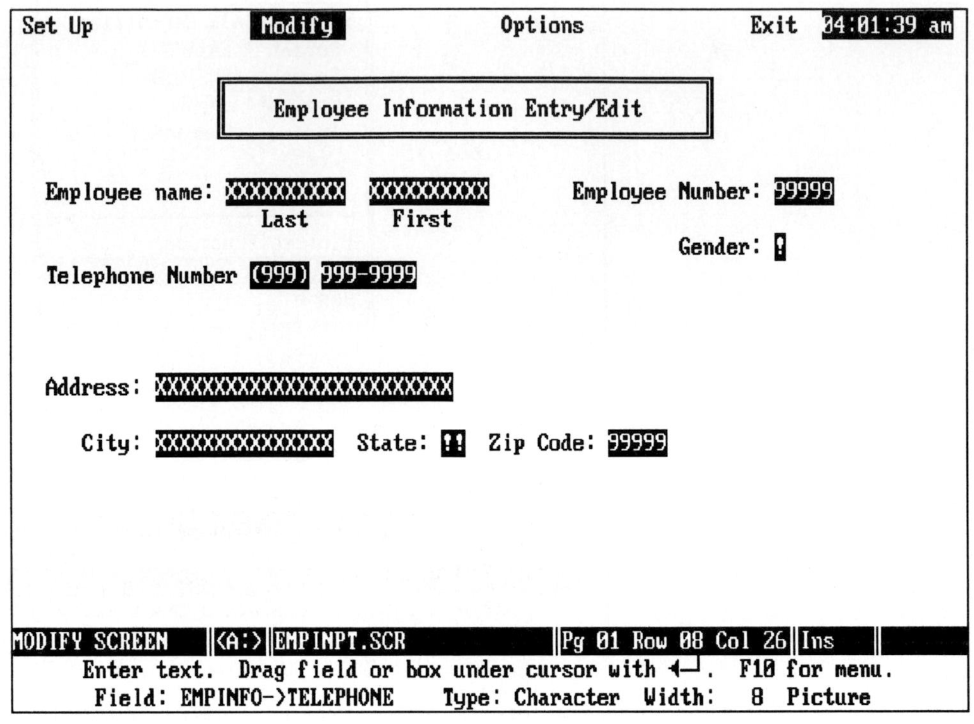

16. Now type F10 to return to the **MODIFY SCREEN** pull-down menus and select the “Exit, Save” command.
17. Next type ‖**SET FORMAT TO** empinpt←┘‖. Then type ‖**APPEND**←┘‖ to begin the operation of adding a record to the database file empinfo.
18. Enter some test data into each field presented on the screen. Try entering letters into the employee number or ZIP code fields. What happens if you try to enter lower-case letters into the gender or state fields? Notice that the user cannot forget to include the parentheses or hyphen in the telephone number.
19. When finished, type Esc to abort adding the record and then use the **TYPE** <file> **TO PRINT** command to print a copy of the empinpt.FMT file on the printer. Next, use the **QUIT** command to exit dBASE III Plus.

EXERCISE 4
Form Letters

This exercise requires that you create a dBASE command file (.PRG file) that, when executed, produces a form letter to be sent to all employees at their home addresses.

Required Preparation

Study the explanations of the **IF...ELSE...ENDIF, TEXT...ENDTEXT, DO WHILE...ENDDO** command structures, as well as the **SET MARGIN, SET PRINT, SET TALK,** and **EJECT** commands found in the dBASE III Plus Operation and Command Summary. Also study the discussion labeled "dBASE III Plus Command Files," pages D-67 through D-68.

Exercise Steps

The general algorithm for the program will be as follows.

1. Initialize: **USE** empinfo, **SET TALK OFF, SET MARGIN TO** 10.
2. Continue executing the following loop instructions until the end of the database file is reached.
   - **A.** Print two blank lines.
   - **B.** If the employee is male,
     - **a.** Print the employee's name with a "Mr." title.
   - **C.** Otherwise,
     - **a.** Print the employee's name with a "Ms." title.

     End If.
   - **D.** Print two blank lines and the letter's salutation.
   - **E.** Begin text.
     - **a.** Print the letter's text.

     End text.
   - **F.** Eject the page.
   - **G.** Move the record pointer to the next record.
3. End of loop instructions.
4. **USE, SET TALK ON, SET MARGIN TO** 0, **RETURN.**

The printed letter for the first record in the database will have the following form.

Mr. John Pratt
1467 S.W. Hill St.
Portland OR 97221

Dear John:

As you may already know, Philip Shear is retiring from his position as chief controller at the end of this month. There will be a reception held in the Cascade room on March 20th at 3:00 P.M. to honor his 25 years of service to the company, and to wish him well in his retirement years.

Your attendance to this important company function will be greatly appreciated.

R.S.V.P. (Regrets only)

Sincerely,

Chip Johnson
Extension 3723
Human Resources Department

1. Write out the commands that will be included in the command file in the order that they will occur before you begin to create the file.
2. Load dBASE III Plus into memory and use the text editing mode of the **MODIFY COMMAND** command to create the .PRG file.
3. Test the program by running it so that the output is displayed on the screen.
4. When the program is functioning correctly, use the **SET PRINT ON** command to send the output to the printer. Then run the program.
5. When finished, type ||**SET PRINT OFF**||. Then use the **TYPE** <file> **TO PRINT** command to print a copy of the program. Next, use the **QUIT** command to exit dBASE III Plus.

EXERCISE 5
Relating Database Files

The following exercise demonstrates the steps involved in bringing two or more database files into use at one time.

Required Preparation

Study the explanations of the **SEEK, SELECT,** and **SET RELATION TO** <expression> **INTO** <alias> commands found in the dBASE III Plus Operation and Command Summary.

Exercise Steps

When creating the record structure of a database, you will want to include one or more fields that uniquely identify a record. For instance, in the database empinfo.DBF there is a field named "empno", which is used to hold the employee number associated with the other data items of the same record. In such a database, you could reasonably assume that no two employees would have the same employee number. Such a field has a special relationship to the other data items in the record and is called a *unique* data item. In exercise 1 you created another database file named "empacct.DBF" which also contained a unique data item. As an intentional element of design, the data in the unique field (also named "empno") of empacct.DBF exactly matches the data found in the empno fields of the empinfo.DBF database file. In other words, the employee numbers were used in each database to uniquely identify the records in which they occurred.

While a complete discussion of concepts pertaining to the nature of data is beyond the scope of this manual, the following exercise demonstrates some basic concepts of database design and presents the steps involved in accessing more than one database file at a time.

1. Load dBASE III Plus into memory.

dBASE allows up to ten database files to be in use at the same time. Each database is opened in its own *work area*.

2. Type the following commands.

	SELECT 1↵	
	USE empinfo↵	
	SELECT 2↵	
	USE empacct↵	

At this time there are two database files in use.

3. Type the following commands to see that each database is now open in its own work area.

	SELECT 1↵	
	DISPLAY ALL↵	
	SELECT 2↵	
	DISPLAY ALL↵	

When more than one database file is in use, each maintains its own record pointer. A command that affects the position of the record pointor (such as the **DISPLAY** command) normally affects only the record pointer for the current database file (the database file residing in the currently selected work area). Commands may reference fields existing in a non-selected database by including the *alias* for the referenced field. It is recommended that you enter an alias field name in the form database file->field name. To better understand how such references can be made, type the following commands shown in gray.

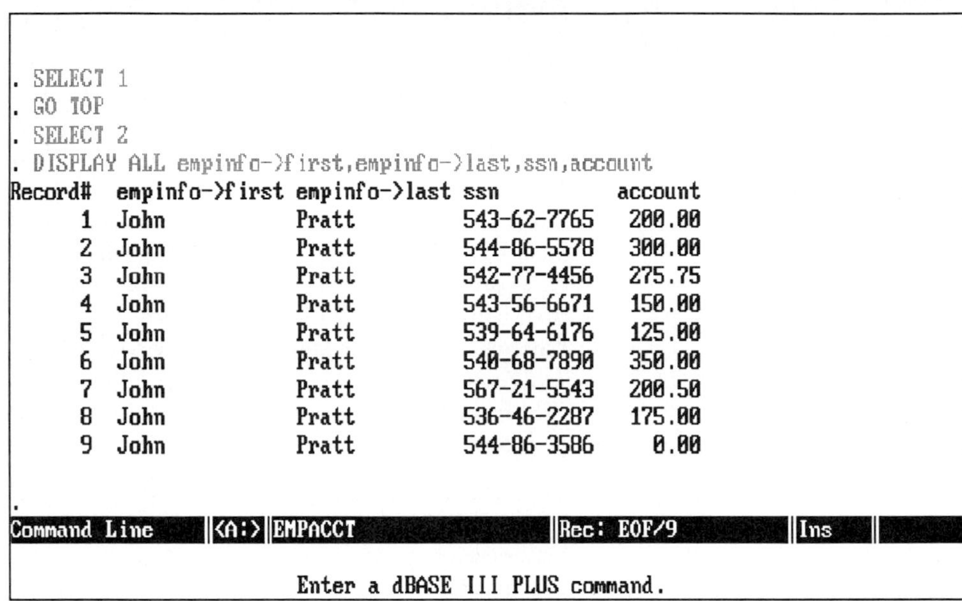

```
. SELECT 1
. GO TOP
. SELECT 2
. DISPLAY ALL empinfo->first,empinfo->last,ssn,account
Record#  empinfo->first empinfo->last ssn          account
      1  John           Pratt         543-62-7765   200.00
      2  John           Pratt         544-86-5578   300.00
      3  John           Pratt         542-77-4456   275.75
      4  John           Pratt         543-56-6671   150.00
      5  John           Pratt         539-64-6176   125.00
      6  John           Pratt         540-68-7890   350.00
      7  John           Pratt         567-21-5543   200.50
      8  John           Pratt         536-46-2287   175.00
      9  John           Pratt         544-86-3586     0.00

.
Command Line  |<A:>|EMPACCT            |Rec: EOF/9        |Ins |

                     Enter a dBASE III PLUS command.
```

Notice that the **ALL** scope used in the **DISPLAY** command affected only the record pointer in the current database, empacct. The record pointer in the empinfo database remained on the first record.

As previously mentioned, the two database files share a logically related primary key, which in this case is held in the field named "empno". In the empinfo database file, the empno field holding the employee number 10126 exists in the record that holds the address information for David Jones. In the empacct database file, the empno field that holds the number 10126 exists in the record that holds the social security number, employed date, and so on, for David Jones. When two or more database files are initially designed to contain matching primary keys in this manner, it becomes possible to link the record pointers in each database so that they will point to the records having related data in them. To give you experience performing such an operation, enter the following commands shown in gray.

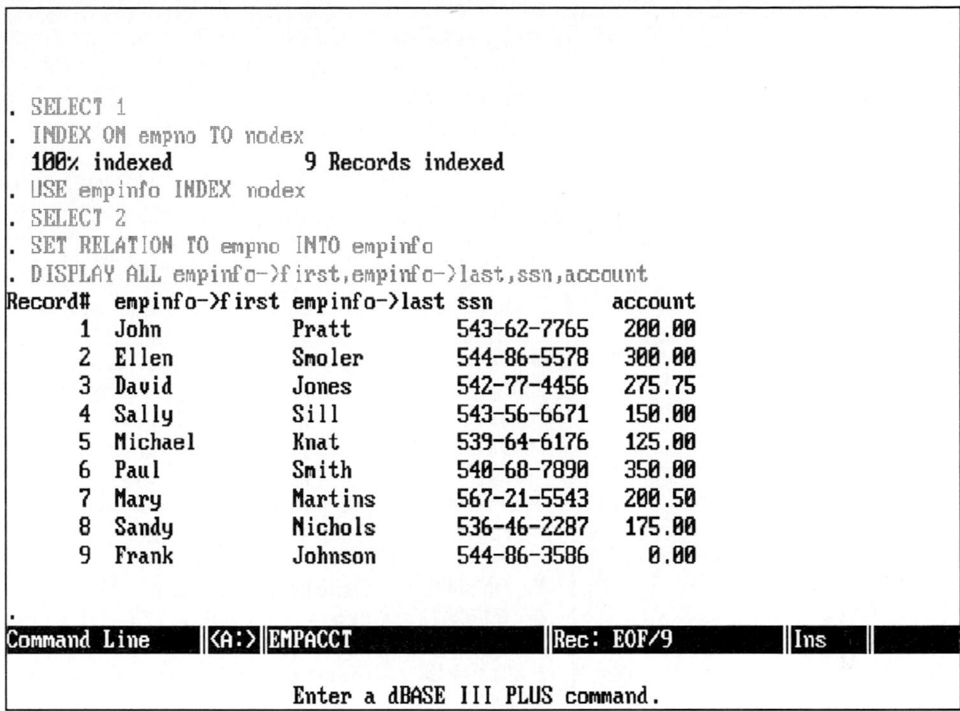

```
. SELECT 1
. INDEX ON empno TO nodex
  100% indexed          9 Records indexed
. USE empinfo INDEX nodex
. SELECT 2
. SET RELATION TO empno INTO empinfo
. DISPLAY ALL empinfo->first,empinfo->last,ssn,account
Record#  empinfo->first empinfo->last ssn          account
      1  John           Pratt         543-62-7765   200.00
      2  Ellen          Smoler        544-86-5578   300.00
      3  David          Jones         542-77-4456   275.75
      4  Sally          Sill          543-56-6671   150.00
      5  Michael        Knat          539-64-6176   125.00
      6  Paul           Smith         540-68-7890   350.00
      7  Mary           Martins       567-21-5543   200.50
      8  Sandy          Nichols       536-46-2287   175.00
      9  Frank          Johnson       544-86-3586     0.00

.
Command Line    ||<A:>||EMPACCT          ||Rec: EOF/9        ||Ins ||

                     Enter a dBASE III PLUS command.
```

In the preceding steps you created a dBASE III Plus relation between the database files named "empinfo" and empacct". In such a relationship, one database is referred to as the *parent* and the other is referred to as the *child*. Here, empinfo would be considered the child database file. The child database must be in use with an index file created on the primary key data item (in this case the field empno). The **SET RELATION TO** <expression> **INTO** <database file> command is issued from the work area in which the parent database resides. The expression specified in the command references data in the parent database and reflects the same expression used to create the child's index file. When fields are used to hold a primary key in two or more database files, it is not necessary for them to have the same name as they do here (empinfo->empno and empacct->empno). For instance, if the field holding the employee numbers in empacct had been originally named "eno", the command used to set the relation would have been **SET RELATION TO** eno **INTO** empinfo. Finally, the database file specified in the command names the child database for the relation.

Once a relation has been made, the record pointer in the parent database becomes the controlling pointer. When the record pointer of the parent database is moved to a record, dBASE evaluates the relation expression and performs a **SEEK** operation on the child database file. The record pointer in the child database file will be positioned at the first record matching the **SEEK** expression. If no such record is found, the record pointer is positioned at the end of the file.

To further demonstrate the use of multiple database files, you next will create a small parent database which will use empacct as its child database. The new database will be used to hold invoice information on purchases made by employees.

4. Type the following.

||**SELECT 3**↵||

||**CREATE** emppur↵||

Next, enter the following record structure for the emppur database.

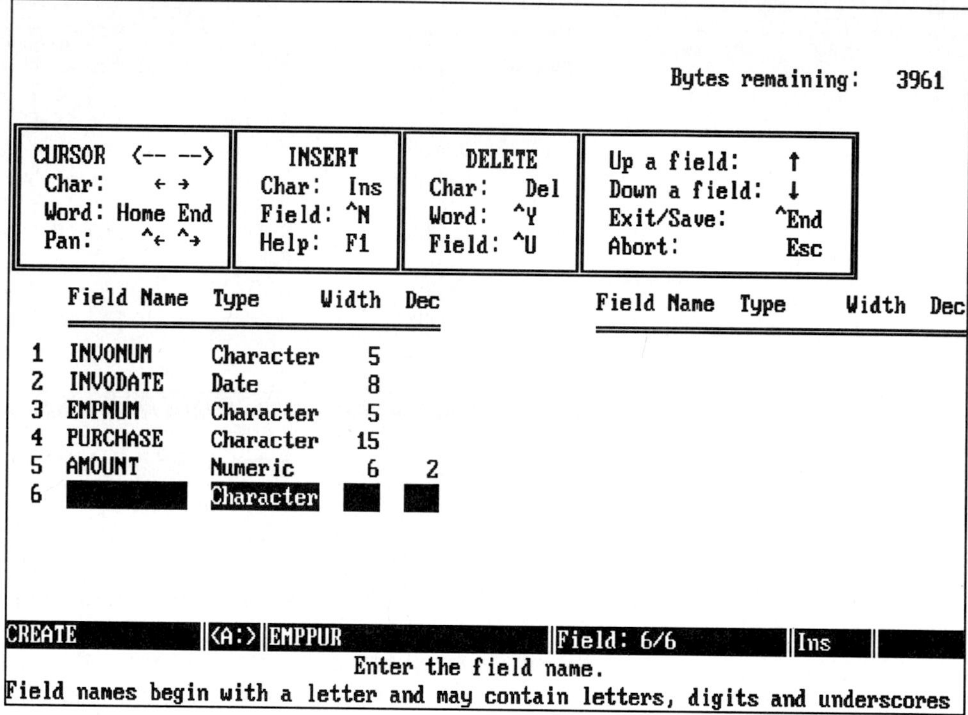

5. When finished, type ||^End,↵,Y|| to end the **CREATE** operation and begin entering records.

The record structure includes a field named "invonum" to hold the invoice number (which serves as the primary key for the emppur database records), a field for the purchase date named "invodate", a field for the employee number of the employee making the purchase (named "empnum" in this database), a field for a short description of the article purchased, and a field for the dollar amount of the purchase.

6. Enter six records into the database to reflect the following information:
   a. Invoice number 10012, date 03/19/90, Mary Martins (employee number 10122) purchased a barbecue on account for $69.00.
   b. Invoice number 10013, date 03/21/90, Paul Smith (employee number 10131) purchased a weed trimmer on account for $59.00.
   c. Invoice number 10014, date 03/21/90, Mary Martins (employee number 10122) purchased three lawn chairs on account for $89.95.
   d. Invoice number 10015, date 03/22/90, Mary Martins (employee number 10122) purchased a croquet set on account for $29.95.
   e. Invoice number 10016, date 03/23/90, Paul Smith (employee number 10131) purchased a hammock on account for $64.00.
   f. Invoice number 10017, date 03/23/90, Frank Johnson (employee number 10137) purchased a picnic table on account for $184.00.

7. When finished, type ↵ on the next record shown (record 7) to stop inputting records.

In the next steps you will relate the parent database emppur with the child database empacct.

8. Type

    ||**SELECT** 2↵||
    ||**INDEX ON** empno **TO** actnodex↵||
    ||**SELECT** 3↵||
    ||**USE** emppur↵||
    ||**SET RELATION TO** empnum **INTO** empacct↵||

Now that all three databases are in use and their record pointers are linked, you may access the fields of related data by using alias field names. For instance, if you wanted to see the invoice number, employee name, invoice amount, and current employee account balance for every invoice record in emppur, you would type the following shown in gray.

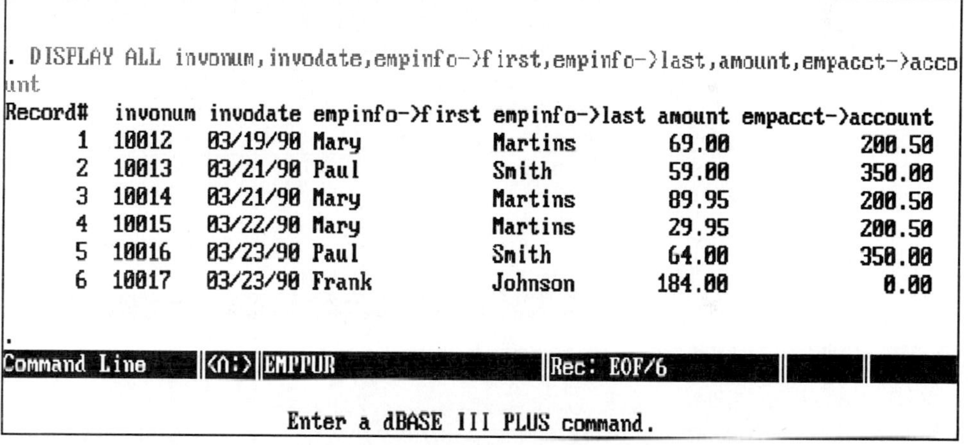

```
. DISPLAY ALL invonum,invodate,empinfo->first,empinfo->last,amount,empacct->acco
unt
Record#  invonum invodate empinfo->first empinfo->last amount empacct->account
      1  10012   03/19/90 Mary           Martins         69.00           200.50
      2  10013   03/21/90 Paul           Smith           59.00           350.00
      3  10014   03/21/90 Mary           Martins         89.95           200.50
      4  10015   03/22/90 Mary           Martins         29.95           200.50
      5  10016   03/23/90 Paul           Smith           64.00           350.00
      6  10017   03/23/90 Frank          Johnson        184.00             0.00

.
Command Line   ||<A:>||EMPPUR            ||Rec: EOF/6        ||   ||

                  Enter a dBASE III PLUS command.
```

9. Now use the **DISPLAY** <scope> <expression list> **FOR** <condition> **TO PRINT** command to produce the following printed information.

    The names, telephone numbers and invoice amounts for all employees having invoice amounts over $60.00.

```
  1  Mary         Martins     (206)    222-2123        69.00
  3  Mary         Martins     (206)    222-2123        89.95
  5  Paul         Smith       (503)    244-1010        64.00
  6  Frank        Johnson     (503)    223-7928       184.00
```

The names, telephone numbers, and invoice amounts for all employees having invoice amounts which, when added to their current account amounts, exceed 20 percent of their monthly salaries.

```
   2  Paul          Smith        (503)      244-1010            59.00
   5  Paul          Smith        (503)      244-1010            64.00
```

10. Use the **DISPLAY STATUS TO PRINT** command to produce a printed copy of the files that are currently open.

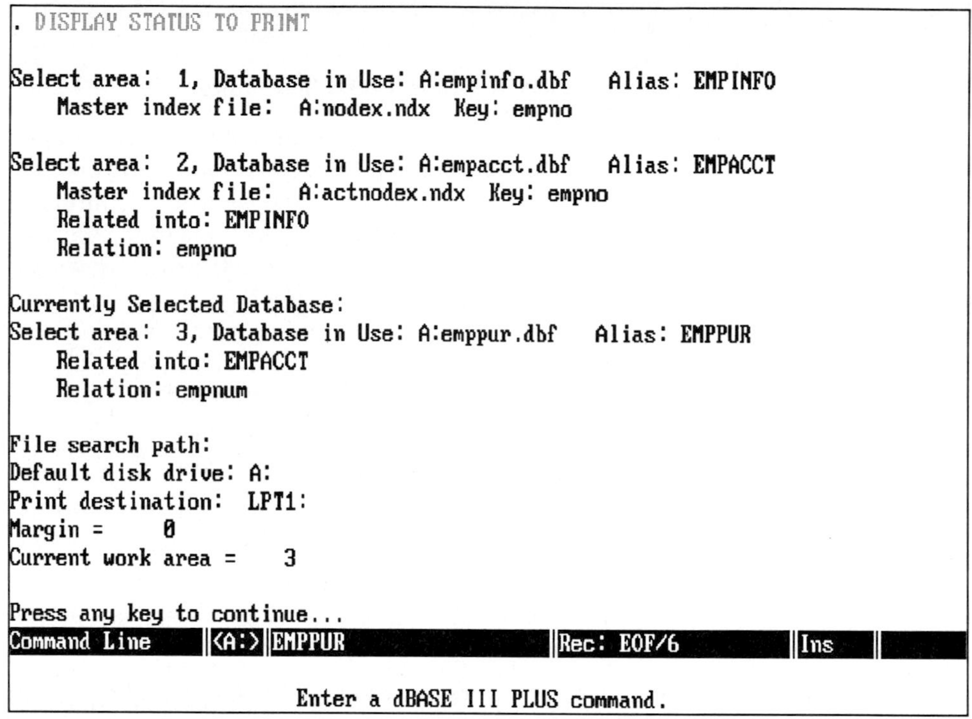

```
. DISPLAY STATUS TO PRINT

Select area:  1, Database in Use: A:empinfo.dbf   Alias: EMPINFO
    Master index file:  A:nodex.ndx  Key: empno

Select area:  2, Database in Use: A:empacct.dbf   Alias: EMPACCT
    Master index file:  A:actnodex.ndx  Key: empno
    Related into: EMPINFO
    Relation: empno

Currently Selected Database:
Select area:  3, Database in Use: A:emppur.dbf   Alias: EMPPUR
    Related into: EMPACCT
    Relation: empnum

File search path:
Default disk drive: A:
Print destination:  LPT1:
Margin =     0
Current work area =    3

Press any key to continue...
Command Line    |<A:>|EMPPUR              |Rec: EOF/6      |Ins |

                    Enter a dBASE III PLUS command.
```

11. Now use the **QUIT** command to properly exit dBASE III Plus.

EXERCISE 6 Employee Invoice Summaries

This exercise requires that you create a dBASE command file (.PRG file) that, when executed, produces invoices of purchases made during the month which will be sent to the appropriate employees at their home addresses.

Required Preparation

You will need to complete Exercise 5 before completing this exercise. Study the explanations of the **IF...ELSE...ENDIF, TEXT...ENDTEXT, DO WHILE...ENDDO** command structures, as well as the **SET MARGIN, SET PRINT, SET TALK,** and **EJECT** commands found in the dBASE III Plus Operation and Command Summary. Also study the discussion labeled "dBASE III Plus Command Files," pages D-67 through D-68.

Exercise Steps

The program will produce printed output for each employee who has had a purchase recorded in the emppur database file. The printed output for the employee named Mary Martins will appear similar to the following.

Ms. Mary Martins
1507 Mill Plain Blvd.
Vancouver WA 98660

Dear Mary:

Here is a list of your account charges for the month of March.

INVOICE #	DATE	ITEM PURCHASED	AMOUNT
10012	03/19/90	Barbecue Grill	69.00
10014	03/21/90	3 Lawn Chairs	89.95
10015	03/22/90	Croquet Set	29.95
			Total - $188.90

Our records show that with the addition of these charges your current account balance is $389.40.

The program will begin by initializing the environment, putting the following database files in use with their associated index files and relations.

Select area: 1, Database in Use: A:empinfo.dbf Alias: EMPINFO
Master index file: A:nodex.ndx Key: empno

Select area: 2, Database in Use: A:empacct.dbf Alias: EMPACCT
Master index file: A:actnodex.ndx Key: empno
Related into: EMPINFO
Relation: empno

Currently Selected Database:
Select area: 3, Database in Use: A:emppur.dbf Alias: EMPPUR
Master index file: A:innodex.ndx Key: empnum
Related into: EMPACCT
Relation: empnum

Notice that the emppur database (work area 3) needs to have an index file (named "innodex") created and in use, and, with that exception, the environment described here is the same one that existed at the conclusion of Exercise 5.

The general algorithm for the program will be

1. Initialize: Open the appropriate database files with their index files in the work areas described, and set the appropriate relations. **SET TALK OFF, SET MARGIN TO** 10.
2. Continue executing the following loop instructions until the end of the emppur database file is reached.
   - **A.** Store the field empacct->account to a variable named b.
   - **B.** Print two blank lines.
   - **C.** If the employee is male,
     - **a.** Print the employee's name with a "Mr." title.
   - **D.** Otherwise,
     - **a.** Print the employee's name with a "Ms." title.

     End If.
   - **E.** Print two blank lines and the letter's salutation.
   - **F.** Begin Text
     - **a.** Print the beginning invoice text and table headings with their underlines.

     End Text.
   - **G.** Store zero to a variable named n.
   - **H.** Store the field empnum to a variable named t.
   - **I.** Continue executing the following loop instructions until the employee number in the field empnum changes.
     - **a.** Print the fields invonum, invodate, purchase, and amount.
     - **b.** Store n plus the value in amount to the variable n.
     - **c.** Move the record pointer to the next record in emppur.
   - **J.** End of loop instructions.
   - **K.** Print the remaining invoice text, total STR(n,6,2), and balance STR(b + n,6,2), and eject the page.
3. End of loop instructions.
4. **CLOSE ALL, SET TALK ON, SET MARGIN TO** 0, **RETURN.**

1. Write out the commands that will be included in the command file, in the order that they will occur, before you begin to create the file.
2. Load dBASE III Plus into memory, put the database file emppur into use, and create an index file named "innodex" on the field empnum.
3. Use the text editing mode of the **MODIFY COMMAND** command to create the .PRG file.
4. Test the program by running it so that the output is displayed on the screen.
5. When the program is functioning correctly, use the **SET PRINT ON** command to send the output to the printer. Then run the program.
6. When finished, type ||**SET PRINT OFF**||. Then use the **TYPE** <file> **TO PRINT** command to print a copy of the program. Next use the **QUIT** command to exit dBASE III Plus.

CASES

CASE 1
University Bookstore

William Davies was recently hired to be textbook manager at the local university bookstore. Each term the bookstore receives requests from faculty members to order textbooks for their classes. Part of Bill's responsibilities includes estimating the number of used books on hand and then ordering the necessary number of new books from publishers to ensure that all students will have texts at the beginning of the term. To help facilitate the ordering process, Bill intends to create a database of textbook orders placed by faculty at the beginning of each term.

In a recent conversation with Paula Cornet, the bookstore manager, Bill said, "I think the time has come to automate at least some of the textbook ordering process around here. There are times when I need to find all orders for a certain book, or all orders made by a certain faculty member. There are other times when I need to find all orders for a particular publisher or all orders made on a certain date. The current manual system we are using makes that part of the job nearly impossible. I know that with a microcomputer database management system we could easily find the order information we are looking for when we need it.

"I realize that the person entering the order records will probably be a part-time, temporary employee and that it will probably be a different person each term. What we need is a simple, easy-to-use system, with a data entry screen that looks like the order form we receive from the faculty. It would also be nice if the system could somehow check to make sure that the employee is entering the right type of data into the right areas on the screen."

Sample Request Form

UNIVERSITY BOOKSTORE
Textbook Request Form

Department	Course #	Section	Expected Enrollment
MGMT	*335*	*002*	*45*

Instructor's Name	Phone #	Date
C. Marshall	*2724*	*02/12/90*

Term	Year
FAL	*90*

Author
L. Ingalsbe

Title	Vol	Edition
Using Computers and Applications Software		*3rd*

#Books Needed	ISBN	Publisher
45	*0-675-21097-6*	*Merrill Publishing Co.*

Data Item Descriptions

Department	Four upper-case letters (MGMT)
Course #	Three-number code (335)
Section	Three-number code (002)
Expected Enrollment	Up to three digits with no decimal (45)
Instructor's Name	Up to 25 characters (C. Marshall)
Phone #	Four-number extension (2724)
Date	Eight character date-type data (02/12/90)
Term	Three letters (FAL,WIN,SPR,SUM)
Year	Two numbers (90)
Author	Up to 25 characters (L. Ingalsbe)
Title	Up to 50 characters (Using Computers and Applications Software)
Vol	Up to three numbers
Edition	Up to four characters (3rd)
# Books Needed	Up to three digits with no decimal (45)
ISBN	13 character code (0-675-21097-6)
Publisher	Up to 35 characters (Merrill Publishing Co.)

CASE 2 Kady's Korner Market

Frank Kady has owned and operated a small grocery store for the past 27 years. Since the time that Kady's Korner Market opened as a typical neighborhood grocery store, Frank has had to make many changes to meet new consumer demands. Today he has to compete with a number of other convenience stores in the area. Frank has recently decided to start renting videotapes of movies to his customers, a service that many of the competing stores in the area offer. With his many years of experience, Frank has a good idea about what is needed to set up a rental service. However, he doesn't know much about new movies, and he has never even operated a video-cassette recorder (VCR).

Frank's nephew, Kevin, who is a sophomore at the local university, has worked for Frank every summer for the past five years. In a recent phone conversation, Frank told Kevin about his plans, and Kevin was enthusiastic about the idea. Kevin said, "I've learned quite a bit about database systems in my business courses here at college, and I think a microcomputer could really help you run the rental service."

Frank has decided to invest in a microcomputer and the software Kevin told him about. When Kevin comes back to work for him next month, Frank is going to suggest that Kevin take charge of the project and set up a recordkeeping system with the microcomputer. He knows that it sometimes takes a while to get the bugs out of these systems, so he'll suggest that Kevin begin by just entering the information for the tapes the store will have in stock. Frank may be able to help Kevin decide what information would eventually be kept in the system. For the time being, though, he wants to keep track of customer rentals with a regular log book.

Frank has checked into the video rental business and collected some information. He has found that the most economical way of offering a variety of movies is to order from one of the distributors in the area that deals with private stores such as his. He can keep a stock of about 200 to 300 tapes at a time, and he may order and return tapes as desired. His system should, therefore, have the ability to add and delete titles, as well as to edit information about the titles in the system.

Frank may stock several copies of more popular movies, while keeping only one copy of movies that are less popular. He also needs to identify certain movies as new releases, for which he can charge a higher rental fee. Long movies may come on two or three separate tapes, but will be rented as one movie. Some of the information available about movies may include the production company, year made, running time in minutes, main actors and actresses, whether color or black and white, rating, and a short synopsis of the movie. He will talk to Kevin about which of this information will be kept in the system.

To have a good variety of movies available, Frank may want to put movies into categories. Some categories that he has seen used in other stores are Action, Adventure, Children's, Comedy, Drama, Foreign Films, Musicals, Mystery, Suspense, War, and Westerns. For the relatively small number of movies he will carry, Frank won't need many categories, but he would like to be able to keep track of how many tapes he has in the different categories at any one time.

Frank has obtained a list of movies scheduled for a second release this month. These movies will be available from the distributor at a reduced rate. He wants Kevin to select from the list those movies which might be good choices to start stocking. He also is relying on Kevin, who has a VCR and has seen or heard of most of the newer movies, to do some research and complete the initial list of movies to stock.

Dangerous Liaisons (1988) (R) (120 min.) Copies to Stock: ?

WARNER HOME VIDEO

Starring: Glenn Close, John Malkovich, Michelle Pfeiffer

Synopsis: Stephen Frears' film won 3 Oscars—Best Screenplay, Art Direction and Costume Design. The sexual power games played by the upper class in 18th Century France are explored, as the Marquise de Merteuil challenges her ex-lover Valmont to seduce the betrothed of her most recent lover. But Valmont has eyes for the virtuous Madame de Tourvel. Oh boy, is this going to get complicated!!!

Mississippi Burning (1988) (R) (127 min.) Copies to Stock: ?

ORION

Starring: Gene Hackman, Willem Dafoe, Frances McDormand, Brad Dourif

Synopsis: Alan Parker's intense drama about the violence and fear during the Civil Rights movement in the '60s in the deep South won an Oscar for Best Cinematography. When three freedom fighters are reported missing, two FBI agents are assigned to the case. Now they have to face the fear and prejudice of people intimidated by the Ku Klux Klan in order to solve it. This one is intense.

Cocoon—The Return (1988) (PG) (116 min.) Copies to Stock: ?

CBS/FOX

Starring: Don Ameche, Steve Guttenberg, Wilford Brimley, Jack Gilford

Synopsis: When last we saw the old folks, they were heading to the planet Antarea in a spaceship. Now they've returned to Florida for a visit, and to try to help save a captive cocoon that was discovered by Earth scientists. Holy homesickness! How will they feel now that they're back with all their loved ones? Hume Cronyn, Jessica Tandy, Maureen Stapleton and Elaine Stritch co-star.

Physical Evidence (1989) (R) (100 min.) Copies to Stock: ?

VESTRON VIDEO

Starring: Burt Reynolds, Theresa Russell, Ned Beatty, Kay Lenz

Synopsis: Joe Paris is a down-on-his-luck cop. Not only has he been suspended from the force for his overly zealous tactics, now he's being accused of first-degree murder. Can he and the beautiful attorney assigned to his case figure out what's really going on? This thriller was produced by Martin (Jagged Edge) Ransohoff, and directed by Michael (Coma) Crichton.

The Boost (1988) (R) (95 min.) Copies to Stock: ?

HBO VIDEO

Starring: James Woods, Sean Young, John Kapelos, Steven Hill

Synopsis: This yuppie couple is searching for the good life and they work hard to get to the top. But when you get to the top, the only way to go is down. Ever since Lenny and Linda Brown moved to the West Coast, he's been hotter than a pistol, selling lucrative real estate. But life in the fast lane includes the deadly lure of cocaine. Will they succumb to drugs and throw it all away?

Daffy Duck's Quackbusters (1988) (G) (76 min.) Copies to Stock: ?

WARNER HOME VIDEO

Starring: Daffy Duck, Bugs Bunny, Porky Pig, Tweety and Sylvester

Synopsis: Daffy's second full-length motion picture finds him going into the exorcism business in order to inherit a fortune. Our wisequacking friend has formed the "Ghosts 'R' Us Paranormal Agency" and the laughs won't stop. This one features his two most recent outings, "The Duxorcist" and "Night Of The Living Duck." And with classic sequences like "The Abominable Snow Rabbit," you can't miss.

Who's Harry Crumb? (1989) (PG-13) (91 min.) Copies to Stock: ?

RCA - COLUMBIA PICTURES

Starring: John Candy, Jeffrey Jones, Annie Potts, Barry Corbin

Synopsis: He's the bumblingest detective ever, that's who. The only reason he's been assigned to a kidnapping case is because his boss doesn't really want it to get solved. But Harry's a master of disguises, and he's going undercover to uncover the truth. There's more going on here than meets the eye, however. Can Crumb find the crumbs behind the crime? Paul Flaherty directed this funny farce.

NOTE: Movie listings reprinted with permission from Vidpix, *vol. 2, no. 1, July 1989.* Vidpix *is a publication of Video Marketing & Publishing, Inc.*

CASE 3 Uptown Delicatessen—Part A

Fritz Cramer owns and operates the Uptown Delicatessen, which is located in a popular shopping mall in the City Center. In addition to his regular line of deli meats and cheeses, Fritz recently began carrying a number of fresh uncooked meat items. He has found that many busy shoppers and people who work in the area find it quicker and more convenient to buy some of these items at the deli than to make an extra trip to the grocery store before going home.

Fritz has a database set up on his microcomputer, which he uses to keep track of inventory and product orders. He has created a database file on which he keeps his fresh meat master product list. The file uses a two-character field, MEATCODE, to identify the type of meat as beef (BF), chicken (CH), or pork (PO). Within each of these groupings, a two-character field, CUTCODE, is used to sequentially number the items carried. For example, beef cut 01 is used for T-bone steaks, chicken cut 01 is used for whole fryers, and chicken cut 02 is used for 8-piece cut fryers. The other fields in this file hold the number of pounds Fritz wants to keep in stock and the average selling price for each item.

The first thing Fritz wants to do is to print a form that can be used for taking a physical inventory of these items. He thinks that this can be accomplished with the database software's report form feature, although he hasn't had time to learn much about it yet. Since he often has one of his part-time employees help him take inventory, Fritz wants the inventory form to be simple, with separate sections for his three fresh meat types coinciding with the way they are separated in his cold storage room. Fritz has typed up an example of how he would like the inventory form to appear.

The Database File

FILE: meatlist.DBF

Record#	MEATCODE	CUTCODE	MEATNAME	CUTNAME	STOCKLVL	AVGPRICE
1	CH	01	CHICKEN	WHOLE FRYERS	150	1.39
2	CH	02	CHICKEN	8-PIECE CUT FRYERS	160	1.49
3	CH	03	CHICKEN	QUARTER-CUT FRYERS	120	0.89
4	BF	01	BEEF	T-BONE STEAKS	75	4.68
5	BF	02	BEEF	RIB EYE STEAKS	40	4.39
6	BF	03	BEEF	ROUND STEAKS	85	1.89
7	BF	04	BEEF	FILETS	115	4.29
8	BF	05	BEEF	SHORT RIBS	140	1.69
9	PO	01	PORK	CHOPS	115	2.89
10	PO	02	PORK	SPARE RIBS	140	1.79
11	PO	03	PORK	ROAST	60	2.69
12	PO	04	PORK	SHOULDER	50	2.09
13	BF	06	BEEF	RUMP ROAST	55	1.98
14	BF	07	BEEF	STEW MEAT	30	1.99
15	CH	04	CHICKEN	BREASTS	80	2.39
16	CH	05	CHICKEN	LEGS	40	1.49
17	CH	06	CHICKEN	THIGHS	80	1.69
18	CH	07	CHICKEN	WINGS	40	0.49
19	PO	05	PORK	CURED HAMS	180	1.89

Example Report Form Output

MEAT INVENTORY ENTRY FORM

INVENTORY DATE: ____/____/____

CODE DESCRIPTION	LBS ON HAND
MEAT TYPE: BEEF	__________
BF01 T-BONE STEAKS	__________
BF02 RIB EYE STEAKS	__________
BF03 ROUND STEAKS	__________
BF04 FILETS	__________
BF05 SHORT RIBS	__________
BF06 RUMP ROAST	__________
BF07 STEW MEAT	__________
MEAT TYPE: CHICKEN	__________
CH01 WHOLE FRYERS	__________
CH02 8-PIECE CUT FRYERS	__________
CH03 QUARTER-CUT FRYERS	__________
CH04 BREASTS	__________
CH05 LEGS	__________
CH06 THIGHS	__________
CH07 WINGS	__________

MEAT TYPE: PORK	________________
PO01 CHOPS	________________
PO02 SPARE RIBS	________________
PO03 ROAST	________________
PO04 SHOULDER	________________
PO05 CURED HAMS	________________

CASE 4 Uptown Delicatessen—Part B

Now that Fritz has an inventory form for his fresh meat items, he needs a way of entering this information into his database system. He also needs a second report that shows the number of pounds of each item he must order to bring his inventory back up to the desired stock level. To test his system, he has set up an inventory file into which he would like to enter his last two physical inventories.

Fritz's inventory file has only three fields. The first field, INVDATE, holds the inventory date. He has decided to make the second field, MEATCUT, a four-character code that is a combination of the two fields MEATCODE and CUTCODE from his master file. This will save space on his disk as well as allowing him to relate this file to the master file when he needs the full name of a particular item. The third field, LBSINV, holds the number of pounds in inventory for each item.

Since Fritz plans to train one of his employees to enter the inventory into the system from the inventory form, he wants to set up a data entry screen that will be easy to use. Since the MEATCUT code (e.g., BF01) is not at all descriptive, he wants the entry screen to display the full cut name for each fresh meat item.

After the inventory amounts have been entered, he wants to be able to produce an order sheet that shows the inventory amounts and average selling prices for each item. In another column he wants these two items multiplied to show the approximate value of his inventory for each item. The final column should show the amount he needs to order for each item, which is his stock level minus the amount he has in inventory. This column, however, should not show any negative values, since that would mean he is already overstocked for an item and shouldn't order any more. Fritz also wants the order sheet report to be organized by meat type, and he would like to see the totals for pounds on hand, value of inventory, and pounds to order for each type of meat. He has typed up an example of how he would like the order form report to appear.

The Database File

File: mtinven.DBF

Record#	INVDATE	MEATCUT	LBSINV
1	02/09/90	BF01	34
2	02/09/90	BF02	45
3	02/09/90	BF03	7
4	02/09/90	BF04	52
5	02/09/90	BF05	157
6	02/09/90	BF06	5
7	02/09/90	BF07	14
8	02/09/90	CH01	0
9	02/09/90	CH02	14
10	02/09/90	CH03	55
11	02/09/90	CH04	90
12	02/09/90	CH05	3
13	02/09/90	CH06	36
14	02/09/90	CH07	45
15	02/09/90	PO01	10
16	02/09/90	PO02	64
17	02/09/90	PO03	67
18	02/09/90	PO04	4
19	02/09/90	PO05	82
20	02/16/90	BF01	35
21	02/16/90	BF02	14
22	02/16/90	BF03	89
23	02/16/90	BF04	53
24	02/16/90	BF05	50
25	02/16/90	BF06	0
26	02/16/90	BF07	14
27	02/16/90	CH01	53
28	02/16/90	CH02	110
29	02/16/90	CH03	55
30	02/16/90	CH04	28
31	02/16/90	CH05	28
32	02/16/90	CH06	37
33	02/16/90	CH07	14
34	02/16/90	PO01	79
35	02/16/90	PO02	65
36	02/16/90	PO03	21
37	02/16/90	PO04	34
38	02/16/90	PO05	83

Example Report Form Output (Inventory Date 02/09/90)

MEAT ORDER SHEET

ITEM CODE	ITEM DESCRIPTION	POUNDS ON HAND	AVG PRICE PER POUND	VALUE OF INVENTORY	MIN LBS TO ORDER
MEAT TYPE: BEEF					
BF01	T-BONE STEAKS	34	4.68	159.12	41
BF02	RIB EYE STEAKS	45	4.39	197.55	0
BF03	ROUND STEAKS	7	1.89	13.23	78
BF04	FILETS	52	4.29	223.08	63
BF05	SHORT RIBS	157	1.69	265.33	0
BF06	RUMP ROAST	5	1.98	9.90	50
BF07	STEW MEAT	14	1.99	27.86	16
		314		896.07	248
MEAT TYPE: CHICKEN					
CH01	WHOLE FRYERS	0	1.39	0.00	150
CH02	8-PIECE CUT FRYERS	14	1.49	20.86	146
CH03	QUARTER-CUT FRYERS	55	0.89	48.95	65
CH04	BREASTS	90	2.39	215.10	0
CH05	LEGS	3	1.49	4.47	37
CH06	THIGHS	36	1.69	60.84	44
CH07	WINGS	45	0.49	22.05	0
		243		372.27	442
MEAT TYPE: PORK					
PO01	CHOPS	10	2.89	28.90	105
PO02	SPARE RIBS	64	1.79	114.56	76
PO03	ROAST	67	2.69	180.23	0
PO04	SHOULDER	4	2.09	8.36	46
PO05	CURED HAMS	82	1.89	154.98	98
		227		487.03	325
		784		1755.37	1015

CASE 5 Albright Ink Company

Leann Holmes works in the production department of Albright Ink Company, a company that manufactures and distributes inks used for printing newspapers and magazines. Albright's sells large quantities of black ink, which is manufactured in a continuous process and is usually delivered by tank trucks. The company also manufactures blue, green, red, yellow, and violet inks in a batch process and sells these inks in five-gallon containers on a much smaller scale.

Leann is primarily responsible for scheduling production runs of colored inks. She is refining the method by which sales of colored inks are forecast and would like to collect and analyze information from daily invoice records. She has spoken with John Hanson, one of the company's sales managers, who is currently receiving files from the data processing department and loading the information into his own database system. John told Leann that although he is only receiving invoice information for his own customers, he is sure that the data processing department could easily supply her with a similar file for all daily invoices. He has given her a copy of the files supplied to him for the last three days. He explained to her that the filename indicates the date for invoice information in the file—for example, the file IN112190.TXT contains invoice information for the date 11/21/90.

Leann has seen a printed copy of the contents of these files and has determined that she will have to perform some manipulation of the data to get the information she needs for her system. For example, the files contain a product code that has two letters for the ink color, followed by a four digit batch number. The files also have sales listed by invoice number. For her system, Leann is not concerned with the batch number, but wants only daily totals of each colored ink sold.

She thinks that once she has set up the structure for her file, the steps used to transfer the data from the daily text files should be routine. She would like to test a procedure using John's files before she makes her own request to the data processing department.

Items in each record of text files (.TXT):

Invoice Number, Customer Number, Product Code, Gallons Sold, Price Per Gallon, Total Dollar Amount

First two characters of product codes indicate ink colors as follows:

BK = Black
BL = Blue
GR = Green
RD = Red
VI = Violet
YL = Yellow

Contents of File: IN112190.TXT

```
"I28659", "16052", "BK8702",   4874,   15.11,   73646.14
"I28659", "16052", "BL6509",     15,   45.01,     675.15
"I28659", "16052", "YL1652",     25,   48.75,    1218.75
"I28660", "07892", "BL6509",     35,   44.95,    1573.25
"I28660", "07892", "GR1648",     10,   52.07      520.70
"I28660", "07892", "RD4586",     20,   45.55,     911.00
"I28661", "09846", "BK8703",    952,   15.12,   14394.24
"I28662", "12546", "BK8703",   4963,   15.11,   74990.93
"I28662", "12546", "BL6510",     45,   45.01,    2025.45
"I28662", "12546", "GR1648",     25,   52.07,    1301.75
"I28662", "12546", "RD4586",     20,   45.55,     911.00
"I28662", "12546", "VI0984",     15,   62.16,     932.40
"I28662", "12546", "YL1652",     20,   48.75,     975.00
"I28663", "05565", "BK8702",   2000,   15.12,   30240.00
```

Contents of File: IN112290.TXT

```
"I28664", "05629", "BK8702",    250,   16.01,    4002.50
"I28665", "10650", "BK8704",    978,   15.45,   15110.10
"I28665", "10650", "GR1648",     25,   52.03,    1300.75
"I28665", "10650", "VI0985",      5,   60.96,     304.80
"I28666", "28659", "RD4586",     35,   45.55,    1594.25
"I28667", "06350", "BK8704",   4826,   15.11,   72920.86
"I28668", "12016", "BK8705",    862,   15.12,   13033.44
"I28669", "07563", "BK8706",   3952,   15.11,   59714.72
"I28669", "07563", "BL6510",     75,   45.01,    3375.75
"I28669", "07563", "GR1648",     35,   52.07,    1822.45
"I28669", "07563", "RD4586",     45,   45.55,    2049.75
"I28669", "07563", "VI0985",     20,   61.12,    1222.40
"I28670", "09852", "BL6511",     30,   45.01,    1350.30
"I28670", "09852", "GR1648",     15,   51.93,     778.95
"I28670", "09852", "RD4586",     35,   45.45,    1590.75
"I28670", "09852", "YL1652",     10,   48.75,     487.50
"I28671", "12025", "BK8706",   4092,   15.12,   61871.04
```

Contents of File: IN112390.TXT

```
"I28972", "05654", "BK8706",    873,   15.12,   13199.76
"I28972", "05654", "GR1648",     65,   52.07,    3384.55
"I28973", "12685", "BL6511",     40,   45.01,    1800.40
"I28973", "12685", "RD4587",     25,   45.55,    1138.75
"I28974", "09846", "BK8707",   1265,   15.07,   19063.55
"I28975", "11618", "BK8707",   5650,   14.72,   83168.00
"I28975", "11618", "BL6511",     25,   44.98,    1124.50
"I28975", "11618", "GR1649",     40,   52.07,    2082.80
"I28975", "11618", "RD4587",     35,   45.55,    1594.25
"I28976", "12502", "GR1649",     25,   49.57,    1239.25
"I28976", "12502", "VI0985",     15,   62.16,     932.40
"I28976", "12502", "YL1652",     10,   48.75,     487.50
```

HINTS AND HAZARDS

FILE HANDLING

HINT The following commands may be used for file maintenance operations when in dBASE's dot (.) prompt mode.

- To obtain a listing of all files on the default drive diskette, use the commands **DIR** *.* or **DISPLAY FILE LIKE** *.*.
- To erase a file on the diskette, use the commands **ERASE** <filename.ext> or **DELETE FILE** <filename.ext>.
- To rename a file, use the command **RENAME** <filename.ext> **TO** <new filename.ext>.
- To make a copy of a file, use the command **COPY FILE** [<*drive:*>]<filename.ext> **TO** [<*drive:*>]<filename.ext>.
- To display the contents of a file without opening it, use the command **TYPE** <filename.ext>.
- To produce a hard copy of the contents of a file without opening it, use the command **TYPE** <filename.ext> **TO PRINT.**

HAZARD Files that are currently open may not be erased, renamed, copied, or typed with the preceding commands.

HAZARD Do not name a database (.DBF) file with the single letter A through J. These letters are reserved as database alias names.

HAZARD dBASE III Plus allows up to 15 files (10 of which may be database files) to be open at once. However, DOS does not automatically allow that many files to be open. To use dBASE to its full capacity, the DOS disk used to load DOS must have a file named CONFIG.SYS in its root directory and the following DOS commands must be included in the file.

```
FILES = 20
BUFFERS = 24
```

The CONFIG.SYS file is an ASCII text file. You can create such a file with a word processor, dBASE's **MODIFY COMMAND** mode, or in the same manner as the .BAT file was created in the introductory Hints and Hazards.

HINT The following commands open/load and close/save the various dBASE file types.

.DBF *Database files.* The **USE** <filename> command opens a database file. To close the file, type **USE** with no <filename> specified.

.FMT *Format files.* Format files are command files with only **@ SAY, @ GET,** and **READ** commands in them. They may be created and saved in the **MODIFY COMMAND** mode, in which case they need to have their extensions specified in the **MODIFY COMMAND** command as <filename.FMT> (or be renamed later to have the .FMT extension). Format files may also be generated from screen files (.SCR) by the **MODIFY SCREEN** command. A format file is opened with the **SET FORMAT TO** <filename> command. Once opened, all commands that invoke full-screen editing of current database fields or memory variables will use the screen display format specified in the format file. Only one format file may be open at a time in a given work area. To close an open format file, use **SET FORMAT TO** with no <filename> specified.

.FRM — *Form files.* The **REPORT FORM** command automatically opens and closes form files. Form files are created with the **MODIFY REPORT** command.

.LBL — *Label files.* The **LABEL FORM** command automatically opens and closes label files. Label files are created with the **MODIFY LABEL** command.

.MEM — *Memory variable files.* The **SAVE TO** <filename> creates memory variable files. They are loaded into RAM with the **RESTORE FROM** <filename> command. These commands open and close the file in a single operation. Memory variables may be erased from RAM with the **RELEASE** or **CLEAR MEMORY** commands.

.NDX — *Index files.* The **INDEX ON** <expression> **TO** <filename> command creates index files and leaves them open. They also may be opened with the **USE** <filename> **INDEX** <index file list> and **SET INDEX TO** <index file list> commands. Open index files may be closed by executing either the **USE** command without the **INDEX** <index file list> clause or the **SET INDEX TO** command without the <index file list> parameter.

.PRG — *Program or command files.* Command files are created and saved in the **MODIFY COMMAND** mode or with a word processing software. They are ASCII text files. A command file is loaded into RAM and executed with the **DO** <filename> command, and remains open until the program is completed. A command file may be automatically loaded and executed when dBASE is loaded by typing ||dBASE <filename>↵|| from the DOS prompt.

.TXT — *Text files.* Text files are ASCII files and may be created several ways. The **COPY TO** <filename> **TYPE SDF** command creates a text file copy of the database in use. The **SET ALTERNATE TO** <filename> command creates a text file. Screen output (except editing mode output) will be written to the file after the **SET ALTERNATE ON** command is executed. **SET ALTERNATE OFF** suspends writing of screen output to the text file, but does not close the file. **SET ALTERNATE TO** with no <filename> specified closes the text file. The **LABEL FORM** and **REPORT FORM** commands will create ASCII text files (.TXT) when the [**TO FILE** <filename>] clause is included. The file is opened and closed by the command.

HINT — The **CLOSE ALL** command closes/saves/erases all files currently open.

HAZARD — Do not remove your files diskette from the disk drive before you type ||**QUIT**↵|| to save all data and close all files. Doing so may result in lost data and/or damaged files.

DATA PROCESSING

HINT The data held in fields and memory variables are literal values. You may not, for instance, **EDIT** a numeric field or variable as shown.

```
75+1200
```

Expressions may be used, however, to put the evaluation of such expressions into fields or variables using dBASE commands. For instance ||**STORE** account + 75 **TO** macct|| or ||**REPLACE** account **WITH** account + 75|| are examples of dBASE commands that use expressions to put a value into a memory variable or field.

HINT Memo fields do not hold record data, but instead hold an address used to access text data that is kept in a memo text file (.DBT) for each record having memo data. dBASE uses (opens) the .DBT file in conjunction with a database file when the database file has a record structure that includes memo fields. Memo data may be accessed for editing by placing the cursor on a memo field and typing Ctrl-PgDn when in the **EDIT** mode.

HAZARD When **MODIFY STRUCTURE** is used to remove any memo fields from a database file's structure, the memo file (.DBT) will be erased. If, however, a memo file (.DBT) is erased with another command without removing the memo field from the file structure, the database file (.DBF) may no longer be opened with the **USE** command. dBASE creates backup copies of .DBT files with a .TBK file extension. If such a file exists on your disk, use the **COPY FILE** command to recreate the .DBT file from the .TBK backup.

If no backup file exists, you may recover from this type of error as follows. Type ||**MODIFY COMMAND** <filename>.DBT↵|| specifying the database file's <filename> and a .DBT extension to re-create the memo file. Immediately type Ctrl-End to save the file, and then use the database file and **MODIFY STRUCTURE** to remove all memo fields. You will no longer have any memo data, but the rest of the database fields will be intact.

HAZARD Since the data in memo fields are not actually part of their associated record, they cannot be processed by dBASE commands. It is not possible, for instance, to search memo data for occurrences of strings; to sort or index records on memo field contents; or to perform batch replacement operations on memo data.

HINT Certain mathematical operations may be performed with date-type data. The following are some examples of "date arithmetic."

`. STORE CTOD("06/15/91") TO date1` `06/15/91`	Place the date-type data for June 15, 1991 into the variable "datel."
`. ? date1 + 90` `09/13/91`	Print datel + 90. September 13, 1991 occurs ninety days after June 15, 1991.
`. STORE CTOD("08/14/91") TO date2` `08/14/91`	Place the date-type data for August 14, 1991 into the variable "date2."
`. ? date2 - date1` `60`	Print date2 minus datel. There are 60 days between June 15, 1991 and August 14, 1991.

HINT String comparisons in expressions must be the same case as well as use the same characters in order for a condition to evaluate as .T. (true). The upper-case function, **UPPER**(<expC>), or the lower-case function, **LOWER**(<expC>), may be used to ensure that a field or variable's string data are compared in the same case. An example is shown below.

```
. LOCATE FOR UPPER(employee)="MARTINS MARY"
Record =       7
```

HAZARD Fields holding string data automatically are padded with spaces (CHR(32)s) which are evaluated as such in expressions. To remove trailing spaces, use the **TRIM** function. You also may remove leading spaces with the **LTRIM** function.

HAZARD Memory variables holding numeric data hold their data to several decimal places of accuracy (the number of decimal places varies between versions of dBASE) regardless of the number of places displayed on the screen. Fields hold numeric data to the number of places of accuracy specified when the record structure for the database was entered. Read through the following commands and their results.

```
. ? 10/3
 3.33

. STORE 10/3 TO test
 3.33

. ? test
       3.33

. ? 3.33 = test
.F.

. ? STR(test,19,15)
 3.333333333333334

. ? 3.333333333333334 = test
.T.

. REPLACE account WITH test
     1 record replaced

. ? account, STR(account,19,15)
    3.33   3.330000000000000
```

HINT You can control the number of decimal places of accuracy for numeric data held in memory variables by using the **ROUND** function.

```
. STORE ROUND(10/3,2) TO test
 3.33

. ? STR(test,19,15)
 3.330000000000000
```

HINT People with programming backgrounds often are initially confused by the dBASE commands used primarily in the dot (.) prompt mode (e.g., **DISPLAY, REPLACE, LOCATE,** and so on) and their parameters <scope>, <field list>, **FOR** <expression>, and **WHILE** <expression>. The commands are complete subroutines with all the fundamental processing operations (assignment, condition, iteration) which are called by the command when it is entered.

dBASE III PLUS FEATURES

HINT The ampersand character (&) may be used for special dBASE III Plus operations called *macro substitution*. When a character-type memory variable holds a character string that has meaning to dBASE, the name of the variable may be preceded by an & to cause dBASE to immediately substitute the contents of the variable in place of the &<memvar> in a command.

This is a very powerful feature of dBASE, but one that requires some practice to be used effectively. Following are some examples of how the macro substitution feature may be used.

- Store logical expressions as character strings to character-type memory variables so that they may then be used with dBASE commands.

```
. STORE "sex = 'F' .AND. salary >= 1650" TO cond1

. STORE "sex = 'M' .AND. salary >= 1800" TO cond2

. DISPLAY MEMORY
COND1       pub   C  "sex = 'F' .AND. salary >= 1650"
COND2       pub   C  "sex = 'M' .AND. salary >= 1800"
   2 variables defined,       64 bytes used
 254 variables available,   5936 bytes available

. DISPLAY FOR &cond1
Record#  EMPLOYEE              TELEPHONE SEX EMPLOYED   SALARY  ACCOUNT
      2  Smoler Ellen          225-3212  F   09/15/83  1650.00   300.00
      4  Sill Sally            224-4321  F   02/15/84  1657.70   150.00

. SET FILTER TO &cond2

. DISPLAY ALL
Record#  EMPLOYEE              TELEPHONE SEX EMPLOYED   SALARY  ACCOUNT
      1  Pratt John            225-1234  M   06/22/82  1949.00   200.00
      5  Knat Michael          221-1235  M   09/15/80  1800.00   125.00
      6  Smith Paul            244-1010  M   11/15/81  2150.50  1050.00
```

- Many programming languages have the ability to define an array of variables. One variable name is used with a number defining the element of an array to use. Although dBASE III Plus does not include array capabilities, arrays can be simulated by using macro substitution to create lists of variables with similar names.

  The following command file demonstrates how an array may be simulated in dBASE III Plus.

```
*  PROGRAM:  Fldarray.PRG  -  stores field employee to variables

USE empfile INDEX namedex
STORE 0 TO cntr

DO WHILE .NOT. EOF()
  STORE cntr + 1 TO cntr
  IF cntr < 10
    STORE "name" + STR(cntr,1) TO varname
  ELSE
    STORE "name" + STR(cntr,2) TO varname
  ENDIF
  STORE TRIM(employee) TO &varname
  SKIP
ENDDO

SAVE ALL LIKE name* TO names
RETURN
```

```
. DO fldarray

. RESTORE FROM names

. DISPLAY MEMORY
NAME1       pub   C  "Johnson Frank"
NAME2       pub   C  "Jones David"
NAME3       pub   C  "Knat Michael"
NAME4       pub   C  "Martins Mary"
NAME5       pub   C  "Nichols Sandy"
NAME6       pub   C  "Pratt John"
NAME7       pub   C  "Sill Sally"
NAME8       pub   C  "Smith Paul"
NAME9       pub   C  "Smoler Ellen"
    9 variables defined,      121 bytes used
  247 variables available,   5879 bytes available
```

HINT The bell that rings during data entry can be annoying. To turn off the bell from the dot (.) prompt mode, type ||**SET BELL OFF**↵||. To turn it back on, type ||**SET BELL ON**↵||.

HINT The error message "Do you want some help? (Y/N)" also can be annoying. To stop the display of this message, type ||**SET HELP OFF**↵|| and to turn it back on, type ||**SET HELP ON**↵||.

HINT The Function keys F1 through F10 are programmed by dBASE to hold the following strings:

F1	HELP;	F6	DISPLAY STATUS;
F2	ASSIST;	F7	DISPLAY MEMORY;
F3	LIST;	F8	DISPLAY;
F4	DIR;	F9	APPEND;
F5	DISPLAY STRUCTURE;	F10	EDIT;

Tapping one of these keys causes the command shown to be typed, displayed on the screen, and entered.

You may change the strings by using the **SET FUNCTION** <expN> **TO** <expC> command. For example, **SET FUNCTION** 2 **TO** "San Diego, CA" will store that city and state in the F2 key. If you want to include an Enter key character (CHR(13)) at the end of the string, add a semicolon at the end of the string "San Diego, CA;".

The Function key F1 is not programmable with the **SET FUNCTION** command.

LIMITS AND CONSTRAINTS

HINT The following are some limits and constraints to various dBASE III Plus data processing operations.

- Maximum filename length—8 characters
- Maximum field name length—10 characters
- Maximum memory variable name length—10 characters
- Maximum characters in a field, memory variable, command file line, report heading or <cstring>—254 characters

- Maximum fields to a record—128 fields
- Maximum characters to a record—4,000 characters
- Maximum current memory variables or @ **GET**s—256
- Maximum file size with **MODIFY COMMAND**—4,096 bytes

dBASE III PLUS OUTPUT

HINT To obtain a hard-copy listing of a command file, use the **TYPE** <filename.PRG> **TO PRINT** command.

HINT To obtain hard copy of screen output generated from the dot (.) prompt mode, use dBASE III Plus's output-generating commands (**DISPLAY, LIST, REPORT FORM, LABEL FORM, TYPE,** etc.) that include the [**TO PRINT**] parameter which causes an echo of screen output to the printer. For commands not having the [**TO PRINT**] parameter, follow the following steps.

1. Make sure your computer is connected and on-line to a printer that is turned on.
2. Either press and hold the Ctrl key and then type the P key, or type ||**SET PRINT ON**↵|| to toggle on the printer echo.
3. Enter the appropriate commands to generate the desired output.
4. Either press and hold the Ctrl key and then type the P key again, or type ||**SET PRINT OFF**↵|| to toggle off the printer echo.

HINT To obtain hard copy of one screen's worth of data while in an editing mode, press and hold a Shift key and then type the key marked PrtSc or Print Screen.

HAZARD If the computer's connection to the printer is not complete or the printer is not turned on, the preceding steps to obtain hard copy may result in the computer locking up until the connection is complete or the printer is turned on.

HINT When you use the **?** command to print field data on the screen, fields holding string data will be displayed with their padded spaces. To eliminate the spaces, use the **TRIM** function.

HINT When you use the **?** command to print memory variables holding numeric data, the data will be displayed with a default length of 11 characters and an accuracy of two decimal places. To control length and displayed accuracy, use the **STR** function. To control just the displayed accuracy, use the **SET DECIMALS TO** command.

HINT The ASCII text files (.TXT) produced by the **SET ALTERNATE** commands and the [**TO FILE** <filename>] clause of the **REPORT FORM** and **LABEL FORM** commands are accessible by word processing software. When text format is important and the text is a one-time product, it usually is more efficient to create a text file with the essential data in it and then use a word processing software to edit it into finished form.

STUDY QUESTIONS

1. Individual data items of a relational database are held in ________________.

2. Related data items of a relational database are held in ________________.

3. To create a database, the ________________ must be defined before any data are entered into the database.

4. Each field of the records in a database is prespecified with an unique ________________, a fixed ________________, and a certain data ________________.

5. If the length of the first field in the first record is known, is the length of the first field in the second record known? Why?
____
____

6. If the length of the data held in the first field of the first record is known, is the length of the data in the first field of the second record known? Why? ____
____

7. Is it possible for one record in a database to have an extra field? Why?
____

8. dBASE III Plus has two editing modes. Direct access to data in fields or memory variables is done in the ________________ mode, and command files are created in the ________________ mode.

9. What event indicates that you are in a mode that allows direct access to data in fields or memory variables? ________________

10. What will be the result of entering 75/100 into a numeric field of a record when you are in an editing mode? Why?
____

11. With a database in use, what will be the result of typing ||**DISPLAY**↵||? ____

12. What are the four possible <scope>s and how do they affect the record pointer? ________________ ________________
________________ ________________

13. Where is the record pointer left after executing a command using the <scope> **ALL**? ________________

14. What command parameter specifies the individual data items in each record for the command to act upon? ________________

15. What is the default <scope> for any command using the **FOR** <expression> parameter? ________________

Given the following database, list the record numbers of the records that will be acted on by the **DISPLAY** commands shown.

Record#	EMPLOYEE	TELEPHONE	SEX	EMPLOYED	SALARY	ACCOUNT
1	Pratt John	225-1234	M	06/22/82	1949.00	200.00
2	Smoler Ellen	225-3212	F	09/15/83	1650.00	300.00
3	Jones David	292-3832	M	06/15/82	1550.00	275.75
4	Sill Sally	224-4321	F	02/15/84	1507.50	150.00
5	Knat Michael	221-1235	M	09/15/80	1800.00	125.00
6	Smith Paul	244-1010	M	11/15/81	1700.00	350.00
7	Martins Mary	222-2123	F	11/01/85	1600.00	200.50
8	Nichols Sandy	229-1111	F	02/15/86	1450.00	175.00
9	Johnson Frank	223-7928	M	03/20/90	1500.00	0.00

16. **DISPLAY FOR** employed < **CTOD**("01/01/84") **.AND.** salary < 1600

____

17. **DISPLAY FOR DTOC**(employed) < "01/01/84" **.AND.** salary < 1600

____

18. **DISPLAY FOR** account < 200 **.AND.** account >= 300

____

19. **DISPLAY FOR** account >= 200 **.AND.** account <= 300

____

20. **DISPLAY FOR** salary < 1550 **.OR.** account > 300

____

21. **DISPLAY FOR SEX** = "F" **.AND.** salary < 1550 **.OR.** account > 300

____

22. **DISPLAY FOR SEX** = "F" **.AND.** (salary < 1550 **.OR.** account > 300)

____

23. **DISPLAY FOR 1=1**

____

24. Describe the differences between the **SORT ON** <field> **TO** <filename> command and the **INDEX ON** <expression> **TO** <filename> commands.

____

____

____

____

25. Describe the differences between the **LOCATE** command and the **SEEK** command.

____

____

____

____

dBASE III PLUS KEY TERM GLOSSARY

Algorithm A step-by-step outline of the program's operation.

Alias An alternate name used for a database file when it is opened. It allows you to reference data from a database file that is open in an unselected work area.

Buffer A small portion of RAM that dBASE uses for temporary storage.

Catalog Files Files that maintain active lists of related files which dBASE treats as belonging to a particular group or set of files.

Child The controlled database when one database is related into another.

Close To remove the file from RAM.

Command Files Files that contain dBASE commands to be executed in sequence. Identical to program files.

Command Parameters Additions to a command that affect the way the command will be executed.

Command-Driven Software Software that responds to commands entered by the user.

Concatenation Combining two or more string data items.

Current Record The record to which the record pointer is currently pointing.

Cursor Control Keys The arrowed keys (up, down, left, and right) used to move the cursor.

Database Data organized in a manner that makes it possible to access specific information.

Database Files Files that hold the records and the record structure of a database.

Database Memo Files Files that hold the memo field information for databases that have a memo field.

Format Files Files that contain dBASE commands used to customize the full-screen editing presentation of fields and/or variables.

Index Files Files that point to records in a database that contain certain information, just as an index in a book points to specific pages.

Key A field in a database that is used to create an index file.

Label Form Files Files that contain user-defined specifications for producing mailing or identification labels from the data in a database.

Macro Substitution The substitution of a character-type memory variable using the & (macro) command.

Memory Variable Files Disk files in which variable names and their contents are saved.

Menu-Driven Software Software that provides menus of commands from which the user selects.

Open The condition of a file that allows changes to the contents of the file.

Parent The controlling database when one database is related into another.

Picture Clause A clause in a format file that prevents the user from entering undesired data.

Program Files Files that contain dBASE commands to be executed in sequence.

Pull-Down Menus Menus that are invoked by selecting options.

Query Files Files that contain user-defined conditions that cause dBASE to affect only certain records during processing of a database.

Record Pointer An unseen pointer that indicates which record is the current record to be processed.

Relational Database A database that contains data organized in records with fields holding related data items.

Report Form Files Files that contain user-defined specifications for producing columnar-type reports from the data in a database.

Screen Files Source files used by dBASE to produce .FMT (format) files.

Text Files Files in ASCII data format that may be processed by other software.

View Files Files that contain the set of working relationships that exist between a group of related files.

Work Area One of ten areas that may be used simultaneously for database processing in dBASE.

dBASE III PLUS OPERATION AND COMMAND SUMMARY

dBASE III PLUS QUICK REFERENCE COMMAND SUMMARY

dBASE III Plus Commands

?/?? [<exp1>[,<exp2>, . . .]]

@ <x1,y1> [**CLEAR**] [**TO** <x2,y2>] [**DOUBLE**]

@ <x,y> **GET** <field/memvar> [**PICTURE** <expC>] [**RANGE** <min>, <max>]

@ <x,y> **SAY** <exp> [**PICTURE** <expC>]

@ <x,y> **SAY** <exp> **GET** <field/memvar>

ACCEPT [<expC>] **TO** <memvarC>

APPEND

APPEND BLANK

APPEND FROM <filename> [**FOR** <condition>] [**TYPE** <file type>]

ASSIST

AVERAGE <expN list> [<scope>] [**FOR** <condition>] [**WHILE** <condition>] [**TO** <memvar list>]

BROWSE [**FIELDS** <field list>] [**LOCK** <expN>] [**FREEZE** <field>] [**NOFOLLOW**] [**NOMENU**] [**WIDTH** <expN>] [**NOAPPEND**]

CALL <module name> [**WITH** <expC> / <memvar>]

CANCEL

CHANGE [<scope>] [**FIELDS** <field list>] [**FOR** <condition>] [**WHILE** <condition>]

CLEAR

CLEAR ALL

CLEAR FIELDS

CLEAR GETS

CLEAR MEMORY

CLEAR TYPEAHEAD

CLOSE <file type> / **ALL**

CONTINUE

COPY FILE [<*drive:*>] <filename.ext> **TO** [<*drive:*>] <filename.ext>

COPY STRUCTURE TO <filename>

COPY TO <filename> [<scope>] [**FIELDS** <field list>] [**FOR** <condition>] [**WHILE** <condition>] [**TYPE** <file type>/**DELIMITED** [**WITH** <delimiter>]]

COPY TO <filename> **STRUCTURE EXTENDED**

COUNT [<scope>] [**FOR** <condition>] [**WHILE** <condition>] [**TO** <memvar>]

CREATE <filename>

CREATE <filename> **FROM** <structure extended file>

CREATE LABEL <filename>

CREATE QUERY <filename>

CREATE REPORT <filename>

CREATE VIEW FROM ENVIRONMENT

DELETE [<scope>] [**FOR** <condition>] [**WHILE** <condition>]

DELETE [**RECORD** <expN>]

DIR [<*drive:*>] [<skeleton>]

DISPLAY [<scope>] [<expression list>] [**FOR** <condition>] [**WHILE** <condition>] [**OFF**] [**TO PRINT**]

DISPLAY HISTORY [**LAST** <expN>] [**TO PRINT**]

DISPLAY MEMORY [**TO PRINT**]

DISPLAY STATUS [**TO PRINT**]

DISPLAY STRUCTURE [**TO PRINT**]

DO <filename> [**WITH** <expression list>]

DO CASE...**ENDCASE**

DO WHILE <condition>...**ENDDO**

EDIT [<scope>] [**FIELDS** <field list>] [**FOR** <condition>] [**WHILE** <condition>]

EJECT

ERASE <filename.extension>

EXIT

EXPORT <filename> **TYPE PFS**

FIND <literal string / &memvarC>

GO <expN> / **TOP** / **BOTTOM**

HELP [<key word>]

IF <condition>...[**ELSE**]...**ENDIF**

IMPORT FROM <filename> **TYPE PFS**

INDEX ON <expression> **TO** <index file> [**UNIQUE**]

INPUT [<expC>] **TO** <memvarN>

INSERT [**BLANK**] [**BEFORE**]

JOIN WITH <alias> **TO** <filename> **FOR** <condition> [**FIELDS** <field list>]

LABEL FORM <filename> [<scope>] [**FOR** <condition>] [**WHILE** <condition>] [**TO PRINT / TO FILE** <filename>] [**SAMPLE**]

LIST [<scope>] [<expression list>] [**FOR** <condition>] [**WHILE** <condition>] [**TO PRINT**] [**OFF**]

LIST HISTORY [**TO PRINT**]

LIST MEMORY [**TO PRINT**]

LIST STATUS [**TO PRINT**]

LIST STRUCTURE [**TO PRINT**]

LOAD <filename>[.<ext>]

LOCATE [<scope>] **FOR** <condition> [**WHILE** <condition>]

LOOP

MODIFY COMMAND <filename>

MODIFY LABEL <filename>

MODIFY QUERY <filename>

MODIFY REPORT <filename>

MODIFY SCREEN <filename>

MODIFY STRUCTURE

MODIFY VIEW <filename>

NOTE or *

ON ERROR / ESCAPE / KEY [<command>]

PACK

PARAMETERS <memvar list>

PRIVATE [<memvar list>] / **ALL** [**LIKE / EXCEPT** <skeleton>]

PROCEDURE <procedure name>

PUBLIC <memvar list>

QUIT

READ [**SAVE**]

RECALL [<scope>] [**FOR** <condition>] [**WHILE** <condition>]

REINDEX

RELEASE [<memvar list>] / **ALL** [**LIKE / EXCEPT** <skeleton>]

RELEASE MODULE

RENAME <filename.ext> **TO** <new filename.ext>

REPLACE [<scope>] <field1> **WITH** <exp1> [,<field2> **WITH** <exp2>, . . .] [**FOR** <condition>] [**WHILE** <condition>]

REPORT FORM [<filename>] [<scope>] [**FOR** <condition>] [**WHILE** <condition>] [**PLAIN**] [**HEADING** <expC>] [**NOEJECT**] [**TO PRINT / TO FILE** <filename>] [**SUMMARY**]

RESTORE FROM <filename> [**ADDITIVE**]

RESUME

RETRY

RETURN [**TO MASTER**]

RUN <command>

SAVE TO <filename> [**ALL LIKE / EXCEPT** <skeleton>]

SEEK <expression>

SELECT <work area / alias>

SET ALTERNATE on / OFF

SET ALTERNATE TO <filename>

SET BELL ON / off

SET CARRY on / OFF

SET CATALOG ON / off

SET CATALOG TO [<filename>]

SET CENTURY on / OFF

SET COLOR ON / off

SET COLOR TO [[<standard>] [,<enhanced>] [,<border>] [,<background>]]

SET CONFIRM on / OFF

SET CONSOLE ON / off

SET DATE [**AMERICAN / ANSI / BRITISH / ITALIAN / FRENCH / GERMAN**]

SET DEBUG on / OFF

SET DECIMALS TO <expN>

SET DEFAULT TO *<drive:>*

SET DELETED on / OFF

SET DELIMITER on / OFF

SET DELIMITER TO <expC> / **DEFAULT**

SET DEVICE TO PRINT / SCREEN

SET DOHISTORY on / OFF

SET ECHO on / OFF

SET ESCAPE ON / off

SET EXACT on / OFF

SET FIELDS on / OFF

SET FIELDS TO [<field list > / **ALL**]

SET FILTER TO [<condition>] [**FILE** <file-name>]

SET FIXED on / OFF

SET FORMAT TO [<format file>]

SET FUNCTION <expN> **TO** <expC>

SET HEADING ON / off

SET HELP ON / off

SET HISTORY ON / off

SET HISTORY TO <expN>

SET INDEX TO [<index file list>]

SET INTENSITY ON / off

SET MARGIN TO <expN>

SET MEMOWIDTH TO <expN>

SET MENUS ON / off

SET MESSAGE TO [<expC>]

SET ORDER TO [<expN>]

SET PATH TO <path list>

SET PROCEDURE TO [<filename>]

SET PRINT on / OFF

SET RELATION TO [<key exp>/<expN> **INTO** <alias>]

SET SAFETY ON / off

SET STATUS ON / off

SET STEP on / OFF

SET TALK ON / off

SET TITLE ON / off

SET TYPEAHEAD TO <expN>

SET UNIQUE on / OFF

SET VIEW TO <filename>

SKIP [–] [<expN>]

SORT [<scope>] **ON** <field1> [/**A**] [/**C**] [/**D**] [,<field2> [/**A**] [/**C**] [/**D**]...] **TO** <new file> [**FOR** <condition>] [**WHILE** <condition>]

STORE <expression> **TO** <memvar list>

SUM <expN list> [**TO** <memvar list>] [<scope>] [**FOR** <condition>] [**WHILE** <condition>]

SUSPEND

TEXT...**ENDTEXT**

TOTAL ON <key field> **TO** <new file> [**FIELDS** <fieldN list>] [<scope>] [**FOR** <condition>] [**WHILE** <condition>]

TYPE <filename.ext> [**TO PRINT**]

UPDATE ON <key field> **FROM** <alias> **REPLACE** <field1> **WITH** <exp1> [,<field2> **WITH** <exp2>, ...] [**RANDOM**]

USE [<filename>] [**ALIAS** <name>] [**INDEX** <index file list>]

WAIT [expC] [**TO** <memvar>]

ZAP

dBASE III Plus Functions

ABS(<expN>) Absolute Value Function

ASC(<expC>) ASCII Code Function

AT(<expC1>,<expC2>) Substring Search Function

BOF( ) Beginning-of-File Function

CDOW(<expD>) Character Day of Week Function

CHR(<expN>) Character String Function

CMONTH(<expD>) Character Month Function

COL( ) Column Function

CTOD(<expC>) Character-to-Date Function

DATE( ) Date Function

DAY(<expD>) Day Function

DBF( ) Database Function

DELETED( ) Deleted Record Function

DISKSPACE( ) Disk Space Function

DOW(<expD>) Day-of-Week Function

DTOC(<expD>) Date-to-Character Function

EOF( ) End-of-File Function

ERROR( ) Error Number Function

EXP(<expN>) Exponential Function

FIELD(<expN>) Field Name Function

FILE(<expC>) File Existence Function

FKLABEL(<expN>) Function Key Label Function

FKMAX( ) Function Key Maximum Function

FOUND( ) Found Function

GETNV(<expC>) Get Environmental Variable Function

IIF(<expL>,<exptrue>,<expfalse>) Immediate IF Function

INKEY( ) Inkey Function

INT(<expN>) Integer Function

ISALPHA(<expC>) Is Alphabetic Function

ISCOLOR( ) Is Color Mode Function

ISLOWER(<expC>) Is Lowercase Function

ISUPPER(<expC>) Is Uppercase Function

LEFT(<expC>,<lenN>) Left Substring Function

LEN(<expC>) Length Function

LOG(<expN>) Logarithm Function

LOWER(<expC>) Lowercase Function

LTRIM(<expC>) Left Trim Function

LUPDATE( ) Last Update Function

MAX(<expN1>,<expN2>) Maximum Function

MESSAGE( ) Error Message Function

MIN(<expN1>,<expN2>) Minimum Function

MOD(<expN1>,<expN2>) Modulus Function

MONTH(<expD>) Month Function

NDX(<expN>) Index File Function

OS( ) Operating System Function

PCOL( ) Printer Column Function

PROW( ) Printer Row Function

READKEY( ) Read Key Function

RECCOUNT( ) Record Count Function

RECNO( ) Record Number Function

RECSIZE( ) Record Size Function

REPLICATE(<expC>,<expN>) Replicate Function

RIGHT(<expC>,<expN>) Right Substring Function

ROUND(<expN>,<decN>) Round Function

ROW( ) Row Function

RTRIM(<expC>) Right Trim Function

SPACE(<expN>) Space Function

SQRT(<expN>) Square Root Function

STR(<expN>[,<lenN>] [,<decN>]) Numeric-to-String Function

STUFF(<expC1>,<startN>,<lenN>, <expC2>) Substring Replace Function

SUBSTR(<expC>,<startN>,<lenN>) Substring Function

TIME( ) Time Function

TRANSFORM(<exp>,<pictureC>) Transform Function

TRIM(<expC>) Trim Function

TYPE(<expC>) Data-Type Function

UPPER(<expC>) Uppercase Function

VAL(<expC>) Character-to-Value Function

VERSION( ) Version Function

YEAR(<expD>) Year Function

IMPORTANT dBASE III PLUS KEYS

Control Keys (Dot (.) Prompt Mode)

Esc key	Erases the current command line or aborts a current operation
^P	Toggles the printer on and off.
^Num Lock	Pauses operations; any key continues.
← (Backspace key)	Backspaces and deletes characters on the current line.

Editing Keystroke Commands

APPEND, CHANGE, and EDIT Modes

Cursor right key	Moves cursor right one character.
Cursor left key	Moves cursor left one character.
Cursor down key	Moves cursor to the next field.
Cursor up key	Moves cursor to the previous field.
PgDn key	Saves current record and advances to next record.
PgUp key	Saves current record and backs to previous record.
Ins key	Toggles between OVERWRITE and INSERT modes.
Del key	Deletes character over cursor.
← (Backspace key)	Deletes character left of cursor.
^T	Erases word to right of cursor.
^Y	Erases field to right of cursor.
^PgDn	Enter the dBASE word processor to edit a memo field.
^PgUp	Exit editing a memo field.
^U	Toggles the record *DEL* mark on and off.
^End	Saves changes and returns to dot (.) prompt.
Esc	Aborts editing of current record and returns to dot (.) prompt.

BROWSE Mode

Cursor right key	Moves cursor right one character.
Cursor left key	Moves cursor left one character.
Home key	Moves cursor to the previous field.
End key	Moves cursor to the next field.
Cursor down key	Saves current record and advances to next record.
Cursor up key	Saves current record and backs to previous record.
PgUp key	Scrolls the screen up 17 lines.
PgDn key	Scrolls the screen down 17 lines.
^Cursor right key	Pans the screen right one field.
^Cursor left key	Pans the screen left one field.
Ins key	Toggles between OVERWRITE and INSERT modes.
Del key	Deletes character over cursor.
← (Backspace key)	Deletes character left of cursor.
^T	Erases word to right of cursor.
^Y	Erases field to right of cursor.
^U	Toggles the record *DEL* mark on and off.
^End	Saves changes and returns to dot (.) prompt.
Esc	Aborts editing of current record and returns to dot (.) prompt.

MODIFY LABEL and MODIFY REPORT Modes

Cursor right key	Moves cursor right one character.
Cursor left key	Moves cursor left one character.
Cursor down key	Moves cursor to the next line.
Cursor up key	Moves cursor to the previous line.
PgDn key	Saves current screen and advances to next screen.
PgUp key	Saves current screen and backs to previous screen.
Ins key	Toggles between OVERWRITE and INSERT modes.

Del key	Deletes character over cursor.
← (Backspace key)	Deletes character to left of cursor.
^T	Erases word to right of cursor.
^Y	Erases field or line to right of cursor.
^U	Deletes current column or line specification.
^N	Inserts new column or line for specification.
^End	Saves changes and returns to dot (.) prompt.
Esc	Aborts all changes made and returns to dot (.) prompt.

MODIFY COMMAND and **MEMO** Field—dBASE Word Processor

Cursor right key	Moves cursor right one character.
Cursor left key	Moves cursor left one character.
Home key	Moves cursor one word to the left.
End key	Moves cursor one word to the right.
Cursor down key	Moves cursor to the next line.
Cursor up key	Moves cursor to the previous line.
PgUp key	Scrolls the screen up 17 lines.
PgDn key	Scrolls the screen down 17 lines.
Ins key	Toggles between OVERWRITE and INSERT modes.
Enter key ↵	Terminates current line. In the INSERT mode, inserts a line below the current line.
Del key	Deletes character over cursor.
← (Backspace key)	Deletes character to left of cursor.
^T	Erases word to right of cursor.
^Y	Erases current line.
^KR	Reads and inserts another file into the current file.
^End	Saves changes and returns to dot (.) prompt.
Esc	Aborts all changes made and returns to dot (.) prompt.

CONVENTIONS AND TERMINOLOGY

Conventions

BOLD UPPER CASE = dBASE III Plus command words.
<lower case entry> = User-supplied information.
[OPTIONAL] = Optional command words or user-supplied information.
... = Additional commands or parameters may be included.
/ = Choice of mutually-exclusive command parameters.

Example

dBASE command words

Optional

DISPLAY [<scope>] [<expression list>] [**FOR** <condition>] [**WHILE** <condition>] [**OFF**] [**TO PRINT**]

User-supplied information

Either form may be used

? / **??** [<exp1>[,<exp2>,...]]

Additional parameters may be included

Terminology

<memvar>	A memory variable of any type (numeric, character, date, or logical).
<field>	The name of a field in an open database file.
<literal>	A literal expression of numeric-, character-, date-, or logical-type data. Also referred to as a constant. Logical-type data is rarely entered as a literal. Numeric-type literals are entered without quote marks (") and may consist of only numerals 0 through 9, a preceding plus (+) or minus (−) sign, and one decimal point. **Examples:** 12648.45 −56 12.7525 Character-type literals are enclosed in quote marks ("), which are referred to as delimiters. **Example:** "This is a literal string" dBASE also recognizes apostrophes (') and bracket pairs ([ ]) as literal string delimiters. This allows a character that is normally used as a delimiter to occur within the literal string. **Example:** [Enter employee's "status" code:] Date-type literals must be entered using the **CTOD** function, which converts a date character string to date-type data. The function name means character-to-date. **Example:** **CTOD**("12/25/91")
<exp> or <expression>	A valid dBASE expression of any type (numeric, character, date, or logical). Expressions may include memory variables, field names, literals, and dBASE functions.
<memvarN>, <fieldN>, or <expN>	A numeric-type memory variable, field, or expression.
<memvarC>, <fieldC>, or <expC>	A character-type memory variable, field, or expression.
<memvarD>, <fieldD>, or <expD>	A date-type memory variable, field, or expression.
<memvarL>, <fieldL>, or <expL>	A logical-type memory variable, field, or expression.
<condition>	A condition is a logical expression <expL>. A logical expression is evaluated as either true (.T.) or false (.F.). Operators in conditions may include: **Relational:** < (less than) > (greater than) = (equal to) <= (less than or equal to) >= (greater than or equal to) < > (not equal to) **Logical:** .NOT. .AND. .OR.

<memvar list>, <field list>, or <exp list> — A list of memory variables, field names, or expressions. The items in the list are delimited with commas (separated by commas).

<filename> — Name of file you wish to create or access.

<key> — An expression that is used to create index files. The expression defines the elements of a record that are used to determine the record's position in the index file.

<scope> — Specifies a range of records to be included in a command operation. <scope> has four possible values:

ALL	All records in file.
NEXT <expN>	Next group of <expN> records in file, beginning with current record.
RECORD <expN>	One record with the record number <expN>.
REST	Records in file from current record to the end of the file.

Default — Default is a term used to define an option that is taken by dBASE when not specified by the user. For example, each command that includes a <scope> parameter has a default <scope>. The default <scope> is **ALL** for some commands, while it is the current record for other commands.

[**FOR** <condition>] — Used to specify a <condition> which must be met in order for a record to be included in a command operation. When [**FOR** <condition>] is included in a command, the default <scope> automatically becomes **ALL** records in the file, and any other <scope> must be used explicitly.

[**WHILE** <condition>] — The next group of records, beginning with the current record, will be included in a command operation as long as the <condition> is evaluated as true. As soon as a record is encountered that is evaluated as false (including the current record), command operation is halted. [**WHILE** <condition>] is normally used only when a file is indexed or sorted so that all records that meet the <condition> are grouped together.

dBASE III PLUS COMMANDS

? / **??** [<exp1>[,<exp2>, ...]]

Displays the evaluation of expressions. The **?** command issues a carriage return/line feed sequence before printing the expression(s) and can be used without an expression to space down a line. The **??** command prints the expression(s) on the current line of the screen and/or printer. The expressions may be of any type and may include field names, memory variables, and literals.

. ? employee Pratt John	field
. ? limit 500	variable
. ? "Credit Available" Credit Available	literal
. ? limit-account,limit>account 300 .T.	expressions
. ? "Credit Available -",employee,limit-account Credit Available - Pratt John 300	combination

@ <x1,y1> [**CLEAR**] [**TO** <x2,y2>] [**DOUBLE**]

The @ command may be used to erase a certain portion of the screen and to draw rectangles with either single or double lines. The x and y values used with the command define a screen coordinate by row (x = 0 to 24) and column (y = 0 to 79). The command may take the following forms.

@ <x1,y1>	Clears the right side of one line on the screen starting at the coordinate specified. For example, @ 5,15 will clear line 5 only, from column 15 to the end of the line.
@ <x1,y1> **CLEAR**	Clears the bottom right portion of the screen from the coordinate specified. For example, @ 5,15 **CLEAR** will clear from row 5 downward and from column 15 to the right.
@ <x1,y1> **CLEAR TO** <x2,y2>	Clears a rectangular portion of the screen from the upper left coordinate <x1,y1> to the lower right coordinate <x2,y2>.
@ <x1,y1> **TO** <x2,y2>	Draws a rectangular box on the screen with a single line. The upper left corner of the box is defined as <x1,y1> and the lower right corner of the box is defined as <x2,y2>.
@ <x1,y1> **TO** <x2,y2> **DOUBLE**	Draws a rectangular box on the screen with a double line. The upper left corner of the box is defined as <x1,y1> and the lower right corner of the box is defined as <x2,y2>.

@ <x,y> **GET** <field/memvar> [**PICTURE** <expC>] [**RANGE** <min>,<max>]

Normally used only in command files, the @ **GET** (at get) command is used with the **READ** command to allow direct access to a field or memory variable for editing. The x and y are numeric expressions designating the screen row (x = 0 to 24) and column (y = 0 to 79) coordinates where data are to be displayed.

When the **READ** command is executed, the cursor jumps to the first field or variable placed on the screen by an @ GET command. The user then may edit the data there with all the keystroke commands of an editing mode. When finished, the edited data replace any previous data that may have been in the field or variable. (See **READ,** page D-176.)

The optional [**PICTURE** <expC>] clause may be used to control the type of data to be entered into the field or memory variable. The character expression defines a template used for data entry control. For example, the clause **PICTURE** "99,999.99" may be used for a numeric entry to include a comma thousands separator and a decimal point. It also may be used to limit data entered to numerals and plus (+) or minus (−) signs. See the dBASE help screens for a list of template characters.

The optional [**RANGE** <min>,<max>] clause may be included to control the upper and lower bounds of a numeric entry. For example, **RANGE** 60,150 will cause an error message to be displayed if an attempt is made to enter a numeric value less than 60 or greater than 150. However, if the value already held in the field or memory variable is outside of the **RANGE** specified, the Enter key may be used to leave the value unedited, and range checking will not occur.

@ <x,y> **SAY** <exp> [**PICTURE** <expC>]

Normally used only in command files, the @ **SAY** (at say) command is used to display an expression on the screen or printer at specified coordinates. When data is displayed on the screen, the x and y numeric expressions designate the screen row (x = 0 to 24) and column (y = 0 to 79) coordinates where data are to be displayed.

When data is sent to the printer, the x and y coordinates designate the printer page row and column (horizontal position) where the data is to be printed. The maximum x and y values used when printing data with an @ **SAY** will depend on the number of lines per page and characters per inch (CPI) horizontally for which the printer is set.

The [**PICTURE** <expC>] clause is used to control the way data is displayed or printed. The character expression defines a template used to format the data. For example, the clause **PICTURE** "***,***.**" will cause the value to be displayed or printed with a comma thousands separator and a decimal point, and with asterisks preceding the number if necessary (i.e., the value 2850.6 would appear as **2,850.60 when displayed or printed). See the dBASE help screens for a list of template characters.

@ <x,y> **SAY** <exp> **GET** <field/memvar>

For data entry screens, the @ **SAY** and @ **GET** commands are often combined into a single command. In this case, one set of coordinates is used to specify where the @ **SAY** expression is to be displayed, and the field or memory variable to be edited with the @ **GET** will appear immediately following the @ **SAY** expression.

The following is a portion of a command file that contains @ **SAY** and @ **GET** commands used separately and in the combined form.

```
CLEAR
STORE 0 TO amt
STORE SPACE(15) TO name

@  3,25 SAY "* * * EMPLOYEE PURCHASES * * *"
@  5, 5 SAY "Employee Name: "
@  5,25 GET name
READ

LOCATE FOR employee = TRIM(name)
IF .NOT. EOF()
  @  5,45 SAY "Record found for: " + employee
  @  9, 5 SAY "Account Balance:"
  @  9,25 SAY account PICTURE "999.99"

  @  9,45 SAY "Purchase Amount:   " GET amt PICTURE "999.99" RANGE 0,500-account
  READ

  @ 11,45 SAY "New Balance:"
  @ 11,65 SAY account+amt PICTURE "999.99"
ELSE
  @  9, 5 SAY "Record not found"
ENDIF
```

When the commands shown are executed, the screen will appear with data displayed at the appropriate screen coordinates, as follows.

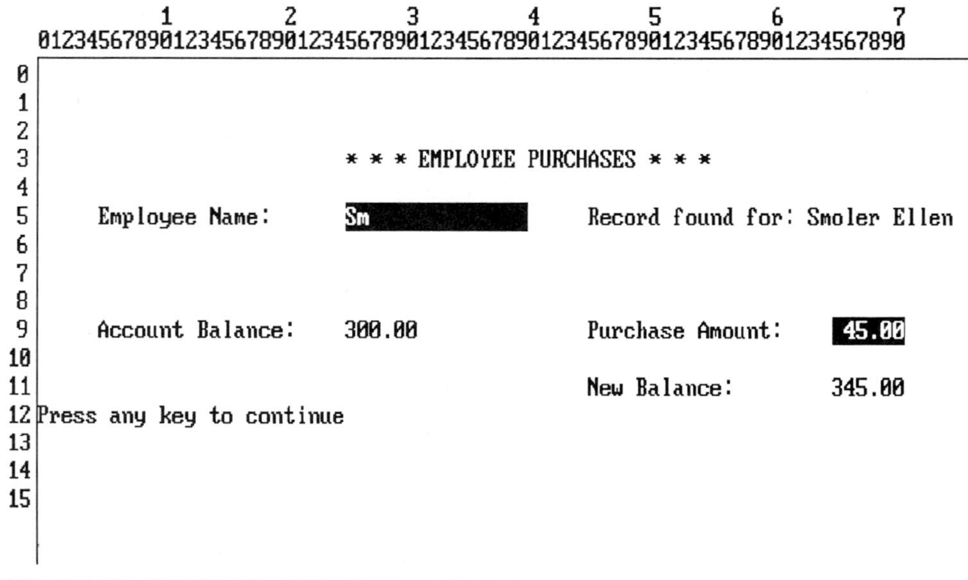

ACCEPT [<expC>] **TO** <memvarC>

Normally used in command files, this command is designed to prompt for a keyboard entry and then place the entry into a character-type memory variable. The optional [<expC>] immediately following **ACCEPT** is a character string used as a prompt to indicate the information to be entered.

```
. ACCEPT "Enter employee's name: " TO name
Enter employee's name: Martin

. ? name
Martin

. LOCATE FOR employee = name
Record =        5
```

APPEND

Appends a blank record to the database file in use and enters the record addition **(APPEND)** editing mode.

APPEND BLANK

Appends a blank record to the bottom of the database file in use.

APPEND FROM <filename> [**FOR** <condition>] [**TYPE** <file type>]

Appends records to the database file in use, either from another database file (.DBF) or from certain other types of files. If the **FROM** file is a .DBF file, any records marked for deletion in the **FROM** file will be appended and become unmarked in the file appended to. Also, if the **FROM** file is a .DBF file, only data in fields with identical field names will be appended to the file in use.

```
. CREATE deptmail
```

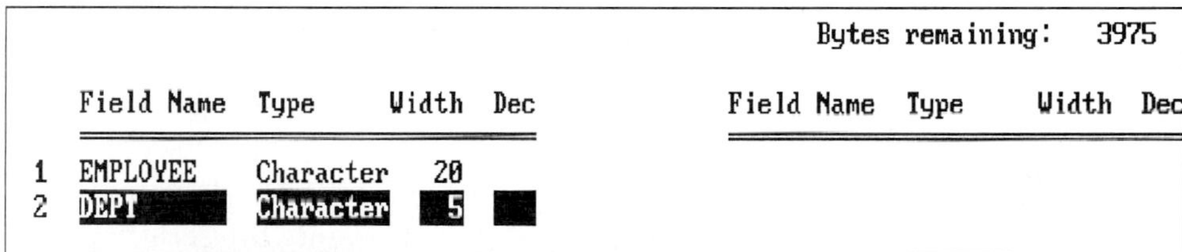

Bytes remaining: 3975

	Field Name	Type	Width	Dec	Field Name	Type	Width	Dec
1	EMPLOYEE	Character	20					
2	DEPT	Character	5					

```
. APPEND FROM empfile
     9 records added

. EDIT 1
```

```
EMPLOYEE    Pratt John
DEPT
```

The [**FOR** <condition>] option may be used to append only records meeting a given condition. Field names used in the condition must be found in the file being appended to.

The [**TYPE** <file type>] option may be used with the following <file type> parameters to append records from other types of files.

SDF	System Data Format (ASCII files).
DIF	A VisiCalc file format.
SYLK	Multiplan spreadsheet format.
WKS	Lotus 1-2-3 spreadsheet format.

ASSIST

Provides a menu-driven mode for execution of dBASE III Plus operations.

AVERAGE <expN list> [<scope>] [**FOR** <condition>] [**WHILE** <condition>] [**TO** <memvar list>]

Computes the averages of the numeric expressions in its <expN list> for records in the database file in use and displays the results. A numeric expression is usually the name of a field. If the [**TO** <memvar list>] option is used, resulting averages are stored to memory variables specified (the two lists must have the same number of entries). The parameters [<scope>], [**FOR** <condition>], and [**WHILE** <condition>] may be used to limit the number of records included in the average calculation. Default <scope> is **ALL** records.

```
. AVERAGE salary,account FOR sex = "F" TO fsal,facct
      4 records averaged
  salary  account
 1551.75   206.38

. DISPLAY MEMORY
FSAL        pub   N        1551.75  (       1551.75000000)
FACCT       pub   N         206.38  (        206.37500000)
    2 variables defined,       18 bytes used
  254 variables available,   5982 bytes available
```

BROWSE [FIELDS <field list>] [**LOCK** <expN>] [**FREEZE** <field>] [**NOFOLLOW**] [**NOMENU**] [**WIDTH** <expN>] [**NOAPPEND**]

Enters the **BROWSE** editing mode. The optional parameter [**FIELDS** <field list>] causes dBASE to display only the fields listed for editing. The fields in the <field list> must be separated by commas. The other optional parameters that may be included when the **BROWSE** command is executed are as follows.

[**LOCK** <expN>]	Prevents the scrolling of the left-most fields when Ctrl-Left or Ctrl-Right is used to pan the screen (scroll horizontally). The <expN> defines how many fields should be prevented from scrolling.
[**FREEZE** <field>]	Allows editing of only the field specified. All other fields are displayed normally.
[**NOFOLLOW**]	Prevents the record pointer from moving with an indexed record when a field that is part of the index key is edited.
[**NOMENU**]	Prevents access to a menu bar that may otherwise be toggled on and off with the F10 key.
[**WIDTH** <expN>]	Limits the display of all character fields to the number of characters defined by <expN>. For fields longer than the width set, the cursor will scroll vertically within the field.
[**NOAPPEND**]	Prevents appending of records in the **BROWSE** mode.

The **LOCK** and **FREEZE** options also may be accessed after entering the **BROWSE** mode by typing F10 to toggle a menu bar on and off. Other options on the menu bar are to move the cursor to the top or bottom of the file or to a specific record number.

CALL <module name> [**WITH** <expC> / <memvar>]

Executes a binary file already loaded into RAM with the **LOAD** command. (See **LOAD,** page D-166.)

CANCEL

Used in a command file, stops command execution and returns to the dBASE dot (.) prompt mode. If execution of a command file was suspended after an error was detected by dBASE or with the **SUSPEND** command, the **CANCEL** command may be used from the dot (.) prompt to cancel the suspended program.

CHANGE [<scope>] [**FIELDS** <field list>] [**FOR** <condition>] [**WHILE** <condition>]

The **CHANGE** command is identical to the **EDIT** command (see **EDIT,** page D-163).

CLEAR

Clears the screen and releases any @ **GET**s that may have been active.

CLEAR ALL

Closes all database files in use and any associated files (.NDX, .DBT, .FMT, .CAT), releases all memory variables, and selects work area 1. (See **USE,** page D-191; **RELEASE,** page D-176; and **SELECT,** page D-180.)

CLEAR FIELDS

Clears any field list previously set with the **SET FIELDS TO** command in all work areas. (See **SET FIELDS TO,** page D-185.)

CLEAR GETS

Releases all active @ **GET** commands without erasing the screen.

CLEAR MEMORY

Releases all memory variables. (See also **RELEASE,** page D-176.)

CLEAR TYPEAHEAD

Used in command files, clears any characters that may be in the typeahead buffer.

CLOSE <file type> / **ALL**

Closes all files of the type specified by <file type> or **ALL** open files. The <file type> may be ALTERNATE, DATABASES, FORMAT, INDEX, or PROCEDURE.

CONTINUE

Resumes a search previously initiated with a **LOCATE** command in the currently selected work area. (See **LOCATE,** page D-166.)

COPY TO <filename> [<scope>] [**FIELDS** <field list>] [**FOR** <condition>] [**WHILE** <condition>] [**TYPE** <file type>/ **DELIMITED** [**WITH** <delimiter>]]

Copies the database in use to another .DBF file which it creates at the time the command is executed. The parameters [<scope>], [**FOR** <condition>], and [**WHILE** <condition>] may be used to limit the number of records copied. The [**FIELDS** <field list>] parameter may be used to create the new database with only specified fields included.

The [**TYPE** <file type>] parameter may be used to create and copy records to another type of file (see the **APPEND FROM** command, page D-153, for a list of <file type> parameters). The [**DELIMITED**] parameter may be used to create and copy records to an ASCII file (extension .TXT) with each record on a separate line, fields separated by commas, and character fields enclosed in double quotes ("). The double quote may be substituted with another character by using the parameter [**DELIMITED WITH** <delimiter>].

```
. COPY TO enplistm FIELDS employee,salary FOR sex = "M" DELIMITED
     5 records copied

. TYPE cmplistm.txt
"Pratt John",1949.00
"Johnson Frank",1500.00
"Jones David",1550.00
"Knat Michael",1800.00
"Smith Paul",1700.00


. COPY TO enplistf FIELDS employee,salary FOR sex = "F" DELIMITED WITH '
     4 records copied

. TYPE emplistf.txt
'Martins Mary',1600.00
'Nichols Sandy',1450.00
'Sill Sally',1507.50
'Smoler Ellen',1650.00
```

COPY TO <filename> STRUCTURE EXTENDED

Converts the structure of the database file into records and copies them to the <filename> specified. The file created has four fields: FIELD_NAME, FIELD_TYPE, FIELD_LEN, and FIELD_DEC.

```
. DISPLAY STRUCTURE
Structure for database: A:EMPFILE.dbf
Number of data records:        9
Date of last update   : 07/26/90
Field  Field Name  Type       Width    Dec
    1  EMPLOYEE    Character     20
    2  TELEPHONE   Character      8
    3  SEX         Character      1
    4  EMPLOYED    Date           8
    5  SALARY      Numeric        8      2
    6  ACCOUNT     Numeric        8      2
** Total **                      54

. COPY TO stfile1 STRUCTURE EXTENDED

. USE stfile1

. LIST
Record#  FIELD_NAME FIELD_TYPE FIELD_LEN FIELD_DEC
      1  EMPLOYEE   C                 20         0
      2  TELEPHONE  C                  8         0
      3  SEX        C                  1         0
      4  EMPLOYED   D                  8         0
      5  SALARY     N                  8         2
      6  ACCOUNT    N                  8         2
```

The file created may be edited and used like any database file and the **CREATE FROM** command may later be used to create a new database file with the structure taken from the records in this file. If this is intended, care must be taken to enter valid field names, types, lengths, and decimals when editing the records of the extended file. (See **CREATE FROM,** page D-158.)

COPY FILE [<*drive:*>] <filename.ext> **TO** [<*drive:*>] <filename.ext>

Makes a copy of any type of file. The first <filename.ext> specified is copied **TO** the second <filename.ext> specified. Data is copied in blocks of 512 bytes and the size of the two files may not match exactly.

COPY STRUCTURE TO <filename>

Creates a .DBF file with the specified <filename> with a record structure that is the same as the current database. No records are copied to the new file.

COUNT [<scope>] [**FOR** <condition>] [**WHILE** <condition>] [**TO** <memvar>]

Counts the number of records in the database in use. The parameters [<scope>], [**FOR** <condition>], and [**WHILE** <condition>] may be used to limit the number of records counted. Default <scope> is **ALL** records. The [**TO** <memvar>] parameter may be used to store the results to a memory variable.

CREATE <filename>

Used to create a new database file (.DBF extension). The record structure is entered in a dBASE editing mode.

CREATE <filename> **FROM** <structure extended file>

Creates a new database file (.DBF) with a structure taken from the records of another database file that has the four fields: FIELD_NAME, FIELD_TYPE, FIELD_LEN, and FIELD_DEC. (See **COPY TO STRUCTURE EXTENDED,** page D-156.)

```
. USE stfile2

. LIST
Record#  FIELD_NAME FIELD_TYPE FIELD_LEN FIELD_DEC
      1  EMPLOYEE   C                 20         0
      2  SALARY     N                  8         2
      3  ACCOUNT    N                  8         2

. CREATE empfile2 FROM stfile2

. USE empfile2

. DISPLAY STRUCTURE
Structure for database: C:empfile2.dbf
Number of data records:       0
Date of last update   : 07/26/90
Field  Field Name  Type       Width    Dec
    1  EMPLOYEE    Character     20
    2  SALARY      Numeric        8      2
    3  ACCOUNT     Numeric        8      2
** Total **                      37
```

CREATE LABEL <filename>

Identical to **MODIFY LABEL.** (See **MODIFY LABEL,** page D-167.)

CREATE QUERY <filename>

Identical to **MODIFY QUERY.** (See **MODIFY QUERY,** page D-168.)

CREATE REPORT <filename>

Identical to **MODIFY REPORT.** (See **MODIFY REPORT,** page D-169.)

CREATE VIEW FROM ENVIRONMENT

Creates a view file (.VUE) from the files currently open. (See **MODIFY VIEW,** page D-174.)

DELETE [<scope>] [**FOR** <condition>] [**WHILE** <condition>]
and
DELETE [**RECORD** <expN>]

Marks record(s) for deletion. Records marked for deletion will not be physically removed from the database until the **PACK** command is executed. The parameters [<scope>], [**FOR** <condition>], and [**WHILE** <condition>] may be used to mark a group of records for deletion. Default scope is the current record. The parameter [**RECORD** <expN>] may be used to mark a specific record for deletion by its record number. Records also may be marked/unmarked with ^U while in edit modes. (See **RECALL,** page D-176, and **PACK,** page D-175.)

DIR [<*drive:*>] [<skeleton>]

Lists a directory of files. **DIR** with no parameters displays the names of all .DBF files on the default drive. The <*drive:*> parameter may be used to specify another disk drive. The <skeleton> parameter is used to display other types of files.

A <skeleton> is made up of filename characters and masking characters that act as "wild cards." The asterisk (*) indicates "Accept any other characters" while the question mark (?) means "Accept any single character in this position." The command **DIR** *.* will list all files on the disk.

```
.DIR *.FRM
FULLREPO.FRM        SALARIES.FRM        ACCTREPO.FRM

   5970 bytes in       3 files

352256 bytes remaining on drive.


.DIR REPORT?.PRG
REPORT1.PRG         REPORT2.PRG

   2048 bytes in       2 files

352256 bytes remaining on drive.
```

DISPLAY [<scope>] [<expression list>] [**FOR** <condition>] [**WHILE** <condition>] [**OFF**] [**TO PRINT**]

Displays information for records in the database file in use on the monitor screen. The expressions in <expression list> may be of any type and may include field names, memory variables, literal values, and functions. The parameters [<scope>], [**FOR** <condition>], and [**WHILE** <condition>] may be used to display information for a group of records. The default scope is the current record. The [**OFF**] parameter suppresses display of record numbers. The [**TO PRINT**] parameter echoes screen output to the printer.

```
. AVERAGE ALL salary TO avgsal

. DISPLAY ALL employee, sex, salary-avgsal, IIF(salary<avgsal,"<--","") OFF
 employee            sex  salary-avgsal IIF(salary<avgsal,"<--","")
 Pratt John          M           315.00
 Smoler Ellen        F            16.00
 Jones David         M           -84.00 <--
 Sill Sally          F          -127.00 <--
 Knat Michael        M           166.00
 Smith Paul          M            66.00
 Martins Mary        F           -34.00 <--
 Nichols Sandy       F          -184.00 <--
 Johnson Frank       M          -134.00 <--
```

DISPLAY HISTORY [**LAST** <expN>] [**TO PRINT**]

Displays the most recently executed commands held in the **HISTORY** buffer. dBASE sets aside a small portion of RAM (a buffer) called **HISTORY** into which it stores previously executed commands. By default, the **HISTORY** buffer holds the last 20 commands executed from the dot (.)

prompt. The buffer allows the user to back up, edit, and then reenter previous commands.

To display a previous command, the cursor up key is typed. Each time the key is typed, dBASE displays the next previous command (scrolls back through the commands in the **HISTORY** buffer). To scroll forward, the cursor down key is typed. When the desired command is displayed, the following keystrokes may be used to edit the command.

Keystroke	Action
Cursor right	Moves cursor right one character.
Cursor left	Moves cursor left one character.
Home	Moves cursor one word to the left.
End	Moves cursor one word to the right.
Ins	Toggles between overwrite and insert modes.
Del	Deletes character at cursor location.
Backspace	Deletes character to left of cursor.
^T	Deletes word to right of cursor.
^Y	Deletes line to right of cursor.
Esc	Aborts any changes made and returns cursor to beginning of command line.

The **DISPLAY HISTORY** command with the [**LAST** <expN>] parameter is used to display fewer commands than may be held in the full **HISTORY** buffer. The [**TO PRINT**] parameter echoes screen output to the printer. (See also **SET HISTORY TO,** page D-186, and **SET DOHISTORY,** page D-184.)

DISPLAY MEMORY [TO PRINT]

Displays names, types, and contents of all current memory variables. The [**TO PRINT**] parameter echoes screen output to the printer.

DISPLAY STATUS [TO PRINT]

Lists files that are open, displaying information about their relationships, **SET** command settings, function key assignments, and other current environment information. The [**TO PRINT**] parameter echoes screen output to the printer.

DISPLAY STRUCTURE [TO PRINT]

Displays field names, types, widths, and decimals (the record structure) of the database in use. The [**TO PRINT**] parameter echoes screen output to the printer.

DO <filename> [**WITH** <expression list>]

Opens and begins execution of the commands in the specified command file. The [**WITH** <expression list>] option is used to pass parameters (expressions) to the command files. (See **PARAMETERS,** page D-175.)

DO CASE
  CASE <condition>
    any commands
  [**CASE** <condition>]
    any commands
  [**CASE** <condition>]
    any commands
  [**OTHERWISE**]
    any commands
ENDCASE

Used only in command files, this command structure is used to select a single set of commands to execute. It is useful when the criteria for command executions are mutually exclusive. When **DO CASE** is encountered, the first **CASE** <condition> is evaluated. If evaluated as true, the commands immediately following are executed and then control passes to the first command following **ENDCASE.** If evaluated as false, the next **CASE** <condition> is evaluated. The process continues until a **CASE** <condition> is evaluated as true or **ENDCASE** is encountered. The [**OTHERWISE**] is optional and its commands are executed when none of the **CASE** <condition>s have been evaluated as true. **ENDCASE** is needed to complete the command structure.

```
USE empfile
CLEAR
STORE " " TO ans
@ 3,25 SAY "      MENU OPTIONS      "
@ 5,25 SAY "  1 - Add a Record      "
@ 6,25 SAY "  2 - Delete a Record   "
@ 7,25 SAY "  3 - Edit Records      "
@ 9,25 SAY "Enter Menu Selection:" GET ans
READ
DO CASE
   CASE ans = "1"
     APPEND
   CASE ans = "2"
     INPUT "Record number of record to delete ? " TO n
     GOTO n
     DISPLAY employee
     ACCEPT "Correct record ? (Y/N)" TO confirm
     IF UPPER(confirm) = "Y"
       DELETE
     ENDIF
   OTHERWISE
     BROWSE NOAPPEND
ENDCASE
CLEAR
RETURN
```

DO WHILE <condition>
  any commands
ENDDO

Used only in command files, the **DO WHILE...ENDDO** command structure creates a program loop. When **DO WHILE** is encountered, the <condition> is evaluated. If evaluated as true, commands between the **DO WHILE** and its **ENDDO** are executed repeatedly until the **DO WHILE**'s <condition> is no longer true.

It is important that within the loop there is something to cause the <condition> to become false at some point. Otherwise, an "endless loop" situation exists—one in which there is no exit from the **DO WHILE**...**ENDDO** loop. In the following example, an end-of-file condition must occur to end the loop process, and **SKIP** is the command that ensures that the record pointer will eventually reach the end of the file.

```
USE empfile
SET TALK OFF
SET PRINT ON

DO WHILE .NOT. EOF()
  IF account > .15 * salary
    ? "To: ",employee
    ? "From:  Accounting"
    ?
    ? "You have exceeded your personal account limit by"
    ? account - .15 * salary, ".  Please make arrangements"
    ? "to pay this amount as soon as possible."
    EJECT
  ENDIF
  SKIP
ENDDO

SET PRINT OFF
SET TALK ON
USE
RETURN
```

Using **LOOP** and **EXIT** in a **DO WHILE**...**ENDDO** Structure

The commands **LOOP** and **EXIT** have meaning only within a **DO WHILE**...**ENDDO** loop. **LOOP** may be used to cause command execution to jump back to the **DO WHILE** <condition> before the **ENDDO** has been reached. The <condition> then is evaluated again to determine if loop processing should continue. **EXIT** causes command execution to jump to the command immediately following the **ENDDO** command (exit the loop) regardless of the evaluation of the **DO WHILE** <condition>.

In the following example, records in the database file are to be processed until an end-of-file condition occurs. The **REPORT FORM** command used with the [**WHILE** <condition>] parameter has the effect of skipping through records of the file until the <condition> is false, at which point the record pointer will already be on the next record. The **LOOP** command is used to avoid executing the **SKIP** command at the end of the loop. The **EXIT** command is used to immediately exit the loop if more than 5 records have been found with invalid data in the sex field, whether or not the end of the file has been reached.

NOTE: The operator $ used in the command line **IF** *sex $ "MF" means "if the value of the field sex is found within the string "MF"." It is roughly equivalent to using the logical operator .OR. in the command* **IF** sex = "M" .OR. sex = "F".

```
USE empfile INDEX sexdex          && file indexed on sex field
STORE 0 TO errcount

DO WHILE .NOT. EOF()
  IF sex $ "MF"
    IF sex = "F"
      REPORT FORM salaryf TO PRINT WHILE sex = "F"
    ELSE
      REPORT FORM salarym TO PRINT WHILE sex = "M"
    ENDIF
    LOOP
  ELSE
    STORE errcount + 1 to errcount
    IF errcount > 5
      ? "Too many gender code errors encountered to produce accurate reports"
      EXIT
    ELSE
      ? "Error - Invalid gender code for " + employee
    ENDIF
  ENDIF
  SKIP
ENDDO

USE
RETURN
```

EDIT [<scope>] [**FIELDS** <field list>] [**FOR** <condition>] [**WHILE** <condition>]

Allows editing of records in the database file in use. Editing may be limited to fields specified with the [**FIELDS** <field list>] option. The parameters [<scope>], [**FOR** <condition>], and [**WHILE** <condition>] may be used to limit the number of records included for editing.

```
. EDIT FIELDS employee,account FOR account > 0
```

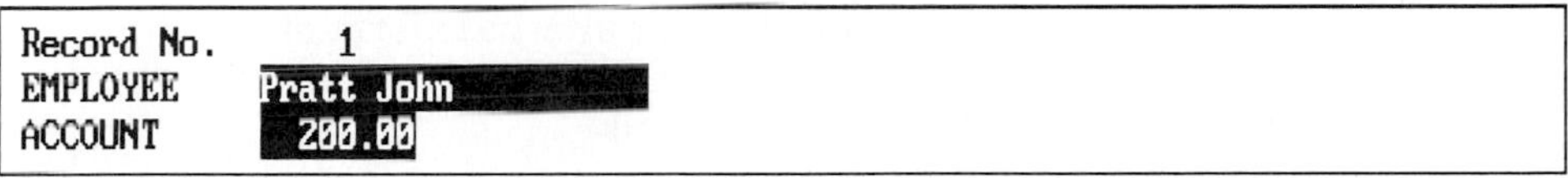

EJECT

Causes printer to form feed (page eject).

ERASE <filename.extension>

Erases a file from the diskette. **ERASE** may not be used to erase an open file.

EXIT

See "Using **LOOP** and **EXIT** in a **DO WHILE**...**ENDDO** Structure," page D-162.

EXPORT TO <filename> **TYPE PFS**

Copies the current dBASE database file and its open format file (.FMT), if any, to a single file named <filename> in the database format used by PFS:FILE.

FIND <literal string / &memvarC>

Used with index files, **FIND** positions the record pointer to the first database record indexed by <literal string / &memvarC>. If a literal string is used, the string is not enclosed in quotations ("), and if a character-type memory variable is used, the name of the variable is preceded by an ampersand (&). (See **SEEK,** page D-179.)

```
. USE empfile INDEX namedex

. FIND Smith P

. DISPLAY
Record#  EMPLOYEE             TELEPHONE SEX EMPLOYED   SALARY  ACCOUNT
      6  Smith Paul           244-1010  M   11/15/81  1700.00   350.00

. STORE "Johns" TO z

. FIND &z

. DISPLAY
Record#  EMPLOYEE             TELEPHONE SEX EMPLOYED   SALARY  ACCOUNT
      9  Johnson Frank        223-7928  M   03/20/90  1500.00     0.00
```

GO <expN> / **TOP** / **BOTTOM**

GO <expN> moves the record pointer to the record with the record number <expN>. **GO TOP** and **GO BOTTOM** move the record pointer to the first and last records in the file, respectively. If an index is in use, **GO TOP** and **GO BOTTOM** move the record pointer to the first and last records in the indexed order. An alternate form of the command is **GOTO.**

HELP [<key word>]

HELP invokes a menu-driven, on-line facility that provides information on various dBASE III Plus commands and operations. If a command or function is specified in the <key word> parameter, **HELP** provides a screen of summary information on that command or function.

IF <condition>
  any commands
ENDIF

Used only in command files, the **IF...ENDIF** command structure permits conditional execution of commands. If the <condition> evaluates as true, the commands between the **IF** and the **ENDIF** are executed; otherwise, the commands are ignored. Each **IF** command used must have a matching **ENDIF.**

IF <condition>
  any commands
[**ELSE**]
  any commands
ENDIF

When the optional [**ELSE**] clause is included, the structure becomes **IF**...**ELSE**...**ENDIF.** If the <condition> evaluates as true, only the commands between the **IF** and the **ELSE** are executed; otherwise, only the commands between the **ELSE** and the **ENDIF** are executed.

IMPORT FROM <filename> **TYPE PFS**

Creates a dBASE database file (.DBF) and a format file (.FMT), both having the same filename, from a PFS:FILE database file named <filename>. At the time a file is imported, dBASE creates a view file (.VUE) that relates the .DBF and .FMT files.

INDEX ON <expression> **TO** <index file> [**UNIQUE**]

Creates an index file (.NDX) for the database in use. The index file is based on key field(s) specified in the <expression>. The <expression> type may be character, numeric, or date. The [**UNIQUE**] parameter causes only the first record of several records having the same key <expression> to be included in the index file.

INPUT [<expC>] **TO** <memvarN>

Normally used in command files, this command is designed to prompt for a keyboard entry and then place the entry into a numeric-type memory variable. The optional [<expC>] immediately following **INPUT** is a character string used as a prompt to indicate the information to be entered.

```
. INPUT "Enter minimum salary to display: " TO minsal
Enter minimum salary to display: 1600

. DISPLAY FOR salary >= minsal
Record#  EMPLOYEE                 TELEPHONE SEX EMPLOYED    SALARY  ACCOUNT
      1  Pratt John               225-1234  M   06/22/82  1949.00   200.00
      2  Smoler Ellen             225-3212  F   09/15/83  1650.00   300.00
      5  Knat Michael             221-1235  M   09/15/80  1800.00   125.00
      6  Smith Paul               244-1010  M   11/15/81  1700.00   350.00
      7  Martins Mary             222-2123  F   11/01/85  1600.00   200.50
```

INSERT [**BLANK**] [**BEFORE**]

The **INSERT** command inserts a record into the database in use immediately after the current record and enters an editing mode for that record. If the [**BLANK**] parameter is used, a blank record is inserted without entering the editing mode for the record inserted. If the [**BEFORE**] parameter is used, the blank record is inserted immediately before the current record.

JOIN WITH <alias> **TO** <filename> **FOR** <condition> [**FIELDS** <field list>]

Creates a new database by combining the records of the .DBF files in use in two work areas. Records are added to a third database (specified by **TO** <filename>). Combined records are created when the **FOR** <condition> evaluates as true for the current record of the current file as it is compared to each record of the <alias> database file. That is, each record of the current file is compared to all records of the <alias> file.

LABEL FORM <filename> [<scope>] **[FOR** <condition>] **[WHILE** <condition>] **[TO PRINT / TO FILE** <filename>] **[SAMPLE]**

Produces labels from the specifications within a label file (.LBL). Label files are created with the **MODIFY LABEL** command. The parameters [<scope>], [**FOR** <condition>], and [**WHILE** <condition>] may be used to limit the number of records for which labels are produced. The default <scope> is **ALL** records.

The [**SAMPLE**] parameter may be used to print test labels to ensure proper label registration. The [**TO FILE** <filename>] parameter may be used to print labels in ASCII format to a diskette file. (See **MODIFY LABEL,** page D-167.)

LIST

The following **LIST** commands are identical to the **DISPLAY** commands except that there are no screen pauses and the default <scope> is **ALL** records when <scope> is part of the command syntax.

LIST [<scope>] [<expression list>] [**FOR** <condition>] [**WHILE** <condition>] [**TO PRINT**] [**OFF**]
LIST HISTORY
LIST MEMORY
LIST STATUS
LIST STRUCTURE

LOAD <filename>[.<ext>]

Loads a binary file into RAM where it may be executed with the **CALL** command.

LOCATE [<scope>] **FOR** <condition> [**WHILE** <condition>]

Moves the record pointer to the first record in the database for which the **FOR** <condition> evaluates as true. If [<scope>] is specified, moves record pointer to the first such record in <scope>. The **CONTINUE** command finds the next such record.

```
. LOCATE FOR salary <= 1500
Record =        8

. CONTINUE
Record =        9

. CONTINUE
End of LOCATE scope
```

LOOP

See "Using **LOOP** and **EXIT** in a **DO WHILE...ENDDO** Structure," page D–162.

MODIFY COMMAND <filename>

Enters dBASE's word processor editing mode to create or edit ASCII files. Normally used to edit command files (.PRG), the **MODIFY COMMAND** mode also may be used to edit .TXT and .FMT files. The maximum file size that **MODIFY COMMAND** can edit is 4,096 bytes.

MODIFY LABEL <filename>

The **MODIFY LABEL** command is used to create or edit a label form file (.LBL) to hold label specifications for use by the **LABEL FORM** command. The label specifications are entered in a dBASE editing mode similar to the **MODIFY REPORT** mode, and the file created is given a .LBL file extension by dBASE.

The **MODIFY LABEL** and **LABEL FORM** commands are primarily designed to produce mailing or identification labels on tractor-fed label stock paper. To produce such labels, the width and height of the labels, left print margin, lines and spaces between labels, and number of labels across a page must be specified. These specifications are made with the Options pull-down menu, which is the first screen the **MODIFY LABEL** command presents.

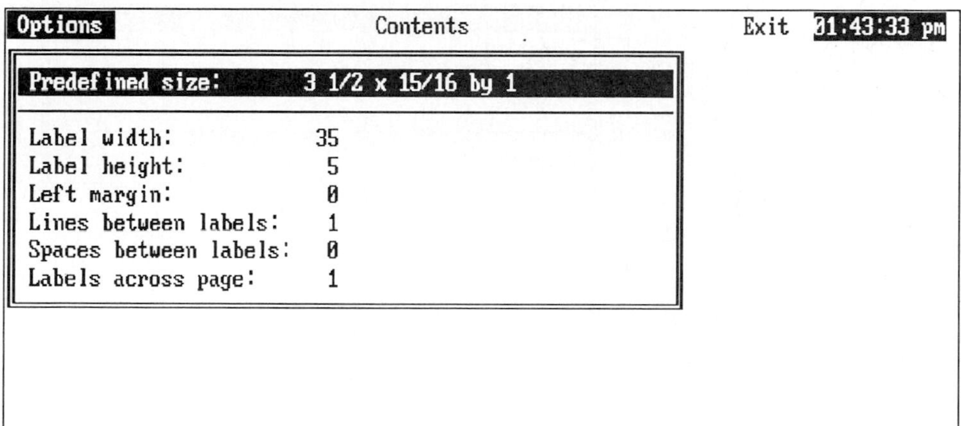

Use the cursor right key to access the Contents pull-down menu, which is used to specify the contents of each line of the label. Move the cursor to the desired line and type the Enter key ↵. Then type an expression list defining the contents for the line (separate expressions with commas if more than one is entered). To include a field name in the contents of a line, you may use the F10 key to select a field from a list in the database file in use.

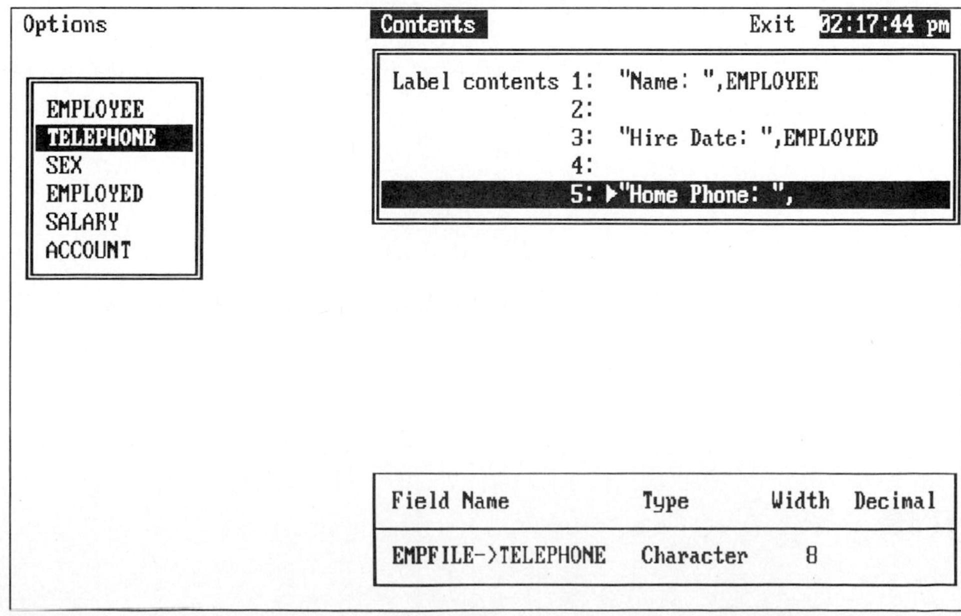

When done entering the line, type ↵. When done defining the label, use the cursor right key to access the Exit pull-down menu. Then select "Save" to save the file or "Abandon" to leave the file as it was before changes were made. To produce labels, see the **LABEL FORM** command, page D–166.

MODIFY QUERY <filename>

The **MODIFY QUERY** command is used to create or change a query file (.QRY) used with the **SET FILTER TO FILE** <filename> command. The **MODIFY QUERY** command uses a full-screen, menu-driven mode for entry of a filter expression.

To set a filter condition to limit records to all men with salaries greater than $1,600 for the database file empfile.DBF, you would first put empfile into use, and then type the **MODIFY QUERY** <filename> command.

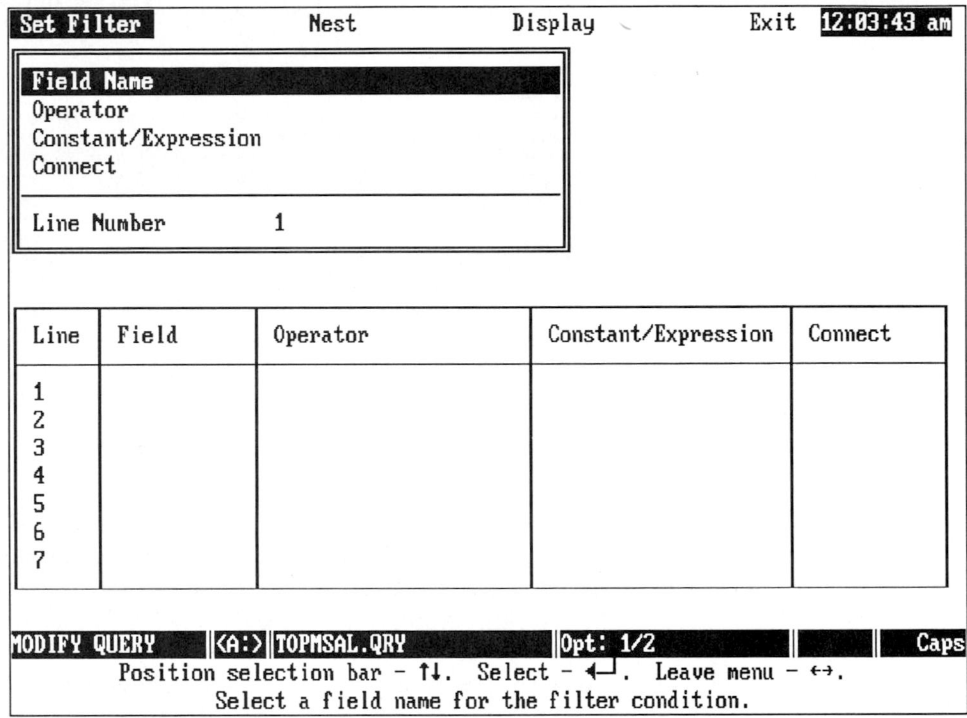

The Set Filter option of the menu bar is used to select fields, relational operators, expressions, and logical operators to form the filter condition (a logical expression). Each item and operator of the condition is selected from a menu.

```
Set Filter          Nest          Display          Exit   12:08:46 am

 Field Name              SALARY
 Operator                More than
 Constant/Expression     1600
 Connect

 Line Number             2
```

Line	Field	Operator	Constant/Expression	Connect
1	SEX	Matches	"M"	.AND.
2	SALARY	More than	1600	
3				
4				
5				
6				
7				

```
MODIFY QUERY  <A:> TOPMSAL.QRY      Opt: 5/5                  Caps
       Position selection bar - ↑↓.  Select - ◄┘.  Leave menu - ←→.
            Enter the line number of the query form to edit next.
```

When finished, the condition(s) specified are described on lines one through seven. The next option of the menu bar, Nest, is used to add parentheses to a logical expression composed of more than two conditions connected with logical operators. Here the positions for parentheses are entered so that they start or stop on a condition, with the start or stop position entered as the condition number according to the order it appears in the logical expression (1st, 2nd, 3rd, etc.).

The Display option of the **MODIFY QUERY** menu bar displays the records of the current database that pass the filter expression currently defined. The Exit option is used to save the .QRY file and return to the dot (.) prompt mode.

Once a .QRY file has been created, the **SET FILTER TO FILE** <filename> command is used to activate the filter expression in it. While the filter is active, only those records passing it will be processed by dBASE. To deactivate a filter, the **SET FILTER TO** command is used without parameters. (See **SET FILTER TO,** page D–185.)

MODIFY REPORT <filename>

The **MODIFY REPORT** command is used to create or edit a report form file (.FRM) to hold report specifications for use by the **REPORT FORM** command. See "Producing dBASE Reports," dBASE III Plus Exercises, for further information.

MODIFY SCREEN <filename>

The **MODIFY SCREEN** command serves as a dBASE program generator. The programs it generates are format files (.FMT) created from screen files (.SCR). Format files are composed of **@ SAY, @ GET,** and **READ** commands—commands used to format screens for data input and output.

MODIFY SCREEN uses a full-screen, menu-driven mode for data entry and provides a blank screen (called the *blackboard*) on which the input/output screen is created. The menus and blackboard are mutually-exclusive data entry modes. The F10 key is used to toggle (switch) from one mode to the other.

The **MODIFY SCREEN** menu bar provides a Set Up option for selecting the fields of data to be displayed on the finished screen. First, a database file is selected from a menu of available database files with the Select Database File option. Then the fields to be included in the screen are selected from a menu generated by the Load Fields option. (A database file also may be created with the Set Up option of **MODIFY SCREEN,** with the structure entered through the Modify option.)

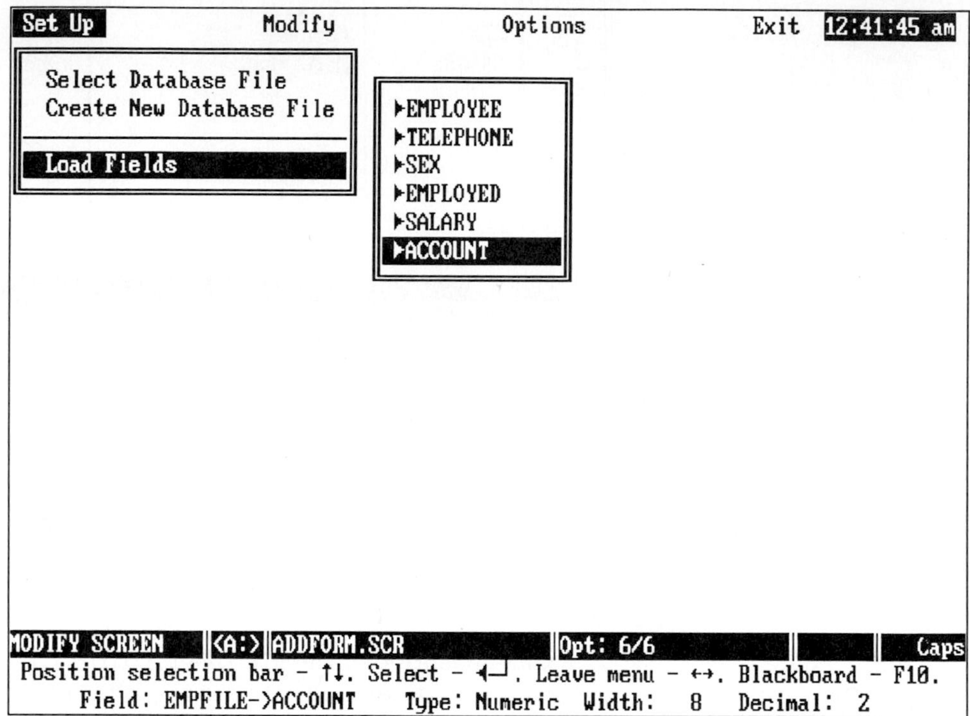

The arrow keys ↓ and ↑ are used to move through the field list displayed, and the Enter key ↵ is used to select fields to be placed on the blackboard. Selected fields are marked with an arrow and may also be unmarked with the Enter key. When the F10 key (or a character key) is typed, the selected fields are placed on the blackboard and are displayed in reverse video next to their field names. The user then is left in the blackboard mode.

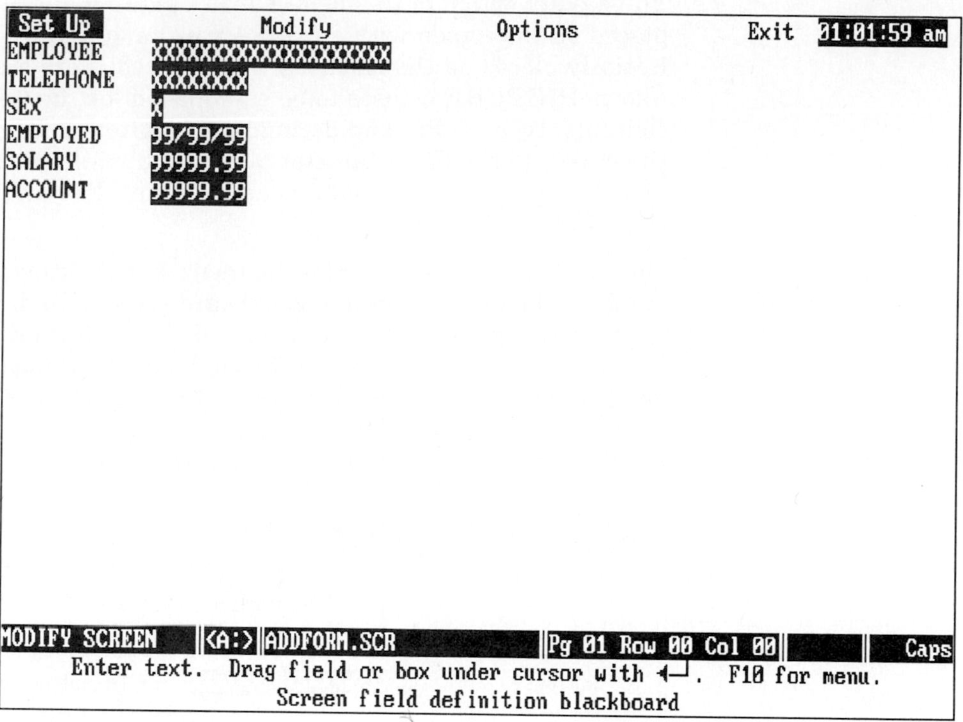

While in the blackboard mode, editing keystrokes similar to those of **MODIFY COMMAND** allow the user to enter screen text. To relocate a field currently displayed on the blackboard, move the cursor to the first character of the field and press the Enter key ↵. Then move the cursor to the new position and press the Enter key again.

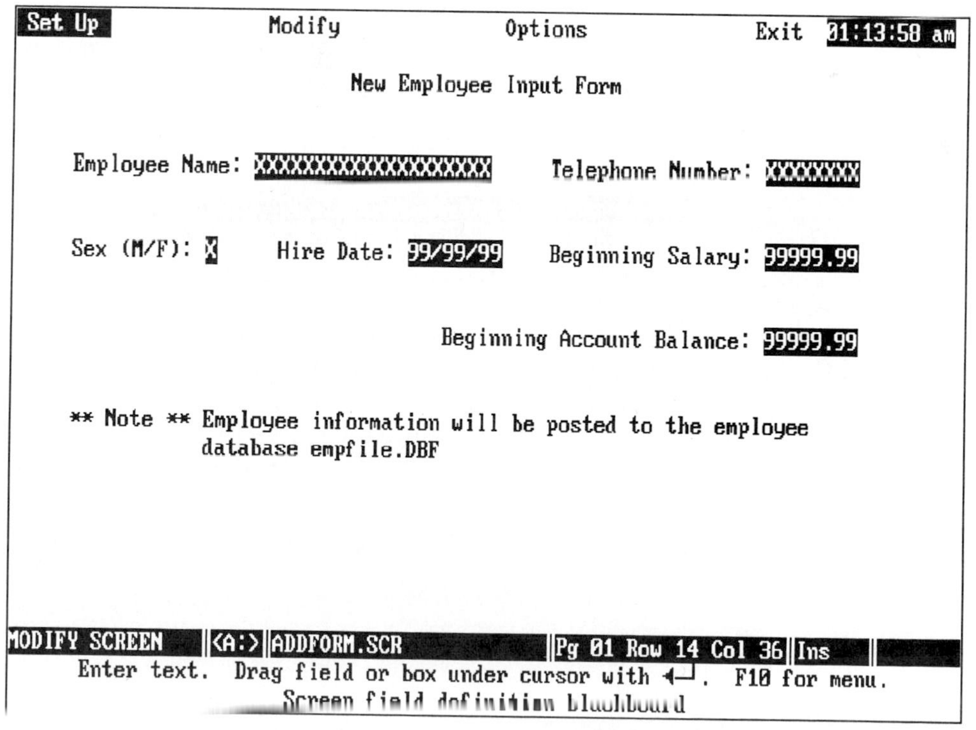

The Modify option of the menu bar is used to determine if a field will be placed on the screen with an @ **SAY** or an @ **GET** command. All fields initially placed on the blackboard are placed there as @ **GET**s. Modify also allows **PICTURE** clauses to be established for the field and permits field contents, type, width, and decimals to be altered. To modify a field, move the cursor to the first character of the field while in the blackboard mode, and then toggle to the menu mode by typing F10 and select the Modify option of the menu bar.

Options may be selected from the menu bar to draw a line or a box with single or double bars on the blackboard screen. To draw a line or box, toggle to the menu mode, select Options, and then select either Single bar or Double bar. The screen will return to the blackboard mode. Move the cursor to one corner of the area to be boxed or lined, type the Enter key ↵, move the cursor to the opposite diagonal corner of the box or the other end of the line to be drawn, and then type the Enter key again.

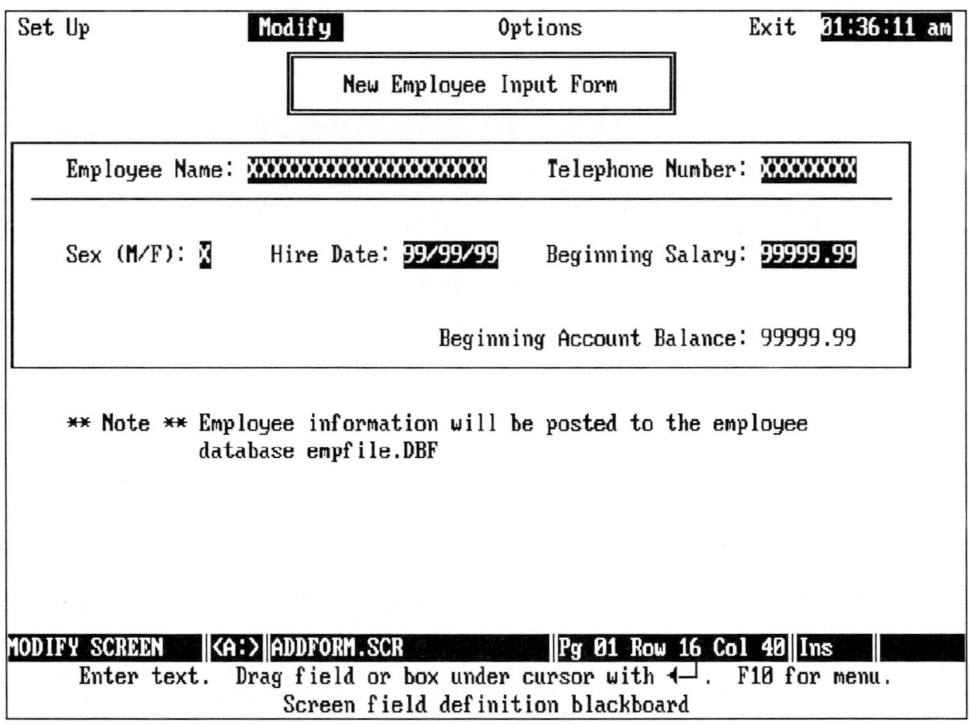

When the blackboard is finished, the Exit option of the menu bar is used to save the .SCR file and generate the .FMT file from it. Both files have the same filename. Later, if the .SCR file is altered with **MODIFY SCREEN,** a new .FMT file is produced when the Exit operation is completed. The following is a listing of the .FMT file created in this example.

```
. TYPE addform.fmt
@  1, 28  SAY "New Employee Input Form"
@  4,  5  SAY "Employee Name:"
@  4, 20  GET  EMPFILE->EMPLOYEE
@  4, 45  SAY "Telephone Number:"
@  4, 63  GET  EMPFILE->TELEPHONE
@  7,  5  SAY "Sex (M/F):"
@  7, 16  GET  EMPFILE->SEX
@  7, 22  SAY "Hire Date:"
@  7, 33  GET  EMPFILE->EMPLOYED
@  7, 45  SAY "Beginning Salary:"
@  7, 63  GET  EMPFILE->SALARY
@ 10, 36  SAY "Beginning Account Balance:"
@ 10, 63  SAY  EMPFILE->ACCOUNT
@ 13,  5  SAY "** Note ** Employee information will be posted to the employee"
@ 14, 16  SAY "database empfile.DBF"
@  0, 23  TO  2, 55    DOUBLE
@  3,  0  TO 11, 75
@  5,  2  TO  5, 73
```

A format file (.FMT) is activated with the **SET FORMAT TO** <filename> command. Once activated, it affects the screen displays for the **APPEND, CHANGE, EDIT, INSERT,** and **READ** commands. For instance, to add a new employee to the database empfile.DBF using the screen display created in the example, you would type the following.

```
. USE empfile
. SET FORMAT TO addform
. APPEND
```

The **APPEND** mode screen would appear as follows.

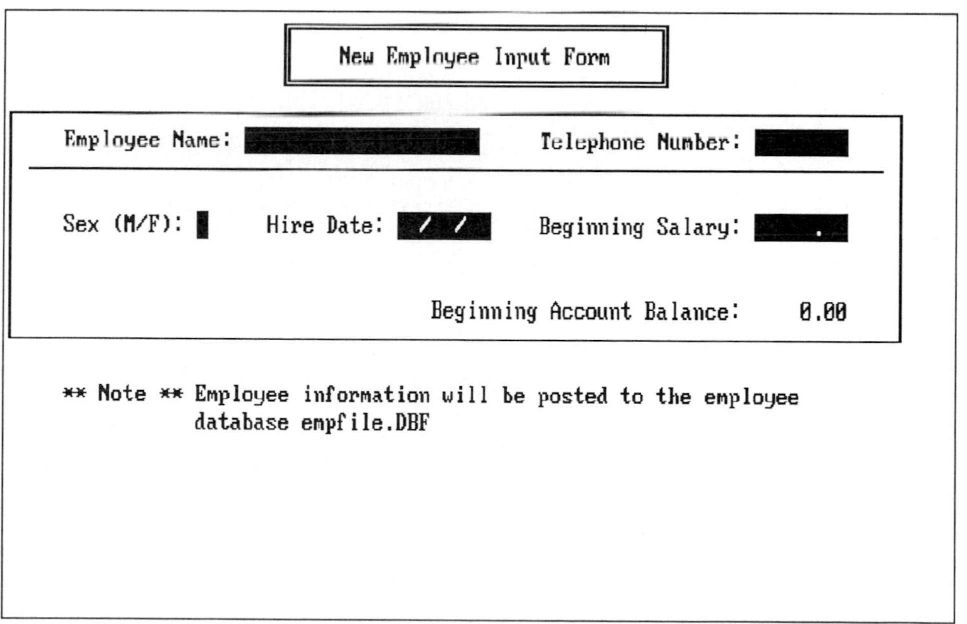

MODIFY STRUCTURE

Alters the record structure of the database in use. The **MODIFY STRUCTURE** command may be used to add new fields or delete fields from the record structure. It also may be used to rename fields or change their lengths. The modifications, however, should be done in separate steps, as listed in the following.

First, use **MODIFY STRUCTURE** to add or delete any fields necessary. Fields may be inserted with ^N or deleted with ^U. Once field additions or deletions are complete, type ^End to exit the **MODIFY STRUCTURE** editing mode.

Next, use **MODIFY STRUCTURE** to change any field names necessary, but do not add or delete any field names or change any lengths. Once field names have been changed, type ^End to exit the **MODIFY STRUCTURE** editing mode. The prompt

```
Should data be COPIED from backup for all fields? (Y/N)
```

will appear at the bottom of the screen. Type Y to leave data in fields whose names have changed or N to erase contents from these fields.

Finally, use **MODIFY STRUCTURE** to change any field widths necessary. Once the new field widths are specified, type ^End to exit the **MODIFY STRUCTURE** editing mode.

MODIFY VIEW <filename>

The **MODIFY VIEW** command is used to create view files (.VUE). View files are used to hold a set of working relationships between dBASE files. **MODIFY VIEW** uses a full-screen, menu-driven mode for data entry. The resulting file records a listing of the databases in use; their active indexes; the work areas in which the databases are in use; any relations between the databases that may exist (see **SET RELATION TO,** page D-188); and the active field list, .FMT file, and/or filter (if any) for each database in use.

Once a view file has been created, it may later be used to reinstate the environment recorded within it through the **SET VIEW TO** <filename> command. (See **SET VIEW TO,** page D-189.)

NOTE or *

Used in command files, this command allows comments to be placed in a command file. **NOTE** and * must begin a line holding a comment. To place a comment to the right of a command and on the same line, use **&&** before the comment.

ON ERROR / ESCAPE / KEY [<command>]

Used in command files, **ON ERROR / ESCAPE / KEY** may be used as an event-trapping command. The three events are **ERROR** (a dBASE error has occurred), **ESCAPE** (the Esc key has been typed), or **KEY** (any key has been typed). When one of these events occurs, and an **ON** command has already been executed for that event, the <command> specified will be executed.

The <command> is normally used to branch program execution to an error-trapping program. The program branched to should first remove the key pressed from the typeahead buffer by executing an **INKEY**() function or **READ** command. Any other commands then may be executed before returning control to the program in which the event occurred. To turn off the feature, use the **ON ERROR / ESCAPE / KEY** command with no <command> parameter.

PACK

Permanently removes (erases) all records marked for deletion in the database file in use. (See also **DELETE,** page D-158, and **RECALL,** page D-176.)

PARAMETERS <memvar list>

Used in programs (command files and procedures), receives parameters passed in the [<expression list>] clause of a **DO** <filename> [**WITH** <expression list>] command and stores each expression to a local (private) memory variable. **PARAMETERS** must be the first executable command in a program.

The number of parameters specified in the **DO** command must be the same as that specified with the **PARAMETERS** command of the program called. The <expression list> passed may include constants, memory variables, or fields. Memory variables passed as parameters will be passed back to the calling program, including any changes made to the variable in the program called. (See also **PRIVATE,** below.)

PRIVATE [<memvar list>] / [**ALL [LIKE / EXCEPT** <skeleton>]]

Used in command files, **PRIVATE** allows use of the same memory variable names as those created in a higher-level command file without affecting the contents of the higher-level command file's variables.

When a command file calls another command file with the **DO** <filename> command, all variables created in the calling program are available in the program called, and changes may be made to these variables in the calling program. Any new variables created in the program called are considered private and will disappear when control is passed back to the calling program (unless declared as **PUBLIC** variables; see **PUBLIC,** page D-176).

The **PRIVATE** command allows certain variables to be treated as private variables in the program called even though they have the same name as variables created in the calling program. The variables in the calling program thus are protected from being changed in the program called.

PROCEDURE <procedure name>

Identifies the beginning of each procedure in a procedure file. A procedure file is a command (.PRG) file that has been declared and opened as a procedure file with the **SET PROCEDURE TO** <filename> command (see page D-187).

Short program subroutines called procedures typically are found within a procedure file. Each subroutine starts with a **PROCEDURE** <procedure name> command and ends with a RETURN command. There may be up to 32 separate procedures in a procedure file.

Procedures are executed with the **DO** command in the same manner as command (.PRG) files are executed. Procedures having the same <procedure name> as that of an existing command file will take execution precedence.

PUBLIC <memvar list>

Declares memory variables as global, allowing them to be used by any program at any level. Memory variables must be declared **PUBLIC** before data are assigned to them. Public memory variables may still be protected from change in a program (command file) by being declared **PRIVATE** within that program. (See **PRIVATE,** page D-175.)

QUIT

Ends a dBASE session and returns to DOS. **QUIT** closes all files and should be typed at the end of each dBASE session to properly exit to DOS.

READ [SAVE]

Allows editing of field or memory variable contents placed on the screen with the @ **GET** command. **READ** normally clears all active @ **GET**s after data have been entered. The **[SAVE]** parameter prevents the **READ** command from clearing (deactivating) the screen's @ **GET**s when editing is finished.

Multiple screens containing @ **GET**s may be produced which allow the user to page back and forth among the screens by typing the PgUp and PgDn keys. The multiple-page screens must be generated from a .FMT file with **READ** commands inserted at the desired page breaks. (See @ **GET,** page D-150.)

RECALL [<scope>] [**FOR** <condition>] [**WHILE** <condition>]

Recalls record(s) marked for deletion ("unmarks" them). The parameters [<scope>], [**FOR** <condition>], and [**WHILE** <condition>] may be used to **RECALL** a group of records. The default <scope> is the current record. (See **DELETE,** page D-158, and **PACK,** page D-175.)

REINDEX

Updates (rebuilds) all active index (.NDX) files in the currently selected work area. (See **USE,** page D-191, and **SET INDEX TO,** page D-187.)

RELEASE [<memvar list>] / **ALL** [**LIKE** / **EXCEPT** <skeleton>]

Erases memory variables from RAM. A <skeleton> is made up of variable name characters and masking characters that act as "wild cards." The asterisk (*) indicates, "Accept all remaining characters," while the question mark (?) means, "Accept any single character in this position."

```
. DISPLAY MEMORY
MALES       pub   N           5  (          5.00000000)
MPAY        pub   N     8499.00  (       8499.00000000)
MACCT       pub   N      950.75  (        950.75000000)
FEMALES     pub   N           4  (          4.00000000)
FPAY        pub   N     6507.50  (       6507.50000000)
FACCT       pub   N      825.50  (        825.50000000)
    6 variables defined,        54 bytes used
  250 variables available,    5946 bytes available


. RELEASE ALL LIKE M*        ← MALES, MPAY, and MACCT will be released.

. RELEASE ALL LIKE MA*       ← MALES and MACCT will be released.

. RELEASE ALL LIKE ?PAY      ← MPAY and FPAY will be released.

. RELEASE ALL EXCEPT F????   ← ALL but FPAY and FACCT will be released.

. RELEASE ALL                ← Erases all variables from RAM.
```

RELEASE MODULE <module name>

Releases a binary file placed in memory with the **LOAD** command. (See **LOAD,** page D-166.)

RENAME <filename.ext> **TO** <new filename.ext>

Used to rename any type of file on the disk from dBASE. Filename extensions must be included. An open file cannot be renamed.

```
. RENAME fullrepo.FRM TO report.FRM
```

REPLACE [<scope>] <field1> **WITH** <exp1> [,<field2> **WITH** <exp2>, . . .] [**FOR** <condition>] [**WHILE** <condition>]

Replaces contents of specified fields with the evaluation of the matching **WITH** <expression> for the records of the database in use. The parameters [<scope>], [**FOR** <condition>], and [**WHILE** <condition>] may be used to make the replacement for a group of records. The default <scope> is the current record only.

REPORT FORM [<filename>] [<scope>] [**FOR** <condition>] [**WHILE** <condition>] **[PLAIN] [HEADING** <expC>] **[NOEJECT] [TO PRINT / TO FILE** <filename>] **[SUMMARY]**

Creates a dBASE report from a report form file (.FRM) and the database file in use. The parameters [<scope>], [**FOR** <condition>], and [**WHILE** <condition>] may be used to limit the number of records included in the report. The default <scope> is **ALL** records. The [**HEADING** <expC>] parameter is used to include the <expC> at the top of each page. The **[PLAIN]** parameter omits page numbers, dates, and any page **[HEADING]** set. The **[NOEJECT]** parameter suppresses the initial page feed before the report is printed with **[TO PRINT]**. The [**TO FILE** <filename>] parameter produces an ASCII text file (.TXT). The **[SUMMARY]** parameter suppresses detail lines to include only total and subtotal lines in the report.

RESTORE FROM <filename> **[ADDITIVE]**

Reads memory variables and their contents into RAM after they have been saved to a memory (.MEM) file with the **SAVE** command. The **[ADDITIVE]** parameter is used to keep currently defined variables in RAM; otherwise, they are erased.

RESUME

Resumes execution of a suspended program (command file or procedure). Programs may be suspended by the **SUSPEND** command in the file, or when **SUSPEND** is selected after dBASE has detected an error.

RETRY

Similar to the **RETURN** command, **RETRY** returns control to a calling command file. With **RETURN,** command execution resumes in the calling program with the line after the last command executed, while returning control with **RETRY** causes the last command executed to be executed again. **RETRY** is most useful for error recovery within a program which uses the **ON ERROR / ESCAPE / KEY** [<command>] command. (See **ON** command, page D-174.)

RETURN [TO MASTER]

Used in command files, the **RETURN** command returns control to the command file which called it or to the dBASE dot (.) prompt. The **[TO MASTER]** parameter returns control to the highest level command file.

RUN <command>

Runs a designated DOS command or executable file (.COM or .EXE) from within dBASE.

SAVE TO <filename> [**ALL LIKE / EXCEPT** <skeleton>]

Saves currently defined memory variables in a memory file (.MEM) so that they may later be called back into RAM with the **RESTORE** command. Without optional parameters, all memory variables are saved. A <skeleton> used with **ALL LIKE** and **ALL EXCEPT** is made up of variable name characters and masking characters that act as "wild cards." The asterisk (*) indicates, "Accept all remaining characters," while the question mark (?) means, "Accept any single character in this position."

```
. DISPLAY MEMORY
MALES       pub   N          5  (         5.00000000)
MPAY        pub   N    8499.00  (      8499.00000000)
MACCT       pub   N     950.75  (       950.75000000)
FEMALES     pub   N          4  (         4.00000000)
FPAY        pub   N    6507.50  (      6507.50000000)
FACCT       pub   N     825.50  (       825.50000000)
    6 variables defined,       54 bytes used
  250 variables available,   5946 bytes available

. SAVE TO vfile ALL LIKE M*         ← MALES, MPAY, and MACCT will be
                                      saved.
. SAVE TO vfile ALL LIKE MA*        ← MALES and MACCT will be saved.

. SAVE TO vfile ALL LIKE ?PAY       ← MPAY and FPAY will be saved.

. SAVE TO vfile ALL EXCEPT F????    ← ALL but FPAY and FACCT will be
                                      saved.
. SAVE TO vfile                     ← Saves all current variables in the
                                      specified file.
```

SEEK <expression>

Used only with files that have been indexed, **SEEK** positions the record pointer at the first database record indexed by the <expression>. **SEEK** is preferable to **FIND** because it may be used with character-type, numeric-type, or date-type index keys, as shown in the following examples. (See **INDEX,** page D-165.)

Examples of using **SEEK** with a character-type index key

```
. USE empfile

. INDEX ON employee TO namedex

. SEEK "Smith P"

. DISPLAY
Record#  EMPLOYEE                TELEPHONE SEX EMPLOYED   SALARY  ACCOUNT
      6  Smith Paul              244-1010  M   11/15/81  1700.00   350.00


. STORE "Johns" TO z

. SEEK z

. DISPLAY
Record#  EMPLOYEE                TELEPHONE SEX EMPLOYED   SALARY  ACCOUNT
      9  Johnson Frank           223-7928  M   03/20/90  1500.00     0.00
```

Examples of using **SEEK** with numeric-type index keys

```
. USE empfile

. INDEX ON salary TO saldex

. SEEK 1600

. DISPLAY WHILE salary <= 1800
Record#  EMPLOYEE                TELEPHONE SEX EMPLOYED   SALARY  ACCOUNT
      7  Martins Mary            222-2123  F   11/01/85  1600.00   200.50
      2  Smoler Ellen            225-3212  F   09/15/83  1650.00   300.00
      6  Smith Paul              244-1010  M   11/15/81  1700.00   350.00
      5  Knat Michael            221-1235  M   09/15/80  1800.00   125.00


. INDEX ON YEAR(employed) TO yeardex

. SEEK 1981

. DISPLAY WHILE YEAR(employed) < 1984
Record#  EMPLOYEE                TELEPHONE SEX EMPLOYED   SALARY  ACCOUNT
      6  Smith Paul              244-1010  M   11/15/81  1700.00   350.00
      1  Pratt John              225-1234  M   06/22/82  1949.00   200.00
      3  Jones David             292-3832  M   06/15/82  1550.00   275.75
      2  Smoler Ellen            225-3212  F   09/15/83  1650.00   300.00
```

Examples of using **SEEK** with a date-type index key

```
. USE empfile

. INDEX ON employed TO datedex

. SEEK CTOD("11/15/81")

. DISPLAY FOR sex = "M" WHILE employed < CTOD("01/01/89")
Record#  EMPLOYEE                TELEPHONE SEX EMPLOYED   SALARY  ACCOUNT
      6  Smith Paul              244-1010  M   11/15/81  1700.00   350.00
      3  Jones David             292-3832  M   06/15/82  1550.00   275.75
      1  Pratt John              225-1234  M   06/22/82  1949.00   200.00
```

SELECT <work area / alias>

dBASE III Plus allows up to ten databases to be used at the same time. When multiple databases are in use, they can be thought of as existing in separate areas of RAM called work areas. Work area 1 (or A) is the currently selected area when you first enter dBASE. To use a database file in another work area, you first must execute the **SELECT** <work area> command to select work area 2 through 10 (B through J), and then execute the **USE** <filename> command. If the **USE** <filename> **ALIAS** <name> command was used to open a database file, the alias <name> may be used with the **SELECT** command.

Each work area maintains a separate database record pointer. Commands affecting the record pointer or which write data to a database file must be executed from the work area in which the intended database for the command resides. Field data from the current record in any work area may be read by preceding the field name with an alias (A through J or alias specified with **USE**) and the characters ->. (See also **SET RELATION,** page D-188.)

```
. USE empfile

. SELECT 2
. USE deptnail ALIAS mail

. DISPLAY ALL
Record#  EMPLOYEE             DEPT
      1  Pratt John           Acct.
      2  Smoler Ellen         Sales
      3  Jones David          Sales
      4  Sill Sally           Acct.
      5  Knat Michael         Pers.
      6  Smith Paul           Acct.
      7  Martins Mary         Sctry
      8  Nichols Sandy        Sctry
      9  Johnson Frank        Sales

. GOTO 2

. ? employee,dept
Smoler Ellen        Sales

. ? A->employee,A->salary
Pratt John           1949.00

. SELECT 1

. SKIP 5
Record No.      6

. DISPLAY
Record#  EMPLOYEE             TELEPHONE SEX EMPLOYED   SALARY  ACCOUNT
      6  Smith Paul           244-1010  M   11/15/81  1700.00   350.00

. ? mail->employee,mail->dept
Smoler Ellen        Sales

. LOCATE FOR employee = mail->employee
Record =       2

. ? employee,mail->employee,mail->dept,salary
Smoler Ellen        Smoler Ellen        Sales  1650.00
```

SET

dBASE has an extensive set of operating features that can be turned on or off, or changed in other ways with **SET** commands. The **SET** commands have two general forms:

SET <parameter> **ON / OFF** or **SET** <parameter> **TO** <option>

The **SET** <parameter> **ON / OFF** commands are shown here with the normal default setting of each indicated in upper-case characters.

SET BELL ON / off (dBASE default setting is **ON**)

In addition to executing **SET** commands from the dot (.) prompt mode or from within a command file, dBASE III Plus provides a full-screen, menu-driven mode for executing many of the **SET** commands. This mode is entered from the dot prompt (.) by using the command **SET** without any parameters.

SET ALTERNATE on / OFF

ON sends all screen output (except full-screen output such as @ **SAY,** @ **GET,** and output of the editing modes) to an ASCII file on the disk. The **SET ALTERNATE ON** command must be preceded by the **SET ALTERNATE TO** <filename> command. **SET ALTERNATE OFF** discontinues output to the disk file, but does not close the file; output to the file may be resumed with **SET ALTERNATE ON.**

SET ALTERNATE TO <filename>

Creates a disk file with a .TXT extension. The file is used for saving screen output (in ASCII format) when the **SET ALTERNATE ON** command is given. **SET ALTERNATE TO** with no filename specified closes the .TXT file.

SET BELL ON / off

dBASE rings a bell at various points during data entry. **OFF** stops the ringing.

SET CARRY on / OFF

The **SET CARRY** command is used when adding records to a database in the **APPEND** or **INSERT** editing modes. When **CARRY** is **SET ON,** data in the fields of the previous record will automatically be copied into like fields of the new record presented. **OFF** leaves all fields of the new record blank.

SET CATALOG ON / off

OFF may be used to suspend updating of the current .CAT file for dBASE files being opened or created. **ON** resumes updating of the .CAT file. (See **SET CATALOG TO,** below.)

SET CATALOG TO [<filename>]

SET CATALOG TO [<filename>] may be used to create a catalog file (.CAT) or to open an existing catalog file. Catalog files are used to record information about files being used. Once the **SET CATALOG TO** [<filename>] command has been executed, the specified catalog file becomes active. Any command entered after this that opens or creates a dBASE file (with the exception of .MEM, .PRG, and .TXT files) causes the opened or created file to become listed in the active catalog file.

A catalog file is actually a database file that is automatically given a .CAT extension (instead of .DBF) at the time it is created. When a catalog file is activated with **SET CATALOG TO,** it becomes an open file in work area 10. To stop the appending of filenames to an active catalog without closing the catalog file, you may type **SET CATALOG OFF.** To resume adding filenames, type **SET CATALOG ON.** While a catalog file is active, dBASE commands that open files may be entered with a ? mark in place of the <filename> parameter to display a menu of filenames from which to select.

To close the current catalog file, use **SET CATALOG TO** with no <filename> specification.

SET CENTURY on / OFF

ON causes the display of date-type data to show all four characters for the year.

SET COLOR ON / off

SET COLOR ON / off is used to switch between color and monochrome displays for systems having both.

SET COLOR TO [[<standard>] [,<enhanced>] [,border]]

Three screen attributes may be altered with the **SET COLOR TO** command: the display of the normal <standard> screen may be changed from its default colors of white on black; the reverse video display <enhanced> of the editing modes may be changed from its default colors of black on white; and the area around the screen <border> may be changed from its default color of black.

The <standard> and <enhanced> color specifications are made in color pairs, with a forward slash (/) separating foreground/background colors. Codes used to specify colors are as follows.

Color	Code	Color	Code
Black	N	Red	R
Blue	B	Magenta	RB
Green	G	Brown	GR
Cyan	BG	White	W
Blank	X		

An asterisk (*) may be used to cause a blinking color, and a plus sign (+) may be used to cause a high-intensity color. For example, the command used to set a <standard> screen of white on blue, <enhanced> screen of bright white on red, and a magenta border would be **SET COLOR TO W/B,W+/R,RB**.

SET CONFIRM on / OFF

In editing modes, when a field or variable has been filled with data, dBASE automatically moves the cursor to the next field or variable for editing. The **SET CONFIRM ON** command disables automatic cursor movement to the next field. The Enter key ↵ must be used to proceed to the next field.

SET CONSOLE ON / off

Used only in command files, **ON** sends output to screen as normal and **OFF** suppresses most output to the screen (@ **SAY**s and @ **GET**s are still displayed).

SET DATE [AMERICAN / ANSI / BRITISH / ITALIAN / FRENCH / GERMAN]

SET DATE is used to alter the display and entry format for date-type data. The format is normally set to **AMERICAN**. For purposes of data transfer, the **ANSI** (American National Standards Institute) format is quite useful. With this format it becomes possible to convert dBASE III Plus date-type data into character-type data (using the **DTOC** function), and then transfer the data with an order of characters more usable to other software. The various formats for date-type data display are as follows.

AMERICAN	mm/dd/yy	**ITALIAN**	dd-mm-yy
ANSI	yy.mm.dd	**FRENCH**	dd/mm/yy
BRITISH	dd/mm/yy	**GERMAN**	dd.mm.yy

SET DEBUG on / OFF

ON sends output created by the **SET ECHO ON** command to the printer. **OFF** sends the output to the screen. (See **SET ECHO,** below.)

SET DECIMALS TO <expN>

Determines the minimum number of decimal places that will be displayed as a result of certain functions and calculations. Applies only to the operation of division and values returned from the functions **SQRT, LOG, EXP,** and **VAL.**

SET DEFAULT TO *<drive:>*

Makes the specified drive the default drive.

SET DELETED on / OFF

On stops dBASE from processing records that are marked for deletion during execution of commands that allow a <scope> parameter, unless the <scope> is specified as **RECORD** <n> or **NEXT** <n> and the first record of the <scope> is deleted. (See **DELETE,** page D-158.)

SET DELIMITER on / OFF

ON causes fields displayed in the editing modes to be delimited by a character string previously specified with the **SET DELIMITER TO** command, or to colons (:) if no **SET DELIMITER TO** command has been executed.

SET DELIMITER TO <expC> **/ DEFAULT**

Assigns a one-character or two-character string (<expC>) for use in delimiting fields displayed in the editing modes. To change delimiters, the **SET DELIMITER TO** <expC> and **SET DELIMITER ON** commands are used. If a two-character string such as "{ }" is used, the first character "{" appears on the left of an entry and the second character "}" appears on the right. To return to the default delimiter of colons (:), the **DEFAULT** parameter may be used.

SET DEVICE TO PRINT / SCREEN

Determines if output from @ **SAY** and @ **GET** commands will be sent to the screen (default device) or to the printer. If sent to the printer, @ **GET** commands are ignored, and any command that would cause the printer to backup causes a page eject.

SET DOHISTORY on / OFF

ON causes commands executed from within a command file (.PRG) to be stored in the **HISTORY** buffer. (See **DISPLAY HISTORY,** page D-159.)

SET ECHO on / OFF

ON displays on the screen the command currently being executed. Used during execution of command files, **SET ECHO ON** allows you to trace the execution of commands in the file. (See **SET DEBUG on / OFF,** page D-184, and **SET STEP on / OFF,** page D-189.)

SET ESCAPE ON / off

ON allows the user to interrupt execution of a command file or dot (.) prompt command with the Esc key; **OFF** disables this feature. When Esc is used to interrupt execution of a command file, the same prompt that dBASE displays when an error is encountered is displayed.

```
*** INTERRUPTED ***
Called from - A:PROGRAM1.PRG
Cancel, Ignore, or Suspend? (C, I, or S)
```

Type C to cancel execution of the program, type I to ignore the interruption and continue execution, or type S to suspend execution. If suspended, the commands **RESUME** or **CANCEL** may be used to later resume or cancel execution.

SET EXACT on / OFF

By default, dBASE allows partial matches of string comparisons in a <condition>. For instance, **DISPLAY FOR** employee = "Smit" will cause dBASE to display the record for Paul Smith in the database empfile. **EXACT ON** requires exact matches in string comparison operations. With **EXACT ON** only **DISPLAY FOR** employee = "Smith Paul" will display the record. (Notice, however, that trailing spaces do not have to be included in the item.)

SET FIELDS on / OFF

Activates or deactivates the field filter in the current work area. The **SET FIELDS TO** <field list> command is used to set a field filter and set fields **ON. OFF** deactivates the field filter and **ON** reactivates it.

SET FIELDS TO [<field list> / **ALL**]

SET FIELDS TO <field list> creates a field filter and sets fields **ON.** A field filter prevents many dBASE commands from processing fields not listed in the <field list>. The **[ALL]** parameter may be used to include all fields of the current database in the field list. **SET FIELDS TO** with no parameters removes all fields from the field list. The field filter may be turned on and off with the **SET FIELDS on / OFF** command. Several precautionary notes are listed in the dBASE III Plus manual about this command.

SET FILTER TO [<condition>] [**FILE** <filename>]

Causes the current database to appear as if it contains only certain records. The <condition> is a logical expression defining the filter. A query file (.QRY) may be created with **CREATE / MODIFY QUERY.** The file contains a filter condition which may then be put into effect with the command **SET FILTER TO FILE** <filename>. **SET FILTER TO** with no condition turns off the filter

```
. SET FILTER TO sex = 'M'

. DISPLAY ALL
Record#  EMPLOYEE                TELEPHONE SEX EMPLOYED   SALARY  ACCOUNT
      1  Pratt John              225-1234  M   06/22/82  1949.00   200.00
      3  Jones David             292-3832  M   06/15/82  1550.00   275.75
      5  Knat Michael            221-1235  M   09/15/80  1800.00   125.00
      6  Smith Paul              244-1010  M   11/15/81  1700.00   350.00
      9  Johnson Frank           223-7928  M   03/20/90  1500.00     0.00
```

SET FIXED on / OFF

When **SET FIXED** is **ON,** all displays of numeric data contain the exact number of decimal places specified by the **SET DECIMALS** command, or two decimal places if the **SET DECIMALS** command has not been executed.

SET FORMAT TO [<format file>]

Opens a format file (.FMT) which dBASE will use to format the screen for **APPEND, CHANGE, EDIT,** and **INSERT** commands. Format files are command files that are made up of @ **SAY,** @ **GET,** and **READ** commands only. They may be created or modified by specifying the file extension (.FMT) with **MODIFY COMMAND** <filename.FMT>. Format files also may be generated along with screen files (.SCR) by using **CREATE / MODIFY SCREEN. SET FORMAT TO** closes any open format file.

SET FUNCTION <expN> **TO** <expC>

Stores the specified character string <expC> to the Function key <expN> (2 through 10). For example, **SET FUNCTION** 2 **TO** "Columbus, Ohio" stores the string to the F2 key. Each time F2 is typed, the string "Columbus, Ohio" will appear on the monitor screen at the location of the cursor just as if it had been typed. A semicolon (;) in the string has the effect of typing ↵ at that point. Type **DISPLAY STATUS** for default function key values. Function key 1 cannot be reprogrammed.

SET HEADING ON / off

OFF removes the column headings for the **DISPLAY, LIST, AVERAGE,** and **SUM** commands.

SET HELP ON / off

OFF disables the "Do you want some help? (Y/N)" message generated by syntax errors.

SET HISTORY ON / off

OFF disables the **HISTORY** buffer so dBASE will not save any previously executed commands.

SET HISTORY TO <expN>

Sets the number of commands held in the **HISTORY** buffer to <expN>. Default is 20 commands. If <expN> is smaller than the current number set, all commands in the buffer are erased. (See **DISPLAY HISTORY,** page D-159.)

SET INDEX TO [<index file list>]

Puts index files (.NDX) in use with the current database file. Records will appear in the order defined by the first index file in the list. Other index files will be updated as changes are made to the database file fields. Essentially the same as **USE** <filename> **INDEX** <index file list>. **SET INDEX TO** without a file list closes all index files in the current work area.

SET INTENSITY ON / off

OFF suppresses reverse video screen displays normally used by dBASE.

SET MARGIN TO <expN>

Sets left margin of printer to <expN> columns.

SET MEMOWIDTH TO <expN>

Adjusts the output width of memo field data to <expN> characters. The default memo output width is 50 characters.

SET MENUS ON / off

ON causes the display of keystroke command menus when in an editing mode; **OFF** suppresses the display of menus. When in an editing mode, F1 may be typed to toggle menus on or off, changing the **ON / OFF** status of **SET MENUS.**

SET MESSAGE TO [<expC>]

Causes the specified character expression [<expC>] to be displayed at the bottom line of the monitor screen. **SET MESSAGE TO** with no parameter removes the display of user-defined messages.

SET ORDER TO [<expN>]

Establishes the controlling index file from the list specified with the **USE** <filename> **INDEX** <index file list> or **SET INDEX TO** <index file list> commands. The <expN>th index file in the <index file list> becomes the controlling index when **SET ORDER TO** <expN> is executed. If <expN> is specified as 0, or **SET ORDER TO** with no <expN> is used, the database file records are processed in natural (unindexed) order. **SET ORDER TO** does not close active index files. (See **SET INDEX,** above.)

SET PATH TO <path list>

Defines alternate DOS directory paths for dBASE to search if a file specified in an operation is not found in the current directory.

SET PRINT on / OFF

ON sends all output not formatted with **@ SAY, @ GET,** or presented in editing modes to the printer. **OFF** stops such output to the printer.

SET PROCEDURE TO [<filename>]

Declares and opens a command file (.PRG) as a procedure file. Only one procedure file per work area may be open at one time. **SET PROCEDURE TO** with no <filename> specified may be used to close a procedure file. (See **PROCEDURE,** page D-175.)

SET RELATION TO [<key exp>/<expN> **INTO** <alias>]

Links the movement of the record pointer in the database file open in the current work area to movement of the pointer in a database file open in another work area. The second database is identified by its <alias>. An <alias> may always be specified by its letter A through J. If the **ALIAS** <name> clause was included in the **USE** command when a database file was opened, the <name> also may be used as the <alias>; otherwise, the <filename> also may be used as the <alias>.

If <key exp> is used, it corresponds to the key of the index file in use with the second database file. If an <expN> is used, it is usually entered as **RECNO( )** and pointer movement is based on record numbers of the second database file, which must not be indexed. Only one relation may be set from each work area. Using **SET RELATION TO** with no parameters removes any relation set in the current work area.

The following example uses a key expression to set a relationship.

Work Area 1
deptmail.dbf

Record#	EMPLOYEE	DEPT
1	Pratt John	Acct.
2	Smoler Ellen	Sales
3	Jones David	Sales
4	Sill Sally	Acct.
5	Knat Michael	Pers.
6	Smith Paul	Acct.
7	Martins Mary	Sctry
8	Nichols Sandy	Sctry
9	Johnson Frank	Sales

Work Area 2
mailrout.dbf (indexed on area)

Record#	AREA	MANAGER	MAILCODE
1	Pers.	Jacobs William	103
2	Sales	Butler John	107
3	Sctry	Branden Julia	101
4	Acct.	Evans Claire	106

```
. SELECT 1

. SET RELATION TO dept INTO mailrout

. LOCATE FOR employee = "Smith P"
Record =       6

. ? mailrout->manager,mailrout->mailcode,"   ATTN: ",employee
Evans Claire    106    ATTN:  Smith Paul

. LIST mailrout->manager,mailrout->mailcode,"   ATTN: ",employee
Record#  mailrout->manager mailrout->mailcode "   ATTN: " employee
      1  Evans Claire      106                    ATTN:    Pratt John
      2  Butler John       107                    ATTN:    Smoler Ellen
      3  Butler John       107                    ATTN:    Jones David
      4  Evans Claire      106                    ATTN:    Sill Sally
      5  Jacobs William    103                    ATTN:    Knat Michael
      6  Evans Claire      106                    ATTN:    Smith Paul
      7  Branden Julia     101                    ATTN:    Martins Mary
      8  Branden Julia     101                    ATTN:    Nichols Sandy
      9  Butler John       107                    ATTN:    Johnson Frank
```

SET SAFETY ON / off

OFF disables the "<filename> already exists, overwrite it? (Y/N)" message.

SET STATUS ON / off

Toggles **ON / off** the status bar displayed on line 22 of the monitor screen.

SET STEP on / OFF

ON aids debugging of a command file by causing dBASE to pause after executing each command in the file.

SET TALK ON / off

dBASE displays various messages associated with the execution of certain commands. **SET TALK OFF** stops display of the messages.

SET TITLE ON / off

Toggles **ON / off** the catalog file title prompt.

SET TYPEAHEAD TO <expN>

Sets the number of characters held in the keyboard buffer to <expN>. Normally 20 characters are held.

SET UNIQUE on / OFF

When **ON,** index files (.NDX) created with **INDEX ON** <expression> **TO** <index file> will include entries for only the first record of several records having the same key <expression>. (See **INDEX ON,** page D-165.)

SET VIEW TO <filename>

Opens a view file (.VUE) and reinstates the environment specified in it. (See **MODIFY VIEW,** page D-174.)

SKIP [−] [<expN>]

Moves the record pointer up or down in the current database file. The number of records to **SKIP** is defined by <expN>. To move backward, specify the [−] parameter. The default **SKIP** value is +1.

SORT [<scope>] **ON** <field1> **[/A] [/C] [/D]** [,<field2> **[/A] [/C] [/D]** . . .] **TO** <new file> [**FOR** <condition>] [**WHILE** <condition>]

Creates a new database file (.DBF) with the same structure as the database file in use and copies records to the new file in order of the data held in the <field>(s) specified. If several fields are used (up to 10), they must be separated with commas. Sorting is done in ascending order unless specified otherwise. The parameters **[/A], [/C],** and **[/D]** are used to specify ascending order, ignore upper/lower case difference, and descending order, respectively. The parameters [<scope>], [**FOR** <condition>], and [**WHILE** <condition>] may be used to limit the number of records sorted and copied to the new file. The default <scope> is **ALL** records.

STORE <expression> **TO** <memvar list>

Stores the value of an expression to one or more memory variables.

SUM <expN list> [**TO** <memvar list>] [<scope>] [**FOR** <condition>] [**WHILE** <condition>]

Computes the sum of the expressions in the expression list for the records in the database file in use and optionally stores the sums to the memory variables in its <memvar list>. The parameters [<scope>], [**FOR** <condi-

tion>], and [**WHILE** <condition>] may be used to limit the number of records summed. The default <scope> is **ALL** records.

```
. SUM salary,account TO fsal,facct FOR sex = "F"
     4 records summed
    salary      account
   6207.00       825.50

. DISPLAY MEMORY
FSAL         pub   N        6207.00  (       6207.00000000)
FACCT        pub   N         825.50  (        825.50000000)
   2 variables defined,        18 bytes used
 254 variables available,    5982 bytes available
```

SUSPEND

Used in command files (.PRG), **SUSPEND** is a debugging command used to temporarily halt the execution of a dBASE program and return to the dot (.) prompt mode. Commands then may be used to display or modify values of memory variables, and so forth. The command file remains open while suspended. **RESUME** may be used to continue suspended program execution. **CANCEL** may be used to cancel execution of the suspended program and close the file.

TEXT
<any data>
ENDTEXT

Used in command fields, allows text to be displayed (or printed) without the use of the @ **SAY** or **?** commands. dBASE treats all data between the **TEXT** and **ENDTEXT** commands as text to be output.

TOTAL ON <key field> **TO** <new file> [**FIELDS** <fieldN list>] [<scope>] [**FOR** <condition>] [**WHILE** <condition>]

Creates a new database file (.DBF) that will have only one record for each unique <key field> in the database file in use. Numeric fields will be totalled for each unique field in the database file in use, and the record in the new database file will hold the total. In the file created, fields of a type other than numeric will hold the data from the first record with the unique field. The database file in use must be indexed or sorted on the <key field> to be specified in the **TOTAL** command.

The [**FIELDS** <fieldN list>] parameter may be used to specify the numeric fields to be totalled to the new file (otherwise all numeric fields are totalled). The parameters [<scope>], [**FOR** <condition>], and [**WHILE** <condition>] may be used to limit the number of records totalled to the new file. The default <scope> is **ALL** records.

```
. USE empfile

. INDEX ON sex TO sexdex
  100% indexed          9 Records indexed

. TOTAL ON sex TO totfile1
      9 Record(s) totalled
      2 Records generated

. USE totfile1

. LIST
Record#  EMPLOYEE              TELEPHONE SEX EMPLOYED    SALARY  ACCOUNT
      1  Smoler Ellen          225-3212  F   09/15/83  6207.00   825.50
      2  Pratt John            225-1234  M   06/22/82  8499.00   950.75
```

TYPE <filename.ext> [**TO PRINT**]

TYPE displays the contents of an unopened file. The **[TO PRINT]** parameter echoes screen output to the printer.

UPDATE ON <key field> **FROM** <alias> **REPLACE** <field1> **WITH** <exp1> [,<field2> **WITH** <exp2>, . . .] **[RANDOM]**

Allows batch update of a presorted or indexed database.

USE [<filename>] [**ALIAS** <name>] [**INDEX** <index file list>]

Specifies a database file (.DBF) to open for processing in the current work area. A database file may be opened in each of ten work areas; however, a file may only be opened in one area at any one time. **USE** <filename> closes any previous file in use in the current work area, and sets the record pointer to the first record in the file just opened. **USE** with no parameters closes the current database.

The [**ALIAS** <name>] parameter is used to specify a <name> which may be substituted for the standard aliases (A through J) when referring to the ten work areas (see **SELECT,** page D-180.) If the **ALIAS** <name> clause is not included, the <filename> is used as the alternate alias <name>. The [**INDEX** <index file list>] parameter may be used to specify previously created index files (.NDX) that are to be opened and in use with the database file (see **INDEX ON,** page D-165).

WAIT [expC] [**TO** <memvar>]

Used in command files, the **WAIT** command pauses execution of further commands in the file until a single keyboard character is typed. The character typed (if printable) is stored in the specified memory variable.

ZAP

Removes all records from the current database. Same as using the command **DELETE ALL** followed by the command **PACK.**

dBASE III PLUS FUNCTIONS

A dBASE function can be described as a shorthand method of accomplishing a specific task. A function is described as returning a value. The value returned often is determined by arguments (expressions) included within the syntax of a function. The general formats for dBASE functions are

NAME(<argument>) **NAME**(<arg1>,<arg2>, . . .) **NAME**( )

Functions begin with the function name, which will be shown here in bold upper-case letters. This is followed by a set of parentheses. If the function requires one or more arguments, the arguments are included inside the parentheses. If more than one argument is used with a function, commas are used to separate the arguments. If no arguments are required, the parentheses are included, but left empty.

Function arguments are valid dBASE expressions, which evaluate to numeric-type, character-type, date-type, or logical-type data, and are specified as <expN>, <expC>, <expD>, or <expL>, respectively, in the function syntax. Most functions require specific types of data as arguments and return a specific type of data. Some functions, however, can accept different data types as arguments and also may return different data types depending upon the arguments used.

Some examples of function syntax are given in the following table.

Function Syntax	Function Description	Data Type Returned
VAL(<expC>)	Character to Numeric conversion	Numeric
RIGHT(<expC>,<expN>)	Right substring	Character
CTOD(<expC>)	Character to Date conversion	Date
EOF( )	End-of-file	Logical
IIF(<expL>,<exp>,<exp>)	Immediate If Function	Any

ABS(<expN>) Data Type Returned: Numeric

Absolute Value function Returns the positive value of a positive or negative numeric argument.

```
. ? ABS(45-55)
10
```

ASC(<expC>) Data Type Returned: Numeric

ASCII Code Function Returns the ASCII code number of the left-most character in the string<expC>. See "ASCII Character Codes" in appendix B for character code numbers.

```
. DISPLAY
Record#  EMPLOYEE                   TELEPHONE SEX EMPLOYED   SALARY  ACCOUNT
     1  Pratt John                 225-1234  M   06/22/82  1949.00   200.00

. ? ASC(employee)                  ←The ASCII code for "P" is 80.
 80

. ? ASC(sex)                       ←The ASCII code for "M" is 77.
 77

. ? CHR(ASC(sex)+32)               ←The ASCII code for any capital letter
m                                    is 32 less than its lower-case
                                     equivalent.
```

AT(<expC1>,<expC2>) Data Type Returned: Numeric

Substring Search Function Returns the integer value equal to the position in <expC2> where the substring<expC1> occurs.

```
. GOTO 7

. DISPLAY
Record#  EMPLOYEE                TELEPHONE SEX EMPLOYED   SALARY  ACCOUNT
      7  Martins Mary            222-2123  F   11/01/85  1600.00   200.50

. ? AT("Mary",employee)
         9
```

BOF( ) Data Type Returned: Logical

Beginning-of-File Function Returns .T. (true) if an attempt has been made to **SKIP** backwards past the first record in a database file. Otherwise, returns .F. (false).

```
. GO TOP

. ? RECNO()
         1

. ? BOF()
.F.

. SKIP -1
Record No.       1

. ? BOF()
.T.
```

CDOW(<expD>) Data Type Returned: Character

Character Day-of-Week Function Returns the day of the week for a date expression argument.

```
. DISPLAY
Record#  EMPLOYEE                TELEPHONE SEX EMPLOYED   SALARY  ACCOUNT
      1  Pratt John              225-1234  M   06/22/82  1949.00   200.00

. ? CDOW(employed)
Tuesday

. ? CDOW(employed + 90)
Monday
```

CHR(<expN>) Data Type Returned: Character

Character String Function Returns the ASCII character 0 through 255 specified by the <expN> argument.

```
. ? CHR(65)
A

. ? CHR(65+32)
a
```

CMONTH(<expD>) Data Type Returned: Character

Character Month Function Returns the month name for a date expression argument.

```
. DISPLAY
Record#  EMPLOYEE                 TELEPHONE SEX EMPLOYED   SALARY  ACCOUNT
      1  Pratt John               225-1234  M   06/22/82  1949.00   200.00

. ? CMONTH(employed + 100)
September

. ? employed + 100
09/30/82
```

COL( ) Data Type Returned: Numeric

Column Function Returns the current screen column position of the cursor.

CTOD(<expC>) Data Type Returned: Date

Character-to-Date Function Returns a date value from a character-type argument that is a valid date representation. The character expression must be in the order mm/dd/yy, but any character can separate the numbers used.

```
. DISPLAY
Record#  EMPLOYEE                 TELEPHONE SEX EMPLOYED   SALARY  ACCOUNT
      1  Pratt John               225-1234  M   06/22/82  1949.00   200.00

. ? employed = CTOD("06-22-82")
.T.

. ? CTOD("01/01/84") - employed
       558
```

DATE( ) Data Type Returned: Date

Date Function Returns the DOS system date.

```
. ? DATE()
07/19/90
```

DAY(<expD>) Data Type Returned: Numeric

Day Function Returns the day of the month of a date expression argument.

```
. DISPLAY
Record#  EMPLOYEE              TELEPHONE SEX EMPLOYED   SALARY  ACCOUNT
     1  Pratt John            225-1234  M   06/22/82  1949.00   200.00

. ? DAY(employed)
 22
```

DBF( ) Data Type Returned: Character

Database Function Returns the filename of the current database file.

```
. ? DBF()
A:empfile.dbf
```

DELETED( ) Data Type Returned: Logical

Deleted Record Function Returns .T. (true) if the current record is marked for deletion.

```
. COUNT FOR DELETED()
     1 record

. LOCATE FOR DELETED()
Record =       7

. RECALL
     1 record recalled

. ? DELETED()
.F.
```

DISKSPACE( ) Data Type Returned: Numeric

Disk Space Function Returns the number of bytes (characters) of available disk space on the current drive.

```
. SET DEFAULT TO a:

. ? DISKSPACE()
  1161216
```

DOW(<expD>) Data Type Returned: Numeric

Day-of-Week Function Returns the day of the week number from a date expression argument. Numbers begin with Sunday = 1 and end with Saturday = 7.

```
. DISPLAY
Record#  EMPLOYEE              TELEPHONE SEX EMPLOYED   SALARY  ACCOUNT
     7  Martins Mary          222-2123  F   11/01/85  1600.00   200.50

. ? DOW(employed)
 6

. ? CDOW(employed)
Friday
```

DTOC(<expD>) Data Type Returned: Character

Date-to-Character Function Converts date-type data to character-type data.

```
. DISPLAY
Record#  EMPLOYEE              TELEPHONE SEX EMPLOYED   SALARY  ACCOUNT
      9  Johnson Frank         223-7928  M   03/20/90  1500.00     0.00

. STORE DTOC(employed+180) TO reviewdate
09/16/90

. ? "Memo: "+employee+" Six month review: "+reviewdate
Memo: Johnson Frank        Six month review: 09/16/90
```

EOF( ) Data Type Returned: Logical

End-of-File Function dBASE holds a dummy record at the end of a database file which has a record number one greater than the last actual record. **EOF**( ) returns .F. (false) if the record pointer is on an actual record and returns .T. (true) if the record pointer is moved past the last actual record to the dummy record.

```
. ? RECCOUNT()
         9

. GO BOTTOM

. DISPLAY
Record#  EMPLOYEE              TELEPHONE SEX EMPLOYED   SALARY  ACCOUNT
      9  Johnson Frank         223-7928  M   03/20/90  1500.00     0.00

. ? EOF()
.F.

. SKIP
Record No.      10

. ? EOF()
.T.
```

ERROR( ) Data Type Returned: Numeric

Error Number Function Returns the dBASE III Plus error number corresponding to the error trapped with an **ON ERROR** command.

EXP(<expN>) Data Type Returned: Numeric

Exponential Function Returns the value of e^x.

```
. ? EXP(1.000)
    2.718
```

FIELD(<expN>) Data Type Returned: Character

Field Name Function Returns a field name in the current database file where <expN> is the number of the field in the database file structure.

```
. ? FIELD(4)
EMPLOYED
```

FILE(<expC>) Data Type Returned: Logical

File Existence Function Returns .T. (true) if the file specified as <expC> exists. The argument <expC> is a character string which holds a file specification "[*drive:*][*path*]*filename.ext*" where the optional [*drive:*] and [*path*], if not specified, will default to the current drive and path.

```
. STORE "empfile.dbf" TO dbfname
empfile.dbf

. ? FILE(dbfname)
.T.

. ? FILE("namedex.ndx")
.T.
```

FKLABEL(<expN>) Data Type Returned: Character

Function Key Label Function Returns the character name of a programmable function key on the current system, where <expN> specifies the number of the function key. dBASE reserves the first function key F1 for the on-line **HELP** facility. Therefore, the first programmable function key is normally F2.

FKMAX( ) Data Type Returned: Numeric

Function Key Maximum Function Returns the maximum number of programmable function keys on the current system.

FOUND( ) Data Type Returned: Logical

Found Function Returns a logical .T. (true) if the previous search operation, **FIND, SEEK, LOCATE,** or **CONTINUE,** was successful.

GETENV(<expC>) Data Type Returned: Character

Get Environmental Variable Function Returns the contents of the operating system variable specified by <expC>.

IIF(<expL>,<exptrue>,<expfalse>) Data Type Returned: Any

Immediate IF Function Returns one of two values depending on the evaluation of a condition. The condition is the <expL> argument. The <exptrue> will be returned if the condition evaluates as true; otherwise, <expfalse> will be returned. The <exptrue> and <expfalse> arguments may be of any data type, but they must both be of the same type. Most useful for including conditional field output in dBASE III Plus **REPORT**s and **LABEL**s, the **IIF** function performs the same type of operation as an **IF... ELSE... ENDIF** structure in a command file.

```
. LIST employee,IIF(account<=.15*salary,"Ok","Over Limit")
Record#  employee          IIF(account<=.15*salary,"Ok","Over Limit")
      1  Pratt John        Ok
      2  Smoler Ellen      Over Limit
      3  Jones David       Over Limit
      4  Sill Sally        Ok
      5  Khat Michael      Ok
      6  Smith Paul        Over Limit
      7  Martins Mary      Ok
      8  Nichols Sandy     Ok
      9  Johnson Frank     Ok
```

You may nest **IIF** functions to create extended conditional tests. An example might be

IIF(<expL>,<exptrue>,**IIF**(<expL>,<exptrue>,<expfalse>))

Here, the <expfalse> of the first **IIF** function is another **IIF** function. This form of nested function works in the same manner as the following **IF** structure

IF condition
  true expression
ELSE
  IF condition
    true expression
  ELSE
    false expression
  ENDIF
ENDIF

In the next example the database empfile.DBF is used. The **IIF** function is one that could be included in a **REPORT** column to produce the following results: if the account amount is less than 12 percent of salary, output nothing; if the account amount is between 12 percent and 15 percent, output "Near Limit"; if the account amount is over 15 percent of salary, output "Over Limit by" x amount. Notice the **STR** function is used to convert the second **IIF** function's <expfalse> into the same data type as all other expressions used.

IIF(account < .12 * salary,"",**IIF**(account >= .12 * salary .AND. account < .15 * salary,"Near Limit","Over Limit by "+ **STR**(account − .15 * salary,5,2)))

INKEY( ) Data Type Returned: Numeric

Inkey Function Returns an integer (the ASCII value) representing the last key typed. This function is used in command files to trap user keystrokes and branch program execution accordingly.

INT(<expN>) Data Type Returned: Numeric

Integer Function Returns the integer value of the <expN> argument.

```
. STORE account/3 TO a

. STORE INT(account/3) TO b

. STORE INT(-4.3678) TO c

. DISPLAY MEMORY
A           pub   N          66.67  (        66.66666667)
B           pub   N          66  (        66.00000000)
C           pub   N          -4  (        -4.00000000)
   3 variables defined,       27 bytes used
 253 variables available,   5973 bytes available
```

ISALPHA(<expC>) Data Type Returned: Logical

Is Alphabetic Function Returns a logical .T. (true) if the character string argument begins with any upper-case or lower-case letter A through Z.

ISCOLOR( ) Data Type Returned: Logical

Is Color Mode Function Returns a logical .T. (true) if dBASE is running in a color mode.

ISLOWER(<expC>) Data Type Returned: Logical

Is Lowercase Function Returns a logical .T. (true) if the character string argument begins with a lower-case character (a through z).

ISUPPER(<expC>) Data Type Returned: Logical

Is Uppercase Function Returns a logical .T. (true) if the character string argument begins with an upper-case character (A through Z).

LEFT(<expC>,<lenN>) Data Type Returned: Character

Left Substring Function Returns the left-most characters of the character string argument <expC>. The numeric argument <lenN> determines the length of the substring to return.

```
. DISPLAY
Record#  EMPLOYEE             TELEPHONE SEX EMPLOYED   SALARY  ACCOUNT
      7  Martins Mary         222-2123  F   11/01/85  1600.00   200.50

. STORE LEFT(employee,7) TO lastname
Martins
```

LEN(<expC>) Data Type Returned: Numeric

Length Function Returns the number of characters in the <expC> argument.

```
. DISPLAY
Record#  EMPLOYEE             TELEPHONE SEX EMPLOYED   SALARY  ACCOUNT
      7  Martins Mary         222-2123  F   11/01/85  1600.00   200.50

. ? LEN(employee)
        20

. ? LEN(TRIM(employee))
        12
```

LOG(<expN>) Data Type Returned: Numeric

Logarithm Function Returns the natural logarithm of <expN>.

```
. ? LOG(2.71828)
1.00000
```

LOWER(<expC>) Data Type Returned: Character

Lowercase Function Returns the <expC> character string with all alphabetic characters converted to lower case.

```
. DISPLAY
Record#  EMPLOYEE              TELEPHONE SEX EMPLOYED   SALARY  ACCOUNT
      7  Martins Mary          222-2123  F   11/01/85  1600.00   200.50

. ? LOWER(employee)
martins mary
```

LTRIM(<expC>) Data Type Returned: Character

Left Trim Function Returns the <expC> character string argument with any leading spaces removed.

```
. ? STR(account)
       200

. ? LTRIM(STR(account))
200
```

LUPDATE( ) Data Type Returned: Date

Last Update Function Returns the system date recorded for the last time the current database was updated.

MAX(<expN1>,<expN2>) Data Type Returned: Numeric

Maximum Function Returns the argument <expN1> or <expN2> that has the highest numeric value.

MESSAGE( ) Data Type Returned: Character

Error Message Function Returns the dBASE III Plus error message corresponding to the error trapped with an **ON ERROR** command.

```
. ON ERROR STORE MESSAGE() TO z

. sdsad
*** Unrecognized command verb.

. DISPLAY MEMORY
Z           pub   C  "*** Unrecognized command verb."
   1 variables defined,      32 bytes used
  255 variables available,  5968 bytes available
```

MIN(<expN1>,<expN2>) Data Type Returned: Numeric

Minimum Function Returns the argument <expN1> or <expN2> that has the lowest numeric value.

MOD(<expN1>, <expN2>) Data Type Returned: Numeric

Modulus Function Returns the remainder resulting from dividing the first argument <expN1> by the second argument <expN2>.

MONTH(<expD>) Data Type Returned: Numeric

Month Function Returns the month number from a date expression argument.

```
. ? MONTH(employed)
 6

. ? CMONTH(employed)
June
```

NDX(<expN>) Data Type Returned: Character

Index File Function Returns the character string *"drive:filename.ext"* for an index file in use in the current work area. The <expN> argument determines which index name to return when several are in use.

OS( ) Data Type Returned: Character

Operating System Function Returns the name of the current operating system.

PCOL( ) Data Type Returned: Numeric

Printer Column Function Returns the current column position of the printer.

PROW( ) Data Type Returned: Numeric

Printer Row Function Returns the current row position of the printer.

READKEY( ) Data Type Returned: Numeric

Read Key Function Returns an integer (the ASCII value) for the last keystroke typed while in a full-screen editing mode.

RECCOUNT( ) Data Type Returned: Numeric

Record Count Function Returns the number of records in the current database.

RECNO( ) Data Type Returned: Numeric

Record Number Function Returns the integer value equal to the current record number.

```
. GO TOP

. LIST WHILE RECNO() < 4
Record#  EMPLOYEE             TELEPHONE SEX EMPLOYED   SALARY  ACCOUNT
      1  Pratt John           225-1234  M   06/22/82  1949.00   200.00
      2  Smoler Ellen         225-3212  F   09/15/83  1650.00   300.00
      3  Jones David          292-3832  M   06/15/82  1550.00   275.75

. ? RECNO()
         4
```

RECSIZE( ) Data Type Returned: Numeric

Record Size Function Returns the record size (number of bytes) for the records in the current database.

REPLICATE(<expC>,<expN>) Data Type Returned: Character

Replicate Function Returns a character string in which the <expC> argument is repeated <expN> number of times.

```
. ? REPLICATE("<>",25)
<><><><><><><><><><><><><><><><><><><><><><><><><>
```

RIGHT(<expC>,<expN>) Data Type Returned: Character

Right Substring Function Returns the right-most characters of the character string argument <expC>. The numeric argument <expN> determines the length of the substring to return.

```
. STORE TRIM(employee) TO name
Sill Sally

. STORE RIGHT(name,5) TO fname
Sally
```

ROUND(<expN>,<decN>) Data Type Returned: Numeric

Round Function Rounds the numeric value <expN> to <decN> number of decimal places. Rounds to the left of the decimal if <decN> is negative.

```
. DISPLAY
Record#  EMPLOYEE              TELEPHONE SEX EMPLOYED   SALARY  ACCOUNT
      3  Jones David           292-3832  M   06/15/82  1550.00   275.75

. ? ROUND(account,0)
  276.00

. ? ROUND(salary,-2)
  1600.00
```

ROW( ) Data Type Returned: Numeric

Row Function Returns the current screen row position of the cursor.

RTRIM(<expC>) Data Type Returned: Character

Right Trim Function Returns the <expC> character string argument with any trailing spaces removed. (Same as the **TRIM** function.)

SPACE(<expN>) Data Type Returned: Character

Space Function Returns a string of spaces equal in length to the <expN> argument.

```
. STORE SPACE(LEN(employee)) TO name

. @ ROW(),45 GET name
. READ
```

SQRT(<expN>) Data Type Returned: Numeric

Square Root Function Returns the square root of the <expN> argument.

STR(<expN>[,<lenN>] [,<decN>]) Data Type Returned: Character

Numeric-to-String Function Returns a character string converted from a numeric expression. The argument <expN> is returned as a character string <lenN> characters long, with <decN> number of decimal places.

Most useful for deleting leading spaces in output of numeric data and/or forcing the display of desired decimal places.

```
. DISPLAY
Record#  EMPLOYEE                TELEPHONE SEX EMPLOYED   SALARY  ACCOUNT
      7  Martins Mary            222-2123  F   11/01/85  1600.00   200.50

. ? employee," - Limit = ",salary*.15
Martins Mary         - Limit =      240.0000

. ? TRIM(employee)," - Limit = ",STR(salary*.15,6,2)
Martins Mary  - Limit =  240.00
```

STUFF(<expC1>,<startN>, <lenN>,<expC2>) Data Type Returned: Character

Substring Replace Function Replaces or inserts the second character string argument <expC2> into the first character string argument <expC1>, starting at position <startN> in <expC1>. The argument <lenN> determines how many characters in <expC1> to replace, if any. The full string <expC2> is inserted, regardless of the <lenN> being replaced.

```
. STORE "This is a test" TO string1
This is a test

. STORE STUFF(string1,10,0,"nother") TO string2
This is another test

. STORE STUFF(string2,9,7,"NOT a") TO string3
This is NOT a test
```

SUBSTR(<expC>,<startN>,<lenN>) Data Type Returned: Character

Substring Function Returns the portion of the character string <expC> argument, beginning at position <startN> and <lenN> characters in length.

```
. DISPLAY
Record#  EMPLOYEE                TELEPHONE SEX EMPLOYED   SALARY  ACCOUNT
      7  Martins Mary            222-2123  F   11/01/85  1600.00   200.50

. ? SUBSTR(employee,9,4)
Mary
```

TIME( ) Data Type Returned: Character

Time Function Returns the system time in the format hh:mm:ss.

TRANSFORM(<exp>,<pictureC>) Data Type Returned: Character

Transform Function Formats the <exp> argument using a **PICTURE** template defined by the <pictureC> argument. Using the same template characters as the @ **SAY** command, this function allows data formatting with other display commands. The <exp> argument may be of any data type.

```
. STORE account - .15 * salary TO ovrlimit
    43.2500

. ? "Your account is over the limit by $" + TRANSFORM(ovrlimit,"999.99") + "!!"
Your account is over the limit by $ 43.25!!
```

TRIM(<expC>) Data Type Returned: Character

Trim Function Returns the <expC> character string argument with any trailing spaces removed.

```
. DISPLAY
Record#  EMPLOYEE                TELEPHONE SEX EMPLOYED   SALARY  ACCOUNT
      7  Martins Mary            222-2123  F   11/01/85  1600.00   200.50

. ? employee,telephone
Martins Mary         222-2123

. ? TRIM(employee),telephone
Martins Mary 222-2123
```

TYPE(<expC>) Data Type Returned: Character

Data Type Function Returns a one-character evaluation "C," "N," "D," "L," "M," or "U" for character, numeric, date, logical, memo, or undefined, respectively, of the <expC> argument. The <expC> must be a literal string enclosed in quotes naming the data item to be checked, or a character expression that evaluates to the name of the data item.

```
. ? TYPE("employee")
C

. ? TYPE("salary")
N

. ? TYPE("account < .15 * salary")
L

. STORE "employed" TO fname

. ? TYPE(fname)
D

. ? TYPE("fname")
C

. RELEASE fname

. ? TYPE("fname")
U
```

UPPER(<expC>) Data Type Returned: Character

Uppercase Function Returns the <expC> character string with all alphabetic characters converted to upper case.

```
. DISPLAY
Record#  EMPLOYEE               TELEPHONE SEX EMPLOYED   SALARY  ACCOUNT
      7  Martins Mary           222-2123  F   11/01/85  1600.00   200.50

. ? UPPER(employee)
MARTINS MARY
```

VAL(<expC>) Data Type Returned: Numeric

Character-to-Value Function Returns the numeric value of numbers held as strings beginning at the first character of the <expC> argument.

```
. ? VAL("7312 S.W. Fulton Park Blvd.")
                   7312.00

. ? VAL("P.O. Box 7312")
         0.00
```

VERSION( ) Data Type Returned: Character

Version Function Returns the version of dBASE III Plus currently in use.

YEAR(<expD>) Data Type Returned: Numeric

Year Function Returns the year number of the <expD> date expression argument.

```
. DISPLAY
Record#  EMPLOYEE               TELEPHONE SEX EMPLOYED   SALARY  ACCOUNT
      7  Martins Mary           222-2123  F   11/01/85  1600.00   200.50

. ? YEAR(employed)
 1985
```

DATA TRANSFER BETWEEN APPLICATIONS SOFTWARE

DATA TRANSFER BETWEEN APPLICATIONS

Suppose you have a report to submit that includes a Lotus 1-2-3 spreadsheet and you want the printed spreadsheet to appear in the body of a text file produced by WordPerfect. Or, maybe you have selected output produced by dBASE III Plus and want that information included in a WordPerfect text file. Perhaps you want to use the editing capabilities of WordPerfect to create a database for dBASE III Plus, or you want to use a Lotus spreadsheet to create the database for dBASE III Plus. What if you want to use WordPerfect or dBASE III Plus to create documentation or data for a Lotus 1-2-3 spreadsheet? All of this and more is possible because you can transfer data between applications software. The examples here use the applications software covered in this manual, but the fundamentals and basic procedures discussed will be similar for other applications software.

ASCII DATA FORMAT

The primary key to transferring data from one type of software to another lies in each software's ability to create and accept data stored in the American Standard Code for Information Interchange or ASCII (pronounced "as-key"). This data format standard was established specifically for the types of tasks mentioned earlier—tasks that involve the interchange of information or data.

For computer users (as opposed to computer programmers or data processing professionals) it is less important to know exactly what ASCII data formatting is than to know how it can be used and how to identify ASCII files.

NOTE: For this section's intended purpose, ASCII files are defined as files including only those characters numbered 13 and 32 to 126 inclusive.

Identifying ASCII Files

The procedure for identifying an ASCII file is straightforward. At the DOS level you use the **TYPE** command to list the contents of the file on the monitor screen. If every character of data that appears on the screen is a standard keyboard character, the file is stored in ASCII data format. If not, it is not stored in ASCII.

Software-Produced ASCII Files

Knowing whether or not you are creating an ASCII file is not as simple as identifying one after it has been created. Different software manuals, commands, and so forth, refer to ASCII files with different terminology. WordPerfect refers to the ASCII files that it creates as being *DOS Text files.* dBASE III Plus refers to ASCII files as being *SDF (System Data Format)* files.

The following is a list of the ASCII files created by the software covered in this manual. It indicates each software's ability to accept files for processing.

Lotus 1-2-3 ASCII Files

Lotus produces only its .PRN (Print files) in ASCII data format. These files are created by printing a range of the spreadsheet to a file using the /**P**rint,**F**ile command. Lotus 1-2-3 readily accepts any ASCII file into its spreadsheets through its /**F**ile,**I**mport command.

WordPerfect ASCII Files

WordPerfect will save its document files in ASCII if the proper procedures are used. The **Ctrl-F5** (Text In/Out),DOS **T**ext,**S**ave command may be used to save the current document in ASCII format.

Any ASCII format file may be directly retrieved into WordPerfect using the **Shift-F10** (Retrieve) command. The file, however, will be immediately converted to WordPerfect data format and rewritten to the current document format settings (margins, line spacing, etc.).

dBASE III Plus ASCII Files

dBASE maintains several of its file types in ASCII format. dBASE .PRG command files are stored in ASCII data format, as are its .TXT files. Its .DBF database files are not kept in ASCII, but a copy of a database in ASCII format can be easily made by using the **COPY TO** <filename> [**SDF**] command. When a copy of a database is made this way, it is given a .TXT extension. In addition, any nonediting screen output generated by a dBASE operation can be written to an ASCII file by using the **SET ALTERNATE TO** <filename> and **SET ALTERNATE ON** commands. The files created in this manner also are given a .TXT extension.

To read ASCII files into a database, the **APPEND FROM** <filename.TXT> [**TYPE SDF**] command is used. In addition, any file dBASE normally maintains in ASCII can be produced by another software and still be used by dBASE III Plus.

In general, the commands of dBASE III Plus are very effective for moving data between dBASE and other software.

DOS ASCII Files

DOS does not actually produce ASCII files itself. However, with versions of DOS 2.0+, DOS can redirect another software's output to an ASCII file as long as the software uses the DOS function calls for its output and does not generate non-ASCII characters as output. This feature of DOS (called "piping") can be most useful for canned programs written in a programming language. To cause this redirection (more accurately called an echo) of output, you use one or two greater than (>) signs followed by the ASCII file's filename when you load the software. A single > erases any previous ASCII file with the same filename, while two >s append output to any previous file with the same filename. For example, typing

A> C:BASICA LINPRO>>testout

loads IBM's BASICA programming language and the BASICA program LINPRO.BAS into RAM, and begins running the program. If the file testout does not yet exist, it is created. As the program LINPRO.BAS runs, all output that occurs on the screen is echoed to (printed to) the disk file testout. If testout previously existed, the data printed to it are appended (added at the bottom). Typing the **SYSTEM** command after the program is through executing completes the printing of data to the ASCII file and closes it.

Data Structure

Understanding the basics of data structure is the second key to transferring data between software. For software able to process both strings and numbers, data structure means incoming data is kept in units of data items. The items are separated from each other (delimited) in a way that differentiates the string-type data from the numeric-type data.

The rest of this section presents procedures for specific types of data transfer between software, and describes instances where the process may prove useful. The section provides details about how the data must be structured in each case. As you progress through the material, many principles of data structure will become apparent, enabling you to perform data transfer operations not covered.

CREATING dBASE .PRG COMMAND FILES USING WORDPERFECT

dBASE .PRG command files may be created using WordPerfect rather than the **MODIFY COMMAND** text editing mode of dBASE.

Benefits

The **MODIFY COMMAND** text editing mode (when compared to the editing mode(s) of a word processing software) is limited and often cumbersome to use. Some features of WordPerfect that are useful when creating .PRG files include the following: the **Alt-F2** (Replace) command for changing variable names throughout a program; the cut-and-paste block operations for making copies of repetitious code; the **Shift-F3** (Switch) command for easily creating two .PRG files at the same time; the **Shift-F8** (Format),**L**ine,**T**ab Set command for setting tabs appropriate for structured style; and, in certain types of .PRG files such as form letters, the **Ctrl-F2** (Spell) command for checking portions of text within the program for spelling errors.

Procedure

After loading WordPerfect, set the left margin to 0" and the right margin to 25.4" by inserting a [L/R Mar:] code at the top of the document with the **Shift-F8** (Format),**L**ine,**M**argins command. Next type the lines of the program. Make sure to end each program line with a hard return by typing ↵. When finished, use the **Ctrl-F5** (Text In/Out),DOS **T**ext,**S**ave command to save the file in ASCII format. When saving the file, include the .PRG filename extension in the specified filename.

Comments

The name you give the file must have the appropriate filename extension (.PRG) for the program to be later executed by dBASE. You either can give the file its appropriate name when you create it, or you can use the **RENAME** command of DOS to change it later. Each line of a dBASE III Plus program written in WordPerfect must end with a hard return (↵).

LOTUS 1-2-3 SPREADSHEETS INTO WORDPERFECT

When the Lotus 1-2-3 /**F**ile,**S**ave command is used, Lotus creates a non-ASCII disk file (.WK1 extension) containing the cell locations and contents of the current spreadsheet. When the Lotus 1-2-3 /**P**rint,**F**ile command is used, Lotus creates an ASCII disk file (.PRN) that contains the output (display) of the current spreadsheet.

Spreadsheet Data File (.WK1)

```
B3: 'Month
C3: "Sales
D3: "COGS
E3: "Net
B4: \-
C4: \-
D4: \-
E4: \-
B5: 'January
C5: 1250
D5: 0.65*C5
E5: +C5-D5
B6: 'February
C6: 1330
D6: 0.65*C6
E6: +C6-D6
B7: 'March
C7: 1410
D7: 0.65*C7
E7: +C7-D7
B8: 'April
C8: 1400
D8: 0.65*C8
E8: +C8-D8
```

Spreadsheet Print File (.PRN)

```
Month          Sales       COGS        Net
----------------------------------------------
January   $1,250.00    $812.50    $437.50
February  $1,330.00    $864.50    $465.50
March     $1,410.00    $916.50    $493.50
April     $1,400.00    $910.00    $490.00
```

The file shown on the left in the above example shows what a Lotus .WK1 file would look like if it were saved in ASCII format. The spreadsheet data file is used by Lotus to reconstruct a saved spreadsheet in RAM each time the file is loaded with the /File,**R**etrieve command. The .WK1 file contains the actual data entered from the keyboard or copied into other cells of the spreadsheet by the user. A file created from the same spreadsheet by using the /**F**ile,**P**rint command to print a spreadsheet to a file is shown on the right. Lotus gives such files a .PRN filename extension. This file contains the processed data, or output, generated by the software. It appears the same in this file as it appears on the monitor screen, or on paper when the spreadsheet is printed. An important difference between the two is that a Print file cannot be loaded back into a spreadsheet by Lotus. It is output that, instead of being printed on a piece of paper, was printed on the disk under its own filename in ASCII data format. If you use a word processor to open the Print file for editing, and then change one of its key values, the rest of the spreadsheet will not recalculate.

With WordPerfect, files can be merged by simply retrieving one file into another. When a file is retrieved, it will be inserted into any existing text at the location of the cursor. Any ASCII file may be inserted into a WordPerfect document in this manner.

Benefits

Using a spreadsheet to produce computed values from formulas, printing the results to a Print file, and then reading them into a WordPerfect text file has many practical applications. Corporate reports, term papers, billings, invoices, budgets, appraisals, and estimates are just some of the instances when such a procedure can be useful.

Procedure

Print the desired area of the spreadsheet to the disk with the /**P**rint,**F**ile command (you may want to set its automatic margins top, bottom, and left to zero). Load WordPerfect and then retrieve the document file into which you want to place the spreadsheet output. Move the editing cursor to the location where the spreadsheet data are to appear and then retrieve the .PRN file. Or, you may simply retrieve the .PRN file and edit around it with WordPerfect. In either case, you will need to specify the whole filename, including its extension, to retrieve the .PRN file for editing.

Comments

It is important to note that when you create a .PRN file using the /**P**rint,**F**ile command of Lotus, you must exit the command by using **Q**uit. Using the Esc key to back out of the /**P**rint commands will result in an empty .PRN file.

dBASE III PLUS DATA INTO WORDPERFECT

dBASE III Plus creates several different types of files, each of which has its own type of filename extension. The .PRG (command files) and .TXT (text files) created by dBASE III are ASCII files. As such, they may be retrieved by WordPerfect for editing and then saved onto the disk in "DOS Format" for use again by dBASE. The procedure is the same as writing a dBASE program in WordPerfect.

dBASE has commands designed specifically for creating ASCII text files (to which it gives a .TXT extension). The files contain copies of screen output created from a dBASE operation, or fields of data in a .DBF database file.

The dBASE commands used to create ASCII files of screen output are

SET ALTERNATE TO <filename>
SET ALTERNATE ON
SET ALTERNATE OFF

First, the .TXT file is created with the **SET ALTERNATE TO** <filename>. After the file is created, the command **SET ALTERNATE ON** will begin writing (echoing) all output appearing on the monitor screen (with the exception of output generated in a full-screen editing mode) to the .TXT file.

The command **SET ALTERNATE OFF** stops the writing of data to the .TXT file. The command **SET ALTERNATE TO,** without a filename specified, or the command **QUIT,** closes the .TXT file.

To create an ASCII .TXT file copy of the fields of data occurring in a database, the following command may be used.

COPY TO <filename> **TYPE SDF**

Once the .TXT file has been created, it may be opened for editing or retrieved into an existing document file with WordPerfect's **Shift-F10** (Retrieve) command.

Benefits

dBASE has commands capable of very precise formatting of output for both the screen and printer, but these commands generally are used in command files for reports produced often. When a single report requiring a specific format is needed, or before you have the time, expertise, and/or patience to write the necessary command file, letting dBASE generate the raw data and then using WordPerfect to manipulate the data into its final form can be the most effective and efficient means of producing the desired product.

Procedure

Type the dBASE commands **SET ALTERNATE TO** <filename> and **SET ALTERNATE ON,** respectively. Type the commands to generate the desired data on the monitor screen, and then use the command **SET ALTERNATE OFF** to stop writing to the .TXT file. To obtain an ASCII copy of a database, type the command **COPY TO** <filename> **TYPE SDF.** Be sure to type **QUIT** to close any .TXT files that may be left open when you are finished with dBASE.

The .TXT file may be opened for editing or retrieved into an existing document file with WordPerfect's **Shift-F10** (Retrieve) command.

Comments

dBASE III Plus seems designed to work quite effectively with word processing software, and few (if any) problems occur when these procedures are followed.

SPREADSHEETS INTO A dBASE III DATABASE

It is possible to use the spreadsheet applications to create records for a dBASE III Plus database. The dBASE command used to read an ASCII file into a database is

APPEND FROM <filename.ext> **TYPE SDF**

When dBASE appends records this way, it looks to the file being appended from for the number of characters equal to the length of the fields defined in that database's record structure. So, if the database's record structure has three fields, each nine characters long, it will append the first nine characters found in the text file into the first field of the first record, the second nine characters found into the second field of the first record, and so on. The text file must have spaces included when the data for a field does not fill the field. With spreadsheet applications this is usually not a problem. Their Print files are text files set up ideally for appending into a database. Each cell in the spreadsheet is read in as a field of data, and the cells are read from the printed spreadsheet, left to right, top to bottom. Using a previous example

Lotus .PRN File

Month	Sales	COGS	Net
January	1250.00	812.50	437.50
February	1330.00	864.50	466.50
March	1410.00	916.50	493.50
April	1400.00	910.00	490.00

an appropriate database structure would be created as

dBASE Record Structure

	Field Name	Type	Width	Dec
1	MONTH	Character	9	
2	SALES	Numeric	9	2
3	COGS	Numeric	9	2
4	NET	Numeric	9	2

Notice that the currency formatting ($ and , characters) were removed from the spreadsheet display before the Print file was created. dBASE requires that numeric data appended to fields in a database are free of such notations. Also notice that the first two rows of labels found in the .PRN file are not what you would want to (or could) enter into the first and second records of the database. Therefore, you either would (1) not print them to the file or (2) retrieve the Print file with WordPerfect, delete the first two rows (lines), and then save the file as a DOS **T**ext File.

From dBASE, after having created the database's structure, typing the command **APPEND FROM** <filename.PRN> **TYPE SDF** would result in a small database with records containing the following data.

Record No. 1

MONTH	January
SALES	1250.00
COGS	812.50
NET	437.50

Record No. 2

MONTH	February
SALES	1330.00
COGS	864.50
NET	465.50

Record No. 3

MONTH	March
SALES	1410.00
COGS	916.50
NET	493.50

Record No. 4

MONTH	April
SALES	1400.00
COGS	910.00
NET	490.00

Benefits

Many of the benefits mentioned in the previous section apply to the reading of spreadsheet Print files into dBASE as records of a database. Operations such as multilevel sorting, substring searches for reporting, and others, are operations that dBASE is designed to do. Also, the use of spreadsheet formulas and the /**C**opy commands often make creating record-type data a quick and easy process, and the ability to more easily edit a database as you create it is often desired.

Procedure

Enter the fields of data into individual spreadsheet cells so that each row in the spreadsheet contains the fields of data for one record. (This arrangement of data is called "row major," and the same organization is used for performing Lotus's /**D**ata,**Q**uery operations.) Set the column widths in the spreadsheet to be the same widths as the intended field widths in the intended database. Usually you will want to write the column width numbers down at this point since it is important that the two widths (column and field) are identical when you create the dBASE record structure. Then use the /**P**rint,**F**ile commands to set the left, top, and bottom margins to 0 and then print only the record data found in the spreadsheet out to a .PRN file.

Load dBASE III Plus. Then use the **CREATE** command to define the intended database's structure. Remember that the field widths must accurately reflect the Lotus column widths. Next use the dBASE command **APPEND FROM** <filename.PRN> **TYPE SDF** to append the spreadsheet data into the database.

Comments

It is important to note that when you create a .PRN file using the /**P**rint,**F**ile command, you must exit the /**P**rint commands by using the **Q**uit command. Using the Esc key to back out of the /**P**rint command results in an empty .PRN file on the disk.

You should note that as long as the data are organized in the same manner as a row major spreadsheet .PRN file, you can use WordPerfect and its **Ctrl-F5** (Text In/Out),DOS **T**ext,**S**ave command to create records for a dBASE database file.

WORDPERFECT FILES INTO A LOTUS 1-2-3 SPREADSHEET

To accept other software's data, Lotus's /**F**ile,**I**mport command is used. The first step in using this command is choosing the option to import a file as either **T**ext or **N**umbers.

Importing Unstructured Data

If **T**ext is specified, the file being imported into the current spreadsheet will be entered into one column of cells, beginning at the current pointer location and continuing down, with each line of the imported file entered as a Label into a cell of the column.

In the case of a WordPerfect DOS Text file, data being imported into Lotus will exist as extended labels in the spreadsheet. For instance, the previous paragraph was made into its own WordPerfect file when it was at the manuscript stage. It appeared in WordPerfect as

```
If Text is specified, the file being imported into the current
spreadsheet will be entered into one column of cells, beginning at
the current pointer location and continuing down, with each line
of the imported file entered as a Label into a cell of the column.
```

The file then was saved with the **Ctrl-F5** (Text In/Out),DOS **T**ext command (adding a .PRN extension to the name when it was saved) and WordPerfect was exited. Next, Lotus was loaded and while the spreadsheet pointer was located on cell A1, the /**F**ile,**I**mport,**T**ext command was used to import the paragraph into the spreadsheet.

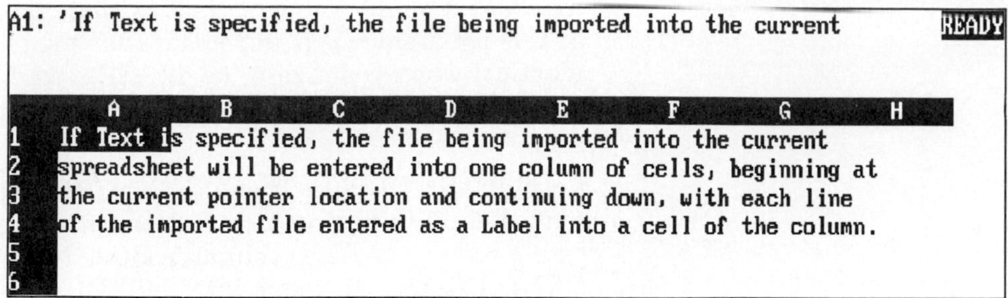

```
A1: 'If Text is specified, the file being imported into the current          READY

     A        B        C        D        E        F        G        H
1  If Text is specified, the file being imported into the current
2  spreadsheet will be entered into one column of cells, beginning at
3  the current pointer location and continuing down, with each line
4  of the imported file entered as a Label into a cell of the column.
5
6
```

The paragraph was imported one line at a time into the cells A1 through A4. Each label extends to the right of the A column as long as the spreadsheet cells to the right remained blank. If spreadsheet data had existed in cells A1 through A4 before the **I**mport command operation, they would have been replaced by the imported data.

The second step of the /**F**ile,**I**mport command requests the filename of the file to import. Lotus will only import a file if it has a .PRN filename extension. Therefore, before attempting to import a file into a Lotus spreadsheet, you may need to use the **RENAME** command of DOS (or a renaming command of another software) to make sure the file you are importing has this file extension.

Importing Structured Data

When the data being imported into the spreadsheet are intended to be separated into different cells, the /**D**ata,**P**arse command may be used after the import operation. The command makes it possible to import ASCII files with a row major organization into the spreadsheet, and then separate the fields into columns of cells having different data types. To demonstrate the operations involved in parsing data, the following example will be used. The example is based on a WordPerfect DOS Text file document listing the names, phone numbers, donations, and donation dates for companies contributing to a charity.

```
Cantrell Industries    (503) 235-7164    $1,000    03/20/90
Allstrong Inc.         (206) 643-1877    $1,500    04/15/90
Willamette Hardware    (503) 227-8739    $1,500    06/08/90
Chase Supplies         (503) 244-9983    $2,000    05/07/90
```

The file is saved as a DOS Text file under the name donors.PRN, or may be renamed later to include the .PRN extension by using DOS's **RENAME** command. The file then is imported into a Lotus spreadsheet using the /**F**ile,**I**mport,**T**ext command. Each line of the file is placed as an extended label into a cell of the A column.

```
A3: 'Cantrell Industries         (503) 235-7164        $1,000      03/20/90          READY

          A          B          C          D          E          F          G          H
1
2
3  Cantrell Industries          (503) 235-7164        $1,000      03/20/90
4  Allstrong Inc.               (206) 643-1877        $1,500      04/15/90
5  Willamette Hardware          (503) 227-8739        $1,500      06/08/90
6  Chase Supplies               (503) 244-9983        $2,000      05/07/90
7
8
```

With the pointer on the top-left cell of the data range (cell A3), the /**D**ata,**P**arse command is next entered. The menu for parsing data includes

```
Format-Line  Input-Column  Output-Range  Reset  Go  Quit
```

The first step in the example is to establish a **F**ormat-Line for parsing the data. When the **F**ormat-Line menu option is selected, the options to **C**reate or **E**dit are given. In the example, **C**reate is selected.

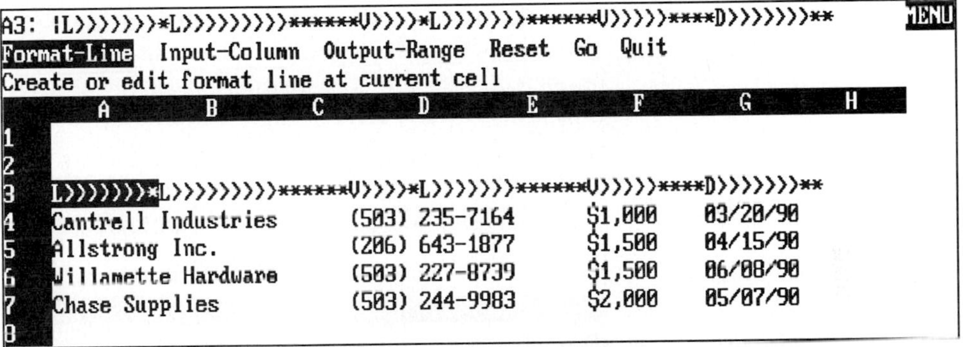

```
A3: |L>>>>>>>*L>>>>>>>>>******V>>>>*L>>>>>>>******V>>>>>****D>>>>>>>**              MENU
Format-Line  Input-Column  Output-Range  Reset  Go  Quit
Create or edit format line at current cell
          A          B          C          D          E          F          G          H
1
2
3  L>>>>>>>*L>>>>>>>>>******V>>>>*L>>>>>>>******V>>>>>****D>>>>>>>**
4  Cantrell Industries          (503) 235-7164        $1,000      03/20/90
5  Allstrong Inc.               (206) 643-1877        $1,500      04/15/90
6  Willamette Hardware          (503) 227-8739        $1,500      06/08/90
7  Chase Supplies               (503) 244-9983        $2,000      05/07/90
8
```

The line inserted by Lotus above the data is a "best guess" format-line based on the first line of data in the range. The format-line is used by Lotus to decide which data will be put in which cell and the type of data it will be (label, value, or date in this example) when the subsequent parsing is complete. The characters of the format-line shown here have the following meaning:

L	The first character of the data block is a label.
V	The first character of the data block is a value.
D	The first character of the data block is a date.
>	The character beneath is the same as the first character in the data block.
*	There is no character beneath, but one may occur in other records.

The second **F**ormat-Line option is to **E**dit. This option may be used to manually edit the characters occurring in a format-line. In the example, the format-line is edited to make the following changes. The first and second names of the companies will be put in the same cell, and the area code will be entered as a label instead of a value and will be put in the same cell as the rest of the phone number.

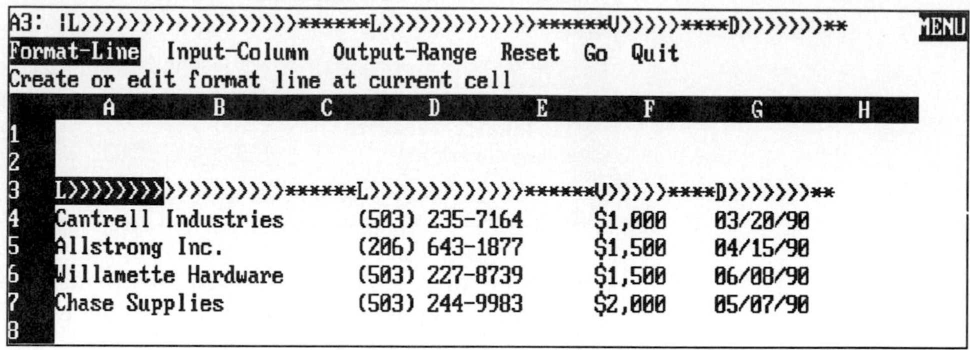

```
A3: |L>>>>>>>>>>>>>>>>>>>******L>>>>>>>>>>>>>******V>>>>>****D>>>>>>>**        MENU
Format-Line  Input-Column  Output-Range  Reset  Go  Quit
Create or edit format line at current cell
        A         B         C         D         E         F         G         H
1
2
3   L>>>>>>>>>>>>>>>>>>******L>>>>>>>>>>>>>******V>>>>>****D>>>>>>>**
4   Cantrell Industries       (503) 235-7164      $1,000    03/20/90
5   Allstrong Inc.            (206) 643-1877      $1,500    04/15/90
6   Willamette Hardware       (503) 227-8739      $1,500    06/08/90
7   Chase Supplies            (503) 244-9983      $2,000    05/07/90
8
```

The next step is to specify the **I**nput-Column for parsing. The input-column is defined as all cells of the column containing the imported record-type data plus the cell containing the format-line. The last range to specify is the **O**utput-Range. The output-range is entered as the top-left cell of the range into which the parsed data will be copied. In this example, the output-range will be cell A10.

Once the steps have been accomplished, the **G**o command of the /**D**ata,**P**arse commands may be executed. The result will be a copy of the data originally imported, placed at the location of the output-range, with each block of data, as defined by the format-line, copied into an individual cell as a specific data type.

```
A3: |L>>>>>>>>>>>>>>>>>>>******L>>>>>>>>>>>>>******V>>>>>****D>>>>>>>**        READY


        A         B         C         D         E         F         G         H
1
2
3   L>>>>>>>>>>>>>>>>>>******L>>>>>>>>>>>>>******V>>>>>****D>>>>>>>**
4   Cantrell Industries       (503) 235-7164      $1,000    03/20/90
5   Allstrong Inc.            (206) 643-1877      $1,500    04/15/90
6   Willamette Hardware       (503) 227-8739      $1,500    06/08/90
7   Chase Supplies            (503) 244-9983      $2,000    05/07/90
8
9
10  Cantrell (503) 235    1000    32952
11  Allstrong(206) 643    1500    32978
12  Willamett(503) 227    1500    33032
13  Chase Sup(503) 244    2000    33000
14
```

Column widths in the output-range may need to be widened to display labels, and range formatting may be necessary to add currency displays. Dates copied to the output-range are copied over as the serial number for the date. A column with such data needs to be formatted for date display.

Benefits

Large spreadsheets often require large areas of documentation explaining the assumptions of the model(s) used, and/or summarizing the information generated by the spreadsheet model(s). When such documentation is required, it may be more convenient for a person knowledgeable with WordPerfect to use that software to produce the necessary text rather than to use the relatively weak word processing capabilities of Lotus to produce the documentation. Additionally, mainframe computers often are able to provide ASCII files containing structured data that, when imported and parsed, can save a microcomputer user many hours of data input.

Procedure

Use WordPerfect to create the DOS Text file or, if necessary, edit an ASCII file provided by another software or computer system. Either name the file initially using a .PRN filename extension or rename the file later to have this extension.

After you have created the ASCII file, load Lotus 1-2-3 and the appropriate spreadsheet into RAM, move the pointer to the top-left cell of the area into which you want the file to be imported, and then use the /**F**ile,**I**mport,**T**ext command to import the file into the current spreadsheet at the location of the pointer. If necessary, use the /**D**ata,**P**arse commands to parse the imported file into separate spreadsheet cells.

Comments

The Lotus Manual states: "Many word processors generate document files which contain special characters. If you attempt to read these files using the /File Import command unpredictable results may occur. Most word processors, however, produce standard ASCII files which should be compatible with 1-2-3."

The words "unpredictable" and "should be" indicate that a more conservative approach to the procedure would be first to import the file into a blank spreadsheet and examine it for peculiar characters. If no such characters are found, continue by importing that file into the intended spreadsheet. If peculiar characters are found, try using 1-2-3's F2 edit mode to delete them, reprint the area to a .PRN file, and repeat the test.

dBASE III PLUS DATABASE RECORDS INTO A LOTUS 1-2-3 SPREADSHEET

The final data transfer operation to discuss is moving dBASE III Plus database records into a Lotus 1-2-3 spreadsheet. In this example Lotus's /**F**ile,**I**mport command will be used with the option to import **N**umbers rather than **T**ext (see "WordPerfect Files into a Lotus 1-2-3 Spreadsheet").

When the **N**umbers option of the /**F**ile,**I**mport command is used, Lotus will import an ASCII file containing both strings and numbers in it, and will automatically put the data items into separate spreadsheet cells, if the data in the imported file are structured correctly. With Lotus, the strings in the file must be delimited with quotes and the data items must be separated by commas.

Using the database created in the dBASE III Plus tutorial lessons, the **COPY TO** <filename> **TYPE SDF** command results in an ASCII file

```
Pratt John          225-1234M19820622 1949.00  200.00
Smoler Ellen        225-3212F19830915 1650.00  300.00
Jones David         292-3832M19820615 1550.00  275.75
Sill Sally          224-4321F19840215 1507.00  150.00
Knat Michael        221-1235M19800915 1800.00  125.00
Smith Paul          244-1010M19811115 1700.00  350.00
Martins Mary        222-2123F19851101 1600.00  200.50
Nichols Sandy       229-1111F19860215 1450.00  175.00
Johnson Frank       223-7928M19900320 1500.00    0.00
```

Another parameter of the dBASE **COPY** command is **DELIMITED WITH** <delimiter>. When used, it will copy the records to an ASCII file with delimiters inserted between the fields of data. When this command specifies a quote as the delimiter, as in the following

COPY TO testfile **DELIMITED WITH** "

the records in the database are copied to the ASCII file testfile.TXT in the form

```
"Pratt John","225-1234","M",19820622,1949.00,200.00
"Smoler Ellen","225-3212","F",19830915,1650.00,300.00
"Jones David","292-3832","M",19820615,1550.00,275.75
"Sill Sally","224-4321","F",19840215,1507.00,150.00
"Knat Michael","221-1235","M",19800915,1800.00,125.00
"Smith Paul","244-1010","M",19811115,1700.00,350.00
"Martins Mary","222-2123","F",19851101,1600.00,200.50
"Nichols Sandy","229-1111","F",19860215,1450.00,175.00
"Johnson Frank","223-7928","M",19900320,1500.00,0.00
```

This organization of data is suitable for importing into a Lotus spreadsheet as Numbers. However, the database field for employment date has been copied to the file as a large number representing the year, month, and day (i.e., 19820622 representing the date 06/22/82). It is typical that date-type data are among the most difficult to transfer between applications software. The general rule for making such transfers is to first convert the date-type data using the commands of the source software into character-type data. Next, make the transfer and then convert the character data back to date-type data using the commands of the destination software. In this case, the procedure would be to use the **MODIFY STRUCTURE** command of dBASE to change the field named "employed" from being date to character type. Then, use the **COPY TO** testfile **DELIMITED WITH** " command to produce the following ASCII file.

```
"Pratt John","225-1234","M","06/22/82",1949.00,200.00
"Smoler Ellen","225-3212","F","09/15/83",1650.00,300.00
"Jones David","292-3832","M","06/15/82",1550.00,275.75
"Sill Sally","224-4321","F","02/15/84",1507.00,150.00
"Knat Michael","221-1235","M","09/15/80",1800.00,125.00
"Smith Paul","244-1010","M","11/15/81",1700.00,350.00
"Martins Mary","222-2123","F","11/01/85",1600.00,200.50
"Nichols Sandy","229-1111","F","02/15/86",1450.00,175.00
"Johnson Frank","223-7928","M","03/20/90",1500.00,0.00
```

Before importing this file into a Lotus spreadsheet it must be renamed to have a .PRN extension instead of the .TXT extension. When Lotus's /**F**ile,**I**mport,**N**umbers command is executed with the pointer on cell A3, testfile specified as the file to import, and the column widths of the spreadsheet changed to make the imported data more easily read, the result is

```
A3: [W15] 'Pratt John                                                READY

          A          B      C    D           E         F        G        H
1
2
3   Pratt John      225-1234 M  06/22/82    1949       200
4   Smoler Ellen    225-3212 F  09/15/83    1650       300
5   Jones David     292-3832 M  06/15/82    1550    275.75
6   Sill Sally      224-4321 F  02/15/84    1507       150
7   Knat Michael    221-1235 M  09/15/80    1800       125
8   Smith Paul      244-1010 M  11/15/81    1700       350
9   Martins Mary    222-2123 F  11/01/85    1600     200.5
10  Nichols Sandy   229-1111 F  02/15/86    1450       175
11  Johnson Frank   223-7928 M  03/20/90    1500         0
12
```

Each field of each record will be entered into an individual spreadsheet cell in the same data type (string or numeric) as it was held in its database field.

To convert the date labels in the spreadsheet to serial date values, you may use the /**D**ata,**P**arse command. Move the pointer to the cell D3 (the first data cell occurring in the D column) and use the /**D**ata,**P**arse,**F**ormat-Line,**C**reate command to produce the following format-line above the column

```
D3: |D>>>>>>>                                                         MENU
Format-Line  Input-Column  Output-Range  Reset  Go  Quit
Create or edit format line at current cell
          A          B      C    D           E         F        G        H
1
2
3                               D>>>>>>>
4   Pratt John      225-1234 M  06/22/82    1949       200
5   Smoler Ellen    225-3212 F  09/15/83    1650       300
6   Jones David     292-3832 M  06/15/82    1550    275.75
7   Sill Sally      224-4321 F  02/15/84    1507       150
8   Knat Michael    221-1235 M  09/15/80    1800       125
9   Smith Paul      244-1010 M  11/15/81    1700       350
10  Martins Mary    222-2123 F  11/01/85    1600     200.5
11  Nichols Sandy   229-1111 F  02/15/86    1450       175
12  Johnson Frank   223-7928 M  03/20/90    1500         0
13
```

Next use the **I**nput-Column command to specify the format-line and all dates below it (D3..D12) as being the input-column, and then use the **O**utput-Range command to specify the cell D4 as being the output-range. Next execute the **G**o command and all date labels in the column will be converted into their serial date equivalents.

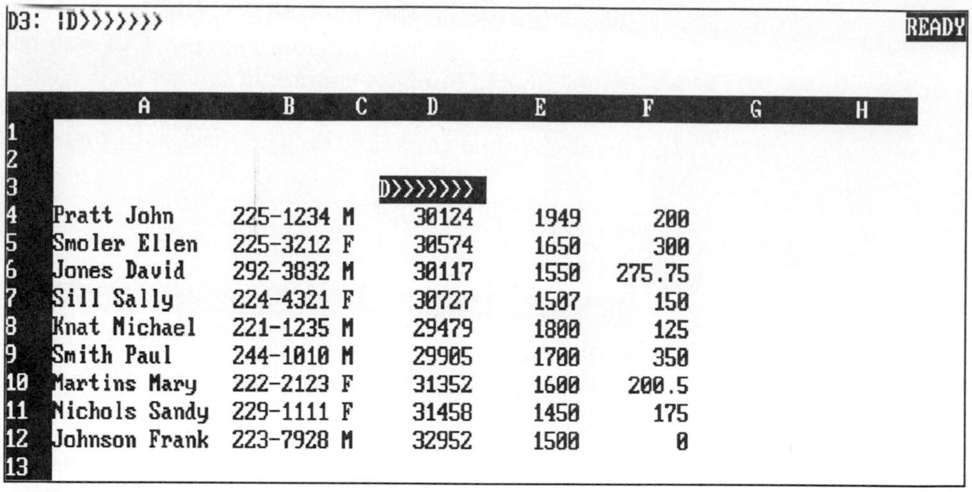

```
D3: |D>>>>>>>                                                     READY

          A           B      C      D         E        F        G        H
1
2
3                                 D>>>>>>>
4  Pratt John     225-1234 M     30124     1949      200
5  Smoler Ellen   225-3212 F     30574     1650      300
6  Jones David    292-3832 M     30117     1550   275.75
7  Sill Sally     224-4321 F     30727     1507      150
8  Knat Michael   221-1235 M     29479     1800      125
9  Smith Paul     244-1010 M     29905     1700      350
10 Martins Mary   222-2123 F     31352     1600    200.5
11 Nichols Sandy  229-1111 F     31458     1450      175
12 Johnson Frank  223-7928 M     32952     1500        0
13
```

Finally erase the format-line, widen the D column, and format the range to display the date format of your choice.

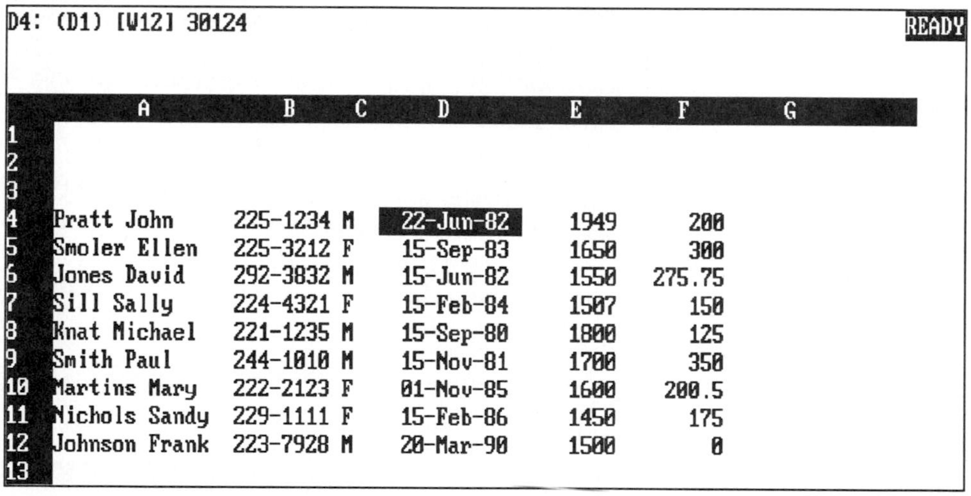

```
D4: (D1) [W12] 30124                                              READY

          A           B      C       D          E        F        G
1
2
3
4  Pratt John     225-1234 M    22-Jun-82     1949      200
5  Smoler Ellen   225-3212 F    15-Sep-83     1650      300
6  Jones David    292-3832 M    15-Jun-82     1550   275.75
7  Sill Sally     224-4321 F    15-Feb-84     1507      150
8  Knat Michael   221-1235 M    15-Sep-80     1800      125
9  Smith Paul     244-1010 M    15-Nov-81     1700      350
10 Martins Mary   222-2123 F    01-Nov-85     1600    200.5
11 Nichols Sandy  229-1111 F    15-Feb-86     1450      175
12 Johnson Frank  223-7928 M    20-Mar-90     1500        0
13
```

Benefits

The greatest strength of a spreadsheet application is its ability to generate formula-based information for decision making. Parametric statistical analysis of an organization's internal data is an example of such information. Database management systems such as dBASE III Plus have the strengths of data maintenance, query, and record organization which are useful for reporting purposes, and provide information relevant to a different type of decision making. When the need for formula-based information from record-type data is required, this transfer of data operation may be very useful, and in fact may provide the only way to obtain the needed information.

Procedure

Use the **COPY TO** <filename> **DELIMITED WITH** " command to create a .TXT ASCII file of the database with the fields of data properly delimited. If necessary, use the **MODIFY STRUCTURE** command to convert all date fields to character fields before creating the .TXT file. Rename the file to have a .PRN filename extension, load Lotus and the appropriate spreadsheet (if any) into RAM, and then move the spreadsheet pointer to the top-left cell of the area into which you want the records imported. Use the /**F**ile,**I**mport,**N**umbers command and specify the appropriate file to import. If necessary, use the /**D**ata,**P**arse commands to convert date labels into their serial date equivalents.

Comments

By now you should see that as long as the data are arranged in an appropriate structure, the source of the ASCII file imported as **N**umbers is not important. WordPerfect, or any software capable of producing a file with data items separated by commas and strings in quotes, could be used to create the ASCII file.

DATA TRANSFER CASE EXERCISE

PRIMARY PAINT CORPORATION

Primary Paint Corporation is a small company that manufactures paint bases for distribution to several well-known paint companies. The paint bases are made to customer specifications and come in the three primary colors (yellow, red, and blue), as well as the base tints white and black. Although small in size, Primary Paint has operated quite profitably for the last several years. A steady increase in sales and a high ratio of assets to debt have made the company a likely candidate for a corporate takeover.

Joel Wilson has worked for Primary Paint Corporation for only a few months. He originally was hired as an assistant to the shipping and receiving manager, but, when management discovered that he knew how to use the microcomputer along with several different applications software, he began being asked to do many tasks outside his normal job description.

For the most part Joel didn't mind the extra work (and recognition) he received from being the company's "computer guru," but early one Friday morning Bill Meyers, the plant supervisor, came to him with a problem that didn't readily lend itself to being solved with any one of the software with which Joel was familiar. Bill said, "Joel, there's a lot of excitement going on upstairs. Evidently Simon Harris, the owner of National Paint, is preparing a friendly takeover tender for the company. A takeover by National would almost certainly mean higher salaries and greater job security for the two of us. Anyway, Harris is coming to the plant Monday morning to ask a few questions about our operations and shipments.

"I haven't a clue about the questions he might have, but I'd like to be prepared to answer all of his questions without missing a beat. If he wants to know how many gallons of yellow paint we shipped in February, or what the dollar sales in the first quarter were for red paint, you and I need to be able to come up with the answer immediately.

"I'd also like to give Harris a one-page summary report of our year-to-date sales along with a first-quarter breakdown of gallon sales for each color of paint base. I want the report to look as professional as possible. Maybe you could include a nice table of dollar sales and a pie chart for the breakdown of first-quarter gallon sales.

"You know, Joel, it's sure good to have someone with your computer talents on our team. I'm leaving early today to get ready for a fishing trip this weekend, so I'll see you bright and early on Monday."

With that, Bill handed Joel a stack of shipping invoices and a wholesale price list and then walked out the door.

Sample Shipping Invoice

Invoice # *A1027*	Invoice Date *02/11/90*	Carrier *Freightliner*
Shipped To: *Northwest Custom Paints*		
Paint Base Color *WHITE* Gallons Shipped *1690*		

Wholesale Price List

WHITE................ $5.25/gal
YELLOW $6.00/gal
RED $6.40/gal
BLUE $6.74/gal
BLACK................ $7.30/gal

Note: In the following case exercises you will see this symbol.

It indicates an opportune time to save your files and quit the tutorial to continue later.

CASE EXERCISE 1
Creating Records of Data Using Lotus 1-2-3

When Joel sorted through the invoices he discovered that they were organized by color/tint. That is, all of the invoices for white paint base were grouped together, as were the invoices for red, yellow, and so on. You will begin solving Joel's problem by creating the dBASE invoice record data using Lotus 1-2-3.

1. Load Lotus 1-2-3 and then enter the following invoice numbers, invoice dates, and gallons shipped data into the appropriate cells. Since the invoice date data is destined to be transferred to dBASE, you will need to enter it as labels (type a single quote and then type and enter the date).

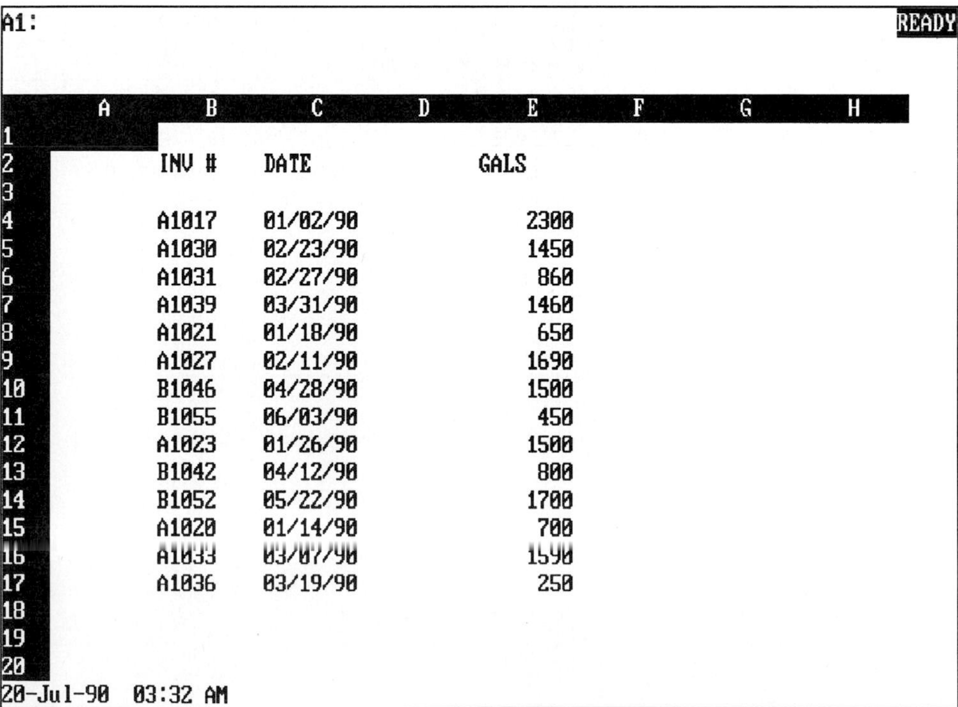

A1: READY

	A	B	C	D	E	F	G	H
1								
2		INV #	DATE		GALS			
3								
4		A1017	01/02/90		2300			
5		A1030	02/23/90		1450			
6		A1031	02/27/90		860			
7		A1039	03/31/90		1460			
8		A1021	01/18/90		650			
9		A1027	02/11/90		1690			
10		B1046	04/28/90		1500			
11		B1055	06/03/90		450			
12		A1023	01/26/90		1500			
13		B1042	04/12/90		800			
14		B1052	05/22/90		1700			
15		A1020	01/14/90		700			
16		A1033	03/07/90		1590			
17		A1036	03/19/90		250			
18								
19								
20								

20-Jul-90 03:32 AM

All of the invoice's records so far are for white paint base, which is currently priced at $5.25/gallon.

2. Move the pointer to cell D4 and enter the label WHITE. Then copy the label into the rest of the cells in that column (you may label the column COLOR). Next move to cell A4 and enter the value 5.25. Then move the pointer to cell F4 and enter the formula +E4*$A$4 and copy the formula into the remaining cells in that column. (You may label the last column EXT).

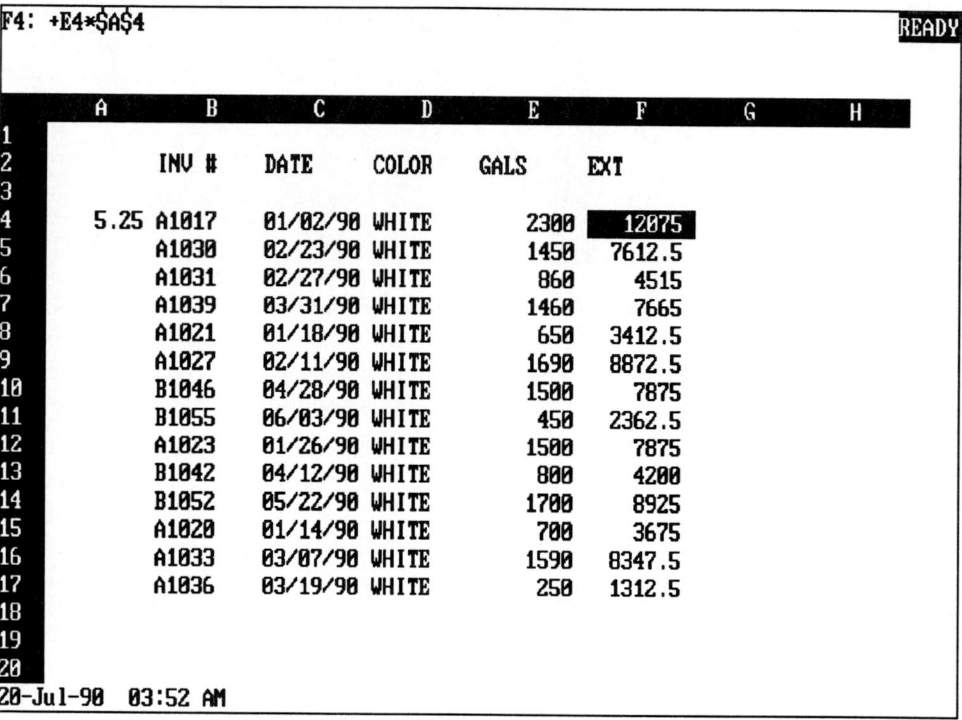

F4: +E4*$A$4 READY

	A	B	C	D	E	F	G	H
1								
2		INV #	DATE	COLOR	GALS	EXT		
3								
4	5.25	A1017	01/02/90	WHITE	2300	12075		
5		A1030	02/23/90	WHITE	1450	7612.5		
6		A1031	02/27/90	WHITE	860	4515		
7		A1039	03/31/90	WHITE	1460	7665		
8		A1021	01/18/90	WHITE	650	3412.5		
9		A1027	02/11/90	WHITE	1690	8872.5		
10		B1046	04/28/90	WHITE	1500	7875		
11		B1055	06/03/90	WHITE	450	2362.5		
12		A1023	01/26/90	WHITE	1500	7875		
13		B1042	04/12/90	WHITE	800	4200		
14		B1052	05/22/90	WHITE	1700	8925		
15		A1020	01/14/90	WHITE	700	3675		
16		A1033	03/07/90	WHITE	1590	8347.5		
17		A1036	03/19/90	WHITE	250	1312.5		
18								
19								
20								

20-Jul-90 03:52 AM

3. Now enter the records for the three primary colors in the same manner. Note that the price/gallon figures are shown in column A.

A37: READY

	A	B	C	D	E	F	G	H
18	6	A1038	03/27/90	YELLOW	175	1050		
19		A1019	01/10/90	YELLOW	220	1320		
20		B1048	05/06/90	YELLOW	155	930		
21		A1028	02/15/90	YELLOW	400	2400		
22		A1032	03/03/90	YELLOW	340	2040		
23		B1050	05/14/90	YELLOW	650	3900		
24	6.4	B1045	04/24/90	RED	165	1056		
25		A1024	01/30/90	RED	230	1472		
26		B1041	04/08/90	RED	200	1280		
27		B1051	05/18/90	RED	275	1760		
28		B1049	05/10/90	RED	150	960		
29		A1029	02/19/90	RED	185	1184		
30	6.75	A1034	03/11/90	BLUE	450	3037.5		
31		A1022	01/22/90	BLUE	120	810		
32		B1053	05/26/90	BLUE	180	1215		
33		A1026	02/07/90	BLUE	210	1417.5		
34		B1047	05/02/90	BLUE	200	1350		
35		B1043	04/16/90	BLUE	210	1417.5		
36		A1037	03/23/90	BLUE	330	2227.5		
37								

20-Jul-90 04:10 AM

4. To finish entering the database records, enter the data for the black paint base as shown here.

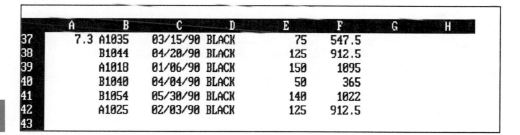

	A	B	C	D	E	F	G	H
37	7.3	A1035	03/15/90	BLACK	75	547.5		
38		B1044	04/20/90	BLACK	125	912.5		
39		A1018	01/06/90	BLACK	150	1095		
40		B1040	04/04/90	BLACK	50	365		
41		B1054	05/30/90	BLACK	140	1022		
42		A1025	02/03/90	BLACK	125	912.5		
43								

CASE EXERCISE 2
Creating Lotus 1-2-3 .PRN Files

Before creating the .PRN file, you will change the spreadsheet column widths to the same lengths as the intended fields of the dBASE database.

1. Use the /**W**orksheet,**C**olumn,**S**et-Width command to make the following changes.

column B	5 characters wide
column C	8 characters wide
column D	6 characters wide
column E	[illegible] characters wide
column F	7 characters wide

Now type the Home key and the screen should appear as

```
A1:                                                              READY

        A      B      C      D     E     F       G       H       I
1
2              INV #DATE     COLOR GALS EXT
3
4         5.25 A101701/02/90WHITE 2300  12075
5              A103002/23/90WHITE 1450 7612.5
6              A103102/27/90WHITE  860   4515
7              A103903/31/90WHITE 1460   7665
8              A102101/18/90WHITE  650 3412.5
9              A102702/11/90WHITE 1690 8872.5
10             B104604/28/90WHITE 1500   7875
11             B105506/03/90WHITE  450 2362.5
12             A102301/26/90WHITE 1500   7875
13             B104204/12/90WHITE  800   4200
14             B105205/22/90WHITE 1700   8925
15             A102001/14/90WHITE  700   3675
16             A103303/07/90WHITE 1590 8347.5
17             A103603/19/90WHITE  250 1312.5
18           6 A103803/27/90YELLOW 175   1050
19             A101901/10/90YELLOW 220   1320
20             B104805/06/90YELLOW 155    930
22-Jul-90  12:11 AM
```

2. Now use the /**F**ile,**S**ave command to save the spreadsheet under the name invrecs (for invoice records).

In the next steps you will use the /**P**rint,**F**ile command to produce an ASCII file of the spreadsheet records.

3. Type ||/**PF**|| to begin the operation, name the file invtemp, and then enter the following specifications

    Print **R**ange: B4..F42 (the record data only)

    Options - **M**argins - **L**eft = 0
    Top = 0
    Bottom = 0

Use the **Q**uit command or the Esc key to return to the /**P**rint,**F**ile menu, use the **A**lign command to set the top of page, and then use the **G**o command to begin printing the output to the file.

To successfully complete printing to a Lotus .PRN file, you **must** exit the /**P**rint,**F**ile menu with the **Q**uit command. You cannot exit the menu using the Esc key.

4. Use the **Q**uit command to end the /**P**rint,**F**ile operation and then exit Lotus 1-2-3 using the /**Q**uit command.

CASE EXERCISE 3
Viewing Lotus 1-2-3 Files from DOS

1. Change the current drive/directory to where your files are kept and use the DOS **TYPE** command to view the file invrecs.WK1.

```
A:\>TYPE invrecs.WK1
 ◘ ♣♦♠      , û *   ♦ ½ ☺ ☺ * ◘ ☺ * ♥ ☺ * ♦ ☺ * ♣ ☺ *  ♥ , / ☺ ☺◘ ☺  ♥ ☺  ♦ ☺
♣ ☺      ☺ ♦ q               ¶              ♦ ♦ H   ♥ ☺  ♥  ♥♥  ♥♦  ♥♣♥  ♀d
                                  G ↓ /Z                        G ↓ \A           ♥
 ; ♥ ;  G ↓ \C              ♦ = ♦ =  G ↓ \X               ♥ = ♥ =  G ↓ \Z
              ↑ ↓                          ↓ ↓                          ◘
A:\>
```

What you see on the screen is an example of what a non-ASCII file may look like when viewed using DOS's **TYPE** command.

2. Now use the DOS **TYPE** command to view the ASCII file invtemp.PRN by typing ‖ **TYPE** invtemp.PRN↵ ‖ .

```
B104805/06/90YELLOW 155    930
A102802/15/90YELLOW 400   2400
A103203/03/90YELLOW 340   2040
B105005/14/90YELLOW 650   3900
B104504/24/90RED    165   1056
A102401/30/90RED    230   1472
B104104/08/90RED    200   1280
B105105/18/90RED    275   1760
B104905/10/90RED    150    960
A102902/19/90RED    185   1184
A103403/11/90BLUE   450 3037.5
A102201/22/90BLUE   120    810
B105305/26/90BLUE   180   1215
A102602/07/90BLUE   210 1417.5
B104705/02/90BLUE   200   1350
B104304/16/90BLUE   210 1417.5
A103703/23/90BLUE   330 2227.5
A103503/15/90BLACK   75  547.5
B104404/20/90BLACK  125  912.5
A101801/06/90BLACK  150   1095
B104004/04/90BLACK   50    365
B105405/30/90BLACK  140   1022
A102502/03/90BLACK  125  912.5

A:\>
```

CASE EXERCISE 4
Editing a .PRN File with WordPerfect

Even though you set the top margin of the .PRN file to 0, Lotus will print three blank lines at the top of the file. Since no Lotus command is capable of preventing the three lines from appearing in the file, and the lines will create three blank records at the top of the dBASE database you will later create, you now may use WordPerfect to remove the lines from the file.

1. Load WordPerfect and then use the **Shift-F10** (Retrieve) command to retrieve the file invtemp.PRN.

```
A101701/02/90WHITE 2300   12075
A103002/23/90WHITE 1450 7612.5
A103102/27/90WHITE  860    4515
A103903/31/90WHITE 1460    7665
A102101/18/90WHITE  650 3412.5
A102702/11/90WHITE 1690 8872.5
B104604/28/90WHITE 1500    7875
B105506/03/90WHITE  450 2362.5
A102301/26/90WHITE 1500    7875
B104204/12/90WHITE  800    4200
B105205/22/90WHITE 1700    8925
A102001/14/90WHITE  700    3675
A103303/07/90WHITE 1590 8347.5
A103603/19/90WHITE  250 1312.5
A103803/27/90YELLOW 175    1050
A101901/10/90YELLOW 220    1320
B104805/06/90YELLOW 155     930
A102802/15/90YELLOW 400    2400
A103203/03/90YELLOW 340    2040
B105005/14/90YELLOW 650    3900
B104504/24/90RED    165    1056
A:\INVTEMP.PRN                                   Doc 1 Pg 1 Ln 1" Pos 1.1"
```

2. Type **Alt-F3** (Reveal Codes) and then use the Backspace and Del keys to remove the [HRt]s, spaces, and [Paper Sz/Typ] code that occur at the top of the file.

```
A101701/02/90WHITE 2300   12075
A103002/23/90WHITE 1450 7612.5
A103102/27/90WHITE  860    4515
A103903/31/90WHITE 1460    7665
A102101/18/90WHITE  650 3412.5
A102702/11/90WHITE 1690 8872.5
B104604/28/90WHITE 1500    7875
B105506/03/90WHITE  450 2362.5
A102301/26/90WHITE 1500    7875
B104204/12/90WHITE  800    4200
B105205/22/90WHITE 1700    8925
A:\INVTEMP.PRN                                   Doc 1 Pg 1 Ln 1" Pos 1"
{ ▲  ▲  ▲  ▲  ▲  ▲  ▲  ▲  ▲  ▲  ▲  ▲  ▲ }  ▲  ▲
A101701/02/90WHITE 2300   12075 [HRt]
A103002/23/90WHITE 1450 7612.5 [HRt]
A103102/27/90WHITE  860    4515 [HRt]
A103903/31/90WHITE 1460    7665 [HRt]
A102101/18/90WHITE  650 3412.5 [HRt]
A102702/11/90WHITE 1690 8872.5 [HRt]
B104604/28/90WHITE 1500    7875 [HRt]
B105506/03/90WHITE  450 2362.5 [HRt]
A102301/26/90WHITE 1500    7875 [HRt]
B104204/12/90WHITE  800    4200 [HRt]

Press Reveal Codes to restore screen
```

3. Next use the **Ctrl-F5** (Text In/Out),DOS **T**ext,**S**ave command to save the file in DOS Text format (ASCII) under the same name. Then exit WordPerfect *without resaving the file.*

CASE EXERCISE 5
Appending ASCII Files into a dBASE Database

You now will create a dBASE record structure for a database that will be suitable for appending the data in the .PRN file.

1. Load dBASE and use the **SET DEFAULT TO** <drive> command to cause dBASE to automatically search your files disk for any files referred to later.
2. Now type ‖ **CREATE** invos↵ ‖ and specify the following record structure for the database.

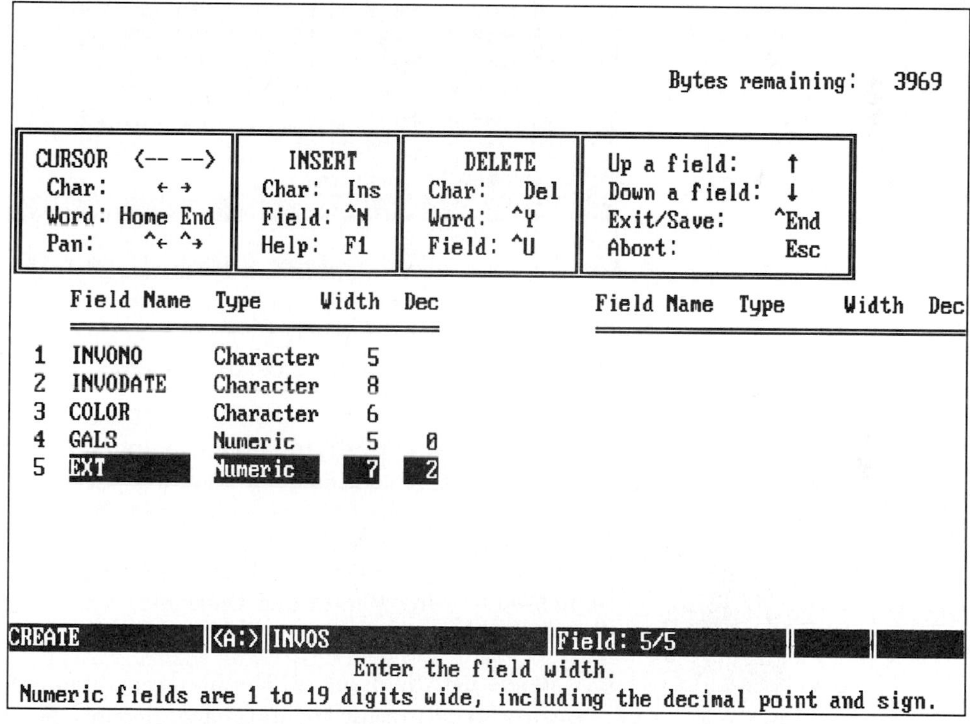

3. When finished, type ‖ **^End**↵**N** ‖ to complete the operation without inputting records now. Then type ‖ **USE** invos↵ ‖ to put the database in use.

Notice that the field lengths, data types, decimals, etc., specified in the record structure exactly match the structure of the data in the .PRN file.

4. Now type ‖ **APPEND FROM** invtemp.prn **TYPE SDF**↵ ‖ . Then type ‖ **DISPLAY ALL**↵ ‖ to see that the data have been appended appropriately.

```
. DISPLAY ALL
Record#  INVONO INVODATE COLOR    GALS     EXT
      1  A1017  01/02/90 WHITE    2300 12075.0
      2  A1030  02/23/90 WHITE    1450 7612.50
      3  A1031  02/27/90 WHITE     860 4515.00
      4  A1039  03/31/90 WHITE    1460 7665.00
      5  A1021  01/18/90 WHITE     650 3412.50
      6  A1027  02/11/90 WHITE    1690 8872.50
      7  B1046  04/28/90 WHITE    1500 7875.00
      8  B1055  06/03/90 WHITE     450 2362.50
      9  A1023  01/26/90 WHITE    1500 7875.00
     10  B1042  04/12/90 WHITE     800 4200.00
     11  B1052  05/22/90 WHITE    1700 8925.00
     12  A1020  01/14/90 WHITE     700 3675.00
     13  A1033  03/07/90 WHITE    1590 8347.50
     14  A1036  03/19/90 WHITE     250 1312.50
     15  A1038  03/27/90 YELLOW    175 1050.00
     16  A1019  01/10/90 YELLOW    220 1320.00
     17  B1048  05/06/90 YELLOW    155  930.00
     18  A1028  02/15/90 YELLOW    400 2400.00
     19  A1032  03/03/90 YELLOW    340 2040.00
Press any key to continue...
Command Line  ||<A:>||INVOS              ||Rec: 39/39     ||     ||

                         Enter a dBASE III PLUS command.
```

The final step in completing the data transfer operation will be to change the invodate field from its current character type to a date-type field.

5. Type ‖ **MODIFY STRUCTURE**↵ ‖, move to the Type area for invodate, and type ‖ D ‖ to make the field a date-type field. Next type ‖ **^**End↵ ‖ to complete the modify operation.

CASE EXERCISE 6 Creating ASCII Files with dBASE

In the following steps you will create two database files designed to hold the requested summary data and then use command (.PRG) files to perform the data reduction operation.

1. Use the dBASE **CREATE** <filename> command to create the following record structure for the database file named "ytdsum" (year-to-date summary.)

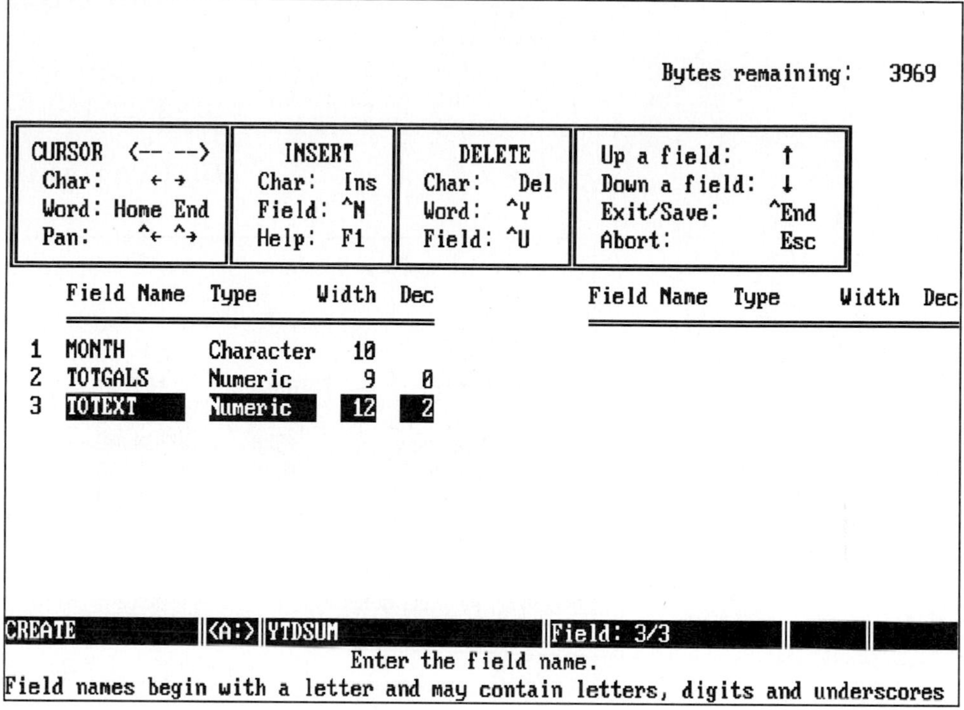

2. When finished type ‖ ^End↵N ‖ to complete the operation without inputting records now.
3. Next use the **MODIFY COMMAND** <filename> command to create the following program named "datasum."

```
Edit: A:datasum.prg

CLOSE ALL
SELECT 1
USE invos
SELECT 2
USE ytdsum
m = 1
DO WHILE m <= 5
  SELECT 2
  APPEND BLANK
  REPLACE ytdsum->month WITH CMONTH(CTOD(STR(m,2,0)+"/01/90"))
  SELECT 1
  SUM gals FOR month(invodate) = m TO total1
  SUM ext  FOR month(invodate) = m TO total2
  SELECT 2
  REPLACE ytdsum->totgals WITH total1
  REPLACE ytdsum->totext WITH total2
  m = m + 1
ENDDO
CLOSE ALL
RETURN
```

4. Use the **DO** <filename> command to execute the datasum program. Then type

	CLEAR↵	
	SELECT 1↵	
	USE ytdsum↵	
	DISPLAY ALL↵	

```
. SELECT 1
. USE ytdsum
. DISPLAY ALL
Record#  MONTH          TOTGALS       TOTEXT
      1  January           5870     31734.50
      2  February          4920     26914.00
      3  March             4670     26227.50
      4  April             3050     17106.00
      5  May               3450     20062.00

.
Command Line    ||<A:>||YTDSUM              ||Rec: EOF/5         ||     ||

                         Enter a dBASE III PLUS command.
```

This small table will appear in the finished report. To create an ASCII file of the screen output, you will next use the **SET ALTERNATE** commands of dBASE.

5. Type the following commands

	SET ALTERNATE TO reptin1↵	
	SET ALTERNATE ON↵	
	DISPLAY ALL↵	
	SET ALTERNATE OFF↵	
	SET ALTERNATE TO↵	

The ASCII file reptin1.TXT containing the screen output of the **DISPLAY ALL** command should now be on your files disk. To continue the exercises, you will next create a database to hold the summary information on the number of gallons sold in the first quarter for each color of paint base.

6. Use the **CREATE** <filename> command to create the following record structure for the database file quartsum.

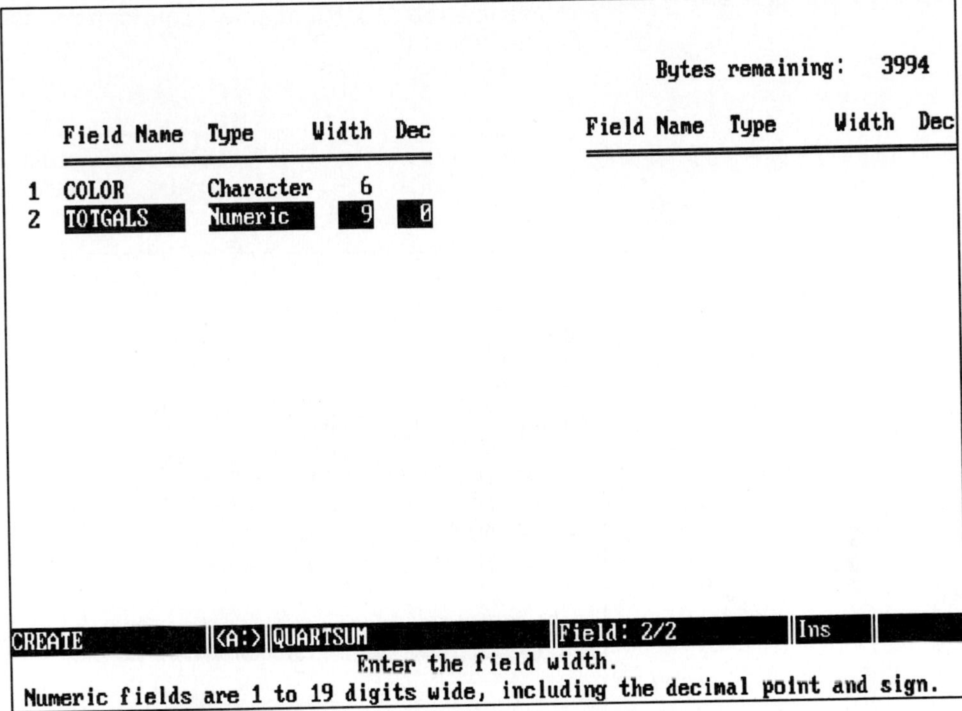

When finished creating the record structure, use the **MODIFY COMMAND** text editing mode to create the following program named "datasum2."

```
Edit: A:datasum2.prg

CLOSE ALL
SELECT 1
USE invos
SELECT 2
USE quartsum
SELECT 1
DO WHILE .NOT. EOF()
  STORE invos->color TO mcolor
  SUM gals FOR month(invodate) <= 3 WHILE invos->color = mcolor TO total1
  SELECT 2
  APPEND BLANK
  REPLACE quartsum->color WITH mcolor
  REPLACE quartsum->totgals WITH total1
  SELECT 1
ENDDO
CLOSE ALL
RETURN
```

7. Next use the **DO** <filename> command to execute the datasum2 program. Then type

	CLEAR↵	
	SELECT 1↵	
	USE quartsum↵	
	DISPLAY ALL↵	

```
. SELECT 1
. USE quartsum
. DISPLAY ALL
Record#  COLOR     TOTGALS
      1  WHITE       12450
      2  YELLOW       1135
      3  RED           415
      4  BLUE         1110
      5  BLACK         350

.
Command Line     ||<C:>||QUARTSUM            ||Rec: EOF/5       ||    ||

                        Enter a dBASE III PLUS command.
```

This data will be used to create a pie chart for the finished report. In order to transfer the data to Lotus for graphing, the **COPY TO** <filename> **DELIMITED WITH** " command will be used. Since the file is destined for a Lotus spreadsheet, and Lotus will only import an ASCII file if it has a .PRN extension, the required extension will be added to the filename when the command is executed. (dBASE would normally attach a .TXT filename extension to the file.)

8. Type || **COPY TO** spreadin.PRN **DELIMITED WITH** "↵ || .

The ASCII file named "spreadin.PRN," containing the field data of the quartsum database file, should now be on your files disk.

9. Now use the dBASE **QUIT** command to exit dBASE III Plus. Then use the DOS **TYPE** command to view the files reptin1.TXT and spreadin.PRN on the screen.

```
A:\>TYPE reptin1.txt

. DISPLAY ALL
Record#  MONTH          TOTGALS       TOTEXT
      1  January           5870     31734.50
      2  February          4920     26914.00
      3  March             4670     26227.50
      4  April             3050     17106.00
      5  May               3450     20062.00

. SET ALTERNATE OFF
A:\>
A:\>TYPE spreadin.PRN
"WHITE",12450
"YELLOW",1135
"RED",415
"BLUE",1110
"BLACK",350

A:\>
```

CASE EXERCISE 7
Importing ASCII Files into Lotus

You now are ready to create the pie chart for the report. To do so, you will import the file spreadin.PRN, created with dBASE, into a Lotus spreadsheet.

1. Load Lotus 1-2-3. Then move the pointer to cell A3 and use the /**F**ile,**I**mport,**N**umbers command to import the file spreadin.PRN into the spreadsheet. Then enter the values shown in cells C3 through C7.

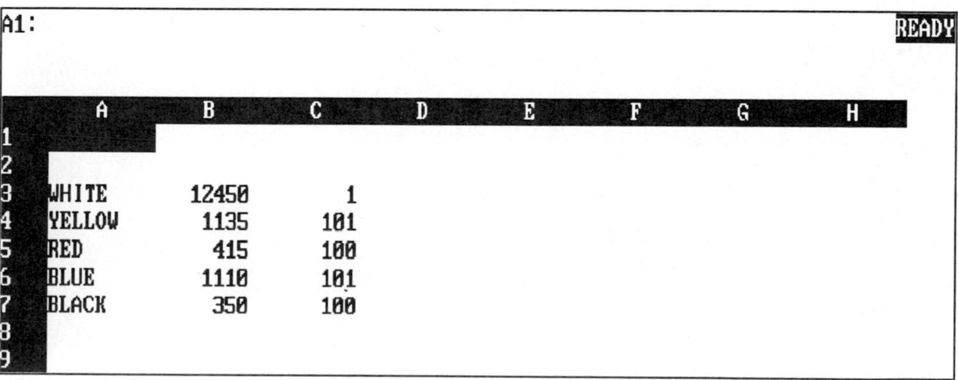
A1: READY

	A	B	C	D	E	F	G	H
1								
2								
3	WHITE	12450	1					
4	YELLOW	1135	101					
5	RED	415	100					
6	BLUE	1110	101					
7	BLACK	350	100					
8								
9								

2. Now use the /**G**raph commands to create a pie chart with the following specifications.

Type = Pie
X data range = A3..A7
A data range = B3..B7
B data range = C3..C7

Then view the graph on the screen.

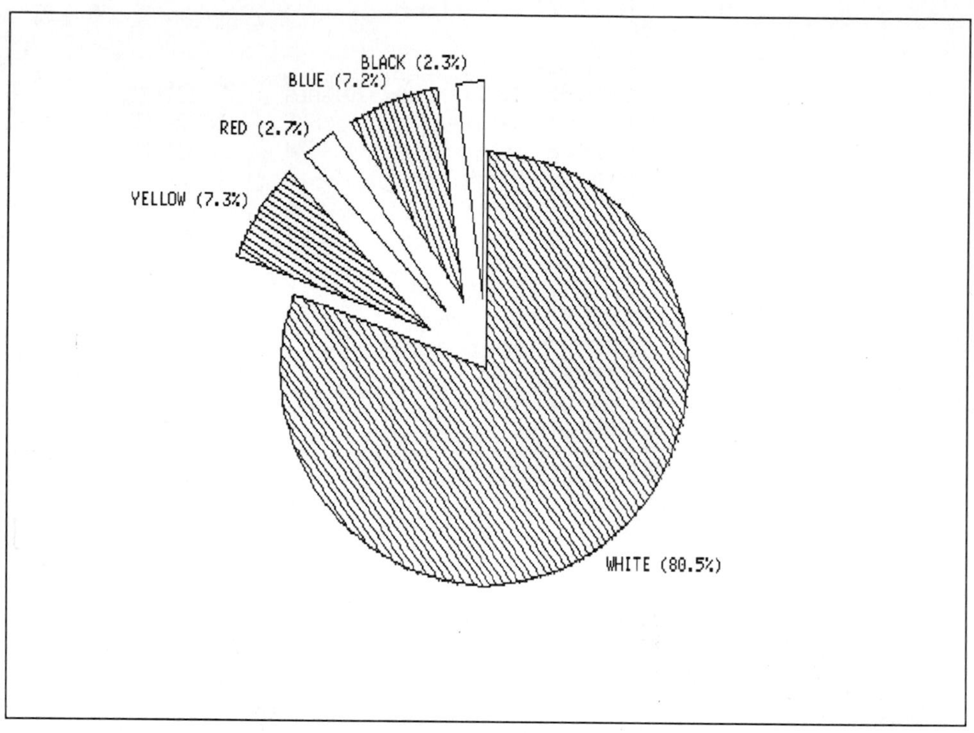

3. Now use the /**G**raph,**S**ave command to save the graph data under the name reptin2 (Lotus will automatically add a .PIC extension to the name). Then use the /**F**ile,**S**ave command to save the spreadsheet data under the name "piedata." Next use the /**Q**uit command to exit Lotus 1-2-3.

CASE EXERCISE 8
Creating the Final Report

You are now ready to create the final report using WordPerfect.

1. Load WordPerfect and then enter the following text. Center the headings and use the **Ctrl-F8** (Font),**S**ize,**L**arge command to make the company's name large font.

```
                    Primary Paint Corporation

            Year-To-Date Sales and Product Mix Report

1990 Dollar Sales

     The first five months of this year have shown a strong
     increase in sales over last year, with the expected seasonal
     down-turn occurring in April:








Typeover                                   Doc 1 Pg 1 Ln 2.83" Pos 1"
```

2. Move the cursor to Ln 3″, Pos 1″ and then use the **Shift-F10** (Retrieve) command to retrieve the file reptin1.txt into the document.

```
                    Primary Paint Corporation

            Year-To-Date Sales and Product Mix Report

1990 Dollar Sales

     The first five months of this year have shown a strong
     increase in sales over last year, with the expected seasonal
     down-turn occurring in April:


. DISPLAY ALL
Record#  MONTH          TOTGALS         TOTEXT
      1  January           5870       31734.50
      2  February          4920       26914.00
      3  March             4670       26227.50
      4  April             3050       17106.00
      5  May               3450       20062.00

. SET ALTERNATE OFF'Z

Typeover                                   Doc 1 Pg 1 Ln 3" Pos 1"
```

3. Next edit the retrieved data (and use the **Ctrl-F3** (Screen),Line Draw commands) so it appears in the document as follows.

```
                    Primary Paint Corporation

            Year-To-Date Sales and Product Mix Report

1990 Dollar Sales

     The first five months of this year have shown a strong
     increase in sales over last year, with the expected seasonal
     down-turn occurring in April:

                              Total        Total
               Month         Gallons      Dollars

               January         5870     $31,734.50
               February        4920     $26,914.00
               March           4670     $26,227.50
               April           3050     $17,106.00
               May             3450     $20,062.00

                                          Doc 1 Pg 1 Ln 1" Pos 1"
```

4. Now move the cursor to Ln 5″, Pos 1″ and type the **Alt-F9** (Graphics) command. Select the **F**igure option and then the **C**reate option. Continue by making the following specifications: **F**ilename is reptin2.PIC; **C**aption is "1st Quarter Sales (Gallons)"; **S**ize is **W**idth (auto height) 4 ″. When finished the Graphics set-up screen should appear as follows.

```
Definition: Figure

     1 - Filename                     REPTIN2.PIC (Graphic)

     2 - Caption                      Figure 1 1st Quarter Sales (Gallons...

     3 - Type                         Paragraph

     4 - Vertical Position            0"

     5 - Horizontal Position          Right

     6 - Size                         4" wide x 2.99" (high)

     7 - Wrap Text Around Box         Yes

     8 - Edit

Selection: 0
```

5. Now type **F7** (Exit) and begin entering the text shown here. Note that WordPerfect will automatically wrap the text around the figure box shown on the screen.

```
Product Percentages          FIG 1

In the first quarter of
the year, white paint
base sustained its normal
80% of sales in gallons.

Yellow and blue paint
bases increased their
product shares slightly
with black and red bases
slipping somewhat from
last quarter's figures.

It is estimated that the
product mix will remain
relatively constant
throughout the remainder
of 1990.  However,
possible shortages of
lead chromate late in the
year may slow production of yellow paint base and create inventory
back-orders for the product at that time.
                                    Doc 1 Pg 1 Ln 0.67" Pos 5.1"
```

6. When finished, use the **Shift-F7** (Print),View Document command to preview the printed document on the screen:

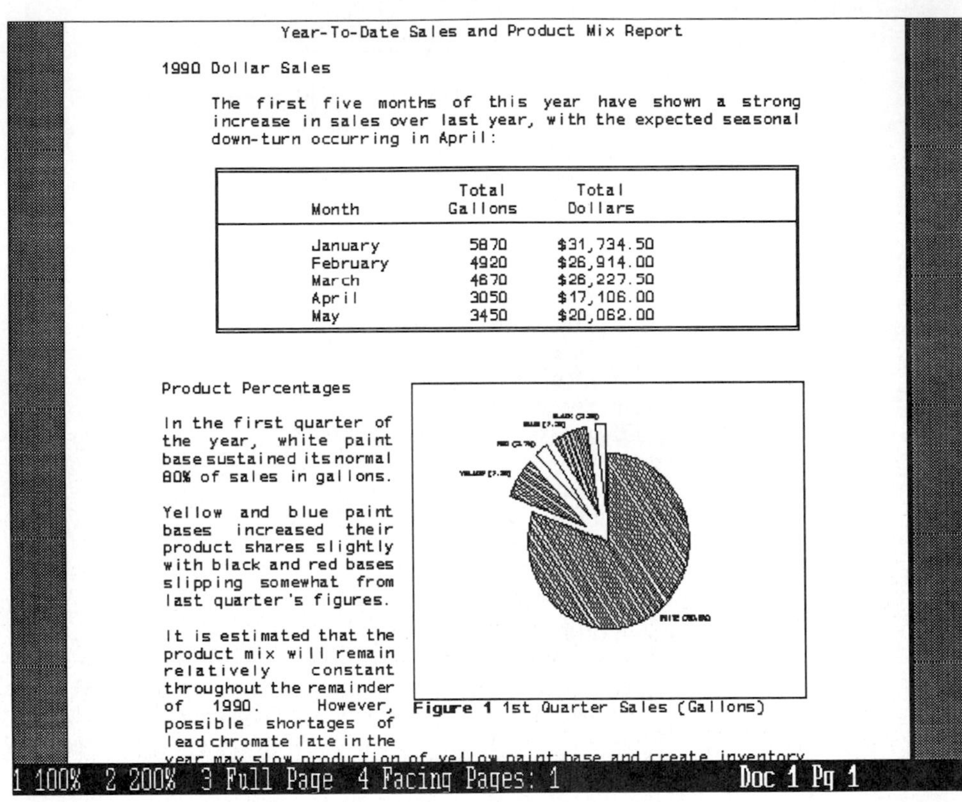

Year-To-Date Sales and Product Mix Report

1990 Dollar Sales

The first five months of this year have shown a strong increase in sales over last year, with the expected seasonal down-turn occurring in April:

Month	Total Gallons	Total Dollars
January	5870	$31,734.50
February	4920	$26,914.00
March	4670	$26,227.50
April	3050	$17,106.00
May	3450	$20,062.00

Product Percentages

In the first quarter of the year, white paint base sustained its normal 80% of sales in gallons.

Yellow and blue paint bases increased their product shares slightly with black and red bases slipping somewhat from last quarter's figures.

It is estimated that the product mix will remain relatively constant throughout the remainder of 1990. However, possible shortages of lead chromate late in the year may slow production of yellow paint base and create inventory

Figure 1 1st Quarter Sales (Gallons)

1 100% 2 200% 3 Full Page 4 Facing Pages: 1 Doc 1 Pg 1

7. Now save the document under the name "fnlrpt", print the document, and then exit WordPerfect.

APPENDICES

APPENDIX A
THE BASICS OF DOS

INTRODUCTION

Before an applications software can be used with the microcomputer, DOS must be loaded (copied) into RAM. DOS performs two basic functions while the microcomputer system is in use. At the DOS operating level, before any other software has been loaded, DOS commands can be used to perform disk and file maintenance operations. At the software operating level, after an applications software has been loaded into RAM, DOS remains in RAM and allows the applications software to perform its input/output operations. Without this DOS interface, most applications software would be unable to access the microcomputer's input/output devices, such as disk drives and printers.

DOS/ROM BIOS—The Operating System

The DOS software includes a set of instructions called the IBM Basic Input/Output (or IBMBIO) which works in conjunction with a set of instructions in ROM called the ROM BIOS. Together, DOS and ROM BIOS constitute the operating system for the microcomputer.

As discussed in the "Fundamentals of Using Microcomputers" section, the operating system is what actually saves your data files onto a disk. In fact, the operating system is designed to handle all input/output device operations for the applications software currently in RAM. The operating system monitors input from the keyboard and then passes the input data to the applications software. It also sends (outputs) data obtained from the applications software to the printer. The operating system also controls the output of characters and graphics to the monitor screen.

Occasionally, an applications software will be written in such a way that it overrides the operating system and performs an input or output operation itself. Lotus 1-2-3, for instance, controls its own output to the monitor screen.

It is not obvious to the user that the operating system is the input/output device controller for the microcomputer system. The following section will explain the role of the operating system and why DOS must be present in RAM before an applications software may be used.

DOS—THE DISK FILE MAINTENANCE SOFTWARE

File maintenance is the ongoing task of keeping data files organized on the disk(s). File maintenance involves operations such as erasing files, copying files, renaming files, and grouping files together. To more fully understand the procedures used in file maintenance, the user needs to know about the microcomputer's disk operating system.

The DOS Disk

The DOS disk and the IBM manual for DOS usually come with the computer when it is purchased. While the packaging and manual suggest that a single software called DOS is on the disk, DOS is, in fact, made up of several different software files.

The software that the microcomputer automatically reads into RAM when the system unit is turned on is composed of three separate software files stored on the disk. Two of the files are "hidden" files—files that will not appear in a directory displayed by the **DIR** command. The two hidden files are named IBMBIO.COM and IBMDOS.COM. The third file, COMMAND.COM, is not a hidden file; it will appear in a **DIR** command directory. In this manual, the three files that are automatically read into RAM are referred to collectively as DOS.

DOS Commands

When the microcomputer is at the DOS operating level, the user may type and enter DOS commands. DOS commands are included in the instruction set of the DOS software. In other words, DOS commands may be entered and the command operations will be performed without the need for additional instructions (software) to be read into RAM. **DIR** is an example of a DOS command.

DOS Programs

In addition to DOS, the disk also contains several small software called DOS utility programs or DOS programs. DOS programs are not automatically present in RAM. The user must type and enter a filename while at the DOS operating level to cause a DOS program to be read into RAM and executed. One such DOS program, FORMAT.COM, is used to format a new disk. To execute the program, the user may type ‖ FORMAT A:↵ ‖ to format a disk in the A: drive. When the DOS program filename is entered, DOS reads the software into RAM memory and the screen appears similar to

```
C>FORMAT A:
Insert new diskette for drive A:
and strike ENTER when ready
```

The microcomputer now is operating at a software operating level. The following model illustrates what is being held in RAM.

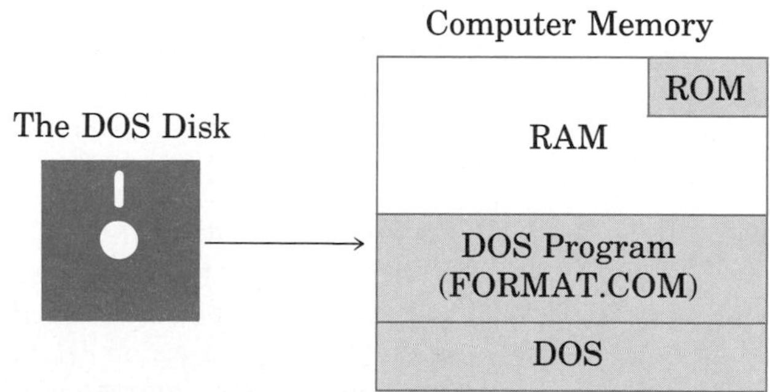

Type the filename of a DOS program: The software is copied into RAM.

DOS programs are generally not used to produce data files. They typically erase themselves from RAM when their particular function or task is complete.

The DOS Default Drive

The microcomputer searches its disk drives for DOS when it is first turned on. After finding DOS and copying it into RAM, the microcomputer's monitor screen will display an A>, B>, or C>. The letter (A, B, or C) displayed in the prompt describes the disk drive device name (A:, B:, or C:) for the drive where DOS was found. The prompt also indicates which disk drive is the current DOS *default drive*. The DOS default drive is the disk drive that DOS will automatically activate to access a disk when it is instructed to read or write data.

For instance, if you type ‖ **DIR**↵ ‖ while an A> appears on the screen, DOS will automatically read the disk in the A: drive and list its directory on the screen. If the A> is on the screen and you enter a software's filename, DOS will automatically search the disk in the A: drive to find the software file you entered.

DOS's default drive stays in effect when the microcomputer system is brought to the software operating level. That is, if the DOS default drive is A: when you use a software's command(s) to save a data file, DOS will automatically write the file onto the disk in the A: drive.

There are two ways to redirect DOS to another disk drive. The first method is to change the current default drive by entering the device name for the desired default drive. At the DOS operating level the default drive may be changed by simply typing the appropriate drive letter, then a colon, and then the Enter key (e.g., **B:**↵). At the software operating level, you must use one of the software's commands to change the DOS default drive.

The other method of redirecting DOS to another disk drive is to override the default drive by including the desired device name in the request for a DOS read/write operation. For instance, with WordPerfect you can answer the "Document to be saved:" prompt by typing ‖ B:REPORT↵ ‖ to save the data file onto the disk in the B: drive. Similarly, at the DOS operating level you can force a listing of the directory of the B: drive by typing ‖ **DIR** B:↵ ‖, or cause DOS to search the C: drive for the WordPerfect software by typing ‖ C:WP↵ ‖.

Since almost all microcomputers have more than one disk drive, the user needs to know how to direct DOS to the appropriate disk drive for its read/write operations.

Formatting a Disk

The first step in disk file maintenance is formatting the disk. All disks must be formatted before software or data files can be stored on them. The DOS program named FORMAT.COM and the microcomputer's ROM BIOS work together to format a disk. *It is important to note that formatting a disk erases all files that may have previously existed on the disk.*

Formatting a disk involves defining a series of concentric rings on the disk (called *tracks*) where the bytes of data will be stored later. The tracks are numbered and divided into sections (called *sectors*). The length of a single track within a sector is able to hold 512 bytes of data (one *block*). The sector groups then are numbered so that a sector section of track may be accessed later by referring to the side of the disk on which it occurs (side 0 or 1), its track number, and its sector group number. Adjacent segments of track called *clusters* are used by DOS in reading and writing data on the disk.

These elements are shown in the following illustration.

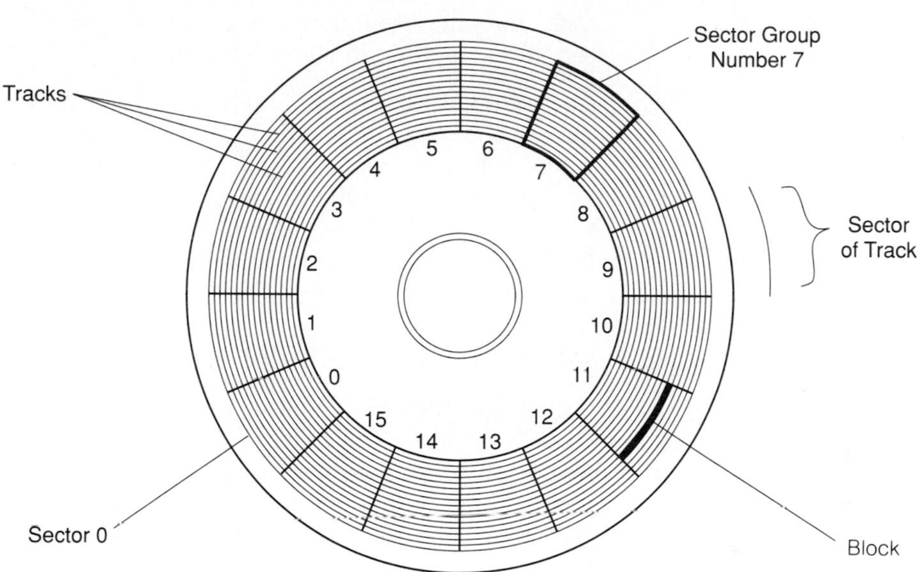

The number of tracks and sectors, as well as the size of the clusters on a disk all depend on the type of disk, the version of DOS, and the hardware being used during the format operation.

After the data storage areas of the disk are physically organized, the format operation checks each sector for errors in the magnetic medium (recording surface). If a sector error is detected, the entire track in which the error occurs is marked "bad" so that DOS will not try to save data on that track.

The format operation also reserves certain sectors of track on the disk for recording specific DOS information about the disk. The reserved sectors are collectively called the *DOS reserved area.* The first sector of data (track 0, sector 0) in the DOS reserved area is called the *boot record.* The boot record contains information about the physical format of the disk (number of tracks, number of sectors per track, number of sectors per cluster, etc.), and the version of DOS that was used to format the disk. The boot record is the first data the microcomputer copies into RAM when it reads a disk. The next information in the DOS reserved area includes the *file allocation tables* (FAT). There are usually two copies of the FAT maintained on a disk. The FAT stores the addresses (locations) of data clusters on the disk that belong to a given file. It is, in effect, a map of data locations keyed to the filenames of the files on a disk. The final major set of information contained in the DOS reserved area is the *root directory.* Every formatted disk has one root directory, and a disk may have one or more *subdirectories* of the root directory. (The root directory and subdirectories will be discussed in greater depth later.) A directory contains the list of filenames, byte sizes, and date/time stamps that are read and displayed by DOS's **DIR** command.

Creating a "Bootable" Disk

The term *bootable disk* refers to a disk that has the three files of DOS (IBMBIO.COM, IBMDOS.COM, and COMMAND.COM) stored on it. Such a disk can be used to bring the microcomputer to the DOS operating level when the system unit is turned on. A bootable disk must have the two hidden files of DOS (IBMBIO.COM and IBMDOS.COM) stored on the sectors that immediately follow the DOS reserved area. Therefore, the files must be saved on the disk in a special manner.

To make a disk bootable, the user should copy the files of DOS onto the disk during the format operation. To do so, the user follows the FORMAT program's filename and disk drive specification with a /S. /S is a *DOS switch*—an addition to a DOS command or DOS program filename that alters the way in which the command or program functions. For example, entering FORMAT A:/S will format the disk in the A: drive and then copy all three DOS files to their appropriate locations on the newly formatted disk.

Compatibility among Versions of DOS

Over time, IBM has released different versions of DOS to keep pace with the advancements in hardware technology used by the microcomputer system. The various versions of any software are numbered so that the latest version has the highest number. For instance, DOS 2.1 was released after DOS 2.0. The user needs to pay attention to which version of DOS is in use because different versions of DOS format disks differently. There are times when the version of DOS currently in RAM may not be able to read or write to a disk because the disk was previously formatted with another version of DOS.

As a general rule, a later version of DOS is able to read or write to a disk formatted with an earlier version of DOS. However, the reverse is not true. That is, an earlier version of DOS in RAM will not be able to read or write to a disk formatted with a later version of DOS.

Dividing a Disk into Subdirectories

With DOS versions 2.0 or later, the user is given the option to organize a disk into separate DOS subdirectories. A DOS subdirectory separates files on a disk into groups of files. The process of creating subdirectories is both mechanical and judgmental—while specific DOS commands are used to create and maintain subdirectories, the user must decide which subdirectories to create and which files to allocate to the subdirectories.

As mentioned earlier, each disk is assigned a directory (called the root directory) at the time it is formatted. Unless the user creates subdirectories, the disk's root directory will hold all files currently stored on the disk.

In the day-to-day use of the microcomputer, users probably will keep copies of files on floppy disks. Each disk may hold files pertaining to different areas or subjects. For instance, one disk might have data files relating to course work prepared for a business management class. The jacket of the disk might be labeled "MGMT213" to help identify the disk. Another disk might have data files relating to a literature class, and it could be labeled "ENG199." When disk files are maintained in this manner, *physical* separation is being used to organize the files.

Another method of grouping files uses DOS *logical* separation of files. With logical separation, DOS treats groups of files on a single disk as if they were stored on separate disks. A logical separation of files on a disk is possible by creating disk subdirectories. While subdirectories may (and often should) be used on a floppy disk, they become particularly important when dealing with hard disks, which have much greater storage capacities.

Preparing a Hard Disk for Subdirectories

When a microcomputer has a hard disk, it is almost always used as the system's bootable disk. Therefore, the first step in preparing a hard disk is to format the hard disk with FORMAT.COM's /S switch. To do so the user places the DOS disk purchased with the computer into the first drive (A:) and turns on the computer and its monitor. After a few moments the A> DOS prompt appears on the screen. The user next types ‖ FORMAT C:/S ‖ to read the FORMAT.COM program into RAM and begin its execution. Since the loss of all files on a hard disk could be disastrous, the program will pause and present a warning about formatting a "non-removable disk." When finished with the format operation, the screen appears similar to

```
A>FORMAT C:/S
WARNING, ALL DATA ON NON-REMOVABLE DISK
DRIVE C: WILL BE LOST!
Proceed with Format (Y/N)?y

Format complete
System transferred

  21170176 bytes total disk space
     79872 bytes used by system
    122880 bytes in bad sectors
  20967424 bytes available on disk

A>
```

These messages indicate that the disk has about 21M of disk space and that 79,872 bytes of it are being used by the three DOS files (the "system"). The format operation identified 122,880 bytes worth of bad sectors and marked them so that data cannot be saved onto the bad tracks. The remaining space (20,967,424 bytes) is available to hold software and data files.

To continue with the example, the user next types ‖ **C:↵** ‖ to change the default disk drive and then types ‖ **DIR↵** ‖ to cause the DOS **DIR** command to read the directory of the C: drive and list it on the screen.

```
C>DIR

 Volume in drive C has no label
 Directory of   C:\

COMMAND  COM     25307    3-17-87   12:00p
        1 File(s)  20967424 bytes free
```

The Disk Root Directory

The directory appearing on the screen was read from the C: disk's *root directory*—the only physical directory on a disk. The file COMMAND.COM appears in the root directory, and, although not listed by the **DIR** command, the files IBMBIO.COM and IBMDOS.COM (the two hidden files of DOS) are also present in the disk's root directory. In order for a disk to be bootable, DOS must be held in the root directory.

When a disk has subdirectories, the user should keep as few files as possible in the root directory of the disk. If the disk is to be bootable, only DOS and a few related files should appear in the root directory.

The **MD** (Make Directory) Command

The DOS command **MD** (Make Directory) is used to create a logical directory, also called a subdirectory. The next step in preparing a hard disk for use is to create a subdirectory into which the files of an applications software, in this example WordPerfect, will be copied.

The user must give a subdirectory a name at the time it is created. A conservative rule to follow when naming subdirectories is the following.

> A subdirectory name is one to eight characters long and is composed of letters and numbers only (no spaces, commas, colons, etc.).

In this example, the name used for the subdirectory will be WORDS.

The user continues by typing ‖ **MD** WORDS↵ ‖ . Although the screen gives little indication that anything has occurred, the user has, in fact, created a subdirectory named WORDS. Assume that the files of the WordPerfect software are now copied from the manufacturer's floppy disks into the WORDS subdirectory. (The process of copying files will be discussed later.)

The **CD** (Change Directory) Command

The DOS **CD** (Change Directory) command causes DOS to "change the logical disk." Here, for example, if the user were to type the DOS command ‖ **CD** WORDS↵ ‖ and then type ‖ **DIR**↵ ‖ the screen would appear similar to the following.

```
C>CD WORDS

C>DIR

 Volume in drive C has no label
 Directory of  C:\WORDS

.            <DIR>       1-17-89  12:39p
..           <DIR>       1-17-89  12:39p
WP       DRS     73688   9-16-88   3:57p
WP       EXE    251904   9-23-88   5:37p
WP       FIL    303478   9-23-88   5:37p
WPHELP   FIL     48459   9-23-88   5:37p
WPINFO   EXE      8192   9-16-88   3:50p
WPRINT1  ALL    321351   9-16-88  12:47p
WP{WP}   SET      2355   1-06-89  11:54a
WP{WP}US LEX    292109   9-16-88   3:55p
WP{WP}US SUP        87  10-22-88   6:28a
WP{WP}US THS    362269   9-16-88   4:02p
       12 File(s)  10405888 bytes free

C>
```

Notice that there are ten filenames listed here. In fact, there are several additional files not shown here that, in total, comprise the WordPerfect software. For the example's sake, however, assume that ten files constitute the entire software.

The user next types ‖ **CD**↵ ‖ and then ‖ **DIR**↵ ‖ . The following directory is read from the disk and displayed on the screen.

```
C>DIR

 Volume in drive C has no label
 Directory of  C:\

COMMAND  COM     25307   3-17-87  12:00p
WORDS         <DIR>      2-22-89   7:30a
        2 File(s)  19303532 bytes free
```

The **CD** command is used to make the root directory the current directory. Notice that the WORDS subdirectory now appears listed in the root directory. The disk's directory organization can be graphically described as follows.

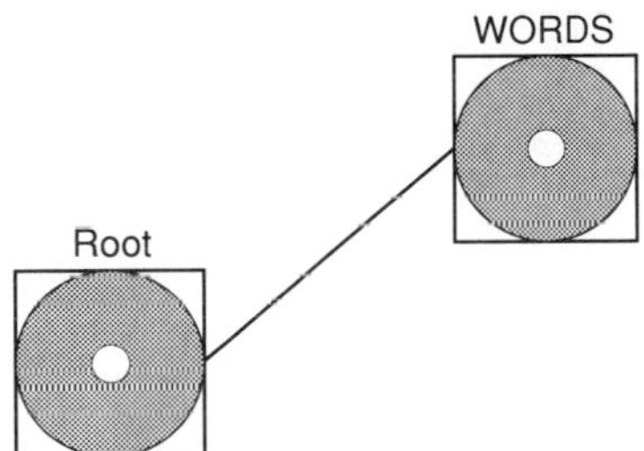

The DOS Default Directory

Like the default drive, DOS maintains a default directory (or current directory). The default directory is the directory that DOS will automatically search when it is instructed to read or write data. For instance, when the DOS command ‖ **DIR**↵ ‖ is typed while the root directory is the current directory, DOS will automatically read the directory of the root directory and display it on the screen.

There are two ways to direct DOS to another directory on the disk. The first method is to change the current default directory. At the DOS operating level, the default directory may be changed by using the **CD** (Change Directory) command. The other method of directing DOS to another directory is to override the default directory by including the directory name in the request for a DOS read/write operation. For instance, in the example, at the DOS operating level with the root directory as the current directory, the user can list the contents of the WORDS directory by typing ‖ **DIR** WORDS↵ ‖ . Like the default drive, DOS's default directory stays in effect when the microcomputer system is brought to the software operating level.

Creating Tree Structured Subdirectories

Assume that, in addition to word processing software, the user in the example intends to use a spreadsheet software and the DOS programs that come on the manufacturer's DOS disk. The user intends, however, to keep the groups of software files separated on the hard disk.

The user continues by typing ‖ **CD**\↵ ‖ to ensure that the root directory is the current directory and then types ‖ **MD** CALC↵ ‖ and ‖ **MD** DOS↵ ‖. The user next copies the files from the manufacturers' disks into the appropriate subdirectories. The organization of directories on the hard disk can now be graphically represented as follows.

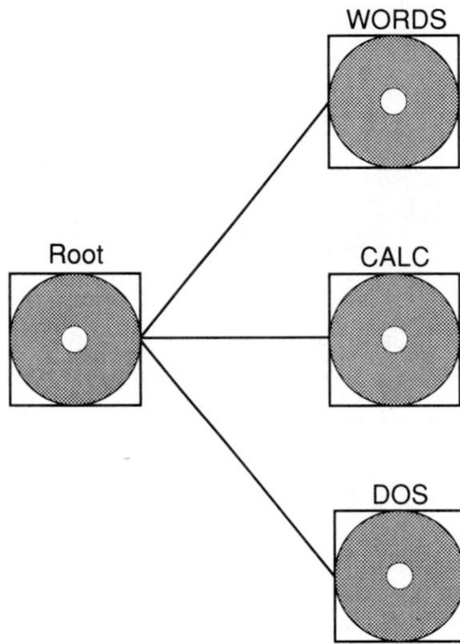

The hard disk now contains DOS in the root directory, two applications software, each in their own directories, and the DOS programs in yet another directory.

The user next is going to create three subdirectories to hold groups of data files. One subdirectory will be used for word processed data files related to a business management class, another subdirectory will hold spreadsheet data files for the same business class, and the final subdirectory will hold word processed data files for a literature class.

Using the DOS **PROMPT** Command

Before the subdirectories are created, the user types ‖ **PROMPT** pg↵ ‖. The user then types ‖ **CD** WORDS↵ ‖ and the screen appears as follows.

```
C:\>CD WORDS

C:\WORDS>
```

The **PROMPT** command may be used to change the display of the DOS prompt. Here the command was used to cause the prompt to display the directory name of the current directory. This prompt display is most useful when subdirectories exist on a disk.

The user next types ‖ **MD** MGMT213↵ ‖ and then ‖ **MD** ENG199↵ ‖ to create the two subdirectories that will be used to hold the word processed data files. The user next types ‖ **CD**\↵ ‖ and then ‖ **CD** CALC↵ ‖ to make the spreadsheet software directory the current directory. The user then types ‖ **MD** MGMT213↵ ‖ to create the subdirectory in which the spreadsheet data files will be held.

The directory organization of the disk can now be represented as follows.

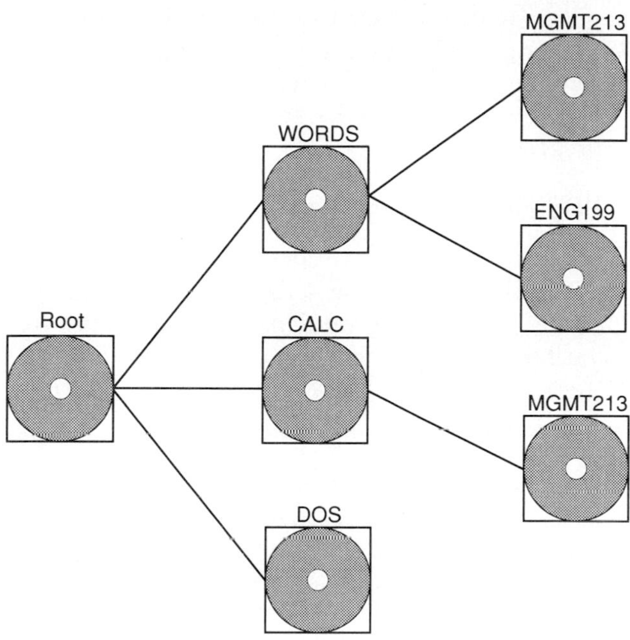

The graphic representation illustrates the concept of *hierarchical* directories—a situation where directories "belong" to each other. The relationship among directories is known as a "parent\child" relationship. Here, the parent directory WORDS has two child directories, MGMT213 and ENG199, and is itself a child directory of the root directory.

Note that there are two directories with the same name, MGMT213. This is possible only because the two directories do not have the same parent directory.

DOS Paths

A DOS path is a list of directory names describing the directories through which DOS must pass to reach a specific directory. The list of directories begins at the current directory. When there are two or more directories included in a DOS path, the directory names are separated by backslashes. For example, if the current directory is the root directory and the user wants to use the **DIR** command to list the directory of the ENG199 subdirectory, he/she types ‖ **DIR**\WORDS\ENG199↵ ‖. However, if the current directory is WORDS, he/she types ‖ **DIR** ENG199↵ ‖. Finally, if the current directory is ENG199, he/she types simply ‖ **DIR**↵ ‖. More precisely stated, the default path for a DOS read/write operation is that path which leads to the current directory. If the path the user needs extends beyond the current directory, he/she must enter the remaining directory names in their parent\child order.

It is important to note that changing the default drive does not change the "logical disk" (directory) of the previous default drive. That is, if the current directory of the C: drive is \WORDS\MGMT213 and the user changes the default drive to A: by typing ‖ **A:**↵ ‖ , the current directory of the C: drive remains the same. If the user then wanted to list the directory for the C:\WORDS\MGMT213 subdirectory, he/she would type ‖ **DIR** C:↵ ‖ .

The discussion so far has focused on how to direct DOS to the appropriate place for it to perform its read/write operation. This knowledge is essential to using DOS at both the DOS and software operating levels. When a DOS command or program is used to read, write, or otherwise affect a file on the disk, the file's filename and extension may be included in the command or program entry.

DOS Filenames and Extensions

The software and data files in a directory are stored there under a name. When the user creates a data file, he/she names the file. Rules about filenames vary among versions of DOS and the software being used. A conservative rule to follow when naming files is the following.

> A filename is one to eight characters long and is composed of letters and numbers only (no spaces, commas, colons, etc.).

A filename *extension* is composed of three characters that follow the filename. A filename's extension is often reserved for the applications software's use. Most applications software use the extension to identify the file type. For instance, when a spreadsheet created with Lotus 1-2-3 is saved, Lotus will add a WK1 extension to the filename the user gives the spreadsheet. WordPerfect is one of the few software that does not normally add extensions to filenames.

Each filename/extension combination in a directory must be unique among the filename/extensions in the directory.

When filenames and extensions are used in a DOS command or program entry, they are separated from each other by a period (.). The default filenames and extensions will vary among different DOS commands or program entries. For instance, the default scope of the **DIR** command is all files in the current or specified directory. Other DOS commands require that the filename and extension be included in the command (they have no default status).

Wild Card Characters

The user may use wild card characters in place of parts or all of the filename and/or extension included in a DOS command or program entry. Two wild card characters are the question mark (?) and the asterisk (*).

When used in a filename, a question mark has the effect of saying to DOS "accept any character here." For example, the command

DIR ?DRAFT.WK1↵

will cause DOS to list the directory for all files beginning with any single letter followed by the five letters "DRAFT" and having a WK1 extension. Examples of such files would include ADRAFT.WK1, BDRAFT.WK1, CDRAFT.WK1, and so on.

When used in a filename, the asterisk has the effect of saying to DOS "accept any remaining characters from this point on." For example, the command

DIR A*.WK1

will cause DOS to list the directory for all files beginning with the letter *A* followed by any letters and having a WK1 extension. Examples of such files would include ADRAFT1.WK1, ACCOUNTS.WK1, and ADS.WK1.

Some common uses of wild card characters and their effects include the following.

.	All files
filename.*	Same filename, any extension
*.ext	Any filename, same extension

DOS Command/Program Syntax

A DOS command or program filename (a word often in verb form) is typed with other elements (drive, path, switch, etc.) that are called *command parameters*. The way the parameters of a DOS command or program entry are put together is referred to as the command's *syntax*. Some parameters of a command or program entry may be optional; however, all parameters included must be typed according to the rules of DOS syntax. DOS identifies optional parameters by enclosing them in brackets [ ] and shows user-defined parameter entries in *italics*. For instance, the standard convention for the DOS **DIR** command is written as follows.

DIR [*d*:][*path*][*filename*[.*ext*]][/P][/W]

All parameters of the **DIR** command (other than the command name itself) are optional. The optional parameters often have default values which are used if the parameter is omitted. For instance, when using DOS commands or programs, the default [*d:*] is always the current drive and the default [*path*] is always the path that leads to the current directory.

The full command convention shown above has the [.*ext*] parameter within the brackets of [*filename*]. This means that a file extension may only be specified if a filename also is specified.

SUMMARY

The DOS software takes time and practice to learn. To help you gain experience using DOS, the following section presents a set of exercises that introduces many DOS commands and programs commonly used to perform file and disk maintenance. The exercises are followed by a brief summary of DOS commands and programs. You may want to review the summary before starting the exercises.

EXERCISES

REQUIRED PREPARATION

The exercises in this section will give you experience using the commands and features of DOS. Before you begin the "hands-on" learning experience, however, you will need to complete a few initial steps and gain some preliminary information to be adequately prepared. Your instructor or laboratory staff will be able to provide you with the following necessary information.

Initial Steps

1. Obtain a floppy disk appropriate for the microcomputer you will be using to complete this set of exercises. You need to know which kind of disk to purchase.

   Size: ____________________

   Sides: ____________________

   Density: ____________________

2. Format your disk to the specifications of the DOS and microcomputer hardware you will be using to complete this set of exercises. **Caution: Formatting a disk erases all files that may exist on the disk.**

   Steps to Format a Disk: ________________________________

   ____

   ____

   ____

   ____

   ____

   ____

3. You will need to copy 40 user files that come with the instructor's manual text onto the newly formatted floppy disk. Your instructor will provide you with the files and the steps required to complete the copy operation.

   Steps to Copy Files onto the Disk: ____________________________

   ____

   ____

   ____

   ____

   ____

4. To read a DOS program into RAM, you will need to know the disk drive and directory that specify where the DOS program(s) are kept.

   Drive: ____________________

   Directory: ____________________

   In these exercises, the location of the DOS programs is referred to as the *DOS directory*. When you see this expression used in an instruction, type and enter the drive\directory you have entered above. For instance, if the DOS programs are kept on the C: drive in the DOS subdirectory and you see the instruction "type *DOS directory*\CHKDSK↵," you will type ‖ C:\DOS\CHKDSK↵ ‖ .

5. Each time you use a DOS command or program to access the floppy disk, you will want to make sure that DOS is directed to the appropriate disk drive.

   Drive: ____________________

   In these exercises, the location of your floppy disk is referred to as the *files drive:*. When you see this expression used in an instruction, type and enter the drive you have entered above. For instance, if your floppy disk is to be kept in the A: drive, and you see the instruction "type DIR *files drive:*↵," you will type ‖ DIR A:↵ ‖ .

Additional Notes on the Exercises

1. DOS commands and filenames may be typed using any combination of upper- or lower-case letters. Upper-case letters are used in the examples here. DOS commands appear in bold type.
2. The term *directory* is used for both the root directory and subdirectories. When a distinction is necessary, the specific terms *root directory* and *subdirectory* are used.
3. When the **DIR** command is used during the exercises, the directory listed on your screen may show byte sizes for the files that are different from those shown in the text. This may be due to differences in floppy disks and/or in versions of DOS being used. The differences will not affect the outcome of the exercises.

REQUIRED MATERIALS

1. An IBM DOS floppy disk (or hard-disk directory containing the DOS software).
2. A formatted floppy disk with the user files on it (your files disk).
3. This manual.
4. Other ____

TUTORIAL CONVENTIONS

During the exercises you will perform many file maintenance operations using DOS commands and programs. The following are the conventions the exercise's instructions will use.

↵	The bent arrow means to type the Enter key located on the right side of the keyboard.
Key-Key	Key combinations using a hyphen indicate that you should press and hold the first key and then type the next key shown.
Key,Key	Key combinations using a comma indicate that you should type the first key and then type the second key.
‖ ‖	Do not type the double lines; type only what is inside them.

HOW TO GET OUT OF TROUBLE

If you want to:	*Then:*
■ Backspace and erase characters to the left of the cursor...	■ Type the Backspace key located on the right top side of the keyboard.
■ Abort a DOS command or program entry...	■ Type the Esc key located on the top left side of the keyboard.

GETTING STARTED

1. Load DOS from a floppy disk or hard disk, or return to the DOS operating level from the current software operating level.
2. Put your files floppy disk into the proper disk drive (drive name ________:).
3. When you see DOS's *drive:*> prompt on the screen, change the current disk drive to where your files disk is by typing ‖ *files drive:*↵ ‖ .

INTRODUCTION TO DOS COMMANDS

DOS is considered a command driven software—one in which user instructions are entered in the form of typed commands. When the microcomputer is at the DOS operating level, a DOS prompt is displayed on the screen to indicate that DOS is waiting for the user to enter a command. After the user types and enters a command, DOS performs the requested command task. When the task is complete, DOS again displays its prompt to indicate that the user can type and enter another command.

The default form of the DOS prompt is an upper-case letter that indicates the current default drive, followed by the > character (e.g., A>, B>, C>, and so forth). A similar prompt should now appear on the screen, indicating that DOS is waiting for a command to be entered. You will begin the exercise by executing a few commonly used DOS commands.

Using DOS Commands

To ensure that your screen matches the examples shown here, you will use the **PROMPT** command to set the DOS prompt to its default form. (If the prompt is already set to its default form, no action will be apparent in this step.)

1. Type ‖ **PROMPT**↵ ‖ to set the DOS prompt to its default form.

The **DIR** command is used to view a list of files in the current directory of the disk in the default drive.

2. Type ‖ **DIR**↵ ‖ to list the directory of files.

```
BLSHEET1 BAK      2031  10-22-89   3:36p
CONBLNC  BAK      2827  10-30-89   3:37p
CONSTMT  BAK      2990  11-06-89   3:38p
DISCOP   BAK      2324  11-12-89   3:33p
ENTRYHLP BAK      2414  11-06-89   3:39p
FCTRANS  BAK      1348  11-21-89   3:40p
INVTS    BAK      1154  11-29-89   3:40p
MEMBDAT1 BAK     13500  11-30-89   3:42p
OPNWSNOV BAK      1002  12-15-89   3:45p
PHONEORD BAK       884  12-02-89   3:43p
RNTEQUIP BAK      1095  12-07-89   3:44p
RPTINTRO BAK      2953  12-17-89   3:46p
RPTSOFTW BAK      7054  12-20-89   3:47p
SILVINTR BAK      1553  12-21-89   3:48p
STCCURR  BAK      3082   1-03-90   3:50p
WORKCAP  BAK      1366   1-03-90   3:50p
WRSIGNAT PCX     19948  11-14-89   3:47p
BOOKVAL  PIC       429  11-14-89   3:42p
CAPEXP   PIC      5948  11-14-89   3:42p
CURRENT  PIC       462  11-14-89   3:42p
DEBTCAP  PIC       462  11-14-89   3:43p
ROA      PIC       457  11-14-89   3:43p
       40 File(s)   1302528 bytes free

A>
```

You may notice that when the directory listing reaches the bottom of the screen, the screen contents begins to scroll up and off the top of the screen. The DOS prompt should now appear below the end of the directory listing at the bottom of the screen. The **CLS** command may be used to clear the screen of all previously issued commands and screen output.

3. Type ‖ **CLS**↵ ‖ to clear the screen.

After the screen is cleared, the DOS prompt is again displayed at the top of the screen. The prompt is always displayed when DOS is waiting for you to type the next command.

The **VER** command is used to display the version of DOS currently in RAM. Because different versions of DOS provide somewhat different operating features and commands, it often is useful to determine which version of DOS is currently being used.

4. Type ‖ **VER**↵ ‖ to display the version of DOS being used.

The screen should now display a message similar to the following.

```
A>VER

IBM Personal Computer DOS Version  3.30

A>
```

So far, assuming you have typed all commands correctly, DOS has performed the task defined by each command. The process of entering DOS commands is quite precise—if the command is not typed in its exact form, it will generate an error message.

5. Now type ‖ **VERSION**↵ ‖ , an unrecognizable command to DOS.

The screen should now display the following.

```
A>VER

IBM Personal Computer DOS Version  3.30

A>VERSION
Bad command or file name

A>
```

The message "Bad command or file name" indicates that the entry is neither a properly typed DOS command, nor a filename for a software on the disk.

User commands such as **PROMPT, VER, DIR,** and **CLS** are features included in the DOS software. When a user entry is not in the form of a DOS command, DOS will search the disk for a software file with a filename that matches the entry. If the software file is found, DOS copies it into RAM and the user is left at a software operating level. Software files are often referred to as "executable" files and have the filename extensions of "COM," "EXE," or "BAT."

The executable files that come with DOS are referred to as DOS programs. One such file, CHKDSK.COM, is a DOS program used to check disk space utilization and system memory availability. The syntax for using the CHKDSK program is

[*d:*][*path*]CHKDSK [*d:*][*path*][*filename*[.*ext*]][/F][/V]

Notice that the syntax for a DOS program usually includes two directory specifications. The first [*d:*][*path*] is used to specify the location of the CHKDSK program. The second [*d:*][*path*] is used to specify the disk location upon which the program is to perform its action.

6. Type ‖ **CLS**↵ ‖ to clear the screen. Then type ‖ *DOS directory*\ CHKDSK↵ ‖ . The screen should now appear similar to the following.

```
A>C:\DOS\CHKDSK

  1457664 bytes total disk space
   155136 bytes in 40 user files
  1302528 bytes available on disk

   654336 bytes total memory
   457616 bytes free

A>
```

In this example, the first [*d:*][*path*] was used to direct DOS to the proper location of the CHKDSK program so that it could successfully read the program into RAM. Since the second [*d:*][*path*] was not entered, the CHKDSK program performed its action on the disk in the default drive.

7. Now clear the screen again by typing ‖ **CLS**↵ ‖ .

In the remainder of the exercises, feel free to execute the **CLS** command whenever you wish to clear the screen. Most of the example screens that follow will show only the screen output resulting from the most recently executed command.

The **DIR** Command

The **DIR** command is used to list the files found in a given directory on the disk in a given drive. The full format for the command is

DIR [*d:*][*path*][*filename*[*.ext*]][/P][/W]

Notice that all parameters for the **DIR** command are optional. If the drive and path are not specified, files in the current directory of the disk in the default drive are listed. If the filename and extension are not specified, all files will be included. The optional parameters [/P] and [/W] are used to modify the way in which the directory is displayed.

When the **DIR** command is executed, the following items are displayed for each file in the directory: the filename; the file extension (if any); a number indicating the size of the file in bytes; and a date and time indicating when the file was created or last modified. Following the listing is the total number of files in the directory and the number of bytes still available on the disk.

In the following steps you will practice using the **DIR** command with various specified parameters.

Using a File Specification with the **DIR** Command

If you want a directory listing to include only specific files, you can follow the **DIR** command with a space and then a specification of the files you want included. The specification may be entered to list files containing certain character patterns in the filename or file extension. The following steps will use filename specifications with the **DIR** command.

8. Type ‖ **DIR** RPTINTRO.BAK↵ ‖ to list a single file.

```
A>DIR RPTINTRO.BAK

 Volume in drive A has no label
 Directory of  A:\

RPTINTRO BAK     2953  12-17-89   3:46p
        1 File(s)   1302528 bytes free

A>
```

9. Type ‖ **DIR** RPTINTRO↵ ‖ . Two files with the same filename but with different file extensions should be listed (one has no file extension).

```
A>DIR RPTINTRO

 Volume in drive A has no label
 Directory of  A:\

RPTINTRO         2953  12-17-89   3:46p
RPTINTRO BAK     2953  12-17-89   3:46p
        2 File(s)   1302528 bytes free

A>
```

10. Now type ‖ **DIR** RPT↵ ‖ . The message "File not found" should be displayed, indicating that no file with this name is found in the current directory.

```
A>DIR RPT

 Volume in drive A has no label
 Directory of  A:\

File not found

A>
```

Using Wild Card Characters in a File Specification

The file specification may also include the characters * and ?, which are referred to as wild card characters. Wild card characters may be used in the specification of a filename or file extension, or in both.

The * is used to accept any characters in the remainder of a filename or extension. For example, the specification "TAX*.WK1" refers to all files with a name beginning "TAX" and with a file extension of "WK1." Therefore, the command **DIR** TAX*.WK1 would include files such as TAX1990.WK1 and TAXTABLE.WK1, but not files such as INC1990.WK1 (does not begin "TAX") or TAX1990.TXT (extension is not "WK1").

The ? is used to accept any character in a given position of a filename or extension. For example, the specification "???1990.WK1" refers to all files with a filename consisting of any 3 characters followed by "1990" and with the extension "WK1." Therefore, the command **DIR** ???1990.WK1 would include files such as "TAX1990.WK1" and "INC1990.WK1," but not files such as "TAX1989.WK1" or "INC1991.WK1."

The following steps incorporate the use of wild card characters in the file specification of the **DIR** command. Example screen displays are shown after each step.

11. Type ‖ **DIR** *.PIC↵ ‖ to list all files with the extension "PIC."

```
A>DIR *.PIC

 Volume in drive A has no label
 Directory of  A:\

BOOKVAL  PIC      429  11-14-89   3:42p
CAPEXP   PIC     5948  11-14-89   3:42p
CURRENT  PIC      462  11-14-89   3:42p
DEBTCAP  PIC      462  11-14-89   3:43p
ROA      PIC      457  11-14-89   3:43p
        5 File(s)   1302528 bytes free

A>
```

12. Type ‖ **DIR** CON*.BAK↵ ‖ to list all files with a filename beginning "CON" and with a file extension "BAK."

```
A>DIR CON*.BAK

 Volume in drive A has no label
 Directory of  A:\

CONBLNC  BAK     2827  10-30-89   3:37p
CONSTMT  BAK     2990  11-06-89   3:38p
        2 File(s)   1302528 bytes free

A>
```

The period (.) in a file specification indicates that what follows is a file extension. To specify only files without an extension, a period must be used to indicate the end of the filename specification. If the period is omitted, DOS assumes that files with any file extension, blank or otherwise, should be included.

13. Type ‖ **DIR** CON*.↵ ‖ to list all files beginning with "CON" and which have no file extension.

```
A>DIR CON*.

 Volume in drive A has no label
 Directory of  A:\

CONBLNC          2827  10-30-89   3:37p
CONSTMT          2990  11-06-89   3:38p
        2 File(s)   1302528 bytes free

A>
```

14. Type ‖ **DIR** CON*.*↵ ‖ to list all files beginning with "CON" and which have any file extension.

```
A>DIR CON*.*

 Volume in drive A has no label
 Directory of  A:\

CONBLNC          2827  10-30-89   3:37p
CONSTMT          2990  11-06-89   3:38p
CONBLNC  BAK     2827  10-30-89   3:37p
CONSTMT  BAK     2990  11-06-89   3:38p
        4 File(s)   1302528 bytes free

A>
```

In the next steps, the ? wild card character will be used to list only files with certain characters in specified positions of the filename.

15. Type ‖ **DIR** ???R*.*↵ ‖ to list files with the letter *R* in the fourth position of the filename and any character following the *R*, and with any file extension.

```
A>DIR ???R*.*

 Volume in drive A has no label
 Directory of  A:\

ANNRPTXT        12015  10-15-89   3:34p
ENTRYHLP         2414  11-06-89   3:39p
FCTRANS          1348  11-21-89   3:40p
ANNRPTXT BAK    12015  10-15-89   3:34p
ENTRYHLP BAK     2414  11-06-89   3:39p
FCTRANS  BAK     1348  11-21-89   3:40p
CURRENT  PIC      462  11-14-89   3:42p
        7 File(s)   1302528 bytes free

A>
```

16. Type ‖ **DIR** ??TR*.↵ ‖ to list files with the letters *TR* in the third and fourth positions of the filename and with no file extension.

```
A>DIR ??TR*.

 Volume in drive A has no label
 Directory of  A:\

ENTRYHLP         2414  11-06-89   3:39p
FCTRANS          1348  11-21-89   3:40p
        2 File(s)   1302528 bytes free

A>
```

Since the * masks all remaining characters in a filename or file extension, the last two examples could have included ? characters in the second part of the filename (that is, "??TR*." is equivalent to "??TR????.").

Using a Drive Specification with the **DIR** Command

Since a drive letter designation has not yet been included in the **DIR** command, all directory listings so far have assumed that the disk is in the default drive. To see a directory listing for a disk in a drive other than the default drive, the drive must be specified in the **DIR** command.

17. Use the **DIR** command to list all of the files in the current directory of your microcomputer's other disk drive. (For example, if the other drive is a C: drive, type ‖ **DIR** C:↵ ‖).
18. Now type ‖ **DIR** *DOS directory**.SYS↵ ‖ to see a listing of files with the extension "SYS" in the DOS directory.

Using Optional Switches with the **DIR** Command

The **DIR** command may be followed by /W or /P to display the directory listing differently. The W and P are referred to as switches. A switch is an option of a command or DOS program that alters the way in which the command or program works.

A directory listing is often too long to be displayed in its entirety on the screen. When the **DIR** command includes the /W switch, the listing is displayed in a wide format. When the command includes the /P switch, the command pauses when the screen is full.

19. Type ‖ **DIR**/W↵ ‖ for a wide directory listing. The screen should appear similar to the following.

```
A>DIR/W

 Volume in drive A has no label
 Directory of  A:\

ANNRPTXT        BLSHEET1        CONBLNC         CONSTMT         DISCOP
ENTRYHLP        FCTRANS         INVTS           MEMBDAT1        OPNWSNOV
PHONEORD        RNTEQUIP        RPTINTRO        RPTSOFTW        SILVINTR
STCCURR         WORKCAP         ANNRPTXT BAK    BLSHEET1 BAK    CONBLNC  BAK
CONSTMT  BAK    DISCOP   BAK    ENTRYHLP BAK    FCTRANS  BAK    INVTS    BAK
MEMBDAT1 BAK    OPNWSNOV BAK    PHONEORD BAK    RNTEQUIP BAK    RPTINTRO BAK
RPTSOFTW BAK    SILVINTR BAK    STCCURR  BAK    WORKCAP  BAK    WRSIGNAT PCX
BOOKVAL  PIC    CAPEXP   PIC    CURRENT  PIC    DEBTCAP  PIC    ROA      PIC
       40 File(s)    1302528 bytes free

A>
```

Notice that in the wide format, the filename and file extension are the only items listed for files.

20. Next type ‖ **DIR**/P↵ ‖ for a directory listing that will pause when the screen is full.

21. At the prompt "Strike a key when ready . . . ," type any key to continue the listing.

The **COPY** Command

The **COPY** command allows you to copy the contents from one or more file(s) to other file(s) having the same or different filename(s). If the copied file is to have the same filename and extension, it must be in another directory. The general syntax for the **COPY** command is

COPY [*d:*][*path*]*filename*[*.ext*] [*d:*][*path*][*filename*[*.ext*]]

There may be two file specifications included in the **COPY** command. The first specifies the source file (the file being copied from) and the second specifies the destination file (the file being copied to). Specification of the destination file is optional, but specification of the source file is required. Since every file in a directory must have a unique filename/extension combination, the filename and extension of the destination file must be different from that of the source file if the locations (drive and path) are the same.

Suppose that you want to make a second copy of the RPTINTRO file. The copy will be in the same directory as the original, so it must have a different filename. Since the copy will be used only to practice DOS file commands, you will name the copy TEMPFILE.

22. Type ‖ **COPY** RPTINTRO TEMPFILE↵ ‖ .
23. Next, type ‖ **DIR**/W↵ ‖ to see that TEMPFILE now appears in the file listing.

The **RENAME** Command

The **RENAME** command may be used to change the filename or extension of an existing file. The format of the command is

RENAME [*d:*][*path*]*filename*[*.ext*] *filename*[*.ext*]

The first file specification is for the file being renamed. The second file specification indicates the new filename and file extension. The **RENAME** command does not change the location (drive and path) of the file; it simply changes the filename or the file extension, or both.

24. Type ‖ **RENAME** TEMPFILE TEMPREPT↵ ‖ to change the name of TEMPFILE to TEMPREPT. Next use the **DIR** command to confirm that the file has been renamed.

The **ERASE** Command

The **ERASE** command is used to permanently remove files from a disk directory. The format of the command is

ERASE [*d:*][*path*]*filename*[*.ext*]

The TEMPREPT file will now be erased from the current directory.

25. Type ‖ **ERASE** TEMPREPT↵ ‖ to erase the file from the directory. Next use the **DIR** command to confirm that the file has been erased.

The specifications for filenames and file extensions used with the **COPY, RENAME,** and **ERASE** commands may also include wild card characters.

This feature is useful for copying, renaming, or deleting several files at once. In the following steps you will create several subdirectories and then copy files from one directory to another using wild card characters with the **COPY** command.

DOS SUBDIRECTORIES AND PATHS

Subdirectories are used to keep files organized by type. For instance, you may wish to keep all word processing document files in one subdirectory and all spreadsheet files in another subdirectory. The following is a partial illustration of how a disk might be organized using subdirectories.

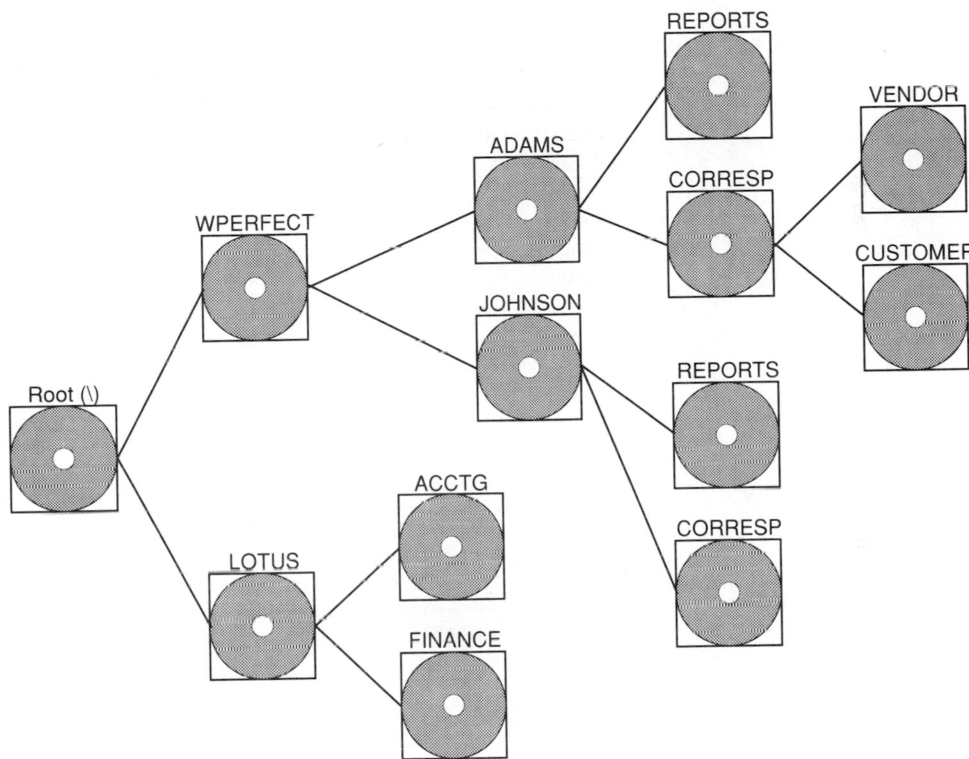

When subdirectories are used, the DOS command or program specification for a file may require that its path be included. The path identifies the directory in which the file is located. The path for the root directory is specified with a single backslash (\) character. Other directories may be specified by their path (either from the root directory or from the current directory).

In the illustration, if ADAMS were the current directory, a file ORDR1231 in the directory VENDOR could be specified as \WPERFECT\ADAMS\CORRESP\VENDOR\ORDR1231 (from the root directory) or as CORRESP\VENDOR\ORDR1231 (from the current directory). A path specification beginning with \ starts at the root directory.

The **MD** (Make Directory) Command

The command used to create a subdirectory is **MD** (Make Directory). The format for the command is

MD [*d:*]*path*

You will now use the **MD** command to make several subdirectories on your floppy disk. Many of the files on the disk are WordPerfect document files. Therefore, the first subdirectory will be named DOCFILES.

26. Type ‖ **MD** DOCFILES↵ ‖ .

DOS does not respond with a message indicating that the directory was successfully created. However, subdirectory names appear as filenames when the **DIR** command is executed. Subdirectories are designated by a <DIR> in the column where the number of bytes is displayed for files.

27. Type ‖ **DIR**↵ ‖ . The directory DOCFILES should now appear in the file listing as shown here.

```
SILVINTR BAK      1553  12-21-89   3:48p
STCCURR  BAK      3082   1-03-90   3:50p
WORKCAP  BAK      1366   1-03-90   3:50p
WRSIGNAT PCX     19948  11-14-89   3:47p
BOOKVAL  PIC       429  11-14-89   3:42p
CAPEXP   PIC      5948  11-14-89   3:42p
CURRENT  PIC       462  11-14-89   3:42p
DEBTCAP  PIC       462  11-14-89   3:43p
ROA      PIC       457  11-14-89   3:43p
DOCFILES     <DIR>       1-15-90  12:14p
       41 File(s)   1302016 bytes free

A>
```

NOTE: The <DIR> date and time displayed on your screen will reflect the DOS system date and time for the microcomputer you are using.

Now suppose that you want to have another subdirectory under the root directory for files with the extension .PIC (Lotus 1-2-3 graphics files).

28. Type ‖ **MD** PICS↵ ‖ to create a subdirectory for these files.

29. Type ‖ **DIR**↵ ‖ to verify that the subdirectory PICS was created.

The **CD** (Change Directory) Command

Once subdirectories have been created, the **CD** (Change Directory) command may be used to make a subdirectory the current directory. You now will make PICS the current directory and then copy files from the root directory to the PICS directory.

30. Type ‖ **CD** PICS↵ ‖ to make PICS the current directory. Then type the **DIR** command. The listed directory should appear as follows.

```
A>DIR

 Volume in drive A has no label
 Directory of  A:\PICS

.            <DIR>       1-15-90  12:16p
..           <DIR>       1-15-90  12:16p
        2 File(s)   1301504 bytes free

A>
```

You next will copy all files having a .PIC extension from the root directory to the current directory (PICS). First review the format for the **COPY** command

COPY [*d:*][*path*]*filename*[.*ext*] [*d:*][*path*][*filename*[.*ext*]]

Since PICS is the current directory, the source file(s) specification must include a path (\ for root directory). However, the path for the destination file(s) is (by default) the current directory, so it does not need to be specified.

31. Now type ‖ **COPY** *.PIC↵ ‖ .

As the files are copied to the PICS subdirectory, the source filenames will be listed on the screen. The **DIR** command may be used to verify that they have been copied to the current directory.

32. Type ‖ **DIR**↵ ‖ . The screen should appear similar to the following.

```
A>DIR

 Volume in drive A has no label
 Directory of  A:\PICS

.            <DIR>       1-15-90  12:16p
..           <DIR>       1-15-90  12:16p
BOOKVAL  PIC       429  11-14-89   3:42p
CAPEXP   PIC      5948  11-14-89   3:42p
CURRENT  PIC       462  11-14-89   3:42p
DEBTCAP  PIC       462  11-14-89   3:43p
ROA      PIC       457  11-14-89   3:43p
        7 File(s)   1293312 bytes free

A>
```

The PICS subdirectory listing shows two <DIR> entries: the first is a single period (.) and the second is a double period (..). Every subdirectory listing will show these two entries. The single period identifies the current directory itself; the double period identifies the parent directory, which in this case is the root directory. The . and .. directory identifiers are sometimes useful as a shorthand notation for directory names.

MULTIPLE PARENT\CHILD SUBDIRECTORIES

Next, suppose that among the WordPerfect document files, you want two further groups of files. The files with the extension .BAK are backup files for the original ("working") files on the disk. .BAK files are not intended to be modified by the user. There are also several files that begin with the letters RPT, which identifies them as parts of a report.

You now will create two additional subdirectories of the parent directory DOCFILES. One of the additional directories will be named "BAKUP" and the other will be named "REPORT." The directory structure of the disk will then appear as follows.

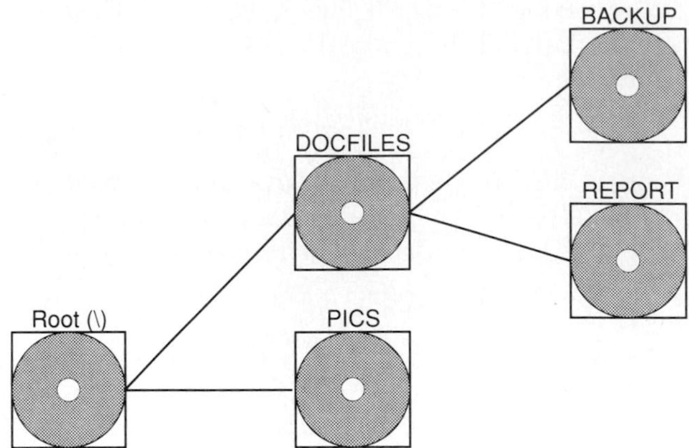

Since PICS is now the current subdirectory, the command MD BAKUP would create a directory BAKUP under the parent directory PICS, not under the correct parent directory DOCFILES. However, like most DOS commands, the **MD** command may be used with a full path specification beginning at the root directory, regardless of the current directory you are in.

33. Type ‖ **MD** \DOCFILES\BAKUP↵ ‖ to create the subdirectory BAKUP.

34. Next type ‖ **DIR** \DOCFILES↵ ‖ to verify that the directory was created.

The screen should now appear as follows.

```
A>DIR \DOCFILES

 Volume in drive A has no label
 Directory of  A:\DOCFILES

.            <DIR>      1-15-90  12:14p
..           <DIR>      1-15-90  12:14p
BAKUP        <DIR>      1-15-90   2:11p
        3 File(s)   1292800 bytes free

A>
```

A subdirectory also may be created under the parent directory DOCFILES by first making DOCFILES the current directory and then executing the **MD** command with only the new directory name. While this involves two commands and even more keystrokes, you may find it easier to keep track of where the new directory is being created if you use this method.

35. Now type ‖ **CD** \DOCFILES↵ ‖ to make DOCFILES the current directory.

36. Next type ‖ **MD** REPORT↵ ‖ to create the new directory REPORT under the current directory DOCFILES.

37. Type ‖ **DIR**↵ ‖ to verify that the directories BAKUP and REPORT now appear under the current directory (DOCFILES).

The screen should now appear as follows.

```
A>DIR

 Volume in drive A has no label
 Directory of   A:\DOCFILES

.            <DIR>       1-15-90  12:14p
..           <DIR>       1-15-90  12:14p
BAKUP        <DIR>       1-15-90   2:11p
REPORT       <DIR>       1-15-90   2:17p
        4 File(s)    1292288 bytes free

A>
```

When using the **CD** command to move among many subdirectories, you may often lose track of the current subdirectory. The **CD** command may be used without a path specification to display the name of the current directory. The **PROMPT** command also may be used with certain parameters to display the current directory as part of the DOS prompt.

38. Type ‖ **CD**↵ ‖ to display the name of the current directory. Then include the path as part of the DOS prompt by typing ‖ **PROMPT** PG↵ ‖ .

The screen should now appear as follows.

```
A>CD
A:\DOCFILES

A>PROMPT $P$G

A:\DOCFILES>
```

The $P parameter included in the **PROMPT** command is used to display the current path in the prompt. The $G parameter is used to include the > character in the prompt. Refer to the DOS command/program summary (pages 000–000) for a list of all parameters that may be used with the **PROMPT** command.

39. Now type ‖ **CD** BAKUP↵ ‖ to change the current directory to BAKUP.

The prompt should now appear as "A:\DOCFILES\BAKUP>," identifying the current directory. You now will copy all files with the extension .BAK from the root directory to the current directory.

40. Type ‖ **COPY** *.BAK↵ ‖ .

You next will copy all files having no extension from the root directory to the directory DOCFILES. Since the current directory (BAKUP) is neither the source nor target directory, the directory path must be specified for each.

41. Type ‖ **COPY** *. \DOCFILES↵ ‖ .

As mentioned earlier, the double period (..) is a shorthand method of identifying the parent directory of the current directory. You will now list the files in the directory DOCFILES using the double period notation.

42. Type ‖ **DIR** ../W↵ ‖ to list files in the parent directory DOCFILES.

The screen should now appear similar to the following.

```
A:\DOCFILES\BAKUP>DIR ../W

 Volume in drive A has no label
 Directory of  A:\DOCFILES

.            ..           BAKUP        REPORT       ANNRPTXT
BLSHEET1     CONBLNC      CONSTMT      DISCOP       ENTRYHLP
FCTRANS      INVTS        MEMBDAT1     OPNWSNOV     PHONEORD
RNTEQUIP     RPTINTRO     RPTSOFTW     SILVINTR     STCCURR
WORKCAP
       21 File(s)    1164288 bytes free

A:\DOCFILES\BAKUP>
```

Since the double period (..) identifies the parent directory DOCFILES, the other subdirectory under DOCFILES may be identified as ..\REPORT. You now will copy all files with a filename beginning "RPT" from the parent directory DOCFILES to its subdirectory REPORT using the double period notation.

43. Type ‖ **COPY** ..\RPT*.* ..\REPORT↵ ‖ .

44. Now change the current directory to DOCFILES by typing ‖ **CD** ..↵ ‖ .

45. Verify the last copy by typing ‖ **DIR** REPORT↵ ‖ .

The screen should now appear similar to the following.

```
A:\DOCFILES>DIR REPORT

 Volume in drive A has no label
 Directory of  A:\DOCFILES\REPORT

.            <DIR>        1-15-90   2:17p
..           <DIR>        1-15-90   2:17p
RPTINTRO         2953  12-17-89   3:46p
RPTSOFTW         7054  12-20-89   3:47p
        4 File(s)    1154048 bytes free

A:\DOCFILES>
```

The **RD** (Remove Directory) Command

You have created subdirectories on the disk to give you experience using DOS directories and path specifications. You now will remove the directories created here with the **RD** (Remove Directory) command. Before subdirectories can be removed, however, they must be emptied of all files and subdirectories. Therefore, you will begin by erasing all files in the current directory DOCFILES.

46. Type ‖ **ERASE** *.*↵ ‖ to erase all files in the current directory. At the prompt "Are you sure (Y/N)?" type ‖ Y↵ ‖ to erase the files.

The prompt "Are you sure (Y/N)?" appears when all files in a directory are about to be erased. DOS commands and programs often display this type of warning when an operation is irrevocable and many data files may be lost.

Another way of erasing all files in a directory is to use the **ERASE** command with the name of a directory.

47. Now erase all files in the directory REPORT by typing ‖ **ERASE** REPORT↵ ‖ and confirm that you want to complete the operation by typing ‖ Y↵ ‖ at the warning prompt.

The REPORT directory may now be removed with the **RD** (Remove Directory) command.

48. Type ‖ **RD** REPORT↵ ‖ to remove the directory. Then verify that the directory has been removed by typing ‖ **DIR**↵ ‖ .

If you try to remove a directory that still has files in it or has further subdirectories beneath it, a message will appear on the screen indicating that the directory may not be removed.

49. Type ‖ **RD** BAKUP↵ ‖ . The following message should be displayed.

```
A:\DOCFILES>RD BAKUP
Invalid path, not directory,
or directory not empty

A:\DOCFILES>
```

DOS normally gives messages indicating that an operation has not been successfully completed. You may have noticed, however, that messages are not normally given to indicate successful completion. Therefore, it is important to pay close attention to any messages displayed when a command is executed.

50. Type ‖ **ERASE** BAKUP↵ ‖ and respond to the warning prompt by typing ‖ Y↵ ‖ .
51. Type ‖ **RD** BAKUP↵ ‖ to remove the directory BAKUP.

You now will erase files in the PICS directory, which is a subdirectory of the root directory, and then remove the PICS directory with the **RD** command.

52. Type ‖ **ERASE** \PICS↵ ‖ and respond to the warning prompt by typing ‖ Y↵ ‖ .
53. Then type ‖ **RD** \PICS↵ ‖ to remove the directory PICS.

The final directory to be removed is the current directory DOCFILES. Although all files in the directory have been erased and the directory no longer has subdirectories beneath it, the current directory may never be removed. To remove a directory, you must first change the current directory to a previous level.

54. Type ‖ **CD**\↵ ‖ to make the root directory the current directory.

55. Then type ‖ **RD** DOCFILES↵ ‖ to remove the subdirectory DOCFILES.

A FINAL NOTE

It should be mentioned that the ability to use the wild card characters * and ? to specify groups of files has implications about how files ought to be named. If you think you might use commands with a group of files (batch operations) at any future time, you should name the files so that the group may be specified with wild card characters. You then can use DOS commands to copy all the files from one directory to another, to make backup copies of all the files, to erase all the files, and so forth.

This completes the DOS exercise. You may refer to the DOS command summary for additional information on commands used in the exercises and for several other DOS commands and programs.

DOS QUICK REFERENCE COMMAND SUMMARY

Device Names

Disk Drives	A:, B:, C:	Monitor	SCR:	Printer 2	LPT2:
Keyboard	CON:	Printer 1	LPT1:		

Commands and Programs

d: Command
Syntax: *drive letter:*

CHDIR or **CD** (Change Directory) Command
Syntax: **CD** [*d:*][*path*]

CHKDSK (Check Disk) Program
Syntax: [*d:*][*path*]CHKDSK [*d:*][*path*][*filename*[*.ext*]][/F][/V]

CLS (Clear Screen) Command
Syntax: **CLS**

COMP (Compare Files) Program
Syntax: [*d:*][*path*]COMP [*d:*][*path*][*filename*[*.ext*]] [*d:*][*path*][*filename*[*.ext*]]

COPY (Copy Files) Command
Syntax: **COPY** [*d:*][*path*]*filename*[*.ext*] [*d:*][*path*][*filename*[*.ext*]]

DATE (Set System Date) Command
Syntax: **DATE** [*mm-dd-yy*], [*dd-mm-yy*], or [*yy-mm-dd*]

DIR (List Directory) Command
Syntax: **DIR** [*d:*][*path*][*filename*[*.ext*]][/P][/W]

DISKCOMP (Compare Floppy Disks) Program
Syntax: [*d:*][*path*]DISKCOMP [*d:*[*d:*]]

DISKCOPY (Copy Floppy Disks) Program
Syntax: [*d:*][*path*]DISKCOPY [*d:*[*d:*]]

ERASE or **DEL** (Erase Files) Command
Syntax: **ERASE** [*d:*][*path*]*filename*[*.ext*]

FORMAT (Format Disk) Program
Syntax: [*d:*][*path*]FORMAT [*d:*][/S][/1][/8][/V][/B]

LABEL (Volume Label) Program
Syntax: [*d:*][*path*]LABEL [*d:*][*volume label*]

MD or **MKDIR** (Make Directory) Command
Syntax: **MD** [*d:*]*path*

PATH (Set Search Directory) Command
Syntax: **PATH** [[*d:*]*path*[[;[*d:*]*path*]]]

PROMPT (Set System Prompt) Command
Syntax: **PROMPT** [*prompt-text*]

RENAME (Rename Files) Command
Syntax: **RENAME** [*d:*][*path*][*filename*[*.ext*]] [*filename*[*.ext*]]

RD or **RMDIR** (Remove Directory) Command
Syntax: **RD** [*d:*]*path*

SYS (System) Program
Syntax: [*d:*][*path*]SYS [*d:*]

TIME (System Time) Command
Syntax: **TIME** [*hh:mm*[*:ss*[*.xx*]]]

TYPE (Contents of File) Command
Syntax: **TYPE**[*d:*][*path*]*filename*[*.ext*]

VOL (Volume) Command
Syntax: **VOL** [*d:*]

DOS CONTROL KEYS

The following keystrokes and keystroke combinations may be used while at the DOS operating level. The convention *key-key* means press and hold the first key shown and then type the second key shown.

NOTE: Refer to the keyboards on page I-4 to help you locate the keys involved in the following keystroke combinations.

KEY COMBINATIONS

Ctrl-Alt-Del Three-key combination. Press and hold the Ctrl and Alt keys, and then tap the Del key. Erases all data from RAM and reloads DOS (reboots the system).

Ctrl-Break Interrupts a DOS command or program operation. Returns to the DOS > prompt.

Ctrl-Num Lock or Pause Pauses a DOS operation. Typing any key will resume the operation.

Ctrl-PrtScr Toggles ON/OFF an echo of screen output to the printer.

Shift-PrtScr Prints the current screen of data.

Enter key Enters the current line into memory for DOS to act upon.

Escape key Aborts the current line without entering it as a DOS command or filename.

F1 key Types out the last entry one character at a time.

F3 key Types out all of the last entry.

F6 key Types out the End of File character ^Z.

IMPORTANT DOS COMMANDS AND PROGRAMS VERSION 3.3

d:
Syntax: *drive letter:*
Type: Command

Changes the current default drive. The drive letter entry specifies the desired disk drive device to make current (usually A:, B:, or C:). The current DOS prompt indicates the letter of the current drive (i.e., A> indicates that the A: drive is the current default drive).

CHDIR or **CD** (Change Directory)
Syntax: **CD** [*d:*][*path*]
Type: Command

Changes the current directory. **CD** used by itself displays the path of the current directory on the screen. **CD** makes the root directory the current directory. **CD..** makes the parent (next previous) directory the current directory.

CHKDSK (Check Disk)
Syntax: [*d:*][*path*]CHKDSK [*d:*][*path*][*filename*[.*ext*]][/F][/V]
Type: Program

The CHKDSK.COM program may be used to search the disk for errors that may have occurred after the disk was formatted, and to report on the status of used and remaining disk space.

Executing the CHKDSK.COM program provides information about the space in use on the disk being checked. The most common form of the program entry is CHKDSK *d:*. An example of the program's output is shown here.

```
C:\DOS> CHKDSK A:

  1457664 bytes total disk space
    52736 bytes in 2 hidden files
   199168 bytes in 46 user files
  1205760 bytes available on disk

   654336 bytes total memory
   457616 bytes free

C:\DOS>
```

The CHKDSK program reports on the total disk space and the disk space remaining (available) on the disk. It also reports the computer's total RAM and the RAM that is still available (total RAM less the RAM being used by DOS). Notice that the CHKDSK program can be used to determine if hidden files exist on the disk.

It is a good habit to use the CHKDSK program to check your disks periodically to avoid running out of disk space in the middle of a save operation.

If the CHKDSK program finds errors on the disk, the output of the program will contain error messages concerning lost clusters.

```
C:\DOS> CHKDSK A:

Errors found, F parameter not specified.
Corrections will not be written to disk.


3 lost clusters found in 1 chains.
Convert lost chains to files  (Y/N)?
```

If such errors occur, the CHKDSK program (with the /F switch) may be executed again to cause the program to convert the lost chains into files. The /V switch may be used to cause the CHKDSK program to display all disk files and their paths.

CHKDSK [*d:*]*.* may be used to produce a report on the disk files which has sectors that are noncontiguous (scattered).

CLS (Clear Screen)
Syntax: **CLS**
Type: Command

The **CLS** command may be used to clear the screen at the DOS operating level.

COMP (Compare Files)
Syntax: [*d:*][*path*]COMP [*d:*][*path*][*filename*[*.ext*]] [*d:*][*path*][*filename*[*.ext*]]
Type: Program

The COMP.COM program compares the contents of files to determine if they are identical. Examples of using the COMP program include the following.

COMP C:file1.ext A:file2.ext Compares file1 on the C: drive with file2 on the A: drive.

COMP \DOCFILES\REPORT \DOCFILES\BACKUP Compares all files in the \DOCFILES\REPORT subdirectory with the files in the \DOCFILES\BACKUP subdirectory.

COPY (Copy Files)
Syntax: **COPY** [*d:*][*path*]*filename*[*.ext*] [*d:*][*path*][*filename*[*.ext*]]
Type: Command

The **COPY** command is used primarily to copy files from one directory to another. The first file specification [*d:*][*path*]*filename*[*.ext*] defines the source file(s) to be copied. The second specification defines the destination for the copied file(s). If the second specification includes only a drive and/or path, the files are copied to the destination with the same filenames and extensions as the source files. Examples of using the **COPY** command include the following.

A> **COPY** report report.bak Copies the file named "report" to a file named "report.bak" into the current directory. (Makes a copy with a different name into the same directory.)

A> **COPY** report.WK1 B: Copies the file named "report.WK1" from the current drive and directory into the current directory of the B: drive, under the same name.

A> **COPY** C:report.WK1 Copies the file named "report.WK1" from the current directory of the C: drive into the current directory of the A: drive, under the same name.

A> **COPY** C:\WORDS\MGMT213 B: Copies all files in the C:\WORDS\MGMT213 subdirectory into the current directory of the B: drive, under the same names.

A> **COPY** C:\WORDS\MGMT213 B:\MGMT213\BACKUP Copies all files in the C:WORDS\MGMT213 subdirectory into the \MGMT213\BACKUP directory of the B: drive, under the same names.

A> **COPY** *.* C: Copies all files in the current directory of the A: drive into the current directory of the C: drive, under the same names.

The **COPY** command may include a hardware device as the source or destination for the copy operation. Examples would include the following.

A> **COPY** report LPT1: Copies the file named "report" to the printer (prints the file).

A> **COPY** CON:test.BAT Copies characters typed on the keyboard to a file named "test.BAT," in the current directory of the A: drive. (Allows you to create an ASCII file from DOS. Typing F6, End of File character, ends the keyboard copy operation.)

DATE (Set System Date)
Syntax: **DATE** [*mm-dd-yy*], [*dd-mm-yy*], or [*yy-mm-dd*]
Type: Command

The **DATE** command is used to change the DOS system date. *mm* specifies a month number (e.g., March = 03), *dd* specifies day number, and *yy* specifies the year number, which is entered as two numbers between 80 and 99 or four numbers between 1980 and 1999. Dashes are used to separate the numbers.

DIR (List Directory)
Syntax: **DIR** [*d:*][*path*][*filename*[*.ext*]][/P][/W]
Type: Command

The **DIR** command is used to display the directory of filenames, extensions, sizes, and date/time stamps for the files in a directory. Examples of using the **DIR** command include the following.

A> **DIR** * .WK1 Lists the directory for all files having a .WK1 extension in the current directory of the A: drive.

A> **DIR** C:\CALC\MGMT213*.PIC Lists the directory for all files having a .PIC extension in the \CALC\MGMT213 directory of the C: drive.

A> **DIR** report.WK1 Lists a directory for the single file named "report.WK1" in the current directory of the A: drive. (May be used to search a directory for a specific file.)

DISKCOMP (Compare Floppy Disks)
Syntax: [*d:*][*path*]DISKCOMP [*d:*[*d:*]]
Type: Program

The DISKCOMP program compares the contents of two floppy disks to determine if they are identical. Examples of using the DISKCOMP program include the following.

A> C:DISKCOMP A: B: Reads the DISKCOMP program from the current directory of the C: drive. The program then compares the contents of the disk in the A: drive with the contents of the disk in the B: drive.

A> C:DISKCOMP A: Reads the DISKCOMP program from the current directory of the C: drive. The program then instructs the user to first insert one disk and then the other into the A: drive in order to compare the two disks.

DISKCOPY (Copy Floppy Disks)
Syntax: [*d:*][*path*]DISKCOPY [*d:*[*d:*]]
Type: Program

The DISKCOPY program copies the contents of one floppy disk onto another floppy disk. The disk being copied from is called the source disk. The disk being copied to is called the target disk. The disks are identical when the disk copy operation is complete. The source and destination floppy disks must be of the same size and density. Examples of using the DISKCOPY program include the following.

A> C:DISKCOPY A: B: Reads the DISKCOPY program from the current directory of the C: drive. The program then copies the contents of the disk in the A: drive onto the disk in the B: drive.

A> C:DISKCOPY A: Reads the DISKCOPY program from the current directory of the C: drive. The program then instructs the user to first insert the source disk and then the target disk into the A: drive in order to perform the disk copy operation.

ERASE or **DEL** (Erase Files)
Syntax: **ERASE** [*d:*][*path*]*filename*[*.ext*]
Type: Command

The **ERASE** command is used to erase one or more files from a directory. Examples of using the **ERASE** command include the following.

A> **ERASE** report.WK1 Erases the file named "report.WK1" from the current directory of the A: drive.

A> **ERASE** *.* Erases all files in the current directory of the A: drive.

A> **ERASE** C:*.WK1 Erases all files having a WK1 extension that are in the current directory of the C: drive.

A> **ERASE** C:\WORDS\MGMT213 Erases all files in the \WORDS\MGMT213 subdirectory of the C: drive.

FORMAT (Format Disk)
Syntax: [*d:*][*path*]FORMAT [*d:*][/S][/1][/8][/V][/B]
Type: Program

The FORMAT program is used to prepare a disk for storing data. *The FORMAT program destroys all data that may already be on a disk.* The various FORMAT program switches have the following effects.

/S Copies DOS onto the disk after the format is complete.

/1 Formats only one side of the disk.

/8 Formats the disk into 8 sector groups (5 ¼″ floppy disks only).

/V Pauses after the format operation to allow you to type and enter a label for the disk. The label then will be listed by the **DIR** command when it reads a directory of the disk.

/B Formats the disk so that DOS may be copied onto it later. See the SYS program for information on copying DOS onto a disk after it has been formatted.

LABEL (Volume Label)
Syntax: [*d:*][*path*]LABEL [*d:*][*volume label*]
Type: Program

The LABEL program is used to enter a label for a disk that will be listed with the directory when the **DIR** command is used. The following example creates a label MYFILES for the disk in the A: drive. The LABEL program in the example is read from a subdirectory named DOS.

C> \DOS\LABEL A:myfiles If the disk already has a label, the LABEL program may be used to change the label. LABEL [*d:*] with no volume label specified may be used to delete a disk's label.

MD or **MKDIR** (Make Directory)
Syntax: **MD** [*d:*]*path*
Type: Command

The **MD** command is used to create a subdirectory on a disk. If the directory being created is a child of the current directory, the directory name is entered immediately after the **MD** command. For instance, if the current directory is \WORDS and you want to create a new directory ACCT335 whose parent directory is WORDS, you type ‖ C:\WORDS>**MD** ACCT335↵ ‖. However, if you want to accomplish the same task while the root directory is the current directory, you type ‖ C:\>**MD**\WORDS\ACCT335↵ ‖.

PATH (Set Search Directory)
Syntax: **PATH** [[*d:*]*path*[[;[*d:*]*path*]]]
Type: Command

The **PATH** command is used to direct DOS to another disk directory if an executable file (software or program) for which it is searching cannot be found in the current or specified directory. For instance, the command **PATH** C:CALC;C:WORDS sets a path to the two software subdirectories. If you then type a software filename command such as WP while the root directory is the current directory, DOS will first search the root directory for the software file. If the file is not found, it will next search the \CALC directory for the file. If the software file is not found there, DOS will continue its search in the \WORDS directory. DOS searches the **PATH** command's directories in the order they were entered when the **PATH** command was entered.

PROMPT (Set System Prompt)
Syntax: **PROMPT** [*prompt-text*]
Type: Command

The **PROMPT** command may be used to change the DOS prompt. Certain letters preceded by a dollar sign ($) may be used to cause the prompt to display certain system information. For instance, the command **PROMPT** pbDate-dg creates a DOS prompt similar to C:\DOS|Date-Sat 1-21-1989> (when the C: drive and the DOS directory are both current). The following is a list of letters and their displayed data that may be included in the **PROMPT** command.

Characters	DOS Prompt Display
$$	$ (dollar sign)
$t	System Time
$d	System Date
$p	The current drive and directory
$v	The version of DOS being used
$n	The current drive only
$g	> character
$l	< character
$b	| character
$q	= character

RENAME (Rename Files)
Syntax: **RENAME** [*d:*][*path*][*filename*[*.ext*]] [*filename*[*.ext*]]
Type: Command

The **RENAME** command is used to rename files in a directory. Examples of using the **RENAME** command include the following.

A> **RENAME** report report.bak   Renames the file named "report" (A: drive, current directory) to be "report.bak" (same drive and directory).

A> **RENAME** C:\WORDS\MGMT213\report report.bak   Renames the file named "report" (C: drive, \WORDS\MGMT213 directory) to be "report.bak" (same drive and directory).

A> **RENAME** *. *.bak   Renames all files having no extension to be files with the same filenames and .bak extensions.

RD or **RMDIR** (Remove Directory)
Syntax: **RD** [*d:*]*path*
Type: Command

The **RD** command is used to remove a subdirectory from a disk. Before a subdirectory can be removed, all of the files in the subdirectory must be erased (see the **ERASE** command for more information on erasing files). A directory may not be removed while it is the current directory. A preceding directory must be the current directory in order to remove a directory. A parent directory may not be removed until all child directories are removed first. A directory containing hidden files may not be removed.

SYS (System)
Syntax: [*d:*][*path*]SYS [*d:*]
Type: Program

The SYS program may be used to transfer DOS onto a disk that has been previously formatted. Unless the SYS program is executed immediately after the disk has been formatted, there is a possibility that there will not be enough room available on the disk where the hidden files of DOS must be stored. See the FORMAT program /B switch for information on how to format a disk in a way that reserves space for the hidden files.

TIME (System Time)
Syntax: **TIME** [*hh:mm*[*:ss*[*.xx*]]]
Type: Command

The **TIME** command allows you to change the system's clock time. Command entries are made: *hh* for hour, 0–23; *mm* for minute, 0–59; *ss* for second, 0–59; and *xx* for hundredths of a second, 0–99.

TYPE (Contents of File)
Syntax: **TYPE** [*d:*][*path*]*filename*[*.ext*]
Type: Command

The **TYPE** command is used to output the contents of a file to the screen. The command is most useful when the file is in ASCII data format. Any non-ASCII contents of a file will be unreadable.

VOL (Volume)
Syntax: **VOL** [*d:*]
Type: Command

The **VOL** command is used to display the volume label of a disk. See the LABEL program for information on how to label a disk volume.

When DOS is first loaded into RAM (booted), the operating system will automatically look for certain files in the root directory. These files, if present, will affect the operations of the microcomputer while it is in use.

AUTOEXEC.BAT

A file given a .BAT filename extension is called a *batch file*. Batch files contain one or more DOS commands and/or executable (program) file filenames. If the filename for an existing batch file is entered at the DOS operating level, DOS will open the file and begin executing the commands/programs within the batch file in the order of their appearance.

.BAT files are ASCII files that can be created by the user with a word processing software (or any other software that will create ASCII files). They can also be created by using a method in which a variation of the DOS **COPY** command is used to create a file directly from the keyboard. This variation of the COPY command has the form

COPY CON:*filename*.BAT

The command simply designates the keyboard (CON:) as the source for the file to copy. When the command is executed, DOS pauses for you to type characters on the keyboard. When finished, you type the F6 Function key to produce the End of File (^Z) character. An example of creating such a file might appear on the screen as follows.

```
A> COPY CON:GO.BAT
 C:\DOS\CHKDSK A:
 PAUSE
 DIR A:
 PAUSE
 C:\WORDS\WP
 ^Z
```

In this example a batch file named "GO.BAT" is created. To execute the file, the user types ‖ GO↵ ‖ at the DOS operating level. When executed, the first line in the file causes DOS to access the C:\DOS subdirectory to load the CHKDSK program and perform a CHKDSK operation on the disk in the A: DRIVE.

The next DOS command, **PAUSE,** typically is used only in batch files. The **PAUSE** command causes the computer to stop executing the commands in the batch file until the user types a key on the keyboard. When the command is executed the message

Strike a key when ready . . .

appears on the screen. The user next types a key and the computer continues by listing a directory of the files found on the disk in the A: drive (DIR A:). It then pauses again.

AUTOEXEC is a special batch file filename that DOS will automatically search for in the root directory when DOS is first booted. If a file named "AUTOEXEC.BAT" is in the directory, DOS will open the file and begin executing the commands/programs within it.

CONFIG.SYS

CONFIG.SYS is another example of a DOS-related ASCII file with a special DOS name. A CONFIG.SYS file may be created in the same manner as a .BAT file, using a software or the **COPY** CON: command. A CONFIG.SYS file also contains DOS commands/programs; however, the commands/programs contained in a CONFIG.SYS file are used to change the default input/output attributes of DOS and so may only be executed at the time when DOS is first booted. At that time DOS will open a file in the root directory named “CONFIG.SYS” and will begin executing the commands/programs within the batch file in the order of their appearance.

Having a CONFIG.SYS file in the root directory of the boot disk is particularly important with newer applications software that maintain several open files while they are being used. In such cases the CONFIG.SYS file should have the following two lines included in it.

```
FILES = 20
BUFFERS = 24
^Z
```

DEVICE = VDISK nnn

Another line you may see in a CONFIG.SYS file is used to load a DOS program (VDISK.SYS) at the time that DOS is booted. The VDISK program creates what is called a “phantom” or RAM disk drive. The program is particularly useful when the microcomputer has only one floppy disk drive in addition to its C: drive. VDISK.SYS configures a portion of the microcomputer’s RAM into what is essentially a temporary disk drive. The program will assign a DOS device name (usually D:) to the RAM drive. You then can use the RAM drive (D:) for temporary storage of data while using the microcomputer.

It is important to note that the RAM drive is not a real disk drive, and any data on it will vaporize the instant the computer is turned off. Therefore, you must copy any data you want to keep onto a real disk before turning off the computer.

The RAM drive reduces the amount of RAM available for processing data. If the software you are using requires a large amount of RAM, you may not be able to use it and the RAM drive at the same time.

To use VDISK.SYS to create a RAM drive at the time the microcomputer is booted, copy the VDISK.SYS program into the root directory. You then must add the following line to your existing root directory CONFIG.SYS file, or create a root directory CONFIG.SYS file with the line in it.

DEVICE = VDISK *nnn*

The *nnn* represents the size of the RAM drive you want to create. For instance, DEVICE = VDISK 256 will create a 256K RAM disk drive.

APPENDIX B
ASCII CHARACTER CODES

The following table lists all the ASCII codes (in decimal) and their associated characters. These characters can be displayed using PRINT CHR$ (*n*), where *n* is the ASCII code. The column headed "Control Character" lists the standard interpretations of ASCII codes 0 to 31 (usually used for control functions or communications).

Each of these characters can be entered from the keyboard by pressing and holding the Alt key, then pressing the digits for the ASCII code on the numeric keypad. Note, however, that some of the codes have special meaning to the BASIC Program Editor. It uses its own interpretation for the codes and may not display the special character listed here.

ASCII Value	Character	Control Character	ASCII Value	Character	ASCII Value	Character	ASCII Value	Character
000	(null)	NUL	032	(space)	064	@	096	`
001	☺	SOH	033	!	065	A	097	a
002	☻	STX	034	"	066	B	098	b
003	♥	ETX	035	#	067	C	099	c
004	♦	EOT	036	$	068	D	100	d
005	♣	ENQ	037	%	069	E	101	e
006	♠	ACK	038	&	070	F	102	f
007	(beep)	BEL	039	'	071	G	103	g
008	◘	BS	040	(	072	H	104	h
009	(tab)	HT	041	)	073	I	105	i
010	(line feed)	LF	042	*	074	J	106	j
011	(home)	VT	043	+	075	K	107	k
012	(form feed)	FF	044	,	076	L	108	l
013	(carriage return)	CR	045	-	077	M	109	m
014	♫	SO	046	.	078	N	110	n
015	☼	SI	047	/	079	O	111	o
016	►	DLE	048	0	080	P	112	p
017	◄	DC1	049	1	081	Q	113	q
018	↕	DC2	050	2	082	R	114	r
019	‼	DC3	051	3	083	S	115	s
020	¶	DC4	052	4	084	T	116	t
021	§	NAK	053	5	085	U	117	u
022	▬	SYN	054	6	086	V	118	v
023	↨	ETB	055	7	087	W	119	w
024	↑	CAN	056	8	088	X	120	x
025	↓	EM	057	9	089	Y	121	y
026	→	SUB	058	:	090	Z	122	z
027	←	ESC	059	;	091	[	123	{
028	(cursor right)	FS	060	<	092	\	124	¦
029	(cursor left)	GS	061	=	093	]	125	}
030	(cursor up)	RS	062	>	094	^	126	~
031	(cursor down)	US	063	?	095	_	127	⌂

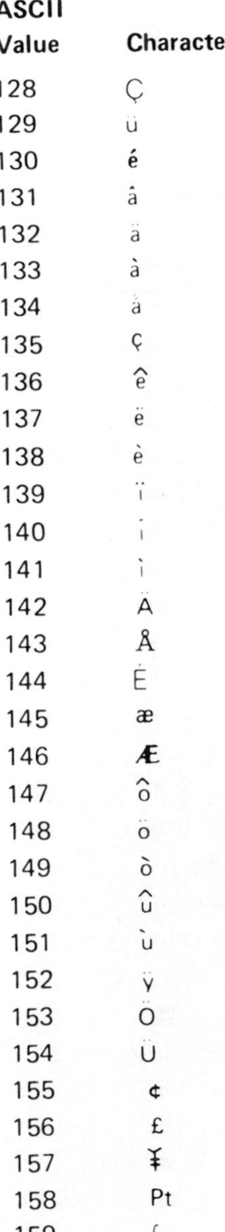

ASCII Value	Character
128	Ç
129	ü
130	é
131	â
132	ä
133	à
134	å
135	ç
136	ê
137	ë
138	è
139	ï
140	î
141	ì
142	Ä
143	Å
144	É
145	æ
146	Æ
147	ô
148	ö
149	ò
150	û
151	ù
152	ÿ
153	Ö
154	Ü
155	¢
156	£
157	¥
158	Pt
159	ƒ

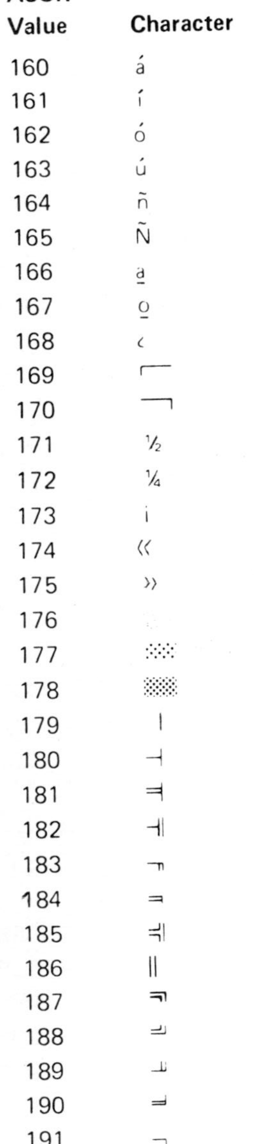

ASCII Value	Character
160	á
161	í
162	ó
163	ú
164	ñ
165	Ñ
166	ª
167	º
168	¿
169	⌐
170	¬
171	½
172	¼
173	¡
174	«
175	»
176	░
177	▒
178	▓
179	│
180	┤
181	╡
182	╢
183	╖
184	╕
185	╣
186	║
187	╗
188	╝
189	╜
190	╛
191	┐

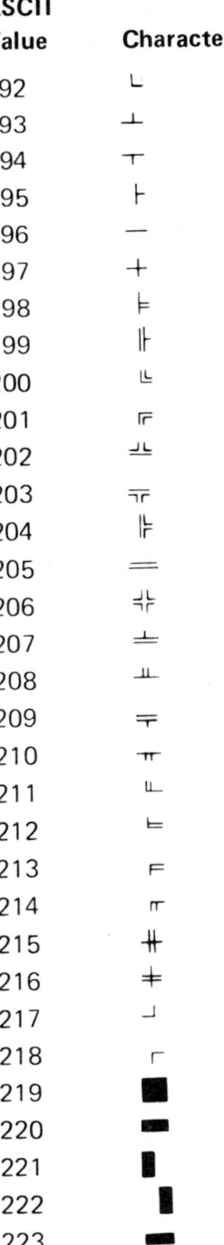

ASCII Value	Character
192	└
193	┴
194	┬
195	├
196	─
197	┼
198	╞
199	╟
200	╚
201	╔
202	╩
203	╦
204	╠
205	═
206	╬
207	╧
208	╨
209	╤
210	╥
211	╙
212	╘
213	╒
214	╓
215	╫
216	╪
217	┘
218	┌
219	█
220	▄
221	▌
222	▐
223	▀

ASCII Value	Character
224	α
225	β
226	Γ
227	π
228	Σ
229	σ
230	μ
231	τ
232	Φ
233	Θ
234	Ω
235	δ
236	∞
237	Ø
238	ε
239	∩
240	≡
241	±
242	≥
243	≤
244	⌠
245	⌡
246	÷
247	≈
248	°
249	•
250	·
251	√
252	ⁿ
253	²
254	■
255	(blank 'FF')

APPENDIX C EXPRESSIONS

Computers can be used to accomplish a wide variety of tasks, many of which may seem fairly complex. However, the computer itself deals with data in a very rudimentary fashion. It is the programming language or applications software that allows for more complex operations through the use of logical expressions. Logical expressions allow the computer to evaluate data, and then perform certain actions based upon that evaluation. To use logical expressions effectively, you must understand the order in which the computer evaluates expressions and the elements that comprise them.

This appendix covers some of the cross-software fundamentals of how computers evaluate expressions. In many cases there are general rules that may or may not be applicable to a particular software, or which may be overridden by a software's own rules. Because this appendix is a general discussion of expressions, color print has been used to call out software-specific interpretations of and exceptions to the general rules for WordPerfect, Lotus, and dBASE.

Almost all applications software include some commands and/or operations that use logical expressions. However, such expressions are used most often in database applications (dBASE). They are used less in spreadsheet applications (Lotus), and even less in word processing applications (WordPerfect). Logical expressions also tend to be used frequently in programming situations, such as those in which dBASE command files or Lotus 1-2-3 macros would be used.

To understand complex logical expressions, you must first understand the various elements that can make up such an expression: constants, variables, fields, numeric and string operators, numeric expressions, string expressions, relational operators, and logical operators.

THE TWO BASIC TYPES OF DATA: NUMERIC AND STRING

In general, computers deal with two distinct types of data, numeric and string. Numeric data are values that can be used in mathematical operations such as adding, subtracting, multiplying, and dividing. String data may also be called values; however, these values simply represent a string of characters (a group of characters arranged in a specific order). String data are typically differentiated from numeric data by the single or double quotation marks that enclose them. These quotes are referred to as delimiters. Examples of the two types of data are shown in the following.

Numeric data	String data
12	"John Smith"
45.876	"1415 S.E. 23rd Avenue"

Computer operations must make a distinction between numeric data items and string data items. The two types of data items cannot be compared to each other in an evaluation (is "John Smith" greater than 45.876?) or combined with each other to form a single item in a command or operation (print "John Smith" + 12). In other words, you cannot "mix" data types.

> Lotus sometimes refers to numeric data items as values and string data items as labels. Lotus allows you to reference string data in a numeric formula (mixed types), but will treat the item as the numeric value zero.
>
> dBASE refers to numeric data items as numeric type and string data items as character type.
>
> WordPerfect typically deals with everything as string data, and any task that performs mathematical operations must, therefore, involve some type of string-to-numeric data conversion.

OTHER TYPES OF DATA

Software sometimes provide (and appear to deal with) data types other than numeric and string. What they actually do, however, is provide a way of identifying specific numeric or string data items that are to be treated in a special manner.

For instance, logical-type data refers to a data item that may hold one of two specific values, such as true or false, yes or no, on or off, zero or non-zero. Logical data is, in fact, numeric data that is interpreted as logical-type data. Software also may appear to deal with date-type data by interpreting, displaying, or otherwise treating certain numeric or string data in a special manner.

> In dBASE you may identify data items as logical or date items. Internally, dBASE stores logical items as numeric data values 1 or 0, but presents the data to the user as .T. (true) or .F. (false), respectively. Similarly, dBASE stores date items as string data such as "19910214", but presents the data to the user in a recognizable format such as 02/14/91.
>
> In Lotus you are not required to identify data items as logical or date items, but you may treat numeric data items as either logical data or date data. Lotus will evaluate any non-zero numeric data as true and the numeric value zero as false, which is actually the way computers make logical (true/false) evaluations of data. In Lotus, you also may cause certain numeric values to be displayed in a recognizable date format. For example, the numeric value 33283 may be used to represent the date 02/14/91.

In general, when you must explicitly identify a data item as being something other than numeric or string, as is the case with dBASE, the rule about not mixing data types applies to all data types identified.

CONSTANTS, VARIABLES, AND FIELDS

Data items used in expressions may be constants, variables, or fields. Constants are values that will never change when the expression is evaluated, while fields and variables are used to identify items that may have different values each time the expression is evaluated.

Constants

A constant is an explicit value, such as the string value "John Smith" or the numeric value 12. Generally, expressions seldom consist of constant values only. Consider, for example, two numeric constants being added and compared to another numeric constant in the following question.

Is 80 + 35 greater than 100?

The evaluation of 80 + 35 will always be 115, and the answer to the question will always be yes.

Variables

The ability to store values to variables is called assignment. Assigning values to variables adds flexibility to computer operations. When a variable is created, a specific location in RAM is allocated to hold a numeric or string data item. The software keeps track of the location and allows you to choose a name with which to identify the data item. A new value may later be assigned to the same variable name, and the computer simply changes the value held in that variable's location.

For example, you might assign the value 80 to a variable named ACCOUNT and assign the value 35 to a variable named PURCHASE. The variable names then could be substituted in the previous question as follows.

Is ACCOUNT + PURCHASE greater than 100?

In this case, the evaluation of the expression depends on the current values of the variables ACCOUNT and PURCHASE. If the variables hold the values assigned above, the evaluation of ACCOUNT + PURCHASE is 115, and the answer to the question is yes. If the numeric value 50 was assigned to the variable ACCOUNT, however, the evaluation of ACCOUNT + PURCHASE would be 85 and the answer to the question would be no.

Fields

A field is one of a group of related data items constituting a record in database operations. A field name is used in an expression to identify which data item is to be evaluated for one or more records in a database. Because an expression is evaluated for only one record at a time, the value specified with a field name in any expression may vary with each record evaluated. New values can also be assigned to fields, which would change the evaluation of an expression for a record. Because of the variable nature of its data, a field can be thought of as a special type of variable. While there are some exceptions, the information held in database fields is stored on disk, while information assigned to variables is held in RAM.

Assume that ACCOUNT is the name of a numeric database field, while PURCHASE is a variable that has been assigned the value 30. Assume further that you have the following database records to consider.

Field names:	NAME	DEPT	PHONE	ACCOUNT	LIMIT
Data types:	*string*	*string*	*string*	*numeric*	*numeric*
Record 1	John Smith	acctg	221-8723	75	100
Record 2	April Miller	acctg	221-8725	42	55
Record 3	Steve Grey	sales	223-5539	90	95

Now look again at the previous example question.

Is ACCOUNT + PURCHASE greater than 100?

You can see that the evaluation of ACCOUNT + PURCHASE and the answer to the question will depend on the record to which you are referring.

LOGICAL EXPRESSIONS

A logical expression is an expression that the computer can evaluate as either true or false. The questions used in the previous examples represented simple logical expressions because they could be answered with a yes or a no. Two or more such questions may be combined into a complex logical expression, just as they could be combined into one sentence, as follows.

Is ACCOUNT + PURCHASE greater than 100?
Is NAME equal to "John Smith"?

Is ACCOUNT + PURCHASE greater than 100 and is NAME equal to "John Smith"?

Although this question could probably be answered without any ambiguity, some complex questions may be difficult to state clearly in the form of a complex logical expression. You must first understand the order in which the computer begins evaluating such an expression to arrive at its true or false determination. Complex logical expressions are evaluated in the following order.

1. All numeric and string expressions and operators are evaluated.
2. All simple logical expressions and relational operators are evaluated.
3. The complex logical expression and all logical operators are evaluated.

This order may be referred to as rules of precedence, where certain evaluation steps always precede others. To give you a clear understanding of these steps, the following sections will discuss numeric expressions, numeric operators, string expressions, string operators, relational operators, and logical operators.

Numeric Expressions

Numeric expressions are single numeric data items, or formulas that use numeric data items and numeric operators that result in single numeric values. Numeric (or arithmetic) operators commonly used in numeric expressions are shown here with their normal order of precedence. The order of precedence indicates which operations will occur first, second, third, and so on.

Operator	Operation	Order of Precedence
−	minus sign	1
^	exponentiation	2
*	multiplication	3
/	division	3
+	addition	4
−	subtraction	4

The normal order of precedence reflects the order in which you would solve a mathematical equation. In addition, parentheses ( ) may be used to override the normal order of precedence. Notice that the minus sign (−) has the highest order of precedence only when it serves to reverse the sign of a numeric value.

The following numeric expression is a formula that uses one numeric constant (.75) and a number of numeric variables (or fields).

−BALANCE/(ACCOUNT−PAYMENT)+BONUS*.75−ALLOWANCE

Assuming the values shown for each variable, the expression will be evaluated by the computer as follows.

ACCOUNT	=	−50
ALLOWANCE	=	65
BALANCE	=	2000
BONUS	=	400
PAYMENT	=	150

The value of each variable is placed in the equation.

−2000/(−50−150)+400*.75−65

Operations in parentheses are performed first.

−2000/−200+400*.75−65

Multiplication and division operations are performed next.

10+300−65

Addition and subtraction operations are performed last.

245

> In WordPerfect all arithmetic operators have equal precedence and formulas are evaluated from left to right. The exponentiation operator (^) is not recognized by WordPerfect.

String Expressions

String expressions are single string data items, or expressions that use string data items and string operators that result in single string values. String operators, also called string concatenators, are used to add one string of characters to another. The operator commonly used to combine two string data items is the plus sign (+), as shown in the following expression.

"Please contact " +NAME+ " at " +PHONE+ " by next week."

This expression concatenates (puts together) two string variables and three string constants (also called literals). The variables and the values that have been assigned to them and the string constants are shown here.

Variables	Assigned Values	Constants
NAME	"John Smith"	"Please contact "
PHONE	"221–8723"	" at "
		" by next week."

The computer's evaluation of the previous string expression would result in the single string data item

"Please contact John Smith at 221–8723 by next week."

dBASE uses the plus sign (+) operator to concatenate strings as shown here, and also uses the minus (−) operator to concatenate strings with trailing blank spaces moved to the end of a combined string.

Lotus uses the ampersand (&) as its string concatenation operator.

dBASE also allows date expressions that use the plus (+) and minus (−) operators together with date values and numeric values. This is an exception to the rule that states that data types must not be mixed in an expression. Only certain types of operations are permitted, however. Examples of allowable dBASE date expressions, the values of variables used, and the resulting data types and values are shown here.

Variable	Data Type	Value
DAY1	date	01/14/91
DAY2	date	02/21/91
DNUM	numeric	10

Expression	Resulting Data Type	Resulting Value
DAY1 + DNUM	date	02/24/91
DAY2 − DNUM	date	02/11/91
DAY2 − DAY1	numeric	7

Relational Expressions

A relational expression is a simple logical expression—one that compares two data items of the same data type using a relational operator. Logical expressions are sometimes referred to as conditions, since they are often used to conditionally perform certain operations. The standard relational operators are shown here.

Operator	**Comparison Operation**
=	equal to
<>	not equal to
>	greater than
<	less than
>=	greater than or equal to
<=	less than or equal to

The computer evaluates a relational expression as either true or false. The following are examples of relational expressions that use constant numeric and string data items. The result of the true or false evaluation is also shown.

Relational Expression	Evaluation
12 = 45.876	false
12 > 45.876	false
45.876 >= 12	true
"John Smith" > "1415 S.E. 23rd Avenue"	true
"John Smith" = "john smith"	false
"John Smith" <> "1415 S.E. 23rd Avenue"	true

Relational operators may be used to make comparisons of two numeric data items or two string data items. When string data are compared, characters are compared according to their ASCII values. Letters at the beginning of the alphabet have lower values than letters at the end of the alphabet ("A" has the value 65 and "Z" has the value 90). Lower-case letters have values greater than upper-case letters ("a" through "z" have the values 97 through 122). Because of these ASCII values, string data items will appear in alphabetical order if they are arranged from lowest to highest.

> dBASE also uses the $ sign as a relational operator; however, it is only used in comparisons of string data items. It determines whether the first data item is found within (that is, it is a substring of) the second data item. For example, "Smith" $ "John Smith" would be evaluated as true.
>
> dBASE also uses relational operators to compare date-type data items in relational expressions such as DAY1 <= DAY2.

Recall the order in which complex logical expressions are evaluated:

1. All numeric and string expressions and operators are evaluated.
2. All simple logical expressions and relational operators are evaluated.
3. The complex logical expression and all logical operators are evaluated.

When a single relational expression is used (no logical operators are included), only the first two types of evaluation are performed to arrive at a true or false evaluation. The following variables and database records will be used in examples of the first two types of evaluation below.

Variable	Data Type	Value
PURCHASE	numeric	30
ALLOWANCE	numeric	65

Field names:	NAME	DEPT	PHONE	ACCOUNT	LIMIT
Data types:	*string*	*string*	*string*	*numeric*	*numeric*
Record 1	John Smith	acctg	221-8723	75	100
Record 2	April Miller	acctg	221-8725	42	55
Record 3	Steve Grey	sales	223-5539	90	95

Consider the following numeric relational expression and the order in which it would be evaluated for the three records of the database.

ACCOUNT+PURCHASE<=LIMIT*1.15-ALLOWANCE/2

Values of variables and database fields are placed in the expression.

Record 1	Record 2	Record 3
75+30<=100*1.5−65/2	42+30<=55*1.5−65/2	90+30<=95*1.5−65/2

Numeric expressions are evaluated according to rules of precedence for numeric operators.

1. Multiplication and division operators are evaluated.

Record 1	Record 2	Record 3
75+30<=150−32.5	42+30<=82.5−32.5	90+30<=142.5−32.5

2. Addition and subtraction operators are evaluated.

Record 1	Record 2	Record 3
105<=117.5	72<=50	120<=110

3. Relational operators are evaluated.

Record 1	Record 2	Record 3
true	false	false

Logical Operators

When logical operators are included in an expression, the expression may be referred to as a complex logical expression. Logical operators are used to combine two or more simple logical expressions (relational expressions) and/or to reverse the true or false evaluation of a logical expression. The relational operators and their normal order of precedence are shown in the following table.

Operator	**Order of Precedence**
NOT	1
AND	2
OR	3

The NOT operator reverses the true or false evaluation of a logical expression in the same way that a minus sign (−) reverses the sign of a positive or negative numeric value. The AND and OR operators are used to combine two logical expressions so that the result is a single true or false answer. A logical expression that combines two logical expressions with the AND operator will evaluate true only if *both* expressions combined evaluate as true. A logical expression that combines two logical expressions with the OR operator will evaluate as true if *either* of the expressions combined evaluate as true.

The following are some examples of how complex logical expressions would be evaluated when they reverse or combine simple logical expressions that have true or false evaluations as shown.

NOT Expressions	AND Expressions	OR Expressions
NOT true = false	true AND true = true	true OR true = true
NOT false = true	true AND false = false	true OR false = true
	false AND false = false	false OR false = false

When a number of logical operators are used in a longer complex expression, understanding the rules of precedence becomes very important. As in the case of numeric expressions, parentheses ( ) may be used to override the normal order of precedence for logical operators.

The following examples have no parentheses included and would, therefore, be evaluated as shown.

Expression	NOT and AND Evaluated	Result
false AND false OR true	false OR true	true
true AND true OR true AND false	true OR false	true
false OR false AND true OR true	false OR true OR false	true
NOT false OR true	true OR true	true

The same expressions yield different results if parentheses are used to override the normal order of precedence.

Expression	Parentheses Evaluated	Result
false AND (false OR true)	false AND true	false
true AND (true OR true) AND false	true AND true AND false	false
(false OR false) AND (true OR true)	false AND true	false
NOT (false OR true)	NOT true	false

The variables and database records used in the example of a simple logical expression evaluation will now be used to illustrate the evaluation of a complex logical expression.

Variable	Data Type	Value
PURCHASE	numeric	30
ALLOWANCE	numeric	65

Field names:	NAME	DEPT	PHONE	ACCOUNT	LIMIT
Data types:	*string*	*string*	*string*	*numeric*	*numeric*
Record 1	John Smith	acctg	221-8723	75	100
Record 2	April Miller	acctg	221-8725	42	55
Record 3	Steve Grey	sales	223-5539	90	95

Consider the following complex logical expression and the order in which it would be evaluated for the first record of the database.

ACCOUNT + PURCHASE< = LIMIT*1.15 – ALLOWANCE/2 OR
DEPT = "sales" AND LIMIT>75

Values of variables and database fields are placed in the expression.

Record 1
75 + 30< = 100*1.5 – 65/2 OR "acctg" = "sales" AND 100>75

Numeric expressions are evaluated according to rules of precedence for numeric operators.

Record 1
105< = 117.5 OR "acctg" = "sales" AND 100>75

Relational operators are evaluated.

Record 1
true OR false AND true

Logical ANDs are evaluated first.

Record 1
true OR false

Logical ORs are evaluated.

Record 1
true

Following are the same evaluation steps for records two and three of the database.

Record 2

42+30<=55*1.5–65/2 OR “acctg”=“sales” AND 55> 75
72<=50 OR “acctg”=“sales” AND 55>75
false OR false AND false
false OR false
false

Record 3

90+30<=95*1.5–65/2 OR “sales”=“sales” AND 95>75
120<=110 OR “sales”=“sales” AND 95>75
false OR true AND true
false OR true
true

Logical operators in dBASE are enclosed in periods (.) and spaces may be used to make logical expressions easier to read. The example expression above might appear in dBASE as

ACCOUNT+PURCHASE <= LIMIT*1.15–ALLOWANCE/2 .OR.
DEPT = “sales” .AND. LIMIT > 75

Logical operators in Lotus are enclosed in score signs (#), and spaces are not allowed in logical expressions. Assuming that named ranges are used for variables, the example expression above might appear in Lotus as

ACCOUNT+PURCHASE<=LIMIT*1.15–ALLOWANCE/2#OR#
DEPT=“sales”#AND#LIMIT>75

INDEX

Concepts

WordPerfect Version 5.1

Lotus 1-2-3 Version 2.2

dBASE III Plus

Data Transfer Between Applications Software

Appendices